# ROUTLEDGE HANDBOOK OF YOGA AND MEDITATION STUDIES

The *Routledge Handbook of Yoga and Meditation Studies* is a comprehensive and interdisciplinary resource, which frames and contextualises the rapidly expanding fields that explore yoga and meditative techniques. The book analyses yoga and meditation studies in a variety of religious, historical and geographical settings. The chapters, authored by an international set of experts, are laid out across five sections:

- Introduction to yoga and meditation studies
- History of yoga and meditation in South Asia
- Doctrinal perspectives: technique and praxis
- Global and regional transmissions
- Disciplinary framings

In addition to up-to-date explorations of the history of yoga and meditation in the Indian subcontinent, new contexts include a case study of yoga and meditation in the contemporary Tibetan diaspora, and unique summaries of historical developments in Japan and Latin America as well as an introduction to the growing academic study of yoga in Korea. Underpinned by critical and theoretical engagement, the volume provides an in-depth guide to the history of yoga and meditation studies and combines the best of established research with attention to emerging directions for future investigation. This handbook will be of interest to multidisciplinary academic audiences from across the humanities, social sciences and sciences.

**Suzanne Newcombe** is a senior lecturer in Religious Studies at the Open University, UK, and Honorary Director of Inform, an independent charitable organisation which researches and provides information about minority religions and is based at the Department of Theology and Religious Studies at King's College London, UK.

**Karen O'Brien-Kop** is a lecturer in Asian Religions and Ethics at the University of Roehampton, UK.

# ROUTLEDGE HANDBOOK OF YOGA AND MEDITATION STUDIES

*Edited by Suzanne Newcombe and Karen O'Brien-Kop*

Routledge
Taylor & Francis Group
LONDON AND NEW YORK

First published 2021
by Routledge
2 Park Square, Milton Park, Abingdon, Oxon OX14 4RN

and by Routledge
52 Vanderbilt Avenue, New York, NY 10017

*Routledge is an imprint of the Taylor & Francis Group, an informa business*



*British Library Cataloguing-in-Publication Data*
A catalogue record for this book is available from the British Library

*Library of Congress Cataloging-in-Publication Data*
Names: Newcombe, Suzanne, editor. | O'Brien-Kop, Karen, editor.
Title: Routledge handbook of yoga and meditation studies / edited by Suzanne Newcombe and Karen O'Brien-Kop.
Description: Abingdon, Oxon ; New York, NY : Routledge, 2020. | Includes bibliographical references and index.
Identifiers: LCCN 2020020123 | ISBN 9781138484863 (hardback) | ISBN 9781351050753 (ebook)
Subjects: LCSH: Yoga. | Meditation.
Classification: LCC B132.Y6 R68 2020 | DDC 181/.45–dc23
LC record available at https://lccn.loc.gov/2020020123

ISBN: 978-1-138-48486-3 (hbk)
ISBN: 978-1-351-05075-3 (ebk)

Typeset in Bembo
by Newgen Publishing UK

MIX
Paper from responsible sources
FSC™ C013985
www.fsc.org

Printed in the United Kingdom
by Henry Ling Limited

# CONTENTS

# EDITORIAL BOARD

# FIGURES

# TABLES

# ACKNOWLEDGEMENTS

All books are collaborative projects – and this one was more collaborative than most. Every chapter has been subject to peer review and we would like to express our gratitude to all the anonymous peer reviewers for their time and generosity in making this volume more rigorous.

We would like to thank our editor at Routledge, Dorothea Schaefter, and our editorial assistant, Alexandra de Brauw, for their patience and guidance on this project.

The SOAS Centre for Yoga Studies, its director, James Mallinson, and project co-ordinator, Martha Henson, have both been invaluable at many stages of this project. We deeply value the collaborative environment and support that has been offered by this Centre.

We are also very grateful for the advice and resources of our Editorial Board, whose expertise we have called upon at several stages of the project as well as all the anonymous peer reviewers who made the work better in numerous ways. Thank you all for participating in the unpaid labour of making academic work better.

The formation of the editorial vision and chapters was deeply impacted by a workshop held at the School of Oriental and African Studies (SOAS) in March 2019. Among those who are not represented by a contributing chapter but nevertheless gave substantial input to the workshop and our thinking about this volume as a whole include: Alp Arat, Christèle Barois, Jason Birch, Graham Burns, Matthew Clark, Jo Cook, Lucy May Constantini, James Mallinson, Elizabeth De Michelis, Mariano Errichiello, Jacqueline Hargreaves, Corinna May Lhoir, Firdose Moonda, Ayesha Nathoo, Daniel Simpson, Daniel Stuart, Leslie de Vries, Richard Williams, Ruth Westoby, Theodora Wildcroft and Amelia Wood. Particular thanks are due to Ruth Westoby, Theodora Wildcroft and Jacqueline Hargreaves who were not only enthusiastic participants at the workshop but also allowed us to employ their skills in recording interviews with participants during breaks.

Financially, the workshop was directly and indirectly supported by the Strategic Research Investment Fund (SRIF) from the Open University's Faculty of Arts and Social Science (FASS), the SOAS Centre for Yoga Studies and the European Research Council Horizon 2020 research and innovation programme under grant agreements No. 639363 (AYURYOG) and No. 616393 (Haṭha Yoga Project). We would especially like to express our gratitude to the Haṭha Yoga Project for their support, encouragement and contributions from their research.

We could not have completed this work without the support and encouragement of our colleagues. Specifically, we would like to thank Dagmar Wujastyk, Principle Investigator of the AYURYOG project, for supporting exploration into the foundations of some of the assumptions about what yoga is and has been through history. Suzanne Newcombe would like to express her gratitude for the support and encouragement of Paul-François Tremlett, Graham Harvey and John Wolffe at the Open University in completing this project. She is also grateful for the patience of Eileen Barker and Sarah Harvey in juggling deadlines as this project was completed. We are both grateful to Jane Cooper for her fabulous and much appreciated editorial assistance. Karen O'Brien-Kop would like to thank Ulrich Pagel at SOAS as well as her newer colleagues at the University of Roehampton whose support has been vital in completing this project, especially Laura Peters, Clare Watkins, Simonetta Calderini and Sean Ryan. Thanks to Richard King and Rupert Gethin for expert support in her research, and to Dan Lusthaus for guidance and encouragement in editing this volume. Special thanks are due to Avni Chag for ongoing academic inspiration and motivation. Finally Karen would like to thank all of her students at SOAS and Roehampton, who have made her a better thinker.

Suzanne Newcombe would like to express her gratitude to Janet Gyatso whose astute challenges to her intellect and character – and pointedly unanswered questions over twenty year ago – have significantly shaped this work and much of her academic exploration. Most of all she would like to express her deep appreciation for the unfailing support of her family – husband Alaric, daughters Ayesha and Kansas, dog Bella, and parents Jim and Susan Hasselle – for quietly putting up with her working at odd times and encouraging her in so many ways. Karen O'Brien-Kop would like to thank family and friends who supported her through this long project – especially Margaret, Thomas and Trevor O'Brien – but her deepest thanks are reserved for her son, Zohar Kop.

This handbook was partially financially supported by the European Union's Horizon 2020 research and innovation programme under grant agreements No. 639363 (AYURYOG) and No. 647963 (Haṭha Yoga Project).

erc

European Research Council

Established by the European Commission

# CONTRIBUTORS

**Andrea Acri** (PhD Leiden University, 2011) is *maître de conférences*/assistant professor in tantric studies at the École Pratique des Hautes Études (EPHE, PSL University, Paris) since 2016. He studies Śaiva and Buddhist tantric traditions in South and Southeast Asia from a text-historical and comparative perspective. He has published the monograph *Dharma Pātañjala* (2011, 2017 and the Indonesian edition 2018) and a number of edited volumes, including *Esoteric Buddhism in Mediaeval Maritime Asia* (2016).

**Daniela Bevilacqua** is a South-Asianist and received her PhD in Civilizations of Africa and Asia from Sapienza University of Rome and in Anthropology from the University of Paris Nanterre. Her PhD research was published by Routledge under the title *Modern Hindu Traditionalism in Contemporary India: The Śrī Maṭh and the Jagadguru Rāmānandācārya in the Evolution of the Rāmānandī Sampradāya*. She is now a post-doc research fellow at SOAS, working for the ERC-funded Haṭha Yoga Project (2015–2020).

**Balbinder Singh Bhogal** is a professor in religion and holder of the Sardarni Kuljit Kaur Bindra Chair in Sikh Studies (Hofstra University, NY, USA). He focuses on Indic religions, specialising in Sikhi(sm). The tensions between hermeneutics and deconstruction, religion and secularism, animal and saint, mysticism and politics, postcolonial and decolonial, animate his work.

**Shameem Black** is a scholar of literary and cultural studies and a fellow in the Department of Gender, Media and Cultural Studies in the College of Asia and the Pacific at the Australian National University. She is the author of *Fiction Across Borders* (2010). Her current work explores the cultural politics of yoga to illuminate paradoxes of national identity and cross-cultural practice in an era of globalisation.

**Sravana Borkataky-Varma,** PhD, teaches at Harvard University and the University of North Carolina-Wilmington. She focuses on the esoteric rituals within the larger space of Hindu Śākta tantra. Her works include 'Red: An Ethnographic Study of Cross-Pollination between the Vedic and the Tantric' in the *International Journal of Hindu Studies* (2019) and 'Taming Hindu

*Śākta* Tantra on the Internet: Online *pūjās* for the goddess Tripurasundarī' in *Digital Hinduism* (2020) ed. Xenia Zeiler, Routledge.

**Gudrun Bühnemann** is a professor in the Department of Asian Languages and Cultures at the University of Wisconsin-Madison, USA. She has published extensively on South Asian iconography and ritual. Her work on yoga includes *Eighty-four Āsanas in Yoga: A Survey of Traditions (with Illustrations)* (2007; Russian translation 2009; 2nd edition, 2011; Korean translation, 2011).

**Mikel Burley** is Associate Professor of Religion and Philosophy at the University of Leeds. His publications include *A Radical Pluralist Philosophy of Religion: Cross-Cultural, Multireligious, Interdisciplinary* (2020), *Rebirth and the Stream of Life: A Philosophical Study of Reincarnation, Karma and Ethics* (2016) and *Classical Sāṃkhya and Yoga: An Indian Metaphysics of Experience* (2007).

**Matylda Ciołkosz** is a scholar of religions and Assistant Professor at the Department of Psychology of Religions, Institute for the Study of Religions, Jagiellonian University in Kraków, Poland. Her doctoral research focused on modern postural yoga and the relation between the embodied experience of *āsana* practice and interpretation of the *Pātañjalayogaśāstra*. As a long-time yoga practitioner, rock climber and musician, she is more broadly interested in the influence of movement practices on the formation of religious concepts and doctrines.

**Florin Deleanu** (PhD, University of Hamburg) is a professor at the International College for Postgraduate Buddhist Studies in Tokyo. His research focuses on the history of Buddhist meditation and the philosophical traditions of Sarvāstivāda, Sautrāntika and Yogācāra. His publications include a monograph on *The Chapter on the Mundane Path in the Śrāvakabhūmi* (2006) and studies on 'Agnostic Meditations on Buddhist Meditation' (2010), 'Meditative Practices in the *Bodhisattvabhūmi*' (2013), 'Reshaping Timelessness: Paradigm Shifts in the Interpretation of Buddhist Meditation' (2017), 'When Gnosis Meets Logos: The Story of a Hermeneutical Verse in Indian Buddhism' (2019), among others. He is currently translating the *Śrāvakabhūmi* and the *Laṅkāvatārasūtra*.

**Philip Deslippe** is a doctoral candidate in the Department of Religious Studies and a teaching associate in the Department of Asian American Studies at the University of California, Santa Barbara, USA where his focus is on Asian, metaphysical and marginal religious traditions in modern America. He has published articles in journals including the *Journal of Yoga Studies* and *Sikh Formations*, and popular venues such as *Tricycle* and *Yoga Journal*.

**Patrick J. D'Silva** is a lecturer in the Philosophy Department at the University of Colorado, Colorado Springs, USA. His research focuses on Sufism and yoga in South Asia. He is the co-author (with Carl Ernst) of the forthcoming volume *Breathtaking Insights: Indian and Sufi Breath Practices from the Kāmarūpančāšikā to Hazrat Inayat Khan* (Richmond, Virginia, Suluk Press). More information is available at patrickjdsilva.com.

**Asaf Federman** is the director of training at Muda Institute, Baruch Ivcher School of Psychology, IDC Herzliya, Israel. Asaf is interested in the convergence between Buddhist meditation and psychology and has published a book in Hebrew on mindfulness. His academic publications on free will, skilful means and the modern history of meditation appeared in *Religion*, *Philosophy East and West*, and *Journal of Buddhist Ethics*.

**Finnian M. M. Gerety** is Visiting Assistant Professor of Religious Studies and Affiliated Faculty Member of Contemplative Studies and the Center for Contemporary South Asia at Brown University, USA. His research interests include sound, mantra and ritual in Indian religions. His forthcoming book, *This Whole World is OM: A History of the Sacred Syllable in India,* is the first-ever monograph of the syllable OM, examining how this syllable came to prominence among Brahmin ritualists and then spread over the religious and cultural landscape of early India. He received a doctorate in South Asian Studies at Harvard University (2015) and completed a post-doctoral fellowship at the Institute of Sacred Music at Yale University (2017–2018).

**Kengo Harimoto** is a faculty member at Mahidol University, Thailand. Prior to working at Mahidol, he worked in the Netherlands and in Germany. His MA is from Kyushu University, Japan, and his PhD is from the University of Pennsylvania, USA. His major research interest is in Indian philosophy, especially classical yoga. His further research interests expand into Buddhist philosophy, history of Indian medicine, popular Sanskrit Hindu literature, and others.

**Ville Husgafvel** is a doctoral student in the Study of Religion at the University of Helsinki and a trained MBSR teacher. In his PhD dissertation, he studies the recontextualisation of Buddhist meditation practices in contemporary mindfulness-based programmes. He has published in *Contemporary Buddhism* ('The "Universal Dharma Foundation" of Mindfulness-Based Stress Reduction: Non-Duality and Mahāyāna Buddhist Influences in the Work of Jon Kabat-Zinn') and *Temenos* ('On the Buddhist Roots of Contemporary Non-Religious Mindfulness Practice: Moving Beyond Sectarian and Essentialist Approaches').

**Andrea R. Jain** is Associate Professor of Religious Studies at Indiana University, Indianapolis (IUPUI), USA, editor of the *Journal of the American Academy of Religion*, and author of *Selling Yoga: From Counterculture to Pop Culture* (2014) and *Peace, Love, Yoga: The Politics of Global Spirituality* (2020). Her areas of research include religion under neoliberal capitalism; global yoga; South Asian religions; sexuality, embodiment and religion; and theories of religion.

**Pamela Jeter**, PhD, is a scientific review officer at the National Center for Complementary and Integrative Health (NCCIH) at the National Institutes of Health, located in Bethesda, MD, USA. Dr. Jeter received her PhD in Cognitive Science (Experimental Psychology) from the University of California, Irvine, where she studied mechanisms of transfer and specificity in visual perceptual learning. She completed her postdoctoral training at the Johns Hopkins Wilmer Eye Institute, where she studied the therapeutic benefits of yoga on fall risk factors in visually impaired individuals. Dr. Jeter also served as Adjunct Faculty at the Maryland University of Integrative Health, where she taught research literacy and academic publishing practices. Dr. Jeter has presented at professional conferences and community-based groups and received recognition for her work on yoga for the blind. As a yoga practitioner, she has studied Ashtanga yoga for many years with senior teachers.

**Sat Bir Singh Khalsa**, PhD, has been fully engaged in basic and clinical research on the efficacy of yoga and meditation practices in improving physical and psychological health since 2001. He has practised a yoga lifestyle since 1972 and is a certified instructor in Kundalini Yoga as taught by Yogi Bhajan. He is the director of yoga research for the Yoga Alliance and the Kundalini Research Institute, Research Associate at the Benson Henry Institute for Mind Body Medicine, Research Affiliate of the Osher Center for Integrative Medicine and Assistant Professor of Medicine at Harvard Medical School in the Department of Medicine at Brigham and Women's Hospital in Boston. He has conducted clinical research trials evaluating yoga interventions for insomnia, post-traumatic stress disorder, chronic stress and anxiety disorders and in both public school and occupational settings. Dr. Khalsa works with the International Association of Yoga Therapists to promote research on yoga and yoga therapy as the chair of the scientific program committee for the annual Symposium on Yoga Research and as editor-in-chief of the *International Journal of Yoga Therapy*. He is medical editor of the Harvard Medical School Special Report: An Introduction to Yoga and chief editor of the medical textbook *The Principles and Practice of Yoga in Health Care*.

**Louis Komjathy** (PhD, Religious Studies, Boston University, USA) is an independent scholar-educator and translator. He researches and has published extensively in Contemplative Studies, Daoist Studies and Religious Studies, with specific interests in contemplative practice, embodiment and mystical experience. He is also founding Co-chair of the Daoist Studies Unit (2004–2010) and the Contemplative Studies Unit (2010–2016) in the American Academy of Religion. In addition to over thirty academic articles and book chapters, he has published nine books to date, including the recent *Taming the Wild Horse: An Annotated Translation and Study of the Daoist Horse Taming Pictures* (2017) and *Introducing Contemplative Studies* (2018). His current work explores cross-cultural and perennial questions related to aliveness, extraordinariness, flourishing, transmutation and trans-temporality. He lives in Chicago, Illinois, USA.

**Hidehiko Kurita** is a lecturer at Aichi Prefectural University, Japan and received his PhD in the Department of Religious Studies in Tohoku University, Japan. In Japanese, he has authored several publications on the history of meditation in modern Japan, and co-edited with Tsukada Hotaka and Yoshinaga Shin'ichi *Kingendai Nihon no Minkan Seishin Ryōhō* (*The Mind Cure Movement in Modern Japan*) (2019).

**Borayin Larios** is an assistant professor at the Department of South Asian, Tibetan and Buddhist Studies of the University of Vienna, Austria. He authored *Embodying the Vedas: Traditional Vedic Schools of Contemporary Maharashtra* published in 2017. His current research focuses on popular religion in urban India.

**JaeGil Lee** is the pastor at St. Paul's United Methodist Church in Newport, RI, USA. He provides support for substance use recovery, counselling, spiritual direction and meditation instruction to his local community. His academic expertise is in the areas of comparative spirituality and interreligious/spiritual dialogue, especially between the contemporary Christian contemplative prayer movement and eastern meditation. This topic is explored in his doctoral dissertation, *Sources and Issues in Contemporary Christian Contemplative Prayer: Thomas Keating's Centering Prayer and John Main's Christian Meditation*. His current interests include the role and place of body in the practice of contemplative prayer and spiritual direction.

**Charles Li** is a postdoctoral fellow at the University of British Columbia in Vancouver, Canada. His research is focused on Indian philosophy, but encompasses philology, comparative literature and the history of ideas. He is currently involved in developing methods and software for producing philological research that is more open, empirically grounded and reproducible.

**Adrián Muñoz** is a lecturer of South Asian Religions at El Colegio de México, and he specialises in yoga literature, hagiography and history. In Spanish, he has authored *La Piel de Tigre y la Serpiente: La Identidad de los Nāth-yoguis a Través de sus Leyendas* (2010) and *Radiografía* *del Hathayoga* (2016), and co-authored *Historia Minima del Yoga* (forthcoming). In English, he co-edited with David N. Lorenzen *Yogi Heroes and Poets: Histories and Legends of the Naths* (2011).

**Suzanne Newcombe** is a senior lecturer in Religious Studies at the Open University, UK, and honorary director of Inform, based in Theology and Religious Studies at King's College London. She has published on topics relating to the popularisation of yoga and ayurveda including the monograph *Yoga in Britain: Stretching Spirituality and Educating Yogis* (2019). She researched the transformations of yoga and ayurveda in modern India as part of the ERC-funded AYURYOG project from 2015–2020.

**Karen O'Brien-Kop** is a lecturer in Asian Religions and Ethics at the University of Roehampton, UK, and was formerly a senior teaching fellow at SOAS University of London. She received her PhD from SOAS, titled *Seed and Cloud of Liberation in Buddhist and Pātañjala Yoga: An Intertextual Study* and continues to research classical Sanskrit texts on yoga and meditation. She has published articles in *Religions of South Asia* and the *Journal of Indian Philosophy* and is currently working on a monograph on classical yoga and Buddhism.

**Kwangsoo Park** is a professor in the Department of *Won*-Buddhism at Wonkwang University in the Republic of Korea. He is now serving as the dean of the Graduate School of Asian Studies, the Dean of Kyohak College and the director of the Research Centre of Yoga Studies at Wonkwang University. He leads academic research both as the president of Korean Association for Religious Studies and the president of Korean Society of Yoga Studies. He received his MA in Religious Studies at the University of Iowa and received his PhD in Buddhist Studies at the University of Wisconsin-Madison in the USA.

**Younggil Park** is a research professor at Geumgang University, Republic of Korea. In Korean, he has authored *A Theory and Praxis of Haṭhayoga* (2013), *Haṭhapradīpikā: An Annotated Translation of Haṭhapradīpikā, Jyotsnā* (2 vols., 2015) and *Haṭhayoga Literature* (2019).

**Samani Pratibha Pragya** is a research assistant at SOAS University of London (UK) working on *Terāpanth* data pertaining to the Jaina-Prosopography project. She received her PhD on *Prekṣā Meditation: History and Methods* from SOAS. Her research interests include the modern development of Jain yoga and meditation. At present, she is head of the Jain World Peace Centre, London, and is an authorised Prekṣā yoga and meditation teacher. She initiated a rural development project at Tamkore, Rajasthan, and established Mahapragya International School there.

**Masoumeh Rahmani** is a lecturer in Religious Studies at Victoria University of Wellington, New Zealand. She previously held a research associate position in the Brain, Belief and Behaviour lab at Coventry University. Rahmani received her PhD from the University of Otago, New Zealand, in 2017. Her research interests include religious conversion and disengagement, meditation groups and Asian religions in non-Asian contexts.

**Olga Serbaeva Saraogi** is an academic associate at the Institute of Asian and Oriental Studies – South Asia, University of Zurich, Switzerland. Her research interests include subjects such as Śaiva tantric texts, *yoginīs*, and computational linguistic methods applied to Sanskrit texts.

**Laura Schmalzl,** PhD, is Associate Professor at Southern California University of Health Sciences, USA. Her research interests lie in furthering our understanding of the mechanisms through which yoga-based practices can impact cognitive functioning, body awareness and emotional self-regulation. She is Editor-in-Chief of the *International Journal of Yoga Therapy*, and also a dedicated yoga practitioner and certified yoga instructor.

**Mark Singleton** is Senior Research Fellow on the Haṭha Yoga Project, SOAS, University of London. His books include *Yoga Body, the Origins of Modern Yoga Practice* (2010), *Roots of Yoga* (2017, with James Mallinson) and several edited volumes of scholarship on yoga.

**Michael Stoeber** is Professor of Spirituality and Philosophy of Religion at Regis College and the University of Toronto, Canada. His current research explores topics on the intersection of spirituality and art, comparative mysticism and issues in meditation, prayer and yoga across religious traditions. Alongside three books, recent essays have appeared in the *International Journal of Practical Theology* ('Theopoetics as Response to Suffering: The Visual Art of Käthe Kollwitz in the Reformation of Practical Theodicy'), in *Hindu-Christian Studies* ('Issues in Christian Encounters with Yoga'), and in *Toronto Journal of Theology* ('Mysticism in *The Brothers Karamazov*').

**Julian Strube** specialises in the relationship between religion, science and politics in the context of esotericism. He has worked on socialist, National Socialist and völkisch relations to esotericism, before focusing on Tantra in colonial Bengal within the context of a global religious history. His current project at the University of Münster revolves around exchanges between Bengali intellectuals and American and British Unitarians.

**Raphaël Voix** is a social anthropologist and research fellow at the National Centre for Scientific Research (CNRS), and a member of the French Institute of Pondicherry (MAEE/CNRS) and the Centre for Indian and South Asian Studies (CEIAS), Paris. His research focuses on sectarian Hinduism in West Bengal. He has co-edited *Filing Religion: State, Hinduism and Courts of Law* (with G. Tarabout and D. Berti) and published in various academic journals and edited books.

**Karen-Anne Wong**, PhD, currently works as a casual lecturer and yoga teacher in Sydney, Australia. Karen completed her PhD in 2017 at The University of Sydney, examining children's yoga practices in Australia. Karen has recently published work on donor conception and race in *The Journal of Bioethical Inquiry* and has a chapter co-authored with Dr. Kerryn Drysdale entitled 'Sensory Ethnography' in the *Sage Encyclopaedia of Research Methods* (2019). Karen's research interests include embodiment, childhood, dis/ableism, gender, sexuality, health and wellbeing practices and ethnography.

**Naomi Worth** is a doctoral candidate in Religious Studies at the University of Virginia, USA. She is a textualist and ethnographer focused on the yoga traditions of Tibet and India and their relationship to mind-body philosophy. She is currently developing a website to compare mind-body philosophies across cultures and disciplines.

# A NOTE ON TERMS AND TRANSLATIONS

We have included transliteration of non-English terms in languages such as Sanskrit, Chinese, Tibetan and Japanese. Some authors have chosen to occasionally employ the script of the languages they work in, such as Devanagari for Sanskrit or logograms for Chinese. Some chapters use Hindi, Prakrit, Pali or Bengali rather than Sanskrit terms in transliteration, which creates some variance in spellings: for example, *āsana* in Sanskrit is *āsan* in Hindi. Where a chapter engages substantially with a non-English technical vocabulary, we have included a short glossary of terms at the end of the chapter. We have reserved diacritics (especially in Sanskrit and Hindi) for chapters where the author employs them because they engage directly with primary sources in original languages.

# PART I

# Introduction to yoga and meditation studies

The overall aim of this section – and the volume as a whole – is to think about what can be gained by reflecting on meditation and yoga *together* as closely related (and overlapping) techniques. Here we highlight some of the main themes and contexts in which the academic study of yoga and meditation currently exists.

In particular, we want to draw attention to the contemporary, global, postcolonial and neo-liberal social contexts and power structures in which we all operate. But, additionally, we want to emphasise the importance of recognising the complex relationships between individual scholars' identities and the construction of academic debates and disciplines.

# 1

# REFRAMING YOGA AND MEDITATION STUDIES

*Karen O'Brien-Kop and Suzanne Newcombe*

## Introduction

The study of yoga and meditation is not new. The techniques that we now associate with the terms 'meditation' and 'yoga' are documented over thousands of years in nuanced explorations by practitioners and theorists. However, the 'outsider' study of these practices is intimately connected with the knowledge construction projects of European modernity. As the Peruvian philosopher Aníbal Quijano (amongst others) has pointed out, modernity was, for the majority of the world, an experience of coloniality; the conceptual frameworks of European modernity co-arise with the experiences, cultural oppressions and transformations of colonisation (Quijano 2000). In many ways our understandings of practices of meditation and yoga, and their popularised meanings, have been filtered and distorted through the epistemic frameworks that have become dominant and globalised during this period. By examining the study of meditation and yoga through a range of disciplines and in a number of specific cultural and historical contexts, we hope to begin a conversation that challenges assumptions created by cultural positioning, disciplinary training and the blind spots to which they almost inevitably give rise.

This volume is aimed at students and educators and aspires to showcase the range, depth and complexity of current, global academic research on yoga and meditation. As such, this volume mostly takes the stance of the 'outsider' perspective to the study of yoga and meditation, although it does include many insider, theological and blended viewpoints. In the past few decades and in line with the rapid expansion of globalised meditation and yoga, there has been a correlative increase in academic studies of yoga and meditation from a range of perspectives. Recent research has been published not only from within established disciplines such as sociology, anthropology, indology, religious studies and medical-based science, but also from newly emerging and interdisciplinary approaches, such as political theory (Kale and Novetzske forthcoming) or critical and cultural race studies (e.g. Gandhi forthcoming). The increased academic interest reflects that yoga and meditation studies is significantly shifting from a submerged sub-field within selected disciplines to a visible field of study in its own right, one that is both multidisciplinary and interdisciplinary and increasingly transregional.

The chapters in this volume not only consolidate the contemporary field of academic knowledge on yoga and meditation, but also push the boundaries of existing research and explore emerging and future directions of study. By investigating the meanings and assumptions behind practices associated with yoga and meditation in a variety of contexts, in specific historical periods and through different theological and disciplinary lenses, the authors of this volume contribute to a breaking up of siloed knowledge and rigid conceptual frameworks.

Historically, the field of yoga and meditation studies has not developed evenly. By the end of the twentieth century, academic study of Buddhism and meditation was firmly established in university departments of area studies and in selected humanities disciplines such as religious studies – and was increasingly a subject of biomedical/psycho-physical studies. However, the academic study of yoga traditions has only just emerged as a distinct category of research in the twenty-first century. This handbook is one of the first attempts to bring into direct dialogue two closely related areas of academic research: meditation and yoga. At times this dialogue has been easier to initiate than at other times – since, for some of the scholars whom we invited, the disciplinary areas of expertise, the questions asked and the assumptions made about their objects of study made it hard to see how their particular scholarly agenda would benefit from being part of interdisciplinary reflections.

In an effort to promote interdisciplinary dialogue and awareness between contributors, we organised an authors' workshop in early 2019, held in London, UK, at the School of Oriental and African Studies (SOAS) with support from the Open University.[1] In this forum, scholars exchanged comments on the first-draft papers, with the intention of creating a more coherent volume. This workshop was closely informed and supported by two interdisciplinary European Research Council funded projects on the history of yoga in South Asia, namely AYURYOG and the Haṭha Yoga Project. Both of these projects sought to cultivate interdisciplinary methods to shine new light on their subjects through *longue durée* lenses. For AYURYOG, this was to examine the histories and entanglements of yoga, ayurveda and *rasaśāstra* (alchemy and iatrochemistry) from the tenth century to the present, focusing on the disciplines' health, rejuvenation and longevity practices. For the Haṭha Yoga Project, the concern was how to identify the origins of both *haṭha* and modern yoga through multidisciplinary approaches of philology, ethnography and cultural history – and at times forging interdisciplinary approaches such as 'embodied philology', the interpretation of historical texts on *āsana* with the aid (and limits) of contemporary practitioner bodies. The diversity of the discussion over the course of these two days was inspiring. We hope that the new perspectives generated will have ripple effects on the framing of many of the participants' research beyond the scope of this particular volume.

Both of the editors of this volume work primarily in the field of yoga studies and, although we have aimed to include a broad range of approaches from the field of meditation and contemplative studies, we acknowledge that the content is slightly more weighted towards the topic of yoga. While some chapters are interdisciplinary (see, for instance, Li, Chapter 26, which integrates philology and digital humanities), other chapters are multidisciplinary (Bühnemann, Chapter 29, combines art history, material culture and religious studies) or cross-disciplinary (Gerety, Chapter 34, in part, employs sound studies to elucidate history of religions).[2] However, in the last section of the book, which focuses on 'disciplinary framings' we also see that the understanding of what yoga or meditation *is* and *does* can shift depending on the questions asked and methods of research. For example, a focus on measurable characteristics in psychophysiology yields a different understanding of yoga and meditation than exploring the social context of yoga with the tools of critical theory. The scope of this volume's essays from scholars around the world ensures that a considerable range of perspectives has been included from across the combined field of yoga and meditation studies and that there is ample opportunity for readers to think and analyse laterally across these complex and intertwined topics, regions, approaches and chronologies.

As editors, we also acknowledge that we are situated in the humanities and social sciences, primarily as scholars of religion. The hard sciences are not represented to the extent that we would have liked, but we have two excellent dedicated science-based chapters, one on biomedicine (Chapter 30) and one on cognitive psychology (Chapter 31), as well as a range of scientific perspectives incorporated in other chapters. It is worth reflecting on the institutionalised structures of knowledge, reward and research finance in this area: many of the scientists that we reached out to were unwilling to commit to publishing in a cross-disciplinary forum and to a publishing format – an edited collection – which is singular to the humanities and social sciences. In the hard sciences, the outputs for hard-won research hours are standard science journal articles (usually by large teams of co-researchers). Often research into health interventions (which is a common focus for yoga and meditation studies in these disciplines) also need to demonstrate the potential to generate or at least to save money in the context of the healthcare market. The academic environment is therefore increasingly driven by constrained research outputs and specific research funding opportunities. An important challenge for social science and humanities researchers going forward is to impress upon both biomedical researchers and the general public the importance of understanding health interventions *in context* – that their healing and meaning-giving potential cannot be reduced to, or fully understood by, biomedical measurements. Conversely, it can also be helpful for humanities and 'soft' science scholars to have a better understanding of how the body is likely to react to certain psycho-physical techniques and what this might mean for the social construction of traditions and ontological understandings of reality.

## Defining meditation and yoga: the challenges

Across this collection, scholars have grappled with central questions, themes and tensions inherent in studying these subjects in the contemporary world and from within the often Euro- and America-centric academic traditions. First and foremost among our projects has been the exploration and problematising of the very definitions of terms such as 'yoga', 'meditation', 'contemplation', and spiritual 'discipline' across chronology, region and religious categories. We have long since moved beyond the twentieth-century view of yoga and meditation as 'timeless' or 'universal' traditions of the 'Mystic East' (see King 1999). Rather, when we probe more deeply, we discover the many nuances of these somewhat general terms and that there are multiple definitions and accounts of yoga and meditation that are particular to specific contexts.

When a scholar sets out to formally define 'yoga' and/or 'meditation' there are many challenges to confront, not least at the basic level of language. For example, scholars encounter translation difficulties, such as which words may reasonably be translated as 'meditation' from different languages. While *dhyāna* in Sanskrit, *jìngzuò* (静坐) in Japanese, and *shouyi* (守一) in Chinese Daoist discourse are often translated into English with the word 'meditation', more technically they denote 'absorption' (*dhyāna*), 'quiet sitting' (*jìngzuò*), and 'guarding the one' (*shouyī*). It is equally possible to assert that these varied practices are entirely disparate and disconnected and should not be grouped under the umbrella term of 'meditation.' The scholar faces similarly challenging philological choices: e.g. did *yogācāra* mean 'discipline of yoga' for classical South Asian Buddhists or something generic such as 'spiritual conduct'? What happens to an experiential categorisation of *samādhi* as a singular type of 'meditative concentration' when some Mahāyāna Buddhist texts note that types of *samādhi*s run, numerically, into the millions? (See Deleanu, Chapter 7.) Furthermore, one has to negotiate semantic change and slippage across time and language: be it within a Sanskrit text or as a borrowed word, what does *yoga* denote in different cultures, languages and eras? Finally, contemporary definitions often eclipse historical definitions and can lead to anachronistic, misinformed or simply skewed understandings of the past discussions of yoga as recorded in textual sources. On the other hand, contemporary definitions of yoga and identities within particular meditative traditions can be weighed down by the ideological anchor of historical 'authenticity' with no room for organic change and development in meaning or understanding.

Then there are the challenges of defining a *practice* of 'yoga' or 'meditation'. Is yoga a means to an end (a set of techniques) or the goal itself (the end state of liberation)? Where does ritual end and meditation begin? (Is lighting a candle a ritual act or a meditative act, or both?) How do we, as scholars, reconstruct past or present practices of yoga and meditation, taking into account the dilemmas of the etic/emic perspectives and the often thorny topic of insider and outsider identities and statuses? Furthermore, what are our presumptions about practice in relation to yoga and meditation? If yoga is understood as primarily characterised by 'visible' practices such as posture and breathing technique, then is meditation understood as an inner or 'invisible' set of techniques? Do the categories of 'meditation' and 'yoga' reproduce a Cartesian dualism of 'mind' and 'body' that is reductive and Eurocentric? Again, our survey of traditions and regions in this volume demonstrates that meditation practice may be just as bodily and demonstrative as any conception of yoga – e.g. Jain walking meditation with fixed gaze (see Pragya, Chapter 13). Indeed, the characterisation of meditation as an 'inner' and silent experience is, in part, a product of the European colonial privileging of Theravāda Buddhist meditation as *the* meditation technique *par excellence* (see Husgafvel, Chapter 3).

A further challenge awaits the scholar in dealing with the field of yoga or meditation studies itself. Since the term 'yoga' has been specifically limited in its application to South Asia and its derived contexts and transmissions, the field of yoga studies is, in many ways, more clearly demarcated. The term 'meditation', however, has a semantic provenance and currency far beyond South Asia, is more culturally neutral, and has been used to define spiritual practices in a range of religions, regions and time periods. As a consequence, the academic field of meditation studies is more difficult to delimit than yoga studies, because it is more disparate culturally. In the case of meditation, all roads do not lead back to South Asia, as they do for yoga. Distinct traditions of contemplation can be traced to ancient Greek concepts of self-care and meditation/contemplation, to the Chinese practices glossed as 'sitting', or to a range of other cultural contexts.

In this volume, we have dealt with a further valence in the definition of yoga in particular. One of the questions that arose was the way in which authors working on different time periods were using the same technical terms. For example, take the case of *haṭhayoga*. This term conveys a different meaning from its early Buddhist mention in South Asian *yogācāra* literature in the c. third century CE (as a 'forceful process' although its method is not explained) (Mallinson 2020: 5), to a medieval context in the fifteenth-century *Haṭhapradīpikā* (indicating the yoga of force, but now encompassing a specific set of techniques), to its popular twenty-first-century anglophone branding as 'gentle stretching in a traditional Indian style.'[3] As editors, we therefore discussed how to differentiate the premodern from the modern referents using a stylistic device.[4] In order to distinguish a modern *haṭhayoga* (indicating post-Vivekānanda, anglophone, asana-focused yoga) from its historical precedents, we opted for the anglicised Hatha Yoga (or more generically hatha yoga). Hatha Yoga is how the term is primarily written in early twentieth-century primary sources in English. In contrast to this borrowed 'Hatha Yoga' in English, we reserve italics and diacritics for the Sanskrit *haṭhayoga* as discussed in premodern South Asian sources, but also for contemporary traditional practices in India that use the term *haṭha*. This indicates a theoretical stance on the need to engage in a constant critical reflection on the meaning of the terms that we employ as scholars, rather than sliding into a comfort zone about what 'yoga' means. This editorial choice also asks the reader to maintain a critical enquiry into the questions of continuity and rupture in traditions of yoga, and it strongly challenges perennialist assumptions of a single yoga that is true for all times, places and people.

We wish to avoid, however, an elision of the entanglements between historical and modern practices of meditation and yoga with this stylistic distinction; it is certainly the case that many 'traditional' forms of yoga and meditation (i.e. historically continuous practices) continue to exist today. Indeed further discussion and deconstruction of the term *haṭha* shows it as unstable and polyvalent even before the *Haṭhapradīpikā* (see Singleton, Chapter 9). Finally, the stylistic intervention that we have applied in this volume to *haṭhayoga* and Hatha Yoga can equally be applied to other relevant terms that have potent cross-linguistic currency and a 'brand value' outside of their original historical contexts, such as *vipassanā* and Vipassana, *aṣṭāṅga yoga* and Ashtanga Yoga, or *āsana* and asana. This nuanced approach points to the unique historical context of South Asian yoga and meditation, and it also highlights singular developments and innovations in transnational yoga and meditation.

Contributors to this volume have also sought to clarify the extent to which concepts and practices of 'meditation' and 'yoga' can be regarded as distinct or overlapping in a particular tradition, context or time period. In some traditions, yoga and meditation have been used synonymously, while in others they are separate. For example, in early South Asia, Patañjali defines yoga as concentration (*samādhi*) (*Pātañjalayogaśāstra* 1.1),[5] indicating that the primary understanding of yoga in this period was as meditative practice. In a contemporary context, Ville Husgafvel (Chapter 3) discusses the relationship between meditation and yoga from a meditation studies point of view, pointing to the many entanglements, such as the inclusion of yoga postures in various Mindfulness-Based Practices (MBPs). In other contexts, however, we see that a stricter demarcation has been maintained between the two disciplines. In Japan, the longstanding historical importance of meditation traditions – inclusive of Daoism, Confucianism, Buddhism, Shinto and more modern interpretations – far outweighs the cultural contact with postural-based yoga in the later twentieth century. Furthermore, in many contexts, practices of yoga and meditation intersect with a broader category of 'asceticism', from which it can be difficult to differentiate discrete concepts of yoga and/or meditation.

Another key question has been the ways in which specific practices of 'yoga' or 'meditation' can lead to unique experiences, effects and understandings. For example, a particular practice of 'meditation' or 'yoga' in one context can look very different to other practices that carry the same label – e.g. *kuṇḍalinī yoga* in medieval Kashmir as explored by Olga Serbaeva Saraogi in Chapter 8, or in contemporary Assam and present-day USA as explored by Sravana Borkataky-Varma in Chapter 25. Equally, we encounter practices, habits and codes in historical traditions that may not be explicitly called yoga or meditation but which appear to entail similar traits and outcomes – e.g. the practices of early Buddhism in South Asia (Deleanu, Chapter 7) or the Sufi breathing techniques of medieval South Asia (D'Silva, Chapter 15). In grouping together various endeavours under an umbrella term such as 'meditation' for the purposes of scholarly analysis, one has to ask whether, in today's world and at the level of experience, there are *any* connections between the contemporary mindfulness of Kabat-Zinn and mantra recitation (*mantar-jap*) in Sikhism, or between yogic jumping techniques (Beps) in Tibetan Buddhism and 'Christian yoga' in the USA, or between Daoist *qi* and yogic *prāṇa*. The artificiality of the analytical categories of 'yoga' and 'meditation' can unintentionally revive and reify the perennialist view all over again. However, this is emphatically not the intention of this volume. Rather than proposing an answer to the above question, the juxtaposition of perspectives here hopes to create more, better and new questions – and to begin to reframe the discussion.

Finally, there is the issue of what is to be regarded as 'yoga' and/or 'meditation': if a practitioner or community defines a particular practice or phenomenon as 'yoga' or 'meditation', even though it appears to be at radical odds with established and traditional forms – witness recent social media discussions about 'goat yoga' or 'beer yoga', for example – should it be dismissed evaluatively as 'non-authentic'? This is a discussion that Andrea Jain takes up in Chapter 5. On the whole, this research handbook seeks to shift the contemporary framing of yoga beyond the limited binary debates of 'tradition' and 'authenticity' versus 'non-tradition' and 'non-authenticity.' Yes, tracing how orthogenetic developments have occurred within and without South Asia is still important (and well covered in section two of this volume), but there are also broader global questions to be asked: In what ways and contexts might yoga and meditation practices cause harm? Is there any yoga on the planet that is not today embroiled in neoliberal capitalism? In what ways are yoga and meditation being weaponised at an international scale as tools of political, religious, racial, economic and cultural hegemony?

## Shifting discussions and emerging areas of research

As editors we are committed to the project of 'decolonising yoga' and have endeavoured to encompass a diversity of views that have the potential to decentre traditional or dominant narratives, be they epistemic, cultural or regional. For example, this volume includes chapters that, for the first time in English, explore developments of yoga and meditation traditions in Korea and in Latin America (see Park and Park, Chapter 22; Muñoz, Chapter 23) – as well as a chapter that introduces new research from Japan (see Kurita, Chapter 21). Additionally, through this collection of studies we are attempting to bring areas of established (but previously niche) research to wider audiences of yoga and meditation studies, such as the significance of yoga and meditation traditions in Insular Southeast Asia (see Acri, Chapter 19). We were able to include theological perspectives in the chapters on yoga and meditation in Jain and Sikh traditions (see Pragya, Chapter 13; Bhogal, Chapter 16). And we have asked all of our contributors to consider insider and outsider implications in their own research, including the complex category of the scholar-practitioner. Furthermore, we also explored how different agendas, questions and interest groups drive current research in our various disciplinary areas of study – a topic thoroughly discussed at the authors' workshop in March 2019. We have therefore aimed to engage in reflexive scholarship on the academic approaches and identities that inform the field. However, shifting the understandings created and maintained by academic power structures and methods of studying is a slow process, and proposing viable alternatives is not necessarily easy or straightforward.

The first step toward creating new assumptions for discussion is to draw attention to what is missing and to those perspectives that have yet to be represented at the table. We regret the limited extent to which we were able to include scholars of yoga and meditation trained at and holding positions at educational institutions in South Asia. Additionally, we were not able to include a chapter that could explore the recent exponential growth of yoga in China or a detailed analysis of the exchange of yogic and meditative practices between China and its neighbours in Asia from the Chinese perspective. Understandings about yoga and meditation in Eastern European and former communist cultures is also a topic that needs more sustained attention in global studies of these techniques and practices. Furthermore, the regional histories and contemporary contexts of yoga and meditation in Africa and the Middle East are vital areas for future, sustained research. Unfortunately, one volume cannot cover everything – but it can highlight and spearhead some important emerging areas for required focus.

One significant area of emerging research is the acknowledgement and analysis of how abuses of power and sexuality have been embedded in many contemporary (and historical) yoga and meditation movements. There are wide-ranging studies of abusive behaviour in many of the groups associated with practices that gained popularity after World War II. Such studies have been undertaken in the context of sociology of religion – particularly in research on 'new religious movements' (NRMs) – and in psychological studies on 'cultic abuse' and (more recently) 'coercive control.'[6] But until the last decade, there was little public discussion of institutionalised abuse, particularly institutionalised sexual abuse. This culture change is facilitating a new framing of research into this important area. Central to future enquiry will be theorisations of race, gender, culture and power and the ways in which intersections of these factors have produced, facilitated and covered up abusive behaviour. This handbook is being produced at the start of a five-year Luce Foundation funded project into 'Sexual Abuse and Religious Movements' which is headed by Amanda Lucia at the University of California-Riverside – and its emerging research agenda promises to include in its publications and output a broad range of groups that have yoga and meditation as central practices. Although several of the contributions in this volume mention the issue of abuse in groups and movements (e.g. Jain, Chapter 5; Wong, Chapter 32), we regret that we were not able to include a substantive chapter on this issue as a stand-alone subject.

Early pioneering work on structural inequalities within both academic and practitioner communities interested in yoga and meditation has been undertaken by scholars working on the intersections of gender and capitalism and research groups such as Race and Yoga[7] (see for example: Jain 2015, 2020; Black 2016; Lucia 2018; Godrej 2017; Gandhi forthcoming). In recent years, there have been key reflections on race, whiteness and Buddhism in the west (e.g. Yancy and McRae 2019; Gleig 2019). Yet critical race theory is still to be integrated and applied within mainstream research in yoga studies. The bulk of the work on race and yoga to date has been produced by women of colour working in the USA, and the burden of drawing attention to social and structural inequities has not yet been shouldered (or discussed reflexively) by significant numbers of white scholars. In line with developments in critical race theory and decolonial approaches, analysis of race in yoga and meditation communities will focus more on whiteness and its cultural manifestations globally. There may also be further scrutiny to ensure that broader demographic and institutional power structures are not automatically replicated in communities of academic scholar-practitioners. A pernicious consequence of colonialism, cultural appropriation and religious exoticism is evident in the fact that while aspects of South Asian culture are pick'n'mixed – from the fashion industry to commercialised yoga – citizens of South Asian heritage are still stereotyped and vilified as terrorists in the global north (see e.g. Bald 2015). Even as yoga reaches the farthest corners of small-town US culture, there are still fundamental misunderstandings of South Asian religion and culture so that Sikhs, for example, are attacked as 'Muslim terrorists' because of their turbans.[8] In many cases, a romanticised and highly selective skimming-off of South Asian cultures has been carried out by white yoga practitioners, to the detriment of engaging with these cultures as integral, living traditions.

Further disciplinary developments in yoga studies will take place in South Asian textual studies related to yoga and meditation, where there has been a firm emphasis on translating Sanskrit texts for the past 200 years. However, there is growing recognition of the many texts yet to be translated and studied in other languages such as Hindi, Urdu and Bengali, and even more so the languages of southern India, such as Tamil, Malayālam and Telugu. Texts and archives in these languages, both premodern and modern, will offer up new information on the history and development of yoga and meditation in South Asia – and steer attention beyond the *Yogasūtra* and *Bhagavadgītā* towards non-elite sources such as songs, poems, tracts, manuals, letters, and popular and literary works. Considerable ground has been gained in acknowledging the diversity of South Asian religious traditions in the development of yoga – including Buddhism, Jainism and Islam – but further work remains to be done in order to develop this body of knowledge. Ongoing rapid developments in digital humanities will continue to alleviate the painstaking burden of creating critical editions of original texts and analysing large corpuses, and such innovations will lead to new insights into old texts at a faster rate.

There is an increasing number of projects that are in various ways connected to the aims of social justice, be it the debates around 'engaged' or 'disengaged' Buddhism or those around 'on the mat/off the mat' activism in yoga. Also growing in number are projects seeking to instigate social change for underprivileged groups – from yoga and mindfulness in prisons, to yoga and meditation for refugees. These developments in political and social activism will also be instantiated in already complex scholar-practitioner identities, leading to new forms of embodied academic critiques, political dissent and socially-engaged knowledge modalities. Finally, an emergent area of interest, on which there is yet to be substantial published research, is the relationship between yoga and technology. The impacts of robot yoga teachers, robot monks chanting in Buddhist temples, digital gurus, meditation headsets and consciousness implants are among the many topics currently under investigation (see Singleton forthcoming).

## Concluding remarks

Interdisciplinary research is vital to the development of yoga and meditation studies. This kind of knowledge exchange is essential to strengthen the field and to make sense of complex and fast-moving global developments. How can lab-based scientists measure the benefits (and potential detriments) of a meditation technique if they do not understand the social contexts in which these practices were developed historically and are presently taught? How can one decode the meaning of historical texts on *haṭhayoga* postures without the referent of embodied interpretation?

We hope that the sheer range of contributions in this volume will help to continue the widening of both academic and practitioner assumptions about the diversity and complexity of traditions of yoga and meditation. Moreover, it is our aim that this collaborative reframing will eventually transform lived understandings beyond the scholars and practitioners who are specifically interested in the techniques of yoga and meditation. The intention of this volume is to generate more nuanced insights into the depth of global traditions of meditation and yoga in order to contribute to a wider reframing of shared understandings of the categories of religion, science, spirituality, politics and culture.

## Notes

1 The workshop 'Disciplines and Dialogue: The Future of Yoga and Meditation Studies' was attended by more than forty international scholars who shared their research; this two-day workshop was generously funded by the Strategic Research Investment Fund at the Open University's Faculty of Arts and Social Science and supported in kind by the Centre of Yoga Studies at SOAS University of London.

2 Interdisciplinarity involves integrating or synthesizing two or more disciplines in a single study to create a new approach; cross-disciplinarity entails using one discipline to examine another; multi-disciplinarity employs a range of disciplinary approaches in one study without attempting to synthesize them. For further discussion, especially on interdisciplinarity, see Graff 2015: 1–19.

3 As one yoga website states: 'Today, the term hatha is used in such a broad way that it is difficult to know what a particular hatha class will be like. In most cases, however, it will be relatively gentle, slow and great for beginners or students who prefer a more relaxed style where they hold poses longer.' www.doyogawithme.com/types-of-yoga. Accessed 11 March 2020.

4 On this subject, we wish to express our gratitude to Mark Singleton for his valuable insights and dialogue with us on the subject.

5 The commentary (*bhāṣya*) to *sūtra* 1.1 states, *yogaḥ samādhiḥ*, 'yoga is concentration'. It also states, *sa saṃprajñāto yoga ity ākhyāyate*, 'That cognitive form [of concentration; of *samādhi*] is called yoga.' (Maas 2006: 2–3; trans O'Brien-Kop).
6 The following references may help to further explore this topic: Caldwell 2001; Crovetto 2008 and 2011; Barker 1987 and 2009; Downing 2001; Jacobs 2007; Lewis 2011; Palmer 2018 and 1994; Palmer and Hardman 1999; Rochford 1998, 2007 and 2011; Masis 2007; Urban 2003 and 2011; van Eck Duymaer van Twist 2014 and 2015; Voix 2008.
7 https://escholarship.org/uc/crg_raceandyoga. Accessed 24 July 2020.
8 See, for example, this news story: https://edition.cnn.com/2016/09/15/us/sikh-hate-crime-victims/index.html. Accessed 11 March 2020.

## Bibliography


Bald, V. 2015. 'American Orientalism'. *Dissent Magazine*, Spring 2015. www.dissentmagazine.org/article/american-orientalism. Accessed 18 March 2020.

Barker, E. 1987. 'Freedom to Surrender with Bhagwan', *Self and Society* 25(5): 209-216.

Barker, E. 2009. 'In God's Name: Practising Unconditional Love to the Death', in Al-Rasheed, M. and Shterin, M. (eds), *Dying for Faith: Religiously Motivated Violence in the Contemporary World*, 49–58. London & New York: I. B. Tauris.

Black, S. 2016. 'Flexible Indian Labor: Yoga, Information Technology Migration, and US Technoculture', *Race and Yoga* 1: 23–41.

Caldwell, S. 2001. 'The Heart of the Secret: A Personal and Scholarly Encounter with Shakta Tantrism in Siddha Yoga', *Nova Religio* 5(1): 9–51.

Crovetto, H. 2008. 'Ananda Marga and the Use of Force', *Nova Religio* 12(1): 26–56.

Crovetto, H. 2011. 'Ananda Marga, PROUT and the Use of Force', in Lewis, J. R. (ed), *Violence and New Religious Movements*, 249–276. New York and Oxford: Oxford University Press.

Downing, M. 2001. *Shoes Outside the Door: Desire, Devotion and Excess at the San Francisco Zen Center*. San Francisco: Counterpoint.

Gandhi, S. forthcoming. *A Cultural History of Yoga in the United States*.

Gleig, A. 2019. *American Dharma: Buddhism Beyond Modernity*. New Haven: Yale University Press.

Godrej, F. 2017. 'The Neoliberal Yogi and the Politics of Yoga', *Political Theory* 45, 772–800.

Graff, H. 2015. *Undisciplining Knowledge: Interdisciplinarity in the Twentieth Century*. Baltimore, Maryland: John Hopkins University Press.

Jacobs, J. 2007. 'Abuse in New Religious Movements: Challenges for the Sociology of Religion', in Bromley, D. G. (ed), *Teaching New Religions*, 231–244. Oxford: Oxford University Press.

Jain, A. R. 2015. *Selling Yoga: From Counterculture to Pop Culture*. New York: Oxford University Press.

Jain, A. R. 2020. *Peace, Love, Yoga: The Politics of Global Spirituality*. Oxford and New York: Oxford University Press.

Kale, S. and Novetzske, C. forthcoming. *The Political Idea of Yoga*. New York: Columbia University Press.

King, R. E. 1999. *Orientalism and Religion: Post-colonial Theory, India and the Mystic East*. London: Routledge.

King, R. E. 2019. 'Meditation and the Modern Encounter between Asia and the West' in Farias, M, Brazier, D. and Lalljee, M. (eds), *The Oxford Handbook of Meditation*. Online. October. https://doi.org/10.1093/9780198808640.013.2. Accessed 21 February 2020.

Lewis, J. R. (ed) 2011. *Violence and New Religious Movements*. New York: Oxford University Press.

Lucia, A. 2018. 'Guru Sex: Charisma, Proxemic Desire, and the Haptic Logics of the Guru-Disciple Relationship', *Journal of the American Academy of Religion*, 86(4): 953–988.

Maas, P. (ed) 2006. *Samādhipāda. Das Erste Kapitel des Pātañjalayogaśāstra zum ersten Mal Kritisch Ediert*. Aachen: Studia Indologica Universitatis Halensis (GeisteskulturIndiens. Texte und Studien, 9).

Mallinson, J. 2020. 'Hathayoga's Early History: From Vajrayāna Sexual Restraint to Universal Somatic Soteriology' in Flood, G. (ed), *The Oxford History of Hinduism: Religious Practices*. Oxford: Oxford University Press.

Masis, K. V. 2007. 'Compassion Betrayed: Spiritual Abuse in an American Zen Centre', in Nowakowski, P. T. (ed), *The Phenomenon of Cults from a Scientific Perspective*, 168–191. Cracow: Dom Wydawniczy Rafael.

Palmer, S. J. 1994. *Moon Sisters, Krishna Mothers, Rajneesh Lovers: Women's Roles in New Religions*. Syracuse, NY: Syracuse University Press.

Palmer, S. J. 2018. '"Guru Pedophiles", Neo-Polygamists, and Predatory Prophets: Exploring the Sex Scandals and Abuse Allegations Concerning "Cults"/NRMs, 1993–2017', in Holtmann, C. and Nason-Clark, N. (eds), *Religion, Gender, and Family Violence: When Prayers Are Not Enough,* 146–162. Leiden: Brill.

Palmer, S. J. and Hardman, C. E. (eds) 1999. *Children in New Religions*. New Brunswick: Rutgers University Press.

Quijano, A. 2000. 'Coloniality of Power, Eurocentrism, and Latin America', *Nepantla: Views from South* 1(3): 533–580.

Rochford, E. B. 1998. 'Further Reflections on Child Abuse within ISKCON', *ISKCON Communications Journal* 6(2): 64–67.

Rochford, E. B. (ed) 2007. *Hare Krishna Transformed*. New York: New York University Press.

Rochford, E. B. 2011. 'Knocking on Heaven's Door: Violence, Charisma, and Transformation of New Vrindaban', in Lewis, J. R. (ed), *Violence and New Religious Movements,* 275–292. Oxford: Oxford University Press.

Singleton, M. forthcoming. *Yoga Machine: Technology, Transhumanism and Transcendence*.

Urban, H. B. 2003. *Tantra: Sex, Secrecy, Politics, and Power in the Study of Religion*. Berkeley: University of California.

Urban, H. B. 2011. *The Power of Tantra: Religion, Sexuality and the Politics of South Asian Studies*. London: I. B. Tauris.

van Eck Duymaer van Twist, A. (ed) 2014. *Minority Religions and Fraud: In Good Faith*. Farnham: Ashgate.

van Eck Duymaer van Twist, A. 2015. *Perfect Children: Growing Up on the Religious Fringe*. Oxford: Oxford University Press.

Voix, R. 2008. 'Denied Violence, Glorified Fighting: Spiritual Discipline and Controversy in Ananda Marga', *Nova Religio* 12(1): 3–26.

Yancy, G. and McCrae, E. (eds) 2019. *Buddhism and Whiteness: Critical Reflections* (Philosophy of Race). Lanham, Maryland: Lexington Books.

# 2
# DECOLONISING YOGA

*Shameem Black*

## Why decolonise?

Does modern yoga need decolonising? And can modern yoga assist with larger projects of decolonisation? The answer to both questions – simultaneously – may be yes. Grappling with yoga through the lens of postcolonial critique can expose the ways in which yogic practice can develop in complicity with imperial configurations, while it can also shed light on how the practice might support emancipatory social projects. Ironically, it is sometimes the very desire to decolonise the practice that can reinscribe yoga within alternative forms of hierarchy. No practice is solely emancipatory, yet no practice is bereft of the potential to liberate. These ambivalences continue to shape yoga today.

This essay addresses three concerns that have acquired increasing salience in the twenty-first century. First, to what extent is the construction of modern yoga a colonial production of orientalist discursive domination? Second, to what extent does the modern practice of yoga beyond South Asian borders constitute a practice of cultural appropriation? Finally, how might the resurgent nationalist Indian interest in yoga decolonise the practice? I address the first question in the section 'Knowledge, body, empire'; the second in 'Travel, positionality, power'; and the third in 'Nationalism, decolonisation, recolonisation'. I end with an invitation for yoga studies scholarship to continue its experiments with decolonising cultural critique in an era of neoliberal globalisation.

In this chapter, yoga signifies a diverse constellation of practices that people call or have called yoga in the twentieth and twenty-first centuries, rather than practices that conform to a foundational philosophical definition. I focus primarily on legacies of British colonialism and India's engagement with western Anglophone countries, where these questions have grown particularly urgent. 'Decolonial', as used in this chapter, refers to the active practice of contesting specific hierarchical configurations of power. A more transformative approach to decolonising yoga would investigate complex histories of yoga, hierarchy and emancipation in other parts of the world, taking us beyond the Eurocentric boundaries reaffirmed by the concept of 'post-colonial'. The need for such scholarship constitutes a key future direction for yoga studies.

While particular presentations of yoga sometimes cultivate an image of being outside regimes of power, the practice has long played diverse political roles. In the twenty-first century, the practice has gained new political vitality. Precisely because yoga has taken on a role as a person-making project and a mode of state theatrics, it becomes important to ask what yoga's rising popularity means for a current understanding of imperial and neo-imperial power relations. By acknowledging more fully how yogic practices have emerged in dialogue with hierarchical formations, we can best cultivate yoga as a practice that challenges, as well as instrumentalises, the neo-imperial projects of our day.

## Knowledge, body, empire

The twenty-first-century scholarly mapping of yoga's modern history from the sixteenth century to the present has revealed that yogic practice communities have long been political. David Gordon White's extensive work in South Asian folkloric traditions exposes the yogi not as a peace-loving practitioner of *āsana*, but instead as a sinister soul-stealer who works close to kingly might (White 2009). Mughal emperors, aiming to bolster support among their Hindu subjects, demonstrated keen interest in yoga and commissioned visual representations of yogic communities (Parikh 2015: 227). Paintings from this era suggest how closely those communities were watched as a potential resource for – and possible threat to – imperial control. Yogic mercenaries, as William Pinch shows, became power brokers in a seventeenth- and eighteenth-century India shaped by British imperial incursions. These groups of organised armed ascetics, knowledgeable in a wide range of military technologies, 'would apply these skills *against* the British in late eighteenth-century Bengal … and *for* the British in Bundelkhand after 1800' (Pinch 2006: 255). This uncertainty around yogic political allegiance leads us to question how yoga has historically been co-created within diverse imperial frames: if not exactly a product *of* empire, then certainly a product *within* and *through* empire.

Common conceptions of yoga are indebted to modes of knowledge production and social ideologies that emerged in dialogue with nineteenth- and twentieth-century colonial norms. Archival scholarship shows how yogis were often recorded in British and European accounts as exotic contortionists who sat outside western conceptions of respectable life (Singleton 2010). This understanding was shared by Indian intellectuals, such as Swami Vivekānanda, who rehabilitated yoga to align with neo-Hindu reform movements and to appeal to a bourgeois western audience. Many key Indian spiritual leaders who popularised such texts as the *Yogasūtra* were influenced by western groups who produced particular ideas of Indian religiosity for their own purposes (White 2014). Histories of breath control in this period reveal how yoga could be constructed both in opposition to and in concert with British ideals of physical cultivation (Green 2008). Yoga thus emerges as the paradoxical product of colonial modernity, transcultural engagement and broader global exercises of western power.

This rehabilitation process made yoga available as an anti-colonial resource to produce indigenous masculinity. The anti-colonial nationalist Aurobindo Ghose, for instance, reimagined the colonial jail cell as a 'revolutionary ashram' (Wolfers 2016: 525). Others, like the Maharaja of the Mysore Palace, saw in yoga the potential for a physical vocabulary that would strengthen the nation's young men. This project appealed to the Rashtriya Swayamsevak Sangh (RSS), where yogic postural practice became aligned – sometimes ambivalently and paradoxically – with the project of making pure, militant and specifically Hindu Indian male bodies (Alter 2004).[1] Hindu nationalists such as V. D. Savarkar drew on articulations of *karma-yoga* in the *Bhagavad Gītā* to develop a Hindu call to arms (Chaturvedi 2010). Framing the practice in opposing terms, Gandhi situated yoga between nonviolent anti-colonial resistance and biomoral public health reform (Alter 2000). These political projects, in all their diversity, used yoga to reimagine anti-colonial masculinities.

Yoga was also to a varying extent supported by western authorities in India. The YMCA was a famous promoter of postural practice, indicating that yoga could be remodulated to serve muscular Christianity and its investment in the ideals of the British empire (Singleton 2010). The yogic body was reshaped in the colonial period in ways that conformed to western ideals of pleasing bodies, featuring sculpted musculature rather than ash-rubbed skin. The practice was sometimes taken up by the British themselves as a supposedly Aryan mode of regenerating imperial masculinity at a time of crisis for the empire (Imy 2016).

More generally, many ideas of yoga in late-nineteenth and twentieth-century Anglophone circuits reaffirmed the orientalist construction of India as a land of exotic religiosity. When defined as India's core strength – a project endorsed by numerous Indian intellectuals, such as Paramahansa Yogananda (Yogananda 1946) – this emphasis on spiritual seeking could be used to justify India's inability to self-govern. This construction of yoga further positioned India as a place ready and willing to save alienated westerners from the failures of industrial capitalist modernity. Western cross-cultural practices of yoga, thus, have emerged within a larger field of knowledge about an imagined 'India' that resonates with Edward Said's emphasis on exotic alterity and political weakness in relation to the West (Said 1979).

While the development of yoga in the late-nineteenth and twentieth centuries cannot be said to be a purely colonial invention or a naked tool of empire, neither can it be understood as a phenomenon divorced from imperial configurations of knowledge and power. The empire perpetuated fantasies of India as an inexpensive source of spiritual raw material for western projects of personal self-development. At the same time, the empire allowed yoga to become useful as an anti-colonial project. This paradoxical genealogy forms one condition of possibility for the practice today.

## Travel, positionality and power

In 1991, India published a series of postage stamps with pictures of *āsana*. This series serves as a fitting emblem to reflect on the twentieth century, an era in which new portraits of yoga began to circulate around the globe with increasing speed. In this century, yoga experienced a mobility sometimes greater than that available to Indians. If the British empire enabled transnational movement for Indians in the nineteenth century, facilitating large migrations to the Caribbean, Southeast Asia, the Pacific and Africa, the twentieth century also witnessed key contractions. Mid-century racially-exclusive immigration policies in places like Australia (the White Australia policy) and the United States (The Immigration Act of 1924) made it challenging for Indians to take up residence in such countries. After World War II, Britain took in large numbers of Indians, but it sharply limited this migration in the 1960s.[2] The Indian state also exercised its own forms of control, since Indians were not guaranteed the right to a passport until the Passport Act of 1967.

This context, in which practices and ideas could travel in ways that sometimes people could not, helped to reshape the politics of yoga by transferring key reproductions of the practice away from Indian communities towards communities associated with privilege and mobility in other countries. To be sure, exceptional figures from India could travel to parts of the West to teach yoga, and they were often highly influential. But the broader restrictions on Indian migration meant that in some parts of the world, relatively few people of Indian descent could shape the practice as it was reconfigured in the West. As Americans and Europeans began to travel in greater numbers to India, their mobility has been seen as crucial to the western popularising of yoga (Goldberg 2015 and 2010). This transformation drew strength from increasingly powerful neoliberal logics that encouraged access to spiritual practices through an open marketplace (York 2001). Under these circumstances, Indian culture could become fetishised in a global market, while privileged communities could freely engage with cultural practices – even and often in respectful ways – without substantial attention to the hierarchies potentially constraining Indian people.

At the turn of the twenty-first century, yoga moved to the mainstream of many parts of the world (especially the West). It did so, as Andrea Jain has argued, by effectively linking religious transformation, personal self-development and ideal body cultivation to capitalist modes of reproduction and emerging norms of personal wellbeing (Jain 2015). As yoga became more popular, many western countries – such as the US, the UK, Australia, France and Germany – began to encourage migration from India. Both of these phenomena emerged within a context of 'expanding Orientalisms' that shaped public culture for migrants and ethnic minorities in the new millennium (Ramaprasad 2018). These patterns have given rise to contemporary concerns in South Asian studies, critical race theory and ethnic studies. First, how do we understand yoga as a South Asian cosmopolitan practice in countries where people of South Asian descent are ethnic minorities? Second, how does the practice of yoga in multicultural societies work to confirm or complicate pre-existing racial, ethnic or gender hierarchies?

A key rhetoric that has risen in urgency in the twenty-first century is whether yoga practised by people who are not of South Asian descent constitutes cultural appropriation. Some of these questions have emerged in popular culture as forms of cultural policing, especially in light of broader demands from conservative Hindu groups for recognition in a transnational public sphere (Ramachandran 2014). These initiatives have tended to focus on socialising new participants into norms of acceptability (how to practise yoga respectfully, for instance) and on consolidating community borders around normative ideals (such as what it means to be a proper Hindu).

Here I focus on a different approach to the question of cultural appropriation within leftist activism that takes decolonising yoga as a political ideal. In these discourses, cultural appropriation is most usefully understood as a term animated for critical purposes when there appears to be a strong inequality between the valuation of cultural practice and the valuation of people associated with that practice. Such an uneven valuation between Indian culture and South Asian people shapes yoga in many parts of the West. Yoga has enjoyed high popularity in the United States, for instance, in a post-9/11 era when many people of South Asian descent face heightened levels of xenophobia, hate crime, state surveillance and detention (Maira 2009). Seen in this context, some members of the Indian diaspora have begun to question why yoga appears more welcome than they are. Critiques of this nature seek to provoke reflection on this broader context, so that individuals may apprehend how their own practices may bolster troubling social patterns that they do not personally endorse. Seen in this light, the question of 'cultural appropriation' is not a call for essentialism or exclusion, but instead an attempt to analyse the place of yoga within larger structures of material privilege, state power and dominant norms.

Theorists of Indo-Chic have argued that the problem posed by cross-cultural practice is that signs of difference, which are often costly for ethnic minorities, are extracted and commodified into signs of cool, which create value for majoritarian subjects. As Anita Mannur and Pia Sahni contend, 'Indianness becomes the simulacrum through which a mainstream American can establish individuality while allowing an embrace of difference on one's own terms' (Mannur and Sahni 2011: 183). Related patterns can also be found in multi-ethnic Europe (Altglas 2014). Yoga analysed in light of Indian global labour markets suggests that political benefits of the practice, once enjoyed mostly by Indian masters, can be widely dispersed to a wide range of cultural positions, yet negative signs remain firmly tethered to Indian subjects (Black 2016). Shreena Gandhi and Lillie Wolff argue that yoga has become desirable because it promises to fix the meaninglessness that emerges when the nourishment of ethnic cultural traditions is traded away for the material benefits of whiteness (Gandhi and Wolff 2017). Seen in this light, yoga may ironically alleviate anxiety for those who benefited the most from settler colonial and imperial enterprises, perfecting the colonial project. Its embrace as a marker of cosmopolitan openness can support neoliberal modes of self-making without cognisance of the politics of race, ethnicity, gender and class (Luhr 2015; Markula 2015). Without stronger critical attention to this condition of possibility, yoga carries the capacity to mask a larger accounting with history.

Diverse new voices in art and activism have emerged to challenge these cultural logics. Chiraag Bhakta, an Indian American visual artist who goes by the working name of *Pardon My Hindi, created a powerful installation, *#WhitePeopleDoingYoga*, to critique the commodification of yoga in the West. His artist's statement declares:

> Brands like Lulu Lemon and Nike have started appropriating and trade-marking phrases, moves and clothing – aligning and embedding themselves in our understanding of yoga, while the South Asian face and voice is relegated to an exotic caricature – cartoons, adoption of South Asian names by white westerners, mystical creatures, Hindu gods.
>
> *(*Pardon My Hindi, n.d.)*

The uneven flow of benefits described in the statement creates a larger context within which the practice of yoga can seem to need decolonising. New initiatives have emerged to argue for South Asian stewardship over yoga in the West to promote positive forms of South Asian visibility (SAAPYA, n.d.). These groups have themselves been critiqued for enacting diasporic dominance and for ignoring yoga's reinforcement of caste and class hierarchies within South Asia (Patankar 2014). These debates suggest how the goals of ethnic and postcolonial activism may be in tension over what decolonising needs to occur.

Ethnic studies has also initiated key conversations around decolonising yoga to explore how yoga makes meaning for other minorities and indigenous peoples. In these analyses, which often join forces with gendered critiques of exclusionary norms (Berila et al. 2016; Horton and Harvey 2012; Klein and Guest-Jelley 2014), one major source of focus is yoga's accessibility. If South Asian studies has critiqued how yoga may be too readily accessible for subjects in positions of privilege, scholars in ethnic studies point out that the benefits of the practice have not been accessible enough for those whose bodies do not fit social norms around a twenty-first-century ideal yoga body. Many ethnic minorities feel isolated, criminalised or fetishized in yoga, and must work to claim space and legitimacy (Manigault-Bryant 2016; Panton and Evans 2017). These emotions speak to racial economies of feeling that enmesh contemporary yoga within broader legacies of slavery, discrimination and the destruction of indigenous communities (Blu Wakpa 2018). Decolonising yoga in this light requires practice communities to confront legacies that go well beyond India's specific histories of colonialism.

As ethnic and feminist studies critique the dystopian use of racial hierarchies, critical race studies has also advocated embedding yoga more deeply within a broader range of social and cultural norms. New initiatives, such as recalibrating yoga as part of the Black Lives Matter movement (Wortham 2016) or mestiza consciousness (Bost 2016), indicate how the practice can be used to confront traumatic hierarchies that govern everyday life for many people. In this respect, decolonising yoga can indicate an alliance project anchored in the specific political concerns and felt needs of minority communities.

## Nationalism, decolonisation, recolonisation

In the twenty-first century, the Indian state has lavished attention on yoga as a vehicle for its soft power aspirations. While this attention may in some respects constitute a project of decolonisation, it also often resembles a process of recolonisation in which nationalist political projects serve very selective parts of India.

Decolonisation, from the perspective of the Indian state, has most powerfully looked like a material project of aiming to protect the economic benefits of yoga for governmental control. India has designated yoga within the category of traditional knowledge subject to protection under the World Trade Organisation by creating a Traditional Knowledge Digital Library (TKDL) in 2001. This process creates new modes of authority-making over yoga (Fish 2014; Sidhu 2017). Through what Anjali Vats has called 'dewesternizing restructuring', the TKDL aims to decolonise yoga by challenging Eurocentric intellectual property classifications and protecting ideals of collective ownership against privatisation (Vats 2016). Economically, India's Ministry of Tourism has singled out yoga as a promising source of revenue within the category of wellness tourism (Ministry of Tourism, Government of India, n.d.). India has thus promoted the monetising of yoga through lifestyle industries. The religious entrepreneur Baba Ramdev, for instance, has encouraged Indians to become yogis and then seamlessly created lifestyle products for them to buy. These practices have aimed to reclaim yoga for Indian legal and economic benefit.

Ironically, this legal and economic decolonisation strategy – one that resonates to some degree with Gandhi's *swadeshi* (self-sufficiency) movement and Nehru's import substitution policies – has also gone hand in hand with a potentially recolonising Indian embrace of western stereotypes about India. While the idea of an exotic spiritual East has been widely bemoaned for decades, Indian government agencies appear to have embraced this stereotype in the hopes of monetising it. In this sense, they draw upon strategies deployed by twentieth-century Indian religious figures who strategically traded on orientalist perceptions of their mystical power (Mukherjee 2017). The long-running twenty-first-century Incredible !ndia campaign has featured yoga in idealised spiritual terms. Taking control of this longstanding western fantasy, India's nation-branding self-orientalises as a marketing strategy.

The second recolonising impulse can be found within the strong and growing link between yoga and Hindutva. Entrepreneurs such as Ramdev are often understood to promote Hindu-centric ideologies through personal self-care (Chakraborty 2007), while social service organisations such as the Vivekananda Kendra enmesh yoga within Hindu nationalist ideals (Pandya 2014). These projects sometimes seek to evacuate India of minorities, to justify caste hierarchies and discrimination based on work and descent and to create a model for aspirational world power. In these projects, yoga can become a tool to assert dominance over specific parts of India's citizenry. The ascendance of Yogi Adityanath as chief minister of Uttar Pradesh signals such a symbolic utility for yoga. Leader of the Gorakhnath Math, Adityanath is notorious for inflammatory comments that allow the ruling party to benefit from Hindutva appeals while protecting national leaders from the stigma of extremism (Kaul 2017). These trends place yoga centrally within concerns that India, celebrating seventy years of democracy, has become increasingly majoritarian and resistant to minority rights (Jaffrelot 2017).

Yoga also potentially gives Hindu nationalist voices a platform within Indian diasporic outreach. In recent years, the Indian state has developed a 'yoga diplomacy' that merges Hindutva-inspired ideals with Nehruvian cultural nationalism (Gautam and Droogan 2018: 19). Organisations such as Sri Sri Ravi Shankar's Art of Living Foundation and the Hindu Students Council in the United States have also pushed such agendas (Sood 2018: 14). In these contexts, yoga can become a vehicle for social groups to promote Hindutva globally as part of consciousness-raising for ethnic minority groups. It can also promote hierarchical and idealised narratives about Hinduism that often rely on the erasure of minority groups (especially Muslim ones) in the post-9/11 war on terror (Chandra 2015). Yoga thus plays a role as a potential and sometimes unwitting conduit for a globalising Hindutva.

The third potential form of recolonisation happening in India reflects the trend that many urban middle-class practitioners take up yoga as a western-legible form of modernity. The external validation that yoga has received around the world has increased its cache domestically. Indeed, this external popularity is at the heart of major government initiatives to capitalise on yoga: the state fears that the material benefits of yoga will be captured by other countries. International validation has made yoga more attractive for some Indian practitioners, while for others, the global popularity of the practice has inspired critical desires to reclaim and reassert an alternative Indian set of traditions (Askegaard and Eckhardt 2012).

While India's intensified interest in yoga in the twenty-first century has brought important decolonising impulses, the nationalist and religious agendas that have woven their way into the promotion of the practice also invite us to consider how diverse forms of yoga remediate influential articulations of hierarchy and control. As Indian governments, teachers and practitioners engage with the practice as a diverse and globalised one, these efforts have the potential to associate the transformative promise of yoga with selective agendas that rely on old and emerging social division. Decolonising yoga, thus, is no simple matter. What looks like 'decolonising' from one point of view may seem, from another angle, like a new imperial configuration.

## Conclusion: towards yoga as critique

For scholars working from postcolonial perspectives, one of the most promising capacities of yoga is its potential to offer not simply an object of knowledge, but a knowledge modality useful for decolonial aspirations. If we conceptualise yoga in hopeful terms as a practical philosophy of transformation that promotes an expanded apprehension of reality, one of the most exciting possibilities is that yoga can give us the tools for better constructive critique. Postcolonial studies is well known for its ability to expose injury and injustice. It is less well known for its ability to articulate a viable way forward.

Yoga alone is unlikely to decolonise habits of thought and action. But, enmeshed with analysis and activism, it offers the possibility for embodied critique. One important twenty-first-century trend links yogic practice to demands for progressive collective action (Training Leaders Worldwide in Social Change, n.d.). While many 'off the mat' actions perpetuate missionary imperialism, it may still be possible for yoga to promote conscious reflection on the larger political orders that shape the world. Farah Godrej suggests that yogic methods can 'encourage attitudes and behaviors that directly counteract neoliberal subjectivity: cultivating a truthful inward gaze that reflects on and problematises the construction of one's own needs, desires, and self-image' (Godrej 2017: 788). To understand how this critical project might take shape, we as scholars need to examine more closely how practices of yoga interweave themselves with analytical and activist frameworks.

Yoga as an alternative form of knowing shapes important ongoing experiments in growing university fields of contemplative studies, where critical first-person pedagogies reanimate yoga's histories of self-experimentation for contemporary knowledge work. Such projects aim to decolonise the traditional Eurocentric scholarly forms of knowing at the heart of the modern university. Yet the price of admission for such decolonising work can be the severing of such contemplative practices from religious and devotional frameworks, so that secularity within a neoliberal paradigm becomes the new master narrative and condition of possibility that shapes yoga's legitimacy. As we as scholars work to cultivate yoga as a critical source of illumination in our writing and our teaching, we do so through intimacy with our own hegemonic forms.

I suggest it is through – not beyond – such uncomfortable intimacies that yoga offers us valuable ways of perceiving the world. Practicing yoga in critically self-reflective ways, in dialogue with analytical and activist voices, can invite us to perceive the invisible layers of power that configure individual subjects and broader social landscapes. Such inquiry can potentially expose, if not escape, the diverse normalised hierarchies that have long shaped the conditions under which yoga transforms lives. Though decolonial projects may never be complete, full or perfected, there is value in their practice.

## Notes

1 The RSS is a large Indian volunteer organisation associated with the promotion of Hindutva, or 'Hinduness', and it is often seen as aligned with the political goals of Hindu fundamentalism.

2 This brief sketch is of course incomplete and does not address key movements, such as the substantial migration of Indians to Gulf states. A welcome direction for future scholarship would investigate further the cultural politics of yoga in the Middle East.

## Bibliography

Alter, J. S. 2000. *Gandhi's Body: Sex, Diet, and the Politics of Nationalism*. Philadelphia: University of Pennsylvania Press.

Alter, J. S. 2004. *Yoga in Modern India: The Body Between Science and Philosophy*. Princeton, NJ: Princeton University Press.

Altglas, V. 2014. *From Yoga to Kabbalah: Religious Exoticism and the Logics of Bricolage*. New York: Oxford University Press.

Askegaard, S. and Eckhardt, G. M. 2012. 'Glocal Yoga: Re-appropriation in the Indian Consumptionscape', *Marketing Theory* 12: 45–60.

Berila, B. Klein, M. and Roberts, C. J. (eds) 2016. *Yoga, the Body, and Embodied Social Change: An Intersectional Feminist Analysis*. Lanham, MD, USA: Lexington Books.

Black, S. 2016. 'Flexible Indian Labor: Yoga, Information Technology Migration, and US Technoculture', *Race and Yoga* 1: 23–41.

Blu Wakpa, T. 2018. 'Yoga Brings You Back to Who You Are: A Conversation Featuring Haley Laughter', *Race and Yoga* 3: 1–11.

Bost, S. 2016. 'Practicing Yoga / Embodying Feminism / Shape-shifting', *Frontiers: A Journal of Women Studies* 37: 191–210.

Chakraborty, C. 2007. 'The Hindu Ascetic as Fitness Instructor: Reviving Faith in Yoga', *The International Journal of the History of Sport* 24: 1172–1186.

Chandra, S. 2015. '"India Will Change You Forever': Hinduism, Islam, and Whiteness in the American Empire', *Signs* 40: 487–512.

Chaturvedi, V. 2010. 'Rethinking Knowledge with Action: V. D. Savarkar, the Bhagavad Gita, and Histories of Warfare', *Modern Intellectual History* 7: 417–435. https://doi.org/10.1017/S1479244310000144

Fish, A. 2014. 'Authorizing Yoga: The Pragmatics of Cultural Stewardship in the Digital Era', *East Asian Science, Technology and Society: An International Journal* 8: 439–460.

Gandhi, S. and Wolff, L. 2017. 'Yoga and the Roots of Cultural Appropriation'. 19 December. Praxis Center. www.kzoo.edu/praxis/yoga/. Accessed 13 March 2020.

Gautam, A. and Droogan, J. 2018. 'Yoga Soft Power: How Flexible is the Posture?', *The Journal of International Communication* 24: 18–36.

Godrej, F. 2017. 'The Neoliberal Yogi and the Politics of Yoga', *Political Theory* 45: 772–800.

Goldberg, M. 2015. *The Goddess Pose: The Audacious Life of Indra Devi, the Woman Who Helped Bring Yoga to the West*. New York: Knopf.

Goldberg, P. 2010. *American Veda: From Emerson and the Beatles to Yoga and Meditation – How Indian Spirituality Changed the West*. New York: Harmony Books.

Green, N. 2008. 'Breathing in India, c. 1890', *Modern Asian Studies* 42: 283–315.

Horton, C. and Harvey, R. (eds) 2012. *21st Century Yoga: Culture, Politics and Practice*. Chicago: Kleio Books.

Imy, K. 2016. 'Fascist Yogis: Martial Bodies and Imperial Impotence', *Journal of British Studies* 55: 320–343.

Jaffrelot, C. 2017. 'India's Democracy at 70: Toward a Hindu State?', *Journal of Democracy* 28: 52–63.

Jain, A. R. 2015. *Selling Yoga: From Counterculture to Pop Culture*. New York: Oxford University Press.

Kaul, N. 2017. 'Rise of the Political Right in India: Hindutva-Development Mix, Modi Myth, and Dualities', *Journal of Labor and Society* 20: 523–548.
Klein, M. C. and Guest-Jelley, A. (eds) 2014. *Yoga and Body Image*. Woodbury, MN, USA: Llewellyn Publications.
Luhr, E. 2015. 'Seeker, Surfer, Yogi: The Progressive Religious Imagination and the Cultural Politics of Place in Encinitas, California', *American Quarterly* 67: 1169–1193. https://doi.org/10.1353/aq.2015.0072
Maira, S. 2009. *Missing: Youth, Citizenship, and Empire after 9/11*. Durham: Duke University Press.
Manigault-Bryant, J. A. 2016. 'Yoga and the Metaphysics of Racial Capital', *Race and Yoga* 1: 40–52.
Mannur, A. and Sahni, P. K. 2011. '"What Can Brown Do for You?" Indo Chic and the Fashionability of South Asian Inspired Styles', *South Asian Popular Culture* 9: 177–190.
Markula, P. 2015. 'Reading Yoga: Changing Discourses of Postural Yoga on the Yoga Journal Covers', *Communication and Sport* 2: 143–171. https://doi.org/10.1177/2167479513490673
Ministry of Tourism, Government of India. n.d. 'Wellness and Medical Tourism'. http://tourism.gov.in/wellness-medical-tourism. Accessed 9 April 2018.
Mukherjee, S. 2017. 'Indian Messiah: The Attraction of Meher Baba to British Audiences in the 1930s', *Journal of Religious History* 41: 215–234.
Pandya, S. P. 2014. 'The Vivekananda Kendra in India: Its Ideological Translations and a Critique of its Social Service', *Critical Research on Religion* 2: 116–133. https://doi.org/10.1177/2050303214534999
Panton, R. and Evans, S. (eds) 2017. 'Sassin' Through Sadhana', *Race and Yoga* 2(1). https://escholarship.org/uc/item/8532c5qr, Accessed 13 March 2020.
*Pardon My Hindi. n.d. '#WhitePeopleDoingYoga Artist Statement'. www.pardonmyhindi.com/wpdy-statement. Accessed 7 October 2018.
Parikh, R. 2015. 'Yoga under the Mughals: From Practice to Paintings', *South Asian Studies* 31: 215–236.
Patankar, P. 2014. 'Ghosts of Yogas Past and Present', *Jadaliyya*. www.jadaliyya.com/Details/30281/Ghosts-of-Yogas-Past-and-Present. Accessed 15 September 2018.
Pinch, W. R. 2006. *Warrior Ascetics and Indian Empires*. Cambridge: Cambridge University Press.
Ramachandran, T. 2014. 'A Call to Multiple Arms! Protesting the Commoditization of Hindu Imagery in Western Society', *Material Religion* 10: 54–75. https://doi.org/10.2752/175183414X13909887177547
Ramaprasad, V. R. 2018. 'Terror, Suspicion and Neo-Liberal Logics: "Expanding Orientalisms" and South Asians in the United States', *South Asia: Journal of South Asian Studies* 41: 87–105. https://doi.org/10.1080/00856401.2017.1349569
SAAPYA. n.d. 'About SAAPYA', *South Asian American Perspectives on Yoga in America*. https://saapya.wordpress.com/about. Accessed 15 September 2018.
Said, E. W. 1979. *Orientalism*. New York: Vintage.
Sidhu, B. K. 2017. 'Yoga as Traditional Medicinal Knowledge: Revisiting the Legal Debate on IPR and Public Domain', *Environmental Policy and Law* 47: 99–105. https://doi.org/10.3233/EPL-170021
Singleton, M. 2010. *Yoga Body: The Origins of Modern Posture Practice*. New York: Oxford University Press.
Sood, S. 2018. 'Cultivating a Yogic Theology of Collective Healing: A Yogini's Journey Disrupting White Supremacy, Hindu Fundamentalism, and Casteism', *Race and Yoga* 3: 12–20.
Training Leaders Worldwide in Social Change. n.d. 'Off the Mat, Into the World'. www.offthematintotheworld.org, Accessed 10 September 2018.
Vats, A. 2016. '(Dis)owning Bikram: Decolonizing Vernacular and Dewesternizing Restructuring in the Yoga Wars', *Communication and Critical/Cultural Studies* 13: 325–345.
White, D. G. 2009. *Sinister Yogis*. Chicago: The University of Chicago Press.
White, D. G. 2014. *The Yoga Sutra of Patanjali: A Biography*. Princeton, NJ, USA: Princeton University Press.
Wolfers, A. 2016. 'Born Like Krishna in the Prison-House: Revolutionary Asceticism in the Political Ashram of Aurobindo Ghose', *South Asia: Journal of South Asian Studies* 39: 525–545. https://doi.org/10.1080/00856401.2016.1199253
Wortham, J. 2016. 'Black Health Matters', *New York Times*, 27 August. www.nytimes.com/2016/08/28/fashion/black-lives-matter-wellness-health-self-care.html, Accessed 13 March 2020.
Yogananda, P. 1946. *Autobiography of a Yogi*. Los Angeles, CA: Self-Realization Fellowship.
York, M. 2001. 'New Age Commodification and Appropriation of Spirituality', *Journal of Contemporary Religion* 16: 361–372. https://doi.org/10.1080/13537900120077177

# 3

# MEDITATION IN CONTEMPORARY CONTEXTS

## Current discussions

*Ville Husgafvel*

### Introduction

Since the counter-culture of the 1960s, the practice of meditation has spread from more marginal spiritual and religious contexts into the western (and increasingly global) cultural mainstream. This is most visible in the introduction of mindfulness-based programmes (MBPs), such as mindfulness-based stress reduction (MBSR) and mindfulness-based cognitive therapy (MBCT), as institutionalised approaches in public and corporate settings (Mindful Nation UK 2015; Wilson 2014).[1] The widespread application of Buddhist-derived mindfulness practices in healthcare, education and the corporate world is supported by a cumulative body of scientific research on their psychological and physiological benefits and the secular reframing of the aims, principles and premises of meditation practice. In recent years, academic research and public interest have created a positive feedback loop, providing increasing funding for mindfulness-related research and, in turn, scientific legitimation for the use of practical mindfulness applications. Reflecting this surge in both academic and general attention, the number of mindfulness-related journal publications has grown from one per year in 1982 to ten in 2000, up to six hundred and ninety-two in 2017 (AMRA Resources and Services 2018). The vast majority of these studies come from the fields of behavioural, cognitive and medical sciences, but lately, research within the humanities and social sciences has increased significantly as well. In addition to standardised mindfulness-based programmes, other Buddhist or Buddhist-derived meditation styles are also attracting large numbers of contemporary practitioners, both within and beyond explicitly religious contexts. Globally, the most popular forms include Tibetan tantric approaches, various forms of Zen meditation and Theravāda-based *vipassanā* practices (taught, for example, by the Insight Meditation Society or the lineage of S. N. Goenka (1924–2013), as well as in more traditional Buddhist contexts).

The first worldwide wave of meditation practice was much indebted to Maharishi Mahesh Yogi's Transcendental Meditation (TM) movement, which included the members of the Beatles as its celebrity evangelists. While TM is still active today, other contemplative practices with Vedic-Brahmanic roots have occupied the global mainstream more recently. In particular, the different forms of modern yoga represent another major driving force in the popularisation of meditation, even if the explicit emphasis on meditative aspects varies greatly between styles (De Michelis 2004). In fact, in both historical and contemporary contexts, drawing too rigid a boundary between 'yoga' and 'meditation' is problematic. Historically, the early roots of yoga and meditation go back to a shared pool of practices, concepts and soteriological structures employed by *śramaṇa* (i.e. Buddhist, Jain, Ājīvika) renunciates (Bronkhorst 2007; Samuel 2008). Instead of distinct 'origins' and clear 'lineages', the early Brahmanic, Buddhist and Jain histories of yoga and meditation are completely intertwined and cross-pollinated (Maas 2018; O'Brien-Kop 2017; Samuel 2008; Wujastyk 2018). In contemporary contexts, the concepts of 'yoga' and 'meditation' may sometimes be equally overlapping, even if in popular imaginaries 'yoga' is more associated with practices involving physical postures and 'meditation' with mental exercises conducted in a paradigmatic cross-legged sitting position (De Michelis 2004: 8). This overlap is evident in the inclusion of yoga postures in the 'mindfulness meditation' techniques of well-known MBPs, such as the MBSR programme (Kabat-Zinn 2005 [1990]: 94–113), or the application of various sitting and lying-down meditation techniques in modern yoga classes (De Michelis 2004: 251–260). Moreover, it requires just a slight shift in orientation to frame some Buddhist-derived sitting meditation techniques as 'postural' practices (see, e.g. Suzuki 1973 [1970]: 25–28) or postural yoga *āsanas* as dynamic forms of 'meditation' (see, e.g. De Michelis 2004: 238–239). Thus, depending on the framing, historical context, and preferred definitions, 'yoga' and 'meditation' may represent two distinct conceptual categories; 'yoga' may be a subcategory of 'meditation practice', 'meditation' a subcategory of 'yoga practice', or the terms can even be used interchangeably.[2]

Besides the formal contexts of modern mindfulness and yoga, meditation practices are often regarded as one signature element in the open-ended cultural formation known as 'New Age' or 'holistic spirituality' (Gilhus and Sutcliffe 2014; Hanegraaff 1996; Heelas and Woodhead 2005). This refers to various ways of life, social networks and cultural products that combine ideas and practices from a wide range of religious, spiritual and philosophical traditions into eclectic combinations of both therapeutic and soteriological significance. While highly visible in the current cultural landscape, the phenomenon is analytically elusive; again, clear definitions and categorisations are difficult. Despite maintaining a certain level of ambivalence – or even distance – in regard to more institutionalised forms of meditation, contemporary 'holistic spirituality' represents one popular cultural milieu for various contemplative practices. However, meditation practice itself should not be regarded as categorically 'spiritual' or associated with 'New Age', as done in some characterisations that lump together practices like '(spiritual) yoga, reiki, meditation, tai chi, aromatherapy, much paganism, rebirthing, reflexology, much wicca and many more' (Heelas and Woodhead 2005: 7). Many scholars and contemporary practitioners of meditation, such as cognitive therapists working in the UK National Health Services (NHS) and using MBCT in their daily work, are likely to find these associations foreign and problematic.

Alongside characteristically contemporary developments, practices that could be referred to as 'meditation' continue to be important elements in many traditional religious and indigenous contexts; various forms of concentration, awareness, recitation, or visualisation practices are found in practically all religions and cultures from the Catholic Church to Amazonian tribal lifeways. This has led some scholars and scientists to make universalist claims about 'meditation' as 'a worldwide practice found in every major religion and in most cultures' (Walsh and Shapiro 2006: 229). However, others are highly cautious about whether collecting a wide range of practices from various geographical areas, cultural milieus and historical eras under the conceptual category of 'meditation' serves any analytical purposes or is just a remnant of outdated 'intellectual trends'. As Lutz, Dunne and Davidson (2007: 500) argue,

> [I]n a typical discussion of this kind [...] practices as diverse as the ritual dances of some African tribes, the spiritual exercises of the desert fathers, and the tantric

> practices of a Tibetan adept are all forms of meditation. Historically, this attempt to categorize diverse practices under the same rubric reflects some intellectual trends in the early 20th century, most especially "perennialism," that argue unequivocally for a certain genre of mystical experience as the essence of religion (Proudfoot, 1985; Sharf, 1998).… [T]he generic use of meditation as applying to such a wide range of diverse practices inevitably trivializes the practices themselves. For example, the unique techniques and context of Sufi *zikr* must be ignored if they are to be considered the same as the Taoist practice of T'ai Chi. In short, to make *zikr* and T'ai Chi describable with the same term, one must ignore a good deal of what makes them radically different from each other. This would be akin to the use of the word "sport" to refer to all sports as if they were essentially the same.
>
> *(citations in original)*

Whatever position one takes on these semantic and conceptual issues, it is worth keeping in mind that labelling something as 'meditation' is often more an argument in need of justification than a natural matter of fact just waiting to be 'discovered'.

In the interest of space and scope, this chapter focuses on Buddhist-derived practices and especially the study of contemporary mindfulness, which dominates recent academic discussions on meditation. Besides the popular appeal of mindfulness training, there is much academic focus on Buddhist styles of meditation in the cognitive neurosciences, and the modernist narrative of Buddhism as a sort of 'inner science of happiness' seems to resonate well with contemporary cultural sensibilities (Lopez 2014; Lutz, Dunne and Davidson 2007; McMahan 2008; McMahan and Braun 2017). I have further narrowed my scope to a handful of themes, including challenges of definition, historical and comparative approaches, research positions and critical discourses. Through these, I hope to provide some insights into the current contributions and challenges of the humanistic and social scientific study of meditation.

## Challenges of definition

Despite being widely used in both popular and academic discourses, there is no universally agreed-upon definition for 'meditation' as a specific category of human activity, and the term has a wide variety of context-dependent meanings and usages. The same applies for 'mindfulness' and much meditation-related terminology, which is usually rooted in the technical language of specific religious-philosophical traditions. When analysed in their 'native' contexts, the meaning of these terms may be defined in rich detail and precision, whether one is discussing the Greek term *melétē* (Latin: *meditatio*) in early Christian asceticism and Stoic philosophy (Rönnegård 2013) or the Pāli *sati* (Sanskrit: *smṛti*, English: *mindfulness*) in certain Buddhist discourses (Dreyfus 2011; Gethin 2011 and 2015). However, problems arise when tradition-specific technical terms are used as signifiers for abstract conceptual constructions and universal categories of human experience.

In order to understand contemporary conceptualisations of 'meditation', it is useful to discern at least four basic stages in its conceptual history: (1) early Greek philosophy (Platonic, Stoic) and Christian asceticism; (2) medieval, premodern philosophy and Christian spirituality; (3) the comparative and historical study of 'world religions' starting in the colonial era (contributing to present-day usages in popular culture and cultural studies); and (4) contemporary medical, behavioural and cognitive sciences. In the first, 'meditation' usually refers to recitation, reflection and visualisation practices based on Biblical passages or other philosophical texts (Rönnegård 2013). In the second, these early usages are formalised in the sophisticated technical terminology of Christian theology. Here, 'meditation' is often seen as a preparatory practice for 'contemplation', which represents a higher, non-discursive form of devotion, prayer and insight (Baier 2009). In the third, many technical distinctions between 'meditation' and 'contemplation' are left aside, so that both terms are adapted for comparative analyses and taxonomies, serving as denominators for a variety of religious-philosophical practices, especially those related to newly 'discovered' Buddhist, Vedic-Brahmanic and Daoist traditions (see, e.g. Burnouf 1844; Müller 1859). This same time period, the late nineteenth century, also witnessed new approaches in western esotericism, such as the influential Theosophical Society, which had distinct ways of characterising 'meditation', building both on indigenous western traditions and influences from Asian religions and philosophies (Baier 2012). In the fourth, the focus is shifted from religions and philosophies to the scientific study of universal neurological, physiological and psychological processes related to meditative techniques and resultant states (see, e.g. Lutz, Dunne and Davidson 2007). While each of these discourses builds their specific definitions and usages on the basis of previous ones, there are significant divergences and gaps between them.

In contemporary discussions, conceptualisations of 'meditation' in Buddhist and cultural studies often differ significantly from the perspectives of medical, behavioural and cognitive sciences, where the focus is mostly on the cognitive, emotional and physiological processes involved. This is evident, for example, in the early work of Daniel Goleman, in which he connects Buddhist *abhidhamma* (Sanskrit: *abhidharma*) philosophy with western psychotherapy and defines meditation as 'the self-regulation and retraining of attentional habits' (Goleman 1976: 44). More recently, Roger Walsh and Shauna Shapiro (2006: 228–229) have continued the dialogue between western psychology and meditative disciplines, suggesting that,

> The term *meditation* refers to a family of self-regulation practices that focus on training attention and awareness in order to bring mental processes under greater voluntary control and thereby foster general mental well-being and development and/or specific capacities such as calm, clarity, and concentration.
>
> *(italics in original)*

Similar reasoning can be found in one of the most cited scientific articles on the definition and typology of meditation by Antoine Lutz et al. (2008: 163):

> Meditation can be conceptualized as a family of complex emotional and attentional regulatory training regimes developed for various ends, including the cultivation of well-being and emotional balance.

Sometimes further methodical details are listed, as exemplified in the following influential attempt at standardisation by Roberto Cardoso et al. (2004: 59):

> To be characterized as meditation, the procedure must contain the following operational parameters: Utilizes a (1) specific technique (clearly defined), involving (2) muscle relaxation somewhere during the process and (3) "logic relaxation": a necessarily (4) self-induced state, using a (5) self-focus skill (coined "anchor").

In all these characterisations, 'meditation' is defined and described in highly technical and individualistic ways with little explicit attention to its cultural and social aspects. This, of course, fits the overall objective of finding universal patterns in human physiology and behaviour which are not dependent on contextual factors.[3] However, when compared to emblematic conceptualisations in Buddhist and cultural studies, the differences are striking.

> Buddhist meditation – as a systematic methodology for uncovering and transforming the basis of our understanding of the world – can be seen as an essentially hermeneutical enterprise ... The various Buddhist meditation techniques are deeply embedded in a larger world view. Buddhist meditation puts into practice the Buddhist understanding of the world.
>
> *(Gregory 1986: 5–6)*

> Contemplative practices are modes of self-cultivation that strive to produce certain experiences and cultivate certain ways of being in a world – a world that contains particular normative understandings of a good life, a holy life, a successful life, as well as conceptions of the person, the mind and its features, the potential for human development and cultivation, and various experiences that meditators will have at different stages on the path.
>
> *(McMahan 2017: 38)*

Here, meditation practice is not seen as an isolated individual enterprise; rather, it is inseparably embedded in history, culture and various socially constructed frames that give purpose and direction for the practice (see also Eifring 2015). Thus, while the intentional self-regulation of attention, awareness and other cognitive-emotional processes represent important technical features of meditation, this is only half of the picture. Without analysing the role of contextual factors, many aspects of meditation remain obscure. This highlights the need for interdisciplinary collaborations, as emphasised by David McMahan, among others:

> The level of analysis that attends only to universal physiological structure and function [...] cannot adequately account for how these practices work in practitioners' lives. If we are to take seriously the first-person perspective of contemplatives, we must understand how they conceive of the meaning, purpose, and significance of their practices in their doctrinal, social, cultural, and cosmic contexts. To understand contemplative practices in a comprehensive way, therefore, scientific study of meditation must work hand in hand with philosophers, anthropologists, sociologists, and scholars of religion who can help articulate these contexts.
>
> *(McMahan 2017: 43–44)*

Even if the focus is purely on measurable and repeatable data in laboratory settings, scholars can help scientists to develop a more nuanced understanding of different meditative approaches in order to better define their research objects and control the many variables involved (see, e.g. Lutz, Dunne and Davidson 2007; Lutz et al. 2008). It is not difficult to understand the problems of making detailed conclusions on the physiological or psychological effects of 'sports' in general, instead of focusing specifically on long-distance running versus bowling, snowboarding and so forth. However, it might still surprise some that the same goes for 'meditation'; there are profound differences, for example, between 'focused attention', 'open-monitoring', or 'compassion' practices (see Hofmann, Grossman and Hinton 2011; Lutz et al. 2008; Pace et al. 2009). Even if these differences are not always outwardly perceptible, they are no less significant, and they need to be understood properly in any meditation-related scientific research.

## Historical and comparative approaches

Mapping the history of specific meditative approaches and analysing their characteristic features represent established approaches within cultural studies. Early on, these descriptions appeared as part of broad introductory books on Buddhism and other Asian religions. Later, they became a topic in their own right, first through general works like Edward Conze's *Buddhist Meditation* (1956), and then gradually with more specific areas of focus in works such as *Mahāyāna Buddhist Meditation: Theory and Practice* (Kiyota and Jones 1991 [1978]), *Theravāda Meditation: The Buddhist Transformation of Yoga* (King 2015 [1980]), and *Traditions of Meditation in Chinese Buddhism* (Gregory 1986). This process of increasing the 'resolution' has continued steadily, and today there is a wealth of studies concentrating on particular techniques, lineages or historical and cultural contexts. Examples abound, such as Sam van Schaik's *Approaching the Great Perfection: Simultaneous and Gradual Methods of Dzogchen Practice in the Longchen Nyingtig* (2004) or Eric Braun's *The Birth of Insight: Meditation, Modern Buddhism, and the Burmese Monk Ledi Sayadaw* (2013).

Outside of discussions in Buddhist studies, Braun's work is frequently cited in the study of contemporary meditation and mindfulness, as influences from Burmese Theravāda Buddhism are nowadays widespread. Many characteristic practices in the Insight Meditation Society, the *vipassanā* tradition of S. N. Goenka or MBSR and related MBPs can be traced back to the practice lineages of Ledi Sayādaw (1846–1923) and his student U Ba Khin (1899–1971) or Mingun Jetawun Sayādaw (1868–1955) and his student Mahasi Sayadaw (1904–1982) (Fronsdal 1998; Husgafvel 2016; Stuart 2018). Burma is also the birthplace of the first large-scale Buddhist lay meditation movement, closely following (and related) to the colonial conquest of Burma in the late-nineteenth century (Braun 2013; Houtman 1990; Jordt 2007; Stuart 2018). However, there is more to the Buddhist origins of current mindfulness-based programmes than these influential lineages and developments.

While scholars are in broad consensus on the overall Buddhist roots of contemporary mindfulness approaches, arguments diverge significantly in more detailed discussions. A common narrative presents modernised Theravāda-based *vipassanā* traditions, such as the aforementioned Burmese lineages and the Thai Forest tradition of Ajahn Chah (1918–1992) (mediated via Insight Meditation Society teachers), as principal Buddhist influences for the pioneering MBSR programme and related MBPs (see, e.g. Bodhi 2016; Braun 2013; Fronsdal 1998; Gethin 2011; R. King 2016; Monteiro, Musten and Compson 2015; Olendzki 2014; Purser and Milillo 2015; Samuel 2016; Sun 2014). However, a number of studies question this approach as one-sided and simplistic. The impact of Theravāda-based *vipassanā* practices should be acknowledged, but attention must also be drawn to direct and formative influences from 'non-dual' Mahāyāna approaches, such as East Asian Chan (Zen/Thiền/Sŏn) schools and Tibetan Dzogchen practice, in both the practical methods and theoretical basis of the pioneering MBSR programme (Braun 2017; Dunne 2011; Husgafvel 2016 and 2018; Watt 2017).

Besides filling an important gap in the history and genealogy of contemporary mindfulness approaches, the recognition of signature Mahāyāna influences has significant implications for comparative approaches, which aim at discerning shared elements between current forms of mindfulness training and more traditional Buddhist practices. For example, a 'world-affirming' orientation or the emphasis on developing 'non-judgemental' awareness, both being characteristic of MBSR practice, are commonly pointed to as disparities in relation to 'classical' or 'traditional' Buddhist practices. However, when one's examination of Buddhist sources is extended beyond the Theravāda tradition and Pāli texts, both of these aspects can be found in established Mahāyāna Buddhist commentaries and practice lineages (Husgafvel 2016 and 2018).

Different understandings about which Buddhist traditions are relevant and a lack of sensitivity towards their differences may partially explain why scholarly discussions have yet to reach consensus on the degree of continuity between Buddhist teachings and contemporary mindfulness practices. Depending on one's viewpoint, MBSR and other MBPs may represent 'the original teachings of the Buddha' in a secular form (Cullen 2011: 189–192), a characteristically American form of socially-engaged Buddhism 'streamlined for a secular clientele' (Seager 1999: 214; see also Wilson 2014), 'stealth Buddhism' with possible covert religious agendas (Brown 2016: 84), or pragmatic mindfulness applications with early Buddhist antecedents (Anālayo 2018 and 2019). However, another common narrative depicts MBSR and related contemporary mindfulness programmes as privatised, de-ethicised therapeutic techniques, which are a far cry from any authentic forms of Buddhist practice (Plank 2011; Purser and Loy 2013; Purser and Milillo 2015; Shonin, Van Gordon and Griffiths 2013).

Similarly, there are difficulties in fitting contemporary MBPs into dominant post-Enlightenment conceptual matrices, which dichotomize 'religion' and 'secular' into clearly distinct, binary categories. While scientific research literature usually presents mindfulness practices as axiomatically secular (Baer 2015; Didonna 2009; Lutz et al. 2008; see also Sun 2014), some scholars argue that they exhibit characteristically religious content (Brown 2016). Others see them as transcending the binary model altogether by sacralising the secular (Arat 2017), enchanting the natural world (Braun 2017), or forming cultural hybrids which are open for both religious and secular interpretations (Frisk 2012).

This ambivalence in scholarly categorisations is mirrored in (and reflects) broader societal discussions. Even if the implementation of mindfulness training in public contexts is generally widely accepted, in some instances this has been contested as a violation of religious freedom and the constitutional separation between church and state. Recently, these claims were made against the Dennis-Yarmouth Regional School District in Cape Cod, Massachusetts, due to the inclusion in public school curricula of an educational mindfulness-based programme called 'Calmer Choice'. A letter written by the lawyer Dean Broyles on behalf of the National Center for Law & Policy (NCLP) and 'concerned parents' states:

> [T]here is a concern that mindfulness meditation involves well-established Buddhist religious beliefs and practices that may undermine rights of conscience and religious freedom because the curriculum may conflict with worldviews or religious beliefs adopted by students and inculcated by parents at home.
>
> *(Broyles 2016)*

These claims repeat arguments of an earlier civil court case on the implementation of a yoga programme based on the Ashtanga Vinyasa Yoga tradition of Pattabhi Jois (1915–2009) in the Encinitas School District (Mayer 2013a; Newcombe 2018) in California. The only major difference was that the more recent perceived danger to religious neutrality in school curricula came from 'stealth Buddhism' instead of 'stealth Hinduism', as framed by Broyles (2017 and 2016). These views follow the arguments of the religious studies scholar Candy Gunther Brown,[4] whom the lawyer uses as his expert witness. Even if the two cases reflect concerns of particular political and religious minorities marked by 'contemporary neo-conservative politics and conservative Christian faith' (Newcombe 2018: 558; see also NCLP 2018), and both school programmes continue with wide support from local communities, these debates are good reminders that academic argumentation is not isolated from the wider society but completely embedded in it – with all the practical, political and ethical implications that follow.

## Research positions

The unique position of each scholar towards his or her objects of study represents another, different example of the inevitable embeddedness of academic research. Besides societal institutions, structures and debates, each argument and study reflects the personal motivations, backgrounds, beliefs and prior understandings of the researcher. Current mindfulness research provides a relevant context for understanding this, as personal religious or ideological backgrounds may sometimes play a considerable role, even if the topic is quite rarely explicitly discussed. (See Rahmani, Chapter 18 in this volume.)

Anyone studying the Buddhist history, ethical dimensions, commercial aspects or religious-secular nature of contemporary mindfulness-based programmes will soon discern some basic standpoints, which frame to different degrees the content and tone of scholarly argumentation. These may include, for example, personal and professional engagement in MBPs, commitment to Buddhist practice, adherence to conservative Christian values and beliefs, or emancipatory motivations based on anti-capitalist, feminist and postcolonial critiques. Thus, a critical reader needs to remain alert to ideological, religious, political or commercial interests and presuppositions potentially at play in various analyses and depictions. For example, a reader could question if and how my scholar-practitioner position as both an academic researcher in the study of religion and a trained MBSR teacher might affect the perspectives or sources I choose and arguments I make in this chapter.

Naturally, personal entanglement in religious practices, yoga and meditation – or the politics and businesses surrounding them – is not in itself a reason to question the integrity or quality of any particular study. Quite the contrary; in many cases the advantages of personal experience and engagement in the field are obvious, as many nuances in both ethnographic and historical source materials can go unnoticed without insight from lived experience. Moreover, despite positivist idealisations of 'objective and value-free' research, it is practically impossible to escape 'subjectivity' in any form of qualitative research (or even the natural sciences, at least when communicated through language). While unique personal positions towards research objects affect how they are perceived and framed, and the language which one uses to form and communicate arguments is only partially shared and understood by others, this does not diminish the value of the scholarly enterprise. It merely puts emphasis on the intersubjective nature of academic knowledge production. Only time and peer discussion (or a lack of it) will determine the value and authenticity of any particular work.

This being said, there are academic conventions that support the transparency of one's position and the reliability of findings from the beginning. When the subjective situatedness or embeddedness of each scholar and 'knowledge product' is recognised, it is necessary to make one's research position and agency explicit and visible. In this way, scholars can provide the reader with the possibility to better contextualise and evaluate the argument being made. These methodological standpoints, based on reflexivity and applied early on in ethnography and anthropology, are already 'a major strategy for quality control' in many areas of qualitative research (Berger 2015: 219). Through the growing trend towards ethnographic approaches in the study of MBPs (Cook 2016; Crane et al. 2015; Drage 2018; Rosch 2015; Wheater 2017), together with critical interdisciplinary discussions on methodology, explicit self-reflection by scholars on their personal research position is hopefully becoming standard procedure also in the study of contemporary mindfulness.

## Critical discourses

While there is a great deal of enthusiasm about the possible positive effects of meditation and mindfulness practices for both individuals and society at large, more and more critical voices are being heard. In scientific critiques of mindfulness and meditation studies, the focus has been on possible positive reporting bias, apparent methodological flaws and a lack of attention towards difficult meditation-related experiences (see, e.g. Coronado-Montoya et al. 2016; Goyal et al. 2014; Lindahl et al. 2017). These issues have contributed to overenthusiastic and exaggerated views on the benefits of meditation, even if empirical evidence in many cases is only promising and in need of further validation. In cultural studies, critical discourses tend to not target research and reporting standards per se, but rather the contemporary approaches and contexts of meditation themselves. Here, the individualisation, secularisation, decontextualisation, commodification, corporatisation and even militarisation of traditional Buddhist meditation practices are problematised and interrogated from various perspectives, including critical theory, postcolonial and feminist studies and also traditional Buddhist positions (see, e.g. Purser, Forbes and Burke 2016). According to these critics, 'denatured' contemporary forms of mindfulness practice may in the service of neoliberal ideologies, corporate profit-making and military objectives become 'tools of oppression' instead of beneficial and liberative practices. While recent 'McMindfulness' debates (Hyland 2015; Purser and Loy 2013; Shonin and Kabat-Zinn 2015) have perhaps gained the most visibility in popular discussions, these arguments can be traced to Slavoj Žižek's much earlier critical (and polemical) takes on 'Western Buddhism' (see also Cook 2016).

> One is almost tempted to resuscitate here the old infamous Marxist cliché of religion as the "opium of the people," as the imaginary supplement of the terrestrial misery: the "Western Buddhist" meditative stance is arguably the most efficient way, for us, to fully participate in the capitalist dynamic while retaining the appearance of mental sanity. If Max Weber were alive today, he would definitely write a second, supplementary, volume to his *Protestant Ethic*, entitled *The Taoist Ethic and the Spirit of Global Capitalism*.
>
> *(Žižek 2006 [2001]: 13)*

Besides Žižek's writings, Michel Foucault's analytical and conceptual tools are widely used in theorising contemporary contemplative practices from critical and philosophical perspectives. Foucauldian ideas on 'governmentality', 'freedom as practice', 'care of self', and 'technologies of the self' open possibilities for perceiving traditional and contemporary forms of meditation as both possibly oppressive techniques of social-political governing and disruptive, emancipatory practices of individual and social liberation, depending on the context and perspective (see, e.g. Ng 2016).

Finally, it may be added that more discussion on methodological issues is also needed in the cultural and historical study of meditation and mindfulness. As has been commonly recognised, the early orientalist works focusing on Buddhism and other Asian religions were dominated by philological approaches, which reflected particular Protestant Christian values and orientations in their focus on 'holy scriptures' as the prime location of religious 'truths' (see King 1999; Samuel 2008: 15–22). In the early study of Buddhism in the west, orientalist presuppositions contributed to problematic value-laden constructions of 'true Buddhism', which prioritised normative canonical texts at the expense of contemporary Buddhist practices (and archaeological evidence) and the Pāli Canon of the Theravāda School at the expense of other Buddhist traditions (King 1999: 143–160; Samuel 2008: 16–17; Schopen 1997: 1–22; Sharf 1995). Even if these dispositions no longer dominate the mainstream study of Buddhism, 'the idea of a "real" Buddhism that can be found in the Pāli Canon rather than the practice of historical and contemporary Buddhists remains alive and well' (Samuel 2008: 17).

The persistence of orientalist ideas in academic research is evident in the study of contemporary mindfulness. Essentialist presentations of 'classical' or 'traditional' Buddhism, Buddhist meditation and Buddhist mindfulness are still commonly based on canonical Pāli texts and

Theravāda commentaries (Husgafvel 2016). Sometimes, these normative ahistorical constructs of 'true mindfulness' are further contrasted with anecdotal ethnographic examples from 'corrupted' contemporary mindfulness approaches (see, e.g. Purser 2015: 32) in ways which repeat classic orientalist patterns (see King 1999: 146). While possibly serving some practical or argumentative purposes, these dispositions omit: the complex interplay between Buddhist textual descriptions and lived practices of meditation, the various versions and editions (i.e. Pāli, Sanskrit, Chinese) of particular Buddhist texts, the different commentarial and practical traditions related to meditation and mindfulness practice (P. *satipaṭṭhāna*, S. *smṛtyupasthāna*) within Tibetan and East Asian Mahāyāna Buddhism and the problems of asymmetrical data when the normative textual descriptions of one tradition (Theravāda Buddhism) are compared to prescriptive ethnographic descriptions of another (MBSR). Thus, the call for more rigorous methodological standards applies not only in the quantitative empirical sciences but also in the historical and comparative study of contemporary meditation and mindfulness, even if on very different grounds.

## Conclusion

It seems appropriate to end this brief discussion on current debates in contemporary meditation studies by sketching possible future developments. Through questions of definition and classification, dialogue between scientific and cultural studies will continue to develop our understanding on the characteristic features of meditation practice in general and on the distinct features of specific contemplative approaches in particular. Attempts at defining 'meditation' as a universal conceptual category may be helpful in drawing the basic outlines of an emerging field of research, but in terms of actual studies the major contributions are likely to deal more with increasing an understanding of context-specific features and terminology than with abstract generalisations. It is precisely due to their contextual understanding of meditation practices and sensitiveness towards problems of essentialism and universalisation that scholars of Buddhism and other meditation-related fields are critically important for – and increasingly being called to collaborate with – cognitive neuroscience and psychological research projects.

While the use of conceptual categories is indispensable in making sense of the world in which we live, they are bound to particular cultural and historical frames, whether emic or etic, scientific or popular, western or Asian. Being aware of the history and limitations of particular semantic and conceptual frames is part of the expertise developed in cultural studies. Research on yoga and meditation does not comprise an exception, but rather the opposite. Both historical and contemporary forms of yoga and meditation occupy many different cultural spheres and spaces simultaneously; while some of these are clearly 'secular', 'religious', 'Buddhist', or 'Brahmanic' when compared to western prototypes or classifications of 'world religions',[5] many others are 'something in-between' and challenge established systems of codification. For more theoretically oriented scholars, empirical data on contemplative practices provides both an impetus and a rich testing ground for much-needed, novel ways of conceptualising cultural phenomena. For everyone in the field – be they more or less entrenched in the use of 'religion', 'secular', 'Buddhism', 'Hinduism', 'yoga', 'meditation', or 'mindfulness' as analytical categories – adopting non-essentialist, discursive, instrumental and situational approaches towards these concepts will likely turn out to be useful or even inevitable (see Masuzawa 2005; Newcombe 2018: 570; Taira 2013; Wilson 2014: 9).

In historical and comparative studies, a more nuanced picture of both contemporary mindfulness approaches, Buddhist meditative traditions, and the many links between them is likely to emerge. Currently, many arguments and assumptions are made about 'contemporary mindfulness' or the 'mindfulness movement' with little sensitivity towards the wide variety of programmes, interventions, applications, products, teachers, motivations and contexts that can be connected to the fuzzy concept of 'mindfulness'. To put it bluntly, when the branding of mayonnaise, clinical cognitive therapy, techniques for increased sexual pleasure and a way of life guided by ethical and philosophical ideals are all gathered under the rubric of 'mindfulness' and treated as 'a movement' (see Wilson 2014), it seems highly questionable whether any shared agendas, identities or arguments can be found. As is the case with meditation and yoga traditions overall, a more clear understanding and sensitiveness to the heterogeneity and subtle differences between (and within) current mindfulness approaches will greatly benefit future discussions.

Finally, while research will continue to be conducted from various points of view, the shadows of positivist idealisations will hopefully no longer haunt scholars and lead them to downplay their subjectivity and agency in argumentation. In order for peer discussion to separate the 'wheat from the chaff', there must be genuine dialogue between scholars, academic disciplines and preferred schools of thought. At the moment, there are many separate 'pillars' or 'bubbles' of knowledge in the study of meditation, mindfulness and yoga, to the detriment of all. Naturally it takes effort to keep track of different discussions and courage to challenge all views (especially one's own), but these are foundational goals if we hope to avoid reducing academic debates and knowledge into parallel monologues of 'alternative truths'. By means of continuing curiosity, self-reflection and critical discussion beyond disciplinary boundaries and personal comfort zones, there is much to learn – for the benefit of academics, practitioners and society at large – about the diverse complex of practices which fall under the rubric of 'meditation' in contemporary contexts.

## Notes

1 Standardised programmes include, for example, mindfulness-based stress reduction (MBSR), mindfulness-based cognitive therapy (MBCT), mindfulness-based mind-fitness training (MMFT), mindfulness-based eating awareness training (MB-EAT), mindfulness-based relapse prevention (MBRP), mindfulness-based childbirth and parenting (MBCP), and mindfulness-based elder care (MBEC).

2 In academia, these historical and contemporary premises question the conceptualisation of 'yoga studies' and 'meditation studies' as two clearly distinct fields of research, and also the earlier field-specific approaches of studying yoga in 'Hindu' (Vedic-Brahmanic) studies and meditation in Buddhist (also Jain, Daoist, etc.) studies. Thus, the name 'yoga and meditation studies' can be seen not so much as indicating a combination of two different research fields but as merely capturing different aspects of one shared field.

3 For a critique of 'context-independent' approaches in the study of meditation within the cognitive sciences, see Thompson 2017.

4 Candy Gunther Brown is an established scholar in religious studies, but her views on the religiosity of yoga and mindfulness appear to be influenced by her ideological and political positioning (see also Newcombe 2018). Brown has repeatedly worked as the main academic expert on behalf of the National Center for Law & Policy (NCLP), a non-profit legal group 'closely associated with ideological positions of contemporary neo-conservative politics and conservative Christian faith' (Newcombe 2018; NCLP 2018) in US court cases and legal concerns against the use of yoga and mindfulness practices in public schools. In the *Sedlock v. Baird* case on the use of yoga in the Encinitas School District, the court explicitly stated that 'Dr. Brown is not objective and not creditable and Dr. Brown is biased' (Mayer 2013a). Moreover, the judge considered Dr. Brown almost 'to be on a mission against Ashtanga yoga' (Mayer 2013b). For Brown's responses and more discussion, see Deslippe 2017 and Brown 2013.

5 On the 'invention of world religions' see Masuzawa 2005.

## Bibliography

AMRA Resources and Services. 2018. *American Mindfulness Research Association Webpage*. https://goamra.org/resources/. Accessed 17 June 2019.

Anālayo, B. 2018. 'Overeating and Mindfulness in Ancient India', *Mindfulness* 9: 1648–1654. https://doi.org/10.1007/s12671-018-1009-x.

Anālayo, B. 2019. 'The Emphasis on the Present Moment in the Cultivation of Mindfulness', *Mindfulness* 10: 571–581. https://doi.org/10.1007/s12671-018-1074-1.

Arat, A. 2017. '"What It Means to Be Truly Human": The Postsecular Hack of Mindfulness', *Social Compass* 64(2): 167–179.

Baer, R. 2015. 'Ethics, Values, Virtues, and Character Strengths in Mindfulness-Based Interventions: A Psychological Science Perspective', *Mindfulness* 6(4): 956–969. https://doi.org/10.1007/s12671-015-0419-2.

Baier, K. 2009. 'Meditation and Contemplation in High to Late Medieval Europe', in Franco, E. and Eigner, D. (eds), *Yogic Perception, Meditation and Altered States of Consciouness*, 321–346. Wien: Österreichische Akademie der Wissenschaften.

Baier, K. 2012. 'Mesmeric Yoga and the Development of Meditation within the Theosophical Society', *Theosophical History* 16(3–4): 151–161.

Berger, R. 2015. 'Now I See It, Now I Don't: Researcher's Position and Reflexivity in Qualitative Research', *Qualitative Research* 15(2): 219–234. https://doi.org/10.1177/1468794112468475.

Bodhi, B. 2016. 'The Transformations of Mindfulness', in Purser, R. E., Forbes, D. and Burke, A. (eds), *Handbook of Mindfulness*, 3–14. Cham: Springer International Publishing. https://doi.org/10.1007/978-3-319-44019-4.

Braun, E. 2013. *The Birth of Insight: Meditation, Modern Buddhism, and the Burmese Monk Ledi Sayadaw*. London: The University of Chicago Press.

Braun, E. 2017. 'Mindful but Not Religious', in McMahan, D. and Braun, E. (eds), *Meditation, Buddhism, and Science*, 173–197. New York: Oxford University Press.

Bronkhorst, J. 2007. *Greater Magadha: Studies in the Culture of Early India*. Leiden: Brill.

Brown, C. G. 2013. 'Yoga Can Stay in School: Looking More Closely at the Encinitas Yoga Trial Decision', *Huffington Post Blog Entry*. 2 July. www.huffingtonpost.com/candy-gunther-brown-phd/what-made-the-encinitas-p_b_3522836.html. Accessed 17 June 2019.

Brown, C. G. 2016. 'Can "Secular" Mindfulness Be Separated from Religion?', in Purser, R. E., Forbes, D. and Burke, A. (eds), *Handbook of Mindfulness: Culture, Context, and Social Engagement*, 75–94. Cham: Springer International.

Broyles, D. R. 2016. 'Legal Opinion Memorandum to Superintendent Carol Woodbury & Members of the Dennis-Yarmouth Regional School District School Committee – Legal & Practical Concerns Regarding the District's Calmer Choice Mindfulness Curriculum'. 2 February. www.nclplaw.org/resources/. Accessed 17 June 2019.

Broyles, D. R. 2017. 'The Dark Side of Mindfulness', *Christian News Journal Blog Entry*. 21 April. http://christiannewsjournal.com/the-dark-side-of-mindfulness/. Accessed 17 June 2019.

Burnouf, E. 1844. *Introduction à l'histoire du Buddhisme indien [Introduction to the History of Indian Buddhism]*. Paris: Imprimerie Royale.

Cardoso, R., et al. 2004. 'Meditation in Health: An Operational Definition', *Brain Research Protocols* 14, 58–60. https://doi.org/10.1016/j.brainresprot.2004.09.002.

Conze, E. 1956. *Buddhist Meditation*. London: George Allen and Unwin.

Cook, J. 2016. 'Mindful in Westminster: The Politics of Meditation and the Limits of Neoliberal Critique', *HAU: Journal of Ethnographic Theory* 6(1): 141–161. https://doi.org/10.14318/hau6.1.011.

Coronado-Montoya, S., et al. 2016. 'Reporting of Positive Results in Randomized Controlled Trials of Mindfulness-Based Mental Health Interventions', *PLOS ONE* 11(4). https://doi.org/10.1371/journal.pone.0153220.

Crane, R. S., et al. 2015. 'Disciplined Improvisation: Characteristics of Inquiry in Mindfulness-Based Teaching', *Mindfulness* 6, 1104–1114. https://doi.org/10.1007/s12671-014-0361-8.

Cullen, M. 2011. 'Mindfulness-Based Interventions: An Emerging Phenomenon', *Mindfulness* 2(3): 186–193. https://doi.org/10.1007/s12671-011-0058-1.

Deslippe, P. 2017. 'Stretching Good Faith: A Response to Candy Gunther Brown', *The Religious Studies Project Blog Entry*. 29 June. www.religiousstudiesproject.com/2017/06/29/stretching-good-faith-a-response-to-candy-gunther-brown-philip-deslippe/. Accessed 17 June 2019.

Didonna, F. (ed) 2009. *Clinical Handbook of Mindfulness*. New York: Springer. https://doi.org/10.1007/978-0-387-09593-6.

Drage, M. 2018. 'Of Mountains, Lakes and Essences: John Teasdale and the Transmission of Mindfulness', *History of the Human Sciences* 31(4): 107–130. https://doi.org/10.1177/0952695118790429.

Dreyfus, G. 2011. 'Is Mindfulness Present-Centred and Non-Judgmental? A Discussion of the Cognitive Dimensions of Mindfulness', *Contemporary Buddhism: An Interdisciplinary Journal* 12(1): 41–54. https://doi.org/10.1080/14639947.2011.564815.

Dunne, J. 2011. 'Toward an Understanding of Non-Dual Mindfulness', *Contemporary Buddhism: An Interdisciplinary Journal* 12(1): 71–88. https://doi.org/10.1080/14639947.2011.564820.

Eifring, H. 2015. *Meditation and Culture: The Interplay of Practice and Context*. London: Bloomsbury Academic.

Frisk, L. 2012. 'The Practice of Mindfulness: From Buddhism to Secular Mainstream in a Post-Secular Society', *Scripta Instituti Donneriani Aboensis* 24(January): 48–61. https://doi.org/10.30674/scripta.67408.

Fronsdal, G. 1998. 'Insight Meditation in the United States: Life, Liberty, and the Pursuit of Happiness', in Prebish, C. S. and Tanaka, K. K. (eds), *The Faces of Buddhism in America*, 163–182. Berkeley, CA, USA: University of California Press.

Gethin, R. 2011. 'On Some Definitions of Mindfulness', *Contemporary Buddhism: An Interdisciplinary Journal* 12(1): 263–279. https://doi.org/10.1080/14639947.2011.564843.

Gethin, R. 2015. 'Buddhist Conceptualizations of Mindfulness', in Brown, K. W., Creswell, J. D. and Ryan, R. M. (eds), *Handbook of Mindfulness: Theory, Research, and Practice*, 9–40. New York: The Guilford Press.

Gilhus, I. and Sutcliffe, S. 2014. *New Age Spirituality: Rethinking Religion*. London: Acumen.

Goleman, D. 1976. 'Meditation and Consciousness: An Asian Approach to Mental Health', *American Journal of Psychotherapy* 30(1): 41–54.

Goyal, M., et al. 2014. 'Meditation Programs for Psychological Stress and Well-Being: A Systematic Review and Meta-Analysis', *JAMA Internal Medicine* 174(3): 357–368. https://doi.org/10.1001/jamainternmed.2013.13018.

Gregory, P. N. (ed) 1986. *Traditions of Meditation in Chinese Buddhism*. Honolulu, HI, USA: University of Hawaii Press.

Hanegraaff, W. J. 1996. *New Age Religion and Western Culture: Esotericism in the Mirror of Secular Thought*. Leiden: Brill.

Heelas, P. and Woodhead, L. 2005. *The Spiritual Revolution: Why Religion Is Giving Way to Spirituality*. Oxford: Wiley-Blackwell.

Hofmann, S G., Grossman, P. and Hinton, D. E. 2011. 'Loving-Kindness and Compassion Meditation: Potential for Psychological Interventions', *Clinical Psychology Review* 31(7): 1126–1132. https://doi.org/10.1016/j.cpr.2011.07.003.

Houtman, G. 1990. *Traditions of Buddhist Practice in Burma*. PhD thesis. School of Oriental and African Studies, University of London.

Husgafvel, V. 2016. 'On the Buddhist Roots of Contemporary Non-Religious Mindfulness Practice: Moving Beyond Sectarian and Essentialist Approaches', *Temenos: Nordic Journal of Comparative Religion* 52(1): 87–126. https://journal.fi/temenos/article/view/55371.

Husgafvel, V. 2018. 'The "Universal Dharma Foundation" of Mindfulness-Based Stress Reduction: Non-duality and Mahāyāna Buddhist Influences in the Work of Jon Kabat-Zinn', *Contemporary Buddhism: An Interdisciplinary Journal* 19(2): 275–326. https://doi.org/10.1080/14639947.2018.1572329.

Hyland, T. 2015. 'McMindfulness in the Workplace: Vocational Learning and the Commodification of the Present Moment', *Journal of Vocational Education & Training* 67(2): 219–234. https://doi.org/10.1080/13636820.2015.1022871.

Jordt, I. 2007. *Burma's Mass Lay Meditation Movement: Buddhism and the Cultural Construction of Power*. Athens, OH, USA: Ohio University Press.

Kabat-Zinn, J. 2005 [1990]. *Full Catastrophe Living: Using the Wisdom of Your Body and Mind to Face Stress, Pain, and Illness*. New York: Bantam Dell.

King, R. 1999. *Orientalism and Religion: Postcolonial Theory, India and 'the Mystic East'*. London and New York: Routledge.

King, R. 2016. '"Paying Attention" in a Digital 3 Economy: Reflections on the Role of Analysis and Judgement Within Contemporary Discourses of Mindfulness and Comparisons with Classical Buddhist Accounts of Sati', in Purser, R. E., Forbes, D. and Burke, A. (eds), *Handbook of Mindfulness*, 27–45. Cham: Springer International Publishing. https://doi.org/10.1007/978-3-319-44019-4.

King, W. L. 2015 [1980]. *Theravāda Meditation: The Buddhist Transformation of Yoga*. University Park: Pennsylvania State University Press.

Kiyota, M, and Jones, E. W. (eds) 1991 [1978]. *Mahāyāna Buddhist Meditation: Theory and Practice*. Delhi: Motilal Banarsidass.

Lindahl, J. R., et al. 2017. 'The Varieties of Contemplative Experience: A Mixed-Methods Study of Meditation-Related Challenges in Western Buddhists', *PLOS ONE* 12(5). https://doi.org/10.1371/journal.pone.0176239.
Lopez, D. S. 2012. *The Scientific Buddha: His Short and Happy Life*. London: Yale University Press.
Lutz, A., Dunne, J. D. and Davidson, R. J. 2007. 'Meditation and the Neuroscience of Consciousness: An Introduction', in Zelazo, D., Moscovitch, M. and Thompson, E. (eds), *The Cambridge Handbook of Consciousness*, 499–554. Cambridge: Cambridge University Press.
Lutz, A., et al. 2008. 'Attention Regulation and Monitoring in Meditation', *Trends in Cognitive Sciences* 12(4): 163–169. https://doi.org/10.1016/j.tics.2008.01.005.
Maas, P. A. 2018. 'Sthirasukham Āsanam': Posture and Performance in Classical Yoga and Beyond', in Baier, K., Maas, P. A. and Preisendanz, K. (eds), *Yoga in Transformation: Historical and Contemporary Perspectives*, 21–48. Göttingen: V&R University Press.
Masuzawa, T. 2005. *The Invention of World Religions: Or, How European Universalism Was Preserved in the Language of Pluralism*. Chicago: University of Chicago Press.
Mayer, J. F. 2013a. *Sedlock v. Baird*. Minute Order, Superior Court of the State of California for the County of San Diego – Central Division.
Mayer, J. F. 2013b. *Sedlock v. Baird*. Statement of Intended Decision, Superior Court of the State of California for the County of San Diego – Central Division.
McMahan, D. 2008. *The Making of Buddhist Modernism*. New York: Oxford University Press.
McMahan, D. 2017. 'How Meditation Works', in McMahan, D. and Braun, E. (eds), *Meditation, Buddhism, and Science*, 21–46. New York: Oxford University Press. https://doi.org/10.1093/oso/9780190495794.001.0001.
McMahan, D. and Braun, E. (eds) 2017. *Meditation, Buddhism, and Science*. New York: Oxford University Press.
De Michelis, E. 2004. *A History of Modern Yoga: Patañjali and Western Esotericism*. London: Continuum.
Mindful Nation UK. 2015. *Report by the Mindfulness All-Party Parliamentary Group (MAPPG)*. www.themindfulnessinitiative.org/mindful-nation-report. Accessed 17 June 2019.
Monteiro, L. M., Musten, R. F. and Compson, J. 2015. 'Traditional and Contemporary Mindfulness: Finding the Middle Path in the Tangle of Concerns', *Mindfulness* 6(1): 1–13. https://doi.org/10.1007/s12671-014-0301-7
Müller, M. 1859. *A History of Ancient Sanskrit Literature So Far as It Illustrates the Primitive Religion of the Brahmans*. London: Williams and Norgate.
NCLP. 2018. *National Center for Law & Policy Official Home Page*. www.nclplaw.org/. Accessed 17 June 2019.
Newcombe, S. 2018. 'Spaces of Yoga – Towards a Non-Essentialist Understanding of Yoga', in Baier, K., Maas, P. A. and Preisendanz, K. (eds), *Yoga in Transformation: Historical and Contemporary Perspectives*, 551–573. Göttingen: V&R University Press.
Ng, E. 2016. 'The Critique of Mindfulness and the Mindfulness of Critique: Paying Attention to the Politics of Our Selves with Foucault's Analytic of Governmentality', in Purser, R. E., Forbes, D. and Burke, A. (eds), *Handbook of Mindfulness*, 135–152. Cham: Springer International Publishing. https://doi.org/10.1007/978-3-319-44019-4.
O'Brien-Kop, K. 2017. 'Classical Discourses of Liberation: Shared Botanical Metaphors in Sarvāstivāda Buddhism and the Yoga of Patañjali', *Religions of South Asia* 11(2–3): 123–157. https://doi.org/10.1558/rosa.37021.
Olendzki, A. 2014. 'From Early Buddhist Traditions to Western Psychological Science', in Ie, A., Ngnoumen, C. T. and Langer, E. J. (eds), *The Wiley-Blackwell Handbook of Mindfulness*, 58–73. Chichester: Wiley-Blackwell.
Pace, T. W. W., et al. 2009. 'Effect of Compassion Meditation on Neuroendocrine, Innate Immune and Behavioral Responses to Psychosocial Stress', *Psychoneuroendocrinology* 34(1): 87–98. https://doi.org/10.1016/j.psyneuen.2008.08.011.
Plank, K. 2011. *Insikt och närvaro: akademiska kontemplationer kring buddism, meditation och mindfulness [Insight and Presence: Academic Contemplations about Buddhism, Meditation and Mindfulness]*. Göteborg: Makadam.
Proudfoot, W. 1985. *Religious experience*. Berkeley, CA, USA: University of California Press.
Purser, R. E. 2015. 'Clearing the Muddled Path of Traditional and Contemporary Mindfulness: A Response to Monteiro, Musten, and Compson', *Mindfulness* 6(1): 23–45. https://doi.org/10.1007/s12671-014-0373-4.
Purser, R. E., Forbes, R. and Burke, A. (eds) 2016. *Handbook of Mindfulness*. Cham: Springer International Publishing. https://doi.org/10.1007/978-3-319-44019-4

Purser, R. and Loy, D. 2013. 'Beyond McMindfulness', *Huffington Post* (blog). 1 July. www.huffingtonpost.com/ron-purser/beyond-mcmindfulness_b_3519289.html. Accessed 17 June 2019.
Purser, R. and Milillo, J. 2015. 'Mindfulness Revisited: A Buddhist-Based Conceptualization', *Journal of Management Inquiry* 24(1): 3–24. https://doi.org/10.1177/1056492614532315.
Rosch, E. 2015. 'The Emperor's Clothes: A Look Behind the Western Mindfulness Mystique', in Ostafin, B. D, Robinson, M. D. and Meier, B. P. (eds), *Handbook of Mindfulness and Self-Regulation*, 271–292. New York: Springer.
Rönnegård, P. 2013. 'Melétē in Early Christian Ascetic Texts', in Eifring, H. (ed), *Meditation in Judaism, Christianity and Islam: Cultural Histories*, 79–92. London: Bloomsbury Publishing PLC. http://ebookcentral.proquest.com/lib/helsinki-ebooks/detail.action?docID=1477396.
Samuel, G. 2008. *The Origins of Yoga and Tantra: Indic Religions to the Thirteenth Century*. Cambridge: Cambridge University Press.
Samuel, G. 2016. 'Mindfulness Within the Full Range of Buddhist and Asian Meditative Practices', in Purser, R. E., Forbes, D. and Burke, A. (eds), *Handbook of Mindfulness*, 47–62. Cham: Springer International Publishing. https://doi.org/10.1007/978-3-319-44019-4.
Schopen, G. 1997. *Bones, Stones, and Buddhist Monks: Collected Papers on the Archaeology, Epigraphy, and Texts of Monastic Buddhism in India*. Honolulu: University of Hawai'i Press.
Seager, R. H. 1999. *Buddhism in America*. New York: Columbia University Press.
Sharf, R. H. 1995. 'Buddhist Modernism and the Rhetoric of Meditative Experience', *Numen* 42(3): 228–283. https://doi.org/10.1163/1568527952598549.
Sharf, R. H. 1998. 'Experience', in Taylor, M. C. (ed), *Critical Terms for Religious Studies*, 94–116. Chicago: University of Chicago Press.
Shonin, E. and Kabat-Zinn, J. 2015. '"This Is Not McMindfulness by Any Stretch of the Imagination"', *The Psychologist*. 18 May. https://thepsychologist.bps.org.uk/not-mcmindfulness-any-stretch-imagination. Accessed 17 June 2019.
Shonin, E., Van Gordon, W. and Griffiths, M. D. 2013. 'Mindfulness-Based Interventions: Towards Mindful Clinical Integration', *Frontiers in Psychology* 4: 1–4. https://doi.org/10.3389/fpsyg.2013.00194.
Stuart, D. M. 2018. 'Insight Transformed: Coming to Terms with Mindfulness in South Asian and Global Frames', *Religions of South Asia* 11(2–3): 158–181. https://doi.org/10.1558/rosa.37022.
Sun, J. 2014. 'Mindfulness in Context: A Historical Discourse Analysis', *Contemporary Buddhism: An Interdisciplinary Journal* 15(2): 394–415. https://doi.org/10.1080/14639947.2014.978088.
Suzuki, S. 1973 [1970]. *Zen Mind, Beginner's Mind*, Dixon, T. (ed). Boston: Weatherhill.
Taira, T. 2013. 'Making Space for Discursive Study in Religious Studies', *Religion* 43(1): 26–45. https://doi.org/10.1080/0048721X.2013.742744.
Thompson, E. 2017. 'Looping Effects and the Cognitive Science of Mindfulness Meditation', in McMahan, D. and Braun, E. (eds), *Meditation, Buddhism, and Science*, 47–60. New York: Oxford University Press.
Van Schaik, S. 2004. *Approaching the Great Perfection: Simultaneous and Gradual Approaches to Dzogchen Practice in Jigme Lingpa's Longchen Nyingtig*. Boston: Wisdom Publications.
Walsh, R. and Shapiro, S. L. 2006. 'The Meeting of Meditative Disciplines and Western Psychology: A Mutually Enriching Dialogue', *American Psychologist* 61(3): 227–239. https://doi.org/10.1037/0003-066X.61.3.227.
Watt, T. 2017. 'Spacious Awareness in Mahāyāna Buddhism and its Role in the Modern Mindfulness Movement', *Contemporary Buddhism: An Interdisciplinary Journal* 18(2): 455–480. https://doi.org/10.1080/14639947.2017.1379937.
Wheater, K. 2017. *Once More to the Body: An Ethnography of Mindfulness Practitioners in the United Kingdom*. PhD thesis. University of Oxford.
Wilson, J. 2014. *Mindful America: The Mutual Transformation of Buddhist Meditation and American Culture*. New York: Oxford University Press.
Wujastyk, D. 2018. 'Some Problematic Yoga Sūtras and Their Buddhist Background', in Baier, K., Maas, P. A. and Preisendanz, K. (eds), *Yoga in Transformation: Historical and Contemporary Perspectives*, 21–48. Göttingen: V&R Unipress.
Žižek, S. 2006 [2001]. *On Belief*. London: Routledge.

# 4

# THE SCHOLAR-PRACTITIONER OF YOGA IN THE WESTERN ACADEMY[1]

*Mark Singleton and Borayin Larios*

## Introduction

This chapter takes as its focus 'scholar-practitioners' of yoga in the western academy; that is to say scholars who research, teach or write about yoga in accredited modern universities, but who also do and/or teach yoga as a practice.[2] It does not consider the category of 'scholar-practitioner' in premodern South Asia nor, except in passing, religious institutions that teach yoga and publish yoga literature. The theoretical notion of the 'scholar-practitioner' is heterogeneous and wide-ranging, and may cover a large variety of positions and approaches to academic work and yoga practice, and to negotiating their relationship. The study arises partly from long consideration of this relationship on the part of the authors – both of whom are in some sense 'scholar-practitioners' of yoga, i.e. professional academics who do and have sometimes even instructed yoga in practice – and from our observation of a renewed and expanded interest in yoga as a subject of academic inquiry in Europe and North America over recent years.[3] It is in one sense therefore itself a work of autoethnographic observation, and while our presentation is necessarily general and schematic, it is rooted in a close knowledge of the various milieux in which yoga is taught and researched as an academic discipline, across departments, disciplines, countries and continents.

The scholar-practitioner of yoga in the western academy is an intriguing historical phenomenon that has arisen from the globalisation of yoga over the past two hundred or so years. Many of the scholars considered in this chapter do not come from traditional yoga-practicing communities, nor from the traditions of knowledge transmission of South Asia (although there are notable exceptions to this). Their position with regard to yoga is therefore, historically speaking, already a complex, multifaceted and evolving one. The category of scholar-practitioner can help us to reflect on the identity, beliefs, agendas, and disciplinary convictions of these scholars, and thus bring into relief one of the most striking outcomes of modern transnational yoga's progress. It can also help to reflect on what constitutes scholarship and what does not, insofar as it is seen to lie beyond the bounds of academic orthopraxis. And finally it can help us to explore the sometimes dynamic relationship between academic methodologies (such as ethnography, religious studies, or philology) and spiritual practice, and the social or professional tensions between academic expectations and spiritual practice in the workplace.

The insider/outsider binary and the allied question of identity and self-representation within the academic community (as well as vis-à-vis one's object of study) have been at the centre of scholarship for several decades now, perhaps especially within anthropology and in religious studies, but also across other disciplines.[4] While the 'academic study of yoga' may imply different theories and methods for different scholars and academic departments, the adjective 'academic' has historically tended to imply (at least in dominant academic discourse) that the topic is based on 'scientific' inquiry and secular reason, and thus that the methods of analysis are neutral, impartial and objective.[5] However, debates around whether such objectivity and critical distance are possible (or indeed desirable) have been going on for many decades now within academia, leading to a variety of new methodological approaches.[6] In recent decades, especially with the emergence of disciplines such as postcolonial studies and 'engaged anthropology',[7] the classical paradigm of objectivity has been openly challenged and claims to neutrality have been treated as naïve and untenable. Also of note in this regard is autoethnography which, rather than claiming objective or 'scientific' knowledge of its subject, emphasises the necessarily un-scientific, messy experience of the researcher-as-subject in particular social settings (Chang 2008; Adams, Holman Jones and Ellis 2015).

While the thorny problem of the 'participant-observer/experiencer' is a fascinating one that may well be relevant for many scholars of yoga – especially for those who conduct ethnographic fieldwork among yoga-practising communities – this problem is not directly the focus of our study, which examines solely how participant or insider status is negotiated within academia. In this regard, the scholars in question are often more closely aligned to the position that Elizabeth Puttick (1997) terms 'insider going outsider, going native in reverse' (Puttick 1997; see also Pearson 2001), that is to say a prior practitioner of yoga who subsequently joins the academy and subjects yoga to academic scrutiny, rather than an ethnographer or social scientist who develops a professional interest in the topic. As we shall see, it is also increasingly the case, particularly perhaps in North America, that these same scholars then take the knowledge and insights from their research back into their practice communities. Such dynamic positionalities are by no means exclusive to scholars of yoga,[8] but they are sufficiently widespread to make the scholar-practitioner of yoga an intriguing object of study. A further complication is that many scholar-practitioners of yoga do not come from a culture that has traditionally practised yoga, having adopted it as a somatic and spiritual practice later in life, often in social and cultural contexts quite different from those of 'traditional' yoga.[9] One of the purposes of this study, therefore, is to begin to examine how scholars who take yoga as a subject of their academic work situate themselves with regard to its practice and, conversely, to examine the degree to which their practice of yoga informs their scholarly work, if at all. This necessarily compressed chapter constitutes a kind of prolegomenon to ongoing research on this topic by the authors.

The varied academic cultures of the study of yoga have been shaped by different agendas, funding structures and disciplinary proclivities within the modern university, and have produced a significant variety in the ways yoga has been approached as an academic subject. There can therefore be distinct regional and disciplinary divides today in the way that yoga practice and yoga scholarship are integrated (or not). German indological traditions, for example, with their roots in nineteenth-century notions of the 'scientific' study of texts, may be uninterested in and even hostile towards scholars who foreground their practitioner status within the academy. Conversely, some scholars may wear their practitioner status more or less on their sleeve, and may derive some level of kudos or prestige from this within their communities. Their practice of yoga (and the philosophico-religious beliefs that go along with it) may even provide the public motive and raison d'être of their academic research. A similar situation can occur in 'contemplative studies' and 'mindfulness' programmes in universities where it may simply be assumed (and/or implicitly required) that professors practise what they teach. In such cases, their work may also comprise elements of pastoral or spiritual guidance.

In other cases, scholars may be practitioners but may prefer to conceal their practice from their peers for a variety of reasons. Still others, who we might think of as 'practitioner-scholars', may operate only marginally within academia and instead assume the role of 'scholar' in public yoga courses and teacher trainings. The category of 'scholar-practitioner' (and of the 'practitioner-scholar'), in its very plurality, thus provides a useful tool for investigating variations in the perceived role of the academic scholar (and its limits) with particular reference to yoga practice. This article seeks to make a first beginning in examining the various modalities of the 'scholar-practitioner of yoga', as well as the political, social and economic forces which act upon them.

Partly as a heuristic exercise for this chapter, we conducted a small survey asking the contributors to this volume to answer a few questions regarding their relationship as scholars to the practice of yoga and meditation.[10] We received a total of eighteen answers out of thirty-four scholars to whom we sent our questionnaire. While this preliminary survey certainly is in no way intended to be representative of the international community of yoga scholars as a whole, it does offer a somewhat representative cross-section of scholars of yoga and meditation. All respondents but two practise (or have in the past practised) some form of yoga or meditation regularly as part of their personal daily routines.[11] The survey was also revealing of how the diversity of academic cultures and disciplines influences a scholar's professional stance regarding the compatibility of yoga as a practice within academia, with some respondents reporting considerable tensions between their lives as practitioners and their lives as scholars, while others reported a seamless, non-differentiated position where practice and research were effectively felt to be the same endeavour.

The 'scholar-practitioner' of yoga is certainly not a recent phenomenon. Some early commentators on the *Pātañjalayogaśāstra*, for example, were clearly practitioners as well as scholars, while others were not; and the eminently practical and philosophy-free *haṭha* tradition (Mallinson 2014) has its own later scholarly tradition, sometimes apparently divorced from actual yoga practice (Birch 2018). In general, however, one could argue that yoga as an academic subject in South Asia belonged to the traditional Sanskrit training in the classical *śāstras* (sciences) of Hinduism. This type of scholarship was based on the apprentice model of the *gurukula,* in which male Brahmin students learned to first memorize by heart and then to interpret or ritually apply the Sanskrit texts they studied. While this type of education has undergone a deep transformation with the introduction of British forms of education in India, Indian universities still rely on what could be called the 'pandit model' of Sanskrit education to study yoga as a *darśana* i.e. philosophical 'point of view'.[12]

In recent years however, and particularly through the establishment of the Ministry of AYUSH[13] in 2014 under Prime Minister Narendra Modi, yoga as a physical practice and an applied discipline has become part of the curriculum of not only higher education institutions[14] but even in public schools.[15] This training is comparable to non-academic teacher trainings in the west, which are often based on yoga styles modelled after charismatic Indian yoga pioneers such as Iyengar, Jois, Sivananda and more recently Baba Ramdev, and is focused on health benefits and wellness rather than on traditional Sanskritic education. As far as yoga is concerned, the 'western' social scientific/religious studies model (which engages with religious and spiritual practice as a sociocultural product) is far less prevalent in Indian universities than its study as a theological or philosophical topic – or more recently as a subject of medical research and as practical training for a yoga teaching qualification. In some respects, this situation is comparable to theology and divinity departments in European universities, in which academic study is often presumed to be vocational. While this is not the place to examine traditional Indian models of education in depth, it will be helpful to keep in mind their divergence from methods such as European indology, social sciences and anthropology, especially in light of certain socio-political tensions that arise from this divergence (see below).

A history of the scholar-practitioner of yoga in the western academy must begin with the early 'Orientalist' scholars of India's religious and philosophical texts. The first studies of yoga by western scholars were produced in the broader context of the colonial use of Sanskrit texts, which were intended to help rule the subjects according to their own laws. This 'constructive orientalism' (Dodson 2002; Singleton 2008) sought to understand Indian religion and philosophy through the philological study of *śāstric* texts (or 'Shaster' in the colonial idiom). In collaboration with local pandits (first in Bengal and later elsewhere) British Orientalists translated a number of texts pertaining to yoga, beginning with Charles Wilkins's *Bhagavadgītā* in 1785. Henry Thomas Colebrooke's 1824 essay 'On the Philosophy of the Hindus' was the first to provide a (partial) English translation of Patañjali's yoga *darśana*. White argues that this 'effectively cut the *Yoga Sutra* free from its Indian moorings' by reading it through a distinctly philosophy-oriented, European classicist's gaze (2014: 60). Shastrideva and Ballantyne's edition of the *Yoga Sūtras* (1885) was explicitly conceived as a pedagogical method to demonstrate the superiority of European philosophy and science to learned Hindus (Dodson 2002). The separation of 'practical yoga' from yoga as a philosophical system allied to Sāṁkhya, as well as an emphasis on textual sources has, arguably, continued to dominate the academic study of yoga until recently.

Concomitantly, in the hands of later Indian and 'western' indologists, the elevation of the *Yogasūtras* as a text of philosophy often went along with the denigration of actual practising yogis in India – usually meaning *haṭhayogis* – insofar as they were seen to be degenerate, corrupt practitioners of this supposedly original philosophical system of yoga's ancient golden age (Singleton 2008). One can trace these attitudes in some of the luminaries of early indology such as Max Müller and M. Monier-Williams, as well as in some early Indian scholars of yoga (Singleton 2010: 41–44).

Initially, '[i]t was Germany's classical philologists who grappled with issues of transmission, corruption, and temporality, and who set the techniques for dealing with them as the methodological core of their science' (Turner 2007: 370). Institutions like the Royal Asiatic Society[16] were founded during this time and soon thereafter influential figures such as Max Müller[17] defined what came to be known as indology. Although yoga was a rather neglected topic among indologists of the time,[18] indological methods shaped the subsequent study of yoga texts, in particular the *Pātañjalayogaśāstra*. The ideals and methodology of this emergent academic discipline, however, were deeply embedded in the Humboldtian principles of the 'university' as an educational system based on unbiased knowledge and analysis, and reflected a deep suspicion of the privileging of revelation over science found in theology faculties.[19] Inden, however, building upon the seminal work of Said (1978), argues that orientalists and indologists in particular assumed that there is a single external reality to which western science has privileged access (what he calls 'Indology's episteme'); that 'rational, scientific thought and the institutions of liberal capitalism and democracy' stem from the nature of Euro-American civilization, and that 'the essence of Indian civilization is just the opposite of the West's' (1990: 402).

Within the category of early scholar-practitioners of yoga we must include scholars affiliated with spiritual and religious organisations producing translations and commentaries on yoga texts in the nineteenth and twentieth centuries. Probably the most significant of these organisations is the Theosophical Society, founded by H. P. Blavatsky and Henry Olcott in 1875, which published many early translations and commentaries on Patañjali's *Yogasūtras* as well as some of the earliest translations of *haṭhayoga* texts. Notable Theosophical authors here include M. N. Dvivedi, Ram Prasad, Annie Besant, William Quan Judge, Judith Tyberg, Walter Evans-Wentz, Paul Brunton, I. K. Taimni, Nilakantha Sri Ram, Charles J. Ryan and Constant Kerneïz. Such authors tend to present themselves openly as practitioners, and often their writings are markedly less academic in terms of scholarly rigour (perhaps because their primary readership was not academic, because they themselves had not been trained in the stricter scholarly environment of the university, and because they were not held to high scholarly standards by their Theosophical peers). Other religious or spiritual organisations producing translations and commentaries on yoga include the Ramakrishna Mission, the Aurobindo Ashram, Kaivalyadhama, the Divine Life Society, the Yoga Publications Trust and the Himalayan Institute.

Somewhere between the category of early textual scholars who spurn practical yoga, and avowed practitioners of yoga who also translate or write studies of yoga texts fall those who lead consciously partitioned, double lives as (public) scholars on the one hand and (secret) practitioners on the other. One of the most striking examples of this is Sir John Woodroffe (1865–1936), who was a High Court judge and scholar of British-Indian law, but also an adept and student of Hindu tantra who, together with a group of Indian pandits, published books on this topic under the pseudonym Arthur Avalon (Urban 2003: 134–147; Taylor 2012 [2001]; see Strube, Chapter 10 for further discussion). Also noteworthy in this regard is the twentieth century's best known non-Indian scholar of yoga, Mircea Eliade, who omitted his own practical knowledge of yoga from his 'scientific' work, but evoked it in his fiction and his journals (Guggenbühl 2008). A similar splitting-off of scholarship and yogic practice is also evident in Eliade's teacher, the great Indian scholar S. N. Dasgupta, who kept his mystical practice a closely guarded 'sacred secret' (ibid.). Of course, scholars may obfuscate or keep secret their own personal experience with yoga or other mystical techniques for many different reasons (such as considerations of scholarly respectability or the conviction that spiritual experience should remain private) but these examples nonetheless point us to an intriguing historical nexus of tension between scholarship and practice.

## Varieties of scholar-practitioner

In discussing varieties of scholar-practitioner, we are well aware that such categories are merely ideal-typical and may not describe any one particular 'scholar-practitioner' of yoga. Scholar-practitioners may straddle two or more categories. They may occupy more than one position over the course of their lives and careers, moving for example from a serious daily yoga practice to no practice at all, or vice versa. And they may be averse (with some justification) to defining themselves as 'types' or particular 'varieties', or consider that the characteristics we describe are too general to be meaningful. Furthermore, what is meant by 'scholar' and 'practitioner' cannot be taken for granted: both are polyvalent terms, resistant to simple definition, and implicated in complex nexuses of power and authority. For example, scholars may not necessarily work, or even have ever worked, in a university (viz. independent scholars, or those working within non- or semi-academic institutions), and some 'practitioners' may do very little by way of formal 'practice', while still considering themselves yoga practitioners by dint of their practice history or spiritual orientation. Furthermore, scholars who are privately funded may come under pressure implicitly or explicitly from their funders to follow particular directions or agendas.[20]

Attitudes among scholars (and indeed across groups of scholars) may also be revealing: one scholar may consider another not to be a 'real' scholar because his or her research methods do not fit their standard of what scholarship means, or because she or he is not accredited by a university, etc. In a similar way, one practitioner may consider that another's practice is not 'real' yoga, and so on. We have tried to take some account of these factors in our description of the varieties of scholar-practitioner of yoga, but it remains a heuristic and provisional model, rather than a description of fixed types that exist in reality.

Nevertheless, these varieties represent identifiable positions that scholars who practise yoga (or yoga practitioners who engage in scholarship) may occupy, and help to illuminate the tensions that can inhere in the way they navigate their relationship between scholarship and the practice of yoga. Broadly speaking, we can divide scholar-practitioners of yoga into two main categories: those who work in formal university settings and those who teach in non-university settings. Of course, this is not a hard and fast distinction: as the academic job market becomes increasingly precarious and as temporary teaching contracts and short-term research scholarships become the norm in higher education, especially for early-career academics, scholars may supplement their income or bridge gaps in university employment with teaching in other, non-academic settings (some of which will be examined below).

University-employed scholar-practitioners of yoga occupy a variety of positions with regard to practical yoga. Some may keep the fact that they practise yoga hidden from their colleagues, perhaps because they consider that if this were openly known it could damage their academic respectability or suggest a lack of detachment and objectivity towards their object of study.[21] This position has some similarities with 'partitioned' scholar-practitioners of previous generations like Woodroofe and Eliade. Or scholars may simply consider their spiritual practice a private affair that need not be discussed in the work environment (as opposed to something that would compromise their professional status), and/or espouse a range of theoretical positions that encourage the separation of personal faith, belief and spiritual practice from academic praxis.[22]

Others, on the other hand, may be overt, active advocates for the practice of yoga, and their teaching may blend 'objective' scholarly work (such as the critical editing of Sanskrit texts) with yoga teaching within the classroom, and even spiritual guidance to students.[23] This latter is perhaps more likely to be the case in faith-based institutions or 'theological' universities, whose institutional remit may even encourage this approach, and in university programmes whose students mainly self-identify as yoga practitioners, such as Loyola Marymount University in Los Angeles, where an MA in Yoga has been running since 2013 (and on which more below).

The blending of normative, mainstream scholarship with spiritual practices is also a key feature of 'contemplative studies' programmes, particularly in the United States, which foreground yoga and meditation techniques as a complement to academic study.[24] In some respects such programmes represent an orientation to practice and scholarship diametrically opposed to that of traditional and present-day European indology, insofar as practice (of yoga or meditation) is no longer simply the object of scholarly attention but also the method, i.e. yoga and meditation are utilised as tools with which to enhance one's experience of reading texts, while reading texts themselves is expected to reinforce one's contemplative practice. Thus Brown University's Contemplative Studies programme offers 'Integrative Contemplative Pedagogy', combining 'traditional' academic methods with contemplative experience in order to create 'a new generation of contemplative humanists, scientists and artists'.[25] Similarly, the University of Virginia's Contemplative Sciences Center offers programmes focused on the exploration of 'contemplative practices, values, ideas, and institutions historically and in contemporary times',[26] as well as practical instruction in yoga.[27] As a final example, the Yoga Studies programmes (up to and including an MA course) offered at the Center for Religion & Spirituality at Loyola Marymount University in Los Angeles, combine the pastoral mission of the broader institution with practical yoga instruction and the academic study of yoga, and are designed with yoga practitioners, rather than academics, in mind. The programmes are intended to 'meet the needs of Yoga students and teachers seeking to enhance their knowledge of the Yoga tradition'.[28]

In these contexts, 'spiritual formation' goes hand in hand with academic formation.[29] As Douglas (2012) remarks, in such environments it becomes very difficult to tell the difference between teaching yoga and teaching about yoga.[30] These programmes stand in marked contrast to some (particularly European) university programmes of study in which blending practical yoga with the academic study of yoga is unusual and may be frowned upon. This may be a reflection of the differing academic histories of Europe and North America particularly, perhaps, in terms of the legacy of 'German' indology (which has had less influence in North America than it does in Europe) and the predominance of religious studies as a discipline in North America. For example, practical yoga is not a formal component of either of the two established European MA yoga programmes, the Masters in Yoga Studies at the University Ca' Foscari in Venice,[31] and the Traditions of Yoga and Meditation MA at SOAS University of London,[32] even though a majority of students may themselves be yoga practitioners.[33]

In other cases, scholars may move between academic environments into which the introduction of practical yoga would be inadmissible (i.e. certain universities), and those in which yoga practice may form an integral part of their teaching (e.g. urban yoga centres), as is the case with some of the contributors to this volume.[34] In such environments, practitioner credentials may be not just tolerated but presumed or solicited alongside one's academic credentials. How such 'interlopers' (or 'multitaskers') manage these roles is a fascinating topic, that is beyond the scope of this short chapter.

Although clearly not 'practitioners', and thus strictly speaking outside the purview of this study, we include here university scholars who write and/or teach about yoga but who are not, never have been and do not intend to be practitioners of it.[35] Related to these, but more complex in terms of their orientation towards practice, are university scholars who used to practise yoga but no longer do, and for whom an initial practical interest in yoga may indeed have led to an academic career in the first place. Similarly, we also include here scholar-practitioners who teach or write in non-university settings. Such scholars may have gained their degrees in universities and then migrated into other milieux, or they may have had a training in non-university institutions, or be self-educated.[36] We include in this category scholars who carry out their scholarship independently of any institution, those who work in non-university institutions that support scholarship and those who teach full-time on the commercial 'yoga circuit'.

Also of note in this regard are 'public yoga intellectuals', who may or may not be professional scholars (i.e. work or have worked in university settings) who are or have been themselves practitioners, and who regularly participate in mostly online public debates. Recent topics have included the 'take back yoga' movement,[37] the introduction of yoga classes in public schools in California,[38] issues of sexual and psychological abuse within yoga communities,[39] the standardisation and the commercialisation of yoga[40] and keeping yoga free from government and corporate interference.[41] Some of these public yoga intellectuals/activists have often actively foregrounded the political within yoga, working on social issues such as power dynamics, trauma and abuse within cults and yoga communities, misogyny, homo- and transphobia, spiritual consumerism, body acceptance, racism, diversity and other related matters.[42] These issues have gained prominence through the use of social media platforms, blogs and other online forums, and have sometimes provoked furious responses by other (most often western) yoga advocates who may see themselves as defending the Indian tradition against the usurpation of a (white) western liberal intellectual elite.[43]

The political engagement of the kind exemplified by such public yoga intellectuals is rarer from academic scholars of yoga, who often prefer to preserve academic objectivity, or simply their precious time.[44] Scholars can and do enter the public sphere in varying degrees, of course. A notable example is the recent Standards Review Project of the US's largest yoga organisation,

Yoga Alliance, in which scholars (including one of the authors of this chapter) participated alongside yoga teachers to reflect on topics such as scope of practice, code of conduct, inclusion, core curricula and teacher qualifications in the context of Yoga Alliance's services to its members.[45] A more troubling example comes from scholars who have been personally attacked or have had their work plagiarised.[46] Indeed, in recent years, academics who study yoga (and indeed Indianist scholars more generally) have increasingly come under attack by right-wing Hindutva critics in India, Europe and the United States, who present these scholars as neo-colonialists trespassing on sacred ground. Commonly in such discourses, scholars who are not born Indian are considered not to have the authority/right (*adhikāra*) to research yoga (a right which is seen to derive from cultural, religious and racial inheritance), and their methods (historical, social scientific, philological, etc.) may be viewed with deep suspicion, or as incompatible with and antithetical to sanctioned, traditional ways of knowing.[47] Indeed, such scholars are often presented in Hindutva discourse as enemies of Hinduism, neo-colonialists or plain 'hinduphobes' whose covert purpose is to destroy Hindu *dharma*.[48] Such attacks often take the form of anti-intellectualism and anti-liberalism. Although yoga is currently a high-profile academic topic, such attacks are not limited to scholars of yoga, but to any scholar of India whose endeavours are seen as antipathetic. It is important to understand that this is not a merely racial or geographical narrative, but an ideological and political one. Indeed, Indian scholars who do not conform to the Hindutva ideological agenda, or who are seen to be adopting 'western' methods, also frequently come under attack.[49] In addition, some non-Indian yoga practitioners have in recent years adopted similar lines of argument against both scholars and their fellow western practitioners of yoga, thus further complicating any simple perceived dichotomy between liberal scholars and Hindutva. Although scholars may brush off these critiques as simplistic, irrelevant to the work at hand, or even delusional, it is important to be aware of them in order to understand the political contexts of yoga scholarship in the academy today, and to consider the possible effects that an increasingly aggressive and widespread critique of yoga scholars from certain quarters may have on research and teaching.[50]

## Conclusion

The category of 'scholar-practitioner of yoga' can provide a useful frame for examining the rapidly expanding field of yoga studies and the variety of disciplinary and personal positions that are deployed within it. Framing the academic study of yoga over the course of the past two centuries as a history which includes scholar-practitioners brings into focus some of the scholarly and individual biases and predilections that have shaped understandings of yoga up to the present. Yoga is not unique in drawing a high proportion of insiders and practitioners to its study, but it is a particularly complex and revealing case which speaks to the varying agendas and disciplinary and (sometimes) religious convictions of those who research and teach about yoga in the modern university. The phenomenon of the contemporary scholar-practitioner is in some respects an outcome of a specific modern, global history of yoga over the past two centuries, in which yoga has been adopted and adapted in a variety of ways and far from its place of birth, along with other 'eastern' physical and metaphysical practices such as Tai Chi. The scholar-practitioner of yoga thus finds him or herself in an intriguing historical position, one in which knowledge of yoga comes not (or not only) from older customary forms of transmission, but also from evidence-based scholarship whose first commitment is to the advancement of knowledge in the professional scholarly community, rather than to cultural or religious traditions.

The category of scholar-practitioner should also encourage us to reflect on what constitutes 'scholarship' and what does not. For example, should we consider writers who do not engage in peer review, do not cite verifiable (nor falsifiable) evidence and do not engage in wider scholarly conversations as 'scholars' (even if they are popularly known or self-identify as such) to be practising scholarship? To what extent is it possible, indeed, to move between evidence-based scholarship and one's faith/practice communities, and what tensions and contradictions are inherent in such manoeuvres? What, moreover, of those popular and influential writers on yoga whose ideological commitments or politico-religious views, combined with creative interpretations of ancient textual or archaeological data, result in the kind of 'desire-driven invention' that Lincoln identifies in certain 'scholars' of myth (1999: 215)? If this 'myth + footnotes' (ibid.) approach cannot be qualified as 'scholarship' in any generally recognised sense (recognised that is, within mainstream western universities), it remains true that many such authors enjoy a reputation as learned, trustworthy scholars among their readership. Indeed, such figures may claim for themselves an intrinsic authority (*adhikāra*) to write on yoga etc. while maintaining a concomitant antipathy towards scholars (Indian or not) who conduct their work according to the norms of academia – itself often judged as intrinsically exclusionary, elitist, colonialist and oppressive. Conversely, scholars may simply disregard such work for not meeting the minimum standards of academic practice. From this situation arises an inherent tension between certain academic and non-academic interpretations of yoga that may in certain respects mirror and amplify tensions already experienced by the scholar-practitioner.

## Notes

1 This chapter was partially financially supported by the European Union's Horizon 2020 research and innovation programme under grant agreement No. 647963 (Haṭha Yoga Project).
2 We would like to thank Suzanne Newcombe, Ann Gleig, Ville Husgafvel and the Routledge anonymous reviewer for their reflections on this chapter.
3 Several international yoga conferences have taken place in the recent past (a few notable examples are: 'Yoga in Transformation, Historical and Contemporary Perspectives on a Global Phenomenon', University of Vienna, 19–21 September 2013; 'Yoga Darśana, Yoga Sādhana: Traditions, Transmissions, Transformations', Jagiellonian University, Krakow 2016; and 'Yoga, Movement, and Space', University of Kyoto, 2–3 November 2018). Between 2015-2020 there were two five-year ERC-funded research projects on yoga: the *Entangled Histories of Yoga, Ayurveda and Alchemy in South Asia* (www.ayuryog.org/) and the *Haṭha Yoga Project* (http://hyp.soas.ac.uk/). There is also a 'Yoga in Theory and Practice Unit' at the American Academy of Religion which has at least one large panel each year at the AAR Annual Meeting. In recent years, other international academic conferences (notably of the European Conference on South Asian Studies, (ECSAS) the European Association for the Study of Religions (EASR) and the Association of Social Anthropologists (ASA)) have often included a panel on yoga as part of their programme.
4 See, for example, McCutcheon (1999); Spickard, Landres and McGuire (2002); Knott (2005); Chryssides and Gregg (2019).
5 In fact, as we write this chapter in late 2018, members of the Yggdrasill German-speaking listserv for scholars of religion have been vigorously revisiting the question of the role of scholars in the production of knowledge, and what our relationship to reality and facts might be. The following article by Kocku von Stuckrad arose from that discussion: www.counterpointknowledge.org/accountability-or-objectivity-being-a-scholar-in-an-age-of-crisis/ Accessed 30 November 2018.
6 See for instance, Knott 2005; the 'Participatory Turn' as proposed by Ferrer and Sherman 2008, or *The Insider/Outsider Debate, New Perspectives in the Study of Religion* edited by George Chryssides and Stephen E. Gregg (2019), who suggest that, 'it has become clear that binary notions of religious belonging, based upon narrow views of religion as a monolithic category of participation, are no longer tenable within the Study of Religion [...] and suggest a new relational continuum approach to the inside/outside issue in the Study of Religion which is reflective of contemporary developments in methodology, focusing in particular on issues of lived religion', www.equinoxpub.com/home/view-chapter/?id=27422. Accessed 30 November 2018.

7 Postcolonial studies has grown to a large field of study. Since Said's critique and coinage of the term 'Orientalism' (1978), other scholars have critically engaged with the relationship between India and the West such as Halbfass (1990), Inden (1990), King (1999), Chakrabarty (2000) to name just a few. For an overview of the approach known as 'engaged anthropology' see Low and Merry (2010).

8 For example, an unpublished study by Michael Aktor and Suzanne Newcombe, based on a non-representative survey of scholars of the religious traditions of Asia, suggests that at least half of professional scholars of Hinduism and Buddhism have 'some kind of personal practice related to the religion they professionally study' (Aktor and Newcombe, unpublished).

9 By 'traditional yoga' we mean yoga as practised in ascetic, monastic and householder settings in South Asia, handed down through a religious lineage and relatively free from the innovations of globalised modern yoga. The term is problematic in that it suggests a kind of hermetic purity that rarely exists in living religious traditions, and a simple binary with 'non-traditional' or 'modern' yoga. We employ the term here simply to highlight the distinct case of the scholar-practitioner in the modern university.

10 We asked the following four questions: (1) Do you practise yoga/meditation regularly and/or have you practised yoga/meditation regularly in the past? What kind(s)? (2) Have you ever taught practical yoga/meditation? (3) Have you ever taught about yoga/meditation in non-academic settings (e.g. centres, studios, teacher trainings etc.)? If so, what is the difference in your experience of teaching in academic and non-academic settings? (4) Do you experience any tension between your academic life and your life as a practitioner of yoga/meditation and do you consciously keep these separate in any way?

11 One of the two respondents who does not currently practise but has tried out some yoga classes feels 'anxiety about his lack of practical experience' and would like to 'delve more deeply into the practice in the future'.

12 In Sanskrit universities and Sanskrit departments all across India, yoga continues to be taught as a *śāstra* in which, typically, students study the *Pātañjalayogaśāstra* along with its commentaries. Yoga is thus part of the curriculum of what would be the equivalent of higher education in 'philosophy'. A list of sixteen Sanskrit universities in India compiled on Wikipedia show that in all of these universities yoga is taught as a subject within the degree of 'Acharya' or 'Shastri' https://en.wikipedia.org/wiki/List_of_Sanskrit_universities_in_India. Accessed on 29 November 2018. As an illustration of this, the Rashtriya Sanskrit Vidyapeetha, Tirupati has its own 'Department of Sankhya Yoga' within the Faculty of Darshanas, http://rsvidyapeetha.ac.in/fd.htm. Accessed on 29 November 2018.

13 An acronym of 'Ayurveda, Yoga and Naturopathy, Unani, Siddha and Homoeopathy'.

14 For example, until fairly recently, yoga was studied at Benares Hindu University as a Sanskrit subject within the philosophy programme. Since 2006, one can also study 'Preventive & Social Medicine and Yoga' within the independently established Department of Swasthavritta and Yoga'. www.bhu.ac.in/ims/swasthayoga/dep_index.html. Accessed on 22 November 2018.

15 Though the Supreme Court of India ruled against making yoga compulsory in public schools, the Human Resource Development Ministry declared that 'Yoga is an integral part of the curriculum of "Health and Physical Education", which is a compulsory subject for Classes 1 to 10. To that extent, yoga has not been neglected'. http://timesofindia.indiatimes.com/articleshow/59967483.cms?utm_source=contentofinterest&utm_medium=text&utm_campaign=cppst. Accessed on 22 November 2018.

16 The Royal Asiatic Society was founded by Colebrooke in 1824. Its academic journal is still being published, with occasional articles on yoga. Currently, this journal has at least one eminent yoga scholar on their editorial board (Carl Ernst). Similarly, other academic journals and institutions that publish research on yoga have an undeniable colonial history, e.g. Société Asiatique, Deutsche Morgenländische Gesellschaft, Brill.

17 Max Müller too, towards the end of his life, published his notes on the 'Six Systems of Indian Philosophy' in which he deals with 'Yoga and Sâmkhya' in Chapter Seven. Not surprisingly, he views yoga as an intellectual exercise mostly devoid of physical exercise. Seated *āsanas* are discussed by him as aids in his subchapter, 'Yogâṅgas, Helps to Yoga' (Müller 1899: 402–473). On Müller's disregard for practical yoga see Singleton 2010: 43.

18 On the lack of interest for yoga within indology and on the history of indological research on the *Pātañjalayogaśāstra* see Maas 2013.

19 'In the Humboldtian ideal the university existed solely to serve truth, science and learning. Reformers looked with suspicion on the "upper" faculties (law, medicine and theology), which ultimately served not *Wissenschaft* but the utilitarian needs of society and state for professional practitioners. Their suspicion fell especially heavily on the faculty of theology. They insisted that if the faculty was to continue to exist

at all as a part of the university, it must abandon its claim to revelatory knowledge transcending science, must treat theology entirely as a branch of *Wissenschaft*, and must abandon or radically de-emphasise the educational task of preparing clergymen for the pulpit and pastoral duties' (Turner 2007: 371).

20 The increased prevalence of private funding in British, European and American universities raises sensitive questions about academic neutrality, especially when funders are wedded to a particular ideology or vision of history, and/or to a particular outcome of the research they pay for. The erosion of public funding in universities increasingly puts pressure on scholars to find money from private sources and, arguably, to adapt their research to the goals of the funder. The privatised university also recreates students as consumers, further impacting teaching and research directions. See Collini 2018.

21 Aktor and Newcombe found in their unpublished survey based on research conducted online in academic discussion groups on the religions of south asia and Buddhism (conducted 2007-8) that 'although many practitioner-scholars have no wish to hide their religious practices and identification, many members in both groups [Buddhist and Hindu 'scholar-practitioners'] voiced anxiety about being subject to discriminatory employment practices and more general negative assessments by colleagues if they identified with their religion of study publicly'.

22 The theoretical work of Donald Weibe (1981)and Russell McCutcheon (1999) are in some respects representative of this position.

23 See Douglas 2012.

24 See Morgan 2012; Barbezat and Bush (eds.) 2014; Simmer-Brown and Grace (eds) 2011; Komjathy 2016.

25 https://brown.edu/academics/contemplative-studies/about. Accessed 31 December 2019.

26 http://csc.virginia.edu/content/mission. Accessed 31 December 2019.

27 https://csc.virginia.edu/activity/spring-2020-yoga. Accessed 14 February 2020.

28 https://academics.lmu.edu/extension/crs/yoga/. Accessed 31 December 2019.

29 As the director of the programme, Christopher Key Chapple, writes: 'Since the 1960s, Loyola University (the name changed to Loyola Marymount University on the occasion of merger with Marymount College in 1974) has been deeply engaged in interfaith dialogue and in various modalities of spiritual formation. Our Yoga Studies offerings build on this long-standing tradition', https://bellarmine.lmu.edu/yoga/people/meetthedirector/. Accessed 31 December 2019.

30 http://yogainhighereducation.blogspot.com/2012/08/north-american-educators-and-use-of.html. Accessed 31 December 2019.

31 https://unive.it/pag/4994/. Accessed 14 February 2020.

32 https://soas.ac.uk/religions-and-philosophies/programmes/ma-traditions-of-yoga-and-meditation/. Accessed 31 December 2020.

33 A roundtable discussion of the convenors of the three extant yoga Master Programmes (Los Angeles, Venice, London) at an academic conference in Krakow in 2016, chaired by one of the authors of this paper (Singleton), made these differences in approach quite apparent, (https://academia.edu/16072001/yoga_dar%C5%9Bana_yoga_s%C4%81dhana_traditions_transmissions_transformations_-_conference_announcement_and_CFP). Accessed 14 February 2020.

34 Fifteen of the respondents to our survey reported having taught or planning to teach at yoga teacher trainings or similar workshops in non-academic settings such as yoga studios or retreats. However, while many teach *about* yoga (i.e. history and philosophy), only about half of them actually teach meditation and/or postural yoga in both academic and non-academic settings.

35 We personally know many scholars who fit this category. All of them are European.

36 American scholars of Siddha Yoga such as Douglas Brooks, Paul Muller-Ortega, William Mahony, Carlos Pomeda, and Sally Kempton each provide interesting (and non-uniform) examples of this phenomenon.

37 https://hafsite.org/takeyogaback. Accessed 5 January 2019.

38 For a treatment of both the case in Encinitas school case and the Hindu American Foundation campaign 'Take Yoga Back', see Jain 2014; Powell 2014.

39 For example, the Yoga Journal published the following article in February 2018, https://yogajournal.com/lifestyle/timesup-metoo-ending-sexual-abuse-in-the-yoga-community. Accessed 10 January 2019; Remski 2019.

40 For example, in North America the Yoga Alliance, following severe critique over the years regarding their yoga teaching standards, decided in late 2017 to launch the 'Standard Review Project', https://yastandards.com/. Accessed 10 January 2019.

41 For example in the UK the Keep Yoga Free movement, http://keepyogafree.co.uk/. Accessed 10 January 2019.

42 Some examples of 'public yoga intellectuals' are Matthew Remski, Carol Horton and Theodora Wildcroft.

43 For example, 'Sri Louise' a disciple of Swami Dayananda Sarasvati who critiques the yoga culture in North America, especially with regards to appropriation, both in her blog and on other social media platforms. An exemplary article published in Indiafacts.org is entitled: 'Denying Yoga Its Roots – Classic Case of Hinduphobia', http://indiafacts.org/darth-yogabecky-hinduphobia-facebook-docu-drama/. Accessed 10 January 2019. Unfortunately, such responses can quickly descend into mere aggressive trolling.

44 Several scholars have privately expressed to us their aversion to public debate of this kind (particularly online) by evoking what Alberto Brandolini, an Italian independent software development consultant, has termed 'Bullshit Asymmetry Principle', which states that the amount of time taken to refute bullshit is exponentially greater than the amount of time taken to produce it, http://ordrespontane.blogspot.com/2014/07/brandolinis-law.html. Accessed on 11 January 2019.

45 See http://yastandards.com/. Accessed on 11 January 2019.

46 Such was the case, for example, with the scholar (of yoga and Hinduism) Andrew Nicholson whose work was plagiarised by Rajiv Malhotra in his 2014 book *Indra's Net*. Nicholson wrote and published this response to the incident in Scroll: https://scroll.in/article/742022/upset-about-rajiv-malhotras-plagiarism-even-more-upset-about-distortions-of-my-work. Accessed on 11 January 2019. Malhotra said in response, 'This syndrome is a subject of my research – namely, the western Indologists plagiarizing from Indians and rewriting in new clever English to claim originality'. In retaliation, he then removed all references to Nicholson from his new edition of *Indra's Net*, replacing them with 'references to the original Indian sources'. As quoted in https://insidehighered.com/news/2016/04/12/scholars-who-study-hinduism-and-india-face-hostile-climate. Accessed on 11 January 2019.

47 See for instance Adluri and Bagchee's critique of German indology in *The Nay-Science: A History of German Indology* (2014). For a critique of this work see Franco (2016 and 2018) and Hanneder 2018. See also the opinion piece 'Claiming Yoga for India' by scholar Andrea Jain (http://religiondispatches.org/claiming-yoga-for-india/. Accessed 11 January 19).

48 See, in particular, Rajiv Malhotra's *Academic Hinduphobia: A Critique of Wendy Doniger's Erotic School of Indology* (2016). For a discussion of the term Hinduphobia in academia see Long 2017. For a critique of Malhotra, see Nussbaum 2009, chapter 7.

49 For example, Malhotra and his allies term such Indian academics '*becharis* ['poor losers']' and 'sepoys [i.e. Indian recruits in the colonial army]', arguing that their motivation is to 'feel superior to ordinary Indians', https://infinityfoundation.com/indic_colloq/papers/paper_malhotra2.pdf. Accessed on 14 December 2018.

50 The case of Patricia Sauthoff is an example of this. Dr. Sauthoff who taught a course entitled 'History and Politics of Yoga' at Nalanda Univerity, was asked by the university to unconditionally apologise for 'her critical comments to the media' after her contract was not renewed without justification. Since the incident in 2017 she has received insults and threats of all kinds on social media, https://thewire.in/education/nalanda-unversity-yoga-patricial-sauthoff-yoga. Accessed 2 December 2018.

## Bibliography

Adams, T. E., Holman Jones, S. and Ellis, C. 2015. *Autoethnography: Understanding Qualitative Research*. New York: Oxford University Press.

Adluri, V. and Bagchee, J. 2014. *The Nay Science: A History of German Indology*. New York: Oxford University Press.

Aktor, M. 2015. 'Asymmetrical Religious Commitments? Religious Practice, Identity, and Self-Presentation among Western Scholars of Hinduism and Buddhism', *Numen* 62(2–3): 265–300.

Aktor, M. and Newcombe, S. [Unpublished]. 'Inside-out in the Closet? Religious Practice, Identity and Self-presentation among Western Scholars of Hinduism and Buddhism.' Research undertaken in online academic lists during 2007–2008.

Barbezat, D. and Bush, M. (eds) 2014. *Contemplative Practices in Higher Education: Powerful Methods to Transform Teaching and Learning*. San Francisco: Jossey-Bass, Wiley.

Birch, J. 2018. 'The Proliferation of Āsanas in Late-Medieval Yoga Texts', in Baier, K., Maas, P. A. and Preisendanz, K. (eds), *Yoga In Transformation: Historical and Contemporary Perspectives*, 101–180. Göttingen: V&R Unipress, Vienna University Press.

Chakrabarty, D. 2000. *Provincializing Europe: Postcolonial Thought and Historical Difference*. Princeton, NJ: Princeton University Press.

Chang, H. 2008. *Autoethnography as Method*. Walnut Creek, CA, USA: Left Coast Press.

Chryssides, G. D. and Gregg, S. E. (eds) 2019. *The Insider/Outsider Debate: New Perspectives in the Study of Religion*. Sheffield: Equinox Publishing.

Colebrooke, H. T. 1824. 'On the Philosophy of the Hindus. Part I', *Transactions of the Royal Asiatic Society of Great Britain and Ireland*, (1): 19–43.

Collini, S. 2018. *Speaking of Universities*. London: Verso.

Dodson, M. S. 2002. 'Re-Presented for the Pandits: James Ballantyne, "Useful Knowledge", and Sanskrit Scholarship in Benares College during the Mid-Nineteenth Century', *Modern Asian Studies*, 36(2): 257–298.

Douglas, L. 2012. 'North American Educators and the Use of Yoga as Pedagogy: Results of a Mixed Methods Study', http://yogainhighereducation.blogspot.fr/2012/08/north-american-educators-and-use-of.html. Accessed 5 April 2018.

Ferrer, Jorge N. and Sherman, Jacob H. 2008. *The Participatory Turn: Spirituality, Mysticism, Religious Studies*. Albany, NY: State University of New York Press.

Franco, E. 2016. 'The Nay Science. A History of German Indology, by Vishwa Adluri and Joydeep Bagchee', *South Asia: Journal of South Asian Studies*, 39(3): 695–698.

Franco, E. 2018. [Unpublished] 'Response to Adluri Bagchee Nay Science', www.academia.edu/31668658/Response_to_Adluri_Bagchee_Nay_Science. Accessed 11 January 2019.

Gosh, T. 2018. 'I'm a Target Because I'm an Outsider: Sanskrit Scholar Sheldon Pollock' *Indian Express*. http://indianexpress.com/article/express-sunday-eye/im-a-target-because-im-an-outsider-sanskrit-scholar-sheldon-pollock-5191995/. Accessed 1 December 2018.

Guggenbühl, C. 2008. Mircea Eliade and Surendranath Dasgupta: the history of their encounter; Dasgupta's life, his philosophy, and his works on Yoga; a comparative analysis of Eliade's chapter on Patanjali's Yogasutra and Dasgupta's Yoga as Philosophy and Religion [Online]. Available at http://crossasia-repository.ub.uni-heidelberg.de/149/.

Halbfass, W. 1990. *India and Europe: An Essay in Philosophical Understanding*. Delhi: Motilal Banarsidass Publishers.

Hanneder, J. 2018. 'Kraut-Indology', www.uni-marburg.de/fb10/iksl/indologie/fachgebiet/mitarbeiter/hanneder/downloads/downloads-varia/krautindology.pdf. Accessed on 1 December 2018.

Inden, R. B. 1990. *Imagining India*. Bloomington, IA, USA: Indiana University Press.

Jain, A. 2014. 'Who Is to Say Modern Yoga Practitioners Have It All Wrong?: On Hindu Origins and Yogaphobia', *Journal of the American Academy of Religion* 82(2): 427–471

King, R. 1999. *Orientalism and Religion: Postcolonial Theory, India and 'the Mystic East'*. London: Routledge.

Knott, K. 2005. 'Insider/Outsider Perspective', in Hinnells, J. R. (ed), *The Routledge Companion to the Study of Religion*, 243–258. London: Routledge.

Komjathy, L. 2016. 'Möbius Religion: The Insider/Outsider Question', in Kripal, J. (ed), *Religion: Sources, Perspectives and Methodologies*. Farmington Hills, MI: Macmillan.

Lincoln, B. 1999. *Theorizing Myth: Narrative, Ideology, and Scholarship* [Online]. Chicago: University of Chicago Press.

Long, J. D. 2017. *Reflections on Hinduphobia: A Perspective from a Scholar-Practitioner*. Prabuddha Bharata.

Low, S. M. and Merry, S. E. 2010. 'Engaged Anthropology: Diversity and Dilemmas', *Current Anthropology* 51(S2): 203–226.

Maas, P. A. 2013. 'A Concise Historiography of Classical Yoga Philosophy', in Franco, E. (ed), *Periodization and Historiography of Indian Philosophy: Twelve Lectures Held at the Fourteenth World Sanskrit Conference (Kyoto, September 1–5, 2009)*, 53–90. Wien: Verein 'Sammlung de Nobili Arbeitsgemeinschaft für Indologie und Religionsforschung' Institut für Südasien- Tibet- und Buddhismuskunde der Universität Wien.

Malhotra, R. 2014. *Indra's Net: Defending Hinduism's Philosophical Unity*. Noida: HarperCollins Publishers India.

Malhotra, R. 2016. *Academic Hinduphobia: A Critique of Wendy Doniger's Erotic School of Indology*. New Delhi: Voice of India.

Mallinson, J. 2014. 'Haṭhayoga's Philosophy: A Fortuitous Union of Non-Dualities', *Journal of Indian Philosophy* 42(1): 225–247.

McCutcheon, R. T. (ed) 1999. *The Insider/Outsider Problem in the Study of Religion: A Reader*. London: Cassell.

Morgan, P. F. 2012. 'Following Contemplative Education Students' Transformation Through Their 'Ground-of-Being' Experiences', *Journal of Transformative Education* 10(1): 42–60.

Müller, M. 1899. *The Six Systems of Indian Philosophy*. London: Longsman Green.
Newcombe, S. [Unpublished Presentation]. 'Identification with Hinduism and the Politics of a Plural World' at the *6th Annual Dharma Association of North American (DĀNAM) Conference*, held in conjunction with the 2008 American Academy of Religion meeting in Chicago, Illinois, USA, 31 October–1 November.
Nussbaum, M. C. 2009. *The Clash Within: Democracy, Religious Violence, and India's Future*. Cambridge, MA: Harvard University Press.
Pearson, J. 2001. '"Going Native in Reverse": The Insider as Researcher in British Wicca', *Nova Religio* 5(1): 52–63.
Powell, S. 2014. *Yoga on Trial: The Imbrication of Yoga and Religion in Sedlock v. Baird*. Unpublished Master's Thesis. University of Washington.
Puttick, E. 1997. *Women in New Religions: In Search of Community, Sexuality and Spiritual Power*. Basingstoke: Macmillan.
Remski, M. 2019. *Practice and All is Coming: Abuse, Cult Dynamics, and Healing in Yoga and Beyond*. Rangiora, New Zealand: Embodied Wisdom Publishing.
Said, E. 1978. *Orientalism: Western Representations of the Orient*. New York: Pantheon.
Shastrideva, G. and Ballantyne, J. 1885. *The Yoga Philosophy, Being the Text of Patanjali with Bhoja Raja's Commentary*. Bombay: Tookaram Tatya for the Bombay Theosophical Fund.
Simmer-Brown, J. and Grace F. (eds) 2011. *Meditation and the Classroom: Contemplative Pedagogy for Religious Studies*. New York: SUNY.
Singleton, M. 2008. 'The Classical Reveries of Modern Yoga: Patañjali and Constructive Orientalism', in Singleton, M. and Byrne, J. (eds), *Yoga in the Modern World: Contemporary Perspectives*, 77–99. London: Routledge.
Singleton, M. 2010. *Yoga Body: The Origins of Modern Posture Practice*. New York: Oxford University Press.
Spickard, J. V., Landres, J. S. and McGuire, M. B. (eds) 2002. *Personal Knowledge and Beyond: Reshaping the Ethnography of Religion*. New York: New York University Press.
Stuckrad, K. von 2018. 'Accountability or Objectivity? Being a Scholar in an Age of Crisis', www.counterpointknowledge.org/accountability-or-objectivity-being-a-scholar-in-an-age-of-crisis/. Accessed 20 June 2019.
Taylor, K. 2012 [2001]. *Sir John Woodroffe Tantra and Bengal*. Hoboken: Taylor and Francis. http://gbv.eblib.com/patron/FullRecord.aspx?p=1047145. Accessed 20 June 2019.
Turner, S. 2007. 'Ideas, Institutions, and Wissenschaft: Accounting for the Research University', *Modern Intellectual History* 4(2): 367–378
Urban, H. B. 2003. *Tantra: Sex, Secrecy, Politics, and Power in the Study of Religion*. Berkeley: University of California Press.
White, D. G. 2014. *The Yoga Sutra of Patanjali: A Biography*. Princeton: Princeton University Press.
Wiebe, D. 1981. Religion and Truth: Towards an Alternative Paradigm for the Study of Religion. The Hague: Mouton Publishers.
Wilkins, C. 1785. *The Bhagvat-Geeta, or Dialogues of Kreeshna and Arjoon: In Eighteen Lectures; with Notes. Translated from the Original, in the Sanskreet, or Ancient Language of the Brahmans*. London: C. Nourse. https://oll.libertyfund.org/titles/2369. Accessed 20 June 2019.

# 5
# NEOLIBERAL YOGA

*Andrea R. Jain*

## Introduction

We have all heard the expression 'you are what you eat'.[1] Historically, the extent of yoga practitioners' concerns about what, when or how a person eats is met only by concerns about with whom, when or how a person has sex, hence attention given in many yoga systems to purifying the body through rigorous control over diet and fasting alongside celibacy. Today, especially among those living in global cities, yoga is as much about what a person buys, another kind of consumption. The majority of yoga practitioners are full participants in the global consumer economy, marking their worth by purchasing expensive brands.

The yoga industry is an enormous one. According to a report by Allied Market Research, the global pilates and yoga studios market was valued at almost $89 million in 2017 and is projected to reach almost $216 million by 2025 (Bhandalkar, Das and Kadam 2019: 14). The yoga industry is also entangled with other large markets. For example, Baba Ramdev, the most famous yoga guru in India, is also the brand ambassador for and CEO of Patanjali Ayurved, a corporation with more than 200,000 outlets, and its sales of health, wellness and food products reached over $1.5 billion in the 2017 fiscal year (Scroll Staff 2017).

This chapter theorises yoga as a social, economic, political, cultural and religious project, locating its disciplines, discourses and institutions within a neoliberal capitalist network. I analyse different and conflicting narratives in order to shed light on the following key aspects of the global yoga industry: capitalist strategies of appropriation and commodification, and a pervasive neoliberal logic whereby control over one's body and personal circumstances is valued and defined as an individual achievement.

When I speak of *neoliberal yoga*, I am referring to the yoga systems that rely on the selective deployment of key assumptions, such as the importance of self-governance and individual responsibility as well as the value of entrepreneurship. In turn, it privileges meritocracy insofar as many activities revolve around discerning and certifying the merit that leads to the envied lifestyle of personal growth, self-care, health, wellness and even liberation. There is a rich archive of this type of yoga, which combines an exhortation for individuals to take responsibility for their conditions with effective commodifying and purchasing strategies and usually marketing endeavours that rely on some kind of nostalgic attachment to the past, valorization of purity and cultural appropriation.

At the same time, the yoga industry has suffered the fate of other areas of culture under the dominance of neoliberal capitalism. Adherents must 'do more with less', cutting costs while meeting ever-greater demands. Yoga teachers, for example, who in much of the world happen to be mostly women, face shrinking wages, and this workforce is increasingly precarious, even as yoga teachers are called on to teach more students than ever before, to do more unpaid *seva* or 'service', and to demonstrate that they are doing it better than ever.

Yoga has undergone rampant change and diversification since its global boom in contemporary consumer culture, yet, even though the extent of this was unprecedented before the late-twentieth century, yoga had always been polythetic in the many pathways of its historical development as a part of South Asian religious history (Jain 2014a: 1–19). Furthermore, although neoliberal capitalist culture's emphasis on self-development through consumer choice – most notably when it comes to tools and regimens for body maintenance – mirrors the yoga industry's devotion to fitness, health and wellness, for many practitioners, yoga's religious qualities have not been eliminated. They have been transformed. So even though neoliberal capitalism birthed the yoga industry, this kind of yoga cannot be reduced to market forces or the dynamics of power, status and money. Rather, it remains deeply religious even in (and in some cases through) acts of appropriation and commodification (Jain 2014a). In fact, yoga consumers share many qualities with what we often imagine as traditional yogic subjects, including demarcating sacred spaces and time, creating communities, posing solutions to the problems of suffering, illness and death, and sharing myths and rituals (Jain 2014a).[2]

Scholars love arguing over the meaning of words, and it is fair to say that *neoliberalism* is one of the most contested terms in our contemporary lexicon. I use the term to refer to a particular modern secular paradigm and mode of governance. Following Wendy Brown, neoliberalism is best understood 'not simply as economic policy, but as a governing rationality that disseminates market values and metrics to every sphere of life … It formulates everything, everywhere, in terms of capital investment and appreciation, including and especially humans themselves' (Brown, 2015: 176). In other words, signs of the rising dominance of neoliberal capitalism are in the increasing monetisation of all public space and the commercialisation of everything.

Since the late 1980s, neoliberalism has increasingly functioned as the 'hegemonic mode of discourse' (Harvey 2005: 3), a discourse that deploys state power 'to reshape society in accordance with market models' (Kotsko 2018: 5). Neoliberalism exercises governance by putting the burden on the individual for their position in society, rendering certain modes of self-governing the 'appropriate' responses to their problems (Burchell, Gordon and Miller 1991; Miller and Rose 2008; Shamir 2008; Hamann 2009). In other words, neoliberal discourses are accompanied by practices and technologies, such as programmes or tools for 'self-care', for individuals to work on themselves. They reframe and reconfigure the conditions of the individual so that their fate depends predominantly on their own choices, actions and abilities. The consequences of the actions, therefore, are borne by the subject alone, who is also solely responsible for them (Lemke 2001: 201). Neoliberal governmentality can be seen at play in discourses of self-sufficiency, which reify the individual, construed as an automaton, ideally self-optimising, self-sustaining and entrepreneurial.

Finally, neoliberalism conflates 'individualism and liberation', along with 'consumption and activism' through its consumer-driven logic (Butler 2013: 46). A person is a good and 'free' citizen when she engages in appropriate consumption. In other words, the shift to neoliberal governance, according to Jess Butler, entails 'the development of discourses that emphasize consumer citizenship, personal responsibility, and individual empowerment' (Butler 2013: 41). A person is liberated insofar as they are free to make consumer choices, to participate in the market economy, hence individuals are expected to be self-reliant and self-disciplining through consumption.

The extension of neoliberal governance into yoga is visible in the discourses and practices of the industry's most powerful corporations and proponents, including the current Prime Minister of India, Narendra Modi, and his spiritual ally and the most famous living yoga guru in India, Baba Ramdev, as well as some of the most popular yoga corporations today, such as Spiritual Gangster (a US-based yogaware company) and Bikram Yoga (the original 'hot yoga'). Neoliberal yoga's discourses and activities are not just a result of the demands of capital, but actually reflect a key part of neoliberal ideology: that we must constantly work on ourselves and call out those who are not doing so properly. They build that ideology as much as market capitalism reproduces them. In other words, even though yoga gets caught in a web of commodification and market exchange, it cannot be reduced to market dynamics; instead it is also reflective of 'good consumer choices', in other words, of discourses and behaviours that construct and uphold a neoliberal ethic.

## Selling yoga

How and when did yoga become a readily available consumer choice in global cities around the world? The postural practice most commonly associated with yoga today underwent popularisation when it began to coincide with certain global developments in the late-twentieth century (Jain 2014a: 42–72). First, increased freedom in physical mobility allowed consumers to travel to other parts of the world and adopt disparate wares and entrepreneurs and proselytising teachers to widely disseminate their teachings or products. Many restrictions on immigration from India to the United States and parts of Europe were lifted in the 1960s. Furthermore, instead of the historically dominant practice of relying on yoga's transmission through the guru-disciple relationship, usually in the isolated context of an ashram, gurus began to actively seek adherents to their yoga systems by 'selling' yoga to large audiences (Jain 2014a: 42–72).

Second, disillusionment with established religious institutions was widespread as many urban dwelling consumers felt threatened by social environments they no longer controlled in light of globalisation and other modern social processes; hence the market for 'alternative' spiritual practices and teachers widened (Kakar 1983: 191–192; Swallow 1982: 123–158). Yoga gurus broke into that increasingly global market with what they prescribed as solutions to the problems of excess and chaos in modern life, drawing large swathes of disciples with their miracles and promises of empowerment and transformation (Jain 2014a: 42–94). Many of these gurus travelled the world, especially in response to the British-American counter-culture, which included audiences – including the high-profile rock band, The Beatles – drawn to spiritual practices and messages distinct from what were perceived as the oppressive, puritanical orthodoxies of the previous generation (Porterfield 2001: 164–165, 203).

Though some scholars suggest that we consider systems of modern yoga as examples of the transplantation of movements from India to Euro-American contexts (for example, see Williamson 2005: 149; Caldwell 2001: 25), many global gurus (for example, Sri Anandamayi Maa; Daya Mata (born Faye Wright); Guru Anjali; Gurumayi Chidvilasananda; Ma Yogashakti; Mata Amritanandamayi or 'Amma'; Muktananda; Maharishi Mahesh Yogi; Bhaktivedanta Prabhupada; Satya Narayan Goenka; and Sathya Sai Baba) developed and maintained prominent Indian followings (Jain 2014a: 46–47; see also the essays in Pechilis 2004; Chapple 2005: 15–35; Raj 2005: 123–146; and Lucia 2014). Their successes testify, not to the 'Americanization' or 'westernization' of yoga, but to the increased visibility of yoga in the late-twentieth century in areas across the globe (Jain 2014a: 65). The entrepreneurial spirit that characterised the global consumer culture landscape influenced these gurus, meaning yoga was commercialised and framed as a practice consumers could select and combine with previously held beliefs or practices according to individual preferences and needs.

When long-term commitment to yoga required adherents to learn Sanskrit, to adopt an inferior position vis-à-vis a guru, or to abstain from a consumer approach to spiritual goods

(Jain 2014a: 65), those systems were less successful in the emergent global yoga market than the ones that thoroughly coincided with the dominant trends of consumer culture. Nonetheless, through acts of cultural appropriation, yoga succeeded when it was perceived to transport the consumer to an authentic ancient landscape – such as 'exotic' or 'ancient' India – independent of actual time and place. Selling yoga, in turn, entailed appropriating and commodifying aspects of South Asian cultures, from Sanskrit terminology to images of Ganesha.

The entrepreneurial spirit was strongest among proponents of postural yoga (Jain 2014a: 65–70). Postural yoga's popularisation is explained in part by the fact that it more often provided quick and direct access to the perceived benefits of yoga, rather than indirect access through the intermediary role of a (far-removed) teacher or text (De Michelis 2004: 250). Increasingly, postural yoga gurus' marketing campaigns attempted to convince people to choose their particular renditions of yoga as one part of individual programmes of self-development. They worked within a market in which wares were most successful when they could be easily fit into individualised lifestyles (Jain 2014a: 65–70). The earliest of these included B. K. S. Iyengar, Selvarajan Yesudian, Sivananda, Boris Sacharow, Vishnudevananda, Indra Devi, Chidananda Sarasvati, Lilias Folan and Richard Hittleman. Many of these yoga advocates abandoned all or many of the rules, such as those dealing with alms, celibacy, scriptural study and retreat from society or social norms, which traditionally separated the yoga practitioner from society so that they could sell yoga as a form of fitness, self-care and wellness (Jain 2014a: 66–67).

With the rise to dominance of neoliberal capitalism in the 1980s, 1990s and 2000s, the yoga market came to feature endless yoga brands whose products were sold for immediate consumption (Jain 2012; Jain 2014a: 73–94). There was a seismic shift in how yoga advocates established and acknowledged authority, which was increasingly vested in certain brand names (Jain 2014a: 74). The market for 'self-care' regimens, which held individuals and their consumer choices accountable for their health, wellness, professional success and other life circumstances, witnessed robust growth. Self-care became a way to signal a consumer's willingness to own up to their responsibility for their wellbeing, and yoga was widely sold as an effective path to get there.

## Neoliberal yoga

There are countless ways neoliberal yoga, that peculiar variant of yoga that incites its adherents to accept full responsibility for their own wellbeing, self-care and liberation by making good consumer choices, is made manifest. Neoliberal yoga is never short on authoritarian prescriptions and prohibitions. Here are just a few examples to consider.

In a *Yoga Journal* article titled 'Kino MacGregor: India Is a Yoga Teacher', the famous white American ashtanga yoga teacher Kino MacGregor appropriates and commodifies India as 'a place where you are free to discover yourself on your own terms'. Here, India itself is the good consumer choice. She encourages yoga consumers to 'go to India and lose all the accoutrements of the Western world to see what's underneath and just be yourself' (MacGregor 2015: para. 4). Such orientalist dialectics or win-win narratives free consumers to purchase yoga without attention to their embeddedness within social structures based on power inequities and histories of colonialism (O'Reilly 2006: 1003), and they are present in a variety of industries.[3] For example, it is precisely this kind of narrative that informs bestselling neoliberal manifestos, such as Whole Foods Market CEO John Mackey's *Conscious Capitalism*, in which the ideal person is construed as atomized, self-optimising and entrepreneurial. Mackey suggests that leadership in 'conscious capitalism' 'integrates Western systems and efficiency with Eastern wisdom and effectiveness' (Mackey and Sisodia 2014: 194). Consider also the Indian Ministry of Tourism's Swadesh Darshan Scheme, launched under the Modi government, which includes a 'spiritual' tourism circuit, arguing that India is 'the land of spirituality' and therefore is in need of 'tourist facilities across the country' to accommodate spiritual travellers (Ministry of Tourism Government of India 2018).

Some yoga consumers respond to the current climate crisis by greenwashing yoga, opting, for example, for the high-end apparel of Satva Living, which offers 'mindfully designed organic fashion'. The company claims to improve the health and wellness of 'conscious consumers' as well as the lives of Indian organic farmers by partnering with Suminter India Organics and working under the model of 'creative capitalism', an approach that ensures that a portion of profits are invested back into the communities and agricultural programmes of the farmers. Satva Living products are sold across India as well as the United States and are available, for example, at Whole Foods Market, where spiritual consumers might also shop for 'eco-friendly' biodegradable paper plates. The multimillionaire entrepreneur Mackey uses the phrase *conscious capitalism,* arguing that capitalism's 'heroic spirit' is the key to creating 'a world in which all people live lives full of prosperity, love, and creativity – a world of compassion, freedom, and prosperity' (Mackey and Sisodia 2014).

The discourses printed across yoga apparel provide more insight into the workings of neoliberal yoga. Yoga pants and t-shirts feature catchy expressions, for example: 'Good Vibes. All Day. Every Day.', 'Good Karma', 'Namaste All Day' and 'Self Love Club'. Spiritual Gangster yogaware is just one articulation of neoliberal yoga, wedding their yoga products to an effort to cultivate universal happiness and freedom. 'Our mission', according to their website, 'is to inspire positivity, generosity, kindness and connectedness with this goal in mind: may all beings everywhere be happy and free'. 'We are connected. We are the same. We are one.' (Spiritual Gangster 2019).

Baba Ramdev similarly espouses a message of 'positive thinking' and 'self-care', which he disseminates across India through speeches, interviews, advertisements and other media platforms. In alliance with Narendra Modi, Baba Ramdev serves a neoliberal regime of power (Andrews, Batts and Silk 2013; Jain and Schulson 2016; Khalikova 2017). There is a paradox in Ramdev's work. On the one hand, Ramdev's stance seems fundamentally nationalist and conservative. He profits from products marketed as traditional, natural foods and ancient medicinal practices, including yoga. In Ramdev, his corporation Patañjali Ayurved has a strong brand ambassador, one credited with bringing yoga as a health practice to the mainstream in India. He has supporters across the country who choose Patañjali Ayurved products because of the yogic authority they invest in its ambassador, as well as the nationalist associations of the brand. Ramdev consistently positions Patañjali Ayurved as a homegrown Indian company fighting global multinational competitors.

Like other entrepreneurs selling yoga and associated products globally, however, Ramdev is also building a massive corporation selling packaged, branded and commercialised products with sleek modern advertising, and he thrives in a modern neoliberal health-and-wellness sector that is growing globally, a sector that calls on consumers to take responsibility for their health, wellness, success and empowerment. Ramdev is helping to accelerate yoga's entry into the twenty-first-century neoliberal capitalist global economy. Entrepreneurial gurus and yoga brands like these might be appealing in part because they successfully appropriate and commodify the 'ancient' ideas and symbols of India, but they also represent one expression of a global shift toward a form of self-care that is deeply exclusionary – creating outgroups who fail when they do not choose the right consumer products. Ramdev, for example, was instrumental in recriminalizing same-sex sex in India, which exacerbated the social and physical vulnerability of LGBTQ Indians. He claimed homosexuality was a 'disease' that could be 'cured' by buying yoga (NDTV 2013).

Another of the most famous neoliberal yoga entrepreneurs is Bikram Choudhury, creator of Bikram Yoga or what is often described as 'the original hot yoga', which he claims maintains and restores health even to those with grave injuries and illnesses. In the 1990s, Bikram began hosting teacher-training programmes in Los Angeles, which would eventually boast upwards of six hundred registrants. The cost for training steadily rose. A 2019 training course, for example, cost $16,600. If, as Kathryn Lofton suggests, 'religion manifests in efforts to mass-produce relations of value' (Lofton 2017: 2), then Bikram Yoga teacher-training programmes represent consumer religion. Teachers who have completed the training have opened more than five thousand yoga studios worldwide (for a more extensive discussion and analysis of Bikram, see Jain 2018 and Jain 2020).

It is not surprising, given the assumption that the best way to bring about happiness and freedom in society is to hold individuals accountable for buying the right self-care regimens, that neoliberal yoga embodies all sorts of contradictions, giving rise to social and political controversies. Bikram, for example, is a multimillionaire who has exploited the cultural cache and economic capital of yoga, all while creating Bikram Yoga, a practice some practitioners deem deeply healing, empowering and transformative. He is also, however, someone who has claimed but failed to secure copyrights on yoga postures, pursued litigation against rival yoga franchises and battled allegations of sexual harassment and even rape by students and employees. In Bikram, we see how neoliberal yoga can betray ritual, mythological and other religious qualities, but it is also an industry that operates by the same logic as multinational corporations.

Bikram is far from the only neoliberal yoga teacher or entrepreneur mired in sex scandals. Since the October 2017 *New York Times* publication of investigative work into the decades of sexual harassment allegations against Hollywood producer Harvey Weinstein (Kantor and Twohey 2017), hundreds of women from the yoga industry stepped forward to say, 'me too'. Most notably, in December 2017, Rachel Brathen collected more than three hundred #metoo stories and posted them on her Yoga Girl website (Yoga Girl 2019). The hundreds of #metoo exposés chronicled (mostly) women's stories in which they accused (mostly) male yoga teachers and gurus, including the famous yoga guru responsible for popularizing Ashtanga Yoga, Pattabhi Jois, of exploitative and sexually violent conduct.

Other contradictions manifest around the International Day of Yoga. For example, consider the closure of the Burrard St. Bridge. In 2015 in Vancouver – home to yoga apparel giant lululemon – a scheduled Yoga Day event threatened to 'divide the city and the local yoga community' due to the $150,000 price tag, corporate sponsors (including lululemon) and the planned seven-hour 'Om the Bridge' closure. The added irony was that the event was largely sponsored by an affluent white Canadian demographic and threatened to eclipse National Aboriginal Day – all while its organisers claimed to celebrate an ancient system of knowledge indigenous to India, that is, yoga. The event was cancelled following a week of protest (see Bramadat 2019). Events for Yoga Day have even sparked controversy in India, where Indian Muslims protested Yoga Day programmes, arguing they serve right-wing Prime Minister Narendra Modi's 'saffron agenda'; that is, his Hindu nationalism (Jain 2014b; see also Jain 2020).

'Personal growth', 'self-care', 'healing', and 'transformation' are just some of the generative tropes in the narrative of what I am calling neoliberal yoga. Huge swathes of consumers in urban spaces all over the world now spend money on yoga, hence the emergence of large multinational corporations, indeed an entire global industry, that produce these products. When yoga practitioners speak about personal growth, self-care or transformation, however, they uphold cultural, religious and economic systems that are less empowering, healing or liberating than implied. Although there is no doubt that yoga practitioners frequently undergo dramatic healing experiences through the practice of yoga, purchasing yoga commodities does not actually challenge or weaken the dominant, oppressive hierarchies or social systems that cause trauma, suffering and sickness to begin with. Much of the industry's products, in fact, are rooted in concerns about preventing deviancy, not only in the form of low productivity but also forms of social deviancy, such as non-conformity to heteronormativity or other gender and sexual norms. The prescriptions for self-care or personal liberation, in other words, have little or nothing to do with societal transformation; rather they denote the requirements for making individuals into more productive, efficient and conforming workers and members of society. As the demands on people to conform to capitalist ideals have increased, so we have seen an increase in yoga teachers, systems and classes, which for the most part claim to enhance productivity and simultaneously conformity to a rigid neoliberal ethical (not to mention racial, gender, sexual and overall bodily) standard (Jain 2020).

Put differently, the yoga industry supports neoliberal capitalism, both in the pursuit of surplus value and ideological control; that is, by reinforcing its structures, norms and values and punishing deviations from them. More specifically, neoliberal yoga creates deviant outgroups – from yoga apparel companies like lululemon or Spiritual Gangster's marketing strategies that present a narrow vision of the ideal (usually white) female body to Baba Ramdev's prescription of yoga as the cure for homosexuality and Modi's political strategies whereby yoga is weaponised against a Muslim minority – claiming that the members of such groups fail to choose the right lifestyle interventions to cultivate self-improvement and public allegiance to the nation (Jain 2020).

Furthermore, there is no doubt that large-scale interest in neoliberal yoga is built on romanticised images of the exotic Other and a distorted view of history. Consumers often ignore context, history and politics when they appropriate and commodify yoga. There are several relevant contexts to consider, including of course the history of white British colonial control of South Asia. The appropriation of South Asian cultural symbols and practices is situated within a history of colonialism and capitalist exploitation. Social inequalities, colonial histories, racism and nationalism all shape our ways of understanding who uses South Asian practices and why. Although many yoga entrepreneurs, corporations and consumers might resist critical reflection on these matters, preferring instead to speak of yoga as if it represents a static essence that can be seamlessly transmitted from one consumer-practitioner to another, transmission is far messier and usually does not take place between social equals (Jain 2020).

Consumers appropriate cultural products because there is something evocative about them (Einstein 2008: 4). Middle- or upper-class white yoga consumers living in the globalised twenty-first century, for example, often imagine themselves as materially rich but spiritually poor and, in turn, see South Asians as materially poor but offering great spiritual wealth or wisdom. In these representations, it becomes clear how capitalism, colonialism, racism, nationalism and orientalism engender and reify one another by discouraging reflection on historical and contemporary systematic forms of oppression.

In addition to the problems of cultural appropriation and orientalism, neoliberal yoga also upholds heteropatriarchy. In fact, gender is central (not peripheral) to its operations, especially insofar as heteropatriarchy shapes the ways authority is demarcated and exercised such that structural transformation is not expected as the solution to gender inequities; rather, resolving those challenges is a burden placed on the shoulders of the most oppressed; that is, women and other gender and sexual minorities. For example, industry leaders call on women, not to subvert heteropatriarchal social structures that obstruct their abilities to parent while fulfilling the demands of a career, but to use yoga as a means of achieving that envied (and maybe impossible) work-life balance. Yoga, in other words, is an individual's tool for breaking the glass ceiling, not dismantling the ceiling so that all women have equal opportunity (Jain 2020).[4]

Genealogies of power, privilege and oppression in neoliberal yoga can be narrated through attention, not only to individual incidents of racism or sexual harassment and assault, but also by reading the texts of popular publications, such as *Yoga Journal*, or listening to widely disseminated yoga discourses, such as those of Baba Ramdev. In these, we learn that single women, queer people, fat people, sick people, people of colour, differently abled and atypical people and poor people are real problems. We learn that yoga practitioners, should they want to survive and thrive, must avoid, call out and regulate those problems. Industry leaders learn that its prescriptions about how to govern bodies has a productive energy that can be harnessed to convince consumers to buy more commodities and therefore support the industry, even when that support also cultivates discrimination, exclusion and abuse. Neoliberal yoga runs only by convincing consumers that they are imperfect and flawed by that same discrimination, exclusion and abuse, and that they can be healed if only they purchase the right products (Jain 2020).

## Conclusion

I suggest we use neoliberal capitalism as a framework for understanding commercial yoga and the generally conservative ethos of the yoga industry. Most significantly, yoga serves as a way to individualise what are fundamentally social and political problems in society. This is obviously cohesive with neoliberal capitalism. It follows an ideology that you need to work on yourself, rather than look to social resources for solutions to your problems or demand structural changes. Through an ethic of self-care, the yoga industry trains consumers not only to believe that their bodily and social conditions are under their control, but to feel ashamed about those parts of their lives that do not comply with cultural ideals. The yoga industry fabricates this neoliberal-individual understanding of self-care and the ideal of the free entrepreneurial individual.

Teachers and entrepreneurs use yoga to advocate for the promise that free markets and for-profits will bring healing and empowerment to those who make the right consumer choices. Many scholars have already offered referenda on commodified spiritualities, such as yoga or mindfulness, suggesting they merely serve as palliatives or coping mechanisms (see note 2). These commodities, in their view, function like a fetish that helps consumers feel as if they have escaped reality. In other words, they offer consumers an escape into an experience (of the present moment, of a romanticised or orientalised Other, or an idealised ancient past), which allows them to imagine themselves as separate from the busyness of everyday life, and by extension disconnected from the social and economic relations of global capitalism.

The solutions to consumers' problems that neoliberal yoga offers do not elide the structural and economic undergirding of the earth's population's greatest threats, for example, pervasive inequalities and environmental destruction. By ignoring that socio-economic and cultural structures shape our lives, they ensure greater conformity to the dominant ideology of neoliberalism and the reigning socio-economic system of capitalism, which are largely responsible for conditions of exploitation and a dehumanizing workplace, assaults against democracy and vast social inequalities. Critical contributions to the study of neoliberal yoga should examine the material and social operations of its commodities, pursued with a sensitivity to subtle – and sometimes not-so-subtle – power dynamics, complicating any straightforward progress narrative about democratization, increased choice or individual autonomy among yoga consumers. This form of yoga ultimately directs its address to the middle- and upper-middle classes, effectively erasing the problems faced by the vast majority of the population from its view. And, since teachers' and entrepreneurs' aim is often bottom-line profit, they are usually uninterested in social justice or mass mobilization, or at least those are not prioritised. Furthermore, as much as individual consumers are not in control of their physical living conditions or places on the socio-economic hierarchy, shopping for yoga and its accoutrements give consumers a sense of control over their lives. A wide range of commodities – mats, apparel, books, classes, workshops – are celebrated as good consumer choices, products that lead to better living outcomes. Adherents of this type of yoga use the notion of *consumer choice* to convince themselves they are in control of their wellbeing, self-care and happiness (Jain 2020).

All of these observations are accurate and notable, yet the commodities of neoliberal yoga also represent cultural, religious and economic systems far more complex than the 'fetish' assessment implies. Critical contributions to the study of neoliberal yoga should also examine how to interpret the dissenting discourses of yoga. Spiritual Gangster's appropriation of 'gangster', for example, could be read as an effort toward dissent, since gang culture is historically a space of Black resistance. According to the Spiritual Gangster website, 'We exercise love as the most powerful form of activism' (Spiritual Gangster 2019). The company also donates an unspecified percentage of every sale to provide food for those living in poverty. What about these neoliberal yoga entrepreneurs and corporations profiting from spiritual commodities that claim to counter the problems of unbridled capitalism with charitable giving or various forms of 'conscious capitalism'?

What should we make of the Indian state's efforts to challenge the imperialism behind western commodifications of yoga, more specifically, the North American multi-billion-dollar yoga industry, by reclaiming yoga for India? Or Baba Ramdev's company, Patañjali Ayurved, which claims to offer alternatives to the products of western corporations with their natural and ayurvedic products, packaged in the orange and green of the Indian flag and marketed as 'Made in Bharat'?

What should we make of the feminist spiritual discourses – the calls for women's empowerment through yoga all while placing the burden of success on individual women and their willingness to work hard under dire circumstances? What should we make of consumers who greenwash yoga in an attempt to counter environmental degradation in the face of capitalism?

When we attend to these contradictions of neoliberal yoga, rather than a mode through which consumers simply ignore or are numbed to the problems of neoliberal capitalism, we find that many yoga commodities, corporations and entrepreneurs do actually acknowledge those problems and, in fact, make efforts to correct them. They are not numbed, in other words, to current social and environmental crises. Yet, from provocative taglines printed across t-shirts or packaging to various forms of charitable giving, commodification serves as a strategy through which the dissent itself is colonised (Jain 2020).

Yoga commodities often enact an orientalist fantasy of enlightenment-ethics that is especially seductive in a world of ever-expanding obligations and needs. In and through its creative usage of capitalist-orientalist tropes, the text of these commodities provides a theoretical model and ideological justification for a neoliberal ethic. Capitalist-individualist understandings of 'progress' or 'freedom' largely stand in place of radical anti-hierarchical, egalitarian and anti-capitalist understandings of liberation (Jain 2020).

In the academic study of yoga and in popular yoga publications themselves, there is often a desire for a narrative of unity, as if there is an essence or core to yoga and to the culture from which participants in the global yoga industry appropriate. But the discomfort that comes with efforts to illuminate the differences, discrepancies and contradictions within and across neoliberal yoga is necessary. Ultimately, attending to these, acknowledging all of the moving parts of neoliberal yoga, will strengthen the collective project to understand not only yoga itself, but also the workings of neoliberalism in contemporary society.

## Notes

1 This chapter draws heavily from my book-length study of neoliberal yoga and neoliberal spirituality at large, *Peace Love Yoga: The Politics of Global Spirituality* (2020). Many of the ideas here also appear in Jain (2014a).

2 Although my work on neoliberal yoga makes the case that the above points are true (Jain 2014a, 2020), this has not been the general consensus among scholars analysing the commercialisation and mass marketing of yoga or spirituality at large. Some studies bemoan the consumer branding, commodification and popularisation of yoga and other spiritual commodities, such as mindfulness, as the loss of an imagined purer, authentic religious practice. Such approaches fit yoga within a framework that pits corrupt commodifications of cultural products against so-called authentic ones. Most notably, Slavoj Žižek (2001) offers such a referendum on modern appropriations of Buddhism, and Jeremy Carrette and Richard King (2005) bemoan the co-optation of spirituality by market forces, arguing that *spirituality*, including the yoga industry, is a 'vacuous cultural trope' that can be mixed with anything (2005: 46) and represents the 'takeover' of religion. Rather than make authenticity claims or otherwise assess the relationship between neoliberal yoga and historical yoga traditions, the current chapter focuses on yoga's relationship to the dominant modes of governance at play under neoliberal capitalism. Of course, my argument that neoliberal capitalism moulds cultures of self-care does accord with the consensus academic position that the present moment's arrangement of culture and ideology shapes the ways people are capable of thinking, even when they seek to think beyond or against the dominant order, it also analyzes those very cultures as religious ones.

3 Edward Said (1978) defines orientalism as 'a system of representations framed by a whole set of forces that brought the Orient into Western learning, Western consciousness, and later, Western empire … a product of certain political forces and activities' (202–203). In the colonial period, orientalist scholarship served to legitimate colonial rule by bifurcating the world into the *Orient* and the *Occident*. The Orient and the Occident were defined in terms of perceived essences, and thus each was perceived as a homogenous, static system. Because orientalist thinkers have defined the Orient vis-à-vis the Occident, the system of representation that Said calls orientalism reveals more about occidental subjectivity than about any reality underlying representations of the Orient. Although these representations do not serve direct colonial rule, the regime of knowledge they support perpetuates divisive attitudes toward colonized cultures.

4 Several studies have addressed these tendencies of the larger 'neoliberal feminist' movement, including H. Eisenstein 2009; Z. Eisenstein 2013; Fraser 2013; Rottenberg 2014; Rottenberg 2018; Kantor 2013; Huffer 2013.

## Bibliography


Andrews, D. L., Batts, C. and Silk, M. 2013. 'Sport, Glocalization and the New Indian Middle Class', *International Journal of Cultural Studies* 17(3): 1–22.

Bhandalkar, S., Das, D. and Kadam, A. 2019. 'Pilates & Yoga Studios Market: Global Opportunity Analysis and Industry Forecast, 2018–2025', *Allied Market Research Report* (April 2019).

Bramadat, P. 2019. 'A Bridge Too Far: Yoga, Spirituality, and Contested Space in the Pacific Northwest.'

Brown, W. 2015. *Undoing the Demos: Neoliberalism's Stealth Revolution*. Cambridge, MA: MIT Press.

Burchell, G., Gordon, C. and Miller, P. (eds) 1991. *The Foucault Effect: Studies in Governmentality*. London: Harvester Wheatsheaf.

Butler, J. 2013. 'For White Girls Only?: Postmodernism and the Politics of Inclusion', *Feminist Formations* 25(1) (Spring): 35–58.

Caldwell, S. 2001. 'The Heart of the Secret: A Personal and Scholarly Encounter with Shakta Tantrism in Siddha Yoga', *Nova Religio: The Journal of Alternative and Emergent Religions* 5(1): 9–51. https://doi.org/10.1525/nr.2001.5.1.9

Carrette, J. and King R. 2005. *Selling Spirituality: The Silent Takeover of Religion*. New York: Routledge.

Chapple, C. K. 2005. 'Raja Yoga and the Guru: Gurani Anjali of Yoga Anand Ashram, Amityville, New York', in Forsthoefel, T. and Humes, C. (eds), *Gurus in America*. Albany: State University of New York Press.

De Michelis, E. 2004. *A History of Modern Yoga: Patañjali and Western Esotericism*. London: Continuum.

Einstein, M. 2008. *Brands of Faith: Marketing Religion in a Commercial Age*. New York: Routledge.

Eisenstein, H. 2009. *Feminism Seduced: How Global Elites Use Women's Labor and Ideas to Exploit the World*. Boulder, CO: Paradigm.

Eisenstein, Z. 2013. '"Leaning in" in Iraq'. Available at www.aljazeera.com/indepth/opinion/2013/03/2013323141149557391.html. Accessed 22 February 2019.
Ellwood, R. and Partin, H. 1988. *Religious and Spiritual Groups in Modern America*. New York: Routledge.
Fraser, N. 2013. *Fortunes of Feminism: From State-Managed Capitalism to Neoliberal Crisis*. London and New York: Verso.
Hamann, T. H. 2009. 'Neoliberalism, Governmentality, and Ethics', *Foucault Studies* 6: 37–59.
Harvey, D. 2005. *A Brief History of Neoliberalism*. New York: Oxford University Press.
Huffer, L. 2013. 'It's the Economy Sister'. Available at www.aljazeera.com/indepth/opinion/2013/03/201331885644977848.html. Accessed 22 February 2019.
Jain, A. R. 2012. 'Branding Yoga: The Cases of Iyengar Yoga, Siddha Yoga, and Anusara Yoga', *Approaching Religion* 2(2): 3–17.
Jain, A. R. 2014a. *Selling Yoga: From Counterculture to Pop Culture*. Oxford: Oxford University Press.
Jain, A. R. 2014b. 'Claiming Yoga for India', *Religion Dispatches*. 15 December 2014. Available at http://religiondispatches.org/claiming-yoga-for-india/. Accessed 13 March 2020.
Jain, A. R. 2014c. 'Who Is to Say Modern Yoga Practitioners Have It All Wrong? On Hindu Origins and Yogaphobia', *Journal of the American Academy of Religion* 82(2): 427–471.
Jain, A. R. 2016. 'Being a Superman Who Can't Be F*$#d With: Bikram Choudhury, the Yoga Industry, and Neoliberal Religion'. *Being Spiritual But Not Religious: Past, Present, and Future(s)*. Conference presentation at Rice University, 2016.
Jain, A. R. 2017. 'The Case of Bikram Yoga: Can "Pop Spiritualities" Be Truly Transformative?' *Tricycle* (Spring 2017). https://tricycle.org/magazine/case-bikram-yoga/. Accessed 13 March 2020.
Jain, A. R. 2018. 'Yogi Superman, Master Capitalist: Bikram Choudhury and the Religion of Commercial Spirituality', in Parsons, W. B. (ed), *Being Spiritual but not Religious: Past, Present, and Future(s)*. New York: Routledge.
Jain, A. R. 2019. 'Namaste All Day', *Harvard Divinity Bulletin* 47(3&4) (Autumn/Winter). Available at https://bulletin.hds.harvard.edu/namaste-all-day/. Accessed 13 March 2020.
Jain, A. R. 2020. *Peace, Love, Yoga: The Politics of Global Spirituality*. New York: Oxford University Press.
Jain, A. R. and Schulson, M. 2016. 'The World's Most Influential Yoga Teacher Is a Homophobic Right-Wing Activist', *Religion Dispatches*, 4 October. Available at http://religiondispatches.org/baba-ramdev/. Accessed 13 March 2020.
Kakar, S. 1983. *Shamans, Mystics and Doctors: A Psychological Inquiry into India and its Healing Traditions*. Boston: Beacon Press.
Kantor, J. 2013. 'A Titan's How-To on Breaking the Glass Ceiling', *The New York Times*, 21 February. Available at www.nytimes.com/2013/02/22/us/sheryl-sandberg-lean-in-author-hopes-to-spur-movement.html?pagewanted=all&_r=0. Accessed 13 March 2020.
Kantor, J. and Twohey, M. 2017. 'Harvey Weinstein Paid Off Sexual Harassment Accusers for Decades', *The New York Times*. 5 October. Available at www.nytimes.com/2017/10/05/us/harvey-weinstein-harassment-allegations.html. Accessed 13 March 2020.
Katju, M. 2017. *Hinduising Democracy: The Vishva Hindu Parishad in Contemporary India*. New Delhi: New Text.
Khalikova, V. R. 2017. 'The Ayurveda of Baba Ramdev: Biomoral Consumerism, National Duty and the Biopolitics of "Homegrown" Medicine in India', *South Asia: Journal of South Asian Studies* 40(1): 105–122.
Kotsko, A. 2018. *Neoliberalism's Demons: On the Political Theology of Late Capital*. Stanford, CA: Stanford University Press.
Lemke, T. 2001. '"The Birth of Bio-Politics": Michel Foucault's Lecture at the Collège de France on Neo-Liberal Governmentality', *Economy and Society* 30(2): 190–207.
Lofton, K. 2017. *Consuming Religion*. Chicago: University of Chicago Press.
Lucia, A. J. 2014. *Reflections of Amma: Devotees in a Global Embrace*. Berkeley: University of California Press.
MacGregor, K. 2015. 'Kino MacGregor: India Is a Yoga Teacher', *Yoga Journal*, 26 March. Available at www.yogajournal.com/lifestyle/kino-macgregor-surrendering-india-teacher. Accessed 6 October 2018.
Mackey, J. and Sisodia, R. 2014. *Conscious Capitalism, with a New Preface by the Authors: Liberating the Heroic Spirit of Business*. Boston: Harvard Business Review Press.
Miller, P. and Rose, N. 2008. *Governing the Present*. Cambridge: Polity Press.
Ministry of Tourism Government of India. 2018. 'Swadesh Darshan', Ministry of Tourism Government of India. Available at http://swadeshdarshan.gov.in/. Accessed 6 October 2018.
NDTV. 2013. 'Is Homosexuality Conflicting with Cultural Values of India?' YouTube Video, 17:37. 12 December. Available at https://youtu.be/9ppftcSAHA4. Accessed 13 March 2020.

O'Reilly, C. C. 2006. 'From Drifter To Gap Year Tourist: Mainstreaming Backpacker Travel', *Annals of Tourism Research* 33(4): 998–1017.

Pechilis, K. (ed) 2004. *The Graceful Guru: Hindu Female Gurus in India and the United States.* New York: Oxford University Press.

Porterfield, A. 2001. *Transformation of American Religion: The Story of a Late-Twentieth-Century Awakening.* Oxford: Oxford University Press.

Raj, S. J. 2005. 'Passage to America: Ammachi on American Soil', in Forsthoefel, T. A. and Humes, C. A. (eds), *Gurus in America.* Albany: State University of New York Press.

Rottenberg, C. 2014. 'The Rise of Neoliberal Feminism', *Cultural Studies* 28(3): 418–437. https://doi.org/10.1080/09502386.2013.857361

Rottenberg, C. 2018. *The Rise of Neoliberal Feminism.* New York: Oxford University Press.

Said, E. W. 1978. *Orientalism.* New York: Pantheon.

Scroll Staff. 2017. 'Patanjali's Turnover for Financial Year 2016–2017 Is Rs 10,561 Crore, Says Ramdev', *Scroll.in – Latest News, In Depth News, India News, Politics News, Indian Cinema, Indian Sports, Culture, Video News.* 4 May. Available at https://scroll.in/latest/836561/patanjalis-turnover-for-financial-year-2016-2017-is-rs-10561-crore-says-ramdev. Accessed 5 October 2018.

Shamir, R. 2008. 'The Age of Responsibilization: On Market-Embedded Morality', *Economy and Society* 37(1): 1–19.

Spiritual Gangster. 2019. Available at https://spiritualgangster.com/. Accessed 13 March 2020.

Swallow, D. A. 1982. 'Ashes and Powers: Myth, Rite and Miracle in an Indian God-man's Cult', *Modern Asian Studies* 16: 123–158.

Williamson, L. 2005. 'The Perfectibility of Perfection: Siddha Yoga as a Global Movement', in Forsthoefel, T. A. and Humes, C. A. (eds), *Gurus in America*, 147–167. Albany: State University of New York Press.

YogaGirl. 2019. Available at www.yogagirl.com. Accessed 13 March 2020.

Žižek, S. 2001. 'From Western Marxism to Western Buddhism', *Cabinet 2.* Available at www.cabinet magazine.org/issues/2/western.php. Accessed 12 June 2018.

# PART II

# History of yoga and meditation in South Asia

In popular global imagination, and in history, the techniques of yoga and meditation are closely associated with the religious traditions of South Asia. This section takes a broadly chronological perspective, looking at the context in which the practices now associated with yoga and meditation developed in the subcontinent. Starting from the ancient and classical periods, the section then explores medieval developments within Indian religious traditions relating to tantra and *haṭhayoga* and highlights some of the transformations of these techniques, as well as the ways in which their significance has been understood.

The final chapters in this section focus on the Indian subcontinent in the modern period, exploring the early modern influences of esoteric and mesmeric thought within India and the growing politicisation of yoga and meditation in the context of colonisation. The final chapter considers how yoga and meditation became closely associated with healthcare provision in contemporary India.

# 6
# HOW YOGA BECAME YOGA
## Yoga and meditation up to the classical period

*Kengo Harimoto*

### Introduction

In this chapter, we discuss diverse topics related to *yoga* and meditation up to, and including, the classical period. For convenience, the author of this chapter tentatively proposes that the classical period of *yoga* begins with the completion of the *Pātañjalayogaśāstra* (PYŚ) i.e. the *Yogasūtra* accompanied by the *Yogabhāṣya*. There is no material reason why one must consider that the classical period started with the *Pātañjalayogaśāstra*. Rather, this periodisation is purely heuristic and is proposed here merely to facilitate a narrative. Dividing periods between before and after the *Pātañjalayogaśāstra* is convenient, as will be shown, because the *Pātañjalayogaśāstra* was influential in defining *yoga* and *yoga* philosophy in subsequent centuries. The *Pātañjalayogaśāstra* attempted to integrate various strands of technique/praxis that its creator considered as *yoga* framed by one coherent philosophy. Apparently, the creator of the text was convinced that there was something in common between those strands, which were incorporated into one idea of *yoga*. This chapter therefore presupposes that even the concept of *yoga* already had a complex history behind it and discusses these elements as 'pre-classical'.

The approach in this chapter is philological and concentrates on the term *yoga*. I distinguish the term *yoga* from the various praxes that might be considered to be *yoga*, even if the latter are not explicitly called *yoga*. As will be shown below, the term *yoga* and the referent of the term evolved organically until the word started to assume meanings familiar to contemporary readers. To sum up the key developments that this chapter will trace: as soon as the word *yoga* appeared in historical contexts, it already connoted 'difficulty' or 'something difficult to do'; then it started to mean 'strife, making efforts'; later, in some circles, *yoga* was juxtaposed with the concept of theory (*sāṃkhya*); gradually, it came to signify spiritual praxes. The *Pātañjalayogaśāstra* was epoch-making in that it provided a system that integrated different yogas into one, accompanied by an intricate philosophical framework.

### Pre-classical period

#### *Prehistoric: the Indus Valley Civilization*

The first recognisable culture evidenced in South Asia is the Indus Valley Civilization (IVC) or, alternatively, the late Harappan Civilization. In most narratives of the history of *yoga* and meditation in South Asia, it has been customary to start from the IVC. Some of the earliest publications about the discovery of the IVC already postulated the existence of *yoga* in the Civilization. British archaeologist John Marshall was the first to report on the Civilization. For him, *yoga* meant as follows:

> Primary, the purpose of yoga was the attainment of union (*yoga*) with the god by mental discipline and concentration; but it was also the means of acquiring miraculous powers, and hence in course of time the *yogī* came to be regarded as a magician, miracle-monger, and charlatan.
>
> (*Marshall 1931, 1: 54*)

Marshall associated two of the most well-known anthropomorphic images from the Civilization with *yoga* praxes. One is the so-called 'Proto-Śiva' seal and the other the so-called 'Priest King'. As for the former, Marshall identified a character in clay seals as a 'Proto-Śiva' figure and he did not hesitate in referring to this figure as 'taking a typical attitude of Yoga' (1931, 1: 52). Regarding the 'Priest King' icon, Marshall (1931 1: 54) mentions the possibility of his being 'portrayed in an attitude of yoga', following a suggestion by his fellow archaeologist, Rai Bahadur Ramaprasad Chanda.

Until recently, speculations on the existence of yogic practice in the IVC were more or less taken for granted (e.g. Eliade 1954/1958), when some scholars, such as Parpola, started to question those identifications (e.g. Parpola 1984: 178–181; White 2009: 48–59): 'the sitting position of 'Proto-Śiva' is an artistic convention borrowed by the Harappans from Proto-Elamite art' (Parpola 1985: 17). Hence, Proto-Śiva is not necessarily an archetype of yogins. As for the 'Priest King', his yogic aspect was not specifically mentioned in Parpola's monograph dedicated to him (Parpola 1985). In fact, we do not know whether yoga-like praxes were already evident in the IVC or whether people there practised some form of meditation. We might one day have more precise information when the symbols they used (the Indus script) are deciphered.[1]

## Early history: yoga in the Vedas

The first surviving texts from South Asia are the Vedas, the composition of which spanned more than one thousand years. For the purposes of this chapter, the only dates we need to foreground are the approximate date of the completion of the compilation of the *Ṛgveda* around 1200 BCE and the period starting from the middle of the first millennium BCE when the Vedic or Principal Upaniṣads were compiled. In the oldest Vedic text, the *Ṛgveda*, the word *yoga* is already in evidence. The word may be considered a noun referring to the actions expressed by the verb √*yuj*. The verb √*yuj* was already part of the Proto-Indo-European vocabulary (Mayrhofer 1976: 21), and its primary meaning was 'harnessing/hitching' of horses to the yoke or *yuga* (Mayrhofer 1976: 21). In the *Ṛgveda*, then, the word *yoga* appears with a rather generic meaning, unrelated to any spiritual praxes. If it has any technical denotation, it would then be related to animal-drawn wheeled vehicles. However, the *Ṛgveda* also contained a further derived meaning of the word *yoga*: that of 'effort'. The derived meaning is prominent when *yoga* is paired with another word, *kṣema* (meaning 'rest, peace, settlement'). Much has been written about this pair, *yoga* and *kṣema*, in Vedic literature, and the meaning of the dual (*dvandva*) compound further evolves in classical Sanskrit (for a recent discussion of the grammar see Pontillo and Neri 2019). In this compound, the meaning of *yoga* is 'hitching up (for battle)', (Jamison and Brereton 2014), 'war' (Jamison and Brereton 2014) or 'battle trip' ('Kriegsfahrt') (Geldner 1951), as opposed to the state of settlement or peace of *kṣema* (also referring to the Vedic pastoralist lifestyle of periodic movement and rest). Even when *yoga* is not paired with *kṣema*, the word is translated as 'enterprise', 'practicing [of custom]', etc. (Geldner 1951). Already in the *Ṛgveda*, *yoga* as a noun had expanded its semantic scope from an original meaning of 'binding one thing to another' to include 'the state that required much effort'.

The Upaniṣads form the youngest layer of the Vedic literature. Although texts classified as Upaniṣads were continuously produced well into the second millennium CE, we generally consider the Vedic or Principal Upaniṣads as those whose existence was presupposed by the early scholars of Vedānta philosophy, such as the author of the *Brahmasūtra* or its early commentator Śaṅkara (whose main task was to interpret the Upaniṣads). Although there are ongoing debates as to how texts predate or postdate each other (e.g. Olivelle 1998; Mallinson and Singleton 2017: xxxix), we can agree that the historical Buddha, the Jina Mahāvīra and the earliest layer of the Upaniṣads belong to a similar time period. In this chapter, we will approach the topic of *yoga* in the Upaniṣads through the eyes of Śaṅkara, who was probably active in the late eighth century CE. His commentary on the *Brahmasūtra*, the basic text of Vedānta philosophy, has become the standard against which all other such commentaries are compared. (In fact, most other commentaries borrow heavily from Śaṅkara's commentary.) He also wrote commentaries on Principal Upaniṣads. It is partly because of this fact that we consider some Upaniṣads early or principal.[2] Another advantage of seeing Principal Upaniṣads through the eyes of Śaṅkara is that he explicitly lists specific passages as teaching 'yoga'. Since Śaṅkara belongs to the classical (post-*Pātañjalayogaśāstra*) period, the way that he identified specific Upaniṣadic passages as 'teaching yoga' sheds light on the developments from the Vedic Upaniṣads to classical yoga. Clearly the composers of the Upaniṣadic passages did not anticipate future *yoga* when they composed them. Reflecting on the original contexts of those passages should give us insights into how classical *yoga* came to be shaped.

In his commentary on *Brahmasūtra* 2.1.3, Śaṅkara raises the issue of *yoga* being taught in the Vedas. Here, Śaṅkara understands that *yoga* is taught in the Vedas as a 'means to acquire the right knowledge (*samyagdarśanopāya*)'. The first passage that Śaṅkara refers to as teaching *yoga* as a means to acquire the right knowledge is from the *Bṛhadāraṇyaka Upaniṣad*, one of the two oldest Upaniṣads. Śaṅkara cites a now-famous phrase, probably the first recorded instance, in which a set of three verbs refers to a process of acquiring knowledge ('hearing *śravaṇa*', 'contemplating *manana*', and 'realising *dhyāna*'[3]): '[Ātman] has to be heard, contemplated, and realized' (*śrotavyo mantavyo nididhyāsitavyaḥ*, BĀU 2.4.5/4.4.21). The word *yoga* does not appear in the vicinity of this passage, so, apparently Śaṅkara understands the process of knowing *ātman* (Self) as *yoga* in this instance. This phrase quoted above imparts *yoga*, according to Śaṅkara, presumably because of the verb behind the expression *nididhyāsitavyaḥ*, especially the root part √*dhyai*. This is the same verbal root behind *dhyāna*, one of the ancillaries (*aṅga*s) of *yoga* in many *yoga* systems. Another point to note is that this third stage of learning – '[*Ātman*] has to be realized (*nididhyāsitavyaḥ*)' – may very well be considered to teach meditative practice. If we look at *Brahmasūtra* 2.3.39 and Śaṅkara's commentary on it, we also learn that *samādhi* (the word is in the *sūtra*) is identified with *ni*-√*dhyai* and √*dhyai* of two Upaniṣadic passages, including the above. For Śaṅkara, *yoga*, *samādhi* and *dhyāna* all belong to the same semantic domain. This does not necessarily mean that this observation held true at the time of the composition of the *Bṛhadāraṇyaka Upaniṣad*, but we can at least say that the meditative practice of realising reality/truth was a concern of the people who composed and used the *Bṛhadāraṇyaka Upaniṣad*, and that they employed verbs such as √*dhyai* to indicate this.

The next Upaniṣad to consider is the *Kaṭha Upaniṣad*. It is another Vedic Upaniṣad and it uses the word *yoga* in a way that appears consistent with our present-day notions. The word *yoga* seems to have acquired a technical sense by the time of the *Kaṭha Upaniṣad* – as a result of a compilation process that might have taken centuries (cf. Hopkins 1901: 333; Bronkhorst

1993/2000: 21–2, etc.). Let us first turn to the *Kaṭha* passage that Śaṅkara cites in that same discussion about the Vedas teaching *yoga*, in which he mentions the *Bṛhadāraṇyaka Upaniṣad*. *Yoga* is explicitly mentioned in this passage: 'They think it, i.e., holding back sense faculties, to be stable yoga' (*tāṃ yogam iti manyante sthiram indriyadhāraṇām*) (Kaṭha 2.3.11 cited in Śaṅkara's commentary on *Brahmasūtra* 2.1.3). In addition to the word *yoga*, another term is worthy of our attention. It is the word *dhāraṇā* in the compound *indriyadhāraṇā* (holding back sense faculties). *Dhāraṇā* is one of the ancillaries of yoga, as in the case of *dhyāna*. However, this *Kaṭha* passage does not teach meditative practice itself; rather, this describes preparation for meditation. This passage is about holding (back) sense faculties (from their objects), similar to how *dhāraṇā* is taught in most later *yoga* texts. And, according to Death (Mṛtyu) – the speaker of the above passage – the wise consider this holding back of sense faculties to be *yoga*.

*Kaṭha Upaniṣad* employs the term *yoga* in other instances. One of them is cited by Śaṅkara again in his same commentary on *Brahmasūtra* 2.1.3: '[Having acquired] this knowledge and the entire precept of *yoga*' (*vidyām etāṃ yogovidhiṃ ca kṛtsnam*, Kaṭha 2.3.18/6.18). This passage, in fact, comes at the end of the entire *Kaṭha Upaniṣad* and thus it could be inferred that anything taught by Death in this text is knowledge (of Brahman, according to Śaṅkara's commentary on the *Kaṭha* itself) and *yogavidhi* (precepts of yoga). *Yogavidhi* here refers to the entire procedure of gaining knowledge. The date of *Kaṭha Upaniṣad* is difficult to determine because of its comprising parts (Olivelle 1998: 372). One could argue that the above passages mentioning *yoga* are relatively young (and perhaps added later) precisely because of the use of the term and concepts expressed in it, or, alternatively, one could also argue that the term, concept and practice of *yoga* are ancient simply because they occur in a Vedic Upaniṣad. Although it is difficult to make a judgement in this regard, one can still note the following: from a relatively early period, the keepers of Brahmanical Vedic culture – the Brahmins – regarded a certain set of teachings regarding the discovery of self as *yoga*. Another point to notice in the above-discussed passages of *Kaṭha Upaniṣad* is the concept of *dhāraṇā* as the restraint of senses, which is a part of the set of teachings.

We shall now continue to follow Śaṅkara in identifying which Upaniṣads contain teachings about *yoga*. He cites the following passage from the *Śvetāśvatara Upaniṣad* as another example of the Vedic teaching on *yoga*. Śaṅkara states: 'Also, in the *Śvetāśvatara Upaniṣad*, multifaceted teaching of *yoga*, starting with the formation of seating positions, etc., is observed in the passage starting from "having stabilized the body straight, with the three (chest, neck, and head) erect"' (*trir unnataṃ sthāpya samaṃ śarīram* [Śvet 2.8] *ityādinā cāsanādikalpanāpuraḥsaraṃ bahuprapañcaṃ yogavidhānaṃ śvetāśvataropaniṣadi dṛśyate*). As Śaṅkara says, the text that follows in the *Śvetāśvatara Upaniṣad* does read like a teaching of yoga. Again, here we see some familiar ancillaries of yoga (*yoga aṅgas*): *Śvetāśvatara Upaniṣad* 2.8 reminds us of 'seating position' (*āsana*) and 'withdrawing senses from objects' (*pratyāhāra*) and 2.9 discusses 'breath control (*prāṇāyāma*)' and 'keeping hold [of mind]' (*dhāraṇā*). *Śvetāśvatara Upaniṣad* is an intriguing Upaniṣad precisely because of the appearance of seemingly advanced teachings on *yoga* and theism. The whole of the second chapter of the *Śvetāśvatara Upaniṣad* is about *yoga* and points back to Vedic verses about uniting/yoking (√*yuj*). In the early Vedic context (see above), the verb √*yuj* (not the noun *yoga*) is used in the sense of firmly fixing one thing onto another. *Śvetāśvatara Upaniṣad* also explicitly uses the noun *yoga*, although there is some incongruence between verses 2.1–5 and 2.8ff.: in the former, the verb √*yuj* is used and in the latter the noun *yoga* is used. In verses 2.12–2.13, when the term *yoga* is used, the meaning is precisely a system of spiritual practice: e.g. 2.11 'revealers in *yoga*' (*abhivyaktikarāṇi yoge*), 2.12 'properties of *yoga*, fire of *yoga*' (*yogaguṇa*, *yogāgni*), and 2.13 'the beginning of *yoga*' (*yogapravṛtti*). As we have already seen, in the *Ṛgveda*, the noun *yoga* was already used in a sense far detached from simply 'uniting, yoking', and meant something in the direction of 'struggle, strife'. This latter meaning, in fact, fits better in the uses of *Śvetāśvatara* 2.11–13 than 'uniting', 'yoking', or 'harnessing'. Thus 'revealers in strife [for ...]' (2.11), 'properties of strife' (2.12), 'fire of strife' (2.12) and 'the beginning of strife' (2.13) appear more meaningful than 'revealers of yoking', and so forth. It would seem the meaning of 'to harness/yoke' of the verb √*yuj* was retroactively applied to the noun *yoga* after a certain period of speculation. That is why we see older Vedic stanzas that use the verb √*yuj* being repurposed in the *Śvetāśvatara Upaniṣad* in a sense different from the original context. A final point to be underlined here is that the *yoga* taught in the *Śvetāśvatara Upaniṣad* consists of those four elements that are mentioned in 2.8 and 2.9, the ones comparable to 'seating positions' (*āsana*), 'withdrawing sense faculties' (*pratyāhāra*)', 'breath control' (*prāṇāyāma*) and 'keeping hold [of mind] (*dhāraṇā*)'.[4] *Yoga*, as a practice, consists of these subsidiaries (*aṅgas*).

Unlike the Upaniṣads discussed above, the *Maitrāyaṇīya Upaniṣad* is not mentioned by Śaṅkara as teaching *yoga*. However, it contains a significant passage that most scholars who discuss early yoga history refer to. Passage 6.18 of what van Buitenen (1962) calls the Vulgate version of the *Maitrāyaṇīya Upaniṣad* states: 'Yoga is said to consist of six subsidiaries; they are: breath control, withdrawing sense faculties, meditation, keeping hold [of mind], and *tarka*'[5] (*prāṇāyāmaḥ pratyāhāro dhyānaṃ dhāraṇā tarkaḥ samādhiḥ ṣaḍaṅga ity ucyate*[6] *yogaḥ*). There is a general consensus among scholars that this and following passages in the Vulgate version of the *Maitrāyaṇīya Upaniṣad* were a late appendix to the text. One of the features that has attracted attention is that *Maitrāyaṇīya Upaniṣad* teaches *yoga* as consisting of six subsidiaries. Though the section may be a later addition to this Upaniṣad, we should still acknowledge that this is one of the earliest textual accounts of *yoga* as consisting of subsidiaries (*aṅgas*). Indeed, we have seen some of the *Maitrāyaṇīya*'s *aṅgas*, or close equivalents, discussed in other Upaniṣads: *prāṇāyāma* (*Śvetāśvatara*), *dhyāna* (*Kaṭha* and *Śvetāśvatara*), and *dhāraṇā* (*Kaṭha* and *Śvetāśvatara*). Even if these passages do not appear in the very oldest Upaniṣads, we are seeing a pattern here: Upaniṣadic *yoga* is about discovery of *ātman*; the process of discovery involves breath control, withdrawing sense faculties from their objects and stabilising *manas* (mind).

There are other concepts that appear in the Vedic literature that are relevant to our discussion of *yoga* or meditation practice. One of these concepts is *tapas,* often translated as 'austerity' or 'asceticism'. The term already appears in the *Ṛgveda,* and yet here it does not mean austerity or asceticism (Hara 1977). By the time of the earliest Upaniṣads, *tapas* as a term refers to something a person can do to achieve a goal. It often appears as a member of a set alongside such practices as *yajña* (sacrifice; *Bṛhadāraṇyaka, Chāndogya*), *dāna* (donation; *Bṛhadāraṇyaka, Chāndogya*), *anāśaka* (fasting; *Bṛhadāraṇyaka*), *adhyayana* (studying/chanting; *Chāndogya*), *brahmacaryā* (celibacy; *Chāndogya, Muṇḍaka, Praśna*), *gurukulavāsin* (living in the master's home; *Chāndogya*), *ārjava* (being honest; *Chāndogya*), *ahiṃsā* (non-harming; *Chāndogya*), *satyavacana/satya* (being truthful; *Chāndogya, Taittirīya, Kauṣītaki, Kena, Śevetāśvatara, Muṇḍaka, Praśna*), *śraddhā* (faith; *Chāndogya, Muṇḍaka, Praśna*), *ṛta* (cosmic order; *Taittirīya*), *dama* (self-restraint; *Taittirīya, Kena*), *śama* (staying calm; *Taittirīya*), *agni* (keeping sacrificial fires; *Taittirīya*), *karman* (ritual; *Kena, Muṇḍaka*), Vedas (*Kena*) and *vidyā* (knowledge; *Praśna*). Also, in *Chāndogya Upaniṣad* 5.10.1, *tapas* is identified with *śraddhā* (faith). In *Taittirīya Upaniṣad* 1.9, *tapas* appears alongside *śama* (staying calm) and *dama* (self-restraint); there, *dama* might be comparable to *pratyāhāra* and *śama* might be comparable to *dhāraṇā*. In a sense, one might say that *Taittirīya Upaniṣad* 1.9 knew a system of *yoga*. In *Taittirīya Upaniṣad* 3.1, *tapas* is taught as a means to learn the identity of *brahman* with various factors such as *tapas* itself, food (*anna*), breath (*prāṇa*), mind (*manas*), consciousness (*vijñāna*) and bliss (*ānanda*). In *Muṇḍaka* 3.1.8, *tapas* is mentioned as a potential but insufficient means to know *ātman* alongside the eye, word, actions/ritual.

Thus in the Upaniṣads, *tapas* is not simply heat, but is something one can do, and it can indeed be a means to achieve a spiritual goal. However, the term *yoga* hardly occurs in proximity to *tapas*, even in those Upaniṣads that show awareness of developed *yoga* practice (consisting of *prāṇāyāma*, *āsana*, *pratyāhāra* and *dhāraṇā*). In this regard, I would like to call attention to the passage just referred to: *Muṇḍaka* 3.1.8. Here, we find the concept of *dhyāna* (*dhyāyamāna*, present participle of the verb √*dhyai*, from which the noun *dhyāna* is formed) as the only possible means to know *ātman*. This stanza hints at the future close connection between *tapas* and *yoga*/*dhyāna*. Hopkins (1901) attempted to show the process of the concept of *tapas* being absorbed in *yoga* in the *Mahābhārata*. One may thus say that the idea of *tapas* as austerity/asceticism was a product of Vedic Brahmanical culture, while we have to wait longer for the concept of *yoga*, which was developing in parallel among the Upaniṣadic authors. Eventually, the meaning *yoga* would develop sufficiently to absorb even the practice of *tapas*.

## *What was the praxis of the Buddha called?*

The Buddha, the founder of Buddhism, and the Mahāvīra, the founder (or more accurately 'restorer') of Jainism, and the philosophers of the oldest Upaniṣads belong to roughly the same time period. Throughout the history of these religions, the most common visual representations of the Buddha and Mahāvīra are as seated meditators. As for meditation, the spiritual praxes of the time around the Buddha and the Mahāvīra included some form of meditative practice (see, for example, Bronkhorst 1993/2000). However, the *Lalitavistara*, the representative life story of the Buddha in Sanskrit, does not apply the term *yoga* to what he practised. Nor does it use the term in a sense related to any spiritual practice. What we see instead are terms such as *dhyāna* (compare this with what we saw in the Upaniṣads). Furthermore, we should note that terms such as *padmāsana* (lotus seat), *bhadrāsana* (auspicious seat), *siṃhāsana* (lion seat), *paryaṅka* (couch/palanquin) appear in the text in relation to seated positions. As will be discussed below in relation to visual representations of the Bodhisattva/Buddha, the text testifies that the names associated with seated positions were already in use perhaps by the second or the third century CE. Another keyword that is interesting is *duṣkaracaryā* (hard penance), the term applied to the practice that would give the Bodhisattva the *samyaksambodhi* (complete enlightenment).

A non-textual source that can inform us about yogic or meditation praxes is the material culture of Gandhara, especially its Buddhist art, a consequence of Alexander's India campaign (from late fourth century BCE). In Gandharan art, we find Siddhārtha as the pre-enlightenment Bodhisattva and as the enlightened Buddha being depicted in human forms, starting around the second century CE. In many sculptures, he is depicted meditating in familiar seated postures. We can even associate seated posture names with those visual representations.[7] In many sculptures the Buddha takes the *padmāsana* (lotus seat) cross-legged posture. In other depictions he is on a seat whose legs are in 'lion' (*siṃhāsana*);[8] or he is on a stool half cross-legged (typically called *paryaṅka*). Those terms are used in textual sources, such as in the *Lalitavistara*, describing the postures the Bodhisattva took. We may deduce from these artefacts that seated postures employed for Buddhist meditation already had names associated with them, or that Buddhist imagery of the meditating Buddha played some role in establishing later posture names.

## **Mahābhārata** *and* **Bhagavadgītā:** **sāṃkhya** *and* **yoga** *(theory and practice)*

There has been much analysis of the use of the terms *sāṃkhya* and *yoga* in pre-classical Sanskrit works. Perhaps the most prominent text that uses the two terms in a contrastive relationship is the *Mahābhārata*, especially the section that is the *Bhagavadgītā*. *Śvetāśvatara Upaniṣad* also contrasts *yoga* and *sāṃkhya*, suggesting a shared background with the *Bhagavadgītā* (see above). The *Mahābhārata* itself is an enormous text, and it is not clear what the chronologies are of various teachings of '*yoga* techniques' or '*sāṃkhya* philosophies'. Most of the teachings related to *yoga* or *sāṃkhya* are found in the 'Mokṣadharmaparvan' of the twelfth book, the *Śāntiparvan*. The *yoga* teachings in the *Śāntiparvan* have much in common with those of the classical *Pātañjalayogaśāstra*. However, the use of the terms *sāṃkhya* and *yoga* in the *Bhagavadgītā* is quite different from that of the *Śāntiparvan* (see e.g. Brockington 2005). This may suggest that the use of the terms *sāṃkhya* and *yoga* in the *Bhagavadgītā* represent an earlier usage. In essence, we can understand the word *yoga* in the *Bhagavadgītā* as 'practice' and *sāṃkhya* as 'theory'. This is concisely expressed in *Bhagavadgītā* 3.3:

> O the spotless one, I have taught before that the goal in this world is two-fold; [it can be achieved] by the practice of knowledge for the Sāṃkhyas [philosophers/theorists] or [it is achieved] by practice of action for those who strive/practice (*loke 'smin dvividhā niṣṭhā purā proktā mayānagha | jñānayogena sāṃkhyānāṃ karmayogena yoginām*).

If one looks at the *Bhagavadgītā* alone, the meaning is straightforward. What is potentially confusing is that: (1) the two terms later start to represent two formal 'philosophical' systems; and that (2) the Sanskrit compound *sāṃkhyayoga* can be a dual (*dvandva*) compound where it means 'sāṃkhya and yoga' or a type of determinative (*karmadhāraya*) compound meaning '*sāṃkhya* (contemplation) as *yoga* (practice)'. Because of the first analysis, when one sees the word *sāṃkhyayoga*, or when *sāṃkhya* and yoga are juxtaposed, one tends to think it is a *dvandva* compound (*sāṃkhya* and *yoga*). Yet as the above-quoted *Bhagavadgītā* 3.3 shows, what Sāṃkhyas engage in is also *yoga*, and the contrast is not between two systems but between knowledge and action. The *Bhagavadgītā* teaches a progression of *yogas*: *jñānayoga* (practice by knowing), *karmayoga* (practice by action), *dhyānayoga**[9] (practice by absorption) and *bhaktiyoga* (practice by devotion). Among these, *jñānayoga* is *sāṃkhya*.

## *The terms* yogāvacara *and* yogācāra *in Buddhist sources*

If we look only at Brahmanical Hindu sources, the emergence of the terms *yoga* and *sāṃkhya*, practice and contemplation, might seem abrupt. However, we may also trace this development in Buddhist sources. In early Buddhist vocabulary, the word *yoga* does not have a positive meaning. Rather it connoted 'torment, suffering'. This meaning was clearly an extension from the ancient twinned concepts of *yoga* and *kṣema* (see above). Yoga to Buddhists was a strenuous situation from which release, a peaceful condition (*kṣema*), was sought. And hence, in Pāli, *yogakkhema* (*yogakṣema,* Skt.) is not a *dvandva* compound meaning 'yoking and rest' (again, on this point see Pontillo and Neri 2019), but a determinative (*tatpuruṣa*) compound, 'peace from torment' (e.g. cf. the Buddhist expression *ayogakṣema*, 'non-release from pain'). The Buddhists also had the expression *yogāvacara* (those who practise yoga) in Pāli and its Sanskrit adaptation, *yogācāra* (see Silk 1997). In this usage, *yoga* is a positive word. As Silk (1997 and 2000) finds out, the word *yogācāra* is best understood as '[Buddhist] practitioner', especially before the term became strongly associated with a philosophical school. The transition from 'trouble' to 'practice' is not hard to conceive. A practitioner is someone who engages in difficult tasks (*yoga*), those who trouble themselves [to achieve something]. *Yoga* is a difficult experience or situation, but is performed in order to reach a spiritual goal.[10] The best evidence of the meaning of *yoga* for Buddhists is the enormous *Yogācārabhūmi* corpus.[11] The *yoga* in the title refers to the whole range (levels/stages or *bhūmis*) of Buddhist practice from the easiest to the most difficult. One remark should be made: the Buddhist practice essentially involves meditation. Two important terms that would be shared with Brahmanical *yoga* in this regard are *dhyāna* and *samādhi*. The transition of the meaning of the word *yoga* that we can observe in Buddhist sources aligns with the development of the meaning of the word *yoga* in the *Bhagavadgītā* and its container, the *Mahābhārata*. *Yoga* indicates struggling, striving, efforts; the performance of difficult acts in order to reach a goal.

## *Hiraṇyagarbha's* Yogaśāstra

A number of Sanskrit texts make statements that Hiraṇyagarbha[12] taught *yoga* and that Kapila taught Sāṃkhya (e.g. *Mahābhārata* 12.337.60). There are also a number of references in philosophical works to plural *yogaśāstras* (e.g. Śaṅkara's commentary on *Brahmasūtra* 4.4.15) that we do not have access to. Furthermore, some philosophical texts incorporate a certain system of *yoga* consisting of subsidiaries (*aṅgas*) (see *Nyāyasūtra/-bhāṣya/-vārttika* 4.2.37ff. and *Vaiśeṣikasūtra* 5.2.16–7). We have also seen above that in some Principal Upaniṣads, such as in the *Śvetāśvatara* and *Maitrāyaṇīya*, there was already a presupposition that *yoga* consisted of subsidiaries. And finally, a commentary on the *Pātañjalayogaśāstra* (the *Vivaraṇa*)[13] knew of at least one *yogaśāstra* (2.29) that might be the same as what is called the *hairaṇyagarbha* (3.40) text that extensively taught *prāṇāyāma* (breath control). If we combine all of this information together, a picture of a *yoga* system emerges. There was a system of *yoga* that consisted of *aṅgas* that commenced with *āsana, prāṇāyāma, pratyāhāra* and *dhāraṇā*. It presupposed the essentially Vaiśeṣika mechanism of perception in which contacts (*sambandha/sannikarṣa/saṃyoga*) between object (*artha*), sense faculty (*indriya*), mind (*manas*) and the self (*ātman*) give rise to a perception (*Pātañjalayogaśāstra* 2.54–55, etc.).[14] Thus, the *yoga* in this system is to leave the contact only between the mind and *ātman* and to realise the truth (*tattva*). This is achieved by cutting contact between the object and sense faculty (*pratyāhāra*) and then cutting the contact between the sense faculty and mind (*dhāraṇā*). It appears that in this system the term *yoga* is explained as *saṃyoga* (union) between *ātman* and *manas* only (*Vivaraṇa* on *Pātañjalayogaśāstra* 1.1; *Vaiśeṣikasūtra* 5.2.16–7). Even though the *yama* and *niyama* of the *Pātañjalayogaśāstra* may not be counted as *aṅgas*, the system may nonetheless have taught them (*Vivaraṇa* on 2.28; see also *Nyāyasūtra/-bhāṣya* 4.2.46).

We do not have enough material to reconstruct details, but it is plausible that at least a variant of the system was compiled in a *yogaśāstra,* since Śaṅkara and the *Vivaraṇa* specifically use the term *yogaśāstra* to refer to non-*Pātañjalayogaśāstra yoga* teachings. This other *yogaśāstra* might well have been ascribed to Hiraṇyagarbha, who was Brahmā, the legendary first teacher of *yoga*. (Brahmā, in fact, is credited as the first teacher of many disciplines.) Here we may hypothetically apply the term 'Hiraṇyagarbha's *yoga*' for this pre-*Pātañjalayogaśāstra* system of *yoga*; it consisted of *aṅgas* (*āsana, prāṇāyāma, pratyāhāra, dhāraṇā, dhyāna,* etc.) and used Vaiśeṣika frameworks to describe the system. Finally, this system of *yoga* comes from the Brahmanical background, or rather the same thinkers who were responsible for producing the Upaniṣads.

## *Pāśupatayoga*

Texts left by early initiatory Śaiva practitioners, the Pāśupatas, also help us to understand the transitional meaning of the word *yoga*. The Pāśupatas referred to the whole of their practice as *yoga*. Thus the *Pāśupatasūtra*, the most fundamental text that teaches their practice, opens with 'Now I will explain the Pāśupata prescription of *yoga* coming from Paśupati (Śiva)' (*athātaḥ paśupateḥ pāśupataṃ yogavidhiṃ vyākhyāsyāmaḥ*) (Sastri 1940: 1). The prescriptions (*vidhi*) given in the *Pāśupatasūtra* are in fact mostly eccentric, anti-social behaviours. The first chapter teaches bathing in ashes alongside general instructions on how to live a mendicant life. The latter include breath control (*prāṇāyāma*), fasting and recitation. At the end of the chapter, the initiate is said to become a great chief retinue (*mahāgaṇapati*) of Śiva. In the remaining chapters, the *Pāśupatasūtra* teaches: behaving in a vile manner (*nindā*, literally 'blame'), pretending to be a fool (*mūḍha*), sustenance on alms (*bhaikṣya*) and recitation of stanzas of choice or the sacred syllable *oṃ*. At the end of the prescribed procedures, the aspirant attains union (*yoga* or *saṃyoga*) with Śiva. Clearly, the author of the text employed two meanings of the word *yoga*: one is 'practice' and the second is 'union'. Here we see the transitioning meaning of the word *yoga* from simply 'practice' to the one that posits an etymological meaning of the masculine noun *yoga*, after perhaps several millennia.

The last ten chapters of the *Skandapurāṇa* preserved in old Nepalese manuscripts[15] are also a source from which we can learn about the *pāśupatayoga*. The ten chapters start by teaching generic *yoga* and in the final four chapters *pāśupatayoga* is taught. In all of the ten chapters, generally, knowledge acquired by praxes is emphasised; this is contrastive against the lack of such emphasis in the *Pāśupatasūtra* and Kauṇḍinya's primary commentary on it. The *pāśupatayoga* taught in the *Skandapurāṇa* gives us the impression of being sanitised and made fit for consumption by – or rather exposure to – uninitiated audiences. Still, eccentric Pāśupata praxes are also mentioned in the *pāśupatayoga* teachings in the *Skandapurāṇa*. The text instructs bathing in ashes and teaches religious suicide (*utkrānti*). The latter is a practice that involves an extreme form of breath control that results in death. The *pāśupatayoga* described in these texts encompasses all aspects of the initiates' practice. One of these aspects is the 'vows of the Pāśupatas' (*pāśupatavrata*), performance of which made the adherents eccentric or even anti-social. In *pāśupatayoga*, we may also observe the idea that *yoga* means union. More importantly, perhaps, the praxes of the Pāśupata initiates (*pāśupatayoga*) is the earliest testimony of Śaiva *yoga* – and we will see its proliferation in the classical period.

## Classical period

Now our discussion enters the classical period. As stated at the outset, this chapter identifies the classical period with the composition of the *Pātañjalayogaśāstra*, the combination of the so-called *Yogasūtra* and its main commentary the *Yogabhāṣya*. This *śāstra* has defined much of what we consider as *yoga*. Many feel a little uneasy if someone tells us that *yoga* in the word *yogācāra* is *yoga*; many take it for granted that 'yoga philosophy' presupposes the Sāṃkhya dualism of *puruṣa* and *prakṛti*, and so on. As seen above, *yoga* simply meant action as opposed to knowledge, and *yoga* was a difficult endeavour to achieve spiritual goals. The framework presupposed in *yoga* consisting of several *aṅga*s was not the Sāṃkhya ontological dualism. All this changed after the *Pātañjalayogaśāstra*.

## *The* Pātañjalayogaśāstra

The text that defines classical yoga is the *Pātañjalayogaśāstra*. The title *Pātañjalayogaśāstra* is, similar to that of many other Sanskrit works, conventional. (It is, however, rather exceptional that a Sanskrit text has an author-designated title.) It consists of the *sūtra*s, often translated as aphorisms, and a commentary, the *bhāṣya* (conventionally the *Yogabhāṣya*). To call the commentary *bhāṣya*, too, appears to be conventional because many other commentaries explaining short, otherwise cryptic *sūtra*s, are given the same designation, e.g *Nyāyabhāṣya*, various *Brahmasūtrabhāṣya*s, etc. Outside of the philosophical genre, the most important *bhāṣya* is the *Mahābhāṣya* by Patañjali on Kātyāyana's critical commentary (*vārttika*) on Pāṇini's *sūtra*s – the definitive authority on classical Sanskrit grammar and the oldest surviving commentary called *bhāṣya*. All the *bhāṣya*s on philosophical *sūtra*s would model themselves after Patañjali's *Mahābhāṣya*.

The authorship of the *sūtras* or the *bhāṣya* part of the *Pātañjalayogaśāstra* is unclear. Traditional ascriptions are to Patañjali for the *sūtra* and to a certain Vyāsa for the *bhāṣya*, although these ascriptions are of late origin. There have been theories that variously ascribe the *bhāṣya* to Bādarāyaṇa (again, traditionally considered the author of the *Brahmasūtra*),[16] or to a Sāṃkhya scholar Vindhyavāsin, etc. (e.g. Bronkhorst 1985; Larson 1969). At this point, however, there may not be much hope that we can recover evidence firmly establishing the authorship of either. The oldest surviving commentary on the *Pātañjalayogaśāstra*, the *Vivaraṇa* (see below), does not mention the name of the authors of either the *sūtras* or the *bhāṣya*. The commentary follows the convention that refers to an author as simply the author (*-kāra*) of such and such. Thus the author of the *sūtra* is 'the author of the *sūtra* (*sūtrakāra*)' or that of the *bhāṣya* 'the author of the *bhāṣya* (*bhāṣyakāra*)'. One further point should be mentioned in relation to the ascription of the *Pātañjalayogaśāstra* to Patañjali. The beginning of the *Pātañjalayogaśāstra* is modelled after that of the *Mahābhāṣya*, and the *Pātañjalayogaśāstra* accepts the *sphoṭa* theory (3.17) that is usually considered the philosophy of Sanskrit grammarians. *Sphoṭa* theory, to put it in the simplest terms, dictates that generally the larger speech unit takes precedence in denoting a meaning (Ihara 1965). Maas also discusses whether the *sūtra* part and the *bhāṣya* part were composed by one person or two (Maas 2006). It does appear that the *bhāṣya* exhibits advanced vocabulary and thoughts that might not always be consistent with what is expressed in the *sūtra*, yet this could be due to the nature of a *sūtra*'s simplicity. In this present chapter, no judgement is made in this regard. Rather I refer to the mind behind the *Pātañjalayogaśāstra* using the expression 'the creator'. The assumption is that, regardless of how the actual composition process took place, at least the finalised version, the version to which we have access, had one consistent consciousness – as opposed to having inconsistent contradictory multiple minds – behind it. The *Pātañjalayogaśāstra* is indeed an apparent attempt to consolidate what its creator felt was or should be *yoga* by joining material mainly from two traditions: Buddhist *yoga* and Brahmanical yoga. In addition, we also find *yoga* practised to obtain supernatural powers, associated more with folk settings. The *śāstra*'s creator made efforts to bind these originally unrelated elements, and it resulted in the creation of a unique philosophy.

The influence of Buddhist teachings in the *Pātañjalayogaśāstra* has long been noted (Jacobi 1929; de La Vallée Poussin 1936; Kanakura 1953, etc.). The first chapter (*pāda*) of the *Pātañjalayogaśāstra* lays down a system that heavily utilises Buddhist terminology and that becomes the backbone of the whole system. Here are just a few examples to show how central a role Buddhist teachings play in the *Pātañjalayogaśāstra*. The text uses the term *dharmamegha* to describe the highest form of *samādhi*. *Dharmamegha* is the tenth stage (*bhūmi*) in the Buddhist system of yoga. The Buddhist concept of the stages (*bhūmis*) is silently present in various contexts (YBh 1.1, 1.30, etc.). The *Pātañjalayogaśāstra* famously incorporates the Buddhist practice of four infinitudes (*brahmavihāras* or *apramāṇas*) (de La Vallée Poussin 1936: 232; Endo 2007): *maitri*, *karuṇā*, *muditā* and *upekṣā*. The parallel between *Pātañjalayogaśāstra* 1.20 on *śraddhā*, *vīrya*, *smṛti*, *samādhi* and *prajñā* and passages in the *Abhidharmakośa* of Vasubandhu has been pointed out (Endo 2007: 111–112). We may also note that the concept of *īśvarapraṇidhāna* is an interesting invention, taking the idea of *praṇidhāna* from the Buddhists, but adapting it in a theistic context. For Buddhists, *praṇidhāna* is typically what a Bodhisattva would do (making a vow to rescue all beings), but in the PYŚ it is more like a prayer so that the practitioner may be successful. A final example is that meditative praxes that generate supernatural powers, discussed in the third chapter, are indicated with the term *samāpatti*, another Buddhist term, incorporated here in a very different sense.

The *Pātañjalayogaśāstra* is meant to be a philosophical text. Over history, the predominant narrative around the *Pātañjalayogaśāstra* is that it is a text that teaches *yoga* based on Sāṃkhya philosophy. However, the creator of the *Pātañjalayogaśāstra* was far more than a Sāṃkhya philosopher. Since his plan was a consolidation of all the *yogas*, he aimed to accomplish it by producing an integral philosophy around *yoga*. Three strands of philosophy were adopted and integrated in the *Pātañjalayogaśāstra*.

The first is Sāṃkhya philosophy. That the *Pātañjalayogaśāstra* teaches a Sāṃkhya philosophy has been widely recognized to the point that some manuscripts of the text are titled *sāṃkhyapravacana* (Maas 2006: xxxix ff.). The *Pātañjalayogaśāstra* uses the term Sāṃkhya isolation (*kaivalya*) to describe the ultimate state achieved by its *yoga*, when *puruṣa* stands alone without *prakṛti*, the former being consciousness and the latter being the material principle in the Sāṃkhya system. The Sāṃkhya concept of three *guṇas* (qualities) is deployed throughout the *Pātañjalayogaśāstra*. Another possible philosophical strand is that of grammarians. As has been noted above, the beginning of the *Pātañjalayogaśāstra* emulates that of the *Mahābhāṣya*. Additionally, the *Pātañjalayogaśāstra* uses the term *citiśakti*, the capacity expressed by the verbal root √*cit* (to cognise),[17] as a synonym of the Sāṃkhya principle *puruṣa*. At other times, the *bhāṣya* simply identifies *puruṣa* with the verbal root √*cit* (1.9). Such discussions indicate that the creator of the *Pātañjalayogaśāstra* was accustomed to philosophical speculations based on Sanskrit grammar, or the philosophy of grammarians.

The third philosophical strand is that of the Buddhists. The *Pātañjalayogaśāstra* does not simply incorporate Buddhist concepts, but it also modifies Buddhist tenets to suit its needs. Here are some examples of philosophical themes that the *Pātañjalayogaśāstra* owes to the Buddhists. YBh 1.7, while defining direct perception (*pratyakṣa*) and inference (*anumāna*), discusses them in terms of their respective objects being specifics (*viśeṣa*) and generalities (*sāmānya*). This may be connected to Buddhist logician Dignāga's definition of them (Takagi 1961). Additionally, the argument for the existence of omniscient Īśvara (God) (*Pātañjalayogaśāstra* 1.24–5) probably has the same inspiration as the argument for the Buddha's omniscience by Buddhist philosopher Dharmakīrti (*Pramāṇavārttika Pramāṇa* 126–133). The theory of modifications (*pariṇāma*) of the mind (*citta*) discussed in *Pātañjalayogaśāstra* 3.9ff. relies heavily on Buddhist material, and textual parallels between the *Pātañjalayogaśāstra* and Vasubandhu's *Abhidharmakośa* found in *Pātañjalayogaśāstra* 3.13 have long been noted (Jacobi 1929; Kanakura 1953; Honda 1978; Maas 2014; O'Brien-Kop 2017, etc. – but especially Kumoi 1985). The system of transformation (*pariṇāma*) in the YBh is complex. Hence, the discussion, despite sounding like Buddhism, opposes Buddhist ideas in some key points. One is that while accepting the identity between *dharmas* (properties) and *dharmin* (property-bearer), as Buddhists do (cf. e.g. Katsura 1978, Dunn 2004: 96, etc.), the *Pātañjalayogaśāstra* delegates *dharmas* to the secondary, unreal side, and promotes *dharmin* as the primary, more real one. For Buddhists, on the contrary, *dharmas* are more real and *dharmin* is less real. This difference is understandable when one sees how Buddhists bring up the issue of the identity of *dharmas* and *dharmin*. When they discuss it, one of the presupposed opponents is Sāṃkhya. Buddhists equate Sāṃkhya's *prakṛti* (non-conscious principle) with *dharmin*, and they do not accept the continuous existence of such a thing. The creator of the *Pātañjalayogaśāstra*, once having basically adopted the Buddhist model of how changes (*pariṇāmas*) through the three times (past, present and future) work, had to tread carefully in dealing with the mind's momentariness (*kṣaṇikatva*), implied in the model. In every moment, the mind goes between two *dharmas* (arisen, *vyutthāna*, and cessation, *nirodha*) but it does not disappear (cf. Larson 1999: 729). The *Pātañjalayogaśāstra* became a rare non-Buddhist system that at least accepted momentary nature of the mind (albeit not disappearing; see also PYŚ 3.52), and asserts that what we identify as the continuous mind is a stream, or flow (*pravāha*), as the Buddhists would say.

One last point to note here is that the *Pātañjalayogaśāstra* in fact appears non-sectarian. While here and there, it makes criticisms of Buddhist ideas, it also accepts many Buddhist ideas. In one case, it might even quote a Buddhist verse in support of its position (YBh 1.47 quotes a Sanskritised version of *Dhammapada* 28; see Kumoi 1985: 15; but there is another variation of the same content in *Mahābhārata* 12.17.19 and 12.147.11). On the other hand, the system of *aṅga* yoga (PYS 2.28ff.) has its roots in Vedic culture (see above). There is even a hint of theistic Hinduism (as in the references to Īśvara). The whole of the *Pātañjalayogaśāstra*, then, is syncretic and, as a result, unique – in that it constructed a philosophy in which various yoga praxes from different traditions can co-exist.

## *Classical period after the* Pātañjalayogaśāstra

The *Pātañjalayogaśāstra* was successful in two respects. The first is that it defined what *yoga* is for a certain audience – scholars who composed culturally significant works in Sanskrit. The second respect is that the *Pātañjalayogaśāstra* created Yoga philosophy. One of the obsessions of Sanskritic civilisation was philosophy and when authors of philosophical works began to refer to the philosophy of yogins, they generally pointed to the *Pātañjalayogaśāstra*.[18] In the meantime, commentaries on the *Pātañjalayogaśāstra* flourished. While its authorship is uncertain, the commentary ascribed to Śaṅkara, the *Pātañjalayogaśāstravivaraṇa*, appears to be the oldest surviving one, and hence could date from the eighth century CE. Other well-known commentators include Vācaspati Miśra (eleventh century) and Vijñānabhikṣu (sixteenth century). There are also commentaries on only the *sūtra* portion of the *Pātañjalayogaśāstra*. The most well-known one is the *Rājamārtaṇḍa* ascribed to Bhoja in the eleventh century, followed by the *Maṇiprabhā* written in the sixteenth century.

While the *Pātañjalayogaśāstra* enjoyed the status of being the authoritative text on *yoga* and Yoga philosophy, other strands of *yoga* did not disappear. For example, a number of Upaniṣads that teach *yoga* were produced throughout the classical period. They are classified as Saṃnyāsa Upaniṣads and Yoga Upaniṣads in various lists. Some of them may have been composed rather recently (up until the eighteenth or even the nineteenth century), but others were composed relatively early. It might be simply arbitrary that Upaniṣads such as the *Śvetāśvatara* or *Maitrāyaṇīya* are classified among the ancient Vedic Upaniṣads, whereas Upaniṣads such as the *Amṛtabindu*, *Jābāla*, etc. are classified as Yoga Upaniṣads. These Upaniṣads are quoted in commentaries on the *Pātañjalayogaśāstra* from the classical period. As may be deduced from classifications, the Saṃnyāsa Upaniṣads teach *yoga* from a mostly Vedānta point of view (*Advayatāraka*, *Tejobindu*). Some place emphasis on renouncer mendicant practice (*saṃnyāsa*). Some Yoga Upaniṣads teach variations of Hiraṇyagarbha's Yoga (*Amṛtanāda*, *Kṣurikā*, *Mahāvākya*). Still others may come from the tantric milieu. Many presuppose the eight *aṅga* system of the *Pātañjalayogaśāstra*, and for most of them the ultimate truth is the identity of the highest being (Brahman [neuter], Śiva or Viṣṇu) and one's self (*ātman*). Although it is hard to know the chronology of composition, we should assume that some of these non-Principal Upaniṣads are early and hence that even when the *Pātañjalayogaśāstra* was being adopted as the authority of yoga (philosophy), there was a wide range of praxes of yoga not based on its philosophy. Finally, we may note the resilience of Hiraṇyagarbha's yoga.

## Conclusion

This chapter has attempted to tell a story of *yoga* and meditation practice, with the noun *yoga* as the main protagonist. The culminating point of the story is the composition of the

*Pātañjalayogaśāstra*. Meditation might have long been part of South Asian culture even before any extant transmitted text or before it was associated with the noun *yoga*. When the noun *yoga* appeared for the first time in the earliest text corpus, it already had an extended meaning beyond simply 'union'. The extended meaning may be translated as 'effort'. The meaning further evolved to encompass practices for a spiritual goal. Some writers distinguished practice (*yoga*) and theory (*sāṃkhya*), and Buddhists called their ideal practitioner a *yogāvacara* (Pāli) or a *yogācāra* (Skt.), the one whose conduct is practice/striving. In the meantime, several systematised practices involving meditation were being formalised, and some were associated with the noun *yoga*. Such practices shared elements, most significantly concepts such as *dhyāna* and *samādhi*, in the early Upaniṣads and Buddhist sources. The *Pātañjalayogaśāstra* is a product of such a time. Its composer integrated practices called *yoga* into one system with a new framework – a formal philosophy. Thus the *Pātañjalayogaśāstra* is a work of philosophy, too. The composition certainly was epoch-making, and text was to remain a key reference point in the ensuing centuries, even until today. Yet, the story of *yoga* does not end with Pātañjala yoga. Despite the unifying effort of Patañjali, various *yogas* still thrived, and the meaning of the term remained flexible. Sequels to our story can be found in other chapters in this volume. Furthermore, the story told here is not the only possible story regarding *yoga* and meditation in the early period. Another author may have told a divergent story by focusing on different facets.

## Abbreviations

| | |
|---|---|
| BĀU | *Bṛhadāraṇyaka Upaniṣad* |
| IVC | Indus Valley Civilization |
| PYŚ | *Pātañjalayogaśāstra* |
| *Vivaraṇa* | *Pātañjalayogaśāstravivaraṇa*, a commentary on the PYŚ |
| YBh | *Yogabhāṣya* |

## Notes

1 For a recent discussion on the relationship between the Proto-Śiva seal and the iconic representations of the Buddha or Jina in arts, including the term lotus position (*padmāsana*), see White (2009: 48–59).

2 Another reason is that interpretations of specific passages from Principal Upaniṣads are the topic of discussions in the *Brahmasūtra*. Even for those passages, we often need Śaṅkara's commentary to know which passages from specific Upaniṣads are the subject of discussion because the *Brahmasūtra* itself consists only of terse sentences.

3 Buddhists use the word *bhāvanā* instead of *dhyāna*.

4 In its first chapter there is also the term *dhyānayoga* (1.3, 14) and *abhidhyāna-yojana* (1.10, 11). *Dhyāna* is also one of the *aṅgas* of *yoga* in many traditions.

5 The meaning of *tarka* in this context cannot be precisely determined. The term usually means analytical thinking, or simply analysis. It can mean logic or logical thinking. There are not many texts that refer to *tarka* as one of the subsidiaries of *yoga* apart from this Upaniṣad.

6 Cowell 1870: 129; van Buitenen 1962: 112 both read *ṣaḍaṅgā ity ucyate*; I consider this to be a typographical error in Cowell adopted uncritically by van Buitenen.

7 See for example Coomaraswamy 1935: 39ff. for the terminology related to the Buddha's throne.

8 *Siṃhāsana* (the lion chair) is a symbol of royalty; a throne. The original association between the Buddha and a throne probably comes from the Buddha's royal status and that of spiritual lord.

9 The asterisk indicates that this is a hypothetical reconstruction, as the term itself is not used in the *Gītā*.

10 The meaning of the word *yoga* in Pāli as 'application, endeavour, undertaking, effort' appears in Pāli dictionaries such as that by the Pali Text Society (1921–1925).

11 Furthermore, the significance of meditation in Buddhism in its entirety and especially in its complex history is a topic that requires dedicated research. Also, the concept and the term *yogācāra* in relation to

the Buddhist philosophical school of so-called Yogācāra-vijñānavāda is a complex matter. Rather than getting into these topics, we focus here only on the meaning of the word *yoga* prior to when the term *yogācāra* was used to refer to a Buddhist philosophical school.

12 Literally 'golden embryo', referring to Vedic cosmogony already found in the *Ṛgveda*, later often a name of Brahmā.

13 There is debate as to whether this commentary can be ascribed to Śaṅkara (discussed below).

14 Note that many systems whose fundamental interest was not to describe how the world works adopted the Vaiśeṣika categories. Such were the Nyāya, Mīmāṃsā and some others.

15 See Adriaensen, Bakker and Isaacson 1998 for the nature of the *Skandapurāṇa*. The first edition of this *Skandapurāṇa* has been published as Bhattarai (1988). The *yogavidhi* chapters are available in Bhatttarai's edition.

16 See Vijñānabhikṣu's commentary on *Pātañjalayogaśāstra* 1.1. (cf. Maas 2006: xiii).

17 The understanding of the term *citiśakti* here follows mainly that in the *Vivaraṇa*. Its explanation is coherent with the use of the term in the *sūtra* and the *bhāṣya*.

18 Some references to *yoga*s or yogins pointing to the *asatkāryavāda* are known. Since Sāṃkhya philosophy is characterized as *satkāryavāda* (the pre-existent effect), those references prompted some speculations. The simple answer is that those references were directed to the system of Hiraṇyagarbha's yoga. While the yoga might be systematic, we do not have to consider that to be a philosophical system.

## Bibliography


Adriaensen, R., Bakker, H. and Isaacson, H. 1998. *The Skandapurāṇa, Volume I, Adhyāyas 1–25, Critically Edited with Prolegomena and English Synopsis*. [Supplement to Groningen Oriental Studies]. Groningen: Egbert Forsten.

Bhattarai, K. P. 1988. *Skandapurāṇasya Ambikākhaṇḍa*. Kathmandu: Mahendra Saṃskṛtaviśvavidyālaya.

Brockington, J. 2005. 'Epic Yoga', *Journal of Vaishnava Studies* 14(1): 123–138.

Bronkhorst, J. 1985. 'Patañjali and the Yoga Sūtras', *Studien zur Indologie und Iranistik*, 10: 191–209.

Bronkhorst, J. 2000 [1993]. *The Two Traditions of Meditation in Ancient India*. Second Edition. Delhi: Motilal Banarasidas.

van Buitenen, J. A. B. 1962. *The Maitrāyaṇīya Upaniṣad: A Critical Essay, with Text, Translation and Commentary*. The Hague: Mouton & Co., Publishers.

Coomaraswamy, A. K. 1935. *Elements of Buddhist Iconography*. Cambridge, MA: Harvard University Press.

Cowell, E. B. 1870. *The Maitri or Maitrāyaṇīya Upanishad, with the Commentary of Rāmatīrtha, edited with an English Translation*. London: W. M. Watts.

Dunn, J. D. 2004. *Foundations of Dharmakīrti's Philosophy*. Boston: Wisdom Publications.

Eliade, M. 1958 [1954]. *Yoga: Immortality and Freedom*. New York: Pantheon Books, Inc. [Originally published in French as *Le Yoga. Immortalité et Liberté* by Librairie Payot, Paris.]

Endo, K. 2007. 'ヨーガ派における慈・悲・喜・捨の修習と四無量 (Maitryādi-bhāvanā in Pātañjala-yoga and Buddhist Four Infinitudes)', *Journal of the Nippon Buddhist Research Association*, 72: 107–117.

Geldner, K. F. 1951. *Der Rig-Veda, aus dem Sanskrit ins Deutsch übersetzt und mit einem Laufenden Kommentar Versehen*. Volumes 1, 2, and 3. Harvard Oriental Series 33, 34, and 35. Cambridge, MA: Harvard University Press.

Hara, M. 1977. 『古典インドの苦行』 *Koten Indo no Kugyo (Tapas in the Mahābhārata)*. Tokyo: Shunjūsha.

Honda, M. 1978. 『ヨーガ書註解—試訳と研究』 *Yōga-sho Chūkai: Shiyaku to Kenkyū* (*The Yogabhāṣya: A Tentative Japanese Translation and Studies*). Kyoto: Heirakuji-syoten.

Hopkins, E. W. 1901. 'Yoga-technique in the Great Epic', *Journal of the American Oriental Society*, 22: 333–379.

Ihara, S. 1965. 'ヨーガ学派のスポータ説 Yoga Gakuha no Sphoṭa Setsu (Sphoṭa Theory of the Yoga School)', 『密教文化 (The Mikkyō Bunka)』 74: 1–11.

Jacobi, H. 1929. 'Über das Ursprüngliche Yogasystem', *Sitzungsberichte der Preußischen Akademie der Wissenschaften, Philsophisch-historische Klasse*. Band 1929: 581–624. (Also in *Kleine Schriften*, 682–725.)

Jamison, S. and Brereton, J. 2014. *The Rigveda: The Earliest Religious Poetry of India*. Volumes 1–3. New York: Oxford University Press.

Johnston, E. H. 1930. 'Some Sāṃkhya and Yoga Conceptions of the Śvetāśvatara Upaniṣad', *Journal of the Royal Asiatic Society* 62(4): 855–878.

Kanakura, Y. 1953. 'ヨーガ・スートラの成立と仏教との関係 (The Formation of the Yoga Sūtra and its Connections with Buddhism)', *Journal of Indian and Buddhist Studies* (『印度学仏教学研究』) 2(1): 1–10.

Karttunen, K. 1997. *India and the Hellenistic World*. Studia Orientalia 83. Helsinki: Finnish Oriental Society.

Katsura, S. 1978. '因明正理門論研究［二］(A Study of the Nyāyamukha (II))', 広島大学文学部紀要 (The Hiroshima University Studies, Literature Department) 38: 110–130.

Kumoi, S. 1985. 'ヨーガ学派と仏教との交渉 (Connection between Yoga School and Buddhism)', 佛教大學研究紀要 (Annals of Bukkyo University) 69: 1–35.

Larson, G. 1969. *Classical Sāṃkhya: An Interpretation of its History and Meaning*. Delhi: Motilal Banarsidass Publishers Private Limited.

Larson, G. 1999. 'Classical Yoga as Neo-Smkhya: A Chapter in the History of Indian Philosophy'. *Asiatische Studien/Études asiatiques* 53: 723–732.

Maas, P. A. 2006. *Samādhipāda: Das Erste Kapitel des Pātañjalayogaśāstra zum ersten Mal Kritisch Ediert/The First Chapter of the Pātañjalayogaśāstra for the First Time Critically Edited*. Aachen: Shaker Verlag.

Maas, P. 2014. 'Sarvāstivāda Abhidharma and the Yoga of Patañjali', Paper presented at the *17th Congress of the International Association of Buddhist Studies*, University of Vienna, Austria. 18–23 August.

Mallinson, J. and Singleton, M. 2017. *Roots of Yoga: A Sourcebook from the Indian Traditions*. London and New York: Penguin Classics.

Marshall, J. (ed) 1931. *Mohenjo-Daro and the Indus Civilization*. Volumes 1, 2 and 3. London: Arthur Probsthain.

Mayrhofer, M. 1976. *Kurzgefasstes etymologisches Wörterbuch des Altindischen*. Volume 3: Y–H. Heidelberg: Carl Winter.

O'Brien-Kop, K. 2017. 'Classical Discourses of Liberation: Shared Botanical Metaphors in Sarvāstivāda Buddhism and the Yoga of Patañjali', in *Religions of South Asia* 11(2–3): 123–157.

Oberlies, T. 1988. 'Die Śvetāśvatara-Upaniṣad. Eine Studie ihrer Gotteslehre (Studien zu den 'mittleren' Upaniṣads I)', *Wiener Zeitschrift für die Kunde Südasiens* 32: 35–62.

Oberlies, T. 1995. 'Die Śvetāśvatara-Upanisad. Einleitung – Edition und Übersetzung von Adhyāya I (Studien zu den 'mittleren' Upaniṣads II – 1. Teil)', *Wiener Zeitschrift für die Kunde Südasiens* 39: 61–102.

Oberlies, T. 1996. 'Die Śvetāśvatara-Upaniṣad: Edition und Übersetzung von Adhyāya II–III (Studien zu den 'mittleren' Upaniṣads II—2. Teil)', *Wiener Zeitschrift für die Kunde Südasiens* 40: 123–160.

Olivelle, P. 1998. *The Early Upaniṣads: Annotated Text and Translation*. New York and Oxford: Oxford University Press.

Parpola, A. 1984. 'New Correspondences between Harappan and Near Eastern Glyptic Art', in Allchin, B. with assistance from Allchin, R. and Sidell, M. (ed), *South Asian Archaeology 1981, Proceedings of the Sixth International Conference of the Association of the South Asian Archaeologists in Western Europe, held in Cambridge University*. 5–10 July 1981.

Parpola, A. 1985. *The Sky Garment: A Study of the Harappan Religion and its Relation to the Mesopotamian and Later Indian Religions*. Studia Orientalia 57. Helsinki: Finnish Oriental Society.

Pontillo, T. and Neri, C. 2019. 'The Case of *yogakṣema/yogakkhema* in Vedic and Suttapiṭaka Sources. In Response to Norman', *Journal of Indian Philosophy* 47: 527–563.

Sastri, R.A. 1940. *Pasupata Sutras with Pancharthabhasya of Kaundinya*. Trivandrum: The Oriental Manuscripts Library of the University of Travancore.

Silk, J. A. 1997. 'Further Remarks on the *Yogācāra* Bhikṣu', in Bhikkhu Tampalawela Dhammaratana and Bhikkhu Pāsādika (eds), *Dharmadūta, Mélanges offerts au Vénérable Thích Huyên-Vi à l'occasion de son soixante-dixième anniversaire*, 233–250. Paris: Éditions You Feng.

Silk, J.A. 2000. 'The *Yogācāra* Bhikṣu', in Silk, J.A. (ed), *Wisdom, Compassion, and the Search for Understanding: The Buddhist Studies Legacy of Gadjin M. Nagao*, 265–315. Honolulu: University of Hawaii Press.

Takagi, S. 1961. 'ヨーガ・バーシュヤとディグナーガとの関係 (Relationship between the Yogabhāṣya and Dignāga)', Journal of Indian and Buddhist Studies (『印度学仏教学研究』) 9(1): 180–183.

Tsuchida, R. 1985. 'Some Remarks on the Text of the Śvetāśvatara-Upaniṣad', *Indogaku-Bukkyōgaku Kenkyū* 34(1): 468–460 (1–9).

de la Vallée Poussin, L. 1936. 'Le Bouddhisme et le Yoga de Patañjali', *Mélanges Chinois et Bouddhiques*, 5: 223–242.

White, D. G. (2009). *Sinister Yogis*. Chicago and London: The University of Chicago Press.

# 7

# BUDDHIST MEDITATION IN SOUTH ASIA

## An overview

*Florin Deleanu*

### Introduction[1]

Few traditions can vie with Buddhism in the scope and depth of its meditative legacy. This comes as no surprise for a practical philosophy that has enshrined the spiritual path (*mārga*) as one of its four noble truths (*catvāry āryasatyāni*).[2] The eight-fold framework of this path includes, or rather culminates in (Vetter 1988: 11–13), right mindfulness (*samyaksmṛti*) and right meditation (*samyaksamādhi*). Spiritual praxis is traditionally conceived as covering three forms of training. Moral cultivation (*adhiśīlaṃ śikṣā*) or the observance of ethical principles and monastic rules provides the basis for training the mind (*adhicittaṃ śikṣā*) through meditative concentration (*samādhi*).[3] This, in turn, lays the foundation for developing wisdom (*adhiprajñaṃ śikṣā*). The attainment of the latter results in awakening and liberation from suffering and the cycle of rebirths.

The essential role played by meditation in the Buddhist tradition has been likened by Conze (1969/1956: 11) to the centrality of prayer in Christianity. Whether all monastic communities throughout history, let alone lay followers, have consistently put this into practice is another issue. What remains sure is that scripture upon scripture, treatise after treatise extols meditation as the quintessential method for attaining *nirvāṇa*. A refrain in one of the earliest accounts of Gotama Buddha's awakening declares that this is attained by the 'ardently meditating' practitioner.[4] In various shapes and hues, the refrain will be repeated throughout the centuries – whether voiced by Buddhist poets such as Āśvaghoṣa (fl. c. 100 CE), comparing the four applications of mindfulness to the arrows shattering the cause of suffering[5] or by great logicians such as Dharmakīrti (c. 570–640 CE) who argued that 'the correct view, well cultivated [through meditative practice], destroys craving and all ensuing [defilements]'.[6]

Covering this bimillennial tradition of meditative theory and practice can hardly be squeezed into a monograph, let alone one chapter.[7] The only thing I can hope to achieve here is a sketchy overview of the main meditative techniques and systems of spiritual cultivation in all major branches of Buddhism, i.e. Mainstream (Śrāvakayāna),[8] Great Vehicle (Mahāyāna) and Tantric (Vajrayāna).[9] To ensure maximum faithfulness, rather than attempting a meta-textual account I have based my presentation on primary sources representative of each tradition.

Three points are important to keep in mind when reading this overview.

1. The meditative practices described under one tradition are not necessarily limited to it. Tranquillity and insight, for instance, represent approaches going back to Early Buddhism, and my account focuses on this approach. The pair remains, however, a salient model in Mahāyāna and Tantric Buddhism as well, sometimes construed according to traditional patterns, sometimes refashioned to accommodate new developments. On the other hand, techniques such as meditation on emptiness or visualisations are not exclusively associated with Mahāyāna or Tantrism, respectively. Their roots can be traced to canonical or Mainstream sources, although it is only centuries later that they come to the fore of the meditative arsenal.
2. Not *all* meditative practices are conceived as leading to awakening. The long (and often winding) road to *nirvāṇa* is basically conceived – pace some rhetorically challenging statements – as a complex process of moral and spiritual progression rather than exclusive reliance upon one particular technique. This makes it essential to view individual methods within the larger context of paths of spiritual cultivation.
3. Frequently throughout Buddhist history the focal (as well as moot) point has been: which particular method or combination of methods should be regarded as conducive to awakening? One meditative strategy may be regarded as central by some traditions, while others will explain it away as ancillary, even unnecessary. The controversial nature of the centrality of one meditative paradigm or another has actually been a major force in the dynamics of change in Buddhist philosophy and spirituality.[10]

## Key terms

Finding precise Indic equivalents for our notion(s) of 'meditation' is a daunting task. Buddhist sources confront us with a vast vocabulary related to spiritual practice. Some of the words match, more or less, the semantic range of the western equivalents, others are too rich in denotations and connotations to be captured in translation. The picture is further complicated by the long history of Buddhist scholastic definitions and semantic innovations. Let us look at just a few generic words related to spiritual praxis.[11]

The most comprehensive terms may be *mārga* 'path' and *pratipad* 'course', the latter often qualified as 'conducive to the cessation of suffering'. Both are, however, blanket terms including not only meditation but also moral and wisdom cultivation. *Bhāvanā*, derived from the verb √*bhū* 'to become, to develop', comes close to 'meditation' construed generically. In this sense, *bhāvanā* is regularly contrasted to *śruta* 'listening to' and *cintā* 'reflection on' Buddhist teachings. *Bhāvanā* or 'meditative/spiritual cultivation' is construed in this context as a superior stage during which the practitioner internalises these teachings.[12] This, however, is not the only usage of the word. In Abhidharma literature, it can also acquire a more specialised sense, on which more will be said later.[13]

Since its dawn, Buddhism shows a tendency to employ particular words for particular meditative methods rather than generic terms. When the context requires more generality, *samādhi* is one of the preferred choices.[14] As defined by the Theravāda exegete Buddhaghosa (fl. c. 370–450 CE), *samādhi* refers to a 'wholesome [act of] focusing one's mind'.[15] The term *samyaksamādhi* 'correct meditative concentration' is an example of a generic use, but even in this case the traditional understanding links it to the practice of the four absorptions (*dhyāna*).[16]

Besides, as mentioned earlier, the eight-fold path also includes right mindfulness (*samyaksmṛti*), a meditative technique known as the four applications of mindfulness (*smṛtyupasthāna*).[17]

The first centuries of the Common Era saw the growing use of another generic word, i.e. *yoga*, conceived first and foremost as 'meditation'. The term is defined by the third-century CE treatise *Śrāvakabhūmi* (*Foundation/Stage of the Disciples[Path]*) as encompassing faith (*śraddhā*), aspiration (*chanda*) for *nirvāṇa*, effort (*vīrya*) and method (*upāya*). The latter is explained as observance of the moral precepts, control of the senses, and, above all, the practice of tranquillity (*śamatha*) and insight (*vipaśyanā*).[18] Around the same time, words such as *yogācāra* 'meditation practitioner' and *yogin* 'contemplative' also begin to be employed in various Northern Buddhist sources.[19] They usually refer to dedicated contemplatives or simply monastics practising meditation (Silk 2000). It will only be later that *yogācāra* will come to denote the famous Mahāyāna school as well.

With the advent of the Great Vehicle movement, both *samādhi* and *dhyāna* come to gain more general meanings. The former becomes *the* quintessential term referring to meditative states (or spiritual ideals) practised by adept bodhisattvas. In keeping with Mahāyāna rhetoric, their number varies from a 'modest' fifty-eight to tens of millions.[20] Without losing its technical sense, *dhyāna* also sees an enlargement of its semantic sphere. The *Mahāprajñāpāramitopadeśa* (*Treatise on the Great Perfection of Wisdom*) declares, for instance, that most meditative techniques, such as the four immeasurable states of mind (*apramāṇa*), meditation on the impure (*aśubhabhāvanā*), the three *samādhi*s, etc. arise in or from the perfection of meditation (*dhyānapāramitā*).[21] According to the *Bodhisattvabhūmi* (*Foundation/Stage of the Bodhisattvas [Path]*), *dhyāna* includes not only meditation practised for blissful experiences in the present life but also meditative techniques for generating bodhisattvic concentration and facilitating altruistic acts.[22]

## Meditation subjects

The *Visuddhimagga* (*Path of Purification*), Buddhaghosa's classic on spiritual cultivation, lists forty subjects (Pali, *kammaṭṭhāna*) for meditation.[23] These include the ten complete concentrations (*dasa kasiṇā*) on earth, water, etc. (mainly suitable for the practice of the meditative absorptions), the contemplation on the ten stages of the impurity (*dasa asubhā*) of a decaying corpse, the ten recollections (*dasa anussatiyo*) on the Buddha (*buddhānusati*), generosity (*cāgānussati*), death (*maraṇānussati*), etc. mindfulness of breathing (*ānāpānasati*), the four sublime states (*cattāro brahmavihārā*) of friendliness (*mettā*), compassion (*karuṇā*), etc.[24]

The Northern traditions generally developed simpler taxonomies. One of the most popular models consists of five meditative objects (*ālambana*). According to the *Śrāvakabhūmi*, these are impurity (*aśubhā*), friendliness (*maitrī*), dependent origination (*idaṃpratyayatāpratītyasamutpāda*), analysis of the elements (*dhātuprabheda*) and mindfulness of breathing (*ānāpānasmṛti*).[25] The choice is made in accordance with the novice's dominant proclivity. Thus, persons dominated by passion will meditate on the impure, i.e. either repellent physiological processes of the body or various stages in the decay of a corpse. If hatred is the prevailing defilement, the novice will focus on friendliness, which is gradually extended to encompass all sentient beings. Those in whom bewilderment is the chief proclivity are taught to reflect upon the fact that all phenomena arise from a complex chain of causation that has neither permanent doer nor eternal experiencer (*niṣkārakavedakatva*). The novices whose minds are dominated by arrogance are supposed to analyse and realise that the human being consists in nothing but six basic elements, i.e. earth, water, fire, wind, space and consciousness/sentience. The mindfulness of breathing is the practice recommended to those badly afflicted with restless thoughts.[26] Other representative subjects of meditation include one's body and various mental functions, the four noble truths, the ultimate reality (*dharmadhātu*) or suchness (*tathatā*), visualised Buddhas, Bodhisattvas, or symbols, mantras, one's inner energy, etc. These will become clear as we unfold the story of the main meditative techniques and paths of spiritual cultivation throughout Buddhist history.

## Main meditative techniques and paths of spiritual cultivation

### *Early and mainstream Buddhism*

#### Tranquillity and insight

Few other techniques in the history of Buddhist meditation have enjoyed such a longevity and versatility as *samatha* and *vipassanā*.[27] The former means 'tranquillity' or 'calm' and is traditionally associated with the four (alternatively, eight or nine) levels of meditative absorption. The latter means 'observing (in detail)', 'distinguishing', or 'insight'. It basically refers to the applications of mindfulness (*satipaṭṭhāna*), hence its modern translation as 'awareness meditation' or 'mindfulness'.[28] Although the meditative methods associated with these terms are very old, the dichotomy itself does not go back to the earliest strata of the Buddhist canon. In one scriptural passage, *samatha* and *vipassanā* are briefly referred to as general approaches rather than detailed techniques. *Samatha* is linked to the cultivation of mind (*citta*) and said to lead to the abandonment of passion (*rāga*), whose cessation is called 'liberation of mind' (*cetovimutti*). *Vipassanā*, on the other hand, is connected to the cultivation of wisdom (*paññā*), which is conducive to the destruction of ignorance (*avijjā*) and results in 'liberation by wisdom' (*paññāvimutti*).[29]

The semantic range of *paññā* (Skt. *prajñā*) goes well beyond the worldly connotations of 'wisdom'. The attainment of correct wisdom (*sammapaññā*) is synonymous with awakening. Typically, in such contexts, *paññā* is defined as a penetrating insight into the essence of phenomena seen as marked by three characteristics, i.e. impermanence, begetting suffering and being neither mine nor myself.[30] Clear evidence concerning the identification of *samatha* and *vipassanā* with concrete meditative techniques comes from later treatises like the *Paṭisambhidāmagga* (*Path of Discrimination*), which seems to have been compiled in the second century CE. The treatise identifies/associates *samatha* with the eight levels of meditative absorption (*jhāna*),[31] and *vipassanā* with the four applications of mindfulness (*satipaṭṭhāna*).[32] Following this equation, we shall now look at the practice of *jhāna* (= *samatha*) and *satipaṭṭhāna* (= *vipassanā*) respectively.

Depending on the number of levels, there are three formulae of practising meditative absorptions. The basic one consists of four stages called *jhāna*. This concatenation can be extended by another four levels. Finally, the most developed pattern adds one more step. The latter part of the sequence goes beyond emotional tranquillity, triggering a process of expanding and then phasing out the scope of awareness. In order to attain meditative absorptions, the contemplative must first free himself/herself from five emotional hindrances: lust, malice, torpor and drowsiness, agitation and remorse [/worry] and doubt. Thus 'he attains and dwells in the first absorption which is entirely separated from sensual pleasures as well as bad, unwholesome factors, being possessed of rough examination (*vitakka*) and subtle investigation (*vicāra*) [of the meditative object]'.[33] This is a state far more peaceful than the pursuit of sensual pleasures, yet the presence of such discursive modes as examination and investigation hampers the attainment of perfect tranquillity. Abandoning them, the contemplative reaches the second level of absorption characterised by joy (*pīti*) and pleasure [/bodily wellbeing] (*sukha*) born of meditative concentration. But emotional states, even if blissful, are fraught with potentially destabilizing factors. The practitioner, therefore, rids himself/herself of the feeling of joy, retaining only a sense of bodily wellbeing. This is the third level of absorption. Eventually, even the sensation of wellbeing is eliminated, and this leads to the fourth level described as 'neither painful nor pleasant, [characterised by] purity of mindfulness due to equanimity (*upekkhāsatipārisuddhi*)'.[34]

Numerous canonical passages end their description of *jhāna*-meditation with the fourth level. Others, however, continue with four more stages known as immaterial stations (*arūppāyatana*) or attainments (*āruppasamāpatti*). In order to achieve them, the contemplative surmounts all perceptions (*saññā*) of matter (*rūpa*) and material resistance, and ignores the variety of the phenomenal world. This induces an unobstructed sense of freedom called the station of the infinity of space (*ākāsānañcāyatana*).[35] The next station of infinite consciousness (*viññāṇañcā-yatana*) is attained as the contemplative realises that the mind can freely reach any corner of the world. Then as awareness is not directed towards any particular object of knowledge, the only perception left is that of 'nothing', a station named 'nothing whatsoever' (*ākiñcaññāyatana*). Finally, without any particular object to rely on, the consciousness fades away into a blurred state called the station of neither perception nor non-perception (*nevasaññānāsaññāyatana*). In some scriptures the concatenation ends here, but in others we see the addition of the cessation of perception and affective reaction (*saññāvedayitanirodha*), or simply attainment of cessation (*nirodhasamāpatti*). Unlike the station of nothing whatsoever, where awareness is still present, though not focused on any particular object, this stage involves a complete halting of all mental functions. This meditative state is one of the most enigmatic experiences in the whole contemplative repertoire, and it has led to various interpretations and doctrinal innovations throughout the history of Buddhism (Schmithausen 1981: 214–219; Griffiths [1986] 1999; Malinowski Stuart 2013).

Let us now turn our attention to insight meditation (*vipassanā*) as described in one of the most famous early sources: the *Satipaṭṭhānasutta* (*Scripture on the Applications of Mindfulness*).[36] Unlike *samatha*-meditation, the applications of mindfulness do not aim primarily at reaching deep contemplative states, let alone complete cessation of the mental flow. Concentration is necessary but only for narrowing the scope of observation and/or reflection on four categories of objects. This allegedly leads to heightened awareness of and ultimately insight into these objects 'as they are in reality' (*yathābhūtam*). The four categories on which the practitioner focuses his/her attention are the body (*kāya*), affective reactions (*vedanā*), mind (*citta*) and doctrinal categories (*dhammā*). The first step is to observe a given phenomenon as it presents itself to the mind, without trying to control the mental flow and its content.[37] The contemplative is then able to become fully aware of their essence and characteristics, especially from the viewpoint of their relation to suffering and liberation.

Body mindfulness begins with observing the respiratory process. 'Breathing in long', the *Satipaṭṭhānasutta* says, '[the contemplative] knows, "I breathe in long". Breathing out long, he knows, "I breathe out long"'. And the same goes for breathing in and out short.[38] This detached observation is then expanded to the entire body, all positions and movements, inner organs (seen mainly under their foul aspect), basic elements making up the body, and finally, to the nine stages of corpse decay. The latter makes the contemplative realise that 'this body [of mine] also has such a nature, it will [eventually] become so, being subject to the [law of death]'.[39] And the refrain tells how the practitioner, whether contemplating arising phenomena or vanishing phenomena, 'abides neither leaning nor clinging to anything in the world'.[40]

Similarly, the meditator observes the affective reactions (*vedanā*), whether they are pleasant, painful or neutral. He/she likewise contemplates the mind (*citta*) with its various states, to wit, being or not affected by lust, hate, bewilderment, etc. Finally, the contemplative turns his/her attention to such doctrinal categories as the five aggregates (*khandha*), the five hindrances (*nīvaraṇa*), etc. up to the noble truths. The contemplation of the latter is conducive to full, non-mediated realisation (*pajānāti*) of the truths as they are (*yathābhūtam*).

Numerous texts, whether Śrāvakayāna, Mahāyana, or Tantric, regard *samatha* and *vipassanā* as ideal counterparts whose balance ensures the awakening.[41] The meditative absorptions usher in a state of serenity unaffected by sensual pleasures (at least for the duration of the practice). Insight meditation, on the other hand, sharpens the cognitive functions generating a heightened awareness and ultimately awakening. In quite a few texts, this is true. But this is not the entire picture.

Early in the history of the Buddhist community, we witness a specialisation and rivalry between, on the one hand, a tranquillity-centred, mystically prone current favouring non-discursive meditative states and, on the other hand, an insight-oriented trend emphatic on reflection and observation conceived as largely discursive mental functions. The Belgian scholar de la Vallée Poussin (1937) called these approaches 'mysticism' and 'rationalism' (see also Schmithausen 1981: 219; Gombrich 1996: 130–131, 133–134). A canonical witness to this rivalry is the *Mahācundasutta*, a text describing two categories of monks, i.e. those devoted to (the study of/reflection on) the teachings/phenomena (*dhammayogā bhikkhū*) and those practising contemplative absorptions (*jhāyī bhikkhū*). Either group despises the other for engaging in allegedly inferior practices.[42] Mahācunda, the protagonist of the scripture, exhorts both groups to respect each other as both approaches have their own advantages.

Mahācunda's advice notwithstanding, not all Buddhists appear to have followed a formula of harmonious blending or impartial assessment of the methods. As intimated above, for traditional meditators (as well as modern researchers), the thorny issue has remained to determine which meditative approach is crucial for attaining liberation. The early Buddhist canon confronts us with three major patterns of treating tranquillity and/vs insight.[43]

1. Clear textual witnesses of tranquillity meditation alone as a path to liberation are not found in the extant sources, but there are traces hinting that such a view may have been held by some groups/authors in the early Buddhist community.[44]
2. Better represented is the opposite idea that insight, understood as the four applications of mindfulness[45] or simply as reflecting on the three characteristics of phenomena,[46] is sufficient to ensure the attainment of liberation.
3. The most common pattern is the combination of tranquillity and insight/wisdom, with the latter often being given the prevailing role. Typically, the contemplative first experiences the four meditative absorptions, and then views them as impermanent, begetting suffering and having no-self.[47] Alternatively, after passing through all nine stages of *samatha*-meditation, the contemplative emerges from the attainment of cessation 'and having seen [the truths] through wisdom (*paññā*), his/her cankers (*āsava*) become completely extinct'.[48]

## The path of spiritual cultivation in Sarvāstivāda Buddhism

The relegation of tranquillity to a subservient, even optional, role becomes even more obvious in the *Abhidharmakośabhāṣya* (*Commentary upon the Abhidharma Thesaurus*). Written by the celebrated philosopher Vasubandhu (c. 350–430 CE),[49] the treatise critically expounds the essentials of the Sarvāstivāda doctrine.[50] Vasubandhu does not reject the entire Sarvāstivādin system, but neither does he regard it as an indisputable authority. He often sets out to criticise it and settles for a position identified as Sautrāntika.[51] At times he goes as far as voicing his own views different from any other tradition. Its idiosyncratic approach notwithstanding, the *Abhidharmakośabhāṣya* has become the most representative compendium of Northern Śrāvakayāna scholastics, a position enjoyed not only in India and Tibet but also across East Asia and continuing into our days.

The Sarvāstivāda path of spiritual cultivation shows the mark of an elaborate systematisation and rearrangement of earlier canonical material alongside unique innovations. Roughly speaking, it comprises five major stages.

1. The practitioner must first fulfil two basic prerequisites:[52] a) develop the wholesome roots conducive to liberation, defined as the resolution to attain *nirvāṇa*;[53] and b) join the lineage of the Noble Ones, i.e. becoming a monastic and living according to its ethical code.[54]
2. The preparatory path (*prayogamārga*) includes three steps:[55] a) the basic meditative training, i.e. cultivation of the impure and/or mindfulness of breathing; b) the four applications of mindfulness (practised according to the canonical formula); and c) the wholesome roots (*kuśalamūla*) conducive to insight (*nirvedhabhāgīya*) into the noble truths. In terms of meditative practice, this refers to contemplating the four truths and perfecting the four applications of mindfulness. According to the degree of internalising the truths, the contemplative advances through four phases: heat (*ūṣmagata*), summit (*mūrdhan*), acceptance (*kṣānti*) and supreme worldly factors (*laukikāgradharma*).[56]
3. The path of vision (*darśanamārga*) marks the full realisation (*abhisamaya*) of the noble truths engendered through pure wisdom (*anāsravayā prajñayā*).[57] The scholastic tradition analyses it into sixteen mental events, but in terms of actual experience, it happens in a single moment. This stage also marks the attainment of the first saintly fruit of the recluse life called 'stream-enterer' (*srotaāpanna*), i.e. one set to reach *nirvāṇa* in no more than seven lives. The path of vision can only stamp out proclivities (*anuśaya*) related to intellectual defilements such as wrong views (*dṛṣṭi*) concerning the existence of a self, etc. The subtler defilements stemming from emotional attachments such as lust (*rāga*) and aversion (*pratigha*) as well as ignorance (*avidyā*) can only be abandoned at the next level.
4. The path of cultivation (*bhāvanāmārga*) is also based on the contemplation of the noble truths, but unlike the preceding step, it involves a long process of repeated meditative efforts gradually eradicating all defilements.[58] It is at this junction that the meditative absorptions (*dhyāna*) come to show their role, albeit not indispensable. The *dhyāna*-practice alone is known as the mundane path (*laukikamārga*) because by itself it cannot lead to a permanent escape from suffering and rebirths. This is contrasted with the supramundane path (*lokottaramārga*), which basically consists of the insight meditation (*vipaśyanā*) directed at the four noble truths. *Lokottaramārga* represents the Buddhist way *par excellence*, at the end of which the practitioner reaches the final liberation. Two scenarios are possible. They are decided by the contemplative's familiarity with the absorptions:
   (a) The contemplative who has not mastered the absorptions has to tread the path of cultivation via the supramundane path alone. This requires only a pre-absorption level of concentration for contemplating the truths. According to Vasubandhu, 'detachment from all [spheres of existence can be obtained] by means of the pure threshold (*anāgamya*)'.[59] The latter refers to a state between the realm of sensual pleasures and the first absorption, which ensures both mental focusing and aloofness. It is precisely this concentrative level that the practitioner needs. The 'threshold' is arguably easier to attain than the altered states of consciousness induced by *dhyāna*-meditation. Though not a deep contemplative level, it can nonetheless ensure the basis for the attainment of arhatship, i.e. the state of a liberated saint. The downside, however, is that it makes the path of cultivation a lengthy, strenuous process.
   (b) The contemplative who has mastered the absorptions during/in parallel to the preparatory path is already detached from the lower categories of defilement linked to sensual pleasures. Upon attaining the path of vision, he/she will therefore obtain higher fruits of the saintly life, i.e. either a once-returner (*sakṛdāgāmin*), who is first reborn in a heavenly sphere and then as a human one more time; or as a non-returner (*anāgāmin*), a holy person who will no longer be reborn in the realm of sensual pleasures. Thanks to *dhyāna*, the contemplative can thus speed up his/her course towards arhatship. On the other hand, focusing exclusively

on the mundane path presents the risk of ending up being reborn in a heavenly world, i.e. high enough but still in the reviled cycle of rebirths. All considered, in spite of its speed-enhancing qualities, the practice of absorption (*dhyāna* = *śamatha*) becomes relegated to an ancillary, optional role.

5. The path requiring no more training (*aśaikṣamārga*) refers to the moment and ensuing state of liberation. Coming to know that all trace of defilement has been eradicated, the contemplative becomes an *arhat* 'a worthy [saint]' who has achieved the supreme awakening.[60]

## *Mahāyāna Buddhism*

### Emptiness and compassion

It is well-nigh impossible to sum up all spiritual facets of a movement as diverse as Mahāyāna Buddhism, but if a broad generalisation is necessary, then no other teachings can rival emptiness (*śūnyatā*) and compassion (*karuṇā*). The Great Vehicle aims at cutting all attachment, even to non-attachment, and transcending all conceptualisation, even of non-conceptualisation. At the same time, the bodhisattva strives to save all sentient beings from the vast ocean of suffering without becoming attached to them or conceptualising their existence. If we were to write the basic equation of the Mahāyāna spiritual path, then it would be something like '$E=mc^2$', where 'E' stands for enlightenment, 'm' for (non-reifying as well as non-reified) meditation, and 'c' for compassion (aplenty, hence squared). (Any resemblance to modern physics is purely coincidental!) In the next pages, we shall take a look at several representative methods designed to interiorise emptiness and compassion through meditative training.

But first a word of caution: we need to pay attention not only to the new techniques developed by Mahāyāna but also to its unique approach toward spiritual praxis. A large part of the meditative arsenal is actually similar, if not identical, to that of Mainstream Buddhism. What matters most is not so much what the bodhisattva practises but how he/she does it, or to put it Mahāyānistically, how to practise without practising.

*Samādhi* or 'contemplation' is one of the trademarks of Mahāyāna literature. The term, however, does not necessarily refer to actual meditative techniques. Quite a few of the *samādhi*s, often exotically dubbed, appear to be emblematic names for doctrinal goals or mental states. Out of the 'tens of millions' of *samādhi*s, the so-called three contemplations stand out as actual practices playing an essential role. Here is how they are described in Prajñāpāramitā literature.[61] By means of the contemplation of emptiness (*śūnyatāsamādhi*), the practitioner examines all phenomena as lacking individual characteristics and becomes aware of their emptiness/unsubstantiality (*śūnyatā*). Through the contemplation of signlessness (*animittasamādhi*), the bodhisattva comes to dwell in a mental state free of phenomenal characteristics. The contemplation of desirelessness (*apraṇihitasamādhi*) leads to the realisation that no phenomenon is worth one's yearning and/or attention.[62]

The set goes back to the Early canon.[63] As such, it does not constitute a novelty. What is innovative is the emphasis on transcending any reification of, and therefore attachment to, meditative states. 'The bodhisattva, the great being, training in the perfection of wisdom, does not connect [his/her practice of] emptiness with "emptiness" [conceived of as a notion], [and thus experiences] no bondage to emptiness'.[64] When properly cultivated, the three *samādhi*s are declared the highest form of practice and thus virtually identical with the perfection of wisdom (*prajñāpāramitā*). The same ideal is discernible in the bodhisattva's meditation on non-attachment to phenomena which excludes any form of verbalisation/ conceptualisation, such as 'I have become concentrated, I shall attain this contemplation, I am experiencing this contemplation,

I have fully obtained this concentration'. The bodhisattva who has mastered this practice attains a state in which 'there exists (*saṁvidyate*) absolutely nothing, in no manner, in no respect'.[65]

The *Bodhisattvabhūmi*, a text compiled in the third century CE and later included in the sacred corpus of the Yogācāra school, gives a more detailed description of the techniques used to obliterate the conceptual content of the consciousness.[66] The contemplative begins with traditional methods such as absorptions, mindfulness of breathing, etc. and then realises that our usual perceptions of meditative objects, to which we attribute a conceptually determinable essence (*svabhāva*), are ultimately nothing but conventions, provisional designations. This superimposition must be relinquished, but the meditator should not go as far as committing the fallacy of reductionism. This would lead to the annihilation of the thing-in-itself (*vastumātra*), identified with the ultimate truth (*paramārtha*). Finally, any perception resulting in conceptual proliferation (*prapañca*) is eliminated. The contemplative 'should consistently dwell on the thing[-in-itself] by a non-conceptualising mental state focused on grasping only the object [perceived] without any [superimposed] characteristics'.[67]

These new approaches are credited with far more efficacy than the Śrāvakayāna techniques from which they have been derived. This tremendous power poses a serious threat to the bodhisattva. They can easily trigger a speedy course towards awakening, and if this is achieved before the completion of the messianic mission, it amounts to falling to the level of a 'Lesser Vehicle' follower who allegedly cares solely for his/her own liberation. In order to achieve the ideal of universal salvation, the bodhisattva must practise these super-potent contemplations while *simultaneously* abiding in friendliness (*maitrī*) directed to all sentient beings.[68]

The Mahāyāna meditative techniques for nurturing friendliness and compassion (*karuṇā*) are traceable to the canonical set of four sublime states of abiding, also known as the four immeasurables, which further include empathetic joy (*muditā*) and equanimity (*upekṣā*). Mainstream Buddhism, however, does not regard these practices as essential for attaining liberation.[69] The importance given to universal salvation in Mahāyāna Buddhism raises the status of friendliness and compassion enormously. The meditative practices associated with them are accordingly re-evaluated.

Kamalaśīla's (c. 740–795) *Bhāvanākrama* (*Course of Spiritual Cultivation*), for instance, declares compassion and its cultivation as the foundation of the bodhisattva's resolution to awakening (*bodhicitta*) and course of practice (*pratipatti*).[70] The latter is described as consisting in the meditative path for perfecting wisdom (*prajñā*) as well as skilful means (*upāya*), first and foremost understood as compassion in action. According to Kamalaśīla, compassion meditation should be based on the realisation that the world is consumed by the flames of suffering.[71] The practitioner then cogitates that all sentient beings dislike suffering as much as he/she himself/herself does, and this fosters feelings of pity. He/she first directs such feelings to the dear ones. Then realising that all living beings are the same and throughout the beginningless cycle of rebirths each of them has been at least one hundred times his/her relative, the yogi's compassion pervades all corners of the world encompassing friends and foes alike. When the meditator comes to spontaneously cherish unbound feelings of pity and genuinely aspires to deliver any single being from suffering, he/she attains the great compassion (*mahākaruṇā*), the very basis and *raison d'être* of the Great Vehicle.[72]

## The path of spiritual cultivation in Yogācāra Buddhism

Alongside Madhyamaka,[73] Yogācāra Buddhism is one of the two major Mahāyāna philosophical schools in India. As implied by its name, it developed in a milieu of contemplatives (*yogācāra*) who gradually came to embrace/formulate idealistic tenets. The tradition is also known as Vijñānavāda 'school/doctrine [advocating the primacy] of consciousness'.[74] It holds that our cognitive paradigm is wrongly based on the postulation of objects existing outside and independent of consciousness. In reality, the world perceived by unenlightened beings can be best described as representation-only (*vijñaptimātra*) or mind-only (*cittamātra*).[75] But even such descriptions are conventional designations. True knowledge, which transcends concepts and language, can only be achieved through a long process of spiritual metamorphosis that hinges on meditation.

This path is first outlined in the *Mahāyānasūtrālaṃkāra* (*Ornament of Mahāyāna Scriptures*), a text going back to the fourth century CE. It comprises five major steps known as stations (*avasthā*) or paths (*mārga*).[76] Structurally as well as terminologically, the model is inherited from the Sarvāstivāda tradition. Its content, however, is drastically revamped. It includes practices and ideals peculiar to Mahāyāna philosophy in general and Yogācāra spirituality in particular.

1. The bodhisattva treading the path of prerequisites (*saṃbhāramārga*) strives for countless aeons to build the foundation of correct knowledge (*jñāna*) and to accumulate merit (*puṇya*). The former involves reflection (*cintā*) as well as the basics of meditative cultivation (*bhāvanā*). This leads to the realisation that all objects of knowledge are dependent upon mental verbalisation (*manojalpa*), i.e. a conceptualising process underlying (and undermining) ordinary cognition.
2. On the path of preliminary practice (*prayogamārga*), the bodhisattva realises that the appearance (*ābhāsa*) of cognitive objects is nothing but mind (*cittamātra*). 'From this point onwards, reaching direct perception (*pratyakṣa*) of the essence/realm of the [supreme] reality (*dharmadhātu*), he/she becomes dissociated from the mark of duality, [to wit,] the mark [of ordinary knowledge which presupposes] a cognising subject (*grāhaka*) and a cognised object (*grāhya*)'.[77]
3. Having apprehended that there is no real object to be grasped, the bodhisattva gains full understanding that '[even] mind-only is non-existent because without an object existing, there is no subject [either]'.[78] Thus the bodhisattva comes to dwell in the essence of reality. This experience is identified as the path of vision (*darśanamārga*).
4. The path of cultivation (*bhāvanāmārga*) marks the attainment of the supreme knowledge. By dint of a non-conceptual cognitive mode (*avikalpajñāna*), the practitioner realises the undifferentiated nature of the underlying reality. The process is accompanied by the eradication of all defilements, technically referred to as noxiousness (*dauṣṭhulya*). This stage is also known as transformation of the basis of existence (*āśrayaparivarta*), a radical transmutation from bondage to liberation.
5. Having become fully awakened to the fact that all perceptions are nothing but imagination (*kalpanāmātrā*) and keeping his/her mind set upon the essence of reality, the contemplative abides now in the path of culmination (*niṣṭhāmārga*), which coincides with Buddhahood itself.

What distinguishes the Yogācāra path of spiritual cultivation is not only the inclusion of the aeon-long accumulation of merit, a distinctly Mahāyānist desideratum, but also the replacement of the predominantly reflective methods of meditation on the noble truths practised in Mainstream Buddhism with non-conceptual forms of contemplation and cognition.

## Tantric Buddhism[79]

### Visualisations and energy control

The visualisation techniques are not a Tantric invention. Their roots go back to the recollection of the Buddha (*buddhānusmṛti*), an exercise aimed at reminding the follower of the quintessential model of practice. Visualisations of various Buddhas, their lands, meditative objects invested with symbolical meanings, etc. appear around the beginning of the Common Era. They enjoy increasing popularity in Mahāyāna Buddhism, and to a smaller degree are also found in several Northern Mainstream traditions. Visualisation techniques will, however, attain their apogee in Tantric Buddhism, which regards them as a chief strategy for attaining Buddhahood in this very life and body.

Here we shall look at a sequence of visualisations described in the *Guhyasamājatantra* (*Tantra of the Secret Community*).[80] The text, which probably reached its present form in the latter half of the eighth century, has been one of the most influential Tantric sources in Indo-Tibetan Buddhism. Traditional Tibetan doxography classifies it as a Supreme Yoga Tantra (*yoganiruttara*[*tantra*]/ **anuttarayogatantra*), the highest of the four classes of Esoteric Buddhism.[81]

Our concatenation starts with contemplating the disc of the full Moon in the midst of the sky and visualising the image of the Buddha. The practitioner embarks then upon the subtle yoga (*sūkṣmayoga*). He/she imagines a mustard seed at the tip of the nose and gradually sees the entire Universe in this seed. This is followed by visualisations of the Sun disc, of a wheel disc, etc. And then the yogi contemplates the union (*saṃyoga*) with the Buddha's eye taking place in a diamond (*vajra*) and lotus (*padma*) – two terms with a wide symbolic spectrum in Tantric Buddhism. The former has an impressive array of meanings from emptiness, identified with the ultimate reality, and non-dual cognition (*jñāna*), which leads to its attainment, to the male sexual organ. The lotus, on the other hand, symbolizes virtues such as empathetic joy (*muditā*) and impartiality (*upekṣā*) as well as the female sexual organ.[82] Their conjunction stands for the fusion of the qualities necessary to attain awakening. Finally, the yogi clearly visualises a chickpea-sized eight-petal lotus at the tip of the nose, then the wheel, etc. until reaching the delightful basis of awakening.

Another practice exclusively associated with the Tantric tradition is the control of inner energy through breathing techniques, yogic postures and sexual practices. Unlike the exoteric mindfulness of breathing, which does not interfere with the physiological process, the Tantric methods aim at controlling respiration and the closely related vital energy (*prāṇa*). The latter is conceived as flowing along a complex web of subtle channels (*nāḍī*), the main ones being central (*avadhūtī*), left (*lalanā*) and right (*rasanā*), and four plexuses (*cakra*) situated in the navel, heart, throat and crown of the head. The role of this arcane physiological approach is better understood in the larger context of the Tantric re-evaluation of the body as the ultimate locus and means for the realisation of the awakening (or rather of the truth of our inherent awakening). A good illustration of this approach is what modern sources call inner heat yoga. Traditionally known as *caṇḍālī* (Tib. *gtum mo*) or 'the fierce one',[83] the technique is one of the six yogas of Nāropā.[84] In the *Vajra Verses of the Tantra [Whispered in] the Ear* (**Karṇatantravajrapāda*), the celebrated Mahāsiddha Nāropā (956–1040) describes *caṇḍālī* as 'the heart of the path'.[85] The method begins with meditation on one's tutelary deity (Skt. *iṣṭadevatā;* Tib. *yid dam*) and viewing the body as an empty shell.[86] Then the yogi visualises the three main channels and the four plexuses as well as the sacred syllables *AḤ* and *HAṂ*.

The exact practice is rather difficult to reconstruct from Nāropā's laconic account. The text simply refers to a blaze of inner fire, *vajra* muttering, meditation on the five basic energies, etc. For more details, we must rely on later sources, many of which have been compiled in Tibet. One of the most authoritative works is Tsong-kha-pa's (1357–1419) *Na ro'i chos drug gi dmigs skor lag tu len tshul* (*Method for Taking a Good Hold of the Practice of Nāropā's Six Yogas*). According to the great Tibetan master, these practices refer to visualisations of mystic syllables in the four plexus combined with the complex technique of 'vase-breathing' (*rlung bum pa can*).[87] This makes the subtle energy enter and dissolve into the central channel. The yogi will then experience the inner heat as it ascends (or descends) along this channel generating four types of bliss at each *cakra*-level. The retention and stabilisation of the energies facilitate the attainment of knowledge. Finally, as the energy and the mind are united in the central channel, the yogi experiences a non-conceptual mode of mentation (*mi rtog pa*). This results in 'the spontaneous pacification of the defilements and an uninterrupted flow of bliss and radiance'.[88]

Energy, and intrinsically the mind, can also be harnessed through numinous sound. This is the medium of another quintessential form of Tantric practice: mantra meditation. Sacred utterances – whether the (initially mnemonic) formulae known as *dhāraṇī* or (not necessarily meaningful) sound sequences called *mantra* – are already attested in Early Mahāyāna,[89] but their use for contemplative purposes is a development chiefly associated with Esoteric Buddhism. Mantra repetition (*mantrajāpa*), which can be either murmured or mentally performed, is often regarded as a preliminary practice, which can be sublimated in higher forms of meditation. The *Mañjuśrīmūlakalpa* (*Mañjuśrī's Root Ritual Manual*), for instance, urges the practitioner to live in the wilderness and repeat his/her mantra three million times. Only then does he/she 'become one who has completed the preliminary training'.[90]

In the *rGyal ba khyab bdag rdo rje 'chang chen po'i lam gyi rim pa gsang ba kun gyi gnad rnam pa phye ba* (*Stages of the Path to the Great Vajradhara, Conqueror and Pervasive Master: Revealing All Secret Topics*), Tsong-kha-pa, extensively drawing on South Asian sources, gives mantra meditation a more prominent role linking it to the obtainment of tranquillity (*śamatha*).[91] Mantra meditation can also concatenate with visualisations. It is thus divided into: (1) observing mantra syllables in the heart of a visualised deity; (2) contemplating mantra syllables in one's own heart; and (3) focusing on mantra sounds.[92] The highest stage of practice, however, involves meditative concentration without 'coarse' mantra repetition, whether whispered or mental. It is in this perfect silence that the yogi attains the 'culmination of the sound' (*sgra'i mtha'*) or the essence of the mantra. Citing the views of the South Asian master Buddhaguhya (eighth-ninth century),[93] Tsong-kha-pa concludes that this coincides with the essence of the supreme reality, and the yogi experiencing it is bestowed liberation.

## The path of spiritual cultivation in the noble lineage of the esoteric community

No choice can do justice to the richness of the Tantric tradition, but to all intents and purposes, we shall focus on the spiritual path described in the *Caryāmelāpakapradīpa* (*The Lamp [Shedding Light] on the Integration of Practices*).[94] The work, attributed to Āryadeva and probably compiled sometime between 850 and 1000 CE, elaborates upon Nāgārjuna's *Pañcakrama* (*Five Stages*),[95] a versified treatise sketching the path of the Noble Lineage (Tib. '*Phags lugs*) of the *Guhyasamājatantra* or *Secret Community Tantra*. The latter contains a model of spiritual progression whose influence goes far beyond its Tantric class.[96] It comprises two major stages: generation (*utpattikrama*) and culmination (*niṣpannakrama*).[97] Nāgārjuna adopts the pattern and divides the level of culmination into five stages.[98] In Āryadeva's interpretation, this is further analysed as a six-step model. Spiced with ample citations from both Vajrayāna and Mahāyāna sources, the *Caryāmelāpakapradīpa* unfolds its presentation as a dialogue between a *vajra*-guru and his *vajra*-disciple.[99]

1. Discernment of body (*kāyaviveka*).[100] The contemplative remodels his/her perception of the body as consisting of five aggregates. Not only is the body a mere accumulation without foundation, but its essence is composed of the same atoms making up the Tathāgathas. The *vajra*-guru reminds the yogi of the *Guhyasamājatantra* verse that declares the five aggregates to be identical to the Five Fundamental Buddhas.[101] The practitioner is now initiated into various *samādhis* that envision the Universe as a wondrous web of holy correlations and

reveal all phenomena as inherently pure. The key to achieving this vision is to eliminate the innate egoism by which we identify ourselves with our ordinary bodies and minds. This narrow 'I'-based perspective fails to understand and enjoy the Buddha-nature with its infinite ramifications. For ridding himself/herself of this existential egoism, the disciple is taught to view all phenomena, no matter how foul, as equally partaking of this intrinsically awakened reality. One's hair, bones, even faeces, become identical to the Cosmic Buddha Vairocana.[102]

2. Discernment of speech (*vāgviveka*). The yogi enters now the stage of culmination. The discernment of speech is qualified as subtle yoga (*sūkṣmayoga*), inaccessible to Vajrayāna practitioners at the stage of generation, let alone exoteric bodhisattvas. It is defined as the mantra reality (*mantratattva*), which can be attained through the practice of breath/energy control (*prāṇāyāma*). The disciple is given detailed instructions about the ten types of subtle wind pervading the body and their correspondence to the Five Buddhas and five senses. The contemplative in full control of the subtle energy can receive the teachings on the mantra reality. The three-syllabled mantra *OṂ ĀḤ HŪM* is revealed as the essence of all numinous utterances. It becomes the object of *vajra* recitation, visualisations making use of the syllable forms, etc. The yogi is thus able to purify the obscurations accumulated through previous karma.[103]
3. Discernment of mind (*cittaviveka*).[104] The *vajra*-guru reveals the subtle structure of the mind, to wit, the triad of consciousness and radiances as well as the eighty primary factors (*prakṛti*). Citing from the *Śrījñānavajrasamuccaya* (*Glorious Gnosis of the Vajra Compendium*), he reveals that the ultimate root of all phenomena is the mind itself. Its transformation into the duality of mental construction (*kalpanādvaya*), which falsely postulates a cognitive subject and object, triggers the evolution of consciousness into the five aggregates, etc. Since consciousness manifests itself though the wind vehicle, the yogi trained in energy control can manipulate mind at its subtlest level. Coupled with his knowledge about the arcane psychology, the great yogi (*mahāyogin*) gains complete understanding of the minds and deeds of all sentient beings, whether in the past, present or future. Without mastering the subtlest workings of the mind, even contemplatives can fall prey to conceptual constructions and remain shackled to the suffering-governed cycle of rebirths. The esoteric path offers a unique locus of experiencing and eventually controlling the process of death and rebirth. This is the intermediate state (*antarabhāva*) between one life and another.[105]
4. Realisation of the conventional/provisional truth (*saṃvṛtisatya*). This marks the moment of self-consecration (*svādhiṣṭhāna*). The yogi combines consciousness with the subtle winds and produces a deity body by dint of sheer gnosis (*jñānamātrena*). A *vajra*-body, endowed with all the Buddha attributes, is thus created. But the contemplative is immediately reminded that all creations, including this phantasm body, indeed the entire Universe and the Buddhas of the ten directions are nothing but a dream. The process of experiencing a created body while being aware of its mirage-like nature is called the phantasmagoric *samādhi* (*māyopamasamādhi*). It is this state that enables the Tathāgatas to remain in the cycle of rebirths as long as it lasts, freely enjoying the objects of sensual pleasures.[106]
5. Realisation of the supreme truth (*paramārthasatya*). Unlike the deity body, which has a phantasmagoric existence, the non-mediated experience of the mind essence, referred to as brilliance (*prabhāsvara*), leads the yogi to the stage of the supreme truth. Following a secret rite of initiation, the disciple is given instructions concerning the two-fold process of enlightenment. The outward process consists in the experience of different types of light at various times of the day. For example, the yogi experiences the radiance of ignorance-darkness at dawn, then pure brilliance bearing the mark of universal emptiness until sunrise

proper, and so on. This is matched by an inner process of experiencing various shades of luminance and ever subtler states of reality. The yogi first sees a five-colour beam of light in the form of a mirage. This is gradually refined until he/she perceives through the eye of gnosis an exceedingly intense brilliance identified as the supreme truth. The yogi enters now a two-fold meditative state which involves first dissolution and then grasping the globe of light. This enables him/her to dissolve into the brilliance of the ultimate reality.[107]

6. The stage of conjoining (*yuganaddha*). The yogi needs to take one more step and unite the phantasm body with this experience of brilliance. As long as he/she still formulates conscious intentions, the contemplative is still bound to latent traces of defilement. 'The state of [supreme] purity is freedom from all [forms of conceptual] mentation', declares Āryadeva.[108] The radiance = consciousness triad is now completely cleansed. The yogi can emerge from the experience of brilliance in reverse order creating a body of supreme bliss. 'Since this [state] is freedom from the bonds of the cycle of rebirths, it is called liberation.'[109] This body also allows the practitioner to continue the messianic spirit of the Great Vehicle. Being able to re-emerge as a transformation body (*nirmāṇakāya*), the Liberated Yogi, now a full-fledged Buddha, can interact with the sentient beings on the most profound levels and effectively lead them to awakening.[110]

## In lieu of conclusion

The impact of Buddhist meditation was deeply felt far across Asia. In one way or another, it moulded new forms of spirituality while undergoing substantial transfigurations to meet the needs of each civilisation it encountered from the Hindu Kush Mountains to the Japanese Islands. It was this exceptionally adaptive power that led to the birth of such diverse and unique systems as the Chan/Zen Buddhism in China or the Dzogchen tradition in Tibet. South Asian Buddhist meditation continues to spin its tale into our days. Whether used for religious practice, psychotherapeutic cure, or mental training, meditation is slowly conquering the modern world. By adapting and reformulating the contemplative repertoire, as illustrated by the development of the modern mindfulness technique, our world is in turn subduing meditation to its own zeitgeist. Whether looking for a quick fix or simple equations linking ancient techniques to modern expectations (both salient features of our zeitgeist), we are prone to forget that traditional Buddhist meditation was not conceived as one or even a series of exercises practised in isolation and functioning like magic bullets. Vasubandhu aptly gives voice to this millennia-long approach:

> First and foremost, verily willing to see the [noble] truths, [the practitioner] must observe the moral precepts. He/she will then grasp [the scriptural teachings to which he/she has] listened [...]. Alternatively, [he/she may] listen to [explanations of their] meaning. Having listened [to these teachings, the practitioner] will reflect [upon them]. Having correctly reflected [upon them], he/she will embark upon spiritual cultivation (*bhāvanā*), [to wit, various forms of] meditative concentration (*samādhi*). From wisdom derived from listening (*śrutamayī prajñā*), the [practitioner] develops reflective (*cintāmayī*) [wisdom]. From reflective [wisdom], he/she develops [wisdom] derived from meditative cultivation (*bhāvanāmayī*).[111]

Meditative praxis is seen as an integral part of a long, gradual process of interiorising an ideal mode of being and knowing. It begins with activities that we would not normally associate with meditation, i.e. observing moral principles, learning about and reflecting upon Buddhist teachings. Only after or in parallel with these steps can the proper meditative training kick in and bring results. Conceived in this way, meditation represents the entire path of spiritual transmutation from suffering and ignorance to liberation and awakening.

## Original sources and abbreviations[112]

AKBh: *Abhidharmakośabhāṣya* (Pradhan ed.)
AN: *Aṅguttara-nikāya* (PTS ed.)
AṣṭaPp: *Aṣṭasāhasrikāprajñāpāramitā* (Wogihara ed.)
BhKr: *Bhāvanākrama* (Tucci ed.)
BoBh: *Bodhisattvabhūmi* (Wogihara ed.)
*Catuṣpariṣatsūtra* (Waldschmidt ed.)
ch.: chapter
CMPr: *Caryāmelāpakapradīpa* (Wedemeyer ed.)
DN: *Dīghanikāya* (PTS ed.)
*Guhyasamājatantra* (Matsunaga ed.)
*Kālacakratantra* (Banerjee ed.)
MahSūtr: *Mahāyānasūtrālaṃkāra* (Lévi ed.)
*Mañjuśrīmūlakalpa* (Vaidya ed. 1964)
MN: Majjhimanikāya (PTS ed.)
P: Tibetan Canon, Peking edition
*Pañcakrama* (Mimaki & Tomabechi ed.)
Paṭis: *Paṭisambhidāmagga* (PTS ed.)
PañcaPp: *Pañcaviṃśatisāhasrikā Prajñāpāramitā* (Dutt ed.)
*Pramāṇavārttika* (Vetter ed.)
PTS: Pali Text Society
*Saddharmapuṇḍarīka* (Kern & Nanjio Bunyiu ed.)
*Saṃdhinirmocanasūtra* (Lamotte ed.)
*Saundarananda* (Johnston ed.)
*Sekoddeśaṭīkā* (Sferra ed.)
Skt.: Sanskrit language/original
SN: *Saṃyuttanikāya* (PTS ed.)
ŚrBh: *Śrāvakabhūmi* (Shukla ed.)
T: Chinese Canon, Taishō edition
Tib.: Tibetan language/translation
ver.: verse
Vin: *Vinayapiṭaka* (PTS ed.)
Vism: *Visuddhimagga* (Warren ed.)

## Notes

1 My sincerest gratitude goes to Drs Karen O'Brien-Kop and Suzanne Newcombe for accepting this modest contribution as well as to the anonymous reviewer for his/her pertinent comments.
2 A more faithful rendering is 'truths of/for the Noble One(s)' (cf. Williams, Tribe and Wynne 2012: 30). The rendering 'noble truths' has, however, the advantage of much wider use. (Unless otherwise indicated, the original terms are provided in Sanskrit.)
3 For canonical passages, see AN I 235; SN I 53; etc.
4 Vin I 2; *Catuṣpariṣatsūtra* 104–108.
5 *Saundarananda* 127, Canto XVII, ver. 25.

6 *Pramāṇavārttika* 162, ch. II, ver. 271cd. Cf. Eltschinger 2009: 179–180. On Dharmakīrti's dates, see Deleanu 2019: 24–39.

7 There is a plethora of introductions to Buddhist meditation in South Asia, but relatively few are based on meticulous historical and philological research. Amongst the most reliable introductions, I would mention Conze [1956] 1969 and Shaw and Hatkis 2009.

8 'Mainstream Buddhism' is an umbrella term encompassing more than thirty schools (see Bareau 1955). Basically conservative in their interpretations of the earlier teachings, these schools began to form from around mid-third century BCE. (The period of roughly two centuries preceding this and going back to Gotama Buddha is referred to as 'Early Buddhism'.) Though not based on an Indic term, 'Mainstream Buddhism' is preferable to the pejorative Hīnayāna, 'Lesser Vehicle', employed by the rival movement of Mahāyāna, 'Great Vehicle', known for its highly innovative, nonconformist interpretations and which appears on the scene in the first century BCE. The appellation used by the Mainstream Buddhists to refer to themselves is Śrāvakayāna 'Disciples Vehicle'.

9 There is no single traditional appellation covering the entire range of Tantric Buddhism, the eclectic esoteric movement which begins to make its presence felt on the doctrinal scene from around the middle of the seventh century CE. Vajrayāna 'Adamantine Vehicle' is often used in modern literature as a generic designation for the movement. The word is attested in South Asian sources, too, but it is not the only one and not necessarily generic. Other terms used to refer to this tradition (or parts of it) include Mantranaya, Mantrayāna, Kālacakrayāna and Sahajayāna (cf. Dasgupta 1958: 52–53, 63–76).

10 The history of South Asian Buddhism is often shrouded in mystery. This makes all attempts to reconstruct a chronology, including the one adopted here, hypothetical as well as controversial.

11 'Meditation' is not a monolithic term in other South Asian traditions or western cultures, for that matter. For an overview of this polysemy, see Bader 1990: 25–44.

12 Depending on how we construe it, 'meditation' might also include mental processes traditionally covered in Buddhism by *cintā* 'reflection'.

13 Abhidharma refers to the scholastic texts, some given canonical status, which comment, interpret and systematise the scriptural teachings. They began to be compiled from around the third century BCE on, and flourish for the next few centuries, mainly in Mainstream Buddhism, most notably in Theravāda and Sarvāstivāda.

14 E.g. DN II 313. For the meaning and place of *samādhi* in the wider context of Indo-Tibetan spirituality, see Sarbacker 2005.

15 Vism p. 68 § 2. The same paragraph leaves, however, no doubt that *samādhi* has a wide semantic range covering many types and various aspects.

16 In Early and Mainstream Buddhism, *dhyāna* (Pali, *jhāna*) usually denotes one or the entire set of four absorptions. There are, however, passages in which the term may have been conceived more generically (e.g. Sn ver. 156–157; ver. 972; Vin I, 2). We also find the word in a compound like *arūpajjhāna* 'immaterial absorption' (e.g. Dhs 56.19; Vism 566.7; Sv I 219.24; 219.27). This refers to the four levels of the so-called immaterial attainments, which follow the four *jhānas*.

17 E.g. DN II 312–313. *Smṛti* (Pali, *sati*) means 'memory' as well as 'mindfulness'. For the semantic range and doctrinal ramifications of the term, see Cox 1992.

18 ŚrBh 275–277.

19 Northern Buddhism is a modern term encompassing Mainstream Buddhist schools such as the Sarvāstivāda, Sautrāntika, etc. as well as the Mahāyāna tradition. They shared not only the same geographical distribution, i.e. the area North of the Deccan Plateau extending into large parts of modern Pakistan and Afghanistan, but also a canonical intertexuality and mutual influences.

20 The *Aṣṭasāhasrikāprajñāpāramitā*, for instance, first lists 58 *samādhis* (AṣṭaPp 940–942) only to speak later of millions of *samādhis* (AṣṭaPp 987). In the *Saddharmapuṇḍarīka* (424), the number of *samādhis* reaches hundreds of thousands of *koṭis* (unit equivalent to ten million).

21 T 25.187c15–18.

22 BoBh 207–208. In Tantric sources, *sādhana* '[spiritual] accomplishment' often refers to/includes meditative techniques, but its semantic sphere is wider. In the *Mañjuśrīmūlakalpa*, for example, *sādhana* comprises 'ritual actions, mantra recitation, fire oblation, visualisation, and worship of enlightened beings' (Wallis 2002: 28–29). See also Sarbacker 2005: 111–126.

23 Theravāda or the School of the Elders represents the oldest and most conservative Buddhist tradition. Its canon, transmitted in Pali, preserves teachings and practices going back to Early Buddhism, but the codification of the Theravāda doctrinal system owes much to later generations of exegetes and scholar-monks, among whom Buddhaghosa is the central figure.

24 The subjects are first listed at Vism 89, § 104, and then each is treated in detail. This paragraph gives mainly Pali forms.

25 ŚrBh 202ff.; 411ff. The five-fold scheme, with some variations in the subjects and the proclivity allotment, is also found in other South Asian sources, mainly associated with Yogācāra. It also enjoyed some popularity in Chinese Buddhism (see Ōminami 1977).

26 ŚrBh 198; 202ff.

27 This section gives mainly Pali forms.

28 It should be noted, however, that the *satipaṭṭhāna* may also be connected to the *samatha* practice and *jhāna* states (see Kuan 2008: 57–80; Gethin 2015: 15–17).

29 AN I 61.

30 MN I 138–139. The latter characteristic is also known as *anattā* 'no-self' (or 'non-self'), a trademark of Buddhist philosophy. This primarily refers to the lack of an unchanging soul as well as, especially in Mahāyāna, the absence of an inherent essence underlying phenomena. Let us add that in its Abhidharmic sense, *paññā/prajñā* is also construed as 'understanding, discernment' (e.g. AKBh 54).

31 Paṭis I.

32 Paṭis I 194–195; Paṭis II p. 93, § 2; Paṭis II 236–242.

33 The description is a stock formula found throughout the canon as well as in later literature. For Pali sources, see DN I 73–75; DN II 313; MN I 21–22, etc.

34 Or 'pure with regard to equanimity and mindfulness' (see Deleanu 2006: 546, n. 207).

35 This, too, is a frequent pericope. See AN IV 410; MN III 27; SN III 237, etc.

36 The Pali canon contains two versions of the text: DN II 290–315 and MN I 55–63. For the traditional understanding of this meditation and its historical background, see especially Schmithausen 1976, Kuan 2008, and Gethin 2015.

37 This step has been the primary source for the modern *vipassanā* movement, an approach summed up by the Thai master Achaan Chah ([1985] 1997: 99) as '[w]hatever arises, just watch'. One must add, however, that the overall aim of the traditional vipassanā is not 'bare awareness'. As aptly pointed out by Sharf 2013, '[t]raditional Buddhist practices are oriented more toward acquiring "correct view" and proper ethical discernment, rather than "no view" and a non-judgmental attitude.' See also Sharf 2015.

38 MN I 56.

39 MN I 58.

40 MN I 59.

41 E.g. *Yogācārabhūmi* (T 30.625a18; id. 810b6), *Saṃdhinirmocanasūtra* (p. 92 § 9 = T 16.698b17–18), **Vijñaptimātratāsiddhiśāstra* (T31.50b10), etc.

42 AN III 355. Traditional exegetes, however, gloss *dhammayogā bhikkhū* as *dhammakathika* 'preachers' (cf. Gombrich 1996: 130).

43 My analysis owes much to the seminal Schmithausen 1981. Other essential studies include Griffiths [1986] 1999, Vetter 1988, Bronkhorst 1993; Gombrich 1996.

44 See SN II 115–118; AN III 355; passages like AN IV 422, etc. The importance attached to the attainment of cessation also hints at this pattern.

45 The *Satipaṭṭhānasutta* concludes that the practice leads to liberating insight (*aññā*), i.e. arhatship, in this very life or, at least, in the state of non-returner (MN I 62–63).

46 MN I 138–139.

47 E.g. AN IV 422.

48 The phrase is found in numerous other texts (e.g. MN I 160, AN IV 451, etc.). On this pattern, see Schmithausen 1981: 214–219.

49 For this dating, see Deleanu 2006: 186–194 and 2019: 12–13.

50 Sarvāstivāda was one of the most influential scholastic traditions and monastic establishments in Northern Mainstream Buddhism. With its main centre(s) in Kashmir, the school thrived during the first centuries of the Common Era, gradually losing pre-eminence to the new scholastic tradition developed by Mahāyāna from the fifth-sixth centuries on. The name of the school comes from its main theory (*vāda*) maintaining that the essence of all (*sarva*) basic factors, i.e. *dharmas*, which constitute the physical and mental reality continue to exist (*asti*) throughout the past, present and future.

51 The Sautrāntikas or 'those following the authority of the canonical texts (*sūtra*)' seem to have represented a broad range of exegetes who favoured flexible interpretations to the strict Sarvāstivādin orthodoxy. Rather than a single group, the Sautrāntikas were more probably individual scholar-monks active within various Mainstream Buddhist communities, some even affiliated to the Sarvāstivāda.

Their common point was a loose core of doctrinal interpretations and a methodology critical of (what was perceived as) Sarvāstivādin dogmatism.

52 Vasubandhu does not give this stage a particular name, but its practice is treated as a distinct phase.

53 AKBh ch.VI ver. 24c. See also AKBh ch. III ver. 44c; ch. IV ver. 124; ch.VII ver. 30; ch.VII ver. 34.

54 AKBh p. 334.

55 Strictly speaking, *prayoga* is used by Vasubandhu for the last sublevel, but the preceding phases can also be taken as part of the preparatory training.

56 AKBh ch.VI ver. 9–25.

57 AKBh ch.VI ver. 25–32.

58 AKBh ch.VI ver. 33–44.

59 AKBh ch.VI ver. 47cd.

60 AKBh ch.VI ver. 45–55.

61 This a corpus of roughly 40 texts whose compilation extends from the earliest strata of Mahāyāna around 100 BCE to late Tantric developments (c. 600–1200 CE) (see Conze 1978). Their central motif is the attainment of the perfection of wisdom (*prajñāpāramitā*) through a non-reifying insight into the emptiness of all phenomena.

62 See PañcaPp 208 (description identical to the *Ekottarāgama*, T 2.630b).

63 Vin III 92–3, DN III 219, SN IV 360, AN I 299; T 2.630b, etc.

64 PañcaPp 48. The same holds true for the contemplations of signlessness and desirelessness.

65 AṣṭaPp 60–61. The collocation *na saṁvidyate* can also mean 'does not perceive [anything]'.

66 BoBh 49–50; 396. The method has canonical roots (AN V 324–326; T 2.235c-236b; T 2.430c-431a), but much of the description here is unique to BoBh.

67 BoBh 396.

68 AṣṭaPp 754.

69 Earliest Buddhist tradition may have given a higher place to these techniques. Their relegation to an inferior or optional place may be a secondary development (see Maithrimurthi 1999).

70 BhKr 187–190 and 229–234.

71 BhKr 189–190. The method is quite similar to the cultivation of friendliness and compassion in Mainstream Buddhism (e.g. Vism 244–262).

72 Lack of space prevents us from looking into other important developments such as friendliness and compassion meditation without [conceptualising the] object (*anālamabana*). E.g. BoBh 241; MSA 121 (Maithrimurthi 1999: 331).

73 Madhyamaka, founded by the famous Nāgārjuna (c. 150–250 CE), pushes the non-substantialism, i.e. emptiness doctrine (*śūnyatāvāda*), advocated in the Prajñāpāramitā literature to its ultimate conclusions developing a dialectical methodology of deconstructivism. It denies the possibility of postulating any real, substantial essences (*svabhāva*) of phenomena. Language/conceptualisation, even by making appeal to such doctrines as 'emptiness', is unable to give account of the nature of the 'ultimate reality' without reifying/mystifying it.

74 Whether Yogācāra is an idealistic philosophy remains a controversial topic. Lusthaus 2002, for instance, argues that the school is closer to a phenomenological approach. My own understanding follows in the footsteps of those scholars, not exactly few in number, who regard Yogācāra-Vijñānavāda as a form of idealism. For a recent and excellent discussion, see Kellner and Taber 2014.

75 *Cittamātra* is another name of the school.

76 For this model, see MahSūtr 90–97 and 23–24 (which I follow below). For the identification of each of the path names, see Sthiramati, *Sūtrālaṃkāravṛttibhāṣya*: P Vol. 108, Mi 89b7-94a39. MahSūtr 65 also contains a model called the five-fold path of spiritual praxis (*pañcavidhā yogabhūmiḥ*), but in spite of the terminological differences, it basically describes a similar spiritual progression.

77 MahSūtr 24.

78 MahSūtr 24 (emended on the basis of the Chinese translation.)

79 It is impossible to give a satisfactory account of the immense repertory of Tantric meditations in a few pages. The relatively small number of edited texts of South Asian Tantric Buddhism makes the attempt even more challenging. For a comprehensive overview, I recommend Ray 2002 (especially pp. 111–325). Though not exactly a historical monograph and relying substantially on Tibetan interpretations, the book is a reliable introduction to the Tantric meditative techniques and path of spiritual cultivation. See also Hopkins 2008.

80 *Guhyasamājatantra* 17–19.

81 In spite of its frequent citation in modern literature, this quadruple classification may not have been so common in South Asia where a number of various models co-existed (see Dalton 2005; Williams et al. 2012: 151–153). It gained popularity in Tibet, from the twelfth century onwards, being mainly associated with the New Schools (*gsar ma*). The Old School (*rnying ma*) favoured a Nine-Vehicle model (see Dalton 2005). The appellation *rnal 'byor bla na med* is often reconstructed as **anuttarayoga*, but the word is not attested in South Asian sources (see Tsukamoto, Matsunaga and Isoda 1989: 55, n. 5; Isaacson 1998: 28; Sanderson 2009 146, n. 337; Williams et al. 2012: 152–153). The closest known term is *yoganiruttara* (e.g. *Yogaratnamāla*, Snellgrove ed. 156; see Tsukamoto et al. 1989: 55, n. 5; Williams et al. 2012: 152–153). (I am indebted to Prof. Harunaga Isaacson for his kind advice concerning **anuttarayoga/ yoganiruttara*.)

82 For this symbolism, see Wayman [1977] 1991 and Dasgupta 1958.

83 *Caṇḍālī* is also the name of the lowest untouchable caste as well as a title given to Śakti in a semiotic code conveying the Goddess's transcendence of impurity (see Wedemeyer 2013: 27–29).

84 The set of six *yogas* (or *dharmas*, in Tibetan: *Na ro'i chos drug*) consists of the techniques of inner heat, illusory body (Skt. *māyākāyā*), [lucid] dream (*svapnadarśana*), clear light (*prabhāsvara*), intermediate state (*antarābhava*) and consciousness transference (*saṃkrānti*). The set is first described in the *Chos drug gi mang ngag* (P Vol. 82 Pu 134b2-135b1), a short text attributed to Tilopa, i.e. Nāropā's master. (For an English translation, see Mullin 2006: 27–29.) The Tantric tradition, Buddhist as well as Hindu, also developed another set of practices similarly named the 'six-fold yoga' (*ṣaḍaṅgayoga*) (e.g. *Guhyasamājatantra* Ch. 18, ver. 157). For a historical overview of this set, see Wallace 2001: 25–30. See also Nāropā's *Sekoddeśaṭīkā*, 109–156.

85 The text is extant only in Tibetan translation: *Snyan rgyud rdo rje'i thigs rkang*; P Vol. 82, Pu 140b1–142b5). For an English translation, see Mullin 2006: 33–41. Unless otherwise indicated, technical terms in this section are given in Tibetan.

86 The qualifications required for initiation into the technique show that the six *yogas* were conceived as an advanced practice in the *Cakrasaṃvara* Tantric tradition.

87 For English translations, see Mullin 1996 and Mullin 2006: 93ff. On the development of Nāropā's contemplative legacy in Tibet, see Kragh 2015. The yoga of inner fire is still practised and taught by modern Tibetan(-trained) masters (see, for instance, Yeshe 1998).

88 P Vol. 82, Pu 140b8.

89 The latter is, of course, a defining feature of the entire South Asian spirituality since Vedic times. For *mantras* and *dhāraṇīs* in Buddhism, see Nattier 1992: 158, 201–202n9. One can also mention in this context the protective formulae (*paritta*) already attested in the Pali canon and the mystical syllabaries (*arapacana*) found in Mahāyāna literature.

90 *Mañjuśrīmūlakalpa* 55.

91 P vol. 161, Wa 1-210a7. For a partial English translation, see Dalai Lama, Tsong-kha-pa and Hopkins [1981] 1987. Cf. also Hopkins 2008: 117ff. for a detailed presentation of mantra meditation.

92 See Dalai Lama et al. [1981] 1987: 141–148.

93 See Buddhaguhya, *bSam gtan phyi ma rim par phye ba rgya cher bshad pa* (**Dhyānottarapaṭalaṭīkā*) (*Commentary on the Manual of the Superior [Stage of] Meditation*), P Vol. 78 Chu 29b6-8. Cf. Dalai Lama et al. [1981] 1987, 161.

94 I rely here on Wedemeyer's (2007) excellent edition, translation and study. Another representative model of Tantric spiritual cultivation, which unfortunately cannot be presented here, is found in the chapter on Spiritual Accomplishment (*Sādhanapaṭala*) of the later esoteric work *Kālacakratantra* (pp. 141–199). For an English translation, see Wallace 2010.

95 These are the so-called Tantric Nāgārjuna and Tantric Āryadeva, different from the Madhyamaka namesakes (see Wedemeyer 2007: 9–14). According to the Tibetan tradition, there are six major lineages based on the *Guhyasamājatantra*, Nāgārjuna's and Buddhajñānapāda's lines of transmission being the major ones (see Sakai 1974: 1, 4, 8–9, etc.).

96 The same paradigm is shared by many texts in the corpus of 'Wisdom Yoga-Mother Tantras' (*Shes rabs rnal 'byor ma'i rgyud*) (see Tsukamoto et al. 1989: 45) and numerous works compiled in Tibet. In his account of the six *yogas*, Nāropā, who follows the *Cakrasaṃvara*, i.e. the Mother-Tantra tradition, also mentions the stage of generation.

97 These are the terms preferred by Nāgārjuna (*Pañcakrama* 1, ver. 2). The *Guhyasamājatantra* uses *utpattika* and *utpannaka* (Ch. XVIII, ver. 84, p. 119) or *sāmānyasādhana* 'general accomplishment' and (*uttama[sādhana]*) 'supreme accomplishment' (ch. XVIII, ver. 139–140, p. 123). The latter stage is said to consist in the six-fold yoga (*ṣaḍaṅgayoga*), i.e. [sense] withdrawal (*pratyāhāra*), meditation (*dhyāna*), control of inner energy (*prāṇayāma*), retention (*dhāraṇa*), recollection (*anusmṛti*) and contemplation (*samādhi*) (for an English translation, see Wayman [1977] 1991: 41–50).

98 *Pañcakrama* 1, ver. 2. The five steps include *vajra*-recitation (*vajrajāpakrama*), mind purification (*cittaviśuddhikrama*), self-consecration (*svādhiṣṭhānakrama*), complete awakening [through/to] bliss (*sukhābhisaṃbodhi*) and conjoining (*yuganaddha*).

99 The polysemic *vajra* 'adamantine', etc. suggests the highest level of Tantric initiation.

100 Wedemeyer translates *-viveka* as 'isolation', i.e. a process that makes the body, speech and mind 'isolated from the ordinary appearances privileged by ordinary pride' (Wedemeyer 2007: 71). This level belongs to the generation stage and is equated with the eighth stage on the bodhisattvic path.

101 See *Guhyasamājatantra* 104, ver. 50. The Five Buddhas are Akṣobhya, Vairocana, Amitābha, Ratnasambhava and Amoghasiddhi.

102 CMPr 350–354.

103 CMPr 369–380.

104 The completion of this level is equated to the tenth stage on the bodhisattva path (CMPr 449), which in Mahāyāna marks the attainment of Buddhahood. The Vajrayāna path goes beyond this exoteric level.

105 CMPr 401–413.

106 CMPr 427–436.

107 CMPr 440–443.

108 CMPr 451.

109 CMPr 453.

110 See Wedemeyer 2007, 66.

111 AKBh 334.

112 Citation/reference conventions. For Sanskrit texts, I note the pages of the modern editions listed below. For Pali texts, PTS edition volume and page number. For Tibetan texts, Peking (P) edition of the canon, volume, traditional folio number, recto(a)/verso(b), line. For Chinese texts, Taishō (T) edition of the canon, volume, page number, segment (a, b, c), occasionally followed by column.

113 In case of reprints, the original date of publication is given in square brackets.

114 The citation is made from the abstract posted online.

## Bibliography[113]


Bader, J. 1990. *Meditation in Śaṅkara's Vedānta*. New Delhi: Aditya Prakashan.

Banerjee, B. 1985. *A Critical Edition of the Śrī Kālacakratantra-Rāja (Collated with the Tibetan version)*. Calcutta: The Asiatic Society.

Bareau, A. 1955. *Les Sectes Bouddhiques du Petite Véhicle*. Paris: École Française D'Extrême-Orient.

Bronkhorst, J. 1993. *The Two Traditions of Meditation in Ancient India*. Delhi: Motilal Banarsidass Publishers.

Chah, A. [1985] 1997. 'Observing Your Mind', in Bucknell, R. and Khan, C. (ed), *The Meditative Way: Readings in the Theory and Practice of Buddhist Meditation*. Richmond, Surrey: Curzon Press.

Conze, E. [1956] 1969. *Buddhist Meditation*. New York and Evanston: Harper Torchbooks.

Conze, E. 1978. *The Prajñāpāramitā Literature*. 2nd edition. Tokyo: The Reiyukai.

Cox, C. 1992. 'Mindfulness and Memory: The Scope of Smṛti from Early Buddhism to the Sarvāstivādin Abhidharma', in Gyatso, J. (ed), *In the Mirror of Memory: Reflections on Mindfulness and Remembrance in Indian and Tibetan Buddhism*. Albany: State University of New York Press.

Dalai Lama, H. H., Tsong-kha-pa, and Hopkins, J. [1981] 1987. *Deity Yoga*. Ithaca: Snow Lion Publications.

Dalton, J. 2005. 'A Crisis of Doxography: How Tibetans Organized Tantra During the 8th -12th Centuries', *Journal of the International Association of Buddhist Studies* 28(1): 115–181.

Dasgupta, S. B. 1958. *An Introduction to Tāntric Buddhism*. Second edition. Calcutta: University of Calcutta.

Deleanu, F. 2006. *The Chapter on the Mundane Path* (Laukikamārga) *in the* Śrāvakabhūmi*: A Trilingual Edition (Sanskrit, Tibetan, Chinese), Annotated Translation, and Introductory Study*. Tokyo: The International Institute of Buddhist Studies.

Deleanu, F. 2019. 'Dating with Procrustes: Revisiting Early Pramāṇavāda Chronology', *Bulletin of the International Institute for Buddhist Studies* 2: 11–47.

Dutt, N. (ed) 1934. *Pañcaviṃśatisāhasrikā Prajñāpāramitā*. London: Luzac & Co.

Eltschinger, V. 2009. 'On the Career and Cognition of *Yogins*', in Franco, E. (ed), *Yogic Perception, Meditation and Altered States of Consciousness*, 169–213. Vienna: Verlag der Östrreichischen Akademie der Wissenschaften.

Gethin, R. 2015. 'Buddhist Conceptualizations of Mindfulness', in Brown, K. W., Creswell, J. D. and Ryan, R. M. (eds), *Handbook of Mindfulness: Theory, Research, and Practice*, 9–41. New York: Guilford Press.

Gombrich, R. F. 1996. *How Buddhism Began: The Conditioned Genesis of the Early Teachings*. London and Atlantic Highlands, NJ: Athlone.
Griffiths, P. J. [1986] 1999. *On Being Mindless: Buddhist Meditation and the Mind-Body Problem*. Delhi: Sri Satguru Publications.
Hopkins, J. 2008. *Tantric Techniques*. Ithaca: Snow Lion Publications.
Isaacson, H. 1998. 'Tantric Buddhism in India (from c. AD 800 to c. AD 1200)', in Johnson, E. H. (ed and trans), *Buddhismus in Geschichte und Gegenwart*. Vol. 2. Hamburg: University of Hamburg.
Johnson, E. H. (ed and trans) 1975 [1928]. The Saundarananda of Aśvaghoṣa. Delhi: Motilal Banarsidass.
Kellner, B. and Taber, J. 2014. 'Studies in Yogācāra-Vijñānavāda Idealism I: The Interpretation of Vasubandhu's *Viṃśikā*', *Asia* 68(3): 709–753.
Kern, H. and Bunyiu, N. (ed) [1908–1912] 1970. *Saddharmapuṇḍarīka*. Osnabrück: Biblio Verlag.
Kragh, U. T. 2015. *Tibetan Yoga and Mysticism: A Textual Study on the* Yogas *of Nāropa and* Mahāmudrā *Meditation in the Medieval Tradition of Dags Po*. Tokyo: The International Institute for Buddhist Studies.
Kuan, T. 2008. *Mindfulness in Early Buddhism: New Approaches through Psychology and Textual Analysis of Pali, Chinese and Sanskrit Sources*. London: Routledge.
Lamotte, É. (ed and trans) 1935. *Saṃdhinirmocanasūtra: L'explication des Mystères*. Louvain: Université de Louvain.
Lévi, S. (ed) 1907. *Asaṅga Mahāyāna-Sūtrālaṃkāra: Exposé de la doctrine du Grand Véhicule selon le Système Yogācāra*. Tome I: Texte. Paris: Libraire Honoré Champion.
Lusthaus, D. 2002. *Buddhist Phenomenology: A Philosophical Investigation of Yogācāra Buddhism and the* Ch'eng Wei-shih lun. London: Routledge/Curzon.
Maithrimurthi, M. 1999. *Wohlwollen, Mitgleid, Freude und Gleichmut: Eine ideen- geschichtliche Untersuchung der vier* apramāṇas *in der buddhistischen Ethik und Spiritualität von den Anfängen bis hin zum frühen Yogācāra*. Stuttgart: Franz Steiner Verlag.
Malinowski Stuart, D. 2013. *Thinking about Cessation: The Pṛṣṭhapālasūtra of the Dīrghāgama in Context*. Vienna: Arbeitskreis für Tibetische und Buddhistische Studien, Universität Wien.
Matsunaga, Y. (ed) 1978. *The Guhyasamāja Tantra*. Osaka: Toho shuppan.
Mimaki, K. and Tomabechi, T. (eds) 1994. *Pañcakrama*. Tokyo: The Centre for East Asian Cultural Studies for Unesco.
Mullin, G. H. (trans) 1996. *Tsongkhapa's Six Yogas of Naropa*. Ithaca and Boulder: Snow Lion Publications.
Mullin, G. H. 2006. *The Practice of the Six Yogas of Naropa*. Ithaca and Boulder: Snow Lion Publications.
Nattier, J. 1992. 'The *Heart Sutra*: A Chinese Apocryphal Text?', *Journal of the International Association of Buddhist Studies* 15(2): 153–223.
Ōminami, R. 1977. 'Go jōshinkan to go monzen', in Sekiguchi S. (ed), *Bukkyō jissen genri*. Tokyo: Sankibō shoten.
Pradhan, P. (ed) 1975. *Abhidharmakośabhāṣya of Vasubandhu*. Patna: K. P. Jayaswal Research Institute.
Ray, R. A. 2002. *Secret of the Vajra World: The Tantric Buddhism of Tibet*. Boston and London: Shambala.
Sakai, S. 1974. *Chibetto mikkyō kyōri no kenkyū*. Revised edition. Volume I. Tokyo: Kokusho kankō-kai.
Sanderson, A. 2009. 'The Śaiva Age', in Einoo, S. (ed), *Genesis and Development of Tantrism*. Tokyo: Institute of Oriental Culture, University of Tokyo.
Sarbacker, S. R. 2005. *Samādhi: The Numinous and Cessative in Indo-Tibetan Yoga*. Albany: State University of New York Press.
Schmithausen, L. 1976. 'Die Vier Konzentrationen der Aufmerksamkeit: Zur Geschichtlichen Entwicklung einer Spirituellen Praxis des Buddhismus', *Zeitschrift für Missionswissenschaft und Religionswissenschaft* 60: 241–266.
Schmithausen, L. 1981. 'On Some Aspects of Descriptions or Theories of "Liberating Insight" and "Enlightenment" in Early Buddhism', in Bruhn, K. and Wezler, A. (eds), *Studien zum Jainismus und Buddhismus. Gedenkschrift für Ludwig Alsdorf*, 199–250, No. 23. Wiesbaden: Alt- und Neu-Indische Studien.
Sferra, F. (Skt. ed) and Merzagora, S. (Tib. ed). 2006. *The* Sekkodeśaṭīkā *by Nāropā* (Parmārthasaṃgraha). Roma: Istituto Italiano per l'Africa e l'Oriente.
Sharf, R. H. 2013. 'Mindfulness or Mindlessness: Traditional and Modern Buddhist Critiques of "Bare Awareness"'. Online lecture, https://vimeo.com/75214495. Accessed 13 March 2020.[114]
Sharf, R. H. 2015. 'Is Mindfulness Buddhist? (And Why it Matters)', *Transcultural Psychiatry* 52(4): 470–484.
Shaw, S. and Hatkis, G. 2009. *Introduction to Buddhist Meditation*. London: Routledge.
Shukla, K. (ed) 1973. *Śrāvakabhūmi of Ācārya Asaṅga*. Patna: K. P. Jayaswal.

Silk, J. 2000. 'The *Yogācāra Bhikṣu*', in Silk, J. (ed), *Wisdom, Compassion, and the Search for Understanding: The Buddhist Studies Legacy of Gadjin M. Nagao*. Honolulu: University of Hawai'i Press.

Tsukamoto, K., Matsunaga, Y. and Isoda, H. 1989. *Bongo Butten no Kenkyū IV: Mikkyō Kyōten-hen*. Kyoto: Heiraku-ji shoten.

Tucci, G. (ed) 1958. *Minor Buddhist Texts*. Part II. Roma: Istituto Italiano per il Medio ed Estremo Oriente.

Vaidya, P. L. (ed) 1964. *Mahāyānasūtrasaṃgraha*. Part II. Darbhanga: Mithila Institute of Postgraduate Studies and Research in Sanskrit Learning.

Vallée Poussin, L. de la 1937. 'Musīla et Nārada', *Mélanges Chinois et Bouddhiques* 5: 189–222.

Vetter, T. (ed and trans) 1984. *Der Buddha und Seine Lehre in Dharmakīrtis Pramāṇavarttika*. Vienna: Arbeitskreis für Tibetische und Buddhistische Studien, Universität Wien.

Vetter, T. 1988. *The Ideas and Meditative Practices of Early Buddhism*. Leiden: Brill.

Waldschmidt, E. (ed) 1957. *Das Catuṣpariṣatsūtra: Eine kanonische Lehrschrift über die Begründung der buddhistische Gemeinde*. Teil II. Berlin: Akademie-Verlag.

Wallace, V. A. 2001. *The Inner Kālacakratantra: A Buddhist Tantric View of the Individual*. Oxford and New York: Oxford University Press.

Wallace, V. A. 2010. *The* Kālacakra Tantra: *The Chapter on Sādhanā, with the* Vimalaprabhā *Commentary*. New York: The American Institute of Buddhist Studies.

Wallis, G. 2002. *Mediating the Power of Buddhas: Ritual in the Mañjuśrīmūlakalpa*. Albany: State University of New York Press.

Warren, H. C. (ed) and Kosambi, D. (rev). 1989 [1950]. *Visuddhimagga of Buddhaghosâcariya*. Delhi: Motilal Banarsidass Publishers.

Wayman, A. (trans) [1977] 1991. *Yoga of the Guhyasamājatantra: The Arcane Lore of Forty Verses*. Delhi: Motilal Banarsidass.

Wedemeyer, C. K. (ed and trans) 2007. *Āryadeva's Lamp that Integrates the Practices (Caryāmelāpakapradīpa): The Gradual Path of Vajrayāna Buddhism According to the Esoteric Community Noble Tradition*. New York: The American Institute of Buddhist Studies.

Wedemeyer, C. K. 2013. *Making Sense of Tantric Buddhism: History, Semiology, and Transgression in the Indian Tradition*. New York: Columbia University Press.

Williams, P., Tribe, A. and Wynne, A. 2012. *Buddhist Thought: A Complete Introduction to the Indian Tradition*. 2nd edition. London and New York: Routledge.

Wogihara, U. (ed) 1932–1935. *Abhisamâylaṃkār'ālokā Prajñāpāramitāvyākhyā (Commentary on Aṣṭasāhasrikā-Prajñāpāramitā), The Work of Haribhadra, Together with the Text Commented on*. Tokyo: The Toyo Bunko.

Wogihara, U. (ed) [1936] 1971. *Bodhisattvabhūmi*. Tokyo: Sankibo Buddhist Book Store.

Yeshe, L. T. 1998. *The Bliss of Inner Fire: Heart Practice of the Six Yogas of Naropa*. Boston: Wisdom Publications.

# 8

# TANTRIC TRANSFORMATIONS OF YOGA

## *Kuṇḍalinī* in the ninth to tenth century

*Olga Serbaeva Saraogi*

### Introduction

This chapter seeks to understand if the terms 'yoga' and 'tantra' can be clearly separated from each other in early South Asian history. When these terms are represented in secondary scholarship as exclusive, the effect is to create a misleading 'invisible wall' between the 'pure' 'classical' yoga, and the black-magic-oriented 'tantra'.[1] I propose to explore this constructed border, and my chosen sources change the picture considerably: the yogic practices of mastering the channels (*nāḍīs*) cannot be worked out from the 'yoga' category of texts, while the early tantras teach precisely this topic. Indeed it is the very basis of the Vidyāpīṭha[2] traditions (Sanderson 1990). I would even go so far as to claim that the early Śaiva-Śākta tantras probably constitute the missing link between Pātañjala yoga and what came to be known as *haṭhayoga*.

This chapter addresses the structure and the meaning of the yogic elements in the Vidyāpīṭha tantric texts, based on the *Jayadrathayāmala* (JY). The *Jayadrathayāmala*, compiled around the tenth century in northern India, was important for the Kashmiri philosopher Abhinavagupta and his school. This text provided the great polymath with the terminology of the subtle body and particular states of consciousness in the context of yogic experience. The JY does not represent a single tradition, but a whole palette, ranging from Pātañjala-like yoga aimed at the cessation of thoughts, to Śaiva yoga with its early forms of visualisation, to *kuṇḍalinī yoga*, which can be found here in its full-blown form. Above and beyond that, the text teaches the yoga of the *yoginīs*, in which the channels are used in the 'vampire techniques' of extracting vital essences (most often blood) from victims.[3] The JY, surviving in more than thirty Nepalese manuscripts, has not been edited or translated, except for small parts. Although the JY does refer to the various yogas, the precise interrelations between Pātañjala yoga and the tantric practices described in the text are yet to be studied.

In a broader sense, yoga, which I define here as 'a method of accessing the divine', pervades the entire JY, and so the material must be delimited. I only concentrate on practices related to the subtle body, which is the ground of all yogic practice in the JY. Although some postures (*āsanas*) and basic breathing (*prāṇāyāma*) techniques are mentioned, they are of no major importance in the visionary, *yoginī*-oriented form of yoga, based on the mastery of channels (*nāḍī*) and the controlled raising of *kuṇḍalinī* at will. Therefore, I only consider the chapters in which the names of the three main channels (*iḍā, piṅgalā* and *suṣumnā*) and *kuṇḍalinī* occur – together or separately.

It is important to note that these terms also appear in iconographical and other non-yoga contexts. On the other hand, many passages in the JY describe channels, *cakras* and *kuṇḍalinī*-like processes without using those specific terms. I do not address these cases here. Having studied this text since 2007, I have arrived at the following preliminary conclusions: although the final compilation of the JY took place sometime around the ninth to tenth century, the earliest available manuscript from Nepal is probably c. twelfth century. The text was known to Abhinavagupta at the end of the tenth century in Kashmir, and it incorporated early evidence of the Krama tradition from c. ninth to tenth centuries, together with much earlier tantras, of which the text lists some four hundred and eighty and actively cites about twenty. When we take the multiple sources of composition of JY into account, we cannot talk about a single yoga, but rather must posit multiple yogas rooted in distinct and traceable traditions preceding the JY. The aim of this chapter is, first of all, to discover how the JY understands the three channels, and what usage it suggests besides the *kuṇḍalinī*-raising context. Secondly, I aim to uncover which yogas are presented in the JY, and to what traditions and texts they are linked. Finally, I would like to define 'yoga' and 'tantra' in the JY, based on the analysis of selected passages.

## *Ṣaṭka* 1

The JY consists of four *ṣaṭkas,* or parts, each supposed to contain six thousand verses. However, the version that came down to us is missing about two thousand verses.[4] Within *ṣaṭka* 1, I discuss chapters 4, 5 and 12. The first two chapters belong to the introductory part of the JY, in which the compiler seems to want to mention everything that he has adopted from the previously existing traditions, such as the Svacchandabhairava and the Tumburu cults (see Sanderson 1990; 2009). Chapter 4 discusses the deity Bhairava, represented as a master of yoga, who is surrounded by various *bhairavas*, *vīras*[5] with their female counterparts, many of whom have yogic names. The *iḍā, piṅgalā* and *suṣumnā* channels are Śaiva deities in this context.[6] This chapter, along with chapter 5, seems to echo the *Svacchandabhairava Tantra* (SVT) (section 10) – a c. seventh-century CE text – and its structures of the yogic Śaiva worlds. In chapter 5, the long lists of *bhairavas* and their female partners illustrate the five principles of consciousness listed at the beginning of the chapter, namely, *dīpikā, mocikā,* etc. '*Mocikā* [is called such because] it liberates the *suṣumnā* stationed in the subtle [body].'[7] The yogic terminology here is taken from the SVT. However, these brief references do not allow us to see the full picture of how the channels are used. It is worth mentioning that in chapter 9, yoga is defined in the style of the *Yogasūtra*, because the 'fluctuations of the mind' (*cittavṛtti*) are said to render the person unconscious (*jaḍaḥ*), while yoga and other practices (*yogādi*) stop the fluctuations.[8]

The compiler addresses this problem of the channels in chapter 12. Its structure and terminology point to the fact that a Saiddhāntika Śaiva yoga[9] text here served as the basis for tantric yoga, the only difference being the addition of the practice of the main goddess of JY: Kālasaṃkarṣiṇī, She Who Retracts Time. The subject of the chapter is practice (*sādhana*), the three supporting feet of which are *yoga, kriyā* and *cārya.* Yoga is defined as the isolated (*kaivalya*) state of the *puruṣa,* which is rather typical Sāṃkhya terminology, and it has the following six limbs: breath control (*prāṇāyāma*), controlled visualisation (*dhāraṇā*), control of the senses (*pratyāhāra*), discernment (*vitarka*), visionary state (*dhyāna*; in which the visions are spontaneous rather than imposed as in *dhāraṇā*) and the final limb being the state of *samādhi*.[10] A similar six-limbed yoga, *ṣaḍaṅga yoga,* was incorporated into the *Mālinīvijayottara*, an early Trika tantra (Vasudeva 2004).

Other verses describe the transformation of the body of the yogi: *prāṇāyāma* purifies the body, and *dhāraṇā* facilitates a state of dissolution at the level of 'the end of the twelve.'[11] Additionally, *dhāraṇā* seems to echo the conquest of the elements as described in the *Mālinīvijayottara* (Vasudeva

2004: 303–330). Starting from the earth and ascending through the hierarchy of the elements, the yogi is supposed to achieve the mastery of space (*vyoma*), and thus to be able to travel in the cosmic *maṇḍala* (*ākāśamaṇḍala*), and to penetrate and control the personal forms (*mūrtis*) of *vyoma*. Seeing one's own mind and realising the karmic and other faults in a particular visual experience is the essence of *pratyāhāra*, i.e. retraction of the sense organs. The next limb (*aṅga*) by order is *vitarka*, but this is not dealt with. Rather the text goes directly to the achievement of non-dual perception and of *samādhi*. In this process the yogic heart is described as having twelve parts (*kalās*).[12] These twelve *kalās* are linked to the 'sun', although not named, while the sixteen aspects discussed next definitely refer to the moon. The lotus of four petals is said to be stationed between the eyebrows. It opens the way to the lotus stationed at the entrance of the 'end of the twelve'[13] under the influence of *samādhi*. Reaching this point means realisation of one's own identity, ascending to the great *vyoma*, by means of riding a single intent (*saṅkalpa*). All in all, this is Śaiva yoga, and it bestows the state of Sadāśiva as the final one.[14]

There is also a list of yogic sounds that arise by means of concentration on one particular place, such as the heart. In addition to the usual changes in sounds – such as have been described in MVT (Vasudev 2004: 276), for example – here the tactile effects are included. The three channels are linked to gods: *iḍā* to Viṣṇu (Hari, the only masculine god here), *piṅgala* to Brahmī and *suṣumnā* to Raudrī.[15] This link facilitates control over time, and was probably the reason for incorporating the whole Saiddhāntika yoga chapter into the practice of the goddess Kālasaṃkarṣiṇī.[16] Time is described as being external and internal, and the latter can be controlled by yoga, since all astronomical junctions are *prāṇa*-related. By joining time to an upward flow of *prāṇa*, liberation is achieved[17] and is to be experienced in this present body.[18] This knowledge is used not only to access special time-junctions that can be seen as rare accelerated moments in the yoga process, but also for black magic (*abhicāra*), which requires mostly the black (lunar) fortnight, and which can be arranged, following the logic of this exposition, from inside of the yogic body.

The deity Bhairava describes the yogic body starting with the place (in the lower body) where *kuṇḍalinī* is said to be stationed prior to awakening: *kanda*.[19] The *nāḍīs* are distributed in all directions from *kanda*, as if forming circles (*cakravat*), and there are seventy-two thousand of these channels. The main one (*pradhānā*) is *suṣumnā*, followed by *iḍā* and *piṅgalā*.[20] There are also ten secondary channels and ten kinds of *prāṇa*. These channels and *prāṇas* are also known from the earlier texts, from as early as the fifth to sixth century CE.[21]

What appears to be new information in the JY is the detailed description of the *kuṇḍalinī* procedure, in which Śiva's power (*śakti*), coming from the *kanda cakra*, enters the multitude of different channels, eventually all seventy-two thousand. This results in complete pervasion (*vyāpti*) and the yogi experiences great pleasure.[22] Verses 154–167 combine a multitude of terms for special psycho-physical states that can be found in the JY in the context of yoga practice, initiation and encounter with the *yoginīs*: going randomly (*bhrama*), being blissfully intoxicated (*ghūrmi*), flaming in the body (*jvala*), falling (*patina*), the supreme state (*parama daśa*), deity possession of the practitioner's body (*āveśa*), horripilation (*roma*), the ability to perform forceful opening (*vedha*) of the central channel to raise *kuṇḍalinī* and attain 'joining' (*yoḍha*) to the highest state, accomplishment in *dhyāna*, realisation of *mudrās*,[23] feeling like a tree burning without fire, accomplishment of bodily perfections (*piṇḍasiddhi*), jumping, flying, spontaneous knowledge of the three times, the ability to control the world, the eight yogic *siddhis* beginning with miniaturisation (*aṇima*), the realisation of all mantras, the opening up of the mantra-activators (*vīrya*) – and the understanding of the functions of all *nāḍīs* by which the state of bliss becomes manifested everywhere. A new psycho-physical ladder is thus formed and linked to *kuṇḍalinī* awakening.[24] Verses 167-181ab affirm that upon exit from this state, one attains *samādhi,* which bestows the mastery over time and death. Among the final and the most spectacular *siddhis* discussed are entry into the bodies of others, burning without fire, distant seeing and such.[25] Besides that, the *sādhaka* will get *aṇima* and other *siddhis*, bind the directions in the practice of the 'night assembly' (*rātrīsaṃcāra*) and break the *cakras* into pieces by joining the channels, starting with *iḍā*.[26]

Until about verse 154 of chapter 12, the JY does not appear to be any different than a Saiddhāntika text. There are very few references to Kālasaṃkarṣiṇī or Vidyāpīṭha or *yoginīs* in this part of the chapter. However, from verse 230 until the end of the chapter, the 'extremely secret' yoga is explained. This consists of a very detailed visualisation of the goddess Kālasaṃkarṣiṇī and her *maṇḍala*. The resulting state (verses 288–299) is the dissolution or melting of the self, visualised as embodying the whole *maṇḍala*. This occurs in various locations of the subtle body, beginning with the navel[27] and continues by riding the upwards flow of *prāṇa*. It confers the ability to see one's own yogic progression with yogic eyes,[28] being fully satisfied with yoga and pleasure (*bhoga*), and thus reaching the state of non-attraction (*virakta*) – likely synonymous with the isolation (*kaivalya)* mentioned at the beginning of the chapter. All of this ensures that the *sādhaka* will not come back again, i.e. be reborn.[29] This visualisation of the goddess constitutes the JY's proper upgrade of the previously described Saiddhāntika yoga.

The next sixty verses describe the six ways (*ṣaḍadhvan*), commonly used in Śaiva initiation.[30] The major aspect of this new yoga is a powerful visionary experience, which manifests when the elements of consciousness (*cit*) expand. Thus the *sādhaka* obtains Śiva, i.e. he realises his own identity with Śiva, and obtains liberation in his own body.[31] He literally sees his own essence as Śiva. By means of becoming stable in *samādhi,* he can enter and live in other bodies, dead or alive, or permanently transfer himself into another body.[32] The basis of the whole process is the expansion of the 'centre', occurring when the energy travels upwards from the root (*mūla*) and that is achieved in a series of particularly blissful psychological states, described in verses 401–418. This process also secures omniscience.

The last forty verses of the chapter describe a step-by-step rising of *kuṇḍalinī*. It is coiled and it moves in the innermost part of the *kanda*. It is in essence a vital breath, because it has five hoods.[33] When it awakens, it resembles a serpent – terrible, because it contains the five knots (*granthis*), and because it is bent upon grasping the universe. It is awakened through the *mahākaraṇa* yoga (yoga of the supreme body), which is the next level from the subtle (*sūkṣma*) body. This yoga requires the adept to adopt a comfortable *āsana* and a slightly opened mouth. By means of manipulation of the right channel, the vital breath is made to enter the *kanda*, and the energy with five hoods awakens in the manner of an arrow, a stick and lightning (*śaravad, daṇḍavad, vidyuvad*).[34] It further provokes powerful psycho-physical effects as it passes each of the five knots, which are positioned along the path of the rising *kuṇḍalinī* in the central channel. The piercing of the first knot results in moving in circles, trembling, swooning and burning of the body. After that great pleasure (*ānanda*) is experienced, such as during orgasm.[35] When the second knot falls open, one experiences expansion, paralysis (*stobha*), endless beauty, possession of various kinds, speaking yogic language and relating the past and the future.[36] When the third knot opens, one jumps like a frog and leaves the ground, goes into *vyoma*, and experiences great pervasion (*mahāvyāpti*), falls into yogic sleep, and feels great pleasure. The yogi obtains omniscience.[37] When the fourth knot falls open, one sees the perfected ones (beings or states). He shakes and horripilates, his eyes move in a random manner, he can attract people, pierce (the knots in the central channel of the other people), and cause descent of the gods and *yoginis*. With his full body shaking, he experiences various sorts of deity possession (*āveśa*), he can extract the six vital essences[38] and he masters the six kinds of revelation.[39] Again he experiences great pervasion.[40] When the fifth knot opens, then all of the aforementioned manifest simultaneously. One realises the sequences of ten, twelve and sixteen (i.e. respectively fire, sun and moon aspects). He reaches the mastery of the 'essence' (*bindu*). He sees the circles of *siddhas* and *yoginīs* and the aerial chariots (*vimāna*). He is omniscient, and having enjoyed all, he becomes like Śiva himself.[41]

From verse 449 to the end of the chapter, the yogic stages are summarised once again by order. The whole yogic procedure is separated into six steps or stages, here called 'clarities' (*vyaktis*), or something that becomes evident. Thus, in stage one the main gods' (*kāraṇendra*) nature is realised.[42] In the second stage, the power behind the mantra becomes clear.[43] It is during the third stage that all *granthi*s fall open, and the *cakras* from *ādhāra* onwards,[44] which are linked to the main deities, become realised. Thus this is the stage relating to *kuṇḍalinī* proper.[45] At stage four, the leader of heroes will be able to hear (gods and revelations). At the fifth stage he realises the five forms of space (*vyomas*).[46] Throughout this process, he achieves 'going in the air', or the state of the *khecarīs*. Moreover, the subtle essence (*rasa*) of each of the five stages, gives rise to the highest state, here called *paramārtha,* in which the yogin realises his non-dual identity, and which is the essence of the *śākta, śāmbhava* and *āṇava* types of pervasion.[47] The yoga that saves one from the terrible *saṃsāra* has thus been explained.[48]

To sum up, in the ninth to tenth-century *Jayadrathayāmala*, which definitely draws on earlier texts, one can already find not only the developed structure of the subtle body with channels and knots, but also a reference to the *cakras*, and to the 'coiled energy' that upon awakening changes the human into god. It is therefore possible to conclude that well-developed *kuṇḍalinī* theory and practice can be found in the Vidyāpīṭha texts in circulation before the ninth tenth century.

## *Ṣaṭka* 2

In *ṣaṭka* 2 there are four relevant chapters, 8, 12–13 and 23. In this section, we do not find Saiddhāntika yoga. Rather enter the domain of the yoga of the *yoginīs*, *yoginīyoga*. To link this yoga to Sanderson's classification of the Śaiva traditions (1990), we are discussing the Kula, a tradition of worshipping goddesses and *yoginīs* arranged into various families or clans (*kula*).

Chapter 8 deals with the goddess named Yantrapramardanī, the Destroyer of the *Yantras*. The list of the effects of her mantra (*vidyā*) includes practices to attract people and to put them under control by manipulating *prāṇas* and channels. These techniques are essentially the same as in the initiation of a disciple (Serbaeva 2010b). In 'putting under control', the *sādhaka* achieves identity with the goddess Bhairavī, and she, having entered the heart of the victim, by repeating 'coming and going' [in a manner of a swing], hooks the essence (*bindu*) of the victim by means of the *mudrā* of *aṅkuśa* and drags it by means of the *mudrā* of *pāśa* (these two *mudrā*s are 'rope' and 'elephant goad'). Having entered the circle of the soul (*jīvacakra*), she takes away the juices of the victim. Having grasped those, s/he quickly returns to her/his own body. By means of this visualisation, s/he can put the moving and immovable world under control.[49] The gender of the actor often clearly switches to the feminine in these passages, as they appear to be originally written for the *yoginīs*. In 'attraction', by means of the same *mudrās* of rope and elephant goad, s/he attracts the triple world. Having expanded the *kauḍilī cakra* (which is probably a corruption of *kuṇḍalinī*) with the flaming elephant goad, s/he provokes great pleasure, and *kuṇḍalinī* goes up decorated with the five serpent hoods (i.e. five *prāṇas*) through the opening in the *suṣumnā*. Thus one does engender attraction. Additionally, by employing the *iḍā* channel, in the practice – in which the head is being stroked by the terrible elephant goad – much pleasure is provoked.[50] The reader will note that the techniques described here are coherent with the stages of the *kuṇḍalinī* awakening in JY.1.12. The blissful and pleasant states that arise spontaneously for a yogi upon awakening are here used to put other persons under control.

Chapter 12 describes a form of Śuṣkā/Karaṅkinī, the Dry One or the Skeleton One, this time rooted in a text called the *Umāyāmala* (verse 10cd).[51] Her *vidyā* provokes paralysis (*stobha*) and raises the hair of the practitioner.[52] The yogic elements occur in the context of initiation, in which the disciple is awakened through the left channel, i.e. *iḍāyoga*. The opening of *vicitra* channel in the blissful state allows plunging the initiand directly into supreme state of *nistaraṅga*.[53]

Chapter 13 is a manual (*kalpa*) of worship of Vātacakreśvarī, the Mistress of the Circle of Wind, in the context of which the goddess requests the revelation of *ṣoḍhāvedhakrama* (verse 35ab) used in initiation. *Ṣoḍhā* refers to purification, *vedha* literally means 'piercing' or forced awakening of the *kuṇḍalinī* and *krama* means 'sequence'.[54] The *śakti* rises up from the hexagram (in the *kanda*), provoking blissful feeling, and everything (i.e. the sequence of world/*tattvas* and states stationed along the central channel) becomes 'pierced'. The yogi experiences himself as being able to do everything, to be omniscient – having eyes, heads and mouths everywhere (i.e. he assumes cosmic form similar to one described in *Bhagavad Gītā* 11.10[55]). He sees his identity with light and bliss. When such experience of a change in identity is achieved, this is known to be the supreme piercing (*vedha*). Other forms of *vedha* include serpent-like (*sarpa-*), sound (*nāda-*) and visible manifestation of the essence (*bindu-*) (Silburn, 1988/[1983]: 17, 87–99).

Chapter 23 describes black magic practices done via channels.[56] In order to kill, the practitioner (*sādhaka*) finds a fitting victim, man or woman. He visualises the goddess in the heart, and repeats her *vidyā* one hundred times. Then, he goes out of his body and enters the victim via the face/mouth by means of the 'coming and going procedure' (*helādolā*). He enters the nectar circle (*maṇḍala*) in the heart of the victim via *suṣumṇā*, and cuts off the heart there. Upon returning to his own body, he offers the extracted lotus of the heart to gods and goddesses as a non-vegetarian offering (*bali*). Contrary to the Siddhānta-based yoga, in which the channels are actively used only once to raise *kuṇḍalinī*, here the channel manipulation constitutes the basis of the initiation and of the 'black magic' procedures. This practice is repeated. It is in the *ṣaṭka* 3 that we shall also find nectar extractions, in which the channels are also used repeatedly. It seems that the two yogas, the Saiddhāntika and the one of the *yoginīs*, have an unsurpassable gap between them, both in aims and in techniques. However, as we shall discover in the next section, according to the JY, this is not at all the case.

## *Ṣaṭka* 3

In the *ṣaṭka* 3 there are four relevant chapters: 8, 15–16 and 29. Chapter 8 is a part of the Trailokyaḍāmarī cycle, i.e. Goddess that Dominates the Three Worlds. The practice of joining the channels (*iḍā* and *suṣumnā*; verses 103ab, 106ab) allows one to reach the states of Śiva, beginning with Sadāśiva, and to fly with the body.[57] These states become available when the four *prāṇas* are blocked, and the type called *udāna* is made to rise up crossing the palate (*tālu*) (verse 106ab).[58] However, the state of Sadāśiva, which was absolute in Saiddhāntika yoga, is superseded by a series of Śiva's forms. Furthermore, the goddess Yogeśvarī is at the top of the new ontological structures. She bestows the highest blessing of the *yoginī* upon the *sādhaka* by giving him her own 'flowers' (*svapuṣpaiḥ, śaktipuṣpāṇi,* verse 131ab), which is a code for menstrual blood throughout the text.

The second reference to the manipulation of the subtle body occurs in a description of the *bhairava-vrata*, in which the *sādhaka* achieves identity with Śiva in the body.[59] In a series of visualisations, the *sādhaka* raises up his consciousness along the *cakras* stationed in the 'weapon' or spear (*śūla*) of the goddess, and merges it into a non-dual visionary state (verse 200–227). Again, this yoga is a mantric one, and it involves *yoginīs*. A further explanation facilitates extracting the soul or life-principle (*jīva*; verse 243ab), and other substances (verse 248–249) from victims.[60] This fuels the further yogic transformation of the *sādhaka* and allows him to fly (*khecarago bhavet*, verse 256ab). Victims who are 'charmed' to the ritual location by yogic procedures are subsequently killed and offered to the gods.

A variant of 'vampire practice' includes the usage of 'doors' linked to the sense organs (*indriyas*), which are also the access points to *suṣumnā*. The substances of a living being are extracted to please the goddesses (verses 290cd-306). This is done via *mudrās* that paralyse the will and body of the victim, and by extending the *mantra* to 'open up' the victim (*paśu*). The text seems to fluctuate between the context of initiation and the extraction of the nectars, because the techniques are essentially similar. However, in this chapter *paśu* means 'victim to be sacrificed' and not 'non-initiated'. The practices of externalisation (*kṛtyā*) and corpse revival (*vetāla*) explicitly require human sacrifices (verses 318–319). Ritual cannibalistic practice (verses 325–328) results in the transformation of the body of the *sādhaka*, who goes to a state called *brahmarākṣasa*, and having enjoyed that goes to Śiva.[61] The main goddess who governs the process and who is encoded also in the *mūla* mantra is called not Kālasaṃkarṣiṇī, but Saṅkariṣṇyā – and that is consistent through chapters 2–8. The extraction of the nectars constitutes the *yoginīyoga*,[62] belonging to the practically unknown traditions of the Kula.

Chapter 15 is entirely dedicated to *kuṇḍalinī* personified here as the goddess Kūṭeśvarī/ Kuṇḍaleśvarī. The goddess is characterised as 'resorting to *kanda*' and going to all *cakras* one by one.[63] When she reaches the middle space of the heart *cakra*, she devours the entire span of time.[64] Her *vidyā* provokes very strong psycho-physical effects: the body trembles, the state devoid of visualisation and its object is achieved, the middle ground between consciousness (*cit*) and unconsciousness (*acit*) is assumed and the vibration of every aspect of *śakti* dissolves in the supreme *vyoma*.[65] In the final stages, the goddess enters the body of the practitioner (*āviśed dehapañjaram*), and the yogi experiences great bliss, becoming the very body of the goddess.[66] The resulting state is equal to *nirvāṇa*. The yogi will be able to cause the descension of the multitude of *yoginīs*, kill gods, etc. and extract the five nectars through that power.[67] In the initiation passage (*dīkṣā*), *kuṇḍalinī* is represented as Kālasaṃkarṣiṇī with five faces (*prāṇas*), eager to devour the universe (verses 74cd-76ab). She is terrible, and yet she joins the disciple with the supreme body (verse 77cd), because, having entered the heart of the disciple, she brings his consciousness up to the 'end of the twelve', making him reach the *visarga* state (verse 79cd) (see Silburn 1988/[1983]: 21, 59). At this point he becomes 'pierced' and somewhat trembles (verse 80cd) and horripilates (verse 81ab). He further experiences the supreme bliss upon realisation of one's own essence, becoming one with consciousness (*cit*) and thus liberated.[68]

The rest of the chapter is a sort of yogic encyclopaedia, in which yogic terms are defined in Krama style (see Sanderson 1990) but through the yogic practice. This includes *ghaṭṭana* (verses 85-90ab) and *nirodha* (verses 90cd-94ab), which is here a yogic visualisation, enabling the cessation of the mind. *Samvitti*, or supreme consciousness, is explained via a practice in which the *sādhaka* stationed in the *kūṭeśvarī cakra*, visualises the moon aspects and drinks the moon nectar, merging his mind with his own supreme consciousness (*svasaṃvitti*). Through this process, the consciousness of the supreme *ātman* can be known, as well as the meaning of *mudrās* and *mantras,* and can be spontaneously realised.

Next we find the definition of three voids, embodying respectively Śiva, *śakti* and *nara* (human) levels. The attainment of these three is linked to the consciousness reaching particular places in the body. It is the heart, which represents the *nara* level, in which the mastery of the lunar aspects is achieved. When the [lunar aspects] attain peace, all in Krama style,[69] then the sun becomes accessible, and that level fits the '*śakti* void', which is not clearly linked to a place in the body. At this point one sees the multitude of deities. The *sādhaka* can perform piercing and joining, and enter into the bodies of dead and alive beings. He can create multiple forms (of himself) and realise the *cakras* (used here in the sense of assembly, group) of *vidyās, mantras* and *mudrās*.[70] Śiva's void includes the other two, namely *nara* and *śakti*, it is beyond definition and language, it is the place where sun and moon dissolve, it is without up and down and does not have the directions of space. It is the supreme consciousness itself. It is Parameśvara. It is void of any expansion or development, and it is inaccessible to the means of knowledge (*pramāṇa*); it is self-conscious, self-manifesting and the identity with that can be obtained through the way shown by the guru. The *sādhaka* becomes endowed with all perfections (*siddhis*) and he himself becomes like Śiva.[71] In brief, via these three voids, the adept masters the *cakras* of sun-moon-fire represented in the Krama tradition by the three eyes of Śiva, but this is not the end.

Finally, the state of the Waveless, (*nistaraṅga*) is defined. It leads to all accomplishments (*siddhis*).[72] In the 'king of the tantras' [JY], liberation can be achieved only through this state. This knowledge is derived from the Krama tradition (*kramāgatam idaṃ jñānaṃ*, verse 128a), it has only been orally transmitted and it is stationed in the mouth of guru.[73] Bhairava says: 'It has never ever been explained by me (*na kasyacin mayā proktaṃ*, verse 129c), I am telling this now to you, o Parameśvarī.'[74] It is the awakening, and the indestructible great bliss.[75] The yogi experiences: 'I am that', 'That is me', 'All volitions (*icchās*) in this world are created by me'[76] and 'All states are mine, and are radiated by me, I create *ātmans* with *ātma*, being the cause of independence (*svatantra*)'.[77] This state appears without beginning or end, void of qualities, including *guṇas*, and yet filling all, and established in peace.[78] When the practitioner enters the circle of Śiva, all manifested elements including Śiva, enter the state of dissolution (*saṃvittir yā śiva sārddhaṃ bhūta pralayage bhavet*).[79] The state of Śiva arises spontaneously in the circle of *śakti*, via *spanda*, and it is the awakening that has always been there.[80] When the practitioner melts in the non-vibrating and becomes established there, then he is Śiva (*nispandane yadā līnā svapratiṣṭhas tadā śivaḥ*).[81] He sees himself as the supreme light stationed above everything,[82] he sees the soul with the soul (*ātmānam ātmanā draṣṭu*),[83] he sees himself as the father and the grandfather of all living beings.[84] Then the grammatical person changes, and we find phrases such as 'I myself Parameśvara see my soul with the soul' (*svayam evātmanātmānaṃ paśyāmi parameśvaraṃ*).[85] This chapter further invites the reinterpretation of the vampire practices that were addressed earlier in a purely internal way:

> I am the non-dual soul, the supreme light, I am awakened (*buddha*), and both supreme and non-supreme. I am the sunlight in the world, appearing from the middle of the sun, [...] extracting the nectar of the sun, he worships the moon elements (*bhūtas*), and having extracted the nectar from those *bhūtas*, he satisfies with offerings to the sun and the moon.[86]

While contemplating the soul, he will see everywhere nothing but the dance of vibration (*spandaṃ nṛtaṃ paśyati sarvaśaḥ*).[87] In brief, *nistaraṅga*, which is further eulogised for some forty verses, is the state where the one and the multiple are merged, and of which there is no higher state. 'I am that', says Bhairava.[88]

This chapter describes the utmost states of yoga in the Krama tradition, as presented in the JY. The other chapters and passages in *ṣaṭkas* 2–4 all seem to draw upon this representation of *kuṇḍalinī*. Krama yoga constitutes the essence of the JY, and it is not impossible that the JY was specifically written to place the Krama at the top of the earlier traditions – since it integrates, digests and embodies all preceding yoga representations, from Siddhānta to the juice extractions performed by the *yoginīs*. Chapter 16 is comparable to chapter 15; the goddess Vāgbhaveśvarī is described here in her standard visualisation (*sakala*) and in the aspectless (*niṣkala*) form, which is linked to the channels. In this respect she closely resembles Kuṇḍaleśvarī.[89] She has the form of sound (*nāda*), and goes up from *piṅgalā*.[90] She is black like smokeless coal, and she is stationed in a peaceful (*śānta*) state in the head. She is that subtle flame of the candle that has the form of awakening, and she is stainless. She pervades the *suṣumnā* unto the top end and appears from the splendour (*tejas*) of Śiva. Riding the mechanism of sound or vibration, she is auspicious and engages in divine deeds. When she is riding the opposite aspect of speech [i.e. a non-discursive state] she devours all time. She is represented thus as *kuṇḍalinī* related to speech.

At the end of the *ṣaṭka* 3 there is a semi-independent section called the *Yoginīsaṃcāraprakara ṇa*. It is a text written for *yoginīs* and *sādhakas* who master the channels in one's own and other bodies to perform various sorts of extractions for one's own transformation, but also to please the deities.[91] Chapter 29 describes a victim reborn seven times only to be killed by *yoginīs* and *sādhakas* in order to obtain *siddhis* (Serbaeva, forthcoming b), and also teaches how to leave the body at will by the manipulation of the channels and to travel around in the manner of the 'space mothers' (*ākāśamātaraḥ,* verse 58ab).[92] This is done through a very detailed raising of *kuṇḍalinī*. After visualising the *cakra* with the syllables, the practitioner should fill up the openings of the channels in the *cakra* by means of controlling wind with breath retention (*kumbhaka).*[93] In the middle of the heart cakra he should visualise the Self shining like Śiva. Having become *bindu,* he should assign at the top of the *bindu* the peaceful and 'unborn' state. Having pierced the left channel, he fills up the *suṣumnā* with the *udāna* kind of *prāṇa*. The knower of mantra, having risen up from the opening of the channels by means of the syllable 'AI', and, having pierced the darkness like a ray similar to lightning, goes up to the place where the cosmic mothers are stationed, by means of *oṃ*.[94] He becomes equal to the *yoginīs*, and reaches the state of the eight heroes (i.e. *bhairavas*). Having obtained that state, he moves on the earth as he pleases.[95] This is, again, represented as *yoginīyoga*. Chapter 35, coming back again to the Krama denies that the identity of the goddess can be fully expressed as *suṣumnā,* or as anything else besides the *nistaraṅga* state (Serbaeva, forthcoming a).

## *Ṣaṭka* 4

In the *ṣaṭka* 4 there are three relevant chapters: 11, 31 and 34. Chapter 11 summarises the structure of the subtle body in the context of initiation. Bhairava says:

> I have already mentioned the 72,000 channels previously. [Among them] three are going verticaly in opposite directions;[96] in the middle of them is the most important one, called *suṣumnā*. It is also called *vicitra,* and *amṛtavāhinī* (bearer of nectar). *Vedha* is when the soul (*ātman*) goes inside of it. [In this case], it is called *viṣuva,* and it is a power that liberates.[97]

Chapter 31 addresses the 'nectar' practices that are secret, called the *yoginīyoga,* which are also protected by the *yoginīs* (*yoginīyogarakṣitaṃ*).[98] This knowledge includes the behaviour and the meeting of *yoginīs* (*yoginīcārasaṃcāra*), knowledge of the vulnerable points (*marmas*) and of the signs of death.[99] These are important for nectar extraction, which becomes possible when *kuṇḍalinī* ascends and reaches the space between the navel and the heart (*amṛtākṛṣṭy[ā] karṣayet*).[100] In the space between the heart and the throat, the *gamāgama* or 'coming and going' is mastered.[101] Having crossed *ghaṇṭikā* and being joined with the *bindu,* which would correspond to the centres higher than the palate, the practitioner abandons the earth and become a space-goer.[102] He can exit from and return to the body via the skull opening called *brahmarandhra*. By means of the destruction of shadow (i.e. one's own subtle body residues that limit one's practice), he will be able to see with the eyes of Brahman, enter the bodies of all others as easy as sun rays enter water.[103] He loses all qualities and liberates himself from all doctrines – he becomes like Bhairava.[104] Without *kuṇḍalinī,* these nectar extractions, being the basis of the *yoginīyoga,* are impossible.

In chapter 34, the goddess asks Bhairava about the clan-liquids (*kuladravyas*), which here stand for the most prominent part of non-dual knowledge and its transmission. Bhairava lists the body products used in rituals, and the women (including close relatives) from whom these can be obtained. All *siddhis* arise from the partaking of nectars,[105] and it also pleases the gods and goddesses of this tradition. At the very end of the chapter, Bhairava converts the previously described external practice to being internal. Having listed eight *śaktis* as low-status women stationed in sacred places all over India, he propounds that the ninth is *kuṇḍalinī* herself. And when she comes out of her *kanda* house, she brings *siddhis* to the eight other places. Without *kuṇḍalinī* the meeting (*melaka*) with *yoginīs* is impossible.[106] Thus, the external sacred site of Prayāga is reinterpreted as the contact point of *iḍā* and *suṣumnā:* the site of Varuṇa is situated between the eyebrows; Kaula corresponds to the uvula (*lambika*); the tip of the nose is Aṭṭahāsa; Jayantī is situated in reality in the opening of the palate (*tāla; tālu*); Caritrā is a place above *bindu*; Ekāmrā is in the navel; Devīkoṭa is the *kanda*. Therefore one does not need to wander: *kuṇḍalinī* includes everything.[107] This chapter is an example of the reinterpretation of antinomian practices by presenting them as being a part of the *kuṇḍalinī* process. Passages such as this appear when the Kula and especially Kaula practices were made to fit a community of practitioners far removed from the literary interpretations of the early tantras.

## Conclusion

The *Jayadrathayāmala* mentions the three main channels, *iḍā, piṅgalā* and *suṣumnā,* in a variety of contexts.

1. These are deities surrounding Bhairava.
2. They appear in the context of a single rising of *kuṇḍalinī* (in *ṣaṭka* 1), incorporating Saiddhāntika yoga, and are linked to initiation.
3. The channels are used in the context of repeated practices of attracting someone, and placing them under control. This is a Śaiva-Śākta yoga, which brings the consciousness of the practitioner to the desired place in the subtle body repeatedly and at will, depending on the supernatural effects s/he aims to achieve.
4. Channels, *marmas* and 'doors' of the organs of senses are used in the context of nectar extraction in the *yoginīyoga*, in which the predators and the victims are clear, but the final state is somewhat blurry. The intermediate state is definitely a transformation into a non-human being – be it a *yoginī,* a *khecarī,* a space mother or even a *brahmarākṣasa* – but what is the final state? What is the identity with the goddess of almost one thousand nine hundred names (mentioned in the JY), which the *sādhaka* is supposed to achieve? This is an open question, but it is related to the Krama tradition with its *nistaraṅga* state.
5. If the Saiddhāntika and the *yoginīyoga* appeared simultaneously in time – and both definitely before the final redaction of the JY around the ninth to tenth century – then Krama yoga, with the *nistaraṅga* state as the highest stage, might have been written down not far away from the moment when the JY was redacted. Here, the already well-known awakening of *kuṇḍalinī* clearly aims to resolve the contradiction between Saiddhāntika yoga and the nectar-extraction yoga, placing both within the play of the absolute consciousness, making them thus purely internal; that is to say 'Krama swallows *kuṇḍalinī*'. A similar strategy, but at a different level was used with Kaula practices of extracting nectar from women (including

in one's family), as recounted in the original passages. Later, in quasi-commentarial passages, these descriptions were reinterpreted as stages of awakening and locations in the subtle body.[108] That is to say: 'antinomian practices are swallowed by the concept of *kuṇḍalinī*'. It is likely that the Kaula reinterpretation preceded the Krama one. The JY should be thus seen as a yogic tree in whose rings of two hundred and two surviving chapters the history of some yogas and their interconnections between the fifth and ninth centuries CE can be traced.

But what about the relation of 'yoga' and 'tantra'? Yoga in the JY means a method of reaching the highest state across the traditions named above; it is not a tradition in itself that has its own aim and philosophy. Yoga here is a 'know-how' and not the goal. Tantra in selected passages means simply 'text', and, depending on which tradition it belongs to – be it Siddhānta, Kula, Kaula or Krama – it might prescribe significantly different aims and methods of yoga. Thus in the ninth to tenth centuries, there is no constructed opposition of 'yoga' and 'tantra' – this distinction would be created much later in history. However, there is a desire to 'digest' the most antinomian tantric elements (i.e. related to *yoginīyoga* and Kaula), such as vampire practices or extracting nectar from women including in one's family, by reconfiguring them as purely internal – and this interiorisation is done in both cases by linking them to *kuṇḍalinī*.

## Glossary

*abhicāra*, black magic
Abhinavagupta, eleventh-century systematiser of the tantras, who lived in Kashmir
*ākāśamaṇḍala*, cosmic *maṇḍala*
*ākāśamātara*, space 'mother', i.e. goddess of the high rank
*amṛtavāhinī*, lit. flow of nectar, synonym of *suṣumnā* in JY
*ānanda*, great pleasure, bliss
*aṅkuśa*, *mudrā* of the elephant goad
*āsana*, body position
*ātman*, self, soul, not entirely equal to *jīva* in JY
*āveśa*, deity possession of the *sādhaka*'s body
*bali*, non-vegetarian offering, often for the demons or tantric deities
*bhairavas*, class of male deities, worshipped in the Mantrapīṭha class of tantras according to the classification of Sanderson 1990
*bhrama*, or going randomly
*bindu*, 'drop', the innermost subtle essence of a living being, sometimes synonymous with *jīva*, i.e. soul, visible to the yogis and the *yoginis*; *jīva* is manipulated in initiation and the vampiric practice
*brahmarākṣasa*, a kind of demonic being, often fond of human flesh, a desirable state in some chapters of the JY
*brahmarandhra*, opening of Brahman, the last 'door' to be opened on the top of the skull, through which the yogi can exit and re-enter
*cakras*, circles of deities that are to be seen; sites within the body, which are sometimes seen as knots to be broken
*cārya*, mode of behaviour required for a particular religious practice
*cit*, consciousness
*dhāraṇā*, controlled visualisation
*dhyāna*, visionary state, in which the visions are spontaneous rather than imposed
*dīkṣā*, initiation. In JY, this includes *vedha* and *yoḍha*

*dīpikā, mocikā, etc.* five principles of consciousness rooted in the *Svacchandabhairava Tantra*, and sometimes seen as goddesses

*gamāgama*, 'coming and going', see also *helādolā*

*ghaṇṭikā*, a small bell, likely the uvula, which is also called *laṃbika*, a particular centre in the region of palate. See also *tālu*

*ghaṭṭana*, part of Śaiva initiation where the guru pretends to beat the disciple to ensure his protection

*ghūrmi*, state of being blissfully intoxicated

*granthi*, knots in the subtle body along the central channel

*helādolā*, coming and going procedure, see also *gamāgama*, both are used in the vampiric practices of the *yoginīs*

*iḍā*, left channel

*Jayadrathayāmala*, ninth to tenth century tantric text, constisting of four ṣaṭkas and two hundred and two chapters, a compilation of around five hundred earlier tantric texts

*jīva*, soul or life-principle, being extracted by guru in initiation, and by the *yoginīs* in the vampiric practices

*jvala*, flaming in the body, heat

*kaivalya*, 'isolation', final state in the Sāṃkhya tradition

*kalā*, part, aspect

Kālasaṃkarṣiṇī, She Who Retracts Time; name of the main goddess of the JY

*kalpa*, manual of worship

*kanda*, the place where the *kuṇḍalinī* is said to be stationed prior to awakening

Kaula, a tradition based on a re-reading of the Kula tradition, according to Sanderson 1990

*khecarī*, 'going in the air', highest rank of *yoginīs* and the state the *sādhaka* tries to achieve

*kriyā*, 'something to be done', a set of required actions in a religious practice

*kṛtyā*, practice of externalisation of an aspect of the subtle body of the practitioner in order to achieve a desired aim. This externalised part is seen as a (semi-) independent being.

Kula, the oldest tradition linked to the *yoginīs*

*kuladravyas*, the clan-liquids, carrying non-dual knowledge and the essence of its transmission, i.e. a mixture of body-products

*kumbhaka*, breath retention

Kuṇḍaleśvarī, Mistress of the Kuṇḍalinī, a personified *kuṇḍalinī*, a goddess in JY

*kuṇḍalinī*, the cosmic energy sleeping as potential in the human body as well as the process of its awakening

*mahākaraṇa yoga*, yoga of the supreme body, which is seen as the next level from the *sukṣma*, or subtle body.

*marmas*, the vulnerable points, often used as doors through which the *yoginīs* and other such beings can enter the human body

*melaka* or *melāpa*, meeting with *yoginīs*

*mudrās*, body positions including gestures and mental states related to them, or being provoked by them.

*mūla, see kanda*

*mūrtis*, in JY personal forms, that have the form of *vyoma*. The forms that *sādhaka* can assume

*nāḍī*, channels, the ways for the *prāṇa*

*nirodha*, limit, in JY it is yogic visualisation, allowing cessation of the mind

*nistaraṅga* state, the supreme state in the Krama, although the term 'waveless ocean' occurs already in the *Svacchandatantra*. Refers to the state manifesting when the consciousness of the practitioner crosses *brahmarandhra* and is close to the 'end of the 12'

*parama daśa*, supreme state, see also *paramārtha*
*paramārtha*, the highest state, sometimes used as synonym of the Krama
Parameśvara, supreme lord, state of Bhairava.
*pāśa*, mudrā of the rope
*paśu*, *animal of burden*, a 'victim to be sacrificed' in JY
*patana*, falling, a mark of a special state in which practitioner may find himself
*piṅgalā*, right channel
*pramāṇa*, means of knowledge
*prāṇa*, vital breath
*prāṇāyāma*, or breath control
*pratyāhāra*, the control of the senses, in JY seeing one's own mind and realising the karmic and other faults
*puruṣa*, the supreme person and state in *Sāṃkhya*, the 25th from 36/37 *śaiva tattvas*
*rasa*, juice, subtle essence
*roma*, horripilation
*ṣaḍadhvan*, six ways used in Śaiva initiation, may also refer to each of the six possible ways that *kuṇḍalinī* may take while rising from the *kanda*
Sadāśiva, 'Ever Auspicious One', main deity of the Siddhānta tradition
*sādhaka*, practitioner
*sādhana*, practice
Saiddhāntika Śaiva yoga, yoga described in the texts of the Śaiva Siddhānta
Śaiva yoga, yoga aiming at the achieving of the state of Śiva, mostly Saiddhāntika
*Śaiva-śākta yoga*, this yoga reflects the state when the Siddhāntika structures started to be filled with the goddesses, but the result is not as independent and radical as in Kula traditions
*śākta*, *śāmbhava* and *āṇava*, types of pervasion, the resulting states of yogic practice and in some cases of initiation
*śakti*, power, sometimes personified as a goddess
*samādhi*, the final limb of the yoga, linked in JY to non-dual perception
Sāṃkhya, one of six philosophical traditions, *darśanas*; the basis of the early Śaiva yoga
*saṃsāra*, world of rebirth
*samvitti*, supreme consciousness, see also *cit*
*saṅkalpa*, single intent
*saptajanmapaśu*, victim reborn seven times only to be killed by the *yoginī*s and *sādhaka*s in order to obtain *siddhi*s
*śaravad*, *daṇḍavad*, *vidyuvad*, manners of rising of the *kuṇḍalinī*, as a stick, serpent, lightning
*siddhi*, supernatural capacities achieved by *yoga*
*ṣoḍhā*, purification
*spanda*, subtle vibration, makes sense for the yogi only once the *bindu* has been mastered. The state where *spanda* stops is the *nistaraṅga*
*stobha*, paralysis, temporary suspension of mind and body, a state necessary for successful initiation in JY
*sūkṣma*, subtle body, also called 'shadow'
Śuṣkā/Karaṅkinī, the Dry One or the Skeleton One, the goddess in JY
*suṣumnā*, central channel
Svacchandabhairava, main deity of the *Svacchandabhairavatantra*
*svatantra*, independence, the state of absolute freedom and non-dependence on anything; state of Bhairava

*tālu*, *palate*
*tantra*, text, often discussing esoteric matters
*tattvas*, refers to worlds and states represented as stationed along the central channel and seen by the yogis
*tejas*, yogic energy, sometimes visible
Trailokyaḍāmarī, Goddess that Dominates the Three Worlds, a goddess in JY
Tumburu, main deity of the Vāma tantras, one of the Bhairavas
*udāna*, the upwards-going kind of *prāṇa*
*Umāyāmala*, a text partly incorporated in JY, probably the same as *Devīyāmala*
Vāgbhaveśvarī, Mistress of the Speech, a goddess in the JY
Vātacakreśvarī, the Mistress of the circle of Wind, a goddess in JY
*vedha* and *yoḍha*, the forceful opening of the central channel, which gives rise to *kuṇḍalinī*, that results in 'joining' (*yoḍha*) to the highest state
*vetāla*, practice of making the deity or spirit enter a dead body and revive it for a short period
*vicitra*, synonym of *suṣumnā* in JY
*vidyā*, *mantra* of the goddess
Vidyāpīṭha, 'seat of *vidyās*', a strand of worship invoking goddesses and not the male Bhairavas within the Mantramārga, according to Sanderson 1990
*vimāna*, aerial chariot
*virakta*, or the non-attraction, likely synonymous with *kailvalya*
*vīras*, heroes, tantric practitioners and sometimes *bhairavas*
*vīrya*, mantra-activator
*visarga* state, the highest state, close to the 'end of the 12'
*viṣuva*, synonym of *suṣumnā* in JY, term is only applicable once *vedha* has been successful
*vitarka*, discernment
*vyakti*, 'clarity', something that becomes evident
*vyāpti*, pervasion
*vyoma*, space, the topmost, the most subtle of the elements
*yantra*, mechanism
Yantrapramardanī, Destroyer of the *Yantras*, a goddess of the JY. She destroys precisely the mechanisms that block the way to the underground worlds, called *patāla*
yoga, method to achieve the absolute state in JY
*yoginī*, feminine being involved in tantric practice
*yoginīyoga*, *yoga* of the *yoginīs*, refers to a set of traditions and texts describing the advanced techniques of the mastery of the channels and *cakras* that are used for the vampire-like extractions of *rasas* from the bodies of other beings

## Abbreviations

| | |
|---|---|
| BG | *Bhagavadgītā* |
| DDŚ | *Devīdyvardhaśatikā,* alias *Śrīsārdhaśatikā* |
| JY | *Jayādrathayāmala* |
| KMT | *Kubjikāmatatantra* |
| KSB | *Kramasadbhāva* |
| NTS | *Niśvāsatattvasaṃhitā* |
| SVT | *Svacchandatantra* |
| YSP | *Yoginīsaṃcāraprakaraṇa* |

## Notes

1 I am referring to the widespread view, although not supported by older Sanskrit texts, that 'yoga' is something pure and respected, while 'tantra' is black magic, employing antinomian means and being radically different from yoga both in aims and methods.
2 This chapter has a substantial glossary for the reader to consult, and so not every term is translated and defined in the main body of the text.
3 These techniques are performed via yogic procedures and from a distance, but preliminary contact between the practitioner and the victim should be established (Serbaeva 2015a).
4 The subchapters of some longer chapters disappeared at an early date and, calculating the length of the surviving subchapters, one comes close to five thousand verses (see Serbaeva in 2007 and 2019).
5 See glossary.
6 JY.1.4.31a. *Suṣumnā* as goddess can be found in JY.1.15.85ab.
7 First noted by Alexis Sanderson, personal communication 2009, see SVT.10.1226. This passage is addressed JY.1.5.5ab.
8 JY.1.9.231.
9 The name of the text is not mentioned in the JY.
10 JY.1.12.5.
11 The yogic body in the JY is not limited by the boundaries of the physical body, and some points, which the consciousness of the yogi is supposed to reach in successful practice, are to be found above his head. One of the most important is called *dvādaśānta*, 'the end of the twelve [fingers above the head]'.
12 JY.1.12.50. This is a rather rare representation, since the usual one would be based on the three eyes of Śiva, standing respectively for the sun-moon-fire and having 12-16-10 aspects.
13 JY.1.12.62ab.
14 For example, JY.1.12.63. The state of Sadāśiva is promised throughout the first part of the chapter, and Sadāśiva is the main deity in the Saiddhāntika tradition, i.e. this chapter can be an adaptation of an early Siddhāntika text on yoga.
15 Silburn, 1988/[1983]: 108. In her sources, the SVT and the *Śaktivijñāna,* these gods are still in masculine.
16 JY.1.12.85cd-86.
17 JY.1.12.104cd.
18 JY.1.12.106cd.
19 *Kanda* is a bulb in which *kuṇḍalinī* is to be found in inactive state, and from which it rises upon awakening.
20 JY.1.12.139cd-140ab.
21 To take only the NTS for example, pp. 101–102, summary, pp. 495–501 translation of NTS.4.119-114b.
22 JY.1.12.151cd-154ab.
23 On *mudrās* in the JY, see Serbaeva 2013b.
24 JY.1.12.155cd-166.
25 JY.1.12.192 further repeated and expounded at JY.1.12.198cd-201ab. The lists of *siddhis* are repeated more than twice in the same chapter and they do not fit each other, which suggests that more than one text was used in compiling this chapter.
26 JY.1.12.204. Further on in the JY there are techniques of opening the central channels, which seems to be done from the junction point between *iḍā* and *suṣumṇā*. Joining of the channel also refers to a particular procedure in the Śaiva initiation, in which the bodies of the guru and of the initiand are connected by a long herb. On that see Brünner, SSP, vol. 3. The *cakras* in this context appear to be a sort of blockage, virtually synonymous with 'knots' or *granthis*.
27 JY.1.12.290cd.
28 JY.1.12.292cd.
29 JY.1.12.299.
30 NTS, pp. 43–44. The fact that *ṣaḍadhvan* appears to be a developed concept in the JY places this part of the JY later than the seventh century CE, according to the evidence of the *Svāyambhuvasutrasangraha*. On the six ways in the Nātha texts, see also Silburn 1988/[1983]: 130.
31 JY.1.12.393-395ab.
32 JY.1.12.396-397ab.
33 JY.1.12.419cd-420. 'Five hoods' or 'five-hooded serpent' is a Śaiva term for five *prāṇas*, used often in the Krama-influenced texts.
34 JY.1.12.421-427ab. One also finds 'in the manner of a serpent' in *Haṭhayogapradīpikā* 3.108ab, which echoes the *Ūrmikaulārṇava* 2.104ab (*sarpavat kuṭilākārā*).

35 JY.1.12.427cd-429ab.
36 JY.1.12.429cd-431.
37 JY.1.12.432-435ab.
38 JY.1.12.438a: *ṣaḍrasākṛṣṭir atulā*. Blood, skin, meat, etc. These are the essences that are being extracted by the *yoginīs* from the victims, and by the *sādhakas* to please the *yoginīs*.
39 JY.1.12.438b *Ṣaḍūrmi śrutir uttamāḥ*. Likely, some of the 'revelations' are mentioned in the TST.6.176–178, namely *upadeśa, saṃpradāya, kaulika*, obtained from various kinds of *yoginīs*.
40 JY.1.12.435cd-439.
41 JY.1.12.440-448.
42 These being Brahmā, Viṣṇu and the three forms of Śiva being present in the knots of the subtle body.
43 JY.1.12.449-452ab.
44 The names of all of the six *cakras* from *mūlādhāra* to *sahasrāra* can be found in the JY, but they are not listed in succession, suggesting that the sequence was already well known and self-evident.
45 JY.1.12.452cd-JY.1.12.453ab.
46 JY.1.12.453cd-454ab. *Ṣaṭka* 3 mentions three *vyomas* only, and these correspond in the names to the three kinds of *āveśa* here. See next note.
47 JY.1.12.454cd-458. On three pervasions JY.1.12.458ab: *evam aikātmyasaṃpattyā śākta śāmbhavam āṇavam*. These three kinds of pervasion were taken into TĀ by Abhinavagupta, see TĀ.1.168–170, etc.
48 JY.1.12.459ab.
49 JY.2.8.27-29.
50 JY.2.8.32cd-35ab.
51 May be identical with the *Devīyāmala*.
52 *Stobha* is a sort of spontaneously occurring suspension of the discursive thought with some bodily effects. It is considered positive, and also happens in the Śaiva initiation. JY.2.12.21.
53 JY.2.12.76cd-78ab. *Nistaraṅga*, or 'waveless' state, is the synonym of the absolute state of consciouness in the Krama tradition. JY has blocks of chapters that propound the Krama in the last three *ṣaṭkas*.
54 The whole passage JY.2.13.39-54. *Paravedam* in verse 45ab is likely *paravedham*. There is a confusion in all Nepalese manuscripts between *vedha-* and *veda-*, i.e. 'piercing' and 'knowledge'. See also 48ab: *prabuddhā vedayet sarvam ābrahma[I ā]bha[I u]vanāntikam*, and 50cd, *tadā vedayate jagat*.
55 BG11.10=MBH.6.33.10a.
56 JY.2.23.70cd-73.
57 JY.3.8.109ab.
58 JY.3.8.107cd-108ab.
59 JY.3.8.193ab.
60 The *sūkṣma* manipulations allow not only to kill or control at a distance, but also to initiate a disciple; see Serbaeva 2010b, and JY.3.8.256-269ab. Similar procedures are further described in JY.3.29.
61 It is a paradoxical chapter, in which the *sādhaka* is supposed to desire to be transformed into a *brahmarākṣasa*, who are seen both in the *purāṇas* and the *tantras* as the monsters of a lower kind, often devouring humans.
62 This expression occurs at least three times in the JY (3.26.110ab and 4.31.24ab and 28cd) and besides that in the Krama texts such as DDŚ.49ab and KSB.5.9ab. The most ancient reference, however, is the NS.13.20cd, discovered by Sanderson.
63 JY.3.15.3cd
64 JY.3.15.11-12.
65 JY.3.15.22ab and 23.
66 JY.3.15.28cd, *śaktipiṇḍaṃs tadā bhavet*.
67 JY.3.15.32cd-33. On liberation and *jīvanmukti* in the JY see also Serbaeva 2010a.
68 JY.3.15.74cd-83ab.
69 Silburn 1975: 111–115 on the twelve Kālīs, each going to a peaceful state, opening the way for the next one in the ancient *Kramastotra*.
70 JY.3.15.109cd-118.
71 JY.3.15.119ab-126ab.
72 JY.3.15.126cd-127ab.
73 JY.3.15.127cd-128ab.
74 JY.3.15.128cd-129ab.
75 JY.3.15.130cd-131ab.
76 JY.3.15.133cd: *so['/]haṃ mayaiva [...] haṃsoham eva ca*. Word play *haṃsa* (swan) - *so['/]haṃ* 'I am that', which shall permeate all later yogic texts.

77 JY.3.15.134cd-135ab.
78 JY.3.15.137cd-138ab.
79 JY.3.15.145cd-146ab.
80 JY.3.15.146cd-147ab.
81 JY.3.15.147cd.
82 JY.3.15.186cd.
83 JY.3.15.187cd.
84 JY.3.15.188ab.
85 JY.3.15.203ab.
86 JY.3.15.214, 215cd-16ab. The switch from 'I' to 'he' is indeed confusing, and can be explained by asserting that two separate texts were combined at this point: one describes the experience of a yogi in *nistaraṅga* state, and the other one tries to justify the practice of nectar extraction, by presenting it as a non-dual and thus uncontradictory transfer of the essence between the world and the beings therein and the principles of sun and moon.
87 JY.3.15.222ab.
88 JY.3.15.261.
89 JY.3.16.28cd-31.
90 Note the preference for the *iḍā-suṣumṇā* junction in the *ṣaṭka* 1.
91 YSP, edited by Sanderson; draft used with permission.
92 JY.3.29.50-51.
93 JY.3.29.55ab.
94 JY.3.29.55cd-58ab.
95 JY.3.29.58cd-59ab.
96 I believe that the central channel is considered to be related to the upward flow of *prāṇa*, while the other two, iḍā and piṅgala, lead the *prāṇa* downwards. Another way to interpret this is simply left (*iḍā*) as opposed to right (*piṅgalā*).
97 JY.4.11.2cd-4.
98 JY.4.31.28.
99 JY.4.31.27. On the technicalities of meeting the *yoginīs* see Serbaeva 2015b and 2013a.
100 The text is *amṛtākṛṣṇakarṣayet* in three surviving manuscripts; the fourth one lacks this passage. Conj ecture: *amṛtākṛṣṭi+[ā]karṣayet*, i.e. *amṛtākṛṣṭyākarṣaet*. *Amṛtākṛṣṭi* is a typical term for this practice in JY, also occurring in JY.2.17.607ab and JY.2.17.667ab, but also in the *Tantrasadbhāva* 3.210ab and the *Ṣaṭsāhasrasaṃhitā* 19.47cd.
101 This is done by a particular eye movement.
102 JY.4.31.29-31ab.
103 JY.4.31.31cd-33ab.
104 JY.4.31.33cd-34.
105 JY.4.34.37ab and 42. Contrary to the practices in *ṣaṭka* 3, which can be in brief be termed vampiric blood extractions, here the nectars are sexual liquids. At least judging from the nectar appellation and the definition of the *yoginīs*, these are not the same traditions.
106 JY.4.34.69-71ab.
107 JY.4.34.71cd-74.
108 See parallel in TST.15 and KMT.25 reinterpreting all cremation ground symbols and objects as being internal and *kuṇḍalinī*-related, and JY.4.34 here.

## Bibliography

### *Primary sources and manuscripts*

Dyczkowski. M. n.d. (prelim. ed). n.d. *Devīdyvardhaśatikā,* alias *Śrīsārdhaśatikā*. MS K: NAK MS no 1242; NGMPP: reel No. A161 DDS.112. MS Kh: NAK MS no. 55184 Śaivatantra 655; NGMPP: reel no. A 161 DDS.114.

Dyczkowski, M. (ed). *Kramasadbhāva*. MS 1–76, *Śaivatantra* 144, A209.23.

Dyczkowski, M. (ed) n.d. *Tantrasadbhāvatantra* partially and provisionally edited by Dyczkowski, M. S. G., MS K 1-1985 śaivatantra 1533, NGMPP A188/22; MS Kh 1–363 śaivatantra, NGMPP A44/1, MS G 5–445 śaivatantra 185, NGMPP A44/2. E-text: Muktabodha. Accessed in 2005.

Goodall, D. (ed) [2015] *The Niśvāsatattvasaṃhitā: The Earliest Surviving Śaiva Tantra*, edited by Goodall, D. et al. Pondicherry, India: Institut Français de Pondichéry.
Goudriaan, T. and Schoterman, J. A. (eds) 1988. *The Kubjikāmatatantra*. Leiden: Brill.
Sanderson, A. n.d. *Niśisaṃcāra Tantra*. Sanderson, A. G. J. S. (ed) [Unpublished variant of 9.10.2004.] MS: NAK 1-1606 *śaivatantra 102*, NGMPP B26/25. Used with permission.
Sanderson, A. (ed) n.d. *(Jayadrathayāmale) Yoginīsaṃcāraprakaraṇam*. [Unpublished variant of 06.10.2004.] Used with permission.
Serbaeva, O. 2019. *Jayādrathayāmala*. Transcript of the full text, based on selected Nepalese manuscripts.
Shastri, M. K. (ed) 1921–1935. *Svacchandatantra*. Vol. 1–6. Bombay: Nirnaya Sagar.
Shastri, M. R. and Shastri, M. K. (eds) 1918–1938. *The Tantrāloka of Abhinavagupta. With Commentary of Rājanaka Jayaratha*. Vol. 1–12. Allahabad and Bombay.
Sukthankar, V. et al. (eds) 1933–1972. *The Mahābhārata,* for the First Time Critically Edited. 19 Volumes. Poona: Bhandarkar Oriental Research Institute.

## Secondary sources

Sanderson, A. 1990. 'Śaivism and the Tantric Traditions', in Hardy, F. (ed), *The World's Religions: The Religions of Asia*, 128–172. London: Routledge.
Sanderson, A. 2009. 'The Śaiva Age: The Rise and Dominance of Śaivism during the Early Medieval Period', in Einoo, S. (ed), *Genesis and Development of Tantrism*, 41–350. Tokyo: Institute of Oriental Culture, University of Tokyo, 2009. Institute of Oriental Culture Special Series, 23.
Serbaeva, O. 2010a. 'Liberation In Life and After Death in Early Śaiva Mantramārgic Texts. The Problem of *Jīvanmukti*', in Bigger, A., Krajnc, R., Mertens, A., Schüpbach, M. and Wessler, H. W. (eds), *Release from Life - Release in Life. Indian Perspectives on Individual Liberation*, 211–233. Bern: Peter Lang.
Serbaeva, O. 2010b. 'When to Kill Means to Liberate: Two Types of Rituals in Vidyāpīṭha Texts', in *Grammars and Morphologies of Ritual Practices in Asia*, 65–84, 2010, 1. Wiesbaden: Harrassowitz.
Serbaeva, O. 2013a. 'Can Encounters with Yoginīs in the *Jayadrathayā*mala be Described as Possession?', in Keul, I. (ed), '*Yoginī' in South Asia: Interdisciplinary Approaches*, 198–212. London: Routledge.
Serbaeva, O. 2013b. 'Mudrās', in Jacobsen, K. A. (ed) with Basu, H., Malinar, A. and Narayanan, V (ass. eds), *Brill's Encyclopedia of Hinduism*, 91–99. Vol. 5. Leiden: Brill.
Serbaeva, O. 2015a. 'Yoga from Yoginīs' Point of View', in *The Journal of Hindu Studies*, 8: 245–262. https://doi.org/10.1093/jhs/hiv019
Serbaeva, O. 2015b. 'The Varieties of *Melaka* in the *Jayadrathayāmala*: Some Reflections on the Terms *Haṭha* and *Priya*', in Olesen, B. W. (ed), *Goddess Traditions in Tantric Hinduism: History, Practice and Doctrine*, 51–73. Oxon: Routledge.
Serbaeva, O. Forthcoming a. 'Avyapadeśyā: Indefinable Kālī, Edition and translation of the chapter 35 of the 3rd *ṣaṭka* of the *Jayadrathayāmala* on Kālī that defies definition', to appear in Slouber, M. (ed), *Garland of Forgotten Goddesses: A Sourcebook*. Oxford University Press.
Serbaeva, O. Forthcoming b. '*Saptajanmapaśu* in Śaiva Traditions and in the *Abhidhānottara*', to appear in Malinar, A. (ed), *The Proceedings of ZICILP 1, Transgression and Encounters with the Terrible in Buddhist and Śaiva Tantras*. University of Zürich.
Silburn, L. (trans and intro) 1975. *Hymnes aux Kālī: la roue des énergies divines: études sur le śivaïsme du Cachemire: école Krama*. Paris: Institut de civilisation indienne.
Silburn, L. 1988 [1983]. *Kuṇḍalinī: The Energy of the Depths: A Comprehensive Study Based on the Scriptures of Nondualistic Kaśmir Śaivism*. Gontier, J. (tr). Albany: State University of New York Press. [Fr. original ed.] Paris: Les Deux Océans.
Vasudeva, S. 2004. *The Yoga of the Mālinīvijayottaratantra. Chapters 1–4, 7, 11–17*. Pondichéry: Institut Français de Pondichery, École Française d'Extrême-Orient.

# 9

# EARLY *HAṬHAYOGA*[1]

*Mark Singleton*

## Introduction

Scholarly uses of the term '*haṭhayoga*' are in some respects constructs used to identify systems of predominantly physical yoga practices such as postures (*āsana*), breath retentions (*kumbhaka*) and yogic seals (*mudrā*) leading to certain psycho-physical results, such as special powers (*siddhi*), physical immortality or liberation from the cycle of samsaric existence (*mukti*, *mokṣa*, *kaivalya*, etc.). None of these practice categories (nor their results) are exclusive to *haṭhayoga*, and many of the practices formative of *haṭha* from the eleventh century onwards had already been in existence for many centuries. Moreover, some of the texts identified by recent scholarship as being constitutive of the early *haṭha* corpus do not refer to their yoga as *haṭha*, and the same is true for later (Brahmanical) assimilations of *haṭha* systems, such as the eighteenth-century Yoga Upaniṣads (see Bouy 1994). Furthermore, taxonomies of yoga types which include *haṭha* that occur in some texts are collapsed and simplified in others, or ignored altogether in favour of the general term 'yoga', and practices not originally considered to be part of *haṭha* are later introduced and synthesised into it. To complicate matters further the meaning of the term *haṭha* – and hence the *sādhana* (pratice) of those who do it – may change, sometimes considerably, according to the context in which it is undertaken. Three examples striking in their differences would be tantric sexual ritual in Vajrayāna Buddhism, renouncer traditions of Hinduism, and modern, globalised yoga, all of which may call their yoga *haṭha*. Finally *haṭha* texts may comprise not only physical techniques but also methods of concentration, meditation and *samādhi*, challenging any straightforward definition of *haṭha* as 'physical yoga'. For example, the c. thirteenth-century *Dattātreyayogaśāstra* integrates the auxiliaries of *pratyāhāra* (withdrawal of the senses) and *dhāraṇā* (meditation) into its discussion of *haṭhayoga*.

Nevertheless, insofar as *haṭha* does exist as a common (if polyvalent) emic term within texts and among practitioners, it points to several key developmental phases in yoga's history, which continue to inform the way that yoga is practised and thought about today both within the traditional yoga-practising lineages of India, and in modern, global contexts. It therefore provides an essential frame for understanding the development of yoga as a whole over the past millennium. For the purposes of this chapter, then, 'early *haṭhayoga*' denotes innovative methods of predominantly physical practice (which may or may not self-identify as *haṭha*), beginning in about the eleventh century CE and continuing up to and including the composition of the *Haṭhapradīpikā* in c. 1450.[2] The *Haṭhapradīpikā* quickly became a popular and influential text, as attested by the large numbers of its manuscripts, and by the assimilation of its verses into later compendia and compilations. The centuries following its composition saw an increasing assimilation of its techniques into mainstream religious practice in India (Birch 2018). As demonstrated by Bouy

(1994) and Mallinson (2014), the *Haṭhapradīpikā* is itself in large measure a compilation of verses from earlier texts, and it is these (Sanskrit) texts that can be said to form the basis for a corpus of 'early *haṭha*'. This corpus has been central to new scholarly understandings of *haṭha*'s history, and it is this history that informs the current chapter.[3]

## Textual criticism and *haṭhayoga*

Key to these understandings is the method of philological textual criticism, which draws on multiple manuscript witnesses of a particular text to create, through careful comparison and editorial judgement, a 'critical edition'.[4] Such editions seek to avoid the reproduction of anomalous elements such as scribal errors in any one particular manuscript and to arrive at the best possible reading of the text. Textual criticism is the basis of the contemporary discipline of Indology, which emerged out of the study of the (Greek and Roman) Classics.[5] Textual criticism of yoga, without regard for other historical sources such as iconography and ethnography, has its limitations. For example, *haṭha* practices that appear for the first time in a particular text may have been well known and practised for a long time previously, passed down orally, and only incorporated into texts at a much later stage. Individually, they do not, therefore, provide more than a sometimes narrow window onto the broader yogic culture of the period. Moreover, it is often difficult to accurately date the texts themselves, and therefore to make conclusive statements about *haṭha*'s chronological development history.

That said, textual criticism remains the best single methodological tool we have for reconstructing yoga's past, especially in combination with art historical sources (e.g. Diamond 2013), archaeology and iconography (e.g. Powell 2018) and early travellers' accounts (such as Tavernier's 1925/1676 account of his travels in India), as well as ethnographies of 'traditional' contemporary practitioners of *haṭhayoga* (e.g. Bevilacqua 2017). What is more, manuscripts are not isolated events but rather intertexual complexes through which continuity, conflict and innovation in yoga traditions can be discerned – such as in the already mentioned borrowing of verses from earlier texts, the importation and assimilation of practices from one religious tradition into another,[6] and criticisms by one lineage of the practices and practitioners of another (see Mallinson and Singleton 2017: 39–45). This enables a detailed and progressively more nuanced picture of yoga's historical development to emerge.

## Precursors of *haṭhayoga*

The non-technical, general meaning of the word *haṭha* is 'forceful' or 'violent', and the compound '*haṭhayoga*' therefore connotes a yoga that is accomplished by forceful methods. Although the authors of *haṭha* texts themselves do not prescribe forceful practices (and, indeed, commonly advise against them, Birch 2011), it is possible for scholars to trace some of the practices of *haṭhayoga* back to ancient ascetic austerities known as *tapas* (lit. 'heat'). Within the Vedic tradition, such austerities are usually intended to develop power, and thereby to force a boon from a god. Many examples of this can be found in stories from the epic and purāṇic literature. In extra-Vedic renouncer traditions dating from the second half of the first millennium BCE – such as the various groups of renunciant ascetics in the 'Magadha' region of northern India known collectively as Śramaṇas[7] – *tapas* practices function to still the fluctuations of the mind or to erase accumulated karma (Bronkhorst 2007; see also Mallinson and Singleton 2017: xiii–xv). Not yet referred to as yoga (itself at this time much more closely associated with meditation practice, or *dhyānayoga*), these techniques (which include *prāṇāyāma* (breath control) methods and practices which foreshadow *haṭhayoga* techniques like *khecarīmudrā*) found their way into later *haṭha* practice as yoga, albeit often adapted and repurposed from the original contexts. Indeed, key practices of *haṭha* such as *āsana* and *prāṇāyāma* are often still referred to as *tapas* in much later yogic contexts (Mallinson and Singleton 2017: 92–94, 129–130), and even today in yoga-practising ascetic lineages in India, *haṭha* is explicitly considered to be a practice of *tapas* (Bevilacqua 2017). Raising and maintaining *bindu* remains an important rationale for *haṭha* practice, both in texts and in contemporary Indian asceticism.

*Haṭhayoga* has close historical ties with Vajrayāna Buddhism. The term *haṭhayoga* first occurs in the fourth-century CE *Yogācārabhūmiśāstra*, but is not defined there. It occurs in multiple Vajrayāna texts between the eighth and the twelfth centuries, where it is predominantly associated with restoration and/or restraint of semen (*vīrya, bodhicitta*) especially during sexual ritual, and is considered a practice of last resort (Mallinson forthcoming). Puṇḍarīka's eleventh-century commentary on the *Kālacakratantra*, the *Vimalaprabhā*, defines *haṭha* as the restraint of semen and raising the breath up the central channel, two features which will continue to be constitutive of *haṭhayoga* in later, non-Buddhist contexts (Birch 2011: 536). However, the sexual ritual constitutive of *haṭhayoga* in Vajrayāna contexts is absent in these later works.

Models of the yogic body deriving from the tantric traditions (mainly Śaiva, Vaiṣṇava and Buddhist, beginning with the fifth-century *Niśvāsatattvasaṃhitā*), and originally tantric practices that manipulate or control that body, became central to many systems of *haṭha*. Although not exclusive to tantric systems, such models of the yogic body are key to understanding how (and on what) *haṭha* practices are intended to work. Tantric yoga often contains complex and multisensory 'visualisations' of a ritualised, divinised body conceived as a microcosmic analogue of the macrocosmic universe or godhead, and typically consists of a network of channels (*nāḍī*) along which move winds (*vāyu*) or vital essences, and various locations (*ādhāras*, *marmans*, *cakras*, etc.) through which the consciousness of the yogi ascends. Yogic bodies are constructed in response to the doctrine of the particular tradition, and are thus enormously varied and often highly complex (Mallinson and Singleton 2017: chapter 5). The physiology of the yogic body in early *haṭha* tends to be much simpler.[8]

One of the most influential tantric models of the yogic body was the six-*cakra* system of the c. tenth-century *Kubjikāmatatantra* of the 'western transmission' of the Kaula cult of the goddess Kubjikā, in which variant forms of Kubjikā and her consort were visualised at various locations (called *cakras*, or 'wheels') along the spine. Thus, *cakras* were originally non-physical loci for meditative practice, rather than the a priori physical entities they became in some later *haṭha* texts.[9] The *Kubjikāmata*'s six-*cakra* model (sometimes, with the inclusion of *sahasrāra* at the crown, counted as seven) later became more widely accepted in yoga compendia that incorporated *haṭhayoga* after the seventeenth century. It is also the best known *cakra* system in modern, global yoga. Also occurring for the first time in the *Kubjikāmatatantra* is the coiled serpent goddess Kuṇḍalinī (there, a manifestation of Kubjikā), who resides at the base of the spine and is made to rise up the central channel through yogic practice. Raising Kuṇḍalinī becomes one of the central aims of yoga practices in early *haṭha* texts that derive from tantric sources, as well as in later syntheses such as the *Haṭhapradīpikā*.

Referring to a '*bindu* model', and a 'Kuṇḍalinī model' of *haṭhayoga*, Mallinson (2011a) discerns two distinct currents in *haṭha*'s development. Certain texts (such as the eleventh-century *Amṛtasiddhi* and the thirteenth-century *Dattātreyayogaśāstra*) present *haṭha* practices as raising and preserving *bindu*, while others (such as the c. thirteenth-century *Gorakṣaśataka*) describe practices that raise Kuṇḍalinī. In subsequent texts, certain practices are even said to work sometimes on *bindu* and sometimes on Kuṇḍalinī, pointing to the synthetic character of later *haṭhayoga*. In the fifteenth-century *Haṭhapradīpikā*, for example, *khecarīmudrā* (described below) is taught twice, first as a method for controlling *bindu* and then as a way to raise Kuṇḍalinī, thus preserving the divergent sources of *haṭhayoga* within the text, but also creating a measure of internal dissonance.

## Early *haṭha*'s textual corpus

We turn now to a brief consideration of the contents of some of the texts of the early *haṭha* corpus.[10] The earliest text in the *haṭha* corpus as identified by Mallinson (forthcoming) is the Vajrayāna *Amṛtasiddhi*, which does not name its practices *haṭha* but which teaches three physical techniques (*mudrā*) that become central to later non-Buddhist *haṭhayoga*: *mahāmudrā*, *mahābandha*, and *mahāvedha*. The function of these practices, as in the *Vimalaprabhā*, is the retention of semen and the forcing of the breath into the central channel. The text also teaches a four-level sequence of practice – beginning (*ārambha*), action (*ghaṭa*), accumulation (*paricaya*), completion (*niṣpatti*) – which is reproduced in subsequent *haṭha* texts such as the *Dattātreyayogaśāstra*; and four levels of aspirant, the first three of which are first found in the c. 450 CE *Pātañjalayogaśāstra*: mild (*mṛdu*), middling (*madhya*), excellent (*adhimātra*) and highly excellent (*adhimātratara*). Finally, the *Amṛtasiddhi* teaches for the first time that the control of semen (*bindu*), breath and mind are all interlinked, such that by controlling one of them, one controls them all. This becomes a key notion in subsequent non-Buddhist *haṭhayoga*. In later manuscripts of the *Amṛtasiddhi* it is clear that the explicitly Buddhist elements in the text have been overwritten with Śaiva references, in a process of trans-sectarian appropriation.[11] Verses from the *Amṛtasiddhi* appear in several subsequent texts of the early *haṭha* corpus, including the *Gorakṣaśataka*, *Vivekamārtaṇḍa*, *Amaraughaprabodha*, *Gorakṣayogaśāstra*, *Śivasaṃhitā* and the *Haṭhapradīpikā*, demonstrating elements of continuity from early Vajrayāna into fully-fledged *haṭhayoga*.

The earliest non-Buddhist texts to teach practices named *haṭhayoga* are the Śaiva *Amaraughaprabodha* and the Vaiṣṇava *Dattātreyayogaśāstra*, twelfth and thirteenth century respectively. Both reproduce the four-fold practice schema and the three *mudrās* of the *Amṛtasiddhi*. The *Dattātreyayogaśāstra* teaches three physical 'locks' or *bandhas* (*jālandhara*, *uḍḍiyāna* and *mūla*) two of which (*jālandhara* and *mūla*) are implicit already in the *Amṛtasiddhi*'s *mahābandha* but not individually explained. The *Dattātreyayogaśāstra* adds the inverted *mudrā viparītakaraṇī* ('reverse maker') and *khecarīmudrā*, in which the tongue is turned back and inserted into the nasopharyngeal cavity. Along with the method of seminal retention by urethral suction called *vajrolīmudrā* that occurs in all texts which call their methods *haṭha* (Mallinson forthcoming), these nine methods constitute the *haṭhayoga* taught in the *Dattātreyayogaśāstra*, which is attributed to the sage Kapila, and which functions to maintain *bindu*. The *Dattātreyayogaśāstra* attempts to adapt *haṭhayoga* for a Vaiṣṇava audience by synthesising these *mudrās* with Yājñavalkya's *aṣṭāṅgayoga*, and this synthesis seems to constitute *haṭhayoga* in the *Dattātreyayogaśāstra*.[12] Two early texts whose verses and practices get assimilated into the *Haṭhapradīpikā* synthesis but that don't call their yoga *haṭha* are the *Vivekamārtaṇḍa* and *Gorakṣaśataka*. Both texts teach the three *bandhas*. In addition, the *Vivekamārtaṇḍa* teaches *mahāmudrā*, *viparitakaraṇī mudrā* and a version of *khecarīmudrā* called *nabhomudrā*; and the *Gorakṣaśataka* teaches a practice called *śakticālanīmudrā* (on which see Mallinson 2011a).

The circa fifteenth-century, South Indian *Śivasaṃhitā* is a compendium of teachings on yoga, framed in the philosophy of the non-dual Śrīvidyā school of tantra. It teaches a system of six-plus-one *cakras* identical in name and location to that of the *Kubjikāmatatantra*; a microcosmic model of the macrocosm within the yogin's body; the four stages of yoga of the *Amṛtasiddhi*; eleven *mudrās* and – in a long final chapter on meditation and ultimate reality – a variety of other practices unusual in texts of the early *haṭha* corpus, including gazing at one's own shadow, and the repetition of mantra. In its section on *mudrā,* the text presents a visualisation of the god Kāma located in the perineum that it calls *yonimudrā.* Although there is a physical element to the practice (a contraction of the perineum similar to *mūlabandha*, and a fixing of the mind there by means of inhalation), it is anomalous among *haṭha mudrās* in that its practice is largely a visualisation.[13] Also unusual is that thereafter the text presents a *separate* group of ten *mudrās*, all of which are familiar from the earlier, above-mentioned *haṭha* sources. Some of the *mudrās* work on Kuṇḍalinī, who breaks through a series of knots (*granthi*) to rise up the central channel (*suṣumnā*), and some on *bindu*.

The locus classicus of *haṭhayoga*, the *Haṭhapradīpikā*, is a highly derivative and synthetic compendium of practices incorporating verses from the sources mentioned above and others. It is the first text to teach *haṭha* as a primary, exclusive practice: that is to say earlier texts had either not called their yoga *haṭha* or had presented it as one among other systems. It defines *haṭha* as consisting of posture (*āsana*), various breath retentions (*kumbhakas*, i.e. *prāṇāyāma*), 'divine procedures' (i.e. *mudrā*) and concentration on the inner sound (*nādānusamdhāna*) (1.56). Not included in this definition of *haṭha,* but also included as preliminary physical cleansing methods are the 'six actions' (*ṣaṭkarma*) for those with an excess of fat or mucus in the body.[14] They appear under the rubric of *haṭha* for the first time in the *Haṭhapradīpikā* (2.20–38), and thereafter become a characteristic component of *haṭha* practice, with new practices being added to their number in later texts such as the seventeenth-century *Haṭharatnāvalī*. Since the *Haṭhapradīpikā* is largely a compilation, it may be that the *ṣaṭkarmas* are borrowed from an earlier, unknown yoga text.

The *Haṭhapradīpikā* describes fifteen postures, eight of which are not simple seated postures; this (slim) majority of non-seated and complex postures therefore represents a departure from earlier yoga traditions in which *āsanas* are intended exclusively as stable and comfortable meditation positions. All the *Haṭhapradīpikā*'s verses on *āsana* are borrowed from other texts, but its presentation of a group of *āsanas* in which the majority are non-seated is a significant moment in the historical development of *āsana* for purposes other than meditation (e.g. for manipulating the fluids and winds of the yogic body, or as remedies for disease; see Birch 2018; Mallinson and Singleton 2017: chapter 3).[15] The *Haṭhapradīpikā* teaches eight *praṇāyāmas*, (four of which are drawn directly from the *Gorakṣaśataka*) which come to constitute a relatively stable set of 'classical' *prāṇāyāmas*.[16] It presents a group of ten *mudrās* (3.6),[17] but adds a description of *yonimudrā*, bringing the total to eleven. As in other *haṭhayoga* texts, *Mahāvedha* is presented as a necessary complement to *mahāmudrā* and *mahābandha,* in which the yogi assumes the three *bandhas* and then strikes his buttocks on the ground in order to force the air into the central channel (3.25–30). As in its descriptions of *āsanas*, the *Haṭhapradīpikā*'s *mudrās* are said to confer mundane health benefits alongside the main aim of raising Kuṇḍalinī. Mahāmudrā, for example, is said to cure consumption, leprosy, constipation, enlargement of the glands and indigestion (3.17). These therapeutic applications are also mentioned in earlier works such as the *Vivekamārtaṇḍa*. The concentration on the inner sound (*nādānusandhāna*), in which the yogi blocks off the sense organs and hears increasingly subtle sounds, is praised (1.43) as the best of the practices of dissolution (*laya*) which, as we shall see, is considered by the text to be a synonym of *samādhi.* It enables one to cheat death and attain liberation.

## Goals of *haṭhayoga*

Broadly speaking, as in other forms of yoga, the ultimate goal of *haṭha* may be the accumulation of supernatural powers (*siddhi*) and/or liberation from the cycle of death and rebirth (*mokṣa, mukti, kaivalya,* etc.), the mechanism and prerequisite for both of which is *samādhi* (see below). *Siddhis* such as making oneself microscopically small or cosmically large, clairvoyance and flight have always been a feature of yoga, whether framed as coveted states that emulate divine cosmic play, or as inevitable but undesirable impediments to liberation.[18] Such powers figure prominently in popular legends and folktales of yogis (White 2009), but are also ubiquitous in premodern yoga texts. Almost one quarter of the sutras of the *Pātañjalayogaśāstra*, for example, consider the topic of special powers and how to attain them. Among all traditions, special powers are perhaps most positively regarded in tantra. To the extent that *haṭha* texts – such as the *Khecarīvidyā* and the *Śivasaṃhitā* – share in this tantric heritage, it is not surprising to find the attainment of *siddhi*s foregrounded in them. However, tantric *siddhi*s with malefic purposes such as entering the body of another do not generally feature in the early *haṭha* corpus, and *siddhi*s are viewed in some texts (such as the *Dattātreyayogaśāstra* and the *Yogabīja*) as a distraction from the main goal.

Practices of *samādhi* in early *haṭhayoga* are often seen to lead the yogi to an insensible, non-cognisant, deathlike state, a process which is somewhat different to the increasingly refined cognitive levels of the *Pātañjalayogaśāstra* (which culminate in the *non-cognitive* state of *asaṃprajñātasamādhi*)[19], as well as to tantric schemata in which *samādhi* is an inferior stage to the apprehension of or merger with the supreme reality of the deity. The *Vivekamārtaṇḍa* (163–168), for example, considers *samādhi* to be a state of non-perception in which the yogi no longer has sensory experience, conceptual understanding or cognition of self or other. This non-cognitive wood- or stone-like trance state becomes a trope in later ethnographic writings in India, where the (*haṭha*) yogin is buried alive as a demonstration of his yogic achievement (Mallinson and Singleton 2017: 327, 342–345). In practice, however, interpretations of *samādhi* vary according to the sectarian and metaphysical affiliation of the text, and insofar as *haṭhayoga*'s heritage is itself various, and its practices shared across a broad range of religious groups, such variation is to be expected.[20] Also of particular note here is the concept of liberation-in-life (*jīvanmukti*), in which the yogin achieves the highest realisation while remaining in his body, and in some cases continues to live and act in the world. While not without ancient precursors, *jīvanmukti* was first celebrated and popularised by the eleventh-century *Mokṣopāya* (later known as the *Yogavāsiṣṭha*) and by the seventeenth century had become a topic of discussion in every school of Hinduism (Mumme 1996: 247). Its appearance and development therefore to some extent mirrors the development of *haṭhayoga*, and *jīvanmukti* is a central goal of *haṭha* texts (Mallinson and Singleton 2017: chapter 11; Birch forthcoming).

In the *Haṭhapradīpikā*, *samādhi* is defined as the union of self and mind (or, as in the *Vivekamārtaṇḍa*, of individual self (*jīvātman*) and supreme self (*paramātman*)) that arises when *prāṇa* stops (i.e. the breath ceases) and the mind dissolves (4.5–7). *Haṭhapradīpikā* 4.4 declares that *samādhi* is a synonym of the terms *laya* and *rājayoga* (among others).[21] The term *rājayoga*, sometimes presented (particularly in modern yoga) as the spiritual or mental counterpoint to physical *haṭhayoga*, itself only starts to appear with frequency in texts at the same time as *haṭhayoga*. The terms *rājayoga* and *haṭhayoga* appear together in texts such as the *Dattātreyayogaśāstra*, the *Amaraughaprabodha*, the *Śārṅgadharapaddhati*, the *Yogabīja* and the *Haṭhapradīpikā* (Birch 2011). The term is used in two distinct ways in these texts: as the final, and highest yoga in a four-fold scheme which also comprises *mantrayoga*, *layayoga* and *haṭhayoga*, and is characterised by the practice of *samādhi*; or as the non-dual, final state achieved through yoga practice (ibid.). Thus, like the term 'yoga' itself, *samādhi* and *rājayoga* are both ambivalent insofar as they can signify practices employed to achieve the final state of yoga, and that state itself. Thus the declaration in *Haṭhapradīpikā* 1.2 that *haṭhayoga* is being explained 'for the sake of *rājayoga* [*rājayogāya*]' should be understood to mean that *haṭha* is for the attainment of the *samādhi*-state of *rājayoga*.[22]

## *Haṭhayoga* after the *Haṭhapradīpikā*

In the centuries following the composition of the *Haṭhapradīpikā*, the methods of *haṭhayoga* enjoyed an increasing influence in mainstream, orthodox religious practice. In the middle of the second millennium CE, the Brahmanical scholar Śivānanda Saraswatī taught methods of *haṭhayoga* alongside those of the *Pātañjalayogaśāstra* in his *Yogacintāmaṇī*, evincing an early acceptance of *haṭha* in Hindu orthodoxy. As Bouy (1994) has demonstrated, in the centuries following the composition of the *Haṭhapradīpikā* a new corpus of Upaniṣads (which later became known as the Yoga Upaniṣads) borrowed wholesale from *haṭha* texts, and cemented the place of *haṭha* techniques in the orthodox religious mainstream. Birch (2018) argues that these centuries represent in some respects *haṭha*'s 'flourishing', with the composition of both larger praxis-oriented and compendious scholarly works which expand significantly on the usually terse descriptions of the early *haṭha* corpus, and also add many new techniques to those of the earlier texts.

## *Haṭhayoga* in contemporary ascetic culture

In contemporary ascetic culture in India, the goals of yoga practice have largely remained those of the historical tradition: the attainment of liberation, and *siddhi*s. Among ascetics, the term *haṭhayoga* is for the most part understood to connote the 'austerities' of *tapas*, or perhaps more precisely the strong intention and determination (*dṛdh saṅkalpa*) that leads to *tapas* (*tapasyā* in Hindi) rather than a separate system of yoga per se, and may not even involve any yoga practice at all (Bevilacqua 2017).[23] Thus *haṭhayoga* can include practices such as only eating fruit or drinking juice, staying in a particular position for long periods of time or strictly following the rules of the ascetic order. This understanding of *haṭhayoga* as effortful or painful practice (sometimes contrasted with 'easy' meditative practices) shows a continuity with the ancient traditions of austerity mentioned above, and the continuing association of yogis with *tapasvins*. The strong intention implicit in these understandings of *haṭhayoga* is seen to be necessary to achieve the difficult goal of liberation. In line with the thirteenth-century *Yogabīja*, contemporary ascetics also sometimes interpret the syllables of *haṭha* to mean the sun (*ha*) and moon (*tha*) of the (*haṭhayogic*) body, and *haṭhayoga* itself as effecting their union.[24] In far fewer cases, *haṭhayoga* is associated explicitly with *prāṇāyāma* practice, itself often considered to be a form of *tapas*. Contemporary ascetics may also identify *haṭhayoga* with the *kriyās* (i.e. *ṣatkarmas*) that, as we have seen, appeared under the rubric of *haṭha* for the first time in the *Haṭhapradīpikā*. For still others, the term signifies physical techniques such as *āsana*s for keeping the body healthy. Unlike in contemporary globalised yoga (see below), ascetics accord little importance to non-seated *āsana*s that are not used as seats for meditation practice.

## *Haṭhayoga* in modern global yoga

The end of the nineteenth century and the beginning of the twentieth century saw an explosion of interest in yoga outside of India, largely due to newly available translations of yoga texts and the influence of teachers from India such as Swami Vivekananda, whose influential 1896 book *Rājayoga* became in some respects the 'blueprint' for many subsequent modern formulations of yoga inside and outside of India, and presents teachings on yoga heavily influenced by western esoteric ideas (De Michelis 2004). Although the physical methods of *haṭha* were dismissed by Vivekananda (and the highly influential Theosophical Society) as inferior to the 'mental' *rājayoga*, by the 1920s and 1930s *haṭha* was beginning to gain prominence in the practical lexicon of globalised modern yoga.[25] In the hands of innovators like Swami Kuvalayananda and Shri Yogendra, the methods of *haṭha* were assimilated into contemporary physical culture and subjected to scientific investigation, a trend which has continued up to the present (see Alter 2004; Singleton 2010). Other globally known teachers such as Swami Sivananda and his disciple Vishnudevananda, T. Krishnamacharya and his disciples B. K. S. Iyengar and Pattabhi Jois have foregrounded the *haṭhayogic āsanas*, which have become virtually synonymous in many places around the world with yoga practice as such. The practices of *haṭhayoga* have undergone significant adaptation over the past century as they have been assimilated into new, diverse cultural contexts, and as yoga's popularity outside of India has swelled enormously. As well as adaptation in practices, the goals of yoga have also often shifted, with the two most common aims of yoga in the Indian tradition – special powers and liberation – commonly being displaced by an emphasis on personal health and wellbeing.

## Notes

1 Thanks to Jason Birch, James Mallinson, Adrián Muñoz, Suzanne Newcombe and Karen O'Brien-Kop for reading and commenting on this chapter. This chapter was financially supported by the European Union's Horizon 2020 research and innovation programme under grant agreement No. 647963 (Haṭha Yoga Project).
2 The text refers to itself as the *Haṭhapradīpikā* ('lamp of *haṭha*') rather than the common title *Haṭhayogapradīpikā* ('lamp of *haṭhayoga*'), by which it is known in some commentaries and in modern publications (see Birch and Singleton Forthcoming).
3 I draw extensively on the ground-breaking research into the early *haṭha* corpus of James Mallinson, and also on Jason Birch's studies of post-fifteenth-century *haṭha*. To a lesser extent, this chapter includes my own research into the wider yoga traditions in Mallinson and Singleton 2017.
4 See Li, Chapter 26 in this volume.
5 On the history of textual criticism in Indology and European philology, see Witzel 2014.
6 Such, as we will see, is the case with the originally Vajrayāna Buddhist *Amṛtasiddhi*, which was later assimilated into a Śaiva context.
7 Bronkhorst 2007; see also Mallinson and Singleton 2017: xiii-xv.
8 Birch (2019) argues that the reason for this simplicity was that early *haṭhayoga* was shaped by its trans-sectarian status as an auxiliary practice for people of various religions. In modern yoga, the term 'subtle body' is often used to refer to these features of the yogic body. However, as a translation of the Sanskrit term *sūkṣmaśarīra*, 'subtle body' does not refer to the features of the yogic body as described in haṭhayogic texts, which may sometimes in fact be gross, physical phenomena. We have therefore chosen the term 'yogic body' to refer to those locations and passages of the body of the yogin through and upon which the methods of *haṭhayoga* work. For further discussion, see Mallinson and Singleton 2017, chapter 5.
9 In the seventeenth-century *Haṭharatnāvalī*, for example, certain *haṭhayogic* methods of cleansing the physical body are also said to purify the *cakras* (1.61).
10 For a more comprehensive treatment of the texts and their contents, see Mallinson forthcoming.
11 On which see the forthcoming critical edition of the *Amṛtasiddhi* by Mallinson and Szántó.
12 Because the *Dattātreyayogaśāstra* adds more techniques and is more syncretic than the *Amaraughaprabodha* it is probable that the *Dattātreyayogaśāstra* is the later text. I thank Jason Birch for this insight.
13 Birch (2018: 107, fn. 13) has argued that the first four chapters and the fifth chaper of the *Śivasaṃhitā* were probably different works, united at some time (perhaps, after the *Haṭhapradīpikā* but before the seventeenth century), which may help to explain these inconsistencies.
14 They are swallowing a long strip of cloth in order to cleanse the stomach (*dhauti*), enema (*basti*), nasal cleansing with thread or water (*neti*), staring until the eyes water (*trāṭaka*), rotating the abdominal muscles to stimulate digestion (*nauli*) and a form of vigorous breathing (*kapālabhāti*).
15 The complex or non-seated postures are *uttānakūrmaka*, *dhanurāsana*, *matsyendrāsana*, *paścimatānāsana*, *mayūrāsana*, *kūrmāsana* and *kukkuṭāsana*.
16 Relative, that is, to *āsanas*. They are, in order of their appearance in the text, *sūrya*, *śītalī*, *bhastrikā*, *ujjāyī*, *sītkārī*, *bhrāmarī*, *mūrcchā* and *plāvinī*.

17 The ten are: *mahāmudrā, mahābandha, mahāvedha, khecarī, uḍḍīyāna, mūlabandha, jālandhara, viparītakaraṇī, vajrolī* and *śakticālana*.
18 The *Dattātreyayogaśāstra* warns that accumulating (and demonstrating) special powers will attract unwanted disciples who will keep the yogi from his practice and turn him into an ordinary man (101–106).
19 Grinshpon (2002) argues that the liberation of the *Pātañjalayogaśāstra* is equivalent to complete ontological death.
20 For a range of interpretations of *samādhi*'s meanings in yoga texts, see Mallinson and Singleton 2017: chapter 9.
21 The text also names the following terms as synonyms: *unmanī, manomanī, amaratva, tattva, śūnyāśunyā, paraṃ padam*.
22 On traditions which understand *rājayoga* to stand in opposition to *haṭhayoga* see Birch 2011.
23 Unless otherwise noted, the statements in this section are all drawn from Bevilacqua 2017.
24 This understanding of *haṭhayoga* first appears in textual sources in the *Yogabīja*.
25 Unless otherwise noted, the statements in this section are drawn from Singleton 2010.

## Bibliography

Alter, J. S. 2004. *Yoga in Modern India: The Body Between Science and Philosophy*. Princeton: Princeton University Press.

Ayangar, C. R. S. 1893. *The Hatha Yoga Pradipika*. Bombay: Tookaram Tatya on behalf of the Bombay Theosophical Publication Fund.

Bevilacqua, D. 2017. 'Let the Sādhus Talk: Ascetic Understanding of Haṭha Yoga and Yogāsanas', *Religions of South Asia* 11(2–3): 182–206.

Birch, J. 2011. 'The Meaning of *haṭha* in Early *Haṭhayoga*', *Journal of the American Oriental Society* 131(4): 527–554.

Birch, J. 2018. 'The Proliferation of *Āsana*-s in Late-Mediaeval Yoga Texts' in Baier, K., Maas, P. A. and Preisendanz, K. (eds), *Yoga in Transformation: Historical and Contemporary Perspectives*, 101–180. Vienna: Vienna University Press.

Birch, J. 2019. 'The *Amaraughaprabodha*: New Evidence on the Manuscript Transmission of an Early Work on Haṭha- and Rājayoga', *Journal of Indian Philosophy*. Published online 2 July. https://doi.org/10.1007/s10781-019-09401-5

Birch, J. forthcoming. 'The Quest for Liberation-in-life in Early Haṭha and Rājayoga', in *The Oxford History of Hinduism*. Oxford: Oxford University Press.

Birch, J. and Singleton, M. forthcoming. 'The Āsana Section of the *Yogacintāmaṇī*.'

Bouy, C. 1994. *Les Nātha Yogin et Les Upaniṣads, Étude d'histoire de la littérature Hindoue*. Collège de France, Publications de l'Institut de Civilisation Indienne. Paris: Édition-Diffusion de Bocard.

Bronkhorst, J. 2007. *Greater Magadha: Studies in the Culture of Early India*. Handbook of Oriental Studies, Section Two, India, Vol. 19. Leiden: Brill.

De Michelis, E. 2004. *A History of Modern Yoga: Patañjali and Western Esotericism*. London: Continuum.

Diamond, D. 2013. *Yoga: The Art of Transformation*. Washington, DC: Arthur M. Sackler Gallery, Smithsonian Institution.

Grinshpon, Y. 2002. 'Silence Unheard: Deathly Otherness in Pātañjala Yoga'. New York: SUNY.

Mallinson, J. 2011a. 'Haṭha Yoga', in Jacobsen et al. (eds), *Brill's Encyclopedia of Hinduism*, Vol. 3: 770–781.

Mallinson, J. 2011b. 'The Original *Gorakṣaśataka*', in White, D. G. (ed), *Yoga in Practice*, 257–272. Princeton: Princeton University Press.

Mallinson, J. 2014. 'Haṭhayoga's Philosophy: A Fortuitous Union of Non-Dualities', *Journal of Indian Philosophy* 42: 225–247.

Mallinson, J. forthcoming. *Yoga and Yogis: The Texts, Techniques and Practitioners of Early Haṭhayoga*. Pondicherry: École Française d'Extreme-Orient.

Mallinson, J. and Singleton, M. 2017. *Roots of Yoga*. London: Penguin Classics.

Mallinson, J. and Szántó, P. forthcoming. *A Critical Edition of the* Amṛtasiddhi.

Mumme, P. Y. 1996. 'Conclusion: Living Liberation in Comparative Perspective', in Fort, A. O. and Mumme, P. Y. (eds), *Living Liberation in Hindu Thought*, 247–270. Albany, NY: State University of New York Press.

Powell, S. 2018. 'Etched in Stone: Sixteenth-century Visual and Material Evidence of Śaiva Ascetics and Yogis in Complex Non-seated Āsanas at Vijayanagara', *Journal of Yoga Studies* 1: 45–106.
Singleton, M. 2010. *Yoga Body, the Origins of Modern Posture Practice*. New York: Oxford University Press.
Sinh, P. 1915. *The Hatha Yoga Pradipika*. Allahabad: Pāṇini Office.
Tavernier, J. 1925 [1676]. *Travels in India*. London: Oxford University Press.
White, D. G. 2009. *Sinister Yogis*. Chicago: University of Chicago Press.
Witzel, M. 2014. 'Textual Criticism in Indology and in European Philology During the 19th and 20th centuries', *Electronic Journal of Vedic Studies* (EJVS), 21(3): 9–90.

# 10

# YOGA AND MEDITATION IN MODERN ESOTERIC TRADITIONS

*Julian Strube*

## Introduction

An exploration of the role of yogic and meditational practices within 'esoteric traditions' poses a range of methodological and historiographical challenges. 'Esotericism' has often been understood in a phenomenological or so-called perennialist sense as a universalist feature of religion, a perspective that resurfaced in the work of influential scholars such as Mircea Eliade. The emergence of esotericism as an institutionalised field of academic study, especially since the 1990s, went hand in hand with a rejection of such approaches, which appeared to carry too much of the 'religionist' baggage from insider-perspective understandings of esotericism (for an overview of these debates, see Hanegraaff 2015, 2012). For this reason, most of the scholarship on esotericism is produced within a field that is called 'western esotericism', which focuses on currents such as Gnosticism, Hermeticism, Rosicrucianism, Spiritualism or occultism in the geographical contexts of Europe and North America since Late Antiquity. On the other hand, esotericism can indeed be understood, for instance from a sociological or anthropological viewpoint, as signifying 'hidden' or 'coded', which would allow for a comparative structural analysis in different cultural, geographical or historical contexts. Perhaps even more importantly, it is anything but clear which boundaries can be drawn on the basis of the notion 'western' from a historical perspective (Asprem 2014; Granholm 2014). This can be exemplified by the highly important transmission of Greek (including Gnostic and Hermetic) sources within Islamicate contexts (Saif 2015) that are, in turn, relevant for an understanding of South Asian contexts.

The present chapter raises important questions about the meaning of 'esotericism' and the definitions and relationship between 'East' and 'West'. As will be argued, the reception of yogic and meditational practice can only be comprehended against the background of 'western esoteric' developments since the end of the seventeenth century, but it would be highly misleading to conclude that such influences were unidirectional. Quite the contrary, the examples that have been chosen for this chapter will serve to demonstrate that the very meaning of 'esotericism' can only be understood in the context of a complex tangle of global exchanges since the nineteenth century. These developments should be seen against the background of debates revolving around the meaning of religion, science, philosophy, national identity and perceptions of the body (Bergunder 2016). Esotericists, such as Spiritualist, occultists or members of the Theosophical Society, played an instrumental and often neglected role in these developments.

This chapter will highlight the role of such esotericists for modern interpretations of yoga and meditation, while at the same time stressing the need to take into account the agency and influence of their South Asian interlocutors, on whose expertise, knowledge and philological skills they depended. Indeed, it will be argued that modern understandings of yoga and meditation can only be fully grasped from a global perspective that investigates these mutual and often ambiguous influences. The chapter will move through the contexts of Mesmerism, Spiritualism, occultism and the Theosophical Society from the nineteenth to the twentieth century, a progression that increasingly saw global entanglements, profound shifts and ambiguous complexities. The heavy focus on the nineteenth century has been chosen because present-day understandings of yoga and meditation are arguably more significantly rooted in that period than in more recent contexts; the fields of youth, hippy or New Age cultures since the 1960s were certainly instrumental in popularising the practice of yoga and meditation, but can themselves only be comprehended against the background of nineteenth-century developments (e.g. Oliver 2014). While the frame and focus of this chapter are unavoidably incomplete, the reader will hopefully find abundant evidence for both the relevance of nineteenth-century developments for present-day yoga and meditation, and for the necessity to look at them from a perspective that questions historiographical dichotomies between 'East' and 'West'.

## Mesmerism

The modern history of yoga and meditation would be incomprehensible without Mesmerism, a theory named after its founder Franz Anton Mesmer (1734–1815) that developed into a range of highly influential currents. Since the publication of his dissertation about the influences of planetary forces on Earth and its inhabitants in 1766, Mesmer propounded a complex theory of an all-pervading 'subtle physical fluid' that manifested in different physical forces such as magnetism, warmth or electricity. In the middle of the 1770s, he developed the notion of 'animal magnetism', which, according to Mesmer, could be employed by trained doctors for therapeutic purposes. These medical implications, although controversially discussed by contemporaries, were enthusiastically received by readers and practitioners who, like many others at that time, were occupied with all-encompassing physical and cosmological theories. It was in this broader cultural context that Mesmerism would exert its largest influence, since its concept of an all-pervading universal fluid provided a basis for attempts to synthesise natural philosophy, the emerging modern sciences and theories about religious experiences. In this context, it was instrumental for the emergence of hypnotism and psychological theories (Crabtree 1993; Gauld 1992).

Central to this was the notion of a subtle energetic body and a concept of sickness relating to blockages of energy and subtle matter. According to Mesmeric therapy, the removal of such blockages could not only lead to a restoration of harmony within the individual body, but also to its unity with the 'Whole', the (re-)establishment of the individual's connectedness with nature and the universe. Such combinations of mechanistic, natural philosophical and religious concepts were not unusual at the time, but Mesmer's insistence on the body as a tool of experience and therapy was. The techniques to achieve this could be learned by cultivating the instinct, or what Mesmer referred to as the inner or sixth sense. The receptiveness of the cosmic fluid, and thus a connection to the Whole, could be increased and was especially effective when the activity of the mind was calmed. The methodical experimentation with calming the mind and inducing altered states of consciousness was an integral part of Mesmeric practice. As Karl Baier has pointed out, Mesmerism thus developed a complex language of contemplative bodily experience that formed a matrix for the later reception of South Asian yogic and meditational practices (Baier 2009: 183). It also exerted a lasting influence on western discourse about religious experience, for instance in the context of Psychical Research and the theories of William James.

The predominance of the religious, 'spiritual' or 'mystical' element made Mesmerism especially attractive within the context of Romanticism (Darnton 1968; Winter 1998). Contemporaries would soon point out Mesmerism's similarity with Neo-Platonic and Hermetic concepts of the World Soul and correspondences or analogies between the bodily microcosm and the universal macrocosm. It is important to emphasise that Mesmerism grew into a highly heterogeneous and eclectic set of currents, rather than representing a unified school of thought. An important step in this process was the activities of the Marquis de Puységur (1751–1825), who stressed the role of the magnetiser's 'will' and thus highlighted the need for the cultivation of the practitioner's individual capabilities. According to Puységur and his followers, it was largely due to the therapist's will that a 'magnetic sleep' could be induced in the patient, leading to 'somnambulistic' states that climaxed in ecstatic experiences. These included the perception of the bodily energy flows along the nerve plexuses, which was described by widely-read authors such as Carl Alexander Ferdinand Kluge (1782–1844) and Joseph Ennemoser (1787–1854). In this context, magnetism was linked to magical practices and gave birth to a veritable 'magnetic historiography' that sought to explain magic scientifically (Hanegraaff 2012: 260–277). It was also seen as a means to establishing contact with the spirit world and the development of clairvoyant abilities, for instance in the famous works of Justinus Kerner (1786–1862) and Johann Heinrich Jung-Stilling (1740–1817).

These authors had openly religious backgrounds and intentions, which were often related to Freemasonry, Swedenborgianism or Rosicrucianism. While Mesmer also had close links to these milieus, he kept them separate from his medical theories, at least in public. This alliance between (esoteric) religious currents and Mesmerism led to several schisms with strands who proclaimed more scientific-medicinal identities. Mesmerism was thus controversially transformed from a therapeutic-medical theory into an integral part of nineteenth-century religious discourse. This went hand in hand with the further elaboration of techniques of 'self-magnetisation' and the control of occult forces through Mesmeric magic. Such syntheses were central to the emergence of modern magical currents, such as French Martinism at the end of the eighteenth century (Viatte 1928; Le Forestier 1970), which were essential for developments in the nineteenth century and remain influential.

It was also in the Romantic context that the idea of animal magnetism at the root of universal religious experience was linked to contemporary theories about the common origin of myths and religion in 'the East' (Baier 2009: 200–221). In his famous Latin translation of the *Oupnek'hat* (1801–1802), the Persian rendering of the Upanishads, Abraham Hyacinthe Anquetil-Duperron (1731–1805) established a correlation between *prāṇa* and magnetism, which was taken up by a number of influential authors. For instance, Joseph Görres (1776–1848) discussed these forces in the context of meditation. Ennemoser claimed that wisdom about magnetism was especially developed in 'the East', and discussed Indian magic in relation to the meditational practices of the Brahmins. In his *Untersuchungen über den Lebensmagnetismus und das Hellsehen* from 1821, Johann Carl Passavant (1790–1857) contemplated travel accounts about fakirs, Sufis and 'yogins' ('Djogis', 'Jauguis'...), linking their practices to magic, somnambulism, clairvoyance, ecstasy, meditation, contemplation or Kabbalah.

In the work of Karl Joseph Windischmann (1775–1839), these connections were particularly elaborated (Baier 2009: 221–243). A professor of philosophy in Bonn who was also a member of the medical faculty, Windischmann had made a Romantic transition from Freemasonry to Catholicism. He specialised in magnetism both from a historical and practical perspective. Due to his close contacts with the Indologists in Bonn, he could draw on significant philological expertise for his unfinished *Philosophie im Fortgang der Weltgeschichte* (1827–1834). Making use of the *Manusmṛti*, several Upanishads and the first German translation of the beginning of the *Yogasūtra* by Friedrich Rosen, Windischmann argued that 'the magnetic life of the soul' was the 'principle of Indian thought' and interpreted Brahmanical doctrines through the lens of animal magnetism. He drew extensive parallels between somnambulism and Indian meditational and yogic practices. According to him, Brahmanical practices were thoroughly determined by 'Joga', a method of contemplation leading to ecstasy and finally to a unification with God. Since such 'magical' practices lay at the foundation of Indian thought, they formed the crucial link to western practices of magic and Mesmerism, a case that Windischmann made, among other things, by an identification of *prāṇa* and the magnetic fluid.

## Spiritualism and early occultism

These developments of Mesmeric theories formed an integral part of the contexts in which nineteenth-century European and North American esoteric currents such as Spiritualism and occultism emerged. Somewhat misleadingly, the history of Spiritualism is often begun in the year 1848 when the young Fox sisters heard 'rappings' in their home in Hydesville, New York, which were interpreted as attempts by spirits to communicate with the living. This prompted a hugely influential fashion of conducting spirit research, holding séances and consulting mediums. The history of Spiritualism, however, reaches back at least to works such as those by Kerner, Jung-Stilling and others. The milieu in which Spiritualism emerged as a movement was largely determined by a mélange of mesmeric theories, Swedenborgianism and early socialist doctrines, most notably Fourierism and Saint-Simonism. This socio-political context is responsible for the radical, progressive character that is associated with nineteenth-century Spiritualism, which was often concerned with social reform, emancipation and feminism. In Europe, the triad Mesmer-Swedenborg-Fourier had been commonplace among radicals in the 1820s until the 1840s (Monroe 2008; Strube 2016; Strube 2017b). Social and physical laws were perceived as inherently intertwined and often expressed in the language of (magnetic) attraction, correspondences and analogies. This combination is also characteristic of the pioneers of US-American Spiritualism such as Andrew Jackson Davis (1826–1910) (Fuller 1982; Albanese 2007). It is important to keep these connections in mind because they also manifested in a concern for alternative forms of healing and diet, new models of communal living and body culture, which paved the way for twentieth-century New Age culture.

The revived interest in the magnetically informed theory and practice of magic came to full fruition in the middle of the nineteenth century and manifested in a new edition of Ennemoser's 1819 work about the history of magnetism, now titled *Geschichte der Magie* (1844, English as *The History of Magic* in 1854), as well as in the widely-read *History of Magic, Witchcraft, and Animal Magnetism* by John Campbell Colquhoun (1851). Most influential, however, were the works of Alphonse-Louis Constant (1810–1875), who, using his new pseudonym Eliphas Lévi, was the first to systematically employ the term *occultisme* from the year 1854 onward. His *Dogme et rituel de la haute magie* (1854–1856), *Histoire de la magie* (1860) and other writings, are still among the most influential esoteric writings ever published. Constant had been a radical religious socialist, exiled Catholic cleric and Romantic artist in the 1840s. It could hardly become more obvious that it was exactly in this context of radical social reform, Spiritualism and heterodox-Romantic Catholicism that Constant's 'occultism' emerged (Strube 2016).

It is important to emphasise that this reflected major debates about the origin of religion and the explanation of religious experiences, rather than esoteric doctrines that could be regarded as culturally marginal. For instance, among Constant's main influences we find the so-called neo-Catholic school around Félicité de Lamennais (1782–1854) that propagated a 'Catholic science' to counter the blossoming historical-critical scholarship. Part of that science was an occupation with Mesmerism, as illustrated by the famous work of Henri Lacordaire (1802–1861) who explained the miracles of Jesus Christ with his command of 'occult' magnetic powers. Most importantly, the neo-Catholics developed the notion of the *révélation primitive*, a common origin of all religions that allegedly became demonstrable through the recent discoveries of orientalist studies, especially in Sanskrit and Persian (McCalla 2009). These ideas were intensely discussed across national borders and exerted a significant influence on contemporary debates about religion. The vast exchanges between French and German Catholics, including Görres, exemplify how these issues were directly linked to the history, theory and practices of magnetism, including its supposed identity with 'Indian magic'.

This Romantic, often Catholic and socialist occupation with Mesmerism and occult traditions of wisdom (often from 'the East') formed the basis of what can be termed 'spiritualist magnetism' (Strube 2016: 375, cf. Monroe 2008: 64–94). Constant was a relatively new member of this heterogeneous group of authors. Much more prominent at the time was Jules du Potet de Sennevoy (1796–1881), who published extensively about his peculiar mix of Martinist-style magic, which involved the use of mirrors, magnetism and socialist ideas. When Constant entered this sphere as Eliphas Lévi, he sharply rejected the practice of Spiritualism and posited himself as a vocal critic of practical magic, whose history and procedures he nevertheless discussed in length. Dismissing the Spiritualists as amateurish dabblers unaware of the true nature of their phenomena, he stressed the importance of the magician's will for the mastery of the universal force that he termed the Astral Light, following Du Potet and the Martinists. This rejection of both Spiritualism and the 'amateurish' practice of magic was an important hallmark in the history of occultism. At the same time, altered states of consciousness, meditation and contemplation were among Lévi's favourite subjects, bearing importance for later occultist appropriation of yogic and meditational techniques. According to Lévi, one of the most important goals of the magician was the mastery of 'self-magnetisation' to induce ecstatic and visionary states. However, he levelled harsh criticism against 'India', which he regarded as a locus of black magic and religious degeneration – citing the *Oupnek'hat* and yogic practices as evidence (Baier 2009: 276). Lévi's discussion of 'India' was mainly informed by contemporary (Catholic) historiographies of religion and did not rely on primary source material. His understanding of Indian 'black magic' that supposedly originated in the 'Gnostic' context of the School of Alexandria mainly served the purpose of promoting his ambiguous and often confusing narrative of 'true' versus 'false' religion (Strube 2017c). It was only later that European esotericists would engage with Indian sources more directly.

## The Theosophical Society

As has become clear by now, Romantic and orientalist images of India or 'the East' formed an important frame of reference for early occultist writings. In contrast to Lévi's negative remarks, later works such as Emma Hardinge Britten's novel *Ghost Land* (1876) presented India as a haven of occult wisdom, although in a very abstract, ahistorical fashion. At that time, India was still mainly an orientalist fantasy rather than a source of information. When occultism became 'institutionalised' in the 1870s and the 1890s, this changed radically. A key factor in that development was the founding of the Theosophical Society in New York in 1875 (Hammer 2013). Growing out of a Spiritualist context and relying on most of the magnetistic, Romantic and occultist authors that have been discussed so far, Theosophy was occupied with an idealised

'East' from the beginning. However, it was Rosicrucianism, Hermeticism, Kabbalah and other 'western esoteric' currents that provided the most relevant references and identity markers for Theosophists. This focus would soon shift towards the east. After the Society's founders Helena Petrovna Blavatsky (1831–1891) and Henry Steel Olcott (1832–1907) had visited Mumbai (then Bombay) for the first time in 1879, the Society permanently moved its headquarters to Adyar near Chennai (then Madras) in 1882.

It quickly established itself, not only as a significant force in the Indian cultural, religious and political landscape, but also as one of the most important platforms for exchanges between India, Europe and North America – and, as becomes increasingly clear, with other parts of the world (Chajes and Huss 2016). Prominent Indian historical figures such as Mahatma Gandhi were influenced by Theosophy, and the election of Annie Besant, president of the Theosophical Society from 1907, as president of the Indian National Congress in 1917 is an illustration of the significant and often ambiguous role of Theosophy within the colonial framework. On the one hand, Theosophists such as Besant were instrumental in the struggle for Indian national identity and independence, providing Indian intellectuals with new means of communication and religious authority; on the other hand, the Theosophical perception of India was thoroughly informed by orientalist notions that more or less implicitly reproduced racially connoted power hierarchies (Bevir 1998; Viswanathan 1998; Bevir 2000; Bevir 2003; Veer 2001: 55–82; Lubelsky 2012; Bergunder 2014; Bergunder 2016). These ambiguities, of which an example will be given below, deserve further scholarship.

Scholars have discussed in some detail how the founders of the Theosophical Society, most prominently the towering character of Blavatsky, gradually directed their attention to the east, and finally to India (Prothero 1993; McVey 2005; Pasi 2010; Hanegraaff 2015). It is important to note that this went hand in hand with a rejection of Spiritualism, which, like in the works of Lévi, was regarded as puerile, superficial and amateurish. Rather, Theosophists stressed the need for initiation and 'traditional' knowledge, meaning that esoteric wisdom cannot simply be accessed and understood by a medium, but requires a learned preparation in esoteric teachings and the means to decipher them. India came to be regarded as the treasure trove of ancient 'Aryan' wisdom that held that required key to occultism. Behind that idea stood the orientalist discovery of the relationship between Sanskrit and European languages, which, during the nineteenth century, first inspired several theories about the origins of religion and 'myths', and received an increasingly biological connotation towards the end of the century. In this context, Yogic and meditational practices were at the core of Theosophical interest in that supposed traditional 'Aryan' wisdom, and as a result, Theosophists gave yoga an unprecedented global attention that formed the basis for later developments in the twentieth century and New Age culture.

This process is inherently intertwined with global debates about the meaning and relationship of religion, science and philosophy (a 'synthesis' of which was promised by Blavatsky in her famous *Secret Doctrine* from 1888), as well as with questions of Hindu religious and national identities. When they entered India, Theosophists found themselves amid existing debates about these issues, which in their own right were already the outcome of intense exchanges between 'East and West'. The Theosophical Society was briefly allied with Dayananda Saraswati's Arya Samaj in 1877 and joined the debates surrounding the Brahmo Samaj. The Theosophical Society rapidly branched out in the 1880s, founding numerous lodges across the subcontinent and providing the Indian intelligentsia with forums such as *The Theosophist*, a journal that opened up a new effective global line of communication for numerous Indians.

The Theosophists' activities were a decisive factor for a revival of yogic practices on the subcontinent. They thus became an integral part of the dynamics often referred to as 'Hindu revivalism', in which the Arya and Brahmo Samaj played a key role. Formed in 1875 and 1828, respectively, these societies tried to renegotiate – or, perhaps more precisely, establish – the meaning of 'Hindu' in the light of western criticism of Indian religious traditions. Part of this heterogenous project were not only concerns about the religious and cultural regeneration of India, but also of physical exercises that should invigorate the Indian body. Yoga played a central part in this context, and the Theosophists would actively contribute to its modern interpretation and popularisation.

A major factor in that was the Theosophical concern for new editions and translations of Sanskrit and vernacular texts: readers will find that many contemporary editions and studies were printed by Theosophical publishing houses. In 1883, Rajendralal Mitra wrote in the translation of *The Yoga Aphorisms of Patanjali* that no pandit in Bengal had made yoga the special subject of his studies (Mitra 1881: xc), which demonstrates the relative lack of interest of western-educated Indians in yoga. Mirroring missionary and orientalist polemics, yoga was often regarded as superstitious, barbaric and dangerous. Not least thanks to the Theosophists, this attitude was beginning to change. One year before Mitra, the Indian Theosophist Tukaram Tatya (1836–1898) had published James R. Ballantyne's translation of the first and second chapters of the *Yogasūtra*, combined with Govindaram Sastri's translation of the third and fourth chapters that had been published in the journal *Pandit*. This book, called *The Yoga Philosophy*, was thus the first English edition of the whole of Patañjali's text. Its introduction was written by Olcott, who explicitly identified yoga with the occultist technique of self-mesmerisation. A second enhanced version was published in 1886, and a revised, more accessible version in 1889 by the leading US-American Theosophist and co-founder William Quan Judge (1851–1896).

The Theosophical occupation with yoga can be observed as early as with the inception of the flagship journal, *The Theosophist*, in an article about 'Yoga Vidya' from October 1879 until January 1880. Therein, yoga is discussed in the light of Mesmerism and Spiritualism, with references to the *Bhāgavata Purāṇa* and the English translation of the *Yogasūtra* from *Pandit*. The year 1880 also marks the first engagement with tantra, which set the stage for a Theosophical reception of *kuṇḍalinī*, *cakras* and related yogic concepts that remains influential up to the present day (Baier 2012; Baier 2016). In what follows, this first encounter with tantra will be put in the context of the western esoteric reception of yoga and meditation, focusing on a selection of key concepts and the role of Indian authors in their transmission into western alternative religious culture.

In January 1880, a western Theosophist using the pseudonym 'Truth Seeker' requested further information about the rising of the Kundalini, about which he had read in an article series from 1853/1854. This practice was supposedly described in the *Jñāneśvarī* and equalled, in the eyes of the Truth Seeker, those of the *Oupnek'hat* as well as those of western mystics. The editors hoped that Dayananda 'would give the world a translation of this work, and also of Patanjali's *Yoga Sastra* …' In the February issue, 'a Bengali friend' penned a first response to this query, pointing out that Dayananda, who was in fact a staunch critic of tantra, was mistaken. He had only seen the '*black* Tantra' and unfairly dismissed the whole tradition, which indeed stood behind the *Jñāneśvarī*. This rejection of Dayananda's judgement is interesting insofar as it represents a criticism of both western-educated Indians as well as missionary and orientalist perspectives on tantra. The Theosophists' eagerness to learn more about this topic would soon be satisfied. After the editors had wondered if 'no one in Bengal care enough for truth and science to send us English translations' of the *Jñāneśvarī*, a range of articles was published on the topic in the same year and the years to follow.

The first to take up the task was the Bengali author Barada Kanta Majumdar, who published a series of articles praising the value of tantra. It is significant that Majumdar would later collaborate with John Woodroffe on the Arthur Avalon project, which produced highly influential books on tantra, as will be discussed below. This collaboration was arguably prepared, at least to a significant extent, by these early exchanges in the 1880s. In 'Tantric Philosophy' and 'A Glimpse of Tantrik Occultism', Majumdar drew parallels between tantric-yogic practices, Mesmerism and Spiritualism. This remarkable identification of 'western' and 'Tantrik Occultism' was further explained by Majumdar in his contribution to Tukaram Tatya's (1836–1898) influential *Guide to Theosophy* from 1887. In 'The Occult Sciences', Majumdar emphasised that western science was only rediscovering what Indian Tantric wisdom had already been practicing throughout the ages. While Theosophists and other esotericists had long claimed the superiority of their synthesis of science, religion and philosophy over 'materialistic' mainstream science and scholarship, this declaration of Indian spiritual-scientific superiority was a key characteristic of the discourse about yoga, meditation and tantra.

These assertions of authenticity and superiority played directly into the inner-esoteric identity struggles revolving around initiation into higher knowledge and the 'competent' practice of magic. It is not least for this reason that the western esoteric reception of Indian concepts was strongly contested, chaotic and often self-contradictory. What can be said with certainty is that western esotericism and Indian traditions became deeply intertwined in the process. The studies by Elizabeth De Michelis (2004), Karl Baier (2009) and Mark Singleton (2010) have demonstrated the importance of these exchanges for new understandings of yoga, both in India and in the West. The hybrid outcomes of these entanglements have often been dismissed as inauthentic. However, instead of regarding them simply as the products of western Theosophical imagination, it is important to consider the agency of the learned Indians on whose information and philological competence western Theosophists relied.

An influential example of this relationship is Sri Sabhapati Swami, who was born in 1840 in Chennai and educated at a Christian missionary school. After having worked in the textile trade, he embarked on a spiritual journey and in 1880 published *Om: A Treatise on Vedantic Raj Yoga*. The text focused on Kundalini Yoga and presented a twelve-chakra system, six of which were located in the head. It saw several editions in the subsequent years and a German translation in 1909. Sabhapati Swami's writings, which were praised by an 'Admirer' in the *Theosophist* in September 1880, exerted a decisive yet controversial influence on western perceptions of Tantric yoga (Baier 2009: 363–369). Blavatsky herself adopted the terminology of chakras in the *Theosophist* in August 1882, referring to a six-chakra system that would later be expanded into seven. In the same year, Olcott lectured about the connection between the chakras and the western technique of 'astral projection', as he saw it taught by Sabhapati Swami's Vedantic Raj Yoga.

Astral projection was an important concept in nineteenth-century esotericism, which can be traced back to the early Mesmeric authors discussed above. Jung-Stilling had already discussed the separation of an 'etheric body' from the material one. While early Theosophical texts discussed this with reference to Mesmeric and ascetic practices, incense or drugs and techniques like magic mirrors as described by Du Potet, Hardinge Britten and others, the shift to Kundalini Yoga for achieving astral projection is a hallmark in the esoteric reception of yoga (Deveney 1997a; Baier 2009: 297–299). Although a footnote in the *Theosophist* from June 1883 was still cautious to distinguish between 'black' and 'white' tantra analogous to black and white magic, several Theosophists were now willing to recognise the value of 'Tantrik Occultism' as the highest form of Indian esotericism – criticising the negative views on it held by adherents of the Arya and Brahmo Samaj.

In 1887, Srish Chandra Basu (1861–1918) published *The Esoteric Science and Philosophy of the Tantras*, a translation of the *Śiva Saṃhitā*. Basu (also spelled Vasu) was a Bengali civil servant and Sanskritist who was closely involved in Theosophical circles. Notably, he edited Sabhapati

Swami's work and appears to have introduced the notion of 'Mesmerism' into it. Basu became a widely-read key actor for 'Hindu revivalism' in the early twentieth century and promoted the values of Indian culture based around the celebration of yogic texts, most notably the *Śiva Saṃhitā* and the *Gheraṇḍa Saṃhitā*, from an early point on. Apart from being hugely popular among esoteric actors, he was also cited by established academics such as Friedrich Max Müller, in his *Six Systems of Indian Philosophy* (1899) (Singleton 2010: 44–53). In March 1888, Basu's younger brother Baman Das Basu (1867–1930) published an article about 'The Anatomy of the Tantras' in the *Theosophist*. While we find a six-chakra system plus the *sahasrāra* in Srish Chandra's translation, Baman Das placed a seventh chakra in the medulla oblongata at the base of the brain; that is below the sixth chakra instead of at the crown of the head. Basu associated the chakras with the nerve plexuses, which was a product of both Theosophical and traditional Indian concepts and an important step in the development of modern systems of yoga. Early Mesmeric theories had already emphasised the importance of the ganglia for interactions between a subtle and a material body through 'fine' forces; this now became an integral point of reference for the explanation of yogic techniques. The association of the nervous system and the chakras is often traced to Vasant G. Rele's *Mysterious Kundalini* from 1927, which however appeared almost forty years after Basu's article.

Another key aspect is the Theosophical reception of *prāṇāyāma*. Blavatsky had already referred to this technique as part of a 'psychological science' in her famous *Isis Unveiled* from 1877 (Blavatsky 1877: 590), but without tangible in-depth knowledge of actual Indian sources. In the 1880s, Theosophists were eager to learn more about pranayama, incorporating it into a variety of contested appropriations of yogic techniques and, in turn, transforming indigenous Indian understandings of it. Instrumental in this regard was *Occult Science: The Science of Breath*, first published in 1884 by Ram Prasad, the president of the Meerut Theosophical Society in Uttar Pradesh. Between 1887 and 1889, it was published as 'Nature's Finer Forces' in *The Theosophist*, followed by an 1890 edition titled *The Science of Breath and the Philosophy of the Tattvas*. It exerted a large influence on a wide readership and had a profound impact on western esoteric practices.

As will be recalled, the question of 'practice' has been a subject of dispute among esotericists at least since the middle of the nineteenth century. Much of what has so far been referred to as 'contested' revolved around the question of whether a practice should be considered as 'white' or 'black', or if it operated on the material rather than the 'spiritual' level. This led to the Theosophical separation between what was perceived as *Haṭha Yoga* and *Rāja Yoga*. Many Theosophists rejected Hatha Yoga as an exoteric, merely physical system that was not only superficial and superstitious, but outright dangerous. This triggered controversial debates, which are reflected in the writings of another highly influential Indian author, Tallapragada Subba Row (1856–1890), who challenged Blavatsky's negative view about Hatha Yoga in the 1880s and remains one the most important sources in the Theosophical context. The controversy is an illustrative example of the ambiguous power relations and claims to authenticity among the different actors within the Theosophical Society and other esoteric currents.

Raja Yoga, in contrast, was hailed by many Theosophical authors as the superior esoteric practice operating on the spiritual level, achieving the practitioner's ascent through asceticism, meditation and spiritual exercises. This distinction was probably mainly inspired by Dayananda Saraswati, although Nobin Chunder Paul's *Treatise on the Yoga Philosophy* from 1851 was also frequently cited as a source. However, these opinions were controversially discussed; in some instances, the front lines appear to reveal inner-Indian rivalries that demand further research. A good example for this is Damodar K. Mavalankar's attack on Sabhapati Swami's Vedantic Raj Yoga. Born in Ahmedabad in 1857, Mavalankar was one of the earliest and most important Indian informants of the Theosophists, since he had met Blavatsky and Olcott in 1879. In a review of Sabhapati Swami's book in *The Theosophist* of March 1884, he strongly denounced the physical exercises described by the author, including the practice of *āsanas*. This criticism was adopted by Blavatsky and Olcott, for instance in the second edition of the Patañjali edition from 1885. Similarly, Blavatsky levelled harsh criticism against the pranayama taught by Ram Prasad, which she regarded as black magical, Tantric and thus harmful.

These quarrels did not end the demand of many Theosophists for practical experiences, and it was for this reason – and, as will be seen, because of competing esoteric societies – that Blavatsky formed an Esoteric Section or Eastern School in 1888 (Baier 2009: 385–395). In this 'Inner Group', members were taught 'practical occultism' including tantric-inspired yoga (Leland 2016: 117–127). Blavatsky designed the lessons for this group, which were published by Besant in the posthumous third volume of the *Secret Doctrine* in 1897. Blavatsky's interpretation of notions like the chakras, nadis, kundalini, etc. were fairly 'creative' and often erroneous from a historical perspective. Clearly, Blavatsky was concerned with harmonising these concepts with her understanding of Theosophy, or with what she termed the 'Trans-Himalayan school, of the ancient Indian Raja-Yogis, with which the modern Yogis of India have little to do' (Blavatsky 1987: 616). In doing so, she increasingly referred to the hidden 'Masters' from whom she supposedly received esoteric instructions, rather than living Indian yogis or historical yogic traditions. This underlines how colonial and racial power dynamics led to an often ambiguous relationship between western Theosophists and their Indian collaborators, as has been indicated above. Apart from this, the tendency of the Theosophical Society to reject the bodily practices of 'Hatha Yoga' left the field open to other currents who became instrumental in preparing the ground for present-day practices of yoga.

## Later Occultism and New Thought

Apart from the clashes about the question of practice, the esoteric landscape was determined by an escalating antagonism between 'eastern' and 'western' esotericism. The Theosophical Society went through several schisms after a crisis in 1886 that questioned the credibility of Blavatsky, the existence of the Masters and by extension the authority of eastern wisdom. In France, where the Theosophical Society had largely stimulated the formation of several occultist groups, a strand of neo-Martinism became increasingly vocal against eastern knowledge and instead proclaimed western Hermeticism, Kabbalah or Renaissance magic (Strube 2017a). This 'Hermetic Reaction' can also be observed in other national – and nationalistic – contexts, most notably in the Anglophone world where influential new societies were founded, such as the Hermetic Order of the Golden Dawn in 1888 (Godwin 1994: 333–362). In Germany, Rudolf Steiner (1861–1925) founded the Anthroposophical Society in 1912, whose decidedly 'Christian', 'Hermetic' or 'Gnostic' orientation subsequently dominated an already fractured scene of Theosophical Societies in the German-speaking countries (Zander 2007; Staudenmaier 2014). At the same time, the emerging current of Traditionalism did retain an orientation towards India, most notably in the work of René Guénon (1886–1951), who exerted a decisive influence on Ananda Coomaraswamy (1877–1947) (Sedgwick 2004).

The most crucial and direct role for modern yogic and meditational practices was played by a heterogenous current called New Thought, which was largely stimulated by the writings of the US-based Mesmeric healer Phineas Quimby (1802–1866) and gained enormous influence in the 1870s and 1880s. According to Karl Baier, it can be considered 'the first modern religious mass movement in the west that was simultaneously a meditation movement' (Baier 2009: 430). The success of Swami Vivekananda (1863–1902) is a good example for New Thought's relevance. It was in this milieu that Vivekananda was especially popular during his activities in the United States since 1893. In turn, it has been pointed out that his outstandingly successful system of Raja Yoga showed significant influences from the context of western esotericism, such as contemplative exercises, focus on bodily health, certain body postures and a concept of prana that was largely informed by Mesmerism (De Michelis 2004: 159–168). It can be argued, however, that Vivekananda's success is not so much due to a spiritual vacuum or 'craving' on behalf of his western admirers (De Michelis 2004: 150). Quite the contrary, the ingredients of his success had already been prepared since the 1880s and were widespread at the time of his arrival. It might therefore be more appropriate to speak of 'welcome structures' (Baier 2009: 485) that were established by Mesmerism, Spiritualism, occultism, Theosophy and New Thought.

As Philip Deslippe has argued, early forms of yoga in the United States were 'not physical or postural, but primarily mental and magical' (Deslippe 2018). With this in mind, it must be noted that New Thought was markedly different to Theosophy in that it was very positive towards bodily practices. At the same time, contrary to occultist organisations who focused on practical occultism, it was neither restricted by elitist structures of initiation, nor was it stigmatised by the more extreme, scandalous practices of sexual magic that will be discussed below. New Thought proclaimed the power of mind over matter and developed systems of 'positive thinking' and 'auto-suggestion' that remain highly influential up to the present day. In the eyes of William James, it represented a system of 'Mind Cure', which he described in the chapter 'The Religion of Healthy-Mindedness' in *The Varieties of Religious Experience* (1902).

The followers of New Thought usually identified as Christian, and the movement itself was closely interwoven with the somewhat rivalling Christian Science, founded by Mary Baker Eddy (1821–1910). Despite its profession of 'esoteric Christianity', New Thought was not secret but open for all, and typically organised in Churches or communities. Nevertheless, New Thought shared common ancestors, narratives and sources, such as Mesmerism, Spiritualism or Christian mysticism. It also became widely successful in Europe, sharing many parallels and having large overlaps with movements such as the German *Lebensreform*. It was concerned with alternative lifestyles, health, body culture, spiritual and personal growth, communal living, art and often socially progressive and feminist tendencies. On both sides of the Atlantic, it was predominantly successful among the white Protestant middle class and developed strong missionary activities, including an unprecedented use of modern media.

Not surprisingly, New Thought had a complicated relationship with Theosophy and soon rose to the rank of its main competitor. This resulted in ambiguous mutual influences. For instance, the popular book *The Primitive Mind Culture* (1884) by the New Thought author Warren Felt Evans (1817–1889) showed influences of Theosophy, and it was through the latter that New Thought quickly opened up to Hinduism and Buddhism, promoting its own forms of yoga and meditation. In turn, Blavatsky's Esoteric School teachings are clearly marked by New Thought concepts. *Meditation*, by the US-American Theosophist Henry Bedinger Mitchell, a pioneering work of an emerging genre of popular literature on meditation (1906, German 1908), is a mix of Theosophy, New Thought and Transcendentalism that does not stress, or even display, Theosophical teachings, initiations or Masters.

These developments laid the foundations for yoga as a mass movement. Its authors became progressively eclectic, such as William Walker Atkinson (1862–1932), who was as much an occultist as a proponent of New Thought. Using the name Yogi Ramacharaka, among numerous others, he focused on an interpretation of Hatha Yoga largely inspired by western body culture and techniques of pranayama that were largely mesmeric. In the early twentieth century, such writings widely disseminated instructions for relaxation, meditation and contemplation, often combined with yogic practices or what was named as such. By the end of World War I, such practices were an integral part of North American and European culture and appreciated not only by those seeking alternative lifestyles.

There were also more deviant and exclusive currents within the occultist fold that not only focused on the refinement of the material, astral or etheric body through postural, meditational or breathing techniques, but also on more scandalous forms of sexual magic (Urban 2006). In 1884, the Hermetic Brotherhood of Luxor made a public appearance. Claiming to be of ancient origin, it propagated the ideas of Pascal Beverly Randolph (1825–1875), an Afro-American occultist who had elaborated a system of magic that tried to harness sexual energies (Godwin, Chanel and Deveney 1995; Deveney 1997b). This magical system was derived from western sources, largely within the context of Spiritualism and Mesmerism, but it should be noted that Randolph's claim to have learned these techniques from fakirs and dervishes in the Near East still awaits scholarly investigation. The year 1888 saw the founding of the more famous Hermetic Order of the Golden Dawn, a training ground for a range of occultists dedicated to more transgressive strands of practical occultism. The Golden Dawn practice of 'Tattwa meditation' in order to achieve 'astral travel' (Owen 2004: 150) is an illustrative example of how Theosophically transmitted writings by Indians found their way into western occultism: its main source were Ram Prasad's writings on 'Nature's Finer Sources' and the 'Science of Breath'.

An occupation with yogic notions in relation to sexual magic arose especially within the Ordo Templi Orientis, whose foundation can be traced back to a collaboration between Carl Kellner (1850–1905), Theodor Reuss (1855–1923) and Franz Hartmann (1838–1912) in the 1890s. The order was probably established between 1906 and 1912 (Pasi 2006; Möller and Howe 1986). Kellner's *Yoga: Eine Skizze über den psycho-physiologischen Teil der alten indischen Yogalehre* (1896) discussed Hatha Yoga practices, while Reuss's 1906 writing, *Lingam-Yoni, oder die Mysterien des Geschlechts-Kultus*, was occupied with sexuality in the comparative history of religions (Baier 2018). Despite the Indianising title, the latter book was a translation of Hargrave Jennings's *Phallicism* (1884) and thus a specimen of the genre of literature about 'phallic worship' that had been popular in the nineteenth century. Reuss did not relate yogic or tantric concepts to sexual magic, and the use of respective terminology was most likely merely superficial (Bogdan 2006). Nevertheless, the Ordo Templi Orientis contributed to the flourishing of yogic terminology, and its influences can be discerned across the alternative religious milieu in Europe and North America, for instance in the work of Rudolf von Laban (1879–1958), the pioneer of modern dancing, whose mélange of dance and sun worship is exemplary of 'Oriental'-inspired bodily practices.

Better known is the occultism of Aleister Crowley (1875–1947), who began his esoteric career in 1898 in the Golden Dawn and soon took over the Ordo Templi Orientis (Kaczynski 2010; Bogdan and Starr 2012; Pasi 2014). It is somewhat unclear to what extent Crowley relied on knowledge about historical Indian traditions for the construction of his immensely influential system called Thelema (Urban 2003; Urban 2006; Bogdan 2006: 223–226; Djurdjevic 2012). While Crowley never claimed to be a 'tantric', he did engage with Indian sources such as Basu's translation of the *Śiva Saṃhitā*. This demonstrates the complex and often ambiguous character of the category 'tantra', not only in esoteric parlance during the period around 1900, but also in light of more recent scholarly attempts to define the category either on certain practices and or on traceable scriptural traditions. In the occultist contexts, these boundaries were frequently blurred, as Crowley's synthesis can illustrate: there is no question that his strong focus on sexual magic led him to adopt a range of tantric vocabulary and yogic practices, which he combined with western esoteric elements – especially those arising from the work of Randolph – but also with contemporary scholarship such as that by William James or James G. Frazer (Asprem 2008; Pasi 2011). Within the system that Crowley called 'Magick', yoga was perceived as an ancient method of psychological and physical self-enhancement that could now be employed in a thoroughly 'scientific' way – notions that clearly mirror the ideas that have been discussed so far.

The same period also saw the works of John Woodroffe (1865–1936), a British judge who worked in Kolkata (then Calcutta) between 1890 and 1922. From 1913 onward, a group of learned Indians and Woodroffe began to publish editions, translations and studies of tantric texts under the pseudonym 'Arthur Avalon' (Taylor 2001). This collaboration almost single-handedly initiated the academic study of tantra and yoga, influencing generations of scholars. Books like *The Serpent Power* (1918) remain popular until today. These texts, which were printed by the Theosophical publisher Ganesh & Co. in Chennai, are a fascinating example of how inherently intertwined the emerging academic study of tantra and yoga has been with the contexts discussed above. Although Woodroffe was no Theosophist and skeptical of contemporary esoteric movements, he drew extensive parallels between New Thought, Christian Science, Theosophy, occultism, etc. and tantric yoga. As Woodroffe wrote in *Shakti and Shakta* (1918), tantra, as 'Indian occultism', shared the same roots and goals as those western movements, which, like the most recent scientific advances, were only rediscovering ancient truths (e.g. Woodroffe 1929: 73–74). These and many similar remarks can only be comprehended in the light of what has been summarised in this chapter. Much of the evidence for this is rather straightforward: it might be recalled that one of Woodroffe's main collaborators was none other than Barada Kanta Majumdar, the very same Bengali who began the *Theosophist* articles about tantra in 1880.

Against this background, mesmeric, New Thought and occultist concepts of 'will power' found their way into the Avalon/Woodroffe writings, as they did into other contemporary publications about yoga, tantra and related topics. Interestingly, there is no evidence that Crowley relied on the work of Woodroffe and his collaborators, but there are clear influences among a diverse range of other esotericists: the Italian fascistic esotericist Julius Evola (1898–1974), who corresponded with Woodroffe, developed this into a veritable 'Yoga of Power' (Urban 2006: 140–161) that aimed at the perfection of the individual and the development of superhuman faculties. All these strands come together in more recent, widely-read esoteric authors and editors such as Gerald J. Yorke (1901–1983), Israel Regardie (1907–1985) and Kenneth Grant (1924–2011), who fused yogic, magical, Kabbalistic and psychoanalytical aspects, especially those of Carl Gustav Jung (1875–1961). These writings form the basis of much of present-day esoteric yogic and meditational practice (Newcombe 2013).

Jung, who was influenced by contemporary esoteric ideas as well as by Romantic Mesmerism, in turn largely relied on the writings of Avalon and Woodroffe in his discussions of yoga. This also applies to Mircea Eliade (1907–1986), another participant of the famous Eranos meetings where distinguished scholars of religion met since 1933 to discuss the history and theories of religions (Hanegraaff 2012: 277–314; Hakl 2013). As the case of the influential Indologist Heinrich Zimmer (1890–1943) illustrates, such ideas formed an integral part of Indological scholarship well into the twentieth century. For Zimmer and many others, Woodroffe's/Avalon's notion about tantra were especially influential for their understandings of Indian philosophy, art and esoteric traditions – aspects that form the core of the latter's writings from the 1910s until the 1920s (Urban 2003: 168–170; cf. Kripal 2007).

## Conclusion

This chapter has pointed towards the manifold and yet interconnected ways that led into the diffuse field of New Age culture, in which present-day yogic and meditational practices took shape. As has become evident, much of what is commonly understood as yoga and meditation was the outcome of a complex tangle of developments since the end of the eighteenth century, when a Viennese doctor pondered the astral influences on the human mind and body. These exchanges between South Asian and western actors call for further exploration, which is thankfully happening within an expanding area of new research. Central challenges include an increased recognition of the historically significant role of historical actors that are marginalised or dismissed in more traditional lines of research – such as the Theosophists and other esotericists. It is also necessary to pay closer attention to the agency and influence of the colonised, which does not only require an increased consideration of vernacular sources but also an awareness of the ambiguities within the colonial framework that have been indicated above. Such an approach would ideally combine research and methodologies from the field of western esotericism and related subjects with those from the area of South Asian Studies and Indology. As the examples in this chapter have shown, such a wider perspective would contribute, not only to an understanding of 'esotericism' but also of larger historical processes since the nineteenth century, whose ambiguities and complexities help to explain modern interpretations of yogic and meditational practices.

## Bibliography


Albanese, C. L. 2007. *A Republic of Mind and Spirit. A Cultural History of American Metaphysical Religion.* New Haven and London: Yale University Press.

Asprem, E. 2008. 'Magic Naturalized? Negotiating Science and Occult Experience in Aleister Crowley's Scientific Illuminism', *Aries* 8: 139–165.

Asprem, E. 2014. 'Beyond the West. Towards a New Comparativism in the Study of Esotericism', *Correspondences* 2(1): 3–33.

Baier, K. 2009. *Meditation und Moderne. Zur Genese eines Kernbereichs moderner Spiritualität in der Wechselwirkung zwischen Westeuropa, Nordamerika und Asien* (2 volumes). Würzburg: Königshausen & Neumann.

Baier, K. 2012. 'Mesmeric Yoga and the Development of Meditation within the Theosophical Society', *Theosophical History* 16(3–4): 151–161.

Baier, K. 2016. 'Theosophical Orientalism and the Structures of Intercultural Transfer. Annotations on the Appropriation of the Cakras in Early Theosophy', in Chajes, J. and Huss, B. (eds), *Theosophical Appropriations. Esotericism, Kabbalah, and the Transformation of Traditions*, 309–354. Beer Sheva: Ben-Gurion University of the Negev Press.

Baier, K. 2018. 'Yoga Within Viennese Occultism: Carl Kellner and Co.', in Baier, K., Maas, P. A. and Preisendanz, K. (eds), *Yoga in Transformation: Historical and Contemporary Perspectives*, 389–428. Vienna: Vienna University Press.

Bergunder, M. 2014. 'Experiments with Theosophical Truth. Gandhi, Esotericism, and Global Religious History', *Journal of the American Academy of Religion* 82: 398–426.

Bergunder, M. 2016. '"Religion" and "Science" Within a Global Religious History', *Aries* 16(1): 86–141.

Bevir, M. 1998. 'In Opposition to the Raj', *History of Political Thought* 19: 61–77.

Bevir, M. 2000. 'Theosophy as a Political Movement', in Copley, A. (ed), *Gurus and Their Followers*, 159–179. Delhi: Oxford University Press.

Bevir, M. 2003. 'Theosophy and the Origins of the Indian National Congress', *International Journal for Hindu Studies* 7(1/3): 99–115.

Blavatsky, H. P. 1877. *Isis Unveiled: A Master-Key to the Mysteries of Ancient and Modern Science and Theology* (2 volumes). London: Bernard Quaritch.

Blavatsky, H. P. 1987. *Collected Writings* (Vol. 12) Second edition. Whaeton: The Theosophical Publishing House.

Bogdan, H. 2006. 'Challenging the Morals of Western Society. The Use of Ritualized Sex in Contemporary Occultism', *The Pomegranate* 8(2): 211–246.

Bogdan, H. and Starr, M. P. (eds) 2012. *Aleister Crowley and Western Esotericism.* New York: Oxford University Press.

Chajes, J. and Huss, B. (eds) 2016. *Theosophical Appropriations. Esotericism, Kabbalah, and the Transformation of Traditions.* Beer Sheva: Ben-Gurion University of the Negev Press.

Crabtree, A. 1993. *From Mesmer to Freud. Magnetic Sleep and the Roots of Psychological Healing.* New Haven: Yale University Press.

Darnton, R. 1968. *Mesmerism and the End of the Enlightenment in France.* Cambridge and London: Harvard University Press.
De Michelis, E. 2004. *A History of Modern Yoga. Patañjali and Western Esotericism.* London: Continuum.
Deslippe, P. 2018. 'The Swami Circuit. Mapping the Terrain of Early American Yoga', *Journal of Yoga Studies* 1: 5–44.
Deveney, J. P. 1997a. *Astral Projection or Liberation of the Double and the Work of the Early Theosophical Society.* Fullerton: Theosophical History.
Deveney, J. P. 1997b. *Paschal Beverly Randolph. A Nineteenth-Century Black American Spiritualist, Rosicrucian, and Sex Magician.* Albany: State University of New York Press.
Djurdjevic, G. 2012. 'The Great Beast as a Tantric Hero. The Role of Yoga and Tantra in Aleister Crowley's Magick', in Bogdan, H. and Starr, M. P. (eds), *Aleister Crowley and Western Esotericism*, 107–140. New York: Oxford University Press.
Fuller, R. C. 1982. *Mesmerism and the American Cure of Souls.* Philadelphia: University of Pennsylvania Press.
Gauld, A. 1992. *A History of Hypnotism.* Cambridge: Cambridge University Press.
Godwin, J. 1994. *The Theosophical Enlightenment.* Albany: State University of New York Press.
Godwin, J., Chanel, C. and Deveney, J. P. 1995. *The Hermetic Brotherhood of Luxor. Initiatic and Historical Documents of an Order of Practical Occultism.* York Beach: Weiser.
Granholm, K. 2014. 'Locating the West. Problematizing the "Western" in Western Esotericism and Occultism', in Bogdan, H. and Djurdjevic, G. (eds), *Occultism in a Global Perspective*, 17–36. London: Acumen Publishing.
Hakl, H. T. 2013. *Eranos. An Alternative Intellectual History of the Twentieth Century.* Abingdon: Routledge.
Hammer, O. (ed) 2013. *Handbook of the Theosophical Current.* Leiden: Brill.
Hanegraaff, W. 2012. *Esotericism and the Academy. Rejected Knowledge in Western Culture.* Cambridge: Cambridge University Press.
Hanegraaff, W. 2015. 'The Globalization of Esotericism', *Correspondences* 3(1): 55–91.
Kaczynski, R. 2010. *Perdurabo. The Life of Aleister Crowley.* Berkeley: North Atlantic Books.
Kripal, J. J. 2007. 'Remembering Ourselves. On Some Countercultural Echoes of Contemporary Tantric Studies', *Religions of South Asia* 1(1): 11–28.
Le Forestier, R. 1970. *La Franc-maçonnerie Templière et Occultiste aux XVIIIe et XIXe siècles.* Paris/Louvain: Aubier-Montaigne/Editions Nauwelaerts.
Leland, K. 2016. *Rainbow Body. A History of the Western Chakra System from Blavatsky to Brennan.* Lake Worth: Ibis Press.
Lubelsky, I. 2012. *Celestial India. Madame Blavatsky and the Birth of Indian Nationalism.* Sheffield and Oakville: Equinox.
McCalla, A. 2009. 'The Mennaisian, Catholic Science of Religion', *Method and Theory in the Study of Religion* 21(3): 285–309.
McVey, G. 2005. 'Thebes, Luxor, and Loudsville, Georgia. The Hermetic Brotherhood of Luxor and the Landscapes of 19th-Century Occultisms', in Gutierrez, C. (ed), *The Occult in Nineteenth-Century America*, 153–181. Aurora: The Davies Group.
Mitra, R. 1881. *The Yoga Aphorisms of Patanjali.* Calcutta: Asiatic Society of Bengal.
Möller, H. and Howe, E. 1986. *Merlin Peregrinus. Vom Untergrund des Abendlandes.* Würzburg: Königshausen + Neumann.
Monroe, J. W. 2008. *Laboratories of Faith. Mesmerism, Spiritism, and Occultism in Modern France.* Ithaca: Cornell University Press.
Newcombe, S. 2013. 'Magic and Yoga: The Role of Subcultures in Transcultural Exchange', in Hauser, B. (ed), *Yoga Traveling. Bodily Practice in Transcultural Perspective*, 57–79. Austria: Springer.
Oliver, P. 2014. *Hinduism and the 1960s. The Rise of a Counter-Culture.* London: Bloomsbury.
Owen, A. 2004. *The Place of Enchantment. British Occultism and the Culture of the Modern.* Chicago: University of Chicago Press.
Pasi, M. 2006. 'Ordo Templi Orientis', in Hanegraaff, W. J., Faivre, A., Broek, Rvd and Brach, J.-P. (eds), *Dictionary of Gnosis and Western Esotericism*, 898–906. Leiden: Brill.
Pasi, M. 2010. 'Oriental Kabbalah and the Parting of East and West in the Early Theosophical Society', in Huss, B., Pasi, M. and Stuckrad, K. V. (eds), *Kabbalah and Modernity. Interpretations, Transformations, Adaptations*, 151–166. Leiden: Brill.
Pasi, M. 2011. 'Varieties of Magical Experience. Aleister Crowley's Views on Occult Practice', *Magic, Ritual, and Witchcraft* 6(2): 123–162.
Pasi, M. 2014. *Aleister Crowley and the Temptation of Politics.* Durham: Acumen.

Prothero, S. R. 1993. 'From Spiritualism to Theosophy: "Uplifting" a Democratic Tradition', *Religion and American Culture. A Journal of Interpretation* 3(2): 197–216.

Saif, L. 2015. *The Arabic Influences on Early Modern Occult Philosophy. Palgrave Historical Studies in Witchcraft and Magic.* New York: Palgrave Macmillan.

Sedgwick, M. 2004. *Against the Modern World. Traditionalism and the Secret Intellectual History of the Twentieth Century.* New York: Oxford University Press.

Singleton, M. 2010. *Yoga Body. The Origins of Modern Posture Practice.* Oxford and New York: Oxford University Press.

Staudenmaier, P. 2014. *Between Occultism and Nazism. Anthroposophy and the Politics of Race in the Fascist Era. Aries Book Series 17.* Leiden: Brill.

Strube, J. 2016. 'Socialist Religion and the Emergence of Occultism: A Genealogical Approach to Socialism and Secularization in 19th-Century France', *Religion* 46(3): 359–388.

Strube, J. 2017a. 'Occultist Identity Formations Between Theosophy and Socialism in Fin-de-Siècle France', *Numen* 64(5–6): 568–595.

Strube, J. 2017b. 'Socialism and Esotericism in July Monarchy France', *History of Religions* 57(2): 197–221.

Strube, J. 2017c. 'The "Baphomet" of Eliphas Lévi. Its Meaning and Historical Context', *Correspondences* 4: 37–79.

Taylor, K. 2001. *Sir John Woodroffe, Tantra and Bengal. An Indian Soul in a European Body?* p. XVI, 319 S. Richmond: Curzon.

Urban, H. B. 2003. *Tantra. Sex, Secrecy Politics, and Power in the Study of Religions.* Berkeley: University of California Press.

Urban, H. B. 2006. *Magia Sexualis. Sex, Magic, and Liberation in Modern Western Esotericism.* Berkeley: University of California Press.

Veer, P. v. d. 2001. *Imperial Encounters. Religion and Modernity in India and Britain.* Princeton: Princeton University Press.

Viatte, A. 1928. *Les Sources Occultes du Romantisme. Illuminisme, Théosophie 1770–1820.* (2 volumes). Paris: Champion.

Viswanathan, G. 1998. *Outside the Fold. Conversion, Modernity, and Belief.* Princeton: Princeton University Press.

Winter, A. 1998. *Mesmerized. Powers of Mind in Victorian Britain.* Chicago: University of Chicago Press.

Woodroffe, J. 1929. *Shakti and Shakta. Essays and Addresses on the Shakta Tantrashastra.* Third edition. Madras/London: Ganesh & Co./Luzac & Co.

Zander, H. 2007. *Anthroposophie in Deutschland. Theosophische Weltanschauung und Gesellschaftliche Praxis 1884–1945.* (2 volumes). Göttingen: Vandenhoeck & Ruprecht.

# 11

# HINDU ASCETICS AND THE POLITICAL IN CONTEMPORARY INDIA

*Raphaël Voix*

## Introduction

This chapter examines the social and political implications of 'ascetic practice' in modern and contemporary India. For the purposes of this analysis, I will consider Indian ascetics who have a meditative and/or yoga practice and who refer to it as a '*sādhana*'. Starting with the assumption that no form of asceticism proposes unambiguous social principles applied to specific contexts, I will examine the way that those who *claim* to practise ascetic disciplines – most notably, those who have renounced their social role as a member of a specific caste and family – relate to and act in the society around them (Barnard and Kripal 2002; Godrej 2016, 2017). Considering the late colonial period up until the beginning of the twenty-first century from an ethnohistorical perspective, I intend to outline various ways in which these individuals render their social conduct compatible or coherent with their ascetic practices.

## The social involvement of modern Hindu ascetics

In South Asian societies, far from the 'theological fiction' of the homeless wandering monk (Olivelle 2003: 274), Hindu ascetics have long constituted communities and represented figures of authority who have played an important – yet overlooked – socio-political role (Thapar 1987: 8, 13, 24). Gathered around charismatic figures, they have formed different institutions or sectarian traditions (*sampradāya*) and looked for public support by attracting lay members and political patronage. Ascetics engaged in different activities, holding positions such as royal advisers, merchants and warriors, with the primary objective often being primarily to maintain the existence of their own order.[1] However, the upheavals generated by colonisation gave rise to important transformations in the way ascetics understood their social role. The emergence, notably among the Indian elites, of a form of socio-political consciousness led to Hindu reformism, a deliberate and concerted activity aimed at a socio-religious change considered 'progress'.[2] In this context, new religious Hindu movements developed. These movements challenged the traditional social role of ascetics and articulated a more modern conception of renunciation which, in order to be socially accepted, had to be portrayed as useful to a larger public.

Although some monasteries *(maṭh)* have a long history of charity, in the nineteenth century critics condemned these institutions as interested mainly in the accumulation of wealth rather than working for the good of the Hindu public at large. Celibate ascetics were denounced as not 'socially responsible'. This criticism, which first appeared in European orientalist discourses, became a common trope among Hindus reformers. Dayananda Saraswati (1824–1883), who founded the Arya Samaj in 1875, severely denounced the 'parasitic' lifestyle and 'egoism' of those preoccupied solely by their own salvation. The idea that an 'authentic' ascetic should be altruistic arose, and with it a reformulation of what renunciation meant in terms of value. Whereas, since the *Upaniṣads* and the *Mahābhārata,* renunciation had been associated with the abandonment of all worldly activity (*nivṛtti dharma*), a sine qua non for obtaining liberation (*mokṣa*) (Bailey 1985: 18), nineteenth-century Hindu reformers insisted that an individual who withdrew from the world must nevertheless act in the service of those who live in the world, leading to the figure of the 'renouncer engaged in the world'. This new figure of a renouncer who could be as active in the world as a householder, while retaining the supreme 'value' of renunciation, can be considered a modern manifestation of what Dumont called 'the dialogue of the renouncer and the man-in-the-world' (1999/1970: 12–13).

At the beginning of the nineteenth century, Sahajananda (1781–1830), founder of the Svāmīnārāyaṇa movement, is believed to be the first to ask his disciples, celibate ascetics like himself, to serve God by serving the people (Williams 1984). He justified this teaching through a reinterpretation of the religious practice of *sevā* (service), a term that has assumed different meanings in various Hindu texts. In Brahmanical texts, *sevā* was primarily associated with ideas of servility and obedience and thus reserved for *śūdra* and women (Beckerlegge 2015: 211). In the medieval devotional traditions (*bhakti*), where a position of humility was praised, *sevā* became a positive religious attitude: anyone serving the Supreme Being could be granted liberation (*mokṣa*). This 'vertical' form of *sevā* was associated with a 'horizontal' one that consisted of giving mutual aid to fellow devotees (Jacobsen 2010: 861–865). However, this form of charity was usually exercised exclusively within a specific community of believers. In contrast, Sahajananda broadened the scope of this belief by no longer limiting it to co-religionists (Pandya 2016). Although this history of the term is not uncontested, it seems that Sahajananda inaugurated a religious practice that became widely popular in the following centuries (Beckerlegge 2015).

When Vivekananda (1863–1902) proposed his 'practical Vedanta' (Halbfass 1995), the idea of socially useful renunciation took definitive shape. Having realised the massive poverty of the population during his many travels around India, Vivekananda thought that celibate ascetics, if properly trained, could be agents of progress far more effectively than householders, since their celibacy made them better adapted to 'social service'. In 1894, in a letter to his brother disciples, he urged them to raise an army of celibate ascetics: 'No disciple householders, please, we want sannyasi. Let each one of you shave a hundred heads. Educated young men, not fools' (Vivekananda in Beckerlegge 1998: 187–188). Vivekananda thus founded a monastic order, the Ramakrishna Mission, and led his disciples in various 'relief activities' which he designated as '*sevā*' (*service*). Vivekananda's commitment to service led to the mobilisation of ascetics in the public sphere in unprecedented forms. Various personalities spread the idea that an ascetic can organise relief operations in the event of famine or natural disaster. Over time *sevā* has thus grown from referring to 'selfless service' to designating 'any voluntary social activity' and become a central concept in contemporary Hinduism, and more specifically within ascetic-led religious groups.

With the entry of the nationalist movement into the decisive phase that led to independence, not only could ascetics engage within society, but they could also be important leaders in nation-building; a 'great potential for political action was attributed to renunciation' (Clémentin-Ojha 2019: 231). This inspired a new figure, that of the 'patriotic ascetic' who would sacrifice his life for his homeland. Bankim Chandra Chatterjee's (1838–1894) novel

*Ānandamaṭha* (*The Monastery of Bliss*, published in 1882), played an important part in this representation. Partly inspired by the so-called *sannyāsin* revolt that the East India Company had suppressed at the end of the eighteenth century,[3] this classic of Indian literature features a group of ascetics who are willing to sacrifice themselves for the love of a highly idealised country, 'Mother India', which is suffering under the yoke of a foreign occupier. Aspiring to a government other than the one in power – a *Moghul* who oppresses his people – they prepare for armed insurrection in the forest where they live. Their purpose is to overthrow the reigning power and, when the time is ripe, to establish a Hindu kingdom.[4]

In 1899, the Maharashtrian Congress leader Bal Gangadhar Tilak (1856–1920) acclaimed this 'new type' of ascetic as not someone 'for whom the world is nothing' but one 'for whom the world is everything and for whom his country and people are dearer than all the world put together' (Tilak in Ganachari 2005: 106). It was in similar vein that, in 1905, the Punjabi Lala Lajpat Rai (1865–1928), also a member of the Congress Party, complained that it was a 'matter of shame' that his party had not 'produced at least a number of *political sannyasis* ready to sacrifice their lives for the political regeneration of the country'.[5] The life of Śraddhānanda (1857–1926), member of the Arya Samaj, could be read as an answer to that call, since he paradoxically engaged himself in politics after he had become a Hindu renouncer (Jordens 1981). Freed from obedience to any organisation, he believed that the act of renunciation had conferred on him a new independence; renunciation enabled him to 'devote [himself] to the service of the world [*loka-sevā*]' (Bhāratīya in Clémentin-Ojha 2019: 218–219). Not only had he 'self-administered' his *saṃnyāsa* but he had also 'self-proclaimed' a moral authority derived from his 'own spiritual depth' (ibid: 219). According to Clémentin-Ojha, Śraddhānanda's life entails the 'secularization' of renunciation, whereby 'renunciation as a Hindu value was given a new lease of life by being seriously envisaged as a mode of intervention in the public sphere' (ibid: 210). Whereas within traditional ascetic milieus, 'politics' had a negative connotation, at the beginning of the twentieth century, a new modality of the renouncer's authority within society emerged through ascetics entering into politics – a mode of intervention in the public sphere that has contemporary heirs, as we will see below.

Originating within the same 'reformist' milieu and in parallel to that of the patriotic ascetic, also emerged figures of laymen who act in the world in the name of ascetic ideals. This immediately calls to mind two major Indian personalities of the twentieth century. The first is Aurobindo Ghose (1872–1950) who, after having instigated the Bengali revolutionary movement, moved to Pondicherry, where from 1910 onwards he led a secluded life as a guru unconnected to any *sampradāya* (Heehs 2008; Wolfers 2016, 2017). The second is Mohandas Karamchand Gandhi (1869–1948), the internationally renowned leader of India's independence movement who became famous for his nonviolent resistance campaigns. While Gandhi and Aurobindo had conflicting views on the means of gaining independence, they were both married men who had internalised the value of renunciation through following 'chastity' (*brahmacarya*), an ascetic practice that they envisioned as being at the foundation of their moral standing (Clémentin-Ojha 2019: 218). Like many in this generation of nationalists, they were inspired by their political reading of the *Bhagavadgītā*, a Hindu text that preaches the possibility of renouncing while remaining in the world through abandoning the desire for the results of one's action (*niṣkāma karma*) (Olivelle 1978: 33). Both Gandhi and Aurobindo envisioned their action in society as a specific 'yoga' that combined the values of renunciation and detachment with those of social and political action. Significantly, with shared inspiration from the *Bhagavadgītā*, both thinkers notably diverged on the acceptability of the use of force: while the young Aurobindo advocated 'violent' action against the British, Gandhi preferred 'non-violent resistance' (Kapila and Devji 2013). Both figures are still an important source of inspiration for the contemporary world.

## Contemporary configurations

The implementation of the Indian Constitution in 1950 drew a separation between a secular domain, which the state can regulate, and a religious one, in which it should not interfere. However, this did not prevent some ascetics from interfering in public life in newly-independent India. Ascetics have continued to engage in society through different means, adapting historical patterns to the new political situation, including the transformations of public Hinduism and the emergence of Hindu nationalism (Kanungo 2015).

It is important also to emphasise that some ascetics present themselves as exclusively dedicated to personal liberation (*mokṣa*): the pursuit of knowledge is the foremost life duty in the face of which all wordly activities are looked upon as illusory. Thus, they cultivate a distance-cum-indifference towards the world and societal matters. Some exemplary ascetic figures in twentieth-century India looked on the world's activity with disdain and assisted others primarily by their mere presence, notably their detached serenity. Widely considered as one who attained liberation while living (*jivanmukti*), Ramana Maharshi (1879–1950) did not belong to any specific lineage, yet he incarnated Shankara's ideal of classical Vedānta, in which the realisation of the identity of *ātman/brahman* makes one totally detached from worldly desires and does not require one to act in the world (Fort 1997: 489–490, 502n4; Barua 2015). This posture is promoted by teachers who lay claim to Maharshi's heritage.[6] Likewise, Anandamayi Ma (1896–1982) also showed a 'complete indifference to politics' (Hallstrom 1999: 11) and conceived the realms of the 'spiritual' and that of the 'social' or 'political' as entirely separated. However, this position does not prevent many ascetics from allowing political dignitaries to meet and pay respects to them. These types of ascetic aim to transform one's relation to the divine and not to the world per se: in fact, as noted by Weber, Hindu sects often disseminate a conviction of 'the unchangeable nature of the order of the world' (Weber 1958: 313). Anandamayi Ma, for example, is known to have supported Indian customs such as *sati* (women's self-immolation on husband's pyre) (Hallstrom 1999: 211–212). While the places where these ascetics and their devotees congregate are not devoid of internal politics (linked to authority and material matters), they are still considered by devotees as places that offer temporary relief from the world.

Although not directly engaged in the transformation of society, some ascetics have been asked to associate themselves with the highest state authorities and to play the role of *éminence grise*. In the former years of Independent India, notably during the years when the agnostic Nehru officiated as prime minister (1947–1964), the absence of any relationship with religious authorities prevailed (Jaffrelot 2012: 82). But during her years as prime minister (1966–1977, 1980–1984), Indira Gandhi sought political mentorship from ascetic figures. She publicly called upon recognised figures, such as the world-famous lecturer Krishnamurti (1895–1986) and more secretly resorted to the services of controversial figures, such as Dhirendra Brahmachari (1924–1994), a *haṭhayoga* teacher who became popular in north India through his weekly TV show in the 1970s. As prime minister (1991–1996), Narasimha Rao also secretly maintained personal connections with ascetics, notably Chandraswami (1948–2017), ex-Youth Congress Leader and self-made tantric guru, who was later accused of various criminal activities (Jaffrelot 2012: 88; Jha 2019: 53). These cases of high-profile politicians seeking advice or supernatural protection from charismatic ascetic figures replicate an old Hindu schema of the renouncer as a 'super-brahmin' counsellor or adviser to the king (Jaffrelot 2012). This relationship can be made public, or not, according to the political benefits one might expect from such an association; for politicians who know how to make use of it, association with an ascetic can reinforce their legitimacy (ibid: 80).

With the rise of a narrow ideology of religious nationalism as defined by the Rashtriya Swayamsevak Sangh (RSS), the ideological parent of the Sangh Parivar (Family of Organisations), in the public sphere from the 1980s onwards and the rise in power of its political arm, the Bharatiya Janata Party (BJP) in the late 1990s, charismatic ascetics have been brought in more than ever to play a public and – almost – official political role (McKean 1996). This is notably the case since the 2014 elections and the rise of the self-made ascetic and businessman, Ramdev (b. 1965). Originating from an Arya-Samaj schooling background, Ramdev gained national fame in the 2000s through his yogic evangelism – a daily public lesson broadcast on TV – and during free camps. His commercialisation of branded ayurvedic products has assured him an outstanding financial success (Chakraborty 2007; Sarbacker 2013; Khalikova 2017). After having brought yoga and ayurveda into the 'mainstream of Indian society [...] in unprecedented ways' (Sarbacker 2013: 352), Ramdev entered the political arena in 2011 during the anti-corruption movement led by Anna Hazare (b. 1937). Hazare staged a public fast that was considerably retransmitted on social media and captured massive attention from the public. Ramdev, who from the start has benefited from solid support from the Sangh Parivar, supported the BJP in the 2014 national elections (Jaffrelot 2011; Pathak-Narain 2017). Since then, he has appeared as a personal ally to the prime minister, Narendra Modi, with whom he shares regular public platforms. Not only has Ramdev probably directly influenced the 'politics of yoga'[7] encouraged by the government by placing yoga and ayurveda at the forefront of public discourse (Worth 2018), but his wide propagation of a Hindu 'somatic' (Chakraborty 2006: 388) or 'biomoral' (Khalikova 2017: 113) nationalism constitutes an invaluable asset for the Sangh Parivar.[8]

In addition to resorting to an ascetic's influence through personal connection, high-profile politicians have for a long time attempted to mobilise the numerous *sādhus* belonging to the different *akhāṛās*. From Gandhi to Nehru, politicians of all sides have seen the Kumbha Melā, a religious fair on which these traditional ascetics reign, as constituting an enviable platform for spreading political messages to the millions of Indian citizens who congregate there every three years. Whereas before Indian independence the ascetics' associations were reluctant to introduce politics to the religious festival (Gordon 1975: 182), after independence, the festival became gradually more political (MacLean 2003: 897). Yet the different parties at stake encountered only limited success until the 1980s when hundreds of RSS militants (*pracharaks*) became ascetics themselves and put forward the Ram temple agenda within the ranks of the ascetics. Following this infiltration, a great number of *sādhus* participated both in the 1989 *yatra* – that the Sangh Parivar had organised in favour of building a Ram temple – and in the 1992 unlawful destruction of the Ayodhya Babri mosque. While political mobilisation of the *sādhus* in the past was usually done on an individual basis (and had an element of instability), the Vishva Hindu Parishad (VHP)[9] promised to give the *sādhus* an 'ecclesiastical status' within a larger Hindu Kingdom, granting them an unprecedented sense of collective importance (Jha 2019). This has enabled the Sangh Parivar to build up a substantial and durable network of patronage within the *akhāṛās*. Among *sādhus* who are also public figures, those opposed such political drift remain exceptions, and even these often support some of the specific claims of the Hindu right.[10]

A more straightforward way for ascetics to influence politics is by standing as candidates in local, regional or national elections. Since India's independence, dozens of them have taken the plunge either through a registered party – Congress, the Hindu Mahasabha, the Janata Party, or the BJP – or through the creation of their own political party. While for most of them this was an individual initiative, there are some new Hindu religious movements based around the cult of a charismatic ascetic that have also attempted to gain power by presenting candidates (laymen or ascetics) under the banner of a specifically created party.[11] In 2017, however, the election of the

BJP candidate Yogi Adityanath (b. 1972) as Chief Minister of Uttar Pradesh changed the game by instituting in India's most populated State 'a form of theocracy' (Jaffrelot 2019: 231). Spiritual and political heir of Swami Avedyanath (1921–2014), whom he succeeded in 1998 as a deputy of Gorakhpur and in 2014 as the abbot (Mahant) of the prestigious Nāth temple-monastery of Goraknāth, Yogi Adityanath distinguished himself in the political arena by his extensive use of 'muscle power'. In 2002 he founded a devoted militia, the *Hindu Yuva Vahini* (Hindu Youth Brigade), aimed at vigilantism which specialised in orchestrating inter-community riots intended to polarise the electorate along religious lines (Bouillier 2016: 277–279). Since his election as chief minister, he has been using 'terror' to govern through police squads that 'under the guise of protecting women, exercise cultural policing' (Jaffrelot 2019: 232). Parallel to his political activity, Yogi Adityanath is also active within his sect where he sponsors publications, defends the sect's yogic heritage and appears at all the important functions where the press is welcome (Bouillier 2016: 278). All kinds of actors – policemen as well as journalists – thus perceive him not only as a politician but as a holyman, routinely bowing at his feet in public (Jaffrelot 2019: 235).

While since the 1960s most of these political ascetics have been functioning in line with the Sangh Parivar, there exist rare but eloquent examples of opponents. Such is the case of Svami Agnivesh (b. 1940) who since the 1970s has been actively campaigning against forced labour, *sati*, the dowry system, consumption of alcohol and abuses of the caste system, both through social work and through being elected multiple times. In keeping with his forefathers in the Arya Samaj, he is a staunch defender of the sanctity of the Vedas. The party he founded, the Arya Sabha, declares its aim as establishing Vedic socialism (*vāidik sāmajvād*), yet he vehemently opposes 'Hindutva politics' which he considers 'a threat to democratic-secular fabric of India but also to the spiritual core of Hinduism.'[12]

The vast majority of ascetics refrain from engaging directly in politics. Yet, many still reflect the broad consensus according to which ascetics must act in the world for its betterment, combining the search for spiritual growth with engagement in social activity. This is notably the case of the contemporary self-made gurus who do not belong to a specific *sampradāya* but have gathered around their personality a huge and often cosmopolitan following. They have founded important religious organisations with many satellite NGOs through which they offer a wide range of social activities. Based on offerings from disciples and state funding, this philanthropic activity has become an ascetic practice in its own right. Since disciples consider that *sevā* is their main *sādhana*, this has also become a way to glorify the movement or its leader. One of the most successful examples of this type of movement is the one founded by Mata Amritanandamayi (b. 1953).[13] Because they are supposed to be free from any kinship attachment, theses gurus are often considered as inherently benevolent, in contrast to politicians who are seen as corrupt. While officially distancing themselves from electoral politics, these gurus nevertheless act as 'Hinduising agents' by bringing back some Hindu pride to the lower and upper urban middle classes from which their followers originate; some of them also openly promote a softcore Hindutva or endorse a position on a particular political issue, such as the cow protection or the Ramjanmabhumi movement. Similarly, traditional ascetics running Hindu monasteries (*maṭha*) often have a strong regional influence. Taking advantage of their significant local following, they are able, in times of natural disasters, to raise funds for relief and reconstruction through which they broaden their local influence. They can also choose to influence the course of politics more directly while at the same time keeping a distance from its 'dirty world'. This explains why politicians often seek support and see their religious organisations as 'vote banks' (Ikegame 2012: 51).

An altogether different way for ascetics to transform society is by radically opposing it through the building of 'practical utopias', that is 'total ideological systems that aim [...] through the transition to practise to radically transform existing global social systems' (Seguy 1999: 117). Whereas the Hindu social order (*varṇāśramadharma*) is based on the acknowledgement of the Veda as revelation (*śruti*), Sanskrit as the unique sacred language and Brahmins as exclusive figures of religious authority, Hindu ascetics follow a revelation of their own that contests these Brahmanical values and affirms that a Supreme Being grants his saving grace to all those who surrender themselves to him. Although these affirmations are theological in nature, they can have certain sociological implications: ideally all persons have direct access to the divine on an equal footing, and therefore they cannot be ranked according to his birth/caste.[14] Whereas for a great majority of these groups their principles of equality exclusively target salvific ends, there exist a few exceptions: groups that intend to produce a real alternative social order through the building of 'ideal cities'. Among the most famous cases, we find the Radhasoami communities at Beas (founded in 1891) and Dayalbagh (founded in 1915) (Juergensmeyer 1982), Ananda Marga's Anandanagar (founded in 1962) (Voix 2011) and the Mother's Auroville founded in 1968 (Minor 1999, 2000). Although most of these movements are also engaged in welfare activities, their objective is not solely to improve society but to develop a new type of humanity. Yet, their success has often been limited. Through a complex socio-religious process, they have gradually lost their radicalism and been co-opted into the caste system by becoming colonies of disciples who have to mingle with the surrounding society.

## Conclusion

Contrary to the popular imaginary of a solitary yogi absorbed in meditation in South Asia, where yoga and contemplative practices originate and where they have a long and varied history, ascetics have never been devoid of temporal preoccupations and have had varying relationships with society. During the rise of nationalism, renunciation (*saṃnyāsa*), which had long been associated with detachment and otherworldliness, was reinterpreted to represent the highest moral ideal of action in the world undertaken for the benefit of others as well as for political aims. This led to the appearance of new ascetic figures who were more fully engaged in the world, such as the 'renouncer engaged in the world', the 'patriotic ascetic' and the contemporary 'political *sādhus*'.

There is a common assumption that yoga should lead to a 'progressive' approach towards society at large, especially in comparison to more classical modes of religious piety. In contrast, this chapter has shown that in contemporary India, renunciant activism has mostly been associated with the dominant Hindu nationalist discourse. This dynamic widely nourishes a narrow Hindutva agenda that aims to reframe the Indian political state. The theological and philosophical background against which actors inscribe their practice of yoga and meditation does have a certain influence on their attitudes towards the world. Yet, this chapter has shown to what extent, more than the practices per se, it is their entrenchment in a particular historical and/or sociological context that defines a specific relation to society. Yoga and meditation traditions, like many other religious traditions, are multiple and sufficiently varied or plastic to justify opposing political or societal choices.

## Notes

1 Following Clémentin-Ojha (2006: 536), I use the term 'ascetic' as a generic term and the term 'renouncer' as a translation of *saṃnyāsī*. This latter Sanskrit term can refer either to the 'twice-born who has entered the fourth Brahmanical stage of life' (*āśrama*) and to a member of an ascetic lineage whose rules of conduct, though modeled on the former's pattern, have integrated later sectarian developments'. This distinction is important since 'not all Hindu ascetics are strictly speaking renouncers'.

2 Although it can be traced back to earlier times, Hindu reformism was most evident in the second half of the nineteenth century, once the political regime following the repression of the Sepoy Revolt (1857–1858) had been established. Literature on Hindu reformism is vast; for a brief synthesis on the upheavals it led to, see Ray (1995) and for an up-to-date bibliography see *OUP Bibliography Online*.

3 On this revolt where ascetics were defending what they considered to be the rights and prerogatives of their sect, see Lorenzen (1978).

4 Although fictional, this novel had a great impact on Indian history: it became a symbol of Indian nationalism and its lyrical ode 'Tribute to the Motherland' (*Vande Mataram*) became the rallying song of many resistance fighters against colonial power (Lipner 2005).

5 My emphasis, published in the report of the twenty-first session of the Indian National Congress, reproduced in Joshi (1966: 101), quoted in Clémentin-Ojha (2019: 227).

6 For example, the Ajatananda Ashram website proclaims that the 'monastic community does not undertake any regular or systematic activities in the world. Rather, the community is designed for those who are called to follow the path of "non-doing", focused on an inner life of silence and solitude (*nirvritti marga*) (sic)' (see ajatananda.org and Lucas 2014).

7 By the 'politics of yoga', I refer to the many decisions that the BJP government has enacted in order to promote yoga nationally and internationally: e.g. the founding of International Yoga Day, annual meetings of the World Ayurveda Congress, introduction of free, semi-compulsory yoga classes for civil servants and most notably for the armed forces (Banerjee 2015).

8 In return, various BJP-ruled state governments granted Ramdev huge discounts on land acquisition, echoing some old habits of kingly patronage (Bouillier 2016), and most certainly nurturing a growing 'crony capitalism' economy (Bhattacharya and Thakurta 2019: 212).

9 VHP is a nationalist organisation founded in 1964 that federalizes different Hindu sects.

10 For example, although the respected Swaroopananda Saraswati (b. 1924), *Śaṅkarācārya* of Dwarka and Jyotish *pīṭhas*, is often considered as a Congress supporter and VHP's enemy (Jha 2019: 132), he supports some political claims that are in line with Sangh Parivar's agenda. For example, he supported the removal of article 370 for Jammu and Kashmir; the reconstruction of a Hindu temple on the premises of the destroyed Babri Masjid; the Ban on the PK movie, etc. (ibid: 169).

11 At local elections in India as well as, in some cases, outside India, the success of these endeavours has been limited and heavily criticised. On the 'Unconquerable India Party' (Ajeya Bharat Party, ABP), founded in 1992 and based on the teachings of Maharishi Mahesh Yogi (1918–2008), see Humes (2005: 70–71, 2013: 513–514). On the Proutist Bloc of India and Amra Bengali, two off-shoots of the Ananda Marga, see Voix (2010: 54–61).

12 This defence of secular India might sound surprising considering the historical role that his organisation played in galvanizing Hindu militancy together with aggravating Hindu-Muslim relations at the end of the nineteenth century and beginning of the twentieth century. As the head of the Arya Samaj he supported the Congress in the 2019 elections (Scroll.in 2019).

13 For studies on her movement, see Warrier 2003a, 2003b, 2005; Lucia 2014a, 2014b. Other important examples are Shri Shri Ravi Shankar (b. 1956), founder of the Art of Living in 1981; H.H. Pujya Swami Chidanand Saraswati (b. 1952), head of the Parmath Niketan ashram in Rishikesh; Jagi Vasudev (alias Sadhguru, b. 1967), founder of the Isha Foundation – to name just three important ones.

14 This explain why many sects, from the time of their first appearance – with early pre-medieval groups such as the Ājivikas, the Jainas and the Buddhists – have often been seen as protest movements contributing to the development of a 'counter-culture' in South Asia (Thapar 1978, 1979).

## Bibliography


Bailey, G. 1985. *Materials for the Study of Ancient Indian Ideologies. Pravṛtti and Nivṛtti*. Torino: Indologica Taurisena.

Banerjee, S. 2015. 'The Yogi as a Pugilist. Psychotherapy-cum-Martial Exercise in the Indian Armed Forces', *Economic & Political Weekly* 50(33): 10–13.

Barnard, G. W. and Kripal, J. J. (eds) 2002. *Crossing Boundaries: Essays on the Ethical Status of Mysticism*. New York: Seven Bridge Press.

Barua, A. 2015. 'The Silences of Ramana Maharshi: Self-Enquiry and Liberation in Sāṁkhya Yoga and Advaita Vedānta', *Religions of South Asia* 9(2): 186–207.

Beckerlegge, G. 1998. 'Swami Vivekananda and Seva: Taking "Social Service" Seriously', in Radice, W. (ed), *Swami Vivekananda and the Modernization of Hinduism*, 158–193. Delhi: Oxford University Press.

Beckerlegge, G. 2015. '*Sevā*: The Focus of a Fragmented but Gradually Coalescing Field of Study', *Religions of South Asia* 9(2): 208–239.

Bhattacharya, A. K. and Thakurta, P. G. 2019. 'Contours of Crony Capitalism in the Modi Raj', in Chatterji, A. P., Hansen, T. B. and Jaffrelot, C. (eds), *Majoritarian State: How Hindu Nationalism is Changing India*. 193–213. London: Hurst.

Bouillier, V. 2016. *Monastic Wanderers. Nāth Yogī Ascetics in Modern South Asia*. New Delhi: Manohar.

Chakraborty, C. 2006. 'Ramdev and Somatic Nationalism: Embodying the Nation, Desiring the Global', *Economic & Political Weekly* 41(5): 387–390.

Chakraborty, C. 2007. 'The Hindu Ascetic as Fitness Instructor: Reviving Faith in Yoga', in *International Journal of the History of Sport* 24(9): 1172–1186.

Chatterjee, B. C. 1993 [1882]. *Ānandamaṭha*. New Delhi: Ḍāyamanḍa Pākeṭa Buksa.

Clémentin-Ojha, C. 2006. 'Replacing the Abbot: Rituals of Monastic Ordination and Investiture in Modern Hinduism', *Asiastische Studien/Etudes Asiatiques* 40(3): 535–573.

Clémentin-Ojha, C. 2019. 'Secularizing Renunciation? Swami Shraddhananda's Welcome Address at the Congress Session of Amritsar in 1919', in Fuchs, M. and Damlia, V. (eds), *Religious Interactions in Modern India*, 209–235. New Delhi: Oxford University Press.

Dumont, L. 1999 [1970]. *Homo Hierarchicus. The Caste System and Its Implication*. London: Oxford University Press.

Fort, A. C. 1997. 'Jīvanmukti and Social Service in Advaita and Neo-vedānta', in Franco, E. and Preisendanz, K. (eds), *Beyond Orientalism. The Work of Wilhem Halbfass and its Impact on Indian and Cross Cultural Studies*, 489–504. Amsterdam: Rodopi.

Ganachari, A. 2005. *Nationalism and Social Reform in Colonial Situation*. Delhi: Kalpaz Publications.Godrej, F. 2016. 'Orthodoxy and Dissent in Hinduism's Meditative Traditions: A Critical Tantric Politics?', *New Political Science* 38(2): 256–271.

Godrej, F. 2017. 'The Neoliberal Yogi and the Politics of Yoga', *Political Theory* 45(6): 772–800. https://doi.org/10.1177/0090591716643604

Gordon, R. 1975. 'The Hindu Mahasabha and the Indian National Congress, 1915 to 1926', *Modern Asian Studies* 9(2): 145–203. https://doi.org/10.1017/S0026749X00004960.

Halbfass, W. 1995. 'Practical Vedanta', in Dalmia, V. & von Stietencron, H. (eds), *Representing Hinduism: The Construction of Religious Traditions and National Identity*, 211–223. Delhi: Sage Publication.

Hallstrom, L. 1999. '*Mother of Bliss*'. *Ānandamayī Mā (1896–1982)*. London: Oxford University Press.

Heehs, P. 2008. *The Lives of Sri Aurobindo*. New York: Columbia University Press.

Humes, C. A. 2005. 'Maharishi Mahesh Yogi beyond the TM Technique', in Forsthoefel, T. A. and Humes, C. A. (eds), *Gurus in America*, 55–78. New York: State University of New York Press.

Humes, C. 2013. 'Maharishi Mahesh Yogi and Transcendental Meditation', in Jacobsen, K. A., Basu, H., Malinar, A. and Narayanan, V. (eds), *Brill's Encyclopedia of Hinduism*. Volume V, 508–514. Leiden: Brill.

Ikegame, A. 2012. 'The Governing Guru. Hindu Maths in Karnataka', in Copeman J. and Ikegame, A. (eds), *The Guru in South Asia. New Interdisciplinary Perspectives*, 46–63. London: Routledge.

Jacobsen, K. A. 2010. 'Sevā' in Jacobsen, K. A., Basu, H., Malinar, A. and Narayan, V. (eds), *Brill's Encyclopedia of Hinduism*. Volume II, 861–863. Leiden: Brill.

Jaffrelot, C. 2011. 'Ramdev: Swami Without Sampradaya', *The Caravan*. 1 July. https://caravanmagazine.in/perspectives/ramdev-swami-without-sampradaya. Accessed 2 March 2020.

Jaffrelot, C. 2012. 'The Political Guru', in Copeman J. and Ikegame, A. (eds), *The Guru in South Asia. New Interdisciplinary Perspectives*, 80–96. London: Routledge.

Jaffrelot, J. 2019. *L'Inde de Modi: National-populisme et Démocratie Ethnique*. Paris: Fayard (Essais).

Jha, D. K. 2019. *Ascetic Games. Sadhus, Akharas and the Making of the Hindu Vote*. Chennai: Antxt.

Jordens, J. T. F. 1981. *Swami Shraddhananda – His Life and Causes*. Oxford: Oxford University Press.

Joshi, V. C. 1966. *Lala Lajpat Rai. Writings and Speeches*. Volume 1, 1888–1919. Delhi: University Publishers.

Juergensmeyer, M. 1982. *Religion as Social Vision: The Movement Against Untouchability in 20th-Century Punjab*. Berkeley: University of California Press.

Kanungo, P. 2015. 'Public Hinduism and Hindutva', in Hatcher, B. A. (ed), *Hinduism in the Modern World*, 245–256. New York: New York University Press.

Kapila, S. and Devji, F. (eds) 2013. *Political Thought in Action. The Bhagavad Gita and Modern India*. London: Cambridge University Press.

Khalikova, V. R. 2017. 'The Ayurveda of Baba Ramdev: Biomoral Consumerism, National Duty and the Biopolitics of "Homegrown" Medicine in India', *South Asia: Journal of South Asian Studies* 40(1): 105–122.

Lipner, J. 2005. *Ānandamāṭh or the Sacred Brotherhood*. New York: Oxford University Press.

Lorenzen, D. L. 1978. 'Warrior Ascetics in Indian History', *Journal of the American Oriental Society* 98(1): 61–75.

Lucas, P. C. 2014. 'Non-Traditional Modern Advaita Gurus in the West and Their Traditional Modern Advaita Critics', *Nova Religio: The Journal of Alternative and Emergent Religions* 17(3): 6–37.

Lucia, A. 2014a. *Reflections of Amma: Devotees in a Global Embrace.* Berkeley: University of California Press.

Lucia, A. 2014b. '"Give Me Sevā Overtime": Selfless Service and Humanitarianism in Mata Amritanandamayi's Transnational Guru Movement', *History of Religions* 53(4): 188–207.

MacLean, K. 2003. 'Making the Colonial State Work for You : The Modern Beginnings of the Ancient Kumbh Mela in Allahabad', *Journal of Asian Studies* 62(3): 873–905.

McKean, L. 1996. *Divine Enterprise: Gurus and the Hindu Nationalist Movement.* Chicago: The University of Chicago Press.

Minor, R. N. 1999. *The Religious, the Spiritual and the Secular: Auroville and Secular India.* Albany, NY, USA: State University of New York Press.

Minor, R. N. 2000. 'Routinized Charisma: The Case of Aurobindo and Auroville', in Yandell, K. E. and Paul, J. J. (eds), *Religion and Public Culture: Encounters and Identities in Modern South India*, 130–148. Surrey: Curzon Press.

Olivelle, P. 1978. 'The Integration of Renunciation by Orthodox Hinduism', *Journal of the Oriental Institute* 28: 27–36.

Olivelle, P. 2003. 'The Renouncer Tradition', in Gavin, F. (ed), *The Blackwell Companion to Hinduism*, 271–287. London: Blackwell Publishing.

Pandya, S. P. 2016. 'Sect Culture and Social Service: The Case of Bochasanwasi Shree Akshar Purushottam Swaminarayan Sanstha', *SAGE Open*. https://doi.org/10.1177/2158244015623996.

Pathak-Narain, P. 2017. *Godman to Tycoon: The Untold Story of Baba Ramdev.* New Delhi: Juggernaut Book.

Ray, R. K. 1995. *Mind Body and Society, Life and Mentality in Colonial Bengal.* Calcutta: Oxford University Press.

Sarbacker, S. R. 2013. 'Swami Ramdev: Modern Yoga Revolutionary', in Singleton, M. and Goldberg, E. (eds), *Gurus of Modern Yoga*, 351–371. New York: Oxford University Press.

Scroll.in. 2019. 'Agnivesh says Arya Samaj supports Congress in 2019 Lok Sabha election campaign', 1 May. https://scroll.in/latest/921939/agnivesh-says-arya-samaj-supports-congress-in-2019-lok-sabha-election-campaign. Accessed 2 March 2020.

Seguy, J. 1999. *Conflit et utopie, ou réformer l'église.* Paris: Les Éditions du Cerf.

Thapar, R. 1978. 'Renunciation: the making of a counter culture?', in Thapar, R. (ed), *Ancient Indian History: Some Interpretations*, 63–104. New Delhi: Orient Longmans.

Thapar, R. 1979. 'Dissent and Protest in the Early Indian Tradition', *Studies in History* 1(2): 177–195.

Thapar, R. 1987. 'Cultural Transaction and Early India: Tradition and Patronage', *Social Scientist* 15(2): 3–31.

Voix, R. 2010. 'Dévotion, ascèse et violence dans l'hindouisme sectaire. Ethnographie d'une secte shivaïte du Bengale'. Unpublished PhD thesis. University of Nanterre-La Défense (550 pages).

Voix, R. 2011. 'Une Utopie en Pays Bengali. De l'idéologie Sectaire Hindoue à l'Édification d'une Alternative Communautaire' in Clémentin-Ojha, C. (ed), *Convictions Religieuses et Engagement en Asie du Sud depuis 1850*, 165–188. Paris: École Française d'Extrême-Orient.

Warrier, M. 2003a. 'Process of Secularization in Contemporary India: Guru Faith in the Mata Amritanandamayi Mission', in *Modern Asian Studies* 36(1): 213–253. https://doi.org/10.1017/S0026749X03001070.

Warrier, M. 2003b. 'The Seva Ethic and the Spirit of Institution Building in the Mata Amritanandamayi Mission', in Copley A. (ed), *Hinduism in Public and Private. Reform, Hindutva, Gender and Sampraday*, 254–289. Oxford: Oxford University Press.

Warrier, M. 2005. *Hindu Selves in a Modern World. Guru Faith in the Mata Amritanandamayi Mission.* London: Routledge.

Weber, M. 1958. *The Religion of India. The Sociology of Hinduism and Buddhism.* Glencoe: The Free Press.

Williams, R. B. 1984. *A New Face of Hinduism: The Swaminarayan Religion.* Cambridge: Cambridge University Press.

Wolfers, A. 2016. 'Born Like Krishna in the Prison-House: Revolutionary Asceticism in the Political Ashram of Aurobindo Ghose', *South Asia, Journal of South Asian Studies* 39(3): 525–545.

Wolfers, A. 2017. 'The Making of an Avatar: Reading Sri Aurobindo Ghose (1872–1950)', *Religions of South Asia* 11(2–3): 274–341.

Worth, R. F. 2018. 'The Billionaire Yogi Behind Modi's Rise', *The New York Times Magazine*, 26 July. www.nytimes.com/2018/07/26/magazine/the-billionaire-yogi-behind-modis-rise.html. Accessed 15 January 2020.

# 12

# YOGA AND MEDITATION AS A HEALTH INTERVENTION[1]

*Suzanne Newcombe*

## Introduction

Yoga and meditation have been increasingly promoted as healthcare interventions by the Indian government. In 2014, a department of Ayurveda, Yoga and Naturopathy, Unani, Siddha and Homoeopathy (AYUSH) was raised to the level of an independent ministry, unambiguously positioning the Indian government as supporting a collection of 'indigenous' traditions as medical interventions. However, this event is predicated on a much longer, but inconsistent history of support for indigenous medical traditions from the government of India, various regional and municipal governments, princely states and ascetic orders.

This chapter is organised into three main sections: the first explains the contemporary structural positioning of yoga and meditation as interventions for health by the Indian government. The second section explores some of the historical entanglements between yogic and meditative traditions as healthcare provision within the subcontinent. The third section will provide insight into contemporary popular experiences of yoga and meditation as health and wellbeing practices.

## Yoga and meditation in AYUSH

During the colonial period and in post-Independence India, government sponsorship of indigenous forms of healthcare in the Indian subcontinent has been inconsistent, with many regional variations (Barois, Newcombe and Wujastyk forthcoming; Brass 1972; Priya 2005). The twenty-first century has seen India's central government more consistently present an ambition for uniting yogic and ayurvedic interventions as well as attempting to achieve more national conformity of content and standards. As Abraham has described, recent developments show that the promotion of Indian indigenous systems of medicine is 'increasingly being driven by narrow political interests and by the dictates of global markets … reflected in the focus on the export' of a few products (Abraham 2005: 211). Attempts to get a grip on the contemporary positioning of yoga as a health intervention in India can quickly become overwhelmed with facts and figures of numbers of institutions, beds and exports (e.g. GOI 2005; Priya 2005). This emphasis on the quantitative in official publications masks the great diversity of provision and experience of healthcare with interventions in this broad area.

Yoga was officially recognised as a component of indigenous medicine in the formation of the Central Council of Research for Yoga and Naturopathy in 1978 (a pairing that will be discussed further below). In 2003, the Ministry of Health recognised a unified Department of Ayurveda, Yoga and Naturopathy, Unani, Siddha and Homoeopathy (AYUSH). With this department being raised to the level of independent ministry in 2014, yoga and ayurveda have become ever-more institutionally intertwined. Contemporary Indian university syllabi for the Bachelors in Ayurvedic Medicine and Surgery (BAMS) require undergraduate syllabuses and graduate programmes to cover a basic understanding of Patañjali's formulation of yoga as well as of therapeutic applications of asana and pranayama (CCIM 2014).[2] This incorporation of asana and pranayama as ayurvedic interventions in government-approved training syllabuses is a contemporary innovation. The change appears to be largely a direct response to global market trends rather than being a natural extension of a historically complex dialogue between yoga and ayurveda. Although there have been many areas of overlap, in general, ayurvedic, siddha and yogic systems of treating bodily suffering offer distinct ontological frameworks and practical techniques. While there is much more consistency within ayurveda and siddha than yogic systems per se, it is extremely important to note that all of these traditions are best understood as being internally plural and diverse (Lambert 2018; Sujatha 2020).

From the nineteenth century, yogis and ascetics have been tested with biomedical tools measuring pulse rates, blood pressure, respiration and more recently with various brain-imaging technologies. Early attempts were an attempt to explore and verify claims of yogic 'attainments' (*siddhis*) and yogic 'cures' by biomedical criteria (early examples include Paul 1851 and Thamotharamphilly 1897). Biomedically-framed measurements of yogic health claims were applied more consistently from the 1920s onwards. This was particularly evident in *Yoga Mīmāṃsā*, the first and longest-running periodical of this nature, which has been published out of Kuvalayananda's Kaivalyadhama Institute in Maharashtra since 1924. For many years this was the primary place in India for biomedical research on the effects of yoga, and the journal had wide circulation among English speakers across the globe (Alter 2004: 73–108; Goldberg 2016: 97–99).

More recently, the Swami Vivekananda Yoga Anusandhana Samsthana (S-VYASA) – the first nationally accredited 'Yoga University' in India (founded in 1986) – has been publishing the results of its research into the efficacy of yoga as therapy in its in-house, open-access journal, the *International Journal of Yoga* (2008–). S-VYASA's journal explores yoga in the paradigm of the 'life sciences', focusing in particular on the mechanisms of yoga, physiological changes and therapeutic benefits (S-VYAS 2020). However, research studies on the efficacy of yoga have been conducted throughout India by many different institutions doing active research into AYUSH. Throughout the history of the Indian state, Abraham notes, government funding has largely gone into institutions and individuals that have an agenda of either: (1) creating more 'scientifically' verified articulations of indigenous systems of medicine (ISM); or (2) rhetorically 'reasserting its traditional roots' (Abraham 2005: 211).

A pivotal figure to capitalise on an international interest in yoga as a health intervention at a global scale was the Maharishi Mahesh Yogi (1918–2008). The Maharishi achieved unheard-of popularity after attracting the attention of the world-famous band The Beatles for a short period in 1967–1968. The Maharishi's teachings in the 1960s were focused on a mantra-based meditation given to initiates in a private 'Vedic' ceremony. Trademarked as 'Transcendental Meditation' or 'TM', these teachings were presented as scientific in promotional materials (Maharishi 1968) and quickly became very popular in the United States, Europe and across the globe (Bainbridge 1997: 188–189). The place of meditation as a central component within the Maharishi's greater revival of 'Vedic' arts was markedly influential – in addition to his unprecedented global success at promoting meditation, yoga and commercial products. The Maharishi's organisations[3] poured significant sums of money into researching and promoting the universal benefits of 'Vedic Science' – which first and foremost rested on the practice of Transcendental Meditation. Research studies, many of which have been conducted and funded by Maharishi-affiliated organisations, have shown Transcendental Meditation practices to have effects on lowering blood pressure, assisting with the management of diabetes and reducing insomnia and feelings of anxiety, among other specific measures (e.g. Forem 1974; Maharishi 1968; Chalmers 1991; Maharishi International University 1998; Balaji, Varne and Ali 2012).

In the United States and Europe, medical attention initially went into exploring the healing potential of meditative techniques. In particular, Herbert Benson and Miriam Klipper's seminal book *The Relaxation Response* (1975) showed how generic meditation and relaxation techniques yielded measurable improvements in lowering blood pressure and reducing feelings of stress. This research was a direct response to the TM-funded research specifically promoting the Maharishi's organisation and established a broader, untrademarked basis of the medical benefits of meditation-based, relaxation interventions.[4] In the United States, this finding resulted in a secondary wave of meditation-focused health interventions, especially in the eventual creation of the highly influential Mindfulness-Based Cognitive Therapy (MBCT). In the next few decades, the majority of biomedical research in the United States on the health effects of meditation shifted interventions from the 'TM/Hindu' intervention to more secular-Buddhist-based interventions.[5] The 1977 US Supreme Court decision that TM was a religious technique which could not be taught in publicly-funded schools firmly established this as a religious, rather than secular biomedical intervention (*Malnak v. Yogi* 1977). This limited the organisations' global expansion, particularly in more overtly secular contexts.

However, the exploration of meditation as a technique for health and healing took on a different focus within the Indian subcontinent. In India, the Maharishi's intervention significantly (re)established 'mental techniques' as the lost heart of 'Vedic Science' – and an essential component of the 'true sense and value' of Indian ayurvedic traditions (Jeannotat 2008: 289). Through the figure of the Maharishi (who was previously a disciple of Śāntānanda Saraswatī (d. 1997), the Śaṅkarācārya of Jyotirmaṭh) the image of the yogi was transformed in the Indian imagination: he represented an India that was simultaneously modern and traditional, scientific and spiritual. The Maharishi attracted international and celebrity interest. Following this trend, in India, meditation has not been framed as an independent healthcare intervention. Rather, from the 1970s onwards, meditation is included by the Indian government as a part of scientific, 'yogic' interventions. This is evident from the headline status given to the work of the Maharishi, Aurobindo and Dhirendra Brahmachari at the 1975 conference on 'Yoga, Science and Man' sponsored by the Indian Government in New Delhi (Kothari 1975).

From the late 1970s, the Maharishi began researching ayurveda and ayurvedic pharmaceuticals and established 'Ayur-Vedic' branded products around 1984 (Jeannotat 2008). From this period onwards, there has been a 'mushrooming of ayurvedic luxury resorts, spas and retreats across many of India's tourist destinations' which offer 'expensive "relaxation" and "rejuvenation" therapy, yoga and meditation sessions, lifestyle advice, as well as beauty treatments, to affluent clients, mostly (though not exclusively) from overseas' (Warrier 2011: 86; see also Zimmermann 1992; Zysk 2001). The Maharishi's commercial and ideological initiatives, promoting the revival of many arms of 'Vedic Science' under the trademarked 'Maharishi' name, associated yoga and ayurveda with international fame and fortune for Indians.

With the Bharatiya Janata Party's rise to power in 2014, the government's enthusiastic promotion of yoga and ayurveda has created an explicit political association of yoga and AYUSH therapies with 'Hindutva' (or 'Hindu-ness') – a term with charged political currency. India is a very diverse nation and yet, far from all the population legally defined as Hindu under Indian family law, identifies as Hindu (Hindu Marriage Act 1955). Meanwhile many Indians who are happy to identify as Hindu might have a complex relationship with the BJP's understanding of Hinduism. This situation creates a politically charged undercurrent to the promotion of yoga and meditation for health and wellbeing, despite unifying and reassuring official rhetoric surrounding these practices. Contemporary AYUSH definitions of yoga combine spirituality and science in a united quest for mind-body unity and transcendent health that incorporates meditation (AYUSH 2017: 5).

This constellation of (biomedical) science, meditation, yoga (or yogis) and Ayurveda, which was largely pioneered by the Maharishi, continues under current AYUSH initiatives. For example, the guru Sri Sri Ravi Shankar (b. 1956) (who was a student of the Maharishi) markets a specific pranayama (Surdarshan Kriya™), a programme of yoga asana as well as a Sri Sri-branded line of ayurvedic remedies. Meditation is subsumed under yogic interventions for health, e.g. Sri Sri Yoga is described as offering:

> a holistic way of life that integrates all elements of ancient knowledge of Yoga, to make a prayerful discipline uniting the body, mind and soul. Along with the series of simple yet effective yoga postures and breathing techniques, a greater emphasis is placed on the inner experience of meditation, for the well-being of mind. The programs quickly restore balance by helping to strengthen the body, calm the mind, regain focus and improve self-confidence.
>
> *(artofliving.org 2015)*

Politically, subsuming the category of meditation-based interventions into state approved 'yogic' ones creates a particular narrative in a charged environment of a very diverse nation. This framing helps to support a vision of (Hindu) national unity and yoga as a promotable export in the healthcare context. In addition to a wide variety of unregulated ingenious health interventions available on the private market, AYUSH-approved forms of yoga may operate as part of an informal fee-based economy, run charitable outreach projects, offer interventions in government-funded hospitals and be subsidised by some private insurance companies within India (PTI 2018).

Within India, yogic therapeutic interventions are typically described as 'Patañjali' or 'Hatha' with a vague idea that all kinds of yoga are 'one'. However, these generic terms might be used to promote specific teachings from a variety of different lineages (both the more 'traditional' and more innovative). Within the broad collection of practices associated with 'yoga' and 'meditation', some techniques will have very different aims and effects than others. This diversity is often in the presentation of yogic interventions in the healthcare context where 'mind-body' integration (however obtained) is often presented as a remedy for pain if not a panacea for all 'dis-ease'.

There are also methodological problems in judging yoga, meditation and other AYUSH traditions as biomedically effective. Considering yoga in particular, there is a lack of standardisation of what exactly a 'yogic intervention' entails as well as a lack of standardisation of 'dose' (how much and how often 'yoga' is prescribed) and a lack of systematic control for 'confounds' or other factors that may be responsible for positive statistical associations suggesting efficacy (Elwy et al. 2014; Jeter et al. 2015; Patwardhan 2016). In the context of indigenous systems of medicine like ayurveda and siddha, any interventions prescribing meditation, asana or pranayama techniques as part of a treatment is likely to also include dietary advice, herbal compounds and perhaps other therapeutic measures such as massages, emetics, steam or oil treatments. As Sujatha and Abraham argue, 'the laboratory is not suitable for evaluating multimodal therapies of indigenous systems of medicine' (2012: 29). Therefore, the emphasis on biomedical 'gold standards' in determining the efficacy of therapies and devising training systems for therapists has led to a distortion of indigenous systems of medicine towards standardised products and services.

## Historical entanglements of yoga, meditation and health

South Asian traditions that promote physical health and liberation (*mokṣa*) have often been in dialogue. Relatively early in the history of Buddhism, the Buddha became associated with the title of 'the great physician', suggesting that his escape from *saṃsāra* was the ultimate cure for both mental and physical suffering. Some of the earliest extant records of medical treatment in the subcontinent were associated with early centres of Buddhist and Jain monasticism; Zysk argues that the early development of what would be systematised in the foundational texts of ayurveda – *Carakasaṃhitā* (first century CE) and the *Suśrutasaṃhitā* (third century CE) – were nascent in and influenced by these early Buddhist and Jain monastic traditions (Zysk 2000/1991: 38–49). This monastic interest in health was both ideological and practical. In both Jainism and Buddhism, there is a moral imperative to avoid and reduce the suffering of other sentient beings. Additionally, when the body is seen as a tool for liberation, it may need to be maintained at a certain standard of health in order to master the meditation techniques necessary for liberation.

Within the Indian subcontinent, ayurveda has historically been the most dominant tradition of knowledge about health and healing. Ayurveda has both preventative and prescriptive aspects; it addresses general practice, surgery, toxicology and paediatrics and also provides guidelines for creating life-prolonging elixirs, virility enhancers and treatment for those possessed by supernatural beings. Strictly speaking, the ayurvedic tradition can be understood as holding a particular canon of Sanskrit texts as authoritative, some of the most important being the *Carakasaṃhitā*, the *Suśrutasaṃhitā* and the *Aṣṭāṅgahṛdyasaṃhitā* (seventh century CE), the latter of which attempts to combine the *Carakasaṃhitā* and the *Suśrutasaṃhitā* into a single coherent text (Wujastyk 2011: 31–42). Although these texts are considered central, it is also important to understand that ayurveda is and always has been a living tradition that makes adaptations to local contexts and new technologies and has included the recognition of new disease categories over time. Additionally, family lineages continue to adapt their own traditional remedies in both oral and manuscript forms.

The *Carakasaṃhitā* contains a chapter on 'The Embodied Person', which describes yoga 'as both spiritual liberation and the means of attaining it', describing various supernatural powers (*siddhis*) that may arise along this path to liberation (Wujastyk 2011: 34). Yet although ayurveda considers mental balance as important to maintaining health, its focus is on the health and healing of the physical body and not on soteriological matters. In ayurveda, disease is usually explained as being caused by an imbalance of the constituent elements of the body: *doṣa* (substances that circulate within the body), *dhātu* (substances whose quality and relationship to each other shape the physical body) and *mala* (substances which leave the body). Most popular presentations of ayurveda speak primarily of the three-dosha theory (*tridoṣa-upadeśaḥ*), namely *vāta*, *pitta* and *kapha*, often glossed into English as air, fire and earth (Benner 2005: 3852–3858). There is a distinct absence of physical postures (*āsana*), breathing exercises (*prāṇāyāma*) or meditation as explicit therapeutic interventions in ayurvedic literature until the modern period (Birch 2018: 1–3). However, mental disturbances such as loss or 'shock' are acknowledged to manifest as illness (Wujastyk 2003: 244–251).

There are other important distinctions between the salubrious ayurvedic tradition and the soteriological yogic system – most notably in their elucidation of distinct models of the body. Early mentions of yoga and yogis are more likely to be associated with the practice of austerities and bodily mortification specifically aimed at liberation and not at all intended to promote health and healing. However, the literature associated with the *haṭhayoga* corpus certainly demonstrates an interest in maintaining health and in curing specific diseases. The 'yogic' body is more generally characterised by networks of energetic channels (*nāḍīs*) and their 'knots' or 'centres' (*granthis*, *cakras* and/or *padmas*), circulating winds (*vāyus* and/or *prāṇas*) and the movement of 'seed/semen' (*bindu*). In the modern period, yogic traditions also describe increasingly subtle 'bodies' (*kośa*) (Mallinson and Singleton 2017: 171–184; in this volume Borkataky-Varma Chapter 25). It appears that conceptual overlap between yoga and ayurveda becomes more common in the textual evidence from the sixteenth century onwards and the role siddha practitioners played in this dialogue is as yet unexplored (Birch 2018: 5; Mallinson and Singleton 2017: 187n2).

Despite these important distinctions, for an individual seeking alleviation from physical pain, there is likely to have always been some overlap between yogic and ayurvedic forms of healing (e.g. Kakar 1982). Nineteenth-century European travelogues suggest that ascetics were sometimes present in the courts of princely states, offering medical advice (e.g. Honigberger 1852: 92–95, 116). It is likely that in Tamil and Telegu-speaking areas from the medieval period until perhaps even the contemporary period, *siddhars* (wandering religious heretics of these regions), acted as roving physicians among the rural population, supplementing settled individuals with medical expertise (Sujatha 2012: 83–84, 2003).

In nineteenth-century Punjab, institutions of learning associated with ascetic orders – including those associated with the Dadupanthi, Nath Yogi and Jain as well as Udasi and Nirmala lineages – were known to teach indigenous medical knowledge in their institutions (Sivaramakrishnan 2006). As in contemporary India, individual *sādhus* probably gained reputations as being able to heal both mental and physical problems through yogic techniques. For example, it appears that a kind of 'sick bay' evolved at the guru Madhavdasji's ashram in Malsar, Gujarat by the beginning of the twentieth century (Rodrigues 2008: 43–44, 47). Further research is needed to determine to what extent ascetic institutions and wandering *sādhus* served as repositories of medical knowledge in other areas of India throughout the Mughal period and into the colonial one (Sujatha 2012, 2020; Narayan 1989; Newcombe 2017b, forthcoming a).

The Usman Report, commissioned in 1923 by the government of Madras, offers an unusual snapshot of ayurveda, unani and siddha practitioners' responses to a set of questions about their practices throughout the subcontinent. The unani medical tradition is associated with Muslim communities and key source texts in Persian and Arabic. Siddha medicine is particularly found in the southern areas of the Indian subcontinent and its key texts are in Tamil and Telegu. Siddha medical knowledge is explicitly connected to yogis and believed to be an 'offshoot of the siddha yogi's experiments in yoga and alchemy towards the achievement of an uninterrupted lifespan and an imputrescible body in this world' (Sujatha 2012: 82). One of the central texts of siddha medicine, the c. twelfth-century *Tirumantiram* (*Sacred Mantra*), is a Śaiva mystico-religious work that combines yoga, medicine and alchemy in an encrypted, poetic language (Kędzia 2017; Weiss 2009).[6] The conception of the body in siddha traditions is distinct from both those of *haṭhayoga* and ayurveda, emphasising both *prāṇa* channels and increasingly subtle bodies (*udampu/koṣa*) (Sujatha 2012: 86–87). Contemporary siddha practitioners in Tamil and Telegu-speaking areas of south India continue the traditional medical treatments attributed to the yogic *siddhars* – which have both distinctive characteristics and many overlaps with ayurvedic practice – although not all siddha practitioners are 'yogis' or wandering medicants (Sujatha 2003, 2012). Yet despite this connection between siddha medicine and yogis, what we now associate with 'yogic' treatment methods (e.g. asana and pranayama) does not appear to be a significant element of the medical practice for any indigenous medical practitioner in the early twentieth century (Barois, Newcombe and Wujastyk forthcoming; Usman 1923).

However, yogic treatment methods that employed asana and pranayama were starting to be institutionalised during the early twentieth century (Newcombe 2017). In 1924, Swami Kuvalayananda founded a research centre that offered yoga techniques both for general improvement of health and as therapeutic intervention for specific conditions (Alter 2004). Kuvalayananda's therapeutic ashram in Lonavala – easily accessible from Mumbai (Bombay) – was able to attract substantial private investment, expanding into a thirty-six bed 'Yogi Hospital' in 1962 (Newcombe 2017: 16). As mentioned previously, Kuvalayananda's guru Madhavdasji offered health cures at an ashram in Malsar at the beginning of the twentieth century. Madhavdasji trained both the young Kuvalayananda and Yogendra, whose Yoga Institute in Santa Cruz (now a suburb of Mumbai) was a pioneer in offering curative yoga therapy to middle-class patrons during the twentieth century (Alter 2014; Singleton 2010: 116–122; Goldberg 2016: 116–122).

The first half of the twentieth century was a dynamic period during which what was understood as yoga – particularly yoga as a health-promoting activity – was rapidly changing. Important figures in this reframing were Bishnu Charan Ghosh (1903–1970) at the Ghosh College of Yoga and Physical Culture in Calcutta (established in 1923), Swami Sivananda (1887–1963) in Rishikesh (from 1936) and Tirumalai Krishnamacharya (1888–1989) who operated a *yogaśāla* in Mysore (1933–1950) and Chennai (Madras) from 1952. The early publications of Swami Sivananda, who was trained as a biomedical doctor, showed interest in health and healing and he opened an Ayurvedic Pharmacy in 1945 (Divine Life Society 2011). Academic studies have noted the innovations and influence of each of these figures in the establishment of what is now understood as 'Modern Yoga', a family of practices shaped by globalised ideas of biomedicine, physical culture, New Thought, esotericism and psychology (among other factors) (Alter 2004; Armstrong 2018; De Michelis 2004; Singleton 2010; Strauss 2005).

But perhaps most influential in the context of yoga as a nationally-supported intervention for promoting health and healing were the interventions of Mohandas Karamchand Gandhi (1869–1948), often called Mahatma or 'great soul'. Gandhi's anti-colonial conception of *swadeshi* (Indian self-sufficiency) included an ideological critique of western medicine, doctors and hospitals, whom he viewed as agents of colonial oppression. Gandhi was also critical of ayurvedic *vaidya*s whom he also saw as largely being part of and serving a metropolitan elite. In a pragmatic and nationalistic response to what he saw as the inability of either ayurveda or western medicine to provide for the majority of the Indian population, Gandhi promoted naturopathy (nature cure) as well as yogic breathing and strengthening and cleansing exercises, in addition to other forms of Indian physical culture (Alter 2000; Priya 2012: 119–120; Sheldon 2020). He emphasised techniques that could be done by poor individuals themselves, without needing to pay for expensive herbal or medicinal compounds (Gandhi 2012 [1948]). He advocated self-discipline and self-help which could build the physical and moral strength needed for an independent India. Because of this strong Gandhian legacy, in early post-independence India, yoga was often paired with naturopathy (and not ayurveda) for promotion by the Ministry of Health (Alter 2018; Brass 1972: 342–371).

However, in other instances, cures conducted by yogis were more specifically associated with ayurveda, as in the well-publicised rejuvenation treatment of the Indian nationalist Madan Mohan Malaviya at the hands of a yogi (an Udasi *sādhu*) in 1938, which received global newspaper syndication (Newcombe 2017b). In line with Gandhi's utilitarian interests for healthcare, the Independent Indian government has been largely focused on being able to improve the health and longevity of the majority of India's citizens: the rural poor (Alter 2000, 2004; Tidrick 2006: 213).

After independence, the Indian government reports show evidence of conflict between wanting to promote indigenous forms of health and healing (especially ayurveda) and a reliance on the demonstrable efficacy and dominance of biomedical models of measuring health and healing. While biomedicine was the dominant force in state-sponsored medical initiatives (Brass 1972; Priya 2012), considerable pluralism in medical care continued among the general population (Sujatha and Abraham 2012: 13–14). Meanwhile, from the 1960s onwards in Europe and the Americas, the dominance of biomedicine was slowly challenged by growing countercultural and feminist movements, which were increasingly identifying limitations and power imbalances (Newcombe 2012).

Responsive to global trends, the Indian government slowly but regularly increased funding and official promotion of both ayurveda and yoga as therapy. In 1970, ayurveda was officially recognised as a national system of medicine by the Indian government, which then set up a council for regulating its practice as well as creating and monitoring standards for ayurvedic education (Leslie 1998). Funding and interest in indigenous or Indian systems of medicine (ISM) began to increase from the 1970s onwards. However, the total amount of support is still at paltry levels when compared to state investment in biomedicine provision for the Indian population (e.g. indigenous medical traditions received only 2.7 percent of health and family welfare spending in 2007–2012) (Priya 2012: 124–125).

## Contemporary experiences of yogic health interventions in India

Perhaps no one embodies the contemporary Indian understanding of yoga for health more than Swami Ramdev. Ramdev shot to national fame in 2003 having purchased airtime on one of India's cable television channels (Pathak-Narain 2017: 56–59). His programmes are simple and accessible for many Indians who were experiencing a poverty of money, time and health. His positive messages, free yoga sessions and relatively affordable products inspired millions of Indians to take up yoga *āsan*, *prāṇāyām* and turn to 'Patañjali products' as a truly Indian form of health and healing (he uses the Hindi versions of the Sanskrit terms). Venera Khalikova (2018) emphasises how Ramdev's rhetoric is well aligned with Hindu nationalist narrative. But Ramdev's vision goes beyond India, and, as Stuart Sarbacker explains, offers yoga as a wish-fulfilling tree that might ultimately answer all the needs of humanity (2014: 369). Using ayurvedic terminology, Ramdev proposes that human beings are essentially the same, composed of the same *doṣas* and *guṇas* (using the ayurvedic model of the body), all suffering from the impressions of past lives; therefore the same balancing programmes of *āsan* and *prāṇāyām* are efficacious for all (Ramdev, 2009: 32). Typically, Ramdev claims numerous specific biomedical benefits attributable to each exercise (Bālakṛiṣṇa 2015; Balkrishna 2007; Ramdev 2009; Poddar 2010).

Ramdev's superlative rhetorical use of scientific language in claims for his methods' results, which do not always hold up to the weight of scientific scrutiny, has been strongly criticised by Meera Nanda in particular (2005 and 2009). Ramdev has been known to make the highly controversial claims that his programmes of yoga and ayurvedic products can cure cancer and homosexuality. However, the extent to which these claims are New-Thought-influenced hyperbole rather than meant to be taken as literal, scientific 'truths' is ambiguous (Newcombe forthcoming b). Rhetorical positivity is paired with the establishment of extensive Ramdev's Patañjali Yogpeeth-funded research institutions in order to prove the biomedical efficacy of his treatment plans.

Perhaps because of – rather than despite – Ramdev's rhetorical exaggerations of yogic and ayurvedic cures, many people experience his interventions as healing and empowering. He is often described as a 'household name' and is very popular among the diasporic Indian population globally, many of whom watch his programmes on satellite television. Ramdev is now one of the most influential promoters of '*swadeshi*' Patañjali Yogpeeth-branded yoga and ayurvedic products throughout India. In 2017, the Patañjali group of companies had the second largest turnover of Fast-Moving Consumer Goods (FMCG) companies in India (Pathak-Narain 2017: 189).[7]

Ramdev has located himself as championing Indian culture and interests in the face of aggressive 'western' multinationals, which selectively exploit and steal from Indian culture, simultaneously stripping Indians of their own powers of self-healing and self-respect. Ramdev and other successful gurus such as Sri Sri Ravi Shankar and Jaggi Vasudev ('Sadhguru' of Isha Inner Engineering) have positioned themselves as revivalists to heal Indian bodies, minds and self-images by using traditionally Indian technologies of health and healing. This language of *swadeshi* nationalism is also associated with the modernisation and pharmaceuticalisation of the production of ayurvedic remedies (Banerjee 2008; Berger 2013; Bode 2008; Zimmerman 2016). Herbal prescriptions, which were once produced personally by the *vaidya* (doctor) or close associates are now mass-produced in factories and bought over the counter in shops.

To some extent, this 'commodification' is in contrast to what many who turn to yoga and meditation as 'therapy' expect from these interventions. Maarten Bode has explained that in the case of what he terms an 'authentic ayurvedic approach' in contemporary India, it 'looks upon the patient as a conscious being who lives his or her disease and gives meaning to treatment by the way he or she responds to it' (2012: 75). This description is echoed by Sujatha's depictions of siddha and tribal medicines in Tamil Nadu (2012 and 2003) as well as by first-hand accounts of many who turn to yoga and meditation as healing interventions globally. These accounts emphasise the subjective transformations of pain and suffering as being at least as important as a biomedically measurable 'cure'. However, those who testify to the power of Ramdev's techniques also emphasise a powerful experience of healing (Newcombe forthcoming a, forthcoming b). As Andrea Jain (2014) has argued for the case of commodified yoga traditions which also represent deeply meaningful, spiritual approaches to life, any apparent contradiction between neoliberal commodification and accessible healing is often not experienced as such by those seeking its benefits.

## Conclusion

Yoga and meditation form growing and dynamic areas of health intervention in contemporary India, enjoying considerable support from both governmental and private initiatives. With the unanimous acceptance of Prime Minster Narendra Modi's proposal for an annual International Yoga Day by the United Nations in 2014, yoga (including meditative practices) is being presented by the Indian government as a potential global panacea for health, wellbeing, world peace and even environmental regeneration. The rhetoric proclaims these practices as simultaneously suitable for everyone, but also rooted in authentic, ancient Indian traditions (United Nations 2014; Modi 2019; McCartney 2019). Contemporary Indian state support for yogic and meditation-based health interventions comes with a particular political agenda. But at the same time millions of Indians are finding their personal experiences of yoga salubrious and empowering.

Significantly, today's world – including India – is characterised by medical pluralism (Lambert 2018). 'Yogic' and meditative healthcare interventions are one of several possible approaches that an individual may try in hopes of alleviating a particular health issue. Patterns of engagement with this diversity of healthcare providers vary in distinctive ways between groups with particular cultures, caste, social class and income levels (Priya 2005, 2012; Sujatha 2020). But despite these structure differences in access and engagement, yoga and meditation interventions are now part of the menu from which individuals may choose in seeking to improve their health and wellbeing. The layers of interaction with and between the specific techniques associated with yogic interventions (including meditation) and the multiplicity of indigenous systems of medicine in India is a fertile area for more in-depth research, as other authors have argued (Sujatha and Abraham 2012). The complexities of practices and identities in contemporary India that relate to yoga, meditation and indigenous medicine cannot be subsumed into the dominant narratives of authentically revived tradition and biomedical efficacy.

## Notes

1 This chapter was financially supported by the European Union's Horizon 2020 research and innovation programme under grant agreement No. 639363 (AYURYOG).
2 There are suggestions that some early ayurvedic institutions might have included Patañjali in their syllabuses for *vaidyas*. For example, the Mumbai-based Prabhuram Ayurvedic College (established in 1896 as the Aryan Medical College), claims to have been teaching this from the late nineteenth century (Ayurved Sadhana 2018).
3 The Maharishi's organisations are vast and varied – at the time of his death he was worth an estimated £2 billion (Webster 2012). Most associated organisations are prefaced by the title 'Maharishi' and or 'Vedic' and or with 'TM/Transcendental Meditation' but there are some notable exceptions, e.g. The Natural Law Party (a political party est. 1992), the Global Financial Capital of New York (established 2007) and the Global Country of World Peace (established in 2000, which currently has physical locations in the USA, Ireland and The Netherlands).
4 For a richer history of relaxation interventions in the biomedical context, which has a much longer genealogy, see Nathoo 2016.
5 For more on the development of MBCT see Chapters 3 (Husgafvel) and 18 (Rahmani) in this volume; for a summary of current physiological and cognitive science research on yogic and meditation interventions see Chapters 30 (Schmalzl et al.) and 31 (Federman) in this volume.
6 This dating is much contested, but I am following Kędzia 2017: 124n16 who follows Goodall 1998 and 2000 in the dating. It is more rhetorically associated with the Siddha medical tradition rather than offering recipies or pratical prescriptions.
7 Priyanka Pathak-Narain (2017) has detailed many allegations of illegal practices associated with Ramdev's rise to power that have not been subject to legal proceedings.

## Bibliography

Abraham, L. 2005. 'Indian Systems of Medicine (ISM) and Public Health Care in India', in Gangolli, L., Duggal, R. and Shukla, A. (eds), *Review of Health Care in India*, 187–223. Mumbai: Centre for Enquiry into Health (CEIH).
Alter, J. S. 2000. *Gandhi's Body: Sex, Diet, and the Politics of Nationalism*. Philadelphia: University of Pennsylvania Press.
Alter, J. S. 2004. *Yoga in Modern India: The Body Between Science and Philosophy*. Princeton, NJ and Oxford: Princeton University Press.
Alter, J. S. 2014. 'Shri Yogendra: Magic, Modernity and the Burden of the Middle-Class Yogi', in Singleton, M. and Goldberg, E. (eds), *Gurus of Modern Yoga*, 60–82. New York: Oxford University Press.
Alter, J. S. 2018. 'Yoga, Nature Cure and "Perfect" Health: The Purity of the Fluid Body in an Impure World', in Baier, K., Maas, P. A. and Preisendanz, K. (eds), *Yoga in Transformation: Historical and Contemporary Perspectives*, 439–462. Göttingen: V&R unipress. www.vandenhoeck-ruprecht-verlage.com/themen-entdecken/theologie/religionswissenschaft/16133/yoga-in-transformation. Accessed 20 February 2020.
Armstrong, J. 2018. *Calcutta Yoga: Buddha Bose and the Yoga Family of Bishnu Ghosh and Yogananda*. Webstrong.
Artofliving.org. 2015. 'The Art of Living joins hands with CCRYN - Ministry of AYUSH'. Press release, 22 May. www.artofliving.org/art-living-joins-hands-ccryn-ministry-ayush. Accessed 13 February 2020.
Ayurved S. 2018. 'About Us'. www.ayurvedsadhana.com/about-us/. Accessed 13 February 2020.
AYUSH. 2017. '2017 Common Yoga Protocol' Government of India. http://ayush.gov.in/genericcontent/common-yoga-protocol-2017. Accessed 13 February 2020.

Bainbridge, W. S. 1997. *The Sociology of Religious Movements*. London: Routledge.
Balaji, P. A., Varne, S. R. and Ali, S. S. 2012. 'Physiological effects of yogic practices and transcendental meditation in health and disease', *North American Journal of Medical Sciences*. October. https://doi.org/10.4103/1947-2714.101980 Accessed 15 January 2020.
Bālakṛiṣṇa, Ā. 2015. *Daily Yogapractice Routine*. Haridvāra: Divya Prakāśana.
Balkrishna, A. 2007. *Yog: In Synergy with Medical Science*. Hardwar: Divya Prakashan.
Banerjee, M. 2008. 'Ayurveda in Modern India: Standardization and Pharmaceuticalization', in Wujastyk, D. and Smith, F. (eds), *Modern and Global Ayurveda: Pluralism and Paradigms*, 201–214. Albany, NY: SUNY Press.
Barois, C. 2017 'Eight Yoga Postures in the Dharmaputrikā', http://ayuryog.org/blog/eight-yoga-postures-dharmaputrik%C4%81. Accessed 20 February 2020.
Barois, C. Draft. 'Medical Practices of Yogins in Medieval India: The testimony'.
Barois, C., Newcombe, S. and Wujastyk, D. forthcoming. 'Introduction to new translations of the Usman Report (1923)', *eJournal of Indian Medicine*.
Benner, D. 2005. 'Healing and Medicine in Ayurveda and South Asia', in Jones, L. (ed), *Encyclopedia of Religion*, 3852–3858. New York: MacMillan.
Berger, R. 2013. *Ayurveda Made Modern: Political Histories of Indigenous Medicine in North India, 1900–1955*. London: Palgrave Macmillan.
Bode, M. 2008. *Taking Traditional Knowledge to the Market: The Modern Image of the Ayurvedic and Unani Industry, 1980–2000*. New Delhi: Orient Blackswan Pvt Ltd.
Bode, M. 2012. 'Ayurveda in the Twenty-First Century: Logic, Practice, Ethics', *eJournal of Indian Medicine* 7: 1–20.
Birch, J. E. 2018. 'Premodern Yoga Traditions and Ayurveda: Preliminary Remarks on Shared Terminology, Theory and Praxis', *History of Science in South Asia* 6: 1–83. https://doi.org/10.18732/hssa.v6i0.25. Accessed 20 February 2020.
Brass, P. 1972. 'The Politics of Ayurvedic Education: A Case Study of Revivalism and Modernization in India', in Rudolph, S. H. and Rudolph, L. I. (eds), *Education and Politics in India*, 342–371. Cambridge, MA: Harvard University Press.
(CCIM) Central Council of Indian Medicine. 2014. 'Ayurveda Syllabus/Curriculum', www.ccimindia.org/ayurveda-syllabus.php. Accessed 20 February 2020.
Chalmers, R. 1991. *Scientific Research on Maharishi's Transcendental Meditation and TM-Sidhi Programme - Collected Papers, Volume 4*. Netherlands: Maharishi Vedic University Press.
De Michelis, E. 2004. *A History of Modern Yoga: Patañjali and Western Esotericism*. London: Continuum.
Divine Life Society. 2011. 'H. H. SRI SWAMI SIVANANDA SARASWATI', http://sivanandaonline.org/public_html/?cmd=displaysection&section_id=1645. Accessed 13 February 2020.
Elwy, A., et al. 2014. 'A Systematic Scoping Review of Yoga Intervention Components and Study Quality', *American Journal of Preventative Medicine* 47(2): 220–232.
Family Law Act. 1955. Government of India. Act No. 25, 18 May. New Delhi.
Forem, J. 1974. *Transcendental Meditation: Maharishi Mahesh Yogi and the Science of Creative Intelligence*. London: George Allen and Unwin.
Gandhi, M. K. 2012 [1948]. Key to Health. Nayan, S. (trans). Ahmedabad: Navajivan Publishing House.
Goldberg, E. 2016. *The Path of Modern Yoga: The History of an Embodied Spiritual Practice*. Rochester, Vermont: Inner Traditions.
Goodall, D. 1998. *Bhaṭṭa Rāmakaṇṭtha's Commentary on the Kiraṇatan-tra*. Volume 1. Pondicherry: Institut Français de Pondichéry, École françaised'Extrême-Orient.
Goodall, D. 2000. 'Problems of Name and Lineage: Relationships between South Indian Authors of the Śaiva Siddhānta', *Journal of the Royal Asiatic Society* 10(2): 205–216.
Government of India (GOI). 2005. AYUSH in India. New Delhi: Planning and Evaluation Cell, Ministry of Health and Family Welfare.
Honigberger, J. M. 1852. *Thirty-five Years in the East: Adventures, Discoveries, Experiments and Historical Sketches relating to the Punjab and Cashmere in connection with Medicine, Botany, Pharmacy and together with an original Materia Medica and a Medical Vocabulary in Four European and Five Eastern Languages*. London: H. Bailliere.
Jain, A. 2014. *Selling Yoga: From Counterculture to Pop Culture*. Oxford: Oxford University Press.
Jeannotat, F. 2008. 'Maharishi Ayur-Ved: A Controversial Model of Global Ayurveda', in Wujastyk, D. and Smith, F. M. (eds), *Modern and Global Ayurveda: Pluralism and Paradigms*, 285–308. Albany, NY: SUNY.
Jeter, P. E., Slutsky, J., Singh, N. and Khalsa, S. B. 2015. 'Yoga as a Therapeutic Intervention: A Bibliometric Analysis of Published Research Studies from 1967 to 2013', *Journal of Alternative and Complementary Medicine* 21(10): 586–592.

Kakar, S. 1982. *Shamans Mystics and Doctors*. Chicago: Chicago University Press.
Kędzia, I. B. 2017. 'Mastering Deathlessness', *History of Science in South Asia* 5(2): 121–142. https://doi.org/10.18732/hssa.v5i2.16 Accessed 20 February 2020.
Khalikova, V. 2018. 'Medicine and the Cultural Politics of National Belongings in Contemporary India Medical Plurality or Ayurvedic Hegemony?', *Asian Medicine* 13(1–2): 198–221.
Kothari, D. S. 1975. 'Seminar on Yoga, Science and Man' 14–16 March. New Delhi: CCRIMH.
Lambert, H. 2018. 'Indian Therapeutic Hierarchies and the Politics of Recognition', *Asian Medicine* 13(1–2): 115–133.
Langford, J. M. 2002. *Fluent Bodies: Ayurvedic Remedies for Postcolonial Imbalance*. London: Duke University Press.
Leslie, C. (ed) 1998. *Asian Medical Systems: A Comparative Study*. Berkeley: University of California Press.
Maas, P. A. 2007–8. 'The Concepts of the Human Body and Disease in Classical Yoga and Āyurveda', *Wiener Zeitschrift für die Kunde Südasiens [Vienna Journal of South Asian Studies]* 51: 125–162.
McCartney, P. 2019. 'Stretching into the Shadows: Unlikely Alliances, Strategic Syncretism, and De-Post-Colonizing Yogaland's "Yogatopia(s)"', *Asian Ethnology* 78(1): 373–401.
Maharishi, M.Y. 1968. *Science of Being and Art of Living, Transcendental Meditation*. New York: Penguin.
Maharishi International University. 1998. *Scientific Research on The Maharishi Technology of the Unified Field: The Transcendental Meditation and TM-Sidhi Program - One Program to Develop All Areas of Life*. Fairfield, IA: Maharishi International University Press.
Mallinson, J. and Singleton, M. 2017. *Roots of Yoga*. London: Penguin Classics.
*Malnak v. Yogi*. 440F. Supp. 1284, 1322 (NJ 1977).
Meulenbeld, G. J. 1999–2002. *A History of Indian Medical Literature*. Groningen: E. Forsten.
Ministry of AYUSH. 2020. 'About the Ministry'. Ministry of AYUSH. http://ayush.gov.in/about-us/about-the-ministry. Accessed 20 February 2020.
Modi, N. 2019. 'Yoga is both ancient and modern. It is constant and evolving: PM Modi', 21 June. www.narendramodi.in/text-of-pm-s-speech-at-the-celebrations-of-5th-international-yoga-day-in-ranchi-545439. Accessed 13 February 2020.
Nanda, M. 2005. 'Perspective: Is India a science superpower?', *Frontline* 22(19): 10–23.
Nanda, M. 2009. *The God Market: How Globalization Is Making India More Hindu*. New York: Monthly Review Press.
Narayan, K. 1989. *Storytellers, Saints and Scoundrels: Folk Narrative in Hindu Religious Teaching*. Philadelphia, PA: University of Pennsylvania Press.
Nathoo, A. 2016. 'Initiating Therapeutic Relaxation in Britain: A Twentieth-century Strategy for Health and Wellbeing', *Palgrave Communications*. Volume 2, 16043. https://doi.org/10.1057/palcomms.2016.43. Accessed 20 February 2020.
Newcombe, S. 2012. 'Global Hybrids? "Eastern Traditions" of Health and Wellness in the West', in Nair-Venugopal, S. (ed), *The Gaze of the West and Framings of the East*, 202–217. New York: Palgrave Macmillan.
Newcombe, S. 2017a. 'The Revival of Yoga in Contemporary India', in *Oxford Research Encyclopaedia of Religion*. https://doi.org/10.1093/acrefore/9780199340378.013.253. Accessed 20 February 2020.
Newcombe, S. 2017b. 'Yogis, Ayurveda and Kayakalpa – The Rejuvenation of Pandit Malaviya', *History of Science in South Asia* 5(2): 85–120. https://doi.org/10.18732/hssa.v5i2.29.
Newcombe, S. forthcoming a. 'Yoga in Modern India', in Salguero, S. and Stanley-Baker, M. (eds), *Religion and Medicine in Asia*. Manchester: Manchester University Press.
Newcombe, S. forthcoming b. 'Working with a Body: Flexible Conceptual Models in Contemporary Yoga' in Baker, E. and Harvey, S. (eds), *Health and Healing in Minority Religions*. London: Routledge.
Pathak-Narain, P. 2017. *Godman to Tycoon: The Untold Story of Baba Ramdev*. New Delhi: Juggernaut.
Patwardhan, A. R. 2016. 'Yoga Research and Public Health: Is Research Aligned with the Stakeholders' Needs?', *Journal of Primary Care & Community Health* 8(1): 31–36.
Paul, N. C. 1851. *A treatise on the yoga philosophy*. Benares: Recorder Press.
Poddar, S. 2010. *Patanjali Yog Part I*. Third edition. Hardiwar: Patanjali Yog Peeth (UK) Trust.
Priya, R. 2005. 'Public Health Services in India: A Historical Perspecitive', in Gangolli, L., Duggal, R. and Shukla, A. (eds), *Review of Healthcare in India* 41–74. Mumbai: Cehat.
Priya, R. 2012. 'AYUSH and Public Health: Democratic Pluralism and the Quality of Health Services', in Sujatha, V. and Abraham, L. (eds), *Medical Pluralism in Contemporary India*, 103–129. Hyderabad: Orient BlackSwan.

PTI. 2018. 'Integration of Ayush in Health Services a Priority in India: Sripad Yesso Naik', *Economic Times of India*, 1 September. https://economictimes.indiatimes.com/news/politics-and-nation/integration-of-ayush-in-health-services-a-priority-in-india-sripad-yesso-naik/articleshow/65637039.cms?from=mdr. Accessed 13 February 2020.

Ramdev, S. 2009. *Prāṇāyāma Rahasya (with Scientific Factual Evidence)*. Hardwar: Divya Prakashan.

Rodrigues, S. 2008. *Life of Shri Yogendra: The Householder Yogi*. Mumbai: The Yoga Institute.

Sarbacker, S. R. 2014. 'Swami Ramdev: Modern Yoga Revolutionary', in Singleton, M. and Goldberg, E. (eds), *Gurus of Modern Yoga*, 351–372. New York: Oxford University Press.

Sheldon, V. 2020. 'Vitality, Self-healing and Ecology: The Flow of Naturopathic Thought Across the United States and India', *Society and Culture in South Asia* 6(1): 121–143.

Singleton, M. 2010. *Yoga Body: The Origins of Modern Posture Practice*. New York: Oxford University Press.

Sivaramakrishnan, K. 2006. *Old Potions, New Bottles: Recasting Indigenous Medicine in Colonial Punjab (1850–1945)*. Hyderabad: Orient Longman.

Slatoff, Z. 2017. 'Seeds of Modern Yoga: The Confluence of Yoga and Ayurveda in the Āyurvedasūtra', *Ayuryog Blogpost*. http://ayuryog.org/blog/seeds-modern-yoga-confluence-yoga-and-ayurveda-%C4%81yurvedas%C5%ABtra. Accessed 20 February 2020.

Sujatha, V. 2003. *Health by the People: Sociology of Medical Lore*. New Delhi: Rawat Publications.

Sujatha, V. 2012. 'The Patient as Knower: Principle and Practice in Siddha Medicine', in Sujatha, V. and Abraham, L. (eds), *Medical Pluralism in Contemporary India*, 77–102. Hyderabad: Orient BlackSwan.

Sujatha, V. 2020. 'Globalisation of South Asian Medicines: Knowledge, Power, Structure and Sustainability', *Society and Culture in South Asia* 6(1): 7–30.

Sujatha, V. and Abraham, L. (eds) 2012. *Medical Pluralism in Contemporary India*. Hyderabad: Orient BlackSwan.

S-VYAS (Swami Vivekananda Yoga Anusandhana Samsthana). 2020. 'About Us: International Journal of Yoga'. www.ijoy.org.in/aboutus.asp. Accessed 13 February 2020.

Thamotharamphilly, C. 1897. *The Comparison of Animal Magnetism or Hypnotism with the Yoga System of the Hindus*. Colombo, Ceylon: Ceylon Independent Press.

Tidrick, K. 2006. *Gandhi: A Political and Spiritual Life*. London: I. B. Tauris.

United Nations. 2014. 'Resolution 69/131. International Day of Yoga'. General Assembly. 11 December. https://undocs.org/A/RES/69/131. Accessed 13 February 2020.

Usman, M. (ed) 1923. 'The Report of the Committee on the Indigenous Systems of Medicine, Madras [1921–1923]'. Madras: Government of Madras, Ministry of Local Self-Government, Committee on the Indigenous Systems of Medicine.

Warrier, M. 2011. 'Modern Ayurveda in Transnational Context', *Religion Compass* 5(3): 80–93.

Webster, N. 2012. 'Maharishi inspired Beatles but died leaving £2b and rape rumours', *The Mirror Online*. 7 Feb 2008. Updated 27 January. www.mirror.co.uk/3am/celebrity-news/maharishi-inspired-beatles-but-died-leaving-292433. Accessed 20 February 2020.

Weiss, R. S. 2009. *Recipes for Immortality: Medicine, Religion and Community in South India*. New York: Oxford University Press.

Wujastyk, D. 2003. *The Roots of Ayurveda: Selections from Sanskrit medical writings*. London: Penguin.

Wujastyk, D. 2008. 'The Evolution of Indian Government Policy on Ayurveda in the Twentieth Century', in Wujastyk, D. and Smith, F. M. (eds), *Modern and Global Ayurveda: Pluralism and Paradigms*, 43–76. New York: SUNY.

Wujastyk, D. 2011. 'The Path to Liberation through Yogic Mindfulness in Early Ayurveda', in White, D. G. (ed), *Yoga in Practice*, 31–42. Princeton: Princeton University Press.

Wujastyk, D. 2015. 'On Perfecting the Body. Rasāyana in Sanskrit Medical Literature', *Aion* xxxvi: 55–77.

Wujastyk, D. and Smith, F. M. (eds) 2008. *Modern and Global Ayurveda: Pluralism and Paradigms*. Albany: SUNY Press.

Zimmermann, F. 1992. 'Gentle Purge: The Flower Power of Ayurveda', in Leslie, C. and Young, A. (eds), *Paths to Asian Medical Knowledge: A Comparative Study*, 209–223. Delhi: Munshiram Manoharlal.

Zimmerman, F. 2016. 'Rasāyana today on the market of proprietary medicines', *AyurYog workshop: Rejuvenation, longevity, immortality. Perspectives on rasāyana, kāyakalpa and bcud len practices*. Held at the University of Vienna.

Zysk, K. 2000 [1991]. *Asceticism and Healing in Ancient India: Medicine in the Buddhist Monastery*. Delhi: Motilal Banarsidass Publishers.

Zysk, K. 2001. 'New Age Āyurveda or What Happens to Indian Medicine When it Comes to America', *Traditional South Asian Medicine* 6: 10–26.

# PART III

# Doctrinal perspectives

## Technique and praxis

The techniques associated with meditation and yoga are understood differently in the context of specific religious traditions. This section highlights a selection of these doctrinal perspectives. The religious traditions of India, particularly those commonly associated with Hinduism and Buddhism, are covered extensively in other sections of this book.

A few of the chapters here are written primarily from an 'etic' perspective of Religious Studies, the multidisciplinary study of religion in the academy. The authors of these chapters may or may not have personal relationships to the religions they are studying (as discussed in the chapter by Singleton and Larios in Part I).

However, several of these chapters, most notably the chapters on Jainism, Sikhism and Christianity, are informed by a Theological perspective, i.e. presenting an evidenced-based position from within the tradition in question. The inclusion of these chapters demonstrates examples of how rigorous analyses of these practices and techniques can be framed within and by specific religious traditions.

The final chapter on secular discursive constructions of the techniques and praxes under discussion highlights the entanglements of secular and religious formations.

# 13

# YOGA AND MEDITATION IN THE JAIN TRADITION[1]

*Samani Pratibha Pragya*

## Introduction

This chapter presents an overview of yoga and meditation praxis in the Jain tradition, from ancient to modern times. It provides selective textual documentation of yogic concepts and theories from early Jain scripture, as well as medieval and modern literature. Ancient and medieval Jain yoga is defined within a soteriological framework. The dualistic philosophical background of Jainism highlights liberation (*mokṣa*) as the final goal of yoga. In a Jain philosophical context, the generic use of the word *yoga* refers to all the physical, vocal and mental activity of the embodied soul.[2] The early Jain term *yoga* has many connotations in the canonical texts, since it is defined in different ways. However, we can assert that practices that we associate with yoga were included in the understanding of asceticism in the Jain scriptures. The early evidence of yoga in Jainism is scattered across many texts, which do not propose a single method. Hence, a wide array of different practices form part of Jain yoga.[3] In the course of this discussion, I will explore the general connotations of compound terms that include *yoga* as well as the key religio-yogic terms that are employed in the ancient Śvetāmbara Jaina scriptures, such as *dhyāna-yoga*, *bhāvanā-yoga* and *svādhyāya-yoga*. This chapter is divided into three parts: ancient Jain yoga, medieval Jain yoga and modern Jain yoga. This chapter is an effort to present a chronological study of typologies, defining the process of Jain yoga and its various models.

## The term *yoga* in early Jain texts

In the early Jain textual sources, the term *yoga* is generally applied to various forms of asceticism. *Sūtrakṛtāṅga-sūtra*, traditionally dated fourth century BCE,[4] employed the term '*jogavaṃ*' (Prakrit),[5] '*yogavān*' (Sanskrit) (Sūs, 1.2.11). Generally, the term *yogavāna* means 'one who performs yoga' but the expression *yogavān* is explained explicitly in *Sūtrakṛtāṅga-Cūrṇī* of Jinadāsa Mahattara (sixth to seventh century CE): yoga means restraint (*saṃyama*) and one who possesses restraint (*yoga*) is a *yogavān*.[6] The meaning of *yogavān*, which implies possessor of *saṃyama*, is an efficient person or a person who has authority in the triad of *jñāna-yoga*, *darśana-yoga* and *cāritra-yoga* (respectively yoga of knowledge, faith and conduct).[7] It is interesting to compare the term *saṃyama*, which is a key term for the Jain yogic field, with that of Pātañjali's *Yogasūtra*, fourth century CE. The *Yogasūtra* also refers to *saṃyama* in association with a triad. However, Patanjali's *saṃyama* triad is different from the Jain *saṃyama* triad. According to the *Yogasūtra* (YS) 'the triad held in praxis together in the one place [i.e. aspirant] is *saṃyama*'.[8] In Patañjali's text, the triad is explained as fixation of thought (*dhāraṇā*), meditation (*dhyāna*) and concentration (*samādhi*). Brought together, they are called *saṃyama*. Thus the Jain triad is related to the religio-ethical praxis, while the *Yogasūtra* is associated with meditative praxis. This underlying Jain emphasis of self-restraint in meditative ventures was already present in ancient religious practices. Jinadāsa explains that one who is always vigilant about the practice of *samiti*, i.e. carefulness, and *gupti*, i.e. restraint, is known as *yogavān*. Explicitly, he uses the term '*svādhīna-yoga*', a practice in which one has self-control over his mind, body and speech.[9] Additionally, he states that while performing an action, someone who engages his mind elsewhere is known as '*a-yoga*'. Here yoga means perfect harmony of mind and body. To sum up, one who keeps mind, body and speech under his control is *yogavān*.

Identical terminology is employed in the *Daśavaikālika-sūtra* too. For example, there we find phrases like '*dhruvajogi*' (DvS, 10.6) and '*saṃjama-dhuva-joga-jutte*' (DvS, 10.10). The term *dhruvayogi* is explained in *Daśavaikālika-Cūrṇī* as

> one who engages his mind, speech and body upon the instruction of *tīrthaṁkara* and follows the rules of inspections of his peripheral accessories (*pratilekhanā*) and obligatory rules (*āvaśyaka*). Furthermore, one who follows the twelve types of limbs (*duvālasaṁga*) which is known as the basket of speeches of the leader (*gaṇipiḍaga*)
> *(DvC(Ag)-10.6)*

*Daśavaikālika-sūtra* presents a compound word for yoga as a practice of self-study: *sajjhāya-joga* (Prakrit) or *svādhyāya-yoga* (Sanskrit) (DvS-Culikā, 2.7).[10] Such contexts present evidence of yoga in an ancient Jain setting. A later formulated text *Samavāyāṃ-sūtra* (SamS) lists thirty-two types of collections of yoga (*yoga-saṅgraha*[11]), which are enumerations of ascetic practices. Just one term '*jhāṇa-saṁvara-joga*' is closely linked with yoga praxis, but the rest of this long list includes those practices that are supportive generally to a Jain ascetic's life.

## Bhāvanā-yoga

The term *bhāvaṇājoga* (Pkt.) or *bhāvanā-yoga* (Skt.) is used to indicate the meditative practice of reflection/cultivation (*bhāvanā*) in *Sūtrakṛtāṅga-sūtra* (SūS, 1.15.5). Here I posit 'cultivation' as an apt translation of *bhāvanā*, and it means 'a serious thought process or consideration'.[12] The term *bhāvanā* (root √*bhū*: 'to bring into being', 'to cultivate', 'to develop') literally means 'becoming', but as coming from the causative form of '*bhū*' it means 'causing to become', i.e. 'producing' or the act of becoming or arising.[13] Cort (2001) translates it as 'intentionally generated meditational sentiment'. The *Sūtrakṛtāṅga-sūtra* states that 'he whose soul is purified by meditating on those cultivations (*bhāvaṇājoga*) is compared to a ship in the water; like a ship reaching the shore, he gets beyond the misery' (SūS, 1.15.5).[14] Here the analogy of 'ship in the water' conveys an ascetic whose psyche is imprinted with pious reflections. Jain canonical texts retained the term *bhāvitātmā*, for those ascetics who have developed themselves by the practice of *bhāvanā*. A *bhāvitātmā*[15] is an ascetic whose soul is permeated with pure thoughts due to the practice of various *bhāvanās*, and he has sublimated his knowledge, faith and conduct.

*Bhāvanā* mainly refers to old ascetic practices that were supplementary to the five great vows. Cultivation (*bhāvanā*) means frequent and prolonged repetition of an idea, a practice that can bring about a radical attitudinal change in the practitioner. This is a technique mentioned in the *Ācārāṅga-cūlā* (ĀSII, 15. 788–791), *Samavāyāṅga-sūtra* (SamS, 25.1) and *Praśnavyākaraṇa-Sūtra*[16] (PVS) as a practice that places emphasis on the purification of the soul. A canonical text enumerates the twenty-five *bhāvanās* of the five great vows (*mahāvrata*). Bhatta discusses these *bhāvanās* critically:

> The 25 *bhāvanās* described in (ĀSII 15) are designed to foster the five *mahāvratas* and help the ascetic gain self-discipline and strengthen his 'right conduct' (*samyak-cāritra*). *Bhāvanā* has a long historical practice in Jainism, mainly related to asceticism but also to householders' practice. The Digambara tradition enumerates a list of 16 *bhāvanās* as a form of meditation. It is clear that these *bhāvanās* are embedded as a part of obligatory ritual (*pratikramaṇa*) of Jain ascetics and repeated in meditative form twice a day at dusk and dawn. This *bhāvanā* package is different from *anuprekṣā* and the Śvetambara formula of 25 *bhāvanās* of five *mahāvratas* (Williams, 1998: 246). At some point, it is confused with *anuprekṣā*. These *bhāvanas* are not to be confused with the 12 *aṇupehās* (*anuprekṣās*).
>
> (Bhatt 1993: 97)

The difference between *bhāvanā* and *anuprekṣā* is very subtle and can be seen through practice. During *pratikramaṇa*, meditation is always followed by *bhāvanā*. It prepares the mind and the body of a practitioner to follow the path of renunciation. According to Jinabhadragaṇī, the 'capacity of meditation comes after the practice of *bhāvanā*.' These are: reflection of knowledge (*jñāna-bhāvanā*), reflection of perception (*darśana-bhāvanā*), reflection of conduct (*cāritra-bhāvanā*) and reflection of renunciation (*vairagya-bhāvanā*).[17] Thus, this paradigm of *bhāvanā* practice means internalisation of those aspects that one has to follow on the soteriological path. *Daśavaikālika-sūtra* (DvS, 8.38) presents a systematised set of counter-states of cultivation (*pratipakṣa-bhāvanā*),[18] and enumerates both the positive and negative states of this *bhāvanā*. A detailed description of *anuprekṣā* is discussed below under the section on *dhyāna-yoga*, since *anuprekṣā* is practised after meditation and *bhāvanā* is practised before meditation (Mahāprajña 2010: 52).

## *Dhyāna-yoga*

Early Jain images are concrete reminders of the importance of 'meditation yoga' (*jhāṇa-joga*, Pkt.; *dhyāna-yoga* Skt.) in the ancient tradition. Among the more visible manifestations are the twenty-four *tīrthaṅkaras*, the ford-makers, who are depicted only in meditative postures, either standing or sitting in a full lotus posture. There is no instance of these figures engaged in non-meditational activities such as sleeping, lying, walking, laughing and blessing – such as we find in Hinduism and Buddhism. There are different kinds of material representations that provide evidence of the importance of 'meditation yoga' in early Jainism. It is argued that throughout the canonical texts, meditation appeared to be a constituent part of ascetic practice or of the practice of austerities (*tapas*), but was not as independent practice. The *Tattvārtha-sūtra* highlights two types of austerities: external (*bāhya*) and internal (*ābhyantara*). Meditation is considered under the sixth sub-type of internal *tapas*.[19] *Dhyāna-yoga* emerged as a part of asceticism or under the umbrella of twelve types of austerities (e.g. SūS, 1.8.27), but it never appeared as an independent practice in the canonical sources.

## Mahāvīra's meditation

The traditional account of Mahāvīra's[20] (599–527 BCE) meditative practice in the ĀSI throws light on the history of Jain practices of meditation. In its eighth chapter,[21] the $\bar{A}S_2$ mentions the meditative techniques that were practised by Mahāvīra during the thirteen years of his non-omniscient time (*chadmastha-kāla*).[22] Bronkhorst states that '[t]he few occurrences of 'meditation' (*jhāṇa*), 'meditate' (*jhāti*) etc. are in *Ācārāṅga-sūtra* (Bronkhorst, 1986: 34). Nonetheless, I would argue that the aphorisms of the ĀS are relevant and may describe Mahāvira's practices because they are traditionally considered *jina-kalpa*[23] practices. These practices imitate those of the victors (*jinas*), which include Mahāvīra, and are the meditative practices undertaken by Mahāvīra, in conjunction with penance (*tava*, Pkt.; *tapas*, Skt.) prior to achieving omniscient knowledge (*kevala-jñāna*).

> Knowing (and renouncing) the female sex in mixed gathering places, he **meditated** finding his way himself: I do not lead a worldly life.[24] Giving up the company of all householders whomsoever, he **meditated.** Asked, he gave no answer; he went, and did not transgress the right path.[25]
>
> *($ĀS_2$, 1.8.1.6)*

> In the resting-places there once, in a night, the single wanderer asked him (who he was and why he was there); as he did not answer, they treated him badly; but he persevered in his **meditation**, free from resentment.
>
> *($ĀS_2$ 1.8.2.11)*

> (Sometimes to avoid greater troubles when asked) 'Who is there within?' he answered, 'It is I, a mendicant.' But this is the best law: **silently to meditate**, even if badly treated.
>
> *($ĀS_2$ 1.8.2.12)*

The above-mentioned passages present the *jina*'s mode of practice (*jina-kalpa*). Here Mahāvīra is stated as meditating in remote places, away from householders, females, in silence and completely engrossed in meditation, which is an important feature of the *jina-kalpa* mode. This practice is different from the elders' mode of practice (*sthavira-kalpa*), in which ascetics remain in the midst of society and play a pivotal role in enhancing religious practices among members of the lay community. These passages may be interpreted as conveying meditative practice as an aspect of daily monastic life and an activity that is consistent with the Jain precept of restraint of action. $ĀS_2$ 1.8 contains a long description of Mahāvīra's solitary meditative method of *trāṭaka* or 'unblinking', fixed-gaze meditation:

> Mahāvīra **meditated** sitting in some posture without distraction. Then he **meditated** (walking) with his eyes fixed on a square before him, on the length of a man and further 'the farsighted one who knows the world, knows its inferior part (hell), its upper part (heaven), its side-long part (the state of brute beasts)' (trans. Jacobi).[26]

According to Jacobi's translation, this *sūtra* presents a meditative practice of Mahāvīra, which Jacobi construes to be a form of walking meditation.[27] The type of meditation Jacobi describes is closest to the Jain ascetic practice of vigilance while walking (*īryā-samiti*).[28] In the above passage, Jacobi follows the meanings given to this passage in the *Ācārāṅga-cūrṇi* (ninth century CE) (pp. 300–301) and the *Ācārāṅga-vṛtti* of *Śīlāṅka* (ninth century CE) (p. 274). It is evident that due to lack of knowledge of other traditional sources such as the *Bhagavatī-vṛtti*, Jacobi's interpretation of the type of meditation that this passage describes differs from that of Mahāprajña. From the above passages of the ĀS, we can conclude that Mahāvīra's method of meditation consisted of perception and concentration in isolated locations, concentration that sought to be unaffected by physical surroundings as well as emotions.

The above discussed forms of meditative practice are an aspect of Mahāvīra's ascetic life and are therefore oriented towards restraint of activity culminating in motionlessness. Motionlessness in early Jain meditation is held to be the only cure for suffering and rebirth, since all activity is karma, i.e. action that leads to rebirth. The goal of such motionless meditation is the attainment of liberation.

## The four *dhyānas*

In the later canonical texts, the phenomenon of meditation was treated systematically. A later *āgamic* text, the *Sthānāṅga-sūtra* gives a short summary of the types of meditation. It introduces a four-fold classification of psychological states or conditions. The first two types of meditation (*dhyāna*) are considered to be mental or psychological states, in which a person can be fully immersed or which may recur. These first two states (*ārtta-dhyāna* and *raudra-dhyāna*) refer to impure psychological conditions responsible for suffering and leading to rebirth particularly in lower life forms. The third and fourth types are pure states of meditative practice and religious conduct, which lead to liberation (*dharmya, śukla-dhyāna*). *Ārtta-dhyāna* may be defined as meditation on sadness; *raudra-dhyāna* as meditation on distress; *dharmya-dhyāna* as meditation on reality and *śukla-dhyāna* as absolutely pure or 'white' meditation (SthāS, 4.60).[29] This four-fold classification of psychological states is extended in later canonical texts such as the *Bhagavatī-sūtra*, (BhS, 25.7.217), the *Uttarādhyāyana-sūtra* (UttS, 30.35)[30], the *Aupapātika-sūtra* (AupS, 30), and the *Āvaśyaka-sūtra* (ĀvS, 4.8).

Bronkhorst states that: 'the nature of these texts brought it about that everything that can be covered by the term *jhāṇa* is enumerated here. This is much more than "meditation" alone; even "thinking" is covered by this term' (Bronkhorst 1993: 151). In other words, this four-fold strategy shows that deep concentration can produce both good and bad results, depending on one's level of spiritual attainment (*guṇasthāna*). Bruhn (2012: 26) adds that the first two types of meditation are mainly 'negative' and the last two are mainly 'positive'. It seems that the first two states involved in meditation refer to the power of concentration and situate meditation within the twelve types of austerity. The same four types of meditation are enumerated by Umāsvāti in the *Tattvārtha-sūtra* (TS, 9.29).[31] The TS combines definition and alignment of meditation with the ladder of fourteen stages of spiritual development (*guṇasthāna*).

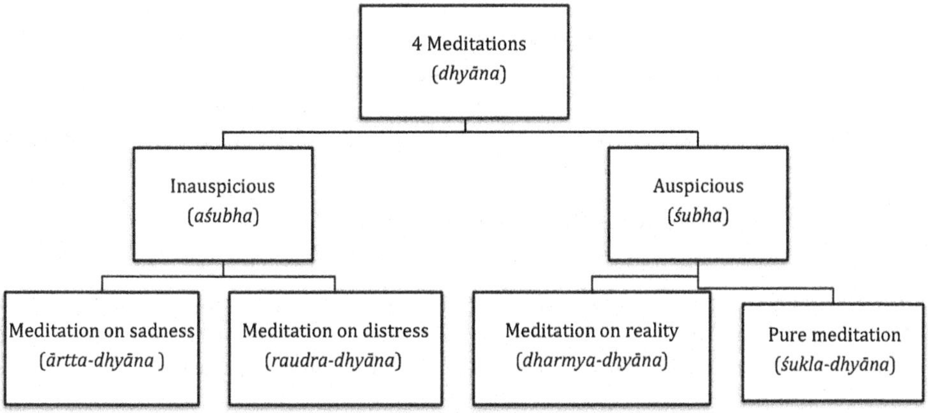


*Figure 13.1* The four *dhyānas*

The first two types of meditation do not refer to spiritual practices, but are included simply for the sake of completeness as types of meditation. They refer to concentration or immersion in a particular mental state that focuses or concentrates on a particular type of emotion; concentration or focus is the broader meaning of *dhyāna* in Jainism. Concentrating upon anguish and anger is not considered penance (*tapas*) because it is not conducive to the development of the self. Nor are these first two psychological conditions of thought and practice helpful in overcoming suffering and rebirth. They are, therefore, omitted in twentieth-century Jain discussions of meditation, which is in line with the contemporary meaning of the term 'meditation' in Jainism. Modern Jain meditation includes only the latter two psychological states that encourage pure states of mind and meditative practice, and form part of the path of liberation (TS 9.30).[32]

## The two meditations: worldly (*saṃsārika*) psychological states

### Ārtta-dhyāna *(anguished meditation)*

*Ārtta-dhyāna* stands for a mental condition of suffering, agony and anguish. A spiritual aspirant must try to overcome this psychological state. *Ārtta-dhyāna* takes place under four conditions, which differentiate the four different types of *ārtta-dhyāna*. These are:

1. Where a person is confronted with an object of desire, and does his utmost to ensure non-separation from that object, hoping for a permanent conjunction with it.
2. Where a person is confronted with a painful ailment, and does his utmost to get rid of it in an attempt to ensure its future non-recurrence.
3. Where a person recalls past enjoyment of certain objects, and does his utmost to ensure non-separation from such enjoyment.
4. Where a person recollects the enjoyment of objects of the past and concentrates fully for such everlasting joy.

The *Dhyāna-śataka* (DhŚ) (sixth century CE) condenses the third and fourth types of meditative practice into one category, only slightly different from the tradition of TS. It then adds a fourth type of *ārtta dhyāna*: intense anxiety for fulfilment of desire (*nidāna*) (DhŚ, 47). This refers to a condition where a person might, for example, be tortured by ambition (born of envy) for superhuman power. The characteristic signs of the person inclined towards *ārtta-dhyāna* are lamenting, a sense of inferiority and helplessness, weeping and mournfulness. A person who is depressed with *nidāna* despises himself and inflicts physical harm upon himself, such as cuts and bruises. This could be seen as psychologically sadistic behaviour. He heaps praise on others, wonders at their supernatural powers, craves these, and directs his energies towards acquiring them for himself (TS, 9.36).

### Raudra-dhyāna *(wrathful meditation)*

*Raudra-dhyāna* is associated with external forms of cruelty. Such *dhyāna* takes place in a person who continuously indulges in sinfulness. His aggressive urges and possessive instincts run deep and are difficult to inhibit. This psychological state manifests in four types of conduct: (1) injurious acts (*hiṁsā*); (2) lying (*mṛṣā*); (3) stealing (*stena*); and (4) protection of possessions (*saṃrakṣaṇa*) (TS 9.36).

Bronkhorst states that the overall four-fold division of Jain meditation into afflicted, wrathful, pious and pure is not reliable. He explains that the four-fold division was made by early systematisers and must initially have been meant to be a division of *dhyāna*, which denotes both 'thought' and 'meditation'. Later, theoreticians mistakenly took it to be a division of meditation only, and this did not fail to influence the later history of Jain meditation (Bronkhorst 2000: 44). I argue that Jain meditation has two aspects under the practice of *dhyāna*: (1) concentration meditation; and (2) thinking meditation. Furthermore, I have included both positive and negative aspects of meditation (*dhyāna*)[33] and cultivation (*bhāvanā*).[34] When concentration is combined with a positive aspect it becomes true meditation and when involved with negative disposition it becomes impure meditation. The positive aspect is to be encouraged and the negative to be avoided. Jain narrative literature has lots of examples embedded in stories of negative meditation.[35] A vast part of Jain meditation is also based on 'thought'. All the processes of reflection (*bhāvanā*) and contemplation (*anuprekṣā*) are deeply associated with thinking about one subject for a long duration of time. These practices are an integral part of Jain asceticism.

## The two meditations: liberating psychological states

*Dharma* and *śukla* are the two types of meditation that have been accepted as conducive to attaining the liberated state in sources from the canonical age to the present day.

## Dharma-dhyāna *(virtuous meditation)*

The word '*dharma*' or '*dharmya*'[36] means 'virtuous' or 'customary' in literature; it is sometimes explained as 'analytical' in a dogmatic rather than a scientific sense, since it is related to the application of the categories of reality (*tattvas*). Jainism, a dualistic religion whose ultimate focus is spiritual development, relies on discriminative knowledge (*bheda-vijñāna*) to achieve the latter. The practice of *dharmya-dhyāna* is analytical, insofar as it analyses and reflects on the various aspects of the soul, the non-soul, the universe and the scriptures.[37] In other words, these varieties of *dharmya* practice encompass a wide spectrum of knowledge. In this so-called meditative state, knowledge and concentration go hand in hand. Śubhacandra explains that *dharma-dhyāna* is predicated on the internalisation and application of the ethico-ontology of the series of *tattvas* that begin with soul and non-soul, bondage by karma (*bandha*) and so on, with liberation (*mokṣa*) as the last ontological category.[38] According to the TS, there are four types of *dharma-dhyāna*:

1. Investigation into the commandments of Jina, *ājñā-vicaya*
2. Investigation into bad consequences, *apāya-vicaya*
3. Investigation into karmic consequences, *vipāka-vicaya*
4. Investigation into the structure of the universe, *sansthāna-vicaya*.

When the mind is concentrating on the 'true' nature of an object, that particular state of the mind is called investigative meditation (*vicaya-dhyāna*). The term *vicaya* has many meanings, such as consideration (*paryālocana*), investigation (*anveśaṇa*), thinking (*anucintana*) and enquiry (*mārgaṇā*).[39] When the mind is contemplating such issues, and investigating the essence of the scriptural commandments, the mind is said to be in the state of *ājñā-vicaya*. When the mind thinks deeply on the causes of suffering in the world, it is said to be in the state of *apāya-vicaya*. Likewise, when the mind ponders upon the fruition of karma, the mind is in the state of *vipāka-vicaya*. When the mind reflects upon the universe and investigates its shape and contents it is called *sansthāna-vicaya*. In fact, all of these involve the four objects of *dharmya-dhyāna* (TS, 9.37).

## Śukla-dhyāna *(pure meditation)*

Pure meditation is the means for the attainment of liberation. The four varieties of pure meditation are:[40]

1. Multiple contemplation (*pṛthaktva-vitarka-savicāra*)
2. Unitary contemplation (*aikatva-vitarka-nirvicāra*)
3. Subtle infallible physical activity (*sūkṣma-kriyā-pratipāti*)
4. Irreversible stillness of the soul (*vyuparata-kriyā-anivarti*).

The first two varieties of pure meditation are said to be attainable only through the knowledge of the scriptural literature called *pūrvas*.[41] However, this literature is no longer existent. Thus, with the *pūrvas* lost, nobody is able to attain this state. Since the time period of between 150 and 350 CE, pure meditation was considered as no longer achievable in this world (Bronkhorst, 1993: 153). According to the Jain tradition, Jambusvāmī was the last person who attained liberation and Bhadrabāhu was the last knower of all the fourteen *pūrva* scriptures (*śruta-kevalin*) (Saṅghamitrā: 2001: 81). However, it is stated in the *Tattvārtha-sūtra* that the first two types of *śukla-dhyāna* are attainable when a person reaches the stage of complete self-restraint with supressed passions (*upaśānta-kaṣāya*) and at the stage of complete self-restraint with eliminated passions (*kṣīṇa-kaṣāya*) (TS 9.40).[42]

However, this problem of non-accessibility of liberation has been solved through cosmography, in that places such as Mahāvideha[43] are not affected by the cycle of time (*kālacakra*). Mahāvideha is divided into thirty-two regions, which are realms of action (*karma-bhūmi*). In these thirty-two *karma-bhūmi* regions, conditions are always suitable for *tīrthaṅkaras* to be born, and liberation is always possible for a human born there. Therefore, pure meditation is also said to be prevalent in these realms (BhS, 20.8). Those who are born in these regions can purify themselves through the performance of *dharma-dhyāna*, which is attainable here. Purification in our realm of birth, plausibly leads towards Mahāvideha in one's next birth where liberation is available.

## Digambara meditation on the soul

To understand the evolution of Jain yogic practices, an examination of works of the Digambara sect of *ācāryas* (leaders of the sky-clad group of ascetics) is essential. The Digambara tradition rejects the authority of the Śvetāmbara *āgama* literature and conveys a different attitude towards meditation. Its main focus is on the self; the body is considered as 'other'. I will examine this conception of meditation in some detail below. There is a long list of traditional Digambara manuals that are devoted to yoga and meditation. Some important Digambara mystical traditional works are those composed by Ācārya Kuṇḍakuṇḍa in the c. second to eighth centuries CE (*Mokṣa-Pāhuḍa, Samayasāra, Pravacanasāra*), which opened new horizons in the field of Jain meditation. These emphasised the 'penetration' of the pure soul. Dundas argues: 'this intense focus on the nature and centrality of the "self" is a defining characteristic of Digambara Jainism as a soteriological path, and its most compelling articulation in the Śaurasenī writings of Kundakunda' (Dundas 2012: 220). Kuṇḍakuṇḍa supports his own view on the soul according to the 'two-truth theory'. The two truths are: the definitive standpoint (*niścaya-naya*) and the empirical standpoint (*vyavahāra-naya*). In the light of these two truths, Kuṇḍakuṇḍa's works represent a movement from the external world towards the inner self in all aspects of thought and practice. What counts as conventional and what counts as ultimate changes as a practitioner progresses on the path. External practices are internalised, so that terms or objects that have an external or a physical significance in the early stages take on an inner significance that is based in the self.

## Contemplation (*anuprekṣā*)

Contemplation (*anuprekṣā*) is an ancient meditative practice. Here *anu* means 'afterwards'; whatever one has perceived during meditation, one can subsequently carry on the thought process afterwards on topics such as transience, etc.[44] This practice is used as a component of *dharma-dhyāna*[45] and *śukla-dhyāna*[46] as well as the third part of *svādhyāya* in SthāS.[47] An early Digambara text attributed to Kundakunda, the *Vārassa-aṇuvekkhā* or 'Twelve Contemplations', elucidates these. Schubring states that the *Uttarādhyayana-sūtra* presents examples within the text for understanding the types of *anuprekṣā*; these are common examples that illustrate transitoriness – such as a falling leaf, or a dangling dew-drop on a blade of grass that survives for a short time. In Schubring's view, these *anuprekṣās* are of a 'pessimistic character' (Schubring 2000: 307).

## *Āsana*

The term *āsana* is formed from the Sanskrit root √*ās* meaning 'to sit' (Āpṭe (2005 [1975]: 90). Thus the early use of *āsana* indicates a sitting position. However, in the Jain context, instead of *āsana* the word used is '*sthāna*'.[48] *Sthāna* is formed from the Sanskrit root √*sthā* which means 'to stay, remain or continue in any condition or action'. Early Jain literature itself does not have a dedicated text on *āsana*, but there are canonical texts in which the *āsana*s are occasionally recorded. The ancient *jina* images shows that *āsana*s in Jainism were used for meditative practices (*dhyānāsana*). Almost all early records of *āsana* are based on ascetic *tapas* practices. In the *Uttarādhyayana-sūtra,* the thirtieth chapter named '*Tava-magga-gaī*'[49] details the twelve types of austerities, which fall under the heading of *cāritra.* In this list of twelve austerities the term *kāyakilesa* (Pkt.), *kāyakleśa* (Skt.), is the practice of various postures – such as *vīrāsana* or *utkaṭāsana* – but this description of the twelve types of *tapas* does not use the term *āsana*.[50]

The Jain practice of *āsana* is based on the conceptual framework of asceticism. The main purpose of *āsana* is purification of the soul. As one progresses in the arena of spiritual practices, one must develop the potential of holding or controlling the energy upsurge that accompanies such progress. If the body is not efficient, it cannot hold the heat generated during meditation. The *Ācārāṅga-sūtra* describes Mahāvīra as practicing certain *āsana*s during his periods of meditation. The ĀSI states that Mahāvīra meditated sitting in the posture called *ukkuḍu*,[51] which means squatting position. *Ācārāṅga Cūrṇi* (first century CE) also mentions the two meditative postures of Mahāvīra, where he engages in squatting (*ukkuḍu*) and the hero's posture (*vīrāsana*). A later text, *Ācārāṅga Cūlā* (ĀSII), suggests that Mahāvīra achieved omniscient knowledge in the squatting position with joined heels, knees high and head low.[52] Finally, at the time of his liberation (*nirvāṇa*), he was in the palanquin (*paryaṅka*)[53] posture. Many canonical texts such as *Sthānāṅga-sūtra*, *Uttarādhyāyana-sūtra* and *Aupapātika-sūtras* present a list of various *āsana*s. Hemacandra also enumerated nine *āsana*s in his *Yogaśāstra* (twelfth century CE): the palanquin (*paryaṅkāsana*), heroic (*vīrāsana*), thunderbolt (*vajrāsana*), lotus (*abjāsana*), blessed (*bhadrāsana*), stick (*daṇḍāsana*), squatting (*utkaṭikāsana*), cow milking (*go-dohikāsana*) and abandonment of the body (*kāyotsargāsana*).[54]

## Medieval Jain yoga

Medieval Jain yoga represented a departure from the earlier canonical tradition and incorporated many new aspects from other yogic schools. It was much affected by Hindu yoga and tantra. In this section I will discuss the main figures who contributed to medieval Jain yoga.

### *Ācārya Haribhadra*

Ācārya Haribhadra (eighth century CE) initiated a shift in the field of yoga. He assimilated elements of Patañjali's *Yogasūtra* and its eight-fold systematisation into his own innovative formulation of Jain meditation – coining new words to describe spiritual progress. Haribhadra also made a valuable contribution to the comparative study of yoga, composing a number of works on the subject. He composed four treatises on Jain yoga – the *Yoga-bindu*, *Yoga-dṛṣṭi-samuccaya* (YDS), *Yoga-śataka* and *Yoga-viṁśikā* (YV) – and introduced changes in the definition and systematisation of yoga. Haribhadra defined Jain yoga in his short treatise *Yoga-viṁśikā*, a Prakrit text of twenty verses: 'all those religious practices, which connect [the self] with liberation is yoga.'[55] In the same text, he also highlighted a five-fold scheme of yoga:[56]

1. Proper posture (*sthāna*)
2. Correct pronunciation of *sūtra* (*ūrṇa*)
3. Proper understanding of meaning (*artha*)
4. Concentration on the image of the *tīrthaṅkara* in his full glory (*ālambana*)
5. Concentration on his abstract attributes (*anālambana*).

Haribhadra does not expand on religious activities (*dharma-vyāpāra*), but his commentator Yaśovijaya (1624–1688) in the *Yogaviṁśikā-ṭīkā* explains that religious activities are related to the ascetic lifestyle such as: (1) residing in one place (*ālaya*); (2) journeys on foot from one place to other (*vihāra*); (3) religious sermons (*bhāṣā*); (4) respect for the guru (*vinaya*); and (5) alms-seeking (*bhikṣāṭanādi*). Tatia elucidates that out of these five, the first two constitute external spiritual practices, which is known to a practitioner as the 'yoga of effort' (*karma-yoga*), while the last three are forms of internal spiritual practices known as the 'yoga of knowledge' (*jñāna-yoga*) (Tatia 1951: 293–294). Haribhadra also presented a model of eight-fold yoga in the *Yoga-dṛṣṭi-samuccaya*, which, as its name indicates, is a collection or overview of various viewpoints on yoga. Patañjali plays an important role here, but the impact ofVedānta and the Buddhist schools is also visible. Chapple states that the yoga system of Patañjali provides the pattern of eight-fold yoga upon which Haribhadra establishes the *Yoga-dṛṣṭi-samuccaya*. Patañjali distinguished eight parts (*aṅga)* of yoga and, similarly, Haribhadra also presents a parallel scheme of Jain yoga through the eight *dṛṣṭis* (Chapple and Casey 2003: 15).

### *Ācārya Śubhacandra*

The Digambara Ācārya Śubhacandra (eleventh century CE) wrote the *Jñānārṇava*, which offers a different form of Jain meditation, a new system of four-fold classification of meditation consisting of the corporeal (*piṇḍastha*), syllable (*padastha*), form (*rūpastha*) and formless (*rūpātīta*) meditations. However, he puts his new four-fold categorisation under the traditional categories of *dharma-dhyāna*. The four virtues of *maitrī* (friendship), *pramoda* (appreciation), *karuṇā* (compassion) and *mādhyastha* (indifference) are recognised as the sustainers of *dharmya-dhyāna* (JñĀ 27.4).[57] Along with *dhyāna*, he also incorporates five *dhāraṇās* into his system of yoga – a *dhāraṇā* is a psychophysiological exercise. Śubhacandra does not use the term yoga to describe his system, but it can be understood through the practices of *bhāvanā*: *dhāraṇā*, *dhyāna*, *āsana* and *prāṇāyāma*. Such formulations shows a clear influence from the Hindu tradition. Ohira notes that in the *Dhyānastava* (DhyS, 24) the four-fold meditations discussed in the *Jñānārṇava* of Śubhacandrara were already present in earlier Hindu tantric texts such as Abhinavagupta's *Tantrāloka* (10.241). She also discusses that the *Jñānārṇava* (Ocean of Knowledge) is the name of a scriptural text of the Śaiva Kaula lineage.[58]

## Ācārya Hemacandra

Ācārya Hemacandra (twelfth century CE) wrote a huge treatise, the *Yogaśāstra*, on Jain yoga. He defined yoga in a parallel way to the path of liberation[59] presented by Umāsvāti in the *Tattavārtha-sūtra* (fourth to fifth century CE).[60] Thus, yoga for Hemacandra is right faith, knowledge and conduct – the famous three jewels (*ratnatraya*). These components of yoga constitute the soteriological path.[61] Qvarnström states (1998) that even though Hemacandra presents *ratnatraya* in the first three chapters of *Yogaśāstra* as Jain yoga, in later chapters he took over the well-known formula of the eight yoga auxiliaries (*aṣṭāṅgayoga*) of Patañjali. Chapter four describes various postures (*āsana*), and chapter five begins with breath control (*prāṇāyāma*). Under the classical form are three breath techniques (*recaka*, *pūraka* and *kumbhaka*), and the remaining two, *uttara* and *adhāra*, are considered a part of tantric activities. It is noted by Qvarnström that the fifth chapter of YŚ (5.5–12) describes seven classical and tantric types of *prāṇāyama*.[62] In the Jain tradition, unlike the classical yoga or tantra traditions, *prāṇāyāma* is not accepted as a path to liberation. However, it is accepted as a means to better health and an aid for meditation. The text also depicts fixation (*dhāraṇā*) and meditation (*dhyāna*) with various mantras and tantric diagrams (*maṇḍala*). The tenth and final chapter explains pure meditation (*śukla-dhyāna*), which can be compared to the state of the highest meditative concentration (*samadhi*).

Hemacandra also deals with other questions: the proper place of meditation, posture, regulation of breath, withdrawal of the mind from the senses and the fixing of the mind on different places in the body. In these matters, he is a close follower of Śubhacandra. Hemacandra also incorporates Śubhacandra's four-fold types of meditation – namely, *piṇḍastha-*, *padastha-*, *rūpastha-* and *rūpātīta-dhyāna* – and considers them to be the objects of virtuous meditation (*dhyeya*) within *dharmya-dhyāna*.[63] The *Yogaśāstra* classifies *dhyāna* as two-fold only: *dharma* and *śukla* – in this respect Hemacandra altered the Jain canonical tradition of four-fold meditation for the first time. Qvarnström's study of the *Yogaśāstra* discusses the impact of 'Kaśmīriyana-Śaiva' traditions on Hemacandra's work. Qvarnström shows that there were multiple causes behind the adoption of mantra and tantric practices in Jain meditation – but the main cause was the influence of the Śaiva king Kumārapāla (1143–1172). Qvarnström suggests that Hemacandra may have foreseen future gains by adapting material familiar to the cultural heritage of the king (Qvarnström, 1998: 42–43). Thus, throughout the medieval period, Jain yogic tradition assimilated many common elements from contemporaneous traditions and 'Jainised' them into suitable forms, perhaps foreshadowing developings in the modern period.

## Modern Jain yoga

The twentieth century opened the worldwide door for yoga in Jain traditions. In more modern interpretations, yoga is not restricted to any specific person or group (such as ascetics), but is understood as incorporating most fields of human endeavour. Many Jains have accepted yoga as part of their lifestyle. During the twentieth and now in the twenty-first century, the Jain Śvetāmbara tradition developed seven new meditation yoga systems.[64] They are: the 'Jain Meditation' of Citrabhānu (b. 1922–2019), the '*Prekṣā-dhyāna-yoga*' of Ācārya Mahāprajña (1920–2010), the '*Arhum Yoga*'[65] (Yoga/meditation on Omniscient) of Ācārya Suśīlakumāra (1926–1994), the '*Samīkṣaṇa Dhyāna*' (Analytical Meditation) of Ācārya Nānālāla (1920–1999), the '*Sālambana Dhyāna*' (Support-Meditation) of Bhadraṅkaravijaya (1903–1975), the '*Ātma Dhyāna*' (Self-Meditation) of Ācārya Śivamuni (b. 1942), the '*Sambodhi Dhyāna*' (Enlightenment-Meditation) of Muni Candraprabhasāgara (b. 1962) and the '*Aśṭamaṅgala Dhyāna*' (Eight Auspicious Symbol Meditation) by Praveen Rishi (b. 1958). The above-mentioned systems were developed by individuals within their sects, but some of them made a worldwide impact.[66] These systems claim that the root of their yoga systems are in ancient Jain texts, while also trying to keep pace with modern scientific approaches.

Here I provide a brief overview of *prekṣā* meditation, which was developed by Ācārya Mahāprajña in 1975, as the culmination of a long period of spiritual research and practice. In the modern period, *prekṣā* meditation became a means of purification rather than a practice for liberation. Mahāprajña explained that the term *prekṣā* is derived from the Sanskrit root √*ikṣa*, which means 'to see'. When the prefix '*pra*' is added, it becomes *pra* + *iksa* = *prekṣā*, which means 'to perceive carefully and profoundly'. Here 'seeing' does not mean external vision, but careful concentration on subtle consciousness by mental insight. *Prekṣā dhyāna* is the system of meditation by engaging one's mind fully in the perception of subtle internal and innate phenomena of consciousness. It presents an eight-fold method of meditation: (1) relaxation with self-awareness (*kāyotsarga*); (2) internal journey (*antarayātrā*); (3) perception of breathing (*śvāsa-prekṣā*); (4) perception of body (*śarīra-prekṣā*); (5) perception of psychic centres (*caitanya-kendra-prekṣā*); (6) perception of psychic colours (*leṣyā-dhyāna*); (7) contemplation (*anuprekṣā*); and (8) cultivation (*bhāvanā*) (Mahāprajña 2010: 59). As Qvarnström and Birch conclude, 'On the whole, this [*prekṣā-dhyāna*] system of yoga is much broader in its scope of practice and theory than most of the systems that are popular in the west today' (Qvarnström and Birch, 2012: 368).

Mahāprajña modernised three traditional practices: relaxation with self-awareness (*kāyotsarga*), cultivation (*bhāvanā*) and contemplation (*anuprekṣā*).[67] The *kāyotsarga* of the modern system of *prekṣā* meditation differs from ancient meditative practice in its non-ascetic and non-ritualistic character. The five stages of Mahāprajña's *kāyotsarga* claim to present a 'scientific interpretation' that uses the terminology of western relaxation techniques, the Hatha Yogic *prāṇa* system and the personal experiences of Mahāprajña.[68] Thus, Mahāprajña mapped the system of 'psychic centres' (*caitanya-kendra*) onto the glandular system and explained the efficacy of this system and its techniques in terms of modern physiological theories of the hormonal system. Mahāprajña's novel use of scientific concepts was an innovative step to modernise Jain meditation. By synthesising original canonical elements with elements from other traditions, and by adding new interpretations, he packaged *prekṣā-dhyāna* as a modern meditation tool geared towards the 'purification of the psyche', the promotion of health and wellbeing, as well as liberation. These aims sought to appeal to both the laity and monastics, and created a 'socio-spiritual' model of meditation that positioned itself at a remove from capitalist culture.[69]

## Conclusion

The textual sources demonstrate the existence of Jain yogic practice in its ascetic tradition dating back to the fourth century BCE. Terms such as *yogavān*, *svādhīna-yoga*, *bhāvanā-yoga*, *dhyāna-yoga*, *dhruva-yoga*, *svādhyāya-yoga*, *samiti* and *gupti* (all discussed above) refer to practices of asceticism. In the canonical texts (fourth century BCE to sixth century CE), the Jain understanding of yoga was an intrinsic part of asceticism, rather than a separate practice. In the medieval period,

Haribhadra, Śubhacandra and Hemacandra's works on Jain yoga demonstrate an influence of Patañjali's *Yogasūtra* and other Hindu tantra literature. Modern Jain yoga has been inclusive of various developments in medieval yoga and related them to modern science. The modern presentation of yoga also incorporates psychological theory, the development of moral conduct, physical fitness and holistic understandings of personality to pave a way to liberation on this earth, away from the day-to-day modern lifestyle-related problems such as anxiety and tension.

## Abbreviations

| | |
|---|---|
| ĀSI, ĀSII | *Ācārāṅga-sūtra, Tulasī* |
| $\bar{A}S_2$ | *Ācārāṅga-sūtra,* Jacobi (Part 1) |
| $\bar{A}S_3$ | *Ācārāṅga-sūtra,* Jacobi (*Sacred Books of the East*) |
| $\bar{A}SBh_1$ | *Ācārāṅga-bhāṣyam 1994* |
| $\bar{A}SBh_2$ | *Ācārāṅga-bhāṣyam 2001* |
| ĀSC | *Ācārāṅga-cūrṇi* |
| ĀSV(Ś) | *Ācārāṁgasūtram Vṛtti* |
| AupS | *Aupapātika-sūtra* |
| ĀvS | *Āvaśyaka-sūtra* |
| BhS | *Bhagavatī-sūtra* |
| DhŚ | *Dhyāna-śataka* |
| DŚ(HV) | *Dhyāna-śataka- Vṛtti* |
| DhyS | *Dhyānastava* |
| DvS | *Daśavaikālika-sūtra 1964–1975* |
| DvS(HVṛ) | *Daśavaikālika-sūtra 1918* |
| DvS(Cū-Ag) | *Daśavaikālika-sūtra* |
| DvC(Ag) | *Daśavaikālika-Cūrṇī* |
| JñĀ | *Jñānārṇava* |
| KS | *Kalpasūtra* |
| PraV(M) | *Prajñāpanā Vṛtti* |
| PvS | *Praśnavyākaraṇa-sūtra* |
| SamS | *Samavāyāṃ-sūtra* |
| SthāS | *Sthānāṅga-sūtra* |
| SūSC | *Sūtrakṛtāṅga-Cūrṇī* |
| SūS | *Sthānāṅga-sūtra* |
| TS | *Tattvārtha-sūtra* |
| UttS | *Uttarādhyayana-sūtra* |
| YDS | *Yoga-dṛṣṭi-samuccya* |
| YS | *Yoga-sūtra* |
| YŚ | *Yoga-śāstra* |
| YV | *Yogaviṃśikā* |
| YVṬ | *Yogaviṃśikā Ṭīkā* |

## Notes

1 Some part of this chapter is taken from my PhD thesis, which I completed at SOAS University of London in 2017. I would like to express my sincere gratitude to Professor Peter Flügel who, as my supervisor, guided me at every stage of my thesis. I would also like to thank Dr. Suzanne Newcombe and Dr. Karen O'Brien-Kop for their suggestions and comments on the early draft of this chapter.

2 SthāS, 3.13. *tivihe joge paṇṇate, taṃ jahā- maṇa-joge, vai-joge, kaya-joge.*
3 These yogic methods include, but are not limited to, abandonment of body (*kāyotsarga*), meditation/ concentration (*dhyāna*), ascetic heat (*ātāpanā*), various stages of renunciation (*pratimā*), cultivation (*bhāvanā*) and contemplation (*anuprekṣā*) on dogmatic subjects.
4 Jain canonical texts present difficulties related to dating and chronology. The final redaction and documentation of the Śvetāmbara canon was attempted around one thousand years after Mahāvīra's liberation (*nirvāṇa*). The redaction of most of them is said to have been completed during the middle of the fifth century CE at the Vallabhi Council under the leadership of Devardhigaṇi. Before this council, the Jain canons are implicit as they were preserved through an oral tradition. For more information see, Dundas ((1992/2002: 22–23).
5 Prakrit is the language of Jain canonical literature.
6 SūC, p. 54. *yogo nāma saṃyama eva, yogo yasyāstīti sa bhavati yogavān.*
7 SūC, p54. *jogā vā jassa vase vaṭṭanti sa bhavati yogavān ṇāṇādīyā.*
8 YS, 3.4.
9 SūC, p 55. *athavā yogavāniti samiti-guptiṣu nityopayuktaḥ, svādhīnayoga ityarthaḥ.*
10 DvS(HVṛ), The term *svādhyāya-yoga* is a specific practice of fasting for scriptural study. It is known as '*yoga-vahana*'. For more detail, see *Hāribhadrīya Vṛtti* (p. 281).
11 SmS, 32.1.
12 Oxford Dictionary, p. 2217.
13 Monier-Williams Sanskrit-English Dictionary, p. 760.
14 SūS, 1.15.5. *bhāvaṇā-joga-suddhappā, jale ṇāvā a āhiyā | ṇāvā va tīra-sampaṇṇā, svva-dukkhā tiuṭṭati | |*
15 A *bhāvitātmā* is a self-cultivated ascetic, who practices various yogic forms. More detailed description about *bhāvitātmā* ascetic can be seen in *Bhagavati-sūtra* (BhS, 3.205).
16 PVS, see detailed description for the *bhāvanā* of the first vow, non-violence (*ahiṁsā*), 6.16–21; the *bhāvanā* of the second vow, truth (*satya*) 7.16–21; the *bhāvanā* of the third vow, non-stealing (*asteya*) 8.8–13; the *bhāvanā* of the fourth vow, celibacy (*brahmacarya*) 9.6.11; and the *bhāvanā* of the fifth vow, non-grasping (*aparigraha*) 10.13–18.
17 DyŚ, 30.
18 DvS, 8.38. See more detail about *pratipakṣabhāvanā* in O'Brien-Kop 2018.
19 TS, 9.19–20.
20 According to Jain tradition Mahāvīra (599-527 BCE) was the twenty-fourth in a series of ford-maker (*tīrthaṅkara*). For more detailed discussion on Mahāvīra's meditation, see Mahāprajña 1978; Bronkhorst 1986, 2000; Sāgaramala 2010; Pratibha Pragya, 2017.
21 The *Ācārāṅga-sūtra*'s eighth chapter was lost and for this reason there is no eighth chapter in the Indian edition, but Jacobi presents the ninth chapter as the eighth chapter in his edition.
22 *chadmastha-kāla* is a period before enlightenment. Here *chadmastha tīrthaṅkara* means a non-omniscient self, who is under the veil of *ghātikarma* and heading to be a ford-maker (*tīrthaṅkara*) in the same life.
23 The term *jinakalpa* denotes a solitary mode of ascetic practice, which is in this current day no longer in practice.
24 $\bar{A}S_2$, 1.8.1.5.
25 $\bar{A}S_2$, 1.8.1.6.
26 $\bar{A}S_3$, 1.8.1.4–5.
27 Jacobi mentions that '*tiriyabhitiṃ*' is left out in his translation. He could not understand the exact meaning of this term and suggests: 'so that he was a wall for the animals' (fn. p.80).
28 ĀSC, p. 301.
29 Ṭhāṇa, 4.60.
30 $UttS_1$, 30.35.
31 TS, 9.28, *ārtta-raudra-dharama-śuklāni.*
32 TS, 9.30, *pare mokṣahetū.*
33 Two negative *dhyānas* are discussed above.
34 There are five *bhāvanās* of malevolence, the behaviour and conduct of one whose psyche is imbued with evil disposition ($Utt_S$, 36.256).
35 There are many examples of afflicted (*ārtta*) and wrathful (*raudra*) meditation available in the *Jñātādharmakathā-sūtra* (e.g. JñāDS, 16.62–63 and JñāDS, 16.67).
36 The third category of meditation has two terms '*dharma*' or '*dharmya*'; *dharma* is used in TS and *Sarvārthasiddhi* employs *dharmya*. Here *dharma* has many meanings such as 'nature of reality' and ten types of *dharma* mentioned in SthāS (10.135).

37 *Tattvārtha-vārtika*, '*dharmādanapetaṃ dharmyaṃ*'. (TS, 9.37. *Tattavārtha-vārtika*, quoted in Maṅgalaprajñā, 2003: 65)
38 JñA, 31.18.
39 *Tattvārthabhāṣyānusāriṇī ṭīkā*, 9.37.
40 TS, 9.42 *pṛthaktvai-katvavitarka-sūkṣmakriyāpratipāti-vyuparatakriyānivartīni.*
41 *Pūrvas* are the collection of fourteen ancient texts in Jain canonical literature (*āgama*). There are numerous ways to define the term '*pūrva*'. Traditionally it means that the chief disciples (*gaṇadhara*) of each *tīrthaṅkara* composed these texts on the basis of knowledge that they gained from *tīrthaṅkaras*. Historically, scholars considered that these texts are teachings of the twenty-third *tīrthaṅkara*, Pārśvanātha. Since Ācārya Bhadrabāhu (I) was the last person who knew all fourteen *pūrvas*, this notion is acceptable in both the traditions of Śvetāmbara and Digaṃbara. Vajrasvāmī was the last *pūrvadhara* who had the knowledge of one *pūrva* (Wiley, 2004: 176).
42 TS, 9.40 *pūrvavidaḥ.*
43 Mahāvidehas are unaffected by the time-cycle and thus there are always *tīrthaṅkaras* in these zones; these areas are known as lands of actions (*karma-bhūmi*).
44 DhŚ, 65.
45 SthāS, 4.68.
46 SthāS, 4.72.
47 SthāS, 5. 220.
48 YVṬī, 2.
49 $UttS_1$, 30.7–8, 29–30.
50 UttS, 30.27.
51 *Ācārāṅga Sūtra* 1.9.4.14.
52 Ācārāṅga Cūlikā (ĀSII) (15.38); Ācārāṅga Cūlikā (ĀSII) (15.25).
53 KS, 146. *saṁpaliyaṁka-nisaṇṇe* ... Also see, *Jñātṛdharmakathāḥ* (JDK, 1.1.6).
54 For further detail on Hemacandra's *āsana* section see Mallinson and Singleton 2017: 101–108.
55 YV, 1 *mokkheṇa-joyaṇāo jogo savvo vi dhammavāvāro. Parisudho vinneo, ṭhāṇāigao viseseṇ.*
56 YV, 1.2.
57 JĀ, 27.4.
58 Śaiva Kaula lineage is a tantric school, also known as a *siddha* tradition.
59 YŚ, 1.15, *caturvarge'graṇīmokṣo, yogas tasya kāraṇam. jñāna-śradhāna-cāritrarūpaṃ ratnatrayaṃ ca sa.*
60 TS, *samyag-jñāna-darśana-cāritraṇi mokṣ-mārgaḥ.*
61 Abhidhāna Cintāmaṇi, 1.77, *mokṣopāyo yogo jñānaśradhāna-caṇātmakaḥ.*
62 See Qvarnström (2002: 102–103). The seven types of *prāṇāyama* are: *pratyāhāra, śānta, uttara, adhara, recaka, pūraka* and *kumbhaka.*
63 $YŚ_1$, 7.8.
64 For more on these modern Jain yoga and meditation systems, see Pratibha Pragya 2017.
65 Although Suśīlakumāra uses *Arhum Yoga* as the term for his method, it does not include many common aspects of yoga. In his book *Song of the Soul*, he noted four practices of meditation.
66 See also Samani Pratibha Pragya's unpublished 2017 thesis on 'History and Method of Prekṣā Meditation' p. 247–303.
67 See detailed textual discussions of *kāyotsarga* and *anuprekṣā* in (Pratibha Pragya 2017).
68 Mahāprajña uses the traditional term *kāyotsarga*, but to appeal to the global audience rendered it as 'relaxation with self-awareness' rather than in its literal meaning 'abandonment of the body'.
69 I have analysed the *prekṣā* meditation through studying its historical development, thus taking a different approach compared to scholars such as Jain 2010, 2014 and Kothari 2013 who analyse capitalism and pop-culture.

# Bibliography

## *Primary literature*

*Ācārāṅga-sūtra*. In Mahāprajña, Y (ed), Aṅgasuttāṇi 1. Vācanā Pramukha: Ācārya Tulasī. Second Edition. Lāḍnūṁ: Jaina Viśva Bhāratī, 1974/1992.

*Ācārāṅga-sūtra* (*The Āyāraṃga sūtra of the Śvetāmbara Jains*). Jacobi, H. (ed). Part 1. London: Oxford University Press Warehouse, 1882.

*Ācārāṅga-sūtra*. Jacobi, H. (trans), Müller, M. (ed), *Sacred Books of the East*. Volume 22, Jaina Sūtras Part 1, 1–213. Delhi: Motīlāla Banārasīdāsa, 1884/1994.

*Ācārāṅga-bhāṣyam*. Text, Sanskrit Commentary, Hindī Translation, Comparative Notes, etc in Mahāprajña, Ā (commentator) and Dulaharāja, M. (trans), *Text and Commentary, Classified List of Topics and Various Appendixes*. Lāḍnūṁ: Jaina Viśva Bhāratī Institute, 1994.

*Ācārāṅga-bhāṣyam*. Mahāprajña, Ā (Sanskrit commentator and Hindī trans) and Dulaharāja, M., Mahendra, M. and Kumāra, M. (English trans). Lāḍnūṁ: Jaina Viśva Bhāratī, 2001.

*Ācārāṅga-cūrṇi*. Jinadāsa Gaṇi (ed unknown). Ratnapura (Mālavā): Keśarīmalajī Śvetāmbara Sāhitya Saṃsthā, 1931.

*Ācārāṁgasūtram Vṛtti*. Silāṁkācārya in Jambūvijayajī, M (ed), *Ācārāṁgasūtram and Sūtrakṛtāṁgasūtram: With the Niryukti* of Ācārya Bhadrabāhu Svāmi *and the Commentary of Silāṁkācārya. The Text Originally Edited by Late Ācārya Sāgarānandasūriji Mahārāja*. Lālā Sundaralāla Jaina Āgamagranthamālā, Volume 1: Delhi: Motilal Banarsidas, 1978.

*Aupapātika-sūtra* (the first Upāṅga written by A Caturdaśa Purvadhara Sthavira). Muni, A. and Surāṇā, S. (eds) and Rājakumāra (English trans). Original Text with Hindī and English Translation, Elaboration and Multi-coloured Illustrations. Delhi: Padma Prakāśana, 2003.

*Āvaśyaka-sūtra*. Mahāprajña, Y. (ed), Nvasuttāṇi. Vācanā Pramukha: Ācārya Tulasī. Lāḍnūṁ: Jaina Viśva Bhāratī, 1987.

*Bhagavatī-sūtra*. Khaṇḍa 1, 4 (Śataka 1, 2, 12–16). Mūla-Pāṭha, Sanskrit Chāyā, Hindī Anuvāda, Bhāṣya Tathā Abhayadevasūri-Kṛta Vṛtti Evaṃ Pariśiṣṭa Śabdānukrama Ādi Sahita. Vācanā-Pramukha: Ācārya Tulasī. Saṃpādaka/Bhāṣyakāra: Ācārya Mahāprajña. Lāḍanūṁ: Jaina Viśva Bhāratī, 2007 [1994].

*Daśavaikālika-sūtra*. Ārya Sayyaṃbhava. Mūla-Pāṭha, Sanskrit Chāyā, Hindī Anuvāda tathā Ṭippaṇa. Vācanā Pramukha: Ācārya Tulasī. Sampādaka Vivecaka: Muni Nathamal. Lāḍanūṁ: Jaina Viśva Bhāratī, 1964/1974.

*Daśavaikālika-sūtra*. Hāribhadrīya Vṛtti by Hāribhadrasūri. Devacandra Lālabhāī Jaina Pustakoddhāra Bhaṇḍāgāra Saṁsthā, Bambaī, Vi.Saṃ, 1918.

*Dhyāna-śataka*. Jinabhadra Kṣamāśramaṇa, in Dulaharāja, M. (ed and Hindī trans), *Jaina Yoga ke Sāta Grantha*, 25–50. Muni Dulaharāja. Lāḍanūṁ: Jaina Viśva Bhāratī, 2006 [1995].

Hāribhadrīya *Dhyāna-śataka-Vṛtti*. Hāribhadrasūri in Dhyānśataka and Dhyānastava. Bālacandra Siddhānta-śāś tri (ed). Dellī: Vīra Sevā Mandira, 1976.

*Dhyānastava*. Bhāskarānaṃdi. Suzuko Ohira (ed). Dillī: Bhāratīya Jñānapīṭha, 1973.

*Jñānārṇava* by Śubhacandra. Pannālāla Bākalivālā (ed with Hindi trans). Agāsa: Śrīmada Rājacandra Āśrama, 1975.

*Kalpasūtra*. Bhadrabāhu, in *Daśāśrutaskandha. Vividha-Varṇaka-Prācīna Citrakalita evaṃ Hindī-Āṅglabhāṣā*. Vinaya Sāgar (ed and Hindī trans), Mukunda Lāla (English trans). Pictorial Illustration: Śrīmatī Candramaṇisingh. Jaipur: Prakrit Bhāratī, 1977/1984.

*Prajñāpanā Vṛtti*. Malayagiryācārya in Malayagirīyā *Prajñāpanā Vṛtti*. Mehasāṇā: Āgamodaya samiti, 1918.

*Praśnavyākaraṇa-sūtra*. In *Aṅgasuttāṇi 3. Vācanā Pramukha: Ācārya Tulasī*. Yuvācārya Mahāprajña (ed). Second edition. Lāḍanūṁ: Jaina Viśva Bhāratī, 1992 [1975].

*Samavāyāṅga-sūtra*. In Muni Nathmal (ed), *Aṅgasuttāṇi 1. Vācanā Pramukha: Ācārya Tulasī*. Lāḍanūṁ: Jaina Viśva Bhāratī. 1992 [1974].

*Sthānāṅga-sūtra. Text, Sanskrit Rendering and Hindī Version with Notes. Vācanā Pramukha: Ācārya Tulasī*. Ācārya Mahāprajña (ed and commentator). Lāḍanūṁ: Jaina Viśva Bhāratī, 1976.

*Sūtrakṛtāṅga-Cūrṇi* of Jinadāsa Mahattara. Śrī Ṛṣabhadevajī Keśarīmalajī Śvetāmbara Saṃsthā, Ratalāma (Mālavā). 1933.

*Sthānāṅga-sūtra*. Text, Sanskrit Rendering and Hindī Version with Notes. Vācanā Pramukha: Ācārya Tulasī. Ācārya Mahāprajña (ed and commentator). Lāḍanūṁ: Jaina Viśva Bhāratī, 1976.

*Tattvārtha-sūtra*. Umāsvāti. In, *That Which Is. Tattvārtha-sūtra of Umāsvāti/Umāsvāmī with the Commentaries of Umāsvāti/ Umāsvāmī, Pūjyapāda and Siddhasenagaṇi*. Nathmal Ṭāṭiā (trans with an Introduction). San Francisco: Harper Collins, 1994.

*Uttarādhyayana-sūtra. Mūlapāṭha, Saṃkṣipta Chāyā, Hindī Anuvāda, Tulanātmaka Ṭippaṇa. Vācanā Pramukha: Ācārya Tulasī*. Sampādaka & Vivecaka: Ācārya Mahāprajña. Third edition. Lāḍnūṁ: Jaina Viśva Bhāratī, 2000 [1967].

*Yoga-dṛṣṭi-samuccya*. Haribhadra. In Chapple, C. K. and Casey, J. T. (eds), *Reconciling Yoga: Haribhadra's Collection of Views on Yoga*. With a new translation of Haribhadra's *Yogadṛṣṭisamuccya*. Albany: State University of New York, 2003.

*Yoga-sūtra*. Patañjali. *With the Commentary of Vyāsa and the Gloss of Vāchaspati Miśra*. Prasāda, R (trans). Allahabad: Munśīrāma Manoharlāla, 1988 [1912].

*Yoga-śāstra*. Hemacandra. *A Twelfth Century Handbook on Śvetāmbara Jainism*. (trans with an introduction by Qvarnström, O). Cambridge, MA: Harvard Oriental Series Vol. 60, 2002.

*Yogaviṃśikā*. Haribhadra. (Pujya Upādhyāya Śrī Yaśovijajī kṛta Sanskrit Ṭīkā nā Gujarātī Anuvāda Sāthe). Mahetā, D. D. (trans). Surat: Dhīrajalāla Ḍāhayālāla Mahetā, 1993.

*Yogaviṃśikā Ṭīkā*. *Yogaviṃśikā* by Haribhadra. (Pujya Upādhyāya Śrī Yaśovijajī kṛta Sanskrit Ṭīkā nā Gujarātī Anuvāda Sāthe). Mahetā, D. D. (trans). Surat: Dhīrajalāla Ḍāhayālāla Mahetā, 1993.

## Secondary literature

Āpṭe, V. S. 2005 [1975]. *The Student's Sanskrit-English Dictionary*. Containing Appendices on Sanskrit Prosody and Important Literary and Geographical Names in the Ancient History of India. Delhi: Motīlāla Banārasīdāsa Publishers.

Bhatt, B. 1993. Ācāra-Cūlās and Niryukti: Studies II (Mahāvīra-biography). In Smet, R. and Watanabe, K. (eds), *Jain Studies in Honour of Jozef Deleu*, 85–122. Tokyo: Hon-No-Tomosha.

Bronkhorst, J. 1986. *The Two Traditions of Meditation in Ancient India*. Stuttgart: Franz Steiner Verlag Wiesbaden GmbH.

Bronkhorst, J. 1993. 'Remarks on the History of Jaina Meditation', in Smet, R. & Watanabe, K. (eds), *Jain Studies in Honour of Jozef Deleu*, 151–162. Tokyo: Hon-No-Tomosha.

Bronkhorst, J. 2000. *The Two Traditions of Meditation in Ancient India*. Delhi: Motīlāla Banārasīdāsa.

Bruhn, K. 2012. 'Two Overviews', in Bruhn, K. and Mevissen, G. J. R. (eds), *Berliner Indologische Studien* 7–36.

Chapple, C. K. and Casey, J. T. (eds) 2003. *Reconciling Yoga: Haribhadra's Collection of Views on Yoga*. With a new translation of Haribhadra's *Yogadṛṣṭisamuccya*. Albany: State University of New York.

Cort, E. J. 2001. *Jains in the World: Religious Values and Ideology in India*. New York: Oxford University Press.

Dundas, P. 1992/2002. *The Jains*. Second revised edition. London: Routledge.

Dundas, P. 2012. 'A Digambara Jain Description of the Yogic Path to Deliverance', in White, D. G. (ed), *Yoga in Practice*, 143–161. Princeton, NJ, USA: Princeton University Press.

Jain, Andrea. 2010. *Health, Well-Being, and the Ascetic Ideal: Modern Yoga in the Jain Terapanth*. Unpublished PhD Dissertation. Houston, Texas: Rice University.

Jain, A. 2014. *Selling Yoga: From Counterculture to Pop Culture*. Oxford: Oxford University Press.

Jain Sāgarmala. 2010. 'The Historical Development of Jaina Yoga System and Impacts of Other Yoga Systems on it: A Comparative and Critical Study', in Balbir, Nalini (ed), *Svasti: Essays in honour of prof. Hampa Nagarajaiah for his 75th Birthday*, 257–269. Krishnapuradoddi: K. S. Muddappa Smaraka Trust.

Kothāri, Smithā. 2013. *Dāna and Dhyāna in Jaina Yoga: A Case Study of Prekṣādhyāna and the Terāpantha*. Unpublished PhD Thesis. Toronto: University of Toronto.

Mahāprajña, Ācārya. 1978/1997. *Jaina Yoga*. Dulaharāja, Muni (ed). Cūrū: Ādarśa Sāhitya Saṅgha.

Mahāprajña, Ācārya 2010. Yātrā Eka Akiñcana kī (Ātmakathā-1). Dhanañjaya Kumāra, Muni and Viśruta Vibhā, Sādhvī (eds). Lāḍanūṁ: Jaina Viśva Bhāratī.

Mallinson, J. and Singleton, M. 2017. *Roots of Yoga*. London: Penguin Classics.

Maṅgalaprajñā, S. 2003. *Ārhatī Dṛṣṭi*. Second edition. Delhi: Ādarśa Sāhitya Saṅgha.

Monier-Williams, D. 1994 [1899]. *Sanskrita English Dictionary* (New enlarged and improved edition). New Delhi: Munshiram Manoharlal.

Pratibha Pragya, S. 2017. *History and Method of Prekṣā Meditation* (PhD thesis). SOAS, University of London.

O'Brien-Kop, K. 2018. '*Pratipakṣabhāvanā*: Yoga as the path of cultivation to overcome the obstacles'. World Sanskrit Conference, University of British Columbia, Vancouver.

Qvarnström, O. 1998. 'Stability and Adaptability: A Jain Strategy for Survival and Growth', *Indo-Iranian Journal* 41: 33–55.

Qvarnström, O. (ed. and trans.) 2002. *A Twelfth Century Handbook on Śvetāmbara Jainism*. Cambridge, MA: Harvard Oriental Series, Vol. 60.

Qvarnström, O. and Birch, J. 2012. 'Universalist and Missionary Jainism: Jain Yoga of the Terāpanthī Tradition', in White, D. G. (ed), *Yoga in Practice*, 365–382. Princeton, NJ, USA: Princeton University Press.
Saṅghamitrā, S. 2001. *Jaina Dharma ke Prabhāvaka Ācārya.* Fourth edition. Lāḍanūṁ: Jaina Viśva Bhāratī.
Schubring, W. 2000. *The Doctrine of the Jainas.* Delhi: Motilal Banarsidass.
Stevenson, A. 2010. *Oxford Dictionary of English.* Third edition. Oxford: Oxford University Press.
Tatia, N. 1951. *Studies in Jaina Philosophy.* Banaras: Jain Cultural Research Society.
Wiley, K. L. 2004. *Historical Dictionary of Jainism.* Historical Dictionaries of Religion, Philosophies, and Movements, 53. Oxford: The Scarecrow Press.
Williams, R. 1991 [1963]. *Jain Yoga: A Survey of the Mediaeval Śrāvakācāras.* Delhi: Motīlāla Banārasīdāsa.

# 14
# DAOIST MEDITATION

*Louis Komjathy*

## Introduction

Along with ritual, meditation has been and remains the primary form of religious praxis in the Daoist tradition. Within the various communities, lineages and movements that comprise the Daoist tradition, adherents have engaged in diverse forms of meditation. These include apophatic meditation, ingestion, visualisation, inner observation and internal alchemy. Such Daoist practices are as diverse, complex and systematised as, say, Buddhist and Christian contemplative practice, but they are largely unknown outside of Daoist communities and academic specialists. One of the challenges here involves the accompanying diversity of views and goals. In the present chapter, I begin with some brief reflections on 'meditation' and 'yoga' as comparative categories, with attentiveness to indigenous Chinese and Daoist terminology. This is followed by a short historical overview of the Daoist tradition and types of meditation. As I have already written various overviews of Daoist meditation (see Komjathy 2013b, 2014a, forthcoming), I focus the majority of this presentation on technical details in a representative sampling of specific practices and techniques, especially Daoist apophatic meditation, visualisation and internal alchemy. The chapter concludes with some information on contemporary Daoist meditation.

## On meditation and so-called 'Taoist yoga'

When approaching 'non-western' traditions like Daoism (Taoism) and Daoist meditation by extension, it is important to recognise that one is engaging with different cultures that use different languages, including 'non-alphabetic' ones. In the case of Chinese traditions, including Ruism ('Confucianism'),[1] Daoism and Sinified or Chinese Buddhism, the primary language is classical/literary Chinese. The latter is a character-based language, with many characters being pictograms and ideographs. On the most basic level, there is no direct equivalent to 'meditation', or 'Daoism' for that matter. It is thus important to investigate indigenous Chinese and Daoist terms approximated by or related to English ones. This may inhibit certain appropriative and domesticating tendencies rooted in colonialist, missionary and orientalist legacies (see Komjathy 2013b, 2015, 2018).

The English term 'meditation', which derives from the Lain *meditatio* ('to think over'/'to consider'), is generally used as a comparative category to designate seated techniques that facilitate transformations of consciousness.[2] In Chinese, these types of practices most often have been designated with the term/graph *zuo* ('sitting'). However, more often than not, one finds tradition-specific technical terms, rather than generalised categories. In the case of Daoism, one of the most influential and common is *shouyi* ('guarding the One'). As explored below, this phrase originally designated classical Daoist apophatic (emptiness-/stillness-based) meditation aimed at mystical union with the Dao. *Shouyi* eventually became used to designate Daoist meditation more generally. In the medieval period, we find the individual terms *cun* ('maintain'), *guan* ('observe'), *si* ('consider') and the composite phrases *zhengzuo* (lit. 'upright sitting') and *jingzuo* (lit. 'quiet sitting'). As in the case of *shouyi*, these terms sometimes designate specific methods. In a contemporary context, *dazuo* (lit. 'undertake sitting') is the most common general term and may be used for any type of meditation, whether tradition-specific or particular methods. Less commonly, *moxiang* (lit. 'deep thought'), as a reverse translation of 'meditation', is used. In my own work and as a viable approach, I accept the use of 'meditation' as a comparative category.

This stands in contrast to 'yoga' (*yoga*), derived from the Sanskrit √*yuj*, meaning 'to yoke' and, by extension, 'to unite' (see Harimoto Chapter 6 in this volume).[3] There is no such indigenous term as 'yoga' in Chinese culture. While there is the Chinese transliteration of *yujia* 瑜珈, that term primarily was used to refer to the Indic notion of *samādhi* and in some later cases to Tantric Buddhism. There is thus no such thing as so-called 'Taoist Yoga'. 'Taoist Yoga' (a.k.a. Tao Yoga) is a misnomer, a mistaken category with no correlation to Daoist technical terms. 'Taoist Yoga' represents a modern appropriation and hybridisation of Indian and Chinese cultural traditions.

Although more research is required, the earliest usage of the western construct of so-called 'Taoist Yoga' appears to be Lu K'uan Yü's (Charles Luk; 1898–1978) *Taoist Yoga: Alchemy and Immortality* (1973), which is a translation of the *Xingming fajue mingzhi* (Illuminating Pointers to the Methods and Instructions of Innate Nature and Life-Destiny; ZW 872) by Zhao Bichen (1860–1942). The latter is a late imperial manual of internal alchemy. The term eventually became part of popular western discourse, wherein it was adopted in the 1980s by early Healing Tao (a.k.a. Universal Tao), Mantak Chia's (Xie Mingde; b. 1940) syncretic and popularised Qigong system, which incorporated some elements of Daoist internal alchemy.[4] In its earliest western usage, 'Taoist Yoga' referred to: (1) Daoist internal alchemy (*neidan*); (2) partnered sexual practices or 'bedchamber arts' (*fangzhong shu*), often misidentified as 'Daoist'; and (3) stretching exercises. In terms of content and practice, there are some parallels between Daoist internal alchemy and Kundalini Yoga and Indian tantra on one hand, and between Daoyin (Guided Stretching) and Hatha Yoga on the other. As I will discuss Daoist internal alchemy below, here I will simply note that Daoyin, often located within larger health and longevity systems (*yangsheng*), usually involves stretching and breathwork that may lend themselves to cross-cultural comparison.

In contemporary popular western discourse, the term 'Taoist Yoga' continues to be used in its three earlier senses. However, it has also been systematised as a specific form of 'yoga' (stretching routines), complete with teacher certification programmes. In that context, it sometimes goes by the names 'Flow Yoga' and 'Yin Yoga'. The latter is said to be softer than 'Yang Yoga' (read: all other forms of yoga) and to focus on the connective tissue, both of which its adherents identify as 'yin'. So-called 'Yin Yoga', like 'Taoist Yoga', is a contemporary form of hybrid spirituality. Yin and yang are indigenous Chinese terms related to traditional Chinese cosmology. They refer to the primary, complementary and dynamic interactive principles or forces of the universe. Yin Yoga adherents not only misidentify yin-yang cosmology as 'Daoist', but also misconstrue the defining characteristics of Daoism (see Komjathy 2013b, 2014a).

At the present time, it is unclear if any of the content of so-called 'Taoist Yoga' derives from Daoist Daoyin practices. Preliminary research suggests that some so-called 'Taoist Yoga' is a modification of Indian practices, while other versions derive from Chinese Wushu and Gongfu (Kung-fu) training exercises. As such, 'Taoist Yoga' is part of what may be referred to as Popular Western Taoism (PWT), a form of New Age hybrid spirituality that appropriates some aspects of the religious tradition which is Daoism in order to increase cultural capital and marketability (see Komjathy 2014a).

## The Daoist tradition and types of Daoist meditation

The Daoist tradition may be understood through what I refer to as the 'seven periods' and 'four divisions' (Komjathy 2013b; 2014a). The seven periods are as follows: (1) classical Daoism; (2) early Daoism; (3) early medieval Daoism; (4) late medieval Daoism; (5) late imperial Daoism; (6) early modern Daoism; and (7) late modern Daoism. There were diverse forms of community and social organisation in these various periods and the associated movements, including eremitic, householder, monastic and so forth. The seven periods roughly correspond to major watersheds for Daoism in Chinese dynastic and post-dynastic history:

1. Warring States (480–222 BCE), Qin (221–206 BCE) and Early Han (202 BCE–9 CE)
2. Later Han (25–220 CE)
3. Period of Disunion (220–589) and Sui (581–618)
4. Tang (618–907), Song (Northern: 960–1127; Southern: 1127–1279), and Yuan (1260–1368)
5. Ming (1368–1644) and Qing (1644–1911)
6. Republican (1912–1949; 1949–) and early Communist (1949–1978).

I in turn divide the modern period into 'early modern Daoism' (1912–1978) and 'late modern Daoism' (1978–present), with the latter including contemporary expressions and developments. These correspond to the sixth and seventh periods, respectively.

Each of these periods saw the emergence of specific communities and movements. Briefly stated, classical Daoism encompasses the diverse communities and 'schools' of the inner cultivation lineages as well as Huang-Lao Dao (Way of the Yellow Emperor and Laozi). Major movements associated with early Daoism include Taiping (Great Peace) and Tianshi (Celestial Masters). Early medieval Daoism consisted of such important movements as Taiqing (Great Clarity), Sanhuang (Three Sovereigns), Shangqing (Highest Clarity) and Lingbao (Numinous Treasure). Late medieval Daoism included a variety of internal alchemy movements, including Quanzhen (Ch'üan-chen; Complete Perfection) and so-called Nanzong (Southern School), as well as new deity cults and ritual movements. Late imperial and modern Daoism was dominated by Zhengyi (Cheng-i; Orthodox Unity; a.k.a. Celestial Masters) and Complete Perfection, though it also saw the emergence of major lineages of the latter as well as new lineages of internal alchemy.

The constituents of global Daoism are a highly complex topic. Briefly stated, from a tradition-based and institutional perspective, global Daoism remains primarily an Orthodox Unity-Complete Perfection tradition. Orthodox Unity Daoism is largely a householder community consisting of married priests (male and female) and family lineages and primarily located in south and southeast China as well as Taiwan. Complete Perfection, including its Longmen (Dragon Gate) lineage, is primarily a monastic community consisting of celibate clergy and monastics (male and female) living in temples and monasteries throughout mainland China, Hong Kong and Taiwan. There are also dynamic (and problematic) recent developments, including mediumistic cult influences, obscure family lineages and diverse organisations.

For simplicity's sake, we might further speak of four basic divisions of Daoism: (1) classical Daoism; (2) early organised Daoism; (3) later organised Daoism; and (4) modern Daoism. The rationale for this grouping is to distinguish historical developments, types of community and distinctive models of practice. It draws our attention to the ways in which the inner cultivation lineages of classical Daoism differ from the householder, ascetic and eremitic communities of early organised Daoism, as the Later Han dynasty witnessed the emergence of Daoism as an organised religious tradition with enduring institutions. Early organised Daoism may be distinguished from later organised Daoism based on the ascendance of a monastic model in the latter and the emergence of new models of practice, especially internal alchemy. As discussed in more detail below, internal alchemy usually involves complex, stage-based physiological (energetic) practices aimed at complete psychosomatic transformation, or 'immortality' in Daoist terms. Modern Daoism corresponds to the end of dynastic rule in China and the increasing influence of western values and political ideologies. In its more contemporary form, it directs our attention towards Daoism as a global religious tradition with worldwide distribution and international adherence.

Here it should be mentioned that Daoism is the object of various western fabrications, fictions and fantasies, which are rooted in colonialist, missionary and orientalist legacies. The most epidemic of these is the inaccurate and outdated distinction between so-called 'philosophical Daoism' and so-called 'religious Daoism', the usage of which should be taken *ipso facto* as misunderstanding concerning Daoism.[5] As herein employed, 'classical Daoism' replaces so-called 'philosophical Daoism', while 'organised Daoism' replaced so-called 'religious Daoism'. This revisionist framework allows individuals to engage the tradition in a more neutral and receptive, a more integrated and sophisticated manner. For present purposes, meditation has been a major form of Daoist religious practice from the beginning of the tradition and throughout its history. By way of background, there are at least five major types of Daoist meditation.

1. Apophatic or quietistic meditation. Designated by various Chinese Daoist technical terms such as 'fasting the heart-mind' (*xinzhai*), 'guarding the One' (*shouyi*), 'sitting-in-forgetfulness' (*zuowang*) and later 'quiet sitting' (*jingzuo*)
2. Ingestion (*fuqi*; lit. 'ingesting subtle breath')[6]
3. Visualisation (*cunxiang*; lit. 'maintaining the image')
4. Inner observation (*neiguan*)
5. Internal alchemy (*neidan*). Also 'female alchemy' (*nüdan*)

Briefly stated, apophatic meditation emphasises emptying and stilling the heart-mind (*xin*), the seat of emotional and intellectual activity from a traditional Chinese perspective, until one becomes empty and still. It is primarily contentless, non-conceptual and non-dualistic (see Roth 1999a, 2015). Ingestion involves taking the energies of the cosmos into one's body and incorporating them into one's being. Typical examples include ingesting solar, lunar and astral effulgences and cosmic ethers or vapours. Visualisation involves visualising (possibly 'imagining' or 'actualising') specific deities, constellations, colours and so forth. There is some overlap between visualisation and ingestion (see Kohn 1989a; Robinet 1989a, 1993). If one were more radical, one might categorise ingestion as a form of Daoist dietetics as well as of meditation. It is also a major Daoist health and longevity technique (see Komjathy 2013b). Adapted from Buddhist *vipassanā* practice, Daoist inner observation generally involves maintaining non-discriminating awareness of all phenomena and/or exploring the body as an internal landscape (see Kohn 1987, 1989c). Finally, internal alchemy utilises complex, stage-based practices aimed at psychosomatic, including physiological and energetic, transformation. It often corporates and systematises the four other types (see Needham et al. 1983; Pregadio and Skar 2000; Komjathy 2007, 2013a, 2013b). Later, methods specifically for women, called 'female alchemy', developed.

These types of Daoist meditation in turn emerged during specific periods and are associated with specific Daoist movements or sub-traditions.

1. Classical Daoism: Warring States (480-222 BCE) to Early Han (206 BCE-9 CE). Texts: *Laozi*, *Zhuangzi* and sections of the *Guanzi*, *Huainanzi*, *Lüshi chunqiu*, etc. Associated movement: Classical inner cultivation lineages

2. Early and early medieval Daoism: Later Han (25–220 CE) to Period of Disunion (220–581). Texts: *Laozi zhongjing*, *Huangting jing*, *Dadong zhenjing*, etc. Associated movements: Taiping, Taiqing and Shangqing
3. Also in the early and early medieval period as (2), although many of the influential texts date from the next period of Daoist history. Texts: *Taiqing fuqi koujue*, *Fuqi jingyi lun*, etc.
4. Late medieval Daoism: Tang (618–907). Texts: *Neiguan jing*, *Dingguan jing* and sections of other Tang-dynasty meditation manuals. Associated movement: Late medieval Daoism (monastic system), specifically later Shangqing
5. Late medieval and late imperial Daoism: Tang to Qing (1644–1911). Texts: *Chuandao ji*, *Wuzhen pian*, *Dadan zhizhi*, etc. Associated movements: Zhong-Lü, Nanzong, Quanzhen, etc.[7]

Apophatic or quietistic meditation is the earliest form of Daoist contemplative practice and is associated with the inner cultivation lineages of classical Daoism. Ingestion and visualisation are particularly connected to the early Shangqing (Highest Clarity) movement of early medieval Daoism, although there are earlier precedents. Inner observation emerged in the context of the fully integrated Tang-dynasty monastic system, although there are earlier precedents in the classical Daoist textual corpus. Finally, internal alchemy, as a developmental stage-based approach, was first articulated in the late Tang and early Song dynasty, with the Quanzhen (Complete Perfection) and so-called Nanzong (Southern School) movements being especially influential. Each of these five types of meditation still exist in contemporary Daoist practice, but apophatic meditation and internal alchemy are most widely practised.

## 'Guarding the One'

*Shouyi*, or 'guarding the One', is a key Daoist technical term for apophatic meditation, that is, emptiness- and stillness-based meditation. This is the earliest form of Daoist meditation. It was the central practice of the inner cultivation lineages of classical Daoism. *Shou* ('guard') suggests protecting a precious substance or condition within oneself, while *yi*, literally the number 'one' and 'oneness/unity/unification' by extension, is an alternative classical Daoist name for the Dao (Tao), the sacred or ultimate concern of Daoists.[8] While the Dao and the One may be used for a technical cosmogonic distinction, the One refers to the Dao as primordial non-differentiation and cosmogonic unity. *Yi* may thus refer to the process of mystical unification and/or the state of oneness/unity. As explored below, 'guarding the One' thus refers to returning to the original and inherent stillness of innate nature (*xing*), which is associated with the Dao-as-Stillness and/or preserving and maintaining it within oneself. *Shouyi* in turn relates to various other classical Daoist technical terms, with *xinzhai* (lit. 'heart fast') and *zuowang* (lit. 'sit and forget') being most influential.[9] These terms appear in chapters four and six of the fourth to second century BCE *Zhuangzi* (*Chuang-tzu*; Book of Master Zhuang), respectively. *Xinzhai*, which may be rendered technically as 'fasting of the heart-mind', directs one's attention to emptying and stilling the heart-mind of excessive intellectual and emotional activity and content. 'Fasting' suggests refraining from unnecessary or harmful consumption patterns (e.g. rumination), while the 'heart-mind' refers to both the actual, physical heart and mind in a more abstract sense.[10] This is a key dimension of 'Daoist anthropology' and 'Daoist contemplative psychology'.[11] *Zuowang*, which may be rendered technically as 'sitting-in-forgetfulness', designates both a physical posture ('sitting'), a meditative method ('forgetting') and a contemplative state ('forgetfulness'). As a method, one forgets everything until one has even forgotten forgetting. Like stillness, forgetfulness may be understood as a state of meditative absorption and mystical union.

The two earliest references to 'guarding the One' appear in the *Neiye* (Inward Training) and aforementioned *Book of Master Zhuang*. The former is a mid-fourth-century classical Daoist text preserved as chapter 49 in the received *Guanzi* (Book of Master Guan) and often identified as one of the so-called 'Xinshu' (Techniques of the Heart-mind) chapters, while the *Zhuangzi* is a multi-vocal anthology that contains historical and textual material from at least the fourth to second century BCE and associated with various lineages of classical Daoism.[12] The *shouyi* reference in the *Zhuangzi* occurs in chapter 11, which is associated with the Primitivists.[13] Both texts provide technical specifics on classical Daoist apophatic meditation.

> Expand your heart-mind and release it.
> Relax your *qi* and allow it to extend.
> When your body is calm and unmoving,
> Guard the One and discard myriad disturbances.
> You will see profit and not be enticed by it.
> You will see harm and not be frightened by it.
> Relaxed and unwound, and yet free from selfishness,
> In solitude you will find joy in your own being.
> This is what we call 'circulating *qi*' (*yunqi*).
> Your awareness and practice appear celestial.
>
> *(Neiye, ch. 24)*

> Come, I will tell you about the perfect Dao. The essence of the perfect Dao is dark and mysterious; the ridgepole of the perfect Dao is obscure and silent. Without looking or listening, embrace spirit (*baoshen*) through stillness. The body will align naturally. You inevitably become still and clear. By not laboring your body or agitating your vital essence, you can live a long life. When the eyes do not see, the ears do not hear, and the heart-mind does not know, then your spirit will guard the body, and the body will attain long life. Be attentive to the internal and seal off the external, because much knowing leads to dissipation. Then I will lead you beyond the great brightness, to the source of utmost yang; I will guide you through the dark and mysterious gate, to the source of the utmost yin. The heavens and earth have regulators; yin and yang have storehouses. You only have only to take care and guard your own body; these other things will be stable on their own. As for myself, I guard this oneness (*shou qi yi*) and abide in this harmony.
>
> *(Zhuangzi, ch. 11; adapted from Watson 1968: 119–20)*[14]

As in other descriptions of classical Daoist apophatic meditation, such as in chapters 10, 16, 20, 28 and 37 of the *Laozi* (Book ofVenerable Masters),[15] these passages encourage aspiring Daoist adepts to disengage sensory perception and decrease psychological activity. As habituated cognitive patterns decrease, one gradually enters a state of deep stillness. One simply sits in silence, which is the ground of one's being. From a Daoist perspective, this is one's innate connection with and manifestation of the Dao. Thus, Daoist apophatic meditation is primarily contentless, non-conceptual and non-dualistic.

In terms of the technical specifics, it is noteworthy that both passages mention the body, which again reveals the psychosomatic characteristics of Daoist practice. This includes the importance of postural alignment and structural integrity in meditation. The *Inward Training* in particular emphasises a four-fold process of alignment: (1) Aligning the body (*zhengxing*); (2) Aligning the four limbs (*zheng sizhi*); (3) Aligning *qi* (*zhengqi*); and (4) Aligning the heart-ind (*zhengxin*) (Roth 1999a, 109). Attentive readers will also note a Daoist critique of 'knowing', in the sense of ingrained opinions, limited perceptions and habituated consciousness states. Daoist meditation results in various 'beyond/non-states', including 'non-knowing' (*wuzhi*). This is a state of open receptivity, especially with respect to the mysterious and numinous nature of existence. There are thus uniquely Daoist views of consciousness and associated contemplative states and traits (see Roth 1991, 1997, 1999a, 2015). In addition, the texts mention what later became known as the internal Three Treasures (*sanbao*), namely, vital essence (*jing*), subtle breath or energy (*qi*) and spirit (*shen*). These generally refer to foundational vitality, energy and consciousness, including 'divine' capacities. In terms of the present volume and the comparative study of meditation, it is especially noteworthy that Daoist anthropology, psychology and theology include an energetic view. From a Daoist perspective, reality is energetic in nature, and the efficacy of meditation manifests in energetic transformation and attunement. There is an energetic signature related to different types of practices, and Daoist meditation results in energetic sensitivity and support.

While retaining its classical technical meaning of apophatic meditation, especially in the sense of 'quiet sitting' (*jingzuo*), *shouyi* eventually became a general term for Daoist meditation. In the early and late medieval period, one finds references to 'guarding the One' in concert with diverse types of meditation (see Kohn 1989b). For example, in the Taiqing (Great Clarity) movement, *shouyi* appears in discussions of visualisation practice.[16] In such discussions, the earlier technical term of *shouyi* now becomes incorporated into an early medieval Daoist system of meditation, which includes visualisation and what might be labelled proto-*neidan*. The latter focuses on the so-called three elixir fields (*dantian*), with *dan* technically designating cinnabar (mercuric sulfide; HgS), a key ingredient in earlier external alchemy formulas. The elixir fields are subtle corporeal locations associated with the Three Treasures. Expressing Daoist microcosmic views and symbolic corporeality, the 'elixir fields' suggest that the body contains 'fields' wherein certain things are cultivated. Framing practice with an agricultural metaphor, one plants, tends, harvests and stores in these interior places. This is the body as landscape and farm. Incorporating an alchemical model, one undertakes a process of alchemical transformation and transmutation. One gathers, coalesces, combines and refines various vital substances in order to concoct 'elixirs' within the body. This is the body as crucible and laboratory (see Komjathy 2008b, 2009, 2011).

## Visualising the dipper

The early medieval period witnessed the emergence and development of Daoist ingestion and visualisation methods, especially in the context of the Shangqing (Highest Clarity) movement of early organised Daoism. In its formative moments, Highest Clarity began in present-day Jiangsu province and largely consisted of disenchanted aristocrats interested in divine communication, ecstatic journeys and self-divinisation (see Robinet 1989a, 1993; Miller 2008). Here visualisation became incorporated into a larger soteriological system aimed at rarefication and self-divinisation. Such Daoist methods are diverse and complex, often involving what might be understood as the 'cosmicisation' of the human body. They thus employ Daoist microcosmic/macrocosmic views of personhood. Some Daoist visualisation techniques parallel ingestion practices by focusing on various Five Phase constituents (e.g. Five Marchmounts, Five Thearchs) as well as the sun, moon and stars. The Five Phases, often referred to as traditional Chinese 'correlative cosmology' or the 'system of correspondences', refer to Wood, Fire, Earth, Metal and Water. These have various associations utilised in Daoist practice, including Wood/spring/east/liver/green, Fire/summer/south/heart/red, Earth/—/centre/spleen/yellow, Metal/autumn/

west/lungs/white and Water/winter/north/kidneys/black (purple).[17] Other forms of visualisation centre on esoteric Daoist pantheons, including inner body-gods associated with various corporeal locations. The latter are frequently described as a somatic landscape, which consists of mountains (spine and head), rivers (meridians), water (*qi* and body fluids), forests (liver) and so forth (see Needham et al. 1983; Schipper 1993; Komjathy 2008b, 2009, 2011).

A representative Daoist visualisation method focuses on the constellations, including the associated 'gods' (divine presences) and astral effulgences. In the *Jinque dijun sanyuan zhenyi jing* (Scripture on the Perfect Ones of the Three Primes by Lord Golden Tower; DZ 253; cf. DZ 1314; see Andersen 1980),[18] part of the original fourth-century Highest Clarity revelations, aspiring adepts are instructed to visualise the Northern Dipper (Big Dipper; Ursa Major) according to the method of 'guarding the One', also referred to as 'guarding the Three Ones' (*shou sanyi*):

> At midnight on the *lichun* (Spring Begins) node [approx. February 2nd], practice aligned meditation facing east. Exhale nine times and swallow saliva thirty-five times.
>
> Then visualise the seven stars of the Northern Dipper as they slowly descend toward you until they rest above you. The Dipper should be directly above your head, with its handle pointing forward, due east. Visualise it in such a way that the stars Yin Essence and Perfect One are just above the top of your head. The two stars Yang Brightness and Mysterious Darkness should be higher up. In addition, Yin Essence and Yang Brightness should be toward your back, while Perfect One and Mysterious Darkness are in front. Though the image may be blurred at first, concentrate firmly and focus it in position.
>
> Then concentrate on the venerable Lords, the Three Ones. They appear suddenly in the bowl of the Dipper above your head. Before long their three ministers arrive in the same way. After a little while, observe how the six gods ascend together Mysterious Darkness, from where they move east. When they reach Celestial Pass, they stop.
>
> Together they turn and face your mouth. See how the Upper Prime supports the upper minister with his hand; how the Middle Prime supports the middle minister; and how the Lower Prime supports the lower minister.
>
> Then take a deep breath and hold it for as long as you can. The Upper Prime and his minister follow this breath and enter your mouth. Once inside they ascend and go to the Palace of Niwan in the head.
>
> Take another breath as deep as you can. The Middle Prime and his minister follow this breath and enter your mouth. Once inside they descend and go to the Scarlet Palace in the heart.
>
> Take yet another breath as deep as you can. The Lower Prime and his minister follow this breath and enter your mouth. Once inside they descend and go to the lower Cinnabar Field in the abdomen.
>
> Next visualise the star Celestial Pass and bring it down to about seven inches in front of your mouth. While this star stands guard before your mouth, the Three Ones firmly enter into their bodily palaces.
>
> With this complete, concentrate again on the Perfected to make sure they are all at rest in their residences. From then on, whether sitting or lying down, always keep them firmly in your mind.
>
> At any point during the practice, if concerns or desires arise in your mind, it will push to pursue them. Then, however much the mind strains to break free, make sure to keep it firmly concentrated on the Three Ones. See that you remain at peace and in solitude. Moreover, if your room is quiet enough, you may continue the practice well into the day.
>
> (*Sanyuan zhenyi jing*, *DZ 253, 6a–7a*)

*Table 14.1* The twelve Chinese zoomorphic zodiac signs and twelve 'double-hours' of traditional Chinese time measurement

| *1* | *2* | *3* | *4* | *5* | *6* | *7* | *8* | *9* | *10* | *11* | *12* |
|---|---|---|---|---|---|---|---|---|---|---|---|
| Zi<br>子<br>Rat<br>11pm–1am | Chou<br>丑<br>Ox<br>1–3 | Yin<br>寅<br>Tiger<br>3–5 | Mao<br>卯<br>Rabbit<br>5–7 | Chen<br>辰<br>Dragon<br>7–9 | Si<br>巳<br>Snake<br>9–11 | Wu<br>午<br>Horse<br>11am–1pm | Wei<br>未<br>Sheep<br>1–3 | Shen<br>申<br>Monkey<br>3–5 | You<br>酉<br>Rooster<br>5–7 | Xu<br>戌<br>Dog<br>7–9 | Hai<br>亥<br>Pig<br>9–11 |

This method begins with a posture of cosmological attunement. *Lichun* (Spring Begins; approximately 5 February) refers to the first of the six energetic nodes of spring. The energetic nodes are twenty-four seasonal and cosmological moments associated with the solar and agricultural cycles; they are divided into four sets of six based on the four seasons. This cosmological dimension is strengthened by facing east, associated with the Wood phase and spring. The more standard temporal correspondence is 3–5am, which corresponds to the terrestrial branch *yin*.[19] The twelve terrestrial branches (*dizhi*) are an ordering system based on observation of the orbit of Jupiter.

This includes the twelve Chinese zoomorphic zodiac signs and twelve 'double-hours' of traditional Chinese time measurement. The time (midnight) utilised in the Dipper visualisation method is the double-hour *zi* (11pm–1am), which technically corresponds to the Water phase and winter/north/kidneys by extension. However, in Daoist meditation, the double-hour *zi* often is central, as it represents the apex of yin and the emergence of yang. Associated with winter solstice, it is thus a time of deep stillness in which spiritual insight and illumination may easily emerge. Another interesting dimension of the initial framing involves exhaling nine times. This probably involves exhaling through the mouth in order to enter a deeper state of relaxation and to expel impurities. The number nine is extremely important in Daoist numerology because it represents 'redoubled' or 'two-fold yang', with three being a 'pure yang' number. Finally, 'swallowing saliva' is a major dimension of Daoist practice more generally. Saliva, and fluids in general, are often associated with the vital essence and the kidneys by extension.[20] That is, one conserves major vital substances, harmonises the entire corporeal system and sets the foundation for deeper meditative practice.

In the main part of the practice, the Daoist adept visualises the Northern Dipper, associated with 'fate' (*ming*) in the Daoist tradition, above his or her head (see Figure 14.1). The seven visible stars are identified as follows (from bowl to handle): (1) Yangming (Yang Brightness); (2) Yinjing (Yin Essence); (3) Zhenren (Perfect One); (4) Xuanming (Mysterious Darkness); (5) Danyuan (Cinnabar Prime); (6) Beiji (North Culmen); (7) Tianguan (Celestial Pass).

The two lower stars of the dipper bowl rest in close proximity to the top of the head, while the handle extends forward so that the seventh star, called Celestial Pass, rests in front of the mouth. One in turn visualises the Three Ones, also known as the Three Primes (*sanyuan*) or Three Purities (*sanqing*), in the dipper bowl. These are the three highest 'gods' (divine/celestial presences) of the standard Daoist pantheon and correspond to three primordial energies of the cosmos. In this visualisation practice, they ascend together to the fourth star, Mysterious Darkness, move to the seventh star, Celestial Pass, and wait there facing towards the adept's mouth. The practitioner then visualises each one in sequence (upper, middle, lower) entering their respective corporeal locations (Niwan [centre of head], Scarlet Palace [heart], Cinnabar Field [navel region]).[21] In this

*Figure 14.1* Visualising the Northern Dipper
Source: *Jinque dijun wudou sanyi tujue*, DZ 765, 16b

way the Three Heavens and their corresponding gods become located in the Daoist adherent's very own body. The text, in turn, advises the Daoist adept to follow the same instructions for the commencements of the other seasons: *Lixia* (Summer Begins; approx. 5 May) facing south; *liqiu* (Autumn Begins; approx. 8 August) facing west; and *lidong* (Winter Begins; approx. 11 November) facing north. The corresponding time seems to be the same, namely, 11pm to 1am. There are thus seasonal, cosmological and theological dimensions to the practice.

In this Dipper method of early Highest Clarity, one notes various features common to Daoist visualisation more generally.[22] These include cosmological, astronomical and energetic dimensions. Numerologically speaking, three and nine are central, and there are various ternary associations. Primary triads include the Three Purities, Three Heavens, Three Fields, Three Treasures and so forth. In the standardised system, they are organized hierarchically, with the highest appearing first (see Table 14.2).

Another distinctive characteristic involves Daoist 'body-gods', including what might be labelled the Daoist 'inner pantheon'. This dimension of the Daoist tradition is complex, as it involves uniquely Daoist cosmological and theological views (see Komjathy 2013b, 2014a). As mentioned, reference to 'gods' and 'deities' may create confusion because, while some Daoists have viewed and do understand these as personal gods, they often correspond to more impersonal cosmic forces and divine presences. Here it is important to note that the indigenous Chinese term is *shen*, also translated as 'spirit', consists of *shi* ('omen') and *shen* ('extend'). It may thus suggest some type of connection to hidden or subtle forces. In the case of the Three Purities, what is one to make of the claim that they exist in both the Three Heavens of the cosmos and the Three Fields of the human body? Thinking through such Daoist views, one discovers the universe in oneself and oneself as the universe. To venerate the Three Purities involves conserving the Three Treasures in the Three Fields, which are, in turn, manifestations

*Table 14.2* Triads common to Daoist visualisation techniques

| *Heaven* | *Deity* | *Field* | *Treasure* |
|---|---|---|---|
| Jade Clarity | Celestial Worthy of Original Beginning | Upper elixir field (centre of head) | Spirit |
| Highest Clarity | Celestial Worthy of Numinous Treasure | Middle elixir field (heart or lower abdomen) | Qi |
| Great Clarity | Celestial Worthy of Dao and Inner Power | Lower elixir field (lower abdomen or perineum) | Vital essence |

or concentrations of the associated three primordial energies. On a deeper level, one may realise that 'divinity' and 'heaven' are within oneself. This may be actualised and/or encountered through Daoist visualisation practice.

## Forming the elixir

In later organised Daoism and in the late medieval period, Daoists began combining the various forms of Daoist meditation into a more comprehensive and integrated system. Although drawing upon methods from earlier Daoist movements like Great Clarity and Highest Clarity, internal alchemy (*neidan*), as a fully developed stage-based process aimed at complete psychosomatic transformation, only emerged at the end of the Tang and beginning of the Song dynasty (see above). Internal alchemy integrated diverse sources, including classical Daoist texts, correlative cosmology, *Yijing* (Book of Changes) symbology,[23] meditational and physical disciplines of Yangsheng, cosmological dimensions and technical terminology of *waidan* (external alchemy), Chinese medical theory and even Buddhist soteriology and Confucian moral philosophy.

Before investigating a specific *neidan* system, let us begin with a brief consideration of what I refer to as the 'Daoist alchemical body' (see Komjathy 2007, 2008b, 2009, 2011). Viewed as a whole, Daoist internal alchemy engages and activates a subtle body, an energetic body within the apparently physical or material body. The constituents of the 'standardised Daoist body' include the following:

- Sun (left eye) and moon (right eye)
- Descending Bridge (tongue), Crimson Dragon (tongue), Twelve Storied Tower (trachea), Sweet Dew (saliva), etc.
- Five yin-organs (*wuzang*)
  - Liver (east/green/dragon), heart (south/red/bird), spleen (centre/yellow/—), lungs (west/white/tiger), kidneys (north/black [purple]/snake-turtle)
- Three elixir fields (*dantian*)
  - Ocean of Qi (lower; navel), Scarlet Palace (middle; heart), Niwan (upper; head)
- Three Treasures (*sanbao*)
  - Vital essence (*jing*), subtle breath (*qi*), spirit (*shen*)
- Meridians (*jing/luo/mai*)
  - 12/8: Governing, Conception, Belt, Thrusting
- Three Passes (*sanguan*)
  - Tailbone Gate (lower; coccyx), Paired Passes (middle; mid-spine), Jade Pillow (upper; occiput)

Most of these are straightforward, but the more esoteric ones require some explanation. As mentioned, Daoist numerology tends to privilege triads. From a Daoist perspective, three is a pure yang number, and multiples of threes, particularly nine (3x3), are prevalent. The latter is often referred to as 'redoubled yang' (*chongyang*) and represents complete alchemical transformation. In the above list, we find the 'three elixir fields' and 'three treasures'. As we saw in the previous sections, 'elixir field' is a Daoist name for subtle body locations. Interestingly, recalling the various influences on internal alchemy, *dan*, more literally 'pill', derives from an ingredient utilised in external alchemy formulas. Specifically, *dan*, designating a colour and being an abbreviation of *dansha*, refers to 'cinnabar', or mercuric sulfide (HgS). As the name indicates, internal alchemy seeks to create an 'inner elixir' through the transmutation of various substances *within the body*. In any case, the standardised Daoist body consists of three elixir fields associated with the internal three treasures. The former may refer to the perineum/navel/head or navel/heart/head. The associations in the former are clearer: perineum/vital essence, navel/*qi* and head/spirit. Also associated with bodily fluids (e.g. saliva, sweat), vital essence is considered the most substantial and corresponds to foundational vitality. The character contains the *mi* ('rice') radical, thus suggesting a more substantial substance. Vital essence is housed in the kidneys and relates to one's constitution, partially indebted to ancestry ('genes'). It is associated with semen in men and menstrual blood in women. While also designating physical respiration, *qi* is a more subtle breath or 'energy' stored in and circulating through the body. The standard character consists of *qi* ('steam') over *mi* ('rice'), thus suggesting a more subtle presence. *Qi* also circulates through the world, universe and all things, and there are many types. For Daoists, the most important is the '*qi* of the Dao' (*daoqi*), which designates a sacred, numinous presence and sometimes corresponds to 'original *qi*' (*yuanqi*). Finally, 'spirit' is the most subtle or rarefied; it is housed in the heart and corresponds to consciousness and divine capacities more generally. The character consists of *shi* ('omen') and *shen* ('extend'). While the latter is usually taken as a phonetic, under one reading spirit suggests the ability to connect to invisible or barely noticeable presences. Simplified and standardised internal alchemy systems tend to frame alchemical transformation in terms of a three-stage process: (1) Transforming vital essence to *qi*; (2) Transforming *qi* to spirit; and (3) Transforming spirit to return to the Void. That is, a process of rarefication, transmutation and even divinisation is at work, which culminates in 'immortality' in Daoist terms. The three elixir fields and internal Three Treasures in turn relate to other triads, including the Three Purities, Three Heavens and external Three Treasures. The meridians, also referred to as 'channels' or 'vessels', are the energy conduits and networks in the body. They are utilised in both Chinese medicine and Daoism, which partially explains the conflation of these traditions in the popular imagination. The standard system consists of the twelve primary organ-meridians and the 'eight extraordinary vessels'. The latter tend to be more central in Daoist training regimens. These meridians are as follows: (1) Governing Channel, which moves up the middle of the spine; (2) Conception Channel, which moves up the centre of the front torso; (3) Thrusting Channel, which moves through the centre of the torso; and (4) Belt Channel, which moves around the waist and is the only horizontal meridian. In Daoist practice, the other four tend to be understood as two moving down the outside and up the inside of the arms, and two following a similar path through the legs.[24] Finally, the Three Passes are the three places along the spine through which it is difficult for *qi* to circulate. Interestingly, and as explored below, they are often imagined as mountain passes and relate to a practice known as the Microcosmic Orbit.

We may now turn to a representative example of a late medieval *neidan* system. One of the most important and influential Daoist movements associated with internal alchemy is Quanzhen (Complete Perfection). In its formative period, Complete Perfection began in present-day Shaanxi and then Shandong province and primarily was a small ascetic and eremitic community centring on alchemical transformation and mystical experience. Among the first-generation adherents, the preferred genres of literary expression were poetry and discourse records (*yulu*). This makes the reconstruction of early Complete Perfection *neidan* practice comparatively challenging. However, there are also two extant technical manuals (see Komjathy 2007, 2013a). Among them, the most systematic discussion appears in the *Dadan zhizhi* (Direct Pointers to the Great Elixir; DZ 244).[25] This manual is attributed to Qiu Chuji (Changchun [Perpetual Spring]; 1148–1227), the youngest first-generation representative, third Patriarch, and eventual leader of the movement. Although this authorial attribution is complex, it appears that the text seems to be a mid- to late-thirteenth-century work, post-dating the death of Qiu Changchun and most of his direct disciples.

In terms of alchemical practice and transformation, the *Dadan zhizhi* is organised as a series of instructions and illustrations with corresponding explanations. On the most fundamental level, *neidan* praxis is presented as a sequence of nine stages.

1. Coupling the Dragon and Tiger and Inverting the Five Phases (1.6a-8b)
2. Firing Times of the Celestial Cycle and Inverting the Five Phases (1.8b-11b)
3. Reversion of the Three Fields and Flying the Gold Essence behind the Elbow (1.12a-14b)
4. Reversion of the Three Fields and the Reverted Elixir of the Gold *Ye*-fluids (1.14b-17b)
5. Five Qi Meeting the Origin and Refining Form into Greater Yang (1.18b-20b)
6. Union of Spirit and Qi and the Consummation of the Three Fields (1.20b-23b)
7. Five Qi Meeting the Origin and Refining Spirit to Enter the Summit (2.1a-3a)
8. Initiating the Fire through Inner Observation and Refining Spirit to Merge with the Dao (2.3a-5a)
9. Casting off the Husk to Ascend to Immortality and Transcending the Mundane to Enter the Sacred (2.8a-11b)

The *Direct Pointers to the Great Elixir* instructs adepts to activate and refine the energies to the five yin-organs (liver, heart, spleen, lungs and kidneys). Specifically, one visualises each organ as an orb of light with the associated colour: liver/green, heart/red, spleen/yellow, lungs/white and kidneys/black (purple). These distinct energies are then combined or 'inverted' (*fan*; *huan*) to become a single, unified energy in the lower elixir field, the navel or lower abdominal region. One then circulates this energy, which has been infused with other vital substances and subtle presences, through the Waterwheel (*heche*) (see Figure 14.2).

Also known as the Celestial Cycle (*zhoutian*), or Microcosmic Orbit in more general discussions, this method involves circulating *qi* up the Governing Vessel, from the perineum towards the occiput and into the head. Then *qi* is normally directed down the Conception Vessel and stored in the lower elixir field. As refinement and transmutation advance through additional techniques, the yang-spirit (*yangshen*) forms. Also known as the 'immortal embryo' (*xiantai*) and 'body-beyond-the-body' (*shenwai shen*), the yang-spirit is the transcendent spirit *created* through internal alchemy, which confirms personal post-mortem survival. The practitioner eventually trains this spirit to exit through the crown-point. This prepares the way for 'casting off the husk to ascend to immortality'. That is, upon death, one leaves behind mundane, physical existence and enters the Daoist sacred realms. This is 'immortality' or 'transcendence' in Daoist terms.

Beyond the simplified formula of refining vital essence and *qi* to eventually become spirit and merge with the Dao, internal alchemy is a complex process of self-refinement and transformation, of rarefication and self-divinisation. For example, refining vital essence, associated with the kidneys, leads to the production of blood, with the assistance of the lungs and heart, and the production of fluids, with the assistance of the spleen and stomach. These fluids in

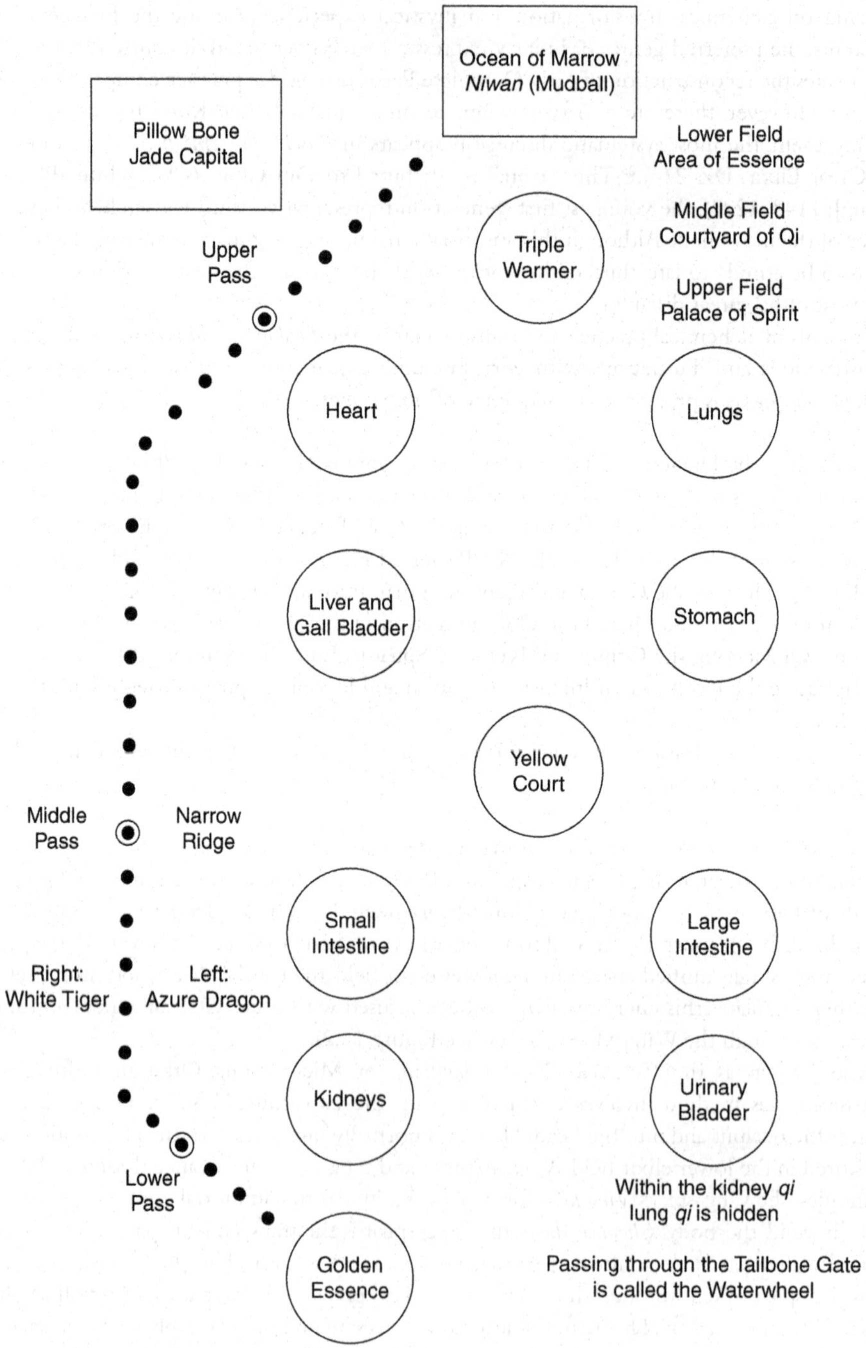


*Figure 14.2* The Waterwheel
Source: *Dadan zhizhi*, DZ 244, 1.11b-12a

turn nourish and moisten the muscles, skin, joints and orifices of the sense organs. In combination with marrow derived from vital essence, the fluids also nourish the brain and spinal cord. Simultaneously, the fluids transferred to the heart become blood, the material basis of spirit. That is, the seemingly simple formula of 'refining vital essence to become *qi*' (*lianjing huaqi*) initiates a complex set of physiological responses. More specifically, producing, conserving and ingesting fluids leads to both a greater resiliency to disease, through increased protective *qi*, and an abundance of spirit, through increased blood and marrow production. Nourishing and attending to the various organs and their related substances initiates a dynamic physiological process. This physiology provides a foundation for the activation and opening of mystical body locations, as well as for the patterning of a pathway for the spirit to transcend the mundane world and become an immortal.

## Sitting in the modern Daoist tradition

The five major types of Daoist meditation, which include aphophatic meditation, ingestion, visualisation, inner observation and internal alchemy, continue to be practised in modern Daoism.[26] Depending on the specific Daoist adherents, associated communities, lineages and movements, there are diverse informing views, goals and ideals. In contemporary Daoism, apophatic meditation, or 'quiet sitting', and internal alchemy are the most prominent, with the latter often integrating the other four. Modern internal alchemy systems frequently begin and end with quiet sitting as both the foundation and culmination of Daoist practice. In terms of posture, Daoists primarily utilise seated ones, usually with the support of a meditation mat and cushion. The so-called modified 'Burmese' posture tends to be the preferred one, but some Daoists sit in full lotus or the earlier *zhengzuo* (Japanese: *seiza*) configuration (see Roth 1999a, 2015). In Daoist practice, which employs Daoist energetic views and emphasises the subtle body, modified 'Burmese' posture involves placing the legs in a position that resembles an inverted triangle, with the vectors of force moving between the sit-bones and knees. Men sit with the right foot behind the left, while women sit with the left foot behind the right. This is because the general Daoist view is that *qi* moves up the left and down the right in men, and up the right and down the left in women. The primary hand-configuration (Chinese: *shouyin*; Sanskrit: *mudrā*) is the *ziwu* gesture. Also referred to as the 'yin-yang *mudrā*', *ziwu* alludes to the above-mentioned terrestrial branches, with *zi* corresponding to midnight (winter solstice), the apex of yin, and *wu* corresponding to noon (summer solstice), the apex of yang. The human hand is, in turn, divided into twelve sections, with *zi* as the base of the ring-finger and *wu* as the tip of the middle-finger.

In the *ziwu mudrā*, men touch all of the tips of the fingers of left-hand to the tip of the left thumb; they then insert the tip of the right thumb through the opening to touch the inside-base of left ring-finger (*zi*), with the tip of the right middle-finger (*wu*) touching the outside-base of the left ring-finger. For women, the hand-configuration is reversed, that is, left-hand encircling right-hand. The latter is the gesture utilised by all Daoists, regardless of gender, in Daoist bowing. One also touches the tip of the tongue to the upper-palate, which joins the Governing and Conception Vessels. The eyes are either completely closed or slightly open. Taken as a whole, this body-configuration facilitates and embodies complete energetic integration. On a more esoteric and ritualistic level, these points also activate specific deities, in this case the Northern Thearch and Southern Thearch, respectively (see, e.g. Saso 1972).

Here a few additional points need to be made. First, while modern Daoists primarily practice seated meditation, there also are contemplative methods that involve standing, walking, lying down and even sleeping. Among these, standing is most common, with 'empty' or 'quiet standing' (*jingzhan*), sometimes referred to as 'post standing' (*zhanzhuang*), being a foundational practice in Daoist Yangsheng (Nourishing Life), or health and longevity techniques. This traditional Daoist practice has some connections to modern Qigong (Ch'i-kung; Energy Exercises), although the latter has a complex history and includes Buddhist, Daoist, medical and even martial systems (see, e.g. Komjathy 2006; Palmer 2007). Empty standing also is used in the so-called Chinese internal martial arts (*neijia*). These parallels help to explain the common conflation and misidentification of practices like Qigong and Taiji quan (T'ai-chi ch'üan; Great Ultimate/ Yin-Yang Boxing) with Daoism as such (see Komjathy 2013b; 2014a). In any case, Daoist quiet standing parallels the previously discussed apophatic meditation. One simply stands in stillness. However, like Daoist postures more generally, this practice also has a strong psychosomatic and cosmological dimension. Specifically, the crown-point (Baihui [Hundred Meetings]; GV-20), associated with the heavens in the human body, is the primary point through which celestial *qi* (*tianqi*) enters the body; the soles of the feet (Yongquan [Bubbling Spring]; KI-1), associated with earth in the human body, is the primary point through which terrestrial *qi* (*diqi*) enters the human body. Thus, standing with postural alignment creates the context for the commingling of these energies and their subsequent circulation through the meridians. Once again, Daoist practitioners literally activate and circulate something else.

In contemporary Daoist communities, Daoist meditation tends to utilise a quietistic and/or alchemical model (see Komjathy 2013a; 2014b). Technically speaking, a quietistic model centres on silence and stillness. Stillness is understood as one's original and innate nature, one's foundational connection to and expression of the Dao. The quietistic model thus involves 'return' and 'dissolution', especially meditative absorption and mystical union with the Dao. One simply disappears into the Dao. This is a transpersonal state that is both an existential approach and response to the inevitability of death. There is no personal death (or post-mortem survival) because separate identity is an illusion. Here we might understand meditation as dying. An alchemical model centres on transformation. Similar to the quietistic model, the alchemical model utilises a composite view of self. However, while in the former death is understood as dissolution, internal alchemists claim another possibility beyond this 'ordinary fate'. Through stage-based practice, which culminates in complete psychosomatic transmutation, one may *create* a transcendent spirit (see above). This results in personal post-mortem survival and eventual entry into the Daoist sacred realms as an 'immortal'. The alchemical model thus involves 'progress' and 'transcendence'. It is more of a participatory vision. Here we might understand meditation as timelessness. These models are often reconceptualised, and complexified, through Buddhism and other traditions. As many, perhaps most, modern Daoists believe in reincarnation, meditation becomes understood as a means to purify defilements, remove obstructions, neutralise karma and make progress on the path to liberation or realisation. That is, unlike traditional Chinese and Daoist views of self, which centre on a composite view (see Komjathy 2013b, 2014a), in the Buddhist-influenced view of meditation, one has some type of enduring personhood. The point of meditation is to facilitate spiritual development.

These various models tend to share the aspiration for meditative absorption and mystical union with the Dao, including numinous pervasion or becoming infused with sacred presence. The diversity of Daoist meditative views and methods in turn lead to different perspectives on and insights into 'union with the Dao'. There are various experiences and accompanying accounts. These include attunement, disappearance, pervasion, vitality and so forth. As chapter one of the *Daode jing* tells us, the Dao is the 'gateway to myriad wonders'. Daoist meditation involves 'entering the Dao' (*rudao*). By opening the door of meditation and finding the gateway to the Dao, another hidden and mysterious landscape opens. This is the landscape explored and discovered in Daoist contemplative practice and contemplative experience. It is a landscape found in/as/through outer and inner worlds.

## Glossary

*Baihui*, Hundred Meetings, 百會
*Baopuzi neipian*, *Inner Chapters of Master Embracing Simplicity*, 抱朴子內篇
*baoshen*, embracing spirit, 抱神
*baoyi*, embracing the One, 抱一
Beiji, North Culmen, 北極
*chongyang*, redoubled yang, 重陽
*Chuandao ji*, *Record of Transmitting the Dao*, 傳道集
cun, maintain, 存
*cunxiang*, maintaining the image; visualisation, 存想
*Dadan zhizhi*, *Direct Pointers to the Great Elixir*, 大丹直指
*Dadong zhenjing*, *Perfect Scripture on Great Profundity*, 大洞真經
*dan*, cinnbar/elixir, 丹
*dansha*, cinnabar, 丹砂/丹沙
*dantian*, elixir field, 丹田
*Danyuan*, Cinnabar Prime, 丹元
Dao; Tao, Way, 道
*Daode jing*, *Scripture on the Dao and Inner Power*, 道德經
*daoqi*, *qi* of the Dao, 道炁
*Daoyin*, Guided Stretching, 導引
*Daozang*, Daoist Canon, 道藏
*dazuo*, undertake sitting; meditation, 打坐
*Dingguan jing*, *Scripture on Concentration and Observation*, 定觀經
*diqi*, terrestrial *qi*, 地氣
*dizhi*, terrestrial branches, 地支
*Duren shangjing dafa*, *Great Methods from the Upper Chapters on Limitless Salvation*, 度人上經大法
*fan*, revert, 反
*fangshi*, formula masters, 方士
*fangzhong shu*, bedchamber arts, 房中術
*fuqi*, ingesting *qi*, 服氣
*Fuqi jingyi lun*, *Discourse on the Essential Meaning of Ingesting Qi*, 服氣精義論
*Gongfu*, Kung-Fu; martial arts, 功夫
*guan*, observe, 觀
*Guanzi*, *Book of Master Guan*, 管子
*heche*, Waterwheel, 河車
*Huainanzi*, *Book of the Huainan Masters*, 淮南子
*huan*, revert, 還
*Huang-Lao Dao*, Way of the Yellow Thearch and Laozi, 黃老道
*Huangting jing*, *Scripture on the Yellow Court*, 黃庭經
*jing*, essence, 精
*jing*, meridian, 經
*jingzhan*, quiet standing, 靜站
*jingzuo*, quiet sitting, 靜坐
*Jinque dijun*, Lord Golden Tower, 金闕帝君
*Jinque dijun sanyuan zhenyi jing*, *Scripture on the Perfect Ones of the Three Primes by Lord Golden Tower*, 金闕帝君三元真一經
*Laozi*, *Book of Venerable Masters*, 老子

*Laozi zhongjing*, *Central Scripture of Master Lao*, 老子中經
*lianjing huaqi*, refining vital essence to become *qi*, 煉精化氣
lichun, Spring Begins, 立春
lidong, Winter Begins, 立冬
*Lingbao*, Numinous Treasure, 靈寶
liqiu, Autumn Begins, 立秋
lixia, Summer Begins, 立夏
*Longmen*, Dragon Gate, 龍門
*luo*, meridian, 絡
*Lüshi chunqiu*, *Spring and Autumn Annals of Mister Lü*, 吕氏春秋
*mai*, meridian, 脈
*mi*, rice, 米
*ming*, fate/life-destiny, 命
*moxiang*, deep thought; meditation, 冥想
Nanzong, Southern School, 南宗
*neidan*, internal alchemy, 内丹
*neiguan*, inner observation, 內觀
*Neiguan jing*, *Scripture on Inner Observation*, 内觀經
*neijia*, internal martial arts, 内家
*Neiye*, *Inward Training*, 内業
*Niwan*, Mudball/Nirvana, 尼丸
*nüdan*, female alchemy, 女丹
*qi*, steam, 气
*qi*, subtle breath, 氣
*Qigong*, Energy Exercises, 氣功
*Quanzhen*, Complete Perfection, 全真
*rudao*, entering the Dao, 入道
*rujia*, Ruism; 'Confucianism', 儒家
*sanbao*, Three Treasures, 三寶
*sanguan*, Three Passes, 三關
*sanqing*, Three Purities, 三清
*sanyuan*, Three Primes, 三元
*Shangqing*, Highest Clarity, 上清
*shen*, extend, 申
*shen*, spirit, 神
*shenwai shen*, body-beyond-the-body, 身外身
*shi*, omen, 示
*shou*, guard, 守
*shou qi yi*, guarding this oneness, 守其一
*shou sanyi*, guarding the Three Ones, 守三一
*shouci*, guarding the feminine, 守雌
*shoujing*, guarding stillness, 守靜
*shouyi*, guarding the One, 守一
*shouyin*, hand-configuration; *mudrā*, 手印
*shouzong*, guarding the Ancestor, 守宗
*si*, consider, 思

*siyi*, meditating on the One, 思一
*Taiji quan*, Great Ultimate/Yin-Yang Boxing, 太極拳
*Taiping*, Great Peace, 太平
*Taiqing*, Great Clarity, 太清
*Taiqing fuqi koujue, Oral Instructions on Ingesting Qi of Great Clarity*, 太清服氣口訣
*Tianguan*, Celestial Pass, 天關
*tianqi*, celestial *qi*, 天氣
*Tianshi*, Celestial Masters, 天師
*waidan*, external alchemy, 外丹
*Wushu*, martial arts, 武術
*wuzang*, five yin-organs, 五臟
*Wuzhen pian*, Chapters on Awakening to Perfection, 悟真篇
*wuzhi*, non-knowing, 無知
*xiantai*, immortal embryo, 仙胎
*xin*, heart-mind, 心
*xing*, innate nature, 性
*Xingming fajue mingzhi, Illuminating Pointers to the Methods and Instructions of Innate Nature and Life-Destiny*, 性命法訣明旨
'*Xinshu*', 'Techniques of the Heart-mind', 心術
*xinzhai*, fasting the heart-mind, 心齋
*Xuanming*, Mysterious Darkness, 玄冥
*Yangming*, Yang Brightness, 陽明
*yangshen*, yang-spirit, 陽神
*yangsheng*, nourishing life, 養生
*Yijing, Classic of Changes*, 易經
*Yinjing*, Yin Essence, 陰精
*Yongquan*, Bubbling Spring, 湧泉
*yuanqi*, original *qi*, 元氣
*yujia*, yoga, 瑜珈
*yulu*, discourse records, 語錄
*yunqi*, circulating *qi*, 運氣
*zhanzhuang*, post standing, 站樁
*zheng sizhi*, aligning the four limbs, 正四肢
*zhengqi*, aligning *qi*, 正氣
*zhengxin*, aligning the heart-mind, 正心
*zhengxing*, aligning the body, 正形
*Zhengyi*, Orthodox Unity, 正一
*zhengzuo*, upright sitting; *seiza*, 正坐
*Zhenren*, Perfect One, 真人
*Zhong-Lü*, 鐘呂
*zhoutian*, Celestial Cycle; Microcosmic Orbit, 周天
*Zhuangzi, Book of Master Zhuang*, 莊子
*ziwu*, *ziwu* branches, 子午
*zuo*, sitting, 坐
*zuowang*, sitting-in-forgetfulness, 坐忘

## Notes

1 Ruism, which derives from the indigenous Chinese *rujia* (Family of the Ru [Scholars/Literati-Officials]), is a closer approximation of the tradition's self-conception. In contrast, 'Confucianism' is a colonialist and missionary construction derived from 'Confucius', which is the Latinised version of the honorific name of Kongzi (Master Kong). The latter was a formative influence on and key representative of Ruism.

2 For my comparative and theoretical reflections on this and related terms see Komjathy 2015; 2018. While beyond this contribution, I utilise praxis, which includes specific forms like meditation, in a technical sense that emphasises the complex interrelationship between views, methods, experiences and goals. Herein I explore the latter in terms of Daoist meditation.

3 As a comparative category, 'soteriology' refers to views about actualisation, liberation, perfection, realisation, salvation or however a given individual or community defines the ultimate purpose of human existence.

4 The history of Qigong, which is a modern Chinese health and fitness movement, and its relationship to Daoism is complex. See, e.g. Komjathy 2006; Palmer 2007.

5 All of this of course begs the question of the meaning of 'philosophy' and 'religion', including the former as referring to disembodied thought and intellectual reflection. For my critical reflections on Daoism as a religious tradition, see Komjathy 2013b, 2014a. For a critical, revisionist perspective on western philosophy as centering on 'spiritual exercises' see Hadot 1995; also Komjathy 2015, 2018.

6 *Qi*, which has some parallels to the Greek *pneuma* and Sanskrit *prāna*, may refer to physical respiration and/or a more subtle breath. It also has been rendered as 'vital breath' and 'energy'. Like Dao and yin-yang, I prefer to leave the term untranslated.

7 For guidance on these various texts see Kohn 2000; Schipper and Verellen 2004; Pregadio 2008.

8 From a Daoist perspective, the Dao, which is impersonal and amoral, has four primary characteristics: (1) Source of everything; (2) Unnamable mystery; (3) All-pervading sacred presence; and (4) Universe as transformative process ('Nature'). In terms of comparative theology (views of the sacred), Daoist theology is primarily monistic (one impersonal reality), panentheistic (sacred in and beyond the world), and panenhenic (Nature as sacred). See Komjathy 2013b, 2014a.

9 Other terms include *baoyi* ('embracing the One'), *shouci* ('guarding the feminine'), *shoujing* ('guarding stillness'), *shouzong* ('guarding the Ancestor') and so forth.

10 I translate *xin* as 'heart-mind' in order to indicate its psychosomatic nature from a traditional Chinese perspective, in which it is considered the psycho-spiritual center of human personhood.

11 Here I use 'anthropology' as a comparative category designating views of human being/personhood and 'psychology' as a comparative category designating views on *psyche* (emotion/mind/spirit/etc.). On 'contemplative psychology', that is psychology derived from and informing contemplative practice, see de Wit 1991; Komjathy 2015, 2018. On Daoist contemplative psychology see Roth 1991, 1997, 1999a, 2015; Komjathy 2013b, 2017.

12 The *Zhuangzi* is one of the most widely translated and interpreted classical Daoist texts. For reliable translations of the *Neiye* see Roth 1999a; Komjathy 2008a, vol. 1. I follow Roth's text-critical edition of the *Neiye*, including his chapter numbers.

13 Revisionist scholars of the *Zhuangzi*, including A. C. Graham, Liu Xiaogan, Victor Mair and Harold Roth, identify various lineages or 'schools' in the received text. For a concise summary see Komjathy 2013a.

14 These instructions are being given by the Daoist Master Guangcheng (Expansive Completion).

15 The *Laozi*, which is attributed to the legendary Laozi (Lao-tzu; Master Lao), is the earliest title of the text that would become known by the honorific title *Daode jing* (Scripture on the Dao and Inner Power). Like the *Zhuangzi*, this work contains material from at least the fourth to second century BCE.

16 Specifically, Ge Hong (Ko Hung; Baopuzi [Master Embracing Simplicity]; 283–343), a key representative and systematiser of Great Clarity, uses the term in his highly influential *Baopuzi neipian* (Inner Chapters of Master Embracing Simplicity; DZ 1185). See, e.g. DZ 1185, 18.1ab.

17 Daoists generally do not visualise 'dark energy' because it is usually associated with illness, injury, negativity, death and the like. On an esoteric level, the black colour of the kidneys becomes purple in practice.

18 Jinque dijun (Lord Golden Tower) was a central deity in early Highest Clarity with strong messianic dimensions. Lord Golden Tower is usually identified as a manifestation of Laojun (Lord Lao), the deified Laozi and personification of the Dao.

19 This differs from the 'organ-meridian times' utilised in classical Chinese medicine, with the liver corresponding to 1–3am.

20 As discussed below, the fluid physiology utilised in Daoist practice is quite complex. It sometimes parallels and sometimes deviates from classical Chinese medical views. On the latter, see, eg, Clavey 1995.
21 Niwan literally means 'mud-ball'. It is generally understood as a transliteration of *nirvana*, but may also derive from an alchemical substance utilised in external alchemy. On a more symbolic level, it recalls the view of realised consciousness as a lotus flower.
22 In point of fact, it is more historically accurate to see Highest Clarity methods as setting some of the foundations for Daoist visualisation practice.
23 The *Yijing* is an ancient Chinese text, neither Ruist ('Confucian') nor Daoist, and consists of sixty-four hexagrams (six-line diagrams), which are also analysed according to the eight trigrams (three-line diagrams). Taken collectively, these are said to describe all of the changes in the universe. Each trigram and hexagram consists of solid or broken lines, which are read from bottom to top and correspond to yang and yin, respectively. In the context of Daoist internal alchemy, these become utilised to designate specific corporeal locations, vital substances and/or psychosomatic transformations. For example, the Gen-mountain ☶ trigram consists of one yang-line above two yin-lines. Under one reading, this represents the stillness of mountains, and meditation by extension. That is, the stability of earth (yin) creates the foundation for the clarity of heaven (yang).
24 Under one view of classical Chinese embryogenesis, the Governing and Conception Channels are the first meridians to form. That is, in the womb and in early stages of foetal development, human beings are a single, unified energy form.
25 A complete annotated translation of this text, with English renderings of the illustrations, is included in Komjathy 2013a.
26 Here I draw upon my 20-plus years of ethnographic study and participant-observation of modern mainland Chinese Complete Perfection monasticism as well as globalised and American Daoism.

## Bibliography


Andersen, P. 1980. *The Method of Holding the Three Ones: A Taoist Manual of the Fourth Century AD*. London: Curzon.

Baldrian-Hussein, F. 1984. *Procédés secrets du Joyau magique – Traité d'alchimie taoïste du XI Siècle*. Paris: Les Deux Océans.

Baryosher-Chemouny, M. 1996. *La quete de l'immortalité en Chine: Alchimie et payasage intérieur sous les Song*. Paris: Editions Dervy.

Bokenkamp, S. 1993. 'Traces of Early Celestial Master Physiological Practice in the *Xiang'er* Commentary', *Taoist Resources* 4(2): 37–51.

Boltz, J. 1983. 'Opening the Gates of Purgatory: A Twelfth-century Taoist Meditation Technique for the Salvation of Lost Souls', in Strickmann, M. (ed), *Tantric and Taoist Studies in Honour of Rolf A. Stein*, Volume 2, 487–511. Bruxelles: Institut Belge des Hautes Etudes Chinoises.

Boltz, J. 1987. *A Survey of Taoist Literature: Tenth to Seventeenth Centuries*. Berkeley: University of California, Institute of East Asian Studies.

Clavey, S. 1995. *Fluid Physiology and Pathology in Traditional Chinese Medicine*. London: Churchill Livingstone.

Darga, M. 1999. *Das alchemistische Buch von innerem Wesen und Lebensenergie: Xingming guizhi*. München: Eugen Diederichs Verlag.

de Wit, H. 1991. *Contemplative Psychology*. Baird, M. L. (trans). Pittsburgh: Duquesne University Press.

Despeux, C. 1994. *Taoïsme et corps humain. Le Xiuzhen tu*. Paris: Guy Trédaniel.

Donner, N. and Stevenson, D. 1993. *The Great Calming and Contemplation: A Study and Annotated Translation of the First Chapter of Chih-i's Mo-ho chih-kuan*. Honolulu: University of Hawaii Press.

Eskildsen, S. 2006. 'Emergency Death Meditations for Internal Alchemists', *T'oung Pao* 92(4/5): 373–409.

Eskildsen, S. 2008. 'Some Troubles and Perils of Taoist Meditation', *Monumenta Serica* 56: 259–291.

Eskildsen, S. 2015. *Daoism, Meditation, and the Wonders of Serenity: From the Latter Han Dynasty (25–220) to the Tang Dynasty (618–907)*. Albany: State University of New York Press.

Gill, S. 2005 (1987). 'Prayer,' in Jones, L. (ed), *Encyclopedia of Religion*, 7367–7372. Second edition. Detroit, MI: Macmillan Reference.

Hadot, P. 1995. *Philosophy as a Way of Life: Spiritual Exercises from Socrates to Foucault*. Hoboken, NJ: Blackwell.

Kohn, L. 1987. *Seven Steps to the Tao: Sima Chengzhen's Zuowang lun*. St. Augustin: Steyler Verlag.

Kohn, L. (ed) 1989a. *Taoist Meditation and Longevity Techniques*. Ann Arbor: University of Michigan, Center for Chinese Studies.

Kohn, L. 1989b. 'Guarding the One: Concentrative Meditation in Taoism', in Kohn, L. (ed), *Taoist Meditation and Longevity Techniques*, 125–158. Ann Arbor: University of Michigan, Center for Chinese Studies.

Kohn, L. 1989c. 'Taoist Insight Practice: The Tang Practice of *Neiguan*', in Kohn, L. (ed), *Taoist L and Longevity Techniques*, 193–224. Ann Arbor: University of Michigan, Center for Chinese Studies.

Kohn, L. 1993. 'Quiet Sitting with Master Yinshi: Medicine and Religion in Modern China', *Zen Buddhism Today* 10: 79–95.

Kohn, L, (ed) 2000. *Daoism Handbook*. Leiden: Brill.

Kohn, L. 2010. *Sitting in Oblivion: The Heart of Daoist Meditation*. Dunedin, FL: Three Pines Press.

Komjathy, L. 2002. *Title Index to Daoist Collections*. Cambridge, MA: Three Pines Press.

Komjathy, L. 2006. 'Qigong in America', in Kohn, L. (ed), *Daoist Body Cultivation*, 203–235. Cambridge, MA: Three Pines Press.

Komjathy, L. 2007. *Cultivating Perfection: Mysticism and Self-transformation in Early Quanzhen Daoism*. Leiden: Brill.

Komjathy, L. 2008a [2003]. *Handbooks for Daoist Practice*. 10 volumes. Hong Kong: Yuen Yuen Institute.

Komjathy, L. 2008b. 'Mapping the Daoist Body: Part I: The *Neijing tu* in History', *Journal of Daoist Studies* 1: 67–92.

Komjathy, L. 2009. 'Mapping the Daoist Body: Part II: The Text of the *Neijing tu*', *Journal of Daoist Studies* 2: 64–108.

Komjathy, L. 2011. 'The Daoist Mystical Body', in Cottai, T. and McDaniel, J. (eds), *Perceiving the Divine through the Human Body: Mystical Sensuality*, 67–103. New York: Palgrave MacMillan.

Komjathy, L. 2013a. *The Way of Complete Perfection: A Quanzhen Daoist Anthology*. Albany: State University of New York Press.

Komjathy, L. 2013b. *The Daoist Tradition: An Introduction*. London and New York: Bloomsbury Academic.

Komjathy, L. 2014a. *Daoism: A Guide for the Perplexed*. London and New York: Bloomsbury Academic.

Komjathy, L 2014b. 'Daoist Clepsydra-Meditation: Late Medieval Quanzhen Monasticism and Communal Meditation', in Eifring, H. (ed), *Hindu, Buddhist and Daoist Meditation*, 185–214. Oslo, Norway: Hermes Academic Publishing.

Komjathy, L. 2014c. 'Title Index to the *Zhonghua daozang* 中華道藏 (Chinese Daoist Canon)', *Monumenta Serica* 62: 213–260.

Komjathy, L. (ed) 2015. *Contemplative Literature: A Comparative Sourcebook on Meditation and Contemplative Prayer*. Albany: State University of New York Press.

Komjathy, L 2017. *Taming the Wild Horse: An Annotated Translation and Study of the Daoist Horse Taming Pictures*. New York: Columbia University Press.

Komjathy, L 2018. *Introducing Contemplative Studies*. West Sussex, England: Wiley-Blackwell.

Komjathy, L. forthcoming a. 'Praxis', in Knepper, T. and Kopf, G. (eds), *Global-Critical Philosophy of Religion*. New York: Springer Publishing Company.

Komjathy, L. forthcoming b. 'Daoist Meditation: From 100 CE to the Present', in Farias, M., Brazier, D. and Lalljee, M. (eds), *The Oxford Handbook of Meditation*. New York: Oxford University Press.

LaFargue, M. 1992. *The Tao of the Tao Te Ching*. Albany: State University of New York Press.

Miller, J. 2008. *The Way of Highest Clarity: Nature, Vision and Revelation in Medieval China*. Magdalena, NM: Three Pines Press.

Needham, J. et al. 1976. *Science and Civilisation in China*. Vol. V: *Chemistry and Chemical Technology*. Part 3: *Spagyrical Discovery and Invention: Historical Survey, from Cinnabar Elixirs to Synthetic Insulin*. Cambridge: Cambridge University Press.

Needham, J. et al. 1983. *Science and Civilisation in China*. Vol. V: *Chemistry and Chemical Technology*. Part 5: *Spagyrical Discovery and Invention: Physiological Alchemy*. Cambridge: Cambridge University Press.

Palmer, D. 2007. *Qigong Fever: Body, Science, and Utopia in China*. New York: Columbia University Press.

Pregadio, F. 2006. 'Early Daoist Meditation and the Origins of Inner Alchemy', in Penny, B. (ed), *Daoism in History*, 121–158. London: Routledge.

Pregadio, F. (ed) 2008. *The Encyclopedia of Taoism*, 2 volumes. London: Routledge.

Pregadio, F. and Skar, L. 2000. 'Inner Alchemy (*Neidan*)', in Kohn, L. (ed), *Daoism Handbook*, 464–497. Leiden: Brill.

Robinet, I. 1989a. 'Visualization and Ecstatic Flight in Shangqing Taoism', in Kohn, L. (ed), *Taoist Meditation and Longevity Techniques*, 159–191. Ann Arbor: Center for Chinese Studies, University of Michigan.

Robinet, I. 1989b. 'Original Contributions of *Neidan* to Taoism and Chinese Thought', in Kohn, L. (ed), *Taoist Meditation and Longevity Techniques*, 297–330. Ann Arbor: Center for Chinese Studies, University of Michigan.

Robinet, I. 1993. *Taoist Meditation: The Mao-shan Tradition of Great Purity*. Pas, J. and Girardot, N. (trans). Albany: State University of New York Press.
Roth, H. 1991. 'Psychology and Self-Cultivation in Early Taoistic Thought', *Harvard Journal of Asiatic Studies* 51(2): 599–650.
Roth, H. 1996. 'The Inner Cultivation Tradition of Early Daoism', in Lopez, D. S. Jr. (ed), *Religions of China in Practice*, 123–138. Princeton, NJ: Princeton University Press.
Roth, H. 1997. 'Evidence for Stages of Meditation in Early Taoism', *Bulletin of the School of Oriental and African Studies* 60(2): 295–314.
Roth, H. 1999a. *Original Tao: Inward Training (Nei-yeh) and the Foundations of Taoist Mysticism*. New York: Columbia University Press.
Roth, H. 1999b. '*Laozi* in the Context of Early Daoist Mystical Praxis', in Csikszentmihalyi, M. and Ivanhoe, P. J. (eds), *Religious and Philosophical Aspects of the Laozi*, 59–96. Albany: State University of New York Press.
Roth, H. 2000. 'Bimodal Mystical Experience in the 'Qiwu lun' Chapter of the *Zhuangzi*', *Journal of Chinese Religions* 28: 31–50.
Roth, H. 2015. 'Daoist Apophatic Meditation: Selections from the Classical Daoist Textual Corpus', in Komjathy, L. (ed), *Contemplative Literature*, 89–143. Albany: State University of New York Press.
Saso, M. 1972. 'On Ritual Meditation in Orthodox Taoism', *Journal of the China Society* 8: 1–19.
Saso, M. 1974. 'On the Meditative Use of the Yellow Court Canon', *Journal of the China Society* 9: 1–20.
Saso, M. 1978. *The Teachings of Taoist Master Chuang*. New Haven, CT: Yale University Press.
Saso, M. 1983. 'The *Chuang-tzu nei-p'ien*: A Taoist Meditation', in Mair, V. (ed), *Experimental Essays on Chuang-tzu*, 140–157. Honolulu: University of Hawaii Press.
Schipper, K. 1993. *The Taoist Body*. Duval, K. C. (trans). Berkeley: University of California Press.
Schipper, K. and Verellen, F. (eds) 2004. *The Taoist Canon: A Historical Guide*. 3 vols. Chicago: University of Chicago Press.
Underwood, F. 2005 [1987]. 'Meditation', in Jones, L. (ed), *The Encyclopedia of Religion*, 5816–5822. 15 volumes. Second edition. Detroit: Macmillan.
Watson, B. 1968. *The Complete Works of Chuang Tzu*. New York: Columbia University Press.

# 15

# ISLAM, YOGA AND MEDITATION

*Patrick J. D'Silva*

One who has seen this cannot remember it, and one who has not seen does not believe it.[1]

*(Amir Khusraw, Nuh Sipihr (1318 CE), writing on amazing deeds by Indian Yogis)*

## Introduction: the issue of permissibility

When discussing the topic of Islam and yoga, one of the first questions that arises for modern readers is that of permissibility: are Muslims *allowed* to study and practise yoga? This question has much more do to with modern conceptions of religion – heavily rooted in European Protestantism (Masuzawa 2005; Nongbri 2013) – and the idea of rigid boundaries between religious communities than it does with the way Hindus, Muslims and others have historically approached yoga. A quick internet search for 'Islam and yoga' produces a series of newspaper and magazine articles written about Muslims who think yoga is permissible, Muslims who think it is not and Muslims who are not sure. As I demonstrate below, these examples taken from the popular press highlight the understanding within modern Muslim communities that there is no singular, definitive yoga, but that instead there are many different yogas. This accords with David Gordon White's description in *Yoga in Practice* that 'yoga can refer to things ranging from the literal yoking of one's animals, to an astral conjunction, to a type of recipe, incantation, combination, application, contact, … and the work of alchemists. But this is by no means an exhaustive list' (White 2012: 2). These debates are not restricted to Muslim communities, for there has been a resurgence in recent years within Hindu groups who claim proprietary ownership over yoga as a quintessentially Hindu cultural and religious 'product'.

## Muslim engagement with yoga

There is a long history of Muslim engagement with *al-Hind* ('India' broadly construed) in general, and yoga in particular. Arab and Persian settlements in South Asia date back to the eighth century CE, with the much-fabled story of Muhammad bin Qassim (d. 715 CE) leading the conquest of Sindh and Multan. More contact took place leading up to the establishment of the Delhi Sultanate in 1206 CE. Lest we are left with the impression that this encounter is of a decidedly military or imperial nature, trade between the Arabian peninsula and western Indian coasts dates back long before the beginning of Islam, and trade (along with the accompanying circulation of people, especially Sufi teachers) served to firmly establish *al-Hind* as an important part of the Islamic imaginary. Turning specifically to yoga, from the outset it should be clear that

Muslims in South Asia during the Delhi Sultanate and Mughal periods were not encountering anything resembling modern postural yoga; instead, they were learning about tantric forms of yoga and tantric-inflected forms of *haṭhayoga*. These latter interactions largely came through the Nāth yogis. The main evidence for this sustained interest in Hinduism generally, and yoga in particular, over the centuries on the part of Muslim scholars are the translations – dating from the fourteenth to nineteenth centuries – from Sanskrit into Arabic and Persian of texts such as Patañjali's *Yogasūtra*,[2] as well as the Upaniṣads and Vedas. The Ghaznavid scholar and court astrologer Abu Rayhan Muhammad ibn Ahmad Biruni (hereafter, Biruni) is undoubtedly one of the most significant Muslim authors who wrote about yoga. Biruni is a key source for developing an understanding of Islamicate views on religion in India. He is best known for his *Taḥqīq ma li'l-Hind min qabūla fi'l-`aql am mardhūla* ('Investigation of What India Says, Whether Accepted by Reason or Refused'), completed in 1030 CE, and often rendered with the shortened title *Kitāb al-Hind* ('Book on India'). He is also known for his translation and analysis of Patañjali's *Yogasūtra*. 'Written in Arabic, the *Hind* may very well be the first systematization of "Indian belief" into one "Indian religion," as Biruni calls it, preceding by almost 900 years the definitions of Hinduism by nineteenth-century European Orientalists' (Kozah 2016: 1). Biruni focused on metempsychosis as the 'banner' of Hinduism, with Patañjali's *Yogasūtra* elevated to its 'Holy Book' (Kozah, 2). His focus on Pātañjala yoga means that he necessarily left out a great deal of information on Hindu learning, traditions with which he nevertheless would have been familiar. Biruni is more open and/or tolerant of the Hindu beliefs he studies in part because he is so clear that they are not Islamic.

Abu'l Hasan Yamin al-Din Khusraw (d. 1325 CE), more commonly known as Amir Khusraw, holds a special place in the pantheon of South Asian Muslim history. A musician and poet, he was a disciple of Nizamuddin Auliya (d. 1332 CE) of Delhi, in whose dargah he is also buried. His family originated in Transoxiana but immigrated to the Delhi Sultanate during the Mongol invasions. Written in 1318 CE, his *Nuh Sipihr* ('Nine Heavens') is a survey of Indian customs composed in Persian as a *masnavī*, or in rhyming couplets. Its contents include sections on Indian food, music and languages, as well as a list of amazing or astonishing things that one finds in India. It also reflects Khusraw's passionate interest in holding up South Asia as a wondrous place. There are several key verses in this selection from the seventh chapter of the fourth *sipihr*. In this chapter, Khusraw focuses on marvels found within India and includes several key lines that directly pertain to the use of the breath for supernatural powers. Later parts of this same chapter contain Khusraw's insights into the importance of occult or magical powers on the part of Indian *jogis*. As to the powers of the breath, he writes:

> Another strange feature is that the Indians are capable of extending the age (of human beings) by different means and methods. It is because everybody has his fixed quota of breaths. One who acquires control over his breath, he would live longer if he takes less breaths. The Jogi (Yogi) who suspends his breath through Yoga in a temple, can live, by this feat, for more than five hundred years. It is wonderful that they (Indians) can spell out omens by distinguishing between the breaths blowing from the two nostrils. By a study of the breath flowing by the right or the left nostril, (thus by distinguishing the open and the closed nostril) they can foretell something of the future. The other thing is that the jogis can send the soul from its own body to another body through their yogic power. Many such jogis live in Kashmir in the mountains and many of them live in the caves.
>
> *(Nath and Gwaliari (trans): 1981: 198)*

Khusraw thus demonstrates that it was popular knowledge in the fourteenth century that Indian ascetics known as *yogīs/jogis* developed particular types of supernatural powers through understanding and controlling their breathing.

Abu `Abdullah Muhammad ibn `Abdullah al-Lawati al-Tanji ibn Battuta (d. 1377 CE; hereafter 'Ibn Battuta') and Wali al-Din al-Rahman ibn Muhammad ibn Muhammad ibn Abi Bakr Muhammad ibn al-Hasan Ibn Khaldun (d. 1406 CE; hereafter 'Ibn Khaldun') combine to provide a key perspective on the spectrum of Perso-Arabic engagement with South Asia. Together they were important authors whose works circulated widely within the Islamicate world. While both hailed from North Africa, both happened to address the subject of India, specifically with regard to yoga. Both Ibn Battuta and Ibn Khaldun made references to the yogis, the former in his *Riḥla* ('Journey'), published *c.*1355 CE, with the latter author relying on the former's account for some of the material found in his well-known work on the rise and fall of civilisations, known generally as the *Muqaddima* (*c.*1379 CE).

Ibn Battuta used the term *siḥr* ('magic' or 'sorcery') to talk about the yogis and their practices (Ibn Battuta 1893–1922: 35). Given that he spent a considerable amount of time in India during his decades of travel, the observations that he records in his *Riḥla* are a valuable (if not always entirely reliable) resource for learning about various practices during his time period. Ibn Khaldun makes references to the yogis' 'many writings', but fails to include any specific information that would reveal what types of sources he has access to or has even heard of. He makes only a few references to yoga in the *Muqaddima*. For example, in his discussion of different kinds of sense perception, he talks about those who engage in exercises (*al-riyāḍa*):

> … such people are the men who train themselves in sorcery (*siḥr*). They train themselves in these things, in order to be able to behold the supernatural and to be active in the various worlds. Most such live in the intemperate zones of the north and the south, especially in India (*bilād al-hind*), where they are called yogis (*wa yusammūna hunālika al-jūkīyya*). They possess a large literature (*kutub*) on how such exercises are to be done. The stories about them in this connection are remarkable (*gharība*).
>
> (*Ibn Khaldun 1967: 85*)

Note that he used the same term here (*al-riyāḍa*) to talk about the spiritual practice or exercises of yoga as he did for the many Sufi practices that came up throughout his massive text. Unfortunately, he did not provide any additional details in terms of what this 'large literature' included.

So far I have addressed major works by Muslim authors who discuss yoga and other aspects of Indian esotericism, but now I turn to direct translations of yogic texts beyond Patañjali's *Yogasūtra*. The *Kāmarū Pančāšikā* is a Persian text on yoga and divination, known by the Hindi name that translates as '50 verses of *Kāmarū*'. While the author is anonymous and the text's date of composition is unknown, excerpts of the text exist in Shams al-Din Muhammad ibn Mahmud Amuli's Persian encyclopaedia of the sciences, the *Nafa'is al-funūn* (Amuli 1961). At one time Amuli held the key position of *mudarris* (literally 'teacher', but here more likely understood as superintendent or principal) at the Sultaniyya madrasa under Ilkhanid ruler Oljeytu (r. 1304–16 CE). Amuli's death date of 1353 CE establishes the latest date by which the *Kāmarū Pančāšikā* could have been written, and the text was most likely written substantially earlier. Carl Ernst's translation of the only full-length manuscript version of this text highlights a number of difficulties, including the scribe's use of numerical ciphers to describe occult practices, as well as the scribe's less than successful attempts at transcribing Sanskrit mantras in Persian.[3] Still, the text 'testifies to the ongoing engagement with yogic materials in Persianate circles over centuries' (Ernst n.d.): 1). In a separate article, Ernst lays out the manuscript's history as a text that Italian traveller Pietro delle Valle obtains in Persia in 1622 (Ernst 2016: 386–400).

The most frequently occurring form of the *Kāmarū Pančāšikā* is a six-chapter abridgement with a brief preface in which the scribe relates a usually very brief story on the circumstances under which he came to a) acquire the text, usually via contact with Indian *jogis*, or b) translate the text from *zabān-i hinduvān* (literally 'the language of the Indians', meaning either Sanskrit or Hindi) into Persian. The chapters for these abridgements are remarkably consistent. The usual line-up includes (1) knowledge of the breath; (2) questioning the questioner; (3) mind-reading; (4) predicting the moment of death; (5) incantation of actions; and (6) love and hate. The order of presentation varies, but the contents of each section are very stable.

Ernst outlines a series of ciphers used in the full-length *Kāmarū Pančāšikā* manuscript. These tend to occur when the author describes spells that have life and death implications for the user and the person(s) towards whom the spells are directed. He states that 'in the translation of a text of occult power from Sanskrit to Persian, the presence of such deliberate esotericism indicates that there were certain subjects that aroused discomfort and hesitation among at least some readers' (Ernst n.d.: 7–8). The use of ciphers and other linguistic means of obscuring or obfuscating intended meaning raises flags because it points to how an author or group of authors responded to a text, and it begs the question of whether or not these types of translations are constrained by limitations based on the scribes' affiliations – be they religious, political or otherwise. For a related example, Hatley (2007) provides examples of medieval Bengali Sufis who developed 'homologies' between the *maqāms* ('stations') found more typically in Sufi texts and tantric conceptions of the subtle body (specifically the *cakras*). Again, I hesitate before imputing that Muslim translators and copyists in any time period or location were unable to render something from one language into another *because of being Muslim*. Taken as a whole, the `*ilm-i dam* corpus is a very large piece of evidence for active and sustained Muslim engagement with practices that were known to have non-Muslim roots. As I demonstrate below, at some points Muslims held up `*ilm-i dam* as worth learning precisely because it was not Islamic, while at other points the techniques were interpreted as being sufficiently domesticated as to be placed along a litany of other esoteric practices. In studying the different `*ilm-i dam* texts, the permeability of the line between translation and interpretation is quite evident. If one author retains references to goddesses and yogis while another excludes them, can these really be understood as approving and disapproving responses to a putative original text? Scholars today can formulate theories to explain the differences between translation and translated, but we must also recognise the very real limits on our knowledge.

The *Kāmarū Pančāšikā*'s contents hold pressing ramifications for understanding the porosity and limits of religious boundaries in the premodern South Asian context. As Ernst has written, this genre of text reflects the extent to which yoga and yogic philosophy is Islamicised, thereby making familiar something that an external observer may expect Muslims to find strange or 'other'. The *Kāmarū Pančāšikā* is a

> text [that] demonstrates an unselfconscious domestication of yogic practices in an Islamicate society. Among the breath prognostications, for instance, one learns to approach 'the *qāḍī* [Islamic judge] or the *amīr* [prince]' for judgment or litigation only when the breath from the right nostril is favorable. Casual references mention Muslim magicians, or practices that may be performed either in a Muslim or a Hindu graveyard (47b), or else in an empty temple or mosque (49b) … [and meant that] for the average Persian reader, the contents of [*Kāmarū Pančāšikā*] fell into the category of the occult sciences, and its Indic origin would have only enhanced its esoteric allure.
>
> *(Ernst 2016: 392–393)*

For scholars of Islam and of India (let alone the combination thereof), discussion of 'esoteric allure' may raise the spectre of orientalist discourse, which many understand as simultaneously a by-product of and a contributing (i.e. legislating) factor in the European colonial project in the eighteenth, nineteenth and twentieth centuries. The notion that Persian readers – especially Muslim Persian readers – would have found texts such as the *Kāmarū Pančāšikā* more exciting or appealing because of the strange and/or exotic nature of their contents raises some important questions about the relationship to difference as defined by religious, linguistic or ethnic identity. Were these texts popular precisely *because* they were exotic, or were they perhaps *not* seen as exotic at all, but rather simply as offering up other means for accessing astral power?

The *Amrtakunda* ('Pool of Nectar') is a no-longer extant Sanskrit work on yoga and breathing techniques that survives in Arabic and Persian translations, which in turn preserve excerpts of the *Kāmarū Pančāšikā*. Both Arabic and Persian translations exist under the title *Ḥawd al-ḥayāt*, literally 'the Pool of Life'.[4] In the mid-sixteenth century, Shattari Sufi master Muhammad Ghaus produced a translation in Persian entitled the *Baḥr al-ḥayāt*, or 'Ocean of Life'.[5] Perhaps not coincidentally, the 'ocean' is much longer and contains much more material than the 'pool'. Additionally, there are also paraphrases and translations found in Bengali called *puthi sahitya*, 'such as the *Yoga Qalandar* of Saiyid Murtada (d. 1662 CE), the *Jñāna Sagara* and the *Jñāna Pradipa* of Saiyid Sultan (d. 1648 CE). Thus, the Sufis incorporated yogico-tantric culture in their own religio-philosophical system through the translations and paraphrases of the [*Ḥawd al-ḥayāt*] and the [*Baḥr al-ḥayāt*]' (Sakaki 2005: 136). Sakaki's presentation here begs the question of whether or not these translations are accurately understood as 'incorporations' of Indian knowledge by Muslims. For example, Ernst demonstrates how Muhammad Ghaus' translation of the now lost *Amrtakunda* makes a noticeable change in chapter 9, in which Ghaus replaces material on summoning *yogini* goddesses with generic Sufi material on *dhikrs* (Ernst 2016, 149–160). This type of alteration marks an area of resistance to the original text. While breath control and related divination practices make it through Ghaus' filter, instruction on summoning goddesses does not. The two texts referenced above serve as case studies, especially for observers interested in a more expansive reading of yoga beyond Patañjali. I now turn from specific texts to high-ranking personas from the Mughal period whose personal interest and study of Indian teachings contributes a great deal to the present inquiry.

Of the Mughal rulers, Abu'l Fatḥ Jalal-ud-Din Muhammad Akbar (b. 1542, r. 1556–1605 CE; hereafter 'Akbar') draws the most attention for his ecumenical outlook and personal engagements with non-Muslim teachings. One key source for examining Mughal engagement with yogic philosophy comes from Akbar's grand vizier, Abu'l Fazl (d. 1602 CE), who composed the *A'in-i Akbari* ('The Institutes of Akbar'), his massive appendix to the *Akbarnama* (biography of Akbar).[6] As David Gordon White notes, the *Akbarnama* depicts Akbar as possessing a divine power that radiated outwards to encompass those in his presence. Not only did this map onto specific Muslim traditions of sacred kingship (Moin 2014), but additionally this

> same supernatural charisma and wisdom also caused the holy men of other Indian traditions, including the yogis, to gravitate toward Akbar's imperial person. In this last case, the attraction was mutual, with Akbar often visiting and holding forth with Hindu holy men, and even building a "City of Yogis" for them on the outskirts of the city of Agra.
>
> *(White 2019: 148)*

His building of the *`Ibādat khāna* ('House of Worship') in 1575 CE at Fatehpur Sikri, to which the ruler invited leaders from various religious traditions, is also held up as a sign of his interest in other traditions. There are a variety of paintings produced, under Akbar's patronage, that document different schools of yogis, particularly the Nāths (Mallinson n.d.). Similarly to the *Baḥr al-ḥayāt*, which furnishes us with the oldest surviving depictions of yoga postures, so too do these painting from Akbar's reign (and subsequent Mughal rulers) provide important historical evidence for the development of different yogic practices and customs.

While the narrative surrounding Akbar is fairly uniformly positive regarding his disposition towards yogis (and other representatives of Indian religious traditions), the waters muddy a bit when turning to his two most famous grandsons, Auragzeb (d. 1707 CE) and Dara Shikoh (d. 1659 CE) – it is worth noting that the former had the latter executed after winning the war of succession for the Mughal throne. The popular (and oftentimes, scholarly) narrative is that where Akbar was disposed towards toleration, Aurangzeb embraced fanaticism, expressed most notably in the destruction of Hindu temples, imposition of the *jizīya* tax on non-Muslims (which Akbar had revoked under his rule) and rejection of Sufism. These claims are all complicated by historical evidence to the contrary. Aurangzeb's final resting place is inside a Sufi shrine in Khuldabad. He employed far more Hindus in his court than any of his predecessors, and he issued edicts protecting Hindu temples and providing support to Brahmins (Truschke 2017: 12). Additionally, Bouillier provides evidence that he engaged directly with representatives of the Nāth Yogis, resulting in their depiction of this ruler as 'a powerful enemy as well as a clumsy devotee' (Bouillier 2018: 525), while Pauwels and Backrach (2018) critique the narrative of Aurangzeb's iconoclasm through Brajbhāṣā Vaishnava accounts regarding images of Krishna from the late 1660s and early 1670s.

In contrast to his brother, Dara Shikoh is remembered for participating in the translation of Indian texts from Sanskrit into Persian, including his rendering of the Upaniṣads as *Sirr-ī Akbar* ('The Greatest Secret'). Alam writes that following a 'critical examination of Hindu religions [Shukoh] found that all religions are identical and lead to the same goal. His work *Majma`* *al-Baḥrain* ("Meeting of the Two Oceans") is devoted to highlighting the similarity between the beliefs and practices prescribed in Islamic *taṣawwuf* and Hindu *yoga*' (Alam 2004: 96). The temptation of later histories of the Mughal dynasty has been to elevate Dara Shikoh as a continuation of Akbar's ecumenism and deep engagement with other religious traditions (especially particular schools of thought within Hinduism), as if this was somehow exceptional. Work by Truschke, Kinra and others on the presence and contributions of Sanskrit scholars at the Mughal court disproves this theory. Mughal rulers and courtiers interacted with yogis and ascetics from various Indian religious traditions on a regular basis. For example, beyond Akbar's famed *`ibādat khāna*,

> Shah Jahan, too, often surrounded himself with mystical consultants, and while he might have inclined more toward 'proper' Sufis, his court was awash with mystically-inclined Hindus like Chandar Bhan Brahman, not to mention various Hindu astrologers and other divines with whom he consulted almost daily.
>
> *(Kinra 2009: 169)*

However, Kinra shows through a close reading of texts by Dara Shikoh's contemporaries, such as Shir Khan Lodi, who includes stories about Dara Shikoh in his *tazkira* written *c.*1690 CE, that there was criticism of the prince for exhibiting a variety of youthful immaturities, including his dabbling with the Vedas, because 'only a childish mind … would be so easily be lured in such heterodoxy' (Kinra 2009: 184). Kinra argues that 'Baba Dara' was thought by many to be too immature to be able to take the throne in the war of succession that he so famously lost to his brother Aurangzeb (Kinra 2009: 190). In short, the popular image of Dara Shikoh as continuing

Akbar's legacy is complicated somewhat when considering the contemporaneous sources that Kinra introduces.

To be clear, not all examples of Sufi–yogi interactions are peaceful. There are many examples of Sufi '*pirs* and *yogīs*' waging spiritual warfare, attempting to out-do one another through performing various amazing feats in order to demonstrate who was more powerful.[7] There is a temptation to read these conflicts as a type of proxy for the political and military struggles of Muslim and Hindu kingdoms against one another. However, such a reading belies the history of alliances between some of these same kingdoms that cross denominational lines. Instead, I suggest that Muslim rulers were very concerned with accessing forms of esoteric power, and that these accounts could be read as efforts by these mystics to maintain and improve their status in the all too real political realm.

What does all of this mean in terms of the original question regarding the permissibility of Muslims to practise yoga? First, it is a mistake to approach the question as if we can retroactively project the modern-day yoga-scape, with studios popping up all over the world, and then anachronistically imagine whether or not members of the Mughal court or other segments of society were flowing through *sūryanamaskār* ('sun salutation'). As other chapters in this volume highlight, the very meaning of yoga has always been quite varied, and past generations' version of yoga focused much more on its techniques for seated meditation. Second, the evidence I introduced above makes it clear that Muslims did engage with yoga in several different ways, especially through translating key texts and exploring these Indian teachings so as to assess their inherent spiritual value and compare them with the Qur'an and other traditional sources of divinely revealed truth.

## *When all breaths are not commensurable:* `ilm-i dam *and* zikr, svarodaya *and* prāṇāyāma

In addition to the question of permissibility, there is also an issue of categorical commensurability. Within Islamic Studies, specifically for those who work on Sufism, there is an expectation that anything associated with paying special attention to the breath is connected with *dhikr/zikr*, the widespread 'remembrance' (of God) exercises that play such an important role in both individual and collective rituals associated with various Sufi communities. Within Hindu or Buddhist studies, I have frequently encountered the expectation that *svarodaya* is somehow linked to *prāṇāyāma*. While perfectly understandable, these connections and associations are also inconsistent.

As mentioned above, *svarodaya* originates in Śaiva tantra sources in Sanskrit, composed as early as the seventh century CE (Arraj 1988). These are typically presented as a dialogue between Lord Shiva and his consort, Parvati. The term translates literally as 'the attainment of voiced breath', and refers to divination practices where the practitioners use knowledge of their breath to predict auspicious moments to engage in various actions, including travelling, waging war, getting married and meeting with one's ruler. In the twentieth century, a series of translations from Sanskrit and Hindi into English occasionally present *svarodaya* using references to *prāṇā*, but more frequent is the retention of the distinction between the two terms for breath (Rai 1980; Ramacharaka 1905; Visaarada 1967). The aforementioned *A'in-i Akbari* provide a clear demarcation between *svarodaya* and *prāṇāyāma* by addressing these practices in separate sections. Amuli's taxonomy in the *Nefais al-funūn* clearly separates the sciences of *tasavvuf* (Sufism) from the natural sciences, within which one finds the material on *`ilm-i dam* in the form of an abridgement of the *Kāmarū Pančāšikā*. This confusion has an earlier precedent. Writing in the nineteenth century, Austrian orientalist Alfred von Kremer places Naqshbandi *zikr* accounts involving specific instructions on breath control directly alongside Amuli's *`ilm-i dam* text, implying that these practices are very similar *because* of the shared interest in the breath, but without even a cursory examination of how the breath is functioning in each case (Von Kremer 1873). Instead, the presence of breath-focused practices plays into von Kremer's real aim, which is arguing for the Hindu and Buddhist origins of Indian Sufism. In the twentieth century, a series of translations from Sanskrit and Hindi into English occasionally present *svarodaya* using references to *prāṇā*, but more common is the retention of the distinction between the two terms for breath.[8]

In addition to the oft-cited *`ilm-i dam*, there are other terms relating to the breath, such as 'holding the breath' *ḥabs-i dam*, 'watching the breath' *pas-i anfās*, or even another way of 'knowing about the breath' *ma`rifat-i dam*. These terms are related in particular ways, but they are also distinct. The challenge is pushing back against the tendency to collapse all of these into a single category that usually invokes Sufism. In my previous work on the translation of Śaiva divination practices from Sanskrit into Persian, I have deliberately placed an emphasis on the texts using the term *`ilm-i dam*, granting those texts pride of place within this iteration of my inquiry into these breathing practices (D'Silva 2018). Future iterations may include broader surveys not just of unambiguously Sufi breathing practices, but also breathing practices found in yoga and other Indian traditions. The main point here is that one should refrain from making automatic links between a reference to the breath in an Islamicate language and then in Sufism. There are, of course, examples of texts on breathing techniques that are clearly linked to Sufi orders, but these are different practices, with different names, and thus must be recognised as such. Whether reading of *svarodaya* or *`ilm-i dam* in the *A'īn-i Akbarī* or in any of the many other sources that range from the fourteenth to nineteenth centuries, the point I want to emphasise is that the user or practitioner employs knowledge of the breath for practical gains. Drawing down power from the cosmos for one's own benefit makes a great deal of sense. Given that nature is by far the most powerful force experienced by humans, it is inherently logical that these actors would seek out the fulfilment of their agency through gaining and utilising knowledge regarding the channelling of all that the universe has to offer. Stellar work by scholars such as Moin (2014) demonstrates how important astrology was within formulations and justifications of Muslim kingship in South Asia (and beyond) during the Mughal period. The breath's importance in Muslim formulations of connections between the body and cosmos are by no means imported or derived from Indic sources. Qur'an 15:28 reads: 'Then your Lord told the angels, "I am making a human being from earth like clay fired and moulded. I have formed him and *breathed* into him of my spirit, so fall before him in prostration"' (emphasis added).[9]

## Meditation

The preceding section focused specifically on Muslim engagement with yoga, a discussion generally framed with yoga as a set of practices essentially different from or foreign to Muslim communities. I have laid out a series of examples that hopefully demonstrate many ways in which Muslims – especially in South Asia – have encountered yoga not necessarily as something exotic, even if they recognise that its roots lie outside of the Qur'an, hadith, sunna and so forth. In this section, I turn to a more challenging question, namely that of Muslim engagement with meditation. Other chapters in this book highlight the vast diversity of meditative practices, both within and outside of 'Indian' traditions (namely Hinduism, Buddhism and Jainism). However, unlike the study of Muslim approaches to yoga, in the case of meditation we must discuss the many meditative and contemplative techniques that Muslims developed from an early point *without any reference to* Indian traditions. If the study of Muslims and yoga always has this sense of syncretism, hybridity and appropriation in the background, then a similar study of Muslims and meditation must be framed in entirely different terms. Despite earlier orientalist scholarship that insisted otherwise, Muslims *did not learn to meditate* from Hindus. The earliest possible example of Muslim meditation is none other than the Prophet Muhammad. Legend holds that the Prophet Muhammad meditated in the cave of Hira, in the mountains near Mecca, and that it was during one of these meditation sessions that the angel Gabriel appeared to him in order to deliver the first of the Qur'anic revelations. While sparse evidence remains that might give modern-day scholars some idea as to the particulars of the Prophet's meditation practice, this aspect of the prophetic example remains deeply woven within the stories Muslim communities preserve and pass down.

Beyond the Prophet Muhammad, Sufi groups have long cultivated a set of practices known as *dhikr*, the 'remembrance' of God. Below I provide some key examples of debates over *dhikr* within Sufi communities in the past and today. It must be said that *dhikr* is a polyvalent term, and that while many – including scholars of Islam – use it as a general catch-all, one should break it down into more specific parts. For example, the weekly group meditative practice commonly referred to as *dhikr* is more accurately termed *hadra* (literally meaning 'presence', but here understood as a meeting). Another facet of *dhikr* is the performance of and listening to music in varied settings, which one could closely associate with *samā`*. Lastly, there is *dhikr*, understood to refer to the recitation of mantras (both aloud and in silence), which technically is termed *wird*. In terms of outer appearance and practitioners' stated understanding of their internal experience, the visualisations and breathing exercises associated with *wird* is probably the closest to meditation for many scholars of related techniques in Hinduism and Buddhism. *Dhikr* often takes the form of chanting the ninety-nine names of God, either silently or aloud, individually or in a group setting. There are many handbooks and other written guides on how to conduct *dhikr* properly depending on one's *tarīqa* (Sufi order).[10]

Beyond *dhikr*, I would add *`ilm al-wahm*, 'the science of imagination', as a form of Islamic meditation. In the *`ilm-i dam* texts referenced above (dating from the fourteenth century CE onwards), many times the authors include a chapter on *wahm*. These sections include instructions for meditation practices designed to aid the practitioner in predicting the moment of their death. For example, one abridged version of the *Kāmarū Pančāšikā* directs the reader to go into the desert and begin meditating. After a time, he will witness a white manifestation of himself. He will then consult the shadow thrown by this projection. By reading the shadow's length, he will be able to predict how much longer he has to live (*Kāmarū Pančāšikā* abridgement, Browne recension). This is a different type of meditation or contemplation, which is not done with the goal of bringing the practitioner closer to God, but instead may be classified more as esoteric or occult technologies for self-knowledge and advancement.

## Contemporary issues

The final section of this chapter focuses on the modern day. The debates over permissibility in the early twenty-first century CE are quite different from those that I discussed earlier. At the same time, we can also find certain lingering threads, which merit explication.

Uzma Jalaluddin sets her 2018 novel, *Ayesha At Last*, in today's Toronto suburbs. A major plot line concerns the mosque that many of the characters attend. In one scene, several key characters attend a yoga class for women offered at the mosque. At no point in the scene is there any debate over the permissibility issue mentioned at the beginning of this chapter. This is a case of fiction reflecting reality, since a quick internet search for 'yoga classes at mosques' yields a number of links describing yoga classes held at mosques in different parts of North America and Europe. This is by no means unique to Muslim communities, for one can also find a wide variety of churches offering yoga classes, at times with similar types of tension over the permissibility issue. In the context of the United States, the *Sedlock v. Baird* case from Encinitas, California, demonstrates one rationale for deciding the question of whether or not yoga is quintessentially Hindu (see discussions in Husgafvel, Chapter 3 in this volume). In this specific case, parents challenged the legality of their children learning yoga while attending public schools on the grounds that doing so violated US federal and California state law. The first amendment to the US Constitution states that 'Congress shall make no law respecting an establishment of religion or prohibiting the free exercise thereof'. Legal scholars have interpreted this to mean that no *single* religious tradition may be 'established' over and above others, which prohibits anyone from declaring an 'official religion' in the USA. In the California legal case, the judge ruled that since yoga has roots in *three* religious traditions, teaching it by definition could not result in the establishment of a *single* religion over others. Yoga's *validity* or *efficaciousness* as a religious or spiritual pursuit is not the subject of critics' investigation (Laine and Laine forthcoming). A key point of contention is whether or not yoga is uniquely Hindu, or whether the physical postures and some type of generic spiritual outlook can be removed from its Hindu background. In 2013 (and subsequently upheld on appeal in 2015), the court ultimately ruled in favour of the defendants, finding that *because* yoga is found in Hinduism, Buddhism and Jainism, the teaching of yoga logically cannot constitute establishing a *single* religious tradition over others.[11]

One gets a different impression when reading Iranian cleric Hamza Sharifi's criticism that those Iranians who practise yoga do not realise it 'is just a sport and insist that it is the road to happiness' (*The Economist* 2014). Hamid Reza Mazaheri-Seif, head of the Spiritual Health Institute in Qom, says: 'The new teachers of yoga are not even Indian ... They're European or American' (*The Economist* 2014). Misbahuddin Mirza's 2017 article in *Islamic Horizons*, 'Does Islam Allow Yoga?' (with the telling sub-heading, 'What Exactly is Yoga?') provides a useful overview designed to assist the average Muslim reader (who may not be familiar with yoga at all) with assessing the permissibility issue. Her article cites a variety of Muslim religious officials in assessing how to respond to this question. The key arguments circle on what yoga is 'really' about, which in these sources' eyes is the pursuit of a particular form of knowledge, namely *jñana yoga*, with an emphasis on *sūryanamaskār* (sun salutation). In reviewing a variety of popular press around the religious decrees, or fatwas, concerning the practicing of yoga, one sees several patterns to the debate. First, there is the notion that chanting *oṃ* and other mantras while practicing yoga is threatening to Muslims' faith. Second, there are questions about whether the *āsanas* are permissible, and enquiries as to how different they are from the physical motions found in *ṣalāt*, the ritual prayer performed five times a day. Third, what role does intention have? If it is just for exercise, then is it permissible? If it is intended for spiritual development, then is the issue that 'there's nothing really there', or is it that 'there is something there, and it leads us astray from the proverbial straight path'? As the popular press reaction to the Indian government's declaration of Yoga Day in 2015 illustrates, this is very much an active debate with a great deal of vibrant interpretation.[12]

## Conclusion

In this all too brief space, I have attempted to provide an introductory sketch of the study of Muslim engagement with yoga and meditation. The endnotes and Bibliography provide a guide for accessing additional resources. From a theoretical point of view, examining how Muslims relate to yoga yields results that push against the received scholarly habits of categorisation, such as the notion that only Hindus, Buddhists and Jains can 'authentically' practise yoga because it is deemed autochthonous to South Asia. In turn, the orientalist discourse insisting on Islam as foreign to

South Asia led to an understanding of Muslims as not really belonging to the region. Put very simply, if one posits that yoga is quintessentially Indian, and that Muslims are not really Indian, then the conclusion emerges that Muslims cannot practise yoga. However, the evidence (textual, archaeological, anthropological, etc.) counters the idea that Muslims only started to look at yoga in the current culturally deracinated and hyper-consumerist mode that has lead to its incredibly strong growth in popularity across the world in the past century. Returning to the *`ilm-i dam* corpus, one scribe who translated a *Śiva-svarodaya* text into Persian comments in the margin that these teachings are 'not the work of the people of Muhammad, it is the action of the yogis, but it is true' (*Kāmarū Pančāšikā* abridgement, Karachi recension). This is marginal only in terms of its physical location on that manuscript page. In truth, it is marginal only if one persists in interpreting religious identity and reading history through prisms conditioned by the European colonial period and subsequent postcolonial angst over preserving the boundaries between religious communities. If one looks at the permissibility issue using primary sources authored by Muslims in the pre- and early modern eras, at a minimum there is more openness to appraising the yogis' techniques with a pragmatic eye: do these techniques work or not? Muslim observers in South Asia – such as Biruni, Amir Khusraw, Muhammad Ghaus and Abu'l Fazl – believed that yoga and other veins of Indic philosophy merited serious examination.[13] Additionally – and perhaps most importantly, in light of the present-day issuance of fatwas or papal decrees advising Muslims and Christians against practising yoga – the Muslim scholars and court officials I just mentioned did not seem to think that learning more about yoga imperilled their status as faithful Muslims. Or, at a minimum I would say that the textual evidence suggests that these 'medieval' Muslims displayed more certitude that invalidating their religious status required a bit more than just learning Sanskrit and working on understanding India's diverse religious and philosophical heritage. As usual, we who style ourselves as moderns have much to learn from our long-gone colleagues.

## Glossary

*dam* (دم), Persian for breath (not to be confused with the Arabic word for blood, which is also *dam*). Used somewhat interchangeably with the Arabic term *nafas*

dhikr (ذكر), Sufi practice dedicated to the remembrance of God, can be performed individually or collectively, silently or vocally

*haḍra* (حضرة), literally 'presence', but a gathering for the purpose of *dhikr*

*`ilm* (علم), Arabic/Persian for 'science', but more generally 'knowledge'

*ma`arifa(t)* (معرفت), Arabic and Persian term for more personal, or sometimes mystical, forms of knowledge

*masnavi* (مثنوی), poem written using rhyming couplets (from Arabic, '*mathnawi*'). Most famous example is the mystical and didactic poem written in Persian during the fourteenth century by Mawlana Jalal al-Din 'Rumi'

*nafās* (نفاس), see *dam*

*riyāḍa/riyāzat* (رياضة), Arabic and Persian term for spiritual practice

*samā`* (سماع), literally 'audition', the ceremony in which Sufi practitioners of certain orders (such as the Mevlevis) use music as part of a *dhikr* practice

*siḥr* (سحر), Arabic/Persian term usually used to mean magic or sorcery

*ta'mal (تأمل),* Arabic for meditation

*Tariqa* (طريقة), literally 'path', but usually used to refer to a Sufi order

*wird (ورد),* daily litany that a Sufi practitioner repeats, similar to a mantra

*zikr*, see *dhikr.*

## Notes

1 Adapted from the translation provided by Nath and Gwaliari 1981: 99, para. 30. The original text reads '*an-keh bidid in sar azu bar nakonad / va an-keh nadid in hameh bavar nakonad*'.
2 A particularly beneficial – and quite accessible – resource is David Gordon White's chapter on Muslim engagement with the *Yogasūtra*, specifically his analysis of the differences between the 'standard' Sanskrit recensions of Patañjali's text that scholars work with today, and the versions that al-Biruni and Abu'l Fazl apparently worked with (White 2012).
3 This translation will be published in D'Silva and Ernst forthcoming.
4 For a detailed review of the translation history of the *Amrtakunda*, see Ernst 2016: 186–228.
5 The *Baḥr al-ḥayāt* is also the oldest extant source for illustrations depicting yogis in various postures. See more examples of Sufis' interactions with yogis as seen in Mughal artwork in Diamond 2013. A groundbreaking study that uses art, architecture and material culture as a means of analysing exchange between Muslims and Hindus during the Delhi Sultanate period is Flood 2009.
6 There are several key editions and translations of the *A'in-i Akbari*. See Gladwin (1777), Abu'l Fazl (1869); Abu'l Fazl (1978). Additionally, Wheeler Thackston translated both volumes of the *Akbarnama* (2015 and 2016, respectively).
7 For several examples of these tales, see Digby 2000.
8 See the following for a representative sampling: Svami 1987; Visaarada 1967; Muktibodhananda 1984.
9 After Kugle's translation, as found in Kugle 2007: 30.
10 For example, the Naqshbandi *tariqa* has a variety of these materials, including translations and audio files with different types of *dhikr*. www.naqshbandi.org. Accessed 31 December 2019.
11 Jain provides an excellent analysis of this issue, distilling the perspectives into two schools of thought, the 'Christian yogaphobic position' and the 'Hindu origins position' (Jain 2014: 131).
12 For a representative sample of reactions, see the following articles: 11 June 2015: 'Darul-Ulum says yoga day is alright because of similarities to namaz': www.indiatoday.in/india/story/darul-uloom-deoband-okay-with-yoga-world-yoga-day-namaz-839259-2015-06-11; 11 June 2015: 'Darul-Ulum says yoga as exercise is acceptable': www.hindustantimes.com/india/darul-uloom-deoband-says-ready-to-accept-yoga-as-an-exercise/story-4VAzxE53ZdD2SIgiS7RptL.html; 19 May 2016, 'Darul-Ulum says that chanting "Om" is not allowed for Muslims, reaffirms that yoga as exercise is permitted': www.asianage.com/india/deoband-fatwa-chanting-om-809. All accessed 31 December 2019.
13 For an example of cutting-edge scholarship that sets new standards for future scholars working on philosophical and theological debates taking place across Sanskrit, Arabic and Persian texts from the Mughal period, see Nair 2020. Nair analyses the translation of the *Laghu-Yoga-Vāsiṣṭha* from Sanskrit into Persian under the sponsorship of future Mughal ruler Jahangir (d. 1627 CE), known in Persian as the Jūg Bāsisht.

## Bibliography


Abu'l Fazl ibn Mubarak ibn 'Allami 1869. *A'īn-i akbari*, ed. H. Blochmann. Calcutta: Baptist Mission Press.

Abu'l Fazl ibn Mubarak ibn 'Allami 1978. *The A'in-i Akbari (Volume III)*, trans H. Jarrett, ed. J. Sarkar. New Delhi: Oriental Books Reprint Corporation.

Abu'l Fazl ibn Mubarak ibn 'Allami 2015. *The Akbarnama* (Vol. 1), trans Wheeler Thackston. Cambridge: Harvard University Press.

Abu'l Fazl ibn Mubarak ibn 'Allami 2016. *The Akbarnama* (Vol. 2), trans Wheeler Thackston. Cambridge: Harvard University Press.

Alam, M. 2004. *The Languages of Political Islam: India 1200-180*. Chicago: University of Chicago Press.

Amuli, S. 1961. *Nafa'is al-funun wa `ara'is al-`ayun. Three volumes.* Tehran: Intitharat Islamiyya.

Arraj, W. J. 1988. 'The Svaddandatantrum: History and Scripture of a Śaiva Scripture', doctoral thesis, University of Chicago.

Ibn Battuta 1893–1922. *Voyages de 'Ibn Batoutah*, trans C. Defrémery and D. Sanguinetti. Paris: Imprimerie nationale.

Behl, A. and Doniger, W. 2012. *Love's Subtle Magic: An India Islamic Literary Tradition, 1379–1545*. Oxford: Oxford University Press.

Bouillier, V. 2018. 'Aurangzeb and the Nath Yogis', *Journal of the Royal Asiatic Society* 28(3): 525–535.

Corbett, R. 2017. 'Dhikr: Remembering the Divine', in Curtis, E. (ed), *The Practice of Islam in America: An Introduction*, 36–59. New York: New York University Press.
D'Silva, P. 2018. 'The Science of the Breath in Persianate India'. Doctoral thesis. Chapel Hill: University of North Carolina at Chapel Hill.
D'Silva, P. and Ernst, C. Forthcoming, *Breathtaking Insights: Indian and Sufi Breath Practices from the Kāmarūpančāšikā to Hazrat Inayat Khan*. Richmond, Virginia: Suluk Press.
Diamond, D. 2013. *Yoga: The Art of Transformation*. Washington, DC: Smithsonian.
Digby, S. 2000. *Wonder Tales of South Asia: Translated from Hindi, Urdu, Nepali and Persian*. Jersey: Orient Monographs.
*The Economist*. 2014. 'The Perils of Yoga in Iran', May 17, p. 14.
Ernst, C. n.d. 'Enigmas of Translation in the Kamaru Panchashika, An Early Persian Work on Yoga', unpublished paper.
Ernst, C. 2016. *Refractions of Islam in India: Situating Sufism and Yoga*. Los Angeles: Sage.
Flood, F. 2009. *Objects of Translation: Material Culture and Medieval Hindu-Muslim Encounter*. Princeton: Princeton University Press.
Gladwin, F. 1886 [1777]. *Ayeen Akbery: Or, The Institutes of the Emperor Akber. Translated from the Original Persian*. Calcutta: William Mackay.
Hatley, S. 2007. 'Mapping the Esoteric Body in the Islamic Yoga of Bengal', *History of Religions* 46(4): 351–368.
Husain, Y. 2003. '*Haud al-Hayat*: The Arabic Version of *Amratkund*', in *On Becoming an Indian Muslim: French Essays on Aspects of Syncretism*, trans M. Waseem. Delhi: Oxford University Press.
Ibn Khaldun. 1967. *The Muqaddimah: An Introduction to History*, trans F. Rosenthal, ed N. Dawood, Princeton: Princeton University Press.
Ibn Khaldun 2013. *Muqadimat ibn Khaldun, kitab al-'abr wa diwan al-mubtada wa'l khabr fi ayyam al-'arab wa'l'ajam wa-l-barbar wa min aasirihim man dhuuwi al-sultan al-akbar*, ed. Sa'id Mahmud 'Aqil. Beirut: Dar al-Jil.
Jain, A. 2014. *Selling Yoga: From Counterculture to Pop Culture*. Oxford: Oxford University Press.
Jalaluddin, U. 2018. *Ayesha at Last*. New York: Harper Avenue.
*Kāmarū Pančāšikā Abridgment, Browne Recension*, Cambridge University Library V. 21, Cambridge. Ff. 59a–66b.
*Kāmarū Pančāšikā Abridgment, Karachi Recension*. National Museum MS-1957.1060/18, Karachi. Ff. 1a–4a.
Kinra, R. 2009. 'Infantilizing Baba Dara: The Cultural Memory of Dara Shekuh and the Mughal Public Sphere', *Journal of Persianate Studies* 2: 165–193.
Kozah, M. 2016. *The Birth of Indology as an Islamic Science: Al-Biruni's Treatise on Yoga Psychology*. Leiden: Brill.
Kugle, S. 2007. *Sufis and Saints' Bodies: Mysticism, Corporeality, and Sacred Power in Islam*. Chapel Hill: University of North Carolina Press.
Laine, J. and Laine, J. Forthcoming. 'Religion/Islam/Hinduism/Sufism/Yoga', in Wheeler B. and Morganstein F. I. (eds), *Words of Experience*. Sheffield and Bristol: Equinox.
Mallinson, J. n.d. 'Yogic Identities: Traditions and Transformations,' *National Museum of Asian Art*, viewed 19 January 2020. https://asia.si.edu/essays/yogic-identities/.
Masuzawa, T. 2005. *The Invention of World Religions: Or, How European Universalism was Preserved in the Language of Pluralism*. Chicago: University of Chicago Press.
Mirza, M. (ed) 1950. *Nuh Sipihr*. Calcutta: Oxford University Press.
Mirza, Misbahuddin. 2017. 'Does Islam Allow Yoga?' Islamic Horizons, August/September: 34–36.
Moin, A. 2014. *The Millennial Sovereign: Sacred Kingship and Sainthood in Islam*. New York: Columbia University Press.
Muktibodhananda, Swami. 1984. *Swara Yoga: The Tantric Science of Brain Breathing*. Bihar: Yoga Publications Trust.
Nair, S. 2020. *Translating Wisdom: Hindu-Muslim Intellectual Interactions in Early Modern South Asia*. Berkeley: University of California Press.
Nath, R. and Gwaliari, F. 1981. *India as Seen by Amir Khusraw*. Jaipur: Historical Research Documentation Programme.
Nongbri, B. 2013. *Before Religion: A History of a Modern Concept*. New Haven: Yale University Press.
Parikh, R. 2015. 'Yoga Under the Mughals: From Practice to Paintings', *South Asian Studies* 31(2): 215–236.
Pauwels, H. and Bachrach, E. 2018. 'Aurangzeb as Iconoclast? Vaishnava Accounts of the Krishna images' Exodus from Braj', *Journal of the Royal Asiatic Society* 28(3): 485–508.
Rai, R. (trans) 1980. *Śivasvarodaya, text with English Translation*. Tantra Granthamala No. 1, Prachya Prakashan.

Ramacharaka, Y. 1905. *The Hindu-yogi Science of Breath: A Complete Manual of the Oriental Breathing Philosophy of Physical, Mental, Psychic and Spiritual Development*. Chicago: Yogi Publication Society.

Sakaki, K. 2005. 'Yogico-tantric traditions in the *Hawd al-Hayat'*, *Minamiajiakenkyu*, Issue 17, 135–156.

Simon, S. 1975. ''Abd al-Quddus Gangohi (1456–1537 AD): The Personality and Attitudes of a Medieval Indian Sufi', in Nizami, K. A. (ed), *Medieval India – a Miscellany*. Bombay: Asia Printing House.

Svami, Rohini-kumara, 1987. *Śivasvarodaya: The Ancient Yoga Science of Bio-pneumatics*. Berkeley, CA: Varnashram Community Inc.

Truschke, A. 2016. *Culture of Encounter: Sanskrit at the Mughal Court*. New York: Columbia University Press.

Truschke, A. 2017. *Aurangzeb: The Life and Legacy of India's Most Controversial King*. Stanford: Stanford University Press.

Von Kremer, A. 1873. *Culturgeschichliche Streifzuge auf dem Debiebte des Islams*. Leipzig: F. A. Brockhaus.

Von Kremer, A. 1976 [1904]. *Contributions to the History of Islamic Civilization*, trans S. Khuda Bakhsh. Leipzig: Accurate Printers.

Visaarada, V. 1967. *Swara Chintamani – Divination by the Breath*. Madras: Kannan Publications.

White, D. 2012. 'Introduction', in *Yoga in Practice*, 1–23. Princeton: Princeton University Press.

White, D. 2019. *The Yoga Sutra of Patanjali: A Biography*. Princeton: Princeton University Press.

# 16

# SIKHI(SM)

## Yoga and meditation

*Balbinder Singh Bhogal*

### Introduction[1]

He Himself is the yogi (*aape jogii*) and the way (*jugati*) throughout the ages.
He Himself is the fearless, absorbed in meditation (*taarii laahaa*).

(*GGS 699 Jaitasarii M4*)

Yoga (*jog*) and meditation (*dhiaan*) abound in the Guru Granth Sahib (hereafter GGS).[2] From the above verse one might think that if God, the True-Guru,[3] is said to be *the* true yogi and 'the way' of yoga itself, then Sikhs would believe in and practise yoga (as commonly understood). But this is not the case.[4] Understanding why this is so is crucial to gain insight into *gur-sikhii* – the way of un/learning guided by the Guru, that Sikhi(sm) fosters.[5]

### Medieval background: Indian renaissance and Gur-Sikh Enlightenment

The GGS includes ideas and terms of yoga (*jog*) and meditation (*dhiaan*) that are found in ancient and medieval soteriological literature. It is, however, important to read these in the wider context of the Sikh Gurus' critique of the Vedas, shastras and smritis, and the ideals of sacrifice, renunciation, asceticism and meditation. Similarly, the GGS's comparative and critically inclusive verses also engage Upanishadic insights, Samkhyan assumptions, Puranic notions of devotion, tantric esotericism and various yoga teachings and practices, reinterpreting *karma*- and *jnana- yogas* in its particular *bhakti/bhagati-jog* as the way of the Name (*naam-maarag*). However, the Sikh Gurus' more immediate context involved direct engagements with the Indian renaissance composed of the ubiquitous and influential Nath Yogis (or Kanphata/Hatha Yogis), but also Buddhist Siddhas, Buddhist and Hindu Tantrikas, Shaiva and Vaishnava Sahajiyas – engaging with their key notions of guru, word (*sabda/shabad*), nirvana (*nirbaan*), impermanence (*anityaa/velaa, calanaa, aavan-jaan*), essencelessness (*shuunyataa/sunn*) and effortlessness (*sahaja/sahaj*), not to mention their shared esoteric vocabulary (*turiiyaa/chauta-pad, sunn-samaadh, dasam-duaar, siv-sakati*). Through this discursive engagement, the GGS questions the exclusive and metaphysical conception of 'God' as well as yoga's ascetic elitism, and thereby rejects the necessity for 'divine' languages and 'esoteric' vocabularies. It elucidates its way via multiple 'vernaculars' taken from a composite people diverse in language, tradition, caste, class, ethnicity and geography. The GGS accepted select songs of non-Sikh 'saints' (*sants/bhagats*) as part of its own pluriversal[6] revelations, marking out the comparative uniqueness of its universally resonant voice.

The GGS speaks of 'a way beyond ways', one that is beyond the techniques, rituals and practices that stabilise the ego. It is inclusive of different paths and expressions, but not without a critique of those paths. To be able to criticise and not dismiss – where the difference of the other is not a challenge to one's own tradition, but a natural expression of life's diversity – and thus to find a resonant pluriversal truth across traditions, is the unique contribution of the Sikh Gurus. This new way of un/learning (de- and reconditioning) brought mantric secrets of the ascetics into the households of the everyday person: Upanishadic and yogic transcendentalism became humanised by the devotee's (*bhagat's*) everyday existentialism; anti-Brahmanic metaphors of relationships between master and student, parent and child, lovers, and friends became the new vocabulary of a soteriological *and* 'worldly' life. Direct communion with the numinous was to be found right there in one's phenomenal existence, via the Guru's guidance.

The affective language of the heart became a new *lingua franca* of expressing the highest conceptual truth: 'knowing' (*jnana*) was thereby recontextualised by 'longing' (*viraha/vijog*, *bhuukh*) for the divine/Name. Communal forms of soteriological practice arose, singing the praises of the divine/Name. Praise itself became the way. This spread of *bhakti* saw the rise of a new religiosity centred around the (only true) universal soteriological forces: the True-Guru, His/his Word and God's Name. However, early modern *bhakti* was largely framed within an apolitical semi-renunciation of the world. Although it had the potential to be revolutionary, it rarely challenged the hierarchy of the prevailing social order. Though it criticised the hypocrisy and ignorance of priestly hierarchies, it rarely instigated political revolution.

Unlike other *bhakti* movements, then, the Sikh Gurus used their notion of direct communion with the numinous in the everyday to launch a socio-political movement, thus forming the Gur-Sikh Enlightenment. This resulted in an epistemic shift from the personal and dualistic to the non-dual and collective – as evidenced by the recontextualisation of scripture within the Guru, mantra within the Word, self-effort (technique) within Other-power (grace), culminating in the democratisation of the Guru (at Baisakhi) into the people's will (*panj piaare*, *khaalsaa*). The Sikh Gurus employ terms, concepts and ideas from multiple traditions to express their own distinct, compound, dialogical and nuanced 'cross-tradition-less tradition'. *Gur-sikhii* involves a reframed and qualified affirmation, one that integrates the vocabulary of opposed traditions through their redefinition, such that 'Sikh *jog*' is simultaneously a critique of all forms of yoga, while affirming a transformed understanding of it.

## Guru Granth Sahib's critique of yoga and meditation

The Gur-Sikh tradition maintains two seats of authority, reflecting two forms of sovereignty: *aasan* and *takhat*. It is important not to confuse Sikh *aasan* with the Upanishads' meditational *āsana*, *haṭhayoga*'s complex *āsana*s, or modern yoga's postural *āsanas*. First, *aasan* (seat, posture) represents a private authority and sovereignty over the ego. *Aasan* elicits a transcendental experience of inner equipoise, illumination and love – it is a form of inner spirituality. In the mastery of the mind the Sikh Gurus repose in the seat (*aasan*) of 'effortless absorption' (*sahaji dhiaan*).[7] Second, *takhat* (throne) represents a seat of authority and sovereignty that chooses governance of the public sphere over tyranny. The Gur-Sikh 'true king' is therefore also a '*jogii*' or saint who sits on the throne of truth, administrating true justice.[8] By occupying both forms of yogic and regal authority, the gurus' invented a new middle way, calling it *raaj-jog*, that was simultaneously private and political.[9] Only those of such a double orientation were considered legitimate administrators of justice.[10] Gur-Sikh *raaj-jog* is a singular notion that contains within it a diversity of different types of union (spanning ascetic-yogic, householder-bhaktic and royal formularies). The two seats together form the Gur-Sikh way of love *as* justice (*raaj-jog*), which updates the Buddhist 'middle way' (*majjhima-patipadaa*). Just as the Buddha found the middle way between kingly indulgence and ascetic denial, so too did the Sikh Gurus solicit the spiritual (*udaas*) within the temporal (*grihast*). The integration of both seats and forms of sovereignty marks Gur-Sikh *jog* as unique, expressing no love without justice, no spiritual transcendence without social responsibility, no saint (*sant*) without soldier (*sipaahi*) and no rule without equality.

Uberoi (1996) argued that the separated and independent domains of the state (*rajyas/kashatriya*), civil society (*grihast/brahmana*) and religion (*sannayas/shramana*) expressed by medieval Hindu and Islamic paradigms (*raajaa/brahman/sannyaasii; sultan/ulemaa/suufii*), were collapsed within and by the Gur-Sikh tradition. This allowed the Guru and Gurmukh to operate in all three seamlessly. Not dividing off the domains into opposed forms of life within *gur-sikhii* represented for Uberoi the first Indian non-dual modernity. Expressed architecturally, the mystical seat (*aasan*) evolved into the Harmandir Sahib (popularly known as the 'Golden Temple'), which brought asceticism (*jogii, udaasii*) into family life (*bhogii, girasat*), forming part of the Indic renaissance of the Siddhas, Sufis, Sahajiyas, Sants and Bhaktas.[11] The latter temporal seat (*takhat*) was formed as the political centre in the building of the Akaal Takhat ('throne of the timeless'). It brings the new ascetic-householder (*jogii-bhogii*) ideal into the realm of governance (*raaj*) and justice (*niaau*) that expresses Gur-Sikh Enlightenment of *raaj-jog*.[12] The Guru/Gurmukh/Khalsa occupies both spaces of loving-saint and just-king, juxtaposing forest, house and battlefield with *ashram, mandir* and *mahal*, making *raaj-jog* a political mysticism rarely developed elsewhere. That is to say, the Sikh tradition proposes nothing short of a double enlightenment: 'spiritual/mystical' and 'social/political' as an 'enlivenment'.[13] This is precisely what allows the inclusive (non-converting) critique of GGS's ideal of what makes a 'true' yogi, qazi and brahmin.[14]

Having considered the proper ascetic-familial, socio-political and religio-political frames of Guru Nanak's vision we are now positioned to ask, of what does the GGS's critique of yoga and meditation consist?

## *Aasan* (spiritual yoga)

First, it is important to recognise that 'critique' (*vicaar, buuj*) in the GGS is not issued from a centre that could be formulated, thus allowing comparisons to a fixed notion of truth. There is nothing fixed at the 'centre' of *gur-sikhii*, not Self (*aatman*), not No-Self (*anaatman*), not God alone nor some impersonal absolute. This is because all centres are metaphysical foils – if not projections of the ego (false centre). The Gur-Sikh 'source' (*ikk-oankaar*), which is 'everywhere everything', is an inexplicable mystery and wonder (*vismaad*) defined only by fungible terms: viz., True One, God, Guru, Word and Name. The GGS's inclusion of Abrahamic and Indic personal deities (Allah, Khuda, Rahim; Hari, Shiva, Devi), and impersonal absolutes (*nirbaan, purush, siv-sakati*) to name *Ikk-Oankaar*, is both affirmative (in not desiring conversion respecting diversity) but also analytical (in requiring transformation to a pluriversal vision).

The Gur-Sikh critique of *yoga* occurs within the broader ideas outlined above. For example:

> That yogi (*jogii*) does not know the way.
> Understand that his heart is filled with greed, attachment, delusion and egotism.
> *(GGS 685 Dhanaasarii M9)*

Here the yogi is criticized for turning yoga into an empty ritual, the by-product of a systematisation of practice over truthful living. The Gur-Sikh way (of the Name and Guru's Word) cannot be captured without the danger of objectification (i.e. the reduction to a thing or technique); *mantras* can be fixed, but not the Word; the Word can include yoga, but yoga is outstripped by the Word. The true yogi is one who looks upon 'gold and iron', 'pleasure and pain' alike,[15] such that the way of the Name (*naam-maarag*) displaces the need for particular techniques (*mantar-jap*), because it is inseparable from an existential praxis of being true (*saciaaraa, sac-kamai*). The Word (*shabad*) is different to itself as it is revealed through an ongoing quotidian encounter where 'Truth' (*sacahu*) is constantly surpassed by the necessity of truthful living (*sacu aacaaru*).[16]

As the following passages show, *naam-maarag* and the practice of the Guru's Word (*gur-shabad kamai*) are not tied to a mantra, ritual or technique delimited by caste hierarchy:

> The root mantra is spiritual wisdom (*giaanu*) for everyone.
> Anyone, from any class (*cahu varanaa*), may chant the Name.
> Whoever chants it, is emancipated ...
> The Name is the panacea, the remedy to cure all ills.
> It cannot be obtained by any religious rituals (*dharami*).
> O Nanak, he alone obtains it, whose karma is so pre-ordained.
> *(GGS 274 Gaurii Sukhamanii M5)*

> Without the Name, all actions are futile, like the magician who deceives through illusions.
> *(GGS 1343 Prabhaatii M1)*

The new Gur-Sikh frame of *naam-maarag* – involving inner recollection (*simaran*) and outer service (*sevaa*) where truthful living requires an orientation towards justice (*niaau*) – formulates an equitable political yoga. I take this to represent a double sovereignty (of self-realisation and social justice) that displaces and reinterprets earlier forms of power, whether martial, Brahmanical or ascetic. As such, the Sikh Gurus emancipated restricted notions of the personal divine or the impersonal absolute.[17] An important strategy used by the Sikh Gurus in their critique is the trope of 'dis-emplotment': to dislodge what each tradition takes as universal and locate it within the Gur-Sikh comparative context of the pluriversal Guru, Word and Name, but without negating the power or relevance of the 'dis-emplotted' term. Those diverse traditional terms are kept but re-employed to express a pluriversal reality of a wholly inclusive existential praxis. The critique of yoga occurs in this manner, for example:

> The Word is yoga, the Word is gnosis [for the yogi]; the Word is Vedas for the brahmin.
> The Word is bravery for the kshatriya; the Word is service to others for the shudra.
> For one who discerns this secret: the Word for all is the One Word (*eka-shabadan*).
> *(GGS 1353 Sahasakritii M1)*

The dis-emplotment and re-emplotment of 'yoga' and 'meditation' follow this major trope of the GGS: diversity is sacred when tied to the Word (*shabad*). 'Yoga', 'Wisdom', 'Vedas', etc., are taken out of the plot in which they claim universal relevance, and replaced within Guru Nanak's pluriversal (cross-traditional, multi-caste, comparative) vision of many namings. Guru-Shabad and Naam work as the inexpressible force behind everything, and remind all that the universal can only be approached through the inclusion of every tradition's imaginations. Guru Nanak is, therefore, not a peddler of specific techniques or mantras but the revealer of an unforeseen pluriversal way that engages key ideas of other paths:

> Meditation of meditators? – good is the meditation on the Name of Hari, Hari.
> Renunciation of renouncers? – good is the renunciation of lust, anger and greed.
> Begging of beggars? – good is the begging for the Lord's praise gained from the Guru.
> *(GGS 1018 Maaruu M5)*

A person may initially practise meditation to overcome greed, anger and lust, however with the likely deferral of the goal the practice may become the goal itself, with the meditator not necessarily cognizant of such a shift having taken place. The treachery of techniques is clear: they replace the transformation that they promised to become the focus themselves. In the GGS all practices – here meditation, renunciation and begging – are reframed, to place the focus on the ego (*haumai*), to unsettle what the ego has always assumed to be efficacious and true.

The GGS as a whole may be understood as a disputation against the efficacy of human techniques (shrines, clothes, rituals, *mantras*, songs, etc.) summed up as '100,000 clevernesses' humans may devise (GGS 1 *Japu* M1). The transformation or the ego-mind-state comes first, not the technique, method or practice. The gurus simply bring us back to the hard work of the real task: disarming and dismantling the common ego – the one that (too easily) makes techniques a part of its progressive arsenal:

> The Digambara may take off his clothes and be naked.
> What yoga (*jogu*) does he practice by having matted and tangled hair?
> If the heart-mind is not pure, [forget] the Tenth Gate (*dasavai duaara*)!
> The fool wanders and wanders, entering the cycle of reincarnation again and again.
> (*GGS 1169 Basant M3*)

How, then, is one to proceed without techniques? Is truth 'a pathless land' (as Krishnamurti claimed)? If (modern) yoga's goal is health of the physical body, no one would argue against its efficacy. But re-emplotted within the context of subjective awakening and political freedom, can physical yoga avoid being humbled, like every other technique or expedient? This is the challenge of the Sikh Gurus' repeated question: what is efficacious?[18] Given that 'God (*hari*) cannot be found by any technique (*upaai*)',[19] without the transformation of the heart-mind (eradicating lust, anger, greed, delusion and pride), what use is any private technique, physical or mental? The devolution of traditions to mere technical specialisms (of vocabulary and ritual) was precisely what the gurus were reformulating into a new synthesis of the Guru's quotidian and existential Word-*praxis*.

## True yoga as *sahaj-jog*[20]

The notion of true yoga and its practitioner, the true yogi, result from the dis-emplotment found within the GGS. A key term used in the GGS is *sahaj*, meaning 'natural, easy; spontaneous; effortless; beatific', and is understood as innate. It relates to a deep yearning of what the body remembers. This makes *sahaj* an 'originary' condition prior to yoga. *Sahaj* as *simaran* – a form of non-egoic 'remembrance' – is beautifully expressed by Namdev: a boy flies a kite while talking to his friends, a girl carries a pitcher laughing with her friends, a mother remembers her child in the cradle whether she works in the kitchen or the field, just as the cow never forgets her calf in a faraway field.[21] Though these symbolise the uneducated, untrained *remembering* of natural beings, for Namdev they become perfect exemplars recalling the Name, valued over the highly trained Siddhas and Nath Yogis and their esoteric knowledge, complex techniques and specialised practices. Unlike the elitism of the yogis, Namdev does not exclude anyone. *Simaran* is not therefore a technical skill but a form of awareness expressed in everyday praxis, open to all to engage spontaneously and effortlessly, almost without thinking. This is *sahaj-jog*, a pluriversal praxis not an idiosyncratic device.

A hymn by Guru Nanak starts with a *kundalini/tantric* trope of the inverted lotus, and the tenth esoteric gate (beyond the nine bodily apertures) from which trickles the ambrosial nectar, but switches quickly to what is really required: not ascetic meditation, not singing, not mantras, not rituals, etc., but the surrender of one's own mind, the 'naughting' of oneself, in order to return home inheriting an infinitely expanded and transformed non-dual vision.[22] *Sahaj* points towards a philosophy of the event of one's existential and moment-by-moment life: 'Whatever the Lord does, look upon that as good; thus, will you obtain the treasure of *sahaj-jog*'.[23] Thus, the mundane world as Word is always already a teaching: the space–time continuum is soteric, hence 'one who understands *hukam* (God's Will, Order, Command, or the inscription of the Word in creation) is called a yogi'.[24] And then 'whatever they speak is wisdom (*giaan*) / whatever they hear is the Name / whatever they see is meditation (*dhiaan*)', they sleep in *sahaj*, awake in *sahaj*.[25] If the yogis (*jogiiaa*), wandering ascetics (*jangama*), renouncers (*sanniaasii*), as well as the 'saints' (*saadhus*) and the virtuous (*gunii*), have tried everything and failed in calming and mastering anger, hatred, desire, then the Sikh Gurus are unlikely to offer yet more techniques.[26] Not only have they failed, they have also wasted their lives, erred and gone astray, leaving behind an inflated sense of egotism (*ahankaar*) and arrogance (*garab*).[27] Guru Nanak implores ascetics and householders to practise true yoga (*saac-jog*), viz., 'subdue the five thieves, and hold your consciousness in its place' and 'discern the Word of the Guru by losing your ego-mind'.[28] Thus, all the Sikh Gurus remain sceptical of any and all answers the ego-mind proffers: 'He alone is a devotee, whom the Lord has united with Himself. Abandoning all devices (*ukati*) and contrivances (*upaavaa*), I have sought the (only real) Renunciate's [God's] Sanctuary.'[29]

Guru Nanak presents an axiomatic sequence: because you do not know, listen (*suniai*); having heard, consider and accept (*maniai*). If you accept, then act, or serve (*sevaa*) with loving devotion (*bhaau*).[30] Techniques and their mastery fool one into believing one's knowledge is superior and unknown by others. But life will not be mastered; rather, only the ego can be humbled. In short, 'by listening one effortlessly enters meditation' (*suniai laagai sahaji dhiaanu*).[31] 'Hearing the Name' (*naai suniai*), only then are 'supernatural powers', 'wealth', 'contentment', etc., received.[32] There is a crucial reversal going on here. It is not that there are techniques so that you can hear the Name, but that one can hear the Name in all techniques, making no one technique better than another; the Name is yoga, but yoga is not the (way to the) Name.

## *Takhat* (political yoga): *raaj-jog*

Guru Arjan sings

> I came to the Guru to learn the way of yoga. The True-Guru has revealed it to me through the Word ... I have brought the five disciples ... under my control ... That place where there is no fear, becomes my seated posture (*aasan*).[33]

And that *aasan* becomes the foundation of political justice:

> One who keeps Naam in his heart attains the immoveable seat (*aasan*).
> One who keeps Naam in his heart is seated on the throne (*takhat*).
> One who keeps Naam in his heart is the true king (*saah*).
>
> *(GGS 1156 Bhairau M5)*

The subjective sovereignty of the mystic state is the true *aasan*, but it is only half the story. The other half is the objective sovereignty of the true king who sits on the true throne (*takhat*):

> It is very difficult to serve the True-Guru: Give your head; lose yourself.
> One who dies through the Word shall never die again; his service is totally approved.
>
> *(GGS 649 Sorathi M3)*

Guru Amar Das captures in four words the double sovereignty of *raaj-jog*[34] in its most pared down form: '*siru diijai aapu gavaai*' – not only the saint's sacrifice of the self (spiritual death of ego-mind), but also of the soldier's head (political death of body). It is this double sacrifice that precludes *sahaj* from being reduced to subjective relativism. In the Gur-Sikh notion of double sovereignty *raaj-jog* does not allow just anyone to be a king – it has to be a saint, or someone that has killed the ego-mind through the Word. Such a one enters not only private realms of bliss but also public realms of justice that *takhat* symbolises:

> The true One's law (*hukam*) is effective everywhere; the Gurmukh merges in its truth.
> He Himself is true, true is His throne (*takhat*), seated, He administers true justice (*niaau*).
> The truest of the true pervades everywhere; the Gurmukh sees the unseen.
>
> *(GGS 949 Raamakalii M3)*

Not only does God make creation His throne,[35] he also establishes that *takhat* within each body (*kaaiaa*).[36] Those 'who can discern the Word' (objectively and subjectively), then, also 'sit upon His throne',[37] for 'The true Lord fashioned the earth for the sake of the Gurmukhs'. Consequently, and without desire or effort, they obtain the eight supernatural powers (*asata siddhii*) and 'all wisdom' (*sabhi buddhii*), knowing fully both worldliness (*paravirati*) and renunciation (*naravirati*).[38] Guru Arjan adds: 'Your consciousness becomes steady and firm (when) forest (*ban*) and household (*grih*) are seen as the same.' The renouncer and the householder are no longer polarised but reframed, such that *raaj-jog* can be practised 'being in the world but not of the world' (*loga alogii*).[39]

## Splitting *raaj-jog* in the conversion to western modernity

In the incalculably violent conversion to Euro–American (globalatinised Christian) modernity, two key historical markers instigated the splitting of *gur-sikhii*'s *raaj* from *jog* (Derrida 2001; 2002; Van der Veer 1996). The first was the colonial encounter with the British, and the second was the invention of India and Pakistan as (modern) 'nations' through the tragedy and trauma of Partition. After two Anglo–Sikh wars, the British annexed the Panjab and de-militarised the Sikh kingdom of Maharaja Ranjit Singh in 1849. Under this colonial subjugation the Gur-Sikh middle way was broken, eventually splintering into opposing Sikh revival and reform movements. Given the run-up to independence and the birth of India as a modern nation state in 1947, the constitutional separation of church and state effectively 'religionised' *sant/jog* in the formation of 'Sikhism' and 'secularised' *sipaahii/raaj* into political movements (Mandair 2013). The secular frame of modernity both rests upon and demands such a polarised duality (i.e. secular vs religious). Furthermore, given the transformative power of nineteenth-century European technologies in India (census, cartography, print, telegraph, railways, roads and canals), various forms of 'Sikh yoga', whether Thind's mental focus or 3HO's physical focus (see below), sought similarly modern techniques. In this shift from premodern *raag-jog* to the technique-isation of the twentieth century, Sikh groups' privatised modes of 'religious' practice became the only form compatible with colonial modernity's political economy; such movements flourished because they could pass unnoticed as apolitical. The 1960s counter-culture furthered this privatisation of religious practice, resulting in the widespread capitalisation and commodification of selling spirituality and yoga: God wore the collar of the dollar whether in the gym or the ashram (Carrette and King 2005; Jain 2015).[40] With Gur-Sikh *raaj-jog*'s sovereignty disarmed, Sikh yoga became malleable to the global market. The capitalist marketplace can countenance spiritualities, and even make their 'spiritual materialism' profitable, but only where stripped of their collective voice of resistance (Trungpa 1987).

Yet, Sikhs from the beginning have understood that 'power concedes nothing without a demand',[41] as evidenced by a long history of resistance movements speaking truth to power (Bhogal 2010; 2011). However, none of these movements are classed under the category of 'Sikh yoga', given the frame imposed by colonial modernity, wherein yoga was to be identified only with *aasan* and *sant*, and not with *takhat* and *sipaahii*. Clearly, the opposite is also true: if *jog* was reduced to 'religion', then *raaj* was similarly reduced to 'politics'. The split augured by modernity led to political movements with no *jog* or *sant* to speak of.[42] Given the teachings of the GGS and the fact that the first and last Sikh Gurus are popularly known as 'Nanak *Shaah-Fakiir*' and 'Guru Gobind Singh *Baadshaah-Dervish*', revealing the inseparability of *raaj-jog*, it is therefore problematic to countenance such contemporary Sikh yoga movements, along with political movements lacking *sant/jog*, as legitimate. Within the contemporary scene all the various 'Sikh yoga' movements reflect such a neutering of Gur-Sikh anti-caste political spirituality into purely subjective forms or privatised practice.

## Contemporary scene: Sikh yoga and meditation movements

We have already noted *gur-sikhii's* critique of yoga and meditation, as well as the gurus' acerbic dismissal of religious spectacle ('outward show').[43] Guru Nanak's oddly familiar critique of the paraphernalia of yogic cults is therefore equally as applicable today as it was five centuries ago.[44] Indeed, the GGS is perhaps the only comprehensive and sustained Indic critique of *jog*, and as such presents a clear lacuna in western scholarship in general and yoga studies in particular. Even recent works charting the history of yoga's invented mental and physical modern forms (from Vivekananda's mid-1890s '*raja yoga*' to the contemporary transnational anglophone 'Hatha Yoga') neglect the GGS.[45] This is partly understandable as *gur-sikhii* and yoga (i.e. not *jog*) are rarely associated by Sikhs. The association is limited to those movements that acquiesced to modernity's bifurcating forces. 'Sikh yoga' is a modern phenomenon that only European, American and Canadian Sikhs have partial familiarity with and Indian Sikhs find offensive and bizarre.

Often in discussions of Sikhism and yoga, two individuals are mentioned: Guru Nanak's son Sri Chand, founder of the Udaasiis (sixteenth century), and Yogi Bhajan, founder of 3HO (twentieth century) and chiefly responsible for the American conflation of 'Sikhism' and 'yoga' (Deslippe 2012; 2016). The former practised a form of ascetic 'yoga' rejected by Guru Nanak's worldly focus. The latter's yoga is inflected by the international physical culture movement as a counter-cultural New Age 'religion/dharma'. Neither could be seriously entertained as having any real relation to Gur-Sikh teachings. Were one to look for figures and movements not related to 'yoga' but to the GGS's '*raaj-jog*', then the list is indeed much longer, including (to varying degrees): Khalsa Singhs, Bandai Sikhs, Akalis, Nihangs, Nirankaris, Namdharis, Singh Sabha reformers, Babbar Akalis, Akali Dal, SGPC, Nanaksar Movement, Bhai Randhir Singh, Akhand Kirtani Jatha, and Babbar Khalsa (Bhogal 1996). None of these, given their integration of *raaj*, are seen as yogic traditions.

Given the two major orientalising discursive formations of Euro–American modernity's appropriation of Asian 'spiritual cultures', as either meditational ('Zen Mind') or postural ('Yoga Body'), the following individuals and groups can be mapped accordingly.[46] The ease of this mapping illuminates the problematic nature of contemporary yoga from the perspective of the GGS, as such apolitical forms reveal their unacknowledged conversion to modernity. Unrelated to *gur-sikhii* is the Radhasoami movement founded by Shiv Dyal Singh in 1861. I mention it because its conceptual vocabulary is largely taken from the GGS – for example, its main focus is *surat-shabd-yoga*. However, this is literally interpreted as a 'sound-current', and 'secret mantras' are used in initiations, which in turn secure a hierarchy of lesser traditions, meditative states and techniques. Their shift away from the Word back to mantra, elitism, initiation, exclusion and dualism reveals a clear divergence from the GGS, a text the tradition purports to interpret. The GGS's non-dual, horizontally inclusivist way contrasts sharply with Radhasoami's literalist, dualistic and hierarchically inclusivist path (Zapart 2020). Unlike particular turn-of-the-twentieth-century movements, such as Nand Singh's (b. 1869) Nanaksar movement (Doabia 1981; Nesbitt 1985; Singh and Barrier 1996) and Bhai Randhir Singh's (b. 1878) Akhand Kirtani Jatha (Singh 1971; Singh 1975; Singh 1983; Singh and Barrier 1996) – who evidence aspects of asceticism, celibacy, ritualism, meditation and literalist fundamentalism – their indigeneity marked them from those who migrated to Europe and the United States during the same period, such as, for example, Bhagat Singh Thind (1892–1967), whose entry into the United States moulded him to shift to a more worldly counter-cultural frame. Both of these types of movements, however, emphasised meditation.[47]

Two twentieth-century movements in the west that retain the 'Zen Mind' meditation but also develop the postural dimension of the 'Yoga Body' are Harbhajan Singh Khalsa's (Yogi Bhajan's) Healthy, Happy, Holy Organization (3HO) and Professor Surinder Singh's *Raj Academy*.[48] Both openly promote yogic techniques, using a vocabulary of *yantra, tantra, mudrā* and *mantra*, as well as actual practices including yogic postures (*āsanas*) – the exact vocabulary displaced and dismissed by the GGS.[49] Surinder Singh further summarises his teaching under the phrase '*naad-yoga*' (yoga of sound), a term also used by others.[50] An alternative yet complementary development to the religious form of 'Sikh yoga' is its alignment to the lucrative self-help, New Age spirituality and corporate mindfulness markets. For example, Davinder Singh Panesar's 'Gurmat Therapy' presents a 'consciousness based psychology', which is a 'Psycho-spiritual approach to optimising mental, emotional, physical & transpersonal health and wellness'. 'Gurmat therapeutic practices, including meditation offer immediate and effective antidotes to stress, anxiety, depression, panic attacks, OCD and other related issues.'[51] 'Gurmat therapy is a latest offering of the highly evolved human development and evidence rich systems from India and the Far East particularly Buddhism, Ayurveda, Yoga, Daoism and Zen.'[52] Under 'Gurmat Psycho-Spiritual Retreats' on the main home page (with a two-minute YouTube video linking each retreat to each of the seven chakras tied to a New Age understanding of 'kundalini yoga'), it claims, 'These highly practical and experiential retreats are designed to enable participants to understand, recognise and cultivate specific states of being, through awareness development practices and techniques… These retreats have enabled many to awaken.'[53] Whether or not this is true, is not the point. But whether this is actually *gurmat* (based on the teachings of GGS) is highly problematic to say the least.[54]

The above movements operate squarely within colonial modernity's Euro–American frame, which permeates their ethos. This frame, because of its coercive vectors of capitalist power (commodification, consumption, technique-isation, orientalism and individualism), gives such movements little choice but to invent 'traditions and techniques'. This can be seen in peculiar interpretations of specific lyrics of the GGS by certain groups like the Akhand Kirtani Jatha and contemporary Kirtan Jathas, that form particular techniques of breathing and chanting (of Waheguru) out of them. Such selective and literalist readings tend to ignore the GGS's emphasis on love and humility as existential modes of being. If the Guru, Word and Name are not particular experiences, but the ground of experience itself, then any experience may trigger that connection. The unavoidable 'arbitrariness' this presents is persistently missed by such groups and their misinterpretations. Contrary to the highly selective readings to extract robust techniques (and thus benefit from claims of authenticity and authority), no specific technique or techniques are given in the GGS. That is to say, nothing additional is required to be compassionate, kind, loving, courageous, etc., for it is a matter of application of these common attributes that we all have, not possessing one technique over others. This is why the gurus switch from the prescription of techniques to the praxis of the way. The way may range from meditation (*jog*) to singing his praise (*bhagati*), but these are still not to be made into techniques for 'without the Name, all would fail'. The inherent deconstructive and existential nature of the Name (as the nameless), Word (as unsystematisable) and Guru (as everywhere there but hidden) will not allow such a reduction to technique that modernity's individualism demands.

## Conclusion

> He is not won over by music, (esoteric) sounds or the Vedas.
> He is not won over by mindfulness (*suratii*), gnosis (*giaanii*) or yoga.
>
> (*GGS 1237 Saaranga M1*)

In the above hymn Guru Nanak goes on to list other actions and ideals that do not align the individual to the One: 'feeling sad', 'beauty, wealth, pleasures', 'being naked', 'shrines', 'charity', 'living alone in the wilderness', 'fighting and dying as a warrior'. On the surface this may seem to contradict the earlier emphasis on all manner of quotidian actions being potential pathways to God, the One. However, there is no contradiction, for both lists offer the same conclusion. One must humble the ego-self such that all actions are infused by love and guided by *gur-shabad* and *naam*. 'The true One is won over by becoming the dust of the masses', that is, 'only by His Name'. The gurus were acutely aware that they made affirmative suggestions (like meditate on Him, praise Him, remember Him, etc.), and hence also sought to undercut any and all suggestions by emphasising the limitless nature of the Name, Word and Guru. This constant deconstructive critique at the heart of the GGS, one that refuses to be tamed into any kind of salve or technique, is the very antithesis of modern consumerism hungry for the next best technique or system.

## Glossary

*aap-gavai*, ego-loss; disciplining, decentring, deconditioning the ego-mind
*aasan*, seat of subjective liberation; inner sovereignty over the ego; posture
*dhiaan*, meditation as remembrance of the One in the Many
*dubidhaa*, duality; otherness; forgetting the One, remembering only the many
*Gurmukh*, S/He who acts with Guru as centre
*Guru*, human guide; God; natural law; true and only Sovereign
*Gur-sikhii*, Guru-directed un/learning
*haumai*, 'I-mind'; ego; individuation
*hukam*, will, order, command; natural law; temporality
*Ikk-Oankaar*, One (before space-time); One as (space–time) Many
*jog*, psychological and physical techniques assumed to aid liberation
*jogii-bhogii*, ascetic-sensuality; union of asceticism with worldly pleasures
*karam*, action; grace
*maaiaa*, delusion generated by the individuation (*haumai*); illusion; dualism
*man*, mind; heart
*manmukh*, S/He who acts with Ego as centre
*mukti*, release; enlightenment; inner liberation and outer liberty
*Naam*, Name of the Nameless, God, The One; the fabric of existence
*naam-simaran*, constant experiential awareness of the One in the Many; unconscious within conscious

*naam-maarag*, way of the Name
*nadar*, grace; favourable glance (of God); 'Other-power'
*niaau*, justice; justice as love (never only as law)
*raaj-jog*, royal-yoga; political mysticism; rule of love as justice
*sacaa-patishaah*, true sovereign; saint as sovereign
*saciaaraa*, one who lives truthfully; performs true deeds (i.e. in harmony with *hukam*)
*sahaj*, equipoise, effortless, natural, spontaneous (becoming of One in Many)
*sant-sipaahii*, saint-soldier; love and justice personified
*sevaa*, devoted care of the other; Selfless love
*Shabad*, Word; hymn; Word of the Guru; Word as Guru
*Sikh*, a being devoted to un/learning, listening, loving
*Sikhism*, Gur-Sikh tradition converted to a 'religion'
*Sikhi(sm)*, decolonial Sikhism aimed at re-creating *gur-sikhii*
*takhat*, throne of objective liberty; outer sovereignty of many as part of the One
*upaai*, stratagem; expedient means; contrivances; technique

## Notes

1 I would like to thank the editors of this volume, Karen O'Brien-Kop and Suzanne Newcombe, as well as Prabhsharanbir Singh, Puninder Singh, Harjeet Singh and especially Sophie Hawkins for their feedback on earlier versions of this chapter.

2 The Guru Granth Sahib, compiled in 1604, contains the songs of six of the ten Sikh Gurus, all sing and sign in the name of 'Nanak': M1 = Guru Nanak (1469–1539), M2 = Guru Angad (1504–1552), M3 = Guru Amar Das (1479–1574), M4 = Guru Ram Das (1534–1581), M5 = Guru Arjan (1563–1606) and M9 = Guru Tegh Bahadur (1621–1675). 'M' stands for *mahala*, the 'palace of God's presence', denoting the Sikh Gurus awakened subjectivity. All translations of the GGS are mine.

3 As part of its engagement with philosophy of language, this chapter employs its own style in capitalizing terms such as 'True-Guru' to render notions of universality and truth. Phonetic transliterations are provided in Gurmukhi and Panjabi.

4 Consequently, very few books have been written on the topic; for exceptions see Kohli (1991) and Nayar and Singh (2007). This is understandable given the critiques of yoga in the GGS that centre on egoism: 'Yogis, householders, pandits, and beggars in religious robes – are all asleep in egotism' (M3). 'Without renouncing egotism, how can anyone be a renunciate? Without overcoming the five thieves, how can the mind be subdued? Whoever I see, is diseased: only my True-Guru-Yogi, remains diseaseless' (GGS 1140 *Bhairau* M5).

5 Elsewhere (Bhogal 2012a; 2014; 2015), I have argued that *gur-sikhii* and Gur-Sikh *dharam* were partially displaced and reframed by British colonisation and classification as a 'religion' named 'Sikhism'. 'Sikhi(sm)', on the other hand, is a decolonial moniker devised to foreground this homogenising translation and recall that pre-colonial *gur-sikhii* was overwritten by Sikhism in the 'conversion' to modernity. The parenthetical term 'Sikhi(sm)' emphasises the importance of retaining indigenous understandings *within* modernity and to seek to understand *gur-sikhii* through its praxis as a verb rather than its conceptual abstraction as a noun. 'Un/learning' refers to the fact that knowledge is often instrumentalised by the ego, group or nation, and thus becomes largely an arbitrary if not false projection, one that should be unlearned.

6 The non-possessable 'pluriversal' (Mignolo 2000; 2007) is a bottom-up concept derived from across many traditions. It *approaches* the universal through truths that resonate *across* traditions – checking the hubris of monolingual narrations, be they Christian, Buddhist or Brahmanic. Only those dedicated to the education required for a pluriversal outlook gain a voice to approach any supposed universal. Mignolo argues 'that modernity occluded the pluriversal under the persuasive discourse of the universal' (Mignolo 2006: 435).

7 GGS 370 *Aasaa* M5; GGS 877 *Raamakalii* M1; GGS 3 *Japu* M1; GGS 942 *Raamakalii* M1; GGS 114 *Maajha* M3.

8 GGS 1156 *Bhairau* M5; GGS 907 *Raamakalii Dakhanii* M1; GGS 1026 *Maaruu* M1; GGS 1087 *Maaruu* M4.

9 See Birch's (2013) historical overview of *rāja yoga*, although it overlooks the Sikh tradition.
10 'The King sits on the throne within the self; He Himself administers justice' (GGS 1092 *Maaruu* M3).
11 'One who sees You is recognised as a householder (*girasat*) and as a renunciate (*udaasii*)' (GGS 385 *Aasaa* M5).
12 'He [M4], seated (as King) upon the Throne of Truth, canopy above His Head, possesses the powers of yoga (*jog*) and the pleasures (of the householder) (*bhog*)' (GGS 1406 *Savaiie mahale chauthe ke* Sala).
13 This term is borrowed from Weber (2019); although there is much in common, important differences remain.
14 GGS 662 *Dhanaasarii* M1.
15 Elsewhere these are expressed as 'joy and sorrow', 'nectar and poison', 'honour and dishonour', 'beggar and king'. The *jiivanmukt* – that one liberated in life – 'amidst all remains unattached' (GGS 274 *Gaurii Sukhamanii* M5).
16 'Truth is higher than everything; but higher still is truthful living' (GGS 62 *Siriiraagu* M1).
17 'God Himself' is the 'great sensualist (*rasiaa*)', 'enjoyer (*bhogi*)', as well as the 'yogi (*jogii*)' residing in the state of 'nirvana' (GGS 1074 *Maaruu* M5), sitting on the throne of Truth (*sachau takhat*) (GGS 1406 *Savaiie mahale chauthe ke* Sala). The divine now unites all three spheres of life: private–asceticism, public–civil society, and political–state: God is the greatest king (*raaj*), yogi (*jogii*), ascetic (*tapiisar*) and sensualist (*bhogii*) (GGS 284 *Gaurii sukhamanii* M5). Not seeing God within, the deluded mind looks outward, yet 'He cannot be found by any device *(upaai)*; the Guru will show you the Lord within your heart' (GGS 234 *Gaurii Puurabii* M4).
18 'When the mind is filthy, everything is filthy; by washing the body, the mind is not cleaned .../ Even if one learns yogic postures of the Siddhas, and holds his senses in check,/ still, the filth of the mind is not removed; the filth of egotism is not eliminated. ||2|| This mind is not controlled by any other discipline, except the Sanctuary of the True-Guru./ Meeting the True-Guru, one is reversed/ transformed beyond description. ||3|| Prays Nanak, one who dies upon meeting the True-Guru, shall be rejuvenated by his Word' (GGS 558 *Vadhansu* M3).
19 GGS 234 *Gaurii Puurabii* M4.
20 Other major Sikh formulations of true yoga are *gurmukh-jog* and *shabad-surat jog*.
21 GGS 972 *Raamakalii* Bhagat Naamdeva jii.
22 GGS 153 *Gaurii* M1.
23 GGS 359 *Aasaa* M1; GGS 68 *Siriiraagu* M3; GGS 139 *Maajha* M2.
24 GGS 908 *Raamakalii* M3.
25 GGS 236 *Gaurii* M5.
26 GGS 219 *Gaurii* M9.
27 GGS 513 *Guuarii kii vaara* M3.
28 GGS 1189–1190 *Basantu* M1; five thieves of the ego: lust, anger, greed, infatuation and pride.
29 GGS 71 *Siriiraagu* M5.
30 GGS 4 *Japu* M1.
31 GGS 3 *Japu* M1.
32 GGS 1240 *Saaranga* M1.
33 GGS 208 *Gaurii* M5; five disciples: the five senses and/or five thieves and/or five elements.
34 Shameem Black (Chapter 2 in this volume) notes this term's politicisation in militant Hindutva discourse.
35 GGS 580 *Vadahansu* M1.
36 GGS 1039 *Maaruu* M1.
37 GGS 1026 *Maaruu* M1.
38 GGS 941 *Raamakalii* M1.
39 GGS 409 *Aasaa Aasaavarii* M5.
40 However, the early stages of the reception of yoga in Europe and North America was to demonstrate its health benefits, scientific viability and relevance to modern people. See Gopal Singh Puri (1974) as a case in point, who together with his wife Kailash Kaur Puri taught meditational and postural yoga. Thanks to Suzanne Newcombe for this reference.
41 On 3 August 1857, Frederick Douglass delivered a 'West India Emancipation' speech at Canandaigua, New York.
42 Figures like Yogi Adityanath, the chief minister of Uttar Pradesh, are a far cry from any actual *jog*, despite being also the head monk/priest at the Gorakhnath Math in Gorakhpur. He is, rather, a crude firebrand

for far-right Hindutva majoritarian politics, and whose youth organization (Hindu Yuva Vahini) has instigated violence against minority, mainly Muslim, communities. The politicisation of such '*raaj-yogiis*' is not my focus here. And though some may argue that Sant Jarnail Singh Bhindranwale was similar (i.e. only political with no saintliness), I offer my rebuttal in Bhogal(2011) and elaboration in Bhogal(2012b). Here *raaj-jog* cannot be divorced from political violence and terrorism whether state-sponsored or from freedom fighters, for the modern nation-state cannot countenance political theologies of the minorities.

43 GGS 556 *Bihaagaraa* M3.

44 'Yoga is not the patched coat [*leggings*], yoga is not the walking stick [*yoga mat*]. Yoga is not smearing the body with ashes [*nor done in 100 degree Fahrenheit rooms*]. Yoga is not the ear-rings [*incense or candles*], and not the shaven head [*six pack abs or the splits*]. Yoga is not the blowing of the horn [*New Age 'spiritual' music*]. Remaining unperturbed amidst worldly seductions – this is the way to attain yoga' (GGS 730 *Suuhii* M1). Such observations can lead to humorous critiques: 'If yoga could be attained by wandering around naked, then all the deer of the forest would be liberated' (GGS 324 *Gaurii* Kabiir jii). The familiarity stems from parallels with nineteenth-century British colonial critique of *jogiis*, internalised by influential Indians (Singleton 2010: chapters 2 and 3).

45 See Eliade 1989 [1958]; De Michelis 2008 [2004]; Phillips 2009; Singleton 2010; Jain 2015; Mallinson and Singleton 2017. Only Feuerstein's 2008 [1998] encyclopedic work contains a short, if problematic, chapter.

46 These terms are taken from Thompson in Horton and Harvey (2012). Others have labelled these 'postural' (Singleton 2010) and 'denominational' (De Michelis 2008) or 'spiritual' (Jain 2015). I use 'Zen Mind' and 'Yoga Body' as monikers denoting large transnational movements (on the one hand, New Thought, Mysticism, Spiritualism, Esotericism, Mantra-Meditation; and on the other, Body Building, Fitness Gym Culture and Modern Postural Yoga, respectively).

47 Deslippe (2012) notes at least eight 'Punjabi Sikh yoga teachers' that travelled to the west during the interwar period.

48 For Yogi Bhajan, see Deslippe (2016).

49 GGS 766 *Suuhii* M1: 'I know nothing of tantras, mantras and hypocritical rituals; enshrining Ram within my heart, my mind is satisfied./ The ointment of *naam* is only understood by one who realises *sach* through *gur-shabad*'; GGS 184 *Gaurii Guaarerii* M5: 'Mantras, tantras, all-curing medicines and acts of atonement, are all in the Name of the Lord (*hari*), the Support of the soul and the breath of life. I have obtained the true wealth of *Hari*'s love.'

50 I have been engaged in a long, ongoing dialogue about this phrase, which does not occur in the GGS, with leading figures within Sikh musicology: Bhai Baldeep Singh (Chairman of the Anād Foundation, founder of Anād Khaṅḍ: Conservatory of Arts, Aesthetics, Cultural Traditions and Developmental Studies, and Dean of Faculty of Humanities & Religious Studies at Guru Nanak Dev University), as well as, and especially with, Dr. Francesca Cassio (Sardarni Harbans Kaur Chair of Sikh Musicology, Hofstra University), about my concerns along the lines of the argument put forth here.

51 www.gurmattherapy.com/, accessed 21 June 2020. Their courses include: 'Mindfulness for Managers', 'Mindfulness & Health Workshops', 'Diabetes Management with Mindfulness', 'Mindfulness (MBCT, MBSR, MBI) 8 Week Courses'; see www.davpanesar.com/services, accessed 21 June 2020.

52 www.gurmattherapy.com/gurmat-therapy-html/, accessed 21 June 2020. Panesar employs a 'groundbreaking combination of tried and tested techniques from many wisdom traditions with cognitive experiential learning exercises', www.betweenyouandmeseva.co.uk/training/davinder-singh-panesar/davinder-singh-panesar, accessed 21 June 2020.

53 www.davpanesar.com/, accessed 21 June 2020. The explanatory text to the video reads: 'The first retreat focuses on Sat, the nature of authenticity … The second retreat focuses on Santokh (contentment) … The third and fourth retreats focus on emotional intelligence and emotional wisdom … The fifth retreat focuses on discovering your specific ethical lifestyle … The sixth retreat focuses on awakening spiritual vision … Our final retreat brings together all the elements of the previous retreats to enable participants to combine their experiences and understanding towards self-actualisation, authenticity, creativity and expression. These retreats have enabled hundreds of individuals to discover their personal path to uncover their sacred self.' Each retreat costs £249; see www.qi-rattan.com/retreats/.

54 https://web.archive.org/web/20181122224653/www.symran.com/about.html (accessed 20 June 2020).

## Bibliography


Bhogal, B. S. 1996. '*Sikhism*', in Shaw, Eliot (ed), *Overview of World Religions*, Part of PHILTAR. Religion, Division of Religion and Philosophy, University of Cumbria. www.philtar.ac.uk/encyclopedia/sikhism/index.html. Accessed 20 February 2020.

Bhogal, B. S. 2010. 'Decolonizations: Cleaving Gestures that Refuse the Alien Call for Identity Politics', *Religions of South Asia*, 4(2): 135–164.

Bhogal, B. S. 2011. 'Monopolizing Violence before and after 1984: Governmental Law and the People's Passion', *Sikh Formations: Religion, Culture, Theory*, 7(1): 57–82.

Bhogal, B. S. 2012a. 'Sikh Dharam and Postcolonialism: Hegel, Religion and Zizek', *Australian Religion Studies Review*, 25(2): 185–212.

Bhogal, B. S. 2012b. 'The Animal Sublime: Rethinking the Sikh Mystical Body', *Journal of the American Academy of Religion*, 80(4): 856–908.

Bhogal, B. S. 2014. 'Postcolonial and Postmodern Perspectives on Sikhism', in Singh, P. and Fenech, L. (eds), 282–297. *The Oxford Handbook in Sikh Studies*. New York: Oxford University Press.

Bhogal, B. S. 2015. 'The Facts of Colonial Modernity & the Story of Sikhism', *Sikh Formations: Religion, Culture, Theory* 11(1–2): 243–265

Birch, J. 2013. 'Rājayoga: The Reincarnations of the King of All Yogas', *International Journal of Hindu Studies* 17(3): 399–442.

Carrette, J. and King R. 2005. *Selling Spirituality: The Silent Takeover of Religion*. London: Routledge.

De Michelis, E. 2008 [2004]. *A History of Modern Yoga: Patanjali and Western Esotericism*. New York: Continuum.

Derrida, J. 2001. 'Above All, No Journalists!' in de Vries, H. and Weber, S. (eds), *Religion and Media*, 56–93. Stanford, CA, USA: Stanford University Press.

Derrida, J. 2002. 'Faith and Knowledge: The Two Sources of "Religion" at the Limits of Reason Alone', in Anidjar, G. (ed), *Acts of Religion*, 40–101. New York: Routledge.

Deslippe, P. 2012. 'From Maharaj to Mahan Tantric: The Construction of Yogi Bhajan's Kundalini Yoga', *Sikh Formations: Religion, Culture, Theory* 8(3): 369–387.

Deslippe, P. 2016. 'Rishis and Rebels: The Punjabi Sikh Presence in Early American Yoga', *Journal of Punjab Studies* 23(1&2): 143–174.

Doabia, H. S. 1981. *Life Story of Baba Nand Singh Ji of Kaleran*. Amritsar: Singh Brothers.

Eliade, M. 1989. *Yoga: Immortality and Freedom*. Trask, W. R. (trans). London: Arkana.

Feuerstein, G. 2008 [1998]. *The Yoga Tradition: Its History, Literature, Philosophy and Practice*. Chino Valley, AZ, USA: Hohm Press.

Jain, A. 2015. *Selling Yoga: From Counterculture to Pop Culture*. New York: Oxford University Press.

Kohli, S. S. 1991. *Yoga of the Sikhs*. Amritsar: Singh Brothers.

Mallinson, J. and Singleton, M. 2017. *Roots of Yoga*. London: Penguin.

Mandair, A. S. 2013. *Sikhism: A Guide for the Perplexed*. London: Bloomsbury

Mignolo, W. D. 2000. *Local Histories/ Global Designs: Coloniality, Subaltern Knowledges and Border Thinking*. New Jersey: Princeton University Press.

Mignolo, Walter D. 2006 [1995]. *The Darker Side of the Renaissance: Literacy, Territoriality, and Colonization*. 2nd ed. Ann Arbor, MI, USA: The University of Michigan Press.

Mignolo, W. 2007. 'DELINKING: The Rhetoric of Modernity, the Logic of Coloniality and the Grammar of De-coloniality', *Cultural Studies* 21(2–3): 449–514.

Nayar, K. E. and Singh S. J. 2007. *The Socially Involved Renunciate: Guru Nanak's Discourse to the Nath Yogis*. Albany, NY, USA: State University of New York Press.

Nesbitt, E. 1985. 'The Nanaksar Movement', *Religion*, 15(1): 67–79.

Phillips, Stephen. 2009. *Yoga, Karma, and Rebirth: A Brief History and Philosophy*. New York: Columbia University Press.

Puri, G. S. 1974 [1972]. *Yoga – Relaxation – Meditation: A Western-Trained Biologist Takes a New Look at an Age-Old Eastern Science*. Liverpool: Self Published.

Singh, B. R. 1975. [1946] *Gurmat Bibek*. 2nd ed. Ludhiana: Bhai Randhir Singh Publishing.

Singh, H. 1983. *Heritage of the Sikhs*. Columbia, MO, USA: South Asia Books.

Singh, P. and Barrier, G. N. (eds) 1996. *The Transmission of Sikh Heritage in the Diaspora*. New Delhi: Manohar Publishers & Distributors.

Singh, T. (trans) 1971. *Autobiography of Bhai Randhir Singh*. Ludhiana: Bhai Randhir Singh Publishing House.

Singleton, M. 2010. *The Yoga Body: The Origins of Modern Posture Practice*. New York: Oxford University Press.

Thompson, N. 2012. 'Bifurcated Spiritualities: Examining Mind/Body splits in the North American Yoga and Zen Communities', in Horton, C. and Harvey, R. (eds), *21st Century Yoga: Culture, Politicis and Practice*. Chicago, IL, USA: Kleio Books.
Trungpa, C. 1987. *Cutting Through Spiritual Materialism*. London: Shambhala.
Uberoi, J. P. S. 1996. *Religion, Civil Society and the State: A Study of Sikhism*. Delhi: Oxford University Press.
van der Veer, P. 1996. *Conversion to Modernities: The Globalization of Christianity*. London: Routledge.
Weber, A. 2019. *Enlivenment: Toward a Poetics for the Anthropocene*. Cambridge, MA, USA: MIT Press.
Zapart, J. 2020. 'The Rādhāsoāmī Theory of Subtle Body as an Expression of Religious Inclusivism'. *International Journal of Hindu Studies* 24: 61–86.

# 17

# CHRISTIANITY

## Classical, modern and postmodern forms of contemplation

*Michael Stoeber and JaeGil Lee*

### Introduction

This chapter outlines significant forms of contemplation, focusing on certain major figures – John Cassian, the author of *The Cloud of Unknowing*, Francisco de Osuna, St. Teresa of Avila, Evelyn Underhill, St. Gregory Palamas, Thomas Keating and John Main. Emphasising the current popular forms of Centering Prayer and Christian Meditation, the chapter illustrates how contemplation in Christianity has evolved in dialogue with various Christian sources, as well as with meditative and other yogic practices of certain Asian religious traditions. It begins by contextualising Christian contemplation within the framework of types of prayer, outlines classic texts and contemplative recollection, and then develops popular contemporary practices and their possible influences.

### Contemplation within the context of Christian prayer

In Christianity, prayer is thought to be communion with God who, as ultimate and eternal Being, is singular, personal, creative and active in the natural world. Such communion takes various forms: adoration (respectful love), thanksgiving (gratitude), confession (moral and spiritual self-discernment and forgiveness), petition (hopeful appeal), intercession (intentional support for others), praise (grateful admiration), lament (expressions of sorrow or anger), meditative *lectio* and *visio divina* (thoughtful reflection on scripture or visual images) and contemplation (*contemplatio* – radical stillness in the presence of God, personal awareness of God or union with God). There are standard ritual forms of these various kinds of prayers as well as openness to creative individual expressions in conjunction with certain sacramental actions or movements, such as bowing, kneeling, genuflection, prostration, performing the sign of the cross and dance.[1] In some contemporary contexts, various types of artistic creativity are regarded in themselves as prayer forms, though traditionally art was only linked as a supportive medium with other forms of prayer.[2]

Some contemporary commentators have criticised hierarchies of prayer and spiritual experience (Jantzen 1995: 12–25; Raphael 1994: 513–515; Stoeber 2015/2017: 10–11, 22–28). However, traditionally Christian prayer has been characterised as having organic and developmental qualities, where one is called to deepen and intensify a fundamental communion with her or his creative Source. Within such contexts, contemplation is clearly marked off. While other types of prayer can involve the senses, imagination, emotions, reflective cognition and/or physical movement, contemplation normally aspires to a relatively passive, static and non-discursive self-opening to God. One traditional classification includes four grades or degrees: discursive, affective, simple and contemplative. (1) Discursive prayer involves the three major faculties of the mind – will, memory and understanding – where the practitioner actively uses these three powers to understand and reflect upon scriptures or other Christian teachings, while raising one's love and adoration towards God. For this reason, it is also called active meditation. As discursive prayer becomes dominated by activities of the will, there is a decrease in thought and reason, and (2) affective prayer is initiated – where feelings are transformed, purified and refined within this devotional context. When there remains only a single aspiration focused on God, it is called (3) the prayer of simplicity or 'simple regard', which culminates in (4) contemplative union (Johnston 1989: 44–50; 1982: 29–30).

This movement has also been classified generally in terms of three levels: vocal meditative and contemplative. When advancing in prayer, one moves from (1) verbal prayer via sound movements, to (2) mental/reflective prayer of the quieted mind, and finally to (3) contemplative prayer, where thoughts and feelings are radically stilled and the felt-sense presence of God becomes prominent (Mursell 2001: 209). Again, these three levels are compatible with the traditional Christian stages of the mystical journey, which was probably first suggested by Origen of Alexandria (185–253) and fully developed by Pseudo-Dionysius (fifth or sixth century): (1) Purgation – which is moral, affective and spiritual transformation through prayer and ascetic practices (such as abstinence, sensory deprivation or flagellation); (2) Illumination – where continued transformative moral, meditative and contemplative practices lead to visions of the divine Presence in various forms; and (3) Contemplation – whereby the mystic is opened to union with this Presence, which inspires and influences her or him creatively (Origen 1954).

## Classics of Christian contemplation

### *John Cassian*

Although Christian prayer develops as an extension of practices already present in Judaism, its Christianisation became more formalised through the development of such texts as the *Didache* (*Teaching*) (first or second century) and the writings of Origen and other early Church Fathers, with John Cassian (360–435) being one of the more significant early authorities on Christian contemplation. His well-formulated written approach to contemplation becomes influential within the western monastic tradition and it later influences contemporary monastic and lay practice, especially through adaptations by John Main (see below), as well as influencing the Jesus Prayer (see below). Cassian attributes its method to Egyptian desert Fathers under whom he and his friend Germanus studied. In *The Conferences* Nine and Ten, he focuses exclusively on the theme of prayer, which is presented in the form of dialogues among Cassian, Germanus and their mentor Abba Isaac. Influenced by Origen and Evagrius of Ponticus (346–399), Cassian held that unmediated communion with God is the highest state of prayer. It aims for liberation from worldly concerns and inner distortions and distractions in attaining perpetual awareness of God. Naturally, then, given God's infinite and transcendent nature, this contemplative state is characterised by ineffability. Cassian called this contemplation 'pure prayer', where one's mind goes beyond itself, becoming free from sounds, concepts and images, within the context of the goal of 'unceasing' practice, where it would become a perpetual state of the heart – where the person ideally remains in permanent communion with God.[3]

Cassian's method – traditionally called 'monologistic prayer' – involves a continual repetition of a short biblical phrase. A specific formula prescribed by Cassian is *Psalms* verse 70:1: 'Come to my help, O God; Lord, hurry to my rescue'. One fixes one's mind and heart on these simple words, passionately reciting this formula as a cry for divine help. The monk constantly pleads for God's assistance as he struggles to transcend his own thoughts, emotional moods and passions. Cassian, following Abba Isaac, claims that this specific verse was chosen from the entire body of scripture because it encompasses essential human affections and emotions: powerlessness, fear, devout sentiment, devotional ardour, burning love and humility. Cassian's method admonishes the monk to exert not only mental but also emotional/affective concentration in reciting the prayer formula.

## *The Cloud of Unknowing*

Another influential text for contemplative prayer in the Christian west is *The Cloud of Unknowing* (1349–1396), which was written anonymously, possibly by a Carthusian priest. An accessible and influential modern translation and introduction was published by Evelyn Underhill in 1912, with a number of others following; other popular writings on meditation have included substantial dependence upon *The Cloud*'s method of prayer, such as Aldous Huxley's *The Perennial Philosophy* (1970: 273–291). Quite apart from the contributions of Centering Prayer to the popularity of *The Cloud* (see below), the book has drawn attention from both Christian and non-Christian spiritual seekers because of its practicality and straightforward simplicity. Influenced by the *apophatic* theology of Pseudo-Dionysius, *The Cloud* also incorporates affective mysticism into the dynamic. In the exercise of contemplative prayer, one not only frees oneself from all images and discursive thoughts (a negative path), but also reaches out to God through 'the blind stirring' of love (an affective path). Contemplative prayer is an action of intentional will, driven by love, and it leads to 'a union of love' (Hodgson 1944: lxii).

To reach out to God, a person is instructed to create two types of meditative conditions in the mind, which are imaged as clouds: the 'cloud of forgetting' and the 'cloud of unknowing'. The cloud of forgetting symbolises the effort to let go of one's learned sense and cognitive reflection on natural phenomena, while the cloud of unknowing is a psychic orientation of radical openness to a purely spiritual Reality that cannot be known in any normal sense. One needs to open one's self to God's presence, apart from the senses, cognitions and feelings. Yet, this contemplative exercise is to be somewhat vigorous and even aggressive, as the author advises the contemplative to 'trample unwanted thoughts' under the cloud of forgetting and to strike the cloud of unknowing with 'the sharp dart of longing love'. Regarding method, the author writes that 'a simple reaching out directly towards God [by a humble impulse of love] is sufficient', without any other means of support. He provides a practical technique, suggesting 'If you like, you can have this reaching out, wrapped up and enfolded in a single word', such as 'God', 'love', 'fire' or even 'sin' (Walsh 1981: 133–134, 195–198). In *The Cloud*, the single prayer-word is referred to as both a 'shield' and a 'spear': a shield which protects from distracting thoughts, and a spear to pierce the cloud of unknowing and reach God beyond. In terms of inner posture, *The Cloud*'s method is categorised as a kind of 'ejaculatory prayer' (McGinn 2012: 412; 1987: 200). The prayer-word is to reflect a fervent and humble longing, expressing the love for God and an appeal for immediate assistance.

## Recollection: St. Teresa of Avila

Along with various contemplative prayer practices influenced by Cassian and *The Cloud*, which evolved in the later middle ages, the 'prayer of recollection' (*recogimiento*) also became popular among some Christian contemplatives in the west by the time of the reformation. This contemplative practice gained modern interest especially due to the popularity of the writings of St. Teresa of Avila (1515–1582) and Evelyn Underhill (1875–1941). The influence of Teresa, who was also declared a doctor of the Roman Catholic church in 1970, extends well beyond her Carmelite order, as she is widely regarded as a spiritual giant; and Underhill was an extremely popular lay Anglican writer, who wrote thirty-nine books and more than 350 articles and reviews on the spiritual classics, mysticism and prayer.

Like Cassian's unceasing prayer and *The Cloud*'s ejaculatory prayer, the prayer of recollection intentionally aims towards a non-discursive experience of God. St. Teresa and Underhill place 'recollection' as the first degree of a prayer dynamic that develops into the prayers of contemplative 'quiet' and 'union'. In her last and most well-known work, *Interior Castle*, Teresa describes an inward-oriented journey, which she symbolises as a movement through seven rooms of a castle, culminating in the direct encounter in the inmost room with God, who resides at the core of the human person, as ultimate creative Source (Teresa 1980).

Of uncertain origin, the prayer of recollection in the west became influential in early-sixteenth-century Spain. Given Teresa's Jewish ancestry, it is interesting that we do find a similar form of contemplative recollection in Jewish sources.[4] In Christian contexts, while medieval popular devotional forms of religious practice were strong, Franciscans also taught recollection to both religious and lay people, though the practice came under Inquisitorial suspicion later that century. At that time in Spain, a few texts on this topic written by Franciscan friars became enormously popular as 'guides to what today would be called contemplative prayer' (Short 2007: 449). One such book was Francisco de Osuna's *The Third Spiritual Alphabet* (1527).[5] Teresa received a copy of this book from her uncle, which she took as her guide for interior prayer and later adapted, as Superior in her reformed Carmelite community, in support of the formation of novices (Teresa 1987: 66–67).[6]

As its name implies, recollection seeks to *re*-collect one's ordinary field of consciousness, which is usually scattered with thoughts, images and emotions. The practice of recollection enables one to narrow and concentrate one's consciousness on a specific object, which gradually becomes a one-pointed focus. It is a typically taxing exercise to hold one's attention on a single object and repeatedly bring that attention back whenever one's mind drifts. Teresa compares the mind to a wild horse; Osuna (1981) likens the process to domesticating a wild bird in a cage. It requires a great deal of effort and perseverance until a habitual state of recollection settles in one's consciousness. The dynamic is complicated by the intrusion of unconscious distortions and vices – negative passions and spirits that resist the transformative opening to the divine Presence. For Osuna and Teresa, the prayer of recollection enables a shift of one's conscious awareness to the centre of one's being, the inmost place of the soul, where the transmuting encounter with God takes place. Teresa writes: 'the soul collects its faculties together and enters within itself to be with its God' (Teresa 1980: 141). Ideally, the process shifts from forms of 'natural contemplation' – where the person works with a spiritual director to remove his or her own distortions and resistances to underlying spirit via moral and ascetic practices – to 'infused contemplation' – where spiritual Reality becomes the active component within a dynamic of passive openness to inspiring and regenerative energies.

Because the goal of recollection is to deepen one's relationship with God, scriptural/religious words or images are used as initial objects of concentration. Osuna instructs his readers to recite a short formula such as 'O God of my heart and my inmost being', or a short phrase from the Lord's Prayer, or to imagine the sacred passion of Christ. Due to her own inability to picture Christ with her imagination, St. Teresa developed a unique way of recollection and taught it to her nuns. She asked them to represent rather than visualise Christ being close to them, as if a person is in a dark room with one's friend, sensing or feeling his presence without seeing him (Teresa 1987: 102; 1980: 133–134). She also suggests incorporating a short prayer formula, particularly from the Lord's Prayer, with such a simple posture of openness to Christ's presence (Teresa 1980: 128–131).[7]

In Osuna and Teresa's recollection, like *The Cloud*'s contemplative exercise, the affective nature of contemplation is potent. Mental concentration is accompanied by the intentional energy of love. It is arduous desire and fervent affection for God that gathers together the dispersed self and enables it to move closer to God. Representing the Franciscan tradition, which stresses affective spirituality, Osuna more keenly emphasises love: 'our love is dispersed throughout human concerns, we must recover it and draw it back, gathering in all our love as payment to God' (Osuna 1981: 418–419). For Osuna and Teresa, the practice of recollection intensifies one's longing and love within the expanding simplification of one's field of consciousness.

## *Recollection: Evelyn Underhill*

Although Evelyn Underhill belongs to the 'modern' period historically, her work is 'classical' in terms of both its sources and its influence. Underhill is one of the most significant early-twentieth-century figures to bring wide public attention to translated Christian spiritual classics for both a religious and a lay audience. She appears to have developed her understanding and method of the prayer of recollection primarily from Teresa, though she draws on others, including the author of *The Cloud*, Jacob Boehme, Richard of St. Victor, Walter Hilton, Meister Eckhart, St. Bernard of Clairvaux and Jan van Ruusbroek (Underhill 1990). She uses the word 'recollection' as an umbrella term to refer to the deliberate and active practice and process of turning inward, which she calls 'introversion'. Through recollection, mystics develop an inner capacity to perceive spiritual realities and deepen an increasing awareness of underlying intimate connection with God. In *Practical Mysticism*, she provides a practical approach to the prayer of recollection, defining it as 'the subjection of the attention to the control of the will' where people seek to obtain 'control of their own mental processes' (Underhill 1914: 46). According to Underhill, recollection is a universal psycho-spiritual practice found in many authentic religions. It works to exercise human consciousness in building the contemplative powers of attention and concentration.

Recollection is a voluntary undertaking that begins by focusing upon a specific object. Religious persons may select a sacred word or image from their religious traditions as a focal point, though Underhill suggests one can choose almost any object from various aspects of life and nature for this exercise. Recollection is a practical method intended to enable a person gradually to move through a process of introversion into her or his underlying spiritual centre or core: first (1) to protect oneself from the typical onslaught of sensory phenomena, then (2) to still the normal processes of conscious imagination and cognition, and eventually (3) to focus one's consciousness directly towards the meditative object, where it completely dominates one's attention, in blissful absorption.

According to Underhill, in both traditional and contemporary Christian contexts, the practitioner is encouraged not to rest in this quietist absorption, however attractive and comfortable this experience might be, but to become open to a transitional shift, where meditative 'Quiet' ideally opens to an awareness of various dynamic spiritual realities, in a movement from 'passive' to 'infused' contemplation.[8] Underhill speaks of eventually coming through this process of self-gathering to recognise one's underlying spiritual Self or Soul:

> you will at last discover that there is something within you – something behind the fractious, conflicting life of desire – which you can recollect, gather up, make effective for new life. You will, in fact, know your own soul for the first time.
>
> *(Underhill 1914: 76–77)*

More significantly, through the regular practice of recollection, the object of meditation gradually transforms into a kind of opening or medium into the spiritual realm. She writes, 'It ceases to be a picture, and becomes a window through which the mystic peers out into the spiritual universe and apprehends to some extent – though how, he knows not – the veritable presence of God'[9] (Underhill 1990: 315).

## *Eastern Orthodox recollection: the Jesus Prayer*

Sources suggest that the 'Jesus Prayer' in Eastern Orthodox Christianity is influenced by a number of early figures, including Gregory of Nyssa (322–398), Evagrius Ponticus, Milus of Ancrya (d. 430) and Diadochos of Photiki (400–486?), but even Origen emphasised the spiritual power of meditating on Jesus' name.[10] The prayer comes to be associated with Christian 'Hesychasm', monastic communities or hermits involved in ascetic practices thought to culminate in a condition of *apatheia*, where virtues are stabilised in an inner peace or stillness – *hesychia* – which enables one to love without the inhibitions of the powerful distorting passions (Palamas, 1983: 117, n.2).

St Gregory Palamas (1296–1359) writes of this ideal in terms of what he called 'unified recollection' – which he understood as 'remembrance of God' – a state of continuous attending to God (1983: 130, n.115). A Hesychast was one who practised the Jesus Prayer and the physical techniques associated with it. The foundational books of Hesychasm are a collection by twenty-five theological masters, written between the fourth and fifteenth centuries, called *Philokalia* (*Love of the Beautiful*). One of these texts, *Life of Abba Philemon* (sixth–eighth century), includes the Jesus Prayer, originally 'Lord Jesus Christ, Son of God, have mercy on me', while later orthodoxy adds 'a sinner' (from Luke 18:13). Repetition of this prayer-form in a series of 50, 100 or 150, supported by a prayer rope, is sometimes accompanied by physical postures – that is, sitting on a nine-inch stool, head and shoulders bowed, back bent, with eyes pointing towards one's heart. Between prayer-series, the practice can also include bowing, signs of the cross and movements of prostration, as well as the coordination of breath with the recitation.

The goal of such prayer is radical humility, which was thought to open the practitioner to the healing, purifying and inspiring presence and power of Jesus, which under normal circumstances people resist in their sin. The prayer supports the orthodox ideal of *theosis*, deification, transformative movement from the human image of God into likeness with the Christ-archetype. For Palamas, and other Orthodox theologians, the idea is to nourish the *transformation* of natural passions rather than their spiritual *transcendence*; the ideal includes the physical body transmuted by and in Christ's purifying energies.

## Popular contemporary Christian contemplation

The Jesus Prayer is still practised today in various forms in Eastern Orthodox traditions,[11] while two of the most popular forms of Christian contemplative prayer in the west today were developed in the 1970s by Thomas Keating (1923–2018) and John Main (1926–1982), named

Centering Prayer and Christian Meditation, respectively. Keating and Main felt the need to provide a simple how-to contemplative method for Christians who sought a deeper relationship with God, in response to the growing popularity of Eastern meditation practices in the west. They claim these practices are renewed forms of a lost contemplative prayer, adapted for present-day Christians in the west, based primarily on Christian contemplative traditions.

## Centering Prayer[12]

In his search for an accessible contemplative prayer method in Christian traditions, Keating, with two other Trappists at St. Spencer Abby – William Menninger and Basil Pennington – found it in *The Cloud*. Because of this, the practice was first called the 'prayer of the cloud'. It later took the more general name 'Centering Prayer', which was suggested by retreatants. Following *The Cloud*'s theological stance, Keating stresses the necessity of the negative path. He claims that although the positive (kataphatic) and negative (apophatic) paths are complementary, the latter is a further movement of one's prayer journey, where, through 'pure faith', one can intuitively experience God (Keating 1997: 5). Keating identifies over-activism and over-intellectualism as major obstacles to one's growth in prayer life. Centering Prayer helps one go beyond the mental level of discursive reflection, to experience God without concepts or images.

'Intention' is the central principle in the practice of Centering Prayer. To cultivate the prayer, a practitioner deliberately consents to the presence and action of God within. Keating claims that, as an 'exercise of intention', Centering Prayer enables a receptive attitude towards God that is different than concentrative methods (e.g. the Jesus Prayer and Christian Zen Prayer), which use 'attention' as the faculty for practice (Keating 2003: 55–58; Bourgeault 2004: 19–21). As a radically receptive method, Centering Prayer requires 'surrender' rather than positive effort. There are only four guidelines given for a twice-daily practice of twenty minutes or longer. Participants (1) choose a sacred word as an expression of one's intention to consent to the divine presence; (2) sit comfortably with eyes closed and introduce the sacred intentional word in silence; (3) when they are distracted by thoughts, gently bring attention back to the sacred word; and (4) following the prayer period, remain in silence with eyes closed for a few minutes, before returning to ordinary consciousness (Keating 1997: 139).[13]

It is important to appreciate the role of the sacred word. The practitioner should not think about the meaning of the sacred word during the time of prayer because it is a symbol that expresses one's intention to surrender to the divine presence. The chosen sacred word is used to renew one's intention to be fully open and receptive to the presence of God. An overall posture of gentleness and effortlessness is a unique feature of Centering Prayer. In the face of distracting thoughts, the practitioner is encouraged to ever so gently return to the sacred word. According to Keating, 'Without effort, without trying, we sink into this Presence, letting everything else go' (Keating 1997: 137). For this reason, Keating claims Centering Prayer is possibly the most receptive method among contemplative prayer forms.

According to Keating, there are three general levels of consciousness. As contemplative attentiveness grows, the practitioner becomes free of the normal flow of ordinary transient thoughts on the surface level of consciousness and enters into a deeper, spiritual level of consciousness, where one experiences oneself as a witness, separate from the concepts, images and feelings of consciousness. There is a therapeutic context to this emotional–spiritual regression, as one overcomes resistances and becomes open to unconscious content and energies. Eventually, sharpened spiritual attentiveness enables one to sense the divine Presence via an even deeper level of consciousness – the source from which one's life unfolds at every moment.

Keating claims that one finds one's true self and happiness, and the meaning of life, in the divine Presence, because it is the source of all life to which everyone is connected.

## *Christian Meditation*[14]

John Main claims that Christian Meditation is rooted in the tradition of John Cassian, from which he relies primarily on *The Conferences* Nine and Ten.[15] In agreement with Cassian, he believes that a deeper state of prayer leads one to wordless and imageless communion with God. While the prayer life of most Christians tends to remain in the domain of reflective and intentional consciousness, the aim of Christian Meditation is to enable the practitioner continuously to renounce thoughts, images and memories so as to attend solely on God, without normal mediating concepts.

'Simplicity' or 'poverty' (the pathway to 'divine stillness') – terms also explored in detail by Evelyn Underhill – are the centrepiece of Main's teaching on contemplative prayer (Main 1984: 26–29).[16] From his view, the strength of Cassian's teaching is found in its 'commitment to simplicity' and 'fidelity to poverty' that enable one to go beyond the complexities of intellect and imagination in encountering God in a more direct fashion (Main 1982: 12). The practical simplicity of Christian Meditation is also shown in its short, plain instruction, which consists of less than 100 words (Main 1989: ix).[17] At the centre of practical simplicity lies what Main calls the 'mantra', which practitioners repeat during the time of prayer. He writes: 'the simplicity that is required' is 'to sit down [...] to close [one's] eyes and to recite the one word from beginning to end' (Main 1984: 28). While Cassian uses a relatively longer verse (Psalm 70:1: 'Come to my help, O God; Lord, hurry to my rescue'), Main recommends a single Aramaic word, *maranatha*, as the mantra, which means 'Come Lord'.[18]

Like Keating, Main instructs one not to think about or reflect on the meaning of the prayer-word while practicing. Rather, the method is to interiorly recite the mantra as four syllables of equal length: *ma-ra-na-tha*. Though not essential, it is suggested to recite it rhythmically, in conjunction with breathing. An effective way of doing this is to gently and silently say every syllable of *ma-ra-na-tha* with the inhalation, while maintaining silence on the exhalation, though what is most important to the meditation is to find one's own rhythm and pace. An interesting and important instruction is to listen to the interior sound of the word: one should listen to it as 'the profoundest and most supreme sound in [one's] being' (Main 2012: 19). The sonic component of the mantra has significance and power.

Main instructs his practitioners to recite the word continuously throughout the entire period of prayer – unless the mantra naturally fades away by itself – which suggests it is more of a concentrative than receptive method of prayer. Yet, like Centering Prayer, the theoretical context of Christian Meditation proposes a progressive shifting from egoic self-awareness to an awareness of one's true Self in union with God. This movement is reflected in Main's description of engagement with the mantra. Initially, the practitioner feels as if the word needs to be recited with one's mind, in the head. At the beginner's stage, being easily distracted by inner chatter, one has to expend enormous effort to maintain meditation. But later, through perseverance, the mantra becomes anchored in one's heart, and it begins to sound rhythmically there, which requires much less effort. Eventually, one comes actually to hear the word sounding in one's heart, instead of working to sound it. Main claims that when one can naturally hear the sound of the mantra, one's meditation *really* begins. In this final stage, one becomes lost in the harmonic sounding and then adrift in the total silence of God (Main 1981: 54–57).

## Postmodern Christian contemplation: non-Christian influences and religious hybridity

Contemporary Christian contemplation has been influenced by non-Christian meditative traditions in significant ways. We have already mentioned Jewish forms of recollection which might possibly have influenced traditional Christian developments. Significant figures in twentieth-century Christian–Hindu dialogue are Jules Monchanin (Parama Arubi Ananda, 1895–1957), Henri Le Saux (Abhishiktananda, 1910–1973), and Bede Griffiths (Swami Dayananda, 1906–1993). Benedictine monks living in India, they studied and learned Hindu sacred texts and yoga practices in integrating certain Indian cultural phenomena – such as language, dress, posture and meditative practices – into their spirituality, which enriched their own Christian understanding and practice of contemplation (Abhishiktananda 1972; Griffiths 1994). Monchanin and Le Saux established Shantivanam Ashram in Tamil Nadu in 1938, and the writings of Abhishiktananda and Griffiths have become influential, though they have not created or promoted concrete forms of contemplative prayer.[19] Similarly, as Paul Pearson observes, the famous Trappist monk Thomas Merton (1915–1968) 'generally writes of his experience of prayer rather than writing of any methods or techniques he might be using', emphasising meditation and contemplation (Pearson 2012: vii,viii). Merton too was keen on interreligious dialogue, especially with Zen and Tibetan traditions of Buddhism (Merton and Suzuki 1968). In his spirituality he stressed an opening to one's inner and underlying self, in intimate union with God, via contemplative and other prayer practices (Merton 1969). He felt that exploring the correspondences and differences of introvertive spirituality among certain non-Christian traditions and Christianity could be mutually enriching.

Main and Keating were aware of the spiritual endeavours and work of such pioneering figures in Christian interreligious dialogue. Also, there is no question that Keating's and Main's understanding of contemplative prayer was influenced by their own experience and practice of certain Asian meditation traditions.[20] As abbot at St. Joseph's Abbey in Spencer, Massachusetts (1961–1981), Keating had invited and learned from meditation teachers from Asian traditions since the 1960s, in particular teachers of Transcendental Meditation and Buddhist meditation: he attended several week-long retreats with Zen teacher Joshu Sasaki Roshi. Keating is quite explicit about this influence: Centering Prayer is the result of the effort to 'harmonize the wisdom of the East with the contemplative tradition of Christianity' (Keating 2003: 12). Also, Main's exposure to Asian meditation preceded his entry into the Benedictine order. In 1955, when he was an officer of the British Colonial Service in Malaya (now Peninsular Malaysia), Main met a Hindu monk, Swami Satyananda, who initiated him into Hindu mantra meditation. Every week for a year and a half, Main visited the swami to meditate; later, in his own teaching, Main frequently credits this teacher for the primary instructions in Christian Meditation.

While Keating and Main claim *The Cloud* and *The Conferences* as their sources for Centering Prayer and Christian Meditation, there are certain features in their teachings that are not part of the traditional Christian contemplative prayer methods. First, for Keating apophatic contemplative prayer can be practised by a person who has not been prepared by kataphatic prayer forms, such as the first three steps of *lectio divina* – reading, reflecting and praying – and other devotional practices (2013: 13–14; 1997: 41). In contrast, traditionally *The Cloud*'s author insists that one should have practised scriptural reading, reflecting and praying as preliminary steps for contemplative prayer. Keating's non-concern about prerequisites for Centering Prayer seems to reflect more the openness in Zen Buddhism and Transcendental Meditation than restrictions one finds in traditional Christian contemplation.

Moreover, while the contemplative prayer forms in *The Cloud* and *The Conferences* integrate human affections and emotional energy into their practices, Keating and Main do not encourage their practitioners to do so. The lack of emphasis on affective longing and emotional needs or wants is a common feature in Transcendental Meditation, Satyananda's Hindu mantra meditation and Zen meditation. Also, the actual meaning of the prayer-word in the two present-day prayer forms is much less significant than it is in their Christian sources. In the traditional prayer methods, the meaning is linked with the passionate intentions of these traditional ejaculatory prayers. In contrast, the meaning of the prayer words in Centering Prayer and Christian Meditation are downplayed or transcended – paralleling their context in Transcendental Meditation and Satyananda's mantra meditation. Indeed, in the case of Christian Meditation it is the sound, not the meaning, of the mantra that matters. Main recalls Satyananda's teaching: 'there must be in your mind no thoughts, no words, no imaginations. The sole sound will be the sound of your mantra. The mantra … is like a harmonic' (Main 1999: 14).

There are also questions surrounding the Asian influences of Ken Wilber's transpersonal theory on Keating's theoretical reflections on levels of consciousness, his articulation of the unitive experience and his treatment of sin.[21] Moreover, even Main's use of the Sanskrit word 'mantra' to describe the prayer-word in Christian Meditation highlights the way in which contemporary Christian contemplative practices have been deeply influenced by non-Christian forms of meditation – to the point where one might argue that all future forms of Christian contemplation will be religious hybrids, to some degree or another. With the growing popularity of yoga in the west, such integrative tendencies will only become more pronounced.

Apart from the many current or lapsed or past Christians in the west who regularly practise different kinds of yoga taught through various contemporary postural yoga schools,[22] there are some Christian groups which claim that the essentials of Yoga – breath work, posture and contemplative meditation – are separable from the religious aspects of Indian religions and so quite compatible with Christianity. These groups have integrated yoga practices with Christian prayer and doctrine, sometimes even excluding all reference to Indian scripture and teaching, such as in the case of Holy Yoga.[23] Both Hindu and Christian authorities have responded with criticism of such formal appropriation, and with caution generally regarding Christian practices of yoga. They accuse integrative tendencies of 'cultural misappropriation', of improperly and even immorally stealing features of non-Christian religious traditions. Or they speak of the traditional practices of yoga being 'commodified' by contemporary business practices, mistreated as an economic item used primarily for material profit. This relates to ethical concerns surrounding the denial or neglect of 'moral prerequisites' in western yoga, which were always aspects of traditional Indian yoga schools, as well as of the classical sources of contemplation in the west. It is also associated with criticisms of the apparent narcissistic attachments to bodily effects present in many western appropriations, where practitioners maintain distorted preoccupation with their own physical attractiveness and achievements. Some Christian critiques go on to emphasise moral/spiritual hazards related to perceived occult dangers, as well as doctrinal differences associated with such religious syncretism, which might impact negatively on orthodox Christian belief and practice.[24]

In response to such concerns, one can argue that many of them are misguided or unjustified, and one can point to the many apparent social and spiritual benefits of such interreligious dialogue and practice. But these criticisms highlight quite effectively the manner in which contemplative meditation in today's world of rapid transportation, mass information, instant communication and religious freedom can no longer be read or comprehended in religious isolation. Moreover, that is to say nothing about the many interesting and significant parallels one finds in the dynamics of contemplation among certain Christian, Buddhist, Hindu, Jewish and

Muslim thinkers in the areas of contemplative exercises and types of experiences, as well as in the proposed resistances, difficulties and associated dangers. Such correspondences would seem to support rather natural coalescences of contemplative practice and theory among different religious traditions in postmodern developments, despite the immense historical, theological and contextual diversity.[25]

## Notes

1 For a comprehensive study on various forms and models of prayer, see Chase (2005). For an account of historical/theological developments of prayer, see Hammerling (2008). For a more traditional understanding of the forms of prayer, see Cassian's *Conferences* (1997: 323–363).

2 For a practical contemporary approach to art as prayer, see Gerding (2001). For a historical overview of art in relation to Christian pastoral practice and theology, see Viladesau (2000).

3 This goal of unceasing prayer follows St. Paul's exhortation in 1 *Thessalonians* 5:17.

4 See, for example, Polen (1994: 4–5 and 159, n. 14). Hasidic Rabbi Shapira outlines a practice of contemplative recollection in *Derekh ha-Melekh* (Jerusalem 1991), which he calls *hashkatah* ('silencing of the conscious mind') (5).

5 Two other influential books on recollection are Bernardino de Laredo's *The Ascent of Mount Sion* (1535) and Bernabé de Palma's *Via Spiritus* (1532). For brief descriptions of these works, see Short (2007: 450–455). Only the former is translated into English (by E. Allison Peers [1950]).

6 For Teresa's discussion of this contemplative practice, see especially Teresa's *Way of Perfection*, (1980: chs 28–31) and *Interior Castle* (1980), first and second mansions.

7 For Teresa, when vocal prayer is sincerely recited with deep and loving attentiveness to whom the prayer is addressed, one can attain contemplation. She writes, ' it is very possible that while you are reciting the Our Father or some other vocal prayer, the Lord may raise you to perfect contemplation' (1980: 130–131).

8 Underhill describes what she calls the dangers of mystical Quietism: 'Pure passivity and indifference were its ideal. All activity was forbidden it, all choice was a negation of its surrender, all striving was unnecessary and wrong. It needed only to rest for evermore and "let God work and speak in the silence"' (1990: 325). St. Teresa also mentions how some of her novices strive to stay immersed in this blissful condition: 'It doesn't seem to them that they are in the world, nor would they want to see or hear about anything other than their God' (1980: 154). Underhill and Teresa insist the mystic needs to become open to other features of spiritual Reality. For Teresa, the danger is to mistake a kind of self-isolated stupor for authentic communal rapture. Rapture is an advanced condition that involves more dynamic elements (1980: 333–334).

9 These comments on Underhill are adapted from Stoeber 2015, especially 38.

10 For a comprehensive and thorough study on the origin(s), history and method(s) of the prayers with the names of Jesus, including the Jesus Prayer, see Hausherr, (1978). His study shows how various short prayers with the name of Jesus started, developed and culminated in the current formula of the Jesus Prayer.

11 For a lively and informative contemporary account of the Jesus Prayer, see Mathewes-Green 2009.

12 Centering Prayer is supported by and spread through a worldwide organisation, named Contemplative Outreach. According to their website, it has more than 90 active chapters in 39 countries, supports more than 800 prayer groups and teaches Centering Prayer to more than 15,000 new people every year. See the website: www.contemplativeoutreach.org/about-us (accessed 8 January 2019).

13 Keating provides complete instruction in a two-page pamphlet, which is available on the website of Contemplative Outreach, whose goal is to promote Centering Prayer and to provide resources for it throughout the world. www.contemplativeoutreach.org/category/category/centering-prayer (accessed 28 December 2018).

14 Christian Meditation, which is supported by the World Community for Christian Meditation, has become a global practice, having spread to more than 120 countries, with approximately 3000 groups around the world. www.wccm.org/content/meditation-groups (accessed 28 December 2018).

15 In 1976, John Main was invited to teach Christian Meditation to the Trappist monks of Gethsemani Abbey in Kentucky. The talks were first published in three consecutive issues of *Cistercian Studies* 12 (1977): 184–90, 272–81; 13 (1978), 75–83, under the title 'Prayer in the tradition of John Cassian'. Later, the collected work was published with a new title, *Christian Meditation: The Gethsemani Talks* (1999).

16 In his writings, 'meditation is the way of simplicity' or similar statements frequently appear. The work of teaching meditation is, according to Main, 'largely taken up with persuading people of the simplicity of meditation' (Main 1982: 17–18).
17 This formal instruction 'How to Meditate' is found right after the 'Contents' of recently published books of John Main. For a slightly longer and different online version of the instruction, see www.wccm.org/content/how-meditate (accessed 28 December 2018).
18 The word *maranatha* is found in two places in the *New Testament*: 1 *Corinthians* 16:22 and *Revelation* 22:20. Main believes *maranatha* is 'one of the earliest recorded Christian prayers' (Freeman 1987: 6).
19 Saccidananda Ashram Shantivanam. www.shantivanamashram.com/about.php. (accessed 19 June 2020).
20 For a critical exploration of the possible influences of Asian meditation traditions on Centering Prayer and Christian Meditation, see Lee 2018, especially 92–139.
21 See, for example, Keating (1997: 27, 140–142, 73–74, 51, 13).
22 Such as: 3HO/Kundalini Yoga, Iyengar Yoga, Ashtanga Vinyasa Yoga, Integral Yoga, Sivananda Yoga, Bihar Yoga and Bikram Yoga.
23 These groups include: Christians Practicing Yoga, (www.christianspracticingyoga.com/), Yoga Faith (https://yogafaith.org/), Holy Yoga (https://holyyoga.net/), Yahweh Yoga (http://yahwehyoga.com/), and Christian Yoga Magazine (https://web.archive.org/web/20080814150734/http://christianyogamagazine.com/) (accessed 28 December 2018). See also the reference to these issues by Candy Gunther Brown in relation to yoga courses given at Wheaton College, a Christian evangelical school in Illinois. She describes the college's position statement on this: 'What redeems yoga at Wheaton is, first, that it is taught by Christians who have signed the Wheaton College Statement of Faith. Second, instructors subtract "ancient (and sometimes religious) words" from pose descriptions and add Christian belief statements: at the start or end of class, they "lead a prayer, offer Scripture or a word of spiritual encouragement."' In her essay Guenther Brown explores questions of cultural appropriation and imperialism, as well as implications related to possible inter-religious influences and practices. Candy Gunther Brown, 'Christian Yoga: Something New under the Sun' (2018: 661).
24 These issues are adapted from Stoeber 2017, especially 5–9. See also Jain's important work focusing on some of these issues, especially that of the cultural appropriation and misuse of yoga by non-Hindus and criticisms of yoga by certain evangelical Christians (2012: 1–8; 2015: 137–140).
25 See, for example, Bakic-Hayden 2008; Clooney 2013; Cole and Sambhi 1993: 139–150; Hisamatsu and Pattni 2015; Matus 1984; Molleur 2009; Justin O'Brien 1978: 23–40; Oden 2017; Stoeber 2015; Unno 2002; Washburn 1995, especially 153–167. Also, we should note in this context that there is some current research in neuroscience that argues there is cross-cultural evidence of a neurological substrate related to contemplative-mystical experience, in terms of corresponding specific electro-chemical brain states (d'Aquili and Newberg 1999; Newberg et al. 2001).

## Bibliography

Abhishiktananda, Swami. 1972. *Prayer*. Revised edition. Philadelphia: Westminister Press.
d'Aquili, E. G. and Newberg, A. B. 1991. *The Mystical Mind: Probing the Biology of Religious Experience*. Minneapolis, MN: Fortress Press.
Bakic-Hayden, M. 2008. 'Two Methods of Contemplation: Yoga and Hesychast Prayer', in *Herald of the Ethnographic Institute of the Serbian Academy of Sciences and Arts*, LV/2: 171–83.
de Bernardino, L. 1952. *The Ascent of Mount Sion*. Peers, A. (trans). London: Faber and Faber.
Bourgeault, C. 2004. *Centering Prayer and Inner Awakening*. Cambridge, MA: Cowley Publications.
Cassian, J. 1997. *John Cassian: The Conferences*. Ramsey, B. (trans). New York: Paulist Press.
Chase, S. 2005. *The Tree of Life: Models of Christian Prayer*. Grand Rapids, MI: Baker Academic.
Clooney, F. 2013. *His Hiding Place and Darkness: A Hindu-Catholic Theopoetics of Divine Absence*. Stanford, CA: Stanford University Press.
Cole, O. W., and Sambhi, P. S. 1993. *Sikhism and Christianity: A Comparative Study*. London: Macmillan.
Contemplative Outreach. 2016. 'The Method of Centering Prayer: The Prayer of Consent'. www.contemplativeoutreach.org/category/category/centering-prayer. Accessed 28 December 2018.
Contemplative Outreach. 2018. 'About Us'. www.contemplativeoutreach.org/about-us. Accessed 8 January 2019.
Francisco de Osuna. 1981. *The Third Spiritual Alphabet*. Giles, Mary E. (trans). New York: Paulist Press.
Freeman, L. 1987. *Light Within: The Inner Path of Meditation*. New York: Crossroad Publishing Company.

Gerding, G. 2001. *Drawing to God: Art as Prayer; Prayer as Art*. Notre Dame, IN: Sorin Books.
Griffiths, Bede. 1994. *The New Creation in Christ: Christian Meditation and Community*. Springfield, Illinois: Templegate Publishers.
Gunther Brown, C. 2018. 'Christian Yoga: Something New Under the Sun/Son'. *Church History* 87(3): 659–683.
Hammerling, R. (ed) 2008. *A History of Prayer: The First to the Fifteenth Century*. Boston: Brill.
Hausherr, I. 1978. *The Name of Jesus*. Cummings, C. (trans). Kalamazoo, MI: Cistercian Publications.
Hisamatsu, E., and Pattni, R. 2015. 'Yoga and the Jesus Prayer – A Comparison between Astanga Yoga and the Yoga Sutras of Patanjali and Psycho-physical Method of Hesychasm', in *Journal of Hindu-Christian Studies* 28(7): 1–21.
Hodgson, P. (ed) 1944. *The Cloud of Unknowing and the Book of Privy Counseling*. London: Oxford University Press.
Huxley, A. 1970. *The Perennial Philosophy*. New York: Harper Colophon Books.
Jain, A. 2012. 'The Malleability of Yoga: A Response to Christian and Hindu Opponents of the Popularization of Yoga'. *Journal of Hindu-Christian Studies* 25: 3–10.
Jain, A. 2015. *Selling Yoga: From Counterculture to Pop Culture*. New York: Oxford Press.
Jantzen, G. 1995. *Power, Gender, and Christian Mysticism*. New York: Cambridge University Press.
Johnston, W. 1982. *The Still Point: Reflections on Zen and Christian Mysticism*. New York: Fordham University Press.
Johnston, W. 1989. *Being in Love: The Practice of Christian Prayer*. New York: Harper & Row.
Keating, T. 1978. 'Contemplative Prayer in the Christian Tradition', in Pennington, M. B., Keating, T. and Clarke, T. (eds), *Finding Grace at the Center*, 35–48. Still River, MA: St. Bede's Publications.
Keating, T. 1997. *Open Mind, Open Heart: The Contemplative Dimension of the Gospel*. New York: Continuum Publishing Company.
Keating, T. 2003. *Intimacy with God: An Introduction to Centering Prayer*. New York: The Crossroad Publishing Company.
Keating, T. 2013. '158. Father Thomas Keating. Interviewed by Rich Archer'. https://batgap.com/transcripts/158_FrThomasKeatingTranscript.pdf. Accessed 21 January 2019.
Larkin, E. E. 1995. 'Contemplative Prayer as the Soul of the Apostolate', in Wicks, R. J. (ed), *Handbook of Spirituality for Ministers*, 456–468. New York: Paulist Press.
Lee, J. 2018. *Sources and Issues in Contemporary Christian Contemplative Prayer: Thomas Keating's Centering Prayer and John Main's Christian Meditation*. PhD Thesis. University of St. Michael. Unpublished.
Main, J. 1981. *Word into Silence*. New York: Paulist Press.
Main, J. 1982. *Letters from the Heart: Christian Monasticism and the Renewal of Community*. New York: Crossroad Publishing Company.
Main, J. 1984. *Moment of Christ: The Path of Meditation*. New York: Crossroad Publishing Company.
Main, J. 1989. *The Heart of Creation: The Meditative Way*. New York: Crossroad Publishing Company.
Main, J. 1999. *Christian Meditation: The Gethsemani Talks*. Tuscon, AZ: Medio Media.
Main, J., and Freeman, L. 2012. 'John Main & Laurence Freeman Respond to Questions on Meditation'. *Meditatio Talks Series*: 1–46. https://issuu.com/meditatio/docs/2012d_questions_on_meditation_-mast. Accessed 21 January 2019.
Mathewes-Green, F, 2009. *The Jesus Prayer: The Ancient Desert Prayer that Tunes the Heart to God*. Brewster, MA: Paraclete Press.
Matus, T. 1984. *Yoga and the Jesus Prayer Tradition: An Experiment in Faith*. Ramsy, NJ: Paulist Press.
McGinn, B. 1987. 'The English Mystics', in Raitt, Jill (ed), *Christian Spirituality II: High Middle Ages and Reformation*, 194–207. New York: Crossroad.
McGinn, B. 2012. *The Varieties of Vernacular Mysticism: 1350–1550*. New York: Herder & Herder.
Merton, Thomas. 1969. Contemplative *Prayer*. New York: Herder and Herder.
Merton, T. and Suzuki, E. T. 1968. *Zen and the Birds of Appetite*. New York: New Directions Publishing Corporation.
Molleur, J. 2009. 'A Hindu Monk's Appreciation of Eastern Orthodoxy's Jesus Prayer'. *Religion East & West* 9: 67–76.
Mursell, G. (ed) 2001. *The Story of Christian Spirituality: Two Thousand Years, from East to West*. Minneapolis, MN: Fortress Press.
Newberg, A. B., et al. 2001. *Why God Won't Go Away: Brain Science and the Biology of Belief*. New York, NY: Ballantine Publishing Group.
O'Brien, J. 1978. *Yoga and Christianity*. Honesdale, PA: Himalayan International Institute.

Oden, A. G. 2017. *Right Here Right Now: The Practice of Christian Mindfulness*. Nashville: Abingdon Press.
Origen. 1954. *Treatise on Prayer: Translation and Notes with an Account of the Practice and Doctrine of Prayer from New Testament Times to Origen*. Jay, Eric George (trans). London: SPCK.
Palamas, Gregory. 1983. *The Triads. Translated by Nicholas Gendle*. Ramsey, NJ: Paulist Press.
Pearson, Paul M. (ed.) 2012. *Thomas Merton on Christian Contemplation*. New York: New Directions.
Polen, N. 1994. *The Holy Fire: The Teachings of Rabbi Kalonymus Kalman Shapira, the Rebbe of the Warsaw Ghetto*. Northvale, NJ: Jason Aronson Inc.
Raphael, M. 1994. 'Feminism, Constructivism and Numinous Experience', *Religious Studies* 30(4): 511–526.
Short, W. 2007. 'Contemplation to Inquisition', in Johnson, Timothy J. (ed), *Franciscans at Prayer*, 449–474. Boston: Brill.
Stoeber, M. 2015/2017. 'The Comparative Study of Mysticism', in *The Oxford Research Encyclopedia of Religion*, 1–40. New York: Oxford University Press.
Stoeber, M. 2015. 'Exploring Processes and Dynamics of Mystical Contemplative Meditation: Some Christian-Buddhist Parallels in Relation to Transpersonal Theory'. *European Journal for Philosophy of Religion* 7(2): 35–57.
Stoeber, M. 2017. 'Issues in Christian Encounters with Yoga: Exploring 3HO/Kundalini Yoga'. *Hindu-Christian Studies* 30(3): 4–20.
Teresa of Avila. 1980. *The Way of Perfection and The Interior Castle*. Vol. 2, *The Completed works of St. Teresa of Avila*. Kavanaugh, Kieran and Rodriguez, Otilio (trans). Washington, DC: ICS Publications.
Teresa of Avila. 1987. *The Book of Her Life*. Vol. 1, *The Completed Works of St. Teresa of Avila*. Kavanaugh, Kieran and Rodriguez, Otilio (trans). Washington, DC: ICS Publications.
Underhill, E. 1914. *Practical Mysticism*. London: E. P. Dutton & Co. Inc.
Underhill, E. 1990 [1911]. *Mysticism: A Study in the Nature and Development of Man's Spiritual Consciousness*. London: E. P. Dutton & Co. Inc.
Unno, T. 2002. 'Jesus Prayer and the Nembutsu', *Buddhist-Christian Studies* 22: 93–99.
Viladesau, R. 2000. *Theology and the Arts: Encountering God through Music, Art and Rhetoric*. New York: Paulist Press.
Walsh, J. (ed) 1981. *The Cloud of Unknowing*. Translated with introduction and notes by James Walsh. New York: Paulist Press.
Washburn, M. 1995. *The Ego and the Dynamic Ground: A Transpersonal Theory of Human Development*. rev. 2nd ed. Albany: SUNY Press.
The World Community for Christian Meditation. *How to Meditate?*. www.wccm.org/content/how-meditate. Accessed 28 December 2018.
The World Community for Christian Meditation. *Meditation Groups*. www.wccm.org/content/meditation-groups. Accessed 28 December 2018.

# 18

# SECULAR DISCOURSE AS A LEGITIMATING STRATEGY FOR MINDFULNESS MEDITATION

*Masoumeh Rahmani*

## Introduction

The secular and scientific reframing of mindfulness meditation, among other things, functions to legitimise and supports the growth of this practice in western mainstream culture. As mindfulness expands the sphere of its influence, an increasing number of scholars have raised concerns about the ethics of implementing mindfulness-based programmes (MBPs) in secular contexts such as healthcare and education. These debates are morally charged and are often hinged on the bedevilling question regarding the nature of the practice: is mindfulness religious or secular?

Within academic circles, and among scholars of religious/Buddhist studies, opinions vary. Some have questioned whether 'nominally secular mindfulness' is actually secular (Brown 2016; 2017; 2019), arguing that even the so-called secularised versions of mindfulness are deeply rooted in Buddhist metaphysical assumptions about the nature of the world and the self (Wilson 2014). Others have argued that the modern application of and selling points of mindfulness are too far removed from the normative Buddhist doctrines, since the purpose of the practice is no longer aimed at cultivating an understanding of the nature of reality as marked by suffering; instead, it has become a panacea, a 'science of happiness' and a method of 'easing the pain of existence' (Lopez 2008; Sharf 2015). Some advocates and promoters of mindfulness, on the other hand, argue that the practice can and should be completely decontextualised from its religious/Buddhist framework and instead recontextualised in secular norms and scientific paradigms (Baer 2015; Crane et al. 2017), with an underlying aim of making the practice more 'accessible' to the non-Buddhist audience.

Conversely, meditation teachers often adopt an entirely different approach and often rhetorically resolve these tensions through fast and loose associations with Buddhism, which essentially allows them to relish the legitimacy associated with the historical Buddha and at the same time relinquish any unfavoured 'religious' connotations associated with the tradition. For instance, a pervasive line of reasoning, commonly used by teachers such as Jon Kabat-Zinn, argues that the technique they teach is not Buddhist but the 'essence' of the Buddha's teachings, which is 'universal' and compatible with science, or that 'the Buddha himself was not a Buddhist'.

These discourses are rooted in the Buddhist reform movements that developed as a resistance to the colonialism, imperialism and missionisation of Southeast Asian counties by European nations during the late-nineteenth century (McMahan 2008). Satya Narayan Goenka (1924–2013) was one of the famous meditation teachers whose rhetorical strategies for disassociating Vipassana meditation from the category of 'religion' has helped to establish and promote these trends globally. Elsewhere, I have systematically analysed Goenka's rhetorical strategies – namely: (1) the rhetoric of experience; (2) meditation as a 'tool'; (3) the 'pure teachings of the Buddha'; and (4) the rhetoric of 'here and now' – and demonstrated how these function to conceal the religious elements of his ten-day Vipassana courses for its committed followers (Rahmani 2017; forthcoming a). Goenka's rhetorical strategies and their interrelated components can also be found in the discourses of mindfulness leaders and, by extension, mindfulness practitioners.[1] In fact, I posit that they are the bedrock upon which contemporary mindfulness leaders have developed their very own constellation of discursive strategies to create legitimacy and to abstract mindfulness meditation from the category of 'religion' in order to facilitate its implementation in secular domains.

This chapter seeks to provide context to these debates by taking a sobering approach: instead of responding to the tiring question about the (religious/secular) nature of mindfulness, it will explore the popular strategies operationalised by meditation teachers to resolve these tensions. In other words, this chapter looks at the most common strategies through which mindfulness has been portrayed as a secular practice by the leading figures[2] of this movement and the extent to which these discursive patterns are adopted by their followers. Similar points can be raised about the language of some contemporary yoga movements, though these are beyond the scope of this chapter.

Drawing from qualitative research, in the following pages I explore several of these strategies in the context of the mindfulness movement – namely: (1) science, scientism and neuroscientism; (2) academisation; (3) the rhetoric of universality; (4) the Buddhist discourse of suffering; and (5) mental health and resilience. Lastly, by taking Oxford Mindfulness Centre (OMC) as a case study, I contextualise the development of these discursive strategies by paralleling them with the evolution of, and the amendments to, this centre's mission statement. Note that in this chapter I am not concerned with assessing the benefits or the shortcomings of mindfulness as a technology of the self: promoters have raised their points in support of the practice, and there is likewise an abundance of criticisms directed at the movement, such as the objections raised by the McMindfulness critiques (Purser et al. 2016). It is also not my intention to discourage readers from engaging with mindfulness, nor do I advocate against the application of MBPs as an optional treatment. Rather, my aim is to showcase the agendas and assumptions that sit beneath the surface of the movement's discourses and, in doing so, further Brown's (2017) call for transparency and informed consent.

## Research method

My arguments are based on my ethnographic fieldwork at various mindfulness conventions and in-depth interviews with thirty-two mindfulness meditators/teachers, as well as secondary sources such as organisational documents. The material presented in this chapter emerged from a two-year, mixed-method, longitudinal study that examined 'unbelief' in the mindfulness subcultures of the USA and the UK, funded by the University of Kent's Understanding Unbelief Programme. The interview participants were recruited based on their identification with non-religious identities/positions (e.g. atheist, agnostic, none, etc.) in our preliminary online survey.[3] Readers should keep these narrow recruitment criteria in mind while drawing conclusions from the findings of this study.

The interviews were semi-structured, steered to some extent by an interview guide that addressed themes such as participants' background, the role of religion in their upbringing, their introduction to mindfulness, their experience and understanding of the practice and examples of its application in their day-to-day lives. The interviews also included conceptual questions, such as the participants' definition of mindfulness, religion and reality, along with a set of provocative issues such as the implementation of mindfulness in the military. Moreover, all interview questions were open-ended in design, allowing for participants to build up their narratives at their own pace and to discuss matters they considered important. The interviews were subsequently transcribed and analysed using a combination of thematic and structural narrative analysis (Riessman 1993). Pseudonyms are used to ensure the anonymity of all participants.

## Science, scientism and neuroscientism

The assertion that mindfulness is secular because it is scientifically validated has been the dominant strategy of the promoters, advocates and practitioners of mindfulness. This pattern of reasoning takes advantage of the authority of science in modern western cultures and its history of perceived opposition with 'religion' since the European enlightenment. Hence, by virtue of associating mindfulness with science, two things are implicitly conveyed: its legitimacy (social approval), and its opposition to 'religion'. This reasoning holds that because the practice is empirically tested, it is therefore not religious. Much like the rhetoric of experience[4] (Rahmani 2017; forthcoming a), this argument rests on a limited Protestant notion of religion as being primarily about beliefs or simply the verbal declaration of transcendent beliefs. According to this line of thought, secularising a technique equates simply with the removal and/or translation of explicit religious language into a secular one (Brown 2017: 53).

It must be noted that this strategic use of the religious/secular binary has been orchestrated from within the mindfulness movement, although some advocates from within academic circles have recently called for a postmodern and 'post-secular' approach and attempt at resolving this tension by erasing the question altogether. Jane F. Compson's (2017) chapter, 'Is Mindfulness Secular or Religious and Does it Matter?' is a fascinating example, whereby the author selectively renders certain categories – 'secular', 'religion', 'Buddhism' – as social constructs in favour of other, supposedly less daunting terms such as 'spirituality', 'suffering' and 'mindfulness'. Subsequently, Compson (2017: 39) suggests that instead of asking if mindfulness is Buddhist or religious, and rather than assessing the nature of mindfulness based on 'outdated' assumptions about the nature of religion and its evolving relationship with science and secularity, 'a better question to focus on is "is mindfulness helpful in reducing suffering?"' – this is precisely the strategic use of the discourse of suffering that I examine later in this chapter.

At a discursive and ideological level, this (re)framing of mindfulness within a scientific narrative, as a means to legitimise the practice and position it under a secular canopy, could be best described as scientism. Scientism is the view that considers scientific knowledge as the only source of real knowledge, placed above and beyond all other branches of learning (Hutchinson 2011; Sorell 1991). This perspective renders all other systems of knowledge (religious, cultural, etc.) inferior 'until granted the imprimatur of empirical verification' (Harrison 2006: 65). Scientism is hence characterised by a tendency to 'extend scientific ideas, methods, practices, and attitudes to matters of human social and political concern' (Olson, 2008). Such dispositions undergird the scientific endeavours of the mindfulness movement, and can also be seen in the discourse of its practitioners. Take, for instance, the following passage from my conversation with Juno:

> Juno [60s, UK]: I'm more keen on science. And with mindfulness the science is evolving. It may be that Jesus and the Buddha had insights into their beings and what made them happy and fulfilled and compassionate to others. And didn't necessarily have the scientific underpinning of that. Whereas I think that's why it's emerging … You know jogging helps the heart. Mindfulness practice, formal mindfulness increases your ability to not get lost in the 'me' and 'I' parts of the brain and I guess that's why I'm more keen on that because there's a lot of scientific basis to it.

Juno's passage encapsulates not only how science is valued (above religious knowledge) but also how crucial this scientific reframing is to the appeal and the perceived legitimacy of the practice.[5] In fact, the scientific representation of mindfulness was an integral factor for the clear majority of the participants in this research (who were atheists, agnostics and 'nones') to experiment with mindfulness in the first place. Further, Juno's comment, 'it may be that Jesus and Buddha had insights … And didn't necessarily have the scientific underpinning of that' is almost suggestive of a perceived shortcoming on the part of Jesus and the Buddha for not formulating their message to the liking of the modern audience – one that is now compensated through the scientific efforts the community.

In a recently published, manifesto-like article, 'What Defines Mindfulness-based Programs? The Warp and the Weft', the leading figures of mindfulness in the USA and the UK took it upon themselves to not only define MBPs and the characteristics of a mindfulness teacher (hence exhorting some kind of monopoly on the marketplace), but also to declare their aim as 'recontextualising' both the content and the theoretical underpinnings of mindfulness into a scientific paradigm so as to safeguard its implementation into mainstream settings (Crane et al. 2017: 992). In other words, they aim to actively unhinge a practice (which we realistically have little scientific understanding of, in terms of its functionality) from its original system of meaning (or, as the authors frame it, its 'religious, esoteric and mystical elements') in order to forcefully recontextualise it in a paradigm that appeals to mainstream western culture (or ironically, as the authors put it, 'ensuring that they [MBPs] are delivered in an inclusive and culturally appropriate way').

This scientisation of meditation is a relatively modern phenomenon that has spread beyond Hinduism and Buddhism, encompassing other Asian traditions such as Jainism. The implication of this scientisation (and academisation; see below) of Asian practices entails a change in the sociological structure of these traditions involving a relegation of the authority of the monastics and ascetics (Aukland 2016). This appeal to science, which we witness in the case of mindfulness, as the means to increase legitimacy is comparable to the well-studied process of the scientisation of Transcendental Meditation by Maharishi, which took place in the 1970s (Farias and Rahmani, forthcoming). In fact, it could be said that Maharishi laid the groundwork for a scientisation model that is now being roughly followed (and expanded upon) by the contemporary mindfulness movement: specifically, Maharishi's active initiative to establish universities, institutes, journals and quasi-academic conferences, and his promotion of devotees with academic (scientific) degrees into higher positions of authority in the TM organisation (Humes 2010: 346). In a sense, both movements turned to 'modern Western science, with its graphs and charts' to vouch for the efficacy of their practices (Lowe 2011: 61).

Yet, other than the rapid accumulation of literature, the evidence for the efficacy of mindfulness is not strong.[6] In fact, within academic circles, studies on mindfulness are commonly known to suffer from various methodological and conceptual issues. In an article published in 2017, for instance, fifteen psychologists and cognitive scientists unanimously raised concerns about the methodological issues undergirding the research on mindfulness. These, according to Van Dam et al. (2018: 7), included:

> (a) insufficient construct validity in measures of mindfulness, (b) challenges to (clinical) intervention methodology, (c) potential adverse effects from practicing mindfulness, and (d) questionable interpretations of data from contemplative neuroscience concerning the mental processes and brain mechanisms underlying mindfulness.

The severity of this situation has led mindfulness leaders to temper some of their enthusiasm in their public talks, particularly those that are tailored to their newly trained teachers.[7] Interestingly, mindfulness leaders place the burden of the mindfulness 'hype' on the shoulders of the media. This was certainly the case for every mindfulness leader/figure whom I watched speak at different conventions and conferences between 2017 and 2018.[8] However, a study by Sumner and colleagues (2014: 4) suggests that most of the exaggerations detected in health-related science news did not originate in the media; rather, inflated claims already existed 'in the text of the press releases produced by academics and their establishments'. Yet, we should not be surprised if, in a few years' time, mindfulness leaders do point fingers at the media for generating further hype, this time in the context of the neuroscience of meditation.

As a sub-genre of scientism, one might consider 'neuroscientism', which is 'the pervasive yet mistaken idea that neuroscience does fully account for awareness and behavior' (Tallis, 2010). Neuro-prefixed terminology – such as neuroplasticity, neurobiology and neurotransmitters – is currently one of the most popular and efficient discursive methods used by mindfulness leaders, teachers and practitioners to make the workings of meditation seem real, tangible and believable, even though this stack of literature lacks a robust understanding of how meditation affects the brain (Dorjee 2017). Here, too, a critique of the neuroscientific study of meditation is emerging from both within and outside this field, and most notably concerns the difficulties associated with the interpretation and the analysis of neuroimaging data (Van Dam et al. 2018), which is said to be analogous to a Rorschach test (Komjathy 2015). While most neuroscientists involved in the field of contemplative studies are aware of these challenges and are taking measures to develop more robust methodologies, such sophistication, as Komjathy notes, 'rarely trickles down to popular publications and discourse, which tend to make sweeping claims about the "scientific benefits of meditation"' (Komjathy 2018: 254). Instead, neuroscientific terminologies are constantly used in mindfulness events and in the programmes tailored to the general public (such as the introductory session of a standard eight-week Mindfulness-Based Cognitive Therapy [MBCT]), without much context or explanation provided as to what is meant by using such terminology.

When used in such vague ways, the sole function of this language is to gain legitimacy, as recent evidence suggests that 'non-experts in neuroscience are more likely to believe explanations if they contain some neuroscience terms' (Dorjee 2018). Indeed, this was the case for many of the mindfulness meditators whom I have interviewed. Most of them referenced not only literature published by various neuroscientists[9] working in this field – among other scientific literature, such as 'that Harvard study'[10] – but also took at face value the anecdotal narratives that these neuroscientists broadcast on various outlets such as online podcasts.

## Academisation as other sources of legitimacy

Legitimacy, like capital, is a resource that businesses and organisations require in order to succeed and survive. Yet unlike money, legitimacy does not have a material form; 'it exists only as a symbolic representation of the collective evaluation of an institution' (Hybels 1995: 243). More importantly, legitimacy is a *dynamic* construct simply because it relies on the expectations, values, beliefs and norms of a community/society, which are not static and change over time. A successful organisation is one that makes an active effort to both create and maintain legitimacy by aligning with, and adapting to, the social norms of the environment in which it operates.

Appealing to science and relying on empirical studies are not the only methods that mindfulness leaders utilise to lend explicit legitimacy to mindfulness and implicit credibility to the claim that mindfulness is secular. As the pool of 'scientific' literature on mindfulness grew in the past couple of decades, new avenues to legitimacy became available to the movement: cementing mindfulness as an academic enterprise. A case in point is the flourishing of MA and PhD programmes, conferences, specific journals and university-affiliated research centres dedicated to different applications of mindfulness. The precise processes involved in the establishment of these centres are beyond the remit of this chapter. Suffice it to note that other than being a source of revenue, they play a crucial role in shaping what mindfulness is, where it should be implemented and how it should be perceived by both the public and the policy makers.

In a keynote speech addressed to hundreds of mindfulness teachers and trainees at the 2018 MiSP event in London, Jon Kabat-Zinn uttered the following:[11]

> The Wellcome Trust has given the Oxford Centre for Mindfulness a very, very large grant to study for I think seven years in a randomised trial the effects of mindfulness in schools. Now, I don't know how many of you actually heard what I just said. The, Oxford, Centre, for Mindfulness. Oxford University has a centre for mindfulness! It didn't always. Twenty years ago, that would've been laughable, inconceivable. And yet, Oxford University, the most august university in the world has a centre for mindfulness. The MIT medical department is big into mindfulness. There are universities all around the world that are doing cutting-edge mindfulness research.

The salient point here is that the movement and its leading figures borrow from the authority of academia and the prestige of their affiliated institutions, arguing implicitly that because these top universities are becoming increasingly invested in mindfulness studies, mindfulness is therefore credible and worthwhile. Another hallmark example involves the birth of the 'Professorship in Mindfulness and Psychological Science' (University of Oxford 2019). This position, which was created in April 2019 by the OMC, is demonstrative of the movement's attempt to solidify and secure the future of mindfulness as an academic discipline.

## Rhetoric of universality

The rhetoric of the universality of mindfulness is a multifaceted discourse that functions to unhinge the practice from the religious, social and historical contexts from which it was derived. In simple terms, when mindfulness is declared as an 'innate human capacity', it cannot be possibly bounded to any tradition, let alone Buddhism. This line of thought, as Sharf (2015: 477) has argued, borrows heavily from 'perennialism', which upholds the universality of mystical experience: the notion that 'there is a singular, transcultural, trans-historical, and spiritual experience' common to all mystics around the world. The following passage from Jon Kabat-Zinn (MiSP Keynote, 2018) illustrates these points:

> It's [mindfulness] a practice, it's a way of being, it's not a philosophy, it's not a catechism, it's not an idea, it's a way of being. And these practices come from all of the ancient meditative traditions of the world. And yet they are universal because they have to do with being human, they don't have to do with being a Buddhist, or a Hindu, or a Yogi, or a Christian, or, or, Islamic or Jewish [...] It's not that you have to get anything in meditation, it's the recognition that we already have everything. We are complete and whole already. So mindfulness is pure awareness. It can't possibly be Asian, or Western, or ancient or modern. It's human. It's in our DNA.

This desire to conceptualise mindfulness as universal was also apparent in the language of most meditators and teachers I have interviewed. However, this is not to say that all of the participants downplayed the Buddhist roots of mindfulness at the expense of portraying it as universal (as was exemplified in the above quote from Kabat-Zinn). See, for instance, the passage below from my interview with Marv:

> Marv [30s; US]: My feeling about the way it's [mindfulness] taught in MBSR-style programs [...] is more that it draws on lessons that come from Buddhism, but are not necessarily true, only of Buddhism. They are kind of like truths of human psychology, or the human condition if you will [...] I don't see those lessons as being tied to any, particular spiritual tradition or faith. I think they're basic truths of the human condition, um, and lessons that anyone could learn from regardless of their background or spiritual tradition.

Moreover, at a functional level, this universalist rhetoric also aims to abstract the ethical underpinnings of the practice from the Buddhist tradition by claiming that ethics are in fact an intrinsic aspect of the practice itself; that mindfulness contains implicit ethics and thus by virtue of practicing mindfulness, one can automatically cultivate virtues such as compassion. These universal claims, as Walsh (2016: 155) has argued, suffer on accounts of having no rational or empirical support and instead function purely on the basis of implicit ideology that serves to strategically ward off criticisms such as the implication and agenda behind introducing mindfulness into the corporate world. This pattern of reasoning is also apparent among the language of meditators and mindfulness teachers. In fact, in response to my question about the application of mindfulness in the US and UK military, almost all participants (30/32) expressed their unbounded support for such interventions, particularly as a method to combat PTSD (see the section 'Mental health and resilience'), while almost half of them (15) seemed convinced that secular mindfulness can/will cultivate compassion and enable soldiers to 'see the humanity in others' in such a way that they *ought* to 'ultimately quit the army' and change their career. Lastly, two participants saw this intervention as deeply problematic and conflicting with what they conceived as the Buddhist ethics of nonviolence. These figures were particularly startling and demonstrative of how these discourses are intertwined with one another – both universalist and mental health (see below) – and how they arguably promote the kind of 'passive acceptance and a suspension of critical reflection' that King (2016: 42) sees as a trend in secular mindfulness practices.

## Buddhist discourse of suffering

In his confession-like article in 2011, Kabat-Zinn notes that in order to facilitate the introduction of mindfulness to western mainstream culture and 'make it acceptable' to non-Buddhists, he 'bent over backward' to select a language that 'avoided as much as possible the risk of it being seen as Buddhist, "New Age," "Eastern Mysticism" or just plain "flakey "' (2011: 282). Such an approach was also mirrored in the early promotion of MBCT in the UK. Ironically, Kabat-Zinn (and, to an extent, his British peers) draws upon Buddhist discourses, most notably 'suffering' as a means to justify his downplaying of the Buddhist roots of mindfulness.

For instance, Kabat-Zinn frames this motivation as being inspired by a ten-second 'vision' that occurred to him during a two-week Vipassana meditation course in 1979. According to his narrative, he envisioned, in a flash of light, Mindfulness-Based Stress Reduction (MBSR) and its far-reaching implications (spreading across hospitals and clinics in the world, sparking scientific investigation, etc.) and took it as his 'karmic assignment' to share the 'essence of dharma' or the teachings of the Buddha with everyone, particularly those who are suffering. Kabat-Zinn thus vindicates his reframing of mindfulness in secular terms on the account of a noble cause: 'to relieve suffering and catalyse greater compassion and wisdom in our lives and culture' (ibid: 285). In fact, similar to Goenka,[12] Kabat-Zinn's (ibid: 281) vision to eradicate suffering has blossomed into a global, evangelical motive, inspiring him to anticipate the current interest in mindfulness leading to

> a multi-dimensional emergence of great transformative and liberative promise, one which, if cared for and tended, may give rise to a flourishing on this planet akin to a second, and this time global, Renaissance, for the benefit of all sentient beings and our world.[13]

This particular use of the Buddhist discourse is not entirely unique to Kabat-Zinn; rather, it can be identified in the language of some proponents – such as Compson (2017: 39), referenced earlier – and other leading figures of this movement. For instance, not only did the Director of the OMC, Willem Kuyken, openly encourage mindfulness teachers to cautiously tailor their language according to the demands of their clients (i.e. avoid Buddhist terminology in promoting mindfulness in the workplace), but he did so by referring to the historical Buddha, arguing that the Buddha himself also changed his language in order to promote the practice to the king – a discursive approach that renders the ethical issues of purposely avoiding Buddhist terminology acceptable.[14]

## Ethics of rebranding: participants' position

All the mindfulness teachers interviewed for this study were very cautious with how they negotiated their position in the marketplace and the language via which they chose to deliver their mindfulness packages (i.e. mindfulness in workplace, mental health, or education, etc.). They frequently spoke about the challenges of selling the practice in ways that appeal to the general public or in ways that do not repel those clients who may not have spiritual leanings. They spoke of the resistance they frequently face from mainstream culture and, more specifically, from their affiliated institutions or colleagues (in the case of those who strived to implement mindfulness in universities or schools as part of the curriculum). Regardless of whether these participants had an affinity towards Buddhism or whether mindfulness fulfilled a spiritual role in their own personal lives, the majority of the teachers and meditators in this study (28/32) were happy to compartmentalise their personal beliefs from their professional approach to teaching mindfulness and did not consider the strategic rebranding as ethically problematic. As Alfred [50s, UK] argued, 'you say potato, I say potāto. You say dukkha and I say discrepancy-based processing.' However, this was not necessarily the case for everyone:

> Penelope [40s, UK]: To take mindfulness into the workplace, it feels like I'm having to use a completely different language again [...] it really clashes with [pause] with the essence of what mindfulness is. So yeah, when we're using words like 'compassion', like 'empathy'. You know 'awareness' is safe. It's ok to use 'awareness'! But anything that has a kind of touchy-feely, um, ambiguous words then, yeah, my fear is that people wouldn't be interested [...] So my challenge is how to get those people in a room, to [pause] introduce them, [pause] to mindfulness! But, [hah] But! without almost [laughs] without using the word mindfulness! But then that goes against, you know [long pause], um, [pause] well, everything that I've learnt, and everything that I believe [long pause] is based on, on, these words.

Several participants (4/32), including Penelope, raised their concerns about the ethics of rebranding mindfulness in secular terminology and/or any intentional lack of transparency about the Buddhist roots of the practice. In short, while they accepted the reality of the marketplace and adopted these marketing strategies themselves, their concerns primarily stemmed from an ambivalence over the role that language and the Buddhist ethical framework played in bringing about the transformative efficacy of mindfulness. In other words, they were concerned that the essence of mindfulness, on which its efficacy rests, could potentially get lost in translation.

## Mental health and resilience

That mindfulness meditators have found something of value in this practice and its teachings to help them better cope with anxiety and improve their mental health is by no means under scrutiny here. In fact, having had the opportunity to speak formally and informally with many mindfulness meditators, I have no doubt about the potential for this practice to bring about positive transformations, particularly in the context of anxiety and depression. Rather, my aim in this section is to shed light on a discursive pattern that is seldom addressed due to the persisting cultural stigmas associated with mental health: that is, using mental health as a *discursive strategy* in specific ways to legitimise the propagation of MBPs in secular spheres (education, military and healthcare), not only at the cost of hiding its Buddhist elements and/or potential spiritual effects, but by means of achieving these ends.

The majority (19/32) of the individuals who participated in this study explicitly framed mental health as their initial motive for engaging with mindfulness (while four individuals highlighted a desire for the self-regulatory benefits as a motive, six arrived through 'serial seekership' (Sutcliffe 2004) and four were introduced to the practice through their networks). Therefore, it was not surprising that their narratives revolved heavily around the theme of mental health and the ways in which meditation had proved helpful in this regard. The significant point is that while most of these individuals started meditation from a non-religious position, with increased participation, the participants' sense of self and the world, their values, and even (for some) their relations with transcendent realities were transformed. In fact, the longitudinal interviews pointed towards a pattern of change in the unbelievers' outlook, such as transit from atheism to (1) secular Buddhism; (2) strong agnosticism; and (3) spirituality (Rahmani, forthcoming b). Take for instance, the following passage from Zoey as an example of the latter pattern of change:

> Zoey [40s; UK]: I've started to deepen my practice, so for about four years I've done it every day. And I've really found probably for the past couple of years, I've found this sense of something greater. Like this, I've got this sense of connection and while I still say I'm not, I'm not a fan of organised religion, but I do think there's more than meets the eye. I meditate sometimes at a Buddhist monastery. I don't count myself as Buddhist. I don't count Buddhism as religion, it's a philosophy to me. Yeah and I actually had, at the monastery, I had what I would class as spiritual awakening. Spontaneously! I, it was very odd and very amazing, and I became one with everything for a couple of hours and that really changed my life [...] since then I've been really on a much more spiritual path. I teach mindfulness in a secular way but myself, I'm much more interested in the spiritual side now [...] I don't think you can have that experience and still consider [yourself] [...] as atheist.

In any case, almost all of the mindfulness teachers I interviewed noted that they actively refrained from divulging their own spiritual approach to the practice, not only in their teachings but also in their conversations with other people. Instead, they simply preferred to use the language of mental health:

> AUTHOR: What is your approach to meditation, and do you categorise it as a religious practice?
>
> VERONICA [40S; US]: No. It's [mindfulness] not a conscious religious practice to me. And when I talk to other people about it, I do it from the perspective of how it helps my physical and mental health. Anything it does for me, spiritually, is very private, and I, I wouldn't discuss it.

Moreover, in these circles, mental health is being used as a discursive strategy to reason the downplay of the religious/Buddhist roots of the practice in order to avoid 'triggering' any trauma or negative memory associated with religion in their clients. This was pointed out to me by Alfred, a trained mindfulness teacher who, like many other participants, utilises mindfulness to improve his mental health. Yet, unlike most of the participants, he noted that he tries to 'live by the *sila*' (the Buddhist code of conduct) and 'follows the dharma' (the teachings of the Buddha) in his life:

> Alfred [50s, UK]: If you read the green book on MBCT, the textbook, as far as I can recall it, it doesn't have any kind of dharma associations or quotations or anything in there. And I think the encouragement at Oxford was to steer clear, um, of those what you might call 'spiritual associations.' For the simple reason that they can be very challenging to people in the group. And an unnecessary challenging to people in the group, particularly a mental health group. So, for example, if you've got a group with clinical indications that they may suffer from depression. For some of those people, their depression may have roots in the religious constrains in their upbringing. And as soon as you bring in any kind of spiritual or religious connotations, those people are going to be instantly turned off [...] if I do talk about *dukkha* to an NHS group in [name of a town] that might just instantly turn some of them off from the whole course. Instantly! Because they feel they're being preached at, and that I'm trying to brainwash them, or evangelise them. So it could be harmful.

Alfred's passage is of interest for three reasons: first, it provides indirect insight into the kinds of rationale that mindfulness organisations provide to their trainees. Second, it depicts the concerns that mindfulness teachers face in delivering their product to the public (note the way Alfred imagines how he might be perceived through the vantage point of his clients). Third, note how Alfred's concerns about repelling his audience with religious terminology morphs into concern about their psychological wellbeing ('harmful'). This particular use of mental health also emerged in the context of several interviews with mindfulness meditators, and in response to provocative questions that challenged their positions (i.e. their context-dependent identities) – for instance, questions about the Buddhist underpinnings of mindfulness or whether a regular practice can be seen as a form of ritual. In these contexts, and instead of responding to these questions directly, those participants who primarily framed their own motivation for practicing mindfulness as a tool to improve their mental health tended to remind me of this fact about their lives (e.g. that mindfulness helps them with their panic attacks) and end any discussion on these topics. In effect, this way of communication tilted the power dynamics between myself and the interviewee in such a way that I often felt both constrained and unwelcome to pursue those specific topics further.

At an institutional level, the strategic use of mental health is evident in the way mindfulness organisations such as the OMC and MiSP have marketed themselves in the UK, secured large research grants, lobbied in the British parliament and justified the promotion of mindfulness in schools; it is mirrored in the movement's legal documents and the mission statements of the OMC (see below); it is reflected in the way these organisations encourage their members and trainees teachers to 'stick with [the] mental health'[15] narrative when they pitch mindfulness to headmasters in schools and to utilise specific language such as 'resilience' and 'grit' when they pitch mindfulness to politicians.[16]

Indeed, a similar critique applies to the buzzword 'resilience', which has gained currency in contemporary socio-political discourse, owing much of its power to the vagueness of the concept that makes it amenable to '(un)intentional scientific justification of particular policies, projects, and practices' (Olsson et al., 2015: 6). In recent years, governments and educational institutions (schools and universities) have invested in programmes that aim to cultivate resilience in students. Notwithstanding the prevalence of such viewpoints among educators, no consensus exists among different educational bodies as to what resilience is, how exactly one develops a resilient student or, indeed, what defines a resilient person? In such contexts, institutions are left to define and supplement a resilience strategy on their own. It was precisely within this fuzzy context that the OMC's Wellcome Trust-funded program, My Resilience in Adolescence project (MYRIAD), introduced mindfulness in British schools. Yet despite hinging this large project on the token of 'resilience', the term has not been adequately defined in the publications emerging from this project, and in fact it is often used interchangeably with 'flourishing' (Kuyken et al. 2017). I therefore consider resilience as the movement's latest discursive strategy to support their promotion of mindfulness in schools.

## OMC history and mission statement

To contextualise the above points and to trace the evolution of the discursive strategies used by the mindfulness movement, we can simply refer to the key developments in the historical timeline of the OMC and the strategic alterations of their mission statement.[17] First and foremost, it should be noted that, contrary to common assumptions, this centre was *not* created within the department of Psychiatry at Oxford University – it attached itself to this department in 2011, when the name of the centre was legally changed to 'Oxford

Mindfulness Foundation'. In fact, the centre was formally founded in 2007 by four members of the Oxford Centre for Buddhist Studies: Geoffrey Bamford, a business man and Oxford graduate in Pali and Sanskrit and an active member of Oxford Centre for Buddhist Studies; Professor Richard Gombrich, a renowned scholar in Buddhist studies; Venerable Khammai Dhammasami, a Buddhist monk and scholar; and Dr. John Peacock, a lecturer in Buddhist studies (Companies House Service [company no. 06144314]). At its inception in 2007, the OMC declared its objective as:

> To advance the education and mental health of the public by both: (1) promoting research into: *traditional Buddhist practices for the enhancement of well-being ('Mindfulness')*; contemporary applications of those practices; and the neuroscientific understanding of their operation and effectiveness; (2) training others in those practices, their applications and relevant neuroscientific research techniques.
>
> *(Companies House 2019; italics added)*

In 2008, the OMC's mission statement remained largely the same, except that the terms 'enhancement of well-being' were replaced with 'achievement and maintenance of psychological balance'.

In 2012, the words 'traditional Buddhist practices' had completely lost their footing in this equation, giving prominence to 'mindfulness', which by now had leapt out of the confinements of parentheses and became an entity of its own standing. Thus, the first component of the above-mentioned mission statement was altered to 'promoting research into the achievement and maintenance of psychological balance through mindfulness'.

In 2017, the mission statement was reconceptualised as '(a) promoting research into (1) *preventing depression* and enhancing human potential across the lifespan and (2) *reducing suffering, promoting resilience* and the realisation of human potential across the lifespan through mindfulness' (ibid; italics added). And finally, in the latest revision of the mission statement in 2018, the OMC stated its aim as:

> To *reduce suffering, promote resilience* and realise human potential across the lifespan through mindfulness. We achieve our mission through rigorous scientific research, maximising the impact of our work through public engagement and dissemination.
>
> *(Companies House 2019; italics added)*

These amendments to the OMC's mission statements are by no means haphazard; they overlap and align with the discursive strategies I have explored above, starting from the scientisation of a traditional Buddhist practice and culminating in a strategic ambiguity.

## Concluding remarks

This chapter has explored several strategies through which mindfulness leaders have created legitimacy for the practice and paved the way for its introduction into and growth in mainstream culture. Most of these strategies are not unique to the mindfulness movement. As noted, comparisons can be drawn between the mindfulness movement, TM, and Goenka's Vipassana movement, particularly in utilising strategies such as the scientisation and academisation of meditation and the secular and universalist rhetoric. A noteworthy exception perhaps concerns the theme of mental health and resilience, which (to my knowledge) are not explicit in Goenka's discourse.[18] Moreover, these discursive strategies are tightly interrelated (e.g. universalism and mental health), as is evident in the interview excerpts and the participants' responses (e.g. mindfulness in the military).

To the extent that these strategies are seen to be operationalised in order to support the growth of mindfulness, a certain critique is due – others may well disagree and reason that such strategies are unintentional. Undoubtedly, this moral criticism has coloured my language, analyses, and presentation of the material provided in this chapter. My critique is specifically directed at the institutional and leadership levels, pertaining to instances where language is manipulated in ways to mask evangelism; where trainee teachers are actively instructed to de-emphasise the spiritual/Buddhist associations of the practice for the sake of appealing to a larger market, leading the very same teachers to feel compelled to conceal their own spiritual leanings; where dishonesty is normalised and mental health is unwittingly trivialised and used to undermine peoples' agency and freedom of choice; and where language obscures ethics and promotes social passivity.

## Notes

1 Framing meditation as a 'tool', for instance, is a common rhetorical strategy that can be seen in the discourse of both Goenka's Vipassana movement and the mindfulness movement. This line of reasoning is empowered by three intrinsically linked ideas that strongly resonate with modern meditators: autonomy (i.e. that an individual is responsible for their own spiritual/personal development), agency (i.e. that an individual should take an active role towards their spiritual/personal development) and practicality (i.e. the specific pragmatic benefits of meditation) – all of which are juxtaposed against the concept of 'empty rituals' (i.e. ritualistically praying to, and relying on, an external force for a desired outcome).

2 By the 'leading figures' of the mindfulness movement, I am referring to a handful of famous mindfulness teachers/academics and directors of key mindfulness institutions, such as Jon Kabat-Zinn and Willem Kuyken.

3 Additionally, for the qualitative dimension of this research, we only included those individuals who scored low on both self-report scales that measured spirituality and religiosity.

4 As an epistemic strategy – that considers embodied experience as a true source of knowledge, overriding intellectual knowledge – this rhetoric undergirds much of Goenka's enterprise for abstracting his teachings of Vipassana from the category of religion. For instance, despite the fact that Goenka's teachings rest on various Buddhist doctrines (including *dukkha*, *anicca*, *anatta*, *sankhara*, *kamma*, reincarnation, etc.), he actively discourages his students from accepting them 'blindly'. Instead, they are advised to accept these insights as 'truths' once they have experienced them for themselves. This rhetoric leads meditators to disassociate these ideas from 'religious doctrine' and the movement from 'religion' simply because they have experienced one of them in an embodied way (*anicca*).

5 For instance, Penelope [40s, UK] noted, 'Now that I've looked into the science of it, now I completely believe that it helps to self-regulate the brain. It self-regulates those hormones.'

6 A widely referenced meta-analysis (Goyal et al. 2014) suggests that mindfulness was only moderately effective in reducing symptoms of pain, anxiety, and depression. However, in this regard, it was not found to be more effective than other active treatments, such as exercise. In the context of other conditions, mindfulness proved to have low or no efficacy.

7 In 2017, I participated in an OMC Master Class, 'Mindfulness-based Interventions in the Workplace: The Role of Theory, Science and Research', led by Willem Kuyken. At this event, I witnessed a lecture room of approximately fifty mindfulness teachers gasp as they were informed about the actual state of scientific literature on mindfulness: that the higher the quality of a mindfulness study is, the positive effects appear lesser.

8 Willem Kuyken at OMC Master Class 2017, Jon Kabat-Zinn at 2018 MiSP and Mark Williams at the Summertown Unified Reformed Church in 2018.

9 See, for example, the final sentence quoted from Juno (i.e. 'in the "me" and "I" parts of the brain …'), where she indirectly draws from the findings of cognitive neuroscience and neurobiology regarding the locality and mechanisms undergirding one's sense of self. The use of neuroscientific explanations (regarding notions of selfhood, etc.) can be seen in the language of Jon Kabat-Zinn (2005: 326, cited in Husgafvel 2018: 290).

10 The most frequently referenced paper by the participants involved the famous article 'A Wandering Mind is an Unhappy Mind' by Killingsworth and Gilbert (2010).
11 Mindfulness in Schools Project. Website: https://mindfulnessinschools.org/. Accessed 30 Dec. 2019.
12 Goenka and Kabat-Zinn both share an evangelical world-saving vision and use this idea as means to frame the promotion of their practice in other countries. In fact, a shared narrative between these two meditation masters is the idea of taking their practice 'back to the land in which it originated': India in the case of Goenka, and China in the case of Kabat-Zinn.
13 Kabat-Zinn's vision of a 'Global Renaissance' is not specifically Buddhist, but a facet of the American New Age movement.
14 Fieldnote from a 'Masterclass' offered by Kuyken at the Oxford Mindfulness Centre in November 2018.
15 Jamie Bristow's presentation at MiSP 2018, London.
16 Katherine Weares' presentation at MiSP 2018, London.
17 The following information is available from the UK government website, Companies House: see https://beta.companieshouse.gov.uk/company/06144314/filing-history?page=4. Charity Commision reference/no. 1122517.
18 This is not to say that Goenka completely avoids promoting Vipassana as a tool to support mental health. In fact, the narrative he tells about his own introduction to Vipassana concerned his struggle with migraine. However, he considers such benefits as secondary in value and frames them as side-effect benefits of Vipassana as opposed to the prime objective.

## Bibliography

Aukland, K. 2016. 'The Scientization and Academization of Jainism'. *Journal of the American Academy of Religion* 84: 192–233.
Baer, R. 2015. 'Ethics, Values, Virtues, and Character Strengths in Mindfulness-Based Interventions: a Psychological Science Perspective'. *Mindfulness* 6: 956–969.
Brown, C. G. 2016. 'Can "Secular" Mindfulness Be Separated from Religion?', in Purser, R. E., Forbes, D. and Burke, A. (eds), *Handbook of Mindfulness: Culture, Context, and Social Engagement, Mindfulness in Behavioral Health*, 75–94. Cham: Springer International Publishing.
Brown, C. G. 2017. 'Ethics, Transparency, and Diversity in Mindfulness Programs', in Monteiro, L. M., Compson, J. F. and Musten, F. (eds), *Practitioner's Guide to Ethics and Mindfulness-Based Interventions, Mindfulness in Behavioral Health*, 45–85. Cham: Springer International Publishing.
Brown, C. G. 2019 *Debating Yoga and Mindfulness in Public Schools – Reforming Secular Education or Reestablishing Religion?* Chapel Hill: The University of North Carolina Press.
Companies House. 2019. *The Oxford Mindfulness Foundation*. https://beta.companieshouse.gov.uk/company/06144314/filing-history?page=4, Accessed 26 February 2019.
Compson, J. F. 2017. 'Is Mindfulness Secular or Religious, and Does It Matter?', in *Practitioner's Guide to Ethics and Mindfulness-Based Interventions, Mindfulness in Behavioral Health*, 23–44. Cham: Springer..
Crane, R. S., et al., 2017. 'What Defines Mindfulness-based Programs? The Warp and the Weft'. *Psychological Medicine* 47: 990–999.
Dorjee, D. 2017. *Neuroscience and Psychology of Meditation in Everyday Life*, 1st ed. London and New York: Routledge.
Dorjee, D. 2018. 'What the Neuroscience of Meditation Does and Doesn't Show'. *Psychology Today*. www.psychologytoday.com/gb/blog/your-meditative-mind/201808/what-the-neuroscience-meditation-does-and-doesn-t-show.
Farias, M. and Rahmani, M. forthcoming. 'The Alchemy of Meditation: Turning Religion into Science and Science into Religion', in De Manning, R. (ed) *Mutual Enrichment: Theology, Psychology, and Religious Life*. London and New York: Routledge.
Goyal, M. et al. 2014. 'Meditation Programs for Psychological Stress and Well-being: A Systematic Review and Meta-analysis'. *JAMA Internal Medicine* 174(3): 357–368.
Harrison, P. 2006. '"Science" and "Religion": Constructing the Boundaries'. *The Journal of Religion* 86(1): 81–106.
Humes, C. A. 2010. 'The Transcendental Meditation Organization and Its Encounter with Science', in *Handbook of Religion and the Authority of Science*. 345–370. Leiden: Brill.
Husgafvel, V. 2018 'The "Universal Dharma Foundation" of Mindfulness-Based Stress Reduction: Non-Duality and Mahayana Buddhist Influences in the Work of on Kabat-Zinn'. *Contemporary Buddhism* 19(2): 275–326.

Hutchinson, I. 2011. *Monopolizing Knowledge: A Scientist Refutes Religion-Denying, Reason-Destroying Scientism*. Belmont, MA: Fias Publishing.

Hybels, R. C. 1995. 'On Legitimacy, Legitimation, and Organizations: A Critical Review and Integrative Theoretical Model'. *Academy of Management Journal* Special Issue: Best Papers Proceedings: 241–245.

Kabat-Zinn, J. 2011. 'Some Reflections on the Origins of MBSR, Skillful Means and the Trouble with Maps'. *Contemporary Buddhism* 12(1): 281–306.

Killingsworth, M. A. and Gilbert, D. T. 2010. 'A Wandering Mind is an Unhappy Mind'. *Science* 330(6006): 932–932.

King, R. 2016. '"Paying Attention" in a Digital Economy: Reflections on the Role of Analysis and Judgement Within Contemporary Discourses of Mindfulness and Comparisons with Classical Buddhist Accounts of Sati', in Purser, R. E., Forbes, D. and Burke, A. (eds), *Handbook of Mindfulness: Culture, Context, and Social Engagement, Mindfulness in Behavioral Health*, 27–45. Cham: Springer International Publishing.

Komjathy, L. 2015. *Contemplative Literature: A Comparative Sourcebook on Meditation and Contemplative Prayer.* Albany: SUNY Press.

Komjathy, L. 2018. *Introducing Contemplative Studies.* Hoboken, New Jersey and Sussex, England: Wiley-Blackwell.

Kuyken, W. et al. 2017. 'The Effectiveness and Cost-effectiveness of a Mindfulness Training Programme in Schools Compared with Normal School Provision (MYRIAD): Study Protocol for a Randomised Controlled Trial'. *Trials* 18: 194.

Lopez, D. S. 2008. *Buddhism and Science: A Guide for the Perplexed.* Chicago: University of Chicago Press.

Lowe, S. 2011. 'Transcendental Meditation, Vedic Science and Science'. *Nova Religio: Journal of Alternative and Emergent ReligIions* 14: 54–76.

McMahan, D. L. 2008. *The Making of Buddhist Modernism.* Oxford: Oxford University Press.

Olson, R. G. 2008. *Science and Scientism in Nineteenth-Century Europe.* Urbana: University of Illinois Press.

Olsson, L. et al. 2015. 'Why Resilience is Unappealing to Social Science: Theoretical and Empirical Investigations of the Scientific Use of Resilience'. *Science Advances* 1: e1400217. https://doi.org/10.1126/sciadv.1400217

Purser, R. E., Forbes, D. and Burke, A. 2016. *Handbook of Mindfulness: Culture, Context, and Social Engagement.* Cham: Springer.

Rahmani, M. 2017. *Drifting Through Samsara: Tacit Conversion and Disengagement from Goenka's Vipassana Movement in New Zealand.* Doctoral Thesis. Dunedin: University of Otago.

Rahmani, M. (forthcoming a) 'Converting to and Disengaging from Vipassana Movement', in Farias, M., Brazier, D., and Lalljee, M. eds. *The Oxford Handbook of Meditation.* Oxford: Oxford University Press.

Rahmani, M. (forthcoming b) 'Understanding Unbelief in the Mindfulness Subculture' in Lee, L., Bullivant, S., Farias, M., and Lanman, J. eds. *Cultures of Unbelief.* Oxford: Oxford University Press

Riessman, C. K., 1993. *Narrative Analysis.* London: SAGE.

Sharf, R. H., 1995. 'Buddhist Modernism and the Rhetoric of Meditative Experience'. *Numen* 42: 228–283.

Sharf, R. H. 2015. 'Is Mindfulness Buddhist? (And Why it Matters)'. *Transcultural Psychiatry* 52(4): 470–484.

Sorell, T. 1991. *Scientism: Philosophy and the Infatuation with Science.* New York: Routledge.

Sumner, P. et al. 2014. 'The Association Between Exaggeration in Health-related Science News and Academic Press Releases: Retrospective Observational Study'. *BMJ* 349: g7015.

Sutcliffe, S. J. 2004. 'The Dynamics of Alternative Spirituality: Seekers, Networks, and "New Age"', in Lewis, J. R., ed. *The Oxford Handbook of New Religious Movements*, 466–490. Oxford: Oxford University Press.

Tallis, R. 2010. 'What Neuroscience Cannot Tell Us About Ourselves: Debunking the Tropes of Neuromythology'. *New Atlantis.* www.thenewatlantis.com/publications/what-neuroscience-cannot-tell-us-about-ourselves. Accessed 20 April 2019.

University of Oxford, 2019. *Future of Mindfulness Research at Oxford Secured with New Professorship.* www.campaign.ox.ac.uk/news/future-of-mindfulness-research-at-oxford-secured-with-new-professorship. Accessed 10 April 2019.

Van Dam, N. T. et al. 2018. 'Mind the Hype: A Critical Evaluation and Prescriptive Agenda for Research on Mindfulness and Meditation'. *Perspectives on Psychological Science* 13: 36–61.

Walsh, Z. 2016. 'A Meta-Critique of Mindfulness Critiques: From McMindfulness to Critical Mindfulness', in Purser, R. E., Forbes, D., and Burke, A. (eds), *Handbook of Mindfulness: Culture, Context, and Social Engagement, Mindfulness in Behavioral Health*, 153–166. Cham: Springer International Publishing..

Wilson, J. 2014. *Mindful America.* Oxford: Oxford University Press.

# PART IV

# Global and regional transmissions

While previous parts have highlighted the chronological and soteriological distinctions between different presentations of yoga and meditation techniques, Part IV explores the unique formulations that can be found in specific global and regional cultures. The cultural 'distancing' of 'other' regional presentations of these techniques and traditions is often under-emphasised, with specialists and the general public alike assuming that their own experience is more representative than it may be globally.

We are excited to offer perspectives from some regional cultures of yoga and meditation for the first time in English: the chapters on yoga and meditation in Latin America, Korea and Japan offer some of the first presentations of this material for English-language audiences. This understanding of how meditation and yoga practices have been understood and developed in specific global regions is an emerging field of study. In particular, high-quality studies on these practices in the context of African, Middle Eastern, Soviet and post-communist contexts are all areas that need further research in order to decentre Euro-American and/or anglophone analytical dominance.

# 19

# YOGA AND MEDITATION TRADITIONS IN INSULAR SOUTHEAST ASIA

*Andrea Acri*

## Introduction

The region of insular Southeast Asia, which for the scope of the present chapter largely coincides with the archipelagic state of the Republic of Indonesia,[1] has been the theatre of the complex and long-lasting phenomenon of linguistic, cultural, and religious transfer called 'Sanskritisation', 'Indianisation'/'Indicisation' or 'Hinduisation', from at least the first half of the first millennium of the current era up to 1500 CE and beyond. While the territories of Indonesia and Malaysia became gradually Islamised from the thirteenth–fifteenth century onwards, Indic cultural and religious elements have continued to be embedded in the local (predominantly Islamic) cultural and religious paradigms, especially in Java. The island of Bali has remained predominantly Hindu to this day, while small enclaves of Hindus and Buddhists (whether 'indigenous' or immigrated) are found in Java, Lombok, Sumatra and other islands. Christianity is the largest religious minority of Indonesia (about 10 per cent of the population). All the above-mentioned religious and cultural elements may be regarded as historical 'layers' resting on a 'substratum' of indigenous or Austronesian elements, which are often difficult to define precisely (beyond the general label of 'shamanism' or 'ancestor cults'), let alone tease out.

An integral part of the phenomenon of Indicisation were the traditions of yoga that originated in the Indian subcontinent – understood here both in the narrow sense of specific philosophical and soteriological traditions described in Sanskrit sources (for example, Pātañjala yoga or tantric *ṣaḍaṅgayoga*) and in the wider sense of inner and outer psycho-physical techniques of self-cultivation, meditation, visualisation, ascesis (*tapas*), etc. Yoga traditions were transmitted to the region by the seventh century at the latest and developed there well beyond the end of the Hindu–Buddhist period into the modern period in Islamic contexts, such as in the Javanese tradition of mysticism (*kejawen*), or in Hindu contexts, for instance in Bali.

The fact that local societies readily adopted these techniques, adapted them to their contexts and concerns, and further developed them suggests that they might already have had a propensity for psycho-physical techniques even before the beginning of Indic influences. In particular, one notes the resilience throughout history in local cultures of practices geared towards the obtainment of physical and spiritual power, supernatural faculties, control of and influence over other people's will, etc.[2] Thus, Indic yoga traditions in Indonesia should not be studied as mere cultural transplants, but as phenomena involving an active Southeast Asian agency. Indeed, according to Wolters (1999: 9), the 'localization' of Indic culture may be regarded as a process that brought 'persisting indigenous beliefs into sharper focus'; this may have been true in the case of 'yogic' psycho-physical techniques. Besides being a worthy object of study in their own right, yoga traditions in Indonesia also enlighten us about dynamics of cultural transfer within the wider transcultural context of the 'Sanskrit Cosmopolis' theorised by Pollock (2006), i.e. a wide cultural-geographical area that included both South and Southeast Asia. Last but not least, they provide an independent – yet parallel – source of data to better understand yoga traditions in South Asia itself.[3]

Our knowledge about yoga traditions in insular Southeast Asia mainly derives from textual documents in Sanskrit and premodern and modern vernacular languages of Java (Old Javanese, Modern Javanese), Bali (Old Javanese, Balinese) and Sumatra (Classical Malay), as well as from sparse art historical evidence and modern and contemporary practices. This chapter will survey this multifarious evidence, focusing mainly on the premodern period and Sanskrit–Old Javanese sources, and include discussions on how Indic traditions have evolved into (predominantly Islamic) modern Javanese and (predominantly Hindu) Balinese religious paradigms and meditative practices. However, I will not elaborate on the contemporary forms of transnational yoga, which are attracting a significant number of followers in Indonesia.

## The earliest literary evidence: the old Javanese *Rāmāyaṇa*

Old Javanese was the translocal literary vernacular (akin to Prakrit(s) in South Asia) used in Java from circa the eighth century to the sixteenth century, and it is still attested in the manuscript tradition and religious lore of Bali to the present day.[4] Zoetmulder's *Old Javanese-English Dictionary* (1982) lists more than two pages of occurrences in Old Javanese literature of dozens of substantival, adjectival and verbal forms based on the root *yoga*. These include, among others, the Sanskrit technical compounds *yogābhyāsa* ('the practice of yoga'), *yogadhāraka* ('concentration of the mind'), *yogajñāna* ('the mind (spirit) in yoga'), *yogakrama* ('method or practice of yoga'), *yogapravṛtti* ('the performance of yoga'), *yogaśāstra* ('the science of yoga'), *yogasiddhi* ('perfection or supernatural power of yoga') and *yogasmaraṇa* ('meditative yoga').[5] Many instances of the word *yoga* and its derivatives are attested in what may be the earliest Old Javanese transmitted text known to us, the poem *Rāmāyaṇa kakavin* (c. ninth–early tenth century CE),[6] where they occur both in the sense of 'magical/creative power' (20.53) and as a psycho-physical meditative technique associated with supernatural prowess and feats (3.38, 20.54), asceticism (1.42, 4.9, 4.13) and release (4.10), along with other technical terms, such as *samādhi* (4.10, 13), *japa* (21.135), *citta* and *dhāraṇā* (24.180). Designations of yogic agents such as *yogin/yogī*, etc., are equally widespread, suggesting that yoga practitioners must have been familiar realities in the *imaginaire* of the ancient Javanese courtly elites (that is, outside of restricted religious circles), and perhaps even of the population at large.

An interesting aperçu on yoga practices and agents in their social contexts is found in the allegorical chapters 24 and 25. Advancing a critique of various ascetic and religious groups mockingly depicted as animals,[7] these chapters contain passages hinting at yoga postures that seem to have derived from Indian prototypes, for instance the observance of hanging upside-down (from trees), carried out by flying foxes (*kalvaṅ*, 24.119, 25.68). This practice seems to have been still in use in modern Java, under the name of *tapa ngalong* or 'the observance of the flying-fox'.[8] A similar practice is attested in South Asia already in the Pāli canon, where it is associated with *tapasvin*s and Ājīvikas practicing the '"bat-penance" (*vagguli-vata*), which is generally assumed to mean suspending oneself upside down from a tree, thus inverting oneself in a fashion not dissimilar to the hathayogic *viparītakaraṇī* mudrā' (Mallinson 2016: 21). It is also mentioned in a number of later Sanskrit sources.[9] According to Mallinson, these austerities may have been linked with techniques practised by celibate ascetics aiming at the preservation of semen, such as those described in early *haṭhayoga* texts.[10] The same chapter of the Old Javanese *Rāmāyaṇa* (25.34) mentions another observance that may have been linked to such techniques: the *asidhāravrata* or 'knife's edge penance' (a form of *coitus reservatus*), found in the Śākta text *Brahmayāmala* (Hatley 2016).

An allegorical reference to what might have been another austerity-oriented (*tapasyā*) precursor of a later postural form of (*haṭha*)*yoga* (i.e., [*ekapāda*]*bakāsana*) is the description, in 24.116 and 117cd (cf. 25.52–60), of a cunning heron (*baka*) standing on one leg and posing as an ascetic to take advantage of the small fishes, which finds exact parallels in Old Javanese texts and temple reliefs, as well as Sanskrit prototypical sources such as the *Pañcatantra* (Acri 2010: 494–498).[11] A panel on the Buddhist monument Borobudur in Central Java (c. late eighth–early ninth century) depicts the bodhisattva Maitreya who is seemingly practising this kind of posture (Figure 19.1).[12] Some reliefs depicting ascetics and deities in *padmāsana* are found at the ninth-century Śaiva sanctuary of Loro Jonggrang in Prambanan, Central Java (Figure 19.2). Still, just like in South Asian tantric milieus throughout the medieval period, postural yoga (intended here as including both *āsana*-based Pātañjala yoga and *haṭhayoga*; see below) never represented the dominant paradigm in Java and Bali, as both the textual sources and living traditions display a clear predilection for internalised practices emphasising meditative processes.

*Figure 19.1* Maitreya carrying out arduous practices; Borobudur, Central Java, c. 8th–9th century. Photo: Andrea Acri

*Figure 19.2* One of the directional manifestations of Śiva at Caṇḍi Śiva, Loro Jonggrang, Central Java, 9th century.
Photo: Andrea Acri.

## Old Javanese Śaiva sources on *aṣṭāṅgayoga* and *ṣaḍaṅgayoga*

Both the Pātañjala yoga of eight auxiliaries or ancillaries (*aṣṭāṅgayoga*) and the tantric form of Śaiva yoga of six ancillaries (*ṣaḍaṅgayoga*) are represented in the Sanskrit–Old Javanese religious literature, mainly formed by the texts known as *tuturs* and *tattvas*. However, it is the latter tradition that is by far the commonest form of yoga found there. This may be due to the fact that the majority of the scriptures from premodern Java and Bali that have survived to us are tantric in nature, and derive from prototypical Sanskrit canons of Śaiva and Buddhist scriptures from South Asia. It is this body of scripture that informed the mainstream religiosity of large parts of South and Southeast Asia from the seventh to the thirteenth centuries and beyond.

Some of the secondary literature published thus far on *ṣaḍaṅgayoga* has mentioned textual evidence from Old Javanese sources:[13] this includes, for example, a widespread verse listing the six *aṅgas* of the Śaiva (and, to a lesser extent, Buddhist) yoga, which features in *Vṛhaspatitattva* 53, *Jñānasiddhānta* 15.1/*Gaṇapatitattva* 3 and *Saṅ Hyaṅ Kamahāyānikan* Śaiva p. 76, and has parallels in several Siddhāntatantras (see Table 19.1; cf. Vasudeva 2004: 376). Many of the Old Javanese sources appear to have inherited the system found in relatively early Saiddhāntika texts, such

*Table 19.1* *Aṅgas* (limbs) of yoga in selected Old Javanese sources

| *Maitrāyaṇīya Upaniṣad* | *Saṅ Hyaṅ Kamahāyānikan (Śaiva)* | *Dakṣasmṛti; Tantrālokaviveka* | *Amṛtanāda Upaniṣad; Rauravasūtrasaṅgraha; Mataṅgapārameśvara; Gaṇapatitattva; Jñānasiddhānta, Tutur Kamokṣan; Vṛhaspatitattva; Sutasoma* | *Guhyasamāja Tantra* | *Mṛgendratantra* | *Tattvajñāna* | *Dhyānabindu Upaniṣad; Gorakṣaśataka; Skanda Purāṇa* | *Yogasūtra; Liṅga Purāṇa; Aji Sangkya; Rsi Yadnya Sankhya dan Yoga* | *Dharma Pātañjala* |
|---|---|---|---|---|---|---|---|---|---|
| | | | | | | | | yama | yama |
| | | | | | | | | niyama | niyama |
| | | | | | | āsana | āsana | āsana | āsana |
| prāṇāyāma | prāṇāyāma | prāṇāyāma | pratyāhāra | pratyāhāra | prāṇāyāma | prāṇāyāma | prāṇasaṃrodha | prāṇāyāma | pratyāhāra |
| pratyāhāra | pratyāhāra | dhyāna | dhyāna | dhyāna | pratyāhāra | pratyāhāra | pratyāhāra | pratyāhāra | prāṇāyāma |
| dhyāna | dhāraṇā | pratyāhāra | prāṇāyāma | prāṇāyāma | dhāraṇā | dhāraṇā | dhāraṇā | dhāraṇā | dhāraṇā |
| dhāraṇā | dhyāna | dhāraṇā | dhāraṇā | dhāraṇā | dhyāna | dhyāna | dhyāna | dhyāna | dhyāna |
| tarka | tarka | tarka | tarka | anusmṛti | anvīkṣaṇa | tarka | | | |
| | | | | | japa | | | | |
| samādhi | samādhi | samādhi | samādhi | samādhi | samādhi | samādhi | samādhi | samādhi | samādhi |
| | | | | | yoga | | | | |

as the *Mataṅgapārameśvara*, the *Kālottara*, the *Kiraṇa*, the *Rauravasūtrasaṅgraha* and the *Parākhya* (ibid.: 377).[14] This system reflects the *ṣaḍaṅgayoga* of the *tarka*-class (emphasising discrimination/reflection), as opposed to the *aṣṭāṅgayoga* of the *āsana*-class (emphasising postures/seats). Besides the omission of *āsanas*, *yamas*, and *niyamas*, which are considered preparatory practices but not ancillaries proper as they are in *aṣṭāṅgayoga*, *ṣaḍaṅgayoga* adds *tarka* (or *ūha*, reasoning), and introduces an important element of theism. An interesting fact is the position of *dhyāna* in the two traditions: it usually appears as second member in early Śaiva sources, whereas in Pātañjala yoga sources – or Śaiva sources influenced by that system – it appears as the penultimate one (see Table 19.1). There are also hybrid lists of ancillaries attempting to bridge *ṣaḍaṅga* and *aṣṭāṅgayoga*, such as the one by the *Tattvajñāna*, including seven ancillaries – i.e. the six standard ancillaries plus *āsana*. This phenomenon reflects an attempt to bridge Śaiva yoga with Pātañjala yoga, and appears to be especially significant in Sanskrit texts composed or (re)compiled at a relatively late date (i.e. after the ninth or tenth centuries).[15] It may reflect either the rising status of the yoga of Patañjali in the Indic world, or an intrinsically eclectic attitude by the Javanese authors, who adopted bits and pieces of what was available to them to perform an operation of textual and doctrinal bricolage.

Indeed, fragments of Pātañjala yoga doctrines interspersed within otherwise eminently Śaiva texts that uphold *ṣaḍaṅgayoga* exist. For instance, a cluster of verses in the *Jñānasiddhānta* (ch. 19.5–7), one of which is borrowed from the Śaiva Saiddhāntika scripture *Kiraṇa*,[16] define the individual soul in the state of *kevala* and final release in a manner that echoes Pātañjala yoga ideas and terminology, which may be traced to the *Pātañjalayogaśāstra* (PYŚ, i.e. the *Yogasūtra* + *Bhāṣya*) 1.24, 2.27 and 4.34 (Acri 2011a). Verse 7 declares that liberation – which amounts to becoming the Spotless Śiva – is achieved via restraint (*saṃyama*), a meditative technique employing fixation (*dhāraṇā*), contemplation (*dhyāna*) and concentration (*samādhi*) mentioned in PYŚ 3.4, as well as lower dispassion (*vāhyavairāgya* [a spelling variant of *bāhyavairāgya*]), higher dispassion (*paravairāgya*) and fixation on God (*īśvarapraṇidhāna*). The couplet *vāhyavairāgya* and *paravairāgya* correspond to *apara*- and *para-vairagya* in *Yogasūtrabhāṣya* 1.15–16, while *īśvarapraṇidhāna* occurs in *Yogasūtra* 2.45.

What is by far the most significant Old Javanese source for our knowledge of yoga (in both the tantric and Pātañjala varieties) in the Archipelago is the *Dharma Pātañjala*, a Śaiva scripture of uncertain date retrieved from a West Javanese palm-leaf *codex unicus* last copied in 1467 CE (Acri 2017). This scripture, arranged in the form of a dialogue between the Lord Śiva (*bhaṭāra*) and his son Kumāra, presents a detailed exposition of the doctrinal and philosophical tenets of the Javanese form of Śaiva Siddhānta. Yet it devotes a long section (c. one-third of its length) – which it calls *yogapāda*, in the manner of Sanskrit Siddhāntatantras – to Pātañjala yoga, thereby providing a unique testimony for the knowledge of this system in premodern insular Southeast Asia. This section apparently follows the first three chapters of the PYŚ, either interweaving a few Sanskrit verses from an untraced versified recension of the *sūtras* with an Old Javanese commentary, or directly rendering into Old Javanese what might have been a likewise unknown Sanskrit commentary. Although the prose section often bears a strong resemblance to the arrangement and formulation of the topics treated in the *Yogasūtrabhāṣya*, it diverges from that commentary in several respects, either presenting specific doctrinal details that are found in other (sub-)commentaries, including the Arabic rendering of the *sūtras*-cum-commentary composed by al-Bīrūnī before 1030 CE, or adding seemingly original elements that are as yet unattested elsewhere. A fresh perspective on some problematic *sūtras* of the PYŚ is provided by the Old Javanese rendering and commentary on 1.10 (on sleep and dream), 1.21–23 (on the categories of yogins) and 2.9 (on *abhiniveśa*, 'obsession') (Acri 2012). Being shaped by an eminently theistic agenda, and imbued with Śaiva (tantric) tenets, the *Dharma Pātañjala* aims at attuning Pātañjala yoga (and philosophy) to Śaiva yoga (and philosophy).

The topics of the *sūtras* are followed in their original sequence (cf. Acri 2017: 482, table 13), opportunely re-arranged and shaped, like the rest of the text, as a commentary in the form of questions and answers. The Sanskrit verses embedded in the text correspond to *Yogasūtra* 1.2 (and *Bhāṣya* 1.28 commenting on it) – the famous definition of yoga as *cittavṛttinirodha*[17] – 1.3 (on the isolated Self's perception of its own nature), 1.24 (on the Lord as a special type of Self) and 1.30 (on the hindrances). The Old Javanese prose is by no means a direct translation of the PYŚ but a paraphrase alternating with more original exegetical passages. The author's priority was apparently to present a synthetic account of the most important doctrinal points and practical techniques of Pātañjala yoga. The section of the *Yogapāda* from pp. 290.1–306.10 generally follows the sequence of the topics treated in the PYŚ up to *sūtra* 1.30, thus covering more than a half of the fifty-one *sūtras* making up the first chapter, the '*Samādhipāda*'. Motifs found in the Sanskrit text are occasionally omitted, presumably in order to avoid the repetition of topics already treated elsewhere in the text. For instance, the text follows the sequence of *sūtras* 1.21–28 characterising the Lord (*īśvara*) while omitting *sūtra* 1.26, where the Lord is said to have been incarnated as a primal sage (Kapila) – the status of the Lord as an incarnated being (e.g. Pātañjala)[18] and universal teacher having been treated already in section 276.2–280.4. Similarly, the parts dealing with karma, latent impressions and cosmology are omitted.[19] Intriguingly, the fourth *pāda* of the PYŚ ('*Kaivalyapāda*') is not reflected in the Old Javanese text. It seems likely that the author did not include it as he was trying to make Pātañjala yoga – an Indic system of yoga that seems to have been relatively marginal in Java – intelligible and useful to the local Śaiva theological milieu, which did not regard isolation (*kaivalya*) as the final goal of yoga (see below). On the other hand, perhaps more tentatively, this omission may also be interpreted in the light of the ongoing debate on the origins and authorship of the PYŚ. That the Javanese author may not have been aware of the '*Kaivalyapāda*' due to the fact that the version of the PYŚ that was transmitted to Java did not (yet) include the fourth chapter is less likely but, at least in theory, not outside the realm of possibility. Indeed, according to Angot (2008: 27–28), the '*Kaivalyapāda*' may be spurious, i.e. a later addition to the text, or in any event not written by the same hand who composed the first three chapters of the PYŚ.[20]

As in the case of the *Jñānasiddhānta*, the *Dharma Pātañjala* makes an attempt to equate the *kaivalya* state of the Self with the Śaiva *summum bonum*, intended as the manifestation of the divine powers of the Lord in the practitioner, who thereby becomes Śiva. For instance, in 298.2–4, the *śloka*-quarter *ātmani cetanaḥ sthitaḥ* [= *sūtra* 1.3: 'Then the Seer is established in his own form' *tadā draṣṭuḥ svarūpe 'vasthānam*], defining the state of *samādhi* and conflating it with *kaivalya*,[21] is glossed as the state where the mind is left behind by the Self and the *yogin* obtains the state of supernatural prowess, adhering closely to the Lord. A polemic on the role of *citta* in yoga may be hinted at in 290.10–11, where the Lord dispels an objection (possibly from the point of view of Pātañjala yoga) as to the identification of the mind with the Soul, remarking that since both have the same object of perception, what is experienced by the opponent (in the state of *kaivalya*) is just the mind, not the Soul. The implication is that stillness or dispassion of the mind alone, belonging to the realm of cognitive absorption, is a necessary but not sufficient condition for the attainment of the final goal of yoga. Stillness of mind is thus a means and should not be confused with its end, as the opponent seems to do. Overall, such passages of the *Dharma Pātañjala* remind me of analogous (albeit more overtly polemic) reinterpretations of Pātañjala yoga by commentators in the Sanskrit tradition of Śaiva Siddhānta, such as Nārāyaṇakaṇṭha (fl. c. 900–950?) in his commentary to *Mṛgendratantra* YP 2a, in which he defines yoga as union with Śiva, as well as Rāmakaṇṭha in his commentary to the *Yogapāda* of the *Mataṅgapārameśvara* (1.1), which regards the teaching of that Tantra as superior to those of Patañjali.[22]

Despite its partial adherence to Pātañjala yoga and the PYŚ, the *Dharma Pātañjala* shares the same stock of tantric yoga as the other texts from Indonesia. *Āsanas*, although included along with *yama* and *niyama* among the preliminaries, just as in South Asian tantric sources, do not play an important role; indeed, their number reflects the standard stock list of early Siddhāntatantras.[23] On the other hand, *samādhi* appears to be the most important ancillary, rather than *tarka*, which is prominent in the Kashmirian non-dual Śaiva sources. A section of the text (pp. 324.7–326.5) describes in detail the practice of *dhāraṇā* to 'conquer' the elements (being equivalent to *bhūtajaya* or 'conquering of the five elements', which is also featured in many South Asian tantric sources, such as the *Mālinīvijaya*; cf. *Saṅ Hyaṅ Kamahāyānikan* Śaiva 28–29). There is nothing specifically Pātañjala in the description of *prāṇāyāma* (p. 316.11–17), which does not follow the *Yogaśāstra* (2.49–52) and is more tantric in character. It revolves around the practice of the breath exercises known in medieval (tantric and non-tantric) Sanskrit texts as *pūraka* 'inhalation', *kumbhaka* 'retention', and *recaka* 'exhalation'. An important doctrinal feature of the *Dharma Pātañjala*, which is also reflected in the majority of Old Javanese Śaiva texts (as well as South Asian Pāśupata Śaiva texts and later *haṭhayoga* and *rājayoga* texts), is the view that liberation can be obtained through yoga and not initiation (*dīkṣā*), as the 'orthodox' Saiddhāntika view would have it.[24] This is indicative of the important role played by yoga in shaping esoteric and mainstream religious traditions of premodern Indonesia. It is, therefore, not surprising that the highest category of (Śaiva) practitioner and epitome of spiritual aspirant is indicated in Old Javanese texts by the term *yogīśvara*, 'leader among yogins', in conformity with the prominence attributed to yoga as the main soteriological means.

Indeed, the majority of the texts of the *tutur* and *tattva* genre may be described as being primarily texts on yoga and, in a wider sense, (tantric) meditation techniques. The most representative practices are visualisations (*dhyānas*), fixations (*dhāraṇās*) and techniques that are reminiscent of the forms of *layayoga* found in Sanskrit texts from South Asia,[25] aiming at dissolving the mind and identifying the practitioner with the supreme reality (see e.g. *Bhuvanakośa* ch. 5). The theistic aspect is prominent, involving visualisations of the Lord and his hypostases (e.g. as the mantra-bodied Sadāśiva in the subtle centre of the heart; as Paramaśiva, Rudra, Mahādeva, etc., cf. *Gaṇapatitattva* 60–61), or constant meditation on, and identification with, Him while eating, sleeping, walking, and standing still (cf. e.g. *Tattvajñāna* 44) – a practice called *caturdhyāna*, whose prototype is well-attested in Sanskrit sources across sectarian boundaries (Acri 2017: 379–382). The idea of the coincidence of the normal state of consciousness with a higher state is reflected in the doctrine, expounded in *Vṛhaspatitattva* 47, of union of the waking state (*jāgra*) with the 'fourth state' (*tūrya*), which has Upaniṣadic parallels and is also found in non-dual Śaivism of Kashmir. Equally widespread is the utilisation of mantras or *akṣaras* of the Sanskrit syllabary to be visualised and emplaced in different parts of the body of the yogin. When the whole syllabary is represented, this practice is called *svaravyañjananyāsa* (Acri 2016). The same interest in gross and subtle physiology that is found in Sanskrit tantric sources also characterises the *tutur* and *tattva* texts, which often include lists of breaths (*vāyus*, *prāṇas*), vessels (*nāḍīs*) and subtle centres (*sthānas*, *padmas*, *cakras*).

References to a practice called (as a Sanskrit *tatpuruṣa* compound) *prayogasandhi* 'esoteric knowledge of the (right) means' or (as two separate words) *prayoga sandhi* 'secret means' are found throughout the corpus. In the *Dharma Pātañjala* (p. 288.10–18), it denotes a form of *samādhi* through which the Lord is made manifest in a human being, like the fire which exists within wood (as the effect in its cause), which comes out as a consequence of rubbing, and like butter in milk, which comes out as a consequence of churning it with a 'tool'. The tool (*upāya*) appears to be a metaphor referring to the six ancillaries of yoga (see p. 308.7–11; *Tattvajñāna* 44). The hymn of the Old Javanese poem *Arjuvavihāha* (c. early eleventh century) declares that the yogin achieves the visible form of the Lord when he carefully 'churns' the consciousness (*amutər tutur pinahayu*). These ideas and practices are likely to be Javanese developments of South Asian Sanskrit prototypes: *Śvetāśvatara Upaniṣad* 1.10–12 equates the body to the slab and the syllable *oṃ* as the upper drill, while *Amṛtabindu/Brahmabindu Upaniṣad* (ninth–twelfth century CE?) 20–21 declares that the realisation of Brahman amounts to the extraction of butter from milk and the production of fire through a churning-stick. An analogous idea is found in the Saiddhāntika Śaiva scripture *Trayodaśaśatikakālottara*. Some bodily and subtle techniques involving the use of *mathana*, 'churning' or 'kindling', are described in the *Kubjikāmatatantra* (12.60–65), which combines yogic techniques and visualisation in the cadre of a sexual intercourse metaphor, and in *Tantrāloka* (5.22–24), which describes a meditation on the 'rubbing' of Soma, Sūrya and Agni as the 'kindling stick' (*araṇī*) in the cadre of an internalised ritual (Mallinson 2007: 27, 208). In other Old Javanese passages, such as *Dharma Pātañjala* p. 328.13–22, *prayogasandhi* is employed to separate the Soul from the enveloping power of the Unevolved Matter (*pradhāna*) and to enter the body of another human being by cutting off its karmic bonds (a practice akin to *paraśarīrapraveśa* in tantric texts as well as the PYŚ).[26] In the Old Javanese Śaiva didactic poem *Dharma Śūnya* 9.2, the aim of *sandhi upāya* (= *prayogasandhi*) is to hold back (or: 'concentrate upon', *rəgəp*) the bad and good actions (*pāpa lavan supuṇya*) with the secret key of yoga (*kuñci rahasya yoga*, seemingly connected with *prāṇāyāma* in Old Javanese texts).

A technique of Indian derivation that is prominently featured in Old Javanese texts is *sadyotkrānti*: 'immediate ascent' ≈ 'immediate (forceful?) expulsion/going out' (of the breath, life-principle or Soul); also *utkrānti* = 'dying'. This practice is attested in the Sanskrit Mantramārga corpus, but it may have been derived from the earlier Pāśupata/Atimārga tradition. In both Indian and Javanese–Balinese contexts, *sadyotkrānti* is a praxis enabling the yogin to precipitate death, which is achieved through the expulsion of the breath. The texts stress the importance of knowing the exact time of the all important moment of physical death, so as not to be unprepared, and to have an empty mind or a mind focused on one's supramundane aim. It is related to the practice of closing the nine bodily orifices with the esoteric/secret key (*kuñci rahasya*) and expelling the breath from the fontanel (cf. Acri 2017: 522–523; Vasudeva 2004: 395–397 and 402–409). Often *sadyotkrānti* is not explicitly mentioned; rather, we find *prāṇāyāma* (*kumbhaka, pūraka, recaka*), and also *(pra)-yogasandhi* (or just *sandhi*). While many passages describing this technique are studiously elliptic and esoteric, it must nonetheless have been widespread, as it constitutes a common literary trope even in the belles-lettres, where it is customarily described as the best way of dying and achieving liberation, such as in *Smaradahana* 8.23 (by Kāma) and *Sumanasāntaka* 10.31–33a (by the king father of the heroine Indumatī).

Insights on this practice come from the modern Balinese tradition, which has appropriated and carried forward this technique from the Old Javanese textual heritage. In yogic practice during life, the adept should unify the syllables *aṃ* and *aḥ*, representing fire and water, Umā and Śiva, *pradhāna* and *puruṣa*, to obtain *amṛta*, the water of eternal life. At the time of death, the two should be kept separated (*rva bhineda*) and their position reversed, so that fire unnaturally moves downward and water upwards (Stephen 2010: 431). The yogin must, therefore, lead the vital principle through the body and expel it through one of the centres, most often the fontanel (*śivadvāra*). Since, depending on the contents of the mind, the soul may go to different abodes, it is crucial to maintain an empty mind as well as a heightened awareness during the time of death. This is a very difficult practice to master, however, and the soul can be brought back and instructed in order to achieve a better goal (ibid.: 446). In the Balinese tradition, this occurs after death itself, during the funerary ritual. Stephen has interpreted the Balinese *pitra yadnya* (funerary ritual) as a 'yogic art of dying', that is, the ritual re-enactment of the resorption of the cosmic principles (*tattvas*) into Paramaśiva. Śaiva Saiddāntika funeral rites (*śrāddha*) seem similar in this regard, insofar that, by bringing the soul back into the corpse and then liberating it, they 'assist the deceased in a process through which he is gradually made to advance into higher levels of liberation, therewith completing the process that had been initiated by the Dīkṣā ritual … bestowing union with Śiva' (Mirnig 2013: 286). However, since, as we have seen above, it is not initiation (*dīkṣā*) but yoga that is deemed to bestow liberation/union with Śiva according to Old Javanese Śaiva texts, it would seem that the Balinese tradition elaborated a post-mortem ritualistic version of an originally yogic practice for the benefit of the lay people.

A genre of Old Javanese manuals on what may be labelled as 'sexual yoga' has been preserved in Bali within the context of the broader Śaiva *tutur* genre (see Creese and Bellow 2002). In these texts (e.g. *Aṅgulipraveśa*, *Indrāṇīśāstra*, etc.), sex is considered a religious practice in which sexual climax and pleasure are central. Some of these texts and ideas may go back to premodern Java, as the demonstrably early belletristic sources convey a widespread idea that the *summum bonum* is attained via sexual union. The textual climax is often represented by the marriage of the hero and heroine and the enactment of 'yoga of the bedchamber', i.e. yogic copulation enjoining meditation and sex, which enables them to identify as the male–female embodiments of Śiva (Ardhanārīśvara), or the human counterparts of Kāma and Rati. That seems to have been understood as the main path of yoga for householders.

## Old Javanese Buddhist sources on yoga

Forms of Buddhist *devatāyoga* existed in premodern Indonesia, where the predominant Buddhist paradigm from the seventh century onwards appears to have been a localised variety of Mantranaya/Mahāyāna Buddhist tantra.[27] While Buddhist and Śaiva tantric traditions – in Java and elsewhere – share a great deal of common concepts, terminology and techniques, a theoretical separation or distinction between the two appears to have existed in the domain of doctrine, ritual and clergy (Acri 2015). For instance, the fourteenth-century Buddhist poem *Sutasoma* by Mpu Tantular describes a 'yogic way of dying' (*parātramārga*, canto 38 and 39) that is in many respects reminiscent of the Śaiva practice of *utkrānti*. Yet it clearly separates the Śaiva way of *ṣaḍaṅgayoga* (canto 40), which leads to the acquisition of supernatural powers, from the Buddhist way of *advayayoga* (canto 41), which leads to liberation (Ensink 1974). The latter yoga is also called *advayajñāna*, and is discussed in connection with the Buddhist deity Prajñāpāramitā and the mantra *aṃ aḥ* (otherwise known as *rva bhineda* in the Balinese Śaiva tradition; see below). Similar passages are found in the Sanskrit–Old Javanese Buddhist manual *Saṅ Hyaṅ Kamahāyānikan*, which is most probably three or four centuries earlier than the *Sutasoma*. A syncretic stance is attested in the Śaiva version of the *Saṅ Hyaṅ Kamahāyānikan*, which contains a variant of the widespread verse on *ṣaḍaṅgayoga* and employs Śaiva rather than Buddhist terminology (Kats 1910: 153–156). The Buddhist version features *samādhi* focused on Vajrasattva, Lokeśvara, Jambāla, Vairocana etc.; a technique called *dhyānapāramitā*; and a four-fold yoga taught by Ācārya Śrī Dignāgapāda: *mūlayoga*, *madhyayoga*, *vasānayoga* and *antayoga*, consisting in the visualisation of a Buddhist deity.

## Classical Malay literature from Sumatra

Evidence of the presence of Indic yoga practices in Sumatra in the sixteenth century – that is, well into the Islamic period – is suggested by some Malay works of Islamic scholars who polemically wrote against certain non-Islamic practices. These are, for instance, the influential eighteenth-century South Sumatran scholar 'Abd as-Samad al-Palimbani (Drewes 1976) and especially the Muslim mystic Hamzah Fansuri, who lived in North Sumatra between the end of the sixteenth and the beginning of the seventeenth century. As shown by Brakel (1979, 2004: 10–11), in a poem Fansuri attacks surviving 'yoga' practices, contrasting 'the jungles of the interior, where such practices frequently occur, with the sea and the Islamized coasts which are open to the world'. Fansuri's critique of the ascetic practices carried out in seclusion by spiritual seekers contains clear echoes of yogic techniques known in the Javano–Balinese tradition; for instance, the statement 'They draw their breath into the brain, Lest their fluids get in commotion' reminds us of the technique of retention of the breath (*prāṇāyāma*), which is described in the Sanskrit–Old Javanese *Vṛhaspatitattva* precisely as the closing of the bodily apertures and the breaking through of the breath from the cranial vault.[28] In a passage of his prose *Asrār al-Ārifin* (Brakel 1979: 74–75), Hamzah admonishes his reader not to localise God in the fontanel (*ubun-ubun*) or on the tip of the nose (*di pucuk hiduṅ*) or between the eyebrows (*di antara keniṅ*) or in the heart (*di dalam jantuṅ*), all of which correspond to the classical subtle centres of the human body described in yogic texts from both the Sanskrit and Javano–Balinese tradition, in which the practitioner should imagine Śiva to reside (e.g. *śivadvāra* = fontanel, *nāsāgra* = tip of the nose, *lalāṭa* = space between the eyebrows, *hṛdaya* = heart). Brakel (1979: 76) concluded that yogic techniques were still current in sixteenth-century Aceh. Braginsky (2004: 144–145) fine-tuned Brakel's analysis and showed that Hamzah's critique included elements of not only *dhyāna* and *dhāraṇā* but also acquisition of supernatural powers through yoga as well as sexo-yogic practices involving the manipulation of the semen. These techniques, of probably tantric derivation, were in fact described in a corpus of syncretic Sufi-tantric mystical literature in Malay from Sumatra focusing on sexual yoga (Braginsky 2004; 2017; 2019). This body of texts represents a clear continuation of the pre-Islamic Indic heritage, owing as it does to hathayogic and tantric practices. As in the case of the Old Javanese and Balinese texts, it lays emphasis on the spiritual practice of married householders through sexual yoga, but reframes it in a thoroughly Islamised religious and sociocultural context.

## Yoga in modern Bali

Today, Bali is considered a mecca for yoga and yoga retreats; however, this phenomenon reflects practices coming from outside (i.e. Indian or globalised/modern postural yoga) and catering to (spiritual) tourists rather than locals. It is still largely centred around Ubud but is now rapidly extending to the main tourist locations across the island. This still-evolving phenomenon will not be dealt with here. Rather, I shall briefly outline the contours of the less-known phenomenon of Balinese yoga(s) and their historical roots.

As I anticipated above, the modern Balinese tradition of yoga may be regarded as a continuation and development of the Old Javanese paradigm, for instance in the case of such central practices as *sadyotkrānti*, the use of mantras and syllables and their imposition on the body, sexual yoga, etc. A ubiquitous practice is the yoga making use of the *daśākṣara* or ten sacred syllables, including the Śaiva *pañcabrahmamantras* (i.e. *sa ba ta a i*) + *na ma(ḥ) śi vā ya*, which are then compressed to the three components of the OṂ – A, U, M –, then *aṃ uṃ maṃ*, *aṅ aḥ*, and finally the meeting and dissolution of the two into *nāda* and Paramaśiva (Stephen 2014: 198). Texts such as the *Aji Sarasvatī* describe the placement of these syllables in the body and correspondences between these and colours, days, directions of the compass, deities, etc. This delineates a process of micro-macro-cosmic absorption within the body of the practitioner that reflects parallel external processes.

According to Stephen, this and other techniques have to be understood as reconfigurations of South Asian ideas and practices. For instance, the last five 'mental' ancillaries of *ṣaḍaṅgayoga* may be linked to the five stages of resorption of the *daśākṣaras*. Further, the visualisation of nectar (*amṛta*) in a precious water vessel located in the brain as flowing down and transforming into the reversed *oṃkāra* located in the upper part of the cranial vault, the tip of the nose, the end of the tongue and then the cavity at the base of the neck (the golden phial) appears to reflect the *haṭhayoga* practice of *khecarīmudrā* (Mallinson 2007). This practice involves the turning backwards of the tongue until it enters the opening located in the back part of the soft palate to release the flow of nectar stored in the head (Stephen 2014; cf. *Dharma Pātañjala*, Acri 2017: 533). The practitioner should also imagine the burning up of the body to ashes and their washing away with nectar flowing from the golden phial (Stephen 2014: 23). This calls to mind the tantric ritual of *bhūtaśuddhi*, in which the elements of the body are purified by fire and water in order to create a divinised body.

A recent series of popular books on yoga deals with the figures of the Kanda Mpat or 'spiritual siblings' accompanying human beings since their birth. This is a widespread and important theme among Balinese Hindu householders who, by building a mystical relationship with their siblings through yoga, aim at attaining not only healing and success in other mundane matters, but also access to the innermost part of their Self. Indeed, the Kanda Mpat frame the theory (and practice) of liberation: the physical origin (birth) and end (death) of the individual finds a counterpart in the spiritual (re)incarnation into a human being and final liberation from the cycle of rebirth, which is achieved through yoga leading to the realisation of the ultimate identity between the Self (represented by the 'fifth' sibling) and the Lord Śiva. This practice and ideology was once represented in Java too, and indeed finds its origin in the Indian tradition, more precisely in the Śaiva Pāśupata doctrine of the four disciples of the incarnation of Śiva and promulgator of Pāśupata Śaivism known as Lakulīśa (Acri 2014).

One notes some sort of tension between the supra-ritualistic yogic attitude of certain categories of religious specialists and textual sources, and the ritualism of lay people and textual genres (mainly practical manuals). Indeed, the Pedanda Śiva, the highest brahmanical ritual specialists, may be regarded more as yogins than (mere) ritualists. Their main ritual practice, the *sūrya sevana*, may be considered a form of yoga aiming to turn, through *prāṇāyāma*, *dhyāna* and the uttering of mantras, the officiant into Śiva,[29] who is then able to produce the holy water (*tīrtha*). Stephen (2015: 96) regards this as a 'daily yogic *sādhanā* of a tantric adept, rather than the recitation of a priestly liturgy or the worship of a deity'. Indeed, during *sūrya sevana* the practitioner assumes a seated yogic posture with his eyes closed, which is more indicative of a meditative rather than a ritual practice.[30] Even lay worship in temples (*sembahyang*) is not characterised by devotion (*bhakti*) and the presentation of offerings to a deity, but rather by the enactment of yoga/seated meditation, framed through the stages of *āsana*, *prāṇāyāma*, *dhyāna* etc., followed by ritualised gestures.

The recent histories of *ṣaḍaṅga* and *aṣṭāṅga* yoga in the religious discourse in modern Bali (and, to a lesser extent, Java) are characterised by both continuities and changes with the precolonial tradition. In Bali, reformist groups have attempted to adopt (and adapt) the canon of neo-Hinduism as a constitutive part of modern Balinese Hinduism since the 1930s. The ideas of the prominent Hindu thinkers such as Vivekānanda, Swami Śivānanda, etc., probably through the medium of Theosophy, which was popular among the political and intellectual elites in Java and Bali, contributed to shape the new paradigm. This is evident from the mimeographed pamphlets and printed booklets in modern (Malay-)Indonesian or Balinese published on Bali from the 1940s, in which Balinese intellectuals and religious leaders were intent upon (re)creating a textual canon that, through the incorporation of elements of Indian Hinduism, would have sanctioned recognition of Balinese religion as a fully fledged, and pan-Indonesian, world religion.

Many such texts, while more or less closely adhering to the doctrinal and yogic paradigm found in Old Javanese Śaiva texts, namely the *ṣaḍaṅgayoga*, reflect an allure for Pātañjala yoga.

For instance, the *Aji Sangkya* by Ida Ketut Jelantik and *Rsi Yadnya Sankya dan Yoga* by Shri Rsi Anandakusuma pay lip service to Patañjali by including the yoga of the eight ancillaries, but maintaining the fundamentally theistic and tantric character of the Old Javanese and Balinese traditions (Acri 2013). Interestingly, the knowledge of Pātañjala yoga by the Balinese authors was not only mediated through the works of the above-mentioned Indian intellectuals, but also through the *Kitab Djoga Soetra Patandjali*, a translation into Malay of a Javanese version (*Serat Yogasūtra Patañjali*) of a Dutch translation of Manilal Nabhubhai Dvivedi's English translation of Patañjali's *Yogasūtra* in 1890, printed in Surakarta, Central Java (probably under the auspices of the local branch of the Theosophical society). The ascendance of Patañjali as the most authoritative voice in the domain of yoga is an ongoing phenomenon, as witnessed by the recent translation into Indonesian of the PYŚ by Balinese scholar Putu Suamba, and by the increasing presence of modern 'Ashtanga' practices in the contemporary Balinese yoga scene.

## Modern Javanese mystical movements

The people of Java were prevalently Hindu and Buddhist until the late fifteenth to early sixteenth century; they have since shifted to Islam. The Islamisation of Java was a long and complex process, which included the – in origin Indic, or India-derived – Javanese psycho-physical yogic techniques. An early-sixteenth-century Portuguese visitor to the north coast of Java, Tome Pires, reported that there were still about 50,000 non-Muslim ascetics (*tapas*) in Java, noting that 'these men are also worshipped by the Moors, and they believe in them greatly; they give them alms; they rejoice when such men come to their houses' (Ricklefs 2006: 11). Indeed, Indic religious elements were absorbed and reconfigured in what is now termed 'Javanism' (*kejawen*), namely a syncretic form of mysticism characterised by a (Sufi) Muslim and Hindu–Buddhist synthesis.

Javanese mysticism is characterised by a doctrinal focus on monism; a belief in karma, reincarnation and deliverance; a practical emphasis on meditative practices and/or ascetic austerities carried out in rivers, cemeteries, caves and forests; periodic fasts; and the acquisition of spiritual and worldly powers. While monism may be ascribed to both Indic and Sufi milieus, the latter seems to be responsible for the idea of total surrender to God (found in, for example, the mystical movements and meditation traditions called Sumarah and Subud). Its various movements and organisations all include, to different degrees, descriptions – through an idiom that freely mixes Indic and Arabic words – of levels of consciousness and subtle centres of the body, repetition of mantras (under the Sufi garb of *dhikr*), initiation, etc., mainly aimed at reuniting the practitioner with the Divine. These aspects of Javanism could indeed be described as a form of yoga in Islamic garb.

As in the ancient Javanese tradition, finding a partner (*jodoh*) and leading the life of a householder (which perhaps implies the practice of sexual yoga) constitute central aspects of spiritual experience. The connubiality between yoga and martial arts that is sometimes found in India also characterises such traditions as the Pencak Silat and Kanuragan, which mix bodily and meditative practices (some of which are clearly connected to the *kanda ampat*) within the context of a broader (nominally Islamic) spiritual dimension to increase spiritual authority and psycho-physical prowess (De Grave 2014). One notes the signs of a revival of mystical groups and a 'nativist' approach to the religious experience in contemporary Central and East Java, including groups identifying as the continuators of the Majapahit tradition of Hindu–Buddhist tantra (whether or not in an Islamic garb). The activities of these groups include rituals and meditation sessions in mountain sites centred around holy water springs and pre-Islamic vestiges (i.e. *liṅgas*, statues, megaliths or temples). Some of these sites have become the destinations of pilgrimages by Balinese Hindus.

All the above practices are in stark contrast with the rising influence of radical, Wahhabi Islam in Indonesia over the past few decades. In spite of this, and in spite of a *fatwa* emanated by the influential Indonesian Ulamas Council in 2009 against the practice of yoga by Muslims (Tedjasukmana 2009), Indic/global contemporary yoga has become a mass phenomenon not only in Java but also in other predominantly Muslim regions of Indonesia. Yoga schools are flourishing in the major urban centres of the country, catering to the middle classes across the boundaries of religious allegiances. Yet, in spite of this growing interest in modern postural yoga, Indonesian mainstream cultural and religious discourses still seem to be largely unaware of the premodern Javanese and Balinese yoga traditions, which makes the task of preserving this heritage in the face of radical Islam and of the cultural onslaught of globalised yoga a particularly difficult one.

## Notes

1 In this chapter I use the term 'Indonesia' for the sake of convenience, bearing in mind that this political entity is a recent (i.e. colonial and postcolonial) phenomenon that is not co-extensive with any polity or culturally homogenous region in the premodern period.

2 These concerns were prominently featured in the Indic socio-religious phenomenon we now call 'tantrism', which exerted a deep and long-lasting impact on the religious traditions of Indonesia.

3 In spite of this fact, and notable exceptions notwithstanding (cf., e.g. Grönbold 1983 and Vasudeva 2004), indological research has often been unwilling to take into account material from Java and Bali. For example, the most recent, authoritative and comprehensive book on yoga in South Asia (including excursuses on Tibet, China and the Islamic world) by Mallinson and Singleton (2017) completely passes over in silence the existence of yoga traditions in Southeast Asia and their relevant textual sources. The same holds true in the case of the voluminous and wide-ranging collection *Yoga in Transformation* (Baier, Maas and Preisendanz 2018).

4 The majority of Old Javanese literature is known to us through the Indic tradition of Balinese palm-leaf manuscripts (*lontar*). A limited oral use of Old Javanese is found, alongside modern Balinese, in elite religious and/or intellectual milieus for mantras and ritualised textual recitation.

5 Some of these Sanskrit terms (such as, for example, the last one) may be only attested in Old Javanese literature, or may have acquired a new meaning due to semantic shift.

6 This is not a direct rendering of the famous Sanskrit epic attributed to Vālmīki, but the local retelling of a later version, the *Rāvaṇavadha* (or *Bhaṭṭikāvya*) by Bhaṭṭi (seventh century CE).

7 This is redolent of stories in the Sanskrit *Pañcatantra,* in which some animals imitate the practices of ascetics for their own gain (see Acri 2010).

8 See *Baoesastra Djawa* (Poerwadarminta 1939), s.v. *ngalong.*

9 See Mallinson 2016: 21 note 98, mentioning, among others, *Vaikhānasasmārtasūtra* and *Mahābhārata.*

10 The upside-down posture seemingly aimed (through the exploitation of gravity) at preventing the downward flow and loss of the life force or *amṛta* (see Mallinson and Singleton 2017: 90). A technique to reabsorb the semen into the body is *vajrolīmudrā* (see Mallinson 2018).

11 Similar practices involving standing on one leg are associated, with positive connotations, with ascetics in other Sanskrit texts, such as the *Mahābhārata* 3.185.4–5: see Mallinson 2016: 21 notes 98 and 107.

12 Fontein (2012: 89) describes the panel as follows: 'Maitreya, standing on one leg in typical yoga fashion, illustrates the words: "he saw how Maitreya carried out arduous practices". This passage seems to occur only in Prajña's Chinese translation (T293, 832, 19)'.

13 See Ensink (1974, 1978), Grönbold (1983), Vasudeva (2004: 367–436) and the notes by Goodall (2004: 351–353).

14 However, Sanskrit verses and their Old Javanese exegeses have not been systematically studied, either individually or in comparison to similar passages from both Indonesia and India.

15 See, for instance, the system of eight ancillaries expounded in *Mṛgendratantra* (*yogapāda*, verse 3), which includes the usual six of Śaiva yoga (with the variant *anvīkṣana* instead of *tarka*, and the same order of the four first auxiliaries, from *prāṇāyāma* to *dhyāna*, as in *aṣṭāṅgayoga* texts) plus *japa* (mantra repetition)

and *yoga* as the final one (Vasudeva 2004: 380); the intermediate system of the *Sarvajñānottara,* teaching six ancillaries without *tarka*; the substitution of *tarka* with *āsana* in the Devakōṭṭai edition of the *Kiraṇatantra* (58.2c–3); and the adherence to Pātañjalayoga in *Suprabhedāgama* (Yogapāda 3.53–56), Īśānaśiva's *Īśānaśivagurudevapaddhati* (ch. 2), *Ajitāgama* (2.29), *Makuṭāgama* (11.1–21) and the Kashmirian *Netratantra* (8.9, 21) (see Vasudeva 2004: 370, note 5; Acri 2013: 94).

16 *Kiraṇatantra, Vidyāpāda* 1.23 (Vivanti 1975: 8). Note, however, that only the half-line 'ab' is present in the Nepalese manuscripts and the commentary of Rāmakaṇṭha, while it appears in later South Indian versions of the text, as well as in Tryambakaśambhu's commentary (Goodall 1998: 221, note 188).

17 This *sūtra* is also attested in the Sanskrit–Old Javanese moralistic-didactic text *Sārasamuccaya* 415.6: *yoga ṅaranya cittavṛttinirodha, kahərətaniṅ manah* ('Yoga is *cittavṛttinirodha,* the restraining of the mind').

18 While the element *Pātañjala* in the title of the text may be a hint to Patañjali, the (legendary) author of the *Yogaśāstra,* it is more likely to refer to the last of the five *pañcakuśikas* or *pañcarṣis,* representing the incarnation of the Lord on earth. This is a reconfigured Pāśupata Śaiva motif, derived from the legend of the Lord's incarnation at Kāyāvarohaṇa as Lakulīśa (Pātañjala's alter-ego), the teacher of the four disciples Kuśika, Kuruṣya, Gārgya, and Maitri (see Acri 2014).

19 Namely, the references to the three kinds of pain as described in the *Bhāṣya* on *sūtra* 1.31 – those having been already defined earlier, in pp. 256.10–260.7; the definition and justification of the mechanism of karma and latent impressions found in *Bhāṣya* 2.13, this having been treated in pp. 272.17–274.18; the long and elaborate cosmographical excursus found in the *Bhāṣya* on 3.26 – cosmography having been treated already in pp. 224.1–226.11.

20 I should like to mention here that the *Dharma Pātañjala,* although of uncertain date, appears to have preserved – much like the other surviving Old Javanese texts of the *tattva* genre – an archaic doctrinal *status quo,* which is detectable in pre-seventh-century Śaiva texts from the Indian Subcontinent, and which has hardly survived in the extant Sanskrit Śaiva Saiddhāntika canon (see Acri 2011b; 2017[2]: 12–14). In this light, although the limited and circumstantial evidence at our disposal does not allow us to draw any conclusions, an analogous point could be made with respect to the form of the PYŚ reflected in the Old Javanese text.

21 In the PYŚ, sūtras 1.2 and 1.3 are generally understood to define *samādhi* and *kaivalya,* respectively, while in the *Dharma Pātañjala,* sūtra 1.3 is quoted in reply to a question by Kumāra about what the absorption of the yogin is like in order to become one with the Lord.

22 This is a prominent theme among the Kashmirian non-dual Śaiva exegetes, too: see, for example, Abhinavagupta's dismissal of the auxiliaries of Pātañjala yoga, and *prāṇāyāma* in particular, in *Tantrāloka* 4.91a (early eleventh century).

23 Cf. *Tattvajñāna* 44 and *Saṅ Hyaṅ Kamahāyānikan* Śaiva pp. 75–76, which enumerate only the few postures common to early Śaivatantras: *padmāsana, vajrāsana, paryaṅkāsana, svastikāsana, vidyāsana* (i.e. *vīrāsana* or *vīryāsana*?), *daṇḍāsana.*

24 A metaphor illustrating this point, found in the *Dharma Pātañjala* and other Old Javanese texts, is that of the fire of yoga burning the impurity (*mala*) sticking to the soul. This differs from the standard Saiddhāntika view that only ritual action (e.g. *dīkṣā*) can burn *mala.* In pp. 306.13–308.12, observances are said to burn maculation (by way of the breath) just like fire burns a piece of dry wood. *Vṛhaspatitattva* 61.14–20 declares that latent karmic impressions (*karmavāsanā*), as well as *mala,* are burnt by yogic fire.

25 These are post-twelfth-century *haṭhayoga* texts, such as the *Amaraughaprabodha, Yogabīja,* etc., where *layayoga* is explicitly mentioned (Mallinson and Singleton 2017: 328–329), but also earlier tantric texts, such as the *Vijñānabhairava* and Vāmanadatta's *Svabodhodayamañjarī* (Torella 2000).

26 See White 2004: 622–623, and *Yogasūtra* (3.38): 'From loosening the fetters of bondage to the body and from awareness of the bodily processes, there is the entering of the mind into another's body'; *bandhakāraṇaśaithilyāt pracārasaṃvedanāc ca cittasya paraśarīrāveśaḥ.* Cf. also al-Bīrūnī's *Kitāb Pātañjal* (Pines and Gelblum 1983: 262).

27 Hardly any traces of Theravāda Buddhism and the meditation techniques associated with it have come down to us from premodern Indonesia.

28 *Vṛhaspatitattva, śloka* 56 and Old Javanese commentary.

29 This corresponds to the stage of *śivīkaraṇa* found in Śaiva Saiddhāntika ritual texts from South India.

30 My conversations with several Balinese Pedanda Śiva have confirmed Stephen's views, as most of them regard this daily procedure as having the same characteristics, and conferring the same benefits, of meditation and yoga.

## Bibliography

### *Primary sources from Java and Bali*


*Adji Sangkya*, by Jelantik, Ida Ketoet. Banjar [no publisher], 1947.

*Arjunavivāha: Arjunawiwāha; Trasformasi teks Jawa Kuno lewat tanggapan dan penciptaan di lingkungan sastra Jawa*, ed. and trans Wiryamartana, I. K. Yogyakarta: Duta Wacana University Press, 1990.

*Bhuvanakośa* [1] Roman transcript, with an Indonesian translation, by a team headed by I Gusti Ngurah Rai Mirsha, printed by PusDok (1991) [2] Lontar MS, Balinese script, LOr 5022, 68 leaves.

*Dharma Pātañjala*: see Acri 2017.

*Dharma Śūnya Kakavin: Dharma Śūnya; Memuja dan meneliti Śiwa*, ed. and Indonesian trans. Dharma Palguna, Ida Bagus Made. Leiden, 1999 [PhD dissertation, Leiden University].

*Gaṇapatitattva: Gaṇapati-tattwa*, ed. and Hindi trans. Sudarshana Devi Singhal. New Delhi: International Academy of Indian Culture, 1958.

*Jñānasiddhānta: Secret Lore of the Balinese Śaiva Priest*, ed. and trans. H. Soebadio. The Hague: Nijhoff, 1971.

*Mahājñāna: Tattwajñāna and Mahājñāna (Two kawi Philosophical Texts)*, ed. and Hindi trans. Sudarshana Devi Singhal. Nagpur: International Academy of Indian Culture, 1962.

*Rāmāyaṇa Kakavin: Rāmāyaṇa Kakawin*, ed. and trans. Santoso, S. New Delhi: International Academy of Indian Culture, 1980. [3 Vols.]

*Rsi yadnya Sankya dan Yoga* by Anandakusuma, Sri Reshi. Singaraja: Toko Buku Indra Jaya, 1973.

*Saṅ Hyaṅ Kamahāyānikan: Sang Hyang Kamahāyānikan; Oud-Javaansche Tekst met Inleiding, Vertaling en Aanteekeningen*, by J. Kats. 's-Gravenhage: Nijhoff, 1910.

*Saṅ Hyaṅ Kamahāyānikan* (Śaiva) (= Kats Ms. C): "Śaiva Version of *Saṅ Hyaṅ Kamahāyānikan*", Lokesh Chandra (ed and trans) in Lokesh Chandra (ed.), *Cultural Horizons of India*, Volume V, 7–101. New Delhi: International Academy of Indian Culture/Aditya Prakashan, 1997.

*Sārasamuccaya: Sāra-samuccaya (a Classical Indonesian Compendium of high ideals)*, ed. and trans. Raghu Vira. New Delhi: IAIC, 1962.

*Smaradahana Kakavin* of Dharmaja: *Smaradahana; Oud-Javaansche tekst met vertaling*, by Poerbatjaraka. Bandoeng: A. C. Nix & Co., 1931.

*Sumanasāntaka: Mpu Monaguṇa's Sumanasāntaka: An Old Javanese Epic Poem, its Indian Source and Balinese Illustrations*, ed. and trans. Peter Worsley, S. Supomo, Thomas Hunter and Margaret Fletcher. Leiden/ Boston: Brill, 2013.

*Sutasoma Kakavin* of Mpu Tantular: *Sutasoma; A Study in Javanese Wajrayana*, ed. and trans. S. Santoso. New Delhi: IAIC, 1985.

*Tattvajñāna: Tattwajñāna and Mahājñāna (Two kawi Philosophical Texts)*, ed. and Hindi trans. Sudarshana Devi Singhal. Nagpur: International Academy of Indian Culture, 1962.

*Vṛhaspatitattva: Wṛhaspati-tattwa; An Old Javanese philosophical text*, ed. and trans. Sudarshana Devi. Nagpur: International Academy of Indian Culture, 1957.


### *Secondary sources*


Acri, A. 2010. 'On Birds, Ascetics, and Kings in Central Java. *Rāmāyaṇa Kakawin*, 24.96–126 and 25'. *Bijdragen tot de Taal-, Land-, en Volkenkunde / Journal of the Humanities and Social Sciences of Southeast Asia* 166: 475–506.

Acri, A. 2011a. 'Re-configuration of Divinity in Old Javanese Śaiva texts from the Indonesian Archipelago (with special reference to *Jñānasiddhānta*, Chapter 19)'. *Travaux de Symposium International: Le Livre. La Roumanie. L'Europe. Troisième édition, Tome III*, 546–65. Bucarest: Éd. Bibliothèque de Bucarest.

Acri, A. 2011b. 'Glimpses of early Śaiva Siddhānta. Echoes of doctrines ascribed to Bṛhaspati in the Sanskrit-Old Javanese *Vṛhaspatitattva*'. *Indo-Iranian Journal* 54: 209–229.

Acri, A. 2012. '*Yogasūtra* 1.10, 1.21–23, and 2.9 in the Light of the Indo-Javanese *Dharma Pātañjala*'. *Journal of Indian Philosophy* 40(3): 259–276.

Acri, A. 2013. 'Modern Hindu Intellectuals and Ancient Texts: Reforming Śaiva Yoga in Bali'. *Bijdragen tot de Taal-, Land-, en Volkenkunde / Journal of the Humanities and Social Sciences of Southeast Asia* 169: 68–103.

Acri, A. 2014. 'Pañcakuśika and Kanda Mpat. From a Pāśupata Śaiva Myth to Balinese Folklore'. *Journal of Hindu Studies* 7(2): 146–178.

Acri, A. 2015. 'Revisiting the Cult of "Śiva-Buddha" in Java and Bali', in Lammerts, C. (ed), *Buddhist Dynamics in Premodern and Early Modern Southeast Asia*, 261–282. Singapore: ISEAS Publishing.

Acri, A. 2016. 'Imposition of the Syllabary (*svaravyañjana-nyāsa*) in the Javano-Balinese Tradition in the Light of South Asian Tantric Sources', in Hornbacher, A. and Fox, R. (eds), *Balinese Letters: Materiality, Efficacy and Scriptural Practices*, 123–165. Leiden/Boston: Brill.

Acri, A. 2017. *Dharma Pātañjala: A Śaiva Scripture from Ancient Java Studied in the Light of Related Old Javanese and Sanskrit Texts*. 2nd ed. New Delhi: Aditya Prakashan. [1st ed.: Gonda Indological Studies XVI, Groningen: Egbert Forsten, 2011]

Angot, M. 2008. *Pātañjalayogsūtram Vyāsabhāṣyasametam; Le Yoga-Sūtra de Patañjali; Le Yoga-Bhāṣya de Vyāsa; avec des extraits du Yoga-Vārttika de Vijñāna-Bhikṣu. Édition, traduction et présentation de Michel Angot*. Paris: Les Belles Lettres.

Baier, K., Maas, P. A. and Preisendanz, K. (eds) 2018. *Yoga in Transformation: Historical and Contemporary Perspectives*. Vienna: Vienna University Press.

Braginsky, V. 2004. 'The Science of Women and the Jewel: The Synthesis of Tantrism and Sufism in a Corpus of Mystical Texts from Aceh,' *Indonesia and the Malay World* 32(93): 141–175.

Braginsky, V. 2017. 'The Manner of the Prophet – Concealed, Found and Regained', *Indonesia and the Malay World* 45(132): 250–291.

Braginsky, V. 2019. 'Through the Optics of Imagination: The Internal Vision of the Science of Women'. *Indonesia and the Malay World* 47(139): 373–405.

Brakel, L. 1979. 'Hamza Fansuri, Notes on Yoga Practice, Lahir Dan Zahir, the Taxallos, a Difficult Passage in the Kitab al-Muntahi, Hamza's Likely Place of Birth and Hamza's Imagery'. *Journal of the Malaysian Branch of the Royal Asiatic Society* 52(1): 73–98.

Brakel, L. 2004. 'Islam and Local Traditions: Syncretic Ideas and Practices'. *Indonesia and the Malay World* 32(92): 5–20.

Creese, H., and Bellows, L. 2002. 'Erotic Literature in Nineteenth-Century Bali'. *Journal of Southeast Asian Studies* 33(3): 385–413.

Drewes, G. W. J. 1976. 'Further Data Concerning 'Abdas-Samad al-Palimbani'. *Bijdragen tot de Taal-, Land- en Volkenkunde* 132: 267–292.

Ensink, J. 1974. 'Sutasoma's Teaching to Gajavaktra, the Snake and the Tigress (Tantular, *Sutasoma* Kakavin 38.1–42.4)'. *Bijdragen tot de Taal-, Land-, en Volkenkunde* 130: 195–226.

Ensink, J. 1978. 'Śiva-Buddhism in Java and Bali', in Bechert, H. (ed), *Buddhism in Ceylon and Studies on Religious Syncretism in Buddhist Countries. Report on a Symposium in Göttingen*, 178–198. Göttingen: Vandenhoeck und Ruprecht.

Fontein, J. 2012. *Entering the Dharmadhātu: A Study of the Gandavyūha Reliefs of Borobudur*. Leiden and Boston: Brill.

Goodall, D. 1998. *Bhaṭṭa Rāmakaṇṭha's Commentary on the Kiraṇatantra*, Vol. 1. Pondichéry: Institut Français de Pondichéry/École française d'Extrême-Orient.

Goodall, D. 2004. *The Parākhyatantra; A Scripture of the Śaiva Siddhānta; A Critical Edition and Annotated Translation*. Pondichéry: Institut Français de Pondichéry/École française d'Extrême-Orient.

de Grave, J.-M. 2014. 'Javanese Kanuragan Ritual Initiation: A Means to Socialize by Acquiring Invulnerability, Authority, and Spiritual Improvement'. *Social Analysis: The International Journal of Social and Cultural Practice* 58(1): 47–66.

Grönbold, G. 1983. 'Materialen zur Geschichte des Ṣaḍaṅga-Yoga I; Der Ṣaḍaṅga-Yoga im Hinduismus'. *Indo-Iranian Journal* 25: 181–190.

Hatley, S. 2016. 'Erotic Asceticism: The Razor's Edge Observance (*asidhārāvrata*) and the Early History of Tantric Coital Ritual'. *Bulletin of the School of Oriental and African Studies* 79(2): 329–345.

Kats, J. 1910. *Sang Hyang Kamahāyānikan; Oud-Javaansche Tekst met Inleiding, Vertaling en Aanteekeningen*. 's-Gravenhage: Nijhoff.

Mallinson, J. 2007. *The Khecarīvidyā of Ādinātha. A Critical Edition and Annotated Translation of an Early Text of Haṭhayoga*. London: Routledge.

Mallinson, J. 2016. 'Śāktism and Haṭhayoga', in Wernicke-Olesen, Bjarne (ed), Goddess Traditions in Tantric Hinduism: History, Practice and Doctrine, 109–140. London: Routledge.

Mallinson, J. 2018. 'Yoga and Sex: What is the Purpose of Vajrolīmudrā?', in Baier, K., Maas, P. A. and Preisendanz, K (eds), *Yoga in Transformation: Historical and Contemporary Perspectives*, 183–222. Vienna: Vienna University Press

Mallinson, J. and Singleton, M. 2017. *Roots of Yoga: Translated and Edited with an Introduction*. London: Penguin Books.

Mirnig, N. 2013. 'Śaiva Siddhānta Śrāddha: Towards an Evaluation of the Socio-religious Landscape Envisaged by pre-12th Century Sources', in Mirnig, N., Szanto, P. D. and Williams, M. (eds),

*Puṣpikā: Tracing Ancient India Through Texts and Traditions: Contributions to Current Research in Indology, Volume 1*, 283–302. Oxford: Oxbow Books.

Pines, S. and Gelblum, T. 1983. 'Al-Bīrūnī's Arabic Version of Patañjali's *Yogasūtra*: A Translation of the Third Chapter and a Comparison with Related Sanskrit Texts'. *Bulletin of the School of Oriental and African Studies* 46: 258–304.

Poerwadarminta, W. J. S. 1939. *Baoesastra Djawa*. Groningen: J. B. Wolters.

Pollock, S. 2006. *The Language of the Gods in the World of Men: Sanskrit, Culture and Power in Premodern India*. Berkeley, CA, USA: University of California Press.

Ricklefs, M. C. 2006. *Mystic Synthesis in Java: A History of Islamization from the Fourteenth to the Early Nineteenth Centuries*. Norwalk: EastBridge.

Stephen, M. 2010. 'The Yogic Art of Dying, Kundalinī Yoga, and the Balinese *pitra yadnya*'. *Bijdragen tot de Taal-, Land- en Volkenkunde* 166(4): 426–474.

Stephen, M. 2014. 'The *Dasaksara* and Yoga in Bali'. *The Journal of Hindu Studies* 7(1–2): 179–216.

Stephen, M. 2015. '*Sūrya Sevana*: A Balinese Tantric Practice'. *Archipel* 89: 95–124.

Tedjasukmana, J. 2009. 'Indonesia's Fatwa Against Yoga'. *Time*, 29 January. http://content.time.com/time/world/article/0,8599,1874651,00.html. Accessed 20 February 2020.

Torella, R. 2000. 'The *Svabodhodayamañjarī*, or How to Suppress the Mind with no Effort,' in Tsuchida, R. and Wezler, A. (eds), *Harānandalaharī: Volume in Honour of Professor Minoru Hara on His Seventieth Birthday*, 387–410. Reinbek: Verlag für Orientalistische Fachpublikationen.

Vasudeva, S. 2004. *The Yoga of the Mālinīvijayottaratantra*. Pondicherry: Institut Français de Pondichéry/École française d'Extrême-Orient.

Vivanti, M. P. 1975. '*Il 'Kiraṇāgama'. Testo e traduzione del "Vidyāpāda"*'. *Annali* 35(3), fasc. 2. Napoli: Istituto Universitario Orientale.

White, D. G. 2004. 'Early Understandings of Yoga in the Light of Three Aphorisms from the Yoga Sūtras of Patañjali', in Ciurtin, E. (ed), *Du corps humain, au carrefour de plusieurs savoirs en Inde. Mélanges offerts à Arion Rosu par ses collègues et ses amis à l'occasion de son 80e anniversaire, Stvdia Asiatica* 4–5: 613–629.

Wolters, O. W. 1999 [1982]. *History, Culture, and Region in Southeast Asian Perspectives*. Singapore: Institute of Southeast Asian Studies.

Zoetmulder, P. J. 1982. *Old Javanese-English dictionary*. With the collaboration of S. O. Robson. Gravenhage: Nijhofff.

# 20
# YOGA IN TIBET

*Naomi Worth*

## Introduction: yoga comes to Tibet

When Tibetan scholars translated the term *yoga* from Sanskrit into Tibetan in the eighth century, they contended with a fundamental philosophical discrepancy between Buddhist and non-Buddhist worldviews. *Naljor* (*rnal 'byor*) is the Tibetan word for 'yoga', and its etymology demonstrates an implicit shift to non-theism, an important distinction between Buddhist and Hindu yoga systems that frequently share practices. Instead of just rendering *naljor* as 'union', the Tibetan etymology literally means 'union with the natural, pristine reality' (Hopkins 2005: 24).[1] In Tibetan Buddhism, contemplative techniques involving body, speech and mind alike are referred to as *naljor*, and the culmination of ascetic practice is union with the fundamental nature of reality itself.

*Naljor* is used broadly in Tibetan Buddhism to mean 'contemplative practice', but its historical usage in tantric literature demonstrates *naljor*'s broad and shifting scope. While a comprehensive history of the term has yet to be written, this chapter captures some important usages of *naljor* and how they are tied to Tibetan Buddhist tantra. First, the etymology of *naljor* highlights the importance of philosophy in contemplative practice. Second, *naljor* was used by early Tibetan scholars who organised the influx of tantras from India to Tibet. Those early scholars delineated tantric doxographical categories that have gone on to define contemplative and ritual practice systems in enduring ways. A third common use of *naljor* is as a moniker for ancillary branch yoga systems, such as Kālacakra's six yogas and the four yogas of Mahāmudrā. These practice traditions demonstrate how tantric philosophy comes to life through practices that constantly refer back to Buddha-nature theory. Special attention in the chapter is thus given to Buddha-nature theory, which maps both emptiness and the fullness of the experience of a Buddha onto the body using tantric embodiment theory. Finally, the chapter ends by turning to *yogis* – *naljorpa* – beginning with an introduction to Tibet's most famous yogi, Milarepa (eleventh century), who used Tibet's emic form of tantric yoga – inner heat – to attain enlightenment. A contemporary case study of Tibetan Buddhist monastics who also practice inner heat yoga as part of a comprehensive contemplative training programme at Namdroling Monastery and Nunnery in South India showcases a continuous yoga practice lineage that reaches back to its clear origins in seventeenth-century Tibet.

## Buddhist philosophy as the foundation of tantra and yoga

If you have visited a Tibetan Buddhist temple or monastery, you may have been surprised to note that, contrary to popular opinion, Tibetan Buddhism is not atheistic per se. The alternatively wrathful and seductive faces of deities are delicately painted on nearly every surface. However, recourse to Buddhist philosophy tells us that even deities must be interpreted according to the doctrine of *emptiness*, the lack of a fixed quality to things. In one of Tibet's most important practices, 'deity yoga' (*lha yi rnal 'byor*), a mainstream tantric technique where the empty self and empty deity are identified as one in contemplative performance, the term 'deity' (*lha*) must be added to *naljor*. In practice, the self-identification is explicitly non-dual. The act of arising as a deity is meant to undermine fixed notions of both the self and the divine. Visualising oneself as a divine being who embodies the Buddhist ideals of wisdom and compassion forges a path of bliss, clarity and non-conceptuality into consciousness by connecting the qualities of Buddhas to ordinary experiences (Jamgön Kongtrul Lodrö Tayé 2007: 106–107).

Buddha-nature theory maps both emptiness and the potential for Buddhahood onto the body[2] as the 'Threefold Buddha Bodies' (*sku gsum*) shared by Buddhas and sentient beings alike. Buddhist yogic practices seek to uncover this Buddha-nature located in the body. In the Ancient Order's (*rNying ma*) interpretation, the *dharmakāya* (*chos sku*), the reality body, is emptiness itself and the foundation of the others. 'Primordially pure' (*ka dag*) and 'free from conceptual elaborations' (*spros pa med pa*), it is the basic voidness that underlies the constantly changing stream of causes and conditions of the manifest world. Its attributive aspect is luminosity, radiance and fullness. The second level of embodiment is the *sambhogakāya* (*longs sku*), the bliss body. In yogic contexts, this is often equated with the network of channels, winds and seminal essences (*rtsa rlung thig le*; Skt.: *naḍī*, *vāyu*, *bindu*) shared with Hindu and other tantric systems. The third level of embodiment, the *nirmāṇakāya* (*sprul sku*), the emanation body, is the result of practice. This level of Buddha-embodiment empowers one to emanate as a Buddha to benefit others (Gyatso 1998).

Tantric literature on winds, channels and seminal essences weave Buddha-nature into the subtlest recesses of the human body in detailed descriptions of tantric anatomy and physiology. Buddhist yogic techniques focus on clearing away the karmic winds, and also train awareness to 'recognise' the natural state of the body, the 'innately real'. When the tantric body is optimised through praxis, the winds enter and abide in the central channel. As the seminal essences (*thig le*; Skt.: *bindu*) travel through the central channel, they break up the *cakras* (*'khor lo*), which causes the practitioner to transcend conditioned reality and experience great bliss (Dudjom Rinpoche 1991). The key difference between flawed embodiment and the flawless embodiment of a buddha is recognition: enlightenment is a matter of perception.

## Tibetan yoga in the three main canons

When early Tibetan scholars translated *yoga* as *naljor*, they included an implicit semantic shift away from theism by adding the prefix *nalma* (*rnal ma*) to the semantic head *jor* (*'byor-* union). In tantric Buddhist philosophy, *nalma* is 'the innate, real condition', and Buddha-nature is what is fundamentally real (Wangchuk 2004). Taken together, Tibetan dictionaries define *naljor* according to its use: 'To be subdued by the authentic path',[3] or 'Contemplation and so forth',[4] or 'Effortlessly connecting the mind to the natural state.'[5]

*Naljor* is a term that exemplifies 'philosophical tantra', where praxis systems are unremittingly entangled with Buddhist philosophy. It showcases Tibetan Buddhist praxis systems' deep commitment to philosophy. Tibetan Buddhism is pervasively tantric yet deeply logical (Germano 2002). Its yogic techniques are so enmeshed in philosophy that the somewhat unconventional twentieth-century translator Herbert Guenther rendered *naljorpa* (Skt.: *yogin*) as 'philosopher' (Bharati 1965). *Naljor* was translated into Tibetan from Sanskrit during the massive translation project from the eighth to the twelfth centuries that catalysed the development of Tibetan Buddhism. As texts were transferred from India to Tibet, scholars faced a dizzying array of literature. In what came to be characteristic of Tibetan Buddhism's propensity to organise its teachings into categories, organisational schemes were established that both reflected and created streams of Buddhist thought. By the fourteenth century, three stable Buddhist collections were redacted, and the term *naljor* was used as a technical term to demarcate tantric doxographies such as Yoga Tantra (*rnal 'byor rgyud*), Anuttara Yoga Tantra (*bla na med pa'i rnal 'byor gyi rgyud*), Mahāyoga (*rnal 'byor chen po*), Anuyoga (*rjes su rnal 'byor*) and Atiyoga (*shin tu rnal 'byor*). In this context, the term explicitly refers to internally oriented contemplative practices, in contrast to earlier forms of tantra focused on external ritual activities.

Buton Rinchen Drup (*Bu ston rin chen grub*, 1290–1364) was an early seminal redactor of the Tibetan Buddhist canons, which came to be divided between the *Kangyur* (*bka' 'gyur*), the words of the historical Buddha in India; and the *Tengyur* (*bstan 'gyur*), a collection of classical Buddhist treatises attributed to various human authors from India. He notoriously excluded the Ancient (*rNying ma*) Order, causing the emergence of a collection of tantras as their own canon, the *Nyingma Gyubum* (*rnying me rgyud 'bum*) (Schaeffer, unpublished work).

In a late edition of the canons from the famous print house in Degé, Kham (Eastern Tibet), 8,815 instances of the term *naljor* appear in the *Kangyur* (c. 1733), with an additional 1,517 entries for *yogin* (*rnal 'byor pa*). In the *Tengyur* (c. 1744), there are 19,712 instances of *naljor*. The preponderance of *naljor* testifies to the long tradition and range of use of the term *yoga* in premodern India (Samuel 2008). The vast proliferation of texts written in Tibet afterward and not included in these canons also frequently refer to *naljor*, with the most common usages discussed next.

## Yoga as a doxographical category: the four-fold and six-fold classes of tantra

Tantra was flourishing in India while Buddhism was being integrated into Tibetan society from the eighth to the twelfth centuries. By the twelfth century, Tibetans recognised that Buddhism was in serious decline in India, and had come to feel responsible for its preservation. In that process, scholars bundled practices, initiations, rituals and contemplative techniques together into increasingly formalised tantric doxographies (Dalton 2005: 116–7). Western scholarship prefers the term doxography, following the ancient Greeks' usage to delineate philosophical schools. The emic category is 'vehicle' (*theg pa;* Skt.: *yāna*), which is likewise divided first and foremost according to the philosophical view (*lta ba*). While all the vehicles lead to the goal of enlightenment, their approaches differ not only in theory, but also in the ritual and praxis techniques used to attain that state (Bstan dzin rgya mtsho 2005: 14). Each vehicle packages rituals, initiations, texts and practices. These early literary organisational schemes gave birth to trends in Buddhist philosophy and praxis that went on to define sectarian lines in enduring ways.

A fundamental division in tantric versions of such doxographies is between the Ancient and New orders of Tibetan Buddhism. The Ancients' nine-vehicle (*theg pa dgu*) system dates back to the eighth century and organises tantra into the last six of the nine vehicles. By the twelfth century, the New Order's (*gsar ma*) popular four-fold classificatory tantra scheme was in place. These tantric doxographies were unprecedented in Indian Buddhism (Dalton 2005: 118). The New and Ancient orders share partially overlapping territory: Unsurpassed Yoga Tantra, the last and highest category for the New orders, roughly maps onto the fourth and fifth categories of the tradition of the Ancients: Mahāyoga and Anuyoga (Dudjom Rinpoche 1991: 34).

## *The Ancient tradition: six classes of tantra culminating in 'Supreme Yoga'*

Only six of the Ancient tradition's nine vehicles (*theg pa dgu*) are tantric, and only the four highest levels are explicitly labelled as types of *naljor*. Some say that the vehicles are divided according to the acumen of practitioners, so that Atiyoga, which is the highest vehicle, serves the most efficient methods to the most intelligent people (Karmay 2007: 146–7). Others assert that each of the nine vehicles address a type of delusion. Yet another explanation of the shades of *naljor* is that the last four vehicles are gradients of concentration (Skt.: *samādhi*) (Dalton 2005: 118). This last explanation resonates with the way *samādhi* is used in Indian religious contexts to describe gnoseological states that are the resultant realisations of the yogic path.

Atiyoga's more common name is Dzokchen (*rdzogs chen*), the 'Great Perfection'. Early forms stress transcendence of all religious practice, including whatever is referred to as yoga. Over time, with the emergence of new traditions by the eleventh and twelfth centuries such as the Seminal Heart (*snying thig*) tradition, such religious practices re-emerge, including somatic yogas such as deity yoga, inner heat yoga and sexual yoga. Atiyoga's predominant motif is the rhetoric of relaxation, where practices aim to drop conceptual thoughts and relax into the natural state of 'self-radiant awareness' (Dudjom Rinpoche 1991: 34). The Dzokchen tradition took models of mind defined by Indian Buddhist philosophers roughly 1,000 years earlier as their basis and added categories such as 'primordial mind' (*ye shes*) and 'open awareness' (*rig pa*). For Dzokchen, because normal conceptuality (*rnam par rtog pa*) – the ongoing stream of thought – indirectly perceives objects through a veil of delusion, it is the cause of human suffering. Atiyoga contemplations use conceptual, indirect perception to navigate toward non-conceptual, direct perception (Komarovski 2015: 47–52).

Atiyoga has its own take on the Threefold Buddha-body theory. The ordinary minds of people have a natural state (*sems nyid*) tantamount to a Buddha's mind that is present throughout the body. This 'primordial awareness' (*ye shes*) of a Buddha flows as embodied awareness through the body's subtle channels. The mind is mapped across the body via three pan-tantric components: channels, winds and seminal essences (*rtsa rlung thig le*; Skt.: *nadī vāyu bindu*). Cosmologically, both karmic winds (*las kyi rlung*) and wisdom winds (*ye shes kyi rlung*) emerge out of the primordial Buddha Samantabhadra (*Kun tu bzang po*), but at the level of the individual the karmic winds obscure the wisdom winds. The yogi's task is to reveal the natural presence of the wisdom winds by clearing away the karmic body through yogic techniques (Higgins 2013: 62–64). Ultimately, the human body is problematised as being made of karma (*las*) and habitual tendencies (*bag chags*; Skt.: *vāsanā*).

## *The New orders of Tibetan Buddhism and the four classes of tantra*

The New orders (Geluk, Kagyu, Sakya and others) have a well-known four-fold classificatory scheme for tantra: Kriyā-, Caryā-, Yoga- and Anuttarayoga. The characteristics vary according to sect, historical time period and even individual interpretation. The following are some examples:

- Kriyātantra (*bya rgyud*) focuses on ritual techniques with an *external support* such as a shrine or visualised image of a deity while philosophically upholding subject–object duality. Of the four traditional tantric empowerment schemes widespread in Tibetan Buddhism (though not universal), only the vase and crown empowerments are given (Tulku Thondub 1995: 118). Such practices reflect pre-eighth-century Indian Buddhist tantra (Dalton 2005: 123). They are for practitioners of the lowest capacity, and enlightenment takes up to seven lifetimes.

- Caryātantra (*spyod rgyud*), aka *Ubhayatantra* (*gnyis rgyud*), has two names, and there is some confusion over whether Tibetan doxographers meant to include this intermediate class of tantra. In practice, it is similar to *kriyā* tantra. Some interpret the two names as dual emphasis on both philosophical view and conduct, but this may be a reflection of the comprehensiveness with which Tibetans invoke hermeneutics, even retroactively. Practices include seed-syllable meditation like *bīja* mantras, *mudrās*, deity meditation and contemplation on ultimate reality without signs. Empowerments include the five tantric Buddhas, and a practitioner can attain enlightenment within five lifetimes (Dudjom Rinpoche 1991: 33). These first two classes are likely extensions of ritual, yogic and devotional practices common in early Indian Mahāyāna Buddhism beginning in the fourth century (Kragh 2015: 68).
- Yoga Tantra (*rnal 'byor brgyud*) shifts the ritual gaze inwardly, into the body and mind of a practitioner, rather than focusing on external ritual actions (Dalton 2005: 124). Practitioners visualise themselves as a deity and 'unite' that with the wisdom that realises emptiness (*stong pa nyid*; Skt.: *śūnyatā*). Empowerments include the five tantric Buddha families, various deities and the master–disciple relationship.
- Unsurpassed Yoga Tantra (*bla na med pa'i rgyud*; Skt.: *Anuttarayogatantra*) philosophically abandons duality (Dudjom Rinpoche 1991: 33). Unsurpassed Yoga Tantra is divided into 'mother' tantras, liturgical practices that emphasise wisdom as the realisation of emptiness, and 'father' tantras, which prioritise the method of *bodhicitta*, the altruistic mind (Bstan dzin rgya mtsho 2005: 24). Its first stage, Generation Stage (*skyed rim*), consists mostly of deity yoga, where one visualises the self arising as a tantric deity while simultaneously contemplating one's own empty nature. In the second phase of practice, completion stage (*rdzogs rim*), techniques centre on the 'body within the body' or 'tantric body'. Empowerments include the widely known four-fold sequence of vase, secret, wisdom and word, and enlightenment is possible within a single lifetime.

## *Naljor* in ancillary branch systems

We now turn to a different use of *naljor* as a moniker for popular Tibetan Buddhist groupings of practices in integrated sequences, such as the famed 'six yogas (*'byor drug*) of the Kālacakra'. These all find a home among the tantric doxographies in the completion stage of Unsurpassed Yoga Tantra (*bla na med pa'i rgyud*). It is noteworthy that the term *naljor* does not actually appear in the bundled families of techniques compiled by Nāropa and Niguma. When twentieth-century scholars erroneously rendered the 'six doctrines of Nāropa' (*Nā ro chos drug*) as the 'six yogas of Nāropa', they left a legacy of confusion (Lopez 2000). They earned their place in this chapter mostly because erroneous modern scholarship popularised them as 'Tibetan yoga'. The rubric instead uses another key term with a wide valence: 'chö' (*chos*), which means 'dharma' or doctrine. While Nāropa and Niguma's groupings of practices are not *naljor* by name, it is easy to see why they were linked: technically, they meet the definition of *naljor* presented here as 'contemplative practices, especially tantric in nature'. These ancillary branch systems share an emphasis on the tantric energy body, the system of winds, channels and seminal essences that locates every aspect of emotion and cognition across the body. A popular Tibetan Buddhist metaphor for the tantric energy body is a horse and rider: the seminal essences represent units of consciousness that 'ride' the body's winds like a lame rider on a blind horse. Being lame, the rider is unable to walk; being blind, the horse unable to see. They depend on each other to move about. In the same way, controlling the breath controls consciousness and harnesses the body's inherent power (Wallace 2010).

## Kālacakra's six yogas

The *Kālacakra Tantra* ('Cycle of Time'; *dus kyi 'khor lo*) is an eleventh Unsurpassed Yoga tantra, characteristic of late Indian Buddhism, with a continuous history of transmission in Tibet documented by a stream of commentaries across the history of Tibetan Buddhism. Nowadays, the Kālacakra initiation is one of the main activities of the 14th Dalai Lama who, in his expanded transmission of Buddhism, brings esoteric yoga into the lives of people worldwide. While some Tibetan Buddhist yogins actually perform Kālacakra six-branch yoga techniques, the vast majority of people receive the Kālacakra initiation as a blessing and way to connect with the Dalai Lama, who links the practice to world peace.

The six yogas of Kālacakra follow a prerequisite contemplative curriculum that consists of the standard foundational practices (*sngon 'gro*) and generation-stage tantra. The six yogas are listed below, following Vesna Wallace's scholarship. Five are identical in name to five of the eight branches of *aṣṭāṅga yoga* in Patañjali's *Yogasūtra*, although the order differs (Wallace 2001: 45).

1. Wind control (*srog rtsol*; Skt.: *prāṇāyāma*) brings the *prāna* and *apāna* winds into the central channel.
2. Retraction (*so sor sdud pa*; Skt.: *pratyāhāra*) is meditative absorption free from mental activity.
3. Meditative stabilisation (*bsam gtan*; Skt.: *dhyāna*) is the single-pointed settling of the mind on empty forms.
4. Concentration (*'dzin pa*; Skt.: *dhāraṇā*) is the dissolution of the winds into the central channel as a continuation of breath control.
5. Recollection (*rjes dran*; Skt.: *anusmṛti*) is the consummation of the winds practices.
6. Concentration (*ting nge 'dzin*; Skt.: *samādhi*) is absorption into unchanging bliss and compassion.

The *Kālacakratantra*'s detailed Indian eleventh-century commentary, *Stainless Light* (*Vimalaprabha*), is divided into two topics: 'sciences' that describe knowledge of the world, and meditation. The Buddhist sciences analyse phenomena in the natural world alongside the doctrine of emptiness to facilitate purification of the physical and mental aspects of human life. The *Kālacakra* connects cycles such as the passage of days, seasons and years to the movement of *prāṇas* in the human body. In that way the individual is a microcosmic representation of the macrocosmos.

The tantra mentions *haṭhayoga* briefly in the section on preserving health with Buddhist tantric medicine. Buddhism has been concerned with physical health from its earliest stages, and this became paramount in tantra where the body is a main condition for the attainment of supernatural powers (*dngos grub*; Skt.: *siddhis*). The *Stainless Light* recommends postures as medical interventions, such as *vajra* posture (*vajrāsana*) to eliminate backaches or headstand (*śīrṣāsana*) as an antidote for diseases caused by phlegm disorders. The *Kālacakratantra* became a repository for alternative healing remedies to be used in conjunction with each other. As complementary disciplines, medical practitioners could draw upon the four sciences – religion, ayurveda, alchemy and medicine – as needed. A healer might prescribe mantras, herbal medications, dietary therapy, *āsana*, *prāṇāyāma*, tantric rites of healing, massage, precious stones, visualisation of deities and/or recommendations based on astrology.

The *Stainless Light* enjoins practitioners to use force (*haṭhena*) to draw the body's vital energies into the central channel, and recommends sexual yoga as a method to do so. Here, yoga is defined as the union of bliss and emptiness, a Buddhist non-dual foregrounding of gnosis that polemically seeks to negate and disparage the Śaiva tantric tradition's emphasis on the Lord (*Īśvara*). Yogins are defined as initiated completion-stage practitioners for whom initiation originates in their own minds, which is justified by tantric embodiment theory. With the gnostic body as the container of Buddha-nature underlying the physical body, access to initiation from a Buddha can be found in the body (Wallace 2001: 6–12).

## *Mahāmudrā's four yogas*

*Mahāmudrā* (*phyag rgya chen po*) literally means the 'great seal', and it uses *naljor* to refer to epistemological states on a contemplative path. The term *mahāmudrā* is featured in both Buddhist and Hindu tantras, as well as in Svātmarama's fifteenth-century *Haṭhapradīpikā*.[6] In Tibetan Buddhism, it is an influential meditation system associated with the New Orders of Tibetan Buddhism with a formidable trail of literature and lineage that dates back to the eleventh century and continues today. It is often compared to Atiyoga. A unique facet of the Mahāmudrā movement is its integration of non-tantric Mahāyāna Buddhism with Unsurpassed Yoga Tantra approaches. The redactors of the system aimed to remove the obstacle that obligatory tantric initiation posed, but also decontextualised meditation from sexual settings prohibited for celibate monastics. The Mahāmudrā movement freed up monastics to take on the life of yogis as opposed to a sole focus on scholastic activities and non-tantric forms of contemplation. Mahāmudrā was radical and timely, and led to the establishment of the Kagyu school ofTibetan Buddhism (Kragh 2015: 30–1).

Mahāmudrā follows a typical organisational scheme for contemplation called base (*gzhi*), path (*lam*) and result (*'bras bu*). The base is the philosophical view, which in tantra is the innate perfection of every experience, tantamount to the *dharmakāya*, the state of mind that is naturally empty and free from conceptual entanglement. The path is the method to uncover that which is already present, i.e. co-emergent emptiness. When practicing Mahāmudrā, thoughts should be seen as 'self-arisen' (*rang snang*) and allowed to dissolve naturally back into their own essence. Guru yoga is the key to circumventing the empowerments: aligning oneself with the guru leads the practitioner to the teacher's level of realisation.

The 'four yogas' (*rnal 'byor bzhi*; Skt.: *caturyoga*) of Mahāmudrā are the result of practice. They are four progressive mental stages of settling into a natural, uncontrived state where every thought and perception is yoked with the *dharmakāya*. They are:

1. Single-pointedness (*rtse gcig*; Skt.: *ekāgra*)
2. Freedom from conceptual entanglement (*spros bral*; Skt.: *niṣprapañca*)
3. One taste (*ro gcig*; Skt.: *ekarasa*)
4. Great meditative absorption (*myna bhat chen po*; Skt.: *mahāsamāhita*).

*(Kragh 2015: 72–73)*

## *Nāropa's six doctrines*

The six doctrines of Nāropa (*na ro chos drug*) is a set of practices that targets states of consciousness governed by the body's natural processes, such as waking, orgasm, dreaming and dying. Among the New Order's four-fold division of tantra, this bundle is also categorised in the completion stage of Unsurpassed Yoga Tantra. Nāropa was a tenth–eleventh-century Indian who received the six-fold instructions from the Bengali yogin Tilopa. They likely represent a collection of tantric teachings current in Bengal in the eleventh century. Tilopa conveyed them to the Indian siddha Marpa, who transmitted them to Tibet (Mullin 1997: 13).

The first three doctrines are foremost because they can be endeavoured during this lifetime. The others, on the bardo, consciousness transference and changing [bodily] residence (S. Harding, personal communication, 3 March 2020), are related to death. Iterations of the list vary, but include:

1a. Inner heat (*gtum mo*) – includes central channel yoga and postural yoga techniques
1b. Sexual consort (*las kyi phyag rgya*)
2. Illusory body (*sgyu lus*)
3. Clear light (*'od gsal*)
4. Dreaming (*rmi lam*)
5. Intermediate state (*bar do*)
6a. Consciousness transference (*'pho ba*) to a Buddhist pure land
6b. Changing residence (*grong 'jug*) – transferring consciousness to another body.

*(Lopez 2000: 3)*

Inner heat and sexual yoga are often treated as alternative techniques to each other because they both train practitioners to manipulate their bodies to produce great bliss. Inner heat can also be used as a preliminary practice for sexual yoga. Control over the body's energy using postural yoga, breath retention and complex visualisations should prepare one to be able to control their mind under the sway of even more powerful sexual energies.

Both inner heat and sexual yoga manipulate the body's energies. The body is said to have 72,000 channels, but it is common in the completion stage to focus on three main channels, or even only one: the central channel. The two side channels represent attachment and aversion, i.e. desire and hatred. When the central channel is not optimised through yogic techniques, it represents ignorance. The *cakras* are psycho-physical centres that relate to personality traits, cognition and bodily processes. However, in practice contexts the *cakras* are visualised as stopping points along the path of the central channel and are used to generate heat. When the winds enter the central channel, the meditator accesses profound states such as the mind of clear light (*'od gsal*), which is the radiance of the *dharmakāya*, the first Buddha-body.

Yogins familiar with the mind of clear light during the day are better equipped to recognise it during sleep, dying and sexual arousal. Nāropa's doctrine on dreaming teaches how to locate and make use of the mind of clear light during sleep (Lopez 2000: 4). The yoga of dying exemplifies how the mind and body are deeply interconnected, and how practitioners can take advantage of that situation. During the process of dying, the body's functions cease to operate in a predictable sequence, and aspects of consciousness come to the foreground in ways not apparent when the body is fully operational. Meditation during life prepares one to recognise the set of luminous apparitions that reveal themselves naturally while dying.

Sexual arousal is yet another powerful mental state that yogins take advantage of in Nāropa's techniques. Such practices that intentionally induce arousal require a high degree of awareness and restraint. That is one reason why these tantric techniques are shrouded in secrecy: most people lack the requisite training and discipline. Carried away by desire, things can easily get out of control. Tibetan Buddhist tantric techniques are meant to be performed accompanied by the altruistic motivation to achieve enlightenment for the benefit of all sentient beings, called *bodhicitta*. If, under the sway of desire, one forgets their compassionate motivation to serve others, the yogin is liable to behave in injurious ways, and the laws of karma that undergird all of Buddhism are just as applicable in tantric practice. In Buddhist cosmology there are special 'tantric hells' for people who break vows when they try to practise tantra but fail.

## *Niguma's six* dharmas

Niguma was a *ḍākinī*, a term varyingly used for celestial beings such as Buddhist goddesses and guardian spirits, but also for real women in their roles as consorts and female practitioners. These paradigmatic female figures are important to the transmission and preservation of texts across generations, as well as male access to them. For example, a sexual encounter with a consort is often required for a treasure revealer (*gter ston*) to understand the secret, coded language in which the hidden texts (*gter ma*) are written – *ḍākinī* code language (*mkha' 'gro 'i brda' skad*).

As a *ḍākinī*, Niguma gave the transmission of her six doctrines to Khyungpa Naljor, and together they became the 'root' of the Shangpa Kagyu lineage. As the root, they support the main practice of Mahāmudrā, making Niguma's doctrines a preliminary practice for that lineage. Like the related six doctrines of Nāropa, these techniques control the tantric body as part of the Completion Phase of Unsurpassed Yoga Tantra. In *Vajra Lines of the Six Doctrines*, Niguma says 'One's own body is the means: three channels and four chakras'. Her six doctrines have much in common with Nāropa's. They are:

1. Inner fire (*gtum mo*)
2. Illusory body (*rgyud lus*)
3. Dreaming (*rmi lam*)
4. Clear light (*'od gsal*)
5. Transference of consciousness (*'pho ba*)
6. Intermediate state (*bar do*).

Niguma was Kashmiri and lived in the tenth or eleventh century. At that time, Kashmir was a centre of tantric activity where Buddhist and Śaiva traditions frequently exchanged philosophy and practices. Little was written down about Niguma compared to her family members and even her disciples, but what is available portrays her as a spiritual virtuoso who had practised for many lifetimes. Niguma was likely Nāropa's sister, and was revered as a highly realised being who attained the rainbow body, the outward manifestation of Buddha-nature obscured within the depths of the tantric body.

Nāropa's disciple Marpa is said to have received teachings from Niguma, but in literary accounts his female teacher is merely referred to as the *ḍākinī* who is 'Adorned with Bone Ornaments', which is not sufficient evidence to claim that this female figure was actually Niguma. Scholar Sarah Harding argues that Niguma has been at the centre of scholarly portrayals that present sexy tales about female figures rather than facts (Harding 2010: 3–17). In Niguma's description of inner heat yoga, she covers the yogin's relationship to food and clothes: 'inner space of fire, the vital point of the body, eating the food of inner heat, wearing the clothing, spreading the seat, receiving the empowerment of existence, naturally liberating obstructing forces, and riding the horse of energy [vital] currents' (Harding 2010: 140). Food and clothes are commonly addressed in Tibetan practices that target energetic blockages made of the network of karmic propensities that permeate the unconscious mind. A mundane way to think about the yogas of food and clothing is that they help yogins in isolated retreat to generate dietary nourishment and warmth when access to supplies is scarce. Alchemy (*bcud len*) in Tibet became the process by which yogins took the essences of substances in order to transform non-traditional sources into biological sustenance. Tibetan yogins have been known to eat stones, herbs, metals, the breath and their own excrement (Germano 1997). We will now turn to practitioners of yoga.

## Tibetan yogis

There is a vast literary record of the life stories (*rnam thar*) of Tibetan yogis who claim to have attained freedom from the cycle of existence, *saṃsāra*, through their contemplative practices. Many went on to become extraordinary teachers, or simply lived out their lives in retreat. What is a Tibetan Buddhist yogi? For modern practitioners, the term *naljorpa* (yogi) has the widest valence. It applies to practitioners engaged in contemplative lifestyles, typically spent in long retreats, whether monastic or lay. Another group called 'yogis' but for whom a more precise translation would be 'tantrists' or 'tantrikas' is the *ngakpas* (*sngags pa*; Skt.: *māntrin*). Literally 'reciters of mantras', the related term *ngakrim* (*sngags rim*) refers to the 'tantric path'. *Ngakpas* are ordained, non-celibate, tantric practitioners. They typically wear red and white robes, sport dreadlocks (or at least never cut their hair) and hold vows that enable them to perform clerical functions for their local communities. They often live in retreat or semi-retreat, but can have families. A final group of *naljorpas* is Tibetan Buddhist monks and nuns engaged in tantric retreats, who are only likely to refer to themselves as such during or after retreats.

Long retreat is a trademark of authentic contemplative engagement in the Tibetan tradition. Buddhist meditation and yoga requires a level of dedication that involves partial or full renunciation of worldly life and isolation from mainstream society in order to achieve the highest goals. Yogis dwell together or alone, typically for periods of months or years. The most well-known format is the traditional three-year, three-month retreat. When no longer forced to entertain the demands of worldly life, ideally the yogin is free to turn their mind inward without distraction. Tibetan Buddhist yogis are dedicated to conquering their negative emotions: anger, jealousy, pride, desire/attachment and misunderstanding or ignorance. They apply a wide range of contemplative techniques.

## *Milarepa, Tibet's most famous yogi*

Jetsun Milarepa (*rje btsun mi la ras pa*; 1028/40–1111/23) is the paradigmatic Tibetan yogi. Milarepa attained enlightenment by means of the yoga of inner heat, the practice that has come to be known as 'Tibetan yoga' in the contemporary period because of its use of postures, breath retention and tantric body theory. With this practice, he was able to control his pulse, stop his heartbeat, arrest haemorrhage, rapidly heal and display many other supernatural powers (*siddhi*) (Quintman 2014). Milarepa defined his success solely by his relationship to his Bengali guru Marpa who lived in Tibet, an irascible man who would be called abusive by contemporary standards. Despite the fact that his guru tested him with great physical and emotional hardships, Milarepa always treated Marpa with respect, humble obeisance and unquestioning devotion. Marpa made Milarepa build and tear down several houses with his bare hands (Mi-la-ras-pa et al. 1972: 4). Milarepa is considered by many to be a Tibetan Buddha, the first to be born and enlightened in Tibet instead of India (Quintman 2014: 9).

## Case study: monastic yogins at Namdroling Monastery and Nunnery in South India

Nowadays, Tibetan yoga practices continue both inside and outside of Tibet. Just two hours from Mysore, Karnataka, which itself is a world-leading hub for modern yoga, sits Namdroling Monastery and Nunnery amidst a dusty and ageing Tibetan refugee camp. Since 1973, Namdroling monks, nuns and Tibetan refugees have quietly been practicing *Sky Dharma* (*gNam chos*), a set of contemplative manuals revealed by Namchö Mingyur Dorje (*gnam chos mi 'gyur rdo* rje; 1645–1667) in Tibet. The modern-day saint and visionary lama Penor Rinpoche (1932–2009) founded Namdroling in 1963, just four years after he undertook the perilous journey on foot from Tibet to India to escape Chinese military rule. He was among the great lamas of the twentieth century instrumental in establishing Tibetan Buddhism outside of Tibet. Along with other Nyingma masters such as Dudjom Rinpoche and Chatrul Rinpoche, they carried the jewel of the dharma across the border from Tibet to India and Nepal in the form of their own education and spiritual realisations. Their mission was to keep the teachings alive, a veritable return home for Buddhism after roughly nine centuries of near absence in India. Namdroling provides a top-notch education in Buddhist philosophy to around 5,000 monastics. The education of monks and nuns is largely equal, an unprecedented phenomenon in the history of Buddhism and a manifestation of modernity; the nunnery was founded in 1993. Namdroling graduates make up a new cohort of teachers who are revitalising Buddhist education and practice in traditionally Buddhist Himalayan regions and across the globe. This includes teachings on Tibetan postural yoga as part of the inner heat practice.

*Sky Dharma* (*gnam chos*) is a three-phase contemplative manual in the Dzokchen tradition that was maintained by the Palyul monastic lineage in Kham, Tibet, one of the Ancient traditions' 'Six Mother Monasteries'. Recently some of the senior Namdroling monks have returned to Tibet to teach at Palyul to contribute to the revitalisation of the lineage in post-Chinese Cultural Revolution Tibet. Book Two of the *Sky Dharma* series is titled 'Winds, Channels, and Inner Heat' (*rtsa rlung gtum mo*), referred to here as 'Tibetan yoga' for short. The book describes the steps of nine *trulkhor* (*'phrul 'khor*), dynamic postural sequences coupled with simultaneous breath retentions, tantric deity yoga and subtle body visualisations. The practices are physically challenging and dynamic, and unfold within the wider context of wisdom teachings on emptiness and method teachings on compassion. The monks and nuns at Namdroling largely hail from traditionally Buddhist regions in the Himalayas of Nepal, India, Tibet and Bhutan that had little access to a scholastically rigorous education until Tibetan Buddhist monasteries were established in exile in India and Nepal. Monks and nuns undertake retreats during their monastic education when they are young (teens to forties, but mostly in their twenties). As students, they only have the opportunity to practise one month out of the year and are not accomplished yogis per se, although some become accomplished through participating in the retreats several times. A handful of monks and nuns teach the yoga practices, some of whom possess a high level of expertise.

Namdroling is having an enormous impact on global modern Buddhism. Each year it sends its highly trained cohort of graduates across the globe as resident teachers in Asia, Europe and the Americas. They teach both Buddhist philosophy and the *Sky Dharma* contemplative training programme. One of the striking features of the Namdroling monks is that they replicate the precise ritual crafts of the monastery when they travel. They bring a professor-type lecturer (*khenpo*), a chanting master (*umse*), sand mandala artists, ritual musicians, ritual dancers and, last but not least, years of training in philosophy, ethics and contemplation.

## The annual retreats

Two weeks after the Tibetan New year, Namdroling hosts its annual, month-long retreats, which follow the *Sky Dharma* manuals word-by-word and have done so since the seventeenth century in Tibet. One must 'sit' the retreats in the order arranged by the manuals. The first book covers the tantric Foundational practices (*sngon 'gro*), which train in basic Buddhist philosophy and the fundamentals of tantric meditation. Practitioners are expected to accumulate 100,000 repetitions of each of the following scripted contemplations, to achieve a total of

500,000 (*bum lnga*): refuge (*kyab 'gro*) in the Three Jewels; the generation of bodhicitta (*byang chub kyi sems*); mandala offering (*maṇḍal 'bul ba)*; Vajrasattva purification (*rdo rje sems dpa'*); and guru yoga (*bla ma'i rnal 'byor*). Transference of consciousness (*'pho ba*) is also taught at the end of the Foundational practices, but one need not accumulate that practice in large numbers. This is the first practice where the tantric body takes centre stage, and it is a preparation for death. Practitioners learn to eject their consciousness from the crown of the head at death, the optimal location for inducing a favourable rebirth. The second phase of contemplative practice is *tsalung tummo*, 'winds, channels, and inner heat', while the third phase covers Dzokchen meditation. In this final stage, the yogin enters in a vision-centred contemplative path. Open-eye meditations such as sky-gazing examine light and form as apparitions of emptiness, and postures are used to aid in the production of visions. The format for each retreat is the three-fold empowerment (*dbang*), transmission (*rlung*) and explanation (*'khrid*) model. The rest of this section will discuss the 'winds, channels, and inner heat' retreat.

## It begins with empowerment

The empowerment takes place on the first morning of the retreat. The social realities of lineage and power in tantric Buddhism are on full display in the empowerment ceremony. *Lamas* (practitioners who have completed three-year retreat), *tulkus* (reincarnated teachers) and *khenpos* (scholars with advanced monastic degrees) arrange themselves hierarchically according to rank – an outer reflection of their inner access to power based on experience in practice, including in past lives. After everyone drinks saffron water for purification to make themselves fit to receive the transmission, the monks walk in a procession carrying holy objects. They gently tap participants on the head with initiation cards, Tibetan texts, vases and statues.

## Motivation setting

Every retreat activity at Namdroling, whether a discourse, meditation or yoga session, begins with the generation of *bodhicitta*: the motivation to liberate sentient beings from the suffering of cyclic existence and lead them to enlightenment. Recognising that motivation wanes over time, a major part of the lamas' job is to keep spirits high and to inspire work towards this higher purpose. Because Namdroling adheres to a Dzokchen philosophical worldview, they add the motivation to drop conceptual thoughts, which is necessary to receive the blessings for successful practice.

Rhythmic group recitation of prayers and texts accompanied by drums, horns and bells takes up a significant portion of the four sessions of each day in retreat. Chanting serves several functions. As a pedagogy, the prayers are philosophically rich and review Buddhist teachings. Socially, one recites the lineage list all the way back to the Buddha, which defines the tantric family and includes the retreatants as the final members. This places the budding yogins in the company of greats and creates a strong group identity. Economically, the prayers are a source of income for the monastery. Lay people sponsor prayers as a way of accumulating merit to support their own practice, either in this lifetime or in the future.

## The yoga practice

Winds, channels and inner heat practice is taught using three pedagogies. First, every three days the most senior *khenpo* (scholar) present at the monastery reads the instruction manual aloud and comments on it to the combined group of male and female participants. There are a total of nine teachings, one for each yoga sequence, and they take place in a large and well-appointed temple/teaching hall on the monks' campus.

The second venue is in gender-separated classrooms in the monastery and nunnery, respectively, which have campuses about two kilometres apart in the fourth camp of Bylakuppe. At the monastery, if the Tibetan yoga lineage holder is present, he demonstrates the posture sequences and offers ample advice on the meditations, breathing techniques and poses. In 2018 at the nunnery, two young nuns who were proficient in the postures but not comfortable giving advice on the inner, contemplative methods led the practice sessions. The following year, the yoga master made several trips to the nunnery despite the gender difference between him and the nuns. These sessions include movement drills, rehearsal of sequences and student-led sessions that serve as exams. The third teaching style consists of open practice periods where experienced practitioners coach newer participants individually or in small groups. Here, participants break movements down into smaller chunks and repeat them until they attain mastery. Some people focus on extending the length of time they can hold the breath. Small, mixed-level breakout groups rehearse the posture sequences to commit them to memory.

## *The sequences*

The postural yoga sequences begin by sitting on the floor in half lotus position on a stuffed cotton mat, which measures around 3 feet x 3 feet and 6 inches high. The exercises share common elements such as:

- Rigorous rubbing along meridian lines
- Circular rotations of the waist
- 'Beps', which are five styles of jumps
- Retention of the inhalation during the entire sequence.

Tibetan yoga is likened to cleaning a dirty pot: when you first add water, it becomes filthy. While Buddha-nature is located in the body, it is not readily apparent because it is obscured by karma (*las*) and mental impressions or habits (*bag chags*). By stirring the pot with postural yoga, *prāṇāyāma* and meditation, the obstacles that karma and mental habits impose are purified. This manifests as physical and mental pain in the Tibetan yoga retreat. Almost everyone takes their turn: practitioners regularly limp, cry and get scared or hopeless. Students are encouraged to see pain as a sign that the practice is working. A main goal of inner heat yoga is the purification of karma. Practitioners typically experience less mental and physical anguish the second time they sit in the retreat, and even enjoy it, much to the dismay of the novice practitioners.

## Conclusion

'Tibetan yoga' is a neologism that situates an ancient tradition in the modern transnational yoga scene. Nowadays, even at Namdroling, the Sanskrit term *yoga* is retroactively applied to *tsalung trulkhor* practice. Monks and nuns are aware that *Sky Dharma*'s dynamic postural techniques have much in common with the form of Indian postural yoga. However, as we have seen, *naljor*'s most common use in Tibetan Buddhism is to describe contemplative practice and the tantric doxographical categories. Tibetan yoga's clear roots in Tibetan Buddhist philosophy harken back to the early meaning of *naljor*: they seek to unite practitioners with emptiness and Buddha-nature. The monastics at Namdroling spend years studying and contemplating these profound concepts, which inform their yoga practice. Tibetan Buddhism's postural yoga practices have remained secret until the present time, including in this chapter.[7] While *tsalung trulkhor* is certainly a type of *naljor*, the wide semantic range of *naljor* is preserved in the Tibetan language, while the Sanskrit term *yoga* nowadays globally refers to contemplative practice involving physical exertion and postures. Prior to the modern period, Tibetan scholars used *naljor* to demarcate tantric systems and practices, many of which had little to do with postural yoga, but much to do with tantric contemplation.

## Glossary

*'byor (jor)*, to unite
*'dzin pa (dzin pa)* (Skt. *dhāraṇā*), concentration
*'pho ba (powa)*, transference of consciousness
*'khor lo (khor lo)* (Skt. *cakra*), chakra; wheel
*'phrul 'khor (trulkhor)*, a set of practices that coordinates postural sequences with breath retentions, deity yoga and subtle body visualisations
*bag chags (bak chak)* (Skt. *vāsanā*), habitual tendencies
*bla ma'i rnal 'byor (la mé naljor)*, guru yoga
*bla na med pa'i rnal 'byor gyi rgyud (la na mé pé naljor gyi gyü)* (Skt.: *Anutarrayogatantra*) Anuttara Yoga Tantra; Unsurpassed Yoga Tantra
*bsam gtan (sam ten)* (Skt.: *dhyāna)*, meditative stabilisation
*bya rgyud (ja gyü)* (Skt.: *kriyātantra*), action tantra
*byang chub kyi sems (jang chup kyi sem)*, the generation of bodhicitta
*chos* (chö) (Skt.: *dharma)*, doctrine
*chos sku (chö ku)* (Skt.: *dharmakāya*), the reality body, the first level of embodiment in the Buddha-body schema
*dngos grub (ngö drup)* (Skt.: *siddhi*), supernatural powers
*dus kyi 'khor lo (dü kyi khor lo)* (Skt.: *Kālacakra*), Cycle of Time
*Kun tu bzang po (Kün tu zang po)*, the primordial Buddha Samantabhadra
*kyab 'gro (kyap dro)* (Skt. *śaraṇa*), refuge in the Three Jewels
*las* (lé), karma
*las kyi rlung (lé kyi lung)*, karmic winds
*lha yi rnal 'byor (lha yi naljor)*, deity yoga
*longs sku (long ku)* (Skt.: *sambhogakāya*), bliss body, the second level of embodiment in the Buddha-body schema
*lta ba (tawa)*, philosophical view
*maṇḍal 'bul ba (mandel bülwa)*, mandala offering
*na ro chos drug (nA ro chö druk)*, six doctrines of Nāropa
*phyag rgya chen po (chak gya chen po)* (Skt.: *mahāmudrā*), the 'Great Seal'
*rdo rje sems dpa' (dor jé sem pa)*, Vajrasattva purification
*rdzogs rim (dzok rim)*, completion stage
*rig pa (rik pa)*, open awareness; the substratum of consciousness
*rjes dran (jé dren)* (Skt.: *anusmṛti*), recollection; remembrance
*rjes su rnal 'byor (jé su naljor)*, Anuyoga
*rjes su rnal 'byor (jé su naljor)* (Skt.: anuyoga), subsequent yoga
*rnal 'byor chen po (naljor chen po)*, Mahāyoga
*rnal 'byor pa (yogin)*, yoga practitioner; yogi
*rnal 'byor rgyud (naljor gyü)*, Yoga Tantra
*rnal 'byor (naljor)*, yoga

*rnal 'byor bzhi* (*naljor zhi*) (Skt.: *caturyoga*), four yogas [of Mahāmudrā]
*rnal 'byor chen po* (*naljor chen po*) (Skt.: *mahāyoga*), great yoga
*rnal ma* (*nalma*) the innate, real condition
*ro gcig* (*ro chik*) (Skt.: *ekarasa*), one taste
*rtsa rlung thig le* (*tsa lung tik lê*) (Skt.: *nadī, vāyu, bindu*), winds, channels, and seminal essences
*rtse gcig* (*tsé chik*) (Skt.: *ekāgra*), single-pointedness
*shin tu rnal 'byor* (*shin tu naljor*), Atiyoga
*shin tu rnal 'byor* (*shin tu naljor*) (Skt.: *atiyoga)*, Dzokchen, the Great Perfection
*sku gsum* (*ku sum*), three [Buddha] bodies
*skyed rim* (*kyé rim*), Generation Stage
*sngags pa* (*ngakpa*) (Skt.: *māntrin*), tantrists or tantrikas; literally, reciters of mantras
*sngags rim* (*ngakrim*), the tantric path
*sngon 'gro* (*ngön dro*), tantric foundational practices
*so sor sdud pa* (*so sor dü pa*) (Skt.: *pratyahara)*, retraction
*spros bral* (*trö drel*) (Skt.: *niṣprapañca*), freedom from conceptual entanglement
*sprul sku* (*nirmāṇakāya*), emanation body
*spyod rgyud* (*chö gyü*) (Skt.: *caryātantra*), conduct tantra
*srog rtsol* (*sok tsöl*) (Skt.: *prāṇāyāma*), wind control; breath control
*stong pa nyid* (*tong pa nyi*) (Skt.: *śūnyatā*), emptiness
*theg pa* (*tek pa*) (Skt.: *yāna*), vehicle
*theg pa dgu* (*tek pa gu*),Ancients' nine-vehicle system for classifying different paths to enlightenment
*thig le* (*tik lê*) (Skt.: *bindu*), seminal essence
*ting nge 'dzin* (*ting ngé dzin*) (Skt.: *samādhi)*, absorption
*ye shes* (*yé shê*), primordial mind; the primordial awareness of a Buddha
*ye shes kyi rlung* (*yé shé kyi lung*), wisdom winds

## Notes

1 'yoga(s) *rnal 'byor*: lit. 'union in fundamental reality" (Dudjom Rinpoche 1991).
2 While this chapter examines various practice systems, this section focuses on the Ancient Order's perspective. Because of significant sectarian divergences, there is no one-size-fits all Buddhist philosophy.
3 *Tshig mdzod chen mo*, 'Yang dag pa'i lam dbang du gyur ba/', 1,577.
4 *Dag yig gsar bsgrigs*, 'Sgom rgyab pa/', 445.
5 *Btsan lha*, 'Bya ba rnal ma la rtsol med kyi ngang gis 'byor/', 141.
6 See chapter 3 of the fifteenth-century yoga manual *Haṭhapradīpikā*, which is on *mudrās*.
7 Most Tibetan Buddhist tantric traditions have been guarded with secrecy for hundreds of years, but that is slowly changing. I have permission from Namdroling to discuss this practice in a general way, but not to provide instructions or mantras.

## Bibliography

Baker, I. 2019. *Tibetan Yoga: Principles and Practices*. London: Thames & Hudson.
Bharati, A. 1965. The Tantric Tradition. New Delhi: B. I. Publications.
Bstan dzin rgya mtsho, Hopkins, J, Tsong-kha-pa Blo-bzang-grags-pa. 2005. *Yoga Tantra: Paths to Magical Feats*. Ithaca, New York: Snow Lion Publications.
Cape, K. N. n.d. 'The Ngakpa Lineage'. www.pemakhandro.org/pema-khandro-ngakpa-lineage/. Accessed 23 February 2020.
Dalton, J. 2005. 'A Crisis of Doxography: How Tibetans Organized Tantra During the 8th-12th Centuries'. *Journal of the International Association of Buddhist Studies* 28, 115–181.
Dudjom Rinpoche. 1991. *The Nyingma School of Tibetan Buddhism: Its Fundamentals and History*. Boston: Wisdom Publications.

Evans-Wentz, W.Y. and Lopez, D. 2000. *Tibetan Yoga and Secret Doctrines: or, Seven Books of Wisdom of the Great Path.* Oxford: Oxford University Press.
Germano, D. 1997. 'Food, Clothes, Dreams, and Karmic Propensities', in Lopez, D. (ed), *Religions of Tibet in Practice*, 293–312. Princeton: Princeton University Press.
Germano, D. 2002. 'History and Nature of the Collected Tantras of the Ancients'. Tibetan & Himalayan Library.
Gyatso, J. 1998. *Apparitions of the Self: The Secret Autobiographies of a Tibetan Visionary.* Princeton: Princeton University Press.
Harding, S. 2010. *Niguma, Lady of Illusion.* Ithaca, New York: Snow Lion Publications.
Higgins, D. 2013. *The Philosophical Foundations of Classical rDzogs chen in Tibet: Investigating the Distinction between Dualistic Mind (sems) and Primordial Knowing (ye shes).* Lausanne: Universite de Lausanne.
Jamgön Kongtrul Lodrö Tayé. 2007. *The Treasury of Knowledge, Book Six, Part Four: Systems of Buddhist Tantra: The Indestructible Way of Secret Mantra.* Ithaca, New York: Snow Lion Publications.
Karmay, S. G. 2007. *The Great Perfection (rdzogs chen): A Philosophical and Meditative Teaching in Tibetan Buddhism.* Leiden: Brill.
Klong-chen rab-'byams-pa. 2007. *The Precious Treasury of Philosophical Systems: A Treatise Elucidating the Meaning of the Entire Range of Spiritual Approaches.* Junction City, CA: Padma Publications.
Komarovski, Y. 2015. *Tibetan Buddhism and Mystical Experience.* Oxford: Oxford University Press.
Kragh, U.T. 2015. *Tibetan Yoga and Mysticism: A Textual Study of the Yogas of Naropa and Mahāmudrā Meditation in the Medieval Tradition of Dags Po.* Tokyo: International Institute for Buddhist Studies.
Mi-la-ras-pa, L. J., Evans-Wentz, W.Y. and He-ru-ka, G. 1972. The Life of Milarepa, Tibet's Great Yogi. London: Murray.
Mullin, G. H. 1997. *Readings on the Six Yogas of Naropa.* Ithaca, New York: Snow Lion Publ
Pill, J. (dir.) 2002. *The Yogis of Tibet.* June Bug Films and JEHM Films.
Quintman, A. 2014. *The Yogin and the Madman: Reading the Biographical Corpus of Tibet's Great Saint Milarepa.* New York: Columbia University Press.
Samuel, G. 2008. *The Origins of Yoga and Tantra: Indic Religions to the Thirteenth Century.* Cambridge: Cambridge University Press.
Thondup, T. and Talbott, H. 1995. *Enlightened Journey: Buddhist Practice as Daily Life.* Boston: Shambhala.
Wallace, V.A. 2010. *The Kalacakra Tantra: The Chapter on Sadhana, Together with the Vimalaprabha Commentary.* New York: American Institute of Buddhist Studies.
Wallace, V. A. 2001. *The Inner Kalacakratantra: A Buddhist Tantric View of the Individual.* New York: Oxford University Press.
Wangchuk, D. 2004. 'The rÑiṅ-ma Interpretations of the Tathāgatagarbha Theory.' *Vienna Journal of South Asian Studies* XLVIII, 171–213.

# 21
# THE POLITICAL HISTORY OF MEDITATION AND YOGA IN JAPAN[1]

*Hidehiko Kurita*

## Introduction

Meditation and yoga are generally considered spiritual, peaceful and harmonic. So how does a meditation group become politically active and even engage in terrorism? For some, the subject of meditation and yoga in Japan may trigger memories of Aum-Shinrikyō. Originally a small yoga circle named *Aum no Kai* (later called *Aum Shinsen no Kai*), it was founded by Asahara Shōkō (1955–2018) in 1984 and then rapidly grew into a conspicuous new religious group, constructing a doctrine based on Esoteric Buddhism and Hinduism. In 1990, it set up its own political party and ran for the House of Representatives election. After the complete defeat of the party's candidates, the group turned to terrorism to achieve its goals. Nevertheless, Aum-Shinrikyō was continuously dedicated to meditation practice. Many scholars have analysed Aum-Shinrikyō from sociological and psychological perspectives. However, to properly supply a politico-religious perspective, we have to go back to the root of the question: What is the relationship between meditation and politics in the case of Aum-Shinrikyō?

Is Aum-Shinrikyō an exceptional case in the history of meditation? Many scholars of Japanese religious history may agree with its exceptionalism. Japan has traditionally been home to many kinds of meditation, including chanting, contemplation, breathing methods and sitting and lying techniques. Buddhism, Confucianism and Shintō all had such physical, mental and spiritual practices. These religions in Japan were close to centres of political power throughout Japanese history and usually played a subordinate or complementary role there; in contrast, Aum-Shinrikyō tried to subvert the state. However, I argue that this conclusion is based on erroneously applying modern assumptions about the nature of 'state', 'politics' and 'religion' (assuming, for example, a separation of religion and politics) to Aum-Shinrikyō and historical Japan. Even in the history of yoga in India, scholars also point out that ascetic groups were sometimes militarised, and yogic ideology was closely associated with the Indian independence struggle (see Voix Chapter 11 in this volume). Therefore, a critical review of these modern concepts and a better understanding of the role meditation techniques have played in Japanese history are essential in understanding the political aspects of yoga and meditation and the nature of Aum-Shinrikyō.

Foucault and Schmitt have re-examined the concept of 'politics', not based on the concepts in modern civil society, but by considering on what basis the modern state was established. By applying Foucault and Schmitt's conceptions of power, we can better understand the political nature of Aum-Shinrikyō as a yoga and meditation-focused group, by exploring three points: (1) meditation techniques are used to create (self) disciplinary power; (2) meditation techniques can be used as a channel for a sovereign (political) power; and (3) specific bodily techniques can be used in aid of us/them or friend/enemy distinctions which are inherently political.

Analysing Daoist meditation, Marcel Mauss, who recognised the social aspects of body techniques, suggested that 'at the bottom of all our mystical states there are body techniques' and that humans imitate actions that have been performed by people with authority and prestige (Mauss 1979: 122). Though Mauss focused on the sociocultural dimensions of body techniques, we can extend this discussion to the political, which Michel Foucault framed as 'discipline', as a form of modern power. According to Foucault:

> [T]he procedures of power that characterized the *disciplines*, centred on the body as a machine: its disciplining, the optimisation of its capabilities, the extortion of its forces, the parallel increase of its usefulness and its docility, its integration into systems of efficient and economic controls.
>
> *(Foucault 1978: 139)*

In this sense, body techniques (including meditation) have a political function: disciplinary power. However, in most modern and contemporary contexts, meditation has rarely been employed by official institutions (e.g. army, schools, prison, etc.) as an explicit technique of power and has remained in unofficial, private or alternative spaces.

Aum-Shinrikyō intended not only to gain legal political power, but also to overthrow the state; its political vision went beyond politics within modern law. Schmitt defines a state 'which is not codified in the existing legal order' as 'the exception' (Schmitt 2005: 6) and asserts that the '[s]overeign is he who decides on the exception' (Schmitt 2005: 5). Asahara, based on predictions from his meditation, judged contemporary society as being in an exceptional situation leading to 'World War III', and insisted that those who will be able to survive the coming war and become members of the next 'millennial kingdom' will be people who have acquired a virtue and a 'transcendental power' through meditative training. In other words, Asahara and Aum-Shinrikyō judged what 'a state of exception' was and identified themselves as the sovereign in the upcoming world. This 'state of exception' is not defined by any codified phenomena, but rather can only be recognised by visioning a world order outside of the visible one. For Asahara and Aum-Shinrikyō, meditation was the channel for that 'outside' order.

What the sovereign does in a state of exception is to establish and maintain order, and thus clarify the structure and limits of this new sovereignty, regardless of existing legal frameworks or national boundaries. In accordance with this order, the 'sovereign' educates and, if education fails, excludes people. Schmitt also argued that 'the concept of the state presupposes the concept of the political', and that the specifically political distinction is between 'friend and enemy', where antagonism has 'the real possibility of physical killing' (Schmitt 2007: 19). The political is thus differentiated from other categories, including the religious, the economical, the ethical and so on, and, at the same time, '[e]very religious, moral, economic, ethical, or other antithesis transforms into a political one if it is sufficiently strong to group human beings effectively according to friend and enemy' (Schmitt 2007: 37). No matter how a meditation envisions a harmonious, peaceful and religious world, a religious movement reaches a friend and enemy antithesis, or 'the political', when it adopts an uncompromising opposition to the current order. Aum-Shinrikyō's violence occurred when its religious distinction of good and evil had intensified to this extent. In this chapter, we examine how these three political natures, exemplified in the example of Aum-Shinrikyō, emerged in the history of meditation and yoga in Japan.

Before going into a detailed historical overview, I will briefly outline each historical period of Japanese history under discussion. The first period I will cover spans both ancient and medieval periods. The ancient period considered here is from the third to tenth centuries. During this time, Buddhism, which is closely related to meditation and yoga, was introduced from Korea and China. In the medieval era, between the eleventh and sixteenth centuries, the social system was based on feudalism and manorialism. In the next section I will cover the early modern era, from the sixteenth to the mid-nineteenth centuries. During this period, one of the samurai families, the Tokugawa family, usurped the feudal system and ruled all over Japan, adopting a foreign policy of national isolation. Around the end of this period, the Tokugawa shogunate dropped its isolationist policy in response to strong demands from western countries. This led to a loss of Tokugawa's authority and political turmoil in Japan. Marking the beginning of the modern period, the shogunate collapsed. A modern, centralised national system was established with a constitutional monarchy and a (restrictive) separation of religion and state. At this point, meditation, including Zen, became popular as a form of personal, spiritual cultivation. Also at this time, Japan embarked on colonial expansion. After World War II, in the midst of rapid economic growth, New Religious Movements (NRMs) flourished in Japan. Following student riots in the 1960s, modern yoga took root in Japan, together with influences from the New Age movement. Aum Shinrikyō was founded in this context.

## Buddhism and meditation from the ancient to medieval periods

Buddhism is an important genealogical source of meditation in Japanese culture. Buddhism was officially introduced through China and Korea in the sixth century. However, during the mid-seventh century full-scale meditative Buddhist philosophy, and most likely its associated practices (Minowa 2015: 75), arrived in Japan by Dōshō (道昭, 629–700), who had studied within the Chinese Buddhist school Fǎxiàng (法相). Fǎxiàng is based in the Indian Yogācāra lineage and is characterised by an epistemological analysis of the means of attaining enlightenment. During the eighth century other Buddhist traditions arrived in Japan, later called Nanto Rokushū (南都六宗). Supported by the Japanese government, these traditions established schools which mainly studied imported Buddhist texts and prayed for the protection of the nation.

Meditative practices have flourished in Japan since the ninth century. Zhiyi (538–597), the founder of the Chinese Buddhist school Tiantai, wrote two influential texts of meditation, *Mohe Zhiguan* (摩訶史観) and *Xiao Zhiguan* (小止観), which were imported by the founder of the Japanese Tiantai (Tendai in Japanese pronunciation) school, Saichō (767–822), into Japan. The Tendai school became the biggest and most integrated centre of Buddhism in the medieval period. At the same time, the founder of the Shingon school, Kūkai (774–835), energetically introduced Esoteric Buddhism, the newest theory in China at that time, which developed by incorporating aspects of Hinduism. In Japanese Esoteric Buddhism, meditative practices including yoga (generally called yuga 瑜伽) were the way to secret truth. By reaching the truth, it was said that the monks were able to obtain supernatural powers, especially the ability to fulfil people's wishes. Their practices of praying for spiritual merit (and thereby health, safety and prosperity) were called *kaji*, a term that originally came from Sanskrit *adhiṣṭhāna*, which refers to the Buddha's power to help people. As a response to this orientation towards meeting people's desires, Esoteric Buddhist meditative *kaji* prayers became popular. The Tendai school and Nanto Rokushū also incorporated this practice, and Esoteric Buddhism flourished in medieval Japan.

Esoteric Buddhist ideologies deeply influenced Japanese thought. Through one of the ideologies, the theory of *honji suijaku* (本地垂迹, which positions Japanese gods as local manifestations of buddhas, bodhisattvas and Buddhist deities), Japanese local gods were for the first time systematically classed as Shintō from the tenth century. What is called Shintō was originally ancestor worship, shamanism, animism various practices (including something meditative) in the Japanese islands and local myths and national myths including *Kojiki* (古事記, *Japan's Ancient Chronicle*) and *Nihonshoki* (日本書紀, *the Chronicles of Japan*). After Esoteric Buddhist ideologies prevailed, Shintō theories and practices were interpreted using Buddhist, or sometimes Daoist, terminology; there was a close syncretism between Japanese gods and buddhas. Therefore, Buddhist influence is pervasive in the development of Shintō's practices and meditations.

Zen schools also appeared in close relationship to Esoteric Buddhism. Yōsai (栄西, 1141–1215), the founder of the Japanese Rinzai (臨済) school of Zen studied in Japanese Tendai schools as well as in the Zen school of Línjì (臨済) in China. He was not only a Zen master but also an Esoteric Buddhist monk and, as his writing named *Kozen gokoku ron* (興禅護国論) shows, set up Japanese Zen Buddhism more for publicly protecting the state than for privately reaching Buddhist truth. Dōgen (道元, 1200–1253), the founder of the Japanese Sōtō school, learned Zen under Yōsai, studied abroad in the Song dynasty and brought a purified Zen style to Japan. Dōgen's Sōtō school is now one of the largest Buddhist groups in Japan, but this achievement is attributed to the second great founder, Keizan Jōkin (瑩山紹瑾, 1268–1325), who also adopted Esoteric Buddhism *kaji* prayers and greatly proselytised to the lower samurai class.

These Zen schools were regarded as heresies in Kyoto (the Japanese capital at that time) by the Tendai school. They therefore courted the patronage of the samurai class, which had recently become dominant in the Kantō district (around Tokyo at present). Since the mid-thirteenth century, leaders of rising military families had founded and patronised the Five Mountain System (a conglomerate of Zen Buddhist temples appointed and sponsored by the government) in the Kantō and Kyoto regions as the centres of Japanese Rinzai Zen Buddhism (imitating the Chinese Five Mountain System). Buddhist monks who studied in and migrated from China (the Southern Song and Ming dynasties) were often appointed as chief priests of these temples and also played a role as diplomatic consultants.

In the medieval era, there was also the development of the meditative practice of Pure Land Buddhism, *nenbutsu* (*nianfo* in Chinese, chanting and recollecting the name of Amitābha). In the Pure Land teaching, if one practices *nenbutsu*, one can rebirth in the Pure Land, equivalent to the attainment of Buddhist enlightenment. The groups of *nenbutsu* monks, who had drifted all over Japan, solicited incentives while spreading *nenbutsu* among the populace in the form of dances and songs, and grew by taking in wanderers who had been driven into giving up their land by poverty. Shinran (親鸞, 1173–1262) emerged from one of those groups (Sueki 1992: 206) and established the systematic doctrine on *nenbutsu*. Shinran's group also became one of the largest Buddhist groups in Japan today, which is called Jōdo Shinshū (Shin Buddhism).

Generally speaking, the ultimate goal of Buddhism is to reach nirvana, understood as a state of freedom from desire and suffering. Accordingly, Buddhism is often considered to be detached from this-worldly things, including politics. Considered from this soteriological end, Buddhism in Japan seems 'this worldly'. However, we have to understand the multi-layered experience of the medieval world. Buddhism also had detached aspects, not only theoretically but also practically. Buddhist temples and territories often had the function of asylum (*asile*). Temple properties had not only the privilege of immunity from taxation but also the privilege of being able to cancel debts and crimes in the secular world (outside the Buddhist temple). From the perspective of secular people, Buddhist temples seemed to enjoy a kind of extraterritorial power and freedom. The historian Amino has argued that at the basis of these functions was the Buddhist principle of 'muen' (無縁) – detachment, non-possession, no-masters and the Buddhist ultimate goals (Amino 1996: 110–124). Under the name of this principle, alliances were formed between the lower class, fugitives and some schools of Zen and Pure Land Buddhism.

Yet, the world of *muen* (detachment) should not be understood as a paradise of freedom or liberation; it was also a world bound by strict disciplines like a 'prison' (Amino 1996: 26–27). In addition, the privilege of *muen* was obtained not only from the patronage of the secular powers but also by the substantial power of the temples themselves. In the medieval era, the political power of temples surpassed that of the samurai and aristocrats. For example, Enryakuji temple, the centre of the Tendai school, had more territory than the Kamakura family, a top samurai family at that time (Itō 2008). Temples' incomes were not only from their agricultural lands, but also from tolls on roads which were constructed by Buddhist monks and their followers as part of relief work; they made enormous profits. In order to extend and protect this land income and privilege, they maintained a large military power composed of *sōhei* (monk soldiers). The Emperor Shirakawa (1053–1129) cited 'monks in Mr. Hiei (the mountain where Enryakuji temple built)' as being beyond his control (Unknown 1623: lvs. 34). The Honganji temple, one of the head temples of Shin Buddhism, organised and led groups of *nenbutsu* (Pure Land) and lay people. Under the leadership of Shin Buddhist priests, these groups took up arms, rioting and setting up independent states in several districts.

In short, Buddhism in the medieval era had an autonomous political power – i.e. sovereign – power. Its authority was embodied in authentic texts, sacred places, symbolic rituals, magical prayers and meditative practices. Buddhism also served as a window for Chinese civilisation, a symbol related to dynastic power. Therefore, the universal state of nirvana, or Buddhist truth, can be understood in the Japanese context as a channel for outside authority. Although the kingship, the ruling power of the Kyoto court, accommodated Esoteric Buddhist activities, protecting these activities was also a way of legitimising the monarch's power by referring to outside authority. Simultaneously, Buddhist monks were understood to maintain the stability of the kingdom through the magical power generated by monks' meditations. Therefore, even in the ancient era, Emperor Shōmu (701–756) regarded himself as 'the slave of the Three Treasures' (i.e. the Buddha, *dhamma* and *sangha*). From around the medieval to the early modern era, an Esoteric Buddhist Anointment rite was part of the enthronement rites of the Emperor of Japan (Taira 1992: 462). The authority of Buddhism even surpassed the kingship authority in some regards, because although Buddhism was legally under the domestic rule of the kingship, it had authority more widely over Asia. Therefore, it was politically advantageous for the kingdom to favour Buddhism. In other words, Buddhism in Japan's medieval period reciprocally supported and was supported by the kingship.[2] For the kingship, Buddhism was a channel for the 'outside' order and, acknowledging the importance of the 'outside' authority, the kingship had to be subject to Buddhism as a 'state of exception'.

## Transformations in the early modern era

In the late fifteenth century, shortly before the Ōnin War (1467–1477), the power balance of the ruling families who sustained the unified state collapsed definitively. This marked the beginning of the Sengoku (Warring States) period. Many local warlords arose, and some Buddhist temples strengthened their forces of *sōhei* (warrior monks). At this time the Honganji (a denomination of Jōdo Shinshū Buddhism), defending its autonomous state, organised guerrilla armies of supporters to attack territories ruled by warlords. It was said that the Honganji group was one of the most formidable enemies of Oda Nobunaga (1534–1582), the most powerful warlord of the time who almost unified and ruled all of Japan. Sueki points out that some schools of Buddhism at this time, including Shin and Nichiren, rejected the existing view that the kingship (which ruled this world) and Buddhism (which had sovereignty over the other world) should maintain mutually complementary relations. This supported a monistic and autonomous view that Buddhist dharma should rule both this and other world orders (Sueki 2010: 22–26). This period was, as Schmitt (2007) describes, 'a state of exception' in which one's own ability to wield power was more important than power derived from acknowledgement by an accepted authority.

However, during this period, Buddhism's military autonomy declined. Eventually, Oda Nobunaga made the Buddhist groups surrender and his successor, Toyotomi Hideyoshi (1536–1598), issued a 'sword-hunting order' to disarm the Buddhist temples. After this, the Tokugawa shogunate ruled local lords in a unified state, marking the beginning of the early modern period, the Edo period, from 1603. The Tokugawa shogunate controlled the Buddhist temples, but entrusted them with the administrative functions of keeping family registers and enforcing anti-Christian edicts. For this reason, Buddhism in the early modern era did not decline, but gained institutional stability and even prospered in its economic and cultural aspects. The Buddhist temples became local 'cultural centres, providing education, entertainment and healthcare' (Sueki 2010: 39). Buddhism become deeply rooted in people's lives, such that even in contemporary Japan funerals are generally held in Buddhist ceremonies. In this way, Buddhism became part of disciplinary power and biopower, which Foucault discusses as a modern technology of power for managing large populations. Buddhism underpinned the Tokugawa regime by playing a part in the education and management of people.

Simultaneously, the political function of Buddhism as a sovereign power was significantly weakened as the Tokugawa shogunate did not rely on an 'outside' power to justify its authority. The Tokugawa shogunate maintained a stable, autonomous and semi-centralised government for almost 250 years. Although it did not totally centralise, it had authority and power over local lords in a kind of absolute monarchism, as well as adopting a foreign policy of national isolation (*sakoku*, 鎖国) (Toby 1984; Ōshima 2006). On the pretext of prohibiting Christian missionary activity, the Tokugawa shogunate banned trade with almost all foreign countries and overseas travel by the Japanese. As exceptions, China and the Netherlands were trading partners, but there was no opportunity to study abroad as medieval Buddhist monks had done. The Tokugawa shogunate cut off its connection with the 'outside' world and Buddhism lost the physical reference of transcendental power. As a result, Buddhism was incorporated into the Tokugawa regime and was 'secularised'. The Tokugawa shogunate did not require acknowledgement from Buddhism, but it desired an enhancement of its own authority. Therefore, a Tendai monk, Tenkai (1536–1643), worked to enshrine the founder of the Tokugawa shogunate, Tokugawa Ieyasu (1542–1616) as a god (Sonehara 2008). Buddhism took a subordinate role in the regime. Meanwhile, Confucianism and Kokugaku were emerging as new ideologies of politics and anti-Buddhism.

## Confucianism and the imperial family line in Japan

Confucianism itself is an ideology for governance. Its political ideal is typically shown by a phrase in the *Lǐjì* (礼記, the Book of Rites): 'those who wish to rule the land must first cultivate their own characters, then manage their families, then govern their states, then bring peace to the world'. Therefore, the goal of Confucianism is to raise the virtue of rulers. Zhu Xi (朱熹, 1130–1200) synthesised the concept of Confucianism, and his philosophy was often called neo-Confucianism. Zhu Xi reinterpreted cultivating one's character as seeking the perfect knowledge of *li* (理), the metaphysical law which is consistent between nature and society, and then controlling *qi* (気), the matter which composes the physical world. The proper state of consciousness was called *gyeong* (敬), meaning reverence, respect or modesty. The investigation of *li* (窮理) and the maintenance of *gyeong* (居敬) were like two sides of the same coin. To achieve these goals, Zhu Xi advocated both reading Confucian texts and practising meditation, or *jìngzuò* (静坐, quiet sitting). Neo-Confucianism became the subject of the higher civil service examination in Chinese regimes.

In medieval Japan, the Rinzai founder Yōsai introduced neo-Confucianism in Rinzai temples. But in the early Edo period, Japanese Confucianism became independent from Buddhism through the work of Hayashi Razan (1583–1657). Razan regarded *li* as the fixed relationship between superiors and inferiors and conceptualised the class system as the ideal social regime. Since it had the capacity to justify the relationship between ruler and ruled under the Tokugawa shogunate, neo-Confucianism was supported by the government. Therefore, Confucianism became a basic educational subject for the ruling class (now the *samurai* class) and quiet sitting was often practised. For example, Satō Issai (1772–1859), a son of a chief retainer's family and a famous Confucian teacher, recommended quiet sitting for personal cultivation. Confucian teachers often criticised Buddhism, warning against indulgence in meditation; they emphasised not transcending but staying in, supporting and reforming this secular world (Nakajima 2012). Therefore, meditation in Japanese neo-Confucian contexts strove to cultivate dutiful and loyal members of the ruling class. Unlike Buddhism in previous generations, neo-Confucianism did not facilitate charismatic authority within the privileged elites through association with an 'outside' authority.

Hayashi Razan argued for the unification of Confucianism and Shintō, thereby separating Confucianism from Buddhism. The founder of the Kimon School, Yamazaki Ansai (1618–1682), went further and developed a neo-Confucian–Shintō theory (垂加神道, Suika Shintō). Focusing on *gyeong*, he interpreted this as the maintenance of Shin (神, god), an ideal unification of *li* and *qi*. Moreover, Ansai drew upon the Japanese creation myth in the *Nihon Shoki* to develop an ideal 'way of Shin'. According to Ansai, maintaining the genealogy of the Emperor of Japan was the 'way of Shin', therefore it was not only the Confucian ideal action but also the Japanese people's ultimate ethical action, i.e. Shintō (the way of gods). The Emperor of Japan began to be viewed as the focus point of Shintō, and the Confucian practice of quiet sitting (*gyeong*) was transformed from an abstract personal cultivation to a concrete ethical action of Shintō which upholds the order of the world (Ushio 2008).

Japanese Confucianism was primarily educational and ethical; it did not have a well-established independent organisation or military authority. However, when its ideology reached the Emperor of Japan, it quickly came into contact with sovereign power. During this period, the Emperor of Japan, who used to be the most powerful and the most elite of the noble families, had been weakened and was under the control of the Tokugawa shogunate. Yet, to preserve appearances, the head of the Tokugawa family was appointed as commander-in-chief by the Emperor. Therefore, the Emperor's authority indirectly appeared to transcend and legitimise Tokugawa's shogunate, even though the Emperor's authority was not directly based on military power. In other words, at the level of Schmitt's 'sovereign power', early modern Japan potentially had a dual power structure. Ansai's Suika Shintō created the possibility of exposing this duality and promoting the cause of the Emperor against the Tokugawa shogunate. Japanese Confucianism, especially the Kimon school, became a source of a political radicalism called *sonnōjōi* (尊皇攘夷, 'revere the Emperor and expel the barbarians') through the Mitogaku (an influential school of Japanese historical studies). Its ideology was broadly shared among those working to overthrow the Tokugawa shogunate at the time of national crisis (another 'a state of exception') at the end of the Edo Period.

## Kokugaku and Daoism

In Japan, the majority of Confucian scholars ran private schools (Unoda 2007). Some of them criticised neo-Confucianism as a concoction by Zhu Xi and different from real Confucianism from the ancient period. After the appearance of Ito Jinsai's Kogigaku (study of ancient meaning) and Ogyu Sorai's Kobunjigaku (study of ancient rhetoric), some scholars questioned the mediating role of language. In other words, the study of Confucianism began to seek 'true' meanings in the more classic texts and, sometimes, beyond the texts themselves. Meditation was often attributed importance for seeking direct truths thought to lie beyond texts. For example, Shingaku (心学, heart learning) was founded by Ishida Baigan (1685–1744) and popularised among the merchant class and wealthy farmers that rose from the mid-to-late Edo period. Shingaku blended Shintō, Confucianism and Buddhism and highly regarded quiet sitting for self-cultivation. The core of its ethics was simple honesty, frugality and diligence – and it was easily adapted to business ethics rather than politics (Bellah 1957), but it was also a practical pursuit of Confucian truth. Takahashi Kōsetsu (1819–1876), the president of the Shingaku association in Edo, went on to the direct pursuit of *li*, and finally approached the Rinzai Zen school (Sawada 2004).

The Rinzai school had stagnated in the early Edo period, but Hakuin (1685–1768) revived it, renewed its training system and widely promoted its Zen ideas. The revival of Rinzai Zen corresponded with a growing interest in valuing truth lying outside of texts. Hakuin is also well known for his books on self-care: *Orategama* (遠羅手釜) and *Yasenkanna* (夜船閑話). These books proposed meditative breathing methods as a way to contribute to good health and composure of mind. Hakuin's medical instructions, which often included ethical and spiritual dimensions, were based on the traditional Chinese concepts of *yin-yang* (陰陽) and *qi* (気) and used in Daoism, Confucianism and some Buddhist contexts. Hakuin's meditative breathing was the mainly Daoist technique of generating *tan* (丹, dān in Chinese), understood as a kind of elixir inside the human body that can be manipulated by controlling *qi* with breathing; internal *tan* is said to be mainly stored in the lower abdomen and called Tanden (丹田). However, Hakuin, probably to enhance his credibility, claimed Tanden breathing techniques were taught by a *hsien* or mountain hermit, Hakuyū (?–1709), who lived in a mountain near Kyoto. This episode shows that although the 'outside authority' was still useful in enhancing legitimacy, this now came from mysterious neighbouring mountains rather than another country with more historical links to Buddhism.

These tendencies were brought into the Kokugaku (the study of Japanese classics) movement. The founder of the movement, Motoori Norinaga (1730–1801), sought to uncover the true meaning of Japanese classics as such *Kojiki*, removing the influences of Buddhism and Confucianism. He identified the Ancient Way (古道), or Shintō, in the first volume of the *Kojiki*. This was understood as just to *let it be*, throwing away any contrived action, including meditative self-cultivation and governing the state. Thereby, an ideal society, where all people are harmonised around the Emperor of Japan, the scion of the universal god Amaterasu, could naturally appear (Motoori 1991). However, in times of serious national crisis, the conservative attitude was able to induce political radicalism beyond Motoori's position.

Hirata Atsutane (1776–1843) described a more concrete worldview of Shintō within the Kokugaku movement. Hirata's worldview had a motley 'outer' world, in which gods, the dead (ancestors), monsters and so on also reside, as in fairy tales. He insisted that the other world adjoined this world through various neighbouring places, especially mountains. Unlike Confucian rationalism, which dismantled wonders, his affirmation of the existence of such things appealed to much of the populace. At the same time, Hirata tried to demonstrate the existence of these non-human forces/beings in the world. To this end, he focused on *hsiens* (the mountain hermits) and interviewed someone who claimed to have lived with a hermit. Hirata argued that *hsiens* were living gods who had supernatural abilities, could move between worlds and had been living in the Japanese mountains since before the arrival of Buddhism (Hirata 2000).

As a doctor Hirata also had interest in *hsien*'s meditative arts for longevity and immortality. As mentioned, *hsien* and these techniques of meditation stemmed from popular Daoism. However, Hirata reinterpreted these techniques as the 'way of gods'. He understood the original Tanden breathing technique as nothing less than the uncontrived, natural breathing of gods. However, he saw his contemporary world as confused by foreign influence; therefore people had to intentionally use the Tanden breathing technique to access 'the way'. Hirata regarded yoga in India, Buddhist asceticism, Daoist practices and other religious beliefs as a partial record of the Tanden breathing technique. In his view, Tanden techniques would produce more than individual longevity and immortality; it was the technique for manifesting an ancient utopia through our bodies.

Thus, during the Edo period, the Hirata School's philosophy reconstructed an external Shintō worldview and positioned Shintō practices, including meditation, as its channels. Through meditative philosophy, Yamazaki Ansai constructed Shintō as a personal ethical system, while Hirata constructed a Shintō worldview of utopian powers and a more-than-human Japanese community. The Kokugaku movement fashioned a utopian social image out of Hirata's worldview and influenced the *sonnōjōi* ('revere the Emperor and expel the barbarians') movement. Moreover, though Hirata's worldview was clearly different from the modern nation state, it became the foundation of the Great Promulgation movement after the Meiji Restoration, as I will describe below. Hirata's utopian philosophy, closely linked to meditative and breathing techniques, continued to inspire a passionate justification for sovereign power at the root of the Japanese modern nation state.

## Meditation and yoga in the modern period

The Meiji Restoration in 1868 had two contradictory aspects: the Restoration of Imperial Rule (王政復古) and Westernisation (文明開化). During the 1850s, western countries pressed the Tokugawa shogunate to stop the national isolation policy and to sign unequal treaties. After the shogunate submitted to this pressure, an extensive anti-foreign movement emerged. Leaders of the movement, who mostly came from the low-level samurai class, supported the Emperor of Japan in order to justify attacking the shogunate, and the idea of *sonnōjōi* became popular. However, leaders of the movement were aware of the powerful military force of western countries and strongly felt a need for westernisation. Modernising their military capability, the anti-foreign factions overthrew the shogunate and established a new centralised administrative framework called the Meiji government.

The Meiji government therefore had to execute both modernisation and restoration – and did so in a dictatorial fashion. In 1868 it established a separation of Shintō and Buddhism and promoted the Great Promulgation campaign, advocating Shintō as a national moral ideology for unifying national identity and facing off against foreign beliefs, especially Christianity, in the tradition of the Hirata School. In 1872, the Meiji government took advantage of Buddhist infrastructure to promote its ideological agenda with the Shintō–Buddhist Joint Propagation (神仏合同布教) – a movement not without its tensions.

Other leaders of the Meiji Restoration believed that a 'modern' model of separation of church and state was necessary in order for Japan to be recognised as a civilised nation. As a result, the Great Promulgation campaign collapsed, and the hard-line followers of Hirata School were purged from the nucleus of the educational (religious) ministry. The government pushed westernisation and even recommended Christianity during the 1880s. Finally, the Meiji Constitution, which was granted by the Emperor in 1889, stipulated religious freedom. The government administratively decided that Shintō was not a religion but national rites. Therefore, official priests in Shintō shrines could no longer be permitted to propagate their teaching. To proselytise, Shintō officials had to operate as one of Shintō's sects (Kyōha Shintō) without direct official support.

It was in this context that the Empire of Japan was established, with the Emperor of Japan as a nominal sovereign. However, the leaders of the most powerful regions at that time, Chōshū and Satsuma, administered power in practice. Additionally, state sovereignty had been limited by the unequal treaties and pressures from 'western' nations. Dissident movements of this time focused on the question of who had sovereignty – the Emperor of Japan, the leaders of Chōshū and Satsuma, or European and US powers? An anti-government movement named the Liberty and Civil Rights movement (自由民, 権運動) gained ground in the 1880s. This movement was highly critical of the despotic government led by Chōshū and Satsuma and demanded civil rights and popular suffrage; it is therefore often viewed as a democratic movement. However, this movement saw suffrage as a means, not an end. The ideological focus was actually on sovereignty, and in the beginning there were also advocates of a direct rule by the Emperor in this movement.

A Rinzai Zen abbot, Imakita Kōsen (1816–1892), had been a key player co-operating with the post-Meiji Great Promulgation campaign, and Okunomiya Zosai (1811–1877), an officer of the educational (religious) ministry, supported Imakita's activities. Okunomiya was an intellectual from the Tosa region (Kōchi prefecture at present) who had been influenced by Confucianism, Kokugaku and western political thought. In 1875, Okunomiya and Imakita began a zazen meditation meeting named Ryomokai (両忘会) (Sugiyama 2013; Kurita 2019). Imakita emphasised the importance of seeking non-textual truth and insisted on a Great Way (大道), which he claimed was coincident with Shintō, Confucianism, Buddhism and Daoism (Imakita 1935: 44–45). In this context, meditation was presented as transcending the doctrinal differences of religions. It likely attracted people who had been sympathetic to the ideals of the Great Promulgation campaign but had become disappointed by internal conflicts.

Interestingly, some of these lay Buddhists later led the Liberty and Civil Rights movement during the 1880s. Important figures were Nakae Chōmin (1847–1901), a famous translator of Rousseau's *Social Contracts*, and Torio Tokuan (1847–1905), a dissident army lieutenant and later pioneer of the Japanese conservative movement. These men were influenced by French political theories, but interpreted them in Confucian and Buddhist terms. For example, Nakae regarded *liberté morale* in French as the idea of the great and prosperous *qi* of *The Discourses of Mencius*, which also corresponded to the 'unyielding mind' in Japanese neo-Confucianism (Kajita 1992). Torio's interpretation of *liberté* was as a moral decision derived from Buddhist and Confucian perspectives (Manabe 2001). Nakae and Torio appealed to the government to establish an elected legislature, introduce civil rights and revise unequal trading treaties. But additionally these political theorists encouraged the population to recover an energetic *qi* of the nation, which was regarded as the foundation of an independent state. In this spirit, the Liberty and Civil Rights movement encouraged the formation of a unified national identity. Imakita's meeting for Zen meditation functioned as an incubator of the new intersectional politico-religious promulgation. For these political leaders, meditation practices function as an independent source of the truth and an ideal of the unified nation, beyond the existing authority or written texts.

This indicates that even in the modern era, meditation has a theoretical and ideological function that was closely associated with 'this worldly', sovereign power. However, the establishment of a modern sovereign state and the modern separation of religions and politics have weakened the power of individual religions to claim political sovereignty. In addition, general acceptance of modern natural science has undermined beliefs in myths and non-human entities. The sovereign power of meditation, however, continued to develop – not through association with individual religious ideologies, but by universally transcending them.

## Psychologisation and universalisation of meditation

Though it had political meaning for some leaders as mentioned above, generally speaking, meditation was often closely associated with self-cultivation and self-care, namely *yōjō*. But westernisation and the introduction of western science changed the context. In 1874, the Japanese government adopted the National Medical License Examination, based on western medicine; religious practices for healing were prohibited if they were regarded as hindrances to medical practice. Historical medical ideas were replaced by biomedical ones and the credibility of *qi*-based theories was radically undermined. Moreover, the Meiji government abolished the class system and asserted that people were able to succeed economically and socially according to their effort. Meditation seemed to decline among 'civilised' people and a translation of *Self Help* (1859) by the Scotsman Samuel Smiles was popular.

However, feeling intensely competitive against Christianity, Buddhist intellectuals presented Buddhism as a rational, scientific or philosophical religion. By doing so, they argued for the usefulness of Buddhism in 'civilising' the population. For example, Inoue Enryō (1858–1919), a Buddhist reformer who graduated from the first modern university of Japan (later called the University of Tokyo), energetically defended Buddhism from philosophical and scientific standpoints, simultaneously criticising Christianity and opposing superstition. In 1887 he established an educational institute named Tetsugakukan (meaning philosophical academy, later named Toyo University) and taught philosophy, psychology and pedagogy for educators and religious leaders (Shimizu 2008).

The curriculum at Tetsugakukan included a course on hypnotism. This was important for Inoue as he saw that hypnotism not only offered psychological explanations for superstition, but also criticised medical materialism and mind–body dualism. He insisted that the mental side of disease should also be treated by religious practitioners who have mastered psychology (Inoue 1923: 34). For Inoue, this was a reformation of Buddhist practices, including meditation and *kaji*. In other words, *kaji* was reframed as hypnotism and Buddhist meditation was reframed as self-hypnotism. In the process, the mixture of psychology and religious explanation brought about a new spiritual movement: the Japanese Popular Mind Cure movement (民間精神療法) (Kurita et al. 2019). As elsewhere in the early twentieth century, New Thought, meditation and breathing techniques were gaining popularity as a way to overcome materialism and mind–body dualism (Albanese 2007; Schmidt 2005).

The international physical culture movement was also influential. Eugen Sandow's (1867–1925) books were translated and sold well in Japan (Zōshikai 1900). Significantly, Paul von Boeckmann, another American physical culture author, influenced the revival of breathing meditation. Boeckmann criticised Sandow's method and insisted that one should train internal organs and muscles rather than external muscles though a breathing method which emphasises controlling the diaphragm (Boeckmann 1906). As tuberculosis and neurasthenia were widely experienced but untreatable with biomedicine at the time, Boeckmann promoted his breathing method as an effective treatment. Boeckmann's book was translated into Japanese by a journalist, Sugimura Sojinkan (1872–1945). Its explanations of breathing methods were completely different from traditional ideas on breathing in Japan.

Sugimura was a lay Buddhist and practised Zen under the instruction of Imakita Kōsen's disciple, Shaku Sōen (Soyen Shaku, 1860–1919). His pupil, Suzuki Daisetsu Teitarō (D.T. Suzuki, 1870–1960), promoted Zen meditation as efficacious not only from a religious perspective, but also as promoting psychological, physiological and ethical growth (Shaku, Suzuki and Seigo 1908). In addition to translating Boeckmann's work, Sugimura also translated excerpts from the American Elizabeth Towne's *Just How to Wake the Solar Plexus* (1907). Sugimura speculated that the solar plexus was equivalent to the Tanden in Hakuin's writing and saw her writings as a scientific explanation of Hakuin's ideas (although Sugimura only partially agreed with Towne).[3]

Fujita Reisai (1868–1957) was another influential figure in the reformist movements of this period. He proposed and systematically propagated what he understood as the original Tanden breathing techniques under the name *sokushinchōwahō* (the way of harmonising mind and breath, 息心調和法). His teachings were synchronistic and universalistic: e.g. Jesus was equated with one of the 'Shinjin' (the Daoist spiritual masters) in the ancient Chinese text *Zhuangzi*. Fujita proposed that his breathing techniques not only maintained health and healed disease but also enabled people to become Shinjin, reaching the Universal Spirit and grasping the essence of religion. His group, Yōshinkai (later Chōwadōkyōkai),[4] was also influenced by foreign spiritual movements, including New Thought (Kurita 2016). His disciple Matsuda Reiyō, a businessman and a leader of the Vancouver branch of Yōshinkai, introduced modern yoga to Japan by translating Yogi Ramacharaka, a pseudonym of the American New Thought writer William Walker Atkinson (1862–1932) (Deslippe 2019).

Fujita's activities went beyond spiritual healing to political activism. In 1917, an auxiliary organisation of the Ministry of Justice asked him to teach his techniques to help prisons reform inmates. From then onwards he observed prisoners' abdomens when he visited prisons and theorised that their belly shape related to character. He said that those with bellies in poor condition had 'abdominal induration' and insisted that they were improved through his breathing techniques. In the 1920s and 1930s, Fujita and his fellows petitioned the Ministry of Education and National Diet to establish a physical education course based on his techniques: the Movement for National Practices of Chōwahō (調和法実修国民運動). This group strongly criticised the Great Japanese Calisthenics (*Dainihon kokumin taisō*), promoted by the Ministry of Health and Welfare, as a 'western' physical education which put too much importance on developing the chest. This framework provided an us/them or 'friend/enemy' opposition by simplifying the West into a 'chest culture' and the East (Japan) into a 'belly culture'. His propagation also extended to China; Fujita hoped that by establishing the Chinese branch of Chōwadōkyōkai in 1925 his techniques would provide East Asian people with the driving force needed to gain prosperity. Needless to say, this vision overlapped with the ideology of 'the Greater East Asia Co-Prosperity Sphere' promoted by the Empire of Japan during its colonising period.

In 1946, Ruth Benedict mentioned that, as the Japanese self-discipline 'builds up the belly', 'enlarges life', and enables one to 'enjoy life', it is totally different from stoic training in the United States and ascetic yogic disciplines in India (Benedict 1946: 227–241). However, in practice, meditation, yoga and belly breathing were already in the United States through New Thought literature; the monistic philosophy of New Thought had travelled across the Pacific. Historical evidence shows that these generalisations were gross simplifications and products of a particular time. Japan was seen as 'the most alien enemy' (Benedict 1946: 1) of the United States in a time of war.

## Political theology on meditation

Other reformers directed their attention to analysing breathing methods from a more universal standpoint. Okada Torajirō, for example, frequently referred to western thinkers and adopted the terms 'inner breathing' and 'outer breathing' from the writings of Emanuel Swedenborg (1688–1772).[5] In spite of the fact that he placed importance on the lower abdomen (*tanden*) as well as on bodies with big bellies (unlike Sandow), he idealised the physical condition of Germans. Though Okada's bodily technique was similar to Zen in several ways, he preferred to identify it with Quaker worship. Simultaneously, he deeply admired Ralph Waldo Emerson (1803–1882), who wrote an essay titled 'The Over-Soul' that is said to have been influenced by Vedānta philosophy. Okada used the concept of selflessness (*muga* 無我), which is usually considered to be a Buddhist term, but he also favoured terms such as 'non-being' and 'zero' to avoid relying on a specific school of thought. Eventually, he advised his disciples just to practise his technique, called *seiza*, without engaging in theoretical discussions (Sasamura 1974).

Although Okada did not write any books, he gained popularity through his adherents' writings. In the background of the popularity of Okada's *seiza* was a period of social disturbance in the late Meiji period – including a pollution scandal at the Ashio Copper Mine and government crackdowns on socialists. There was a tension between questioning modernisation and asserting that traditional ways had to change. Through his meditative method, Okada provided a possibility between the binaries of 'modernisation vs tradition' and 'western vs eastern'. His techniques attracted a wide spectrum of adherents: from students and teachers in universities, to socialists and right-wing activists; from artists and journalists to politicians and *zaibatsu* (financial business conglomerate) families. Among his disciples was Sahoda Tsuruji (1899–1986), one of the earliest promoters of yoga in modern Japan.

Okada's quiet sitting was believed to enable autonomy – that is, to practise by oneself the way (rule, order). During World War II, the leader of a war-time national education centre, Satō Tsūji (1901–1990), thoroughly developed Okada's practical philosophy of autonomy and, like Yamazaki Ansai, interpreted loyalty to the Emperor as Japanese autonomous action (Satō 1941). According to him, the ultimate identity of Japan transcended modernisation and tradition and was not about the people, constitution and lands, but hinged upon loyalty to the Emperor. Therefore, even as other Japanese leaders secretly began to work towards ending the war from 1944, he became part of a group that planned to launch a coup d'etat and exercise the Emperor's prerogative in fighting out the Decisive Battle in mainland Japan (Akazawa 2017: 84–105). As shown by his close connection to a German psychologist of meditation, Karlfried Dürckheim (1896–1988), who was an ex-member of Nazi Germany's *Sturmabteilung* and lived in Japan during World War II (Baier 2013), he also had an international or universal standpoint through meditation. He no longer directly adopted a dichotomy between 'modernisation and tradition' or 'western and eastern', but, in terms of how much a nation state is ruled by economic desire which is supposed to be overcome by meditation, he created another antithesis of 'friend and enemy': the Axis and the Allied powers between capitalism and communism.

## Postmodern meditation and yoga

After Japan's 1945 defeat in World War II, the ideal of the Greater East Asia Co-Prosperity Sphere collapsed. General Headquarters (GHQ) occupied Japan and put responsibility for the Asia–Pacific War on 'State Shintō', banning official support for Shintō shrines. In 1952 the occupation ended; Japanese state sovereignty was 'recovered', nominally shifting from the Emperor to the Japanese people under a new constitution. But this sovereignty is different from Schmitt's sovereignty: Schmitt's sovereign 'stands outside the normally valid legal system' and is the entity which 'all tendencies of modern constitutional development point toward eliminating' (Schmitt 2005: 7). From the normal legal standpoint, no one knows where sovereignty in this sense lurks now or will appear in the future.

After World War II, new religious groups flourished in Japan, termed by the American scholar McFarland 'the rush hour of the gods' (McFarland 1967). There were many conspicuous groups, such as Soka Gakkai, Rissho Kosei-kai and the Church of Perfect Liberty. However, Seicho-no-ie, founded by Taniguchi Masaharu (1893–1985) has been particularly important as a trans-sectarian group for meditation and self-cultivation, promoting a meditation technique for healing called *shinsōkan* (Seicho-no-ie-honbu 1959). The group also operates a religious publishing house producing Taniguchi's own books as well as translations of New Thought literature, and it introduced Paramahansa Yogananda's writings to Japan. It also actively promotes anti-communist and nationalistic policies.

Nihon Shingaku Renmei (the Japanese Shintō Theologians League), which publishes *The Japanese Shintō Theology* journal, also introduced a form of yoga into Japan in the 1950s. Sekiguchi Nobara (1888–1967), a Christian socialist, was a particularly influential member of this group who developed a theology uniting Christianity, Shintō, New Thought and the teachings of Yogananda, arguing that meditation was the core of all religions' esoteric roots. An important aim of Sekiguchi and the group has been to positively revive Shintō, reversing the negative associations as being the ideology of the Asia–Pacific War. Until the 1970s, especially from a standpoint of reformists, meditation might be understood as having an affinity to conservative or reactionary political movements.

Another interesting figure was Oki Masahiro (1921–1985), who was actively teaching in the late 1950s and 1960s. He practised a disciplined communal life incorporating yoga and meditation – arguing that Buddha, Jesus and Muhammad were enlightened by yoga. He was originally an intelligence agent and insisted that he, through these activities, learned yoga from the leader of the Myanmar independence movement, a Buddhist monk Sayadaw U Ottama (1879–1939) and Mahatma Gandhi (1869–1948). His yoga connoted a close relationship with the pre-war Pan-Asianist network and also attracted a small number of followers in Britain.

As the global counter-culture encouraged a widening interest in yoga and meditation, a similar influence was felt in Japan. In the late 1960s and 1970s, the Japanese New Left (shinsayoku, 新左翼) sought a third way against the United States and the Soviet Union and also opposed the Japanese conservative party and the communist party. After New Leftists were defeated in student riots, some of the New Leftists, especially Maoists and non-sectarian radicals, theoretically turned their backs on modernism and soviet Marxism. Influenced by the American New Age movement, practices of 'eastern' medicine and meditation were often combined with social reformation beliefs. Some of these activists gained popularity in the media: for example, Nakazawa Shin'ichi (1950–), whose book *Niji no kaitei* (*The Step of the Rainbow* (1981)) became one of the publications that deeply influenced Asahara Shōkō, the guru of Aum Shinrikyō, and his leading disciples.

As Suga has argued, in the postmodern and postcolonial situation, boundaries between right-wing and left-wing discourses have blurred, and thick subculture discourses have emerged (2006: 192). The post–World War II New Age and indigenous Japanese movements were broadly critical of modernism and had affinities to both postmodernism and reactionary nationalism. From the 1970s, meditative and yogic practices gained popularity among young people critical of aspects of modern Japanese society and a new wave of religious innovation occurred – i.e. the '"new" new religions'(新新宗教), including the GLA (God Light Association), Agon Shū and Aum Shinrikyō (Shimazono 2001: 13).

The year 1995 was pivotal in Japan. In this year, Aum Shinrikyō committed the Tokyo subway sarin gas attack, retrospectively seen as the beginning of 'a fight against terrorism'. However, since this period, yoga and other meditative practices have become overwhelmingly associated with private, apparently apolitical practices for promoting health and fitness.

Neoliberal capitalist ideology appears to be expanding across the globe, relegating both religion and physical embodiment to the personal. Yoga and meditation are now seen as primarily providing possibilities for psychological resilience within the system rather than revolution. As elsewhere in the world, the popularity of the mindfulness movement suggests that meditation is a universal way of approaching personal knowledge rather than a resource for political power.

## Conclusion

Meditation in Japan has a long and complicated history, and is intimately entwined with politics. Buddhism was a significant autonomous 'worldly' power in the medieval era which competed against (and was interdependent with) other secular powers. In the early modern period, meditation was understood not only as a disciplinary power but also as a way of criticising textual knowledge, including scriptures, laws and treaties. In this capacity, its deconstructive character critiqued the established order and encouraged change.

In modern Japan, meditative self-cultivation has been associated with various practical ideologies, including anti-American, anti-British, anti-communist thought, Asian solidarity, loyalty to the Emperor and the Pact between Japan and Germany, as well as having been strongly recommended as a practice during the Asia–Pacific War. After World War II, self-cultivation became a channel for the 'third' political standpoint and was associated with reactionism, the New Left and the New Age. In this chapter, I have argued that this link between politics and meditation in Japan can be better understood by exploring how meditative traditions have served as a channel for 'sovereign power', justifying and giving authority to political sovereignty.

To conclude, we find that the political development of Aum-Shinrikyō is, in light of the political history of meditation in Japan, not a deviation from meditation's inherent nature, but an intensification of its political nature. Aum-Shinrikyō tried to establish an alternative power with violence and to confront global capitalism by relying on the function of meditative techniques as a channel for sovereign power. Its indiscriminate terrorism was inextricably linked to the fact that modern society has evolved to thoroughly eliminate 'a state of exception'. Since Aum-Shinrikyō's incidents, the manifestation of the 'sovereign' and 'a state of exception' through meditation seems totally suppressed in most advanced countries.

It could be argued that the effect of meditation is not to create in the practitioner harmony with the world and the universe, but rather to separate practitioners from the existing world, and then to manifest another world in their disciplined bodies. In this sense, meditation is a form of elitism. If the division between this meditative elite and the other is ideologically emphasised, the more clearly the practitioner-elite perceive their autonomy, and a corresponding right to sovereignty. Conversely, if this division is less marked, the elitism of the practitioners can be incorporated as part of a hierarchical discipline reinforcing the authority of the existing society. Aum-Shinrikyō appears to be a definitive example of the former. Now that ideology of 'freedom' and 'diversity' is sweeping globally through modern society, meditation and yoga is primarily providing a tool to discipline subjects within society and to maintain the existing social order.

## Notes

1 I would like to make a most cordial acknowledgement and appreciation to my reviewer and editors.

2 A historian, Kuroda Toshio, theorised this Japanese medieval ruling order as *kenmon taisei* (system of ruling elites), in which powers of military families, noble families and temple families were mutually dependent and sometimes conflicted (Kuroda 1994).

3 The lay Buddhist Katō Totsudō (1870–1949) was also influenced by Boeckmann and Towne's breathing methods: his book *Meisōron* (1905) proposes meditations for self-cultivation and self-care called *shūyō* (修養).

4 Members of Yōshinkai included Murai Tomoyoshi (1861–1944), a Christian sociologist; Ōkuma Shigenobu (1838–1922), the ex-Prime Minister of Japan; and Ōkawa Shūmei (1886–1957), an activist of Pan-Asianism.

5 Emanuel Swedenborg was influential in western esotericism and New Thought. From 1910 to 1914, T. D. Suzuki translated Swedenborgian books into Japanese and wrote a biography of Swedenborg (Yoshinaga 2014).

## Bibliography

Akazawa, S. 2017. *Tokutomi sohō to dainihongenronhōkokukai*. Tokyo: Yamakawashuppansha. (赤澤史朗2017『徳富蘇峰と大日本言論報国会』山川出版社)

Albanese, C. L. 2007. *A Republic Mind and Spirit: A Cultural History of American Metaphysical Religion*. London: Yale University Press.

Amino, Y. 1996. *Muen, Kugai, Raku*. Tokyo: Heibonsha. (網野善彦1996『無縁・公界・楽』平凡社)

Asahara, S. 1995. *Hiizurukuni wazawai chikashi: Asahara Shōkō senritsu no yogen*. Tokyo: Aum. (麻原彰晃1995『日出づる国、災い近し—麻原彰晃、戦慄の預言』オウム)

Baier, K. 2013. 'The Formation and Principles of Count Dürckheim's Nazi Worldview and his interpretation of Japanese Spirit and Zen'. *The Asia-Pacific Journal* 1(48) no. 3: 1–34.

Bellah, R. N. 1957. *Tokugawa Religion: The Cultural Roots of Modern Japan*. New York, Free Press.

Benedict, R. 1946. *The Chrysanthemum and the Sword: Patterns of Japanese Culture*. New York: Houghton Mifflin Harcourt.

Boeckmann, P. von. 1906. *Kyōhaijutsu: Saishin shiki tairyoku yōseihō, the Revised and Expanded Edition*. Sugimura, K. (trans). Tokyo: Keiseidōshoten. (パウル・フヲン・ベークマン1906『強肺術最新式—体力養成法(改訂増補版)』杉村広太郎訳、鶏聲堂出版).

Deslippe, P. 2019. 'William Walker Atkinson as Yogi Ramacharaka', in Kurita, H., Tsukada, H. and Yoshinaga, S. (eds), *Kingendai nihon no minkanseishinryōhō: okaruto enerugii no shoos*, 79–108. Tokyo: Kokushokankokai. (デスリプ, フィリップ2019「ウィリアム・ウォーカー・アトキンソン—別名、ヨギ・ラマチャラカ」栗田英彦・塚田穂高・吉永進一編『近現代日本の民間精神療法—不可視なエネルギーの諸相』国書刊行会)

Foucault, M. 1978. *The History of Sexuality Volume 1: An Introduction*. Hurley, R. (trans). New York: Random House, Inc.

Gebhardt, L. 2001. *Japans Neue Spiritualität*. Wiesbaden: Verlag Otto Harrassowitz.

Hirata, A. 2000. *Senkyō ibun; Katsugorō saisei kibun*. Tokyo: Iwanami shoten. (平田篤胤2000『仙境異聞・勝五郎再生記聞』岩波書店)

Imakita, K. 1935. *Zenkai Ichiran*. Tokyo: Iwanami shoten (今北洪川1935『禅海一欄』岩波書店)

Inoue, E. 1923. *Yōkaigaku kōgi*, Vol. 3. Tōkyō: Daitōkaku. (井上円了1923『妖怪学講義』第三巻、大鐙閣)

Itō, M. 2008. *Jishaseiryoku no chūsei*. Tokyo: Chikumashobō (伊藤正敏2008『寺社勢力の中世』筑摩書房)

Kajita, A. 1992. 'Seinan senso izen no gensetsu Jōkyō: Shizokuminkenron o meguru "Ki" no mondai nit suite'. *Bulletin, Study on the Japanese Culture in Relation to the Imperial Family and Court* 43: 15–37. (梶田明宏1992「西南戦争以前の言説状況—士族民権論をめぐる「気」の問題について」『書陵部紀要』第43号)

Katō, T. 1905. Meisōron. Tokyo: Tōadō. (加藤咄堂1905『冥想論』東亜堂)

Kurita, H. 2016. 'Modernity in Japanese Breathing Techniques: Fujita Reisai and his Activities'. *Ronshū* 43: 1–24. [in Japanese] (栗田英彦「腹式呼吸の近代—藤田式息心調和法を事例として」『論集』43号)

Kurita, H. 2019. 'Seikyōbunri, Jiyūminken, ki no shisō'. In Kurita, H., Tsukada, H. and Yoshinaga, S. (eds), *Kingendai nihon no minkanseishinryōhō: okaruto enerugii no shosō*, 111–143. Tokyo: Kokushokankokai. (栗田英彦2019「政教分離・自由民権・気の思想」栗田英彦・塚田穂高・吉永進一編『近現代日本の民間精神療法—不可視なエネルギーの諸相』国書刊行会)

Kurita, H., Tsukada, H. and Yoshinaga, S. (eds) 2019. *Kingendai nihon no minkanseishinryōhō: okaruto enerugii no shosō*. Tokyo: Kokushokankokai. (栗田英彦・塚田穂高・吉永進一編『近現代日本の民間精神療法—不可視なエネルギーの諸相』国書刊行会)

Kuroda, T. 1994. *Kenmon taiseiron*. Kyōto: Hōzōkan. (黒田俊雄1994『権門体制論』法藏館)

McFarland, H. N. 1967. *The Rush Hour of the Gods: A Study of New Religious Movements in Japan*. New York: Macmillan.

Manabe, M. 2001. 'Kindai kokka keiseiki ni okeru dentō shisō: Torio Koyata Ōhōron no hyōka o megutte'. *Wasedadaigakudaigakuinbunngakukennkyūkakiyō* 4(47): 67–79. (真辺将之2001「近代国家形成期における伝統思想—鳥尾小弥太『王法論』の評価をめぐって」『早稲田大学大学院文学研究科紀要』第4分冊47号).

Mauss, M. 1979. *Sociology and Psychology: Essays*. Brewster, B. (trans). London: Routledge & Kegan Paul.

Minowa, K. 2015. 'Jōzabukkyō to daijōbukkyō no meisō: sono kyōtsūsei.' Kokusai tetsugaku kenkyū bessatsu 6: 60–79. (蓑輪顕量2015「上座仏教と大乗仏教の瞑想—その共通性」『国際哲学研究』別冊6)

Motoori, N. 1991. *Uiyamafumi; Suzuya tomonroku*. Tokyo: Iwanami shoten. (本居宣長『うひ山ふみ・鈴屋答問録』岩波書店)

Nakajima, R. 2012. *Seiza: Jissen Shisō Rekishi*. Tokyo: Kenbun shuppan. (中嶋隆蔵2012『静坐—実践・思想・歴史』研文出版)

Nakazawa, S. and Khetsun, S. 1981. *Niji no kaitei : Chibetto mikkyō no meisō shugyō*. Tōkyō : Hirakawa Shuppansha.

Ōshima, A. 2006. 'Acceptance of "Sakoku-ron" translated by Shizuki Tadao in latter half of early modern times Japan'. *Annals of the Society for the History of Western Learning in Japan* 14: 1–32. (大島明秀2006「近世後期日本における志筑忠雄訳『鎖国論』の受容」『洋学史学会』14号)

Sahoda, T. 1929. 'Okada sensei sanzaroku: Jyō'. *Seiza* 3(4) 11–13. (佐保田鶴治1929「岡田先生参坐録(上)」『静坐』3巻4号)

Sasamura, S (ed) 1974. *Seiza: Okada Torajirō sono kotoba to shōgai* [privately printed book]. (笹村草家人1974『静坐——岡田虎二郎その言葉と生涯』私家版).

Satō, T. 1941. *Kōdōtetsugaku*. Tokyo: Asakurashoten. (佐藤通次1941『皇道哲学』朝倉書店).

Sawada, J. T. 2004. *Practical Pursuits: Religion, Politics, and Personal Cultivation in Nineteenth-century Japan*. Honolulu: University of Hawai'i Press.

Seicho-no-ie-honbu. 1959. *Seicho-no-ie sanjū nen shi*. Tokyo: Nihonkyōbunsha. (生長の家本部1959『生長の家三十年史』日本教文社)

Schmidt, L. E. 2005. *Restless Souls: The Making of American Spirituality*. New York: HarperCollins.

Schmitt, C. 2005. *Political Theology*. Schwab, G. (trans). Chicago: University of Chicago Press.

Schmitt, C. 2007. *The Concept of the Political: Expanded Edition*. Schwab, G. (trans). Chicago: University of Chicago Press.

Shaku, S., Suzuki, D. and Seigo, H. 1908. *Seiza no susume*. Tokyo: Kōyūkan. (釈宗演・鈴木大拙・棲梧宝嶽1908『静坐のすすめ』光融館)

Shimazono, S. 2001. *Posutomodan no shinshūkyō*. Tokyo: Tōkyōdōshuppan. (島薗進2001『ポストモダンの新宗教—現代日本の精神状況の底流』東京堂出版)

Shimizu, T. 2008. 'Kyōikushisō no hensen to testugakukan, toyōdaigaku niokeru shinrigaku, kyōikugaku: Kamoku tantōsha o chūshin to shite'. *Annual report of the Inoue Enryo Center* 17: 53–88. (清水乞2008「教育思想の変遷と哲学館・東洋大学における心理学・教育学—科目担当者を中心として」『井上円了センター年報』17号).

Sonehara, S. 2008. *Shinkun Ieyasu no tanjō: Tōshōgū to gongensama*. Tokyo: Yoshikawa Kōbunkan. (曽根原理2008『神君家康の誕生—東照宮と権現様』吉川弘文館)

Sueki, F. 1992. *Nihon Bukkyōshi: Shisōshi toshiteno apurōchi*. Tokyo: Shinchōsha. (末木文美士1992『日本仏教史—思想史としてのアプローチ』新潮社)

Sueki, F. 2010. *Kinsei no bukkyō: Hanahiraku shisō to bunka*. Tokyo: Yoshikawakōbunkan. (末木文美士『近世の仏教—華ひらく思想と文化』2010、吉川弘文館)

Suga, H. 2006. *1968 nen*. Tokyo: Chikumashobō. (絓秀実2006『1968年』筑摩書房)

Sugita, M. 1932. 'Okada sensei goroku: Shōzen'. *Seiza* 6(8): 12–16. (杉田正臣1932「岡田先生語録(承前)」『静坐』6巻8号)

Sugiyama, T. 2013. *Research of Okunomiya Zosai: Mainly in Meiji Era*. Tokyo: Waseda University (doctoral dissertation). [in Japanese] (杉山剛『奥宮慥斎の研究—明治時代を中心にして』早稲田大学審査学位論文)

Taira, M. 1992. *Nihon chūsei shakai to bukkyō*. Tokyo: Hanawashobō. (平雅行1992『日本中世社会と仏教』塙書房)

Toby, R. P. 1984. *State and Diplomacy in Early Modern Japan: Asia in the Development of the Tokugawa Bakufu*. Princeton: Princeton University Press.

Towne, E. 1907. *Just How to Wake the Solar Plexus*. Holyoke: Elizabeth Towne Co.

Unknown. 1623. *Heike monogatari*, Vol. 1. [publisher unknown]. (著者不明1623『平家物語』巻第一、出版社不明[元和9年版])

Unoda, S. 2007. 'Jyusha', in Yokota, F. (ed), *Chishiki to gakumon o ninau hitobito*, 17–43. Tokyo: Yoshikawakobunkan. (宇野田尚哉2007「儒者」横田冬彦編『知識と学問をになう人びと』吉川弘文館)

Ushio, H. 2008. 'On the Explanation of Jing zuo (静坐) and Ju jing (居敬) in Zhu zi's Thought and Learning'. *Studies in Chinese Philosophy* 34: 1–22. [in Japanese] (牛尾弘孝2008「朱子学における「静坐・居敬」の解釈をめぐって」『九州大学中国哲学研究会』34号)

Yoshinaga, S. 2014. 'Suzuki Daisetsu and Swedenborg: A Historical Background', in Hayashi, M., Ōtani, E. and Swanson, P. L. (eds), *Modern Buddhism in Japan*, 112–143. Nagoya: Nanzan Institute for Religion and Culture.

Zōshikai (ed).1900. *Sandau tairyoku youseihō*. Tokyo: Zōshikai. (造士会編1900『サンダウ体力養成法』造士会)

# 22
# YOGA AND MEDITATION IN KOREA

*Kwangsoo Park and Younggil Park*

## Introduction

Many historical records and writings mention mind and body practices for physical and spiritual wellness, and these days in Korea it is easy to find centres for the practice of yoga, meditation, breath control and nurturing vital energy. This, along with Koreans' exposure to other beliefs – such as Christianity, for example – means that contemporary Korea 'offers individuals a vast array of goals and techniques to choose from when they embark on a spiritual quest' (Baker 2008: 144). First, under the broad topic of yoga and meditation in Korea, we will briefly review the various traditions of practice and meditation in their historical context. This chapter will then examine the acceptance and development of yoga in Korean society, such as the current status of research in colleges, the activities of associations related to yoga studies, trends in yoga federations, and the challenges and outlook for yoga and meditation in Korean society.

'Yoga' and 'meditation' have various meanings, with the applications of the latter term being manifold. Meditation generally implies mentally observing, contemplating and analysing a particular object or target in the mind. However, this is a narrow interpretation since it tends to exclude all practices beyond the acts of observing, thinking or analysing. For the purposes of this chapter, a more comprehensive conception of meditation is required – one that encompasses the practice of the mind beyond analytic language and the world of reflecting. Thus, various forms of practice could be included under 'meditation', such as *śamatha* and *vipaśyana* (지관, 止觀, 'tranquillity and insight') to reach *nirvāṇa* (열반, 涅槃) in early Buddhism, silent prayer in Christianity or Sufi dance in Islam.

## Traditions of practice and meditation in Korea

Although Asian religions share some teachings and practices, Buddhism, Confucianism and Daoism value human nature in different ways and have developed their own unique philosophies and practices.

### *Confucianism in Korea*

Confucianism was introduced into Korea during the Three Kingdoms period (57 BCE–668 CE) in the fourth century CE, which eventually came to provide the framework for individual and social ethics. During the Joseon dynasty, neo-Confucianism, as the state religion, was firmly established as the political and ideological foundation of the Korean government for nearly 500 years and its values permeated all aspects of society (Park 1997).

The Confucianism of Confucius (孔子) and Mencius (孟子) was systematically developed by Zhu Xi (朱熹, 1130–1200) into neo-Confucianism (性理学) and by Shou-jin Wang (王守仁, 1472–1528) into the Yangming school of philosophy (阳明学) (Zhu Xi 2010). The Confucian academic focus on the mind is called Mind Studies (心学); this is the common link between neo-Confucianism and the Yangming school of philosophy. In general, neo-Confucian scholars criticised the attitude and ideas of Buddhism, while the Yangming school accepted the Buddhist concept of the mind and developed a system of Mind Studies. The Mind Studies of Confucianism considered the mind as the central pillar of the behavioural functions of the body. Confucianism tends not to view human emotions such as joy and sorrow negatively, but pursues happiness by 'following nature' (*solseong* 솔성, 率性) and controlling the mind and emotions by following a path of moderation (中庸). In chapters 1–4 of his book *Tong Shu* (通書), Dunyi Zhou (周敦頤, 1017–1073) viewed sincerity as the source of wisdom and the original creative force (C. qianyuan, 乾元) (Chan 1963: 465–480). In relating the sources of the cosmos and sagacity to sincerity, he proposed a way of practice based upon his philosophy.

Korean Confucian scholars, i.e. Hwang Yi (이황, 李滉, 1501–1570) and I Yi (이이, 李珥, 1536–1584), considered sincerity and reverence to be important virtues in cultivating oneself and attaining the learning of the sages. Regarding the interaction between sincerity and reverence, I Yi asserted that 'reverence is the way to accomplishment, and sincerity the ground to harvest it; thus sincerity can be attained from reverence' (Yi 2007). He viewed sincerity as the basis of reverence, and reverence as the application (용, 用) of sincerity in practice. Conversely, Hwang Yi stressed the close relationship between sincerity and reverence but placed more emphasis on reverence. Yi's ideas on the origins of the mind were construed from the Theories on Nature and Conduct (성명론, 性命論), and the correlation between the nature of the mind and the seven emotions was identified in the debate of *Sadanchiljeong* (사단칠정론, 四端七情論, the Four Beginnings and the Seven Emotions) in Korean Confucianism. In particular, Hwang Yi promoted these spiritual values and practical and ethical principles. In *The Ten Diagrams of the Sages' Learning* (*Seong-hak Sip-do*, 聖學十圖) he emphasised that one could come to respect everyone by cultivating an attitude of reverence as if one is present before the Lord on High (Kalton 1988: 178). Therefore, it is important for the Confucian practitioner to practise sincerity and reverence as important virtues in cultivating oneself and attaining the learning of the sages.

During the eighteenth and nineteenth centuries, ruling conservative Confucian scholars tried to preserve their traditional governing system in the face of reform efforts. The academic Confucian Silhak movement aimed to modernise the social institutions of the Korean Confucian literati. In doing so, these pioneering neo-Confucians expected the prevailing social and political structures in Korea to be changed as well. However, the Silhak movement's campaign was ultimately rejected by an entrenched elite resistant to change. At that time, the government of the Joseon dynasty considered Catholicism to be a heterodox and anti-government organisation that was tied to western imperialism. For that reason, they began to persecute Catholics. There was a massacre in 1866, which included some famous Silhak Confucian scholars (Park 1997: 11). Although Confucianism lost its strong influence in contemporary Korea after the fall of the last Joseon dynasty (1910), the legacy of Confucianism is still found in Korean customs and values. Also, many renowned Confucian private schools or communities, called 'Seowon' (서원, 書院)', are found throughout the country, either for education or for rituals to honour distinguished Confucian scholars and statesmen.

## Daoism in Korea

Daoism, unlike Confucianism and Buddhism, values not only the mind but also the vital force (정기, 精氣) in the body, which is viewed as the power that maintains life. In the *Tao Te Ching* (道德經, *The Book of the Way and its Virtue*), Laozi (老子) said, 'You could become soft like a new-born baby if you focus on your vital force' (精氣致柔能嬰兒乎). The body is the house of the vital force (정, 精), which is closely related to Heshang Gong's (河上公) interpretation of the body in the *Tao Te Ching*. In the *Commentary of Heshang Gong on the Tao Te Ching* (老子道德經河上公章句), Laozi states there are five types of spirits (신, 神) that exist within the organs in the human body. In *Spirit of the Valley Does Not Die* (곡신불사, 谷神不死), he explained that 'the liver and bowels keep the soul (혼, 魂); the lungs, vigour (백, 魄); the heart, vital spirit (신, 神); the kidneys, vital force (정, 精); and the spleen, aspiration (지, 志). If the five organs are ruined, the five spirits will leave your body' (Lee 2005: 63). According to Laozi's Nature of Non-Action (무위자연, 無爲自然) principle, Daoism values life in harmony with nature, and aims to reach the state of perennial youth and long life (불로장생, 不老長生) or perennial youth and immortality (불로불사, 不老不死) by maintaining the spirits in the body through training (양생법, 養生法).

The traditional techniques of Buddhism, Confucianism and Daoism that were popular in Korea mostly focused on *prāṇāyāma* (breath control) – with the method of cultivation in Chinese Daoism or *qigong* (기공, 氣功) also emphasised. This method of cultivation is based on the theory *ohaeng* (오행, 五行): the movement of five elements. *Ohaeng* is a theory that addresses changes in Mother Nature, the human body and the mind, based on the incompatibility and interdependence between the five elements that make up the universe, including wood (목, 木), fire (화, 火), soil (토, 土), iron (금, 金) and water (수, 水). According to this theory, a weak water energy, for example, can be supplemented with controlled breathing. Some of these ideas, along with a belief in improving one's health by breath training and retreats to the mountains, still resonate in Korea today, along with the concepts of *dosa* (도사, 道士), *qi* (기, 氣) and practice (수행, 修行).

The concept of *dosa* – 'one who practices the Way (*Tao*)' in nurturing the mind and body – reflects the Korean view of practice or practitioners well. Although there is no historical link, the concept of *dosa* is very similar to those people understood as *nātha* and *siddha* in medieval India. *Dosa* took hold in modern times, after the Joseon dynasty and its dominant Confucian social order had ended. Stories about *dosa* who chanted spells like '*surisurimasuri*' (*śrīśrīmahāśrī*) and performed Daoist magic were passed down orally across the countryside until the 1970s. There was a feeling of admiration toward *dosa* (*siddha*) and *sinseon* (신선, 神仙, *ṛṣi*), which is corroborated by the fact that the *seonmudo* (선무도, 禪武道) of Buddhism were popular among college students in the 1970s. Methods of practice such as *kukseondo* (국선도, 國仙道) and *danhak* (단학, 丹學) gained tremendous popularity in the 1980s, and books on the topic were bestsellers. The reverence for practitioners also extends to the places where *dosas* stayed or practised, which are viewed as sacred. Gyeryongsan, a mountain in the central region of South Korea, is still perceived as a place where Confucian, Buddhist and Daoist adherents practise (to achieve spiritual enlightenment), a place to meditate or a place where *dosas* reside.

## Buddhism in Korea

Buddhism was formally introduced to Korea during the Three Kingdoms period (372 CE in Goguryeo; 384 CE in Baekje; and formally recognised in 527 CE in the Shilla kingdom, after the martyrdom of Ichadon). Yogācāra and Madhyamaka are the significant transmissions to Korean Buddhism. In Korea, Woncheuk (원측, 圓測, 613–696) developed Yogācāra in a new way through books such as the *Commentary of Samdhinirmocanasūtra* (解深密經疏). Wonhyo (원효, 元曉, 617–686), who represents Korean Buddhism, embraced pan-Buddhist philosophies and practices including Hue-yen, T'ien-tai and Pure Land philosophies. He systematised the *ilche-yusim* (일체유심, 一切唯心, everything depends on the mind) philosophy during the Unified Shilla dynasty (seventh to tenth centuries). During the Goryeo dynasty (고려, 高麗, 918–1392), Buddhism was declared the state religion, which served as a catalyst for it to be developed across Korea. Jinul (지눌, 知訥, 1158–1210), the National Preceptor (보조국사, 普照國師), contributed to the establishment of Seonjong (선종, 禪宗, *dhyāna* school) (Buswell 1983). He elaborated on the practice of mind cultivation, called *sushim* (수심, 修心), and gave teachings on methods such as *ganhwaseon* (간화선, 看話禪, word contemplation meditation) and practices such as *dono* (돈오, 頓悟, sudden enlightenment) and *jeomsu* (점수, 漸修, gradual cultivation).

Although Buddhism was regarded as the state religion during the Goryeo dynasty (918–1392), its viability was seriously challenged when Confucianism was declared the state religion in the Joseon period (1392–1910). The Joseon dynasty placed restrictions on Buddhist properties, and Buddhist monks were expelled from the capital to the mountains. Although there were a few kings, such as Sejong and Sejo, who favoured Buddhism, it was generally persecuted. Despite this, Buddhist beliefs remained strong among the mass population, particularly among women (Nahm 1996: 108–109).

When Korea was invaded by the Japanese between 1592 and 1598, the Buddhist Master Seosan (西山), Hyujeong (休靜) and other Buddhist monks organised warrior monks to defend against the Japanese, based on the spirit of bodhisattva and the desire to improve the status of Buddhism. Hyujeong is considered the central figure in the revival of Buddhism during the Joseon dynasty, and his followers maintained Buddhist thought and practice until the end of nineteenth century. When the Joseon dynasty was unstable during the late nineteenth and early twentieth centuries, it was forced to open the country, beginning with the Treaty of Kanghwa Island (*Ganghwado-joyak*) with Japan in 1876, the United States in 1882 and with other European nations shortly afterwards. The Joseon dynasty collapsed after Japan's victory over Russia in 1904/5 and the entire country was annexed to Japan in 1910 and was colonised and controlled by the Japanese Governor-General until 1945 (Park 1996: 1–2). During this period, Buddhist leaders tried to modernise Buddhism. Buddhism owes its prolificacy in Korea in part to the continuity and resonance of its teachings, but also to its willingness to adopt traditional myths, legends, shamanist beliefs and folk religions. This fusion can be seen at Buddhist temples where shrines have been built to commemorate the Mountain Spirit, the Three Gods and other local deities.

Today, there are several modern revival Buddhist orders in Korea, including Jogye, Taego, Cheontae and others that inherited the Mahāyāna Buddhist traditions. The Jogye Order (조계종, 曹溪宗) that represents Korean Buddhism is Seonjong (Dhyana school), which focuses on *ganhwaseon* for contemplation meditation. *Ganhwaseon* is the most ancient practising tradition in Korea, but it is generally for Buddhist monks. A master and his disciples exchange questions and answers, and publicly recognised topics (*Gongan*, 공안, 公案) are used as points of meditation (*hwadu*, 화두, 話頭) to search for the wisdom of enlightenment. In general, Korean Buddhist monks cut themselves off from the outside world and train their minds through meditation. They gather in a meditation room (선방, 禪房) designated by each order during a three-month summer meditation retreat (하안거, 夏安居) and a winter meditation retreat (동안거, 冬安居). For example, during the winter meditation retreat in 2018, a total of 2,032 monks gathered at ninety-four meditation temples. Buddhist monks were highly respected during the Three Kingdoms period and the Goryeo dynasty, and many sons of the ruling class became Buddhist monks and influential spiritual leaders in Korean society. However, when Buddhism was supressed during the Joseon dynasty, few became Buddhist monks and nuns and their social status was one of the Eight Socially Degraded Groups (*Pal Ban*). Nowadays, Buddhist monks and nuns are generally revered, and the temples provide meditation programmes for Koreans and foreigners, who can easily join meditation retreats.

## Won Buddhism as a new religion in Korea

Won Buddhism (원불교, 圓佛敎) has been one of the most successful new religious movements in Korea (Cozin 1987: 171). It was established by Jungbin Pak (박중빈 朴重彬, 1891–1943, aka Sotaesan) as a new religious movement in 1916. The relationship between Buddhism and Won Buddhism is a complex one. While Won Buddhism clearly finds resonance in Buddhism, it is also careful to differentiate itself from traditional Korean Buddhism. Sotaesan's main purpose in the reformation of Buddhism was to apply Buddhism to the contemporary secular world. He proposed (1) to open up Buddhism from the few to the majority; (2) to reform the monastic system to make Buddhism accessible for monks and lay devotees; and (3) to eradicate gender discrimination in Buddhism.

Won Buddhism maintains a visible presence in the modern Korean religious landscape (Baker 2008: 128). Sotaesan believed that one way to find the path to salvation and to realise paradise in the mind (심낙원, 心樂園) is to find the Buddha-nature within the inner world of each individual and to reveal it (Park 1997: 22–34). Sotaesan approached deliverance from a social perspective. He sought to lead those who suffer into the paradise of the *Great Opening of Subsequent Heaven* (*hucheon-gaebyok*, 후천개벽, 後天開闢). He foretold the coming of 'a truly civilised world' where moral philosophy and science are advanced together, and individuals, families, societies and nations open their boundaries and are 'interfused' with one another. The *Threefold Study* in Won Buddhism comprises three methods for 'completing' an individual's personality. It places great importance on the following practices: cultivating the spirit (정신수양, 精神修養), enquiry into human affairs and universal principles (사리연구, 事理硏究) and choice in action (작업취사, 作業取捨). Cultivating the spirit can be achieved through reciting the Buddha's name (念佛) and seated meditation (좌선, 坐禪). Enquiry into human affairs and universal principles (사리연구, 事理硏究) can be attained through scriptures (경전, 經典), lecturing (강연, 講演), conversation (회화, 會話), cases for questioning (의두, 疑頭), and the principle of nature (성리, 性理). Choice in action can be carried out using methods such as keeping a daily diary (상시일기, 常時日記), heedfulness (주의, 注意) and attention to deportment (조행, 操行) (Park 2007; Won Buddhism 2016).

In general, the reformative focus in Won Buddhism is evident in its practices, which is where it most differs from traditional Buddhism. The iconography of traditional Buddhism – such as statues of buddhas and bodhisattvas – is replaced with the simple form of a circle, a symbol called *Irwon-sang*. Won Buddhism's clerical system differs from traditional Korean Buddhism as well. Won Buddhism rejects the age-based hierarchy of Buddhist clergy; while a hierarchical structure of leadership is maintained, it is based on spiritual achievement and leadership ability. Won Buddhism also rejects gender discrimination between nuns and monks. Whereas nuns in traditional Buddhism have a greater number of vows and seem to be subject to a 'glass ceiling' when it comes to leadership roles, priests and nuns in Won Buddhism are perceived as equals and are required to keep the same number of vows (Park 1997: 240–276). Furthermore, as Cozin comments, Won Buddhist nuns have advanced to esteemed positions, and in fact outnumber priests (Cozin 1987: 171). Won Buddhism is also actively involved in the social and educational spheres and is widespread in Korea.

## Yoga in Korea

Although yoga has flourished in Korea in the twenty-first century, it is not a recent phenomenon. Yoga techniques based on *āsana*, *prāṇāyāma* and *mudrā* were established in the 1980s and 1990s, when the yogi in the Korean public imagination was not so much an 'asana practitioner' as a 'breathing practitioner' or a 'meditation practitioner'. Yoga techniques that came into the spotlight around 2000 were mostly centred on postures, but it is the professional structures of transnational globalised forms of yoga which particularly contribute to their popularity in contemporary Korean culture. Popular Korean breathing techniques concentrate on the lower abdomen, such as such as *bosikhohup* (복식호흡, 複式呼吸, abdominal breathing) and *danjeonhohup* (단전호흡, 丹田呼吸, hypogastric breathing). Using *bosikhohup*, the abdomen rises when inhaling, and the stomach becomes flat when exhaling. Using *danjeonhohup*, the lower abdomen (around five centimetres below the belly button) rises when inhaling, and the stomach is further lowered when exhaling. It is deemed important to pull air (*apānavāyu*) upward, but this is believed to cause side effects called '*sanggi-byeong*' (상기병, 上氣病), the abnormal rising of *qi* (氣), the vital energy. For this reason, Korean techniques mostly focused on concentrating energy in the lower abdomen. However, some breathing practices appear to have been influenced by yogic techniques, such as *ūrdhvaretas*: vital air (*prāṇa*) is concentrated on the lower abdomen and is pulled upward through the spine to fill the crown of the head. In the 1980s, *haṭhayoga* techniques such as *jalaṃdhara*, *mūlabandha* and *uḍḍīyanabandha* were also widely adopted. As new light was shed on Korea's traditional breath-based practices, books related to *danjeonhohup* (hypogastric breathing) entered the bestseller lists. During this period, publications by modern Indian philosophers such as Krishnamurti, Ramakrishna and Maharishi also became commercially popular. These books contributed to the boom in Koreans travelling to India in the 1990s and to the increased popularity of yoga in the 2000s. From the 1990s onwards, Vipassana, a Theravada meditation technique used in Myanmar and Thailand, also took hold in Korea. Vipassana was first introduced by graduates who majored in Theravada Buddhism at university and who then had short-term monastic training. They offered programmes that, although small-scale, eventually yielded high numbers of practitioners.

There is debate about when yoga was first introduced to Korea. Some say that yoga was introduced by the Beobsang School (법상종, 法相宗) in the Unified Shilla dynasty (seventh to tenth centuries), a Buddhist state; others argue that interest in yoga occurred spontaneously in the early twentieth century as Koreans became exposed to foreign literature. In a narrow sense, yoga appears to have been introduced in the 1950s, and the first yoga centre was opened in Seoul in 1955. There were several pioneers and associations, and Taehyuk Jeong (1922–2015) in particular contributed greatly to the popularisation of yoga and was highly influential in the field (Sim 2015: 18–21). Jeong undertook Buddhist studies and indology in Japan between 1961 and 1966. During that time he exchanged ideas with Masahiro Oki (J. 沖正弘) and Sahoda Tsuruji (J. 佐保田鶴治), and seemed to have taken the opportunity to learn about yoga. Furthermore, his studies were likely influenced by publications from Indra Devi and Sivananda. After returning from abroad, Jeong published multiple translations and books, and operated a yoga centre in Seoul (Sim 2015: 27–30). He also worked as a professor in the Department of Indian Philosophy at Dongguk University, mentoring students who majored in *sāṃkhya* and *pātañjalayoga*.

The tradition of yoga introduced by Jeong was further developed by one of his disciples: Taeyoung Lee promoted hatha yoga focused on asana, pranayama and *mudrā*. Until the 1980s, most organisations had taught *ṣaṭkarma* and asana only. Lee developed a yoga programme composed of fifty minutes for asana, five minutes each for *kapalabhāti* and *nāḍīśodhana* and 30 minutes for *bhastrikakumbhaka. Bhastrikakumbhaka* is a practice of doing *mūla, jalandhara* and *uḍḍīyāna* simultaneously in the *siddhāsana* posture (Lee 2004: 115–160). The organisation, led by Lee, expanded this programme to about thirty branches across the county by 2010. However, it seems to be less popular at the present time as a variety of posture-centred yoga practices have come into vogue. The yoga programme developed by Lee is relatively faithful to the *Haṭhapradīpikā* of Svātmārāma.

At the time of writing, there were at least ten large-scale nationwide yoga federations in Korea, and they pursue various types of yoga, such as therapy yoga, Hatha Yoga and hot yoga. Federations that preside over at least 100 training centres include the Korea Yoga Federation, the Korea Yoga Association, the Daehan (Korea) Yoga Association, the Korea Therapy Yoga Association, the Korea Yoga Masters Association and the Korea Yoga Instructor Association. There are other small-scale organisations that have propagated their own yoga practices, such as Yogakorea, the Korea Dhammayoga Association and the Korean Branch of the Association of Himalayan Yoga Meditation Societies International. Aside from these, yoga programmes are provided in after-school classes in elementary schools in Korea, and 'yoga classes for citizens' operate in almost every community centre and city hall cultural centre. The discussion of 'yoga' here is directly related to Indian traditional thought and practices of yoga meditation. One also finds the term 'Dhan Yoga' in Europe and the United States, which, although originating from Korea, is not really 'yoga' but rather a syncretic adoption of traditional Korean Daoist practice. The term 'Dhan Yoga' is generally not used in Korea and is not considered to be traditional yoga.

Common issues shared by national yoga organisations include establishing a system of state-certified yoga instructors and offering yoga classes as a regular subject in elementary, middle and high schools. Resolving such issues is essential for the development and future of yoga in Korea, but – considering that the philosophy and practice principles of yoga have yet to be firmly founded – the horizontal integration of these organisations in society will take some time. In addition, there is no standard to integrate the various modified techniques of modern yoga. Recently, however, a body of literature on *haṭhayoga* has been translated, and related studies have been conducted, which requires further academic discussion. Yoga in Korea is generally commercial and secular. Of course, health and therapy are important, but there are only a few organisations that adhere to the main goal of traditional yoga practice: *mokṣa* (liberation). Most organisations only emphasise on 'secular prosperity', which could be attributed to a lack of study and discussion of historical *haṭhayoga* in Korean.

## Current status of academic study of yoga in Korea

At the time of writing, there were a total of seven colleges and graduate schools in Korea that opened yoga departments or courses to train yoga specialists. One of them is the Department of Indian Philosophy at Dongguk University. The department has designed its curriculum to focus on reading Sanskrit texts. It has produced graduates who majored in the six ('orthodox') systems in Indian philosophy (*ṣaḍdarśana*) – including *vedānta*, *nyāya* and *yoga* – and Indian Buddhism and Tibetan Buddhism such as Abhidharma, Madhyamaka and Yogācāra. When Jeong translated the *Yogasūtrabhāṣyā* of Vyāsa into Korean in 2010, the influence of the department increased. The department has also produced PhD graduates in Śaivism and Tantrism, although its overall focus has been on *pātañjalayoga* and not on *haṭhayoga*. In 2000, when yoga in Korea was becoming widespread, Wonkwang University opened its Department of Yoga under the Graduate School of Asian Studies in order to research yoga and to educate practitioners. The department has produced a large number of graduates from its master's degree programme within a short period of time, and some graduates have pursued doctoral research. In its early years the curriculum focused on ayurveda and related studies based on classical Indian philosophy, but recently the department has added Sanskrit classes and produced researchers and translators who can read original texts in Sanskrit. Other graduate schools that provide courses related to yoga include the Department of Mind-body Healing at Seoul University of Buddhism; the Department of Naturopathy at Dongbang Culture University; and the Department of Naturopathy at Sunmoon University. For undergraduates, the Department of Yoga Meditation at Wonkwang Digital University and the Department of Yoga at Choonhae College of Health Science offer courses related to yoga. The number of master's and doctoral degree theses that were attained before the year 2000 did not exceed thirty, and they were mostly studies on religion related to *pātañjalayoga* and mysticism (Kwak 2018: 125–128). Since 2000, graduate theses have branched out into areas including physical education, social science and natural science. However, the share of philosophical and philological graduates has been low, and among doctoral degree theses this discrepancy has been even more pronounced. Remarkably, the number of doctoral theses on original yoga texts has decreased over this same period.

Academic research on yoga dates back to 1986 when the Korean Society for Yoga Studies was first established. Back then, however, the organisation was more of a social community of yoga instructors and specialists of texts such as *pātañjalayoga*, *Bhagavadgītā* and Vedic Upaniṣads. Except for a few lectures, other academic activities were barely organised. In the 2000s, however, as yoga's popularity rapidly grew, the number of those who majored in yoga in graduate schools also increased, which created a need for specialist journals. In 2006, the Korean Society for Yoga Studies declared the re-foundation of the society, and held various symposiums, facilitating a forum for academic discussion on yoga. As a result, the first issue of the *Journal of Yoga Studies* was published in 2011, and twenty issues have now been published (as of October 2018). As this journal was ranked high in the evaluation of journals based on the citation index, which was performed by the National Research Foundation of Korea (NRF) under the Ministry of Education, its status was raised to 'an approved journal'. Aside from the *Journal of Yoga Studies*, essays on yoga have been published in other approved journals on liberal arts, sociology, medicine, etc. The following table shows the number of papers that were published from 2011 to 2017 (Kwak 2018: 125–128):

As the statistics in Table 22.1 show, yoga has been researched in various fields, but many of these studies were in yoga studies itself – or rather, they were conducted in physical education or other related areas. Limited numbers of papers on yoga philosophy have been published in the *Korean Journal of Indian Philosophy*, the *Critical Review for Buddhist Studies*, the *Journal of Yoga Studies*, the *Journal of Indian Studies* and the *Journal of Buddhist Studies*. Studies on *haṭhayoga* are now at an early stage in Korea, and as yet there are only a few philological research projects.

In recent years academic interest in yoga has sharply increased. Numerous yoga practitioners and instructors have been to graduate school to investigate the philosophical or textual origins of their practice, with a primary interest in *pātañjalayoga*. In 2015, however, the publication of '*An Annotated Translation of Haṭhapradīpika-based on Brahmānanda's Jyotsnā*' – translated with the support of the Korea Research Foundation – shifted the attention of graduate students from *pātañjalayoga* to historical literature on *haṭhayoga*. Accordingly, the most immediate challenge for Korean academia today is to translate, research and introduce more published research on *haṭhayoga*. Still, it is encouraging to see that the Korean Society for Yoga Studies has strengthened its support for translating Sanskrit texts into Korean, and that Wonkwang University has led efforts to fill gaps through academic exchanges with the Haṭha Yoga Project (SOAS University of London). At the time of writing, a total of eight books on *haṭhayoga* are being translated

*Table 22.1* Academic papers on yoga published in Korean (2011–2017)

| *No. of published papers by area (2011–2017)* | | | | | | | |
|---|---|---|---|---|---|---|---|
| | *2011* | *2012* | *2013* | *2014* | *2015* | *2016* | *2017* |
| Physical education | 13 | 12 | 15 | 15 | 23 | 9 | 4 |
| Dance | 5 | 3 | 0 | 3 | 4 | 2 | 0 |
| Philosophy | 1 | 6 | 9 | 2 | 10 | 11 | 6 |
| Other liberal arts | 0 | 2 | 2 | 0 | 3 | 1 | 2 |
| Social science | 3 | 5 | 5 | 3 | 3 | 3 | 1 |
| Medicinal science, pharmacy | 2 | 3 | 1 | 1 | 0 | 1 | 0 |
| Combined | 1 | 1 | 2 | 4 | 3 | 2 | 3 |
| Natural science | 1 | 0 | 2 | 0 | 1 | 0 | 1 |
| Others | 3 | 1 | 0 | 2 | 1 | 0 | 0 |
| Total | 29 | 33 | 36 | 30 | 48 | 29 | 17 |

Note: This chart is a revised version of material found in Kwak 2018: 125–128.

into Korean, supported by individuals, yoga associations or yoga federations: (1) *Gorakṣaśataka*; (2) *Amaraughaprabodha*; (3) *Yogaśāstra of Dattātreya*; (4) *Haṭharatnāvalī*; (5) *Yogayājñavalkya*; (6) *Śārṅgadharapaddhati* (part thereof); (7) *Kumbhakapaddhati*; and (8) *Jyotsnā of Brahmānanda*. These are scheduled to be published from 2020. In addition, there are critical editions and Korean translations of the *Yogabīja* and *Siddhasiddhāntapaddhati* in progress. Furthermore, Sanskrit classes are slowly growing in number, as is the publication of Sanskrit grammar books for non-academic audiences who want to read primary sources in Sanskrit. Recently, a number of scholars of Buddhism have been translating the Pali Buddhist scriptures. Indeed, many Buddhist and yoga practitioners are publishing general or popular books on the practice of meditation and yoga. However, only a few professional scholars in yoga studies are involved in the translation of the classical yoga literature. Academic networks for researchers of yoga and meditation thus need to be expanded globally to promote joint studies between researchers at home and abroad, and to facilitate further academic developments.

## Bibliography

Baker, D. 2008. *Korean Spirituality*. Honolulu: University of Hawai'i Press.

Buswell, R. E. Jr. 1983. *The Korean Approach to Zen: The Collected Works of Chinul*. Honolulu: University of Hawaii Press.

Chan, W. (trans) 1963. *A Source Book in Chinese Philosophy*. Princeton: Princeton University Press.

Cozin, M. 1987. 'Won Buddhism: The Origin and Growth of New Korean Religion', in Kendell, L. and Dix, G. (eds), *Religion and Ritual in Korean Society* 171–184. Berkeley, CA, USA: University of California Press.

Kalton, M. C. 1988 (trans. and ed., with commentaries). *To Become A Sage: The Ten Diagrams on Sage Learning by Yi T'oegye*. New York: Columbia University Press.

Kwak, M. 2018. 'A Study on the Domestic Recent Research Trends in Related to Yoga' (국내 요가관련 분야의 최신 연구동향). *Journal of Yoga Studies* (요가학연구) 20: 113–145.

Lee, S. (trans). 2005. *Commentary of Heshang Gong on the Tao Te Ching* (老子道德經河上公章句). Seoul: Somyong.

Lee, T. 2004. *Kundaliniyoga* (쿤달리니요가). Seoul: Yeorae.

Nahm, A. C. 1996. *A History of The Korean People*. Elizabeth, NJ, USA: Hollym.

Park, E. 1996 *Zhou Lianxi-ui Taegukron-e Gwanhan Yeon'gu* (*Study on Zhou Lianxi's Theory of the Supreme Ultimate*). SungKyunKwan University. PhD dissertation.

Park, J. 2007. 'The Won Buddhist Practice of the Buddha-Nature', in Buswell, R. E. Jr. (ed), *Religions of Korea in Practice*, 476–486. Princeton, NJ, USA: Princeton University Press.

Park, K. 1997. *The Won-Buddhism (Wonbulgyo) of Sotaesan: A Twentieth-Century Religious Movement in Korea*. San Francisco; London; Bethesda: International Scholars Press.

Sim, J. 2015 'The Identity and Origin of Korean Yoga' (한국요가의 기원과 정체성 검토). *Journal of Yoga Studies* (요가학연구) 14: 9–37.

Won Buddhism. 2016. *The Scriptures of Won-Buddhism* in *the Doctrinal Books of Won-Buddhism*, Iksan: Wonkwang Pub.

Yi, I. 2007. *The Complete Works of Yulgok* (율곡전서 栗谷全書) (Korean translated version), Vol. 6. Seongnam, South Korea: The Academy of Korean Studies.

Zhu Xi, 2010. *Commentaries on Great Learning and Doctrine of the Mean*, Seong, B. (trans), Vol. 3. Seoul: Institute of Traditional Culture.

# 23

# YOGA IN LATIN AMERICA

## A critical overview

*Adrián Muñoz*

### Introduction

This chapter seeks to offer a comprehensive overview of the history and present state of important yogic trends in Latin America, including not only physical methods but also meditative approaches. It draws on the idea that yoga is a perfect example of a 'transnational flow of ideas about spirituality, health, and well-being' (Hauser 2013: 6). This flow evidently transcends linguistic worlds and frontiers and is itself subjected to cultural translation in particular regional and cultural worlds.

To begin with, it is worth noticing that the Hispanosphere comprises a vast cultural world, made up of more than twenty countries in Latin America, plus Puerto Rico, Spain, Equatorial Guinea and Western Sahara, all of which amounts to more than 500 million speakers. It would be virtually impossible to cover all of these regions in one general article. It would also be misleading to believe that there has been one single, uniform trajectory of yoga in this vast region. As in the case of France (Ceccomori 2001: 10), for example, there have been a number of pioneers who introduced yoga in Latin America, sometimes in almost complete isolation, sometimes within esoteric circles that were strong in specific regions. For this reason, this chapter will predominantly derive information from one exemplary case (the Mexican one), so as to shed light on what sort of agents and features have occurred in the history of yoga in this geo-cultural world. Nevertheless, the chapter will also try to offer a more general balance of the wide presence of yoga and some meditation groups in different Latin American locations. This overview does not attempt to cover cases of Spanish-speaking countries beyond the American continent.

There is one crucial process that we need to recognise so as to assess the history of yoga in the Latin American context. A major difference between the ways in which Asian or 'Oriental' cultures were incorporated in Europe or North America and in Latin America in general is concomitant with the existence or absence of a tradition of orientalist research (a topic I have no space to pursue in this chapter). Obviously, many of the contemporary schools and centres for yoga practice and teaching in Mexico and elsewhere are intimately tied to centres located primarily in the United States and, secondarily, in nations such as the United Kingdom. This is the case for many Ashtanga, Vinyasa and hatha-based yoga studios; this is also evidently the case of, for example, Bikram Yoga or Shadow Yoga.[1] Also, a constant flow of practitioners partakes of the so-called yoga tourism and pays systematic visits to India in order to continue their training or simply to 'be in touch' with spiritual India and the so-called original, pure yoga. The two most popular destinations by far are Mysore and Rishikesh.

## Understandings of 'yoga'

The term yoga implies a wide range of meanings, both in the present and in the past. We should bear in mind that yoga is understood and presented in different ways 'depending on the requirements of particular social or physical locations' (Newcombe 2018: 569). Thus, yoga can at the same time be deemed religious or secular, depending on specific contexts. By paying attention to its different expressions and the various ways in which practitioners resort to it worldwide, 'yoga' can denote a certain set of physical techniques oriented to improve wellbeing and health or a rigorous discipline of meditative methods directed toward spiritual growth and inner contentment. Also noteworthy is the fact that due to its wide polysemic possibilities, yoga can imply various things in different places, while at the same it can only mean specific things associated with a so-called 'true' or 'authentic' yoga (Newcombe 2018: 552, 563–567).

To a large extent, yoga in Latin America responds to a generalised image of hatha yoga, that is, a 'gentle, recreational, feminized, pacifist, and non-competitive practice [that] reflects discursive strands rather than any inherent and/or elemental features of yoga' (Hauser 2013: 5). This partly represents the 'ecumenical possibilities' of yoga that Gerald Larson has pointed out (in Alter 2004: 9). Joseph Alter further notes that technically yoga 'is not a religious system'; moreover, 'in a very important sense, Yoga is a step beyond religion in terms of soteriological conceptualization' (Alter 2004: 13). Also, some specialists observe that contrary to more 'traditional' understandings of yoga, modern yoga expressions entail public performance and demonstrations (Newcombe 2018: 556). All these approaches and understandings have been present in Latin America, but yoga has not always been a blunt copy of developments elsewhere. There have been interesting chapters and agents in the framing of yoga in this huge territory. They comprise a field to be studied more properly; in this chapter I will offer introductory vignettes to some of these issues

Here, as elsewhere, the role of Patañjali's *Yogasūtra* has been a bedrock for the yoga community at large. Although it is eminently a philosophical – and introspective – work, the yoga community has taken the *Yogasūtra* to be a foundational text for contemporary hatha yoga too, a more physical form of yoga and rather less inquisitive in nature. In part, the misperception derives from Swami Vivekananda's stance on both *haṭhayoga* and what he termed *rājayoga* in the late nineteenth and early twentieth centuries, an issue that has been discussed by some scholars (e.g. De Michelis 2005; Alter 2004; Singleton 2010). Even though the *Haṭhapradīpikā* and the *Gheraṇḍasaṃhitā* are sometimes also invoked and read, they lack the authorial status of Patañjali's work in most Latin American yoga centres. Alongside Vivekananda's Neo-Vedanta philosophy, the Theosophists provided a strong interpretive framework for yoga in French language sources. In the early twentieth century, France still was a major cultural influence in the Mexican intelligentsia. Therefore, it is unsurprising that many cultural and intellectual items (including yoga and Indian ideas) entered the culture from French sources. No doubt, here methodologies from global history can prove very useful to probe into this sort of cultural transference across regions.

It is also worth noting that – almost since its inception in countries such as Mexico, Brazil or Venezuela – yoga has been paired with meditation and spiritual yearnings. For this reason, it has not been uncommon to encounter offers of yoga and Buddhist meditations in the same contexts. Indeed, the general public (those not practising) would identify Buddhism mainly with meditation and would not so easily discern a difference between meditation and yoga.

But even among sympathisers, to practise yoga would inherently imply a form of meditation; within the postural variants, then, yoga would be understood as a sort of *motional meditation*, so to speak. Different forms of mediation became increasingly popular in the region after the so-called Buddhist boom that took place in the United States from the 1960s onwards. The Vipassana methods became available in a number of large cities, sometimes also establishing ad hoc places for retreat outside of the cities. An example of this phenomenon extending into Latin America is the Dhamma Vihara, a Theravada monastery located within a forest in Veracruz State on the southeast Mexican coast. Established in 1999, the Dhamma Vihara was led by Burmese monk U Silananda until his death and is now run by Bhikku Nandisena, a former Argentinian ordained by U Silananda in the United States in 1991. The Vihara offers general courses on Buddhist tenets, as well as retreats – for either individuals or groups of people – destined to enhance meditation.

Yoga has been variously understood in Latin America as a philosophy, a belief, a practice, a religious path and a health-improving technique (Muñoz 2018). In a preliminary, cursory survey that I launched in January 2019, respondents had to answer this question, among others: *In a few words, how would you describe 'yoga'?* Out of sixty-nine answers, I highlight the following ones:

- 'A complete method, with multiple variants, intended to achieve mental stability and based on a philosophical system.'
- 'Yoga is both integral health and a lifestyle.'
- 'Practice entails union with oneself, [and] our immediate environment at different levels – physical, energetic, mental, empathic, and including the spiritual.'
- 'Pretzel-shaped union.'
- 'It is a tool for life; it helps raise awareness of physical, emotional, and sometimes also psychological conditions.'
- 'One gram of practice is worth more than tons of theory.'
- 'An ancestral discipline that, by means of psycho-physical techniques and self-enquiry methods, leads us to self-realisation.'
- 'I would describe it as a meditative tradition. I would highlight that it aids the realisation of the human being.'
- 'Yoga is the art of uniting mind, body, and emotions by means of breath, movement, and meditation. It is not just about subjecting the body to postures. It's about the body being able to find a way to feel good.'
- 'It is a state of health and balance.'
- 'Education of peace, resilience, love.'
- 'It is a method for human and transpersonal development.'

Respondents belong to nine different Latin American nationalities. Physical practices, inner and mental welfare and the notion of union are central in most of the answers. They also summon ideas of transcendent improvement and efficient ways to deal with anxiety, stress and grief. Indeed, many sympathisers would claim that yoga comprises a refined set of techniques for the betterment of the individual, through both perfection of physical movements and the improvement of health. Thus, it is very common to find venues and gyms that offer sessions of physical fitness systems as well as some style of yoga. It is not surprising, then, that there is an increasing offer of 'restorative yoga' and yoga for pregnant women. More often than not, therefore, adherence to one of the various yoga forms entails the adoption of a healthy, nonviolent diet and the alleged cultivation of ethical behaviour: lifestyle and ethical choices are closely associated with an 'ideal' yoga practitioner.

Not wholly separated from this, yoga also summons ideas of mind-calming methods and the procurement of inner wellbeing. Usually this yoga mentality draws near some sort of religious self-identification, mainly Hindu-oriented, but there are important Buddhist- and Sikh-related positions too (Kundalini Yoga, for example). This greatly depends on the actual practitioner or studio that 'teaches' yoga, and on what type of yoga it is. Hence, it is common to find workspaces where yoga is advertised along with meditation, mindfulness and even Kabbalah. For this reason, notions such as 'spirituality', 'transcendental', 'purity' and the like are usually invoked in yogic circles. This presumed religiosity is of a very peculiar nature, for it can constantly negotiate with secular demands from the modern, urban world, the setting where most yoga centres are located in Latin America.

A very significant contribution in the general and early understanding of yoga in the region was Yogananda's *Autobiography of a Yogi* (1960). This book has circulated widely in Latin America; one of the first translations into Spanish dates from 1951, about five years after the original publication in English. Apart from Yogananda's own words, it is also important to pay attention to the phrasings of the translator, as most readers will receive both discourses while reading the volume. In the very first chapter, footnote 2 explains a yogi as 'Someone who practices yoga (union), ancient Indian science about meditation on God' (Yogananda 1960: 19).[2] There are three key elements in Yogananda's gloss: (1) It conceived yoga as a 'science', something that is somehow on a par with Theosophical and Spiritualist attempts to reshape and explain their own methods to the modern audience; (2) Yoga is meditation, that is to say that it does not involve physical work; (3) The meditative process has God as a goal, which is a comfortable tactic to make the Christian public accept this yogic message.

One could object that these are the translator's words and not Yogananda's, but Cuarón's translation was authorised by the Self-Realization Fellowship (SRF). Likewise, Kriya Yoga is explained as a 'yogic technique by means of which sensory turmoil is silenced, granting man a greater and enhanced sense of identification with cosmic consciousness' (Yogananda 1960: 24). This is in consonance with the guru's own exposition, which comes in chapter 26, where Yogananda also conceives of Kriya Yoga as a science, one that enables the yogi to get rid of *karma*, the law of causation (Yogananda 1960: 209). The 'scientific method', so to speak, is expounded as a pyscho-physiological technique that decarbonises the blood and draws in an input of fresh oxygen. This process brings rejuvenation, purification and awareness. According to Yogananda, the god Krishna, the poet Kabir, Jesus Christ, the prophet Elijah and apostles John and Paul all mastered and transmitted this technique (Yogananda 1960: 209–10). SRF sympathisers would embrace such understandings of yoga.

Regardless of the yoga trend they adhere to, practitioners usually style themselves as 'yogis', especially those engaged in postural forms. More often than not, these so-called (postural) yogis have not received any initiation from a guru, much less undertaken vows of renunciation.[3] A significant identity-formation process takes place here, and it should be adequately scrutinised. Some basic notions to take into account are: (1) modern yogis in Latin America are urban-based; (2) they may or may not formally belong to a religious path or affiliation; (3) they all still participate in social interaction *as* social individuals (i.e. they are not *sādhus* or renunciates); (4) most of them observe dietary customs, such as vegetarianism; and (5) they sponsor, at least nominally, the tenets of nonviolence towards both human beings and animals. The aforementioned traits make it possible that, despite being instructors and not religious mendicants, leaders or sages, they can still see themselves as yogis. In other words: by performing a physical practice (usually that of asana) and upholding some ethical tenets, they locate themselves within a discipline or path of yoga. Also, more often than not, sympathisers with some form of yoga do not consider the study of yogic scriptures, Hindu lore or Sanskrit language a necessary requirement for success.

Out of idealistic notions, modern yogis in Latin America imagine themselves in an idyllic scenario that summons the mysterious halo and beatitude of India. This mysteriousness is fuelled in part by an inherited orientalist imagery (Asia as a fountain of ancient wisdom), itself nourished by Christian ideas of spatial sacrality. This does account for a sense of wellness. And, interestingly enough, this sense is a fascinating enactment of religious feeling within a secular space, as most urban places and cities in the contemporary world pretend to be secular, non-confessional and progressive. Curiously, this liberality leads to an open-mindedness that allows for accommodation of religious imagery and ideas in both the public and private metropolitan spheres.

Evidently, the centres and studios of postural yoga cannot be deemed equivalent to churches or temples. Yet, there is an internal dynamic that recalls how some religious congregations work, especially due to the pious, spiritual aura that permeates such spaces. Notice that most Iyengar and Ashtanga Vinyasa yoga sessions habitually begin with the recitation of the salutatory stanzas to Patañjali. This is done in an entirely devout way, an atmosphere that is enhanced because the stanzas are composed in the Sanskrit language. The bulk of the practitioners have no knowledge of Sanskrit utterances, so the recitation of an alien, 'enchanted' language adds to the numinous environment; it consecrates the space, so to speak, before the actual physical practice begins. An enchanted aura is not present in all yoga spaces, of course; the contemporary world accommodates the religious and the secular without necessarily ruling out the 'spiritual'. As elsewhere, in Latin America there are different, apparently opposing views, especially within urban spaces. Yet, as Suzanne Newcombe argues, these views are in constant interplay. Drawing from the spatial analysis developed by Kim Knott, she concludes that

> although some positions, or actors, in yoga may present themselves as antagonistic to other actors, close analysis can show that both positions are created through relationship with the other, and many positions also depend on relationships which are much less antagonistic.
>
> (*Newcombe 2018: 562*)

## Forerunners and diffusors

In the case of Mexico, there are four significant moments in the early phases of yoga reception: (1) 1887–1913, when Francisco I. Madero made recurrent – if oblique – references to Indian philosophy; (2) 1900, when the infamous Aleister Crowley visited Mexico and became immersed in yoga; (3) 1920–1945, when, just after the end of the Mexican Revolution, José Vasconcelos became a major agent in modernisation and education campaigns nationwide; and (4) 1929, when Paramahamsa Yogananda visited Mexico for a few months. These moments are by no means the most influential ones, or the only ones; nor do they necessarily suggest a chronological development, but they are noteworthy and illustrative of key processes at the turn of the century.

In this brief outline it is possible to pay heed to the influence of two political and intellectual Mexican figures, on the one hand, and two sporadic, unrelated episodes of two prominent foreign figures visiting the country, on the other. Each of these four cases bears distinct features, but it is significant that they more or less coincided in time. The reasons why that happened were probably a response to issues of global networks through which cultural and ideological artefacts travelled far and wide. Other actors were also active at more or less the same time in other places of the continent. There was no single channel for the transmission of ideas or practices, but rather a multifaceted network from the very onset. There are two paradigmatic cases, but these are by no means unique. De la Ferrière, discussed below, is one. A second case is Krishnamacharya's disciple Indra Devi, who there is no room to discuss here. After long periods in Russia and the United States, she eventually moved to Latin America: first to Mexico in 1961, and finally settling in Argentina, where she died in 2002. She inaugurated a strong tradition of yoga practice which continues to this day (Goldberg 2015).

The first case alluded to in the beginning of this section is an unforeseen episode in the introduction of Indian ideas to Mexican soil. Francisco I. Madero (1873–1913) was a defender of democracy and, therefore, a key promoter of the Mexican Revolution.[4] Madero's political career was centred on social justice and democratic values, and he is justly remembered as one of the chief architects of anti-reelectionist politics in Mexico. Madero opposed the regime of Porfirio Díaz, who ruled over a period of thirty-one years, from 1876 to 1880 and from 1884 to 1911. Díaz was understandably viewed by some liberals as a dictator that had to be deposed. Madero played a major role in this mission, and this, in turn, ignited the Revolution. To this day, Madero is considered one of the most relevant political figures in Mexican history and is still invoked by some politicians as an example of virtue and honesty. Yet, Madero has also caused amazement and discomfort among some scholars due to his sympathies with Spiritualism. After a long stay in France in the 1880s, he became an ardent follower of Allan Kardec's ideas and began to practise Spiritualism.

It is interesting to note that Madero's political career was not divorced from his spiritualist leanings; on the contrary, he usually derived decisiveness from his conversations with spirits and from his readings of the *Bhagavadgītā*. In fact, he even authored a commentary on the Hindu text. The edition of the *Gītā* that Madero used was printed in Barcelona in 1896, a translation into Spanish done by Theosophist Roviralta Borrell. Yet, Madero's sympathy for Indian ideas was not limited to the *Gītā*; he referred time and again to Indian philosophy and ethics. In his *Spiritualist Handbook* (1910), for example, he claims that the theories of Spiritualism have been proved by the 'philosophies from Hindustan' as well as by astronomers. Madero's apparent eclecticism was, during this period, a fairly common attempt to understand the edges of human knowledge and advancement, e.g. identifying and negotiating between the belief in spirits and reliance on matter, between 'Eastern' philosophies and Christian values, between religious feelings and trust on scientific advancements, and between occultism and human improvement. In other words, neither the scientist nor the occultist 'believe[d] in miracles but in natural laws, yet expand[ed] the scope of the latter, for there are hidden laws liable to be uncovered by imaginative reason' (Chaves 2008: 110). Some thirty-five years earlier, in 1875, Madame Blavatsky had founded the Theosophical Society, one of the most notorious enterprises in this line. Although not in accord with Theosophical tenets, Spiritualism somehow partook of similar trends, as also did some other organisations and groups. In the case of Madero, human improvement implied ethical conduct, and this in turn conveyed correct political action.

In this sense, some prominent characters from magic and occultist milieus moved widely, not only travelling from Europe and/or the United States (the 'West') to Asian countries, but also to some destinations in Latin America (both cultural regions shaping an ambiguous epistemological 'East'). Thus, in 1900 the infamous magician Aleister Crowley went to Mexico, a visit he recorded in his autobiographical writings. Tellingly, he compares the strength and beauty of the Mexican landscape to some places in India. Also noteworthy is the fact that it was precisely while in Mexico that Crowley took an earnest interest in yoga through acquaintance with Oskar Eckenstein, a fellow mountaineer with whom Crowley was to travel and climb some Mexican peaks. It appears that because of this episode, he decided to go to Ceylon between 1901 and 1902 in order to further enhance his knowledge of yoga, as well as different aspects of both Hinduism and Buddhism (Urban 2006: 116).

Information is very scanty, and it is not at all clear whether Crowley or Eckenstein had any followers or sympathisers who may have kept up a yogic practice in Mexico. However, Crowley projected his yogic practice at the time onto what was for him an idyllic, enchanted setting. In other words it was both a romantic and an orientalist experience, exoticising both an Indian methodology and a Latin American territory, permeated with pre-Hispanic culture.

Crowley's visit has to be read along Madame Blavatsky's, who allegedly also visited Mexico and Honduras between 1851 and 1852, that is, some twenty-five years before the foundation of the Society. It is in her rather obscure biography (penned by Theosophist collaborator A. P. Sinnet) that she claims to have visited Mexico and Central America, after having been to Canada and the United States. However, the actual details about her supposed visit to Mexico are not reliable; there are hardly any records of her impressions of the Mexican landscape and context. It is somewhat suspicious that she did not provide faithful records, especially taking into account that both Crowley and Yogananda did, and quite effusively for that matter. Why, then, should she have tried to claim such a travel? Blavatsky did mention Mexican ancient civilisations, especially in her *Isis Unveiled* (1877) and *The Secret Doctrine* (1888). These two books were written more than twenty and thirty years, respectively, after her supposed travel to Mexico. Here, Blavatsky equates Aztec and Mayan cultures with the civilisation of ancient Egypt and Indian culture, by means of the affinities and resemblance she finds in the pyramids and the Ellora caves (Chaves 2008: 116). We should note that these are not the accounts of a tourist, but the notions of an occultist, conceived at a distance. In other words, it was the mythical Mexico that she was fantasising about, in very much the same way that she exotised the 'Orient' (she also made travels to Greece, Lebanon, India, Sri Lanka and Tibet, among other destinations). Maybe it was an effect of this romanticisation that different personages were attracted to Mexico and other Latin American destinations: 'During the last quarter of the nineteenth century esoteric ideas became so widespread in educated circles both East and West that historians of religion can hardly avoid coming across one or another of their manifestations' (De Michelis 2005: 67). In this sense, it is historically interesting that almost simultaneously with Crowley, around 1899 and 1900 Katherine Augusta Westcott Tingley arrived in Latin America from the United States, with the specific purpose of teaching Raja Yoga in the light of Theosophy and Freemasonry (Simões 2018). Tingley was a disciple of Blavatsky, so she may have felt attracted to this region in part because of Blavatsky's romantic visions of Pre-Hispanic cultures in the Americas. Tingley's main base was in Havana, Cuba. Unfortunately, there is almost no critical work on this interesting figure.

There was another noteworthy figure, whose activities focused in the southernmost parts of the American continent: Léo Alvarez Costet de Mascheville, a French man who went to Argentina, Uruguay and Brazil between 1924 and 1947 (Simões 2018). This latter year also marked the arrival of another key figure in yoga dissemination in the region: Serge Raynaud de la Ferrière, who I discuss below. Costet de Mascheville took the initiate name of Swami Servananda and followed the tenets of the 'Independent Group of Esoteric Studies', dedicated to Kabbalah, astrology, occultism and Buddhism. Most probably, Costet's main stronghold was in Rio de Janeiro. It is worth mentioning that among Costet's fervent followers was General Caio Miranda, who displayed great efforts in promoting yoga in Brazil. Yet, the diffusion of yoga was rather slow and discreet, and in lusophone Latin America and neighbouring countries it was also undertaken by Cesar Della Rosa, an Italian-born Francophile who popularised Indian religiosity in South America. Allegedly, this entrepreneur founded the first International Federation of Yoga in 1936–1941, with seats in France, Uruguay and Argentina. These two characters have received no substantive attention from scholars to date, but attest to a very interesting link between French and Latin American intellectuals.

At roughly the same time, in 1929, the illustrious Paramahansa Yogananda payed a visit to Mexico. This event is of utmost significance since it was one of the first visits of an Indian guru to Latin America. In some senses, his stay reproduced some of the features of Crowley's trip, especially because of the huge impact that the Mexican landscape made on the Indian yogi. Like Crowley, Yogananda not only stayed in Mexico City, but also wrote eulogically about mountains, uplands and lakes elsewhere. At some point, Yogananda even compared some hills to Kashmir and other places in India. Unlike Crowley, however, Yogananda gave some private and public lectures, the content of which are yet to be found in the historical record. His visit was recorded in Mexican newspapers, and he was even welcomed by the then president, Emilio Portes Gil. Despite being a holiday, Yogananda's was an official visit of sorts. It coincided with the establishment of Mexican branches of his Self-Realization Fellowship, founded less than ten years earlier and with a base in Los Angeles, California. Through this organisation, Yogananda set himself up to teach and spread the principles of his Yogoda (a term that implied harmony, union and human improvement through a sense of self-realisation) and Kriya Yoga (a set of techniques of respiration and mantras meant to awaken the individual's spiritual development). The Mexican branch is still functioning. It constantly offers meditation retreats and visits to Lake Chapala in Jalisco state, a freshwater lake for which Yogananda wrote a heart-felt praise in verse. Yogananda's visit somehow paved the path for the incursions that would later take place.

Readers can imagine that there have been many other actors in this history. They cannot all be accounted for in such an introductory overview as this. Brief sketches of more figures can be found in Simões 2015, but detailed and thorough studies on individual actors are still needed. A notable exception is Siegel 2014, a detailed and well-documented critical biography of Serge Raynaud de la Ferrière, discussed below.

## Typologies 1: yoga, meditation and bodywork

As in many other parts of the globe, the history of yoga in the Hispanosphere is concomitant with the history of meditation currents. An important number of these place a strong emphasis on devotion. In significant ways, faith through veneration and devotion towards a deity or master are enactments of *discipline*, one of the many meanings of 'yoga'. We will take a brief look at some key examples in Latin America. I have discussed the main understandings of yoga above. Let me here reiterate that 'yoga' can signify various things, even if we were to only deal with physical forms; trying to pin it down to one single conception would be misleading and equivocal. As Singleton (2010: 15) has aptly put it: 'A more valid and helpful way of thinking beyond such unproductive positions might be to consider the term *yoga* as it refers to modern postural practices as a *homonym,* and not a *synonym,* of the 'yoga' associated with the philosophical system of Patañjali' and the other theoretical versions. Yet, we should not lose sight of the fact that for many practioners both yogas converge and, sometimes, are even equivalents.

Traditionally, Latin America has been conceived as a predominantly Catholic region. However, at least since the 1990s there has been an ongoing change from Roman Catholicism to Protestantism and, more recently, to Pentecostal denominations, where Evangelical activity has been very intense, especially in Central America and Brazil (De la Torre 2018: 161–162). Few countries in the region have specific and efficient tools to measure religious change; hence, it is difficult to gauge the accurate numbers of followers of religions other than Roman Catholicism. One phenomenon that seems to take place is the overlap of faith and observation, whereby despite recognising oneself as a Catholic, a person can still resort to beliefs or practices from other religious systems (usually, meditation and yoga are epistemologically placed within non-Christian religious systems in Latin America). Combinations of religious identity and praxis can also involve Spiritualism, New Age ideas and indigenous beliefs, among others. This hybrid practice is recognised as 'mutant' or 'non-exclusive religious' (De la Torre 2018: 166). Like Buddhism itself, yoga in Latin America shares with other originally Asian religions in the region (International Society for Krishna Consciousness, Daoism, Siddha Yoga and so forth) the fact that it is primarily undertaken by converts. The participation from Asian immigrants is comparatively small. In Argentina, for example, Buddhism is practised by some 5,000 Asian migrants or descendants, in contrast to the 35,000 Argentinian converts (Carini Catón 2018: 42). Many among them could have participated in different Asian methods, from Reiki through martial arts to yoga (Carini Catón 2018: 44).

Probably the most notable group is that of the Hare Krishnas, more properly known as the International Society for Krishna Consciousness, or ISKCON. In Latin America, more often than not, the Hare Krishnas do not undertake physical forms of yoga, but rather endorse a devout course of action through life. For them, this approach entails an ethical discipline that they call yoga, a discipline decidedly based on the *Bhagavadgītā*, the famous Hindu text. This is one of the most cherished texts for this society, alongside the *Bhagavatapurāṇa* and the writings of Srila Prabhupada, who founded the ISKCON in New York in 1966. Prabhupada visited Mexico in 1972 and established a long-lasting footing there and in other parts of Latin America. From the *Bhagavadgītā*, the Hare Krishnas especially endorse the path of love and devotion (*bhaktiyoga*) towards God, whose real, universal form is Krishna. Devotion to Krishna is exclusivistic. Thus, the ISKCON is unmistakably a monotheistic religious group; it cannot be combined with participation in another religious denomination. It also places a strong emphasis on a vegetarian diet and on abstinence from drugs, alcohol consumption and pre-marital sex. Although it claims to follow the philosophical tenets of Bengali Vaishnavism, its practice is mainly devotional, preferring chanting and congregational sharing to the study of Sanskrit and Hindu scriptures. The followers have a clear penchant for proselytism, and they tend to pay visits to different public spaces so as to draw attention and generate followers. ISKCON's success in Latin America is evidenced by the many branches and temples it has established in a wide number of countries, such as Argentina, Bolivia, Brazil, Chile, Colombia, Costa Rica, Dominican Republic, Ecuador, El Salvador, Guyana, Mexico, Panama, Paraguay, Peru, Surinam, Uruguay and Venezuela. In some cases, former followers, to ensure the continuity of the society's activity, have donated facilities and houses for temples.

Another school of devotional yoga that has been successful in some Latin American countries is Siddha Yoga, the group that evolved around the teachings of Swami Muktananda, originally from Karnataka and later based in Maharashtra. He allegedly received initiation from his guru Bhagavan Nityananda in 1947. After mystical experiences and gathering followers, he launched a missionary journey between 1970 and 1980; this activity led him to the United States, where he formally founded the group in 1975. His activities outside India were centred on the 'Intensives', i.e. massive initiatory gatherings-cum-rituals. In 1982, Muktananda chose Swami Chivilasananda, popularly known as Gurumayi, as his successor. She is currently running the Siddha Yoga Dham Associates, or SYDA Foundation. Directed toward developing spirituality in human beings, Siddha Yoga does not demand full renunciation, but the gaining of ever-increasing awareness of the innate human perfection. The adept is thus called a 'perfect' (*siddha*) being. In 1975, Muktananda visited Mexico and founded the Centro de Siddha Yoga de la Ciudad de México (Cross 2018); this centre was established just a few months after the first US centre. The Mexico City ashram is still operating and has a somewhat diminished, but loyal, cohort of followers. Probably the more stable SYDA centres in the region are those in Argentina, Brazil, Mexico, Uruguay and Venezuela. They partake of meditation, chanting (especially of the *Gurugītā*) and mantra recitation (notably the *oṃ namaḥ śivaya*). Besides the meditation centres, in some countries (such as Mexico) there are also Casa de Estudios ('Study Residence', also known as Home Study), with a view to reinforcing the practice of *sādhana*, partly through the propagation of interest and study in the Sanskrit language and the Trika philosophy associated to Kashmirian philosopher Abhinavagupta (tenth to eleventh century).

Buddhism has played an important role in spreading meditation. It has also been an appealing item for both sympathisers and academia (albeit in smaller numbers). The presence of Zen and Vipassana groups is notable. Especially significant is the presence of insight and mindfulness meditation, which may very well exemplify general understandings of meditation, Buddhism, Hinduism and yoga. In Latin America, both academic and practical Buddhism is a transplant of North American Buddhism, but it is also received through the filter of exoticist expectations (Gómez Rodríguez 2019: 17). This not only implies Latin American imaginings of 'ancient', 'mysterious' Asia, but also the notion that meditation is *the* key element in all Buddhist schools, something that cannot be proved by factual and textual evidence in Asia throughout history (Gómez Rodríguez 2019: 21–22). Mindfulness in North America bloomed in particular between the 1960s and the 1990s, after a long and interesting history of development, translation and adaptation, until it also became a favourite topic in psychotherapy. This accounts for the pervasive influence of what we may well call 'Anglophone Buddhism'.

Despite this huge influence, there are some Zen/Chan groups in Latin America which aspire to have connections with and transmission from Asian teachers (usually, but not exclusively, Japanese). In the particular case of Mexico, Ezer May May has identified two conjunctions that mark the trajectory of Buddhism: namely, international policies from the nineteenth century, and ecumenical policies from the twentieth (May May 2015). The first is reflected in migrations from China and Japan in 1875 and 1897, respectively, especially in Northern Mexico. Nevertheless, the immigrant impact of Buddhism in Mexico – as in Argentina, and probably in most countries in the region – was rather weak, an issue that lies beyond the scope of this article. The second 'conjunction' depended on a comparative and pragmatist approach. It was partly fuelled (at least in Mexico and Central America) by rationalism, Theosophy, universalism and a dialogical relationship between Buddhism and Christianity. In recent decades, Buddhism has been further popularised by Tibetan Buddhism. The 14th Dalai Lama has paid visits to Mexico, where the Casa Tibet has been operating relentlessly since 1989, more or less. It has become a renowned place for meditation and prayer, and is probably more visible in the media than other Buddhist centres or groups.

Meditation in the region was also boosted by the Transcendental meditation movement founded by Mahesh Prasad Varma, aka Maharishi, in 1955 in Madras. Twenty years later after its foundation, the Maharishi foundation established centres in different locations in Argentina, Brazil, Peru, Mexico and Uruguay (De Oliveira 2015: 1–2), but also paid regular visits to Cuba. Personal development is underpinned through breath control, which is expected to activate inner energies.

Even though some forms of devotional and meditational yoga can be found all over the region, without a doubt it is the more physical forms that prove to be all-pervading nowadays. They have become more popular and are fast growing. The most conventional schools of postural yoga are well established in most Latin American places, as well as some of the newer forms. From a cursory view, it becomes clear that the most popular forms of yoga are hatha yoga, Vinyasa, Iyengar, Ashtanga, Kundalini and Bikram. There are other forms that have gained popularity more recently, namely Anusara, Aeroyoga and Naamyoga, all of which have been non-Indian developments and which often involve Kabbalistic symbolism or terminology, as is the specific case of Naamyoga. These are recognisable asana-based manifestations of yoga.

A common phenomenon is the opening of yoga studios bearing the word 'yoga' in their name (X yoga, N yoga …). Quite often there is an overlapping of the name with a yoga style, and the name of the head of said studio. Without a doubt, yoga has become a brand-enhancing label; it definitely helps to boost the impact of a given style or studio. Even when a person has developed a completely different methodology that bears little connection with recognisable forms of yoga (however difficult and disputable this can be), using the label 'yoga' makes the set of techniques derive both epistemological and commercial benefit ('Laughter' or 'Beer yoga', for example). By calling it 'yoga', it is set apart from other practices that are more clearly and undeniably circumscribed in the field of sports, fitness and athletics, including trending ones such as pilates or zumba.

## Typologies 2: Latin American yoga

It is no surprise that many yoga trends in Latin America largely continue North American and British schools, or 'Anglophone yoga', a phenomenon labelled in such fashion by some specialists (e.g. Singleton 2010: 9–10; Beatrix Hauser 2013; see also Newcombe and Deslippe, Chapter 24 in this volume). At the same time, apart from regional divergences, there are some more or less detectable traits in Spanish-speaking countries and Brazil, a Portuguese-speaking country. This means that some important actors were influential on either side of the linguistic divide, but usually not simultaneously in both until more recently. Simões (2015) formulates a five-phase scheme to account for the implantation of yoga in Latin America, partly inspired by De Michelis's typologies expounded in her seminal work (2005). According to Simões, the phases are: (1) Mystic-esoteric yoga; (2) Latin American journey to India; (3) Indian yoga settlements in Latin America; (4) Seeking of identity and singularity in Latin American countries; and (5) Strain between 'traditional' and 'hybrid' yoga. Although the scheme is helpful, I am not sure it can provide us with precise insight into the developments and intricacies of the history of Latin American yoga, partly because it presupposes a chronological development, as though in the first phases there was a single understanding of yoga. I do not think that is the case, as is hinted in the earlier section on 'Forerunners and diffusors'. Nonetheless, the scheme may well be used as a reference point for further research.

As elsewhere, most yoga trends in Latin America are not directly linked to traditional yogas in South Asia, but are more or less dependent on North American or European developments. The most obvious exceptions are the Iyengar Yoga and Jois's Ashtanga Vinyasa Yoga lineages, which systematically receive visitors with a view to extend formative processes and issue official certifications for the practice and instruction of these yogas. One possible phenomenon, still to be further examined, is the alleged fact that Latin American yoga was somewhat isolated for about eighty years (*c.*1900–1980) and remained a spirituality without any legitimation from an Indian figure or group (Simões 2018). In countries such as Argentina, the inception and acceptance of yoga and meditation has had to negotiate with more established religions, notably Christianity. Yoga and meditation also benefited from New Age discourse:

> The different price options and ways of practicing it, the appropriation and acceptance among Catholics and physicians, the idea of exercising the body in a delicate way, and the possibility of enjoying its benefits not having to adopt a new lifestyle mark it as a preferential option.
>
> (*Saizar 2015: 1*)

Roberto Simões speculates that the lack of continuity and homogeneity may have been a result of a linguistic barrier, with the Spanish and Portuguese languages preventing Indian gurus (usually more at ease with English) from possible and frequent visits to the Latin American continent (Simões 2015: 3) Therefore, the introduction of yoga was undertaken by non-Asians first: people who could handle the two main languages in the region. Understandably, there were some people in Spain and France that could do so (and, to a lesser degree, but due to political and economic interests, in the United States as well). However, it is worth remembering that Paramahansa Yogananda visited Mexico at a rather early stage. This and other visits suggest that some countries in Latin America were seen as promising and potential places to 'spread the word of yoga', as it were.

The introduction of physical yoga in the region owes a great deal to the notorious Serge Raynaud de la Ferrière, a French self-styled spiritual leader and philosopher. He claimed to have encountered a Dalai Lama who appointed him as a *bodhisattva* and entrusted him with the mission of becoming a 'messiah' of the New Age not in the Old World, but in the New one, specifically the Americas (Gutiérrez Zúñiga 2015: 2). This new era, the Age of Aquarius, allegedly began on 21 March 1948, when he was already in Latin America. De la Ferrière had various interests, among them parapsychology, metaphysics, theology and esotericism. He emphatically promoted vegetarianism, peace-preaching, psycho-physical gymnastics and abstinence from alcohol, tobacco and drugs (Siegel 2014: 344). He planned to found a great non-sectarian congregation, for which purpose he went first to the United States in 1947. However, he soon left for Guatemala and then arrived in Venezuela a year later to found the Gran Fraternidad Universal, or GFU (Great Universal Brotherhood). To this end, the GFU established ashrams so as to encourage both 'exoteric movement' and 'esoteric elevation' (Gutiérrez Zúñiga 2015: 2). The success of the GFU has been explained as the result of its presence in cultural events and not just within the inner precincts of the group, thus strengthening a strong process of synthesis and fostering a growing interest in the ideas and practices promoted by the GFU (Gutiérrez Zúñiga 2015: 2–3).

A prolific writer, De la Ferrière authored many books on religion and his own views on Freemasonry, Buddhism and other traditions. He was especially famous for his *Yug, yoga, yoghismo* (1969), his personal take on the yoga path and psychology. In fact, he called himself 'Mahatma Chandra Bala', the pen-name he used to author this volume. Like De la Ferrière himself, most elders in GFU are known as *maestres* (masters) and dress all in white. Critical and reliable information about De la Ferrière's study of yoga, Indian philosophy and other fields is rather scanty; even De la Ferrière's wife did not seem to have any recollection of her husband's alleged intense study of Indian traditions (Siegel 2014: 39, 280, 287). This did not prevent him from becoming a successful forerunner in Latin America. As with Tingley, Costet de Mascheville and Della Rosa, De la Ferrière's yoga was of an esoteric type, yet in most GFU branches there has been a constant and increasing offer of other forms of yoga, such as hatha or prenatal yoga.

The GFU was very successful and soon established roots in other countries, significantly Mexico and Costa Rica, where Nicaraguan Adaluz de Lake spread De la Ferrière's ideas as well as yoga practice. Many followers also authored sundry books, such as the Venezuelan José Rafael Estrada, who wrote *Enseñanzas de la Nueva Era* (*Teachings of the New Age*), where he spoke on behalf of the fraternity among all Latin American peoples, itself the axis of the New Age of Aquarius. The book deals with yoga, meditation, kung-fu, breath control, gymnastics and nutrition (Siegel 2014: 262). Another publication, by Antonio Renato Henriques, explains some key concepts from Vedic cosmology, the caste system and classical Indian philosophy, as well as yoga and psychoanalysis. It also provides some information on Brazilian yoga schools (Siegel 2014: 266). Despite the fact that the GFU has managed to thrive in the region, it has also experienced various schisms, mainly emanating from Mexico, Colombia and Venezuela (Siegel 2014; Gutiérrez Zúñiga 2015).

As in other regions of the globe, yoga is present in both independent and semi-corporate contexts. There are a vast number of instructors and practitioners not easy to include in a census.

There are also some organisations and/or associations that seek to represent and account for the diverse varieties of yoga within regional boundaries. Although there are representations of transnational corporations and/or branches (Iyengar Yoga, Yoga Alliance, Bikram Yoga, etc.) in most Latin American cities, there are also regional associations, such as the International Association of Yoga and Yoghism, the Mexican Federation of Yoga, the Mexican Institute of Yoga, the Argentinian Yoga Association, the Argentinian Federation of Yoga, the Latin American Union of Yoga, the Venezuelan Association of Yoga, AsoYoga-Costa Rican Association of Yoga Teachers and the Colombian Association of Yoga. As can be deduced from this list, there is at least one national yoga association for each country. Also, there is vast array of places that offer retreats for yoga training. Many of these places of retreat are located in touristic and idyllic scenarios, most notably on appealing beaches or in well-preserved forests.

In an ongoing survey, I collected some basic statistics worth mentioning. So far, sixty-nine people have responded to the survey: forty-seven females and twenty-seven males. Forty-three of the respondents are from Mexico; the remaining twenty-six are resident in Argentina, Bolivia, Brazil, Chile, Colombia, Costa Rica, Cuba, Nicaragua, Peru and Venezuela. The survey attempted to identify the most practised forms of yoga; respondents had to choose from twenty-one options, including an 'Other' option. Many respondents adhered to more than one form of yoga. According to the responses, the most practised varieties are: Hatha Yoga (62.3%), Vinyasa (39.1%), Iyengar (36.2%) and Ashtanga (34.7%). Power Yoga and Kundalini Yoga tied for fifth place (11.5%), well below the other four varieties. Acroyoga, Aeroyoga, Anusara, Bikram, ISKCON's *bhaktiyoga*, Jivamukti, Kripalu, Shadow, Siddha Yoga and Yogananda's Yogoda were each reflected in a very small number of adherents (7.2% or less). However, these figures may change as data is collected from a larger number of people. It will be helpful to mention some data in order to supplement my current statistics. According to Saizar (2015: 2), Hatha yoga is the most widespread form of yoga in Argentina, although it remains unclear whether she makes a distinction between Ashtanga, hatha and other postural modalities. May May states that the Buddhist population in Mexico is predominantly female and middle-class, presumably because the practice 'enables them to modulate their economic life'(2015: 1, 4).

## Concluding remarks

When dealing with yoga and yoga-related systems in Latin America, it must be stressed that they reflect modern forms and transmissions. It is not possible to claim that they are continuous with or equal to the methods and soteriologies practised in South Asia 500 or 1,000 years ago (Muñoz 2018). In general, we can observe that modern yoga 'seeks its legitimacy as spiritual path under the aegis of scientific rationality and new religious movements in the West' (Simões 2015: 1). As in the rest of the world, yoga and meditation systems are modern expressions. All of them were developed or mediated by western agents, interested in Indian religions from around the mid-nineteenth century and mainly situated in urban contexts (De Michelis 2005: 2). If there is one successful globalised cultural item, it is indeed yoga. As Beatrix Hauser writes:

> If one considers globalization in terms of cultural flows rather than economic markets, yoga provides rich source materials for understanding the process of knowledge transfer – preached, exported, translated, appropriated, touted, assimilated, and modified at various stages along its world-wide journey.
>
> *(Hauser 2013: 2)*

The forms of yoga and meditation that we encounter in Latin America nowadays are the product of a rich combination of factors. It has been impossible to summarise them all in this text, but suffice it to say that this mixture involves a blend of aspirations, ideals, idealisations, projections, misrepresentations and adaptations. It is especially noteworthy that the Latin American expressions of yoga and meditation are largely, yet not exclusively, an inheritance of the developments in North America and Europe. As a result of this influence, many varieties of these systems greatly emphasise the refinement of bodily postures. Additionally, there are a great number of centres and styles that prescribe meditation and ethical behaviour above other aspects. Finally, there are some schools that foreground devotion; Patañjali is usually venerated and, in like manner, both classic and modern gurus are revered. Their role as guides in different yogic paths is understood as essential.

Nevertheless, the European and North American influence has not ruled out regional innovations, such as syncretic forms of yoga, meditation and pre-Hispanic purificatory rituals in places such as Mexico, Brazil or Peru. New Age thought has been an undeniable agent in spreading meditational and yogic ideas in the region. This has been far more than just an inheritance from the Anglophone world after the second half of the twentieth century. On the contrary, a great number of Theosophists, Freemasons, Rosicrucians, Spiritualists and the like have come to countries such as Argentina, Brazil, Cuba and Mexico since the nineteenth century with a view to implementing the realisation of a New Age promise for the betterment of the world in the New World; this was later reinforced by the counter-cultural movements in the 1960s and 1970s (Gutiérrez Zúñiga 2018: 425). The New Age sensibility has then allowed for a revaluation of indigenous practices. Popular traditions and Latin American ethnicities have become special hybrid entities for New Age movements, while at the same time offering a fresh, promising environment for a global spirituality (Guitérrez Zúñiga 2018: 466). To aptly sketch this map of transcultural flow will require much archival research and field work. Yet, it is hoped that this critical overview has offered a compact prospect of the history and modern developments of yoga and meditation in the region. Indeed, there is a broad scope for future research and investigation into the Latin American avatars of yoga – do they reinforce, negate or complement other stories of yoga in the modern world?

## Notes

1 In general, I use lower case for generic modes of yoga and uppercase for branded forms.
2 My translation. I am quoting from an Argentinian edition.
3 However, it is worth noting that the primarily meditation-focused tradition of Siddha Yoga is also visible in Mexico (although now clearly less popular than postural yoga). These practitioners also refer to themselves as 'yogis' after undertaking a formal initiation from an authorised guru of their tradition.
4 The Mexican revolution was a major armed struggle that spanned more than a decade (roughly, 1910–1920). It brought about significant changes in politics, culture, economy and education.

## Bibliography

Alter, J. 2004. *Yoga in Modern India. The Body Between Science and Philosophy*. Princeton and Oxford: Princeton University Press.

Carini Catón, E. 2018. 'Budismo en Argentina', in Blancarte, R. (ed), *Diccionario de las Religiones en América Latina*, 42–48. México: Fondo de Cultura Económica.

Ceccomori, S. 2001. *Cent ans de yoga en France*. Paris: Edidit.

Chaves, J. R. 2008. 'Viajeros Ocultistas en el México del Siglo XIX'. *Literatura Mexicana* XIX (1): 109–122.

Cross, E. 2018. 'Siddha Yoga: El Sendero de Śaktipata'. Paper presented at the Symposium 'Yoga en Latinoamérica: Historia, Recepción y Praxis de un Fenómeno Globalizado', XVI Congreso Internacional de la Asociación de Estudios de Asia y África (ALADAA). Lima, Peru.

De la Torre, R. 2018. 'Diversidad Religiosa' in Blancarte, Roberto (ed), *Diccionario de las Religiones en América Latina*,161–166. México: Fondo de Cultura Económica.

De Michelis, E. 2005. *A History of Modern Yoga. Patañjali and Western Esotericism*. London: Continuum.

De Oliveira, A. G. C. 2015. 'Transcendental Meditation', in Gooren, H. (ed), *Encyclopaedia of Latin American Religions*. Living edition. Switzerland: Springer International Publishing. https://doi.org/10.1007/978-3-319-08956-0

Goldberg, M. 2015. *The Goddess Pose. The Audacious Life of Indra Devi, the Woman Who Helped Bring Yoga to The West*. New York: Alfred A. Knopf.

Gómez Rodríguez, L. O. 2019. *Las Religiones de Asia a partir de la Modernidad: El Ejemplo de la Meditación Budista*. México: El Colegio de México. (Jornadas 175).

Gutiérrez Zúñiga, C. 2015. 'Gran Fraternidad Universal', in Gooren, H. (ed), *Encyclopaedia of Latin American Religions*. Living edition. Switzerland: Springer International Publishing. https://doi.org/10.1007/978-3-319-08956-0_31-1

Gutiérrez Zúñiga, C. 2018. 'New Age', in Blancarte, R. (ed), *Diccionario de las Religiones en América Latina*, 421–428. México: Fondo de Cultura Económica.

Hauser, B. (ed) 2013. *Yoga Traveling. Bodily Practice in Transcultural Perspective*. Austria: Springer.

Lorenzen, D. N. 2011. 'Religious identity in Gorakhnath and Kabir. Hindus, Muslims, Yogis, and Naths', in Lorenzen, D. N. and Muñoz, A. (eds). *Yogi Heroes and Poets. Histories and Legends of the Naths*, 19–49. Albany, NY: State University of New York Press.

May May, E. R. 2015. 'Buddhism in Mexico', in Gooren H. P. P. (ed), *Encyclopedia of Latin American Religions*. Switzerland: Springer International Publishing. https://10.1007/978-3-319-08956-0_128-1

Muñoz, A. 2018. 'Yoga', in Blancarte, R. (ed), *Diccionario de las Religiones en América Latina*, 669–676. México: Fondo de Cultura Económica.

Newcombe, S. 2018. 'Spaces of Yoga: Towards a Non-Essentialist Understanding of Understanding of Yoga', in Baier, K., Maas, P., and Preisendanz, K. (eds), *Yoga in Transformation. Historical and Contemporary Perspectives*, 549–573. Götingen: Vienna University Press.

Siegel, P. 2014. *Serge Raynaud de la Ferriere: Aspectos Biográficos*. São Paulo, Brazil: Universidade Estadual de Campinas.

Saizar, M. 2015. 'Yoga and the New Age Movement in Argentina', in Gooren, H. (ed), *Encyclopedia of Latin American Religions*. Switzerland: Springer International Publishing. https://doi.org/10.1007/978-3-319-08956-0_92-1

Simões, R. 2015. 'Yoga in Latin America', in Gooren, H. (ed), *Encyclopedia of Latin American Religions*. Switzerland: Springer International Publishing. https://doi.org/10.1007/978-3-319-08956-0

Simões, R. 2018. 'As Raízes do Yoga Latinoamericano'. Paper presented at the Symposium 'Yoga en Latinoamérica: Historia, Recepción y Praxis de un Fenómeno Globalizado', XVI Congreso Internacional de la Asociación de Estudios de Asia y África (ALADAA). Lima, Peru.

Singleton, M. 2010. *Yoga Body: The Origins of Modern Posture Practice*. Oxford and New York: Oxford University Press.

Urban, H. 2006. *Magia Sexualis. Sex, Magic, and Liberation in Modern Western Esotericism*. California: University of California.

Yogananda, Paramahansa. 1960 [1955]. *Autobiografía de un Yogi Contemporáneo*. Preface by Evan-Wentz, W. Y.; Cuarón, J. M. (trans). Buenos Aires: Ediciones Siglo Veinte.

# 24

# ANGLOPHONE YOGA AND MEDITATION OUTSIDE OF INDIA

*Suzanne Newcombe and Philip Deslippe*

## Introduction

'Modern Yoga', as defined by Elizabeth De Michelis (2004) and assumed in most academic works on yoga, has been influenced by the English-speaking world and the medium of English (e.g. Hackett 2017; Jain 2015, 2020; Newcombe 2009, 2019). It is true that many of those who popularised yoga as Indian physical culture and a tool of nationalism in the early twentieth century did not speak English – and this is an under-researched area of yoga studies (Newcombe 2017; Alter 2004). But many Indian teachers did speak English, especially those who gained an international following. English was influential to the extent that when Mark Singleton decided to trace the construction of 'modern yoga', he also specified his object of study as 'transnational anglophone yoga' (Singleton 2010: 10).[1]

English was the language of the British Empire and became the common second language for many within India, which has hundreds of indigenous languages. In this role, English within India has continued to be influential after independence. English has had specific influence on the transmission of various religious and spiritual ideas both within and from India to the world; Srinivas Aravamudan (2005) identified 'Guru English' as a register of English that was used to transmit Indian spiritual wisdom to the wider world from the Romantic Orientalism of the late-eighteenth century to the more recent spirituality of New Age and global commercialisation.

English has become a global language with a reach that extends beyond the imperial and political influences exerted by Britain and the United States from the nineteenth to twenty-first centuries. In 2019, English was the most spoken language in the world (taking into account its use as a second or third language) (Ethnologue 2019). As Aravamudan points out, 'English dominates by virtue of its stranglehold on global organisations as an international auxiliary or link language', such as the strong links English has to international exchanges with 'computers, medicine, business, media, higher education, and communications' (2005: 1–2). To some extent these domains are largely features of the lives of a globalised elite – those working in these sectors tend to have more disposable income, higher education levels and greater access to travel than other workers. This demographic also holds true with the majority of global yoga practitioners outside of India.

Originally the language of empire (both British and US), King has argued that English was also the medium through which the modern binary assumptions of mind/body and science/

religion have come to dominate global articulations about the nature of meditation and yoga (King 2019: 5). Yet English has been more than the cosmopolitan language of power and the coloniser (Pollock 2002). The 'colonised' also extensively use the language to 'talk back' and articulate their experiences (Rushdie 1982; Said 1978; Spivak 1988). In the context of globalised modern yoga, these roles are complex and often mixed, since individuals promoting yoga wish to maximise the spread of their message while depicting yoga as a means of resisting some aspects of the dominant Anglo-European cultures. The complexities of global cultural and information exchange in the twentieth century is only beginning to be analysed, even as technology transforms our global communications networks in ways we are just starting to comprehend.

What exactly yoga *is* in this context – what practices and ideas are transmitted – has both transnational 'universalised' and localised elements (Newcombe 2018; Pollock 2002). In trying to define yoga and meditation within the specific location of the medium of English, we hope to highlight some broad themes in the various local creative expressions of yoga (many of which also use the medium of English). It is intended that this may contribute to the 'consensual dissensus' of what yoga and meditation is and has been, which has the potential to contribute to the articulation of new kinds of cosmopolitanisms – acknowledging and validating both the universal and particular simultaneously in modern and contemporary formulations of yoga (Breckenridge et al. 2002).

## Early modern and nineteenth-century networks and translations

Europeans (re)discovered India, and to some extent yoga, during the European 'Age of Discovery' which covers the fifteenth to eighteenth centuries. Although there were overland trade routes in antiquity, and limited trade continued by land in the early years of this millennium, advances in sea travel and trade ambitions during this period made India an attractive place to source valuable imports. While most European travellers were primarily focused on establishing beneficial trade relationships, missionaries also accompanied these exploratory ships. Both types of traveller sometimes published travelogues of 'exotic' cultures. The behaviours of ascetics, associated with 'yoga' and meditation practices, can be found in attempts to catalogue the unfamiliar beliefs and practices of the 'pagan natives' and to justify missionary activity. In northern India, would-be British colonial powers felt it necessary to disrupt the militarised Nāth (Hindu ascetic) orders who had developed allegiances with local rulers. During most of the colonial period, living yoga and yogis were largely regarded with contempt and suspicion (Pinch 2006; White 2009).

Even while living Indian 'yogis' were being denigrated by British propaganda and policies, Sanskrit literature was being explored and acclaimed. Colonial bureaucrats hoped to find a better basis for government; idealists and historians hoped to find the origins of European languages and religions in Sanskrit. The founding of the Asiatic Society of Bengal in 1784 by the British polymath and judge Sir William Jones (1746–1794) established a formal study of India's languages and cultures (Banerji 2016: 555–556; see also Rocher 2002). In this context, yoga became closely associated with the explanations given by Kṛṣṇa in the *Bhagavad Gītā*, which began to appear in translation in European languages in the early 1800s (Marshall 2002[1970]). Largely through translations of the *Bhagavad Gītā*, interest in yoga became acceptable for the upper classes of society interested in cultural and mystical exploration and the frontiers of human knowledge. The *Gītā* has perhaps been the most frequently read text by those involved in the yoga revival, not least due to Mahatma Gandhi citing it as an inspirational text, having encountered it first as a law student in London during the 1880s (Newcombe 2020).

Buddhism, in turn, was also explored initially through texts, and the Pali Canon in particular. The 1880 publication of Edwin Arnold's *The Light of Asia*, a popular English verse account of the life of the Buddha, met with widespread popularity and critical acclaim among liberal elites. Victorians imagined Buddhism in ideal terms without reference to institutional power struggles or the needs and expectations of everyday people. The question of whether Buddhism was a religion or a philosophy was debated. However, for many, no system that professed atheism could be considered a religion (Almond 1988: 94). In the nineteenth century a philosophical Buddhism became articulated in European and American intellectual discussions as distinct from the 'idol-worshipping Hindus', and the foundations for secular 'mindfulness' movements were established (Tweed 2005). In 1881 the Pali Text Society was established in Britain by Professor Rhys Davids (1843–1922), who translated many volumes of the Buddha's teaching into English, promoting Buddhism as a compelling model for daily living. Davids later founded the more public-facing Buddhist Society for Great Britain and Ireland in 1907 (Oliver 1979: 34 and 49).

## The Theosophical Society

The Theosophical Society was founded in 1875 in the United States by the American Henry Steel Olcott (1832–1907) and the Russian Helena Petrovna Blavatsky (1831–1891). It quickly became a multinational and multilingual organisation dedicated to the exploration of esoteric religiosity that also reinterpreted and championed Indian religions and was an important element in defining the first international understandings of both yoga and meditation in anglophone contexts (see also Albanese 2007; Clarke 1997). English was central for its international communications, which continued through the relocation of its headquarters to Adyar just outside Madras (now Chennai) in India in 1879. The society's dissemination of materials throughout the English-speaking world was extremely influential (Dixon 2001; Sand and Rudbog 2020; Godwin 1994; Lubelsky 2012). However over time, different cultures and linguistic groups emphasised distinct aspects of the Theosophical interventions (see Acri, Chapter 19 and Muñoz, Chapter 23 in this volume).

Not only did the Theosophical Society produce texts, but its reading rooms and distribution houses provided a place for broad religious explorations; its speaking forums allowed specific Indian individuals to more easily promote their own teachings of yoga (Newcombe 2019: 9–11, 19). As De Michelis (2004) has argued, Vivekananda's invitation for Americans and Europeans to identify with Indian yoga was made in a Theosophically saturated milieu. Early English translations of the *Yogasūtra*, which has become an important point of reference for many modern and contemporary yoga practitioners (Singleton 2008; White 2014), were produced in a relatively accessible format by the Theosophical Society. The Theosophical Society was also crucial in the initial global popularisation of Buddhism, and it translated and published Buddhist texts and made them available in public reading rooms wherever 'lodges' were established. This interest inspired some British people to take ordination as Buddhist monks and nuns in the early twentieth century.

## Early twentieth-century publications

The turn of the century saw the publication of several key yogic texts in English along with the emergence of print networks of publishers and retailers. These connections spread yogic texts and ideas throughout the anglophone world and beyond. In addition to the books of

Vivekananda (De Michelis 2004), two of the most important figures in the Indian yoga revival of the early twentieth century merged yoga practice with physical culture and medical science to shape what is recognised as yoga today. Shri Yogendra (Manibhai Desai, 1897–1989) and Swami Kuvalayananda (Jagannatha Ganesha Gune, 1883–1966) published extensively in English, including their respective journals *Yoga* and *Yoga-Mīmāṃsā*. Many of these early successful popularisers of yoga had high standards of English education: Yogendra was educated in the medium of English at Amalsad English School and then St. Xavier's College in Bombay, and Kuvalyananda, although coming from a poor family, excelled at school and mastered English. Swami Vivekananda attended the Presidency University in Bengal which taught in English. Sri Aurobindo was privately educated in England and attended Cambridge University. All of these early pioneers were well placed to 'talk back' to the British Empire in its own language by encouraging a universalisation of yoga as an ideal practice.

There is evidence that the earliest forms of postural practice in the United States arrived through printed materials rather than lived traditions. Vivekananda taught some postures in his small, private classes in New York during the late-nineteenth century (Goldberg 2016: 54–55). Yet it appears these courses were designed by Vivekananda based on texts sent to him (Deslippe 2018: 34). During the 1920s, Rishi Singh Gherwal transposed material from the pages of *Yoga-Mīmāṃsā* into his pamphlet *Practical Hatha Yoga* for distribution in the United States (Deslippe 2018: 33–34 and 7n1). Based in the United States from the 1920s, Paramahansa Yogananda (1893–1952) also pioneered a form of yoga teaching which involved physical postures, drawing from physical culture as well as other contemporary literature (Singleton 2010: 132).

An important example of the power and diffusion of print is the works of William Walker Atkinson (1862–1932), a Baltimore-born attorney who wrote under the pseudonym of Yogi Ramacharaka from 1903 to 1912. His yogic writings combined New Thought, Theosophy and physical culture, and were first published in the United States as a series of mail-order lessons and then books by the Yogi Publication Society of Chicago. These 'yoga' teachings were republished through a special distribution arrangement in London by L. N. Fowler & Co. and became available through booksellers in major South Asian cities such as Allahabad, Delhi, Lahore and Mumbai, as well as through the Latent Light Culture of Tinnevelly. They were also sold in Australia and New Zealand no later than 1911; in the 1930s several of the South Asian yoga teachers in the United States presented the Yogi Ramacharaka exercises to US audiences as ancient Indian yogic practices. Through the transnational global networks of English-language print material, the US-born Atkinson, who never travelled to India, wound up influencing Indian understandings of yoga and beyond (Deslippe 2019). Even if Ramacharaka's teachings have little (if any) historical continuity with Indian forms of yoga, his ideas and practices have become central to the framing of many modern yoga traditions in both cosmopolitan contexts and Indian ones (e.g. Bharati 1970). The Ramacharaka books were quickly translated into other languages and provide an example of how exchanges within the anglophone world often went global (Deslippe 2019). Like Theosophy, Ramacharaka had a global and multilingual spread, but the distinct presentation of 'yoga' arrived out of an anglophone context.

Another incredibly important influence is that of Swami Sivananda (Kuppuswami Iyer 1887–1963). Before turning to yoga, Sivananda trained as a 'western' biomedical doctor and ran an English-language medical journal in Tamil Nadu called *The Ambrosia*, demonstrating a good command of English language and culture. While studying classical yoga texts for his PhD with the philosopher Dasgupta in Kolkata during the 1930s, the Romanian scholar Mircea Eliade (1907–1986) heard of an 'English-speaking swami in Rishikesh' with an authentic yoga practice and travelled to learn from him. English was a second language for both Sivananda and Eliade, but it facilitated a communication between the two men.

Moreover, Sivananda was a prolific writer (of easily posted pamphlets and books) and corresponded in English. Strauss argues that Sivananda's 'cosmopolitanism, fluency in English and congenial attitude brought him wide recognition' (Strauss 2005: 40). She goes on to argue that Sivananda's communications in English, like the literature produced by Vivekananda before him, created a global 'imagined community' of yoga practitioners in Benedict Anderson's (1983) sense – a 'community of people who, though they are rarely acquainted in the face-to-face sense, nevertheless feel themselves connected through their shared interest in and practice of yoga' (2005: 40–1). The English-language publications sent out worldwide from Sivananda's Divine Light Society (founded in 1935) had a vital role to play in the creation of a globalised modern yoga.[2]

## Anglophone physical culture and yoga

One of the major forces to shape modern yoga was the modernist physical culture movement that promoted physical health and strength training through military drills, competitive games, calisthenics and gymnastics. Physical culture was influential throughout Europe (particularly in Prussia and later Germany) and the anglophone world. Singleton (2010) has argued that the global popularity of these exercises for health likely influenced the development of posture-oriented yoga in the modern period, while in the later twentieth century doing and teaching yoga became socially acceptable for women partially due to precedents within movement traditions for women in Europe and the United States (e.g. Newcombe 2007). While physical culture and yoga have resonances in many different cultural–linguistic contexts, the medium of English was particularly helpful in the transfer of ideas. Social Darwinism and eugenics became intertwined with calls for nationalism, while military readiness and physical culture was seen as a remedy to these concerns (Singleton 2007).

Although originating in imperial urban metropolises, these concepts were also integrated into independence movements, particularly in India. Indian nationalists promoted a distinctly Indian physical culture for 'Indian bodies' and in the Indian *akhāṛā* (gymnasium). In this context, yoga *āsana* was added to a repertoire of Indian 'physical culture' that included indigenous martial arts, wrestling warm-up exercises (*dands*), *sūrya namaskāra*, Indian club exercises and *mallakhamba*, i.e. exercises on a pillar or ropes (Alter 2004; McCartney 2019a; Mujumadāra 1950; Singleton 2010). The connections between the yoga revival and physical culture show just how dynamic and numerous exchanges were within the anglophone world. Yogendra was not only influenced by physical culture (and titled one of his earlier books *Yoga Physical Education*), but also spent a half-decade in the United States where he worked with several US health reformers. Kuvalayananda hosted a professor of physical education from Columbia University at his centre in India, in addition to physicians and academics (Alter 2004: 73–108; Goldberg 2016: 80–87.)

Courses on 'yoga' and the development of psychic control could be found in the advertisement sections of physical culture journals that circulated from the interwar period into the 1950s and became part of mainstream exercise culture. Physical culture magazines in the United States during the late 1930s noticeably heralded the arrival of postural forms of yoga as a new import (Deslippe 2018: 7). In Britain, Mary Bagot Stack's Women's League of Health and Beauty, which was very popular among middle-class women from the 1930s through the 1950s, directly incorporated some yoga asanas, which the founder reported learning while living in India with her husband in 1912 (Newcombe 2007; Singleton 2010: 150–2). This emphasis on yoga asana as part of physical culture increasingly came to define yoga as asana-focused in the second half of the twentieth century.

## Immigration, English and empire

A significant number of Indian guru figures travelled during the early years of the twentieth century, making influential visits to both the United States and Britain (and often other anglophone countries such as Canada). They included Swami Vivekananda (1863–1902) and Swami Abhedananda (1866–1939) of the Vedanta Society, Swami Rama Tirtha (1873–1906), Swami Prabhavananda (1893–1976), Yogananda (1893–1952), Yogendra Mastanami (1897–1989), Premananda Baba Bharati (1857–1914) and the more obscure Tiger Mahatma (dates unknown). In the early twentieth century, Britain was visited by Jiddu Krishnamurti (1895–1986 – who lived most of his life in California, visiting Europe regularly), Ananda Acharya (1881–1945), Hari Prasad Shastri (1882–1956), Meher Baba (1894–1969) and Swami Avyaktananda (dates unknown), originally representing the Ramakrishna Vedanta Centre (Beckerlegge 2020). Some of these figures visited only briefly, but their teachings were likely incorporated into others' English-language presentations of yoga and meditation. There was a particular ease of travel between member states of the British Commonwealth, including India; before 1962 there were no restrictions on empire citizens (e.g. Indians) resettling in Britain, provided they had the funds to get there.

Several observers in both India and the United States noted that English served as a 'critical dividing line' in the arrival of yoga to the United States at the turn of the century, and that the swamis and yogis who came from India to America had a common proficiency in the language and a background of English-style education (Deslippe 2018: 21). Ironically, it was a restriction of movement that saw a major increase in the dissemination of yoga in the United States during the interwar decades of the 1920s and 1930s. Legal decisions rendered South Asians as 'ineligible for citizenship', and a wave of denaturalisation proceedings that left many without any citizenship at all led several dozen South Asians in the United States who were unable to leave the country or otherwise establish themselves to take up the profession of travelling yoga teacher and metaphysical lecturer. They would move from city to city, often in a regular, circuit-like pattern, and offer the public a series of free lectures that led into private lessons and dyadic services for a fee (Deslippe 2018). In the early years of the twentieth century, outside of general ideas of being mental and magical, there was no singular or stable idea as to what 'yoga' was, and these peripatetic instructors would freely borrow and modify ideas and practices from New Thought, Spiritualism and occultism and present it to US audiences as ancient yogic wisdom from India.

The global elite of empire and the ease of global travel for English-speaking people into global contexts can be illustrated by several unusual individuals. The life story of the Latvian-born, multilingual Indra Devi (born Eižēnija Pētersone, 1899–2002) highlights how global these flows of ideas and people could be: Devi was born in the capital of Latvia, Riga, and trained as an actress in Russia before deciding to travel to India, having been inspired by the writings of Yogi Ramacharaka and a Theosophically led camp of the Order of the Eastern Star in The Netherlands, which presented the young Jiddu Krishnamurti as a world teacher in 1926 (Goldberg 2015: 65–67). Devi eventually travelled to India, where she learned yoga from Krishnamacharya, Kuvalayananda and likely from Sivananda, as well as later in life being strongly influenced by Sathya Sai Baba and Swami Premananda (Goldberg 2015: 239–243). Devi made a career of teaching yoga. She influenced understandings of yoga among expatriates in Singapore, then the Hollywood elite in the 1950s, and in later life settled and taught in Argentina. Although Devi was an accomplished linguist (and actor) herself, in many of these global contexts English was very often the primary means of communication to individuals of a range of nationalities. Her broad influences highlight the variety of teachings and understandings associated with yoga.

## Adult education and mass media

As yoga and meditation continued to grow in size and reach, they largely expanded through pre-existing networks in the anglophone world – and texts published in English were no exception, both in quantity and in influence. Two complementary and sequential bibliographies identified an exponentially growing number of works on yoga published in English between 1950 and 2005: more than 4,000 books, journal and magazine articles, instruction manuals, translations, dissertations and theses, and periodicals were dedicated to the topic (Jarrell 1981; Callahan 2007, see also Newcombe 2019: 10). Particularly influential was the *Autobiography of a Yogi*, published in 1946 and allegedly authored by Paramahamsa Yogananda, which helped to fix India as a mystic and miraculous land for western seekers for decades following its release (Williamson 2010: 56, 138). Similarly, *Light on Yoga* (1966), written by B. K. S. Iyengar (1918–2014) and first published in English in 1966, has often been described as 'the bible of modern yoga'. It has sold millions of copies and was translated into at least seventeen other languages. It is notable that an Englishman who was deeply conversant with Buddhism, Theosophy and Alistair Crowley's teachings, Gerald Yorke, had a significant role in shaping the (English) language used in the original publication and, in particular, the introduction to the volume (Newcombe 2019: 28–38).

In Britain, yoga became integrated into a network of publicly funded adult education classes during the 1960s and 1970s. In this context, yoga was (usually) expected to be secular, and to promote health and fitness as part of the vision of the social welfare state and post-war recovery.[3] It was likely in this adult education context that the first yoga teaching certificates were issued in the late 1960s, as the directors of adult education centres wanted some measure of quality control over those teaching on taxpayers' money (Newcombe 2014). Particularly influential in the adult education context was the creation by B. K. S. Iyengar of a standardised teaching system of asana that could be transmitted largely in the absence of a charismatic guru (Newcombe 2014).

B. K. S. Iyengar struggled with formal English to some extent, failing his school matriculation examination in English and not progressing to further formal education. However, English was also key to his first yoga teaching posts; in an autobiographical reflection, Iyengar describes being sent to Pune by his brother-in-law Krishnamacharya because he was one of the few students available to take up the appointment, which required instruction in English (Iyengar nd).[4] While teaching in Pune, a practical, auto-didact English became Iyengar's means of transmission and precise asana-focused instruction. One long-term student recalled that Iyengar described English as 'the best language in which to teach yoga because you could always find an appropriate word when teaching pupils: not only was it a very technical language but its expressiveness was a powerful teaching tool' (Ward 2019). The systematised and exacting articulations in the Iyengar method of teaching (Ciołkosz 2014) are likely to have facilitated and strongly influenced the spread and nature of anglophone presentations of yoga.

In the United States, popularisation was largely carried out through mass media, including paperback books and long-playing records. In second half of the twentieth century, the media with the longest reach for presenting yoga in the United States (and soon internationally) was television. The first yoga teacher in United States with a television programme was Richard Hittleman, whose *Yoga for Health* began airing in 1961 and was then broadcast nationally for decades. Hittleman's style was imported into British television programming from 1971–1974, and Lynn Marshall continued to present yoga on television until 1983 (Newcombe 2019: 186–194). Lilias Folan, inspired by Hittleman, started her own show, *Yoga and You*, in 1970 and recorded 500 episodes that aired on public broadcasting stations across the United States for almost three decades.

## Movement of gurus and the counter-culture

The counter-culture of the late-1960s was another significant moment in the development of yoga and meditation in the anglophone world and beyond. The combination of a period of geopolitical stability, inexpensive travel and the comparatively low cost of living in Asia allowed journeys to India via the overland 'hippy trail' through Turkey, Iran, Afghanistan and Pakistan, allowing some 'westerners' to live in India for months at a time (Oliver 2014). Significantly, many yoga teachers and their students were able to successfully negotiate both sides of the era's drug culture by promoting yoga and meditation as both the ultimate 'high' or 'trip' while simultaneously being part of a healthy, drug-free lifestyle. The engagement between the counter-culture and 'eastern spirituality' allowed yoga and meditation to spread through the networks and varied milieus of the hippies and to grow through metropolitan centres, university campuses and 'college towns', health food stores and communes. This was not an exclusively English-language phenomenon, but the ubiquity of English-language pop culture and particularly the popularity of musicians who were closely associated with 'eastern spirituality' during this period did much to spread ideas about yoga and meditation globally (Goldberg 2010).

The United States passed sweeping changes to its immigration laws in 1965 that ended four decades of exclusionary policies and allowed immigrants from Asia to arrive in significant numbers. While this is often seen as a turning point in the reception of yoga and meditation, the connection between the two is more a matter of conventional wisdom. There were other factors preceding and beyond immigration policy that generated interest in these practices and shaped them for wider consumption, and many of the figures that are associated with the 'turn East' – including Swami Prabhupada of the Hare Krishnas and Maharishi Mahesh Yogi of Transcendental Meditation – arrived before the 1965 Immigration Act.

While the counter-culture of the 1960s marked a distinct period in the popularisation of a variety of 'eastern' religions and spiritualities in the global context, its influence has often been overestimated. The 'hippy trail', alternative religions and mind-altering practices were explored by occultists in the early twentieth century and the Beats in the 1950s (Baker 2008; Pearlman 2012). The events of the late 1960s – such as the appearance of Swami Satchidananda at Woodstock in 1969 – marked a 'widening of the road' rather than the paving of new ground (Newcombe 2019: 142). Likewise, the shifting foci towards consumerism and individualism at the end of the twentieth century did not mark the end of counter-cultural communities, camps and festivals that use yoga and meditation as integral parts of their identity (e.g. Lucia 2020; Wildcroft 2020).

## The arrival of scientific meditation

Yoga and meditation became more acceptable after World War II, as teachers in South Asia, Europe and the United States presented it as physical, practical, scientific and accessible to westerners. In the United States, meditation and Buddhism were popularised in a way that was both later than and different to yoga (Mitchell 2016). In Europe, most of the direct immigration from Buddhist-majority countries happened after World War II. Early Buddhists in Britain were from Theravadin countries (Sri Lanka, Thailand and Burma), followed by Japanese, Chinese, Vietnamese, Korean and Tibetan Buddhists (Baumann 2002). But as meditation techniques were 'anglicised' in the United States in the post-war period, they have had a strong influence on British and European ideas of 'meditation' and 'mindfulness'. Since English was one of the primary languages of global publication in the biomedical sciences, this trend was accelerated, as was the influence in English-speaking areas and beyond.

There were a handful of Zen teachers from China and Japan on the west coast of North America in the nineteenth and early twentieth centuries. But meditative techniques such as visualisation and contemplative 'going into silence' were mostly associated with New Thought and early forms of yoga in the United States. The Buddhist immigrant communities faced persecution and largely served as support groups for the community rather than teaching others about Buddhism (Matthews 2002; Seager 2002). The mass internment of more than 100,000 Japanese citizens on the west coast of the United States during World War II accelerated a process of Anglicisation and Americanisation of Japanese Buddhism in North America in the post-war period (Seager 2002: 106–109; McMahan 2002).

Using English, Daisetsu Teitaro Suzuki (1870–1966) helped to popularise Zen Buddhism during the interwar decades with a series of published essays and then, after World War II, as a lecturer and a professor in the United States. During this time, Zen was further popularised by the writers of the counter-cultural Beat movement and Alan Watts. This nascent interest helped the Soto Zen monk Shunryu Suzuki to form the San Francisco Zen Center and the Tassajara Zen Mountain Center, incorporated and completed in 1962 and 1967 respectively (Seager 2002: 110–101; Chadwick 1999). In the late 1960s, Tibetan Buddhists fleeing the Chinese occupation of Tibet began to arrive in Europe and North America and offered tantalising and popular tastes of secret and exclusive teachings, believed to be untainted by modernity (Wallace 2002: 44–46).

In the 1960s, the promotion of the Maharishi Maheshi Yogi and his Transcendental Meditation as scientific was hugely influential in creating scientific interest in the biological effects of meditation, and later yoga. The 1975 book *The Relaxation Response* by Herbert Benson and Miriam Klipper presented Transcendental Meditation to the public in an accessible and scientifically supported form, and was cited in a 1986 survey reported in the *New York Times* as the most-recommended book by clinical psychologists to their patients (Harrington 2009; Hickey 2019).

The practice of mindfulness developed in Buddhist communities, but quickly expanded in the 1980s as teachers such as Jon Kabat-Zinn and Thich Nhat Hanh developed models for teaching meditation and published books that offered mindfulness as an accessible technique with practical benefits. By the 1990s mindfulness had established itself outside of a Buddhist context, and it became part of the mainstream self-help milieu as it was applied to everything from performance in sports, weight loss and workplace efficiency (Wilson 2014: 36–42).

Several students of South Asian teachers who came to the United States in the 1960s made inroads in rendering yoga and meditation as better known and more palatable to mainstream America in the 1980s and 1990s. Dean Ornish, a physician who studied with Satchidananda for several decades, became an influential advocate for reversing heart disease through changes in diet and lifestyle, including yoga and meditation. Another physician, the Indian-born Deepak Chopra, studied Transcendental Meditation and was initially associated with Maharishi Mahesh Yogi and his organisations. While Chopra has frequently been the target of criticism and mockery, his book sales and high public profile have nonetheless made his ideas, and thus his techniques, well known – including yoga, meditation and ayurveda (Warrier 2019; Reddy 2004).

## Early 1980s to the present

Yoga and meditation, like many of the practices and beliefs that were largely associated with the New Age movement of the 1970s and 1980s, underwent a rapid expansion in popularity and mainstream acceptance; by the turn of the millennium they were so common as to be often unremarkable (Deslippe 2015a). This was in no small part a product of the effort of many schools of yoga and meditation who began to institute teacher-training programmes and continued to expand and promote themselves.

Yoga during this time was further popularised and influenced by the introduction ofVHS tapes in the 1980s and then DVDs in the 1990s. Like the syndicated television shows that preceded them, VHS tapes and DVDs allowed for many people not only to practise yoga in the privacy of their own homes, but to do so at their convenience. Pre-recorded classes freed teachers from the limitations of a television studio and allowed them to create better-produced classes with specialised instruction for specific audiences. Later surveys would show that a large percentage of all yoga practitioners in the United States saw their practice as something that was not done in a studio, but at home in front of their television. Yoga also received a boost from the fitness 'boom' and rapid expansion of gyms and health clubs in the United States during the 1980s that allowed for wider reception of health and fitness and provided a common venue for yoga teachers as the popularity of yoga dramatically increased in the following decade (McKenzie 2013).

After the turn of the millennium, yoga and meditation in the United States, Britain and Australia found popularity and mainstream acceptance. All these areas showed similar practitioner demographics in ways that suggest strong similarities within the anglophone world (Ding and Stamatakis 2014; Birdee 2008; Penman et al. 2012; Yoga Journal and Yoga Alliance 2016). However, these demographic studies and surveys also show how complicated an understanding of these practices might be. The widely touted large number of anglophone yoga practitioners reached by these surveys might not represent a stable population engaging in a spiritual practice, but rather may mostly consist of a steady flow of people who take it up for physical fitness and wellbeing and then leave it for other forms after some time, to be replaced by others who take up yoga for the first time (Yoga Journal and Yoga Alliance 2016).

A prominent case that shows how much these practices have grown and gained mainstream acceptance is the death in 2011 of Apple co-founder Steve Jobs, after which several obituaries, posthumous tributes and biographies looking for the sources of his success and innovation pointed to his travels in India as a young man, his reading of Yogananda's *Autobiography of a Yogi*, and the influence of Zen Buddhism on his aesthetic sense (Segall 2013; Issacson 2001). Such a glowing association with yoga and meditation would not only have been unthinkable for someone in such a position of power even a few decades earlier, it was actually used to discredit a sitting governor and potential vice-presidential candidate in the United States (Deslippe 2015b).

As the size and influence of yoga and meditation shows no sign of lessening in the anglophone world and beyond, there are serious and complicated issues involving how yoga and meditation are defined and represented. Critics of cultural appropriation have attacked what they see as the commercialised and ill-informed inclusion of Hindu elements into western yoga classes, while those who have taken up what Jain has called the 'Hindu origins' position (2014) have criticised those who do not fully and openly embrace yoga as Hindu. Debates on the teaching of yoga and meditation in American public schools have hinged on whether or not these practices should be understood as inherently religious. Promoters of yoga and meditation practices from the Maharishi Mahesh Yogi to the 'Encinitas School District Yoga' have presented these practices as nondenominational and secular. Meanwhile (mostly) Christian advocates have insisted on these practices having an integral spiritual nature with unavoidable effects on practitioners (Brown 2013; Newcombe 2018). These debates also have political consequences. In 2014, the Indian prime minister, Narendra Modi, made yoga a key part of India's exercise of diplomatic soft power on the global stage, particularly with the creation of the International Day of Yoga in which he described – in English – the practice of yoga to the United Nations

General Assembly in his first major international speech as Prime Minister as 'an invaluable gift of India's ancient tradition' (Modi 2014).

However, there are also signs of the limitations of English as a language of transmission for yoga in contemporary India. The most popular television guru in India, Swami Ramdev, teaches almost entirely in Hindi and is closely associated with Hindutva nationalism (McCartney 2019b). B. K. S. Iyengar used English to popularise yoga throughout the world, collaborating with native English speakers in his published written work to ensure comprehension for his intended audience of initially British, then US, then global English-as-second-language audiences. In contrast, his son Prashant describes the English language as 'inadequate for the teaching of Yog' (using the Hindi term) (Ward 2019). Prashant's use of English is more creative and postcolonial, playing with the limits of English and creating new words that sound foreign to many of the native and second-language English speakers from around the world who attend his teachings.

According to many critics, the assessment of mindfulness and other meditation techniques through scientific study caused these traditions to develop more in line with western capitalist and neoliberal values and become removed from their ethical roots (Lau 2000; King 2019; Carrette and King 2004). In the most extreme cases, the perceived 'positive' and 'negative' outcomes of meditation techniques, such as increased productivity and engagement with one's work and detachment from the world, have been positioned in direct contradiction to core Buddhist teachings. However, as Jain has pointed out, commodification of spiritual and religious practices does not preclude a meaningful and religious engagement with these practices by individuals (Jain 2015). There are also divides between the meditation practices of western converts to Buddhism and communities of Buddhists that have multi-generations of affiliation with Buddhism and are often first- and second-generation immigrants to English-speaking cultures. An emphasis on meditation practices by the former has served to diminish the role of ritual, merit-making, and the importance of Buddhism in preserving other languages and cultures in the latter (Cheah 2011).

Yoga schools and studios are increasingly engaging in the profitable enterprises of destination retreats and teacher-training programmes. Ironically, the desire to engage in yoga tourism – as part of a wellness vacation, spiritual retreat or a residential teacher-training – as an attempt to be more spiritual or authentic about yoga practice, often strengthens the commercialised, neoliberal and globalised nature of the yoga industry as well orientalist constructs about a mystic India (Lehto et al. 2006; Maddox 2015; Bowers and Cheer 2017; McCartney 2020). A growing number of people are training to be yoga teachers, with some trainings demonstrating an unsustainable Ponzi-like model of two aspiring yoga teachers for every one that is currently active (Einstein 2017).[5] The proliferation of teachers also points to issues that have arisen around standards and accreditation, such as who should be considered a teacher of these practices, what would qualify someone to be such a teacher and what role accrediting institutions should play in establishing standards and enforcing codes of conduct.

Recent decades have seen the unearthing of a staggering number of scandals involving yoga and Buddhist gurus and meditation teachers who engaged in sexual misconduct, abusive behaviour and exploitation of their students (e.g. Bell 2002; Remski 2019).[6] In some cases, this has caused the restructuring of organisations or the reappraisal of their history. Some critics have argued that these cases of abuse and misconduct are facilitated by, or even inherent to, the deference and authority within the traditional *guru–śiṣya* or teacher–student model of mentorship and should be abandoned for more democratic and open structures. It is not clear what further changes the role of guru, which has already undergone substantial shifts over the last century, will see in the future. It is possible that the model of the guru as a gatekeeper of traditional wisdom and object of ritual devotion largely will be overtaken by other structures, even if it persists in some contexts (Lucia 2018; Goldberg and Singleton 2014).

One of the subtexts in the dozens of guru scandals has been the role played by the internet and social media, which has allowed for the amplification of victims' voices and the rapid and open sharing of information in a way that was not possible in previous decades. It is sure to be one of many ways that technology will shape the future of yoga and meditation. The recent array of meditation and mindfulness apps, as well as yoga routine apps, for smartphones are likely to dramatically increase not only the already expanding number of those who meditate, but also further establish meditation and mindfulness techniques as individual pursuits done for specific pragmatic benefits, divorced from religious traditions, ethics or communities.

## Conclusion

In the anglophone context, yoga and meditation hold unique and flexible forms of cultural power and influence. In the United States, Britain and Commonwealth countries these practices receive the benefits of being perceived as spiritual, but without the negative connotations associated with organised religion. They are viewed as simultaneously progressive and innovative, but still ancient and traditional. They can be undertaken for individual betterment and practical benefit, while also being perceived as universal and altruistic. They can be supported by medical science but are not dependent on it. Yoga can have an unquestioned place in either a health club or an individual's description of their spiritual life, just as mindfulness and meditation can effortlessly move from hospitals and schools to corporate seminars and retreats.

Although many academic commentators have noted that they have been researching 'modern *anglophone* yoga', the distinguishing features and historical context of the anglophone aspect of this phrase has yet to be expanded as an analytic category. We would suggest that a more linguistic-based analysis of the structure of English as a medium of translation and pedagogy might also prove fruitful and produce innovative understandings of the transformations of yoga and meditation practices in the modern period. However, this task is complicated by the fact that English is used as both a *lingua franca* of the transnational, cosmopolitan elite and as a vernacular language used for specifically local expressions and actions aimed at subverting dominant narratives and practices. It might be fair to say that the physically focused, often commercialised and 'branded' yoga forms of neoliberal yoga described by Jain (2015) characterise the majority of contemporary, cosmopolitan anglophone yoga. However, English is also the medium used within localised resistances to the dominant culture (e.g. Wildcroft 2020) and is sometimes vernacularised in a postcolonial reframing of yoga (e.g. Ward 2019).

It is hoped that this brief outline might serve as a critical jumping-off point for analysis of which themes and influences are distinctive in presentations of yoga and meditation in English, beyond the medium of presentation. We have highlighted the influence of Theosophy and New Thought (in the form of Yogi Ramacharaka), physical culture, adult education, the counterculture of the 1960s and 1970s, English as a language of medicalisation and the accelerated commodification of these practices from the 1980s onwards in the English-speaking world. Although these trends broadly follow the linguistic binary framings of mind/body and science/religion as identified by King (2019), the pervasive popularity and diversity of yoga and meditation during the modern period in anglophone contexts also points to the limitations of these binaries in accurately expressing how people are experiencing the world through these practices.

## Notes

1 For *Yoga Body*, Mark Singleton defined the object of his study more specifically as 'forms of yoga that were formulated and transmitted in *a dialogical relationship between India and the West through the medium of English*' (2010: 9–10; emphasis in the original).

2 Sivananda's influence was also strong through the English-as-a-second language correspondents Boris Sacharow (1899–1959) in Germany and Harry Dickman (born Harijs Dīkmanis, 1895–1979) in Latvia, who both further extended his influence (Fuchs 1990; McConnell 2016).

3 Adult education structures were also influential in several other European nations including Germany and Bulgaria (Jacobsen and Sardella 2020).

4 The first language of the Iyengar family was Tamil, and they also spoke Kannada.

5 A 'Ponzi scheme' or pyramid scheme is a common form of fraud where the initial investors profit off the 'training' of subsequent investors, with all the profit being made from other individuals hoping to profit from the training rather than by sales of a product to another audience.

6 More historical data about scandals involving particular groups and teachers were well-documented by media and academics, particularly in the 1970s and '80s in the emerging field of 'New Religious Movement' studies within sociology of religion. Some of this literature is detailed in Newcombe (2009).

## Bibliography


Albanese, C. L. 2007. *A Republic of Mind and Spirit: A Cultural History of American Metaphysical Religion*. London: Yale University Press.

Almond, P. C. 1988. *The British Discovery of Buddhism*. Cambridge: Cambridge University Press.

Alter, J. 2004. *Yoga in Modern India: The Body Between Science and Philosophy*. Princeton, NJ: Princeton University Press.

Anderson, B. 1983. *Imagined Communities: Reflections on the Origin and Spread of Nationalism*. London: Verso.

Aravamudan, S. 2005. *Guru English: South Asian Religion in a Cosmopolitan Language*. Princeton, NJ: Princeton University Press.

Arnold, E. 1880. *The Light of Asia: Or the Great Renunciation being the Life and Teaching of Gautama*. London: Trubner & Co.

Baker, D. 2008. *A Blue Hand: The Beats in India*. London: The Penguin Press.

Banarji, S. C. 2016. *A Companion to Sanskrit Literature*. New Delhi: Motilal Banarsidass.

Baumann, M. 2002. 'Buddhism in Europe: Past, Present, Prospects', in Baumann, M. and Prebish, C. (eds), *Westward Dharma: Buddhism Beyond Asia*, 85–105. Berkeley: University of California Press.

Bharati, A. 1970. 'The Hindu Renaissance and Its Apologetic Patterns'. *The Journal of Asian Studies* 29(2): 267–87.

Beckerlegge, G. 2020. 'Ramakrishna Vedanta in Europe', in Jacobsen, K. and Sardella, F. (eds), *Hinduism in Europe*, 422–461. Leiden: Brill.

Bell, S. 2002. 'Scandals in Emerging Western Buddhism', in Baumann, M. and Prebish, C. (eds), *Westward Dharma: Buddhism Beyond Asia*, 230–244. Berkeley: University of California Press.

Benson, H. with Klipper, M. 2001 [1975]. *The Relaxation Response*. New York: HarperCollins.

Birdee, G. S., Legedza, A., Saper, R., Bertisch, S., Eisenberg, D., and Phillips, R. 2008. 'Characteristics of Yoga Users: Results of a National Survey'. *Journal of General Internal Medicine* 23(10): 1653–1658.

Bowers, H. and Cheer, J. 2017. 'Yoga Tourism: Commodification and Western Embracement of Eastern Spiritual Practice'. *Tourism Management Perspectives* 24: 208–216.

Breckenridge, C. A. et al. 2002. 'Cosmopolitanisms', in Breckenridge et al. (eds), *Cosmopolitanism*, 1–14. London: Duke University Press.

Brown, C. G. 2013. *Healing Gods: Complementary and Christian Medicine in Contemporary America*. New York: Oxford University Press.

Callahan, D. 2007. *Yoga: An Annotated Bibliography of Works in English, 1981–2005*. Jefferson: McFarland & Company.

Carrette, J. and King, R. 2004. *Selling Spirituality: The Silent Takeover of Religion*. London: Routledge.

Chadwick, D.1999. *Crooked Cucumber: The Life and Zen Teaching of Shunryu Suzuki*. New York: Broadway Books.

Cheah, J. 2011. *Race and Religion in American Buddhism: White Supremacy and Immigrant Adaptation*. Oxford: Oxford University Press.

Ciołkosz, M. 2014. 'The Quasi-Linguistic Structure of Iyengar Yoga Āsana Practice. An Analysis from the Perspective of Cognitive Grammar'. *Studia Religiologica* 47(4): 263–273.

Clarke, J. J. 1997. *Oriental Enlightenment: The Encounter Between Asian and Western Thought.* Abingdon: Routledge.

De Michelis, E. 2004. *A History of Modern Yoga: Patañjali and Western Esotericism.* London: Continuum.

Deslippe, P. 2015a. 'New Age', in Cardin, M. (ed), *Ghosts, Spirits, and Psychics: The Paranormal from Alchemy to Zombies*, 176–179. Santa Barbara: ABC-CLIO.

Deslippe, P. 2015b. 'The American Yoga Scare of 1927: How Traveling Yogis Toppled the Oklahoma State Government'. *Tides, The Magazine of the South Asian American Digital Archive.* www.saada.org/tides/article/20150910-4457. Accessed 21 January 2020.

Deslippe, P. 2018. 'The Swami Circuit: Mapping the Terrain of Early American Yoga'. *Journal of Yoga Studies* 1: 5–44.

Deslippe, P. 2019. 'William Walker Atkinson as Yogi Ramacharaka', in Kurita, H., Tsukada, H. and Yoshinaga, S. (eds) *Kingendai nihon no minkanseishinryōhō: okaruto enerugii no shoos,* 79–108. Tokyo: Kokushokankokai. (デスリプ, フィリップ2019「ウィリアム・ウォーカー・アトキンソン—別名、ヨギ・ラマチャラカ」栗田英彦・塚田穂高・吉永進一編『近現代日本の民間精神療法—不可視なエネルギーの諸相』国書刊行会)

Ding, D. and Stamatakis, E. 2014. 'Yoga practice in England 1997–2008: Prevalence, Temporal Trends, and Correlates of Participation'. *BioMed Central Research Notes*, 7(172): 1–4.

Dixon, J, 2001. *Divine Feminism: Theosophy and Feminism in England.* Baltimore, MD: Johns Hopkins University Press.

Einstein, J. C. 2017. 'CorePower Yoga Pays $1.4M in Class-Action Lawsuit'. *Martindale Legal Library Online.* 30 October. www.martindale.com/legal-news/article_shulman-rogers-gandal-pordy-ecker-pa_2503267.htm. Accessed 21 January 2020.

Ethnologue. 2019. 'What are the Top 200 Most Spoken Languages?' www.ethnologue.com/guides/ethnologue200. Accessed 21 January 2020.

Fuchs, C. 1990. *Yoga in Deutschland: Rezeption, Organisation, Typologie.* Berlin: Verlag W. Kohlhammer.

Godwin, J. 1994. *Theosophical Enlightenment.* Albany, NY: SUNY Press.

Goldberg, P. 2010. *American Veda: From Emerson and the Beatles to Yoga and Meditation – How Indian Spirituality Changed the West.* New York: Harmony Books.

Goldberg, M. 2015. *Goddess Pose: The Audacious Life of Indra Devi, the Woman Who Helped Bring Yoga to the West.* New York: Corsair.

Goldberg, E. 2016. *The Path of Modern Yoga: The History of an Embodied Spiritual Practice.* Rochester, VT: Inner Traditions.

Goldberg, E. and Singleton, M. 2014. 'Introduction', in Goldberg, E. and Singleton M. (eds), *Gurus of Modern Yoga*, 1–14. Oxford: Oxford University Press.

Hackett, P. (ed) 2017. *The Assimilation of Yogic Religions through Pop Culture.* New York: Lexington Books.

Harrington, A. 2009. *The Cure Within: A History of Mind-Body Medicine.* New York: W. W. Norton & Company.

Hickey, W. S. 2019. *Mind Cure: How Meditation Became Medicine.* Oxford: Oxford University Press.

Isaacson, W. 2001. *Steve Jobs: A Biography.* New York: Simon & Schuster.

Iyengar, B. K. S. n.d. Typewritten autobiographical manuscript (an account from birth to 1954, but certainly written after 1958) in the archives of Maida Vale Iyengar Yoga Institute, London.

Iyengar, B. K. S. 1966. *Light on Yoga.* London: Allen & Unwin.

Jacobson, K. and Sardella, F. (eds) 2020. *Handbook of Hinduism in Europe.* 2 vols. Leiden: Brill.

Jain, A. 2014. 'Who Is to Say Modern Yoga Practitioners Have It All Wrong? On Hindu Origins and Yogaphobia'. *Journal of the American Academy of Religion* 82(2): 427–471.

Jain, A. 2015. *Selling Yoga: From Counterculture to Pop Culture.* New York: Oxford University Press.

Jain, A. 2020. *Peace, Love and Yoga: The Politics of Global Spirituality.* New York: Oxford University Press.

Jarrell, H. R. 1981. *International Yoga Bibliography, 1950 to 1980.* Metuchen, NJ: The Scarecrow Press.

King, R. 2019. 'Meditation and the Modern Encounter between Asia and the West', in Farias, M., Brazier, D. and Lalljee, M. (eds), *The Oxford Handbook of Meditation*, 1–24. Oxford: Oxford University Press. https://doi.org/10.1093/oxfordhb/9780198808640.013.2. Accessed 20 February 2020.

Lau, K. 2000. *New Age Capitalism: Making Money East of Eden.* Philadelphia, PA: The University of Pennsylvania Press.

Lehto, X., et al. 2006. 'Yoga Tourism as a Niche Within the Wellness Tourism Market'. *Tourism Recreation Research* 31(1): 25–35.

Lucia, A. 2018. 'Guru Sex: Charisma, Proxemic Desire, and the Haptic Logics of the Guru-Disciple Relationship'. *Journal of the American Academy of Religion* 86(4): 953–988. https://doi.org/10.1093/jaarel/lfy025

Lucia, A. 2020. *White Utopias: The Religious Exoticism of Transformational Festivals*. Berkeley: University of California Press.

Lubelsky, I. 2012. *Celestial India: Madam Blavatsky and the Birth of Indian Nationalism*. Sheffield: Equinox.

Maddox, C. B. 2015. 'Studying at the Source: Ashtanga Yoga Tourism and the Search for Authenticity in Mysore, India'. *Journal of Tourism and Cultural Change* 13(4): 330–343. https://doi.org/10.1080/14766825.2014.972410

McCartney, P. 2019a. 'Mallkhamb: A Preliminary Sketch of the Relations between Hatha Yoga and the "Wrestlers Pole"'. Presentation given at the Haṭha Yoga Project conference *Yoga and the Traditional Physical Practices of India: Influence, Entanglement and Confrontation*, at SOAS, The University of London on 9 November. www.youtube.com/watch?v=GnEVnlFICZw&feature=emb_logo. Accessed 21 January 2020.

McCartney, P. 2019b. 'Stretching into the Shadows: Unlikely Alliances, Strategic Syncretism, and De-Post-Colonizing Yogaland's "Yogatopia(s)"'. *Asian Ethnography* 78(2): 373–401.

McCartney, P. 2020. 'Yoga-scapes, Embodiment and Imagined Spiritual Tourism', in Palmer, C. and Andrews, H. (eds), *Tourism and Embodiment*, 86–106. New York: Routledge.

McConnell, M. M. 2016. *Letters from the Yoga Masters: Teachings Revealed through Correspondence from Paramhansa Yogananda, Ramana Maharshi, Swami Sivananda and Others*. Berkeley: North Atlantic Books.

McKenzie, S. 2013. *Getting Physical: The Rise of Fitness Culture in America*. Lawrence: University of Kansas Press.

McMahan, D. L. 2002. 'Repackaging Zen for the West', in Baumann, M. and Prebish, C. (eds), *Westward Dharma: Buddhism Beyond Asia*, 218–229. Berkeley: University of California Press.

Marshall, P. J. 2002 [1970]. *The British Discovery of Hinduism in the Eighteenth Century*. Cambridge: Cambridge University Press.

Matthews, B. 2002. 'Buddhism in Canada', in Baumann, M. and Prebish, C. (eds), *Westward Dharma: Buddhism Beyond Asia*, 120–138. Berkeley: University of California Press.

Mitchell, S. A. 2016. *Buddhism in America: Global Religion, Local Contexts*. London: Bloomsbury.

Modi, N. 2014. Statement by H. E. Narendra Modi, Prime Minister of India for the general debate of the 69th session of the United Nations General Assembly. 27 September. New York. www.un.org/en/ga/69/meetings/gadebate/pdf/IN_en.pdf

Mujumadāra, D. C. 1950. *Encyclopaedia of Indian Physical Culture: A Comprehensive Survey of the Physical Education in India, Profusely Illustrating Various Activities of Physical Culture, Games, Exercises, etc., as Handed Over to us from our Fore-fathers and Practised in India*. Baroda: Good Companions.

Newcombe, S. 2007. 'Stretching for Health and Well-being: Yoga and Women in Britain, 1960–1980'. *Asian Medicine, Tradition and Modernity* 3(1): 37–63.

Newcombe, S. 2009. 'The Development of Modern Yoga: A Survey of the Field'. *Religion Compass* 3(6): 986–1002.

Newcombe, S. 2014. 'The Institutionalization of the Yoga Tradition: "Gurus" B. K. S. Iyengar and Yogini Sunita in Britain', in Singleton, M. and Goldberg, E. (eds), *Gurus of Modern Yoga*, 147–167. Oxford: Oxford University Press.

Newcombe, S. 2017. 'The Revival of Yoga in Contemporary India', in *Oxford Research Encyclopaedia*. https://doi.org/10.1093/acrefore/9780199340378.013.253

Newcombe, S. 2018. 'Spaces of Yoga: Towards a Non-essentialist Understanding of Yoga', in Baier, K., Maas, P. A. and Preisendanz, K. (eds), *Yoga in Transformation: Historical and Contemporary Perspectives*, 551–73. Wiener Forum für Theologie und Religionswissenschaft. Göttingen: V&R University Press.

Newcombe, S. 2019. *Yoga in Britain: Stretching Spirituality and Educating Yogis*. Sheffield: Equinox.

Newcombe, S. 2020. 'Yoga in Europe', in Jacobsen, K. and Sardella, F. (eds), *Hinduism in Europe*, 555–587. Leiden: Brill.

Oliver, I. P. 1979. *Buddhism in Britain*. London: Rider & Company.

Oliver, P. 2014. *Hinduism in the 1960s*. London: Bloomsbury.

Pearlman, E. 2012. *Nothing and Everything: The Influence of Buddhism on the American Avant Garde: 1942–1962*. Berkeley: North Atlantic Books.

Penman, S., et al. 2012. 'Yoga in Australia: Results of a National Survey'. *International Journal of Yoga* 5(2): 92–101.

Pinch, W. R. 2006. *Warrior Ascetics and Indian Empires*. Cambridge: Cambridge University Press.

Pollock, S. 2002. 'Cosmopolitan and Vernacular in History', in Breckenridge, Carol A., Pollock, S., Bhabha, H. K. and Chakrabarty, D. (eds), *Cosmopolitanism*, 15–53. London: Duke University Press.
Rocher, R. 2002. 'Sanskrit for Civil Servants 1806–1818'. *Journal of the American Oriental Society* 122(2): 381–390. https://doi.org/10.2307/3087633
Reddy, S. 2004. 'The Politics and Poetics of "Magazine Medicine": New Age Ayurveda in the Print Media', in Johnston, R. D. (ed), *The Politics of Healing: Histories of Alternative Medicine in Twentieth-Century North America*, 207–30. London: Routledge.
Remski, M. 2019. *Practice and All Is Coming: Abuse, Cult Dynamics, and Healing in Yoga and Beyond.* Rangiora: Embodied Wisdom Publishing.
Rushdie, S. 1982. 'The Empire Writes Back with a Vengeance'. *The Times* (London) 3 July, p. 8.
Said, E. 1978. *Orientalism.* London: Pantheon Books.
Sand, E. and Rudbog, E. (eds) 2020. *Imagining the East: The Early Theosophical Society.* New York: Oxford University Press.
Seager, R. H. 2002. 'American Buddhism in the Making', in Baumann, M. and Prebish, C. (eds), *Westward Dharma: Buddhism Beyond Asia*, 106–119. Berkeley: University of California Press.
Segall, L. 2013. 'Steve Jobs' Last Gift'. *CNN Business Online.* 10 September. https://money.cnn.com/2013/09/10/technology/steve-jobs-gift/index.html Accessed 25 January 2020.
Singleton, M. 2007 'Yoga, Eugenics and Spiritual Darwinism in the Early Twentieth Century'. *International Journal of Hindu Studies* 11: 125–146.
Singleton, M. 2008. 'The Classical Reveries of Modern Yoga: Patañjali and Constructive Orientalism', in Singleton, M. and Byrne, J. (eds), Yoga in the Modern World: Contemporary Perspectives, 77–99. London: Routledge.
Singleton, M. 2010. *Yoga Body: The Origins of Modern Posture Practice.* New York: Oxford University Press.
Spivak, G. C. 1988. 'Can the Subaltern Speak?', in Nelson, C. and Grossberg, L. (eds), *Marxism and the Interpretation of Culture*, 271–313. London: Macmillan.
Strauss, S. 2005. *Positioning Yoga: Balancing Acts Across Cultures.* Oxford: Berg.
Tweed, T. 2005. *The American Encounter with Buddhism, 1844–1912: Victorian Culture and the Limits of Dissent.* Chapel Hill: University of North Carolina Press Books.
Wallace, B. A. 2002. 'The Spectrum of Buddhist Practice in the West', in Baumann, M. and Prebish, C. (eds), *Westward Dharma: Buddhism Beyond Asia*, 34–50. Berkeley: University of California Press.
Ward, R. A. 2019. 'Prashantji's Use of English'. *Yoga Rahasya*, 26(4): 62–67.
Warrier, M. 2019. 'Ayurveda and Mind-Body Healing: Legitimizing Strategies in the Autobiographical Writing of Deepak Chopra'. *International Journal of Hindu Studies* 23: 123–145
White, D. G. 2009. *Sinister Yogis.* Chicago: University of Chicago Press.
White, D. G. 2014. *The Yoga Sutra of Patanjali: A Biography.* Princeton, NJ: Princeton University Press.
Wildcroft, T. 2020. *Post-lineage Yoga: From Guru to #MeToo.* Sheffield: Equinox.
Williamson, L. (2010) *Transcendent in America: Hindu-Inspired Meditation Movements as New Religion.* London: New York University Press.
Wilson, J. 2014. *Mindful America: The Mutual Transformation of Buddhist Meditation and American Culture.* Oxford: Oxford University Press.
*Yoga Journal* and Yoga Alliance. 2016. 'Yoga in America Survey'. www.yogajournal.com/page/yogainamericastudy. Accessed 25 January 2020.
Yogananda, P. 2003 [1946]. Autobiography of a Yogi. New Delhi: Sterling Publishers.
Yogendra. 1956 [1928]. Yoga Physical Education. 7th ed. Santa Cruz, Bombay: The Yoga Institute.

# 25

# THE YOGIC BODY IN GLOBAL TRANSMISSION

*Sravana Borkataky-Varma*

## Introduction

The practices discussed in this chapter (including yoga, *cakra*, *Kuṇḍalinī* and *kuṇḍalinī yoga*) are highly complex and historically entrenched. By themselves or in combination, each brings forth materials that are not only rich in content but also provide a challenging landscape for scholars to navigate. The meta-objective of this chapter is to bring forth the complexity of the various transmissions through a comparative study of *kuṇḍalinī yoga*, specifically by comparing its practice in an esoteric environment with its practice in exoteric settings. Conversations from a temple in Kāmākhyā, India, provide the primary data for esoteric interpretations of *kuṇḍalinī yoga*, while exoteric explanations of the practice draw from interviews conducted in the United States.

Over a period of four years, the study asked eleven research participants in each of the two contexts to reflect on a range of questions that included: What is *kuṇḍalinī*? Where does it reside in the body? How do you activate the *kuṇḍalinī*? How does it feel when it rises? What practices or rituals do you follow as part of your *kuṇḍalinī yoga* practice? (This latter question included specific questions for male and female partners). In Kāmākhyā, all interviews occurred within the guru–disciple rubric. In other words, research participants were all either gurus who teach *kuṇḍalinī yoga* or their disciples. Research participants in the United States, meanwhile, included authors who publish books on *cakra* and *kuṇḍalinī yoga*, gurus, yoga studio owners, 3HO (Healthy, Happy, Holy Organization) instructors and online teachers. The names of all interviewees have been changed in order to protect their identities.

As a result of this comparative study, I conclude that exoteric and normative understandings of *kuṇḍalinī yoga* are being increasingly popularised both in Kāmākhyā and in the United States. The esoteric – which in Kāmākhyā is believed to be more 'authentic' – is tightly confined within the teacher–disciple-initiation (*dīkṣā*)-secret (*gupt*) matrix. The chapter's first section, 'Context and Terms', offers a broad overview of the four key terms used here: 'yogic body', '*cakra*', '*Kuṇḍalinī* and *kuṇḍalinī yoga*'. The second section, 'Behind the veil', discusses *kuṇḍalinī yoga* in the context of the Kāmākhyā temple. The third section, 'Public *Kuṇḍalinī*', discusses *kuṇḍalinī yoga* as practised in the United States and contrasts it with understandings of *kuṇḍalinī* that emerged from the Kāmākhyā temple.

## Context and terms

### Yogic body

The objective of *kuṇḍalinī yoga* practice is to raise the *kuṇḍalinī* in the yogic body, though this objective is often obscured in practice. As Mallinson and Singleton note, 'The predominance of scientific and medical realism in popular yoga discourse has tended to obscure or displace more traditional visions of the body, and has thereby, mutatis mutandis, reshaped the perceived function of the yoga practices themselves' (Mallinson and Singleton 2017: 171). Studies on the yogic body began before the common era: 'Some of our earliest Indian sources, dating from the early first millennium BCE, already posit the existence of several bodies, some spiritually constructed, some physically, some psychologically' (Wujastyk 2009: 190). Texts such as the *Taittirīya Upaniṣad* posit five bodies, or '*ātmans*': *annamaya*, or the physical body derived from food; *prāṇamaya*, or the body of the vital breath or airs; *manomaya*, or the self of the mind; *vijñānamaya*, or the self as a locus of knowledge; and *ānandamaya*, or the self made of joy (Olivelle 1996: 298–311). In later yogic and tantric traditions from the late first millennium CE, however, a whole 'alternative' anatomy evolved. Simply articulated, the body of the yogi now was largely understood as a network of psycho-physical centres (*cakras*, *granthis*, etc.) linked by channels (*nāḍīs*) that carry air and vital forces (*vāyus*, *kuṇḍalinī*, etc.). This understanding of the body has varying levels of empirical existence. For example, in the context of *kuṇḍalinī yoga*, the *cakras*, *nāḍīs* and *kuṇḍalinī* are visible in the earlier stages of the practice and become progressively corporeal, which enable the practitioner to manipulate them at will. We will return to this progression later in the chapter.

Understandings of the yogic body can vary considerably across different time periods and traditions. Some are comparable and some are vastly different (for example, the body in Āyurveda). Mallinson and Singleton argue that

> this is in part because yogic bodies arise according to the particular ritual, philosophical or doctrinal requirements of the tradition at hand, and because they are expressions of these requirements, rather than descriptions of self-evident, empirical bodies common to all humans.
>
> *(2017: 172)*

Within the framework of *kuṇḍalinī* yoga, *cakras* and *nāḍīs* are believed to be vital to the practice.

### Cakras

The study of *cakra* and its representations have been brought into popular culture both by academic and non-academic writers. In addition to the scholars mentioned above, Kurt Leland (2016), David Gordon White (2003) and Dorothea Maria Heilijgers-Seelen (1994) are all widely cited scholars of this topic. In popular culture, writers such as Cyndi Dale (e.g. 2018, 2016, 2009), Ambika Wauters (e.g. 2017, 2002, 1997), and Kristine Marie Corr (2016) are just a few of the successful names. Having said that, the study of *cakras* and the yogic body is still fairly underdeveloped – a scholar and/or practitioner must stitch together a historical narrative from the various sources that are most relevant to their practice and/or lineage.

While the genealogy and history of *cakra* are obscure to many people (including practitioners), most can articulate an explanation of *cakras* as a group of energy centres placed along the central axis of the human body. Historically speaking, there are many systems of *cakras*, and no single description fits them all. 'Every school, sometimes every teacher within the school, has had their own *cakra* system. These have developed, over time, and an "archaeology" of the various configurations is in order' (White 2003: 222). White traces the *cakra* system back and forth between texts written sometime between the eighth and the twelfth centuries CE across two religious traditions: Hindu and Buddhist. In the eighth century, two Buddhist texts, the *Caryāgīti* and the *Hevajra Tantra*, 'locate four *chakras* within the human body at the levels of the navel, heart, throat, and head' (White 2003: 224).

By the latter half of the first millennium CE, the four *cakras* would develop into the vertical configuration with six (occasionally seven) *cakras* aligned along the spine. The *Bhāgavata Purāṇa* (eighth–tenth CE) mentions six *cakras* along with their respective locations: 'navel (*nābhī*); heart (*hṛd*); breast (*uras*); root of the palate (*svatālumūlam*); place between the eyebrows (*bhruvorantaram*); and cranial vault (*mūrdhan*)' (White 2003: 224). The next significant phase in the understanding of the *cakras* came with the understanding of the yogic body in the Nāth Sampradāya. 'The earliest references to the Nāth ascetic order as an organized entity date to the beginning of the seventeenth century, but its first historical gurus, Matsyendranātha and Goraksanātha, lived much earlier, probably in the ninth and twelfth centuries, respectively' (Mallinson 2011: 1). The religious views of the Nāth *siddhas* are obscured by a lack of reliable evidence. However, the *Kaulajñānanirṇaya*, which is attributed to Matsyendranātha (Mukhopadhyay: 2012), lists seven linear energy centres along the spine: '(1) the secret place (genitals), (2) navel, (3) heart, (4) throat, (5) mouth, (6) forehead, and (7) crown of the head' (White 2003: 225).

The modern-day transmissions on *cakra* have also borrowed extensively from '*Ṣaṭcakranirūpaṇa*', the sixth chapter of *Śrītattvacintāmaṇi*. The *Ṣatchakranirūpaṇa* is a large work written by the Bengali tantra practitioner Purnananda sometime in the sixteenth century. The Sanskrit text was first published in 1858 together with a translation into Bengali (Blumhardt 1886: 85). A second Bengali translation and commentary were published in 1860, with a second edition printed in 1869 (Baier 2016: 313). This text rose to international fame in the late nineteenth and early twentieth centuries.

In his comments on the *Ṣaṭcakranirūpana*, Sir John Woodroffe (writing under the name Arthur Avalon; see Chapter 10 in this volume) notes that there are six centres in the body: the spinal centre of the regions below the genitals (*mūlādhāra*), the spinal centre of the region above the genitals (*svādhiṣṭhāna*), the spinal centre of the region of the navel (*maṇipūra*), the spinal centre of the region of the heart (*anāhata*), the spinal centre of the region of the throat (*viśuddha*) and the centre of the region between the eyebrows (*ājñā*) (Avalon 1978: 141). This linear understanding of the *cakra* system led to several pictorial representations. Applying this model to human anatomy, Woodroffe connects the six chakras to nerve plexuses, thereby bringing the yogic body into conversation with the western biomedical body.

This blended yogic–biomedical body soon became an integral element of American metaphysical discourse and, eventually, counter-culture and popular culture. Beginning in 1880, the Theosophical Society played a significant role in the import of the *cakras* to the west and the construction of modern yoga.

> Theosophical constructions of yoga were profoundly influential in shaping contemporary ideas, and [Helena Petrovna] Blavatsky's claim in 1881– that 'neither modern Europe nor America had so much as heard' of yoga, until the 'Theosophists began to speak and write', while hyperbolic, is not made without reason.
>
> *(Singleton 2010: 77)*

Other notable figures from this group include Annie Besant (1874–1933) and Swami Vivekanada (1863–1902), who added to the popularity of *cakras* in this time period.

The twentieth century saw a proliferation of scholarship and literature on *cakras* from figures such as James Morgan Pryse (1859–1942), Alice Bailey (1880–1949) and the Sikh guru Bhagat Singh Thind (1892–1967), along with a burgeoning of small and large institutes such as the Esalen Institute. For example, Kripal (2008: 6) notes that 'Eranos [conferences by C. J. Jung in Europe] and Esalen are related European and American counter-culture weavings of radical religious experimentation, technical scholarship, and popular culture that provided the intellectual substance for broad cultural transformations.' Having mapped the global transmissions of *cakras*, let us now look at the understandings of *kuṇḍalinī* and the transmissions of *kuṇḍalinī yoga*.

## Kuṇḍalinī *and* kuṇḍalinī yoga

The transmission of *Kuṇḍalinī* and *kuṇḍalinī yoga* follow a similar trajectory to the *cakras*. We begin with two texts from the thirteenth and the fourteenth centuries that discuss *kuṇḍalinī*. The first is *Jñāneśvari*, written by the poet-saint Jnandev (1275–1293), who is considered to be one of the founders of the Maharashtrian *Vārkarī* or the 'pilgrim' movement. The second is the story of Cūḍāla and Śikhidhvaja from the *Yogavāsiṣṭha*, a philosophical text attributed to Valmiki (although the real author is unknown; see Chapple 1984: ix–x).

*Jñāneśvari* is 'a commentary on the *Bhagavadgītā* of about 9000 verses in old *Marāṭhī*, most probably completed in 1290 AD' (Kiehnle 2004–2005: 447). *Kuṇḍalinī* is discussed in chapter 6 of *Jñāneśvari*. Since *Jñāneśvari* is a commentary on the *Bhagavadgītā*, it follows the same format: that is, Lord Kṛṣṇa instructing Arjuna. Jnandev dedicates seventy poetic verses to describing the effects of *kuṇḍalinī* rising (6.222–6.292). Jnandev begins his description of *kuṇḍalinī* as an infant snake, bathed with saffron, curled up asleep in exactly in three and a half coils, with her head downward. As a result of breath entering the stomach of the practitioner, the *kuṇḍalinī* serpent awakens from her sleep. She softly loosens her coils and rises out of her relaxed body, like a seed sprouting. Having sprouted from its seed of long slumber, *kuṇḍalinī* is now famished. With her flaming mouth, she starts to devour the yogi's flesh. She takes a morsel out of each body part that is covered in flesh and draws the essence out from the nails and the feet before becoming one with the skeleton of the practitioner. She then takes a big gulp of the seven constituents of the body, resulting in the production of an intense and dry heat in the yogi's body. The yogi's body is now on fire. The practitioner must endure the intense heat and not let it break his yogic one-pointed concentration. If he is successful in maintaining his concentration, the outside of his body will slowly start to cool down and a type of new body (yogic body) gets constructed. At this point, the practitioner is blessed with *siddhis*: 'perfections' or 'magical powers' (Kiehnle 2004–2005: 485). Dependent on the yogic breath, she then enters the yogi's heart. It is at this point that the intellect is transformed into pure consciousness, and at this stage the male yogic body transforms into a feminine principle. While Jnandev does not provide commentary on the feminine body rising in a male body, we can see the appearance of the androgynous man. The *tattvas* or the 'elements' begin to dissolve, and finally air, the subtlest of the elements, leaves the yogic body.

Jnandev stops using the term *kuṇḍalinī* after she leaves the heart, and he chooses to call her *mārutī*, 'belonging to the wind'. *Mārutī* remains *śakti* (*Śākta* and *śakti* are both derived from the Sanskrit verbal root √*śak*, 'to be able') which suggests ability, capacity and energy. The word *śakti* means energy or power, but when written as *Śakti*, it signifies the 'embodied form of *śakti* as a goddess' (Kinsley 1997: 285) until she merges into her final destination, Śiva *tattva* (thatness, truth, reality). The serpent's journey from resting in the body of the yogi to becoming one with

Śiva now comes to an end. By way of conclusion, at the end of chapter 6 Kṛṣṇa tells Arjuna that yogis who are successful in this *sādhana* are equal to Kṛṣṇa himself: 'Those who did with their bodies just this *sādhana* which we told, became experts [and] equal to me' (Kiehnle 2004–2005: 490). In other words, such yogis achieve a divine status.

In the second text, *Yogavāsiṣṭha, kuṇḍalinī* is mentioned in the story of Cūḍāla and Śikhidhvaja in the *pūrvārdha* section of Book VI called *Nirvāṇa-prakaraṇa*. This is the only text known to scholars where *kuṇḍalinī yoga* is shown practised by a woman, Cūḍāla. Cūḍāla is a princess of extraordinary beauty who was married in her youth to a neighbouring prince, Śikhidhvaja. She will eventually become his spiritual teacher. Cūḍāla studied meditation, gaining a deep calm and insight that left her husband bewildered. Śikhidhvaja, on the other hand, ignored Cūḍāla's advice by renouncing his kingdom and retreating to a distant forest. In his absence, she ruled the country. One day, she took the form of a young ascetic, appearing before her husband as he wandered in the forest and offering herself as his teacher. She instructs him in meditation and mind control, and it is at this point of the story that we find mention of the *kuṇḍalinī*.

Like *kuṇḍalinī* in *Jñāneśvari*, in *Yogavāsiṣṭha* she is again described as a coiled sleeping serpent. She is present in all living beings as the supreme power (*paramā śakti*). The text also uses the same analogy of the sprouting germ as the *Jñāneśvari*. Further, in the *Yogavāsiṣṭha*, her vibration is compared to a bee in a lotus. It touches (*sparśa*) the yogic body ever so softly, vibrating from within, giving rise to looming sensations and desires (Maderey 2017: 248). Once she rises, her journey to the heart and beyond is similar to the *Jñāneśvari*.

Discussion on *kuṇḍalinī* is incomplete without the mention of Kashmir *Śaivism* and Abhinavagupta. In this system, *kuṇḍalinī* is 'nothing but vibration – the vibrant undulation of emanation, the more and more subtle vibration of reabsorption – a high-frequency vibration' (Silburn 1988: 6). For us to understand what vibration really means here, we have to first quickly arrive at an understanding of the Sanskrit word *spanda*, 'vibration'. The best place to get a good grasp of divine vibration is to look at the *Spandakārikās*. The most popular commentary on the *Spandakārikās* was written by Abhinavagupta's cousin and pupil, Kṣemarāja. The word *spandana* comes from √*spand*, which means to tremble, quiver, vibrate, throb or move. So what is this movement?

> Spanda is the spontaneous and recurrent pulsation of the absolute objectively manifest as the rhythm of the arising and subsidence of every detail of the cosmic picture that appears within its infinite expanse. At the same time, Spanda is the inner universal vibration of consciousness as its pure perceptivity (*upalabdhṛtā*) which constitutes equally its cognizing subjectivity (*jñātṛtva*) and agency (*kartṛtva*).
>
> *(Dyczkowski 1980: 24)*

In other words, *spanda* is a throb, a heaving of spiritual rapture in the essential nature of the divine, which excludes all succession. Simply put, in this schema the entire cosmos emerges from the pure consciousness of Śiva. Thus, the dynamic movement of Śiva is understood to be the *causa sine qua non* of all movements (Singh 1980: xvi).

To return to our discussion on *kuṇḍalinī*, for Abhinavagupta, *kuṇḍalinī* is the rippling manifestation of Śiva's throb, both in the universe and the individual. Thus, the objective of *kuṇḍalinī* yoga in Kashmir Śaivism is for the yogi to make an inward turn by which he can be attuned to and finally identify and recapture the primordial pulsation of Śiva. When the yogi successfully identifies the primordial throb within him, he progresses from duality to unity. Having looked at the transmission of the terms, let us now focus on *kuṇḍalinī yoga* in the Kāmākhyā temple.

## Behind the veil

In terms of age, the temple of Kāmākhyā surpasses most of the shrines in India, and even more in eastern India. While it is difficult to date its historical origins, numerous sculptures and the oldest stratum suggest the existence of temples in the seventh century, with a larger temple complex dating back to the Pāla dynasty (Bernier 1997: 23).

The goddess Ṣoḍaśī (also known as Tripurasundarī) is the heart of Kāmākhyā. Ṣoḍaśī is understood to be a 'beautiful young girl of sixteen with a red complexion. She is sometimes shown astride Śiva in sexual intercourse. [...] Sometimes she is said to sit on a lotus that emerges from the navel of Śiva, who is reclining below her. Her four arms hold a noose, goad, bow, and arrows' (Kinsley 1997: 11). Ṣoḍaśī is associated with *rajas guṇa*: 'energy qualities'. In Kāmākhyā, the central ritual (*pūjā*) for Ṣoḍaśī is the *kumārī pūjā*. The meta-narrative is that after performing the *pūjā* in the sanctum sanctorum of the temple and completing the circumambulation, *parikramā*, one must offer *kumārī pūjā* (ideally a Brahmin girl between five and ten years old) in order for the visit to the temple and the wish to be complete. In further questioning during fieldwork, however, practitioners articulated benefits of *kumārī pūjā* that corresponded to the text *Devī Bhāgavata Purāṇa*. For example, it is believed that the worship of a two-year-old led to the extinction of misery and poverty, *pūjā* to a five-year-old provided a cure to diseases, *pūjā* to a six-year-old destroyed enemies, and so forth (Banerjee Mukherjee 2016: 153).

Another *pūjā* relevant to our discussions here is ritual for the goddess Rājarājeśvarī. The *Śakta* tantra initiates and the *Śakta* tantra practitioner (*sādhaka*) perform the Rājarājeśvarī *pūjā* during the festival of *Chaitra Navratri* (March–April). While Ṣoḍaśī in Kāmākhyā is kept in the exoteric, Rājarājeśvarī is understood as existing in the realm of *Kamakalā-vilāsa*, where the meaning of the goddess is explained within the context of sexual fluids: 'Red being the female sexual fluid; white, semen, [and] the union of the two' (Kinsley 1997: 121). Offerings of the *pañcamakāra* or the five substances – *madya* (wine), *māṃsa* (meat), *matsya* (fish), *mudrā* (parched grain) and *maithuna* (sexual intercourse) – are central to the ritual space (Interviews conducted by the author with Sarma in 2013). The practitioners perform this ritual with their wives and often to the *Guptasādhanā-tantra* – a text that

> directs the adept to worship his wife, or the wife of another, by washing her feet with water, then worshipping her forehead, face, throat, heart, navel, breasts, and vagina by repeating one hundred mantras of his chosen deity. At the time of ejaculation, the *sādhaka* is to offer his semen to Śiva and imagine the *śakti* as his chosen deity.
>
> *(Kinsley 1997: 248)*

*Kuṇḍalinī yoga* is taught and learned within the frameworks of the Rājarājeśvarī *pūjā*. Specific instructions on *kuṇḍalinī yoga* are still believed to be *guru mukhi vidyā* – that is, 'face-to-face wisdom from the spiritual teacher' that is meant to be kept secret by the initiate. This often raises the question of how the data presented in this chapter was acquired.[1]

All *kuṇḍalinī* yoga practitioners have a *bīja mantra* or 'seed mantra', which is chanted at the beginning of the practice to awaken the *kuṇḍalinī*. It takes several years of dedicated studies and acumen in bodily practices before an individual can be initiated in the larger space of *kuṇḍalinī yoga*. Hence, the population of adepts who practise *kuṇḍalinī* yoga in Kāmākhyā is rather small. They are also hard to locate, since there are no websites, visiting cards or resumes that practitioners or their respective gurus offer to the outside world to list their accomplishments or their practices. A formidable degree of access is required to be accepted into these tight-knit, highly secretive communities.

*Kuṇḍalinī yoga* practitioners in Kāmākhyā begin the practice with a variety of cleansing practices (*dhauti*) and purification of the nerve system (*nāḍīśuddhi*). This is followed by invoking the *iṣṭa devatā/devī* or 'patron god/goddess', followed by the guru who taught the practice. Raising the *kuṇḍalinī* involves the application of bodily locks (*bandhas*) as well as sexual intercourse, whether real or imagined. In reference to the *bandhas*, while there are many locks that the adepts perform as a daily ritualistic regimen, there are three locks that are vital to the *kuṇḍalinī* practice: *mūlabandha*, *uḍḍiyāna-bandha* and *jālaṁdhara-bandha*. Successful application of these *bandhas* affects the nervous (*snāẏutantrēra*), circulatory (*saṁcaraṇaśīla*), respiratory (*śbāsayantrēra*) and endocrine systems (*antaḥsrābī sisṭēma*) and – most important of all – the system of internal energy or *prāṇa* (Interviews conducted by the author with Ashok in 2013 and 2014). Further, the three *bandhas*, when performed as a triad, create a vacuum inside the physical body, trapping air and bodily fluids. This in turn creates pressure in the cranial vault (*larōṭisaṅkrānta khilāna*), which compresses the *cakras*.

The objective of *kuṇḍalinī yoga* is to endure the discomfort felt due to this increased pressure and to allow the *śakti* to keep moving upwards – that is from the *mūlādhāra* to *svādhiṣṭhāna* to *maṇipūra*, and so on. All eleven interviewees reported that for the longest time (the number of years varied), they failed in completing all three *bandhas*. However, they were eventually successful through diligent and regular practice. In addition to the *cakra*s and the *bandha*s, ritualised sexual intercourse also came up as an important facet – especially in the initial stages of the practice. The practitioner needs to get some fluids absent in their bodies. For example, female fluids (vaginal) for a male practitioner and vice versa. The successful combination of these fluids leads to an 'accelerated stir of the *kuṇḍalinī* in the *mūlādhāra*' (Interviews conducted by the author with Mai in 2012, Ashok in 2013 and 2014, and Nirupama in 2015). It is imperative to note that several interviewees emphasised the need to differentiate sexual activities undertaken for pleasure or procreation from those performed as ritual sexual acts, which are essential at the early stages of the training, akin to an orientation exercise. The objective is for the practitioner (both men and women) to avoid releasing their bodily fluids immediately after a climax. Instead, the practitioner must mindfully use the *mūlabandha* to store the sexual fluids within his or her body.

So, what is *kuṇḍalinī* for practitioners of *kuṇḍalinī yoga* in Kāmākhyā? *Kuṇḍalinī* is a 'kind of light' (*jyoti*), which gets activated when one seeks to genuinely know the mysteries of the divine (Interview by author with Mai in 2012). Upon further probing, Mai explained the visualisation of the light as akin to a white dot. The white dot is *kuṇḍalinī*, the cosmic power that has created the entire universe and is planted as a seed in all human beings. It is the agent in the nervous system that remains dormant for most people, yet *kuṇḍalinī* can be raised with determination and single-pointed concentration. Once it rises, it is systematically absorbed into the body and blends in with the 'entire nervous system', which in turn activates each cell in the body. This eventually leads to a formation of a 'new body', a yogic body.

A second definition that emerged from interviews with practitioners is that '*Kuṇḍalinī* is the energy of the *iṣṭa devī* that rises within the body of the practitioner. In other words, it is the true presence of the divine within the human body' (Interview by author with Nirupama in 2014). The arrival of the divine and the process of taking abode simultaneously converts the practitioner's body from being profane to being sacred. When *kuṇḍalinī* rises, *cakra* to *cakra*, the practitioner is blessed with certain special abilities, such as the ability to see into a person's past, to communicate with a departed soul and other abilities similar to those we see with mediums and psychics in the west. It is only from the transformed sacred body that the practitioner can exhibit these *siddhis* or 'special powers'.

A third definition that emerged through interviews was that '*kuṇḍalinī* is red and is like a coiled snake residing in the *mūlādhāra cakra*, which is present in everyone's body. It is the *brahmāṇḍa* in us. This energy must be raised from the *mūlādhāra cakra* to the *sahasrāra cakra*.' The objective of *kuṇḍalinī yoga* is to successfully 'identify the presence of *tattva*s in one's body and be able to channel the elements' (Interviews by author with Ashok in 2013, 2014 and 2015). When *kuṇḍalinī* rises through each *cakra*, the practitioner's internal energy generated from the elements (*tattva*) is transmitted back to the cosmos (*brahmāṇḍa*). As this happens, the dross material in the body is shed, and the physical body is transformed into a pure body. Ashok uses the example of a car:

> If you have not started a car for a long time, it gets rusty. After the initial preparations, when you start the engine, some rusted dust particles and dried oil residue will fall off the engine. In the same way, when *kuṇḍalinī* rises, the dross elements from the body are flushed out. A strange kind of *śakti* called 'creator power' (*sṛṣṭi śakti*) starts to appear, and a kind of heat gets generated. When this happens, it is very important to have a guru. It can be a very scary stage since people will not necessarily know how to deal with this intense experience.
>
> *(Interview by author with Ashok in 2014)*

To summarise the three sample definitions and the remaining eight discussions from the Kāmākhyā temple, *kuṇḍalinī* is mostly understood as the divine energy planted and present in men and women alike. Esoteric yogic practices often grouped under the rubric of *kuṇḍalinī yoga*, then, are used to raise the divine energy and to activate it. This form of ritualised yoga is followed by a select few under the strict guidance of their gurus. It is almost never offered and practised in a secular space. Furthermore, the practice is closely interconnected to the goddess, the *śākti*, and understood as a highly evolved tantric practice. And finally, in the Kāmākhyān worldview, *kuṇḍalinī* allows for *siddhis*. When an adept can successfully raise their *kuṇḍalinī*, they are able to provide insights and solutions for life situations. So, what are the esoteric practices that are understood as *kuṇḍalinī yoga* in Kāmākhyā? Although they map well to the definitions provided for *kuṇḍalinī*, *kuṇḍalinī yoga* practices are also somewhat different.

Mai and Ashok provided the most detailed (though somewhat differing) interviews. The remaining nine interviewees either agreed with Mai or with Ashok. Mai's understanding of *kuṇḍalinī yoga* mapped to her interpretation of three kinds of practitioner: unmarried men, married men and married women. In her view, for any man (whether single or married), 'a female partner is essential for the practice of *kuṇḍalinī yoga*' (Interviews by author with Mai in 2012 and 2013). Mai strongly advocated *kuṇḍalinī yoga* to be practised only by married men: 'A man cannot proceed on this path unless he is married and has a devoted wife who will practise with him. Therefore, success comes to married men only' (ibid.). Practicing outside the rubric of marriage is problematic, since a majority of people do not understand the relationship between a practitioner and a 'spiritual partner' (Interview by author with Mai in 2013). In reference to women practicing *kuṇḍalinī yoga*, Mai said that women do not require the support of anyone because they already have all the energies that are required. They do not need a male partner or a husband for the energy to rise or for the practice to bear fruit. If a woman has self-will, determination and blessings from the goddess, she will succeed.

In the context of the practice itself, Mai's practice included a variety of *dhauti* and *bandha*s as discussed above. However, she emphasised the importance of the heart *cakra* (*anāhata cakra*).

According to Mai, *kuṇḍalinī* rises in the heart and extends progressively through the rest of the body, altering the yogic body permanently:

> After *kuṇḍalinī* has risen, it creates a new inner body. The new body is formed, each cell in the body, each nerve gets charged; there is a distinct sensation, almost like a vibration, like goose bumps, but the goose bumps surface internally and not externally. Every cell in the body will have bumps. Not a single cell is left untouched. One will have no desire or energy left to move away from this state. Once individuals – male or female – get *kuṇḍalinī* to rise, they are never the same again. Something alters within the individual permanently.
>
> *(Interviews by author with Mai in 2012 and 2013)*

Mai's description of *kuṇḍalinī*, the accompanying description of the physical sensations and the feeling of being altered forever are similar to Gopi Krishna's narration of his experience of *kuṇḍalinī* rising (Krishna 1970), which I will return to in the Conclusion. Mai also makes some significant claims about the occurrence of the 'new body'.

Ashok's *kuṇḍalinī* yoga practice, meanwhile, rested on the physical body and *tattva* (element). He used the classic definition for *tattva* as found in *Śākta Tantra*. There are five *tattvas* that create global energy cycles of *tattvic* tides: spirit *tattva* (*ākāśa*), air *tattva* (*vāyu*), fire *tattva* (*tejas*), water *tattva* (*āpas*) and earth *tattva* (*pṛthivī*). Most people live their entire life without coming to any realisation of how the *tattvas* affect the constitution of the human body and nature, whereas for a *kuṇḍalinī yoga* practitioner, the identification and wilful activation of the *tattvas* is significant (Interviews by author with Ashok in 2013, 2014 and 2015). With dedicated practice, the *kuṇḍalinī* yoga practitioner gets better at identifying and taking command of the *tattvas*. This results in experiencing the presence of *kuṇḍalinī*. In order to do so, a man or woman must have a guru, a deep desire to activate the *kuṇḍalinī*, a commitment to the yoga practice and a partner. This is a significant difference in understanding between Mai and Ashok.

For Ashok, the process involves three steps: identifying the guru, initiation (*dīkṣā*) and identifying a partner. For *kuṇḍalinī* to rise, 'one must experience ultimate pleasure, climax, and, for that, one needs three people: the guru, the disciple, and the partner' (Interview by author with Ashok in 2015). The role of the partner is largely to physically draw the 'bodily fluids from the other sex into one's physical body'. He further stated that 'a male practitioner takes help from his female partner (wife) until the time he is able to identify and channel the feminine energy latently present in him. Once the practitioner masters the art of channelling the feminine, he is barred from using a woman as part of *kuṇḍalinī yoga*' (Interview by author with Ashok in 2015).

Since Ashok repeatedly switched between the terms 'partner' and 'wife', I probed more deeply on the distinction between the two. Ashok clarified that:

> Most men practitioners are married, and the wife almost always takes *dīkṣā* with the husband and performs her duties every day as prescribed. However, there are unmarried practitioners who need the presence of women consorts. In some tantric traditions, unmarried women are frowned upon. But in Kāmākhyā, unmarried women who aid adepts in their *sādhana* are not looked down upon. They are fewer in numbers and are well accepted. It is much easier if the practitioner is married, as no one asks questions. Similarly, a woman practitioner may be allowed a male consort.
>
> *(Interview by author with Ashok in 2015)*

The above claim is by no means simple or well known in the exoteric space in Kāmākhyā. Further research is required to understand the role of male and female consorts. We now turn to the third section, 'Public *kuṇḍalinī*'.

## Public *kuṇḍalinī*

In the United States, a large number of people are willing to speak about *kuṇḍalinī yoga* in the broader yoga community, and the number of definitions for *kuṇḍalinī* is equally large. The following are some definitions that capture the essence of all eleven definitions selected for this chapter: (1) '*Kuṇḍalinī* is a life energy, which is typically considered feminine. When activated in the body, it stirs the *cakras*, which cleanses the body, thereby leading to enlightenment. This helps the person to express her true self on an everyday basis' (Interview by author with Sandra, 2014). (2) '*Kuṇḍalinī* is the creative power of the individual. An active *kuṇḍalinī* helps with what you do in life and your energy balance' (Interview by author with Kaur, 2014). (3) '*Kuṇḍalinī* is a metaphor. It is a metaphor for the life essence of nature and the individual' (Interview by author with Janet, 2015). (4) '*Kuṇḍalinī* is the presence of *Śiva* and *Śaktī*. *Kuṇḍalinī* is our individual power. It is not awake because of *ahaṃkāra*, or 'ego'. *Ahaṃkāra* makes us experience life in 'separation', but once *kuṇḍalinī* rises, we experience 'oneness'. The binary existence comes to an end' (Interview by author with Swami Ji, 2016). (5) '*Kuṇḍalinī* is the past. It is the vibration from inside that enables us to fulfil our life purpose' (Interview by author with Frieda, 2016).

There is a common pattern in these definitions. Almost all interviewees in the United States defined *kuṇḍalinī* in the context of the American metaphysical religion and human potential movements rather than the goddess narrative (except for Swami Ji, an Indian American who maps his lineage to Kashmir Śaivism). For the majority, the practice of *kuṇḍalinī* is a secular type of yoga that exists outside the tight clutches of a guru, initiation rites and the temple. A majority of research participants in the United States also spoke to the 'spontaneous arising of the *kuṇḍalinī*', which did not come up even once in the Kāmākhyā interviews.

The objectives of *kuṇḍalinī yoga* practice that emerged in interviews with US-based research participants included making money, heightened sexual experience, completing writing projects, evocative art, success in sports such as baseball and football, etc. It is important to note that in each interview, research participants repeatedly emphasised sexual fulfilment and/or heightened sexual experience as a benefit of the practice. For example, Paulo said:

> *kuṇḍalinī yoga* is a great practice for men. *Kuṇḍalinī yoga* generates a strong sense of bliss, which arises from the cessation of the mundane. There is an [outpouring] of happiness, joy, a kind of 'high', which when performed with a woman helps break the ego. To be able to share the bliss stimulated in the genitals with a woman partner is a useful vehicle to realize the non-boundary between you and the other, thereby destroying the ego.
>
> *(Interview by author with Paulo, 2016)*

Janet and Sandra spoke at length about how *kuṇḍalinī yoga* practice brought them closer to their own sexual desires and needs, 'sort of like being raw and feeling emotions and expressing pleasure without inhibitions' (Interviews by the author with Sandra, 2014). Further, only two out of the eleven US interviewees shared that they were initiated by a guru whose lineage was mapped to India. These two individuals had an *iṣṭa devī*, a *bīja mantra* as discussed by the practitioners in Kāmākhyā. The rest stated that they were introduced to the *kuṇḍalinī* practice in their yoga studio, by a friend, the internet, a book, social media and streaming services.

In the United States, the 3HO movement encapsulates the understandings of the most popular form of *kuṇḍalinī yoga* practice in the United States. Practitioners used a wide range of mantras, including 'sa-re-sa-sa', 'sat-na-a-ma' and 'oṃ, oṃ nama śivāy'. While three interviewees had not heard of the 3HO, a large majority was at least aware of it or had accessed or attended 3HO workshops. 3HO was founded in 1969 by a Punjabi Sikh, Harbhajan Singh Puri, later known as Yogi Bhajan. He began teaching Kundalini Yoga classes in Los Angeles to largely white, middle-class audience of Americans. There are currently hundreds of 3HO yoga studios across the United States coast to coast (see their website: 3ho.org). *Cakras* remain central to *kuṇḍalinī yoga* practice in the United States, but there are substantive differences between this setting and Kāmākhyā in terms of how *cakras* are understood to be activated. While the large majority activated the *cakra* from *mūlādhāra* going all the way to *svādhiṣṭhāna* (crown of the head), for some, the practice began from *svādhiṣṭhāna* and settled into the *mūlādhāra*. By contrast, beginning from the crown never came up in Kāmākhyā. Finally, there was a wide disparity between the rigour in training. In Kāmākhyā, training is rooted in the Rājarājeśvarī *pūjā* ritual, which is governed by the guru, *guru mukhi vidyā*, *iṣṭa devī*, *bīja mantra*, *bandhas*, *tattva*, and so forth (as discussed above). The socio-religious power structures continue to shield *kuṇḍalinī* practice from the public eye. The centuries-old patriarchal culture of Hindu India is a meta-narrative, and this narrative yields a meta-power structure, which in turn confines the practice of *kuṇḍalinī yoga* to a select few and keeps the practice shrouded in secrecy. In the United States, on the other hand, terms such as ego, individual, clairaudience, subtle body, creativity, life purpose and sexual fulfilment drive popular narratives. This allows for the practice to be accessible to anyone who may be interested, which in turn allows for more flexibility in terms of who (men and women, initiated or not), where (studio, online, private), and how (crown *cakra* to root, or root to crown) the practice will be taught. A *kuṇḍalinī yoga* teacher may stick to a tradition, as seen by 3HO teachers, or have the complete freedom to create their own practice, which invariably is borrowed from various traditions and styles.

## Concluding remarks

Carl Gustav Jung (1875–1961) gave a series of four lectures in the autumn of 1933 in response to a talk presented by the Indologist Jakob Wilhelm Hauer titled 'Der Yoga, im besondern die Bedeutung des Chakras': that is, 'Yoga, in particular the Importance of the *Cakras*'. Hauer was a missionary to India and later became a professor of religious studies at Tübingen, Germany. He founded a new religion called the Deutsche Glaubensbewegung (Hauer, Heim and Adam 1937). Jung's use of terms such as 'suprapersonal', 'Soter' and 'the Saviour Serpent of the Gnostics', interspersed with Sanskrit words such as '*mūlādhāra*' and '*sūkṣma*', perfectly exemplifies the cultural fusions and translations that would come to define 'the serpent' – that is, *kuṇḍalinī* in the twentieth century. *Kuṇḍalinī* managed to capture the minds of many twentieth-century thinkers and philosophers around the world, and serpent-inspired interactions between these western intellectuals and their Indian counterparts yielded a vast and rich collection of materials. We must deal with and try to better understand these cross-cultural fusions and hybridities and do so without immediately rendering them as 'appropriations'. After all, the same processes can be seen throughout India and throughout the history of Indian religions.

In a short span of time, the consensus view of *kuṇḍalinī* in the counter-culture and contemporary yoga scene became 'evolutionary'. In addition to Jung and Blavatsky, Gopi Krishna also a made notable contribution to this understanding. Krishna's construction of *kuṇḍalinī* and his interpretive model is drawn from Aurobindo Ghose and Woodroffe (Krishna 1970). Ghose himself drew on earlier sources (Aurobindo 2003) and evolutionary biology in the same way that Woodroffe drew on theosophy and western physiology (Avalon 1978). In short, all were doing something similar, and the meaning of *kuṇḍalinī* shifted over the course of the twentieth century through each writer.

To paraphrase Kripal's definition, such a hermeneutic can be understood as a disciplined practice of reading, writing and interpreting through which intellectuals come to experience the religious dimensions of the texts they study. What they study in the texts somehow crystallises or linguistically embodies the forms of consciousness of their original authors. In many ways, this is a kind of virtual initiatory transmission (Kripal 2001). Jung, Blavatsky, Aurobindo, Woodroffe, Krishna and other authors went through a similar process of mystical hermeneutics. All of them started on a personal quest, and somewhere along the way the authors they read, the gurus they spoke with and the bodily disciplines they practised resulted in a fusion of life and text. Evidence of the results of this amalgamation can be found in the vast volumes of written literature they produced in their lifetimes. This literature is rich in preserving some of the primary texts. It also provides a modern-day commentary that helps the reader comprehend a complex practice. In addition, the personal narratives that weave these authors' works together make them approachable and understandable to a contemporary audience.

Mapping the various transmissions shows that emic descriptions of *kuṇḍalinī* and *kuṇḍalinī yoga* essentially have three distinct features. First, *kuṇḍalinī* yoga practitioners assume the presence of a yogic body. For many of these practitioners, there do not appear to be any necessary ontological dilemmas surrounding the existence of *cakras*, for example. In many of these esoteric anatomies, the physical or material human body as seen by the naked eye is merely a shell, and it is the yogic body that really drives spiritual enlightenment. Second, *kuṇḍalinī* is understood to be both a feminine energy and a type of spiritual energy. Third, it is believed that *kuṇḍalinī* resides coiled in the human body and ordinarily in a state of deep slumber.

In Kāmākhyā, *kuṇḍalinī* is not connected to any organ or to a specific neurological centre in the human body. While most gurus state that *kuṇḍalinī* resides in the lower recesses of the human body, there are a few practitioners who believe that *kuṇḍalinī* resides in the heart. In the United States, by contrast, *kuṇḍalinī* is connected to the *mūlādhāra*. Irrespective of the placement of this feminine energy within the human body, *kuṇḍalinī* is believed to be the 'seed' of the divine, present in all humanity. The latter universalism is seldom, if ever, articulated as such, but it is almost always implied.

Interviews with *kuṇḍalinī yoga* practitioners make it clear that *kuṇḍalinī* is both a physical experience and a psychological or spiritual event. It is at once psycho-spiritual and psychosomatic. *Kuṇḍalinī* can awaken either through intentional practice or spontaneously. Ritually speaking, it is understood that one experiences awakening of *kuṇḍalinī* when there is controlled and channelled movement of bodily fluids and breath. The *bandhas* or 'locks' are an essential aspect of this practice. For *kuṇḍalinī* to awaken and possibly rise, one must successfully and swiftly apply the *bandhas*. There is a complex esoteric anatomy at work in the modern practices. Basically, there are three *bandhas* that are vital to *kuṇḍalinī*, as discussed earlier in the chapter.

Regarding someone experiencing *kuṇḍalinī* spontaneously or outside an intentional practice, it can be said that the individual unknowingly but successfully applied the *bandhas*. Irrespective of the geography, a raised *kuṇḍalinī* is an achievement that few have been able to accomplish. An awakened *kuṇḍalinī*, on the other hand, is considered relatively simpler to attain, and many in the *kuṇḍalinī* yoga community are reported to have stirred the 'Serpent'.

## Note

1 I am from Assam. I was first initiated in Kāmākhyā at the age of fifteen. I am a scholar-practitioner and I define myself as an insider with an outsider's lens.

## Bibliography

Aurobindo, S. 2003. *The Complete Works of Sri Aurobindo.* Vol. 1. Pondicherry: Sri Aurobindo Ashram Publication Department.

Avalon, A. 1978. *Shakti and Shākta.* New York: Dover Publications.

Baier, K. 2016. 'Theosophical Orientalism and the Structures of Intercultural Transfer: Annotations on the Appropriation of the Cakras in Early Theosophy', in Chajes, J. and Huss, B. (eds), *Theosophical Appropriations: Esotericism, Kabbalah, and the Transformation of Traditions*, 309–354. Beer Sheva: Ben-Gurion University of the Negev Press.

Bernier, R. 1997. *Himalayan Architecture.* Madison: Farleigh Dickinson University Press.

Blumhardt, J. F. 1886. *Catalogue of Bengali Printed Books in the Library of the British Museum.* Hertford: Stephen Austin and Sons.

Chapple, C. 1984. 'Introduction', in Venkatesananda, S. (trans), *The Concise Yoga Vāsiṣṭha*, Albany: State University of New York Press.

Corr, K. M. 2016. *Chakras: A Complete Guide to Chakra Healing: Balance Chakras, Improve your Health and Feel Great.* Amsterdam: Maven Publishing.

Dale, C. 2009. *The Subtle Body: An Encyclopedia ofYour Energetic Anatomy.* Louisville: Sounds True.

Dale, C. 2016. *Complete Book of Chakras: Your Definitive Source of Energy Center Knowledge for Health, Happiness, and Spiritual Evolution.* Woodbury: Llewellyn Publications.

Dale, C. 2018. *Awaken Clairvoyant Energy.* Woodbury: Llewellyn Publications.

Dyczkowski, M. S. G. 1980. *The Doctrine of Vibration: An Analysis of the Doctrines and Practices of Kashmir Shaivism.* Delhi: Motilal Banarsidass.

Dyczkowski, M. S. G. 2017. *The Subtle Body Coloring Book: Learn Energetic Anatomy –from the Chakras to the Meridians and More.* Louisville: Sounds True.

Hauer, W., Heim, K. and Karl, A. 1937. *Germany's New Religion: The German Faith Movement.* London: George Allen & Unwin Ltd.

Heilijgers-Seelen, D. M. 1994. *The System of Five Cakras in Kubjikāmatatantra 14–16.* Groningen: Forsten.

Kiehnle, C. 2004–2005. 'The Secret of the Nāths: The Ascent of Kuṇḍalinī according to Jñāneśvari 6.151–328'. *Bulletin Des Études Indiennes*, no. 22–23.

Kinsley, D. 1997. *Tantric Visions of the Divine Feminine.* Berkeley: University of California Press.

Kripal, J. J. 2001. *Roads of Excess, Places of Wisdom: Eroticism and Reflexivity in the Study of Religion.* Chicago: The University of Chicago Press.

Kripal, J. J. 2008. *Esalen: America and the Religion of No Religion.* Chicago: The University of Chicago Press.

Krishna, G. 1970. *Kuṇḍalinī: The Evolutionary Energy in Man.* Boston: Shambhala.

Leland, K. 2016. *Rainbow Body: A History of the Western Chakra System from Blavatsky to Brennan.* Lake Worth: Ibis Press.

Maderey, A. L. F. 2017. 'Kuṇḍalinī Rising and Liberation in the Yogavāsiṣṭha: Story of Cūḍāla and Śikhidhvaja'. *Religions* 8: 248. https://doi.org/10.3390/rel8110248.

Mallinson, J., and Singleton, M. (eds) 2017. *Roots ofYoga.* USA: Penguin Classics.

Mallinson, J. 2011. 'Nāth Saṃpradāya', in Jacobsen et al. (eds), *The Brill Encyclopedia of Hinduism*, Vol. 3. Leiden: Brill

Mukherjee, C. B. 2016. *Kūmarī Pūjā: A Religious Custom.* Kolkata: Jadavpur University.

Mukhopadhyaya, S. and Dupuis, S. (eds) 2012. *The Kaulajñānanirṇaya: The Esoteric Teachings of Matsyendrapāda (Matsyendranātha) Sadguru of the Yoginī Kaula School in the Tantra Tradition.* New Delhi: Aditya Prakashan.

Olivelle, P. 1996. *Upaniṣads.* New York: Oxford University Press.

Silburn, L. 1988. *Kuṇḍalinī: The Energy of the Depths.* Albany: State University of New York Press.

Singh, J. 1980. *Spanda-Kārikās: The Divine Creative Pulsation.* Delhi: Motilal Banarsidas.

Singleton, M. 2010. *Yoga Body: The Origins of Modern Posture Practice.* New York: Oxford University Press.

Wauters, A. 1999. *Chakras and Their Archetypes: Uniting Energy Awareness and Spiritual Growth.* Toronto: Crossing Press.

Wauters, A. 2002. *The Book of Chakras: Discover the Hidden Forces Within You*. New York. B. E. S. Publishing.
Wauters, A. 2017. *Angel Oracle: Working with the Angels for Guidance, Inspiration and Love*. London: Eddison Books.
Wauters, A. 2019. *Essential Chakra Meditation: Awaken Your Healing Power with Meditation and Visualization*. San Antonio: Althea Press
Wauters, A. and Gerry, T. 1999. *Principles of Colour Healing: The Only Introduction You'll Ever Need*. London: Thorsons.
White, D. G. 2003. *Kiss of the Yoginī*. Chicago: The University of Chicago Press.
Wujastyk, D. 2009. 'Interpreting the Image of the Human Body in Premodern India'. *International Journal of Hindu Studies* 13: 189–228. https://doi.org/10.1007/s11407-009-9077-0.

# PART V

# Disciplinary framings

Not only do understandings of yoga and meditation techniques change depending on historical and social context as well as soteriology, but what these techniques *are* can look very different depending upon the methods and questions we bring to investigate them.

In this section, we offer a selection of different academic disciplines and asked our authors to explore what unique perspectives their chosen discipline can bring to the study of meditation and yoga. What questions do they ask? What problems do they seek to solve? What sources do they look at to consider what these practices are and what they might do to people?

Some of these disciplinary perspectives are well-established, such as philology, philosophy, art history and anthropology. Other chapters offer new and emerging – even multidisciplinary – lenses, such as critical theory, sound studies, material culture or movement studies. In this section we also explore the more 'hard science' perspective of psychophysiology and cognitive science on the practices of yoga and meditation. As well as single and multidisciplinary approaches, some chapters offer integrated interdisciplinary insights.

By reading chapters from an unfamiliar discipline, we hope that readers may experience a widening of perspective and a re-evaluation of some of the assumptions that they might have had about what yoga and meditation are and how they work on the human body and mind.

# 26

# PHILOLOGY AND DIGITAL HUMANITIES

*Charles Li*

## Introduction

For many practitioners of the diverse traditions of yoga and meditation, the study of texts might not form a significant part of their practice, if at all. The kind of mental training involved in meditation, for example, seems almost impossible to learn from a text. And as B. K. S. Iyengar writes in his preface to Edwin Bryant's translation of the *Yogasūtra*, 'Pātañjala Yoga is a practical subject and not a discursive one' (Bryant 2009: ix). Yet, immediately following that statement, Iyengar shows how deeply he has studied the text, debating the interpretation of various Sanskrit terms and disputing the commentaries of medieval philosophers; it is clear that his yoga practice involves a serious engagement with textual scholarship. Moreover, as David Gordon White has pointed out, no matter how far removed contemporary yoga practices are from the ancient texts that they purport to derive from, teacher training in the United States often still includes mandatory instruction in the *Yogasūtra* (White 2014: 1). It seems that many of today's yogis still appeal to the authority of a text, and the ongoing conversation between contemporary practitioners and the knowledge of the distant past would be impossible without the work of textual scholars.

Yet as a practitioner, one might not consider some of the fundamental questions that a textual scholar would ask, namely: Where and when does the version of the text that we are reading really come from? How different is the text we have now compared to what the author wrote, hundreds or thousands of years ago? What other versions of the text exist, apart from the one that we consider to be authoritative? Research into these issues, which forms part of the discipline termed philology,[1] can give us valuable insights into the intellectual history of yoga as it evolved and diversified in South Asia and beyond.

## Reconstructing an ancient text

> No quería componer otro Quijote – lo cual es fácil – sino "el" Quijote.
> ('He did not want to compose another Quixote – that would be simple – but *the* Quixote.')
>
> *(Borges 1996: 19)*

Typically, when we talk about an ancient text such as 'the *Yogasūtra* of Patañjali', we are tacitly referring to an original, unified work by a definite author, composed at a definite point in time. All three of these assumptions are often highly contentious. Many texts are stratified – consisting of many layers composed at different times. At which stratum should we consider the text to be *the Yogasūtra?* Philipp Maas, for example, has argued that the *Yogasūtra*, together with its *Bhāṣya* commentary, should be considered a single text, which – in manuscript sources as well as in commentaries and later works referring to it – is titled the *Pātañjalayogaśāstra* (Maas 2013a).[2] In addition, even if we have an estimate of when the text – in the form in which we have it now – was composed, we usually do not have manuscripts that are that old. But none of these problems have stopped scholars from continuing to study ancient texts. And while the 'ideal but impossible desideratum'[3] of reconstructing an original work is out of reach, we can reconstruct a version of the text that is as close as possible to the original, based on the extant manuscript evidence. In this endeavour, we are not strictly limited by the date of the oldest manuscript; that is, we do not simply take the oldest manuscript and consider that to be the best text available to us.[4] By comparing all known manuscripts, we can usually reconstruct a version of the text that is older than any single manuscript. But since each manuscript contains a slightly different version of the text, we need some method to choose between variant readings.

When there is sufficient evidence, perhaps the most common approach used to reconstruct a text from manuscripts is 'Lachmann's method', named after the ninteenth-century German philologist, Karl Lachmann:

> To make a long story short, the method of Lachmann, or 'common errors' method, as theorized by Paul Maas (Maas 1957), came about in the historicist/positivist context of the nineteenth century, as a way of analyzing the textual variation in manuscripts in genealogical/hierarchical terms: mistakes produced in the course of the copying process are transmitted in the subsequent copies, which add their own mistakes etc.
>
> *(Bausi et al. 2015: 336)*

In order to do this, we represent the genealogical relationships between manuscripts – that is, our hypothesis of how the text was transmitted through repeated copying – as a family tree, or *stemma codicum*. For example:

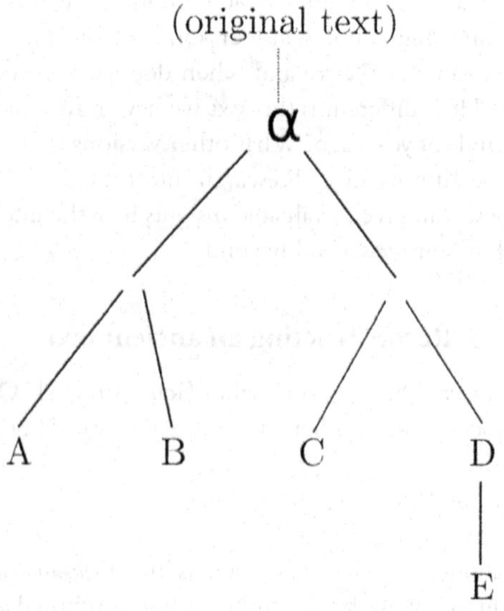


*Figure 26.1* A sample stemma codicum

In this stemma, A, B, C, D and E represent manuscripts. α represents the *archetype*[5] – that is, the hypothetical common ancestor of our surviving manuscripts, the oldest possible version of the text that we can reconstruct based on that evidence. The relationship between this archetype and the original is not clear. In our hypothesis, A and B derive from a common source, as do C and D. E is a direct copy of D, and therefore it is not useful for reconstruction purposes. Theoretically, it contains the text of D, but with additional errors. Having established a stemma, the work of reconstructing the archetype can proceed, resulting in what we call a *critical edition* of the text.

However, in practice, for any given text, the situation is rarely so simple or straightforward. The extant manuscripts might be fragmentary, or 'contaminated' – that is, one manuscript may be copied from more than one source – or a scribe may have actively tried to 'correct' the text they were copying.[6] It may be impossible to construct a stemma.[7] Moreover, a stemma is only a hypothetical model to help guide the reconstruction; it usually does not represent a true, complete and historical account of how the text was transmitted, simply because we usually do not have access to every single manuscript of the tradition. For example, in reality, E could have been copied from another, lost, manuscript which was copied from D, but in the absence of evidence for that lost manuscript, the stemma presents the most *parsimonious* hypothesis of how the text was transmitted – that is, it hypothesises the lowest possible number of lost intermediate copies between the archetype and the surviving manuscripts.

Another common issue is that the archetype itself may already contain many errors. Depending on the age of the surviving manuscripts, the oldest reconstructible archetype might be hundreds of years younger than the original text, and, in many cases, the archetype may be so corrupt that a careful editor will need to emend it. This is where the 'positivist' ideal of Lachmann's method gives way to the expert judgement of the editor, who must be well-versed in the language and culture of the presumed original as well as how that language and culture are transformed each time the text is transmitted into a new context, e.g. as it crosses boundaries of script, dialect, religion, polity, etc. Moreover, we can also look to quotations and references in later texts as 'secondary' witnesses, which may quite possibly preserve a version of the text that is older than the manuscripts of the text itself. Although there are many handbooks to the work of editing a text in general,[8] each particular case ultimately requires careful consideration of the evidence at hand and its historical, cultural and material context.[9]

## Against reconstruction

> For a long time people have been aware of differences in local recensions or traditions but it has not occurred to them that these differences should be accounted for in terms of historical change. … The only conclusion which suggests itself is that any locally accepted version is authoritative in its own right.
>
> *(Biardeau 1968: 122)*

Against this method of textual genealogy are scholars who believe that a critical edition gives a false sense of authority to the text as reconstructed by the editor. As opposed to a reconstructed text, we know that the text of any given manuscript was really read by someone – at the very least, by the scribe in the act of copying. The manuscript also has a temporal, geographical and cultural context, whereas the reconstructed text exists in a nebulous, hypothetical past. Some critics have gone so far as to describe a critical edition as 'the invention of the editor' (Schoening 1995: 180; see the reply in Adriaensen et al. 1998: 39). Moreover, as Biardeau has pointed out, different versions of a text are authoritative in their own right – that is, people base their practices and beliefs on them – without referring to any hypothetical original. Biardeau considers these versions to be different *recensions.* The recension of the *Yogasūtra* that Iyengar studied, for example, contains fifty-six *sūtras* in the third chapter, whereas medieval commentators accepted fifty-five *sūtras* (Bryant 2009: xi). Even if, in the process of producing a critical edition, an editor concluded that Iyengar's extra *sūtra* was a later addition, it does not make Iyengar's version any less important. For a scholar studying contemporary yoga practices, Iyengar's version is likely to be much more relevant than any presumed original.

Along with a shift from print publishing to online publishing, this critique of critical editing has given rise to what Elena Pierazzo terms 'digital documentary editions':

> an edition of a text based on a single document, which attempts to reproduce a certain degree of the peculiarities of the document itself, even if this may cause disruption to the normal flow of the text presented by the document.
>
> *(Pierazzo 2014: 2)*

This impetus to reproduce a document rather than to edit it is not new; especially in the case of texts that exist in a single manuscript witness, scholars have produced 'diplomatic editions' which simply reproduce the text as it is found. However, with a structured format like TEI XML, scholars can now easily encode much more information about a document than before, such as page and line breaks, additions and corrections, marginal annotations, changes of the scribal hand, etc., in a machine-readable format. A number of digital editions of multi-witness texts also take this approach[10] – that is, they reproduce, in as much detail as possible, the text of the physical documents themselves, rather than attempt to reconstruct a hypothetical text based on those documents, resulting in an archive of careful transcriptions rather than a single, authoritative text.

Another recent development, also linked with the use of new technologies, is the conceptualisation of text-genealogical relationships not as hierarchical trees but as unrooted trees, without the presumption of an original text from which all others descend. This is an approach inspired by the application of phylogenetic software, used in evolutionary biology, to the study of texts. A phylogenetic approach – in which relationships between manuscripts are inferred from their common traits – typically suggests a hierarchical tree, and, indeed, phylogenetic software has been used to reconstruct textual archetypes (See Maas 2009; Maas 2013b; Graheli 2015; Apple 2019). But, as Wendy Phillips-Rodriguez has argued, there may be cases where the textual transmission is so complex that it would be too presumptuous to reconstruct an archetype; instead, an unrooted tree – which shows the relationships between text versions without suggesting which version is closer to the original – can help us understand each version as 'separate interpretations, each with its particular history of evolution' (Phillips-Rodriguez 2012: 228).

Another way of representing relationships between texts – the split network – is also useful for detecting contamination: whereas in a tree each manuscript is only connected by a single branch, a split network uses sets of parallel edges to represent 'incompatible and ambiguous signals in a data set' (Huson and Bryant 2006: 255). These edges can be used to infer situations in which one manuscript has been copied from more than one exemplar (Phillips-Rodriguez 2007: 102ff).

Both the rise of documentary editions and the tendency towards a less hierarchical understanding of the relationship between text versions can be understood as part of an umbrella movement termed 'New Philology', in which 'the wickedly complex, seemingly endless textual variations engendered by manuscript copying and circulation [...] suddenly became not a jungle to be tamed but the source of critical fertility' (Cohen 2017). In Lachmann's method

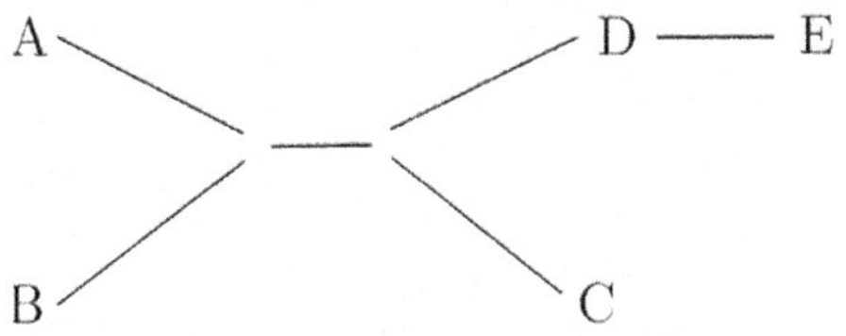


*Figure 26.2* An unrooted tree

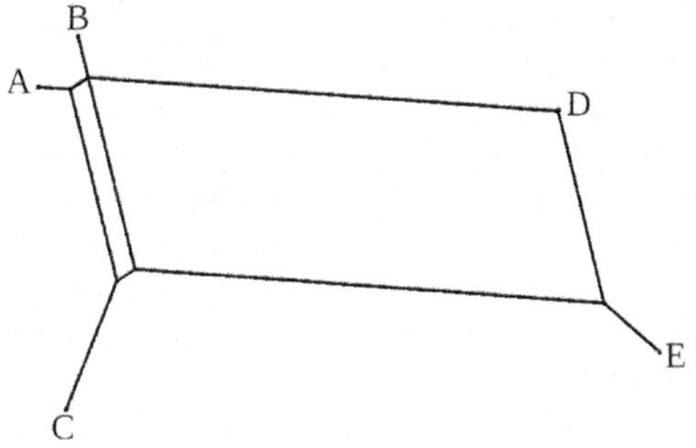


*Figure 26.3* A split network

of reconstruction, the copying mistakes that a scribe makes are considered only in as much as they provide evidence for what the original text might be. But the variation that an editor encounters, the accumulated errors that one tries to correct when reconstructing the text, are important pieces of information that can also help us to piece together the history of the text's transmission and reception, hundreds of years after its composition, as in the case of Iyengar's *Yogasūtra*. As Peter Robinson writes, this could redefine what an edition is: 'a narration of the whole history of a work, from its conception, through its production and first and later publication, and then its reception among all its readers right to the present' (2016: 198).

## Having your cake and eating it too[11]

Yet there is no necessary opposition between critical editions and diplomatic, documentary editions; in fact, they can be mutually supportive endeavours. Critical editions can benefit from the meticulous documentation and diplomatic transcription of its manuscript witnesses. Documentary editions, on the other hand, can benefit from the connections that a critical text draws between multiple documents, placing a single manuscript in a broader context. Ideally, a digital edition would be critical, diplomatic *and* documentary, comprising a digital archive of carefully transcribed documents as well as one or more critical texts, which make an argument about the genealogical relationship of those documents to one another.[12] With such a wealth of information, the digital edition should also provide tools to help the reader make sense of that data, to analyse the distribution of textual variation and test scholarly hypotheses about it.[13] In this way, we can address some of the concerns around the opacity of critical, editorial decisions: every reading in the critical text can be easily traced back to its source.[14] Naturally, this ideal is not limited to digital editions; the critical apparatus of a traditional, printed edition is meant to achieve the same aim. However, a digital edition can capture much more detail than has ever been produced on the printed page, and that data can be easily reused and reinterpreted by other scholars.

## Interpreting manuscripts

> It's a little like reading – the bedrock reality is black marks on a page, and those marks are nothing like the world, but your mind insists on making sense of them. The illusion is seamless, and thus hard to escape. Every inconsistency gets explained away.
>
> *(Mason 2017: 276)*

The amount of detail that a digital edition contains depends, essentially, on the degree of diplomacy that the editor employs in the transcription of the source documents. This can range from, on the one hand, 'ultra-diplomatic' transcription (D'Iorio 2010: 52) – taking care to reproduce, typographically, the placement of each character on the page – to, on the other hand, the regularised spellings often found in a critical apparatus, without any reference to where a reading occurs on the page at all. In any case, some amount of interpretation is inevitable; transcription is, at its most fundamental, the mapping of a messy, material reality to a fixed set of characters in a writing system. Every transcription, no matter how diplomatic, embodies some assumptions about what the text is and how it was meant to be used.[15] But, generally speaking, the more diplomatic the transcription, the more useful it will be as data.

However, for a digital edition, it is perhaps more useful to think in terms of *specificity* rather than *diplomacy*. In transcribing documents, it is often preferable to make some undiplomatic, editorial interventions to specify how the text should be interpreted, since these can easily be ignored at the data analysis stage. For example, Sanskrit manuscripts are usually written in *scriptio continua*, with no spaces between words. While an ultra-diplomatic transcription would reproduce this, for the purposes of a digital edition, it is much more useful for the editor to add spaces; this adds a layer of interpretation that makes it much easier to compare manuscripts. Moreover, it is simple to remove those spaces automatically at the data analysis stage, but very difficult to add them in. Another example: some manuscripts do not distinguish between *va* and *ba*, writing both of them as *va*. Diplomatically, one would transcribe this as *va* in all cases; however, it is much more useful for the editor to transcribe this as *va* or *ba* depending on how one interprets it. Again, it is simple to change all *ba*-s to *va*-s at the data analysis stage, if one does not want to use this information. For a human reader, these undiplomatic gestures also make it much easier to use the text; it gives some indication about how the transcriber has understood the text, and does not burden the reader with the work of, for example, splitting up a line into individual words.

Once the documents – containing different versions of the same text – have been transcribed, they can be compared in order to come up with a hypothesis about the relationship between the versions. Since the documents have been transcribed diplomatically, taking care to reproduce orthographic variations (e.g. *patañjali* could also be written *pataṃjali*), the transcriptions first need to be processed in order to filter out variants that we do not consider to be informative. In the past, when text versions were collated by hand, an editor would discard such variations at the collation stage: that is, the editor would simply go through each manuscript, comparing it to some vulgate text, and note down 'substantial' variant readings, ignoring, for example, the difference between *patañjali* and *pataṃjali*. However, working with diplomatic transcriptions, we can do this work automatically, expressing our text-critical principles – our rules for deciding whether or not a variant is substantial – as computer algorithms.[16]

## Case study: a quotation from the *Pātañjalayogaśāstra*

In my work on Helārāja's *Prakīrṇaprakāśa*, a tenth-century commentary on Bhartṛari's *Vākyapadīya*, I came across a quotation from the *Pātañjalayogaśāstra* that was significantly different from the text as printed in the 1904 edition of K. S. Āgāśe. I hypothesised that Helārāja had falsified the quotation, changing it to fit the argument that he was trying to make (Li 2018: 43ff). But in order to be sure that my understanding of Helārāja's text was not merely due to a scribal error, it was important to critically edit the passage in question. Thus, I diplomatically transcribed this passage from sixteen manuscripts and three printed editions of the *Prakīrṇaprakāśa*. No *significant*

*Table 26.1* An 'insignificant' variant

| | *with virāma* | *no virāma* |
|---|---|---|
| *ṣaḍ vi-* | षड्वि | षड्वि |
| *ṣaḍ avi-* | षडवि | |

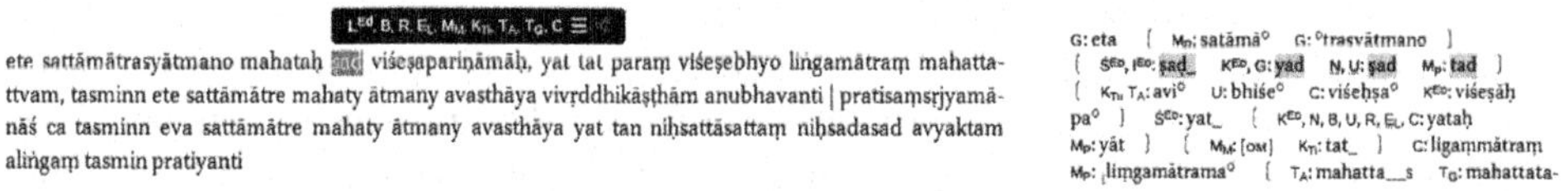
$L^{Ed}$, B, R, $E_L$, $M_M$, $K_{Tr}$, $T_A$, $T_G$, C

ete sattāmātrasyātmano mahataḥ viśeṣapariṇāmāḥ, yat tat paraṃ viśeṣebhyo liṅgamātraṃ mahattattvam, tasminn ete sattāmātre mahaty ātmany avasthāya vivṛddhikāṣṭhām anubhavanti | pratisaṃsṛjyamānāś ca tasminn eva sattāmātre mahaty ātmany avasthāya yat tan niḥsattāsattaṃ niḥsadasad avyaktam aliṅgaṃ tasmin pratiyanti

G: eta [ $M_n$: satāmā° G: °trasvātmano ]
[ $Ś^{ED}$, $I^{ED}$: ṣaḍ_ $K^{ED}$, G: yad N, U: ṣad $M_p$: tad ]
[ $K_{Tr}$, $T_A$: avi° U: bhiśe° C: viśeḥṣa° $K^{ED}$: viśeṣāḥ pa° ] $Ś^{ED}$: yat_ [ $K^{ED}$, N, B, U, R, $E_L$, C: yataḥ $M_p$: yāt ] [ $M_M$: [OM] $K_{Tr}$: tat_ ] C: ligaṃmātraṃ $M_p$: limgamātrama° [ $T_A$: mahatta__s $T_G$: mahattata-

*Figure 26.4* The digital edition, with *virāmas* considered as significant variants. In the apparatus on the right, only the two recent printed editions, $Ś^{Ed}$ and $I^{Ed}$, use the virāma

variation was found. But what about variant readings that would, traditionally, be considered insignificant? One particularly important phrase from this quotation is, in the Āgāśe edition, *ṣaḍ aviśeṣapariṇāmāḥ* (षडविशेषपरिणामाः) (1904: 85), 'the six unparticularized transformations'. Helārāja's reading, according to all manuscripts and printed sources, is *ṣaḍ viśeṣapariṇāmāḥ*, 'the six particularized transformations'.[17] In the printed editions, this is printed as षड् विशेषपरिणामाः or *ṣad_ viśeṣapariṇāmāḥ*, with a virāma – here represented by an underscore (_) – applied to the *ḍ*. In a Devanāgarī manuscript, it is very easy for a scribe to misinterpret this: a virāma is very small, and could easily have crept into the text through careless copying. On the other hand, if the manuscripts use a conjunct character rather than a virāma, it would look like this: षड्विशेषपरिणामाः. It is much more difficult to go from Āgāśe's reading, षडविशेषपरिणामाः, to षड्विशेषपरिणामाः unintentionally.

Traditionally, a critical edition would not record this type of orthographic variation, i.e. the use of a virāma versus a conjunct character. And in my digital edition of this passage, the default behaviour is to ignore such differences. However, since the digital edition is built on diplomatic transcriptions of the manuscript sources, we can easily ask the software not to ignore virāmas and display an apparatus which considers a virāma as a variant reading.[18] Sure enough, the resulting display shows that only the printed editions use the virāma; all manuscripts use a conjunct character.

This becomes even more significant when we take into account the fact that the manuscript sources are in Devanāgarī, Malayālam and Telugu script. Like Devanāgarī, both Malayālam and Telugu have a distinct conjunct character for *ḍvi*, which is what we find in the manuscripts. This small, previously insignificant variation – which a scholar, only a few decades ago, would have ignored – lends some support to the hypothesis that the reading in Helārāja's text is intentional, rather than a scribal error. Naturally, this is only one piece of a larger body of evidence that points to Helārāja's intentional misquotation. But the more carefully we document our sources, the better equipped we are to answer these questions, and we have shown how diplomatic transcriptions can work together with the flexibility of the digital edition in order to facilitate our scholarly investigations into the history and transmission of a text.

## Artefacts in time and space

Ideally, we would also have a digital, critical and diplomatic edition of the *Pātañjalayogaśāstra* to work with, comprising both diplomatic transcriptions of the available manuscript witnesses and printed texts, as well as a critically edited reconstruction. With more and more texts edited this way, the possibilities for new avenues of research become enormous: we can begin to investigate the relationships not only between different texts, but also between different versions of different texts. Is Helārāja's peculiar quotation of the *Pātañjalayogaśāstra* attested in any of the *Pātañjalayogaśāstra* manuscripts themselves? If so, can we then begin to hypothesise a stemma codicum that spans across the manuscripts of both the *Pātañjalayogaśāstra* and the *Prakīrṇaprakāśa*, understanding their evolution not as two isolated traditions, but rather, perhaps, as texts embedded within broader philosophical trends evolving over time?

Apart from variations in the text itself, we can also begin to look at the temporal, geographical and cultural contexts in which these variations arise. A diplomatic transcription should – in addition to transcribing the text – document the particular material features of each manuscript. By correlating the genealogy of the text itself with metadata on the provenance of the manuscripts, features of their format and any information about the scribes and scribal practices that we have, what more could we discover? How does cultural contact shape the transmission of a text across time and space? What kind of intellectual networks existed to transmit knowledge across those boundaries, and how do they correlate with trade routes or migratory patterns? We absolutely have the technology to wrestle with these questions; now, as ever, we need scholars to do the careful, meticulous and unglamorous work of diplomatically transcribing and documenting manuscripts.

## Notes

1 Many scholars have offered definitions and re-definitions of this term; for examples, see Nichols 1990, Said 2004 and Pollock 2009. Michael Witzel has defined philology as 'the study of a civilization based on its texts', with the aid of other disciplines such as history, anthropology, religious studies, palaeography, zoology, etc. (Witzel 2014, 16).

2 Federico Squarcini, on the other hand, argues for the *Yogasūtra* as an independent text (Squarcini 2015: cxi onwards).

3 As V. S. Sukthankar puts it; his critical edition of the *Mahābhārata* has been one of the most monumental works of textual reconstruction ever attempted. See Sukthankar 1933: cii–ciii.

4 However, see the criticisms below, as well as Joseph Bédier's method of 'best-text' editing (Trovato 2014: 77ff).

5 The term *archetype* has been used to mean slightly different things by textual scholars; for details, see Trovato 2014: 63ff).

6 For examples of these issues in yoga texts, see the stemmata of the *Pātañjalayogaśāstra* (Maas 2006: lxxiii) and the *Khecarīvidyā* (Mallinson 2007: 11).

7 For an interesting example of this, in which editors have posited that the author himself revised the text, see Coulson and Sinclair 1989: xxx.

8 See, for example, Katre and Gode 1941, West 1973, or Trovato 2014.

9 As Trovato writes, 'Actually, almost all existing manuals of textual criticism are useful, because they reflect the experiences of different scholars' (Trovato 2014: 29).

10 See Robinson 2016: 196.

11 This strange proverb has been traced back to 1546, in which, *originally*, it states: 'Would you both eat your cake, and have your cake?' (Zimmer 2011)

12 For texts with very meagre manuscript evidence, this is also possible in a print format; for example, see Steinkellner and Krasser 2016.

13 As Peter Robinson has noted, few digital editions actually offer such tools, and thus are not so differentiated from print editions (2016: 193).

14 For a discussion of this ideal, see Buzzetti and McGann 2007.

15 Transcribing a manuscript assumes that the text was meant to be read; this is not necessarily true. For example, consider the practice of sealing manuscripts inside Buddhist statues.

16 See Li 2017 for an overview of this technique; Li 2018: 151ff contains a full list of filtering rules for Sanskrit texts.

17 Apart from a couple of sources which read *yad*.
18 For more information on how the software works, and for a digital edition of one chapter of the *Prakīrṇaprakāśa*, see https://saktumiva.org/.

## Bibliography


Adriaensen, R., Bakker, H. T., and Isaacson H. 1998. *The Skandapurāṇa*. Groningen: Egbert Forsten.

Āgāśe, K. Ś. (ed) 1904. *Pātañjalayogasūtrāṇi*. Pune: Ānandāśramamudraṇālaye.

Apple, J. B. 2019. 'Digital Filiation Studies: Phylogenetic Analysis in the Study of Tibetan Buddhist Canonical Texts', in Veidlinger, D. (ed), *Digital Humanities and Buddhism: An Introduction*, 209–226. Berlin: de Gruyter.

Bausi, A., Borbone, P. G., Briquel-Chatonnet, F. et al. (eds) 2015. *Comparative Oriental Manuscripts Studies: An Introduction*. Hamburg: COMS.

Biardeau, M. 1968. 'Some More Considerations about Textual Criticism'. *Purāṇa* 10(2): 115–121.

Borges, J. L. 1986. *Ficciones – El Aleph – El Informe de Brodie*. Caracas: Biblioteca Ayacucho.

Bryant, E. F. 2009. *The Yoga Sutras of Patañjali: A New Edition, Translation, and Commentary*. New York: North Point Press.

Buzzetti, D. and McGann J. 2007. 'Electronic Textual Editing: Critical Editing in a Digital Horizon'. *Text Encoding Initiative*. www.tei-c.org/About/Archive_new/ETE/Preview/mcgann.xml.

Cohen, M. 2017. 'The New, New, New Philology'. *electronic book review* 5 February. https://electronicbookreview.com/essay/the-new-new-new-philology/.

Coulson, M., and Sinclair R. 1989. *A Critical Edition of the Mālatīmādhava*. Delhi: Oxford University Press.

D'Iorio, P. 2010. 'Qu'est-ce qu'une édition génétique numérique?' *Genesis: Manuscrits-Recherche-Invention* 30:,49–53. https://genesis.revues.org/116.

Graheli, A. 2015. *History and Transmission of the Nyāyamañjarī: Critical Edition of the Section on Sphoṭa*. Wien: Verlag der Österreichischen Akademie der Wissenschaften.

Huson, D. H. and Bryant, D. 2006. 'Application of Phylogenetic Networks in Evolutionary Studies'. *Molecular Biology and Evolution* 23(2): 254–267.

Katre, S. M. and Gode P. K. 1941. *Introduction to Indian Textual Criticism*. Bombay: Karnatak Publishing House.

Li, C. 2017. 'Critical Diplomatic Editing: Applying Text-critical Principles as Algorithms', in Boot, P., Cappellotto, A., Dillen, W., et al. (eds), *Advances in Digital Scholarly Editing*, 305–310. Leiden: Sidestone Press.

Li, C. 2018. 'Limits of the Real: A Hypertext Critical Edition and Translation of Bhartṛhari's Dravyasamuddeśa, with the Commentary of Helārāja'. PhD thesis, University of Cambridge.

Maas, P. 1957. *Textkritik*. 3rd ed. (Verbesserte und Vermehrte Auflage). Leipzig: Teubner.

Maas, P. A. 2006. *Samādhipāda: Das Erste Kapitel des Pātañjalayogaśāstra zum ersten Mal Kritisch Ediert*. Aachen: Shaker Verlag.

Maas, P. A. 2009. 'Computer Aided Stemmatics: The Case of Fifty-Two Text Versions of the Carakasaṃhitā Vimānasthāna 9.67–157'. *Wiener Zeitschrift für die Kunde Südasiens* 52–53: 63–119.

Maas, P. A. 2013a. 'A Concise Historiography of Classical Yoga Philosophy', in Franco, F. (ed), *Periodization and Historiography of Indian Philosophy*, 53–90. Vienna: De Nobili Research Library.

Maas, P. A. 2013b. 'On What to Do with a Stemma – Towards a Critical Edition of the Carakasaṃhitā Vimānasthāna 8.29', in Wujastyk, D., Cerulli, A. and Preisendanz, K. (eds), *Medical Texts and Manuscripts in Indian Cultural History*, 29–61. New Delhi: Manohar.

Mallinson, J. 2007. *The Khecarīvidyā of Ādinātha: A Critical Edition and Annotated Translation of an Early Text of Haṭhayoga*. London: Routledge.

Mason, Z. 2017. *Void Star: A Novel*. New York: Farrar, Straus & Giroux.

Nichols, S. G. 1990. 'Introduction: Philology in a Manuscript Culture'. *Speculum* 65(1): 1–10.

Phillips-Rodriguez, W. J. 2007. 'Electronic Techniques of Textual Analysis and Edition for Ancient Texts: An Exploration of the Phylogeny of the Dyūtaparvan'. PhD thesis, University of Cambridge.

Phillips-Rodriguez, W. J. 2012. 'Unrooted Trees: A Way Around the Dilemma of Recension', in Brockington, J. (ed), *Battle, Bards, Brahmins (Papers of the 13th World Sanskrit Conference)*, 217–230. Delhi: Motilal Banarsidass.

Pierazzo, E. 2014. 'Digital Documentary Editions and the Others'. Scholarly Editing: The Annual of the Association for Documentary Editing 35. http://scholarlyediting.org/2014/pdf/essay.pierazzo.pdf.

Pollock, S. 2009. 'Future Philology? The Fate of a Soft Science in a Hard World'. *Critical Inquiry* 35(4): 931–961.

Robinson, P. 2016. 'The Digital Revolution in Scholarly Editing', in Crostini, B., Iversen, G. and Jensen, B. (eds), *Ars Edendi Lecture Series IV*, 181–207. Stockholm University Press.

Said, E. W. 2004. 'The Return to Philology', in *Humanism and Democratic Criticism*, 57–84. New York: Columbia University Press.

Schoening, J. D. 1995. *The Śālistamba Sūtra and its Indian Commentaries, Volume I.* Wien: Universität Wien.

Squarcini, F. 2015. *Yogasūtra*. Torino: Einaudi.

Steinkellner, E., and Krasser, H. (eds) 2016. *Dharmakīrti's Hetubindu*. Beijing: China Tibetology Publishing House/Austrian Academy of Sciences.

Sukthankar, V. S. 1933. *The Ādiparvan, Being the First Book of the Mahābhārata, the Great Epic of India, for the First Time Critically Edited*. Poona: Bhandarkar Oriental Institute.

Trovato, P. 2014. *Everything You Always Wanted to Know about Lachmann's Method*. Poole, F. (trans). Padova: liberiauniversitaria.it.

West, M. L. 1973. *Textual Criticism and Editorial Technique*. Stuttgart: Teubner.

White, D. G. 2014. *The Yoga Sutra of Patanjali: A Biography*. Princeton: Princeton University Press.

Witzel, M. 2014. 'Textual Criticism in Indology and in European Philology During the 19th and 20th Centuries'. *Electronic Journal of Vedic Studies* 21(3): 9–90.

Zimmer, B. 2011. 'On Language: "Have your Cake and Eat it Too"'. *The New York Times*, 18 February. www.nytimes.com/2011/02/20/magazine/20FOB-onlanguage-t.html.

# 27

# OBSERVING YOGA

## The use of ethnography to develop yoga studies[1]

*Daniela Bevilacqua*

### Introduction

Ethnography as a method can be defined as an approach to social research based on first-hand experience. As a methodology, it intends to create an epistemology that emphasises the significance and meaning of the experiences of the group of people being studied, thereby privileging the insider's view. A researcher using ethnography employs mostly qualitative methods (Pole and Morrison 2003: 9), such as interviews (that can be non-structured, structured or casual conversation), participant observation, field notes, etc.

Participant observation can be considered as a distinctive feature of ethnography; within this method the researcher adopts a variety of positions. As Atkinson and Hammersley have noted (1994: 248), the researcher can be: a complete observer when the researcher is a member of the group being studied who conceals his/her researcher role; an observer as participant when s/he is a member of the group being studied and the group is aware of the research activity; a participant as observer when s/he is not a member of the group but is interested in participating as a means for conducting better observation; or a participant non-member of the group who is hidden from view while observing. These typologies work differently according to other variables (Atkinson and Hammersley 1994: 249): what is known about the research and by whom; in which activities the researcher did and did not engage, and how this locates the researcher in relation to the various conceptions of category and group membership used by participants; what the orientation of the researcher is and how completely s/he consciously adopts the orientation of insider or outsider; and so on. These variables, which influence the collection of data and therefore their analysis, should be clear to the researcher while writing (through an attentive reflexive examination), and to the reader who, taking them into consideration, can better understand, contextualise and evaluate the background and the content of the work.

The final product of the ethnographic research should incorporate the views of the participants (emic perspective) as well as the analysis of the researcher (etic perspective). This portrait can open up understanding and interpretation that goes beyond what quantitative research can do, sometimes challenging or highlighting notions that are taken for granted. For this reason, although ethnography was pioneered in the biological, social and cultural branches of anthropology, it has also become popular among those disciplines that decide to observe social practices and interactions of cultural groups of people, such as social sciences, sociology, religious studies, history and, of course, yoga studies.

## Ethnography as a method within yoga studies

Given the diffusion of yoga and meditation all over the world, and the constantly increasing number of people practicing one of the various typologies of yoga, it was inevitable that scholars from various disciplines and branches of knowledge would eventually address these practices and their resulting transcultural/transnational communities.[2] However, such scholarly interests only properly developed after Elizabeth De Michelis (2004) published her study on 'Modern Yoga' and its various sub-categories, providing the input and the general theoretical substratum needed for the development of yoga studies.

The presence of yoga studies as a new field of academic inquiry 'shows how the emergence and diversity of today's postural yoga provides rich source material for understanding the process of cultural diffusion and knowledge transfer' (Hauser 2013b: 1). Indeed, yoga has been evaluated for its transnational aspect, since it is taught and practised at a global level, and for its transcultural aspect, since practices and theories are negotiated and adjusted according to various, local contexts. Looking at yoga in relation to these two aspects

> provides useful terms and descriptive categories that help one grasp more fully the mutual influence of the varying schools of yoga, the competing ways in which yoga has been circulated, and the twists and turns in yoga's overall orientation [...] The concept of transcultural flows also provides a frame of reference that can locate and connect individual research results to larger perspectives, statements, representations, and developments.
>
> *(Hauser 2013b: 23)*

These two aspects also correspond to a transdisciplinary approach that many scholars have adopted: in dealing with modern yoga, scholars engage in different methods, and one of these is the ethnographic. This is evident when we consider the scope of some recent edited volumes published within the field of yoga studies.

In 2005 Knut A. Jacobsen published *Theory and Practice of Yoga*, with the purpose of evaluating yoga 'as a historical and pluralistic phenomenon flourishing in a variety of religious and philosophic contexts' (2005: 3). Although the majority of the articles are based on textual or historical evidence, a few show an interest in the contemporary context and are extensively based on fieldwork data. Ramdas Lamb, for example, provides information about the practice of Rāmānandī ascetics (323–330), while Tracy Pintchman (355–362) points to female yogic practices based on *kartik vrat* (vows during the Indian month of Kartik) and *pūjā*.

In 2008, Mark Singleton and Jayne Byrne edited *Yoga in the Modern World*, which offers 'a range of perspectives on yoga's contemporary manifestations' with contributions that 'span a number of disciplines in the humanities, including anthropology, philosophy, studies in religion and Asian studies, offering a range of entry points to the issues involved in the study of the subject' (2008: 1).

On a similar track and using a comparable range of specialists, in 2013 Singleton and Goldberg presented *Gurus of Modern Yoga*, which explored the role that modern international gurus have had in the formation of practices and discourses of modern, transnational yoga in India and elsewhere. Ethnography was one of the methods used by contributors to explore this subject in the volume.

In the same year, Beatrix Hauser edited *Yoga Travelling*, resulting from a 2009 meeting held in Heidelberg University in which an interdisciplinary group of scholars from Europe and the United States discussed 'the specifics of present-day yoga and its global appeal' (2013b: 5).

The research questions behind this meeting are similar to those present in several studies that manifest an ethnographic approach:

> For what reasons do people engage in yoga classes? How did particular social environments shape the practice of yoga and how did these situated practices in turn influence the perception and experience of body and self? In what ways has the spread of yoga served as a social and cultural incentive that inspires and reorients general ways of thinking about health and human well-being?
>
> *(Hauser 2013b: 5)*

Taking these questions as starting point, this chapter initially provides an outline of the studies in which ethnography is 'naturally' embedded so as to demonstrate how it emerges as a preferred method for yoga studies. Following this, the chapter focuses on the ethnographic work that I have been conducting since 2015 among ascetic practitioners of yoga in India. I provide an analysis of data from my own fieldwork, demonstrating how ethnographic work, used together with other methods, can help in understanding not only present situations, but also their historical developments. In conclusion, the chapter argues for the importance of the ethnographic method itself in order to understand contemporary yoga and meditation practices.

## Dealing with yoga and meditation from an ethnographic perspective

Ethnography traditionally required spending long periods of time in the field. However, much contemporary ethnography, which can be sided or multi-sided, has now moved 'out from the single sites and local situations of conventional ethnographic research designs to examine the circulation of cultural meanings, objects, and identities in diffuse time-space' (Marcus 1995: 96). Many studies of contemporary yoga movements incorporate an element of ethnographic fieldwork to explore the significance and meaning of the activity to practitioners.

To give a few examples of authors who have conducted single-sided fieldworks in a particular location: Suzanne Hasselle-Newcombe (2005) supplemented a quantitative case study by using participant observation among British practitioners of the Iyengar Method of Yoga; Verena Schnäbele (2010) combined ethnographic observation with in-depth interviews of thirty-four individuals representative of the major styles of yoga regularly practised in group classes in Hamburg. Other recent studies on yoga incorporating fieldwork methods include Mans Broo (2012), who analysed Finnish practitioners and their relationship with practice; Laura Mandelbaum who, in her research conducted tegether with Sara Strauss (2013), worked on Ashtanga practitioners in Toronto; and Theodora Wildcroft's (2020) exploration of the lived experience of contemporary, transnational yoga practices in Britain.

Other studies adopt a multi-sited ethnography in order to 'follow the paths of transnational cultural flows of ideas, practices and people' (Strauss 2005: xix). Sara Strauss did her fieldwork among practitioners attending classes at the Sivananda Ashram in Rishikesh, India, and in their country (i.e. Germany and USA) to explore how they integrated yoga in their everyday life and, consequently, transformed it and its practices. Veronique Altglas highlights that the 'advantage of cross-national approaches is that they avoid generalizing what may be specific to a case study in one location' (2014: 21). For her research, between 1999 and 2005 she conducted participant observation and collected eighty non-directive interviews with the leaders and members of Siddha Yoga and Sivananda Centres in London and Paris, and semi-structured interviews with those involved in the management of religious diversity in both countries (2014: 18–19). Benjamin Smith (2004) conducted ethnographic research on the practice of Ashtanga Vinyasa

Yoga among western practitioners in Australia, India and other locations to reflect on the embodied experience of asana practice. Klas Nevrin (2008) conducted ethnographic research with people doing yoga in environments inspired by Krishnamacharya, primarily in Sweden but also in India. (See also Ciołkosz, Chapter 33 in this volume). Another interesting multi-sided research was conducted by Andrea Jain (2014) on the propagation of *prekṣā dhyāna*, a yoga and meditation practice established by the Jain Terapānth group, in Rajasthan and Houston.

Pagis Michal (2010) collected data through two years of participant observation of *vipassana* meditation practices in Israel and the United States. As Gustaaf Houtman argues in his study on Buddhism in Burma, the location of a fieldwork can produce remarkable differences in findings. He stresses the variations that he found while researching meditation in a monastery and in a meditation centre: 'While in the monastery knowledge can be received in a social context and transmitted between people, in the meditation centre knowledge is not conceived in its "received" form but only as an experiential knowledge derived from lengthy private dedicated "work"' (Houtman 1990: 156). Those meditating in the centre would not have the time or the inclination to talk to the anthropologist, since social pleasantries are a distraction from meditation. Houtman admits that neither his personal experience nor his anthropological training had equipped him to approach such intrinsically anti-social activity. This clearly exemplifies the nature of fieldwork: a 'place' can be a source of information but can also be a black hole for the researcher, who has to face circumstances and events that cannot be anticipated in advance and may depend on his/her interaction and involvement in the field. This also explains why, in a successful fieldwork, participant observation can be a fundamental tool to collect original, qualitative data.

Strauss argues that, for her, 'participation in yoga classes was absolutely essential, not only to gaining credibility in the eyes of the community, but also to the personal bodily understanding of the transformations these practices make possible' (2005: 60).[3] Joanna Cook (2010) even decided to become ordained and to practise meditation in order to understand what it is like to be a monastic and the way in which monastic identity is formed through ascetic practice. In so doing, she also wanted to experience the effects of religious practice on her own feelings and sense of self. She combined in-depth and long-term participant observation with formalised research methods: she conducted surveys and questionnaires, conducted formal and informal interviews, collected life-histories and documented rituals, but she also undertook regular intensive meditation retreats to cut attachment to a sense of self. As she argues, 'intensive embodied practice of this sort provided a way of understanding abstract concepts of "truth" in the field while remaining "true" to the roles of *mae chee* (nun) and meditator adopted in the field' (2010: 20–22).

Scholars might, indeed, become 'insider going outsider, going native in reverse' (Pearson 2001: 57), which means a practitioner of yoga may decide to join the academy to study topics related to yoga and then take this new knowledge and insights back into their practice communities (see Singleton and Larios, Chapter 4 in this volume) As we will see in the final part of this chapter, such a position could be 'dangerous' if not supported by an attentive, reflexive approach.

## Data from fieldworks

In recent decades, scholars involved in yoga studies have tried to understand why people engage in yoga, also focusing their attention on the premises and the consequences of that. A general conclusion of these studies is that modern lifestyles have created conditions in which people are overwhelmed by stress and therefore are looking for balancing strategies. Since yoga 'is praised as a relaxing, healthy body technique' it has become increasingly popular (Schnäbele 2013: 143).

Practitioners are part of global health ideas according to which one has to keep oneself fit and free of physical and mental diseases thorough emotional balance, mental flexibility and self-care (Hauser 2013a: 111). That is why, as Nevrin (2008: 119) highlights, the experiences of the body are 'essential [...] to understand the effects of yoga practice and to explain its increasing popularity'. The work of Ann Koch is exemplary in that respect: most of her informants reported that they started yoga because of back problems. Practicing yoga gave them more flexibility and mobility, and some started taking more care of their body, changing their body perception and, in general, their mode of paying attention, which deeply influenced their everyday life (2013: 236). Schnäbele (2010) considers how and in what ways the awareness of the body is shaped in and by yoga practice in contemporary Germany. She claims that in contemporary yoga practice the human body is generally structured by the experience of limits (of personal strength and flexibility) and by 'an inside versus outside perspective of the body' that would result in a 'useful body', a body that develops a more refined awareness of itself and 'becomes an agent of its own' (2010: 161).

As several studies have stressed, this awareness supported by the yoga practice leads practitioners towards a feeling of empowerment, self-confidence and self-transformation (Nevrin 2008; Smith 2004, 2007, 2008; Burger 2006). However, this transformation would not remain in the physical–attitudinal sphere. The intermingled researches of Laura Mandelbaum and Sara Strauss have revealed that nearly two thirds of their respondents considered yoga as a source of discipline and a trigger for a work ethic (2013: 185). Furthermore, Sidnell interprets the daily practice of *āsana* in Ashtanga Yoga as a form of ethics, in so far as *āsana*s are not solely bodily techniques but meditative ones (given the precise coordination of breath and the attention required) whose purpose is 'the cultivation of self', through which the individual is stimulated to become a good or a better person (2017: 15–16). The importance of discipline in Ashtanga Yoga had been already stressed by Smith (2008: 140), who emphasised that the practice of *āsana*s inflames in teachers and dedicated practitioners a physical discipline that is comparable to *tapas*, so that the 'heated effort' of ascetic practice becomes the sweating and bodily heat of modern yoga. Likewise, Lars Jørun Langøien reveals that the practice of Ashtanga Yoga may become 'an embodiment of religio-spiritual practice, which for the dedicated practitioner is an encompassing disciplining of both body and mind' (2012: 27). This inner dimension of yoga has been the subject of investigation by Sarbacker (2014: 20), who notes that many contemporary yoga practitioners adopt contemplative or spiritual practices from Hindu and Buddhist philosophy, and that this mystique and spiritual appeal would be one of the reasons why one 'feels great' after a yoga session (2014: 102).

But is this feeling the result of the practice of yoga in itself? Hauser has questioned the role that habitual language used in yoga tutorials has in shaping 'the experience of yoga practitioners, their perspective of the body and its potential for self-development' (2013: 29). Using case studies from Bikram Yoga classes (a 'style' of yoga which required the teachers to follow a specific class script verbatim) and *Yoga for Everyone* promoted by Kareen Zebroff in Germany, Hauser stresses how 'speech conventions have tremendous influence on how the regular performance of yoga exercises changes the subjective perspective of the body and its potential for self-development' (2013a: 112). This would mean that, whether intended or not, it is suggested to practitioners how they should feel and think about their corporeal self during and after practising yoga. Therefore, one could wonder whether there is a kind of placebo effect in the practice of yoga and whether the expectations of practitioners are such that they necessarily get what they are looking for.[4]

However, not all practitioners engage in yoga with the same intensity, or for the same reasons. For example, Mimi Nichter (2013: 221), in her fieldwork in Mysore, recognises four typologies of practitioners: the yoga tourist or 'yoga lites'; the yoga traveller; the yoga practitioner 'going to the source'; and the yoga professional. As part of her research, she also describes the response of the local Indian community, which manifests in 'Indian entrepreneurs and cultural brokers who flourish on the edges of the yoga school and interface with foreign yoga students' (2013: 201), trying to exploit them. This topic demonstrates how ethnographic fieldworks based on direct observation enable researchers to expand the area of interest by bringing to light often overlooked consequences of the spreading of yoga practices and schools – thereby expanding the field of yoga studies.

For this reason, it is not surprising that the modern practitioner has been also analysed as a consumer, and yoga analysed as a product in which branding processes highly develop. In effect, as Anne Koch argues (2013: 245), although the core doctrine of detachment and relaxation in modern yoga can be interpreted as a reaction to our society, the self-enhancement of yoga-body practices does not entail resistance to modern economic systems. Jain (2012c; 2015; see also Jain, Chapter 5 in this volume) examines several yoga brands – Iyengar Yoga, Siddha Yoga and Anusara Yoga – and demonstrates that they can be contextualised in the social milieu of contemporary consumer culture, being subject to a sequential branding process of selection, introduction, elaboration and fortification (2012c: 4). Since yoga is seen as a method for self-development, it 'can be consumed in combination with other worldviews and practices', making it 'attractive to large target audiences of consumers who do not want to go to an Indian ashram nor seek out a proselytizing guru in order to "do yoga" as it is colloquially put' (2012c: 6). According to Jain, branded yoga products – mats, pants, styles, teachers, services – have to contain the self-developmental needs of the consumers so that they feel personally connected to them. Yoga becomes a tool that enables '*consumers* to become better people through physical and psychological transformation' (Jain 2015: 78 (my emphasis)). Offering another layer of analysis of yoga practitioners as consumers, Mandelbaum and Strauss (2013: 182) conducted an internet survey of retreats, vacations and trainings offered to yoga consumers, through which they reveal that the prices of these events transform the practice of yoga into a luxury that creates class distinctions.

A doubt might arise, then, as to whether this '"me-oriented" spiritual quest, marked by a discourse of 'nailing' poses and pushing through to practice higher series of āsana practice'[5] can still be considered yoga (Nichter 2013: 221). Indeed, questions about authenticity have been crucial for practitioners and scholars. However, scholars today are unanimous in asserting that it is impossible to draw a line that divides those practices that are legitimate from those that are not (Alter 2008: 47). According to Samuel, those 'syncretic, (post)modern and transnational phenomena that are termed "yoga" today should not be dismissed or condemned simply on account of their dislocation from the perceived tradition' (2008: 178). They should indeed be critically historicised, and all claims of both originality and orthopraxy scrutinised 'so as to understand why the claims are made rather than whether they are true' (Alter 2008: 47). Using such scrutiny, Altglas (2005, 2014) claims that transnational Siddha Yoga and Sivananda centres tell us 'more about religious attitudes in western societies today, than about Hinduism itself' (2011: 240) since they underwent a process of westernisation caused by western disciples who adopted and appropriated practices and values as tools to answer 'the urge for self-development characterizing large sections of western societies' (2011: 240).

This westernisation of yoga is not left uncriticised. Jain (2012b: 4) discusses how postural yoga has Hindu opponents because it is perceived as the 'product of a profit-driven market featuring the co-optation and corruption of an otherwise authentic, Hindu system'. However, in the same article she shows that postural yoga also has Christian opponents because it is perceived as too Hindu, hence in conflict with Christian doctrine and therefore an obstacle on the path to salvation. It is the case that movements based on yogic practice have attracted such a number of followers as to be considered religious movements. Lola Williamson (2010: ix) explores the experiences, views and lifestyles of people who have been participating in Self-Realization Fellowship, Transcendental Meditation and Siddha Yoga. She analyses how these movements produced a new hybrid form of religion which 'combines aspects of Hinduism with Western values, institutional forms, modes of teaching, and religious sensibilities'. She explores the contours of these movements and their implications for American culture through personal, historical and cultural lenses. Williamson's work provides modern examples that support Jain's claim that the long history of yoga is made of interactions of various traditions and that, therefore, 'there is no "legitimate", "authentic", "true", or "original" tradition, only contextualized ideas and practices organized around the term yoga' (2012b). A syncretic perspective through which to interpret contemporary yoga is also supported by Kenneth Liberman (2008), who argues that in modern times, yoga and *bhoga* (sensual enjoyment) are not easily distinguishable.[6] The narrative that contemporary practice derives from an original, ancient and pure yoga, he continues, belies the true syncretism of contemporary yoga and limits the exploration of some of the effects that yoga has on practitioners, such as the development of emotional and imaginative poise and existential empowerment (2008: 129–130).

As revealed by Wildcroft's (2020) research, which included ethnographic observations of a yoga subculture in Britain, there are practitioners who actively support the ongoing evolution of the practice by maintaining communities where practitioners from many lineages and none came together. Wildcroft's work stresses that most individuals have found their own way to relate to the post-lineage[7] network in practice, authority and knowledge through a series of revelations and disillusionments, each shared by a few and supported by the many. Disillusionment may be the result of exploited power relationships. This occurs especially when a search for spirituality ends because of misconducts and sexual scandals, as the recent developments of the #MeToo campaign has shown. Unfortunately, these are not new concerns. In 2001, Sarah Caldwell used a reflexive methodology to dig into and interpret the dimensions of power and uses of sexuality in the religious context of the Siddha Yoga movement in relation to the person of Swami Muktananda. Furthermore, Jain (2012c) has analysed the scandals surrounding the founder of Anusara Yoga.

As this section has shown, there has been an increasing amount of recent scholarship based on data collected through ethnographic work. Nevertheless, attention towards more non-international scenarios in India remains scarce. Exceptions are the works of Joseph Alter (2008) and Raphaël Voix (2008), which provide interesting information on the reinterpretation of yoga in contemporary India. In his explanation of the organisation of the yoga *śivir* (campus), Alter demonstrates that also in India 'yoga becomes a means to develop morals, standards of good character, and civic-mindedness', while the 'performativity of the shivir lends itself very well to advocacy for social and moral reform based on the "virtues" of yama and niyama' (2008: 44). Voix, instead, demonstrates the dangerous results that the new interpretation of yoga can assume. He analyses the case of the Ananda Marg and its reinterpretation and codification of the *Yogasūtra* as 'a higher type of spiritual discipline called "extraordinary yoga" (*biśesa yoga*)', a practice that is kept secret and that can lead the most advanced to 'psychic clash': a state of profound despair which is considered an integral part of the Ananda Marga spiritual path (2008: 17).[8]

More grounded in fields that deal with meditation among 'traditional' orders in South and Southeast Asia are – to mention just a few – the works of Houtman (1990), Cook (2010) Jordt (2007) and Cassaniti (2018), while the works of Mallinson (2005, 2011a, 2012, 2013, 2018) and Lamb (2005, 2012) provide original hints about the yoga practice of Vaiṣṇava and Nāth *sādhus* in India. It is noteworthy that although the yoga practice of more traditional India-based ascetics has been described by the aforementioned scholars and finds space among the paragraphs of a few others (see, for example, Gross 1992; Hausner 2007; Bouillier 2017), an ethnographic study focused entirely on this issue has never been carried out before. This is quite surprising considering that, probably, yogic techniques developed in ascetic contexts.

## Ethnography among *sādhus* in India

When I started to work on the yoga practices of ascetics in present-day India for the Haṭha Yoga Project in 2015, I was surprised by the paucity of ethnographic works dealing with average ascetics belonging to deep-rooted lineages who learn yoga practices through oral transmission.[9] The purpose of my ethnographic research was to remedy this lack of information by engaging in fieldwork among *sādhus* belonging to the main *sampradāyas* (religious orders) connected with yoga practice, i.e. Nāgā Daśanāmīs, Rāmānandīs, Nāths, Udāsīns and also some *vairāgīs* from the Rāmānūjī *sampradāya*. I aimed to reconstruct an emic understanding of yoga and *haṭhayoga* among *sādhus*, and I reported on their present practice through interviews, casual conversations, photos or videos of practitioners. I undertook extensive fieldworks in India in various holy cities, attending religious gatherings in search of ascetic practitioners and moving between *āśrams* and religious centres to spend time with *sādhus* and to allow them to know, recognise and trust me and my research.

Compared to the ethnographic studies outlined above, my fieldwork presents two fundamental differences: the difficulty of being a practitioner, and the fact of being a woman. We have seen that in various ethnographic works among yoga practitioners outside of India, scholars were often part of the practice, a practice that involves the intensive participation of women.[10] In my case, during four fieldworks from October 2015 to March 2019 covering various regions

*Figure 27.1* Phalahari Baba, a Rāmānandī *tyāgī*, performs *dhūnī tap*. Allahabad, February 2019. Credit: Daniela Bevilacqua.

and religious orders mostly in North India, there were just two female informants. Although it is said that there is not a gender distinction in the *sādhu* society, in reality it is a male one in which conventional gender roles still operate and in which the female presence is very limited. Together with cultural and traditional discouragement about female asceticism, one strong reason why ascetics prefer to limit the female presence is that *brahmacārya* (celibacy) is very important. Therefore it is preferable to keep women at a distance or to maintain limited contact with them, and this is quite possible in India because the patriarchal society is such that it is unlikely that unmarried women will go to talk with *sādhus* or spend time with them. When this happens, specific behaviours are maintained, and I had to learn how to behave properly in front of a *sādhu* to be considered a respectable woman. However, the fact that I was a foreigner, a researcher and that I can converse in Hindi created that curiosity and respect which helped to break the wall of distrust and suspicion.

The difficulty of being a practitioner in this context stems from the fact that *sādhus* give proper teachings only to those who are initiated into their orders.[11] My decision to not be initiated in any tradition was both ethical and practical: it was awkward for me to take initiation (with the requisite duties and the faith around which such duties revolve) only in order to obtain information about practices,[12] and I did not consider it appropriate to acquire an esoteric knowledge that was not supposed to be shared with non-initiated audiences. From a practical point of view, to get initiated into a specific order would have meant remaining close to a single guru, at least during the religious festivals, limiting the time spent with *sādhus* from other *sampradāyas*.

Ascetics understand yoga as a *sādhana* (religious discipline), which slowly proceeds towards the development of detachment to realise a communion with God. Therefore, according to many ascetics, since yoga is an inner practice that happens on a level of reality indescribable by words, it cannot be shared, only experienced.

A similar argument is put forth by Cook (2010: 20) in investigating meditation in Thailand. She writes:

> the emphasis placed upon the experiential dimension of meditation makes it a particularly thorny challenge for anthropology: in many ways research about meditation is an attempt to 'eff' the ineffable [...] some questions were met with responses such as 'acknowledge' or meditate and you will know.[13]

Additionally, Houtman (1990: 156) declares that he had to work mostly with informants who were '"improvising" meditators' because they were 'the ones most forthcoming in talking of their experiences', while monks replied to him to engage in three months of full-time meditation for twenty hours a day without talking or writing to obtain results. Fortunately, since in my case the research focuses on *haṭhayoga* practices (*ṣaṭ karma, āsana, prāṇāyāma, mudrā, bandha*), and since *sādhus* do not have particular restrictions in talking about some techniques of the physical part of their yoga *sādhana*, it was possible to collect data. In the next section, I select a few topics to practically demonstrate how ethnography can provide fundamental hints to inform research into yoga, its history, its practices and further development.

## Analysing ethnographic data

As I have written elsewhere (Bevilacqua 2017), the simple question 'what is *haṭhayoga*?' addressed to *sādhus* allowed me to reconstruct an emic understanding of the meaning of *haṭhayoga*. Although the word *haṭha* has been generally understood as a system of physical techniques (*ṣaṭ karma, āsana, prāṇāyāma, mudrā, bandha*) supplementary to yoga, in my conversation with ascetics four different meanings were attributed to the label: *haṭhayoga* was strictly connected with *tapasyā*, i.e. it was the mental determination that helps in performing and keeping austerities; *haṭhayoga* was linked to the esoteric meaning of the union of *ha-* the sun and *-ṭha* the moon, intended as the union of *iḍā* and *piṅgalā nāḍī* in the *suṣumṇā*; *haṭhayoga* was connected to practices for controlling and suppressing *prāṇa*; *haṭhayoga* was the practice of *kriyā*s, especially inner, difficult *kriyā*s. I was able to verify that although these various meanings are scattered in textual sources belonging to different religious contexts, these texts are, nevertheless, not mentioned by ascetics. Therefore, confronting ethnographic evidences with textual sources, I demonstrated that the *haṭhayoga* tradition was not a monolithic one but was connected to various contexts and developed probably from the teachings of various gurus. Such gurus elaborated, shared and spread practices that could be universally useful for individuals on the path of yoga *sādhana*. However, the data also demonstrates that *sādhu*s do not use Sanskrit texts systematically. In effect, in the ascetic context the main source of knowledge is the teaching of the guru. These teachings are secret and are the key for getting the *ras*, juice, of the practice. They can be hidden in texts, but only the guru can explain them; therefore *sādhu*s consider texts as conveyors of a knowledge that everybody can access, but it is a general knowledge. I met very few ascetics who had read books about yoga. Sometimes they can recite *śloka*s (verses or lines), but the origin of the source is not clear to them.

This ethnographic data encouraged an enquiry into the role of medieval *haṭhayoga* manuscripts and their audience. Taking as a starting point Birch's argument that the late literature on *haṭhayoga* should be divided in the two etic categories of 'extended works' and 'compendia', I suggest a third category of vernacular texts – unfortunately largely unstudied. Prescriptive texts in vernacular languages were probably produced inside *sampradāya*s, circulating therefore in the *sampradāyik* milieu for the individual practice of its ascetics. However, as an article by Birch (forthcoming) demonstrates, in texts such as the *Jogapradīpakā*, the word *haṭhayoga* is not used. Larger collections in Sanskrit were probably written by Brahmin followers of particular gurus, 'working' under specific patrons to promote yoga teachings (see, for example, Mallinson 2019). It is likely that such texts had a purpose similar to that of yoga books today: to attract people and their economic support with practices that could lead to *dhyāna* yoga. Probably because they were looking at a wider audience, these Sanskrit texts leave aside austerities, i.e. *tapasyā*, properly practised only by ascetics.

Ethnographic data on the ascetic practice of *āsana*s also provides interesting information. Often, different *āsana*s or *kriyā*s are learned from different *sādhus*, who are expert in specific practices, during pilgrimages or during religious gatherings. Questioning *sādhus* about *āsanas* revealed that there are two ideas of *āsana*s in the ascetic milieu. On the one hand, there are *āsana*s used as stable, seated positions for practicing *dhyāna*, in particular *sukhāsana*, *siddhāsana* and *padmāsana*. Then, there are those temporary *āsanas* whose purpose is to keep the body healthy by preventing diseases, and to make it *sthir*, stable, consequently to stabilise the mind to facilitate meditation. The interviews collected show that *sādhu*s focus on one *āsana* at time and only when this is perfected do they start to practise another one. Interestingly, sharing this information with Jason Birch, we were surprised to recognise a similar attitude in the *Jogapradīpyakā*, probably written by a Rāmānandī *sādhu*. As Birch related to me in a personal communication, the *Jogapradīpyakā* contains similar recommendations about the practice of *āsana*s: for example, it suggests that *Paścimotānāsana* (*Jogapradīpyakā* 70–78), requires a special preparatory diet, is practised for a period of 168 days and is held continuously for the last eighty-four days of this period (see also Birch and Hargreaves forthcoming). In contemporary practice, when temporary *āsana*s became *siddh* (perfected/accomplished), *sādhu*s stop practicing them systematically unless they need to, i.e. to alleviate physical problems or to maintain their physical shape, but not more than few minutes a day. Despite this temporary use, *āsanas* are an initial fundamental step for meditative practice: to practise one *āsana* for a long time increases the perseverance and the intention of the practitioner, so that he will be able to use the same persistence to accomplish and follow religious aims.

This attitude of ascetics towards *āsanas* could be 'captured' through the ethnographic method. Furthermore, it was useful to understand some contents of the *Jogapradīpakā* and to relate present with past traditions. It would be interesting to compare *sādhus*' descriptions of theories and practices with the understanding that modern practitioners have. While in the first case we have knowledge – whose origin is probably lost in time – that primarily derives from an oral transmission strictly connected to the presence of a guru and given only if the disciple is considered apt, in the second case we may have 'spiritual wanderers', empowered practitioners who may form their 'own opinion cognitively by reading and attending lectures, and through (embodied) experience of spiritual methods' (Koch 2013: 247). Similar discussions demonstrate how direct conversation with ascetic practitioners can lead to observations that help us in outlining the historical development of physical yogic practices, also creating a comparison with modern yoga, its practices and its transmission.

## Challenges and conclusions

This chapter demonstrates how scholars are becoming interested in understanding the practices, aims, results and environments that influence practitioners who belong to one of the various postural yogic or meditative movements spread all over the world. To fully understand these new topics, scholars often turn to ethnographic methods. Considering, in fact, that yoga is an experiential discipline (as *sādhana* and as physical training), ethnography provides useful tools (especially participant observation that in some cases becomes co-participation) to dig into and interpret diverse nuances. However, the researcher and the reader should be aware of the challenges and the ambiguities inherent to this approach. Hammersley has argued that 'the idea that ethnographic accounts are simply descriptions of reality "as it is" is misleading' (1990: 607), because for any phenomenon 'there is an infinity of factors that played a role in its production', and we, as scholars, 'select from that range those factors that are relevant to the purposes that our explanation is intended to serve'. Therefore, one should take into consideration that the description and the explanation of data is influenced by the figure of the researcher and his/her value.

In the field of yoga studies, wherein many researchers are also privately involved in the practice, there is also the risk of what Hammersley defines as 'the potential to turn ethnographic description into an ideological device in which an account shaped by particular values is presented as if it were the only description or explanation possible' (1990: 609). That is why we should not only attempt to be as reflexive and honest as possible in the production of our results, but also try 'to understand the context and form of practice', of the 'many different ways in which yoga can be performed and taught' (Alter 2008: 47). This means confronting ethnographic data with other sources because, as Alter suggests,

> it is also important to understand the way in which yoga, as represented in the classical and medieval literature – which reveals differences and delineations in the form, structure, and meaning of practice – tends to get blurred together with modern and postmodern formulations.

As my ethnographic work among ascetics demonstrates, to maintain a synchronic and diachronic approach while analysing the studied realities is useful and fruitful to understand present situations and, through them, to interpret past contexts.

Given the fact that the topics and issues of investigation will most likely increase in the future of yoga studies, we can expect further ethnographic research among the numerous Indian religious orders and transnational yoga groups. Such systematic multidisciplinary research enquiry will overcome the challenges and problems that accompany the ethnographic method, helping to broadly reconstruct the history and the development of yogas in India and abroad.

## Glossary

*bandha*, lock
*kriyā*, action
*iḍā* and *piṅgalā nāḍī*, left and right channels
*kartik vrat*, vows during the Indian month of Kartik.
*prāṇa*, breath
paramparā, traditional lineage
*pūjā*, worship
*sādhana*; religious discipline
*sadhu*, holy man
*sampradāya*, religious order
tapas, inner spiritual fire
tapasyā, austerity
*suṣumṇā nāḍī*, central channel

## Notes

1 This chapter was financially supported by the European Union's Horizon 2020 research and innovation programme under grant agreement No. 647963 (Haṭha Yoga Project).
2 For an overview of yoga scholarship undertaken by indologists and historians of religion, see Hauser (2013b: 11–16) and Newcombe (2009).
3 Wildcroft (2020) defines this as 'co-practice.'
4 On the other side, Pagis' ethnographic data on meditation illustrates how 'despite the absence of direct verbal communication, the practice of meditation still holds important intersubjective dimensions'. He suggests that 'covert mechanisms of silent intersubjectivity play an important role in everyday social life and require further ethnographic attention' (2010).
5 According to Schnäbele (2013: 221), the flow of yoga students to Mysore is increasing, but the reasons why they are going has changed over the decades: in the 1960s and 1970s those who went to study with Pattabhi Jois demonstrated a more devotional attitude, while today's younger students have a more 'me-oriented' attitude.
6 Yoga and *bhoga* have been sharply distinguished in history. *Bhoga*, understood as the experience of supernatural pleasures, was the aim of Śaiva groups who were followers of the Mantramārga (Sanderson 1988: 667). Mallinson notes that with the development of *haṭhayoga* systems the main tendency was to preserve the seeker of liberation rather than the seeker of enjoyment. Therefore, although *haṭhayoga* incorporated various traditions that can refer to the Mantramārga, it did away with 'their complex and exclusive bhoga-oriented systems' (2011b). The *Haṭhapradīpikā*, for example, claims that *bhoga* (enjoyments) are the greatest of all impediments for yoga.
7 Post-lineage yoga consists of 'a re-evaluation of the authority to determine practice, and a privileging of peer networks over pedagogical hierarchies, or saṃghas (communities) over guru-śiṣya (teacher-adept) relationships' (Wildcroft 2020).
8 As Voix mentions (2008: 17), a theoretically similar technique of shock seems to be used in other contemporary religious groups inspired by tantrism, as described by Sarah Caldwell concerning alleged sexual abuses involving Swami Muktananda and his Siddha Yoga (2001: 9).
9 If we look instead at works which take into consideration international or modern *sādhus*, the production is wide and detailed. See, for example: the work of Strauss (2005) on Swami Sivananda; the works of

Persson (2007; 2010) and Pankhania (2008) on Swami Satyananda; Aveling (1994) on Swami Satyananda and Osho; and the work of Khalikova (2017) and Longkumer (2018) on Baba Ramdev.

10 A 2012 survey by *Yoga Journal* found that of the 20.4 million people who practise yoga in the United States, only 18 percent of them are men. (www.yogajournal.com/blog/new-study-finds-20-million-yogis-u-s. Accessed April 2019).

11 In my case, I could not spend time on personal practices, since the results would not have been of any interest for my research, and given the time needed to attain a sufficient level to be shared or compared with that of *sādhus*, the five years of the project would have not been enough.

12 Joanna Cook (2010) became a Buddhist nun committed to ordination and meditation. However, the members of the monastery were aware that her ordination would be limited to one year in which she would undertake anthropological research. Another case is that of Ingrid Jordt (2007), who also became a Buddhist nun for several years, focusing her attention on *vipassana* as a diplomatic link between Burma and the rest of the world.

13 This practical approach has been testified also by scholars working with the founders of modern transnational yoga. For example, Smith reports that Pattabhi Jois used to claim: 'Ninety-nine percent practice, one percent theory [...] practice and all is coming' (2008: 153).

## Bibliography


Alter, J. 2004. *Yoga in Modern India: The Body Between Science and Philosophy*. Princeton: Princeton University Press.

Alter, J. 2008. 'Yoga Shivir: Performativity and the Study of Modern Yoga', in Singleton, M. and Byrne, J. (eds), *Yoga in the Modern World: Contemporary Perspectives*, 36–48. London and New York: Routledge Hindu Studies Series.

Altglas, V. 2005. *Le Nouvel Hindouisme Occidental*. Paris: Éditions du CNRS.

Altglas, V. 2011. 'Yoga and Kabbalah as World Religions? A Comparative Perspective on Globalization of Religious Resources,' in Huss, B. B. (ed), *Kabbalah and Contemporary Spiritual Revival*, 233–50. Beer Sheva: Ben-Gurion University of the Negev Press.

Altglas, V. 2014. *From Yoga to Kabbalah: Religious Exoticism and the Logics of Bricolage*. Oxford and New York: Oxford University Press.

Atkinson P., and Hammersley, M. 1994. 'Ethnography and Participant Observation', in Denzin, N. K. and Lincoln, Y. S. (eds), *Handbook of Qualitative Research*, 248–261. Newbury Park: Sage.

Aveling, H. 1994. *The Laughing Swamis: Australian Sannyasin Disciples of Swami Satyananda and Osho Rajneesh*. Varanasi: Motilal Banarsidass Publisher.

Bevilacqua, D. 2017. 'Let the Sādhus Talk. Ascetic Understanding of Haṭha Yoga and *Yogāsanas*'. *Religions of South Asia* 11(2): 182–206.

Birch, J. 2020. 'Haṭhayoga's Floruit on the Eve of Colonialism', in Goodall, D., Hatley, S., Isaacson, H. and Raman, S. (eds), *Śaivism and the Tantric Traditions: Essays in Honour of Alexis G. J. S. Sanderson*. Leiden: Brill.

Birch, J. and Hargreaves, J. (forthcoming). 'Distinct Regional Collections of *Āsanas* in Eighteenth and Nineteenth-century India'. *Journal of Yoga Studies*.

Bouillier, V. 2017. *Monastic Wanderers, Nāth Yogi Ascetics in Modern South Asia*. New Delhi: Manohar.

Broo, M. 2012. 'Yoga Practices as Identity Capital, Preliminary notes from Turku, Finland'. *Scripta Instituti Donneriani Aboensis* 24: 24–34. https://doi.org/10.30674/scripta.67406

Burger, M. 2006. 'What Price Salvation? The Exchange of Salvation Goods between India and the West'. *Social Compass* 53: 81–95.

Byrne, J. and Singleton, M. (eds) 2008. *Yoga in the Modern World: Contemporary Perspectives*. New York: Routledge Hindu Studies Series.

Caldwell, S. 2001. 'The Heart of the Secret: A Personal and Scholarly Encounter with Shakta Tantrism in Siddha Yoga'. *Nova Religio* 5(1): 9–51.

Cassaniti, J. 2015. *Living Buddhism: Mind, Self, and Emotion in a Thai Community*. Ithaca: Cornell University Press.

Cassaniti, J. 2018. *Remembering the Present, Mindfulness in Buddhist Asia*. Ithaca, NY, USA: Cornell University Press.

Cook, J. 2010. *Meditation in Modern Buddhism: Renunciation and Change in Thai Monastic Life*. Cambridge: Cambridge University Press.

De Michelis, E. 2004. *A History of Modern Yoga*. London: Continuum.
Goldberg, E. and Singleton, M. (eds) 2013. *Gurus of Modern Yoga*. Oxford University Press.
Gross, L. R. 1992. *The Sadhus of India, A Study of Hindu Asceticism*. New Delhi: Rawal Publications.
Hammersley, M. 1990. 'What's Wrong with Ethnography? The Myth of Theoretical Description'. *Sociology* 24(4): 597–615.
Hasselle-Newcombe, S. 2005. 'Spirituality and "Mystical Religion" in Contemporary Society: A Case Study of British Practitioners of the Iyengar Method of Yoga'. *Journal of Contemporary Religion* 20(3): 305–321.
Hauser, B. 2013a. 'Touching the Limits, Assessing Pain: On Language Performativity, Health, and Well-Being in Yoga Classes', in Hauser, B. (ed), *Yoga Traveling, Bodily Practice in Transcultural Perspective*, 109–134. Heidelberg: Springer.
Hauser, B. 2013b. *Yoga Traveling, Bodily Practice in Transcultural Perspective*. Heidelberg: Springer.
Hausner, S. 2007. *Wandering with Sadhus: Ascetics in the Hindu Himalayas*. Bloomington: Indiana University Press.
Houtman, G. 1990. *Traditions of Buddhist Practice in Burma*. PhD thesis, SOAS, University of London.
Jain, A. 2012a. 'The Dual-Ideal of the Ascetic and Healthy Body: The Jain Terāpanth and Modern Yoga in the Context of Late Capitalism'. *Nova Religio* 15(3): 29–50.
Jain, A. 2012b. 'The Malleability of Yoga: A Response to Christian and Hindu Opponents of the Popularization of Yoga'. *Journal of Hindu-Christian Studies* 25: 3–10.
Jain, A. 2012c. 'Branding Yoga. The Cases of Iyengar Yoga, Siddha Yoga and Anusara Yoga'. *Approaching Religion* 2(2): 3–17.
Jain, A. 2014. *Selling Yoga: From Counter-Culture to Pop Culture*. New York: Oxford University Press.
Jordt, I. 2007. *Burma's Mass Lay Meditation Movement: Buddhism and the Cultural Construction of Power*. Ohio University Press.
Khalikova, V. R. 2017. 'The Ayurveda of Baba Ramdev: Biomoral Consumerism, National Duty and the Biopolitics of "Homegrown" Medicine in India'. *South Asia: Journal of South Asian Studies* 40(1): 105–122.
Knut, A. J. 2005. *Theory and Practice of Yoga: Essays in Honour of Gerald James Larson*. Leiden: Brill.
Koch, A. 2013. 'Yoga as a Production Site of Social and Human Capital: Transcultural Flows from a Cultural Economic Perspective', in Hauser, B. (ed), *Yoga Traveling, Bodily Practice in Transcultural Perspective*, 225–248. Heidelberg: Springer.
Lamb, R. 2005. 'Rāja Yoga, Asceticism, and the Rāmānanda Sampradāy', in Jacobsen, K. A. (ed), *Theory and Practice of Yoga: Essays in Honour of Gerald James Larson*, 317–331. Leiden: Brill.
Lamb, R. 2012. 'Yogic Powers and the Rāmānanda Sampradāy', in Jacobsen, K. A. (ed), *Yoga Power. Extraordinary Capacities Attained Through Meditation and Concentration*, 427–457. Leiden: Brill.
Langøien, L. J. 2012. 'Yoga, Change and Embodied Enlightenment'. *Approaching Religion* 2(2): 27–37.
Liberman, K. 2008. 'The Reflexivity of the Authenticity of Haṭha Yoga', in Singleton, M. and Byrne, J. (eds), *Yoga in the Modern World: Contemporary Perspectives*, 100–116. New York: Routledge Hindu Studies Series.
Longkumer, A. 2018. '"Nagas Can't Sit Lotus Style": Baba Ramdev, Patanjali, and Neo-Hindutva'. *Contemporary South Asia* 26(4): 400–420.
Mallinson, J. 2005. 'Rāmānandī Tyāgīs and Haṭha Yoga'. *Journal of Vaishnava Studies* 14(1): 107–121.
Mallinson, J. 2011a. 'Nāth Sampradāya', in Jacobsen, K. A., Basu, H., Malinar, A. and Narayanan, V. (eds), *Brill Encyclopedia of Hinduism Vol. 3*, 407–428. Leiden: Brill
Mallinson, J. 2011b. 'Haṭha Yoga', in Jacobsen, K. A., Basu, H., Malinar, A. and Narayanan, V. (eds), *Brill Encyclopedia of Hinduism Vol. 3*, 770–781. Leiden: Brill.
Mallinson, J. 2012. 'Yoga and Yogis'. *Nāmarūpa* 3(15): 2–27.
Mallinson, J. 2013. 'Yogic Identities: Tradition and Transformation'. *Smithsonian Institute Research Online*, https://eprints.soas.ac.uk/17966/. Accessed 12 March 2020.
Mallinson, J. 2018. 'Yoga and Sex: What is the Purpose of Vajrolīmudrā', in Baier, K., Maas, P. A. and Preisendanz, K. (eds), *Yoga in Transformation, Historical and Contemporary Perspectives*, 181–222. Vienna: V&R Unipress.
Mallinson, J. 2019. 'Kālavañcana in the Kokan: How a Vajrayāna Haṭhayoga Tradition Cheated Buddhism's Death in India'. *Religions* 10(4): 273. https://doi.org/10.3390/rel10040273.
Marcus, E. G. 1995. 'Ethnography in/of the World System: The Emergence of Multi-Sited Ethnography'. *Annual Review of Anthropology* 24: 95–117.
Nevrin, K. 2008. 'Empowerment and Using the Body in Modern Postural Yoga', in Singleton, M. and Byrne, J. (eds), *Yoga in the Modern World: Contemporary Perspectives*, 119–139. New York: Routledge Hindu Studies Series.

Newcombe, S. 2005. 'Spirituality and "Mystical Religion" in Contemporary Society: A Case Study of British Practitioners of the Iyengar Method of Yoga'. *Journal of Contemporary Religion* 20(3): 305–321.
Newcombe, S. 2009. 'The Development of Modern Yoga: A Survey of the Field'. *Religion Compass* 3(6): 986–1002.
Newcombe, S. 2018. 'Spaces of Yoga: Towards a Non-Essentialist Understanding of Yoga', in Baier, K., Mass, P. A. and Preisendanz, K. (eds), *Yoga in Transformation: Historical and Contemporary Perspectives*, 551–573. Vienna: Vienna University Press.
Newcombe, S. 2019. *Yoga in Britain. Stretching Spirituality and Educating Yoga*. Sheffield: Equinox Publishing.
Mandelbaum, L., and Strauss, S. 2013. 'Consuming Yoga, Conserving the Environment: Transcultural Discourses on Sustainable Living', in Hauser, B. (ed), *Yoga Traveling, Bodily Practice in Transcultural Perspective*, 175–200. Heidelberg: Springer.
Nichter, M. 2013. 'The Social Life of Yoga: Exploring Transcultural Flows in India', in Hauser, B. (ed), *Yoga Traveling, Bodily Practice in Transcultural Perspective*, 201–223. Heidelberg: Springer.
Pagis, M. 2010. 'Producing Intersubjectivity in Silence: An Ethnographic Study of Meditation Practice'. *Ethnography* 11(2): 309–328.
Pankhania, J. 2008. *Encountering Satyananda Yoga in Australia and India: Reflections of a Complex, Postcolonial, Gendered Subject*. PhD dissertation, University of Western Sydney. Centre for Cultural Research.
Pearson, J. 2001. '"Going Native in Reverse": The Insider as Researcher in British Wicca', *Nova Religio* 5(1): 52–63
Persson, A 2007. 'Intimate Immensity: Phenomenology of Place and Space in an Australian Yoga Community'. *American Ethnologist* 34(1): 44–56.
Persson, A 2010. 'Embodied Worlds: A Semiotic Phenomenology of Satyananda Yoga'. *Journal of the Royal Anthropological Institute NS* 16(4): 797–815.
Pintchman, T. 2005. 'Raising Krishna with Love: Maternal Devotion as a Form of Yoga in a Women's Ritual Tradition', in Jacobsen, K. A. (ed), *Yoga Power. Extraordinary Capacities Attained Through Meditation and Concentration*, 351–362. Leiden: Brill.
Pole, C. and Morrison, M. 2003. *Ethnography for Education*. London: Open University Press, McGraw-Hill Education.
Samuel, G. 2008. *The Origins of Yoga and Tantra*. Cambridge: Cambridge University Press.
Sanderson, A. 1988. 'Śaivism and the Tantric Traditions', in Sutherland, S., Houlden, L., Clarke, P. and Hardy, F. (eds), *The World's Religions*, 660–704. London: Routledge and Kegan Paul.
Sarbacker, S. R. 2008. 'The Numinous and Cessative in Modern Yoga', in Singleton, M. and Byrne, J. (eds), *Yoga in the Modern World: Contemporary Perspectives*, 161–183. London: Routledge.
Sarbacker, S. R. 2014. 'Reclaiming the Spirit through the Body: The Nascent Spirituality of Modern Postural Yoga'. *Entangled Religions Interdisciplinary Journal for the Study of Religious Contact and Transfer*, 1: 95–114.
Schnäbele, V. 2010. *Yoga in Modern Society*. Hamburg: Verlag Dr. Kovac.
Schnäbele, V. 2013. 'The Useful Body: The Yogic Answer to Appearance Management in the Post-Fordist Workplace', in Hauser, B. (ed), *Yoga Traveling, Bodily Practice in Transcultural Perspective*, 135–154. Heidelberg: Springer.
Sidnell, J. 2017. 'Ethical Practice and Techniques of the Self at a Yoga School'. *Anthropology Today* 33(4): 13–17.
Singleton, M. and Byrne, J. (eds) 2008. *Yoga in the Modern World: Contemporary Perspectives*. New York: Routledge Hindu Studies Series.
Sjoman, N. E. (1999). *The Yoga Tradition of the Mysore Palace*. New Delhi: Abhinav Publications.
Smith, B. R. 2004. 'Adjusting the Quotidian: Ashtanga Yoga as Everyday Practice'. in *The Online Proceedings from Everyday Transformations; The 2004 Annual Conference of the Cultural Studies Association of Australasia*. https://openresearch-repository.anu.edu.au/handle/1885/80667. Accessed 12 March 2020.
Smith, B. R. 2007. 'Body, Mind and Spirit? Towards an Analysis of the Practice of Yoga'. *Body & Society* 13(2): 25–46.
Smith, B. R. 2008. '"With Heat Even Iron Will Bend": Discipline and Authority in Ashtanga Yoga', in Singleton, M. and Byrne, J. (eds), *Yoga in the Modern World: Contemporary Perspectives*, 140–160. London: Routledge.
Strauss, S. 2000. 'Locating Yoga: Ethnography and Transnational Practice', in Amit, V. (ed), *Constructing the Field*, 162–194. New York: Routledge.
Strauss, S. 2002. '"Adapt, Adjust, Accommodate": The Production of Yoga in a Transnational World'. *History and Anthropology* 13(3): 231–251.

Strauss, S. 2005. *Positioning Yoga, Balancing Acts Across Cultures*. Berg: Berg Publishers.
Van Maanen, J. 1996. 'Ethnography', in Kuper, A. and Kuper, J. (eds), *The Social Science Encyclopedia*, 263–265. London: Routledge.
Voix, R. 2008. 'Denied Violence, Glorified Fighting: Spiritual Discipline and Controversy in Ananda Marga'. *Nova Religio: The Journal of Alternative and Emergent Religions*, 12(1): 3–25.
Wildcroft, T. 2020. *Post-lineage Yoga: From Guru to #MeToo.* Sheffield: Equinox Publishing.
Williamson L. 2010. *Transcendent in America: Hindu-Inspired Meditation Movements as New Religion.* New York: New York University Press.

# 28

# YOGA AND PHILOSOPHY

## Ontology, epistemology, ethics

*Mikel Burley*

### Introduction: philosophy in a global context

It is routinely acknowledged by philosophers that 'What is philosophy?' is itself a challenging philosophical question. In western philosophical contexts, this question has often been addressed in ways that marginalise or exclude non-western philosophies, giving little, if any, attention to sources and traditions outside the western canon. But such parochial approaches are coming under increasing pressure in today's globalised world, a world in which information about many non-western forms of philosophical inquiry is more readily available than ever before. Increased knowledge about non-western traditions inevitably shapes what philosophy is understood to be.

Within the Indian philosophical milieu, the concept of yoga and multiple concepts related to meditation have had a prominent place. Indeed, the term *Yoga* is commonly treated as the name of one of the major *darśana*s (roughly, 'schools' or 'ways of seeing') of classical Indian philosophy. When treated in this way, *Yoga* normally denotes the system of philosophy attributed to Patañjali and adumbrated primarily in the *Pātañjalayogaśāstra* (*c.* fourth or fifth century CE), comprising the series of terse statements customarily referred to as the *Yogasūtra* plus the commentary called either the *Yogabhāṣya* or *Vyāsabhāṣya*. Central to this system are forms of meditative practice geared towards the reduction and eventual elimination of mental activities (*citta-vṛtti*), and the practical instructions for promoting this end are integral to a philosophical vision that includes ontological, epistemological and ethical dimensions. The Yoga system of Patañjali is in turn closely aligned with the school of philosophy known as Sāṃkhya, whose hallmark is the rigorous analysis of the constitutive conditions of experiential life. At the heart of both Sāṃkhya and Yoga is the aspiration – shared especially with Buddhism – to eradicate the causes of 'dissatisfactoriness' (*duḥkha*) by coming to realise that none of the modes of desire, feeling and emotion, or of experience tout court, are essential to who one really is. Unlike most forms of Buddhism, however, Sāṃkhya and Yoga do not deny the existence of an ultimate self. For Sāṃkhya and Yoga, this self is *puruṣa* (the authentic 'person', identified with pure consciousness) or *draṣṭṛ* (the 'seer' or subject). Never itself becoming an object of consciousness, this self stands in opposition to the fundamental source of everything objective, namely that which is 'seeable' (*dṛśya*) or 'procreative' (*prakṛti*).

My purpose in this chapter is neither to supply a comprehensive exposition of the philosophies of Sāṃkhya and Yoga, nor to offer a survey of the many other philosophies that have been associated with the practices of yoga and meditation (including not only Brahmanical and

Buddhist philosophies, but also those of Jainism, Sikhism and certain non-Brahmanical Hindu schools). Rather, my purpose is to examine some of the ways in which philosophy has been utilised as a disciplinary approach to the study of yoga and meditation. To provide a manageable focus, however, Sāṃkhya and Yoga will constitute central reference points for each of the three main themes that the chapter discusses, and other philosophical schools will be mentioned along the way. The first of the themes, 'Yoga and ontology', is concerned with competing interpretations of what, according to classical Yoga, exists. The second, 'Yoga and epistemology', concerns what, according to Yoga and other meditative traditions, can be known and, more specifically, what it might mean to speak of a state of 'pure consciousness'. Third, under the heading of 'Yoga and ethics', will be a discussion of how ethical aspects of Yoga praxis have been interpreted in the light of normative moral theories. Rounding off the chapter will be some thoughts about the future prospects for philosophical approaches to yoga and meditation.

## Yoga and ontology

Ontology (from the Greek *ontos*, 'being') is the branch of philosophy that enquires into what *is* or what *exists* or into the nature of *being*. Among yoga- and meditation-related traditions, there is a wealth of ontological systems, from the respective monisms of, for example, Advaita Vedānta and Kashmir Śaivism to the ontological pluralisms of Nyāya and Vaiśeṣika. Both Yoga and Sāṃkhya, when treated as schools of classical Indian philosophy, are normally labelled as ontologically dualist, but this basic classification leaves much interpretive work still to be done. The task of interpreting Yoga ontology is itself a philosophical enterprise that involves trying to formulate an interpretation that supplies the most coherent result. This in turn normally requires not only close attention to the original sources but also a degree of comparative analysis with other systems of philosophy, for the purpose of discerning both similarities and differences. It is this interpretive philosophical task that will be the main topic of this section.

A central question pertaining to Yoga philosophy is whether the various entities that constitute Yoga's overall ontology are best understood in cosmological terms or in terms that might be described as psychological or phenomenological. In this context, a cosmological interpretation is one that identifies the entities in question as constituents of the world as it exists 'in itself', independently of anyone's experiencing it. Such an interpretation may also be referred to as *realist*, in the specific philosophical sense that it understands Yoga to be offering an account of a mind-independent reality, as opposed to an idealist account, which treats the world as in some way dependent upon mental states or activities. A psychological or phenomenological interpretation, meanwhile, identifies the components of Yoga's ontology as either a set of psychological faculties or as constitutive features of experience – or, in some instances, a mixture of these two categories.

The question of whether a realist-cosmological or a more psychologically or phenomenologically oriented interpretation is most plausible arises largely as a consequence of Yoga's alignment with Sāṃkhya, an alignment sufficiently close for certain interpreters to have opted to use the combined term 'Sāṃkhya–Yoga'. Indeed, the *Yogabhāṣya* refers to itself as an 'explanation of Sāṃkhya' (Larson 2008: 23), thereby designating Yoga as a form of Sāṃkhya. What Sāṃkhya is most renowned for is its system of twenty-five 'principles' or 'essences' (*tattva*s), and Yoga is commonly assumed to adopt this same system, with the exception that it adds a twenty-sixth principle, namely 'the Lord' (*īśvara*). Whether the latter should be treated as a distinct principle is, however, doubtful, given that *īśvara* is defined in *Yogasūtra* 1.24 merely as a 'special self' (*puruṣa-viśeṣa*) rather than as a separate ontological category (Jacobsen 2012). Meanwhile, when defining what is *not* the self, namely the 'seeable', both Yoga and Sāṃkhya characterise it as comprising three co-fundamental 'strands' (*guṇas*), which are identified, respectively, as 'illumination, activity and stability' (*Yogasūtra* 2.18). *Yogasūtra* 2.19 proceeds to name four different 'levels' or 'divisions' (*parvāṇi*) that are formed by these three *guṇas*, and the *Yogabhāṣya* subdivides the four levels in such a way as to yield unmanifest *prakṛti* plus all twenty-three of the principles that, according to Sāṃkhya, emerge from it. Thus, if the commentary's exposition is accepted, Yoga endorses the Sāṃkhya ontology. By the same token, the problem of whether to construe the ontology in cosmological or in psychological–phenomenological terms is inherited by interpreters of Yoga.

Provided care is taken not to simply impose western philosophical models on the Indian material, the interpretive project can be assisted by means of comparisons with ideas from western philosophy. Since the ontology common to Sāṃkhya and Yoga appears to consist in a basic dualism between a centre of consciousness (*puruṣa*) – or, more precisely, a multiplicity of centres of consciousness (see *Sāṃkhyakārikā* 18; *Yogasūtra* 2.22) – and the productive source of experienceable phenomena (*prakṛti*), it is tempting to compare it with other dualist ontologies, such as the substance dualism of René Descartes. Despite certain superficial similarities, however, what this comparison reveals is that, unlike Descartes's ontology, the dualism advanced by Sāṃkhya and Yoga is not well characterised in terms of mind versus matter. This is because, for Descartes, both the mind and matter exhibit several 'modes', such as perceiving, willing, sensing, emoting and desiring in the case of minds, and position, shape, movement and divisibility in the case of matter (Descartes 1985 : Part 1, §§48, 53). *Puruṣa* is not a mind in this sense, for it is held by Sāṃkhya and Yoga to be inactive and without modes. By contrast, *prakṛti*, in its – or 'her' – manifest form, is not only thoroughly active, but is the source of all the mental modes as well as the material ones. This is why philosophical interpreters have characterised Sāṃkhya and Yoga ontology as, for example, a dualism between 'individual consciousness' and 'the unconscious world' (Larson 1969: 47) or between 'consciousness' and 'mind' (Schweizer 1993; Perrett 2001: 11) rather than between mind and matter. None of these characterisations is, however, unproblematic. While *puruṣa* is certainly, in some sense, consciousness, *prakṛti* is not straightforwardly an 'unconscious world', unless (implausibly) the term 'unconscious world' is understood to include things such as sensations and mental states; but neither is *prakṛti* simply 'mind', for it is, in its unmanifest state, ontologically prior to the emergence of mental capacities and experiential phenomena.

My own interpretive work has included comparisons between the ontology of Sāṃkhya and Yoga, on the one hand, and certain aspects of both western philosophy and Indian Buddhist philosophy, on the other (Burley 2007). In the area of western philosophy, I have borrowed ideas from the transcendental idealism of Immanuel Kant and the phenomenological philosophies of Franz Brentano and Edmund Husserl; from Buddhism, I have drawn upon prevalent interpretations of Abhidharma philosophy. Though, of course, other comparisons are possible, it is these that I shall elaborate in the remainder of this section.

What Kant seeks to provide in his critical philosophy is an analysis of the transcendental conditions of possible experience – 'transcendental' in the sense that the conditions at issue are not themselves possible objects of experience, precisely because they are what must be in place for experience to occur. On Kant's account, these conditions include space and time, which he regards as formal characteristics of sensory experience (or 'pure forms of intuition') rather than features of the world as it is in itself (Kant 1998: 155–192), plus a total of twelve 'concepts of pure understanding' (201–266), which may be divided into concepts of quantity, quality, relation (including causality) and modality. In the case of Brentano and Husserl, they offer, in their respective ways, accounts of 'mental phenomena in general' (Brentano 2015: Bk 2) and 'the invariant essential structure of the total sphere of pure mental process' (Husserl 1999: 326). And in the case of Abhidharma Buddhism, a number of interpreters have emphasised the extent to which its account even of the four 'great elements' (*mahābhūtas*) – namely earth, water, fire and air – is concerned not with a physical world entirely independent of consciousness, but rather with 'the physical world as experienced by a sentient being' (Gethin 1986: 36).

The comparison with Abhidharma Buddhism is especially instructive, for Sāṃkhya and Yoga share with Buddhism the fact that they are soteriological or liberative disciplines whose ontologies may reasonably be presumed to complement the practice of sustained meditation. If we were to adopt what I above referred to as a realist-cosmological interpretation of the respective ontological systems, then the relevance of those systems to meditative practice would remain obscure. If, however, we treat the ontological systems as the outcome of analyses of *experience*, then their soteriological relevance becomes evident. In the case both of Sāṃkhya and Yoga and of Buddhism, meditative practice is geared towards the realisation that the various constituents of experience, whether they be cognitive, affective or conative in nature, are not to be identified with one's true self. From the standpoint of most forms of Buddhism, the very idea of a true self is illusory, whereas for Sāṃkhya and Yoga the self is conceived of as *puruṣa*; but the negative enterprise of disidentifying with the components of experience and their conditioning factors is common to Buddhism and to Sāṃkhya and Yoga.

The comparisons with Kant and with the phenomenological philosophies of Brentano and Husserl are helpful inasmuch as they further illuminate how a philosophical inquiry might move from the observation of particular experiences towards a progressively abstract classification of the necessary conditions of any possible experience. Just as, for example, Kant identifies the 'synthetic unity of apperception' – meaning (roughly) the coherence of all the thoughts and experiences of a given individual within a holistic gestalt possessed by a single 'I' – as necessary for the undergoing of any experience at all, so Sāṃkhya affirms that the capacity to identify oneself as an 'I', namely *ahaṃkāra* (literally 'I-maker'), is what enables the emergence of both the capacities for sensation, on the one hand, and the contents of sensory and perceptual experience, on the other. Virtually the same idea occurs under the term *asmitā* ('I-am-ness') in Yoga. And just as, for Brentano and Husserl, one of the fundamental characteristics of consciousness is intentionality – meaning directedness towards an object or the possessing of a given content – so, for Sāṃkhya and Yoga, there is an intentional relation between the 'instrument' (*karaṇa*), comprising the capacities for awareness, egoity, sensation and sensory synthesis, and the 'object' (*kārya*), comprising the sensory contents and the five perceptible 'elements' (*bhūtas*) (see, e.g. *Sāṃkhyakārikā* 32).

An important disanalogy between the position of Sāṃkhya and Yoga, on the one hand, and that of Kant and the western phenomenologists, on the other, is that Sāṃkhya and Yoga insist that it makes sense to speak of nonintentional as well as of intentional consciousness. *Puruṣa* is defined as consciousness without qualities, and the highest state of meditation to be aimed for is one in which no experiential content is present. But it is precisely because of disanalogies such as this, in addition to the partial analogies, that cross-cultural comparative philosophy can be illuminating. Whether the idea of nonintentional, or contentless, consciousness is viable is a significant epistemological and conceptual issue that will receive further attention in the next section.

## Yoga and epistemology

Epistemology (from the Greek *epistēmē*, 'knowledge') is concerned with questions of what can be known and how we can know it. Corresponding terms in Sanskrit include *pramāṇa vidyā* and *pramāṇa śāstra*, the 'study of knowledge and of the means of knowing'. Traditional schools of Indian philosophy take various positions on what counts as a means of knowing. Classical

Sāṃkhya and Yoga are among those that initially list three – namely, perception, inference and verbal (or scriptural) testimony – but also admit the possibility of what is often termed 'yogic perception' (*yogi pratyakṣa*). This, which is held to be a special means of knowing available only to those who have mastered heightened states of meditation, is also recognised by other schools of Indian philosophy, such as Nyāya, Vaiśeṣika and the sundry Vedānta schools, as well as by Buddhism and Jainism (Sinha 1934: 335). It is held, for example, that certain practices of prolonged meditation can deliver knowledge of otherwise inaccessible matters, such as one's former lives (*Yogasūtra* 3.18; *Visuddhimagga* 13.13–71). It is also believed by at least some representatives of these philosophical schools that meditation can lead to a state of consciousness that is so rarefied as to be best characterised in terms of 'pure consciousness' – the 'aloneness of seeing', as Patañjali puts it (*Yogasūtra* 2.25), or consciousness 'without form' (*nirākāra*), as certain proponents of Yogācāra Buddhism have described the state of Buddhahood (Williams 2009: 101–102). Whether the notion of pure consciousness makes sense is a controversial question that has received considerable attention from scholars of mysticism in particular. Insofar as it bears upon the issue of the necessary conditions for knowledge and experience, it is an epistemological question. But it is also a conceptual question, given that it involves inquiring into the limits of sense. It is upon the debate over pure consciousness that I shall concentrate in this section.

The modern debate over pure consciousness was sparked in large part by the publication in 1978 of an edited volume entitled *Mysticism and Philosophical Analysis*, which contains an extensive essay by Steven Katz, the volume's editor, called 'Language, Epistemology and Mysticism'. In that essay, Katz takes as his point of departure a broadly Kantian 'epistemological assumption', namely that, as Katz emphatically puts it, '*There are* NO *pure* (*i.e. unmediated*) *experiences*. ... That is to say, *all* experience is processed through, organized by, and makes itself available to us in extremely complex epistemological ways' (1978: 26). From this starting point, Katz contends that even in cases where the practitioners of a style of meditation maintain that it culminates in a state of *un*mediated consciousness, such descriptions must be false, for Katz's basic epistemological assumption precludes it. With reference to Yoga, for instance, Katz asserts that, '[p]roperly understood', it 'is *not* an *un*conditioning or *de*conditioning of consciousness, but rather it is a *re*conditioning of consciousness, i.e. a substituting of one form of conditioned and/or contextual consciousness for another' (1978: 57). Like all meditative traditions, Katz insists, what 'mediates' or 'conditions' the states of consciousness arrived at by means of Yoga practice is, precisely, the forms of language and ways of thinking embodied in Yoga texts and discourse; these linguistic and conceptual factors establish certain expectations on the part of the practitioner, and the expectations influence or 'condition' the resulting experience. Even when the results of meditation do not conform precisely to the practitioner's expectations, someone who adopts Katz's position is liable to argue that there must have been *something* in the practitioner's cognitive makeup that gave to the experience the specific form that it has, since this is simply 'the sorts of beings we are' (Katz 2013: 5).

Katz's preferred term for his position is *contextualism*, since it hinges on the claim that experience is invariably conditioned by contextual elements, especially the background presuppositions of the experiencer. Others have termed his position *constructivism* on the grounds that it asserts that experience is 'constructed' by linguistic and conceptual factors. Unsurprisingly, the sort of position exemplified by Katz has not gone unchallenged. A notable antagonist has been Robert Forman, who refers to his own position as *perennialism* in order to indicate an affinity with the doctrine of *perennial philosophy*, that there is an essential truth uniting all major religions and that this truth, despite being ineffable, may be directly encountered or 'realized' in mystical experience (cf. Huxley 1946: 29). Forman coined the term 'pure consciousness event' to denote the ineffable state of realisation – 'a wakeful but objectless consciousness', which, he maintains, 'should be viewed as *decontextualized*' (1998: 7). For as long as the 'event' lasts, the mind is devoid of content, yet following the event 'one knows that one has been aware continuously for some time' (ibid.). This conception of a heightened meditative state requires an understanding of consciousness as something that can persist even in the absence of anything that one is conscious of. It thus entails a rejection of the standard view taken by phenomenological philosophers, which is that consciousness is necessarily intentional, in the sense that it is always consciousness *of* something. Understandably, Forman's critics, such as Katz, have questioned the intelligibility of the idea that one can be 'aware continuously' without being aware of anything, including the passing of time. And even if one thinks the idea is intelligible, critics have also taken issue with the contention that one could ever *know* that one has undergone an episode of pure consciousness, for there would be literally nothing to remember that could differentiate it from a period of mere unconsciousness (Gellman 2005: 148). In response, Forman admits that the idea is paradoxical, but insists that pure consciousness events nevertheless occur, that he has undergone one and that what is disclosed through these events is precisely what mystics have alluded to with phrases such as 'ground of the soul' (1998: 7; 1990b: 28; 1990a).

An interesting dimension of the debate over pure consciousness is the way in which it intersects with debates concerning the 'gendered' nature of religious discourse. From a feminist standpoint, Katz's contextualist approach has been endorsed for its rejection of the idea of any epistemic position that is unaffected by sociocultural factors, including gender. On this view, the notions of neutrality and objectivity are fictions that operate to conceal 'male partiality' (Jantzen 1995: 337). They also, it has been claimed, serve to privilege a conspicuously disembodied conception of mystical states that is unlikely to coincide with the more bodily forms of religious experience often reported by female mystics (Raphael 1994: 522).

Whatever we make of the disagreements between contextualists and their perennialist opponents, it has to be admitted that, at the level of textual exegesis, something like a pure consciousness event does seem to be what the authors of sources such as the *Pātañjalayogaśāstra* and *Sāṃkhyakārikā* are alluding to as the goal of meditative practice. That goal, termed 'aloneness' (*kaivalya*), is described, for example, as 'the abiding of the power of consciousness (*citi-śakti*) in its own form' (*Yogasūtra* 4.34) and as the 'singular and conclusive' result of the complete cessation of the activities of the *guṇa*s (which are the fundamental constituents of everything that is experienceable) (*Sāṃkhyakārikā* 68). So if one's primary philosophical task is the hermeneutic one of interpreting what is being described in the original texts, then Forman's idea of 'a wakeful but objectless consciousness' seems close to the mark, a point that has not gone unnoticed by certain scholars of Sāṃkhya and Yoga (e.g. Chapple 1990; Pflueger 1998). If, however, one maintains, with Katz and others, that there are irremediable conceptual and epistemic problems with such an idea, then one will be forced to conclude that the purported soteriological goal of Sāṃkhya and Yoga is itself incoherent. Since some contributors to the debate, such as Forman himself, claim to have first-hand experience on their side, whereas those on the other side suppose that they have a priori reasons for denying the possibility of what Forman claims to have undergone, it is far from obvious how the debate might be resolved.

Amid the more abstract moments in the debate, it is important not to lose sight of the textual sources that constitute much of the raw material for the study of mysticism and meditative traditions. As Jason Blum (2015) has argued, the project of understanding these texts, and of analysing them in comparison with one another, is unlikely to benefit from imposing upon them a preformed epistemological theory. Instead, what is called for is close attention to the experiential accounts in relation to multiple contextual factors, such as the rest of the text within which they occur plus (where available) other writings by the same author and within the same tradition. Such holistic interpretive procedures provide a firm basis from which to pursue comparison across the various traditions of meditation and mysticism without simply presupposing either that there must be a common essence that all of them share or, contrariwise, that every tradition, by virtue of its being a distinguishable tradition at all, must generate experiences that are incommensurable with those of any other.

## Yoga and ethics

Ethics (from the Greek *ēthos*, 'character' or sometimes 'custom, habit'), though often equated with morality and hence with issues such as which actions are right and which are wrong, may also be concerned with broader matters of how to live one's life. The most comprehensive of ethical theories will thus typically include a vision of the ultimate goal (or goals) of life, along with some prescription for how best to make progress towards its fulfilment. When ethics is construed in these broad terms, the various philosophies associated with yoga and meditation can in most instances be understood as having a strong ethical dimension. They can often also be described as soteriological, inasmuch as their respective formulations of the ultimate goal are ones that consist in spiritual salvation or liberation. In the case of Buddhism, for example, the goal is generally said to be *nirvāṇa* (however that might be understood), and, as has been discussed above, the goal specified in classical Sāṃkhya and Yoga is *kaivalya*.

With regard both to Buddhism and to Sāṃkhya and Yoga, the methods for achieving the ultimate goal are multiple. They include adherence to moral principles, or precepts, but also activities that are less obviously morally focused such as, prominently, extensive periods of meditation. Buddhism is well known for its noble eight-fold path, which comprises two principles of 'wisdom' or 'insight' (*prajñā*) and three of 'meditative absorption' (*samādhi*) alongside three of 'morality' (*śīla*). And the best known portion of the *Pātañjalayogaśāstra* is that which expounds the 'yoga of eight limbs' (*aṣṭāṅga-yoga*), the first two 'limbs' of which are each made up of five regulative precepts, with the subsequent six 'limbs' consisting of instruction in correct posture, breathing techniques and progressively internalised modes of single-pointed meditation. The *Sāṃkhyakārikā*, for its part, says little about actual practice, which is one of the reasons why Sāṃkhya is frequently assumed to advocate a 'rationalistic' or 'purely intellectual' method (Feuerstein 1980: 113; Koelman 1970: 237). But a perusal of the traditional commentaries indicates that meditation is as central to Sāṃkhya as it is to Yoga; in fact, as I noted above, Patañjali's Yoga system has been regarded by the commentarial tradition as itself a version of Sāṃkhya. Here, for reasons of space, I shall focus on the Yoga system and on how it has been interpreted in relation to theories of ethics or moral philosophy.

For a start, there has been disagreement over whether Yoga should be regarded as a moral or ethical system at all. While recognising that there is an obvious sense in which the five 'restraints' (*yamas*) and five 'observances' or 'lesser restraints' (*niyamas*) do constitute a set of ethical principles, some interpreters have regarded these as playing a merely instrumental role within the system as a whole, and hence as conveying a sense of extrinsic rather than intrinsic value. Georg Feuerstein, for example, points to *Yogasūtra* 4.7 – which states that the actions of a yogin are 'neither black nor white' – as indicative of the fact that yoga's purpose is, ultimately, to transcend morality. Although the implication of this is not that the accomplished yoga practitioner is free to perform acts that would be deemed immoral by conventional standards, it does entail that yogic meditation should 'be understood as an *a-moral* process' (Feuerstein 1989: 81). Gerald Larson, too, observes, with reference to both Sāṃkhya and Yoga, that the goal of *kaivalya* is (in Nietzsche's phrase) 'beyond good and evil' – 'a non-moral or a-moral intuition that arises through an extraordinary modality of knowing'; hence, although the world may have some extrinsic value for the practitioner insofar as it provides the setting within which the goal can be sought, neither the world nor moral theorising is of any value in its own right (Larson 1987: 151).

Comparable to the 'a-moral' interpretation just outlined is the view that the moral outlook of Sāṃkhya and Yoga is best categorised as *consequentialist*, for adherence to the 'first-order moral precepts' of these systems is enjoined merely as a self-purificatory exercise that contributes to the supremely sought-after consequence, namely *kaivalya* (Perrett 2007: 152–153). If we are to call this a version of consequentialism, its divergence from what has normally been referred to as consequentialism should be acknowledged.

Consequentialism is normally defined as the view that (in simple terms) what determines the moral rightness of an action is the goodness of the consequences, and hence that what ought to enter chiefly into moral decision-making are considerations of how one's actions are likely to impinge upon not only oneself but upon sentient beings in general. By contrast, when someone such as Roy Perrett defines the moral perspective of Sāṃkhya and Yoga as consequentialist, the relevant consequences are exclusively self-directed: it is one's own liberation from the suffering that permeates the ongoing flow of life, death and rebirth that is at issue.

Opposed to these a-moral and consequentialist readings is the view that Yoga's contribution to moral theory is in fact a highly developed one that offers an advanced alternative to standard western theories such as those of deontology, consequentialism and virtue ethics (Ranganathan 2017: 177). Ian Whicher, for example, describes the way of life promoted by Yoga as a process of 'sattvification', by which he means the continuous refinement of one's state of mind so that the quality of *sattva* (roughly, 'intelligence', 'purity') predominates over the qualities of *rajas* ('activity', 'energy') and *tamas* ('darkness', 'inertia'). Internal to this process is 'the cultivation of moral virtues such as compassion (*karuṇā*) and nonviolence (*ahiṃsā*)' (Whicher 1998: 285), and hence there is something dubious about picturing Yoga's moral requisites as mere means to some further end that transcends morality altogether; rather, the goal of ego-transcendence is itself a moral end. In this respect, Whicher's vision of Yoga's aspirations in fact comes to resemble a version of virtue ethics, according to which one's aim is to develop a virtuous character and live a flourishing life. Controversially, Whicher interprets *kaivalya* not as a realisation of *puruṣa*'s absolute isolation from *prakṛti*, but as 'an integration of both principles' (Whicher 1998: 303). Despite its revisionary flavour, this interpretation is apt to appeal to many modern yoga enthusiasts since it places the emphasis firmly on purification, understood in both moral and cognitive terms, as opposed to a total cessation of activity and experience.

Even if one remains doubtful that a vision of *kaivalya* as 'an integrated, embodied state of liberated identity' (Whicher 1998: 301) is well supported by the original sources, there are good reasons for questioning the view of Yoga's moral precepts as serving a merely instrumental function. The *Pātañjalayogaśāstra* makes it explicit that the five restraints (*yamas*), with *ahiṃsā* ('nonviolence', 'non-harming') as their foundation, are thoroughly unconditional. To commit oneself to abiding by them is to take the 'great vow' (*mahāvrata*), which is not qualified by factors such as caste, place or time (*Yogasūtra* 2.31). If it were qualified in these ways, then, as *Yogabhāṣya* 2.31 observes, someone who catches fish for a living might be excused from causing harm to fish, or someone might vow to abstain from killing living beings only in sacred places or at certain auspicious times, and so on. Contrary to such conditional commitments, the great vow is deemed to be categorical. Exactly what its implications are in practice remains, no doubt, open to interpretation. For example, Jainism, which has the same five-fold great vow as Patañjali's Yoga, is renowned for the strictness with which its mendicant practitioners follow the principle of nonviolence. But even in Jainism there is room for differing interpretations, with the monks and nuns of certain sects (most notably the Sthānakvāsīs and Terāpanthīs) constantly wearing a cloth over their mouths to avoid harming microorganisms in the air, whereas others either wear such a cloth only when performing rituals and speaking or do not wear it at all (Cort 2001: 41–42). Such stringency is not typically assumed to apply in the case of Patañjali's Yoga, though it has been argued that, even in this case, the vow of nonviolence minimally demands 'the unconditional renunciation of all flesh eating' and could also be extended to encompass withdrawing one's consent from non-vegetarian social practices more generally (Dickstein 2017: 620).

Notwithstanding the latter considerations, it could still be contended that Yoga's moral principles in general and its principle of nonviolence in particular fail to demonstrate a commitment to the intrinsic value of living beings. This contention may be strengthened if one takes seriously the comparison with Jainism, for the Jain ethic of nonviolence, at least as it applies to mendicants, is commonly interpreted as forming part of an overarching strategy for disconnecting oneself from a world that is irredeemably mired in violence. One cultivates detachment not for the sake of the world and its inhabitants, but for the sake of one's own spiritual purity (Vallely 2002: 29–32): nonviolence is, as James Laidlaw provocatively expresses it, 'an ethic of quarantine' (1995: 159). One way of countering this interpretation, however, is to point out that abstaining from harming living beings would not even have the purifying effect that is attributed to it if it were the case that the lives of such beings are of no intrinsic value, for it is precisely their having that kind of value that makes harming them detrimental to one's spiritual progress. With regard to Yoga, an argument along these lines is supportable by means of careful elaboration of certain claims made within the *Pātañjalayogaśāstra* itself. By analysing several passages (esp. *Yogabhāṣya* 2.13–15, 2.34 and 4.11), Christopher Framarin has argued that the text at least implicitly asserts that pleasure and a relatively long life have positive intrinsic value, that pain and a relatively short life have intrinsic negative value, and that these positive and negative types of value apply to living beings across the board (including non-human animals and even plants), as does the intrinsic positive value of certain further capacities that may be acquired as a consequence of virtuous behaviour in previous lives. On this basis, Framarin concludes that Yoga does indeed accord intrinsic value and, hence, 'direct moral standing' to humans, animals and plants (Framarin 2014: ch. 8).

Although it is beyond the scope of my present discussion to enter into the details of Framarin's analysis, it is notable that he situates it within a more general appraisal of the relevance for environmental ethics of ideas contained in traditional Hindu texts. Despite his making a strong case for the contention that the texts in question, including the *Pātañjalayogaśāstra*, ascribe moral standing to individual creatures, there is no suggestion in the texts that value is being accorded to collectivities such as species or ecosystems, and hence the application of the conclusions to environmental ethics remains limited.

## Future prospects for the philosophical study of yoga and meditation

The foregoing sections have examined a selection of ways in which yoga and meditation have been approached philosophically. In relation to each of the three topics I have discussed, a broad distinction can be made between two orientations, which we might call a *hermeneutical* orientation and a *critical* orientation, respectively. By 'hermeneutical', I mean an orientation that prioritises the task of exegesis: seeking to interpret and understand what the original sources are saying. The pursuit of this task may occasionally require admitting that it is simply impossible to make sense of a given text, perhaps because it is incoherent or confused. In these cases, a hermeneutical approach cannot avoid passing judgement upon the text; but, for the most part, the approach emphasises understanding over evaluation. What I am here calling a critical orientation, meanwhile, places the emphasis more on critical and argumentative engagement with the textual sources. Of course, a critical approach cannot be pursued in the absence of a hermeneutical one, since one can hardly hope to engage critically with philosophical ideas if one does not know how to interpret them. But a critical emphasis will view the hermeneutical enterprise as something merely preliminary and subordinate to the evaluative project. In considering future prospects for the philosophical study of yoga and meditation, it is helpful to bear in mind this distinction between hermeneutical and critical orientations.

The philosophical investigation of yoga and meditation in a hermeneutical mode remains an ongoing venture, with regard both to texts that are already well known and to those that have been newly discovered or newly translated. The *Pātañjalayogaśāstra* and *Sāṃkhyakārikā*, for example, have both been studied extensively, and yet questions about how best to interpret them have not been fully resolved. In the past, many interpreters sought to distinguish Yoga from Sāṃkhya on the grounds that its methods of inquiry involve 'direct experience' in contrast to the 'rationalistic' methods of Sāṃkhya, but, as I suggested above, such a distinction appears crude in the light of the recognition that the *Pātañjalayogaśāstra* articulates a form of Sāṃkhya and that significant commentaries on the *Sāṃkhyakārikā*, such as the *Yuktidīpikā* (*c.*680–720 CE), describe Sāṃkhya's methods as including a combination of non-attachment (*vairāgya*) and meditative practice (*tattva-abhyāsa*) highly resemblant of that which is recommended in the *Pātañjalayogaśāstra*. These observations facilitate further exploration of the intriguing relations between rational analysis and meditative insight not only in the context of Sāṃkhya and Yoga in particular, but also, by means of comparative study, in connection with Indian soteriological traditions more generally. The scope for further cross-cultural or inter-traditional comparative research is also substantial, having the potential to disrupt simplistic assumptions about, for example, the supposedly more rational nature of western philosophy vis-à-vis the more 'mystical' philosophies (or 'wisdom traditions') of Asia.

My notion of a 'critical orientation' to the philosophical study of yoga and meditation is really a placeholder for a rich melange of philosophical approaches. The demand is growing, both from within academic philosophy and from outside, for professional philosophers to do justice to the full range of philosophical traditions throughout the world in their teaching and research, as opposed to remaining sequestered in a monocultural silo dominated by a relatively narrow canon of western philosophers. No one is expecting those who teach philosophy to become experts in all the philosophical traditions of India, China, Africa, Native American communities and so on, but merely to look seriously at ways of incorporating non-western material into the philosophy curriculum (see, e.g. Van Norden 2017). This can be done in various ways, including drawing upon ideas and arguments from one tradition to supplement or modify a position in another, or showing how philosophical considerations from tradition A undermine or refute certain positions in tradition B.

With regard to traditions with a specifically meditative component, attempts at bringing them into engagement with western philosophy have been most prevalent in the case of Buddhist philosophy. Mark Siderits, for instance, has championed what he terms 'fusion philosophy', which he views as a successor to the sort of comparative exercises that seek merely to expose similarities and differences between perspectives arising from two or more philosophical traditions. In contrast to these 'merely' comparative approaches, fusion philosophy applies methods or theories from one tradition to philosophical problems that occur in another. Siderits himself has made notable contributions to the philosophy of personal identity by deploying ideas from Buddhist debates concerning the non-existence of a permanent self (Siderits 2015), and further contributions to this and related topics have been made by others (e.g. Ganeri 2007; Garfield 2015). Although the themes of yoga and meditation are not uppermost in such studies, they nevertheless infuse the practical and conceptual background out of which notions such as the Buddhist conception of no-self emerge. As Jay Garfield remarks in a discussion of Śāntideva's account of ethics, meditation plays a central role, 'for it is through meditation that one embeds discursive knowledge into one's character' (2015: 307). If this role for meditation in cultivating an ethical life at first appears alien to western philosophy, it may cease to do so when one recalls the long tradition of 'philosophy as a way of life' (Hadot 1995), which stretches back to the ancient Greeks and routinely combines various 'spiritual exercises' with more overtly discursive forms of reasoning in the philosophical quest. One benefit of attending to yoga- and meditation-related philosophies of Asia (and elsewhere) can thus be the reminder that is thereby offered of the fact that philosophy has frequently – indeed, predominantly – been pursued not as a purely academic exercise, but as a means of overcoming genuine difficulties in life and, ultimately, advancing towards some ethical or spiritual ideal.

There is, then, enormous potential for continuing and expanding the philosophical study of yoga and meditation, both as a field of philosophical inquiry in its own right and as part of the development of increasingly globally aware perspectives on philosophy as a whole.

## Glossary

Abhidharma, a body of Buddhist scholastic teachings that attempts to systematise doctrinal material from discourses attributed to the Buddha

Advaita Vedānta, a school of Indian philosophy, best known for its monist (or 'non-dual') conception of reality; most famously propounded by Śaṅkara (*c.*8th–9th centuries CE)

*ahiṃsā*, nonviolence, non-harming

a priori, prior to and independent of experience

*aṣṭāṅga-yoga*, eight-limbed yoga

Brentano, Franz (1838–1917), German philosopher and psychologist, a seminal influence on the development of phenomenological philosophy

*citta-vṛtti*, mental activities

contextualism, theory that mystical states of consciousness are 'mediated' by contextual factors such as language, culture and conceptual scheme

*darśana*, Indian philosophical school; way of seeing

Descartes, René (1596–1650), early modern French philosopher

*draṣṭṛ*, seer; also a synonym of *puruṣa*

*dṛśya*, seeable; that which can be experienced

*duḥkha*, dissatisfactoriness, pain, suffering

epistemology, branch of philosophy that studies what knowledge is and how we can have it

*guṇa*, quality, constitutive property; lit. strand

hermeneutics, branch of study concerned with interpretation – especially of texts

Husserl, Edmund (1859–1938), German philosopher, generally regarded as the founder of phenomenological philosophy

idealism (in philosophy), ontological theory that the whole of reality is mental or ideational in nature

*īśvara*, the Lord

*kaivalya*, spiritual liberation; lit. aloneness

Kant, Immanuel (1724–1804), an influential German philosopher, well known for his 'Critical' philosophy

*karuṇā*, compassion

Kashmir Śaivism, a school of Indian philosophy, most famously propounded by Abhinavagupta (10th–11th centuries CE)

monism, ontological theory that the whole of reality is reducible to one ultimate principle
Nyāya, a school of Indian philosophy, originally propounded in Gautama Akṣapāda's *Nyāyasūtra* (*c.*100 CE)
ontology, branch of philosophy that studies what exists or the nature of being; an ontology can also be a taxonomy of basic categories of entity
*Pātañjalayogaśāstra*, term for the *Yogasūtra* plus *Yogabhāṣya*
Patañjali, purported author of the *Yogasūtra*
perennialism, theory that states of pure consciousness are common to multiple mystical or meditative traditions
pluralism (ontological), ontological theory that reality comprises multiple categories of entity
*prakṛti*, nature, matter; lit. that which procreates
*puruṣa*, self, centre of consciousness; lit. man, person
realism (in philosophy), ontological theory that some designated class of entities exists independently of anyone's perceiving of thinking about them
Sāṃkhya, a school of Indian philosophy, expounded in the *Sāṃkhyakārikā*
*Sāṃkhyakārikā*, principal text of 'classical Sāṃkhya', composed by Īśvarakṛṣṇa (*c.*4th–5th century CE)
Śāntideva (late 7th to mid-8th century CE), Indian Buddhist philosopher-monk whose works include *Bodhicaryāvatāra* ('Guide to the Bodhisattva Way of Life')
*tattva*, essence, entity, principle
*Vaiśeṣika*, a school of Indian philosophy, originally propounded in Kaṇāda's *Vaiśeṣikasūtra* (*c.*100 BCE)
*Yogabhāṣya*, earliest and most influential commentary on the *Yogasūtra*, traditionally attributed to Vyāsa
Yogācāra, a school of Mahāyāna Buddhist philosophy, normally defined as idealist but sometimes as phenomenological
*Yogasūtra*, principal text of 'classical Yoga', attributed to Patañjali (*c.*4th or 5th century CE)

## Bibliography


Blum, J. N. 2015. *Zen and the Unspeakable God: Comparative Interpretations of Mystical Experience.* University Park, PA: Pennsylvania State University Press.

Brentano, F. 2015 [1874]. *Psychology from an Empirical Standpoint.* Abingdon: Routledge.

Buddhaghosa, Bhadantācariya 2010. *The Path of Purification (Visuddhimagga)* [5th century CE]. Ñāṇamoli, Bhikkhu (trans), 4th ed. Kandy: Buddhist Publication Society.

Burley, M. 2007. *Classical Sāṃkhya and Yoga: An Indian Metaphysics of Experience.* Abingdon: Routledge.

Chapple, C. 1990. 'The Unseen Seer and the Field: Consciousness in Sāṃkhya and Yoga', in Forman, R. K. C. (ed), *The Problem of Pure Consciousness: Mysticism and Philosophy*, 53–70. New York: Oxford University Press.

Cort, J. E. 2001. *Jains in the World: Religious Values and Ideology in India.* Oxford: Oxford University Press.

Descartes, R. 1985. *Principles of Philosophy* [1644], in Cottingham, J., Stoothoff, R. and Murdoch, D. (trans), *The Philosophical Writings of Descartes*, Vol. 1, 177–191. Cambridge: Cambridge University Press.

Dickstein, J. 2017. 'The Strong Case for Vegetarianism in Pātañjala Yoga'. *Philosophy East and West* 67(3): 613–628.

Feuerstein, G. 1980. *The Philosophy of Classical Yoga.* Manchester: Manchester University Press.

Feuerstein, G. 1989. *The Yoga-Sūtra of Patañjali: A New Translation and Commentary.* Rochester, VT: Inner Traditions India.

Forman, R. K. C. 1990a. 'Eckhart, *Gezücken*, and the Ground of the Soul', in Forman, R. K. C. (ed), *The Problem of Pure Consciousness: Mysticism and Philosophy*, 98–120. New York: Oxford University Press.

Forman, R. K. C. 1990b. 'Introduction: Mysticism, Constructivism, and Forgetting', in Forman, R. K. C. (ed), *The Problem of Pure Consciousness: Mysticism and Philosophy*, 3–49. New York: Oxford University Press.

Forman, R. K. C. 1998. 'Introduction: Mystical Consciousness, the Innate Capacity, and the Perennial Psychology', in Forman, R. K. C. (ed), *The Innate Capacity: Mysticism, Psychology, and Philosophy*, 3–41. Oxford: Oxford University Press.

Framarin, C. G. 2014. *Hinduism and Environmental Ethics: Law, Literature, and Philosophy*. Abingdon: Routledge.

Ganeri, J. 2007. *The Concealed Art of the Soul: Theories of Self and Practices of Truth in Indian Ethics and Epistemology*. Oxford: Oxford University Press.

Garfield, J. L. 2015. *Engaging Buddhism: Why It Matters to Philosophy*. Oxford: Oxford University Press.

Gellman, J. I. 2005. 'Mysticism and Religious Experience', in Wainwright, W. J. (ed), *The Oxford Handbook of Philosophy of Religion*, 138–167. Oxford: Oxford University Press.

Gethin, R. M. 1986. 'The Five *Khandhas*: Their Treatment in the *Nikāyas* and Early Abhidhamma'. *Journal of Indian Philosophy* 14(1): 35–53.

Hadot, P. 1995. *Philosophy as a Way of Life: Spiritual Exercises from Socrates to Foucault*, Davidson, A. I. (ed) and Chase, M. (trans). Oxford: Blackwell.

Husserl, E. 1999 [1927]. 'Phenomenological Psychology and Transcendental Phenomenology', in Welton, D. (ed), *The Essential Husserl: Basic Writings in Transcendental Phenomenology*, 322–336. Bloomington, IN: Indiana University Press.

Huxley, A. 1946. *The Perennial Philosophy*. London: Chatto & Windus.

Jacobsen, K. A. 2012. 'Songs to the Highest God (Īśvara) of Sāṃkhya-Yoga', in White, D. G. (ed), *Yoga in Practice*, 325–336. Princeton, NJ: Princeton University Press.

Jantzen, G. M. 1995. *Power, Gender and Christian Mysticism*. Cambridge: Cambridge University Press.

Kant, I. 1998 [1781/1787]. *Critique of Pure Reason*, Guyer, P. (trans) and Wood, A. W. (ed). Cambridge: Cambridge University Press.

Katz, S. T. 1978. 'Language, Epistemology and Mysticism', in Katz, S. T. (ed), *Mysticism and Philosophical Analysis*, 22–74. New York: Oxford University Press.

Katz, S. T. 2013. 'General Editor's Introduction', in Katz, S. T. (ed), *Comparative Mysticism: An Anthology of Original Sources*, 3–22. Oxford: Oxford University Press.

Koelman, G. M. 1970. *Pātañjala Yoga: From Related Ego to Absolute Self*. Poona: Papal Athenaeum.

Laidlaw, J. 1995. *Riches and Renunciation: Religion, Economy, and Society among the Jains*. Oxford: Clarendon Press.

Larson, G. J. 1969. 'Classical Sāṃkhya and the Phenomenological Ontology of Jean-Paul Sartre'. *Philosophy East and West* 19(1): 45–58.

Larson, G. J. 1987. '"Conceptual Resources" in South Asia for "Environmental Ethics" or the Fly Is Still Alive and Well in the Bottle'. *Philosophy East and West* 37(2): 150–159.

Larson, G. J. 2008. 'Introduction to the Philosophy of Yoga', in Larson, G. J. and Bhattacharya, R. S. (eds), *Yoga: India's Philosophy of Meditation* (Encyclopedia of Indian Philosophies, Vol. 12), 21–159. Delhi: Motilal Banarsidass.

*Pātañjalayogaśāstra* [including *Yogasūtra* and *Yogabhāṣya*]. Śrī Nārāyaṇa Miśra (ed) 1992. *Pātañjalayogadarśanam. Vācaspatimiśraviracita-Tattvavaiśāradī Vijñānabhikṣukṛta-Yogavārtikavibhūṣita Vyāsabhāṣyasametam*. Dillī and Vārāṇasī: Bhāratīya Vidyā Prakāśana.

Perrett, R. W. 2001. 'Computationality, Mind and Value: The Case of Sāṃkhya–Yoga'. *Asian Philosophy* 11(1): 5–14.

Perrett, R. W. 2007. 'Sāṃkhya-Yoga Ethics', in Bilimoria, P., Prabhu J. and Sharma, R. (eds), *Indian Ethics: Classical Traditions and Contemporary Challenges*, Vol. 1, 149–159. Aldershot: Ashgate.

Pflueger, L. W. 1998. 'Discriminating the Innate Capacity: Salvation Mysticism of Classical Sāṃkhya-Yoga', in Forman, R. K. C. (ed), *The Innate Capacity: Mysticism, Psychology, and Philosophy*, 45–81. Oxford: Oxford University Press.

Ranganathan, S. 2017. 'Patañjali's Yoga: Universal Ethics as the Formal Cause of Autonomy', in Ranganathan, S. (ed), *The Bloomsbury Research Handbook of Indian Ethics*, 177–202. London: Bloomsbury Academic.

Raphael, M. 1994. 'Feminism, Constructivism, and Numinous Experience'. *Religious Studies* 30(4): 511–526.

*Sāṃkhyakārikā* of Īśvarakṛṣṇa, in M. Burley 2007. *Classical Sāṃkhya and Yoga: An Indian Metaphysics of Experience*, 163–179. Abingdon: Routledge.

Schweizer, P. 1993. 'Mind/Consciousness Dualism in Sāṅkhya-Yoga Philosophy'. *Philosophy and Phenomenological Research* 53(4): 845–859.

Siderits, M. 2015. *Personal Identity and Buddhist Philosophy: Empty Persons*, 2nd ed. Farnham: Ashgate.

Sinha, J. 1934. *Indian Psychology: Perception*. London: Kegan Paul, Trench, Trubner & Co.

Vallely, A. 2002. *Guardians of the Transcendent: An Ethnography of a Jain Ascetic Community*. Toronto, ON: University of Toronto Press.

Van Norden, B. W. 2017. *Taking Back Philosophy: A Multicultural Manifesto*. New York: Columbia University Press.

Whicher, I. 1998. *The Integrity of the Yoga Darśana: A Reconsideration of Classical Yoga*. Albany, NY: State University of New York Press.

Williams, P. 2009. *Mahāyāna Buddhism: The Doctrinal Foundations*, 2nd ed. Abingdon: Routledge.

# 29

# ON 'MEDITATIONAL ART' AND *MAṆḌALAS* AS OBJECTS OF MEDITATION[1]

*Gudrun Bühnemann*

> The Buddhist art of Nepal and Tibet is a visual system of presenting symbols of enlightenment and also the way of inducing the experience of enlightenment.
>
> *(Kramrisch 1960: 23)*

## Introduction

Buddhist art from Tibet and Nepal has become widely known through display in museums and exhibitions. Images of esoteric deities, *maṇḍalas* and ritual objects, previously seen only by practitioners, have been exposed to the public's gaze. Tibetan art has attracted particular attention and has been idealised as 'meditational' and 'enlightenment art'. Although for the past two decades scholars have exposed such western fantasies about Buddhist art, these notions are still prevalent, especially in popular books. The *maṇḍala* is a case in point. Mainly used in tantric initiation rituals in the past as a surface whereon to invoke divinities, it has more recently been described too uniformly as a tool for meditation. It has entered still other contexts – being interpreted, for example, by psychologists and art therapists – and correspondingly has taken on new meanings.

In this chapter I will explore the widespread association of art from the Himalayan region with meditation and enlightenment – as evidenced, for example, by the opening quote by art historian Stella Kramrisch (1896–1993). In particular, I will critically examine the notion that the *maṇḍala* necessarily serves as a tool for meditation. In the first part I will interrogate the notions of 'meditational art' as presented in some exhibition and sales catalogues. In that connection, I will briefly discuss techniques used in displaying religious art in museums in ways that seek to create a sense of the numinous for the museum-goer. I will then turn to some widespread misconceptions regarding Tibetan (and Newar Buddhist) art. These include the notion that it necessarily constitutes sacred art, is sublime and transcendent in nature, and has been created by an artist who is himself a mystic. In the second part of this chapter I will present a case study of the *maṇḍala*.

## On the notion of 'meditational art'

Exhibitions of Tibetan and Nepalese art regularly attract large numbers of visitors. The shows usually display a wide range of objects, including statues of Buddhas belonging to esoteric tantric traditions, exotic objects such as skull-cups and ritual daggers and, inevitably, scroll paintings featuring divinities and colourful *maṇḍala*s. Art from Tibet is especially popular. Often classified as sacred art in exhibition or sales catalogues, it has been idealised as 'meditational' and 'enlightenment art' (Rhie and Thurman 1999: 15).

Objects of the lesser-known Tantric Buddhist art of the Newars in Nepal were the focus of an exhibition jointly organised by the Los Angeles County Museum of Art and the Columbus Museum of Art in 2003 and 2004, and memorialised in the volume *Circle of Bliss: Buddhist Meditational Art* (Huntington and Bangdel 2003). While the main title, *Circle of Bliss*, is explained as one interpretation of the tantric deity Cakrasaṃvara's name, the expression 'meditational art' requires clarification. Did the art objects (or artefacts) function as supports for the meditation practices of practitioners? Or did they serve even more saliently as objects of practitioners' meditation? Or did the mere viewing of them perhaps induce a meditative state? Or else were the works of art created by artists while they themselves were immersed in meditation?

The catalogue explains that 'meditational art' denotes art works which are of central importance 'in the context of Buddhist meditations' (Huntington and Bangdel 2003: 12) and which 'reflect the religious practices that lead to … [an] illumined state of being' (ibid.: 19). In other words, these art works are objects relevant to (or tools used by) practitioners while engaged in meditation in pursuit of enlightenment. As is evident from the illustrations in the catalogue, 'meditational art' is a term used to designate, for instance, statues of divine beings, *maṇḍala*s and ritual implements. The last of these, which are not created for mere aesthetic enjoyment, could perhaps better be classified as artefacts. As is often the case, the word meditation remains a term not clearly defined in the voluminous exhibition catalogue. The context suggests that the word is used to refer to Buddhist tantric rituals that involve the use of external objects as well as complex visualisation practices in which practitioners create a mental image of a divinity.

The exhibition set itself an ambitious goal, namely to mediate a religious experience and bring the visitor face to face with the deepest realisations of Tantric Buddhism. Thus, we are told that '[t]he art is a subtle vehicle of teaching and guidance' for practitioners 'along the meditative path': 'Combined with practices transmitted through textual and oral traditions, the artistic works serve to express both conceptual and non-conceptual realizations. These realizations, achieved through Tantric Buddhist meditation, are the subject of this exhibition' (Huntington and Bangdel 2003: 21).

We further learn that the show was 'not about the works of art as material objects so much as how the art communicates both the process and goal of attainment', namely 'the process and aesthetics of human perfection' (Huntington and Bangdel 2003: 19). In other words, the exhibition's 'aim has been to convey the beauty of the envisioned goal of Tantric Buddhist practice and the means by which the art communicates and guides the practitioner in this quest for perfection' (ibid.: 19). Thus, the 'Circle of Bliss' show, exhibiting Newar (and many Tibetan) art objects in the secular space of a museum, sought to convey the highest goal of tantric Buddhism to persons outside the tradition who had little familiarity with the specific religious framework and ritual context of these objects. Its aim was to mediate an experience of transcendence by relying on the objects' aesthetic appeal and the way they were arranged in the exhibition space.

The exhibition had a similar goal to, and was likely inspired by, the large 'Wisdom and Compassion' show, which was first mounted in San Francisco in 1991, travelled to London in 1992 and – in a reorganised and enlarged form – continued on around the world from 1996 to 1997. That show aimed to 'introduce Tibet's compelling and mysterious art *on its own terms*' (Rhie and Thurman 2000: 12), a goal the curators sought to reach by arranging the exhibits in a specific way, inspired by the structure of the Kālacakra ('Wheel of Time') *maṇḍala*.

## Issues concerning the display of religious art in museums

The general approach captured in the exhibition *Wisdom and Compassion* conforms to a trend in contemporary museum practice which seeks to bring objects to life. It is only in recent decades that scholars of museum studies and museum anthropology, reflecting on techniques of display in museum spaces, have acknowledged that art installations entail interpretations and evaluations of art in so far as the selection of the objects, the lighting used and the ways in which objects are arranged in the galleries to tell visitors a particular story are concerned. In the past, museums exhibited objects stripped of their cultural contexts – as carefully labelled lifeless museum pieces. Staff classified them by applying standard art historical approaches that focused on the identification, provenance, style and date of objects. The decontextualisation of exhibits, sometimes referred to as museumification or museumisation, went hand in hand with the aestheticisation of these redefined objects, namely, the process in which exhibits are presented in an aesthetic rather than social or religious context, and so acquire the status of art objects. In contrast, contemporary museum practice seeks to recreate the objects' cultural context through settings, carefully selected sounds, light effects, colour patterns or even scents. The aim is to provide an immersive and multisensory experience, beyond mere vision, that engages visitors and enables them to experience the objects more fully.

More recently, discussions have focused specifically on strategies that might be appropriate for the display of religious objects in museums. As a result of these considerations, many museums have moved away from a purely aesthetic, art historical presentation of religious objects which fails to acknowledge the fact that they are objects used in devotional practice, treats them as 'the other' and does not engage with them (Paine 2017: 218). Instead, museums now often make efforts to recreate the ritual context of the exhibits through sophisticated display techniques that are designed to bring these objects to life, thereby seeking to engender a sense of the numinous for the museum-goer. Curators and exhibition designers working for state-supported museums, however, face some challenges, having to tread a fine line between the secular and the sacred (Sarma 2015: 28). Moreover, some critics have characterised such installations as 'theatrical' shows that lack a scholarly component (Durham 2015: 83) and promote a 'voyeur spirituality for outsiders' (ibid.: 92).

While the general display strategies of 'Wisdom and Compassion' thus align with the goals of contemporary museum practice, the specific portrayal of Tibetan Buddhist art in the exhibition catalogue has provoked considerable criticism.[2]

## Misconceptions about Tibetan art and the role of the artist

In their catalogue, M. M. Rhie and R. A. F. Thurman explicate Tibetan art and its significance for the general public. In that context, they frequently offer idiosyncratic interpretations, introducing concepts such as 'archetypes' (Rhie and Thurman 2000: 15) and 'Tibetan depth psychology' (Thurman in ibid.: 36). Speculating about the nexus between art and meaning, they ascribe to Tibetan art the potential 'to break the 'veil of illusion' and offer a complete, instantaneous vision of the radiant beauty and power of pure reality' (Rhie in ibid.: 39). The authors even hold out the prospect of an enlightenment experience through an encounter with Tibetan art. Thus, Rhie asserts that

> [t]he aesthetics of Tibetan Buddhist art is based upon revealing the Buddhist understanding of the way things truly are. Because of this, Tibetan art … possesses an intensity, a power, and a reality that appear more penetrating, more beautiful, and

> greater than ordinary. Deities whose forms have been revealed to those whose minds have a purified, clear vision are portrayed to assist others in attaining this same vision and thereby become acquainted with the possibility of complete enlightenment.
>
> *(Rhie in ibid.: 39)*

Interpreting an image of the tantric deities Cakrasaṃvara and Vajravārāhī in sexual union, Thurman suggests that '[i]f we let ourselves observe and experience this image as Tibetans do, we can be inspired about the possibility of attaining enlightenment for ourselves' (Thurman ibid.: 18).

Scholars have criticised these and similar statements for constructing an idealised notion of Tibetan art as sublime, transcendent, therapeutic, as 'a delight for the eyes or a balm for the troubled soul' by overstating the link the art has to 'spirituality and psychological improvement' (Harris 2012: 21). In the past, religious statues were installed in shrines and temples as objects of worship. They were not, however, expected to function as catalysts for an enlightenment experience. Frequently, they were commissioned to generate merit on behalf of deceased family members, to cure illnesses or to ameliorate the effects of unfavourable astrological constellations (Lopez 1998: 150). While one will not want to deny the affective power of Buddhist images, their ability to evoke emotions and uplift people, the viewing of a religious object in a museum or art gallery will at most evoke an aesthetic emotion, but is unlikely to lead to a religious experience, such as a vision of ultimate reality or an experience of enlightenment. Thus, the art historian P. Pal subtitled his 2003 exhibition of art from the Himalayan region more cautiously, as 'an aesthetic adventure'.

Focusing in more general terms on widespread misconceptions about Tibetan culture, Lopez observed that 'Tibet and Tibetan Buddhism have long been objects of Western fantasy' (1998: 3). In his seminal study *Prisoners of Shangri-la*, the author devotes one entire chapter to misconceptions pertaining to Tibetan art, which range from portrayals of wrathful tantric deities as monstrous figures to notions about male and female deities in sexual union functioning as symbols of a transcendent reality (1998: 140). Critiquing art historical engagement with Tibetan art, Lopez identified

> some of the assumptions and interpretative flights of fancy that were launched when Tibetan works came under the art historical gaze during the present century, flights of fancy that through the power of repetition came to acquire the status of knowledge.
>
> *(Lopez 1998: 136)*

In particular, this author challenges the following assumptions, again encountered in the 'Wisdom and Compassion' and 'Circle of Bliss' exhibition catalogues, namely

1. that meditation is 'the motivating aesthetic of Tibetan painting, rendering it somehow more sublime than other art forms' (ibid.: 139);
2. that Tibetan art is 'an evocation of (and hence a conduit to) a transcendent reality, inexpressible in words but not in art' (ibid.: 143);
3. that the statues of divine beings are merely symbols (ibid.: 143–145), an assumption contradicted by textual records that provide clear evidence that a statue becomes the deity through a ritual of animation; and the assumption that the *maṇḍala* 'is ultimately neither Tibetan nor even Buddhist, but a symbol of something ancient, universal, and timeless' (ibid.: 147);
4. and, finally, that the Tibetan artist is also a mystic (ibid.: 144)[3].

Despite the criticisms by Lopez, Harris and other scholars, misconceptions and misrepresentations regarding Tibetan (and also Newar Buddhist) art and its meaning and function persist. Thus, Paine observes in his recent study, *Religious Objects in Museums*, that '[i]n Tibetan Buddhism, the purpose of art is to aid devotees in their search for enlightenment'. The author further asserts that Buddhist images 'are intended to help others to share the artist's or patron's meditation experience' (Paine 2013: 62, paraphrasing Reedy 1992: 42). These statements reflect the still widespread notions of this art as 'meditational' and 'enlightenment art' created by artists who are also mystics. In a similar vein, the 2019 exhibition at the Virginia Museum of Fine Arts titled 'Awaken: A Tibetan Buddhist Journey Toward Enlightenment' invites the visitor to 'join a voyage into the visionary art of Tibetan Buddhism' and 'also to take part in the narrative it presents of a quest for enlightenment'.[4] The exhibition catalogue reiterates the familiar statement that 'Tibetan Buddhist art is meant to catalyze awakening' (Rice and Durham 2019: lx).

## Case study: the *maṇḍala*[5]

### *Introduction*

The *Wisdom and Compassion* and *Circle of Bliss* volumes and the corresponding exhibitions have provided the general public with unprecedented access to images of esoteric Buddhist deities and ritual objects. Exhibiting such objects in public, however, is at odds with traditional tantric notions of secrecy, which require that sacred objects be placed in private spaces such as shrine rooms, where they can only be seen by practitioners who have received the tantric initiations. Some of these secret objects of veneration that were exposed to the public's gaze have become widely known, reinterpreted and been assigned new functions. *Maṇḍalas* are a case in point. Mainly used in the past as a surface to invoke divinities down upon in tantric initiation rituals, they have been described too uniformly as a tool for meditation. Furthermore, interpreted by psychologists, art therapists and others, they have been drawn into extraneous contexts and have taken on new meanings.

*Maṇḍalas* from the Tibetan and Newar Buddhist traditions painted on canvas surfaces have been displayed in exhibitions worldwide. The 2014 show 'Enter the Mandala: Cosmic Centers and Mental Maps of Himalayan Buddhism' in San Francisco's Asian Art Museum provided visitors with an opportunity not only to view such *maṇḍalas*, but also to experience them as three-dimensional architectural constructs.[6] The curator thereby sought to simulate the experience of a skilled practitioner who has perfected his ability to visualise *maṇḍalas* after many years of meditative training. This show was perhaps an extreme example of an attempt to recreate what was assumed to be the original context of *maṇḍalas* and the experience of the numinous as part of contemporary museum practice (discussed above), which in this case served to perpetuate certain stereotypes about the function of *maṇḍalas*.

In recent decades, Tibetan Buddhist monks have constructed the Kālacakra ('Wheel of Time') and other *maṇḍalas* from coloured grains of sand in a large number of museums and galleries around the world. This laborious process has been interpreted as a form of meditation (Paine 2013, caption to figure 6). These performances, accessible to a wide audience of non-initiated individuals (Figure 29.1), contributed to the appropriation and commodification of *maṇḍalas*. It is now possible to construct small sand *maṇḍalas* at home 'for meditation, healing, and prayer' (Rose and Rose Dalto 2003), using commercially available kits. Brauen has termed these kits as 'misused ritual objects', noting that '[w]hat was hitherto reserved for trained monks can now be produced by every Tom, Dick and Harry: a personal sand mandala' (Brauen 2004: 201, 202).

*Figure 29.1* A sand *maṇḍala* for the goddess Tārā, created by Geshe Palden Sangpo as part of the Asia Week 2017 celebration at the University of North Carolina at Chapel Hill.
Photo courtesy of David Strevel.

Admired for their captivating designs with a central focal point, *maṇḍala*s have become popular tourist souvenirs in Nepal, with new patterns emerging at regular intervals. Once appropriated by popular culture, they began to appear on T-shirts and bags, and to serve as body tattoos and home decor wall art. As we will consider more closely below, popular uses now also include the colouring of templates in *maṇḍala* colouring books, part of the recent adult colouring book trend. These developments have led to entirely new interpretations and a wide application of the term *maṇḍala*.

## *Basic characteristics of* maṇḍalas

In Buddhist tantric traditions, the word *maṇḍala* generally refers to a structured space into which Buddhas, Bodhisattvas and other divine or semi-divine beings are invoked and made present by means of the recitation of mantras. The basic structure of many *maṇḍala*s calls for an image or symbolic representation (an attribute or a seed syllable) of a Buddha in the centre, surrounded by his court like a king. The figures in his entourage, usually emanations, attendants and protectors, are grouped around him in one or several concentric circles or enclosures, and are arranged in a specific order. Important figures are placed close to the centre, while others, such as gatekeepers, are positioned further away on the periphery. In this way the *maṇḍala* structure functions as an important device for representing a hierarchy in a pantheon of divinities of a certain doctrinal system or school. The number of residents within a *maṇḍala* depends on the teaching of a specific school, but the directional orientation is – in addition to the hierarchical order – a standard feature of all schools when it comes to the act of invocation. A basic *maṇḍala* structure may feature one central deity with four surrounding deities placed in the four cardinal directions. This pattern can be expanded by adding four divine beings in the intermediate directions. Maṇḍalas depicting a seated Buddha surrounded by eight Bodhisattvas are among the earliest examples of *maṇḍala*s, and were popular in Dunhuang between the eighth and tenth centuries.[7] In complex *maṇḍala*s, several hundred or even more than one thousand deities can be invoked. There are certain common patterns found in *maṇḍala* structures. In some *maṇḍala*s, the divine figures inhabit a palace structure with four entrances and outer courtyards; in others, they are invoked onto the petals of a large eight-petalled lotus flower, into an eight-spoked wheel or into a grid with nine panels (Tanaka 2018: 263–266). The *maṇḍala* space is enclosed by an outer circumferential line, separating the divine from the mundane sphere.

A *maṇḍala* is the realm of one particular deity and not a timeless universal symbol, as often claimed in secondary sources. As Lopez noted:

> When the art historian portrays the mandala as an abstract symbol of an archetypal universe, he ignores the fact that a mandala is a particular palace of a particular deity who occupies the central throne, a palace decorated in a particular way and inhabited by particular buddhas, bodhisattvas, gods, goddesses, and protectors, that there are many different mandalas, and that the initiate seeks to memorize the palace in all of its aspects in order to become that particular deity.
>
> *(1998: 147)*

Some Buddhist tantric authorities distinguish between the *maṇḍala* structure, which functions as the locus of or receptacle for divinities, and the actual group of divine beings which are invoked and placed in it – that is, the *maṇḍala*'s inhabitants. Most authorities, however, use the term *maṇḍala* with reference to the animated surface that includes the divinities as an integral part. For them, the *maṇḍala* provides a surface onto which divinities are invoked, their assumed presence transforming the *maṇḍala* into a sacred space. Thus, *maṇḍala*s should not be considered as merely colourful designs.

In the course of time, Buddhist authorities began associating various theological and philosophic concepts with the *maṇḍala*. By the eleventh century many different interpretations were in circulation, with texts displaying considerable sophistication in the way they distinguished between different categories of *maṇḍala*s, depending on their ritual use.

In exhibition catalogues and popular books, we encounter widespread confusion regarding the use of *maṇḍala*s, which are too uniformly designated as tools for meditation, although visualisation of them (a practice discussed below, which can be subsumed under the term meditation) is among their uses. In fact, *maṇḍala*s have been employed in a variety of ways within tantric traditions. They can decorate sacred spaces, such as the interior walls or ceilings of temples and caves; they can be visualised in rituals, as explained below; and they can become the objects of veneration by laypeople. Most importantly, however, *maṇḍala*s are used in initiation or empowerment (*abhiṣeka*) rituals.

In one of these rituals, known as the garland empowerment (*mālābhiṣeka*) in (Indian) tantric Buddhism, the blindfolded disciple is made to cast a flower (or flower garland) onto the *maṇḍala*, into which a pantheon of divinities has already been invoked. The blindfold, symbolic of the practitioner's nescience, is then removed and the practitioner finds himself beholding the *maṇḍala*. The viewing of the *maṇḍala* constitutes the climax of that initiation. It is the dramatic moment in which the initiate comes face to face with the *maṇḍala* as the realm of the Buddhas. The ideal viewing of a *maṇḍala* entails not merely beholding its design or appreciating its beauty, but rather seeing and experiencing the *maṇḍala* as an animated sacred space. To return to a distinction referred to above, it is the experience of the *maṇḍala* not as a mere locus of or receptacle for divinities to be invoked into, but as the structured space animated by the *maṇḍala*'s inhabitants. The ritual of the garland empowerment often entails an identification of the initiate with the *maṇḍala* deity. In later tantric texts, the candidate's Buddha family is determined on the basis of the deity who resides in the section of the *maṇḍala* where the flower has fallen.

This ritual also forms part of East Asian Buddhist traditions and is documented, in particular, for the Japanese Shingon and Tendai schools. In the contemporary practice of the Shingon school, the *kechien kanjō*, as it is called, is an entry-level initiation meant to 'establish a bond' or a connection between the candidate and a divinity inhabiting one of the two great Shingon *maṇḍalas*: the Diamond-Realm (*vajradhātu*, Sanskrit; *kongōkai*, Japanese) and the Matrix- or Womb-Realm (*garbhadhātu*, Sanskrit; *taizōkai*, Japanese) *maṇḍalas*. The ritual is performed at the central temple complex of the Shingon school on Mount Kōya near Osaka for laity once a year for each of the two great *maṇḍalas* (Nicoloff 2008: 175–177; Winfield 2012). The ritual of casting a flower onto a *maṇḍala* is attested in Śaiva and Vaiṣṇava texts from India and can thus be considered both trans-sectarian and transregional.

One noted Indian scholar and authority on *maṇḍalas*, Abhayākaragupta (late eleventh to early twelfth century), presents a breakdown into two kinds of *maṇḍalas*. He distinguishes *maṇḍalas* for visualisation, on the one hand, and powder *maṇḍalas*, which are drawn or painted *maṇḍalas*, on the other. His work *Niṣpannayogāvalī* focuses on the three-dimensional forms of these *maṇḍalas* for visualisation, in which a large number of divinities are envisioned, each with distinct iconographic characteristics. Such visualisations can be subsumed under the rubric meditation, understood as the practice of creating a mental image and holding it in one's mind. In contrast, the author's *Vajrāvalī* explains the construction and ritual use of two-dimensional *maṇḍalas*, which are drawn or painted on the ground and used for initiation. In the drawn *maṇḍalas*, the divinities are usually only represented by corresponding symbols.

The visualisation of divine figures (occasionally in three-dimensional *maṇḍalas*) is a constituent part of tantric *sādhanas*, which are methods employed for the worship of particular divinities. They are described in *sādhana* texts, such as the collection of short texts published under the title *Sādhanamālā*. Three-dimensional *maṇḍalas*, however, have not only been visualised; they have also been made – in different sizes and using different materials, such as wood or metal – for ritual purposes. Two-dimensional *maṇḍalas* painted on a canvas surface are known as *paṭa* (Sanskrit), *thaṅka* (Tibetan) or *paubhā* (Newari) (Figure 29.2). They were (and still are) often commissioned in order to gather merit for a deceased relative.

As an organisational principle, the *maṇḍala* concept has also had an impact on town planning, and has been projected onto natural landscapes. *Maṇḍalas* have been conceptually applied to the human body as well; these are then spoken of as body *maṇḍalas*.

## *Interpretations by psychologists and the use of* maṇḍalas *in therapy*

For the modern understanding of the *maṇḍala* concept in the West, the interpretations of C. G. Jung (1875–1961) have been particularly influential. The Swiss psychologist is well known for his studies on what he termed 'archetypes' (primordial images) and the 'collective unconscious'. He was familiar with selected *maṇḍalas* from the Tibetan Buddhist and Hindu traditions, and included among them auspicious designs drawn by women in South Asia on the ground in front of buildings (Jung 1959: 71). Jung was not concerned with the development and function of *maṇḍalas* in a historical context. For him, the *maṇḍala* is 'the psychological expression of the totality of the self' (1959: 20) and a therapeutic tool that he tried out himself. Thus, he reports that

*Figure 29.2* A two-dimensional *maṇḍala* painted on a canvas surface, showing the goddess *Mahāpratisarā* at the centre.
56-deity Pañcarakṣāmaṇḍala commissioned by Lhachog Sengge (1468–1535 CE) of Ngor Monastery, Tibet. See Himalayan Art Resources (HAR) no. 8049. Photo courtesy of Sanjay Kapoor, Kapoor Galleries Inc.

> I had painted the first mandala in 1916 ... In 1918–19 ... I sketched every morning in a notebook a small circular drawing, a mandala, which seemed to correspond to my inner situation at the time. With the help of these drawings I could observe my psychic transformations from day to day ... My mandalas were cryptograms concerning the state of the self ... In them I saw the self – that is, my whole being – actively at work ...
>
> *(Jung 1965: 195–196)*

Jung had noted that Tibetan Buddhist *maṇḍala*s served 'to assist meditation and concentration' (Jung 1959: 3). This understanding of the *maṇḍala*'s function is later reflected in the writings of Jungian analysts, such as von Franz, who – speaking of 'the contemplation of a mandala' – characterises *maṇḍala*s and *maṇḍala*-like paintings as devices 'to enable one to plunge into deep meditation' (von Franz 1964: 230); or Jaffé, who calls *maṇḍala*s 'instruments of meditation' (Jaffé 1964: 267).

Influenced by Jung's psychology, the Tibetologist G. Tucci (1894–1984) wrote his widely known study, *The Theory and Practice of the Maṇḍala*, subtitled 'with special reference to the modern psychology of the subconscious'. The scholar describes the *maṇḍala* as 'a support for meditation' (Tucci 1961: 37) and as 'a means of reintegration' (ibid.: 21) He also referred to it as a 'psycho-cosmogram' (ibid.: vii), a term which he explains as 'the scheme of disintegration from the One to the many and of reintegration from the many to the One' (ibid.: 25). Tucci's interpretations, sometimes in the form of generalisations, have influenced many later authors who follow him in calling the *maṇḍala* a 'cosmogram'. Although applicable in certain contexts, these labels are often misleading. It is essential to distinguish between types of *maṇḍala*s, their specific ritual functions and the interpretations of the term *maṇḍala* offered by individual Buddhist authorities in different time periods.

Also influenced by Jung's depth psychology are Thurman's interpretations of Tibetan art in the 'Wisdom and Compassion' exhibition catalogue. Thurman presents us with idiosyncratic translation choices, such as 'archetype deity' for Sanskrit *iṣṭadevatā* (chosen deity) (Rhie and Thurman 1999: 27, 37; 2000: 15).

Inspired by Jungian ideas of individuation, J. Kellogg (1922–2004) promoted the use of *maṇḍala*s in art therapy. She was mainly concerned with the diagnostic interpretation of colours, shapes and the placement of shapes in the *maṇḍala*s that her clients drew. Based on her experiences with clients, Kellogg developed her own therapeutic tool, the 'Mandala Assessment Research Instrument' (MARI®) in the form of the MARI® Card Test©. Her system, in its mature form, distinguishes thirteen stages of 'The Great Round of Mandala' and thirty-nine design cards. Each stage is associated with a specific mental state and 'illustrated by three designs of the MARI® Card Test©' (Kellogg 2001: 49). She instructed patients in hospitals to draw a circle and '[m]ake something in the center, put something there, then meditate on it or think about it' (ibid.: 17). Kellogg placed the creation of a *maṇḍala* in 'an almost contemplative framework' (ibid.: 15) and handled the patients' *maṇḍala*s 'in a very sacred way' (ibid.: 17). As a result of her work, *maṇḍala*s have now become tools used in art therapy settings.

In addition to Jung and his followers, proponents of New Age spirituality have played an important role in the reinterpretation of the *maṇḍala*. Critiquing these adaptations of the *maṇḍala* to new contexts, Lopez has spoken of the 'psychologization' of the *maṇḍala* (1998: 146), and Davidson of its 'idealization' (2002: 131).

## *A typology of modern* maṇḍala *meditation*

Described too uniformly as aids to or tools for meditation and designated as 'meditation diagrams' and 'meditational art', *maṇḍala*s have indeed become central to the various kinds of modern *maṇḍala* meditation (Bühnemann 2017). In popular writing on *maṇḍala* meditation, however, neither the term *maṇḍala* nor the word meditation is clearly defined. The word *maṇḍala* is broadly used in the sense of a geometric pattern with a central focal point, and variously understood to represent or relate to the cosmos, the subconscious or unconscious. Usually no distinction is made between Buddhist and Hindu *maṇḍala*s, or between them and *maṇḍala*-like designs said to derive from Native American or other traditions, or from non-traditional sources. The word meditation is mostly understood to refer to an activity that focuses and calms the mind, leading to a state of relaxation, concentration or contemplation. The term *maṇḍala* meditation, finally, is used to designate a range of activities involving different uses of *maṇḍala*s, focusing on the structures' designs (without an invocation of divine beings into their parts). The activities most commonly include the following (Bühnemann 2017: 267–268):

1. The slow and attentive process of drawing, painting or creating a *maṇḍala* design
2. The colouring of a *maṇḍala* template
3. The focusing and resting of one's gaze upon a *maṇḍala* design

In the present typology, the first category comprises free-form *maṇḍala*s. These were highly valued by Jung and are now often created in art therapy settings. The therapeutic intervention may involve the spontaneous drawing or painting of a *maṇḍala*, which is then analysed and interpreted by both client and therapist.

The activity in the second type, the colouring of a template featuring a *maṇḍala*-like design, often from a *maṇḍala* colouring book, is widespread. It can be considered part of the larger and recent adult colouring trend, which uses templates with different types of patterns and designs. *Maṇḍala* colouring has also been taught in many schools. However, in recent years the practice has come under criticism and efforts have been made to remove it from school curricula since some parents consider it religious indoctrination,[8] along with mindfulness and yoga (Brown 2019: 1). In South Korea, big companies such as Samsung hire instructors to teach employees and their family members relaxation techniques to manage work-related stress. The stress management activities include the colouring of (not necessarily Buddhist) *maṇḍala* templates.[9]

The colouring of traditional Tibetan or Newar Buddhist *maṇḍala* templates sketched by a teacher is a more specialised activity, currently taught as a meditative process by some individuals in Asia, Europe and North America. As one instructor asserted, '[d]rawing a Mandala … is a meditation in itself and creates inner peace and joy'.[10] The format is usually that of a workshop providing instruction to small groups. Each participant colours one template, working mostly in silence for up to several hours a day over the duration of about one week (Figure 29.3). One artist[11] reported that she teaches her students to paint or colour in *maṇḍala*s while being aware of their inhalation and exhalation (but not to hold the breath while drawing a line, as is sometimes taught). She emphasised that she feels a profound inner peace when drawing *maṇḍala*s and that her students experience the week-long activity of *maṇḍala* colouring as a deeply transformative process.

For many people, colouring in *maṇḍala*s is a more accessible activity than formal sitting meditation. It does not require the same amount of discipline and patience as counting or observing breaths or repeating a mantra, and enables practitioners to focus their attention and centre themselves more easily without experiencing mental fatigue and exertion.

*Figure 29.3* Participant of a *maṇḍala* meditation workshop
Photo courtesy of Renuka Gurung.

One practice involving colouring in *maṇḍala*s can be compared to the 'image copying' (*shabutsu*) currently taught to laypeople in some Buddhist temples in Japan. The practitioner places thin copying paper on the image of a Buddha or Bodhisattva or divine figure and traces the lines. The practice is advertised not only as 'a form of meditation, to clear the mind and focus on beauty'[12] but also as an easy way to relax. The practitioner buys a package, which includes the entrance fee to the temple and the use of the drawing tools required for the session. The activity lasts between thirty minutes and two hours, depending on the complexity of the image. At the beginning a religious text, usually the Buddhist *Heart Sūtra*, is recited, and at the end of the session, green tea and a sweet are served.

The teaching of *maṇḍala* colouring or painting as a meditative activity has been criticised by some. It has been argued that a painter, given his lack of religious authority, is not qualified to pass on tantric teachings, including those pertaining to the structure of Buddhist *maṇḍala*s into which tantric deities are invoked. Even if the painter were empowered to dispense such esoteric teachings, he would not be allowed to instruct individuals who have not received the required initiations. Furthermore, some painters consider the painting of *maṇḍala*s (and of images of divinities) a craft unrelated to meditation and criticise the activity of colouring or painting of *maṇḍala* designs by persons outside the tradition as an inauthentic New Age practice that has no precedents in the past. This point of view finds support in a statement from the Tibetan meditation master Chögyam Trungpa (1938–1987), who discussed painted images on a canvas surface – known as *thaṅka*s (Tibetan) – and concluded with the following observation:

> It is widely thought that thangka painting is a form of meditation. This is not true. Though all the thangkas have religious subjects, most of the artists were and are lay people ... Naturally, also, artists have a sense of reverence for the sacredness of their work. Nevertheless, the painting of thangkas is primarily a craft rather than a religious exercise. One exception is the *nyin thang* ('one-day thangka') practice in which, as part of a particular sādhana, while repeating the appropriate mantra, uninterruptedly, without sleeping, a monk paints a thangka in one twenty-four hour period.
>
> *(1975: 18)*

Trungpa's statement is of particular interest since it addresses the role of the artist, who has been idealised as some sort of mystic or yogin in western art historical literature, as in the following statement by Thurman:

> The artist has to be a person who is open enough to enlightenment to serve as a selfless vessel for its manifestations; who has to participate in the creation of a work of art out of dedication to the higher realm, and not primarily for fame and profit.
>
> *(Thurman in Rhie and Thurman 2000: 37)*

The notion that the Tibetan artist, or rather – applying a modern distinction – craftsman, is also a meditator or even mystic has been challenged by scholars such as Lopez (1998: 149–150) and is addressed above. But the matter is more complex, since some texts specify in considerable detail how an artist should prepare himself before creating a work of religious art – a process that entails receiving an initiation, taking a bath, observing a specific diet, etc.[13] It appears, though, that these prescriptions were rarely followed (Lopez 1998: 150), due to the pressures and time constraints of everyday life. In short, while some meditators have also been artists, few artists have been meditators.[14] An example in the first category is the Sherpa monk, hermit and *thaṅka* painter Ngawang Lekshey, known as Au Leshi/Leshey (*c.*1900–*c.*1978) (Berg 2002).

The third category of *maṇḍala* meditation, the focusing and resting of one's gaze upon a *maṇḍala* design, is described in the literature as follows: The practitioner's gentle gaze focuses on a *maṇḍala* design, specifically its centre, while the body stays relaxed. Whenever the mind wanders, one gently refocuses one's concentration on the *maṇḍala*. When the eyes get tired, one shuts them while attempting to create a mental image of the *maṇḍala*. After a period of rest, one resumes the practice of gazing at the *maṇḍala*. The time recommended for this practice ranges from five to thirty minutes a day. Dahlke (2001: 201) recommends that practitioners spend fifteen minutes gazing at a *maṇḍala* while listening to music, and provides the following instructions:

> Put up the colored mandala about two yards away from you, direct a strong light onto it, and then gently gaze down to its center. Listen to some appropriate meditation music. You will soon feel that the mandala is alive and can hold you under its spell. Allow about fifteen minutes for this excursion to the center of being ..

This author claims that '[t]here is evidence that, due to its shape and a person's readiness to be drawn into it, the mandala can actually put people in a trance when they are meditating on it or even just coloring it' (Dahlke 2001: 28).

One author summarised the benefits of *maṇḍala* gazing in the following statement:

> As we rest our gaze upon a mandala, the mind becomes as still as the surface of a pool of water. From the profound depths of tranquillity emerge insights that help us to tap into and develop our innate healing powers.
>
> *(Tenzin-Dolma 2008: 9)*

This description is particularly interesting, since the author claims in the first sentence the outcomes that calmness or tranquillity (*śamatha*) meditation is assumed to produce, while she cites the benefits commonly attributed to the practice of insight (*vipaśyanā*) meditation in the second sentence.

It is very likely that '*maṇḍala*-gazing' meditation developed from the notion of the *maṇḍala* as an instrument with which to meditate, as discussed above. This practice must have been popular already in the 1970s, since Chögyam Trungpa dismissed it as non-traditional in 1975, asserting that '[i]t should be understood that mandala representations are not used as objects of contemplation in an attempt to bring about certain states of mind' (1975: 23). Citing Trungpa's statement, two decades later Lopez asserted that: '[t]he mandala is not, then, a diagram that one stares at to induce altered states' (1998: 146). In other words, *maṇḍala*s do not constitute designs that serve as foci of concentration with the aim of bringing about meditative equipoise.

Technically, one could classify '*maṇḍala*-gazing meditation' as a type of tranquillity (*śamatha*) practice. It could be considered a technique in the tradition of the *kasiṇa* (Pali, 'sphere') devices of early Buddhism, as described, for example, in the *Visuddhimagga* ('Path of Purification') by Buddhaghosa (c. 370–450 CE). This work details how the practitioner perfects concentration and attains different absorption (*jhāna*, Pali) stages by gazing at a disk until he is able to reproduce a mental image of it. *Maṇḍala* gazing could also be compared to some extent to the meditation on the a-syllable (*ajikan*, Japanese), which has a profound meaning in Buddhism. The syllable is written on a disk and gazed at by practitioners of the Japanese Tendai and Shingon schools of Buddhism. Historically, however, *maṇḍala* gazing is not related to these practices.

## Conclusion

In this chapter I have explored the notion of art from the Himalayan region as 'meditational' and 'enlightenment art', often invoked in museum catalogues and popular books and created during museum exhibits, sometimes with new display techniques that may contribute to reinforcing such stereotypes. In this context I critically examine widely held misconceptions regarding Tibetan art and the role of the artist. The case study of the *maṇḍala* sheds light on the intersection of tradition and modernity. Here I provide an overview of the traditional use and significance of Buddhist *maṇḍala*s and show that the modern, widespread understanding of *maṇḍala*s as solely tools for meditation fails to characterise adequately the complexity of their functions. Although the visualisation of *maṇḍala*s in tantric Buddhism can be subsumed under the term meditation, there are many other uses of *maṇḍala*s, most frequently in initiation rituals. The case study further addresses the discourse on *maṇḍala*s in Jungian psychology, the *maṇḍala*'s use in art therapy and in popular culture, and the *maṇḍala*'s commodification. I also introduce a typology of modern *maṇḍala* meditation.

When one contrasts the contemporary use of *maṇḍala*s with traditional applications of Buddhist *maṇḍala*s, it becomes obvious that modern *maṇḍala*s serve very different purposes to those forming part of Buddhist tantric practice. The interpretation of *maṇḍala*s has clearly undergone significant change over time, and one goal of this chapter is to trace these new developments in their historical and cultural contexts. Another goal is to highlight modern misconceptions, distortions and stereotypes regarding the significance and function of *maṇḍala*s. However, I do not want to write them off as deviations from some static, ancient and original concept underlying *maṇḍala*s. Already in the eleventh century, Buddhist authorities were providing more than a single interpretation of *maṇḍala*s.

Considering the contribution of art historians and curators to the study of *maṇḍala*s, one can note that the display of *maṇḍala*s in museums and art galleries and the depiction and description of them in art books and exhibition and sales catalogues has, despite some shortcomings, stimulated an interest in these objects in the general population.

Art historical study, focusing on the structural patterns of *maṇḍala*s and on the figures depicted in them across different regions and time periods, has contributed significantly to our knowledge of the development of the pictorial forms. Here the discipline has favoured the study of the objects' provenance, identification, function, style, date and their material and social context (such as questions of patronship and the implications of trade routes). Some of these issues are equally relevant to and overlap with current discussions in Material Religion. This subdiscipline of Religious Studies explores religion within the framework of material culture, by examining the interaction between humans and objects used in religious practice. A mere art historical approach, however, can provide only a limited understanding of the significance and function of *maṇḍala*s. It needs to be supplemented by a study of the rich extant textual material that can shed light on the theological interpretations and uses of *maṇḍala*s in Buddhist tantric traditions in different regions and time periods.

## Notes

1 I would like to thank friends and colleagues for help and suggestions while writing this chapter (in alphabetical order): Lok Chitrakar, Finnian M.M. Gerety, Renuka Gurung, the Lumbini International Research Institute and its director Christoph Cüppers, Suzanne Newcombe, Karen O'Brien-Kop and Philip Pierce

2 Several scholars (including Jackson 1993; McLagan 1997: 75–81; Lopez 1998: 147–149; Harris 1999: 37–39; and Harris 2012: 19–20) have criticised the text of the exhibition catalogue authored by Rhie and Thurman; for an assessment of the exhibition, see Stoddard 2001.

3 On the 'mystification' of the Tibetan artist, see the discussion below.

4 See the text describing the show: www.vmfa.museum/exhibitions/exhibitions/awaken/. Accessed 20 June 2019.

5 Part of this paper is based on Bühnemann 2017.

6 On this exhibition, see https://exhibitions.asianart.org/exhibitions/enter-the-mandala-cosmic-centers-and-mental-maps-of-himalayan-buddhism/. Accessed 22 June 2019, and Durham 2015.

7 For a recent study of the Maṇḍala of the Eight Great Bodhisattvas, see Wang 2018.

8 For a discussion, see Brown 2019: 64, 96–97, 121, 205.

9 Interview with Kim Tae Hee, a researcher at the Research Center of Yoga Philosophy, Won Kwang University, Iksan, Korea, 5 June 2018. Hee instructs Samsung employees in *maṇḍala* colouring.

10 Quoted from Carmen Mensink's description of a course held in Venice. See www.tibetan-buddhist-art.com/italy-venice-thangka-weekend-course. Accessed 31 October 2018.

11 Interview with Dr. Renuka Gurung, a *paubhā* painter from Kathmandu who leads *maṇḍala* meditation retreats/workshops; Kathmandu, 10 August 2018.

12 The activity is taught at the Bishamondo Shourinji Temple in Kyoto; see www.veltra.com/en/asia/japan/kyoto/a/110834. Accessed 29 September 2018.

13 For extracts from texts in translation, see Dagyab 1977: 27–28 and Wang 2018: 43, 46. For a summary of the prescriptions in the *Mañjuśrīmūlakalpa*, see Wallis 2002: 115–125.

14 See Kapstein 1995: 258, 260; for a discussion of Kapstein's ideas, see Wallis 2002: 92–95.

## Bibliography

Berg, E. 2002. 'Cultural Change and Remembering: Recording the Life of Au Leshey'. *European Bulletin of Himalayan Research* 23: 5–25.

Brauen, M. 2004. *Dreamworld Tibet: Western Illusions*. Willson, M. (trans). Trumbull, Connecticut: Weatherhill.

Brown, C. G. 2019. *Debating Yoga and Mindfulness in Public Schools*. Chapel Hill: The University of North Carolina Press.

Buggeln, G., Paine, C. and Plate, S. B. (eds) 2017. *Religion in Museums: Global and Multidisciplinary Perspectives*. London: Bloomsbury.

Bühnemann, G. 2017. 'Modern Maṇḍala Meditation: Some Observations'. *Contemporary Buddhism* 18(2): 263–276.

Dagyab, L. S. 1977. *Tibetan Religious Art: Part I: Texts*. Wiesbaden: Otto Harrassowitz.

Dahlke, R. 2001. *Mandalas for Meditation*. New York: Sterling Publishing.

Davidson, R. M. 2002. *Indian Esoteric Buddhism: A Social History of the Tantric Movement*. New York: Columbia University Press.

Durham, J. 2015. 'Entering the Virtual Mandala: Transformative Environments in Hybrid Spaces', in Sullivan, B. M. (ed), *Sacred Objects in Secular Spaces: Exhibiting Asian Religions in Museums*, 80–93. London and New York: Bloomsbury.

von Franz, M.-L. 1964 [1977]. 'The Process of Individuation', in Jung, Carl G. et al. *Man and His Symbols*, 157–254. New York, New York: Dell Publishing (16th printing).

Harris, C. 1999. *In the Image of Tibet: Tibetan Painting after 1959*. London: Reaktion Books.

Harris, C. E. 2012. *The Museum on the Roof of the World: Art, Politics, and the Representation of Tibet*. Chicago: The University of Chicago Press.

Huntington, J. C. and Bangdel, D. 2003. *The Circle of Bliss: Buddhist Meditational Art*. Chicago: Serindia Publications.

Jackson, D. 1993. 'Apropos a Recent Tibetan Art Catalogue'. *Wiener Zeitschrift für die Kunde Südasiens und Archiv für Indische Philosophie* 37: 109–130.

Jaffé, A. 1964 [1977]. 'Symbolism in the Visual Arts', in Jung, Carl G. et al. *Man and His Symbols*, 255–322. New York: Dell Publishing (16th printing).

Jung, C. G. 1959 [1972]. *Mandala Symbolism*, Hull, R. F. C. (trans). Princeton, New Jersey: Princeton University Press, 1972.

Jung, C. G. 1965. *Memories, Dreams, Reflections,* recorded and edited by A. Jaffé. Translated from the German by R. and C. Winston. New York: Vintage Books (rev. ed.).

Kapstein, M. T. 1995. 'Weaving the World: The Ritual Art of the Paṭa in Pāla Buddhism and Its Legacy in Tibet'. *History of Religions* 34(3): 241–262. Reprinted in Kapstein, M. T. 2001. *Reason's Traces: Identity and Interpretation in Indian and Tibetan Buddhist Thought*, 257–280. Boston: Wisdom Publications.

Kellogg, J. 2001. *Mandala: Path of Beauty*. Belleair, Florida: ATMA, Inc. (3rd ed., 2nd printing).

Kramrisch, S. 1960. 'The Art of Nepal and Tibet'. Philadelphia Museum of Art Bulletin 55(265): 23–38.

Lopez, Jr., D. S. 1998. *Prisoners of Shangri-La: Tibetan Buddhism and the West*. Chicago: The University of Chicago Press.

McLagan, M. 1997. 'Mystical Visions in Manhattan: Deploying Culture in the Year of Tibet', in Korom, F. J. (ed), *Tibetan Culture in the Diaspora: Papers Presented at a Panel of the 7th Seminar of the International Association of Tibetan Studies Graz 1995*, 69–89. Vienna: Österreichische Akademie der Wissenschaften.

Nicoloff, P. L. 2008. *Sacred Kōyasan: A Pilgrimage to the Mountain Temple of Saint Kōbō Daishi and the Great Sun Buddha*. New York: State University of New York Press.

*Nispanna-Yogāvalī*. 2015. *Sanskrit and Tibetan Texts*, with English Translation by Lokesh Chandra and N. Sharma. New Delhi: International Academy of Indian Culture/Aditya Prakashan.

Paine, C. 2013. *Religious Objects in Museums: Private Lives and Public Duties*. London: Bloomsbury.

Paine, C. 2017. 'Rich and Varied: Religion in Museums', in Buggeln, G., Paine, C. and Plate, S. B. (eds), *Religion in Museums: Global and Multidisciplinary Perspectives*, 213–223. London: Bloomsbury.

Pal, P. 2003. *Himalayas: An Aesthetic Adventure*. Chicago: The Art Institute of Chicago.

Reedy, C. L. 1992. 'Religious and Ethical Issues in the Study and Conservation of of [sic] Tibetan Sculpture'. *Journal of the American Institute for Conservation* 31(1): 41–50.

Rhie, M. M. and Thurman, R. A. F. 1999. *Worlds of Transformation: Tibetan Art of Wisdom and Compassion*. New York: Tibet House.

Rhie, M. M. and Thurman, R. A. F. 2000. *Wisdom and Compassion: The Sacred Art of Tibet.* Expanded edition. New York: Harry N. Abrams ['published on the occasion of the third incarnation ofWisdom and Compassion: The Sacred Art ofTibet'].

Rice, J. H. and Durham, J. S. 2019. Awaken: *A Tibetan Buddhist Journey Toward Enlightenment.* New Haven: Yale University Press.

Rose, E. M. and Rose Dalto, A. 2003. *Create Your Own Sand Mandala: For Meditation, Healing, and Prayer.* Alresford, Hampshire: Godsfield Press.

*Sādhanamālā.* 1925–1928. 2 volumes. Bhattacharyya, B. (ed). Baroda: Oriental Institute.

Sarma, D. 2015. 'Under the Gaze of Kali: Exhibitionism in the Kalighat Paintings Exhibition at the Cleveland Museum of Art', in Sullivan, B. M. (ed), *Sacred Objects in Secular Spaces: Exhibiting Asian Religions in Museums*, 26–34. London and New York: Bloomsbury.

Stoddard, H. 2001. 'The Development in Perceptions of Tibetan Art: From Golden Idols to Ultimate Reality', in Dodin, T. and Räther, H. (eds), *Imagining Tibet: Perceptions, Projections, and Fantasies*, 223–253. Boston: Wisdom Publications.

Sullivan, B. M. (ed) 2015. *Sacred Objects in Secular Spaces: Exhibiting Asian Religions in Museums.* London/New York: Bloomsbury.

Tanaka, K. 2018. *An Illustrated History of the Maṇḍala: From its Genesis to the Kālacakratantra.* Somerville, MA: Wisdom Publications.

Tenzin-Dolma, L. 2008. *Healing Maṇḍalas: 30 Inspiring Meditations to Soothe Your Mind, Body and Soul.* London: Duncan Baird Publishers.

Trungpa, C. 1975. *Visual Dharma: The Buddhist Art of Tibet.* Berkeley: Shambhala.

Tucci, G. 1961. *The Theory and Practice of the Maṇḍala. With Special Reference to the Modern Psychology of the Subconscious.* Translated from the Italian by A. H. Brodrick. London: Rider & Company.

*Vajrāvalī of Abhayākaragupta.* Edition of Sanskrit and Tibetan Versions by M. Mori. 2 volumes. Tring, UK: Institute of Buddhist Studies, 2009.

Visuddhimagga: The Path of Purification, the Classic Manual of Buddhist Doctrine and Meditation. 2010. Translated from the Pali by Bhikkhu Ñāṇamoli. Kandy: Buddhist Publication Society (fourth edition).

Wallis, G. 2002. *Mediating the Power of Buddhas: Ritual in the Mañjuśrīmūlakalpa.* Albany, New York: State University of New York Press.

Wang, M. C. 2018. *Maṇḍalas in the Making: The Visual Culture of Esoteric Buddhism at Dunhuang.* Leiden and Boston: Brill.

Winfield, P. D. 2012. 'Coronation at Kōyasan: How One Woman Became King and Learned about Homeland Security and National Health Care in Ancient Japan', in Harding, J. S. (ed), *Studying Buddhism in Practice*, 11–24. New York: Routledge.

# 30

# THE PSYCHOPHYSIOLOGY OF YOGA

## Characteristics of the main components and review of research studies

*Laura Schmalzl, Pamela Jeter and Sat Bir Singh Khalsa*

### Introduction: yoga as a multicomponent practice

As the prevalence of yoga practice is now surpassing 14% of the US adult population (Clarke et al. 2018), yoga practices are being implemented in mainstream institutions. Yoga instruction is appearing in educational institutions and in occupational and healthcare settings. Biomedical research on the psychophysiology of yoga and its therapeutic potential is critically important for the justification of such implementation. Yoga instructors and therapists increasingly need to acquire a basic understanding of biomedical and scientific research in order to justify the efficacy and cost-effectiveness of yoga within these mainstream societal venues. This research is also of interest to yoga practitioners who want to increase their understanding of the synergistic mechanisms of yoga as a multicomponent practice. An otherwise healthy yoga student may find benefit from any number of yoga classes. However, a yoga student or patient seeking yoga as therapy for a specific condition, whether it be mental health or chronic pain conditions, is likely to achieve greater benefit from understanding the evidence base and consulting with an expert.

It is important for the research and clinical community to have a fundamental understanding of the contemporary, social and historical context in which the evolving practices are conducted. For example, modern yoga-based practices originate from various schools and lineages. Most of them are multifaceted in nature, typically involving a combination of specific postures or movement sequences, breath regulation, deep relaxation and meditative techniques, as well as spiritual teachings (Gard et al. 2014a; Schmalzl et al., 2015; Sullivan et al. 2017). The way these components are taught and the emphasis on each element differs across styles, which in turn impacts psychophysiological effects. As a clinician or scientist, it is key to understand the purported benefits of specific components or combinations of techniques that is applied in a research setting for evaluating specific mechanisms or effects on clinical conditions. Often the delivery of the yoga intervention in research studies is highly standardised to improve validity and rigour, but this may not be generalisable to real-world yoga classes. An emerging discipline is that of yoga therapy, which requires more specialised training (>600 hours) than for the average yoga teacher; one growing certification credential is offered by the International Association of Yoga Therapists (IAYT). A yoga therapist is more likely to deliver an individualised yoga approach that is best suited to the client's specific health needs.

This chapter summarises what is currently known about the psychophysiology of the main components of yoga-based practices (including meditation) and how they are proposed to work in synergy. The primary emphasis will be on a selection of basic, mechanistic studies, as well as some clinical research studies examining psychophysiological aspects of yoga as a multicomponent practice. Although the focus on the psychophysiological lends itself to an emphasis on underlying biological or physical mechanisms, this chapter will also discuss the potential for these mechanisms to influence or co-occur with psychological and clinical outcomes. While yoga may affect physiological parameters, this may not necessarily translate to a beneficial outcome for treating a clinical condition. Reviewing the wide range of existing clinical yoga research studies on specific disease conditions is, however, beyond the scope of this chapter. It is also important to note that while the emerging field of yoga research has been rapidly evolving, some of the currently published literature has methodological limitations, which we will address in the final section of this chapter.

## *The movement component*

In modern western contexts, yoga-based practices typically have a strong emphasis on postures and movement sequences. The movement component of yoga can range from large and intense to small and subtle motion and may even include purely internal motion or motor imagery (Schmalzl et al. 2014). Some traditions primarily involve series of static individual postures that are held for a prolonged period of time (up to several minutes), some involve more dynamic and continuous physical movement and some employ a combination of static postures and flowing movement sequences.

Across different yoga styles there are numerous individual yoga postures and variations. Broadly speaking, they can be divided into categories that include standing postures, seated postures, supine postures, forward folds, backbends, lateral bends of the spine, twists, hip-openers and inversions. Individual postures are mostly instructed using very precise alignment cues, and when practices involve dynamic sequencing of movements they are typically performed in a slow, rhythmic and symmetric manner that is synchronised with the breath. Independently of the specific style, yogic movement is typically aimed at increasing range of motion, strength, endurance, flexibility and balance, as well as promoting relaxation and wellbeing.

An important characteristic of posture practice is the emphasis on cultivating awareness of interoceptive, proprioceptive, kinesthetic and spatial sensations, and using them to adjust and fine-tune one's positioning and movements. Typically, there is a focus on obtaining and maintaining a balanced muscle tone that supports a quality of movement that is grounded and stable, yet light and fluid. Some postures are characterised by hypertonic (e.g. arm balances that require a high level of muscle tension) or hypotonic (e.g. a supine relaxation pose) muscle activation, but the general aim is that of obtaining a state of eutony or 'well-balanced tension' (Alexander 1985). This is often facilitated by engagement of interior muscle groups, which supports the stability of core musculature and the maintenance of breath regulation while moving through the postures.

Even though there is such a strong emphasis on the physical component of yoga-based practices in modern contexts, to date little is known about the specific effects of the postures and movement sequences in and of themselves. One of the challenges that research faces in isolating the effects of the movement component per se is that the postures are typically instructed in combination with some type of breathing and/or meditation techniques. That said, a number of studies have characterised general aspects of the movement component. Compared to more vigorous forms of exercise, such coordinated movement of moderate intensity has been proposed to help promote parasympathetic tone (Payne and Crane-Godreau 2013). It has also been suggested that movement sequences such as sun salutations, in which joint load is mostly kept at submaximal levels, support bone remodelling and osteogenesis (Omkar et al. 2011). Furthermore, one study suggests that the musculoskeletal demands vary across different yoga poses, such as chair or tree pose, which has implications to inform individualised yoga therapy and rehabilitation goals (Wang et al. 2013).

Movement-based yoga practices have been reported to positively impact muscular strength and endurance, flexibility and cardiorespiratory fitness (Tran et al. 2001). In addition, studies comparing yoga-based movement with other forms of physical exercise have suggested that yoga can be equally effective for improving fatigue, self-esteem and quality of life (Taspinar et al. 2014). Corroborating the claim that the benefits of posture practice extend beyond the physical realm, it has been reported that yoga can be as effective as conventional exercise in improving mood and decreasing anxiety (Streeter et al. 2010). When it comes to energy expenditure (Ray et al. 2011) and certain pulmonary functions (Gupta and Sawane 2012), yoga-based practices are generally considered to be at a lower level compared to other types of aerobic exercise in young healthy adults. Unless practices incorporate a substantial amount of dynamic movement sequences such as vigorous or rapid sun salutations (Hagins et al. 2007), yoga practice may often not meet the criteria recommended for improving or even maintaining cardiovascular fitness and pulmonary function in the general population (Beutler et al. 2016). Although yoga may not improve aerobic exercise capacity in young healthy adults, there is some evidence to suggest an improvement in respiration regulation at rest, which may have implications for sedentary or clinical populations (e.g. those with cardiovascular risk factors) in future research.

Yoga-based movement has been proposed to affect, and mediate, several neurophysiological and neurocognitive mechanisms. One of these relates to the biomechanical behaviour of the connective tissue or fascia, which is particularly affected by deep stretching. Stretching of the connective tissue causes fibroblasts to expand by actively remodelling their cytoskeleton, which in turn contributes to a change in extracellular fluid dynamics that prevents swelling and tension. If stretching is prolonged it can cause the overall compactness of the connective tissue in a given area to decrease, promoting the flow of fluid from the capillary bed into the extracellular space. In a recent study in mice, it was shown that stretching activates inflammation-regulating mechanisms within connective tissues (Berrueta et al. 2016). These mechanisms are proposed to play an important role in the regulation of tissue fluid, metabolic homeostasis and even immune surveillance (Langevin et al. 2013).

A second proposed mechanism is the promotion of afferent signaling by the vagus nerve (Porges 2001). The vagus nerve is one of the key components of autonomic regulation (Porges 1995), with its afferent fibres communicating peripheral information about bodily states to the brain (Berthoud and Neuhuber 2000). While vagal tone is said to be primarily impacted by the slow and rhythmic breathing employed in yoga-based practices (Brown and Gerbarg 2005), the movement component may also contribute to it through enhancing the depth of the breath (e.g. active expansions/contractions of the rib cage during back/forward bends), further strengthening core diaphragmatic muscles and increasing baroreceptor sensitivity (Strongoli et al. 2010). Moreover, the interior muscle activation and abdominal tone emphasised in many yoga postures can promote peripheral vagal stimulation and afference (Ritter et al. 1992).

A third proposed mechanism relates to functional characteristics of neural circuits involving the basal ganglia (BG) (McHaffie et al. 2005). BG circuits consist of semi-independent loops originating from specific cortical areas, passing through functionally corresponding portions of the

BG and returning to the same cortical areas via the thalamus (Alexander 1994). Functions that are supported by these cortico-BG-thalamic loops, and that are all implicated in the movement aspect of yoga-based practices, include body awareness, motor coordination and procedural learning. Additional functions supported by BG loops include more complex higher-order cognitive functions as well as social behaviour (Arsalidou et al. 2013). Recent neuroimaging work found that a group of expert yoga practitioners showed more widespread functional connectivity within BG circuits compared to controls (Gard et al. 2015). This finding can be interpreted to suggest that yoga-based practices may potentially promote increased connectivity within, and dynamic shifting between, motor, cognitive and emotional circuits, with subsequent beneficial effects for mind–body integration and self-regulation.

Lastly, it has been proposed that selective physical postures and movements can be used to target specific psychophysiological effects, and impact not only physical functioning but also psychological states. For example, it has been suggested that physical posture can affect pain tolerance, neuroendocrine levels and even risk propensity. Adopting a dominant, as opposed to a submissive or neutral, physical posture has been shown to positively affect pain tolerance (Bohns and Wiltermuth 2012). Similarly, 'high-power' postures characterised by and suggestive of high degrees of expansiveness, openness, assertiveness and confidence, have been associated with decreased levels of cortisol, increased levels of testosterone and enhanced feelings of psychological power (Carney et al. 2010). It has also been suggested that upright postures favour the generation and recall of positive thoughts (Wilson and Peper 2004), whereas assuming a slumped posture may promote higher degrees of perceived helplessness (Riskind and Gotay 1982). With specific reference to yoga postures, preliminary evidence suggests that backbends may be associated with greater increases in positive mood compared to forward folds or standing poses (Shapiro and Cline, 2004). This observation is intriguing and calls for further studies comparing the differential efficacy of selective yoga postures for clinical populations affected by mood disorders.

## The breathing component

A multitude of breathing practices exist within yoga traditions, and they can be practised alone or in the context of postures and movement sequences. In some practices, breathing patterns are instructed in conjunction with postures and movement sequences, and specific emphasis is put on linking the breath and the movement. In other practices there is simply a focus on maintaining an even rhythm of inhalations and exhalations, or the breath can also merely serve as an object of attention as in many meditation practices. Depending on the type of breathing that is emphasised, breath regulation can have a number of different physiological effects (Brown and Gerbarg 2005). While slow and rhythmic breathing is proposed to promote parasympathetic dominance, more forceful breathing practices can actually promote sympathetic activation (Beauchaine 2001). The most common yogic breathing practice is a slow and rhythmic abdominal breathing pattern, with a frequency of about six breaths per minute or slower. This so-called diaphragmatic breathing, in which there is an emphasis on involving the entire abdominal cavity as opposed to just the chest, has long been adopted by many western therapists as it ensures a deeper breath with a larger tidal volume.

One of the most common slow breathing techniques used in modern yoga-based practices is the so-called '*ujjayi* breath' (Brown and Gerbarg 2005). It is a deep, slow and rhythmic diaphragmatic breath performed through the nostrils which in some traditions also includes the concomitant narrowing of the glottis, creating a soft and soothing sound. It can involve visualising the breath as rising from the lower belly, through the ribcage, to the upper chest and throat during inhalations, and follow the opposite order during exhalations. Inhalations and exhalations are typically of equal length, and their duration can be gradually expanded with practice. Additional common yogic breathing techniques include '*kapālabhāti*' (rapid abdominal breathing involving short and forceful contraction of the anterior abdominal wall), '*bhastrikā*' (rapid thoracic breathing using intercostal and accessory muscles), '*sītalī prāṇāyāma*' (slow breathing through puckered lips with a curled tongue), '*nāḍī śodhana*' (alternate nostril breathing), and '*kumbhaka*' (retention of the breath for various durations either after inhalations, exhalations or both).

Breathing practices have been associated with several psychophysiological effects (Sovik 2000;Vinay et al. 2016; Critchley et al. 2015; Nivethitha et al. 2016; Russo et al. 2017; Steffen et al. 2017). In fact, the view that emotional states can be expressed in breathing patterns, and that breath regulation can consequently influence emotional states, is supported by both yoga traditions and biomedical science on respiratory physiology (Boiten et al. 1994; Brown and Gerbarg 2005; Henje Blom et al. 2014). A common autonomic response to stress, for example, is rapid thoracic breathing, which can lead in turn lead to hyperventilation and a change in tidal volume (Laffey and Kavanagh 2002).

Slow and rhythmic yogic breathing with a frequency of about six breaths per minute has been reported to decreases chemoreflex sensitivity (Spicuzza et al. 2000) and oxidative stress (Sharma et al. 2003), increase cardiac-vagal baroreflex sensitivity (Esposito et al. 2015) and promote the release of prolactin and oxytocin, which are associated with feelings of calmness and social bonding (Torner et al. 2002).

As noted above, one of the main mechanisms through which slow breathing is said to impact autonomic regulation is by promoting vagal afference (Porges 2001).Vagal tone is proposed to be reflected by heart rate variability (HRV), i.e. the variability of the inter-beat intervals of the heart (Porges 2001), and especially mirrored by respiratory sinus arrhythmia (RSA), i.e. the HRV within the frequency of respiration (Calabrese et al. 2000). In addition, there is a correlation between breathing frequency and both HRV and arterial baroreflex sensitivity, with slower breathing rates increasing both of these indices (Bernardi et al. 2001).

In terms of specific yogic breathing techniques, *ujjāyī* breath has been proposed to be particularly effective in stimulating somatosensory vagal afferents to the brain (Nivethitha et al. 2017) (primarily via contraction of laryngeal muscles) (Brown and Gerbarg 2005) and consequently promoting autonomic regulation (Calabrese et al. 2000). Alternate nostril breathing has also been associated with increased parasympathetic nervous system activity as measured by heart rate parameters and orthostatic tolerance (Sinha et al. 2013), increased HRV and decreased systolic blood pressure (Telles et al. 2014, Telles et al. 2017), as well as changes in the P300 auditory evoked potential, which is a neural marker for sustained attention (Telles et al. 2013). Moreover, some studies have documented laterality effects, with breathing through individual nostrils affecting brain responses and autonomic regulation in specific ways. Examples include differential effects of left and right nostril breathing respectively on oxygen consumption (Telles et al. 1994) and blood pressure parameters (Raghuraj and Telles 2008), as well as the P300 auditory evoked potential, which was found to be more affected in the contralateral brain hemisphere (Telles et al. 2012).

While most of the published literature focuses on the positive effects of slow breathing, it is worth noting that more rapidly paced breathing can have specific benefits as well. For example, pulmonary deficiencies that require strengthening of the respiratory system may improve more rapidly with breathing techniques that require a higher rate of respiratory muscle activity and breath coordination (Dinesh et al. 2015). Moreover, it has been proposed that fast breathing may positively impact working memory and sensory-motor performance (Sharma et al. 2014).

## *The relaxation component*

A fundamental aspect of most yoga practices is deep relaxation. Relaxation techniques can constitute a practice in their own right (e.g. in restorative yoga) or be included at various points of a practice session to complement more vigorous movement or breathing exercises. Independently of the practice style, individual sessions typically end with a supine relaxation pose called corpse pose or *śavāsana*, which can involve explicit instructions for systematic progressive relaxation throughout the body's musculature. A well-known relaxation practice is *yoga nidra* (Miller 2005). It consists of a gradual progression from deep relaxation to a near sleep-like state in which individuals remain aware of their surroundings, which can be accompanied by a change in brain waves (Lou et al. 1990). It typically includes relaxation, breath awareness, meditation and guided imagery (Parker et al. 2013).

Modern medicine and clinical psychology have been using relaxation techniques such as progressive muscle relaxation for decades (McGuigan and Lehrer, 2007). Relaxation techniques are an easily accessible nonpharmacological approach for a variety of populations and clinical conditions and lend themselves very well to being integrated in various community, educational and hospital settings (Klainin-Yobas et al. 2015). Clinical conditions for which progressive relaxation has been implemented and studied include anxiety-related disorders, as well as psychosomatic conditions such as insomnia and chronic pain (Manzoni et al. 2008). Studies investigating the specific effects of *śavāsana* have documented that it can promote reductions in HRV, blood pressure (Pal et al. 2014), respiration rate and oxygen consumption (Sarang and Telles, 2006), energy expenditure (Ray et al. 2011) and symptoms of anxiety (Subramanya and Telles, 2009). The practice of *yoga nidra* has been found to reduce symptoms of stress, depression and anxiety, and promote states of mindfulness (Eastman-Mueller et al. 2013). Moreover, there is preliminary evidence from electroencephalography (EEG) studies that the practice may be associated with increases in both alpha and theta waves (Kjaer et al. 2002; Kumar and Joshi 2009; Lou et al. 1990). It should be noted, however, that so far, most published studies on *yoga nidra* are confounded by a lack of empirical consistency (Parker et al. 2013).

## *The meditation component*

Contemplative practices – including various forms of meditation – broadly refer to practices involving sustained and non-analytic attention and/or deep consideration of an object of interest. Individual practices differ in terms of their specific techniques, but what they typically share is a disciplined process of becoming reflectively attentive to experience (Schmalzl et al. 2014) and the cultivation of a state of equanimity (Desbordes et al. 2015). Recent theoretical accounts of meditation practice have defined it as a process that develops self-awareness (awareness of one's own physical, emotional and mental states), increases self-regulation (the ability to effectively modulate one's physiological responses and behaviour) and promotes self-transcendence (a progressive and positive shift from predominantly self-focused to increasingly decentred and prosocial views of the world) (Vago and Silbersweig 2012).

Meta-cognitive awareness refers to the conscious monitoring of one's own mental processes (Teasdale 1999) and is emphasised in many meditative practices. The specific role of meta-cognitive awareness can differ depending on the style of meditation (Fox and Christoff 2014; Irrmischer et al. 2018; Lutz et al. 2016; Tomasino and Fabbro 2016). In forms of meditation practice characterised by focused attention (FA), also referred to as concentrative, closed-focus or single-point-focus meditation, it includes the activity of noticing drifts from a selected single object of attention, and subsequently redirecting attention towards it when the attention wanders. In forms of meditation practice characterised by open-monitoring attention (OM), also referred to as open-focus or mindfulness meditation, it can have the role of monitoring one's stream of thought or sensation while attempting to maintain detachment and refrain from any cognitive elaboration, analysis or judgement (Lutz et al. 2008). Some of the meditative techniques employed in yoga-based practices emphasise FA and include body-scan meditation (Mirams et al. 2013), guided imagery meditation or Transcendental Meditation (TM) (Balaji et al. 2012). If no specific meditative technique is employed, however, and there is simply a general emphasis on cultivating awareness to present-moment experience, yoga practitioners may gradually transition from a predominantly FA to a more OM approach as they progress in their practice. While practitioners may initially only be able to allocate their attention to a single element of the practice at the time, they may eventually become skilled at simultaneously monitoring movement, breath and any accompanying interoceptive and exteroceptive sensations that may arise.

Cultivation of attention to bodily sensations and sensory experience, including interoceptive, proprioceptive, kinaesthetic and spatial awareness, is another central characteristic of many meditative techniques in the context of yoga-based practices (Farb et al. 2015). Body awareness is primarily cultivated by directing attention to sensations arising from the movement and breath components of the practice, and there is increasing consensus that it is of substantial significance for health and self-regulation. Enhancing body awareness can increase one's ability to detect bodily signals of emotional states as they arise, and consequently facilitate self-regulatory responses to them (Baas et al. 2004).

Lastly, a putative general mechanism through which cultivating attention may account for psychological wellbeing across various forms of meditation practices is by decreasing mind-wandering and rumination (Brandmeyer and Delorme 2018; Hasenkamp et al. 2012; Wolkin 2015). Mind-wandering is defined as spontaneous and undirected thought processes that mostly occur unintentionally, and rumination refers to a repetitive process of dwelling upon predominantly negative thoughts and emotions that are frequently self-focused. High levels of mind-wandering have been shown to correlate with negative mood states (Killingsworth and Gilbert 2010), and high levels of rumination have been found to constitute a risk factor for the development of depression and depressive relapse (Smith and Alloy 2009). It has been reported that both mind-wandering and rumination may decrease by engaging in meditative practices that promote the ability to decentre and disentangle one's self-identification with negative thoughts (Segal et al. 2002).

Several preliminary studies have documented positive effects of meditation on cognitive and health-related functions, including attention (Jha et al. 2007), interoceptive awareness (Farb et al. 2013; Sharp et al. 2018), somatosensory processing (Kerr et al. 2013), self-regulation (Tang et al. 2014), stress (Jain et al. 2007), immune function (Infante et al. 2014), blood pressure (Bai et al. 2015), chronic pain (La Cour and Petersen 2015) and sleep (Nagendra et al. 2012).

Recent research has also focused on investigating the neural mechanisms underlying meditative practices. Neuroimaging investigations using functional magnetic resonance imaging (fMRI) (Manna et al. 2010) seem to suggest that, broadly speaking, FA predominantly engages right frontal brain areas, whereas OM predominantly engages left frontal brain areas. With respect to FA specifically, recent neuroimaging work has proposed the existence of four distinguishable phases that naturally occur during practice, and that are supported by partly independent neural networks (Hasenkamp et al. 2012). The consecutive phases include mind-wandering, the awareness that one's mind has wandered, the redirecting of attention to the chosen object of meditation and the active maintenance of sustained attention on that object. Mind-wandering engages brain regions associated with the so-called default mode network (DMN) (Raichle et al. 2001), the activation of which is increased during wakeful rest and attenuated during goal-directed behaviour. Brain areas involved in the DMN include the posterior cingulate cortex, the medial prefrontal cortex, the posterior parietal/temporal cortex and the parahippocampal gyrus. The awareness of mind-wandering engages a subdivision of the so-called salience network, which is generally associated with supporting conflict monitoring and error detection and includes the anterior insular cortex and anterior cingulate cortex. The redirecting of attention to the object of meditation engages the so-called executive network, which includes the lateral prefrontal cortex and the lateral inferior parietal cortex. Lastly, sustained attention on the object of meditation also may engage a portion of the executive network, with selective clusters in the dorsolateral prefrontal cortex. With respect to OM, neuroimaging studies have also documented activation changes in both DMN and meta-cognitive networks, which is again indicative of concomitant presence of mind-wandering as well as attentional processes (Fox and Christoff 2014). Since OM meditation does not involve selected focus on a discrete single object of meditation, however, the attentional component relies less on brain regions involved in engaging or sustaining attention. Instead, it primarily engages brain regions involved in monitoring, vigilance (Telles et al. 2017) and processing of sensations related to present-moment experience (Lutz et al., 2008), which include higher-order prefrontal regions (Fleming and Dolan, 2012), the anterior cingulate cortex and the insular cortex (Critchley 2005).

Neuroimaging studies have also shed light on the neural underpinnings of cultivating attention to bodily sensations and sensory experience in the context of meditation practices, and both structural and functional brain changes have been reported. According to a meta-analysis (Fox et al. 2014), structural brain changes associated with meditation practices have been repeatedly found in the insular cortex, primary and secondary sensorimotor cortices, and the anterior precuneus. These areas are thought to be involved in interoceptive awareness, the processing of tactile and proprioceptive sensations, and higher-order body awareness, respectively. Similarly, a meta-analysis looking at functional brain changes associated with meditation practices (Fox et al. 2016) also revealed changes in a number of regions involved in the processing of bodily signals. These include the posterior parietal cortex, the right supramarginal gyrus and, again, the insular cortex.

A further aspect of interest to neuroimaging studies is the reported reduction of rumination, and consequent enhancement of psychological wellbeing, associated with meditation practices (Wolkin 2015). It has been proposed that on a neural level this is supported by a shift away, and repeated disengagement, from DMN activity (Hasenkamp et al. 2012). Apart from mind-wandering, the DMN is also said to be involved in the construction of the autobiographical self, which involves the assessment of stimuli for their relevance to one's mentally constructed and sustained image of oneself. DMN activity change during meditative states has therefore been suggested to underlie a shift to less self-centred and more objective awareness of interoceptive as well as exteroceptive present-moment experience (Brewer et al. 2011). This theory is corroborated by studies showing that increased DMN activity is associated with negative mental health outcomes (Sheline et al. 2009). Recent research also suggests that mindfulness interventions in stressed adults can be associated with alterations in DMN coupled with reductions of the inflammatory marker interleukin-6 (Creswell et al. 2016). Moreover, it has been shown that meditation can reduce depression vulnerability, thereby reducing trait rumination and negative bias (Paul et al. 2013).

## The spiritual experience component

An interest in spirituality has been a quantifiable reason why some yoga and meditation practitioners have reported adopting a yoga practice (Park et al. 2015; Quilty et al. 2013).

Specific experiences have often been reported and described by adherents of religious and contemplative practices which can be conceptualised as directly affecting spirituality. Cross-tradition explorations have described this experience generally as a transcendent immersive unitive state, in which the universe is experienced all at once in a complete state of oneness with no sense of duality (Wahbeh et al. 2018). Other descriptions include a noetic quality in which one appears to appreciate the ultimate truth of reality, a positive mood state typically involving peace, serenity, joy and ecstasy, a sense of timelessness, as well as a sense of the holy, sacred or divine. A common consequence of these profound types of experiences is a psychological transformation of the individual, in which one's sense of life purpose and meaning have been permanently changed in a positive direction. Long-term practitioners of yoga and meditation will use phrases such as 'yoga changed my life' to describe this transformation (Ross et al. 2014).

From a biomedical perspective, there is evidence that these experiences are likely a consequence of the activation of specific brain regions (Newberg 2014). Support for this comes from recent research conducted on hallucinogenic agents, which can generate these experiences in most individuals (Barrett and Griffiths 2018). Historically, it has been suggested that the prevalence of psychedelic experiences in the 1960s counter-culture may have been related to the increased interest in contemplative practices such as yoga (Richert and DeCloedt 2018).

Studies of meditators and yoga practitioners have reported increases in experiences consistent with unitive transcendent states as well as overall spirituality. These have often used outcome measures designed to capture detailed accounts of mystical experiences, transcendence and spirituality (MacDonald and Friedman 2009), and yoga practitioners have been found to score highly on these measures (Fiori et al. 2014). A systematic review (Wahbeh et al. 2018) identified twenty-five studies related to transcendence over a wide variety of contemplative practices and investigative techniques including neuroimaging, psychophysiological measurements and qualitative accounts. The review concluded that 'transcendence most commonly describes an experience associated with deeper stages of meditation and across traditions' (Wahbeh et al. 2018: 33).

Some studies have shown that duration and intensity of yoga practice are positively correlated with the experience of this unitive state and its positive consequences. A study of yoga practitioners in an ashram community setting undergoing regular practice as part of a yoga lifestyle showed that higher percentages of practitioners reported experiences of oneness (83%) and being in touch with the divine or spiritual (91%) than did a control group of non-practitioners (40% and 43%, respectively) (Wilson and Spencer 1990).

There is also evidence that transcendent experiential characteristics are directly correlated with both intensity and duration of practice. An internet survey study of older female yoga practitioners showed statistically significant correlations between transcendence (as measured by the transcendence subscale of the WHO Subjective Well-Being Inventory) and three self-reported yoga practice measures (current hours per week, total lifetime hours and total calendar years) (Moliver et al. 2013). These data suggest that longer duration of practice is more likely to yield transcendent experiences, as one would expect with mastery of practice increasing over time. Another recent internet survey of yoga practitioners divided them into three categories of marginal, moderate and high levels of involvement with yoga practice (Gaiswinkler and Unterrainer 2016). Scores on the Multidimensional Inventory for Religious/Spiritual Well-Being measure showed a statistically significant relationship to yoga practice intensity, with high levels of involvement having the highest scores. Scores on subscales of this questionnaire assessing connectedness, immanent hope, transcendent hope and experiences of sense and meaning showed a similar trend with the level of yoga involvement.

While one would expect that transcendent experiences and spirituality are more likely to occur over a longer time frame, there are studies suggesting that these changes can take place over a short period as well. A recent controlled study of a four-week yoga intervention showed statistically significant increases in transpersonal characteristics in the yoga group (Gobec and Travis 2018). The flow state, as measured with the Dispositional Flow Scale, before and after only six weeks of yoga in young adult musicians showed significant increases as compared with controls (Butzer et al. 2016). The Autotelic Experience subscale of this questionnaire, which is a direct measure of the transcendent experience, also showed statistically significant negative correlations with music performance anxiety, suggesting the possibility that yoga is facilitating flow by inhibiting the interference from compromising mood states. Another yoga study showed that yoga practitioners, non-practitioners and metabolic syndrome patients all showed increases in the flow state following yoga practices lasting less than one hour, with the yoga practitioners showing the greatest increase and highest scores (Tyagi et al. 2016).

Although this field of inquiry has very little biomedical research at present, it represents an important area of investigation into the deeper benefits of yoga practices. Yoga practice, especially over the long term and with a meditative component, likely leads to significant improvements in important quality of life measures, including spiritual wellbeing, transcendence, flow, and life meaning and purpose (Sullivan et al. 2017). These qualities are viewed as inherently valuable and desirable and are becoming increasingly more important in both modern medicine and in society as a whole.

## Yoga practice as a whole

The model in Figure 30.1 depicts the major areas by which yoga practices impact psychophysiological states and ultimately modify experience and behaviour. In line with the previous sections of this chapter, the top box defines yoga as a multicomponent practice that includes postures/movement sequences, breathing techniques, deep relaxation practices and meditation – and that leads to the skills and attributes listed in the boxes below. Physical and respiratory components of yoga practice improve physical functioning, including flexibility, strength, endurance and balance, as well as respiratory function, which ultimately leads to improved physical self-efficacy. Through the meditative component in particular, practitioners enhance their ability to regulate and sustain attention on both physical (sensations) and mental (thoughts and emotions) events. This leads to enhanced mind–body awareness which includes mindfulness, concentration and cognitive functioning, as well as self and social awareness. Self-regulation, especially when it comes to stress responses and emotion regulation, is likely impacted by all components of yoga practice. Increased self-regulation in turn leads to improved resilience, stress tolerance, equanimity and, ultimately, psychological self-efficacy. Lastly, a sustained regular yoga practice together with living a lifestyle based on yogic principles can impact an individual's spirituality, promote feelings of unity and transcendence, and enhance a sense of meaning and purpose. The arrows between the boxes indicate that the aspects described in the three boxes are all mechanistically linked. Together, all of the listed skills and attributes work together synergistically to improve a multitude of behaviours, mental states and health-related aspects that are all depicted in the bottom box. In sum, the model outlines how yoga ultimately works in a global and holistic manner to improve human functioning on multiple levels and domains.

Yoga-based practices have been documented to affect a series of physiological parameters that impact physical health, including stress hormones, inflammatory markers and cardiovascular indices. It has been suggested that yoga can reduce cortisol levels more than common exercise (Rocha et al. 2012), that reductions in cortisol may be evident even after just a single yoga session (Kamei et al. 2000) and that both movement-focused and breath-focused yoga practices can reduce cortisol levels alike (Schmalzl et al. 2018). Yoga practice has also been found

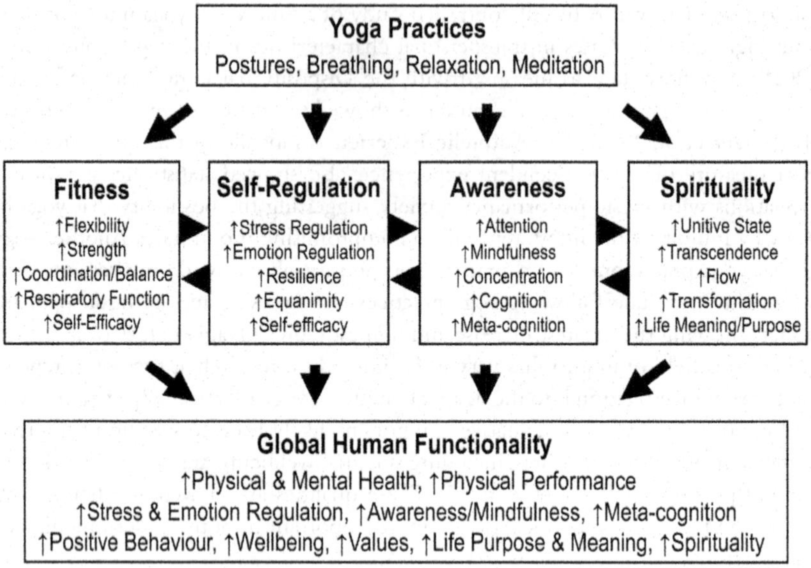


*Figure 30.1* A logic model describing the main aspects by which yoga practices develop behavioural skills, change psychophysiological state and modify behaviour and experience.

to increase levels of y-aminobutyric acid (GABA), an inhibitory neurotransmitter that tends to be reduced in several clinical conditions, including epilepsy (Streeter et al. 2012). Lastly, yoga can elicit measurable changes in several cardiovascular indices, including total peripheral resistance (TPR), arterial compliance (CWK), stroke volume (SV) and cardiac output (CO) (Parshad et al. 2011), as well as HRV (Papp et al. 2013), which is one of the primary indicators of balanced nervous system activity.

## *Body awareness and mindfulness*

As mentioned earlier, body awareness is a multidimensional construct that entails a combination of proprioceptive and interoceptive awareness (Mehling et al. 2012). Early studies of yoga-based practices have documented increases in self-reported body awareness following a three-month programme (Rani and Rao 1994). More recently it has been reported that self-reported levels of body awareness in advanced yoga practitioners seem to be related to the character trait of self-transcendence (reflecting an individual's inclination to perceive a strong connection between themselves and all other forms of life) (David et al., 2014). An elegant study employing both sensory testing and neuroimaging techniques showed that advanced yoga practitioners exhibited increased pain tolerance compared to controls with no yoga experience, and that this increase was correlated with structural brain differences in brain regions supporting body awareness, including the insular cortex, the cingulate cortex and parietal areas (Villemure et al. 2014). Similarly, a recent neuroimaging study found a positive correlation between trait mindfulness and pain tolerance, which was in turn associated with greater deactivation of the posterior cingulate cortex, which is known to be involved in the affective appraisal of stimuli (Zeidan et al. 2018). Mindfulness and self-compassion have also been shown to increase with yoga-based practices. For example, a study evaluating the effects of a residential yoga programme on quality of life found that attendees exhibited reduced perceived stress, which was statistically demonstrated to be mediated by increased levels of mindfulness and self-compassion (Gard et al. 2012). The authors proposed that this finding indicates that yoga and mindfulness-based interventions share underlying mechanisms. Another study found that the amount of yoga practice implemented in a mindfulness-based stress reduction (MBSR) programme which also included sitting meditation and body scan was significantly correlated with increases in mindfulness (Carmody and Baer 2008). The view that yoga increases mindfulness is further corroborated by additional investigations with novices (Bowden et al. 2012), advanced yoga practitioners (Brisbon and Lowery 2011) and yoga teacher trainees (Büssing et al. 2012).

### *Self-regulation*

Improvements in stress and emotion regulation are a hallmark of the effects of yoga-based practices (Li and Goldsmith 2012; Riley and Park 2015; Sharma 2014). The idea that yoga as a multicomponent practice enhances self-regulation is not surprising given that both meditation and breathing practices alone can improve stress regulation and impact autonomic functioning. Early studies documented positive effects of yoga programmes on self-reported levels of subjective wellbeing (Sell and Nagpal 1992), as well as vitality (e.g. perceived levels of alertness, sleepiness, enthusiasm, sluggishness, calmness, nervousness, etc.) (Wood 1993). More recent studies found self-reported levels of stress to decrease in individuals participating in residential programmes involving daily yoga classes and didactic coursework focusing on the integration of yoga practices into daily life activities (Gard et al. 2012). Lastly, reduced levels of self-reported stress have also been reported in military populations participating in yoga programmes, which is of particular significance given the high levels of stress that these individuals are exposed to on a daily basis (Rocha et al. 2012).

### *Cognitive functioning*

A growing body of research has investigated the effects of yoga-based practices on cognition, including attention, memory and executive functioning. In terms of visual attention, studies have reported measurable improvements in the ability to detect subtle changes in visual stimuli (Telles et al. 1995) as well as colour discrimination (Narayana 2009). A recent study investigating the differential effect of movement-focused and breath-focused yoga practices suggested that only the breath-focused practice yielded specific improvements in visual sustained attention and response inhibition (Schmalzl et al. 2018). With respect to memory, improvements have been documented for short-term and long-term memory (Rocha et al. 2012), as well as working memory (Gothe et al. 2013). In relation to executive functioning, yoga has been suggested to positively impact problem-solving ability (Manjunath and Telles 2001), and potentially to promote neuroplastic changes in neural systems that support executive functioning (Froeliger et al. 2012a; Hernandez et al. 2018). It has also been documented that yoga practitioners more efficiently activate cognitive control brain networks in the presence of emotionally salient stimuli (Froeliger et al. 2012b). Lastly, it has been reported that, compared to controls, experienced yoga and meditation practitioners exhibit less age-related decline in fluid intelligence (a set of abilities involved in coping with novel environments and abstract reasoning) (Gard et al. 2014b).

## Limitations of current research on yoga-based practices

From the previous sections of this chapter it is clear that yoga research has witnessed strong growth during recent decades (Jeter et al. 2015). That being said, it is important to draw awareness to the fact that some of the currently published research studies on yoga-based practices have methodological limitations that undermine our ability to make conclusive claims about their findings.

Some common weaknesses in the literature include the use of self-selected populations and, often, inappropriate control groups. Many of the currently published studies have been conducted on either advanced practitioners (David et al. 2014; Villemure et al. 2014) or individuals participating in residential yoga programmes (Gard et al. 2012; Telles et al. 1995), whereas control groups often consist of individuals with no yoga experience. It can therefore not be precluded that some of the observed physiological or behavioural differences may therefore be driven by pre-existing characteristics of individuals who are naturally inclined to practise yoga (Gard et al. 2014b). In addition, several studies did not have an active control group, which prevents the evaluation of comparative effectiveness of yoga compared to other interventions (Fiori et al. 2014; Froeliger et al. 2012a).

Another limitation is that many of the studies evaluating the effect of yoga-based practices on stress and emotional states are exclusively based on self-report measures (Malathi et al. 2000; Wood 1993). This is problematic in the context of contemplative practices in particular, as an individual's perception and judgement of their own coping mechanisms can actually change as a result of the practices themselves. In addition, there is a danger of biased responses towards expecting, believing and reporting beneficial effects, due to common beliefs about the positive impact of yoga on one's overall wellbeing (Grossman 2008). Future research employing complementary assessment of behavioural, physiological, neural and cognitive changes is highly desirable.

Additionally, in many of the currently published research studies the protocols of the yoga interventions are not described with the necessary detail to allow experimental replication. (Narayana 2009; Rani and Rao 1994). Given the multifaceted nature of yoga-based practices, it will be of particular importance for future research to improve in this aspect. Only carefully designed studies with detailed intervention protocols will allow researchers to further deconstruct the role of the individual component parts and elucidate whether their effect is cumulative or synergistic in nature (Payne and Crane-Godreau 2013).

Finally, there is continued need for further studies outlining specific mechanistic hypotheses about the physiological and neural processes underlying the reported effects of yoga-based practices. While some recently published theoretical frameworks are an encouraging step forward (Gard et al. 2014a; Schmalzl et al. 2015; Sullivan et al. 2018), many of the proposed mechanistic hypotheses refer to general mechanisms known to underlie the effect of mindfulness-based practices (Froeliger et al. 2012b; Gard et al. 2012; Villemure et al. 2014). Further research testing the hypothesised interaction between bottom-up physiological and top-down cognitive processes will be of particular relevance, and will require multidisciplinary studies across the domains of physiology, neuroscience and psychology.

Prior to this body of published research, it was not possible for yoga instructors and therapists to justify and convey the benefits of yoga practice for mainstream society and in a biomedical context. In general, yoga instructors and therapists are highly appreciative of this new biomedical research information. It provides greater credibility for yoga's benefits and allows for a professional presentation of yoga's effects and mechanisms; we are seeing an increasing implementation of psychophysiological research literacy in yoga teacher and yoga therapist training programmes and schools (e.g. Khalsa et al. 2016).

## Acknowledgement

The content of this chapter is largely based on Chapter 4 of the textbook *The Principles and Practice of Yoga in Health Care*, entitled 'Research on the Psychophysiology of Yoga' (Schmalzl et al. 2016).

## Bibliography

Alexander, G. 1985. *Eutony: The Holistic Discovery of the Total Person.* Great Neck, NY, USA: Felix Morrow.

Alexander, G. E. 1994. 'Basal Ganglia–Thalamocortical Circuits: Their Role in Control of Movements'. *Journal of Clinical Neurophsysiology* 11: 420–431.

Arsalidou, M., et al. 2013. 'The Centre of the Brain: Topographical Model of Motor, Cognitive, Affective, and Somatosensory Functions of the Basal Ganglia'. *Human Brain Mapping* 34: 3031–3054.

Baas, L. S., et al. 2004. 'An Exploratory Study of Body Awareness in Persons with Heart Failure Treated Medically or with Transplantation'. *Journal of Cardiovascular Nursing* 19: 32–40.

Bai, Z., et al. 2015. 'Investigating the Effect of Transcendental Meditation on Blood Pressure: A Systematic Review and Meta-analysis'. *Journal of Human Hypertension*, 29(11): 653–62.

Balaji, P. A., et al. 2012. 'Physiological Effects of Yogic Practices and Transcendental Meditation in Health and Disease'. *North American Journal of Medical Sciences* 4: 442–448.

Barrett, F. S. and Griffiths, R. R. 2018. 'Classic Hallucinogens and Mystical Experiences: Phenomenology and Neural Correlates'. *Current Topics in Behavioral Neuroscience* 36: 393–430.

Beauchaine, T. 2001. 'Vagal Tone, Development, and Gray's Motivational Theory: Toward an Integrated Model of Autonomic Nervous System Functioning in Psychopathology'. *Development and Psychopathology* 13: 183–214.

Bernardi, L., et al. 2001. 'Slow Breathing Reduces Chemoreflex Response to Hypoxia and Hypercapnia, and Increases Baroreflex Sensitivity'. *Journal of Hypertension* 19: 2221–2229.

Berrueta, L., et al. 2016. 'Stretching Impacts Inflammation Resolution in Connective Tissue'. *Journal of Cellular Physiology* 231: 1621–1627.

Berthoud, H. R. and Neuhuber, W. L. 2000. 'Functional and Chemical Anatomy of the Afferent Vagal System'. *Autonomic Neuroscience* 85: 1–17.

Beutler, E., et al. 2016. 'Effect of Regular Yoga Practice on Respiratory Regulation and Exercise Performance'. *PLoS One* 11: e0153159.

Bohns, V. K. and Wiltermuth, S. S. 2012. 'It Hurts When I Do This (or You Do That): Posture and Pain Tolerance'. *Journal of Experimental Social Psychology* 48: 341–345.

Boiten, F. A., et al. 1994. 'Emotions and Respiratory Patterns: Review and Critical Analysis'. *International Journal of Psychophysiology* 17: 103–128.

Bowden, D., et al. 2012. 'A Comparative Randomised Controlled Trial of The Effects of Brain Wave Vibration Training, Iyengar Yoga, and Mindfulness on Mood, Well-Being, and Salivary Cortisol'. *Journal of Evidence Based Complementary and Alternative Medicine* Article ID: 234713.

Brandmeyer, T. and Delorme, A. 2018. 'Reduced Mind Wandering in Experienced Meditators and Associated EEG Correlates'. *Experimental Brain Research* 236: 2519–2528.

Brewer, J. A., et al. 2011. 'Meditation Experience is Associated with Differences in Default Mode Network Activity and Connectivity'. *Proceedings of the National Academy of Sciences of the United States of America,* 108: 20254–20259.

Brisbon, N. M. and Lowery, G. A. 2011. 'Mindfulness and Levels of Stress: A Comparison of Beginner and Advanced Hatha Yoga Practitioners'. *Journal of Religion and Health* 50: 931–941.

Brown, R. P. and Gerbarg, P. L. 2005. 'Sudarshan Kriya Yogic Breathing in the Treatment of Stress, Anxiety and Depression: Part I - Neurophysioloigc Model'. *The Journal of Alternative and Complementary Medicine* 11: 189–201.

Büssing, A., et al. 2012. 'Development of Specific Aspects of Spirituality During a 6-month Intensive Yoga Practice'. *Journal of Evidence Based Complementary and Alternative Medicine,* Article ID: 981523.

Butzer, B., et al. 2016. 'Yoga Enhances Positive Psychological States in Young Adult Musicians'. *Applied Psychophysiology and Biofeedback* 41: 191–202.

Calabrese, P., et al. 2000. 'Cardiorespiratory Interactions during Resistive Load Breathing'. *American Journal of Physiology - Regulatory, Integrative and Comparative Physiology* 279: 2208–2213.

Carmody, J. and Baer, R. A. 2008. 'Relationships between Mindfulness Practice and Levels of Mindfulness, Medical and Psychological Symptoms and Well-being in a Mindfulness-based Stress Reduction Program'. *Journal of Behavioral Medicine* 31: 23–33.

Carney, D. R., et al. 2010. 'Power Posing: Brief Nonverbal Displays affect Neuroendocrine Levels and Risk Tolerance'. *Psychological Science* 21: 1363–1368.

Clarke, T. C., et al. 2018. 'Use of Yoga, Meditation, and Chiropractors Among US Adults Aged 18 and Over'. *NCHS Data Brief* 325: 1–8.

Creswell, J. D., et al. 2016. 'Alterations in Resting-state Functional Connectivity link Mindfulness Meditation with Reduced Interleukin-6: A Randomized Controlled Trial'. *Biological Psychiatry* 80: 53–61.

Critchley, H. D. 2005. 'Neural Mechanisms of Autonomic, Affective, and Cognitive Integration'. *Journal of Comparative Neurology* 493: 154–166.

Critchley, H. D., et al. 2015. 'Slow Breathing and Hypoxic Challenge: Cardiorespiratory Consequences and their Central Neural Substrates'. *PLoS One* 10: e0127082.

David, N., et al. 2014. 'Susceptibility to the Rubber Hand Illusion does not tell the Whole Body-awareness Story'. *Cognitive, Affective and Behavioral Neuroscience* 14: 297–306.

Desbordes, G., et al. 2015. 'Moving beyond Mindfulness: Defining Equanimity as an Outcome Measure in Meditation and Contemplative Research'. *Mindfulness* 6: 356–372.

Dinesh, T., et al. 2015. 'Comparative Effect of 12 Weeks of Slow and Fast Pranayama Training on Pulmonary Function in Young, Healthy Volunteers: A Randomized Controlled Trial'. *International Journal of Yoga* 8: 22–26.

Eastman-Mueller, H. et al. 2013. 'iRest Yoga-nidra on the College Campus: Changes in Stress, Depression, Worry, and Mindfulness'. *International Journal of Yoga Therapy* 23: 15–24.

Esposito, P., et al. 2015. 'Trained Breathing-induced Oxygenation Acutely Reverses Cardiovascular Autonomic Dysfunction in Patients with Type 2 Diabetes and Renal Disease'. *Acta Diabetologica* 53(2); 217–26.

Farb, N.A. S., et al. 2013. 'Mindfulness Meditation Training alters Cortical Representations of Interoceptive Attention'. *Social Cognitive and Affective Neuroscience* 8: 15–26.

Farb, N., et al. 2015. 'Interoception, Contemplative Practice, and Health'. *Frontiers in Psychology* 6: 763.

Fiori, F., et al. 2014. 'Processing of Proprioceptive and Vestibular Body Signals and Self-transcendence in Ashtanga Yoga Practitioners'. *Frontiers in Human Neuroscience* 8: 734.

Fleming, S. M. and Dolan, R. J. 2012. 'The Neural Basis of Metacognitive Ability'. *Philosophical Transactions of the Royal Society of London* 367: 1338–1349.

Fox, K. C., et al. 2014. 'Is Meditation Associated with Altered Brain Structure? A Systematic Review and Meta-analysis of Morphometric Neuroimaging in Meditation Practitioners'. *Neuroscience and Biobehavioral Reviews* 43: 48–73.

Fox, K. C. R. and Christoff, K. 2014. 'Metacognitive Facilitation of Spontaneous Thought Processes: When Metacognition helps the Wandering Mind find Its Way', in Fleming, S. M. and Frith, C. (eds), *The Cognitive Neuroscience of Metacognition*, 293–319. Berlin, Germany: Springer.

Fox, K. C. R., et al. 2016. 'Functional Neuroanatomy of Meditation: A Review and Meta-analysis of 78 Functional Neuroimaging Investigations'. *Neuroscience and Biobehavioral Reviews* 65: 208–228.

Froeliger, B. E., et al. 2012a. 'Yoga Meditation Practitioners Exhibit Greater Gray Matter Volume and Fewer Reported Cognitive Failures: Results of a Preliminary Voxel-based Morphometric Analysis'. *Journal of Evidence Based Complementary and Alternative Medicine* 2012: 821307.

Froeliger, B. E., et al. 2012b. 'Neurocognitive Correlates of the Effects of Yoga Meditation Practice on Emotion and Cognition: A Pilot Study'. *Frontiers in Integrative Neuroscience* 6: 48.

Gaiswinkler, L. and Unterrainer, H. F. 2016. 'The Relationship between Yoga Involvement, Mindfulness and Psychological Well-being'. *Complementary Therapies in Medicine* 26: 123–127.

Gard, T., et al. 2012. 'Effects of a Yoga-based Intervention for Young Adults on Quality of Life and Perceived Stress: The Potential Mediating Roles of Mindfulness and Self-compassion'. *The Journal of Positive Psychology* 7: 165–175.

Gard, T., et al. 2014a. 'Potential Self-Regulatory Mechanisms of Yoga for Psychological Health'. *Frontiers in Human Neuroscience* 8: 770.

Gard, T., et al. 2014b. 'Fluid Intelligence and Brain Functional Organization in Aging Yoga and Meditation Practitioners'. *Frontiers in Aging Neuroscience* 6: 76.

Gard, T., et al. 2015. 'Greater Widespread Functional Connectivity of the Caudate in Older Adults who Practice Kripalu Yoga and Vipassana Meditation than in Controls'. *Frontiers in Human Neuroscience* 9: 137.

Gobec, S. and Travis, F. 2018. 'Effects of Maharishi Yoga Asanas on Mood States, Happiness, and Experiences during Meditation'. *International Journal of Yoga* 11: 66–71.
Gothe, N., et al. 2013. 'The Acute Effects of Yoga on Executive Function'. *Journal of Physical Activity and Health* 10: 488–495.
Grossman, P. 2008. 'On Measuring Mindfulness in Psychosomatic and Psychological Research'. *Journal of Psychosomatic Research* 64: 405–408.
Gupta, S. S. and Sawane, M. V. 2012. 'A Comparative Study of the Effects of Yoga and Swimming on Pulmonary Functions in Sedentary Subjects'. *International Journal of Yoga* 5: 128–133.
Hagins, M., et al. 2007. 'Does Practicing Hatha Yoga Satisfy Recommendations for Intensity of Physical Activity which Improves and Maintains Health and Cardiovascular Fitness?' *BMC Complementary and Alternative Medicine* 7: 40.
Hasenkamp, W., et al. 2012. 'Mind Wandering and Attention during Focused Meditation: A Fine-grained Temporal Analysis of Fluctuating Cognitive States'. *NeuroImage* 59: 750–760.
Henje Blom, E., et al. 2014. 'Adolescent Girls with Emotional Disorders have a Lower End-tidal $CO_2$ and Increased Respiratory Rate Compared with Healthy Controls'. *Psychophysiology* 51: 412–418.
Hernandez, S. E., et al. 2018. 'Gray Matter and Functional Connectivity in Anterior Cingulate Cortex are Associated with the State of Mental Silence during Sahaja Yoga Meditation'. *Neuroscience* 371: 395–406.
Infante, J. R., et al. 2014. 'Levels of Immune Cells in Transcendental Meditation Practitioners'. *International Journal of Yoga* 7: 147–151.
Irrmischer, M., et al. 2018. 'Controlling the Temporal Structure of Brain Oscillations by Focused Attention Meditation'. *Human Brain Mapping* 39: 1825–1838.
Jain, S., et al. 2007. 'A Randomized Controlled Trial of Mindfulness Meditation versus Relaxation Training: Effects on Distress, Positive States of Mind, Rumination, and Distraction'. *Annals of Behavioral Medicine* 33: 11–21.
Jeter, P., et al. 2015. 'Yoga as a Therapeutic Intervention: A Bibliometric Analysis of Published Research Studies from 1967 to 2013'. *Journal of Alternative and Complementary Medicine* 21: 586–592.
Jha, A. P., et al. 2007. 'Mindfulness Training Modifies Subsystems of Attention'. *Cognitive, Affective, and Behavioral Neuroscience* 7: 109–119.
Kamei, T., et al. 2000. 'Decrease in Serum Cortisol during Yoga Exercise is Correlated with Alpha Wave Activation'. *Perceptual and Motor Skills* 90: 1027–1032.
Kerr, C. E., et al. 2013. 'Mindfulness Starts with the Body: Somatosensory Attention and Top-down Modulation of Cortical Alpha Rhythms in Mindfulness Meditation'. *Frontiers in Human Neuroscience* 7: 12.
Khalsa, S. B., et al. (eds) 2016. *Principles and Practice of Yoga in Health Care.* East Lothian, UK: Handspring Publishing.
Killingsworth, M. A. and Gilbert, D. T. 2010. 'A Wandering Mind is an Unhappy Mind'. *Science* 330: 932.
Kjaer, T. W., et al. 2002. 'Increased Dopmanine Tone during Meditation-induced Change of Consciousness'. *Cognitive Brain Research* 13: 255–259.
Klainin-Yobas, P., et al. 2015. 'Effects of Relaxation Interventions on Depression and Anxiety among Older Adults: A Systematic Review'. *Aging and Mental Health* 19(12): 1–13.
Kumar, K. and Joshi, B. 2009. 'Study on the Effect of Pranakarshan Pranayama and Yoga Nidra on Alpha EEG and GSR'. *Indian Journal of Traditional Knowledge* 8: 453–454.
La Cour, P. and Petersen, M. 2015. 'Effects of Mindfulness Meditation on Chronic Pain: A Randomized Controlled Trial'. *Pain Medicine* 16: 641–652.
Laffey, J. G. and Kavanagh, B. P. 2002. 'Hypocapnia'. *The New England Journal of Medicine* 347: 43–53.
Langevin, H. M., et al. 2013. 'Cellular Control of Connective Tissue Matrix Tension'. *Journal of Cellular Biochemistry* 114: 1714–1719.
Li, A. W. and Goldsmith, C. A. 2012. 'The Effects of Yoga on Anxiety and Stress'. *Alternative Medicine Review* 17: 21–35.
Lou, H. C., et al. 1990. 'A 150-H20 PET Study of Meditation and the Resting State of Normal Consciousness'. *Human Brain Mapping* 7: 98–105.
Lutz, A., et al. 2008. 'Attention Regulation and Monitoring in Meditation'. *Trends in Cognitive Sciences* 12: 163–169.
Lutz, J., et al. 2016. 'Altered Processing of Self-related Emotional Stimuli in Mindfulness Meditators'. *NeuroImage* 124: 958–967.
MacDonald, D. A. and Friedman, H. L. 2009. 'Measures of Spiritual and Transpersonal Constructs for use in Yoga Research'. *International Journal of Yoga* 2: 2–12.

McGuigan, F. J. and Lehrer, P. M. 2007. 'Progressive Relaxation: Origins, Principles, and Clinical Applications', in Lehrer, P. M., Woolfolk, L. and Sime, W. E. (eds), *Principles and Practice of Stress Management*, 57–87. New York: Guilford Press.

McHaffie, J. G., et al. 2005. 'Subcortical Loops through the Basal Ganglia'. *Trends in Neurosciences* 28: 401–407.

Malathi, A., et al. 2000. 'Effect of Yogic Practices on Subjective Well Being'. *Indian Journal of Physiology and Pharmacology* 44: 202–206.

Manjunath, N. K. and Telles, S. 2001. 'Improved Performance in the Tower of London Test following Yoga'. *Indian Journal of Physiology and Pharmacology* 45: 351–354.

Manna, A., et al. 2010. 'Neural Correlates of Focused Attention and Cognitive Monitoring in Meditation'. *Brain Research Bulletin* 82: 46–56.

Manzoni, G. M., et al. 2008. 'Relaxation Training for Anxiety: A Ten-years Systematic Review with Meta-analysis'. *BMC Psychiatry* 8: 41.

Mehling, W. E., et al. 2012. 'The Multidimensional Assessment of Interoceptive Awareness (MAIA)'. *PLoS One* 7: e48230.

Miller, R. 2005. *Yoga Nidra: The Meditative Heart of Yoga*. Boulder, CO, USA: Sounds True.

Mirams, L., et al. 2013. 'Brief Body-scan Meditation Practice Improves Somatosensory Perceptual Decision Making'. *Consciousness and Cognition* 22: 348–359.

Moliver, N., et al. 2013. 'Yoga Experience as a Predictor of Psychological Wellness in Women over 45 Years'. *International Journa of Yoga* 6: 11–19.

Nagendra, R. P., et al. 2012. 'Meditation and its Regulatory Role on Sleep'. *Frontiers in Neurology* 3: 54.

Narayana, N. V. V. S. 2009. 'The Effect of Yoga on Visual Reaction Time'. *Indian Journal of Social Science Research* 6: 63–70.

Newberg, A. B. 2014. 'The Neuroscientific Study of Spiritual Practices'. *Frontiers in Psychology* 5: 215.

Nivethitha, L., et al. 2016. 'Effects of Various Pranayama on Cardiovascular and Autonomic Variables'. *Ancient Science of Life* 36: 72–77.

Nivethitha, L., et al. 2017. 'Heart Rate Variability Changes During and After the Practice of Bhramari Pranayama'. *International Journal of Yoga* 10: 99–102.

Omkar, S. N., et al. 2011. 'A Mathematical Model of Effects on Specific Joints during Practice of the Sun Salutation – A Sequence of Yoga Postures'. *Journal of Bodywork and Movement Therapy* 15: 201–208.

Pal, G. K., et al. 2014. 'The Effects of Short-term Relaxation Therapy on Indices of Heart Rate Variability and Blood Pressure in Young Adults'. *American Journal of Health Promotion* 29: 23–28.

Papp, M. E., et al. 2013. 'Increased Heart Rate Variability but no Effect on Blood Pressure from 8 Weeks of Hatha Yoga – A Pilot Study'. *BMC Research Notes* 6: 59.

Park, C. L., et al. 2015. 'Who Practices Yoga? A Systematic Review of Demographic, Health-related, and Psychosocial Factors Associated with Yoga Practice'. *Journal of Behavioral Medicine* 38: 460–71.

Parker, S., et al. 2013. 'Defining Yoga-nidra: Traditional Accounts, Physiological Research, and Future Directions'. *International Journal of Yoga Therapy* 23: 11–16.

Parshad, O., et al. 2011. 'Impact of Yoga on Haemodynamic Function in Healthy Medical Students'. *West Indian Medical Journal* 60: 148–152.

Paul, N. A., et al. 2013. 'Psychological and Neural Mechanisms of Trait Mindfulness in Reducing Depression Vulnerability'. *Social Cognitive and Affective Neuroscience* 8: 56–64.

Payne, P. and Crane-Godreau, M. A. 2013. 'Meditative Movement for Depression and Anxiety'. *Frontiers in Psychiatry* 4: 71.

Porges, S. W. 1995. 'Orienting in a Defensive World: Mammalian Modification of our Evolutionary Heritage. A Polyvagal Theory'. *Psychophysiology* 32: 301–318.

Porges, S. W. 2001. 'The Polyvagal Theory: Phylogenetic Substrates of a Social Nervous System'. *International Journal of Psychophysiology* 42: 123–146.

Quilty, M. T., et al. 2013. 'Yoga in the Real World: Perceptions, Motivators, Barriers, and Patterns of Use'. *Global Advances in Health and Medicine* 2: 44–49.

Raghuraj, P. and Telles, S. 2008. 'Immediate Effect of Specific Nostril Manipulating Yoga Breathing Practices on Autonomic and Respiratory Variables'. *Applied Psychophysiology and Biofeedback* 33: 65–75.

Raichle, M. E., et al. 2001. 'A Default Mode of Brain Function'. *Proceedings of the National Academy of Sciences of the United States of America* 98: 676–682.

Rani, N. J. and Rao, P. V. K. 1994. 'Body Awareness and Yoga Training'. *Perceptual and Motor Skills* 79: 1103–1106.

Ray, U. S., et al. 2011. 'Hatha Yoga Practices: Energy Expenditure, Respiratory Changes and Intensity Of Exercise'. *Journal of Evidence Based Complementary and Alternative Medicine* Article ID: 241294. https://doi.org/10.1093/ecam/neq046.

Richert, L. and DeCloedt, M. 2018. 'Supple Bodies, Healthy Minds: Yoga, Psychedelics and American Mental Health'. *Medical Humanities* 44(3): 193–200.

Riley, K. E. and Park, C. L. 2015. 'How Does Yoga Reduce Stress? A Systematic Review of Mechanisms of Change and Guide to Future Inquiry'. *Health Psychology Review* 1–30.

Riskind, J. H. and Gotay, C. C. 1982. 'Physical Posture: Could it have Regulatory or Feedback Effects on Motivation and Emotion?' *Motivation and Emotion* 6: 273–298.

Ritter, S., et al. 1992. *Neuroanatomy and Physiology of Abdominal Vagal Afferents.* Boca Raton, FL, USA: CRC.

Rocha, K. K., et al. 2012. 'Improvement in Physiological and Psychological Parameters after 6 Months of Yoga Practice'. *Consciousness and Cognition* 21: 843–850.

Ross, A., et al. 2014. '"I am a Nice Person When I Do Yoga!!!" A Qualitative Analysis of How Yoga Affects Relationships'. *Journal of Holistic Nursing* 32: 67–77.

Russo, M. A., et al. 2017. 'The Physiological Effects of Slow Breathing in the Healthy Human'. *Breathe* 13: 298–309.

Sarang, P. S. and Telles, S. 2006. 'Oxygen Consumption and Respiration During and After Two Yoga Relaxation Techniques'. *Applied Psychophysiology and Biofeedback* 31: 143–53.

Schmalzl, L., et al. 2014. 'Movement-based Embodied Contemplative Practices: Definitions and Paradigms'. *Frontiers in Human Neuroscience* 8: 205.

Schmalzl, L., et al. 2015. 'Neurophysiological and Neurocognitive Mechanisms Underlying the Effects of Yoga-based Practices: Towards a Comprehensive Theoretical Framework'. *Frontiers in Human Neuroscience* 9: 235.

Schmalzl, L., et al. 2016. 'The Psychophysiology of Yoga', in Khalsa, S. B., Cohen, L., Mccall, T. and Telles, S. (eds), *Principles and Practice of Yoga in Health Care.* East Lothian, UK: Handspring Publishing.

Schmalzl, L., et al. 2018. 'The Effect of Movement-focused and Breath-focused Yoga Practice on Stress Parameters and Sustained Attention: A Randomized Controlled Pilot Study'. *Consciousness and Cognition* 65: 109–125.

Segal, Z. J., et al. 2002. *Mindfulness-Based Cognitive Therapy for Depression: A New Approach to Preventing Relapses.* New York: Guilford Press.

Sell, H. and Nagpal, R. 1992. *Assessment of Subjective Well-Being.* New Delhi, India, World Health Organization – Regional Office for South-East Asia.

Shapiro, D. and Cline, K. 2004. 'Mood Changes Associated with Iyengar Yoga Practices: A Pilot Study'. *International Journal of Yoga Therapy,* 14: 35–44.

Sharma, H., et al. 2003. 'Sudarshan Kriya Practitioners Exhibit Better Antioxidant Status and Lower Blood Lactate Levels'. *Biological Psychology* 63: 281–291.

Sharma, M. 2014. 'Yoga as an Alternative and Complementary Approach for Stress Management: A Systematic Review'. *Journal of Evidence Based Complementary and Alternative Medicine* 19: 59–67.

Sharma, V. K., et al. 2014. 'Effect of Fast and Slow Pranayama Practice on Cognitive Functions in Healthy Volunteers'. *Journal of Clinical and Diagnostic Research* 8: 10–13.

Sharp, P. B., et al. 2018. 'Mindfulness Training Induces Structural Connectome Changes in Insula Networks'. *Scientific Reports* 8: 7929.

Sheline, Y. I., et al. 2009. 'The Default Mode Network and Self-referential Processes in Depression'. *Proceedings of the National Academy of Sciences of the United States of America* 106: 1942–1947.

Sinha, A. N., et al. 2013. 'Assessment of the Effects of Pranayama / Alternate Nostril Breathing on the Parasympathetic Nervous System in Young Adults'. *Journal of Clinical and Diagnostic Research* 7: 821–823.

Smith, J. M. and Alloy, L. B. 2009. 'A Roadmap to Rumination: A Review of the Definition, Assessment, and Conceptualization of this Multifaceted Construct'. *Clinical Psychology Review* 29: 116–128.

Sovik, R. 2000. 'The Science of Breathing – The Yogic View'. *Progress in Brain Research* 122: 491–505.

Spicuzza, L., et al. 2000. 'Yoga and Chemoreflex Response to Hypoxia and Hypercapnia'. *The Lancet* 356: 1495–1496.

Steffen, P. R., et al. 2017. 'The Impact of Resonance Frequency Breathing on Measures of Heart Rate Variability, Blood Pressure, and Mood'. *Frontiers in Public Health* 5: 222.

Streeter, C. C., et al. 2010. 'Effects of Yoga Versus Walking on Mood, Anxiety, and Brain GABA levels: A randomized controlled MRS study'. *Journal of Alternative and Complementary Medicine* 16: 1145–1152.

Streeter, C. C., et al. 2012. 'Effects of Yoga on the Autonomic Nervous System, Gamma-aminobutyric-acid, and Allostasis in Epilepsy, Depression, and Post-traumatic Stress Disorder'. *Medical Hypotheses* 78: 571–579.

Strongoli, L. M., et al. 2010. 'The Effect of Core Exercises on Transdiaphragmatic Pressure'. *Journal of Sports Science and Medicine* 9: 270–274.

Subramanya, P. and Telles, S. 2009. 'Effect of Two Yoga-Based Relaxation Techniques on Memory Scores and State Anxiety'. *Biopsychosocial Medicine* 3: 8.

Sullivan, M., et al. 2018. 'Yoga Therapy and Polyvagal Theory: The Convergence of Traditional Wisdom and Contemporary Neuroscience for Self-regulation and Resilience'. *Frontiers in Human Neuroscience* 12: 67.

Sullivan, M. B., et al. 2017. 'Toward an Explanatory Framework for Yoga Therapy Informed by Philosophical and Ethical Perspectives'. *Alternative Therapies in Health and Medicine* 24(1): 38–47.

Tang, Y. Y., et al. 2014. 'Meditation Improves Self-regulation over the Life Span'. *Annals of the New York Academy of Sciences* 1307: 104–111.

Taspinar, B., et al. 2014. 'A Comparison of the Effects of Hatha Yoga and Resistance Exercise on Mental Health and Well-being in Sedentary Adults: A Pilot Study'. *Complementary Therapies in Medicine* 22: 433–440.

Teasdale, J. D. 1999. 'Metacognition, Mindfulness and the Modification of Mood Disorders'. *Clinical Psychology and Psychotherapy* 6: 146–155.

Telles, S., et al. 1994. 'Breathing through a Particular Nostril Can Alter Metabolism and Autonomic Activities'. *Indian Journal of Physiology and Pharmacology* 38: 133–137.

Telles, S., et al. 1995. 'Improvement in Visual Perception Following Yoga Training'. *Journal of Indian Psychology* 31: 30–32.

Telles, S., et al. 2012. 'Yoga Breathing through a Particular Nostril is Associated with Contralateral Event-related Potential Changes'. *International Journal of Yoga* 5: 102–107.

Telles, S., et al. 2013. 'Changes in P300 Following Alternate Nostril Yoga Breathing and Breath Awareness'. *Biopsychosocial Medicine* 7(1): 11.

Telles, et al. 2014. 'Blood Pressure and Heart Rate Variability During Yoga-based Alternate Nostril Breathing Practice and Breath Awareness'. *Medical Science Montiro Basic Research* 20: 184–193.

Telles, S., et al. 2017. 'Alternate-nostril Yoga Breathing Reduced Blood Pressure while Increasing Performance in a Vigilance Test'. *Medical Science Monitor Basic Research* 23: 392–398.

Tomasino, B. and Fabbro, F. 2016. 'Increases in the Right Dorsolateral Prefrontal Cortex and Decreases the Rostral Prefrontal Cortex Activation after 8 Weeks of Focused Attention Based Mindfulness Meditation'. *Brain and Cognition* 102: 46–54.

Torner, L., et al. 2002. 'Increased Hypothalamic Expression of Prolactin in Lactation: Involvement in Behavioural and Neuroendocrine Stress Responses'. *European Journal of Neuroscience* 15: 1381–1389.

Tran, M. D., et al. 2001. 'Effects of Hatha Yoga Practice on the Health-related Aspects of Physical Fitness'. *Preventive Cardiology* 4: 165–170.

Tyagi, A., et al. 2016. 'Heart Rate Variability, Flow, Mood and Mental Stress During Yoga Practices in Yoga Practitioners, Non-Yoga Practitioners and People with Metabolic Syndrome'. *Applied Psychophysiology and Biofeedback* 41: 381–393.

Vago, D. R. and Silbersweig, D. A. 2012. 'Self-awareness, Self-regulation, and Self-transcendence (S-ART): A Framework for Understanding the Neurobiological Mechanisms of Mindfulness'. *Frontiers in Human Neuroscience* 6: 296.

Villemure, C., et al. 2014. 'Insular Cortex Mediates Increased Pain Tolerance in Yoga Practitioners'. *Cerebral Cortex* 24: 2732–2740.

Vinay, A. V., et al. 2016. 'Impact of Short-term Practice of Yoga on Heart Rate Variability'. *International Journal of Yoga* 9: 62–66.

Wahbeh, H., et al. 2018. 'A Systematic Review of Transcendent States across Meditation and Contemplative Traditions'. *Explore* 14(1): 19–35.

Wang, M. Y., et al. 2013. 'The Biomechanical Demands of Standing Yoga Poses in Seniors: The Yoga Empowers Seniors Study (YESS)'. *BMC Complementary and Alternative Medicine* 13: 1–11.

Wilson, S. R. and Spencer, R. C. 1990. 'Intense Personal Experiences: Subjective Effects, Interpretations, and After-effects'. *Journal of Clinical Psychology* 46(5): 565–573.

Wilson, V. E. and Peper, E. 2004. The Effects of Upright and Slumped Postures on the Recall of Positive and Negative Thoughts. *Applied Psychophysiology and Biofeedback* 29: 189–195.

Wolkin, J. R. 2015. 'Cultivating Multiple Aspects of Attention through Mindfulness Meditation Accounts for Psychological Well-being through Decreased Rumination'. *Psychology Research and Behavior Management* 8: 171–180.

Wood, C. 1993. 'Mood Change and Perceptions of Vitality: A Comparison of the Effects of Relaxation, Visualization and Yoga'. *Journal of the Royal Society of Medicine* 86: 254–258.

Zeidan, F., et al. 2018. 'Neural Mechanisms Supporting the Relationship between Dispositional Mindfulness and Pain'. *Pain* 159(12): 2477–2485. https://doi.org/10.1097/j.pain.0000000000001344.

# 31

# MEDITATION AND THE COGNITIVE SCIENCES

*Asaf Federman*

## Introduction: defining meditation for scientific analysis

Three developments have fuelled cognitive interest in meditation in the past decade. The first was the development of mindfulness-based interventions (MBI) in medicine, psychotherapy and education. This has created pressure to both explain mindfulness meditation in non-traditional ways, and to scientifically evaluate its merit. Of course, from a sociological point of view, the popularity of mindfulness must also depend on research outcomes that support its effectiveness. It is therefore better to describe a feedback loop in which cognitive research promotes MBI's popularity and that popularity encourages further research.

The second development was the successful dialogue between scientists and the Tibetan spiritual leadership. This was primarily the work of a dozen dedicated individuals who have been very successful in creating influential social and scientific structures. The fourteenth Dalai Lama is, of course, one of them. A group of scientists – including Richard Davidson and Daniel Goleman, to take two prominent examples – endeavoured to create a mutually respectful dialogue with meditation experts. Their very successful careers in neuroscience and science journalism, respectively, definitely helped to validate the dialogue and to promote a cognitive-neuroscientific outlook on meditation. One of the major institutions that arose from this dialogue was *Mind and Life*, which funds conferences, dialogues and research on meditation. The third development was of brain-imaging technologies that allowed investigation of the neural activity of meditators in more detail than had previously been possible. The nuanced images of brain functions in meditation and of experienced meditators (even when they are not practicing) are informative both to the understanding of meditation itself and to the study of the human brain in general.[1] The result of these developments is rich scientific research of meditation that, although far from being conclusive, has made huge steps forward in terms of describing and explaining what meditation is and how it works with concepts from cognitive science and clinical psychology.

During the historical process of researching meditation, the term 'meditation' has gradually become problematic. It describes very different forms of human activity, each of which on its own deserves an entire study/project in cognitive science. The scientific literature covers anything from adept Tibetan meditators who practise compassion meditation to novices who learn to focus attention on their breath. In 2007 neuroscientists Antoine Lutz and Richard Davidson, along with Buddhist scholar John Dunne, suggested a model for grouping and analysing meditation in ways that would begin to address the problem of definition and help cognitive scientists to define their subject of study. To begin with, they defined meditation as any cognitive practice that (1) produces distinctive, reproducible states that can be phenomenally reported; (2) leads to a development or changes in specific traits; and (3) includes progression in the practice from the novice to the virtuoso (Lutz, Dunne and Davidson 2007). Based on further cognitive research, they later identified two main families of practice: focused attention and open-monitoring meditation (Lutz et al. 2008). More recently they expanded this typology (without Dunne) and suggested grouping meditations into three families: attentional, constructive and deconstructive (Dahl, Lutz and Davidson 2015). As explained below, these families partially overlap with the three psychological processes that are outlined in this chapter: *attention control*, *approach* and *meta-cognition*, respectively. In all cases the explaining concepts are derived from psychology, not Asian traditions, while the *explananda* are the different types of meditation: both traditional and modern.

To briefly expand on the topic, the **attentional** family of meditation would include practices that mainly train conscious awareness, and result in a better controlled awareness. This would include both focused attention (on breath, body or mantra, to give a few examples), and open-monitoring awareness that does not have a particular object. The main cognitive process operating in this family would naturally be *attention control*. The **constructive** family of meditation would include the active cultivation of attitudes like loving-kindness and compassion. The expected result, again, would be increased compassion as a trait. The characteristic cognitive process in this case would be *approach*. The **deconstructive** family would include analytical meditation, mindfulness practices, *vipassanā* and koan practices that are assumed here to have the common purpose of exposing the reality about the dynamics of self and the world. These practices lead to liberating insight and reduced grasping, obsessions and destructive thinking patterns. In spiritual traditions these aim at counteracting or deconstructing the current view of the self and the world, and opening up the potential of transcendence. In the case of therapeutic meditation, these would include distancing from negative thinking patterns and seeing them as 'not myself'. The characteristic cognitive process in this case would be *meta-cognition*.

Critics of this mapping exercise may point out its bias towards the cognitive aspects of Buddhist meditation. This is true. Almost the entire field of research is biased towards Buddhist practices, and, more specifically, their therapeutic modern adaptations. To overcome this problem Komjathy suggests a phenomenological approach to mapping the field of practices, casting the net much wider to also include non-Buddhist practices. His sole criteria for inclusion is what he calls 'family resemblances' (Komjathy 2015: 4). His approach results in no less than twenty-four types of practices without a predetermined organising criteria. Indeed, it is more inclusive, and allows a comparison between different types of contemplative practices, including prayer, meditative reading, ecstatic dance, as well as crossed-legged sitting meditation on various objects. But as a typology, it is weak exactly because it is deliberately loose. Some practices are groups by their being 'communal', others by being 'secular', 'solitary', 'attentional', 'mantric' and so on (Komjathy 2017: 36). Note how practices in these examples are grouped by either social aspects (communal), by ideology or philosophy (secular), by cognitive function (attentional) or by object (mantric). The value of this approach is clear for mapping the entire field of contemplative practices for the social sciences, but less helpful for cognitive neuroscience. For the purpose of this chapter, the analytical and cognitive approach is more appropriate as it captures the actuality of psychological research in the past twenty years – research that is indeed focused heavily on Buddhist meditation and its modern therapeutic derivatives.

It is within that research context that the three cognitive processes of meditation emerged: *attention control*, *meta-cognition* and *approach*. As we shall see, these processes are extremely informative for describing the differences between meditation techniques, and for explaining how each practice brings about its psychological benefits. While this is certainly the case for the modern Buddhist- and Hindu-inspired therapeutic meditations, it may also become helpful for understanding the psychological aspects of traditional practices.

## Attention control

### *Transcendental Meditation: focused attention breaks the train of distracting thoughts*

Transcendental Meditation (TM) arrived in the west during the 1960s and was initially linked with the counter-culture movement and its interest in altered states of consciousness, creativity and drugs. The Beatles and other celebrities were attracted to the ashram of the Maharishi Mahesh Yogi in India, whose modern Hindu teachings aimed at the spiritual regeneration of the western world. The main vehicle was his mantra meditation – adapted from the Vedic tradition to suit modern life. The framing was initially not scientific in particular. The reformed mantra practice was said to help students to 'draw attention to those higher beings or gods living [in some other worlds]' (Harrington 2008: 211), and to experience 'pure consciousness', a blissful state that transcends the individual and is the basis of waking, dreaming and dreamless sleep. But in the early 1970s the encounter with science changed the discourse.

Herbert Benson was a Harvard physiologist studying stress (in monkeys, mainly). He was persuaded by TM practitioners in the United States to study their alleged ability to control physiological aspects linked to stress – namely blood pressure and metabolism. Teaming up with Robert Keith Wallace, who had discovered earlier that TM practitioners alter their brain activity while practicing meditation (Wallace 1970), they embarked on a research project that culminated with a bold statement: stress response can be downward-regulated, at will, by the practice of meditation. The *stress response* was an already accepted construct in physiology. It describes the natural physiological changes that occur when facing a threat, and that develop into chronic stress if prolonged. Benson's encounter with TM brought about a new construct of an opposite direction: 'the relaxation response' is the activation of reduced metabolism and increased calm. It can be deliberately activated by meditation and thus counteract the health risks that come with chronic stress.

For Benson and the scientific community this, and not TM meditation per se, was the important news. He discovered that meditators could reduce their metabolism, blood pressure and heart rate. This was the first time that the medical world fully acknowledged that meditation had scientific and therapeutic value, and that a cognitive practice has measurable influences on the body. The findings were published in the journal *Science* (Benson et al. 1971). Benson, however, did not endorse the religious philosophy of the TM movement and he 'got into an enormous argument with the TM people', as he put it later (Harrington 2008: 217). He went on to publish a bestseller on the technique of the relaxation response, in which he mentions TM, but emphasises that 'the various physiologic changes that accompanied Transcendental Meditation were part of an integrated response opposite to the fight-or-flight response and that they *were in no way unique to Transcendental Meditation*' (Benson 1976: 94. Italics are in the original). Vedic mantras with transcendental aspiration were now replaced with neutral English words and simple breath-counting that evokes 'decreased activity of [the] sympathetic nervous system' (ibid.). Benson argued that, in fact, concentration on any object – be it visual, auditory, a movement or a word – would elicit the relaxation response. The editor of the *Harvard Business Review*, William Nolen, wrote on the back cover of the book that he was delighted that 'someone has finally taken the nonsense out of meditation' (Harrington 2008: 220).

The medicalised understanding of meditation allowed it to penetrate society more widely, but it also created a new way of looking at the practice of meditation and describing how it works within the newly debated phenomena of chronic stress in medicine. Meditation was now understood to produce the opposite effect of stress. What are the cognitive mechanisms by which this process happens? Benson describes it simply as cutting through the chain of thoughts. As stress is maintained by stressful thoughts, worries and anxieties, and as the mind cannot hold two thoughts at a time, the repetition of the 'mantra' (be it sacred religious syllables or not) naturally leads to decreased stressful thinking patterns and the physiological relaxation follows. In Benson's words: 'the repetition of the word or phrase is a way to help break the train of distracting thoughts' (Benson 1976: 160).[2]

## *Mindfulness: attending and discerning the wandering mind*

The second wave of medicalised meditation entered the scene about ten years later with the mindfulness movement. It emerged from an integration of a few Buddhist traditions that had recently immigrated to the United States. The story of Jon Kabat-Zinn, who is considered by many to be one of the founders of the secular mindfulness movement, illustrates it well. Kabat-Zinn was a graduate student in microbiology at MIT when he encountered yoga and meditation, and he became a dedicated practitioner of both. After graduation he taught at the medical school of the University of Massachusetts, and in his free time he taught yoga, had strong ties with an American Korean Zen centre and practised *vipassanā*. In 1979 he managed to persuade officials at the medical centre to allow him to teach a relaxation programme for patients who had chronic illness. The programme was initially called the Stress Reduction and Relaxation Program; it later changed its title to Mindfulness-Based Stress Reduction (MBSR) before gaining unprecedented popularity throughout the world.

Kabat-Zinn defines mindfulness as the 'awareness that emerges through paying attention on purpose, in the present moment, and non-judgementally to an unfolding of experience moment-by-moment' (Kabat-Zinn 2003). The first part of the definition is clearly about attention control, and researchers agree that mindfulness meditation includes a component of attentional training (Malinowski 2013). In cognitive theory, attention is thought of in terms of three main cognitive functions: *alerting*, which is responsible for the level of arousal, alertness and attentional engagement; *orienting*, which is responsible for stimulus selection and focusing; and *executive*, which is responsible for top-down control of attention and is associated with self-regulation of attention.[3] Recent evidence suggests that the executive system is far more complex than previously assumed, and is responsible for error detection, conflict management between different competing tasks and choosing to which channel to attend (e.g. sensory or emotional) and more. This led some to sub-divide this function, and to suggest a fourth function – *salience* – which is involved in the detecting of salient events, such as changes in bodily states, sensory input and emotions.

In meditation, *alerting* is linked with any attentional process – for example, focusing on the breath as the object of meditation. *Salience* is associated with noticing changes that are subjectively meaningful – for example, when the mind wanders, or an emotion is experienced. *Executive* comes to action with the decision to shift attention, and the shifting itself will be the function of *orienting*.

It is impossible to describe meditation without referring to mind-wandering, which has also gained unprecedented scientific interest in the past twenty years. The discovery of the Default Mode Network (DMN) in the brain opened up a possible neural description of what happens in mind-wandering, and to even hypothesise what its function(s) may be. In short, the DMN refers to vast areas of the brain that function collectively when the person is resting or not busy with any difficult task. Research has demonstrated that it is closely associated with the reported levels of mind-wandering, and also with autobiographical memory, planning the future and theory of mind. Its function is therefore hypothesised to include 'perspective taking of the desires, beliefs, and intentions of others and in remembering the past as well as planning the future. All of these putative functions are self-referential in nature' (Sheline et al. 2009: 1942). In other words, the function of DMN may be to create and sustain an image of the self from pieces of past memories and future projections. When we are not doing anything in particular, especially during rest or automatic and boring activities, this function increases and is experienced as mind-wandering into past events and into thoughts about the future.

With these cognitive functions at hand, the process of attentional meditation could now be described as follows:

> Motivation is set to focus one's attention, be alert and notice the object of meditation. Sustained alertness would be the basic function. Then, probably because the task is not particularly rewarding or interesting, and because it induces relaxation and rest, DMN increases its activity in what is experienced as mind-wandering. In most cases thoughts would be about past events (autobiographical memory, i.e., events involving oneself in the past) or future planning (i.e., self-related events that one wishes happened or be avoided). Then, the meditator recognizes mind-wandering. Beginners may recognize mind-wandering when a teacher makes a vocal reminder, but with time these reminders are internalized. This would be the function of *salience*. The *executive* would be responsible for the decision to disengage from mind-wandering and return to the meditation object. The *orienting* function is responsible for completing this shift of attention back to the breathing.

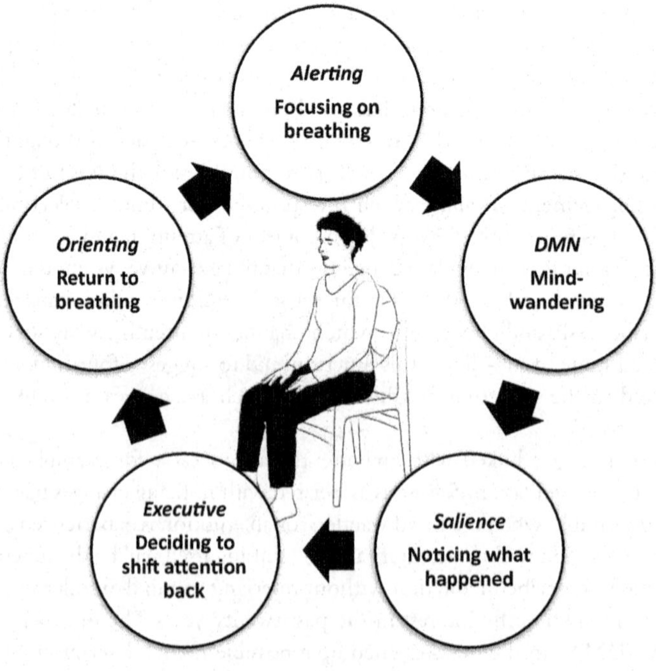


*Figure 31.1* Cognitive functions in attentional meditation.
Based on Malinowski (2013).

In these cognitive models, meditation is understood as a process of repetitive disengagement from self-referential thinking (DMN), and re-orienting attention back to the meditation object. In mindfulness courses, the object is typically breathing and bodily sensations. But the cognitive description is valid for any meditation object, including TM mantra and visual objects such as the Theravāda Buddhist *coloured kasiṇa* (Pali; class of visual object).

Typically, for people untrained in meditation, bodily sensations feed into the process of self-referential thinking that is associated with DMN. It is experienced as judging, worrying, planning or ruminating about bodily sensations. To take a simple example, discomfort in the belly may lead to thinking about the previous meal and quickly into a chain of thoughts about food, weight, regret, health, medical examinations and so forth. But in meditation training, the present-moment sensation is prioritised over these mind-wandering processes. Because the brain is plastic (its structure is changed with experience), it is predicted that as meditators become more experienced, their brain function and eventually their brain structure would change, too. Remarkable evidence on this came from a 2007 study that showed that DMN brain areas reduced their activity pronouncedly after an eight-week MBSR course (Farb et al. 2007). Experienced meditators expressed lower DMN activity and higher activity in attention control areas of the brain. Phenomenologically, they were better at suppressing *thinking about* what they felt, and better at *sustaining attention on the feeling itself.*[4]

### *Attention is not enough*

In cognitive language, negative and repetitive self-referential thinking processes are called *rumination*, and are considered a risk factor for developing depression and anxiety (Hamilton et al. 2015: 224). It has been known since the year 2000 that Mindfulness-Based Cognitive Therapy (MBCT) helps to prevent major depression for patients with three or more episodes in their past (Kuyken et al., 2016). Is attention control the function that mediates this outcome? There is some reason to believe that it is not, and that other cognitive functions must be involved. Indeed, people with major depression disorder typically show increased levels of DMN activity that are associated with *higher* levels of maladaptive and depressive rumination. However, cutting through the train of ruminative thinking brings about only temporary relief. Once meditation is over, self-referential thinking resumes. In fact, DMN must be associated with adaptive and helpful thinking processes as much as with destructive processes (Hamilton et al. 2011); its activity is probably value-free and is simply associated with self-referential memories and planning, regardless of whether they are positive or negative (in many cases these are actually constructive and adaptive patterns of thinking that contribute to planning). If attention control itself solved the negative impact of rumination, we would expect that any type of meditation would lead to the same outcome and help prevent depression. But this seems not to be the case.[5] Something else is helping to prevent depression for people who learned to practise mindfulness meditation.

## Meta-cognitive insight: another way to work with automatic thoughts

Meta-cognition is a cognitive process that reflects on, monitors and controls another cognitive process. It is phenomenologically rather easy to understand – human beings seem to be naturally good at thinking about thinking, and to be aware of internal processes such as emotions, feelings and motivations. Such awareness is often used to manipulate or better control these processes, especially when they are perceived to be in conflict with personal goals or views that are generally held by the person. If being angry or having a particular thought about the world are defined as first-layer mental activity, being aware of these as belonging to the self (I know that I am angry) would be defined as second-layer meta-cognition. One can better manipulate these emotions, thoughts and behaviours once they are clearly brought under the light of awareness and stopped from operating automatically and subconsciously. As we have seen, not all meta-cognitions are necessarily supportive of wellbeing. Rumination, for example, can be seen as a meta-cognitive process that includes awareness and a wish to manipulate certain thoughts and emotions. Thinking about one's thoughts of despair is a meta-cognitive strategy that generally fails, as it sustains in awareness the negative thoughts it seeks to eliminate.

Meditation, and some practices of mindfulness in particular, are thought to enhance a different type of meta-cognitive process. The psychologist John Teasdale, one of the developers of MBCT, explained that meta-cognitive insight is distinctly different from meta-cognitive knowledge (Teasdale 1999). The latter is propositional, and is similar to intellectually acquired knowledge that has no direct influence on emotions. It can be acquired 'vicariously' from others, from books, and without personal experience. Meta-cognitive *insight*, on the other hand, is implicational and is acquired by some form of experiential learning. According to Teasdale's model it emerges from 'sensory features, such as tone and loudness of voice, or proprioceptive feedback (e.g. from bodily sensations related to posture or facial expression)' (Teasdale 1999: 148).

This foundational distinction was made already after Teasdale and his colleagues had encountered mindfulness meditation and began to investigate how it may differ from other cognitive trainings that have been central in cognitive therapy. Crucially, knowing that certain thoughts are not true (and therefore should not be uncritically accepted as true) is not the same as experiencing thoughts as mental events that pass through the mind. Only the experience of thoughts as impersonal mental events that come and go is considered meta-cognitive *insight*. Such insight has profound implications for the relationship between self and thoughts. It creates a distance, or de-fusion, between the thoughts and the self, and can be particularly therapeutic when the thought's content is negative and self-harming.

Observing-thought meditation that is common in *vipassanā* and mindfulness training courses teaches the skill of 'decentring', a meta-cognitive process that disconnects the identification with views and reduces the absorption in their emotional content. The key features of these practices are non-identification and non-reaction to thoughts that arise moment after moment. Rumination, in this case, is counter-activated not by distracting attention into focusing on another object (e.g. breathing) but by developing a distant point of view – a meta-cognition – in which the contents of ruminative thinking are marginalised and attention is given to structural features such as the ever-changing nature of thoughts (they come, go, change) or their form (thoughts about the past, thoughts of planning, many thoughts, little thoughts). The distance helps to defuse the negative emotional tone that accompanies rumination, and eventually reduces rumination itself as its emotional fuel is gradually exhausted.

## Approach

The third and final cognitive construct that emerges in research as central to the understanding of meditation is *approach*. It is easy to understand by looking at its opposite, *withdrawal* (or avoidance) and its role in creating mental suffering.

Both depression and anxiety are increased by withdrawal and avoidance attitudes and behaviours. In anxiety, avoidance is the behaviour of disengaging from activities that are perceived (wrongly) as dangerous. But it also manifests cognitively as avoiding certain thoughts that may evoke unpleasant emotional reactions (e.g. thoughts about illness, catastrophe or past events). Depressed individuals tend to feel isolated and lonely and experience emotions of guilt, shame and rejection. These are withdrawal emotions, but they are coupled with another cognitive withdrawal – that which seeks to eliminate and escape from the emotions themselves. When this happens, rumination begins – i.e. thinking recurrent, self-reflective and uncontrollable thoughts that focus on the depressed mood and its causes and consequences.

As described above, *controlled attention* meditation may help to temporarily reduce the intensity of ruminative thinking, which can be relaxing for those who experience anxiety and depression. *Meta-cognitive* decentring may increase awareness of the rumination itself and help to reduce the emotional fusion with the negative thoughts. But to some extent, as long as the *withdrawal* continues, rumination will come back and the affect will continue to be coloured by the feeling of isolation or fear. The solution, therefore, could involve deliberately evoking *approach*, as the opposite of the *feeling of withdrawal*. The latter part of the definition of mindfulness by Kabat-Zinn captures this attitude with the term 'non-judgementally', which hints that attention control and detached awareness are accompanied by something else (Kabat-Zinn 2003). In other places, Kabat-Zinn insists that mindfulness is not an attention control technique but an attitude about 'love and loving life' (in Dunne and Harrington 2015: 629).[6] He lists seven other attitudinal foundations that are part of what is cultivated: 'beginners mind', patience, non-judging, trust, curiosity, non-striving, acceptance and letting go (Kabat-Zinn 1990). At least three of these can be associated with *approach* attitudes: *curiosity*, which requires getting closer and growing interest and motivation; *acceptance*, which entails openness and willingness to experience whatever arises in the moment; and *non-judging*, which means reducing self-criticism and not rejecting unpleasant experiences.[7]

Meditations that seek to cultivate *approach* attitudes more explicitly are generally referred to by scientists as 'loving-kindness' or 'compassion' (Kok and Singer 2017). In Buddhist traditional terms they are part of a four-fold group of practices and qualities: loving-kindness, compassion, sympathetic joy and equanimity. Here, in contrast to the detached observation stance of meta-cognitive mindfulness, practitioners strengthen feelings of warmth and care through the visualisation of others, and sequentially extend these feelings. Longitudinal studies have found that meditators who practise these increase in trait positive emotions and feelings of closeness to others (Kok et al. 2013).

The cognitive theory suggests that experiential avoidance is a key feature in the preservation of depression and anxiety and that the remedy is meditation that includes attention control, meta-cognitive awareness and a cultivation of an *approach* mode. The latter seems particularly important for anyone who experienced strong depressive moods in the past, because the strong negative experience (negative thoughts and unpleasant sensations) would evoke a strong urge to avoid it at any cost. Rumination and withdrawal are counterproductive strategies to escape from one's own feelings and thoughts. To begin with, it is impossible to avoid the internal experiences of loneliness and isolation by activating a withdrawal attitude. Moreover, it leads to increased rumination about the depressed mode, which only prolongs it, and adds a layer of helplessness and despair.

Initially, the developers of MBCT called their intervention (designed specifically for the prevention of depression) 'attention control training'. The idea was that, by controlling attention, participants will be able to decentre from negative thinking patterns and break the cycle of rumination. However, mixed results forced them to rethink the active component. What was missing in their training was the aspects of 'welcoming and allowing' (Segal et al. 2013: 56). Only when participants learned to also get closer and befriend unpleasant emotions and sensations was the full effect of the training manifested.[8]

The therapeutic theory here is closely linked to cognitive research that had identified the motivational systems of approach and avoidance, and their neural correlates. Simply put, approach motivation is defined as 'the energization of behavior by, or the direction of behavior toward, positive stimuli' (Elliot 2013: 8); Avoidance motivation is 'the energization of behavior by, or the direction of behavior away from, negative stimuli' (Elliot 2013: 8). Some evidence suggests that they are associated with different frontal lobe activation in the brain: higher right activation (compared with left activation) is associated with avoidance and depression. Well-cited research on MBSR showed that after eight weeks, asymmetry is changed and moved leftward, as self-reported measures also show reduction of depression and anxiety symptoms for course participants (Davidson et al. 2003).

This line of research points to a crucial characteristic of modern medicalised meditation training. To bring about the therapeutic benefits, the training of attention should include a particular attitude towards experience: not that of a detached observer, but that of a friendly companion that is actively seeking to approach, allow, welcome and accept experience. The approach system is naturally activated towards pleasant experiences, but in learning meditation individuals begin to activate it towards the unpleasant as well.

A similar process happens in constructive meditations, largely derived from Buddhism, that explicitly train compassion and loving-kindness. In compassion, the meditator evokes both the suffering of others (or of oneself) and the wish to approach and help. In loving-kindness the context of suffering is less pronounced, but approach is clearly and deliberately evoked with the wishes for care, happiness and ease – directly towards oneself and towards others. In both traditional and therapeutic frameworks, the activation of approach towards what is not pleasant is closely related to kindness and compassion.

> Whether mindful awareness enables a fundamental shift in how we relate to what is arising in the external or internal world depends on whether friendliness and compassion can be brought to those elements of present-moment experience to which we attend.
>
> (*Segal et al. 2013: 137*)

The attitude of approach is therefore central to the psychological understanding of meditation and how it works. It also helps to differentiate between mindfulness, as understood in this particular modern and therapeutic context, and other forms of meditation. TM, for example, seems to not emphasise this particular aspect of the practice, while compassion meditation, loving-kindness and self-compassion would take it even further and more explicitly than the mindfulness taught in MBSR and MBCT.

## Conclusion

The picture that arises from the cognitive study of meditation includes three main processes that operate within meditation. *Attention control* is required for almost any type of meditative practice, regardless of what the object of attention may be. What perhaps had been known intuitively by practitioners has been now articulated in scientific terms: different cognitive mechanisms and (their correlative neural systems) function even within the simplest event of mind-wandering and returning to the meditation object. Mindfulness of breathing and mantra meditations can now be described as involving cycles of activating the cognitive functions of alerting, mind-wandering, salience, executive and re-orienting attention back to the object. *Meta-cognition* helps to identify additional processes that involve insight into one's own mental events, and in particular creates deliberate distance between oneself and one's thoughts and emotional turbulence. Much of what we normally call 'awareness' or 'self-awareness' may now be described as meta-cognition, as long as it involves the internal reflective process of mental events themselves. Lastly, *approach* is pointed out as crucial for understanding the motivational aspect of meditation. It is the 'warmth' component that is linked to the cultivation of friendliness and compassion that also bring about therapeutic benefits. While these three are clearly cognitive concepts which are well situated within the scientific and clinical literature, they become helpful to our understanding of what meditation is and how it works.

This certainly applies to types of meditation that were subject to scientific research, such as TM and modern mindfulness. Moreover, it helps to deconstruct the umbrella term 'mindfulness' into several components that function sequentially and simultaneously. An MBSR course, for example, includes training of controlled attention as well as a good portion of meta-cognition, each expressed in a different phase of the course. The approach element is less explicit, perhaps, but is clearly embodied in the accepting and gentle attitude of the course leader who is skilled in demonstrating approach towards participants and their difficult experiences.

The same analysis could apply to traditional forms of meditation, even those that are less researched. To take a few examples, devotional practices may be understood as involving a strong aspect of *approach* as they are encouraging heightened motivation for getting close, appreciating and serving the object of devotion. This almost begs further empirical research. Zazen (in the sense of *shikantaza*, 'just sitting') could be understood as an attentional practice that emphasises the role of the *alerting* system, and is less bothered with executive control and the redirecting of attention to a particular object. *Vipassanā* as taught by S. N. Goenka involves executive attentional control (scanning the body) and the entire cycle of disengaging from mind-wandering. It also includes meta-cognition when it encourages insight into impermanence of all mental and physical sensations. These are only snippets of possible descriptions that require further research, but they demonstrate the utility of using the above-mentioned empirically based cognitive models for the study of many other forms of meditation.

## Glossary

Decentring: A meta-cognitive process that disconnects the identification with views and reduces the absorption in their emotional quality.

Default Mode Network (DMN): vast areas of the human brain that function collectively when the person is resting or not busy with any difficult task. Closely associated with the reported levels of mind-wandering, and also associated with autobiographical memory, planning the future and theory of mind. Hypothesised to be the correlate of mind-wandering in meditation.

MBCT: Mindfulness-Based Cognitive Therapy. An eight-week programme based on MBSR, which was originally designed for the prevention of major depression. Research demonstrates that it reduces the risk of recurrent depression for those who had a few previous episodes. Now part of what the National Health Service (NHS) in Britain offers patients.

MBSR: Mindfulness-Based Stress Reduction. An eight-week programme that teaches meditative yoga in a non-religious setting. Founded by Jon Kabat-Zinn in 1979.

Meta-cognition: A cognitive process that reflects on, monitors and controls another cognitive process.

Relaxation Response: Coined by the physiologist Herbert Benson. The activation of reduced metabolism and increased calm. The opposite of Stress Response. Can be activated by meditation.

Rumination: Negative and repetitive self-referential thinking. Considered a risk factor for depression and anxiety.

Stress Response: The natural physiological changes that occur when an organism is facing a threat.

Transcendental Meditation: A modern mantra meditation technique, introduced to western culture by the Maharishi Mahesh Yogi in the 1960s. One of the first techniques to be scientifically studied.

*Vipassanā*: (Pali) clear sight or insight. Also, a form of Buddhist meditation that has gained popularity in modern times, and in the west.

## Notes

1 For a summary of Davidson's life-long scientific research into meditation, see Goleman and Davidson 2017. *Mind and Life* has published several volumes that document the dialogues between the Dalai Lama and scientists. Notably: Goleman 1997; Harrington and Zajonc 2006; Kabat-Zinn and Davidson 2012. For the development of Mindfulness-Based Cognitive Therapy and its psychological theory, see Segal et al. 2013.

2 A Theravāda fifth-century commentary on mindfulness of breathing gives a similar outlook: 'for counting, by cutting off thoughts which cling to external things, serves the purpose of establishing mindfulness in the in-breaths and out-breaths as object' (Ñanamoli 1952: 27).

3 For a detailed discussion of attentional system in the brain, see Peterson and Posner (2012).

4 Evidence from neuroscience suggests that it is not only brain function that is altered soon after a meditation training course, but also that more stable structural changes can be detected in experienced meditators (Fox et al. 2014)

5 Mindfulness meditation has moderate strength of evidence (SOE) for improvement in anxiety, depression and pain, but the SOE effect of TM on depression is insufficient according to a detailed report that investigated the impact of meditation on psychological stress and wellbeing (Goyal et al. 2014. See in particular p. viii and table at page ES-12).

6 Kabat-Zinn himself refused to give his definition a higher status than that of a practical working definition, and has claimed that what he teaches is in fact *dharma* (Kabat-Zinn 2011).

7 *Approach* is included in the two last items that are measured in the Five Facet Mindfulness Questionnaire (FFMQ), which is used in research to measure levels of mindfulness. The five are: observing, describing, acting with awareness, non-judging of inner experience and non-reactivity to inner experience (Baer et al. 2006).

8 'Habitual patterns of experiential avoidance are one of the key planks that trigger and maintain depression. A distinctive feature therefore of MBCT is its emphasis on learning how to notice and then intentionally transform these patterns through choosing to turn towards or "approach" experience' (Crane 2017: 39).

## Bibliography

Baer, R. A., Smith, G. T., Hopkins, J., Krietemeyer, J., and Toney, L. 2006. 'Using Self-Report Assessment Methods to Explore Facets of Mindfulness'. *Assessment* 13: 27–45.

Benson, H. 1976. *The Relaxation Response* (1st ed.). New York: Avon Books.

Benson, H., et al. 1971. 'Decreased Systolic Blood Pressure Through Operant Conditioning Techniques in Patients with Essential Hypertension'. *Science* 173(3998): 740–742.

Crane, R. 2017. *Mindfulness-Based Cognitive Therapy: Distinctive Features*. London: Routledge.

Dahl, C. J., Lutz, A., and Davidson, R. J. 2015. 'Reconstructing and Deconstructing the Self: Cognitive Mechanisms in Meditation Practice'. *Trends In Cognitive Sciences* 19(9): 515–523.

Davidson, R. J., Kabat-Zinn, J., Schumacher, J., Rosenkranz, M., Muller, D., Santorelli, S. F., and Sheridan, J. F. 2003. 'Alterations in Brain and Immune Function Produced by Mindfulness Meditation'. *Psychosomatic Medicine* 65(4): 564–570.

Davidson, R., Lutz, A. and Ricard, M. 2014. 'Mind of The Meditator'. *Scientific American* November: 39–45.

Dunne J. and Harrington, A. 2015. 'When Mindfulness Is Therapy: Ethical Qualms, Historical Perspectives'. *American Psychologist* 70(7): 621–631.

Elliot, A. J. 2013. *Handbook of Approach and Avoidance Motivation*. New York: Psychology Press

Farb, N. A. S., et al. 2007. 'Attending to the Present: Mindfulness Meditation Reveals Distinct Neural Modes of Self-Reference'. *Social Cognitive and Affective Neuroscience* 2(4): 313–322.

Fox, K. C. et al. 2014. 'Is Meditation Associated with Altered Brain Structure? A Systematic Review and Meta-Analysis of Morphometric Neuroimaging in Meditation Practitioners'. *Neuroscience and Biobehavioral Reviews* 4: 48–73.

Goleman, D. ed. 1997. *Healing Emotions: Conversations with the Dalai Lama on Mindfulness, Emotions, And Health*. Boston: Shambhala Publications.

Goleman, D. and Davidson, R. J. 2017. *Altered Traits: Science Reveals How Meditation Changes Your Mind, Brain, And Body*. New York: Penguin.

Goyal, M., Singh, S., Sibinga, E. M., Gould, N. F., Rowland-Seymour, A., Sharma, R., … and Ranasinghe, P. D. 2014. 'Meditation Programs for Psychological Stress and Well-Being: A Systematic Review and Meta-Analysis'. *JAMA Internal Medicine* 174(3): 357–368.

Hamilton, J. P., Farmer, M., Fogelman, P., and Gotlib, I. H. 2015. 'Depressive Rumination, the Default-Mode Network, and the Dark Matter of Clinical Neuroscience'. *Biological Psychiatry* 78(4): 224–230.

Hamilton, J. P., Furman, D. J., Chang, C., Thomason, M. E., Dennis, E., and Gotlib, I. H. 2011. 'Default-Mode And Task-Positive Network Activity In Major Depressive Disorder: Implications For Adaptive And Maladaptive Rumination'. *Biological Psychiatry* 70(4): 327–333.

Harrington, A. 2008. *The Cure Within: A History of Mind–Body Medicine*. New York: W. W. Norton & Company

Harrington, A. E. and Zajonc, A. E., 2006. *The Dalai Lama at MIT*. Cambridge, MA: Harvard University Press.

Kabat-Zinn J. 1990. *Full Catastrophe Living: The Program of the Stress Reduction Clinic at the University of Massachusetts Medical Center*. New York: Delta.

Kabat-Zinn J. 2003. 'Mindfulness-Based Interventions in Context: Past, Present, and Future'. *Clinical Psychology Scientific Practice* 10: 144–156.

Kabat-Zinn J. 2011. 'Some Reflections on the Origins of MBSR, Skillful Means, and the Trouble with Maps'. *Contemporary Buddhism* 12(01): 281–306.

Kabat-Zinn, J. and Davidson, R. eds. 2012. *The Mind's Own Physician: A Scientific Dialogue with the Dalai Lama on the Healing Power of Meditation*. Oakland, CA: New Harbinger Publications.

Komjathy, L. 2015. 'Approaching Contemplative Practice', in Komjathy, L. (ed), *Contemplative Literature: A Comparative Sourcebook on Meditation and Contemplative Prayer*, 3–52. Albany, NY: SUNY Press.

Komjathy, L. 2017. *Introducing Contemplative Studies*. New Jersey: John Wiley & Sons.

Kok, B. E., et al. 2013. 'How Positive Emotions Build Physical Health: Perceived Positive Social Connections Account for the Upward Spiral Between Positive Emotions and Vagal Tone'. *Psychological Science* 24(7); 1123–11322.

Kok, B. E., and Singer, T. 2017. 'Phenomenological Fingerprints of Four Meditations: Differential State Changes in Affect, Mind-Wandering, Meta-Cognition, and Interoception Before and After Daily Practice Across 9 Months of Training'. *Mindfulness* 8(1): 218–231.

Kuyken, W., Warren, F. C., Taylor, R. S.,… Dalgleish, T. 2016. 'Efficacy of Mindfulness-Based Cognitive Therapy in Prevention of Depressive Relapse: An Individual Patient Data Meta-Analysis from Randomized Trials'. *JAMA Psychiatry* 73: 565–574.

Lutz, A., Dunne, J. D., and Davidson, R. J. 2007. 'Meditation and the Neuroscience of Consciousness: An Introduction', in Zelazo, P. D., Moscovitch, M., and Thompson, E. (eds), *The Cambridge Handbook Of Consciousness*, 499–551. Cambridge: Cambridge University Press.

Lutz, A., Slagter, H. A., Dunne, J. D., and Davidson, R. J. 2008. 'Attention Regulation and Monitoring in Meditation'. *Trends In Cognitive Sciences* 12(4): 163–169.

Malinowski, P. et al. 2013 'Neural Mechanism of Attentional Control in Mindfulness Meditation'. *Frontiers In Neuroscience* 7: 1–11.

Ñanamoli Bhikkhu (trans) 1952. *Mindfulness of Breathing (Anapanasati)*. Kandy: Buddhist Publication Society.

Petersen, S. E. and Posner M. I. 2012. 'The Attention System of the Human Brain: 20 Years After'. *Annual Review Of Neuroscience* 35: 73–89.

Segal, Z. V., Williams, M., and Teasdale, J. 2013. *Mindfulness-Based Cognitive Therapy for Depression*. New York: Guilford Publications.

Sheline, Y. I., et al. 2009. 'The Default Mode Network and Self-Referential Processes in Depression'. *Proceedings of the National Academy of Sciences of the United States of America* 106(6): 1942–1947.

Teasdale, J. D. 1999. 'Metacognition, Mindfulness and the Modification of Mood Disorders'. *Clinical Psychology & Psychotherapy: An International Journal Of Theory & Practice* 6(2): 146–155.

Wallace, R. K. 1970. 'Physiological Effects of Transcendental Meditation'. *Science* 167: 1751–1754.

# 32

# INCLUSIVE IDENTITIES

## The lens of critical theory

*Karen-Anne Wong*

### Introduction

Modern yoga would appear to be all-inclusive. From flow yoga to gentle yoga, power yoga, yin yoga, seniors' yoga, children's yoga, teen yoga, special needs yoga, prenatal yoga, postnatal yoga, baby yoga, chair yoga, workplace yoga, prison yoga, paddleboard yoga, yoga with goats, chocolate yoga, drunk yoga, disco yoga, meditation classes, kirtan and chanting – the list goes on, and the market seems to have created a space for every kind of body within the yoga classroom. However, the sheer prevalence and variety of yoga classes on offer to modern practitioners obscures the fact that there are social and logistical barriers to participating in yoga, such as class, race, gender, age and ability. Despite the aspirations of many yoga practitioners to be more inclusive, there are still many ways in which contemporary yoga reproduces exclusion and marginalisation. This chapter will examine several ways in which yoga classes have the potential to be empowering for non-mainstream identities, while also highlighting ways in which they may fail to do so. I will examine several disciplines that create discourses around yoga, and argue that critical theory is one register that has significant potential to represent yoga as inclusive and empowering. I will highlight the discipline of critical theory for its ability to describe and critique society, often questioning forms of authority and normative values. Following this, I will focus specifically on disability and gender as two areas of inclusion that yoga may address. To conclude, I will use a case study to illustrate how Modern Postural Yoga (MPY) could function as an inclusive practice within institutionalised settings, in this case within a preschool environment. This case study uses the example of children as a deliberate way of addressing how children's identities, as minors, may form another kind of marginalisation, which multiplies exclusion when combined with identities such as disability or queerness.

In this chapter I claim that specific practices of yoga involve particular experiences, effects and understandings which are unique to the practice, context and individual. This means that although yoga and meditation practices may operate under similar labels, they vary widely in how they approach identity and inclusion. Understanding the nuance and specificity of individual classes is essential to understanding that not all yoga is created equal – and not all bodies may be understood as equal within it. While many yoga practitioners hope that yoga may be all-inclusive, non-mainstream identities are often alienated when faced with representations of yoga which focus on the white, middle-class, feminine, flexible, slim, youthful, able body as an ideal yoga body (at least within the western world [Markula 2001]). However, some practices can combat these dominant representations and create classes where students feel included, and even celebrated for their differences, in productive and empowering ways.

In this chapter the concept of inclusivity is derived from, and is an extension of, ideas defined within a specific version of critical theory: critical disability studies. Critical disability studies as a discipline emerged out of critical theory and uses many similar techniques in applying philosophy to social experience. Critical disability theorists such as Kuppers have aimed to define inclusion through readdressing the social and environmental barriers that signal differences between bodies and prioritise 'mainstream … bodies and their need' (2011: 4). The concept of inclusion proposed by Kuppers, and taken up here, understands difference as the norm, and approaches the pedagogy of yoga classes from that perspective. Kuppers bases this model on Gilles Deleuze and Felix Guattari's notion of the rhizome, in which internal and external experiences of difference 'mix and merge' and there is a refrain from juxtaposing 'pain and pleasure or pride and shame', making way for transformation and 'a coming into being' (2011: 95). This version of inclusivity offers new paths towards plurality, complexity and difference which resist normalisation and seek out new forms of empowerment. In the context of yoga these new forms of empowerment would take us beyond the binaries of normalisation that are so easy to slip into, such as good/bad, strong/weak, fit/unfit, flexible/stiff. It aims to 'extend into new territory' and perhaps even 'productively critique' the limitations of other concepts of difference (Shildrick 2012: 32).

Certain identities may feel more welcome in yoga classes than others. Recent surveys in Australia and the United States have shown that yoga practitioners in these countries are most often female, are on average around forty years old, are tertiary educated and have a greater likelihood of being white, non-Hispanic and Caucasian (Telles et al. 2017; Lewis 2008; Markula 2014; Ross et al. 2013). This is not necessarily the main demographic for yoga practitioners across the world (as a recent survey in India showed, where most practitioners were male [Telles et al. 2017]), but indicates how identity is often represented in western practices of MPY. For the purposes of this chapter I will focus on western practices and their representations of identity, as the issues of transnationality, race, class and ethnicity are dealt with elsewhere in this volume. I argue that MPY practices are often invested in ideals of social inclusion yet also maintain specific barriers and instances of exclusion. This is a similar perspective to that presented by Smith and Atencio (2017), who have found that MPY participants often believed that 'exclusion and barriers to practise could be overcome by individual choice-making'; that is, people thought that they were excluded from yoga practices because they had not forced themselves to overcome the social, financial and logistical barriers that prevented them from participating (Telles et al. 2017: 1167). This demonstrates that yoga participants are often 'invested in and reproduce ideals of individualism and meritocracy relative to normative neo-liberal yoga discourses' (Telles et al. 2017: 1167). When people are alienated from yoga, the discursive formation surrounding the practice suggests that it is the fault of the individual for not including themselves, rather than being due to any lack of social inclusion practices within yoga. This is problematic because it removes the onus on MPY to position itself as more inclusive, and encourages the individual to see themselves as failing rather than the system failing them. Similar findings have been made in aerobics and other fitness settings that are invested in socially accepted values of self-government and self-regulation (Markula 1995; McLaren, Rock, and McElgunn 2012), indicating that yoga operates in this way as part of a broader health and wellbeing industry.

## Yoga discourses and research methodologies

Yoga has been and is currently studied in a variety of registers and disciplines. Since the 1990s, one of the primary modes in which it has been studied is through the lens of clinical trials and medical efficacy. The disciplines of medicine, (neuro)biology, physiology, public health and allied health all produce specific forms of medical literatures about MPY. Each of these disciplines seeks to use yoga to make patients' bodies measure as closely as possible to an imagined 'normal' body and/or to optimise its functioning and wellbeing (e.g. Ross et al. 2013; Pelt 2011; Powell et al. 2008; Jensen 2004). Medical literature on yoga creates a narrative of legitimacy around MPY by demonstrating quantifiable benefits and has been a major driving force in the increased popularity and acceptability of yoga practices. Medical literature has harnessed MPY as one of many physical activities that promotes '"health" (as absence of illness)' and has 'become aligned with minimization of health risks, individualized healthy lifestyle, and self-care' (Markula 2014: 146). Further, this 'literature perpetuates the notion that yoga is inherently healthy, and thus good for everyone' (Smith and Atencio 2017: 1181). Medical literature also frames expectations of MPY – for example, that it reduces stress, increases physical fitness and treats mental illness. However, as I will explain below, medical literature also functions by coding and judging particular behaviours within yoga, so that some bodies and identities are deemed to be doing yoga 'well' while others are not – including some and excluding others.

When studied via medical disciplines, yoga is often (though not exclusively) researched using quantitative methods. This largely consists of researchers identifying and coding bodily markers that can indicate yoga's measurable effects on the body, as understood in medical terms. One of the major advantages of this approach is its clarity: coding bodily markers within a numeric scale (where one end is 'bad' and the other 'good') distils information to present clear conclusions. However, the disadvantage is that in simplifying data in this way, there is a risk of misinterpretation or omission of the complexity and nuance of individuals' practices. The only things that can be measured are those that are specifically sought, predicted and tested for – there is little room for exploration. This is particularly problematic within the context of yoga, which, like many embodied practices, is by its nature undelineated and sensual: the effects of the practice are most often *felt* rather than measured (even if a yoga practitioner has defined goals, such as relieving back pain or releasing stress). Coding and categorising an individual's yoga practice forces the body to be representative, a sign of whatever is under scrutiny, such as emotional regulation, athletic performance or mental health. There must always be a process of selection, synthesis and categorisation.[1]

Within these parameters quantitative research approaches have been productive in collecting certain types of information about yoga practices. However, it has also judged some individuals' practices as less effective or less functional than others. The necessary by-product of quantifying bodies is that some bodies will measure up better than others. Further, since biomedicine is aligned with the (twenty-first century) state, as MPY has gained legitimacy within the medical profession, state institutions such as schools, hospitals, workplaces and prisons have had more opportunity to fund MPY as an increasingly accepted form 'of health care [where] the division of labour' is 'formally underwritten by the state' (Saks 2005: 2). In acknowledging this alignment of biopower and the state, it is important to remember that '[b]iopower and its various mechanisms' are 'productive, in the sense that disciplinary techniques make us who we are' (Barcan 2008: 16). But it is also a mechanism through which the state exerts control over individuals and can include or exclude based on how well an individual is able to perform as a 'normal' (able, youthful, non-transgressive) body. This means that as yoga has been institutionalised, it has become a mechanism through which the state controls individuals, even as it is a mechanism through which individuals produce themselves and develop identity – in often 'pleasurable' ways (Barcan 2008: 15).

Large-scale quantitative medical literature has the power to bring together multiple representations of individuals and gather a more complex picture of yoga's effect in their lives. For example, Slovacek, Tucker and Pantoja's (2013) comprehensive study integrated survey data from 405 child yoga students with exam results, attendance rates, fitness test scores and reports from teachers. They were able to synthesise an understanding of yoga's effect as it applied to many areas of children's lives: academic performance, physical fitness and behaviour. Much medical literature – including Slovacek, Tucker and Pantoja (2013) – asks whether yoga can produce optimised 'normal' individuals (emotionally regulated, academically or professionally successful, physically healthy), and values yoga only if it is successful in this. In comparison, qualitative approaches have the opportunity to ask more exploratory questions regarding what exactly MPY does, without assuming that producing optimised 'normal' individuals (or any other kinds of individual) will be beneficial or not. Qualitative approaches also often understand MPY as deeply emplaced and contextual; it is not assumed that any findings may be applied as broad generalisations to other yoga practices, though they may be suggestive or indicative and can be compared to similar studies in other contexts to demonstrate similarities and differences.

One set of approaches that relies on qualitative methodologies centres around critical theory. Critical theory approaches typically analyse yoga and the ways it is discussed in self-reflexive ways, often considering how identity and inclusion are employed and represented in yoga practices. Critical theory approaches to yoga have emerged out of the significant amount of work done in the humanities on yoga, particularly within the disciplines of Indian studies, history, religion, philosophy and, to a certain extent, sociology and cultural studies. In recent decades these disciplines have used yoga as an example of practices that have the potential to offer non-normative ways of understanding the body, knowledge, ritual and experience.

One of the earliest significant engagements with yoga from a philosophical perspective occurred in Marcel Mauss's paper 'Techniques of the Body' (1931). Mauss developed a theory of the body out of anthropological observations, and yoga appears briefly at the end of his essay as an exemplum of a body practice that unites education, culture, psychology and physical movement in a 'socio-psycho-biological' nexus (Mauss 1931: 475). Since then, philosophy of the twenty-first century has dynamically changed how yoga is approached as a topic of study. Philosophical approaches to yoga now often embrace its potential as an embodied practice to 'integrate Eastern elements' into a habitually western 'manner of thinking' (Irigaray 2008: 44–45). The obvious risk of these approaches is their potential for orientalism (as first described by Edward Said), romanticising eastern philosophy as non-dualist and embodied in comparison to western philosophy's dualism and preoccupation with the mind. Further, such approaches rarely engage with any significant detail in the content or context of MPY, and 'yoga' almost certainly has very different meanings for different philosophers. Feminist philosopher Luce Irigaray's phenomenological approach teeters on this edge as she specifically credits her own bodily practice with changing her thought processes; she claims that yoga provides her with 'a greater liberty in the unfolding of my thinking', where her 'thoughts take place in a wider space' (Irigaray 2008: 45). Irigaray is critical of 'our [Western] tradition' for its inattention to the body. She writes that western philosophy lacks 'language capable of expressing our bodily and sensible experiences' while claiming to 'overcome bodily and gender dimensions' (ibid., 50). Yoga offers Irigaray a non-dualistic way 'to rethink the categories of subjectivity and objectivity' that exists beyond 'the masculine Western subject' (41). Valuable as this philosophical analysis is, it does not address any of the sociocultural contexts or political import of yoga as a contemporary western practice. Irigaray's perception of yoga is limited by its lack of acknowledgement that MPY has been commercialised as 'a Western fitness practice increasingly governed by the neoliberal rationale' (Markula 2014: 143). MPY's endorsement of an 'individualised healthy lifestyle' may encourage practitioners to look for self-empowerment within only specific, limited parameters, rather than extend beyond them (ibid., 146). There seems to be an increasing trend for both scholars and practitioners of MPY to try to resolve the ironies, contradictions and paradoxes at its heart. As Markula has put it, scholars are now asking whether it is 'possible to change the discursive construction' of fitness practices such as MPY, so that they 'do not build docile bodies' (2010: 66). The answer that seems to be emerging in this set of disciplines is yes, but determining whether a single body is produced as docile in any moment is rather complicated.

Despite the potential problems with Irigaray's understanding of yoga, her approach is representative of a fundamental shift in the ways yoga is studied. In the twenty-first century, western 'scholar-practitioners' of yoga have conducted 'rigorous academic reflection' of MPY (Newcombe 2009: 2).[2] No longer purely an object to be scrutinised, yoga also became an actively subjective mode of operating in and understanding the world. The mode has produced a significant body of additional research on yoga enthusiasts/practitioners/teachers (Atkinson 2010; Bost 2016; Buckingham and Degen 2012; Heyes 2007; Lea 2009; Smith 2007) and yoga classes (Augenstein 2013; McInnes 2015; Morgan 2012; Lewis 2008). Through this kind of rigorous reflection Suzanne Bost concluded that '[y]oga is intellectually thick' and can be a critical lens that sees 'corporal heterogeneity' rather than embodied differences (2016: 191 and 193). Yet Markula identified a potential pitfall of this approach, in that yoga's religious grounding demands to be 'analyzed as a discursive construction and disciplinary production of its own' before any kind of 'problematization of the westernized production of identity and individualism can take place' (2010: 68). Few scholars have undertaken this kind of comprehensive deconstruction of yoga, its traditions and contemporary practices, limiting the claims that can be made about MPY and its place in the modern world.

Accepting these limitations, there have been many scholars who have expanded upon the notion of MPY as more than an object of study, such as Cressida Heyes, who has approached yoga through a sharply socially oriented critique. Heyes argues that yoga provides 'not just an alternative to contemporary Western gym culture and exercise regimens, but also models of self-care and self-development' (2007: 128). Heyes's version of MPY casts it as a potential antidote to the neoliberal imperative that Markula, and Heyes herself, have witnessed *within* MPY. For Heyes, MPY can constitute a 'personal counterattack to the teleology of corporeal normalization', but this potential is not fully realised by most practices 'of yoga in the West, especially in its casual and attenuated forms' that are 'hardly separate from overtly normalizing pressures' (ibid., 129). Heyes's perception of MPY is significant because it suggests that there are ways of engaging in normalising practices that do not produce limitations upon on the body. Heyes does not 'prescribe yoga as the antidote to normalization' but suggests that practitioners may undertake their 'own yogic labor, without seeking to meet particular targets' of normalised discipline (ibid., 129). Yoga could both enable and restrict, include and exclude, provide benefit and harm and produce conformity to normalisation and alternatives to it.

The difference between critical theory and/or socially oriented philosophical approaches to yoga and other studies of yoga has tended to be their approach to relationality and the self. Medical and historical literatures on yoga do not take the researchers' own experiential sensation of yoga as a significant starting point for research. There is little focus on the researchers' own intervention into the social phenomenon of yoga. This includes interdisciplinary work between studies of religion, history and philosophy, such as Alter's examination of *haṭhayoga* and sacrifice (2012). Other philosophical and phenomenological approaches can focus almost entirely on the internal sensation of the researcher, in an auto-ethnographic mode similar to Irigaray's work or that of McInnes (2015). Heyes's socially oriented philosophy has much more in common with ethnographic accounts of yoga, such as that by Patricia Morgan, who has considered the embodied relationship between researcher and researched when analysing sensory learning and the nature of contemplation (2012). Of course this is a highly oversimplified categorisation, and there are many other commonalities and differences between approaches than can be mentioned here, but the salient point is that critical theory neither removes the researcher entirely nor focuses solely on the self as subject. Within these parameters, Heyes's understanding of yoga as a process of and resistance to normalisation reveals that yoga has the potential to transform, while also subscribing to normative corporealisation. This means that MPY practices are often a complex mixture of accepting and including different identities while simultaneously attempting to normalise bodies (for example, cure or treat disability). These two goals can also be in competition with one another.

The disciplines of critical theory and socially oriented philosophy have intervened in studies of yoga with new methodologies, accessing new kinds of information about individuals' embodied practices. Heyes has worked with other researchers to experiment with inserting this into institutional frameworks, teaching yoga at a tertiary level and publishing research based on the experience as a strategy against normalisation. However, she found that despite the intention of teachers, 'students of yoga sometimes use[d] the physical practice against itself – perhaps as another opportunity for self-criticism or one-upmanship, or to entrench less than-optimal physical and mental habits' (Helberg et al. 2009: 265). For Helberg, Heyes and Rohel, squeezing yoga into the demands of tertiary education seemed to counter the edict (from contemporary 'yogic philosophy') that 'one should accept one's own capacities without constantly judging those capacities as deficient' (ibid., 270). The ideological clash between the views of various forms of yoga, its teachers and the institutions in which they are housed (such as the modern university) is particularly pertinent when individuals are excluded from practice. For example, as I will discuss further in this chapter, for individuals with disabilities the notion of 'deficiency' is highly potent. Heyes's approach and critical theory more generally ground yoga within social relations, revealing it to be an institutionalised, contextualised strategy that may or may not counteract normalisation, inclusion and exclusion, depending on its circumstances.

Studying MPY through the lens of critical theory has revealed the complex relationship that yoga has to normalisation. When a practice such as yoga produces normalisation, it excludes non-mainstream bodies and identities that are unable or unwilling to meet the terms of existing power relations. At a basic level, normalising practices exclude some bodies which are not deemed to be able, gendered or raced in normative ways. Practices that create alternatives to normalisation seek to include these non-mainstream identities. Yet the process of normalisation can also be more complex than this when we consider how MPY may intervene in individuals' lives as care of the self. The discipline of normalisation happens through surveillance, and MPY is one of many fitness and wellbeing practices which encourages intense scrutinisation of the self. Cultural studies scholar Ruth Barcan has observed this in alternative therapies more generally, where both the internal and external self are subjected to vigorous surveillance, and 'the vigilance of external bodies is supplemented to greater or lesser degree by *self*-monitoring, *self* "management," *self*-surveillance' (2008: 15). Indeed, it seems that many yoga practices provide practitioners with tools for coping with the stresses of everyday life, sustaining them in those stresses, rather than challenging them. Sarah Sharma found this in her research of yoga within office environments, where it operated as one of many 'cultural technologies for capitalism to produce docile and productive bodies' (2014: 84). This means that yoga can function as a way of 'training and treating' bodies 'in order to develop a form of capitalistic endurance', rather than encouraging practitioners to scrutinise social structures such as class and gender, which empower and disempower in multifaceted ways (ibid., 100). However, when individuals engage in MPY as a practice of self-surveillance, this does not necessarily mean acceding to the 'intensification of disciplinary power'; MPY's mode of self-surveillance can be embraced as a way of developing new capacities and abilities and a powerful tool for care of the self, without producing docility (Heyes 2006: 127). In these instances, individuals can learn poses, breathing practices and mindfulness techniques as ways of 'changing old patterns' and producing 'embodied effects' that enable 'acts of self-transformation' (ibid., 128). This could also mean that yoga becomes more inclusive of different abilities and different kinds of bodies, as part of 'an alternative picture in which increasing capabilities are closely tied' to reformulations of power relations (ibid., 131). In contrast to purely normalising practices, MPY may offer rewards to those who do more than just cede to existing power relations – it may create alternatives and embrace new identities, even as it demands certain kinds of normalised movement or functioning of individual bodies.

## Disability

Imagine a physically disabled boy who practices yoga with his peers at a mainstream school. The yoga class may both teach this child new ways of using his body, making him less dependent on his mobility aids and developing techniques of care of the self that provide further inclusion within mainstream institutional life, while simultaneously excluding him from certain poses or practices that mark him as different and unable to meet the demands of a normalised body. This example is a reasonably common occurrence in schools and serves to show how MPY can both be inclusive and exclusive, normalising and transforming all at once.

Disability is one form of identity that I focus on in this chapter in order to examine how inclusion and exclusion may operate in MPY classes. I use the term 'disability' in this chapter for want of a better term. 'Disability' denotes ways in which particular bodies are socially coded as less able than other bodies, without suggesting that all will be synonymous or equal, as there are marked differences between how each form of disability is socially coded on individual bodies and how they are physically experienced. As already mentioned, in this chapter I follow critical disability studies scholars, such as Julie Allan and Petra Kuppers, in how I use terms such as 'inclusion' and 'disability', with the understanding that many specific conditions are contentiously debated as constructions of biological and social discourse. However, Kuppers reminds us that the dominant way of viewing disability is 'as culturally negative: defective, in need of accommodation, other-than-whole' (Kuppers 2016: 93). Popular and medical discourses of MPY often view disabilities as diagnosable and potentially or partially treatable (Wong 2017a).

Literature on yoga conducted with disabled individuals is almost exclusively limited to medical and popular registers. Within medical literature, clinical trials, like those with 'normal' individuals, test the efficacy of yoga in 'treating' disability and assume that normalisation is in their best interests (e.g. Jensen 2009; Hawkins et al. 2012; Shailaja et al. 2014; Steiner et al. 2013). Popular literature on yoga conducted with disabled populations largely includes how-to manuals, very similar to other popular books on yoga, which instruct specific exercises that the authors recommend for specific disabilities (Sumar 1998; Goldberg 2013; Williams and White 2010). This popular literature often highly values inclusivity and pays careful attention to how yoga may be adapted to suit different needs. Yet these two registers, medical and popular, are rarely in deep dialogue with one another: both medicalised versions of disability and practitioners' approaches to it only refer in the vaguest sense to each other's work. For example, while practitioners' books on yoga with disabilities place enormous emphasis on which exercises to do and how to do them, clinical trials, such as that by Steiner et al. (2013), rarely give details of class content (as is true of the vast majority of research literature on MPY). Steiner et al. simply state that 'yoga sessions were taught by certified yoga instructors experienced in yoga instruction' and '25% of each session was spent on initial relaxation, 50% of each session on yoga exercises and group activities, and 25% of each session on closing visualization/meditation' (2013: 817–818). There is an assumption that all yoga sessions, teachers and institutions will be the same or similar. This assumption is highly problematic because the broad range of yoga philosophies, brandings of yoga, individual teachers' approaches and requirements of institutions means that each individual yoga practice approaches disability in its own way.

Very often, both medical and popular registers are directed at analysing and treating disability in children specifically, since children's disabilities, more so than adults', are understood as treatable and potentially 'curable' (that is, able to be eradicated to produce a normalised, less disabled body). As I have discussed elsewhere, children's disabilities are also heavily loaded, since their diagnosis often burdens children, teachers and parents with the responsibility to 'overcome' and minimise deviation from 'standard' child development (Wong 2017a). More so than adults', children's disabilities have the pressure of temporality, as adults often hope that children will 'correct' as soon as possible, returning to the standardised trajectory of childhood growth.

Drawing on concepts of critical disability studies, I suggest that for yoga to be inclusive it must dispute representations of disability as lacking, and dominant 'embedded assumptions that conceptualise disability as misfortune' (Devlin and Pothier 2005: 2). That is, MPY needs to free itself of the imperative to *cure* or *treat* disability. Concepts of adequacy and competency need to be re-evaluated by critiquing the institutions and discourses that determine usefulness and efficacy, and we need to consider, in every yoga practice, who is 'represented', 'who "sees" or "hears" whom, and how and why' (Lesnik-Oberstein 2015: 3–4). Critical disability studies aims 'not to construct a universal theory, but to position disability as figuring an irreducible provocation to the normative desire' (Shildrick 2012: 37). This points to one of greatest challenges for yoga practice: avoiding the presumption that disabled people have the desire to be normative and 'impl[ying] judgements of good and bad, of what ought and what ought not to be' (Watson 2012: 99). It is also potentially unsettling to 'both sides of the putative divide between disabled and non-disabled' since it re-imagines disability and its purpose in the lives of non-disabled people (Barnes 2012: 35). Yoga practices need to engage with the kinds of judgements that are made about disabled bodies and the notion of their agency. Individuals need to be given the opportunity and 'individual capacity to challenge or alter those structures' that construct a body as 'disabled' (Watson 2012: 100).

So far I have focused on disability as one form of identity that may be included or excluded, in multifarious ways, throughout MPY classes. In the next section I will examine gender. In connecting the two, I here briefly draw attention to the ways in which disability and gender intersect. All individuals are navigating gender and sexuality stereotypes, and those labelled 'disabled' are no exception. Yet disabled genders and sexualities are complicated because '[t]he disabled sexual body is, in many ways, oxymoronic' (Beckman 2011: 90). Yet we could also think of yoga as an opportunity to complicate representations of both disability and gender, as part of a wider project of analysing and understanding difference. By exploring different ways of becoming masculine, feminine and disabled we can identify practices that demarcate particular bodies as on the outside, unable to conform to a normalised set of standards. Yoga could become a place for individuals to find equality, rather than an attempt to cure or care for nonconforming bodies. This would free some individuals from the 'oppressive' discussion, 'profound disincentives and few rewards' attached to identifying as disabled or gender transgressive (Garland-Thomson 1997: 347). In the current social climate, MPY classes may pressure individuals to choose between 'coming out' as disabled or attempting to 'pass'. The pressure may be applied as a student enrols in a class and signs an indemnity form detailing medical disclosure and insurance policies, and may extend into the delineation of populations into classes labelled 'general', 'accessible' or 'special needs'. Both the option to 'come out' and the option to 'pass' are problematic, since, like racial, gender and queer passing, the option of passing as non-disabled potentially serves up certain privileges alongside a sense of misrecognition and internal dissonance. 'Coming out' or identifying as disabled (if the disability is non-visible enough that this is an option) risks being reduced to stereotypes or having one's body work devalued or dismissed entirely. Since most disabilities are non-visible the choice may be 'between passing and performing the dominant culture's stereotypes of disability' (ibid., 326).

This is parallel to the choice to 'come out' as gender transgressive – gender stereotypes are as heavily policed as concepts of ableism, by teachers, students and institutions of yoga alike. As in many fitness settings, MPY classes require a gender/disability transgressive person to navigate the expectations others place on them while in close, sweaty, physical proximity to their evocatively stretching, moving body. Further, the transgressive individual must usually make a choice to use either gendered/non-disabled change rooms or seek access to disabled bathrooms in order to secure privacy while changing. For this reason, it may be useful to think of both individuals' dis-abilities and gender transgressions as forms of alternative embodiments – boldly enacted against dominant power structures that seek to disenfranchise them. The choice between passing and transgressing, however, carries with it a heavy neoliberal burden on the individual, which new concepts of inclusivity could help assuage by changing our social structures and environments so that individuals were not forced to choose between the two. As it is, yoga students sometimes cede to what Heyes calls 'normalizing desires', by choosing to pass as a normalised body and effectively 'assuage the suffering' of a transgressive body (Heyes 2007: 121). Meanwhile, individuals who perform alternative embodiments within MPY classes continue to defeat and diversify the ways we think about identity and inclusion.

## Gender

MPY is highly feminised within the context of other fitness and wellbeing practices and within the context of historical representations of yoga. There is a dominant representation and perception of yoga that 'one must have a flexible (white) feminine body to practise' and that women's bodies 'are more suitable for yoga' (Smith and Atencio 2017: 1178). This perception potentially excludes many individuals from participating in MPY classes. In western imaginations, yoga is understood as a relatively 'gentle, recreational, feminised, pacifist, and non-competitive practice', and all of these attributes are 'fairly recent discursive strands rather than any inherent and/or elemental features of yoga' (Hauser 2013: 5). Certainly, today's feminised version is a more *feminist* version than it was in the early twentieth century (Syman 2010). Yoga, as feminised, can also be hard, sweaty and aerobic – but it does not feature the overt emphasis on violence and competition of masculinised sports such as rugby or boxing.

One of the major criticisms levelled at MPY is that it emphasises the visual and reinforces mainstream imperatives to have or achieve the 'right' kind of body: youthful, slim and normatively beautiful. Particularly, MPY is problematic if it reinforces the dominance of a male gaze over predominantly female participants. Several MPY communities have attempted to combat this representation, such as The Yoga and Body Image Coalition, which aims to develop and promote yoga that is 'accessible, body positive and reflects the full range of human diversity' (Cummings 2016). Similarly, in 2017 and early 2018, the #MeToo and #TimesUp campaigns in the entertainment and political industries spread to MPY, as fresh allegations of sexual abuse and harassment shed light on the gender imbalances that have structured MPY practices since (at least) the twentieth century (Taylor 2018). Perhaps most infamously, Sri K. Pattabhi Jois and Bikram Choudhury, the founders of Ashtanga and Bikram yoga respectively, have been accused of performing sexually inappropriate adjustments and treating women with condescension and even contempt, throughout the 1980s and 1990s. In 2016 and 2017, there were seven separate lawsuits in the California courts against Bikram, alleging violation of women, including those under his tutelage and his former attorney, with 'accusations ranging from racial discrimination to gay slurs to harassment to rape' (Fagan 2018). In December 2017, Rachel Brathen collected more than 300 #MeToo stories which were anonymously submitted online by yogis around the world who related their experiences of abuse, harassment, misogyny and assault within MPY communities (Brathen 2017). Brathen, like The Yoga and Body Image Coalition, has been involved in calls for the MPY industry to confront the ways it has institutionalised patriarchy and maintained power imbalances between genders, most particularly between male teachers and female students, and created conditions in which such extensive abuse and harassment could take place. Undeniably, this must be one of the most important imperatives faced by the MPY industry today.

These instances of misconduct exist within a broader culture that determines how women think about themselves and their bodies. MPY communities, predominantly made up of women, function as spaces for women to come together (although they are not usually female-only spaces) and to shape their identities and imagined futures. Indeed, there is historical evidence that since coming to the West, yoga has played this important role in women's lives (Newcombe 2007; Singleton 2010: 51). According to cultural theorist Catherine Driscoll, thoughts about identity and the future are at the crux of these kinds of cultures, where women 'say who they are and want to be' through a 'set of stylistic choices', such as, for example, choosing to attend yoga or buying and wearing yoga clothing (Driscoll 1999: 189). Yoga in this context is one of many things in broader consumer culture that women 'can do, be, have and make' (ibid.), which is 'produced both for and about' women and circulates popularly among them, even though both men and women are involved in producing and using yoga as a form of women's culture (ibid., 114). In this understanding yoga teachers form one part of a 'range of experts' that help define yoga's 'contents and margins', as part of women's culture, among other experts such as 'magazine writers and fashion designers' (Driscoll 2014: 130). In the age of social media this is more instantaneous and visible than ever, as students follow and like particular teacher profiles, producing them as a kind of 'objec[t] circulated', in a way not dissimilar to how selfies of Kim Kardashian and Taylor Swift circulate (ibid., 130). Yoga classes, the teacher's body and the attention given to students are all commodities that are traded throughout this feminised consumer culture.

This form of women's culture is part of a broader consumer culture which operates within a heteronormative structure. Women are often self-conscious about their appearance in yoga classes and aware of being gazed upon, whether by men or other women. Even in MPY practices where students are encouraged to practise with their eyes closed (as is not uncommon), the choice to close one's eyes is a choice to temporarily *ignore* the gaze or 'turn it inwards', accepting its very prevalence, rather than an elimination of the gaze and its power. As women gaze upon each other and are gazed upon, they perpetuate competitive homosociality – projecting sexualities onto their own and others' bodies and producing embarrassment and vulnerability along with desire and transgression. Bodies cannot escape the gaze; dominant and alternative sexualities are visible (and whether those with alternative sexualities choose to pass or not, the representation they choose is still visible), and there is often little alternative to heteronormative competition between women. Susan Bordo has written of how women's use of their bodies is affected by constant awareness of being gazed upon. Bordo writes that under the scrutiny of the gaze an individual is 'shamed' by the 'looseness' of a 'soft, bruised' body (1999: 68–69). In some cases, such as that aimed for by The Yoga and Body Image Coalition, MPY may help women to challenge this perception, and find ways to 'radiat[e] independence, toughness, emotional imperviousness', a feeling of being 'armoured' by the body (ibid., 68–69). Yet as Bordo acknowledges, the difference between these two responses is often murky and muddled, as women oscillate between shame and defiance of those feelings. Further, the idea that women must be 'hard' in order to be allowed to be 'soft' perpetuates gender stereotypes, as women want 'to obtain the feminine body' and yet do so by 'appreciating the masculine characteristics of physical strength and skill' (Markula 2006: 29). Women not only practise yoga to reinvent and maintain their bodies as heteronormatively desirable; they also feel a feminist urge to defy the need to do so and seek to use MPY classes as an escape from the constant demands of being gazed upon. Yet, paradoxically, the gaze is often an embedded and important pedagogical tool in all MPY classes (whether self-surveillance or external surveillance). The teacher often gazes upon the student (even in self-practice) in order to develop learning. The student often also gazes upon the teacher as poses are demonstrated. The gaze searches, observes and judges, as it 'also touches, dominates and controls' (Synnott 1993: 227).

In this context, some critical theorists and MPY scholars have claimed that yoga has the potential to break free of the demands of a masculinised, patriarchal gaze and focus on somaesthetics as an alternative. Shusterman suggests that somaesthetics grants 'the body more careful aesthetic attention not only as an object that externally displays beauty … but also as a subjectivity that perceives these qualities and that experiences attendant aesthetic pleasures somatically' (2012: 6). Shusterman attempts to separate aesthetics out from the terrain of the visual, in order to grant it sensuality. If MPY were to function in this way, it must separate out 'the reflective and cognitive dimensions of somaesthetics', intimacy with one's own bodily sensations and 'meditative experiences of beautiful inner feelings' (ibid., 11). Shusterman witnesses this in 'Hatha Yoga' when 'somatic postures and movements' penetrate 'beneath skin surfaces and muscle fibre to realign our bones and better organise the neural pathways through which we move, feel, and think' (ibid., 43). For Shusterman this means that yoga has both representational and experiential rewards because 'there is a basic complementarity of representation and experience, outer and inner' (ibid., 44).

Shusterman claims that MPY could realign visual and experiential perception, redefining 'right and wrong' bodies. Less based on conventional standards of physical beauty, 'right and wrong' within yoga could refer to alignment within poses, meaning that there are 'beneficial' and 'unsafe' ways of using the body. However, just as 'beautiful' and 'ugly' bodies are often associated with moral and ethical judgements (for example, that an overweight person might be seen as lazy or unmotivated), having a 'right' or 'wrong' body within yoga could be laden with values, such as strong, weak, flexible, stiff, healthy, unhealthy, focused, distracted, experienced or beginner. Further, if a student is seen to be either normatively self-conscious, or self-aware, these qualities are also value-laden; as Karen Hanson has suggested, to be self-conscious is to be vain and lacking in self-esteem, to be self-aware is to be happier, more 'grounded' and mature (1993). Not least of those who observe a body in yoga is the teacher; as already mentioned, surveillance and self-surveillance are unavoidable in-built forms of objectification ever-present in most if not all MPY practices. Yet this form of objectification also possibly coexists with an invitation and encouragement to find alternative ways of gazing, working 'to find an appropriate stance on the relation between the individual and social norms' and 'learn how to participate happily, deriving appropriate if ephemeral satisfactions' from the body (ibid., 240). This is a decidedly feminist project, meditating the lived body as both an observed object and an influential subject. Yoga becomes a socially conditioned experience of interoception ('all sensations of the viscera, that is internal organs'), exteroception ('five senses open to the external world') and proprioception ('balance, position, and muscular tension') (Leder 1990: 39). It builds upon 'tactile perception' and 'kinesthetic' and 'sensational awareness' to affect how individuals experience themselves, perhaps opening up new gender and other identities (Bermúdez et al. 1995: 176, 271).

## Case study: yoga and queerness in institutionalised preschool education

At this point it will be useful to turn from an examination of what the potential of yoga could be and examine a brief, real-life example of how an MPY practice could reshape how particular identities could be included within institutions and pedagogical practice. This example focuses on a preschool environment in Sydney, Australia, where very young people are coming to terms with their sexualities in the twenty-first century, and being confronted with '[t]he future [a]s queerness's domain' (Muñoz 2009: 1). One of the most pertinent questions in the lives of these young people is whether 'the future [can] stop being a fantasy of heterosexual reproduction' and how queerness could offer 'futurity and hope' (ibid., 49, 11). This case study is a small extract from a larger ethnographic research project on children's yoga in Australia (Wong 2017b). I have deliberately used an example here that features children, since in most social structures today children's identities are minoritised and marginalised in comparison to those of adults (James, Jenks and Prout 1998: 4). In the twenty-first century, disabled, raced and queer children are often even more excluded and marginalised than disabled, raced and queer adults.

In September 2016, Roger, the director of a preschool at which I had taught children's yoga for years, informed me that preschool policy had changed so that teachers were no longer allowed to praise children with the words 'good boy' or 'good girl' (or similarly gendered variations). Instead, teachers were encouraged to compliment children on the specific task at hand – in the case of yoga: 'well done stretching', 'excellent balance' or 'you're very strong today'. This change had been instigated by one of the students, Alex. Alex, who was four years old, had been assigned female sex at birth, but was not identifying as female. Alex wore 'boy' clothes, had predominantly male friends and played 'boy' games. The news that Alex was not identifying as female came as no surprise to any of the teachers or staff at the preschool (including myself). Alex was constructing a gendered identity that misaligned with what Robinson calls 'socio-cultural narratives' about what it meant to be an 'authentic' or 'appropriate' girl (Robinson 2013: 82). Alex's parents had also begun to recognise this and were working to find ways to allow Alex to express a more reflective gender identity. However, Alex continued to have long hair and retained the same gendered name given at birth (I have deliberately used a non-gendered pseudonym; Alex's real name is an identifiably 'girl' name). Alex's teachers and parents were negotiating Alex's gendered identity yet struggling 'with whether and how to distinguish childhood self-knowledge from adult identity' (Meadow 2014: 58). They were not ready to commit to Alex's chosen gender (by allowing a name change or haircut) and labouring 'to determine if gender is ever fluid or stable, unfinished or finished' (ibid., 58). By December 2016, while still in preschool, Alex was preparing to transition to 'big school' and took to wearing 'big school's' unisex uniform every day. This was not unusual; many children similarly wore their 'big school' uniforms (or older siblings' uniforms) in term four of their last year at the preschool. Yet in Alex's case the unisex uniform also provided freedom from gender dichotomy. Alex's uniform was one of many 'micro moments and experiments' that provided 'glimpses of freedom – proto possibilities that emerge as becomings' and demonstrated Alex's inventiveness in finding ways to 'survive and momentarily transcend' the hegemony of gender dichotomy (Renold and Invinson 2015: 252–253). Similarly, many of the children who did identify as girls found that wearing their school uniforms (shorts) during yoga provided freedom, since they no longer were concerned about their skirts falling away when they were upside down, or revealing any part of their bodies. This is demonstrative of how even three- and four-year-olds were aware of the dominance of a heteronormative gaze in their yoga practices.

The preschool community, led by its director, Roger, were very supportive of Alex's choices. This was important because labelling a child as transgender (rather than, in Alex's case, a 'tomboy') potentially represented what Meadow sees as a 'shift in social category' and/or signified how other people understood Alex's 'history' (Meadow 2014: 58). Roger was also an openly gay man, in a long-term monogamous relationship. Roger's own gendered and sexual identity was important in this context, not just because he was the only man employed at the preschool, and in a position of power over women and children, but because in a social climate of 'alert around children, because of their perceived vulnerability to sexual danger', the figure of the gay man has become the epitome of 'the homosexual as the sexual predator' (Robinson 2008: 116, 127). The association of queer with paedophilic is historic, specific and persistent, as moral panics have repeatedly surrounded both male and female queer teachers and childcare workers in Australia (Riggs 2011: 245). Roger was highly aware of his own ethical responsibility to the children in his care, no doubt fuelled by 'paranoia about falling victim to false allegations of inappropriate behaviour' (Robinson 2008: 126). Yet Roger's sensitivity to the subject of sexuality did not translate into an avoidance of the subject. Instead, he became more highly aware of how he could enable children to be active agents in the negotiation of their sexualities and develop critical literacies in their relationships.

During the same conversation in which he informed me of the change in 'good girl/boy' policy, Roger also told me that 'one of our parents is also transitioning' and emphasised the importance of supporting Alex's, and other children's and adults', gender choices 'because we could be saving their lives'. Roger was committed to establishing ethical and respectful relationships between adults and children and made this 'an integral part of the early education agenda' at his preschool (Robinson 2013: 85). He acknowledged children's active sexualities and encouraged both adults and children at the preschool to develop 'sexual literacy' (ibid., 85). He wanted to eliminate all active and passive forms of 'stigma and abuse' that could be 'attached to transgressing gender norms' (ibid., 82). Yoga was part of this mammoth task, which Roger was trying to institutionalise, and was one of the many ways in which he imagined he could help children and adults to be more aware of their bodies and the language they used in 'respectful, ethical, and competent' and inclusive ways (ibid., 85).

For the children in this preschool yoga was a project of inclusion, one that embraced queer modernity. Yoga was not a wondrous unicorn, solving all anti-normative and/or liberatory problems for its participants. Yet it was a step, just one among many, that lifted adult and child participants out of the ways they thought and used their bodies and into new modes of being. It was able to hook into desires and needs that children already had for new forms of embodiments and new ways of doing queerness – for a new generation. Not all yogas with children, or all yogas in the twenty-first century, or all yogas in Australia, will be able to do this. It depends on the framing of the practice, within national and local settings, and the content of the practices themselves. Yet, as this case demonstrates, yoga can be a good place to start. As Heyes reminds us, body practices such as these are important 'first step[s]' toward creating grander queer projects and constitute 'useful forms of counterattack against corporeal normalization' (2007: 136). 'Although setting out to change the body is risky', and perhaps for no one more so than children, 'there remain real possibilities for a life of greater embodied freedom', and particularly in the twenty-first century, 'for people of all genders and genders not yet imagined' (ibid., 136). For young people like Alex, who needed embodied ways of addressing gender and sexuality, yoga provided one avenue for exploring greater freedom, and did so in a way that allowed for sensory perception and conscious ways of relating between the self and other.

## Conclusion

Individuals who participate in yoga today experience it as a complex mixture of discipline, freedom, pressure, comfort, normalisation, healing, limitation and learning. Like many practices and behaviours, yoga is embodied, surrounded by ethics, and a constant negotiation of power relationships. Sometimes MPY succeeds in 'build[ing] docile bodies' (Kennedy and Markula 2011: 64). At other times MPY challenges popular and dominant representations of identity and inclusion, questioning assumptions about what a body 'should' be able to do and how to achieve wellbeing. I have suggested that MPY has the potential to offer new ways of approaching difference, particularly for those with disabilities and non-heteronormative identities, as it can provide a space for exploring and embodying alternatives to dominant presumptions. Critical theory has provided one approach to yoga which has allowed for these kinds of conversations to become available, influencing discussion to move beyond the judgements and normalising pressures that continue to prevail. In this context, no two yogas are ever the same. The institutional environment of a class, its teacher and its participants are all major influencing factors on the kinds of ethics, pedagogies and philosophy that are employed within it. Further, it would be difficult to distil whether any particular moment in a classroom were wholly inclusive, empowering, dis-enabling or normalising for any given individual – every moment contains such a complex mixture of power structures that there are usually several ways of interpreting the kinds of subjectivities that are produced. Docility, engagement and non-compliance could all be ways of enacting different kinds of enabling and/or disenfranchised subjectivities at any one time depending on the context of the moment. For this reason, MPY practices, institutions and researchers must pay attention to the details and nuances of their practices and the thoughts of their participants – with the goal of consistently finding new and alternative ways to include all forms of identity.

## Notes

1 It should be noted that in certain ways the same can be said for qualitative research, but a qualitative approach often allows space for information that exists beyond the limits of any researchers' expectations, hypotheses and quantified measurements.

2 Other examples of scholar-practitioners' engagements with yoga on global and local levels can be found in Alter (2012), Black (2016), Lewis (2008), Atkinson (2010), Smith (2007), Lea (2009) and Chapple (2016), among others.

## Bibliography

Allan, J. 2014. 'Inclusive Education and the Arts'. *Cambridge Journal of Education* 44: 511–523.

Alter, J. S. 2012. 'Sacrifice, the Body, and Yoga: Theoretical Entailments of Embodiment in Hathayoga'. *South Asia: Journal of South Asian Studies* 35: 408–433.

Atkinson, M. 2010. 'Entering Scapeland: Yoga, Fell and Post-sport Physical Cultures'. *Sport in Society* 13: 1249–1267.

Augenstein, S. 2013. 'The Introduction of Yoga in German Schools: A Case Study', in Hauser, B. (ed), *Yoga Traveling: Bodily Practice in Transcultural Perspective*, 155–172. Heidelberg: Springer International Publishing.

Barcan, R. 2008. 'Alternative Therapies as Disciplinary Practices: The Uses and Limitations of a Foucauldian Approach', in Anderson, N. and Schlunke, K. (eds), *Cultural Theory in Everyday Practice*, 14–27. South Melbourne, Victoria: Oxford University Press.

Barnes, C. 2012. 'Understanding the Social Model of Disability', in Thomas, C., Roulstone, A. and Watson, N. (eds), *Routledge Handbook of Disability Studies*, 12–29. New York: Routledge.
Beckman, F. (ed) 2011. *Deleuze and Sex*. Edinburgh: Edinburgh University Press.
Bermúdez, J. L., Marcel, A. J. and Eilan, N. 1995. *The Body and the Self*. Cambridge, MA: MIT Press.
Black, S. 2016. 'Flexible Indian Labor: Yoga, Information Technology Migration, and US Technoculture'. *Race and Yoga* 1: 23–39.
Bordo, S. 1999. *The Male Body: A New Look at Men in Public and in Private*. New York: Farrar, Straus and Giroux.
Bost, S. 2016. 'Practicing Yoga/Embodying Feminism/Shape-Shifting'. *Frontiers: A Journal of Women Studies* 37: 191–210.
Brathen, R. 2017. '#Metoo – The Yoga Stories'. *Yoga Girl*, 6 Dec. www.yogagirl.com/read/metoo/me-too-the-yoga-stories-part-1. Accessed 21 June 2020.
Buckingham, S. and Degen, M. 2012. 'Sensing Our Way: Using Yoga as a Research Method'. *The Senses and Society* 7: 15.
Chapple, C. K. 2016. *Yoga in Jainism*. London, Routledge.
Cummings, N. 2016. *Yoga and Body Image Coalition*, http://ybicoalition.com/. Accessed 19 June 2019.
Devlin, R. and Pothier, D. 2005. *Critical Disability Theory*. Vancouver: UBC Press.
Driscoll, C. 1999. 'Girl Culture, Revenge and Global Capitalism: Cybergirls, Riot Grrls, Spice Girls'. *Australian Feminist Studies* 14: 173–193.
Driscoll, C. 2014. *The Australian Country Girl: History, Image, Experience*. Farnham: Ashgate Publishing Ltd.
Fagan, K. 2018. 'Bikram Yoga's Moral Dilemma'. *ESPN*, 23 May, www.espn.com/espnw/culture/feature/article/23539292/after-serious-allegations-founder-bikram-yoga-practitioners-crossroads. Accessed 20 June 2019.
Garland-Thomson, R. 1997. *Extraordinary Bodies: Figuring Physical Disability in American Culture And Literature*. New York: Columbia University Press.
Goldberg, L. 2013. *Yoga Therapy for Children with Autism and Special Needs*. New York: W. W. Norton & Company.
Hanson, K. 1993. 'Dressing Down Dressing Up: The Philosophic Fear of Fashion', in Hein, H. S. and Korsmeyer, C. (eds), *Aesthetics in Feminist Perspective*, 229–242. Bloomington: Indiana University Press.
Hauser, B. (ed) 2013. *Yoga Traveling: Bodily Practice in Transcultural Perspective*. New York: Springer.
Hawkins, B. L., Stegall, J. B., Weber, M. F. and Ryan, J. B. 2012. 'The Influence of a Yoga Exercise Program for Young Adults with Intellectual Disabilities'. *International Journal of Yoga* 5: 151–156.
Helberg, N., Heyes, C. J. and Rohel, J. 2009. 'Thinking Through the Body: Yoga, Philosophy, and Physical Education'. *Teaching Philosophy* 32(3): 263–284.
Heyes, C. J. 2006. 'Foucault Goes to Weight Watchers'. *Hypatia* 21: 126–149.
Heyes, C. J. 2007. *Self-Transformations: Foucault, Ethics, and Normalized Bodies*. Oxford, Oxford University Press.
Irigaray, L. 2008. 'Conversations', in Pluháček, S. (ed), *Interviews. Selections*, 73–84. London: Continuum.
James, A., Jenks, C. and Prout, A. 1998. *Theorizing Childhood*. Cambridge: Polity Press.
Jensen, P. 2004. 'The Effects of Yoga on the Attention and Behavior of Boys with Attention-Deficit/Hyperactivity Disorder (ADHD)'. *Journal Of Attention Disorders* 7(4): 205–216.
Jensen, P. 2009. *Yoga as an Adjuvant Therapy for Students Enrolled in Special Schools for Disruptive Behaviour*. PhD dissertation [Ed. Discipline of Behavioural and Social Sciences in Health], University Of Sydney.
Kennedy, E. and Markula, P. 2011. *Women and Exercise: The Body, Health and Consumerism*. New York: Routledge.
Kuppers, P. 2011. *Disability Culture and Community Performance*. Basingstoke: Palgrave Macmillan.
Kuppers, P. 2016. 'Diversity: Disability'. *Art Journal* 75: 93–97.
Lea, J. 2009. 'Liberation or Limitation? Understanding Iyengar Yoga as a Practice of the Self'. *Body & Society* 15: 71–92.
Leder, D. 1990. *The Absent Body*. Chicago: University of Chicago Press.
Lesnik-Oberstein, K. (ed) 2015. *Rethinking Disability Theory and Practice*. Basingstoke: Palgrave Macmillan.
Lewis, C. S. 2008. 'Life Chances and Wellness: Meaning and Motivation in the "Yoga Market"'. *Sport in Society* 11: 535.
Markula, P. 1995. 'Firm but Shapely, Fit but Sexy, Strong but Thin: The Postmodern Aerobicizing Female Bodies'. *Sociology of Sport Journal* 12: 424–453.
Markula, P. 2001. 'Beyond the Perfect Body: Women's Body Image Distortion in Fitness Magazine Discourse'. *Journal Of Sport & Social Issues* 25: 158–179.
Markula, P. 2006. 'Deleuze and the Body without Organs: Disreading the Fit Feminine Identity'. *Journal of Sport & Social Issues* 30: 29–44.

Markula, P. 2010. '"Folding": A Feminist Intervention In Mindful Fitness', in Kennedy, E. and Markula, P. (eds), *Women And Exercise*, 60–79. Proquest Ebook Central: Taylor and Francis.

Markula, P. 2014. 'Reading Yoga: Changing Discourses of Postural Yoga on the Yoga Journal Covers'. *Communication & Sport* 2: 143–171.

Marcel, M. 1992 [1931]. 'Techniques ofThe Body', in Crary, J. and Kwinter, S. (eds), *Incorporations*, 455–477. New York: Zone.

McInnes, D. 2015. 'Yoga: Cultural Pedagogy and Embodied Ethics', in Watkins, M., Noble, G. and Driscoll, C. (eds), *Cultural Pedagogies and Human Conduct*, 201–216. New York: Taylor and Francis.

McLaren, L., Rock, M. J. and McElgunn, J. 2012. 'Social Inequalities in Body Weight and Physical Activity: Exploring the Role of Fitness Centers'. *Research Quarterly For Exercise and Sport* 83: 94–102.

Meadow, T. 2014. 'Child'. *Tsq: Transgender Studies Quarterly* 1–2: 57–59.

Morgan, P. F. 2012. 'Following Contemplative Education Students' Transformation Through Their "Ground-Of-Being" Experiences'. *Journal of Transformative Education* 10: 42–60.

Muñoz, J. E. 2009. *Cruising Utopia: The Then and There of Queer Futurity*. New York: New York University Press.

Newcombe, S. 2007. 'Stretching For Health and Well-Being: Yoga and Women in Britain, 1960–1980'. *Asian Medicine* 3: 37–63.

Newcombe,. S. 2009. 'The Development of Modern Yoga: A Survey of the Field'. *Religion Compass* 3: 986–1002.

Pelt, J.V. 2011. 'Yoga and Children's Mental Health'. *Social Work Today* 11(6): 8.

Powell, L., Stapley, J. and Gilchrist, M. 2008. 'A Journey of Self-Discovery: An Intervention Involving Massage, Yoga and Relaxation for Children with Emotional and Behavioural Difficulties Attending Primary Schools'. *European Journal of Special Needs Education* 23(4): 403–412. https://doi.org/10.1080/08856250802387398

Renold, E. and Invinson, G. 2015. 'Mud, Mermaids and Burnt Wedding Dresses: Mapping Queer Becomings In Teen Girls' Talk On Living With Gender And Sexual Violence', in Renold, E., Ringrose, J. and Egan, R. D. (eds), *Children, Sexuality and Sexualisation*, 239–255. Palgrave Macmillan.

Riggs, D. W. 2011. '"What About the Children!" Homophobia, Accusations of Pedophilia, and the Construction of Childhood', in Scherer, B. and Ball, M. (eds), *Queering Paradigms Ii: Interrogating Agendas*, 245–258. Bern: Peter Lang Ag, Internationaler Verlag Der Wissenschaften.

RMIT. 2018. 'Introduction to Body, Breath and Movement', *RMIT University*. http://www1.rmit.edu.au/courses/041294. Accessed 19 June 2019.

Robinson, K. H. 2008. 'In the Name of "Childhood Innocence": A Discursive Exploration of the Moral Panic Associated with Childhood and Sexuality'. *Cultural Studies Review* 14: 113–129.

Robinson, K. H. 2013. 'Building Respectful Relationships Early: Educating Children on Gender Variance and Sexual Diversity. A Response to Damien Riggs'. *Contemporary Issues in Early Childhood* 14: 81–87.

Ross, A., Friedmann, E., Bevans, M. and Thomas, S. 2013. 'National Survey ofYoga Practitioners: Mental and Physical Health Benefits' *Complementary Therapies in Medicine* 21: 313–323.

Saks, M. 2005. *Orthodox and Alternative Medicine: Politics, Professionalization and Health Care*. London: Sage Publications Ltd.

Shailaja, U., Rao, P. N., Girish, K. J. and Arun Raj, G. R. 2014. 'Clinical Study on the Efficacy of Rajayapana Basti and Baladi Yoga in Motor Disabilities of Cerebral Palsy in Children'. *Ayu* 35: 294–299.

Sharma, S. 2014. *In the Meantime*. Duke University Press.

Shildrick, M. 2012. 'Critical Disability Studies', in Thomas, C., Roulstone, A. and Watson, N. (eds), *Routledge Handbook Of Disability Studies*, 30–41. New York; Routledge.

Shusterman, R. 2012. *Thinking Through the Body*. Cambridge University Press.

Singleton, M. 2010. *Yoga Body: The Origins of Modern Posture Practice*. Oxford, Oxford University Press.

Slovacek, S. P., Tucker, S. A. and Pantoja, L. 2003. 'A Study of the Yoga Ed Program at The Accelerated School'. *Yoga Ed*, Nov, https://www.inschoolyoga.com/Yoga-Ed-Program-Study.pdf. Accessed 22 July 2013.

Smith, B. R. 2007. 'Body, Mind and Spirit? Towards an Analysis of the Practice of Yoga'. *Body & Society* 13: 25–46.

Smith, S. and Atencio, M. 2017. '"Yoga is Yoga. Yoga is Everywhere. You Either Practice or You Don't": A Qualitative Examination ofYoga Social Dynamics'. *Sport in Society* 20: 1167–1184.

Steiner, N. J., Sidhu, T. K., Pop, P. G., Frenette, E. C. and Perrin, E. C. 2013. 'Yoga in an Urban School for Children with Emotional and Behavioral Disorders: A Feasibility Study'. *Journal of Child And Family Studies* 22: 815–826.

Sumar, S. 1998. *Yoga for the Special Child: A Therapeutic Approach for Infants and Children with Down Syndrome, Cerebral Palsy, Learning Disabilities.* New York, Special Yoga Publications.

Syman, S. 2010. *The Subtle Body: The Story of Yoga in America.* New York, Farrar, Straus and Giroux.

Synnott, A. 1993. *The Body Social: Symbolism, Self, And Society.* London: Routledge.

Taylor, M. 2018. '#Timesup: Ending Sexual Abuse in the Yoga Community'. *Yoga Journal*, 12 Feb., https://www.yogajournal.com/lifestyle/timesup-metoo-ending-sexual-abuse-in-the-yoga-community. Accessed 19 June 2019.

Telles, S., Sharma, S. K., Singh, N. and Balkrishna, A. 2017. 'Characteristics of Yoga Practitioners, Motivators, and Yoga Techniques of Choice: A Cross-Sectional Study'. *Frontiers in Public Health* 5: 184.

Watson, N. 2012. 'Researching Disablement', in Thomas, C., Roulstone, A. and Watson, N. (eds), *Routledge Handbook of Disability Studies*, 93–106. New York: Routledge.

Williams, N. and White, L. 2010. *Yoga Therapy for Every Special Child: Meeting Needs in a Natural Setting.* London: Singing Dragon.

Wong, K.-A. 2017a. 'Minor Bodies: How Disability Is Figured in Children's Yoga Classes'. *Continuum* 31: 93–103.

Wong, K.-A. 2017b. *Child's Pose: Children's Yoga and the Complexities of Normalisation.* Dissertation/Thesis, University of Sydney.

# 33

# YOGA: BETWEEN MEDITATION AND MOVEMENT[1]

*Matylda Ciołkosz*

## Introduction

The main aim of this chapter is to advance a particular methodological approach to the study of yoga and meditation. While the major part of yoga-related scholarship has been philological and historical, with ventures into ethnography, sociology and psychology, I would like to discuss the possibilities of studying yoga practice – as well as 'yoga philosophy' – from the perspective of movement.

At the outset, a clarification is in order. While the experience of movement is central to being human, the concept of movement is not at all self-explanatory and may be defined from different vantage points. We may talk of movement from the physical perspective, in terms of Newtonian mechanics. When describing the movement of living organisms, we may refer to biomechanics, but we may also discuss it from the perspective of biology as such – describing its physiological causes, effects and correlates. In this regard, we may discuss the movement of the skeleto-muscular system (let us call it 'movement *of* the body'), the movement of single cells, tissues, organs, and fluids or solids of external origin ('movement *within* the body'), as well as the relation between the two. Because a moving being is immersed in an environment, we can talk about movement, or displacement, in relation to this environment (as in running in circles, climbing up mountains, or running down a road), or about movement without displacement, involving changes in the relative positioning of different body parts (as in performing *āsana*).

Moreover, we can interpret human movement as a cultural or social phenomenon, as sociologist Marcel Mauss did in 1931 when he talked about *techniques of the body* (see below). Finally, we could approach movement – within the body, of the body, featuring displacement in the environment, transmitted culturally or not – from the perspective of phenomenology, as a first-person *experience* of a particular moving subject. It is this last approach that is the main theme of this chapter.

## Phenomenology as a research method

Although we may take it for granted as socialised, well-behaved and thoughtful adults, movement is our primary – and primal – experience. As philosopher and dance scholar Maxine Sheets-Johnstone put it, '[w]e come straightaway moving into the world' (Sheets-Johnstone 2011: 117). We are born 'wiggling, stretching, opening our mouths, swallowing, kicking, crying, and so on' (ibid.). It is through the increasing variety of movements that enter our repertoire in infancy that we establish our concept of space, of our presence and identity in that space, of effort, cause and effect, and even of time. However, our kinetic activity is largely spontaneous. In most cases, it does not undergo analytical scrutiny. Unless we are faced with unusual kinetic tasks as adults – regaining our basic motor capacities after a serious injury, learning how to dance or play a new sport – we are more or less oblivious of the complexities of our own bodies in motion.

In order to study movement, however, we need to *experience* it in a phenomenological sense – not only to be aware of it, but also to be able to deconstruct it. Edmund Husserl's phenomenology – as a proposal of an infallible philosophical method – assumes a subject's ability to not only clearly discern the object of intentional focus, but also to tell apart the object as 'a thing itself', as it appears in direct experience, from any pre-judgements and preconceptions the subject might have about it. It is this 'thing itself' that is the *phenomenon* to be examined. Husserl's method also assumes the ability to abstract the singular instances of those 'things themselves' – with their incidental features – from their non-incidental, eidetic aspect. Finally, it assumes the subject's ability to tell themselves apart from themselves – to distinguish the naïve 'I' immersed in the world from the unbiased phenomenological subject, as well as from the transcendental subject, capable of attributing meaning to the observed phenomena.

Phenomenology as a method is 'a disciplined approach to human experience' (Varela 1996: 330). Therefore, engaging in phenomenology of movement requires the researcher to adopt and to rigorously retain a three-fold stance: of the actual mover immersed in their own kinaesthesia, of an unbiased observer witnessing this kinaesthesia as 'a thing itself' – a sheer feeling of movement, uninfluenced by any preconceptions or expectations – and, finally, of the critical analyst of these observations, capable of interpreting them. As researchers of movement we should be 'practicing phenomenologists' who, 'having kinaesthetic experiences, can examine them, paying rigorous attention to what is actually there, sensuously present in our experience, and in turn validating or disarming what a phenomenological account discloses' (Sheets-Johnstone 2011 [1999]: 121).

Naturally, yoga is not simply about movement. Yoga is a historical and cultural phenomenon encompassing a variety of practices, including those involving movement and the cessation thereof. Such conventionalised methods of moving and rendering oneself motionless are what Mauss calls *techniques of the body*, 'the ways in which from society to society men know how to use their bodies' (1973 [1931]). Some techniques of the body – like gaits, birthing positions or ways to dance at weddings – may be shared across entire societies and acquired with relative spontaneity through typical socialisation. Other techniques – like yogic practices – are specific to more exclusive groups and require special training.

In techniques of yoga, bodies are used in inventive, rigorously prescribed ways. They are also used for a clearly prescribed purpose: attaining, or at least facilitating, liberation. This conventional and systematic aspect of yogic techniques – their artificialness, as opposed to the spontaneity of the kinetic skills we acquire as infants – makes them more available for phenomenological scrutiny. A skilled researcher, while becoming familiar with yogic ways of moving and feeling the body, might find it easier to observe their own experience from an ex-centric, unbiased perspective. At the same time, however, they have to be capable of relating this experience and observation to the doctrinal system to which the studied techniques are related, as well as to the overall cultural and historical context in which they are embedded.

To sum up, this chapter proposes a research method in the form of a systematic survey of the experience of movement during yoga practice – movement within the body and of the body, featuring spatial displacement or not – and of the meaning-making potential of this experience. How does the yogin's feeling of their body in motion (or stillness) relate to concepts of liberation? How does it relate to the broader religio-philosophical context in which particular practices develop and transform? Below, I will suggest possible ways of answering these questions.

## We move before we think

How does the yogin's feeling of their body in motion relate to concepts of liberation? Below, I start the discussion of yoga, meditation and movement by listing the meanings given to yoga in writing. I do so, because I endorse the view held by groups of scholars across various disciplines: that human kinaesthetic experience – or, more broadly, human sensorimotor experience – is a key substratum for concept formation and language.

In the words of Sheets-Johnstone (2010: 166), 'language is and should be regarded as post-kinetic'. What this means is that our experience of being immersed in a world, of moving within it and interacting with it, provides us with embodied representations of this world that we may abstract concepts from. Before we formulate a general notion of a 'near' or 'far', we try to reach objects within our sight as infants, sometimes successfully, and sometimes not. Before we construe a general concept of a container and learn that it is called so, we put things in boxes or in our mouths. Before we can understand yoga as holding the mind still, we experience holding objects in our hand and realise that if a thing is held tight, it may not be displaced.

Among the foregoing examples, the last one is especially significant. 'Yoga' is a polysemous term, and an abstract concept – it is not an object we can touch, move or squeeze. And yet it is often construed in terms of holding. In fact, thinking of abstract concepts in terms of tangible experiences is as common as it can be. As linguist George Lakoff and philosopher Mark Johnson famously argued in 1980, formulating what is known as the *theory of conceptual metaphor*, the most salient domains of our lived experience provide the metaphors we use to represent those concepts that are difficult, or impossible, to represent directly. Because we experience our bodies as oriented in space, we can think and talk about our mood in terms of our placement in relation to the vertical axis: our spirits are *up* when we are happy, and bad news is a *downer.* Because we deal with many different containers in our everyday life, we can think about events in terms of containers, like when we say 'He got himself *into* a difficult situation' (like we may enter *into* a crowded room) or 'She is *stuck in* a loveless marriage' (like an object may be *stuck in* a container that was too small to begin with). Because we know how it feels to hold something firm in our hand, we can call a state of yogic meditation, involving focusing attention on a single object, *dhāraṇā*, i.e. 'holding'.

Below, I will attempt to connect some of the concepts related to yoga with the various kinds of kinaesthetic experience that have possibly informed them. In this way, I hope to show that phenomenology of yogic movement may get us further than just the movement itself, and into the realm of 'yoga philosophy'.

## Yoga: journeying towards stillness

The verbal root √*yuj*, from which the noun *yoga* stems, was first applied in writing in the *Ṛg Veda* to refer to the yoking of the horses to a chariot (Mallinson and Singleton 2017: xiii). Although yoking implies constraining the movement of a previously autonomous creature, it is in fact more than that. It is just an initial stage of a longer process, during which the creature's movement is controlled and directed, so that the creature, the vehicle it is yoked to and the driver arrive at a chosen destination. In other words, the yoking is just the beginning of a journey, and it is not until the journey is over that movement can actually cease. As Vedic scholar

Joanna Jurewicz (2018) explains, in the *Ṛg Veda*, the term *yóga* refers to a period of journey in the nomadic Aryans' life, as opposed to the period of peaceful settling (*kṣema*). The experience of a journey involved yoking horses to a chariot, controlling the movement of those horses with the reigns, moving across different territories on even or bumpy roads, encountering various obstacles and possibly enemies to fight, and, finally, arriving at a point of destination. The noun *yóga*, 'yoke', denoting an object put on a horse's neck at the outset of a journey, came to metonymically[2] represent the experience of a journey in its entirety (Jurewicz 2018: 26–27). Later, when yoga came to be understood as a soteriological pursuit, the experience of journeying – with its varieties of movement including holding the reins, controlling the movement of the horses, being displaced in space along a linear trajectory and stopping at a point of arrival – came to represent metaphorically various aspects of yogic practice.

In the *Kaṭha Upaniṣad*, yoga is defined as *sthirāmindriya dhāraṇā*, holding the senses steady (KU 6.11). An earlier part of the text provides a context for the definition, when mental control is likened to driving a chariot. The horses are the senses (*indriya*), the reigns are the mind (*manas*), and the charioteer is the intellect (*buddhi*). It becomes clear that the notion of *dhāraṇā* (from √*dhṛ* – 'to hold', 'to maintain', 'to keep'; Monier-Williams 1899: 519) has its origins in the experience of constraining the movement of the horses with the reigns.

The concept of *dhāraṇā* recurs in the *Pātañjalayogaśāstra* as one of the last three auxiliaries of *aṣṭāṅgayoga*. These three auxiliaries, best understood as gradually limiting one's cognitive activity, are called jointly *saṃyama* (PYŚ 3.4) – a term also suggesting holding or keeping together (with √*yam* meaning 'to hold up', 'to support', or 'to wield'; Monier-Williams 1899: 845).

While the first stage of *saṃyama* – *dhāraṇā* – involves the binding (*bandhana*) of the consciousness (*citta*) to a particular object (PYŚ 3.1), *dhyāna* (lit. 'thought', 'reflection', 'meditation'; Monier-Williams 1899: 521) implies unidirectionality (*ekatānatā*) of attentiveness (PYŚ 3.2). Once *citta* is bound and constrained (similarly to a horse), it can be steered in a preferable direction (linear movement ensues). During the following stages of *samādhi* (lit. 'putting together', 'combining with' or 'joining with'; Monier-Williams 1899: 1159), this goal is gradually attained, as the object of meditative focus is deconstructed and the cognising subject itself – the passive, i.e. motionless *puruṣa* – is experienced. Ultimately, motion ceases when the last available reference point for movement – the object of meditation – is removed. The point of arrival, the point of ultimate stillness, is the one and only *puruṣa* – deprived of the power to move and, hence, deprived of notions of spatiality.

As the foregoing terminology suggests, the stilling of *citta* in *saṃyama* is construed in terms of applying force through holding, tying or placing – as if to control and stop the movement of consciousness, a counter-movement needed to be applied. This construal is questioned in some later interpretations of yogic meditation. The medieval *rājayoga* tradition, first attested in writing in the twelfth-century CE *Amanaska*, explains the meditative cessation of cognitive processes as effortless. According to the *Amanaska*, *samādhi* is a 'natural state' (*sahajāvasthā*) attained when a yogin's mind simply stops wandering, like an elephant freed from its goad (see Birch 2013). Here, the notion of restraining the movement of an animal to steer it towards a goal is discarded and a different metaphor is applied, derived from an observation of another animal that, when simply let loose, stops at a preferred spot.

What this short discussion has hopefully shown is that the notion of movement is present at the very outset of the conceptualisation of yoga. Although the goal of yoga is stillness, the means to achieve this goal is displacement attained by forceful constraint. In this case, the experience of movement used to construe this process is not related to yogic practice as such. However, certain techniques of the body already in use in the Upanishadic period could have been conducive to a similar experience.

## The inward journey: yoga and movement within the body

It seems that techniques of breath control and retention have a long history in India, with a classification of different breaths present already in the *Atharva Veda* (AV 15.16–18; see Mallinson and Singleton 2017: 137). In the *Pātañjalayogaśāstra*, the practice of *prāṇāyāma* is defined as the cutting (*viccheda*) of the movement (*gati*) of the inhalation and exhalation (PYŚ 2.49). The breath may be stopped after exhalation or after inhalation, or both the inbreath and the outbreath may be stopped. The yogin may observe the displacement of the locus where the breath occurs, the length of the breath and the number of breaths (PYŚ 2.50).

Having previously adopted a seated *āsana*, the yogin practicing *prāṇāyāma* experiences solely the movement of the breath. They may control this movement, slowing it down or stopping it at will. Just like riding a chariot, controlled breathing is the source of an experience of using force to constrain, direct and stop motion. And this experience is also used to construe the notion of mental constraint. As breathing and thinking occur simultaneously, there is a metonymic association of the breath with the mind, like in the *Chāndogya Upaniṣad* (ChU 6.8.2), where it is said that the mind is tied to the breath and therefore it cannot fly off.

The medieval *haṭha* techniques are a true exploration of the movement within the body, with a set of techniques able to produce intense proprioceptive and interoceptive[3] experience, and a theoretical model of the body corresponding to this experience. In *haṭha* literature, varieties of breath-retention practices, called *kumbhaka*, are presented next to *bandhas* ('ties', 'bonds'; Monier-Williams 1899: 720) and *mudrās* ('seals', 'stamps'; ibid.: 822). The latter two involve mostly selective contraction of the pelvic and abdominal muscles to produce a feeling of vacuum inside the abdominal cavity and of ensuing upward movement (see Mallinson 2011; 2018). Some of these techniques (like *mahāmudrā*) involve intense pressing of the heel against the contracted perineum – a practice that, as Thomas McEvilley has argued, may produce 'a flow of nerve sensation upward from the base of the spine' (McEvilley 1981: 60).[4] When this experience is taken into consideration, it is not surprising that the *haṭha* practices were believed to result in the lifting of *bindu*, the essence of life, along the central duct of the body (*suṣumnā nāḍī*) back into its receptacle in the head.[5] In this process, control of the vital breaths (mainly *prāṇa* and *apāna*) was considered instrumental, as they were the medium in which *bindu* was believed to move.

*Haṭha* practices were not aimed at attaining the ultimate yogic stillness of consciousness directly. They were a preparation for meditative practices (now subsumed as *rājayoga*), and their goal was to inure the yogin's body against death and disease. Nonetheless, they involved a notion of controlled, directed movement culminating in more or less abrupt 'arrival' (to a point located in the head). Importantly, this notion seems to correspond to the experience of the movement within the body during actual *haṭha* practices.

## Posturing for liberation: movement and motionlessness in asana

The remaining part of this chapter focuses mainly on modern postural yoga (MPY). Arguably the most visible and accessible category of yoga practices nowadays, MPY – called so by Elizabeth De Michelis – encompasses 'styles of yoga practice that put a lot of emphasis on *āsanas* or yoga postures; in other words the more "physical" or gymnastic-like type of yoga' (De Michelis 2004: 4). Of all the yogic practices, *āsana*, or at least the MPY variety of asana, is mostly about movement. The practitioner puts their body through a sequence of complex postures, doing so more or less dynamically and more or less in synchrony with the breath. Nonetheless, many practitioners put a lot of effort in arguing that the 'gymnastic-like' quality of their pursuits is only apparent. Modern asana practice is expected not only to be meditative in character, but also to lead to a deep transformation of one's identity – a modern version of liberation. As I will argue, notions of this transformation are very much inspired by the kinds of movement and stillness experienced during asana practice.

The understanding of posture practice in MPY reflects an attempt to reconcile the transformation of the concept of *āsana* across centuries with its definition provided by Patañjali a millennium-and-a-half ago. Late *haṭha* literature attests to growing complexity of *āsana* practice, with an increasing number and variety of prescribed postures (see Birch 2018). The *āsanas* of late *haṭhayoga* – including balancing and inverted poses as well as dynamic repetitions of strenuous movements – required significant physical prowess. In twentieth-century India, *āsana* practice was influenced by forms of physical culture, both indigenous and European (Sjoman 1996; Singleton 2010; Armstrong 2018). This influence turned postural yoga into a demanding physical drill and a kind of spiritualised gymnastics that it remains until today.

At the same time, however, the key reference point for construing asana in MPY has been a passage from *Pātañjalayogaśāstra* defining it as 'a steady and comfortable posture … [that arises] either from the slackening of effort or from merging meditatively into infinity' (Maas 2018: 56). As a result, the challenging posture sequences of acrobatic nature are expected to be performed with the same comfort and effortlessness that Patañjali attributed to the seated postures recommended for *prāṇāyāma*.

This attempt to enact Patañjali's definition of *āsana* determines the kinds of kinaesthetic experience sought during MPY practice. Different systems seek different ways of attaining the feeling of effortlessness, stillness and meditative constraint of activity. In Iyengar Yoga, for example, meditative stillness is attained through great focus on detail and gradual increase of proprioceptive awareness. Each posture, maintained for a prolonged time, is broken down into multiple units – relative positioning of small body parts. The practitioner controls these units first sequentially, and then simultaneously, ideally becoming aware of the relative alignment of countless parts of the body at once. B. K. S. Iyengar construed this process of ongoing observation and alignment in terms of an inward journey 'from the skin to the core and back again' (Iyengar 2002: 103). This journey is aimed not only at feeling one's body throughout, but also at experiencing one's own psyche and spirit. The point of arrival is believed to be the merging of consciousness with the Universal Self (*puruṣa/ātman*), encountered not only in the 'core' of one's being, but in fact in each and every bodily cell. Although maintaining the asana requires a lot of isometric effort (of 'holding' the muscles in a state of prolonged contraction), the ultimate experience is expected to be that of effortlessness, attained through a kind of cellular *samādhi*.

On the other hand, asana practice in the tradition of K. Pattabhi Jois is very dynamic, with smooth transitions between postures in the form of so-called *vinyāsa*, and very little time given to maintain each particular pose. However, the permanent isometric contraction of abdominal muscles (through the *haṭha* techniques of *mūla* and *uḍḍīyāna bandha*), combined with rhythmical audible breathing and the fixing of gaze, are conducive to a trance-like state that one of Jois' former students calls 'movement meditation' (Maehle 2006: 4). A sense of decreased agency is also to be experienced, when the body seems to be moving effortlessly on its own, observed from the vantage point of its robust, motionless core.

As these two brief examples show, despite the athletic character of modern postural yoga, the kind of movement engaged in during MPY asana practice is interpreted in terms of yogic cessation of motion. In case of Iyengar Yoga, the performance of asanas is in fact believed to enable the attainment of *samādhi*. This latter case indicates that kinaesthetic experience may indeed be applied to represent in embodied terms certain abstract concepts. Understanding this experience may hence be a gateway to explaining why particular 'yoga philosophies' receive the kind of interpretative treatment they do.

## Yoga scholars in action: scholarship on yogic movement so far

Engaging in phenomenology of movement requires a reconsideration of the researcher's position. A phenomenologist is not just a distanced observer describing and evaluating the object of their enquiry from an external perspective. They have to engage fully in the practices they are investigating. A particular challenge of such an approach lies in the fact that the researcher's body needs to become a research tool, which requires the kind of sensitivity that may not be available just by virtue of being human. Unless we cultivate them deliberately, our kinetic capacities are not the subject of our special attention. This is all the more true for academics, who are trained specifically to suppress their urge to move and pay attention to their bodies' basic needs, for the benefit of focused intellectual work (see Carp 2001: 99). Being an academic is a particular technique of the body, involving dissociation from one's sensorimotor presence in the world.

Such academically disciplined bodies may not only be incapable of immediate engagement in complex movement practices. They may also be oblivious to the significance of kinaesthesia in human life. Even Husserl himself did not grasp this significance, reducing the body to 'a freely moving organ (or system of such organs) by means of which the subject experiences the external world' (Husserl 1989: 168). It was not until a few decades later that Maurice Merleau-Ponty acknowledged the body as an actual centre of a lived experience. Similarly to Husserl, who distinguished between the phenomenological and the naïve subject, Merleau-Ponty (1962) identified the objective physical body as distinct from the subjective lived body. Both of these aspects of the body, he claimed, are a part of the human experience, and they both have to be acknowledged in a phenomenological pursuit. This means that a phenomenologist has to not only acknowledge the importance of movement as an external fact, they also have to develop the skill of becoming consciously engrossed in their own kinaesthesia. They need to simultaneously objectify their movement and make their moving, feeling bodies the centre of their experience. I also believe that they have to develop a 'transcendental body' (a counterpart of Husserl's transcendental self) that would enable them to attribute meaning to their own kinaesthesia.

For yoga scholars this task should be relatively easy, since many of them are actual yoga practitioners (see Singleton and Larios, Chapter 4 in this volume). Having arisen from their desks and trained themselves in various yogic techniques, they already know how to pay attention to their movement. What remains to be done is to scrutinise the subjective experience they are already more or less proficient in.

First-person experience does implicitly inform some of the major works on modern yoga. It resonates clearly when Norman Sjoman – a former student of B. K. S. Iyengar – describes *āsana* as 'movement and stillness' that 'begins with effort, matures into stretching to reach an ultimate position, then recedes from that to attain balance which is thus a form of transcendence or revelation' (Sjoman 1996: 42, 45). It resounds when Elizabeth De Michelis – also experientially familiar with a variety of contemporary yoga practices – describes Swami Vivekananda's interpretation of yoga in terms of a 'proprioceptive journey' (De Michelis 2004: 153). Personal experience also underlies the extensive study of *haṭhayoga* by James Mallinson, who is an initiated *haṭha* practitioner. Nonetheless, although the listed studies draw on their authors' experiences, they are not studies *of* these experiences. And the latter are not many to behold.

A few minor papers attempt to discuss the phenomenology of yogic movement. Philosopher of science Sundar Sarukkai (2002) departs from Merleau-Ponty's interpretation of depth, dimensionality and the inner/outer body to argue that the yogic practices of *āsana* and *prāṇāyāma* are a means to gain control over the inner body. Relying mostly on the *Haṭhapradīpikā* and B. K. S. Iyengar's *Light of Yoga*, he proposes that the alleged health benefits of *āsana* and *prāṇāyāma* are a result of the inner body becoming accessible, or 'visible' (Sarukkai 2002: 470), to the practitioner. He suggests that the practitioner's experience of the body fosters a sense of control over their physiology.

In a slightly earlier paper, psychologist James Morley (2001) refers to the system of yoga practice developed by T. K.V. Desikachar. He argues that the practice of pranayama and asana, by enhancing proprioception, breaks the practitioner's alienation from their own body and allows them to recognise it as 'inhabited, psychical space' (ibid.: 76). In the words of Merleau-Ponty, it transports them from thc objective to the lived body.

Klas Nevrin, a pianist holding a degree in the study of religions, remarks that asana practice exposes students to novel ways of moving the body, resulting in a change of kinetic patterns and heightened sensory sensitivity (Nevrin 2008). More importantly, he acknowledges the significance of the context of yoga practice, noting that students move in particular surroundings, accompanied by members of a particular social group. He argues that the combination of learning new kinetic skills and engaging with a supportive community may result in existential and social empowerment of the practitioner. Important in this account is the implicit assumption that the experience of the body in motion is meaningful and that it influences the way humans perceive the world and themselves as a part of it. However, Nevrin's conclusions are rather general and vague and, just like those of Morley and Sarukkai, are more of an introduction to the phenomenology of yoga practice than systematic phenomenological accounts as such.

Perhaps the most in-depth analyses are those of Benjamin R. Smith. A practitioner of Ashtanga Yoga in the tradition of K. Pattabhi Jois, he provides a fairly detailed summary of the particularities of his practice. He describes the Ashtanga Yoga asana sessions step by step, as they are experienced by a student. He offers accounts of his personal experience, including his emotional evaluation of the elements of the practice. He talks about being 'overwhelmed by anxiety or physical effort' (Smith 2007: 26), about his attention being 'drawn into [the] body' in face of his teacher's invasive manual adjustments.[6] These small ventures into autoethnography provide information about asana practice that is nowhere to be found in yoga manuals, historic or contemporary – that it is lived, personal experience.

Smith also hints at the meaning-making potential of asana practice by briefly discussing the connection between this practice and the interpretation of the concept of *tapas* (Smith 2008). He draws a parallel between the association of the term with increased heat and the experience of heating up during Ashtanga Yoga sessions. His account of the cleansing (*śodhana*) of the body through yoga refers directly to the experience of a yogin's body in motion as well. Smith also interprets the manual adjustments in Ashtanga Yoga practice (the pressing, pulling and lifting of the students' body parts by the teachers in order to help them attain a difficult posture) as a form of 'haptic communication' (Smith 2007: 35), i.e. transmitting the tradition through touch[7]. This point seems particularly significant, as it presents movement as a form of direct communication.

Nevrin and Smith's papers are side projects of academically bent practitioners rather than systematic studies. Nonetheless, they direct our attention to an important prospect: that the experience of asana performance, the experience of moving in a very specific way and in a very specific context, has a meaning-making potential. It can transform the practitioner and influence the way they think about themselves, the world, and even about fairly abstract concepts. Moreover, it is what makes a practitioner a participant in a living tradition – a tradition transmitted through movement more so than through text.

A much more systematic approach to yogic movement – though not phenomenological as such – is that of Jason Birch and Jacqueline Hargreaves. As a Sanskritologist working on *haṭha* and *rājayoga* manuscripts, Birch has direct access to original descriptions of yogic techniques of the body. Having attempted these techniques themselves, and in order to popularise their findings,[8] he and Hargreaves began to offer experiential sessions to other yoga practitioners, e.g. by teaching them the *āsana*s as described and illustrated in late *haṭha* manuals. Birch and Hargreaves' work culminated in their decision to reconstruct on film the practice attested in the eighteenth-century *Haṭhābhyāsapaddhati*. In cooperation with Mark Singleton, having enlisted seasoned yoga practitioners from India and the United Kingdom, they recorded the performance of more than 100 *āsana*s described in the manual. Helpful in this pursuit were the graphic representations of these postures, found in the nineteenth-century *Śrītattvaniddhi*. The final version of the production is being edited as this chapter is being written.[9]

The specificity of the *āsana*s of the *Haṭhābhyāsapaddhati* is that they are often dynamic. They are not merely postures, or ways of putting the body into postures – they feature repetitive movement performed with the use of props (a wall, a rope), and sometimes even with the help of a partner. This dynamicity provides the missing hermeneutic link between the motionless *āsana* of the *Pātañjalayogaśāstra* and the motion-full asana sequences of MPY. A film is one way to capture this dynamicity and to provide material for further study.[10]

## Yoga philosophy in motion

The *Haṭhābhyāsapaddhati* film project is not yet a phenomenological pursuit. It is, at its current stage, an attempt to reconstruct as objectively as possible the techniques of the body as they were engaged in more than two centuries ago. However, it does open these techniques for phenomenological scrutiny. What was the kinaesthetic and proprioceptive experience of the performers of the *āsana*s? How did it compare to their experience of other forms of *āsana* practice? How did it influence their lived bodies? How did it transform their understanding of *haṭhayoga* and yoga in general? Obtaining first-person accounts of the practitioners, in the form of extensive interviews, would be an appropriate first stage of a phenomenological enquiry. Engaging in the recreated practices personally to experience their kinaesthesia – to reconstruct a late *haṭhayoga* body in motion – would be the second step. The last step would be to verify whether this experience finds its reflection in the narratives produced in the milieus in which these practices developed. In this way, by trying to mimic the bodies of eighteenth- and nineteenth-century *haṭha* practitioners, we might be able to create a gateway into their minds.

The pursuit summarised above is essentially what I engaged in during my own research, though related to MPY (Ciołkosz 2019). Through a regular, prolonged practice of Iyengar Yoga, Ashtanga Yoga of K. Pattabhi Jois and the yoga of T. K.V. Desikachar, I became familiar with the kinaesthetic experience of these practices and I described it in detail. Then, applying the theories concerning the meaning-making significance of kinaesthesia – including those of Lakoff and Johnson summarised above – I sought to identify traces of this experience in the 'yoga philosophies' propagated by Iyengar, Jois and Desikachar. By analysing the three teachers' written interpretations of the categories of *Pātañjala yoga*, with their specific conceptual metaphors and other tropes, I managed to prove a correspondence between how the body is felt during yoga practice and how abstract concepts such as *duḥkha*, *samādhi* or *īśvara* are interpreted. I believe that a similar method, combining phenomenological insight into particular techniques of the body with linguistic analysis of textual sources produced by the practitioners of these techniques, may be a means to better understand other yogic and meditative traditions, both contemporary and – provided enough material – historical.

## Conclusion

Throughout this chapter I have attempted to explain the importance of movement for the understanding of the development and transformation of the concept of yoga. I argue that yoga practices have always involved a negotiation between movement and stillness. I propose what kinds of experienced movement inspired particular interpretations of yoga as a soteriological method, and I suggest that the study of yogic movement – most particularly from the phenomenological, experiential perspective – is a relevant methodological approach that may provide a better understanding of what yoga is.

I hope that this brief discussion has shown that movement matters. Not only as a way to get around in the world, not only as a means to acquire particular goals of mental stillness or physical prowess, but also as a way to make sense of various facets of existence. We explain our lives, with its sources of joy and fear, with its contingencies and paradoxes, by referring to the most basic experience we have: that of moving beings in a tangible environment. The most elaborate soteriological systems in history – the ways of providing a sense of order, purpose and security in a largely unpredictable world – emerged from the kinaesthetic experience of their creators. Yoga is by all means one such system, and embracing this fact will open a way to better understanding.

## Notes

1 I would like to thank Lucy May Constantini, Theodora Wildcroft, Suzanne Newcombe and Karen O-Brien-Kop for their comments on the first draft of this chapter.

2 According to Lakoff and Johnson (1980), metonymy is a conceptual operation in which a part of a given domain of experience represents the entire domain. When we say that we 'jumped on a bike to get to work as fast as possible', we make the moment of mounting a vehicle stand metonymically for the entire journey from point A (possibly 'home') to point B ('work'). In fact, even the term 'work' is used metonymically in this context – the action performed at the place where one realises the terms of one's employment ('working') stands for the place itself.

3 The term *proprioception* refers to the sensing of the positioning of the body in space, of the relative position of body parts, as well as of their movement. *Interoception* refers to the sensing of internal organs and, generally, the internal state of the body.

4 A possibly similar sensation is referred to as *udghāta* in some texts (see Mallinson and Singleton 2017: 144).

5 Later texts also mention the upward movement of *kuṇḍalinī* from the base of the spine towards the crown of the head.

6 The issue of manual adjustments in modern postural yoga is a relevant topic in itself, especially in light of the current discussion of abuse (physical, sexual, but also verbal) on the part of Ashtanga Yoga and Iyengar Yoga instructors. Manual adjustments involve directing the movement of the practitioner by applying more or less forceful touch. This notion of constraint and control of one agent's movement by another agent is in line with the early, Upanishadic construal of yoga. However, more relevant in this context is how touching a person and controlling their movement through force influences the social relations between the controller and the controlled, the boundaries of their identity as individuals ('personal space'), as well as the enactment of power and social hierarchy. The issue of manual adjustments and their potentially abusive nature is strongly tied to the understanding of the authority of the teacher (*guru*) in Indian traditions, and the interpretation of this authority in translational systems of yoga practice. While extensive discussion of this topic exceeds the scope of this chapter, its signalling seems necessary in the context of yogic movement and its meaning. For an in-depth analysis of sexual abuse in Ashtanga Yoga and its social dynamic, see Remski 2019.

7 Such 'transmission through touch' may involve not only imparting the rules of *āsana* performance through tactile guidance, but also communicating the traditional relations between the *guru* (the teacher) and the *śiṣya* (the student). The absolute, unquestioned authority of the *guru* and the expectation for the *śiṣya* to faithfully submit to this authority are expressed through forceful control of the movement of the *śiṣya*'s body (see previous endnote).

8 For short popular summaries of Birch and Hargreaves' work, see www.theluminescent.org/.
9 See http://hathabhyasapaddhati.org and Birch and Singleton (2019) for details.
10 Although it may not be the case with the *Haṭhābhyāsapaddhati* project – as it is a reconstruction of a now-defunct system of practice – film may become a way for participants in an ongoing tradition to transmit it effectively. Finnian Gerety, who has done research among contemporary representatives of the *Sāmaveda* tradition (the Nambudiri brahmins of Kerala), observed that both the teachers and their students use digital video recordings of Sāmavedic hymns for reference. Although written transmission is out of bounds in the case of Vedic lineages, video materials seem to be accepted – a fact that Gerety associates with the kinaesthetic character of Vedic recitation. During performance, the practitioners not only modulate their voices, but also move their torsos and heads and use a variety of gestures for the sake of accurate memorisation. It is the use of the movement of the body as a mnemonic device that guarantees unadulterated transmission of the ancient hymns. Hence film, providing an accurate representation of the sonic and kinetic patterns of correct recitation for the purpose of mimicry, becomes an accepted medium (see Gerety 2018).

## Bibliography


Armstrong, J. 2018. *Calcutta Yoga: Buddha Bose & the Yoga Family of Bishnu Ghosh and Yogananda*. Webstrong LLC Publishing.

Birch, J. 2013. '*Rājayoga*: The Reincarnations of the King of All Yogas'. *International Journal of Hindu Studies* 17(3): 401–444.

Birch, J. 2018. 'The Proliferation of *Āsana*-s in Late-Medieval Yoga Texts', in Baier, K., Maas, P. A. and Preisendanz, K. (eds), *Yoga in Transformation: Historical and Contemporary Perspectives*, 101–180. Vienna: Vienna University Press.

Birch, J. and Singleton, M. 2019. 'The Yoga of the *Haṭhābhyāsapaddhati*: Haṭhayoga on the Cusp of Modernity'. *Journal of Yoga Studies* 2: 3–70.

Carp, R. M. 2001. 'Integrative Praxes: Learning from Multiple Knowledge Formations'. *Issues in Integrative Studies* 19: 71–121.

Ciołkosz, M. 2019. *Thinking in Āsana: The Kinaesthetic Experience of Post-Krishnamacharyan Yoga Practice and Its Influence on Formation of Religio-Philosophical Concepts.* Unpublished doctoral dissertation.

De Michelis, E. 2004. *A History of Modern Yoga: Patañjali and Western Esotericism*. London: Continuum.

Gerety, F. M. M. 2018. 'Digital Guru: Embodiment, Technology, and the Transmission of Traditional Knowledge in Kerala'. *Asian Ethnology* 77(1–2): 3–31.

Iyengar, B. K. S. 2002 [1993]. *Light on the Yoga Sūtra of Patañali*. London: Thorsons.

Husserl, E. 1960. *Cartesian Meditations: An Introduction to Phenomenology.* Cairns, D. (trans). The Hague: Martinus Nijhoff.

Husserl, E. 1989. *Ideas Pertaining to a Pure Phenomenology and to a Phenomenological Philosophy: Book 2 (Ideas II)*. Rojcewicz, R. and Schuwer, A. (trans). Boston: Kluwer Academic Publishers.

Jurewicz, J. 2018. 'The Metaphor of Journey in Early Indian Thought', in Stasik D. and Trynkowska, A. (eds), *Journeys and Travellers in Indian Literature and Art. Volume I: Sanskrit and Pali Sources*, 15–33. Warsaw: Dom Wydawniczy Elipsa.

Lakoff, G. and Johnson, M. 1980. *Metaphors We Live By.* Chicago: The University of Chicago Press.

Maas, P. A. 2018. '"*Sthirasukham Āsanam*": Posture and Performance in Classical Yoga and Beyond', in Baier, K., Maas, P. A. and Preisendanz, K. (eds), *Yoga in Transformation: Historical and Contemporary Perspectives*, 49–100. Vienna: Vienna University Press.

Maehle, G. 2006. *Ashtanga Yoga: Practice and Philosophy*. Innaloo City: Kaivalya Publications.

Mallinson, J. 2011. 'Haṭha Yoga', in Jacobsen, K.A., et al. (eds), *Brill's Encyclopedia of Hinduism*. Volume III, 770–781. Leiden: Brill.

Mallinson, J. 2018. 'Yoga and Sex: What is the Purpose of *Vajrolīmudrā*?' in Baier, K., Maas, P. A. and Preisendanz, K. (eds), *Yoga in Transformation: Historical and Contemporary Perspectives*, 181–222. Vienna: Vienna University Press.

Mallinson, J. and Singleton, M. 2017. *Roots of Yoga.* London: Penguin Classics.

Mauss, M. 1973 [1931]. 'Techniques of the Body'. *Economy and Society* 2(1): 70–88.

McEvilley, T. 1981. 'An Archaeology of Yoga'. *Res* 1: 44–77.

Merleau-Ponty, M. 1962. *Phenomenology of Perception*. Smith, C. (trans). London: Routledge.

Monier-Williams, M. 1899. *A Sanskrit-English Dictionary*. Oxford: Clarendon Press.

Morley, J. 2001. 'Inspiration and Expiration: Yoga Practice through Merleau-Ponty's Phenomenology of the Body'. *Philosophy East & West* 51(1): 73–82.

Nevrin, K. 2008. 'Empowerment and Using the Body in Modern Postural Yoga', in Singleton, M. and Byrne, J. (eds), *Yoga in the Modern World: Contemporary Perspectives*, 119–139. London: Routledge.

Remski, M. 2019. *Practice and All is Coming: Abuse, Cult Dynamics, and Healing in Yoga and Beyond*. Rangiora: Embodied Wisdom Publishing.

Sarukkai, S. 2002. 'Inside/Outside: Merleau-Ponty/Yoga'. *Philosophy East & West* 52(4): 459–478.

Sheets-Johnstone, M. 2010. 'Thinking in Movement: Further Analyses and Validations', in Stewart, J., Gapenne, O., and Di Paolo, E. A. (eds), *Enaction. Toward a New Paradigm for Cognitive Science*, 165–182. Cambridge, MA: MIT Press.

Sheets-Johnstone, M. 2011 [1999]. *The Primacy of Movement*. Amsterdam, Philadelphia: John Benjamins Publishing Company.

Singleton, M. 2010. *Yoga Body: The Origins of Modern Posture Practice*. Oxford: Oxford University Press.

Sjoman, N. E. 1996. *The Yoga Tradition of the Mysore Palace*. New Delhi: Abhinav Publications.

Smith, B. R. 2007. 'Body, Mind and Spirit? Towards an Analysis of the Practice of Yoga'. *Body and Society* 13(2): 25–46.

Smith, B. R. 2008. '"With Heat Even Iron Will Bend": Discipline and Authority in Ashtanga Yoga', in Singleton, M. and Byrne, J. (eds), *Yoga in the Modern World: Contemporary Perspectives*, 140–160. London: Routledge.

Varela, F. J. 1996. 'Neurophenomenology: A Methodological Remedy for the Hard Problem'. *Journal of Consciousness Studies* 3(4): 330–349.

# 34
# SOUND AND YOGA[1]

*Finnian M. M. Gerety*

## Introduction

What is the significance of sound for understanding yoga?[2] And yoga for sound? The answers depend on practice, practitioner and context. Imagine the range of sounds at a postural yoga studio: the teacher's voice and footsteps; students' breaths, grunts and sighs; bodies and yoga-wear shuffling; the handling of blocks and props; recorded chanting and music; live voices intoning the sacred syllable OM and other Sanskrit mantras; singing bowls droning; a smartphone's muffled vibration; doors opening and closing; people murmuring outside; the distant drone of traffic. Some of these sounds are intentional and cultivated, while others are incidental and intrusive. The constant ebb and flow makes up the acoustic environment of a given practice – what we might call the 'soundscape' of yoga (Schafer 1993 [1977]).[3] Yet there is more to yogic soundscapes than external, audible sound. Sound in yoga also encompasses internal, silent and embodied realms of vibration, with practitioners listening to their own breath, tuning in to inner sounds, or meditating on the flow of sonic energy within the subtle body. This chapter treats the diverse manifestations of sound and listening in yoga and meditation, focusing on the quintessential sonic instrument in these traditions: the Sanskrit mantra.

### *Theorising sound*

The field of sound studies offers a useful frame for thinking about yoga and sound. Sound studies

> is a name for the interdisciplinary ferment in the human sciences that takes sound as its analytical point of departure or arrival. By analyzing both sonic practices and the discourses and institutions that describe them, it redescribes what sound does in the human world, and what humans do in the sonic world …
>
> *(Sterne 2012: 2; cf. Pinch and Bijsterveld 2012)*

A central concern is to understand the ways sound and listening have formed *auditory culture* – the aural analogue of visual culture. In this vein, Bull and Back advocate a stance of 'deep listening', which involves 'attuning our ears to listen again to the multiple layers of meaning potentially embedded in the same sound' (2003: 4) in order to 'rethink' relations of community, place and power. In approaching auditory culture, the relations between sounds are also important: hence, Sterne's imperative 'to think across sounds, to consider sonic phenomena in relationship to one another' (2012: 3). The domains of sound and listening resonate with particular force in sacred contexts; indeed, as Kapchan has observed, 'listening to sound creates sacred affect and identity' (2004: 70). Against this stance that our understanding of sound is always mediated by human culture, other scholars have theorised sound as a universal phenomenon with its own materiality and ontology that can only be revealed through sound itself. For Goodman, 'the sonic is a phenomenon of contact' (Goodman 2009: 10, cited in Kane 2015: 5) – vibration transmitted materially from one body to another. According to Cox, sound art, because it eschews representation and brings attention to sound as such, 'broadens the domain of the audible and discloses a genuine metaphysics of sound' (Cox 2009: 25, cited in Kane 2015: 8). In a recent critique of this 'ontological turn', Kane argues that such claims to universalism can never be severed entirely from their cultural context: 'a "sound studies" without "auditory culture"...crucially ignores the constitutive role that auditory culture plays in determining its object of study' (Kane 2015: 16). Echoing Kane's critique, this chapter contends that the histories of sound, listening and yoga in India – rich veins of auditory culture stretching back thousands of years – ultimately serve to constitute the theories of yogic sound ascendant in any given context. Yogic sound, notwithstanding its claims of transcendence, can never entirely transcend the cultures that reveal it.

Sound studies has pushed back against 'the assumed supremacy of the "visual" in accounts of the social' (Bull and Back 2003: 3) by asserting 'the primacy of sound as a modality of knowing and being in the world' (Feld 2003: 226). The emergence of sound studies on the academic scene – quite recent, when compared with visual culture studies and sensory studies – leads James Lavender to articulate the goal of sound studies with equal parts urgency and succinctness: 'to make sound thinkable, *at last*' (Lavender 2017: 246). This is a common sentiment in sound studies: that somehow or other, the academy has neglected the sonic and the aural. For Sterne, the most damning evidence is on the tips of our tongues: 'While visual experience has a well-developed metalanguage, sonic experience does not ... [T]here are very few abstract words in common English for describing the timbre, rhythm, texture, density, amplitude, or spatiality of sounds' (Sterne 2014: 60). Lavender goes further still, suggesting that critical theory to date has been inadequate to the task of thinking sonically. Thus, sound 'is not merely another object for thought ... rather, it is a demand posed to thought by that which it has yet been unable to think' (Lavender 2017: 246).

In the face of these debates over sound's universality, cultural embeddedness and even imperviousness to thought and expression, yoga studies has something to offer. Indian religions, which furnish the context for the earliest constructions of yoga, have a long and highly developed history of 'thinking sound'. This history includes refined metalanguages and sophisticated traditions of critical and philosophical reflection. It also includes ancient sonic ontologies and theologies, elaborate practices of sounding and listening and dynamic auditory cultures. So even as we consider the potential for recent academic scholarship about sound to illuminate yoga, we must also do the reverse: draw on Indian accounts of yoga to illuminate sound.[4]

## *Yoga as a technique of listening*

Sound studies and yoga studies alike are concerned with 'techniques of listening' (Sterne 2014). Calling the body 'man's first and most natural instrument', Mauss made the case that human activity is based on 'techniques of the body' – repertoires of actions imparted through training and socialisation (Mauss 1935; 2006) (see Ciołkosz, Chapter 33 in this volume). Such techniques run the gamut from habitual, apparently natural activities such as walking, sleeping and sex to more obviously self-conscious, culturally constructed ones like dancing, swimming and writing. Arguing that listening is likewise a bodily technique, Sterne charts a genealogy of techniques of listening in modernity, with an emphasis on technology. Sterne's main interest is 'headset culture', which he defines as the separation of listening from other sensory techniques in order to intensify audition; the examination of sound on its own terms, through analysis of acoustic content; and the technological transformation of acoustic space from a collective ambience to an individualised cocoon. The pervasiveness of headset culture should be obvious to anyone who moves through cosmopolitan space in the world today, be it a shopping mall, train station or apartment: earpieces, smartphones and headsets sequester individuals within invisible walls, immersing them in interior soundscapes, permitting them to be 'alone together' (Sterne 2014: 69).

Indian traditions of yoga and meditation possess many highly cultivated techniques of the body, as Mauss himself – a trained Indologist and close reader of yoga texts in Sanskrit – observed (Mauss 1935; Noland 2009: 35–37). Alongside techniques of posture and breath, yoga possesses elaborate techniques of sounding, most notably the recitation of mantras in various registers. What may be less apparent, however, is that some of yoga's most powerful bodily techniques are techniques of listening. Such techniques need not be centred on the ears, just as techniques of sounding mantras need not be centred on the voice. Yogic sound may be entirely embodied and interiorised – *and still be sound*. Where an ordinary person might hear silence, the practitioner of yoga perceives a continuum of vibration that extends from gross to subtle, connecting the outside phenomenal world with the innermost recesses of the body – what the *Chāndogya Upaniṣad* calls the 'space within the heart' (8.1.3; trans. after Olivelle 1998).

Drawing on the auditory culture school of sound studies, let me suggest that yogic sound is above all a domain of *deep listening*.[5] The practitioner voices a mantra out loud – or silently chants it – then listens carefully to every phase of its emanation, resonance and decay. In this way, mantras originating within the body become sonic instruments for entering into contemplative states and revealing esoteric layers of meaning. Other bodily techniques can deepen listening further, as the *Maitrāyaṇīya Upaniṣad* attests: 'By fixing (*yoga*) the thumbs on the ears, practitioners listen to the sound in the space within the heart' (6.22; trans. after van Buitenen 1962). Modern postural yoga has its own techniques of deep listening: practitioners are often enjoined to 'listen' to their bodies and emotions, attending to areas of flexibility, injury, stress and so on. Sustained listening in this way allows yoga practitioners in a group to be *alone together* in a way that resembles headset culture. With the body as their primary instrument – and usually without any external apparatus such as headsets – practitioners of yoga have cultivated their own interior soundscapes for centuries. Yoga offers an auditory path to aesthetic states of aloneness, whether it is the radical 'isolation' (*kaivalya*) of Pātañjala yoga or everyday contemplation on a yoga mat.

## Sound, listening and yoga in India: entangled histories

Sound and listening have been central to yoga throughout its history. The rest of this chapter surveys the entangled histories of sound, listening and yoga from the earliest Indian texts up through the transnational movements of today, with the goal of articulating an overarching theory of yogic sound. This diachronic approach comes with limits and risks. We should abandon any hope of being comprehensive. Like all human culture, yogic sound is a domain of tradition and innovation, shaped equally by the authority of earlier models and by adaptations to new doctrines, media and social facts. To the extent that an all-encompassing theory of yoga and sound is possible, it can only be formulated by taking stock of this dynamic interplay over the *longue durée*. What is the significance of sound for yoga, yoga for sound? We now take up the practitioners and practices, texts and contexts that will help us answer these questions.

## Vedic sacred sound

Indian discourses of sacred sound begin with the *Vedas*, a corpus of mantras and texts composed without the aid of writing in the late second and early first millennium BCE – and orally passed on ever since within lineages of Brahmin priests (Jamison and Witzel 2003). The agency of Brahmins in the construction of yogic sound can hardly be overstated: most sonic traditions of yoga bear the imprint of Brahmanical ideologies and practices. Although the Vedas were eventually written down and have had a parallel existence in manuscripts and books for the last thousand years, the efficacy and authority of Vedic mantras depend on sound. Already in the ancient period, practitioners described the Vedas as 'that which is heard' (*śruti*), thereby casting orthodox religiosity as *listening* to the echoes of an eternal auditory revelation. As the seminal work of Padoux (1990) has demonstrated for Vedic and Hindu Tantric traditions, sacred sound – manifesting as the 'goddess Speech' (*vāc*) – inspires a range of cosmologies, theologies and soteriologies based on phonemes, words and language. This intertwining of sound, language and metaphysics is not limited to *vāc* alone – van Buitenen points out that Indian religion and philosophy furnish numerous examples of single terms that denote spoken utterances while simultaneously representing transcendent principles. *Brahman* – at once a 'sacred formulation' and a name for absolute reality (Thieme 1952) – is a signal instance. Another is *akṣara*, a polyvalent term that denotes both a grammatical 'syllable' and the great syllable that Vedic poets regard as the inexhaustible source of sound, speech and the cosmos (van Buitenen 1959).

### *Sound, sacrifice, solar ascent*

Vedic sacrifice, the premier ritual system of ancient India, was crucial for the development of early ideas about sound and mantra. Sound is fundamental to the soteriological efficacy of sacrifice: the recitation of mantras helps the patron to attain immortality. The types of mantra include 'verse' (*ṛc*), 'melody' (*sāman*) and 'formula' (*yajus*) – such is the three-fold knowledge that comprises the sacrificial portions of the Vedic corpus: *Ṛgveda*, *Sāmaveda* and *Yajurveda* (Caland and Henry 1907). For the most part, Vedic mantras are verbal praise directed to the gods in heaven. In this respect, the gods are the main audience for ritual performance: the sound of the mantras attracts their attention to the feast of offerings. Beyond this sacrificial milieu, later Hindu Tantric and yogic traditions venerate certain Vedic mantras for their auspiciousness and power: the signal example is the *sāvitrī* mantra (*Ṛgveda* 3.62.10; also dubbed the *gāyatrī* because it is a verse in the *gāyatrī* metre), which celebrates the inspiration of the sun-god.

Vedic authors conceive the pursuit of immortality as an ascent to the sun that carries practitioners across the three worlds of earth, atmosphere and heaven. This paradigm is another way that Vedic traditions shape yoga – David White calls solar ascent the 'episteme of Indic soteriologies' (White 2009: 60). The vertical trajectory may be encoded in sonic terms. For instance, a common expiatory formula articulates ascent by arraying the terms 'earth, atmosphere, heaven' (*bhūr bhuvaḥ svar*) in a sonic sequence. Another example is the structure of the Vedic liturgies themselves: on the last day of sacrifice, the number of syllables in the mantras and their respective metres increases with successive rounds, thereby constructing a liturgical ascent that climaxes in the final rounds of chanting (Gerety 2015: 252n8). Yet the most fundamental expression of ascent through sound is the sacred syllable OM, whose utterance leads to 'the heavenly world' (*Aitareya Brāhmaṇa* 5.32; see Gerety 2015: 156). As the *Chāndogya Upaniṣad* says of a dying man: 'But when he is departing from this body, he rises up along those same solar rays. He goes up with *om*. No sooner does he cast his mind towards it than he reaches the sun' (8.6, trans. after Olivelle 1998).

## *The sacred syllable OM*

OM emerges in Vedic texts as a multifarious recitational technique: variants of the syllable are added to other mantras to augment their efficacy in performance. These variants run the gamut from the pure *o*-sound to the nasalised *oṃ*/ *oṁ* to the labial *om*; sometimes, the *o* is held out for three or more beats, notated as *o3ṃ*.[6] In the 'humming' (*praṇava*), the most frequent of OM's many uses in sacrifice, the '*om*-sound' (*oṃkāra*) is substituted as a resonant flourish for the final syllable of a Ṛgvedic mantra.[7] Whether in the *praṇava* or in some other application, the practice of adding variants of OM to mantra recitation is so frequent that the syllable comes to characterise the acoustic environment of Vedic ritual performance: hence, the Upaniṣadic statement of cosmic holism – 'this whole world is OM' (*Taittirīya Upaniṣad* 1.8; trans. after Olivelle 1998) – can also be read as a description of the soundscape of sacrifice, where OM is heard to ring out constantly. By the middle of the first millennium BCE, OM symbolises the essence of the Vedic corpus: millions of syllables articulated in a single, elemental sound.

Although some scholars have argued that the primary meaning of OM is 'yes' (Parpola 1981), OM as a symbol represents the potency of sound prior to and beyond language; like *brahman*, the syllable is constitutive of language but never constrained by it. The way that OM is vocalised emphasises its elemental nature. As Staal reminds us: 'the most natural order of sound production is an opening of the mouth followed by its closure' – and this, in turn, is 'a very apt description of the mantra *oṃ*' (Staal 1989: 274–275; see also Jakobson 1962: 541 and Gerety 2016: 186–187). Already by 800 BCE, Vedic authors had analysed the sequence of constituent phonemes that make up OM's articulation, explaining the syllable as the euphonic combination of the phonemes *a*, *u* and *m* (*Aitareya Brāhmaṇa* 5.32; Gerety 2015: 156). The practitioner opens the mouth, and the breath engages with a slight catch in the throat as the vocal cords begin to resonate (*a*). The sound wells up and moves across the tongue into the roof of the mouth (*u*), lingering with a tickle below the nose and finishing with the resonant closure of the lips (*m*). There is momentum from breath to voice, inside to outside, silence to sound, opening to closure. The analysis of OM's phonemes proves to be a fertile theme in the construction of yogic sound. The *locus classicus* of *a-u-m* reflections is the *Māṇḍūkya Upaniṣad*, where the three phonemes correspond to the three Vedas, the three worlds, the three states of consciousness, the past, present and future, and so on. The authors of this work supersede these triads by adding what Wendy Doniger calls a 'transcendent fourth' (2014: 27, 29–31) – silence. The fame of the *a-u-m* analysis is such that many scholars and practitioners hold that '*aum*' is the original form of the sacred syllable. Yet the reverse is true: *aum* is derived from ancient phonemic analysis of OM.

## *Vedic mantras: between sound and silence*

As a counterpoint to audible sound, silence is woven throughout Vedic soundscapes. The interplay between sound and silence is encoded in the very term *mantra*, which derives from the Sanskrit root 'to think' (√*man*-), and is cognate with Indo-European words for the faculty of thought, from Sanskrit *manas* to Latin *mens* to English *mind*. Although *mantras* frequently entail chanting, murmuring and other forms of audible sound, this etymology shows that they are also 'instruments of thought' (Thieme 1957). The Vedic expression 'yoked to the mind' (*manoyukta*) describes how a priest mentally engages with mantra (White 2009: 60–63). Whether or not it is recited out loud, a mantra in Vedic traditions always presupposes the *silent* activity of the mind; this idea is only strengthened in traditions of yoga.

While most recitations in sacrifice must be 'loud' (*uccaiḥ*) and 'distinct' (*nirukta*), other vocal registers are also important. Total silence is sometimes called for: the *brahman* priest, who flags mistakes made by other priests, must often 'restrain his speech', that is, remain silent (Renou 1949; Bodewitz 1983). *Japa* refers to the repetitive 'muttering' of mantras, usually in a 'quiet' (*upāṃśu*) way through the mouth, but sometimes using a 'mental' (*mānasa*) approach in which the lips do not move at all and the chant is delivered 'silently' (*tūṣṇīm*; on these technical terms, see Renou 1949; 1954). In the style of chant called 'unexpressed' (*anirukta*), the words of the mantras are replaced entirely by the non-lexical syllables *o* and *vā*, which represent the syllable OM and the goddess of speech, Vāc. As the priest chants these syllables out loud, he must mentally recite the original words in silence. In the Jaiminīya school of Sāmaveda, this kind of chanting includes a rite called the 'yoking' (*yukti*), in which the seated practitioner controls his breath, attends to his senses, and visualises his chant shining in the sky. According to Vedic authors, unexpressed chanting preceded by the *yukti* allows the sacrificer to ascend to the sun and win immortality (Fujii 2004). Especially in view of the fact that the term *yukti* is cognate with *yoga*, this Sāmavedic ritual sequence may offer a crucial antecedent for yogic mantra meditation (Gerety 2015: 255–256).

## Personal recitation and murmuring

In later Vedic texts, authors elevate quiet, internal forms of recitation over the loud and external. This sonic predilection corresponds to the broader 'inward turn' (White 2009: 76) of Vedic religiosity in the middle of the first millennium BCE, when ritualists experimented with the interiorisation of ritual and its components – including mantra. Malamoud's study of the daily practice of 'personal recitation' (*svādhyāya*; Malamoud 1977), which consists of orally reviewing Vedic texts for mastery, offers insights into this development and suggests another paradigm for yogic mantra meditation. According to a key early passage on *svādhyāya* analysed by Malamoud (*Taittirīya Āraṇyaka* 2.3–8), after sunrise the practitioner leaves his village and seeks out a secluded place where the rooftops are no longer visible. There, he sits down facing east on strewn grass with his legs crossed, right foot propped on the left knee. Holding a ring made of two blades of grass, he positions his hands so that the right rests on top of the left. To complete the posture, he fixes his gaze on the horizon where the sky meets the earth (or else closes his eyes). He then performs the *svādhyāya* proper by murmuring the syllable *om* followed by other mantras. This is the origin of the practice of beginning Vedic instruction with OM (see, e.g. *Mānava Dharmaśāstra* 2.74–75). (Remarkably, this longstanding convention is still evident in modern settings: recitations in Hindu temples today begin with OM – as do many yoga classes.) In contrast with external sacrifices, which involve loud mantras and material offerings to the gods, *svādhyāya* is considered a 'sacrifice to the absolute' (*brahmayajña*) – the quiet offering of mantras for the practitioner's liberation.

Because *svādhyāya* is conducted in a murmur, Vedic authors also refer to it as the 'sacrifice of *japa*' (*japayajña*). The authors of the *Mahābhārata*, the Sanskrit epic, emphasise *japa*'s interiority and efficacy for attaining liberation. By undertaking *japa*, meditating on the absolute and devoting himself to a supreme deity, the *japa* practitioner (*jāpaka*) can achieve release as surely as the *yoga* practitioner (*yogin*) (*Mahābhārata* 12.193). The contrast between the two pursuits in the epic is striking, perhaps anticipating the decreased importance of mantra in some later streams of yoga, as Mallinson and Singleton have argued (Mallinson and Singleton 2017: 258, 262). Brockington (2012) suggests that *japa* in the epic offers a bridge between Vedic practices and the devotional practice of murmuring the name of God repeatedly. In the *Bhagavad Gītā*, Kṛṣṇa seems to allude to such a practice when he announces 'of all the sacrifices, I am the sacrifice consisting of *japa*' (7.8). Yoga in the *Gītā*, which encompasses a range of practices from asceticism to devotional worship, makes mantra-muttering a central feature of its soteriological repertoire. In one striking passage, Kṛṣṇa counsels Arjuna to combine 'devotion' (*bhakti*), 'yoga-power' (*yogabala*) and OM into a contemplative praxis that ensures liberation at the moment of death (*Bhagavad Gītā* 8.12–13):

> Shutting all the gates of his body and confining his mind in his heart; keeping his breath in his head, absorbed in concentration through *yoga*; uttering *om* – *brahman* in a single syllable – and calling me to mind; when he sets forth, leaving his body – such a man goes along the highest path.

In Upaniṣads composed before the early centuries CE, we can trace the emergence of a system of mantra meditation that involves OM, *yoga* and contemplative techniques such as 'meditation' (*dhyāna*) or 'fixation' (*dhāraṇā*). Showing that sonic practices *are* contemplative practices (and vice versa), these Upaniṣads employ sound to soteriological ends. For instance, the *Kaṭha Upaniṣad*, an influential work that contains an early definition of *yoga*, teaches that OM is the best 'support' (*ālambana*; 2.17) for meditating on the self and transcending death. In the *Muṇḍaka Upaniṣad* (2.2.3), OM is the bow that propels the arrow of the self into the target of the absolute, so that the practitioner becomes immersed in *brahman*. The *Praśna Upaniṣad* recommends 'meditating' (*abhi* + √*dhyai*-; 5.1) on the syllable OM at death. The liminality of sound – the way it crosses the physical boundaries of the practitioner's body – is a key factor in these discourses about transitions to metaphysical states. Thus, the *Śvetāśvatara Upaniṣad* codifies 'the discipline of meditation' (*dhyānayoga*) by teaching how to 'grasp both god and primal matter within the body by means of the *praṇava*' (1.13; trans. after Olivelle 1998), a technique that is compared to igniting a fire.

## Sound and mantra in early yoga: the *Pātañjalayogaśāstra*

Let us turn now to the *Pātañjalayogaśāstra*, the influential system of yoga articulated in terse *sūtras* and an accompanying auto-commentary, all likely composed in the third to fourth centuries CE (Maas 2006). Although this work is known primarily for its codification of yoga as silent meditation, it also incorporates mantra-based practices. The Vedic influence is evident: Patañjali's list of 'observances' (*niyama*) includes *svādhyāya* (2.44; see Carpenter 2003: 29–34): 'From personal recitation arises union with one's chosen deity' (trans. after Mallinson and Singleton 2017). The commentary adds: 'one practised in recitation sees the gods, sages, and adepts, who help him in his task'. Given the central role played by Brahmins in the formation of this text, it seems likely that the *svādhyāya* referred to here is an adaptation of earlier models: daily recitation of Vedic mantras as a contemplative practice (see Bryant 2009: 273).

A related mantra practice is attested in Patañjali's codification of 'meditative worship of the Lord' (*īśvarapraṇidhāna*; 1.23 ff.), which Oberhammer considers the prototype of theistic meditation in yogic traditions (Oberhammer 1989). Two *sūtras* prescribe *japa* based on OM as a way to realise *Īśvara*, the 'Lord' of yoga. While the Vedic technique of reciting the *praṇava* adds emphasis to a verse and attracts divine attention, Patañjali teaches that the *praṇava* should be murmured quietly on its own, drawing the practitioner's attention inward (1.27–28). Echoing terminology used by early Sanskrit grammarians, the *praṇava* is the 'verbal signifier' (*vācaka*) of Īśvara (Angot 2008: 249). Yet the *praṇava* here has a ritual function that transcends everyday language – it is the sonic means by which the practitioner realises the deity, not unlike the use of OM as a contemplative 'support' (*ālambana*) in some Upaniṣads (Bryant 2009: 109). As Malinar observes, 'OM is used to evoke … the god on which the concentration of the yogin is fixed' (2007: 141).

Also relevant is the 'auditory dimension of meditation' (Beck 1993: 100) in the *Pātañjalayogaśāstra*. The work's third section on 'special powers' (*vibhūti*, *siddhi*) resulting from yoga includes a heightened sense of 'listening' (*śrāvaṇa*), which enables the 'audition of divine sounds' (*divyaśabdaśravaṇam*). Additionally, contemplation of the connection between the ear (*śrotram*) and the primary medium of sound, 'space' (*ākāśa*), leads to 'divine hearing' (*divyaṃ śrotram*; 3.41). Since this section deals with the acquisition of powers with external effects, we may surmise that these *sūtras* refer to suprasensory audition, capable of picking up sounds at great distances, or extremely quiet stimuli. Such teachings remind us that techniques of listening in yoga do not always guide the practitioner's perception inward for soteriological purposes – sometimes they pertain to the world outside the body.

## Mantra meditation in the *Maitrāyaṇīya Upaniṣad*

The *Maitrāyaṇīya Upaniṣad*[8] (*c.*600–700 CE) synthesises a wide array of Upaniṣadic teachings on yogic sound. A key mantra-based technique is 'supreme fixation' (*parā dhāraṇā*; 6.18), which involves turning one's tongue back on the soft palate, fixing the breath (*prāṇa*) in the central channel and chanting *om* (6.21). The paradigm of the yogic body (Padoux 2011: 103–11; 2017: 73–86; Samuel and Johnston 2013), emerging around this time, contrasts the subtle (*sūkṣma*) anatomy with the gross (*sthūla*) form of the physical body. The *Maitrāyaṇīya Upaniṣad* extends this notion to sound, which takes gross and subtle forms. Audible sounds are physical, material, discrete, inferior; subtle sounds are ethereal, immaterial, immanent, superior. Subtle sound emanates from the central channel (*suṣumnā*), which conducts breath from the heart to the head. In a new take on the ancient episteme of ascent through sacrifice, this upward progression constitutes the soteriological ascent of sound through the yogic body: by using mantras in increasingly subtle forms, the practitioner moves upward towards liberation in the crown of his head.

Whereas earlier texts tend to employ technical terms (e.g. *mantra*, *japa*, *praṇava*) when discussing sonic practices, the authors of the *Maitrāyaṇīya Upaniṣad* engage broadly with sound as an aesthetic and soteriological category. In one section, they teach meditation (*abhi* + √*dhyai*) on the absolute (*brahman*) in two forms: 'sound' (*śabda*) and 'non-sound' (*aśabda*). OM, *brahman* in sonic form, is the contemplative support for attaining the non-sonic *brahman*: 'Having risen up by means of OM, the practitioner reaches the syllable's ending in non-sound' (6.22). Another technique involves plugging the ears with the thumbs to make it possible to listen to the 'sound within the space in the heart'. Using an array of descriptive sonic terms – several of them onomatopoetic in Sanskrit – the authors compare this inner soundscape to 'the sound of rivers, or a bell, or a brass vessel, or a wheel, or the croaking of frogs, or rain, or a sound heard in a still place' (6.22; trans. after van Buitenen 1962).

## Tantric *mantraśāstra* and yogic sound

The second half of the first millennium CE witnesses the emergence of rich discourses on sacred sound in the early Hindu tantras (*c.*500–900 CE). In this period, yogic and tantric approaches to sound mutually influence each other to the point of overlapping – in the formulation of Padoux (2011: 1), yoga becomes 'tantricized'. While maintaining continuities with Vedic ideology and practice, tantric 'teachings on mantra' (*mantraśāstra*) boast many new elements. Tantric mantras not only invoke deities, as in Vedic sacrifice – tantric mantras *are* deities in sonic form. Another innovation is the use of script: through diagrams (*yantras*, *maṇḍalas*), writing practices and syllabaries, the graphic forms of mantras are central to tantric *mantraśāstra*.[9] And as in yoga, the body remains a crucial site for pursuing liberation: the practitioner undertakes elaborate internal visualisations and places mantras including potent seed syllables (*bīja*) on the energy centres (*cakra*) of the yogic body.

Tantric authors regard the entire cosmos as the emanation of the power (*śakti*) of *kuṇḍalinī*, a feminine energy that animates sound and produces the constituents of language from which the universe springs. The cosmogonic emanation moves in a sonic sequence from the subtle arising to the audible sounding, and from the decaying resonance to the silent resorption. This macrocosmic trajectory finds its microcosmic counterpart in the practitioner's 'utterance' (*uccāra*) of the mantra, which moves up the central channel with the breath, from the base of the spine through the heart to the palate to the crown of the head (Padoux 1990: 140–42). Conceived as an ascent within the practitioner's body, the mantra is enunciated in its gross form as audible sound, then rises into subtle forms including the 'vibration' (*nāda*), the reverberation of the mantra, and the 'drop' (*bindu*), its concentrated essence (as well as the written dot representing the nasal *anusvāra*). Beyond these is silence – the highest sonic state, correlated with the absolute. The circulation of 'breath' (*prāṇa*) is central to speculations about sound and speech in yogic and tantric texts alike, with breath's movement conceived as a 'goose' in flight (*haṃsa*).[10] Yogic and tantric authors divide the word *haṃsa* into two syllables, *haṃ* and *sa*, identified with inhalation and exhalation. In this way the practitioner's every breath, waking and sleeping, gives voice to the mantra. Repeated in a cycle, the syllables change through euphonic combination to yield *so 'haṃ*, which can be understood as 'I am that', identifying the practitioner with the absolute or with a supreme deity such as Śiva (Padoux 2011: 140).

## Sound and listening in *haṭhayoga* traditions

Influential exponents of the synthesis of tantra and yoga were the Nāthas, characterised by Bouy as blending yogic asceticism with tantric and Vedantic traditions (Bouy 1994: 5). Mallinson and Singleton have noted the lesser role of mantra among the Nāthas and other groups associated with *haṭhayoga*, suggesting that the emphasis on physical techniques over sacred sound is partly due to the influence of non-Brahmanical renouncers (*śramaṇa*), who opposed mantra cultures based on the Veda (Mallinson and Singleton 2017: 262–63). However, specific texts belonging to the *haṭhayoga* milieu show divergent attitudes to mantra, with some incorporating tantric mantra practice and others dismissing it as the lowliest of yogic techniques.[11] Among the former, the muttered repetition (*japa*) of mantras and seed syllables – tens of thousands, hundreds of thousands, and even millions of times – can confer special powers, grant access to worldly pleasures and lead to liberation. For instance, the practitioner who chants the formula *aim klīṃ sauḥ* becomes irresistible to women with 100,000 repetitions, bends kings to his will with 600,000, gains a divine body and levitates with 1,800,000, becomes the equal of the great god Rudra with six million, until finally, 'with ten million repetitions the great yogi is absorbed into the absolute' (*Śivasaṃhitā* 5.232–251). Knowledge of mantras is jealously guarded: in the *Khecarīvidyā*, certain mantras are not given explicitly and instead must be extracted using coded instructions (1.38–39).

As in earlier traditions, there remains a close connection between mantra and breath: take, for example, the familiar *haṃsa* mantra, which is dubbed the 'unmuttered' *(ajapā) gāyatrī* because its utterance arises naturally through respiration (*Vivekamārtaṇḍa* 28–30). Other authors question the efficacy of endless repetitions, suggesting that the subtle sounding of OM trumps myriad rounds of *japa*. Consider this verse of the fourteenth-century Kashmiri poet and mystic Lallā, one of the very few female voices in premodern yoga and tantra (*Lallāvākyāni* 2.34):

> What use are a thousand mantras for one who has, by means of holding the breath, regularly moved from the navel the single mantra called *oṃ* up to the skull and who has made the mind to have *oṃ* as its only essence?

For Lallā, however, even *oṃ* is merely a stopgap – the penultimate step before the final, emancipatory 'worship of the Lord with the mantra called Silence' (*Lallāvākyāni* 2.40; all translations in the above section by Mallinson and Singleton 2017: 273–276).

Alongside mantra techniques in various forms, auditory practices are also attested in *haṭha* traditions. A signal example is a technique of deep listening that pertains to *layayoga* as codified by the *c.*fourteenth-century *Śivasaṃhitā* (5.36–37, trans. Mallinson 2007; see also Powell 2018):

> When the *yogin* restrains the wind by tightly closing his ears with his thumbs, his eyes with his index fingers, his nostrils with his middle fingers, and his mouth with his ring fingers, and intently carries out this practice, then he immediately sees himself in the form of light.

Through this technique, the practitioner discerns 'vibration' (*nāda*) in its subtle forms and reaches a point of cognitive 'dissolution' (*laya*; *Śivasaṃhitā* 44–45).

The *Haṭhapradīpikā*, the influential fifteenth-century anthology of Svātmārāma, codifies two auditory practices under the rubric of 'concentration on inner sounds' (*nādānusandhāna*; Powell 2018). One approach entails the manual closing of eyes, ears, nose and mouth so as to attune oneself to the movement of *nāda* within the central channel. The practitioner then hears a fourfold sequence of internal musical sounds, corresponding to his progress through the four stages of *yoga* and culminating in the emancipatory state of *rājayoga* (*Haṭhapradīpikā* 65–77). In the other, the practitioner blocks his ears so as to discern ten types of natural and musical sounds within – from the waves of the ocean to the beat of a kettle drum to the buzzing of a bee. As he concentrates on this sonic progression from gross to subtle, his mind attains *samādhi* and becomes absorbed in the maximally subtle 'noise of the unstruck sound' (*anāhatasya śabdasya dhvanir*) – a vibration produced by no material impetus. Dissolved in this way, he attains the absolute, called 'the soundless' (*niḥśabdam*) (*Haṭhapradīpikā* 78–101).[12]

## Deep listening and silence in the *Yoga Upaniṣads*

The blending of tantric and yogic practices finds its fullest expression in the *Yoga Upaniṣads*, medieval works on mantra meditation. Composed in north India in the first centuries of the second millennium CE – and later transmitted in expanded form in the south up through the early modern period – these works synthesise the non-dualist soteriologies of Vedānta, the *nāda* teachings of Nātha traditions and tantric approaches to sound and the yogic body, as Ruff has shown (2002). Although they are heterogeneous texts composed by different authors, most *Yoga Upaniṣads* share an interest in the cosmology, physiology and soteriology of sacred sound. Engaging the subtle manifestations of OM, *haṃsa*, *nāda* and *bindu*, the texts codify sonic practices that include visualisations, breath control and the body's energy centres. In common with earlier texts, sound is instrumental to the attainment of *brahman* (*Amṛtabindu Upaniṣad/ Brahmabindu Upaniṣad*, trans. Ruff 2012: 114): 'Gaining union with the boundless by means of the sound *oṃ*, one enjoys the highest reality.'

The *mantrayoga* codified by these works includes contemplation of subtle sound as it culminates in the 'point' – the concentrated essence of mantra (*Dhyānabindu Upaniṣad*, trans. after Ruff 2012: 115):

> The point (*bindu*) is more important than the syllables, it is more important than the reverberation (*nāda*). When the syllables and sound cease, then silence is the most amazing state.

This silence reverberates in the space within the heart: it is the constant and eternal sound, generated without material contact – again we encounter the 'unstruck sound' (*anāhata nāda*). Meditation on this inaudible, embodied sound leads to gnosis of the supreme self.

## Sound, language and revelation: the Veda and beyond

All of the discourses examined so far assume a fundamental overlap between sacred sound and a particular language: Sanskrit. Vedic mantras represent Sanskrit in its purest form, unmediated by human authors (*apauruṣeya*). In the Vedic ideology of *śruti*, sages gain access to this revelation through powers of insight and then pass it on orally and aurally to their descendants. This outlook informs the orthodox stance of Brahmanical exponents of grammar (*vyākāraṇa*) and ritual theory (*mīmāṃsā*): Sanskrit is the 'root language' (*mūlabhāṣya*), 'the only language that was capable of making its meaning known directly' (Granoff 1991: 17), and hence the only acceptable language for ritual and learned discourse. This is not only a social claim, but also an ontological one: as the language of the Vedas (and later, the Tantras), Sanskrit is regarded as the universal, eternal language – and the one closest to absolute reality. In the system of the grammarian Bhartṛhari (*c.*fifth century CE), mastery of Sanskrit leads to liberation (Beck 1993: 65–66). As Filliozat (2006) argues, the practice of *yoga* for grammarians entails purifying speech of its imperfections until it is completely 'perfected' (*saṃskṛta*) and distilled to its sonic essence (*śabda*), which in turn leads to revelation of its meaning (*sphoṭa*). For grammarians, this mode of inquiry brings the self into communion with the absolute.

## Sacred sound in early renunciatory traditions

From this orthodox perspective, languages other than Sanskrit are deviations from the direct relation between perfected speech and absolute reality – and hence useless as a means to salvation. This position presented a challenge to the non-Brahmanical renunciatory traditions – the precursors of Buddhism and Jainism – whose early discourses were mostly conducted in Middle Indo-Aryan languages, including Ardhamāgadhī, Pāli, and various Prakrits; and whose founders – Siddhārtha and Mahāvīra in particular – are represented as preaching and conversing in these vernaculars. These same charismatic founders also criticised Brahmins and Vedic culture, including sacrifice and the use of Sanskrit mantras.

To navigate this terrain, as Bronkhorst (2015) has argued, some Buddhists and Jains came to think of the liberated founders as sonically disseminating wisdom in ways that did not require language – Sanskrit or otherwise. According to some accounts, these omniscient teachers used a 'monotone' (*ekasvara*) or 'divine sound' (Sanskrit *divyadhvani*; Prakrit *divvajhuṇī*) that would automatically be intelligible to anyone listening, or else would require disciples to translate (Bronkhorst 2015). Lamotte (1970: 1380 n1, cited in Bronkhorst 2015: 14) argues that the Buddha's preaching is sometimes conceived as a unitary sound, compressed vocally into a single instant – this sound expressed the *dhamma* in its entirety, pervaded all the worlds, and conferred liberation. Castro-Sánchez adduces a similar account showing that the perfection of Buddha's speech, also known as 'the voice of Brahmā' (*brahmasvara*), spiritually transforms his listeners (Castro-Sánchez 2011: 23). In some Jain texts, sound flows without interruption from the liberated being's body and diffuses everywhere; moreover, it is 'sound' (*dhvani*) as distinguished from language: 'The speech of a *tīrthaṅkara* has the form of sound, because it does not consist of syllables, and for this reason it is single' (*Dhavalā* 1.1.50, trans Bronkhorst 2015: 12).[13] Masefield has made a case for the broader affinity between what he calls the '*dhamma* of sound' in the Pāli canon – liberation through hearing the Buddha's preaching first-hand – and Vedic *śruti* (Masefield 1986).[14] Thus, in spite of their differences and mutual contestations, early Brahmanical, Buddhist and Jain traditions can also be seen as partaking in a shared sensibility when it comes to sound, language and revelation.

## Mantras and *dhāraṇīs* in early Buddhism

Notwithstanding this deep-seated affinity for sonic and auditory revelation, the instrumental use of mantras for soteriological purposes is strikingly absent from the earliest Buddhist and Jain traditions. Early on, non-Brahmanical traditions tended to emphasise 'meditation' (*dhyāna*) and 'austerity' (*tapas*) in the pursuit of liberation – pointedly excluding mantra-based practices. Nevertheless, early Buddhists and Jains did employ protective incantations and spells (*rakṣā*, *paritta*) to protect against snakebite or malevolent supernatural forces, or to gain special powers and effect magical transformations (Skilling 1992). Later testimony shows that some authorities prohibited such incantatory practices, especially when undertaken by monks on behalf of the laity to earn money (Davidson 2009: 113; Castro-Sánchez 2011: 21–22; Gough 2015: 82; Shah 1947: 114–15).

Yet already by the first centuries of the Common Era, Mahāyāna texts attest a sea-change in favour of mantra practices, spurred by widespread adoption of Sanskrit in this stream of Buddhist tradition. According to Castro-Sánchez, 'a mastery of the Sanskrit grammar became one of the hallmarks of Bodhisattva training, [for one] who wanted to "acquire the skill in the cognition of sounds" (*rutajñānakauśalya*)' (*Mahāprajñāpāramitāsūtra* 162; Castro-Sánchez 2011: 26). Some Buddhist authors theorised mantras as the 'word of the Buddha' (*buddhavacana*) – and hence fulfilling mundane and supramundane goals alike (Castro-Sánchez 2011: 23). The sonic instrument of choice in Mahāyāna and Vajrayāna traditions was the *dhāraṇī*, functionally equivalent to mantra and akin to other types of formula known as *vidyā* ('knowledge') and *hṛdaya* ('heart') (Davidson 2009; Castro-Sánchez 2011). As Davidson has argued, *dhāraṇī* denotes not only a particular formula but also the cognitive faculties of memory, thought and speech: thus, a *dhāraṇī* is 'a syllable/letter or word that represents the potential for unlimited, inexhaustible meaning in a concentrated form ...' (2009: 122).[15] These Buddhist innovations in mantra culture made extensive use of script to encode sound: thus, *dhāraṇīs* are represented graphically in manuscripts, amulets, and syllabaries (2009: 120–23; Copp 2014).

By the second half of the first millennium CE, Buddhist authors codified fixed repertoires of *dhāraṇīs* and other such formulas, a trend that is embedded in the broader turn of these traditions towards tantric *mantraśāstra*. The *Kāraṇḍavyūha Sūtra*, a Śaiva-influenced disquisition on *oṃ maṇi padme hūṃ*, celebrates this Buddhist mantra as 'the six-syllable great formula' (*ṣaḍakṣarī mahāvidyā*). Knowledge of this formula, the text promises, ensures the practitioner a desirable rebirth in the body of the *bodhisattva* Avalokiteśvara (Studholme 2002: 61–62). In these and other tantricised contexts, the vocalisation of mantras and syllables has the effect of manifesting deities in sonic form, while their inscription in various media – diagrams, writing and the subtle body – fosters the practitioner's visualisation and embodiment of the deity.

## Mantras and meditation in Jain traditions

A similar rapprochement between renunciatory asceticism and mantra practice also occurred in Jain traditions, as Jain authors and ritualists developed their own distinctive brand of *mantraśāstra* (Gough 2015; see also Dundas 1998). Recent work by Gough (forthcoming) on mantras in Jainism offers insights into the role of sound in Jain yoga and meditation. Unlike Brahmanical authors of the first millennium CE, for whom chanting OM was the premier sonic practice, Jain authors from that period forward promoted the recitation of the *pañcanamaskāra*, a litany in praise of the Five Supreme Lords, with the rationale that praise of enlightened beings leads to the eradication of *karma*. By the tenth century CE, when Jains start to use OM in ritual for soteriological purposes, this background shapes their approach: instead of emphasising recitational practices with OM, Jain authors instead focus on diagrams (*yantra*) linked to the Five Supreme Lords and employed in 'virtuous meditation' (*dharmyadhyāna*). Hemacandra's twelfth-century *Yogaśāstra* (8.31), for instance, codifies meditation on a multicoloured OM diagram, whose various colours represent negative qualities to be destroyed through meditation, and whose overall form gives expression to the pure soul of the Jina. The *Yogapradīpa*, a later Jain text on yoga, echoes the Brahmanical *Dhyānabindu Upaniṣad* in emphasising meditation on OM as the 'unstruck sound' (*anāhata nāda*). This refers to the subtle sonic resonance of OM, but perhaps also to the spiraloid representation of the syllable found in Jain *yantras*. Gough concludes that in Jainism, the 'sounding … of *oṃ* is far less important than focusing one's mind on a physical representation of it' (forthcoming: 18). Thus, Jains reimagine the continuum between sound and silence in their own way.

## Islamic traditions of yoga and sound

Moving into the early modern period, the nexus of sound, listening and yoga becomes important in some Islamic contexts. While there is no space to delve into these developments – which speak to generative exchanges between Sufis, Nātha Yogis and Sikhs – we can mention a few key instances. Ernst (2003) brings our attention to an early description of yogic sound in the Sufi milieu, the *c.*thirteenth-century *Amrtakunda* ('The Pool of Nectar') – an Arabic text that recontextualises Sanskrit mantras in Islamic terms and gives rise to many subsequent translations and adaptations. As Gandhi (2018) has demonstrated, the Mughal prince Dara Shukoh studied Indian esoteric practices, including breath control and mantra meditation, under the tutelage of Sufi preceptors. Dara Shukoh's writings mention the *ajapā gāyatrī* of yogic and tantric texts, equating the utterance *so 'ham* ('I am that') with the Sufi practice of divine remembrance (*ẕikr*) by reciting *huwa allah* ('He is God'). According to Vaudeville, the encounter between Islam and yoga also took other forms, such as the doctrine of the transcendent 'word' (*śabda*) shared by Gorakhnath, Kabir and the early Sants, which prizes internal revelation over scriptural authorities such as the Vedas or the Qur'an. Another instance is the repeated murmuring of god's name in devotional prayers (often called *jap*), which Kabir, among others, advocated as a path to liberation (Vaudeville 1993: 98–99). This cross-pollination of Sufism and yoga continued well into the British colonial period, as Green has shown with reference to the late-nineteenth-century circulation of printed pamphlets about contemplative breathing techniques, which encode 'the intimate sounds of the history of colonialism' (2008: 315).

## Sound, chanting and mantra meditation in modern transnational yoga

The above survey is a highly selective account of how sound and yoga have mutually influenced each other in Indian religious traditions over the centuries. Can we extract an overarching theory of yogic sound from this bricolage of historicised accounts? Let us jump forward in time to briefly consider how today's transnational yoga movements have received premodern ideas of yogic sound. Even as exponents of modern transnational yoga have approached mantra in new ways, they have simultaneously emphasised the authority of classical Indian paradigms.

The most high-profile of the transnational yoga movements focused on mantra emerged in the mid-twentieth century through the interactions of Indian gurus and western practitioners. Founded by Maharishi Mahesh Yogi and inspired by a fusion of Vedic, yogic and ayurvedic ideals, Transcendental Meditation (TM) teaches the practitioner to silently meditate on a personal mantra (acquired at initiation) so as to foster serenity and stress reduction (Williamson 2010). Championed by celebrities from the Beatles to Jerry Seinfeld, TM has disseminated its techniques to millions of people and has sought to validate its health benefits through scientific studies (Lowe 2011). Systematised by the Sikh teacher Yogi Bhajan with reference to premodern discourses on *kuṇḍalinī* energy (Deslippe 2012) and practised mostly by American Sikhs in conjunction with Sikh Dharma International (Khalsa 2012), Kundalini Yoga is a fusion of modern postural yoga, breath control and Sikh mantras. Chanting is a central feature: a typical sequence might include assuming a pose, breathing in a rhythmic fashion and repeating the formula *sat nam*. Perhaps the most visible of all the transnational mantra movements is the International Society for Krishna Consciousness (ISKCON), or the Hare Krishna movement, founded by Bhaktivedanta Swami Prabhupada to promote Gaudiya Vaishnavism around the world. Sound – especially the chanting of devotional songs (*bhajan*) in praise of Krishna – is the preferred way for Hare Krishna adherents to practise the yoga of devotion (*bhakti*) and transmit 'Krishna consciousness' to others (Bhaktivedanta Book Trust 1983). Practitioners also undertake daily personal regimens of *japa*, muttering the Hare Krishna mantra repeatedly while keeping count using prayer beads (Rochford 2007).

We finish this survey of sound and yoga back where we began: the modern yoga studio. Mantras are a core component of many contemporary practices, especially to begin and end a practice. On the teacher's cue, practitioners utter a given formula together, whether it is the invocation of Patañjali, variations of the *gāyatrī* mantra, the *lokāḥ samastāḥ* formula or simply OM (Nevrin 2004). Perusing major yoga magazines and online platforms reveals a host of articles, courses and workshops on using sacred sound in postural and contemplative practice (e.g. Creel 2018; Moroz Alpert 2017). Another recent trend in transnational yoga culture is the sound bath, in which a sound artist uses acoustic and electronic instruments to create an immersive soundscape to clear energy blockages, reduce anxiety and promote wellbeing (e.g. Kercher 2015; Mazurek 2017). Also worth mentioning is the global popularity of *kīrtan*, a call-and-response form inspired by Indian devotional traditions (Graves 2017), in which singers, musicians and participants collectively perform songs of prayer or praise (Jacobs 2017).

## Conclusion: the unstruck sound

From the Vedas through sound baths, the examples we have considered herein demonstrate the richness and diversity of yogic approaches to sound and listening, bringing in a wide array of doctrines, practices and media. Notwithstanding the prominence of Brahmins and the authority of Sanskrit texts, other voices have found ways to shape thinking on sound and yoga. And in spite of the fact that universalist claims are central to this discourse, yogic sound has never been monolithic, but always multiform – adherence to tradition has gone hand in hand with innovations and ruptures. At the same time, however, our survey suggests remarkable continuities across millennia. Yoga has always been a strategy for cultivating sacred soundscapes: the attentive engagement of mantra, mind and body in pursuit of supramundane states characterises most traditions. And yoga is fundamentally a technique of deep listening: the practitioner strives to perceive sounds – mantras, syllables and vibrations in gross and subtle forms – that are perpetually immanent but not always manifest.

By way of conclusion, consider once again the unstruck sound, that cosmic vibration undetectable by the human ear yet perceptible to the practitioner who listens to the sound within his heart. This embodied sound offers a path to liberation, in that it serves as a support for meditating on the self and its relation to a supreme deity or the absolute. Yet the unstruck sound also constitutes the condition of liberation, in that to hear it is to be fully absorbed in a transcendent condition. Returning finally to the questions posed at the start of this chapter –'what is the significance of sound for understanding yoga? And yoga for sound?' – I offer this formulation: yoga is meditation *through* sound (understood as a technique of chanting that supports contemplative states), meditation *on* sound (as a technique of listening that leads to emancipatory absorption) and meditation *towards* sound (as the highest soteriological goal, identical with the self, the highest deity or the cosmic absolute).

## Glossary

*agni*,Vedic god of fire, kindled at sacrifice
*ajapā gāyatrī*, the unmuttered version of the *gāyatrī* mantra; esoteric name for the *haṃsa* mantra
*akāśa*, space; the medium in which sound moves
*akṣara*, imperishable; syllable; the absolute
*ālambana*, support; mantra or other technique used to cultivate contemplative states
*anāhata nāda*; *anāhata śabda*, unstruck vibration, unstruck sound; name for internal, subtle sound, representing the cosmic absolute
*anirukta*, indistinct, unexpressed; mode of chanting mantras so that the words are replaced by non-lexical syllables
*anusvāra*, nasalisation of vowel; represented in script by a dot
*apauruṣeya*, not of human origin; reference to Veda as divine revelation
Ardhamāgadhī, Middle Indo-Aryan language of some Jain texts
*AUM*, esoteric variant of the sacred syllable OM based on analysis of its constituent phonemes
*bhajan*, devotional song in Hindu traditions
*bhūr bhuvaḥ svar*, earth, atmosphere, heaven; expiatory formula chanted in Vedic sacrifice
*bindu*, dot, point, drop; the concentrated essence of a mantra; nasalisation of a syllable, represented in script by a dot
*bīja*, seed syllable; the most potent and concentrated form of mantra
*brahman*, poetic formulation; the cosmic absolute; name for the supervisory priest in Vedic sacrifice
*cakra*, circle; energy centre in the yogic body
*dhamma*, the Buddha's teaching
*dhāraṇā*, fixation; contemplative practice of fixing one's attention on a mantra or other support
*dhāraṇī*, mantra or formula in Tantric Buddhism
*dhvani*, sound
*dhyāna*, meditation
*divyam śrotram*, divine hearing; suprasensory audition
*divyadhvani*, divine sound; name for suprasensory sound that emanates from the Jina
*haṃsa*, goose; esoteric name for formula *haṃ so 'haṃ so 'haṃ sa* ..., which corresponds to the breath
*japa*, muttering, murmuring; characteristic register of chanting mantras in yoga
*jāpaka*, practitioner of *japa*
*kaivalya*, isolation; the soteriological aim of Pātañjala yoga
*kīrtan*, call-and-response song in devotional traditions of yoga and Hinduism
*kuṇḍalinī*, coiled; feminine power associated with the upward flow of breath and energy in the subtle body
*mānasa*, mental; mode of silently meditating on mantras
*maṅgala*, benediction; auspicious formula in Jain traditions

*mantra*, formula, usually in Sanskrit, used in chanting or meditation
*mantraśāstra*, the knowledge of mantra, associated with Tantric traditions
*nāda*, reverberation, vibration; subtle sound arising in the resonance of the chanted mantra
*nirukta*, distinct; mode of chanting mantras so that their meaning is understood clearly
OM (*om*, *oṃ*, *oṁ*), sacred syllable of Indian religions; essence of the Vedas; supreme seed syllable and mantra
*oṃ maṇi padme hūṃ*, the six-syllabled formula of Avalokiteśvara; supreme mantra of early Buddhism
Pāḷi, Middle Indo-Aryan language of some Buddhist texts
*pañcanamaskāra*, a litany in praise of the Five Supreme Lords of Jainism
Prakrit, Middle Indo-Aryan language(s) of some Jain and Buddhist texts
*paritta*, spell in Buddhist and Jain texts
*praṇava*, humming; recitational technique of adding *om* to Ṛgvedic mantras; generic name for OM as a sacred syllable
*prāṇa*, breath
*ṛc*, verse belonging to the *Ṛgveda*
*Ṛgveda*, one of four Vedas; corpus of mantras and interpretations pertaining to reciting verses in Vedic sacrifice
*sāman*, melody belonging to the *Sāmaveda*
*Sāmaveda*, one of four Vedas; corpus of mantras and interpretations pertaining to chanting melodies in Vedic sacrifice
*śabda*, sound; word; distillation of language
*śakti*, feminine power of mantras, syllables, script, language
*siddhi*, supernatural power acquired through yoga
*sphoṭa*, burst; intuition of sound or word's meaning
*śravaṇam*, faculty of hearing; audition
*śruti*, that which is heard; Veda as aural revelation
*sthūla*, gross; external aspects of body or utterance, perceptible to normal senses
*sūkṣma*, subtle; internal aspects of body or utterance, imperceptible and suprasensory
*sulṭān al-ẕikr*, emperor of divine remembrances; contemplative technique that includes suprasensory audition in Sufi traditions
*suṣumnā*, gracious; name for central channel of subtle body through which breath and energy flow
*svādhyāya*, personal recitation of mantras for mastery, worship, or meditation
*tūṣṇīm*, silently; mode of internally chanting mantras
*uccaiḥ*, loudly; mode of chanting mantras
*uccāra*, rising; utterance of mantra in Tantric traditions, conceived as ascent of sound through the body
*upāṃśu*, quiet; mode of muttering mantras
*vāc*, Vedic goddess of speech; language
*Veda*, knowledge; mantras and prose texts forming the sacred corpus of Brahmanical traditions
*vibhūti*, supernatural power acquired through yoga
*vidyā*, knowledge; mantra or formula in Tantric traditions
*Yajurveda*, one of four Vedas; corpus of formulas and interpretations pertaining to making offerings in Vedic sacrifice
*yajus*, prose formula belonging to *Yajurveda*
*yantra*, ritual diagram used in Tantric traditions
*yukti*, yoking, union; Sāmavedic rite of uniting practitioner's mind with the liturgy through mantra meditation

## Notes

1 I am grateful to the editors of this volume, the participants in the 'Disciplines and Dialogue: The Future of Yoga and Meditation Studies' workshop at SOAS, and Richard Williams for their thoughtful engagement with this chapter.
2 While this chapter uses 'sound' as shorthand for sonic practices and auditory practices *together*, certain sections contrast sound as sonic vibration with listening as auditory modality. Moreover, in this chapter 'yoga' (without italics) denotes the general category of yogic doctrines and practices; while *yoga* (with italics) denotes the term as used in specifics texts and contexts. Unless indicated otherwise, all unattributed translations of Sanskrit terms and passages are my own.
3 R. Murray Schafer defined 'soundscape' in broad terms as 'any aural area of study' (1993 [1977]: 7). Yet as Ari Kelman has shown, the term's subsequent popularity has often elided Schafer's 'ideological and ecological messages about which sounds "matter" and which do not' (2010: 214) – Kelman suggests that Schafer's soundscape is fundamentally prescriptive, 'favoring the ideal over the actual, and the interior over the exterior' (ibid.: 223). As such, the term soundscape is well suited to yoga, which privileges ideal, interiorised practices of sound and listening; notably, Schafer himself compares yogic mantra meditation to 'headphone listening' (1993 [1977]: 119).
4 Previous scholars have fruitfully explored the crossroads of sound and Indian religions. To name a few key works: Staal 1986 and 1989 examine the 'sound of religion' and the theory, practice, and interpretation of mantras; Beck 1993 argues for 'sonic theology' in classical Hindu traditions of ritual, grammar and theology; Wilke and Moebus 2011 examine the interplay between sound, meaning and aesthetics in Sanskrit texts; O'Brien 2018 sheds light on the reception of Indian religion and philosophy in 1960s minimal music; and Cox 2018 theorises 'sonic flux' and the metaphysics of sound art with reference to Indian doctrines.
5 Alongside Bull and Back's use of the term, Becker's use of 'deep listening' (2004) to refer to the practice of entering into trance states through music is also relevant to yogic sound.
6 For convenience, this chapter will refer to the syllable in general with the capitalised form 'OM', while using the lowercase, italicized variants in discussions of specific passages.
7 Thus, the verse ending *dhenūnām iṣudhyasi* (*Ṛgveda* 8.69.2) is transformed in performance to *dhenūnām iṣudhyaso3m* (*Aitareya Āraṇyaka* 5.1.6; see Gerety 2015: 81).
8 According to van Buitenen (1962: 13, 21–24), the various recensions of this text have gone by different names related to the Yajurvedic Maitrāyaṇīya school, including *Maitrāyaṇīya*, *Maitrāyaṇa*, *Maitrāyaṇī*, *Maitri*, *Maitrī* and *Maitreya Upaniṣad*.
9 On *maṇḍalas* and meditation, see Bühnemann, Chapter 29 in this volume.
10 The high-flying goose symbolises breath already in the *Kaṭha Upaniṣad* (5.3). As Vogel 1962 convincingly demonstrates, *haṃsa* denotes a goose (not a 'swan' as frequently translated).
11 Texts such as the *Khecarīvidyā* and *Śivasaṃhitā* teach tantric mantra practices, while others like the *Dattātreyayogaśāstra* circumscribe mantra practice or dismiss it entirely; Mallinson and Jason Birch, personal communication.
12 According to Mallinson and Birch (personal communication), the *Haṭhapradīpikā*'s teachings on *nāda* derive from two different streams of *haṭha* textual tradition. The first (70–77) is from the *Amaraughaprabodha*, which in turn takes its teachings from the *Amṛtasiddhi*; the second (78–99) is untraced but seems to incorporate material from various Śaiva Tantras.
13 It seems tempting to conceive this unitary divine sound as OM – yet the evidence for this is lacking.
14 This idea is affirmed by Castro-Sánchez (2011: 23n22), who observes that the concept of Buddha's perfected speech may be understood as a Buddhist adaptation of the twin Upaniṣadic doctrines of speech as the embodiment of absolute reality and of the identity of speech and *dharma*.
15 Like the yogic technique of *dhāraṇā* ('fixation') – also derived from the Sanskrit verb root √*dhṛ*- 'to hold' – *dhāraṇī* conveys the idea of 'holding' something in mind; see Davidson 2009: 111.

## Bibliography

Akers, B. D. 2002. *The Hatha Yoga Pradipika*. Woodstock, NY: YogaVidya.com.
Angot, M. 2008. *Le Yoga-Sūtra De Patañjali: Le Yoga-Bhāṣya De Vyāsa: Avec Des Extraits Du Yoga-Vārttika De Vijñāna-Bhikṣu*. Indika; 1. Paris: Les Belles Lettres.
Beck, G. L. 1993. *Sonic Theology: Hinduism and Sacred Sound*. Columbia, SC: University of South Carolina Press.

Becker, J. 2004. *Deep Listeners: Music, Emotion, and Trancing*. Bloomington: Indiana University Press.
Bhaktivedanta Book Trust, attributed to A. C. Bhaktivedanta Swami Prabhupāda. 1983. *Chant and Be Happy...* Mumbai, India: Bhaktivedanta Book Trust.
Bodewitz, H.W. 1983. 'The Fourth Priest (the Brahmán) in Vedic Ritual', in Kloppenborg, R. (ed), *Selected Studies on Ritual in the Indian Religions: Essays to D. J. Hoens*, 179–191. Leiden: E. J. Brill.
Bouy, C. 1994. *Les Nātha-yogin et les Upaniṣads: étude d'histoire de la Littérature Hindoue*. Paris: Édition-Diffusion De Boccard.
Brockington, J. 2012. 'How *Japa* Changed between the Vedas and the *Bhakti* Traditions: The Evidence of the *Jāpakopākhyāna* (MBh 12.189–93)'. *Journal of Hindu Studies* 5(1): 75–91.
Bronkhorst, J. 2015. 'Divine Sound or Monotone? *Divyadhvani* between Jaina, Buddhist and Brahmanical Epistemology', in Soni, Luitgard and Soni, Jayandra (eds), *Sanmati: Essays Felicitating Professor Hampa Nagarajaiah on the Occasion of his 80th Birthday*, 83–96. Bengaluru: Sapna Book House.
Bryant, E. 2009. *The Yoga Sūtras of Patañjali*. New York: North Point Press.
Bull, M, and Back, L. 2003. 'Introduction: Into Sound', in Bull, M. and Back, L. (eds), *The Auditory Culture Reader*, 1–18. Sensory Formations Series. Oxford, UK; New York: Berg.
Caland, W. and Henry, V. 1907. *L'Agniṣṭoma: Description Complète de la Forme normale du sacrifice de soma dans le culte védique*. 2 vols. Paris: Ernst Laroux.
Carpenter, D. 2003. 'Practice Makes Perfect: the Role of Practice (*abhyāsa*) in Pātañjala yoga', in Whicher, I. and Carpenter, D. (eds), *Yoga: The Indian Tradition*, 25–50. London and New York: RoutledgeCurzon.
Castro-Sánchez, P. M. 2011. 'The Indian Buddhist *dhāraṇī*: An Introduction to its History, Meanings and Functions'. MA thesis, University of Sunderland.
Copp, Paul. 2014. *The Body Incantatory: Spells and the Ritual Imagination in Medieval Chinese Buddhism*. Sheng Yen Series in Chinese Buddhist Studies. New York: Columbia University Press.
Cox, C. 2009. 'Sound Art and the Sonic Unconscious'. *Organised Sound* 14(1): 19–26.
Cox, C. 2018. *Sonic Flux: Sound, Art, and Metaphysics*. Chicago, IL: University of Chicago Press.
Creel, B. 2018. '10 Top Teachers Share Their Go-To Yoga Mantras'. *Yoga Journal*. www.yogajournal.com/yoga-teachers-people/top-teachers-share-their-go-to-yoga-mantras. Accessed 23 May 2019.
Davidson, R. 2009. 'Studies in Dhāraṇī Literature I: Revisiting the Meaning of the Term Dhāraṇī'. *Journal of Indian Philosophy* 37(2): 97–147.
Deslippe, P. 2102. 'From Maharaj to Mahan Tantric: The Construction of Yogi Bhajan's Kundalini Yoga', *Sikh Formations: Religion, Culture, Theory* 8(3): 369–387.
Doniger, W. 2014. *On Hinduism*. Oxford and New York: Oxford University Press.
Dundas, P. 1998. 'Becoming Gautama: Mantra and History in Śvetāmbara Jainism', in Cort, J. (ed), *Open Boundaries: Jain Communities and Cultures in Indian History*, 31–52. Albany, NY: State University of New York Press.
Ernst, C. 2003. 'Islamization of Yoga in the "Amrtakunda" Translations'. *Journal Of The Royal Asiatic Society* 13: 199–226.
Feld, S. 2003. 'A Rainforest Acoustemology', in Bull, M. and Back, L. (eds), *The Auditory Culture Reader*, 223–239. Sensory Formations Series. Oxford, UK; New York: Berg.
Filliozat, P. 2006. 'La parole et le yoga de la parole selon Bhartṛhari'. *Rue Descartes* 54, Les Rationalités De L'inde (Novembre): 35–46.
Fujii, M. 2004. *The Jaiminīya-Upaniṣad-Brāhmaṇa: A Study of the Earliest Upanisad, Belonging to the Jaiminīya Sāmaveda*. Publications of the Institute for Asian and African Studies 4. Helsinki: Valopaino Oy.
Gandhi, S. 2018. 'OM/Allah: Mantras and Translation in Early Modern India'. Paper given at the 'Mantras in South Asia' panel, Religions in South Asian Program Unit, Annual Meeting of the American Academy of Religion, Denver. PDF accessed 15 January 2019.
Gerety, F. M. M. 2015. 'This Whole World Is OM: Song, Soteriology, and the Emergence of the Sacred Syllable'. PhD thesis, Harvard University.
Gough, E. 2015. 'Making a Mantra: Jain Superhuman Powers in History, Ritual, and Material Culture'. PhD thesis, Yale University.
Gough, E. forthcoming. 'Picturing Oṃ in Jainism'. *Material Religion*.
Goodman, S. 2009. *Sonic Warfare: Sound, Affect, and the Ecology of Fear*. Cambridge, MA: MIT Press, 2009.
Granoff, P. 1991. 'Buddhaghoṣa's Penance and Siddhasena's Crime: Remarks on Some Buddhist and Jain Attitudes Towards the Language of Religious Texts', in Shinohara, K. and Schopen, G. (eds), *From Benares to Beijing: Essays on Buddhism and Chinese Religions in Honour of Prof. Jan Yün-Hua*, 17–34. Oakville; New York; London: Mosaic Press.
Graves, E. 2017. 'The Marketplace of Devotional Song: Cultural Economies of Exchange in Bengali Padāvalī-Kīrtan'. *Ethnomusicology* 61(1): 52–86.

Green, N. 2008. 'Breathing in India, c. 1890'. *Modern Asian Studies* 42(2–3): 283–315.

Jacobs, S. 2017. 'Yoga Jam: Remixing Kīrtan in the Art of Living'. *Journal of Religion and Popular Culture* 29(1): 1–18.

Jakobson, R. 1962. 'Why "Mama" and "Papa"?' In *Selected Writings, Vol. I: Phonological Studies*, 538–545. The Hague: Mouton.

Jamison, S. and Witzel, M. 2003. 'Vedic Hinduism', in Sharma, A. (ed), *The Study of Hinduism*, 65–113. Columbia, SC: University of South Carolina Press.

Kane, B. 2015. 'Sound Studies without Auditory Culture: A Critique of the Ontological Turn'. *Sound Studies* 1(1): 2–21.

Kapchan, D. 2009. 'Learning to Listen: The Sound of Sufism in France'. *World Of Music* 51(2): 65–89.

Kelman, A.Y. 2010. 'Rethinking the Soundscape: A Critical Genealogy of a Key Term in Sound Studies'. *The Senses and Society* 5(2): 212–234.

Kercher, S. 2015. 'Sound Baths Move from Metaphysical to Mainstream'. *New York Times*, 15 August. www.nytimes.com/2015/08/16/fashion/sound-baths-move-from-metaphysical-to-mainstream.html. Accessed 23 May 2019.

Khalsa, S. K. 2012. 'Yogi Bhajan and the Emergence of Sikh Dharma International'. *Sikh Formations* 8(3): 389–401. https://doi.org/10.1080/17448727.2012.752652

Lamotte, E. 1970: *Le Traité de la Grande Vertu de Sagesse de Nāgārjuna (Mahāprajñāpāramitāśāstra)*. Vol. III. Louvain: Institut orientaliste.

Lowe, S. 2011. 'Transcendental Meditation, Vedic Science, and Science'. *Nova Religio* 14: 54–76.

Lavender, J. 2017. 'Introduction: Sounding/Thinking'. *Parallax* 23(3): 245–251.

Maas, P., ed. 2006. *Samādhipāda: Das Erste Kapitel Des Pātañjalayogaśāstra Zum Ersten Mal Kritisch Ediert*. Indologica Halensis, Aachen: Shaker Verlag.

Malamoud, C., ed. 1977. *Le Svādhyāya: récitation personelle du Veda. Taittirīya-Āranyaka livre II: texte*. Paris: Institut de civilisation indienne.

Malinar, A. 2007. *The Bhagavadgītā: Doctrines and Contexts*. Cambridge; New York: Cambridge University Press.

Mallinson, J. 2007. *The Shiva Samhita: A Critical Edition and an English Translation*. Woodstock, NY: YogaVidya.com.

Mallinson, J, and Singleton, M. 2017. *Roots of Yoga*. Penguin Classics. London: Penguin Books.

Masefield, P. 1986. *Divine Revelation in Pali Buddhism*. Colombo; London: Sri Lanka Institute of Traditional Studies; Allen & Unwin.

Mauss, M. 1935. 'Les Techniques du Corps', *Journal de Pscychologie* 32: 271–93. [Translated by B. Brewster. 1973. *Economy and Society* 2(1): 70–88.]

Mauss, M. 2006. *Techniques, Technology and Civilisation*, edited by N. Schlanger. New York: Durkheim Press/Berghahn Books.

Mazurek, B. 2016. 'Giving Peace A Chance'. *Billboard*, 30 July; Arts Premium Collection, 37–38. PDF accessed May 23, 2019.

Moroz Alpert, Y. 2017. '13 Major Yoga Mantras to Memorize'. *Yoga Journal*. www.yogajournal.com/yoga-101/13-major-mantras-memorize. Accessed 23 May 2019.

Nevrin, K. 2004. 'Performing the Yogasutra: Towards a Methodology for Studying Recitation in Modern Hatha Yoga'. Revised version of paper presented at the conference 'Ritual Practices in Indian Religions and Contexts', Lund, 9–12 December 2004. PDF accessed 23 May 2019.

Noland, C. 2009. *Agency and Embodiment: Performing Gestures/Producing Culture*. Cambridge, MA: Harvard University Press.

Oberhammer, G. 1989. 'The Use of Mantra in Yogic Meditation: The Testimony of the Pāśupata', in Alper, H. (ed), *Understanding Mantras*, 204–223. Albany, NY: State University of New York.

O'Brien, K. F. 2018. 'Experimentalisms of the Self: Experiments in Art and Technology, 1966–1971'. PhD thesis, Indiana University.

Olivelle, P. (ed and trans) 1998. *The Early Upaniṣads: Annotated Text and Translation*. New York: Oxford University Press.

Padoux, A. 1990. *Vāc: The Concept of the Word in Selected Hindu Tantras*. Translated by J. Gontier. Albany: State University of New York Press.

Padoux, A. 2011. *Tantric Mantras: Studies on Mantraśāstra*. Routledge Studies in Tantric Traditions. Abingdon, Oxon; New York, NY: Routledge.

Padoux, A. 2017. *The Hindu Tantric World: An Overview*. Chicago: University of Chicago Press.

Parpola, A. 1981. 'On the Etymology and Primary Meaning of the Sacred Syllable OM', in Parpola, A. (ed), *Proceedings of the Nordic South Asia Conference, Helsinki 1980*, 195–214. Studia Orientalia 50. Helsinki: Finnish Oriental Society.
Pinch, T. J., and Bijsterveld, K. 2012. 'New Keys to the World of Sound', in Pinch T. J. and Bijsterveld, K. (eds), *The Oxford Handbookof Sound Studies*, 3–35. New York: Oxford University Press.
Powell, S. 2018. 'Yogic Concentration on the Inner Sounds: *Nādānusandhāna* in Haṭhayoga Literature'. Conference paper given at 'Yogic Traditions and Sacred Sound Practices in the United States', Boston University, 6 April 2018. PDF accessed January 2019.
Renou, L. 1949. 'La Valeur du Silence dans le Culte Védique'. *Journal of the American Oriental Society* 69(1): 11–18.
Renou, L. 1954. *Vocabulaire du Rituel Védique.* Collection de Vocabulaires Techniques du Sanskrit I. Paris: Libraire C. Klincksieck.
Rochford, E. B. 2007. *Hare Krishna Transformed.* New York: New York University Press.
Ruff, J. 2002. 'History, Text, and Context of the "Yoga Upanisads"'. PhD thesis, University of California Santa Barbara.
Ruff, J. 2012. 'Yoga in the *Yoga Upaniṣads*: Disciplines of the Mystical OṂ Sound', in White, D. G. (ed), *Yoga in Practice*, 97–116. Princeton, NJ: Princeton University Press.
Samuel, G. and Johnston, J. 2013. *Religion and the Subtle Body in Asia and the West: Between Mind and Body.* Routledge Studies in Asian Religion and Philosophy 8. Abingdon; New York: Routledge.
Schafer, R. M. 1993 [1977]. *The Tuning of the World.* New York: Knopf.
Shah, U. P. 1947. 'A Peep into the Early History of Tantra in Jain Literature', in Radhakumud Mookerji, Radha Kumud Mookerji Lectureship Committee (ed), *Bhārata-Kaumadī: Studies in Indology in Honour of Radha uomud Mookerji*, II, 839–854. Allahabad: The Indian Press, Ltd.
Skilling, P. 1992. 'The Rakṣā Literature of the Śrāvakayāna'. *Journal of the Pāḷi Text Society* 16: 109–182.
Staal, F. 1986. 'The Sound of Religion'. *Numen* 33(1–2): 33–64; 185–224.
Staal, F. 1989. *Rules Without Meaning: Ritual, Mantras and the Human Sciences.* New York: Peter Lang.
Sterne, J. 2012. 'Sonic Imaginations', in Sterne, J. (ed), *The Sound Studies Reader*, 1–17. New York: Routledge.
Sterne, J. 2014. 'Headset Culture, Audile Technique, and Sound Space as Private Space'. *Tijdschrift Voor Mediageschiedenis* 6(2): 57–82.
Studholme, A. 2002. *The Origins of Oṃ Maṇipadme Hūṃ: A Study of Kāraṇḍavyūha Sūtra.* Albany, NY: State University of New York Press.
Thieme, P. 1952. 'Bráhman'. *Zeitschrift der Deutschen Morgenländischen Gesellschaft* 102(27.1): 91–129.
Thieme, P. 1957. 'Vorzarathustrisches Bei Den Zarathustriern Und Bei Zarathustra'. *Zeitschrift Der Deutschen Morgenländischen Gesellschaft* 32(1): 67–104.
van Buitenen, J. A. B. 1959. '*Akṣara*'. *Journal of the American Oriental Society* 79(3): 176–187.
van Buitenen, J. A. B. 1962. *The Maitrāyaṇīya Upaniṣad: A Critical Essay, with Text, Translation and Commentary.* Disputationes Rheno-trajectinae VI. 'S-Gravenhage: Mouton & Co.
Vaudeville, C. 1993. *A Weaver Named Kabir: Selected Verses with a Detailed Biographical and Historical Introduction.* French Studies in South Asian Culture and Society 6. Delhi; New York: Oxford University Press.
Vogel, J. P. 1962. *The Goose in Indian Literature and Art.* Leiden: E. J. Brill.
Wayman, A. 1977. *Yoga of the Guhyasamājatantra: The Arcane Lore of Forty Verses, A Buddhist Tantra Commentary.* Delhi: Motilal Banarsidass.
White, D. G. 2009. *Sinister Yogis.* Chicago: University of Chicago Press.
Wilke, A. and Moebus, O. 2011. *Sound and Communication: An Aesthetic Cultural History of Sanskrit Hinduism.* Berlin: De Gruyter.
Williamson, L. 2010. *Transcendent in America: Hindu-Inspired Meditation Movements as New Religion.* New York: New York University Press.

# INDEX

*Note*: Page numbers in *italics* refer to figures; those in **bold** refer to tables.